The Television Studies Reader

The Television Studies Reader offers a roadmap to contemporary issues in the expanding and dynamic field of television studies. Thirty-eight cutting-edge essays lay out a wide array of approaches to the study of the changing phenomenon that is 'television' around the world.

The *Reader* pushes television studies well beyond the traditional equation of 'television' with terrestrial broadcasting, showcasing exciting new work on the wide variety of ways that television is experienced around the world and addressing issues of technology, industry, genre, representation, circulation, reception and audiences, production and ownership. It brings together contributions from leading international scholars to provide a range of perspectives on current television forms and practices, acknowledging both the status of television as a global medium, and the many and varied local contexts of its production and reception. A general Introduction situates these important scholarly contributions to our understanding of contemporary television within the history of the academic study of television.

Essays are grouped in themed sections, each with an introduction by the editors:

- Institutions of Television
- Spaces of Television
- Modes of Television
- Making Television
- Social Representation on Television
- Watching Television
- Transforming Television

Editors: **Robert C. Allen** is James Logan Godfrey Professor of American Studies, History and Communication Studies at the University of North Carolina, Chapel Hill. He is the editor of *To Be Continued . . .: Soap Operas Round the World* (1994) and *Channels of Discourse Reassembled: Television and Contemporary Criticism.* (1992).

Annette Hill is Reader in Communication at the Communication and Media Research Institute, University of Westminster. She is the author of *Shocking Entertainment: Viewer Response to Violent Movies* (1997) and, with David Gauntlett, *TV Living: Television, Audiences and Everyday Life* (1999). She is also the author of *Reality TV* (2004).

The Television Studies Reader

Edited by

Robert C. Allen and Annette Hill

Routledge
Taylor & Francis Group

LONDON AND NEW YORK

First published 2004
by Routledge
11 New Fetter Lane, London EC4P 4EE

Simultaneously published in the USA and Canada by Routledge
29 West 35th Street, New York, NY 10001

Routledge is an imprint of the Taylor & Francis Group

Typeset in Perpetua and Bell Gothic by RefineCatch Ltd, Bungay, Suffolk
Printed and bound in Great Britain by TJ International Ltd, Padstow, Cornwall

British Library Cataloguing in Publication Data
A catalogue record for this book is available from the British Library

Library of Congress Cataloging in Publication Data
The television studies reader / edited by Robert C. Allen and
Annette Hill.
        p. cm.
Includes bibliographical references and index.
    ISBN 0–415–28323–X — ISBN 0–415–28324–8 (pbk.)
1. Television broadcasting.   2. Television.   I. Allen, Robert
Clyde, 1950–   II. Hill, Annette.
    PN1992.5.T375 2004
    384.55—dc22
2003015086

ISBN 0-415-28323-X
ISBN 0-415-28324-8

Contents

Notes on Contributors   ix

Acknowledgements   xv

Robert C. Allen

FREQUENTLY ASKED QUESTIONS: A GENERAL INTRODUCTION TO THE READER   1

PART ONE
Institutions of Television

INTRODUCTION TO PART ONE   27

1 Richard Collins
'ISES' AND 'OUGHTS': PUBLIC SERVICE BROADCASTING IN EUROPE   33

2 Laurie Ouellette and Justin Lewis
MOVING BEYOND THE "VAST WASTELAND": CULTURAL POLICY AND
TELEVISION IN THE UNITED STATES   52

3 David Hutchison
PROTECTING THE CITIZEN, PROTECTING SOCIETY   66

4 Tom O'Regan
AUSTRALIA'S TELEVISION CULTURE   79

5 Eileen R. Meehan and Jackie Byars
TELEFEMINISM: HOW LIFETIME GOT ITS GROOVE, 1984–1997   92

PART TWO
Spaces of Television

INTRODUCTION TO PART TWO   105

6   Scott Robert Olson
    HOLLYWOOD PLANET: GLOBAL MEDIA AND THE COMPETITIVE
    ADVANTAGE OF NARRATIVE TRANSPARENCY   111

7   John Sinclair
    GEOLINGUISTIC REGION AS GLOBAL SPACE: THE CASE OF LATIN
    AMERICA   130

8   Colin Sparks
    THE GLOBAL, THE LOCAL AND THE PUBLIC SPHERE   139

9   Stuart Cunningham
    POPULAR MEDIA AS PUBLIC 'SPHERICULES' FOR DIASPORIC
    COMMUNITIES   151

PART THREE
Modes of Television

INTRODUCTION TO PART THREE   163

10 Jason Mittell
    A CULTURAL APPROACH TO TELEVISION GENRE THEORY   171

11 Jérôme Bourdon
    LIVE TELEVISION IS STILL ALIVE: ON TELEVISION AS AN
    UNFULFILLED PROMISE   182

12 Derek Paget
    CODES AND CONVENTIONS OF DRAMADOC AND DOCUDRAMA   196

13 Margaret Morse
    NEWS AS PERFORMANCE: THE IMAGE AS EVENT   209

14 John Corner
    ADWORLDS   226

15 Robert C. Allen
    MAKING SENSE OF SOAPS   242

16 Albert Moran
    THE PIE AND THE CRUST: TELEVISION PROGRAM FORMATS   258

PART FOUR
Making Television

INTRODUCTION TO PART FOUR 267

17 John Ellis
TELEVISION PRODUCTION 275

18 John Thornton Caldwell
MODES OF PRODUCTION: THE TELEVISUAL APPARATUS 293

19 Jane Roscoe
BIG BROTHER AUSTRALIA: PERFORMING THE 'REAL' TWENTY-FOUR-SEVEN 311

20 Sonia Livingstone and Peter Lunt
STUDIO DISCUSSIONS 322

21 Nick Couldry
MEDIA PILGRIMS: ON THE SET OF *CORONATION STREET* 332

22 Eric Freedman
PUBLIC ACCESS/PRIVATE CONFESSION: HOME VIDEO AS (QUEER)
COMMUNITY TELEVISION 343

23 Brian Larkin
HAUSA DRAMAS AND THE RISE OF VIDEO CULTURE IN NIGERIA 354

PART FIVE
Social Representation on Television

INTRODUCTION TO PART FIVE 367

24 Julie D'Acci
TELEVISION, REPRESENTATION AND GENDER 373

25 Ron Becker
PRIME-TIME TV IN THE GAY NINETIES: NETWORK TELEVISION,
QUALITY AUDIENCES, AND GAY POLITICS 389

26 Victoria E. Johnson
WELCOME HOME?: CBS, PAX-TV, AND "HEARTLAND" VALUES IN A
NEO-NETWORK ERA 404

27 David Morley
BROADCASTING AND THE CONSTRUCTION OF THE NATIONAL FAMILY 418

28 Timothy Havens
'THE BIGGEST SHOW IN THE WORLD': RACE AND THE GLOBAL
POPULARITY OF *THE COSBY SHOW* 442

PART SIX
Watching Television

INTRODUCTION TO PART SIX   457

29   Ellen Seiter
     QUALITATIVE AUDIENCE RESEARCH   461

30   Hannah Davies, David Buckingham and Peter Kelley
     IN THE WORST POSSIBLE TASTE: CHILDREN, TELEVISION AND
     CULTURAL VALUE   479

31   Anna McCarthy
     TELEVISION WHILE YOU WAIT   494

32   Matt Hills
     DEFINING CULT TV: TEXTS, INTER-TEXTS AND FAN AUDIENCES   509

33   John Hartley
     DEMOCRATAINMENT   524

PART SEVEN
Transforming Television

INTRODUCTION TO PART SEVEN   535

34   Arild Fetveit
     REALITY TV IN THE DIGITAL ERA: A PARADOX IN VISUAL CULTURE?   543

35   Jon Dovey
     CAMCORDER CULTS   557

36   Will Brooker
     LIVING ON DAWSON'S CREEK: TEEN VIEWERS, CULTURAL
     CONVERGENCE, AND TELEVISION OVERFLOW   569

37   Mark Poster
     POSTMODERN VIRTUALITIES   581

38   Don Slater
     SOCIAL RELATIONSHIPS AND IDENTITY ONLINE AND OFFLINE   596

     Caroline Dover
     SUGGESTIONS FOR FURTHER READING   615

     Index   625

Notes on contributors

Robert C. Allen is James Logan Godfrey Professor of American Studies, History, and Communication Studies at the University of North Carolina at Chapel Hill. He is the author of *Speaking of Soap Operas* and the editor of *To Be Continued: Soap Operas Around the World*, *Channels of Discourse* and *Channels of Discourse, Reassembled*.

Ron Becker is a graduate student in the Department of Communication Arts at the University of Wisconsin-Madison. He is interested in the relationships among industrial practices, social forces, and television programming.

Jérôme Bourdon is Senior Lecturer at the Department of Communications, Tel Aviv University. His latest publications include *Introduction aux médias* and 'Is television a global medium? A historical view' (in *Transmissions: Technology, Media, Globalization*). He is working on a cultural history of European television and on the coverage of the Israeli-Palestinian conflict in the Western media.

Will Brooker is Assistant Professor in Communication at Richmond, the American International University in London. He has published widely on popular texts and their audiences, with a particular focus on fandom, interpretation and cultural power. His most recent work includes *Batman Unmasked*, *Using the Force* and *The Audience Studies Reader*.

David Buckingham is Professor of Education at the Institute of Education, University of London, and Director of the Centre for the Study of Children, Youth and Media. He is the author of numerous books, including *Children Talking Television*, *Moving Images*, *The Making of Citizens*, *After the Death of Childhood*, and *Media Education: Literacy, Learning and Popular Culture*.

Jackie Byars is Associate Professor in the Department of Communication at Wayne State University in Detroit, MI, USA. Author of *All That Heaven Allows*, on feminist film theory and criticism and on 1950s Hollywood melodramas, Byars writes on American film and television.

John Thornton Caldwell is a Professor of Television Studies at the University of California at Los Angeles. His books include *Televisuality: Style, Crisis, and Authority in American Television*,

Electronic Media and Technoculture and *New Media: Digitextual Theories and Practices* (co-edited with Anna Everett). He is also the producer and director of documentary films *Rancho California* (*por favor*) (2002) and *Freak Street to Goa: Immigrants on the Rajpath* (1989).

Richard Collins is Professor of Media Studies at the Open University in the UK. His books include *Culture Communication and National Identity: The Case of Canadian Television, New Media. New Policies* (with Cristina Murroni) and *From Satellite to Single Market*.

John Corner is a Professor in the School of Politics and Communication Studies at the University of Liverpool. His recent work includes *Critical Ideas in Television Studies,* an edited collection on political culture, *Media and the Restyling of Politics* (with Dick Pels) and articles on aesthetics, history, documentary and media power in a number of international journals.

Nick Couldry is Lecturer in Media and Communications at the London School of Economics and Political Science, and Director of the MSC programme in Media and Communications Regulation. He is the author of three books: *The Place of Media Power, Inside Culture* and *Media Rituals: A Critical Approach,* as well as numerous articles on media culture and media power.

Stuart Cunningham is Professor and Director of the Creative Industries Research and Applications Centre (CIRAC), Queensland University of Technology. He is the author of *The Australian TV Book* and *The Media and Communications in Australia* (with Graeme Turner). His recent projects include *Floating Lives: The Media and Asian Diasporas* and international studies of 'borderless' education and its implications for Australian higher and further education.

Julie D'Acci is a Professor of Media and Cultural studies at the University of Wisconsin-Madison. She is the author of *Defining Women,* the co-editor, with Charlotte Brunsdon and Lynn Spigel, of *Feminist Television Criticism,* and author of various articles on television and cultural studies.

Hannah Davies was a Research Officer at the Institute of Education. She is the co-author (with David Buckingham, Ken Jones and Peter Kelley) of *Children's Television in Britain.*

Caroline Dover is a Research Fellow in Media, currently working in the Communication and Media Research Institute, University of Westminster. She completed her doctoral thesis ('British documentary television production: tradition, change and "crisis" within a practitioner community') at Goldsmiths College, London in 2001.

Jon Dovey is a writer, producer and lecturer in the School of Cultural Studies at the University of Bristol. Publications include *Freakshow – First Person Media and Factual Telelvision* and the co-authored *New Media – A Critical Introduction.*

John Ellis is Professor and Head of the Media Arts Department, Royal Holloway University of London. He is the author of *Visible Fictions* and *Seeing Things.* From 1982 to 1999 he ran Large Door Productions, producing television documentaries, including *Visions* (1982–85), *The Holy Family Album* (1991) and *Riding the Tiger* (1997 and 1998).

Eric Freedman is an Assistant Professor in the Department of Communication at Florida Atlantic University. An independent video artist and former public access producer, he is has written on the aesthetics and politics of public access cable television in *The Television Studies Book* and the journal *Television and New Media*. His experimental video work has shown at such venues as the American Film Institute, and Ars Electronica in Linz, Austria.

Arild Fetveit is a research fellow at the department of media and communication, University of Oslo. He has worked in reception studies, reality TV and digitalisation of film and photography. Now he is writing a book on the problem of defining documentary and on the discursive possibilities between documentary and fiction film.

John Hartley, FAHA, FRSA, is Dean of the Creative Industries Faculty, Queensland University of Technology in Australia. He is author of many books and articles in media and cultural studies, journalism and cultural history. His recent books include: *Popular Reality: Journalism, Modernity, Popular Culture, Uses of Television, The Indigenous Public Sphere: the Reporting and Reception of Aboriginal issues in the Australian media* (with Alan McKee) and *A Short History of Cultural Studies*.

Timothy Havens is Assistant Professor of Communication and Humanities at Old Dominion University in Norfolk, Virginia. His research explores how the international television business handles expressions of cultural difference. His research has appeared in *Critical Studies in Media Communication*, the *Journal of Broadcasting and Electronic Media*, and *Media and Society*.

Annette Hill is Reader in Communication at the Communication and Media Research Institute at the University of Westminster. She is the author of *Shocking Entertainment: Viewer Response to Violent Movies, TV Living: Television, Audiences and Everyday Life* (with David Gauntlett) and *Reality TV: Television Audiences and Popular Factual Entertainment*, as well as a variety of articles on audiences and popular culture.

Matt Hills is Lecturer in Media and Cultural Studies at Cardiff University. He is the author of *Fan Cultures* and *The Pleasures of Horror*. Matt is the co-editor of *Intensities: The Journal of Cult Media* (available at www.cult-media.com). He has recently contributed to *Teleparody: Predicting/Preventing the TV Discourse of Tomorrow* and *Red Noise: Buffy the Vampire Slayer* and *Critical TV Studies*.

David Hutchison teaches at Glasgow Caledonian University. He is the author of *Media Policy* and *The Modern Scottish Theatre*, and has a particular interest in the Canadian media. He was formerly a member of the BBC's General Advisory Council and of the Scottish Film Council.

Victoria E. Johnson is Assistant Professor in the Program in Film Studies and Visual Studies at the University of California, Irvine. She has published several articles regarding the politics of place, race, and the construction of community in popular American television and film.

Peter Kelley was a Research Officer at the Institute of Education. He is the co-author (with David Buckingham, Ken Jones and Hannah Davies) of *Children's Television in Britain*.

Brian Larkin is Assistant Professor of Anthropology at Barnard College. He is co-editor of *Media Worlds: Anthropology on New terrain* (with Faye Ginsburg and Lila Abu-Lughod). He writes on issues of media and urbanisation in Nigeria.

Justin Lewis is Professor of Communication at the Cardiff School of Journalism, Media and Cultural Studies. He is the author of *Constructing Public Opinion, Art, Culture and Enterprise: the Politics of Cultural Industries,* and *The Ideological Octopus: An Exploration of Television and its Audience.*

Sonia Livingstone is Professor of Social Psychology at the London School of Economics and Political Science. She has published widely on the subject of media audiences, particularly audience reception of television genres (talk shows, soap opera, crime media). Books include *Making Sense of Television, Mass Consumption and Personal Identity* and *Talk on Television* (both with Peter Lunt), *Young People, New Media* (with Moira Bovill), *The Handbook of New Media* (with Leah Lievrouw) and *Young People and New Media.*

Peter Lunt is a Social Psychologist at University College London. His research interests include the media psychology, consumption research and the link between social psychology and social theory. His publications include *Mass Consumption and Personal Identity* and *Talk on Television* (both with Sonia Livingstone) and *Economic Socialization* (with Adrian Furnham).

Anna McCarthy teaches in the Department of Cinema Studies at New York University. She is the author of *Ambient Television: Visual Culture and Public Space* and co-editor, with Nick Couldry, of *Media/Space: Place, Scale and Culture in a Media Age.*

Eileen R. Meehan is the Garrey Carruthers Chair in Honors at the University of New Mexico for the academic year 2002–3. Along with Janet Wasko and Mark Phillips, she was a co-principle investigator for the *Global Disney Audiences Project* and co-editor of its report *Dazzled by Disney?* She co-edited *Sex and Money: Feminism and Political Economy in the Media* with Ellen Riordan. Meehan's research focuses on the connections between economic structures and expressive styles in the media.

Jason Mittell is an Assistant Professor of American Civilization and Film and Media Culture at Middlebury College. He has published essays in *Cinema Journal, The Velvet Light Trap, Television and New Media, Film History* and a number of anthologies. He is currently writing a book on television genres.

Albert Moran is Senior Lecturer at the Australian Key Centre for Cultural and Media Policy, Griffith University, Australia. He is the author of *Copycat TV: Globalisation, Program Formats and Cultural Identity, Film Policy: International, National and Regional Perspectives* (ed.), and *Public Voices, Private Interests* (edited with Jennifer Craik and Julie James Bailey).

David Morley is Professor of Communications in the Department of Media and Communications, Goldsmiths College, London University. Among his publications are: *Everyday Televison: Nationwide* (with Charlotte Brunsdon), *The Nationwide Audience, Family Television, Television, Audiences and Cultural Studies, Spaces of Identity* (with Kevin Robins), *Stuart Hall: Critical Dialogues in Cultural Studies* (co-edited with Kuan-Hsing Chen) and *Home Territories: Media, Mobility and Identity.*

Margaret Morse is a Professor of Film and Digital Media at the University of California at Santa Cruz. She has published widely, including the books *Virtualities: Television, Media Art and*

Cyberculture and *Hardware, Software, Artware,* as well as numerous theoretical and critical articles on subjects in media, art and culture ranging from aerobics and sport to electronic empathy and virtual war.

Scott Robert Olson is Professor of Speech Communication at Minnesota State University. Olson's many publications include *Hollywood Planet: Global Media and the Competitive Advantage of Narrative Transparency,* and *Komunikacja w Organizacji i Zarzadzaniu* ('Business and Management Communication').

Tom O'Regan is Professor of Film, Media and Cultural Policy in the Faculty of Arts, Griffith University, Brisbane and the Australian UNESCO-Orbicom Chair of Communications. His books include *Australian National Cinema* and *Australian Television Culture.* He is a co-author of *The Future of Local Content?* for the Australian Broadcasting Authority and is co-editor of *Mobilising the Audience.*

Laurie Ouellette is Assistant Professor of Media Studies at Queens College, City University of New York. She is the author of *Viewers Like You? How Public TV Failed the People.*

Derek Paget is Visiting Fellow in the Department of Film, Theatre and Television at the University of Reading. He is author of *True Stories?: Documentary Drama on Radio, Screen and Stage* and *No Other Way to Tell It: Dramadoc/docudrama on Television.*

Mark Poster is Director of the Film Studies Program at the University of California, Irvine and a member of the History Department. He is a member of the Critical Theory Institute. His recent books are: *What's the Matter with the Internet?: A Critical Theory of Cyberspace, The Information Subject, Cultural History and Postmodernity, The Second Media Age* and *The Mode of Information.*

Jane Roscoe is Head of Screen Studies at the Australian Film, Television and Radio School, Sydney, Australia. She has published extensively in the areas of documentary, mock-documentary, audiences and new television hybrids. She is the author of *Documentary in New Zealand: An Immigrant Nation,* and she is co-author (with Craig Hight) of *Faking It: Mock-Documentary and the Subversion of Factuality.*

Ellen Seiter is Professor of Communication at the University of California, San Diego, where she teaches media studies and critical gender studies. She specializes in the study of children and the media and is the author of *Television and New Media Audiences* and *Sold Separately: Children and Parents in Consumer Culture* and co-editor of *Remote Control:Television, Audiences and Cultural Power.*

John Sinclair is a Professor in the Department of Communication, Language and Cultural Studies at Victoria University of Technology in Melbourne, Australia. His published work covers various dimensions of the globalization of the media and communication industries, and includes the books *Images Incorporated: Advertising as Industry and Ideology, Latin American Television: A Global View,* and the co-edited, co-authored works *New Patterns in Global Television: Peripheral Vision* and *Floating Lives: The Media of Asian Diasporas.*

Don Slater is Reader in Sociology at the London School of Economics and Political Science. He has written extensively about the Internet and new media, from an ethnographic perspective. His publications include *The Internet: an Ethnographic Approach* (with Daniel Miller), *Consumer Culture and Modernity* and *Market Society: Markets and Modern Social Thought* (with Fran Tonkiss).

Colin Sparks is Professor of Media Studies and Director of the Communication and Media Research Institute at the University of Westminster. He has written widely on the mass media, most recently on tabloidization and on media and democracy in post-communist countries. His publications include *Communism, Capitalism and the Mass Media, Television, Democracy and Eastern Europe* and *Tabloid Tales* (with John Tulloch).

Acknowledgements

The following articles have been reproduced courtesy of the authors and publishers involved:

Allen, Robert C. (ed.), 'Introduction', in *To Be Continued: Soap Operas Around the World*, London and New York: Routledge: (1995) 1–26.

Becker, Ron, 'Primetime TV in the Gay Nineties: Network Television, Quality Audiences and Gay Politics', *The Velvet Light Trap* 42 (1998): 36–47. Copyright 1998 University of Texas Press.

Bourdon, Jérôme, 'Live Television Is Still Alive: On Television as an Unfulfilled Promise', *Media, Culture, and Society* 22, 5 (2000): 531–56. Copyright 2000 Sage Publications Ltd.

Brooker, Will, 'Living on *Dawson's Creek*: Teen viewers, cultural convergence and television over-flow', *International Journal of Cultural Studies*, 4, 1 (2001): 456–72. Copyright 2001 Sage Publications Ltd.

Caldwell, John T., 'Modes of Production' in *Televisuality: Style, Crisis and Authority in American Television*, New Brunswick, New Jersey: Rutgers University Press (1995): 73–102. Copyright 1995 John Thornton Caldwell.

Collins, Richard, 'Public Service Broadcasting' in *From Satellite to Single Market: the Europeanisation of Television 1982–1992*, London: Routledge (1998): 51–74.

Corner, John, 'Adworlds' in *Television Form and Public Address*, London: Arnold (1995): 105–33. Reprinted by permission of the publisher.

Couldry, Nick, 'Media Pilgrims: on the set of *Coronation Street*' in *The Place of Media Power: Pilgrims and Witnesses of the Media Age*, London: Routledge (2000): 65–87.

Cunningham, Stuart, 'Popular Media as Public "Sphericules" for Diasporic Communities', *International Journal of Cultural Studies* 4, 2 (2001): 131–47. Copyright 2001 Sage Publications Ltd.

Davies, Hannah, Buckingham, David, Kelley, Peter, 'In the Worst Possible Taste: Children, Television and Cultural Value', *European Journal of Cultural Studies* 3, 1 (2000): 5–25. Copyright 2000 Sage Publications Ltd.

Dovey, Jon, 'Camcorder Cults' in *Freakshow: First Person Media and Factual Television,* London: Pluto Press (2000): 55–77.

Fetveit, Arild, 'Reality TV in the Digital Era: A Paradox in Visual Culture?', *Media, Culture, and Society* 21, 6 (1999): 787–804. Copyright 1999 Sage Publications Ltd.

Freedman, Eric, 'Public Access/Private Confession: Home Video as (Queer) Community Television', *Television and New Media* 1, 2 (2000): 179–92. Copyright 2000 by Sage Publications Inc.

Hartley, John, 'Democratainment' and 'Clueless? Not! DIY Citizenship', in *Uses of Television*, London: Routledge (1999): 154–65, 177–88.

Havens, Timothy, ' "The Biggest Show in the World": Race and the Global Popularity of *The Cosby Show*', *Media, Culture and Society* 22 (2000): 371–91. Copyright 2000 Sage Publications Ltd.

Hutchison, David, 'Protecting the Citizen, Protecting Society', in *Media Policy: An Introduction*, Oxford: Blackwell (1999): 103–21.

Johnson, Victoria, 'Welcome Home?: CBS, PAX-TV, and "Heartland" Values in a Neo-Network Era', *The Velvet Light Trap* 46 (2000): 40–55. Copyright 2000 University of Texas Press.

Larkin, Brian, 'Hausa Dramas and the Rise of Video Culture in Nigeria', in Jonathan Haynes (ed.) *Nigerian Video Films,* Athens, Ohio: Ohio University Press (2000): 209–41. Reprinted with the permission of Ohio University Center for International Studies.

Livingstone, Sonia, and Lunt, Peter, 'Studio Discussions: Social Spaces and Postmodernity' in *Talk on Television: Audience Participation and Public Debate*, London: Routledge (1993): 162–80.

McCarthy, Anna, 'Television While You Wait', in *Ambient Television*, Durham: Duke University Press (2001): 195–223. Copyright 2001 Duke University Press. All rights reserved.

Meehan, Eileen R. and Byars, Jackie, 'Telefeminism: How Lifetime Got its Groove 1984–1997', *Television and New Media* 1: 1 (2000): 33–51. Copyright 2000 Sage Publications Inc.

Mittell, Jason, 'A Cultural Approach to Television Genre Theory', *Cinema Journal* 40, 3 (2001): 3–24. Copyright 2001 University of Texas Press.

Moran, Albert, 'The Pie and the Crust: Television Program Formats', in *Copycat TV: Globalisation, Program Formats and Cultural Identity*, Luton: University of Luton Press (1998): 13–23.

Morley, David, 'Broadcasting and the Construction of the National Family' *Home Territories: Media, Mobility and Identity*, London: Routledge (2000): 105–27.

Morse, Margaret, 'News as Performance: The Image as Event' in *Virtualities: Television, Media Art and Cyberculture*, Bloomington and Indianapolis: Indiana University Press (1998): 36–67.

O'Regan, Tom, 'Australian's Television Culture', in *Australian Television Culture*, Sidney: Allen and Unwin (1993): 1–21.

Olson, Scott, R., Chapter 1, in *Hollywood Planet: Global Media and the Competitive Advantage of Narrative Transparency*, Mahwah, N.J.: Lawrence Erlbaum Associates (1999): 1–29.

Ouellette, Laurie, and Lewis, Justin, 'Moving Beyond the Vast Wasteland: Cultural Policy and Television in the United States', *Television and New Media* 1,1 (2000): 95–115. Copyright 2000 Sage Publications Inc.

Paget, Derek, 'Codes and Conventions' in *No Other Way to Tell It*, Manchester: Manchester University Press (1998): 61–89.

Poster, Mark, 'Postmodern Virtualities', in *Arena Journal*, Melbourne, Australia: Arena Printing and Publishing (September 1994).

Roscoe, Jane, 'Big Brother Australia: Performing the 'Real' Twenty-Four-Seven', *International Journal of Cultural Studies*, 4, 1 (2001): 473–88. Copyright 2001 Sage Publications Ltd.

Seiter, Ellen, 'Qualitative Audience Research', in *Television and New Media Audiences*, New York: Oxford University Press (1999): 9–32.

Sinclair, John, 'Geolinguistic Region as Global Space: the Case of Latin America' in Georgette Wang, Jan Servaes and Anura Goonasekera (eds), *The New Communications Landscape: Demystifying Media Globalization*, London: Routledge (2000): 19–32.

Slater, Don, 'Social Relationships and Identity Online and Offline', in Leah A. Lievrouw and Sonia Livingstone (eds), *Handbook of New Media: Social Shaping and Consequences of ICTs*, London: Sage (2002): 533–46.

Sparks, Colin, 'The Global, the Local and the Public Sphere', in Georgette Wang, Jan Servaes and Anura Goonasekera (eds), *The New Communications Landscape: Demystifying Media Globalization*, London: Routledge (2000): 74–95.

Every effort has been made to obtain permission to reproduce copyright material. If any proper acknowledgement has not been made, we would invite copyright holders to inform us of the oversight.

ROBERT C. ALLEN

FREQUENTLY ASKED QUESTIONS
A General Introduction to the Reader

H OW ARE YOU DEFINING "TELEVISION" FOR THE PURPOSE OF THIS
BOOK?

Let's start with some of the ways that television has been and might be defined and studied.

- Television is a changing set of technologies for electronically capturing images and sounds; recording, manipulating and arranging images and sounds; (sometimes) transmitting images and sounds through space (via radio waves, through coaxial cable, bounced off satellites, over the internet); and displaying images and sounds thus captured, recorded, manipulated, arranged, and (sometimes but not always) transmitted from one place to another.
- Television is the aggregate of all the images and sounds "carried" by television and produced, organized, and experienced as television programming.
- Television is a set of formal, narrative, and representational structures and capacities—some of which it shares with other media, modes of representation, and art forms; some of which enable it to incorporate aspects of these other forms; and some of which mark out television as a distinctive or unique experience. For example, many critics and scholars have identified the quality of aural and visual "liveness" (the perceived simultaneity of image capture and reproduction at millions of geographically dispersed locations) historically as one of the defining qualities of broadcast television.
- Television is a set of institutions and relationships among institutions: production companies, broadcasters, networks (and the corporations that own them), state television systems (in the case of public service television), program distributors, advertisers (in the case of commercial television), equipment manufacturers, government regulators, international trade and cultural agencies, the institutions of other media (cinema, publishers, radio, the internet, computers, etc.), universities, and public advocacy groups, among them.
- Television is the social experience associated with producing, viewing, listening, talking about, reading about, being captured by, appearing on, and being influenced and affected by television.

So are you saying that the definition of television used in this book is "all of the above" and that the essays included in this book will cover all of these aspects of television?

There are geographic and historical factors that further complicate defining television as an object of study and television studies as a field.

The ways in which the various features of television enumerated above (and perhaps others I left out) coalesce into "television" vary from country to country, from region to region, and from home to home/person to person within a particular locality. Because every country in the world regulates terrestrial broadcasting (television carried over radio waves, as distinct from television programming carried by cable or satellite services) in some way, there is still a national character to broadcast television. A few national regimes still regard broadcast television as the exclusive prerogative of the state. Others are mixed systems of government-run or -funded broadcast television services and advertiser-supported broadcasting with the latter being subject to greater or lesser levels of regulation. Since the 1980s, television increasingly has also been carried via cable and satellite. Each country's policies toward and levels of uptake of these new technologies vary. In some countries television is a national, centralized, monolingual, and metropolitan cultural force. In other countries television is local (or regional), national, and international — as television from adjacent countries bleeds across borders. In some countries television is strictly a broadcast medium. In others, television is delivered via radio waves, cable, and satellite signals.

Another factor that complicates our attempts at formulating a concise and universally-applicable definition is the dynamism of television *as* a set of technologies, complex of institutions, menu of program options, constellation of formal possibilities, and range of viewing experiences. As television has changed over the nearly sixty years since its establishment as a mass medium in Europe and North America (roughly fifty years in Australia and New Zealand), so has the research and scholarship changed in the way television is understood, the features of television that have been singled out for special attention, and the theories and methodologies that have been applied to it.

Calling this book "The Television Studies Reader" would suggest that there is an academic discipline called "television studies." Is this the case?

Despite the fact that television is now taught in universities around the world, particularly in the English-speaking world, and that each year hundreds of scholarly books and articles are published about television (including this one), the study of television does not have anything approaching the disciplinary coherence of, say, history or biology. One reason for this is that there has never been a general consensus among scholars as to why or how television should be studied or even whether television should be the object of scholarly inquiry at all. As a consequence, at any given university in the US, the UK, Australia, Canada, or New Zealand you might find television included in syllabi for courses in departments of literature, sociology, political science, psychology, art, communication, cultural studies, or media studies, but you will *not* find very many departments calling themselves television studies departments. And at many colleges, particularly smaller ones, not a single scholar would identify him or herself as a "television studies" scholar — as opposed to a literature or film or sociology or political science scholar who sometimes teaches *about* television.

But we would argue that over the past twenty-five years or so there has emerged — particularly in the English-speaking academic world but outside it as well — a field of inquiry called television studies, which is recognizable through the organization of courses on television and through a now substantial, international, and cross-referencing body of scholarly literature. In 1998, British television scholar Charlotte Brunsdon argued that although its object of study was by no means self-evident or agreed upon, it was possible to identify television studies as "the relatively recent, aspirationally disciplinary name given to the academic study of television." Her American colleague Lynn Spigel noted in 2000 that "we are [now] able to teach our students a history of scholarly reading protocols, theoretical assumptions, debates, . . . [and] 'ideas' " that together constitute something that can be called television studies.[1] But you should be aware that not everyone who teaches or researches or writes about television would see themselves as belonging to this "field" of television studies. Although there are increasing points of interconnection among disciplines that take television as one of their objects of study, it is still the case that some scholars in journalism, mass communication, psychology, and other fields would see the study of television as representing a very different research agenda and as being constituted by a very different set of courses and body of scholarly literature.

How did this "field" of television studies come to be?

As for how this still rather unstable and by no means universally recognized field of television studies came to be, there is not one, single "history of the field" that would apply — even across international academic cultures that share a common language and similar ways of organizing knowledge. Because the character of television itself is in many respects nationally specific, the history of its study is also to some degree nationally specific, even though there has been considerable international circulation of ideas, theories, methods, emphases and scholars themselves within television studies over the past twenty years or so. All I can offer here is a very subjective, necessarily schematic, and in some respects, I'm sure, idiosyncratic account of how I see and saw the formation of the field of television studies. Warning: for readers outside the US, this account will have a distinctly American odor about it.

British television scholar John Corner has argued that "the overwhelming rationale for most research into television has undoubtedly been anxiety about its influence."[2] The nature of this anxiety has differed from country to country, but the rapid growth of television systems after World War II and the location of the experience of television in the home provoked concerns regarding its influence on political processes, social relations, and cultural values.

My students groan whenever I begin a sentence in this way, but when I began studying television as a graduate student in the US in the early 1970s, perhaps the dominant focus of research on television was its possible influence on the attitudes and behaviors of children. Research on the effects of television viewing on children was itself heavily influenced by a set of assumptions, research goals, and techniques derived from the social sciences. As such it was informed by the "scientific method" used in the natural sciences, by quantitative methods of analysis, and by statistical techniques of data representation and interpretation.

There was significant pressure in the 1950s and 1960s — academic, social, and political — for US researchers to attempt to make research on television conform to the protocols of "scientific" inquiry. The use of radio and movie newsreels for propaganda purposes during World War II prompted researchers to ask how television might affect the attitudes, beliefs, and behaviors of post-war audiences. Commercial television's targeting of the huge cohort of Baby-Boom children (76 million of us born between 1946 and 1964!) as an audience in the 1950s and 1960s, combined with social anxiety over a perceived increase in "juvenile delinquency" encouraged researchers to devise experimental paradigms for measuring the "effects" of television viewing on children's behavior. Paradoxically, of course, commercial television was predicated upon television's ability *to* influence particular attitudes and behaviors—those associated with consumerism—*and* upon the quantitative measurability of that influence.

In 1969, the US Senate asked the Surgeon General to commission a major research project designed to produce "definitive information regarding the existence of a causal relationship between televised crime and violence and antisocial behavior." It was probably the largest and best funded academic study of television viewing ever undertaken in any country, and it certainly drew upon the resources and expertise of the largest and richest scientific research community in the world. Two years later, the Scientific Advisory Committee on Television and Social Behavior issued a six-volume summary of its findings, concluding that there was "modest relationship between exposure to television viewing and aggressive behavior or tendencies, *as the latter are defined in the studies at hand* [italics added]." However, the committee admitted that there were two possible explanations for this connection: that watching violence on television did cause aggressive behavior in children, or that "both aggression and violence viewing may be joint products of a third condition or set of circumstances." The committee's report concluded that "a good deal of research remains to be done before one can have confidence in these conclusions."[3]

I entered graduate school in the fall of 1973, the year following publication of the committee's report, and I was assigned to read a number of the violence studies in classes on research methods in mass communication. Like many of my fellow graduate students who had come to the study of television from undergraduate backgrounds not in the social sciences but in literature, philosophy, history, theater, cinema studies, and other fields in the arts and humanities, I was struck by the limited and equivocal nature of the studies' conclusions in relation to the questions they sought to answer—despite having large research budgets, the resources of the US government, and the full arsenal of scientific methods and apparatus at their disposal. After all, the Surgeon General appointed his television violence committee the same year that a US astronaut became the first man to walk on the moon! It seemed to me that if finding a causal connection between televised violence and aggression in children was the social science equivalent of a moon landing, what the best social "science" of the time was able to produce was a sub-orbital chimp flight.

Furthermore, by focusing so narrowly on the imitation of violence associated with viewing particular acts in particular programs and by making causality the holy grail of "effects" research, the scholarly debate over television violence left undisturbed the institutional structures and aims of the American commercial broadcasting system. The research paradigm wouldn't accommodate someone asking, for example, whether using television to subject very young children to the persuasive powers of huge corporations was itself a form of violence *against* children. By the time social scientists reached a general consensus that allowing children to watch large amounts of televised violence over a long period of time was probably encouraging some of them to try out violence as a way to solve problems on the playground, the landscape of television had changed enormously, and the attention of parents and politicians had shifted to violent video games and movies and violent and misogynistic rap lyrics.

Politicians and social scientists were not the only ones who were concerned about the influence of television. In a 1985 reflection on the development of television studies, American television scholar Horace Newcomb argued that the general tenor of American critical and journalistic discourse about television in the 1960s was overwhelmingly negative. Television was represented as a problem and a threat: "a potential danger to morals, ethics, to behavior, to politics, and to religion."[4] Within a decade of its widespread adoption by American consumers, television had become the poster-child for critics and commentators on the left and the right of American cultural politics who argued that the mass media in general exercised an unequivocally pernicious influence on modern society. One of the first anthologies of critical essays on the media I ever purchased was Alan Casty's 1968 *Mass Media and Mass Man*. The first sentence of the first essay in the collection, Ernst van den Haag's "Of Happiness and of Despair We Have No Measure," read: "All mass media in the end alienate people from personal experience and, though appearing to offset it, intensify their moral isolation from each other, from reality and from themselves. One may turn to the mass media when lonely or bored. But mass media, once they become a habit, impair the capacity for meaningful experience." If you disagreed with Professor van den Haag's cheery assessment of the effects of mass media, the next essay by critic Dwight MacDonald provided yet another set of reasons to hate television and reasons *not* to take it seriously except as a threat to culture. Mass Culture is "fabricated by technicians hired by business; its audiences are passive consumers, their participation limited to the choice between buying and not buying. The Lords of *kitsch*, in short, exploit the cultural needs of the masses in order to make a profit and/or to maintain their class rule — in Communist countries, only the second purpose obtains." Somehow I doubt that either of them was charter members of the *I Love Lucy* fan club.[5]

This makes it sound as if there was an unequivocal animosity between commercial broadcasting interests and academics and journalists in the 1960s. But as Lynn Spigel has argued, the relationship between journalistic and academic writing on television and the television industry has always been complicated and ambivalent. No more so than in the 1960s, when the study of television was just getting established in the American academy and when the commercial broadcasting industry was defending itself against charges that its programming practices had created a vast cultural wasteland and that its reliance upon violence as a means of attracting audiences had deleterious effects upon children. One of the first published collections of television criticism, *The Eighth Art* (Shayon 1962), was underwritten by a commercial television network (CBS). One of the first journals devoted to television scholarship and criticism in the US, *Television Quarterly*, was, as Spigel puts it, in part intended as a " 'publicity' machine for the industry."[6] To an extent that we would probably find surprising, the agenda of academic writing on television in the 1960s and early 1970s in the US was framed, in part at least, by what kinds of knowledge would be of benefit to broadcasters.[7] The strand of television research presumed to represent the parallel interests of academic researchers and the television industry even had a name: administrative research. Furthermore, it should be remembered that many university programs in broadcasting or mass communication had strong links to the commercial broadcasting industry and saw training students for jobs in the industry as a part of their mission.

The early 1970s saw the gradual emergence of a different paradigm for the study of television in the US, a paradigm that we can now see as underwriting a new "field" of television studies. This paradigm was, in the first instance, distinguished by what it was not. It was not informed by the assumptions or methods of scientific or administrative research. It was also qualitative rather than quantitative in its methods of interpretation, focused on the pleasurability of the experience of television viewing rather than upon its possibly pernicious cultural and social effects, and interested in exploring the complexities of the fictional worlds created by television rather than comparing those worlds with the "real" world outside television.

To an extent, the emergence of television studies in the US, at least, reflects a generational shift in television scholarship. In order to be in a position to have been selected to undertake one of the television violence studies commissioned in 1969 or to have had a critical essay anthologized the year before, for example, a critic or academic television researcher would almost certainly have been born before World War II and therefore to have been a child of radio and newspapers, not television. Those of us who came to the study of television as undergraduates or graduate students in the 1970s, however, were a part of the same generation of TV children legislators were so concerned about. We were among those who watched an average of two hours of TV each day throughout our childhoods, including, in my case at least, lots of sadistic *Three Stooges* routines and *Tom and Jerry* cartoon mayhem. There was no anterior moment in our remembered life histories *prior to television* in relation to which the effects of our watching television might be compared. Our intellectual interest in television as an object of study was grounded in our own experience as a part of the television audience, and in the sometimes guilty pleasures we found in front of the set.

You felt guilty about studying television?

I said the pleasures of television were "guilty pleasures." Here's what I mean by that. Reading the social science literature on television, I wondered if the scholars conducting these studies actually watched television themselves at all or if their interest extended only to why other people watched TV and whether those "other" viewers were influenced by it. Certainly, as I've noted, the protocols of empiricist social science, with its demand for investigatory objectivity, argued *against* research being in any way influenced by the scholar's own experiences as a television viewer. On the other hand, the reason some of my colleagues in the emergent field of cinema studies in the 1970s decided to devote their professional lives to watching, writing about and teaching about movies was that they genuinely *loved* movies and believed that cinema was as much an art form as literature, painting, or theater. Traditions of European art cinema, as well as experimental and documentary filmmaking tied cinema to other strands of twentieth-century aesthetic innovation (modernism, surrealism, expressionism, naturalism, etc.). Even some films made in the factory-like environment of the Hollywood studio system, when subjected to the proper forms of analysis, could be shown to exhibit formal complexity, coherence, and power of aesthetic effect that elevated them above the merely commercial.

I can think of few of my generation of television scholars drawn to its study because of an unalloyed tele-philia or belief that television represented *the* art form of the second half of the twentieth century, however. Nevertheless, the development of television studies in the 1970s was driven by a fascination with television programming *and* with television's ability to recruit *us* as viewers. With US television policies dominated so thoroughly by the demands of advertisers, television culture so pervaded by consumerism, and programming strategies so driven by network imperatives to attract and hold the largest possible fraction of the viewing audience, our pleasure in particular moments of television was shadowed by the recognition that this pleasure implied an uncomfortable complicity with the institutions of commercial television. When we pay to see a movie in a theater, it is the movie that is being sold to us. When we watch a program on commercial television, on the other hand, it is our attention to the commercials that interrupt the program that is being "sold" to advertisers. Some television scholars have argued that watching television is not really leisure, but labor: it is our voluntary work as compliant viewers that produces value for commercial broadcasters. Thus, I think, television studies was propelled in part by a desire among some scholars (and I'll include myself here) to figure out why *we* watch television as much or more than by a determination to establish why other people do.

Furthermore, as Charlotte Brunsdon (1998) reminds us from the perspective of the mid-1990s and as the van den Haag (1968) and MacDonald (1968) essays made abundantly clear at the time, the study of television has had to contend not only with the charge that it is not worthy of the same kind of degree of scholarly scrutiny that academics routinely applied to other modes of culture but also with the belief (frequently thought but less frequently articulated by our colleagues in more respectable fields) that even watching television was an activity that no self-respecting intellectual would admit to. As Brunsdon puts it, "Debate about the significance and value of television persists, and much academic and popular writing about the medium is haunted by anxiety about the cultural legitimacy of watching television."[8]

The emergence of television studies in the 1970s, then, was also a part of a more general process by which universities, scholarly journals, academic publishers, and research-funding entities began to come to terms with what might be called "the popular." This process is still being played out in university faculty meetings, hiring committees, and tenure and promotion panels. The question of what to "do" with television and other popular forms remains a contentious one at the level of secondary education as well. School boards, state education authorities, and testing bodies struggle to make "media literacy" an educational goal without being at all sure what that term actually means or which teachers should teach what about television. But to return to our story, in the US, the political, social, and intellectual turmoil of the 1960s led to a questioning of the boundaries and hierarchies by which knowledge was organized and circumscribed within university curricula. "Relevance" became the watchword of students (and a few professors) who questioned the absence in university curricula of those things that had become essential aspects of their culture and everyday lives: popular music, graphic art, and films, among them. The new field of American Studies began to embrace (too slowly for some) dime novels as well as Melville. In both North America and the UK, television studies followed in the wake of and developed in relation to cinema studies, which by the early 1970s had brought to bear upon seemingly inconsequential Hollywood genre films sophisticated analytical approaches derived from linguistics, cultural anthropology, political philosophy, and psychoanalysis. The *Journal of Popular Culture* began publication in 1967, and a professional organization and annual conference devoted to popular culture were organized in 1969. Conference papers and published essays developed out of attempts to apply to television theories and methods that had been found to be productive in the analysis of popular cinema, literary texts, myths and folk tales.

In my own case, I wondered how narrative theory might explain a story-telling form—the US daytime soap opera—that seemed to lack one of the defining features of traditional narrative structure: an ending. Other scholars examined the organization of commercial television output into distinctive genres: the situation comedy or the crime drama, for example, which seemed to possess generic conventions every bit as important to the viewer as those that had been identified in relation to the western film or melodrama. Attention was paid to the fact that the viewing of commercial television was organized not just by individual programs (as was the case with movies) but by the "flow" of the network schedule, which attempted to secure the viewer's interest and hold it across a carefully sequenced span of programs, commercial messages, and promises of more viewing pleasure to come. And then there were the forms of commercial television that seemed to overturn the conventions of Hollywood cinema. Many television advertisements and some forms of programming (wrestling, for example) addressed the audience directly and called attention to their own status as rhetorical constructs, neither of which Hollywood films did very often.

Although I experienced the emergence of television studies primarily in relation to the American academy and American television in the 1970s, the field was also being shaped by academic engagements with other forms of television in other countries. In Britain, one of the contexts within which television studies emerged was a much older and more general debate over the role of popular or "mass" culture in contemporary British society and the place of the popular in the academy, particularly the humanities. John Hartley has argued that television studies in the UK has been shaped by a powerful " 'textual tradition' of denunciation" of popular culture dating back to the 1920s, which reflects "a quite straightforward fear of and hostility to the democratization of taste." These debates were much less focused on the role of television as an instrument of consumer culture, however, than they were in the US. As Brunsdon notes, when British journalists, critics, and academics talked about "television" in the 1960s and 1970s they did so in relation to a media landscape dominated by the BBC and its publicly-funded mission of enlightenment and culturally elevating entertainment. "Television" was presumed to address the viewer as citizen and not merely as consumer.[9]

As in the US, one strand of television studies in the UK grew out of cinema studies. Inspired by the embrace of popular cinema by French intellectuals in the 1950s, British cinema studies developed in the 1960s and early 1970s through a re-examination of forms of popular cinema that had been previously dismissed by critics: westerns, gangster films, melodramas, musicals, etc., and the filmmakers whose careers were spent making these pictures for mass audiences (Alfred Hitchcock, Howard Hawks, and John Ford, among them). By the mid-1970s, cinema studies in the UK had achieved what seemed to us in the US an enviable institutional solidity and visibility: British scholars, journals, and book series were enormously influential on the development of cinema studies throughout the English-speaking world. In some ways and to some degree television studies emerged in the UK in the mid-1970s by both drawing upon and separating itself from the institutions, theories, and agendas of British cinema studies.[10]

Equally or more important to the development of television studies in the UK, Canada, Australia, and New Zealand was the work of scholars associated with the Center for Contemporary Cultural Studies at the University of Birmingham. What characterized this work, which began to be published in the mid-1970s, was, as John Fiske has noted, a focus on three aspects of television. First, it examined television as a complex system for representing the world, not a transparent window on reality. Second, this work asked how the viewer was positioned in relation to television's representation of the world. And third, it located its analysis of television in a larger social and political context and, specifically, in a consideration of the social and political interests served by television. Charlotte Brunsdon, whose work on television grew out of the cultural studies "movement" in the UK, sees Anglo-American television studies coalescing around three slightly different areas of interest: defining and analyzing the nature of the texts of television, analyzing the social worlds constructed in television, and investigating the audiences for various forms of television programming.

As Brunsdon's (1998) genealogy of television studies suggests, a new type of television audience research emerged within the cultural studies paradigm. It began by challenging the notion (still dominant in cinema studies) that the viewer was effectively locked into a complicit relationship with "the text" (the film or television program), which, in turn, merely reproduced the ideology and class interests of those groups in positions of power (presumably represented in the texts of commercial mass culture). Interviews with viewers of the same news program, for example, revealed a range of interpretations, which seemed to line up roughly with the class position of viewers. Interpretations ranged from overall agreement with the ideological values and norms expressed in the program, through degrees of partial agreement, to outright opposition or simply a refusal to find the program and its ideas relevant at all. Further studies underscored the interpretive openness of popular texts and the importance of social factors—race, ethnicity, gender, and class—to the ways in which meanings and pleasures were generated by viewers.

As Ellen Seiter discusses in her essay in Part Six, this strand of audience research turned to cultural anthropology for its inspiration and for some of its methods. Within cultural anthropology, ethnography attempts not so much to produce comprehensive causal explanations of complex social phenomena as it does "thick descriptions" of social and cultural practices, achieved through direct observation and a variety of interview techniques. Studies of the family dynamics of television viewing, the role of gossip in interpreting and taking pleasure from soap operas, the distinctive qualities of fan culture, the gendered nature of television technology (Who programs the VCR? Who controls the remote?) all pointed to the socially conditioned and socially situated nature of television viewing as well as the complex relationship between viewing and other features of everyday life.

The early and continuing influence of the Center for Contemporary Cultural Studies upon television studies in the UK and, in the 1980s, well beyond the British Isles gave it a social, and, indeed, a sociological emphasis that was not a prominent feature of either British or American cinema studies. As John Caughie has put it, the social ubiquity of television "seemed to demand recognition of a sociology of audiences, institutions, etc." For John Fiske a key moment in the formation of television is when the study of television's texts is linked with the study of its institutions and audiences.[11] While work on the institutional nature of television from the cultural studies perspective tended to concentrate on the development of theoretical accounts of the relationship among individuals, social groups, and political and social institutions, other scholars were also examining the more concrete implications and effects of television's institutional character.

As I have suggested above, some television scholars in the US saw their interests and those of commercial broadcasters to be compatible if not identical. This cozy relationship between the academy and broadcasters in the first decades of commercial television in the US was reinforced by the curricula in many departments being geared toward training students for careers in broadcast production and management. Such perceived commonality of interest did not tend to lead to a questioning of the principles upon which the American system of broadcasting was predicated. Other scholars in the US, Britain, Canada, and Australia diverted sharply from this tradition of "administrative" research in American mass communication scholarship precisely by raising the questions about television—as a powerful social institution, a profit-seeking business enterprise, and an extension of governmental policy interests—that administrative research tended to marginalize. In short, this strand of television research focused on what has come to be called the political economy of television (about which more will be said in the introduction of Part One). Scholars outside the US were in a particularly advantageous position to observe and analyze the consequences of the export of the American system of commercial broadcasting to other countries, particularly to what used to be called the "developing world." The installation of American-style television cultures in countries in Latin America, for example, had the effect of marginalizing public service broadcasting, depressing the production of local programming (because US programming could be bought for much less than it cost to produce equivalent programming), and greatly increased the influence and power of US consumer products in those countries.

The relocation of a number of British media and cultural studies scholars to Australia after the 1970s, including John Fiske, John Hartley, Tony Bennett, and John Tulloch, among others, influenced the development of television studies there. But it is certainly not the case that television studies in Australia developed simply as the application of methods derived from British cultural studies to Australian television. As Tom O'Regan notes in his essay in Part One, both television and the study of television in Australia have been shaped by local political, social, and geographic factors, on the one hand, and the strong influence of both US and UK television cultures on the other. If the latter produced "close family resemblances" between Australian television and that imported from the US and the UK, the former made "Australian television subtly and distinctively different."

For two decades after the advent of broadcast television in Australia in 1956, imported programs and program forms "tended to define particular program categories" of Australian television, as O'Regan puts it (see Chapter 4). Because it was cheaper than producing such programming in Australia, commercial broadcasters imported the bulk of their dramatic programming from the US and the UK. If there was an "Australian" presence in Australian television of the 1950s, 1960s, and early 1970s it was, as Australian television scholar Albert Moran has argued, more to be found in the variety and quiz show genres than in drama or comedy.[12]

Australian television culture changed markedly after 1975, however. Color programming was introduced in 1976. Regulations that mandated minimum levels of "Australian" program content and gave a higher weighting to dramatic programming were also reaffirmed that year. Australian television experienced what Moran (1993) has called "cinematisation" in the late 1970s as the decline of the Australian film industry prompted film producers to develop projects for television, particularly mini-series, more than one hundred of which were produced in Australia in the ten years after 1978. The serial, or soap opera, a form that had been a part of Australian broadcasting since radio days, flourished in the late 1970s and 1980s. In the early 1980s television audiences in other parts of the English-speaking world began to become aware of Australian serials and mini-series for the first time, as the international marketing of Australian television began in earnest. In 1980, Australia began its extraordinary (certainly by US standards!) experiment in multi-lingual and multi-cultural television programming with the launch of SBS, the Special Broadcasting Services channel.

During what Moran (1993) has termed the "Golden Years" of Australian television drama (1976–86), television scholars, journalistic critics, and the public at large responded to what O'Regan (1991) has termed the "indigenisation" process, by which Australian television producers adapted, localized, and transformed what might have been imported television forms (the serial, the mini-series) into "Australian" television. In the process, Moran says, television became a "textually worthy object." Television scholarship moved away from attempts to measure the deleterious effects of television viewing to analyses of Australian-produced television forms and studies of the relationship between television culture and national identity.

As Graeme Turner has pointed out, the development of television studies in Australia in the 1970s and 1980s is also linked to changes in the tertiary education sector in Australia, particularly the establishment in the early 1970s of a new tier of post-secondary institutions (Colleges of Advanced Education). Designed to prepare students much more directly for the world of work than were research universities, these colleges also were fertile ground for the formation of interdisciplinary programs in the humanities and social sciences and for the introduction of subject areas (such as media studies and journalism) that were ignored or marginalized in more elite institutions.[13]

Much more so than in the US or the UK, television studies in Australia has been organized around issues of national identity and of the similarities and differences between indigenous and imported television. As O'Regan notes, Australia is a culturally-diverse, geographically dispersed, medium-sized Anglophone television market and culture, whose programming strategies, regulatory policies, critical agenda, and audience responses need to be situated in relation to the power and influence of non-Australian television—in this case that of the UK and the US.

Critical and academic discourse about television in Canada has been similarly shaped by that country's relation to another country's television institutions and programming. As Canadian television scholar Paul Attallah has pointed out, television viewing came to Canada before the first television program was broadcast *in* Canada. With most Canadians living close enough to the US border to receive television broadcasts from US stations, both the history of Canadian television and the development of television studies have been profoundly influenced by the presence of US television culture *within* Canada. Furthermore, one must speak of television culture*s* in Canada: a nation-wide English-language television culture serving some 22 million English-speakers, and a French-language television culture principally serving the French-speaking majority in Quebec. "Both groups," says Attallah, "are largely ignorant of each other's media."[14]

Richard Collins, whose essay on European public service broadcasting appears in the Institutions of Television section, has also written on the distinctive television cultures of Canada. He points out that the impact of television has been very different within francophone culture than within anglophone culture. In the former, intellectuals have perceived television as "an agency of national integration and unity," while in English-speaking Canada the availability and popularity of US programming makes television into "the pre-eminent threat to national integrity."[15]

So, getting back to my earlier question, how, exactly, are you defining television and television studies for the purposes of this reader?

We're arguing that the field of television studies began to take shape in the 1970s and early 1980s in the US, the UK, and elsewhere in the English-speaking academic world as the constellation of research and teaching arising from three main areas of investigation: television programming (including the organization of programs into genres, narrative and representational strategies, television's distinctive modes of address, advertisements, scheduling, etc.); the political economy of television; and the experience of watching, writing and talking about television. So, "television studies" as it is represented here does not attempt to encompass all of the ways in which television has been or might be studied or taught, although we did cast our net pretty widely: the previously-published essays reprinted here were chosen from among dozens of books and more than 3,000 journal articles in several hundred different journals published since 1995.

The Television Studies Reader showcases work produced within or informed by the now twenty-year tradition of teaching and research that we are calling television studies, which emerged in the 1970s and 1980s as described above. One of the terms that distinguishes this notion of television studies both from older traditions and from other ways television continues to be studied is "critical." Television studies produced within this broad paradigm regards television as a diverse, dynamic, and hence unstable set of technologies, businesses, and cultural and social practices. Television studies is reflexive about (and hence critical of) its own assumptions, methods, values, and goals. It aims to help viewers of television become more "critical" themselves, as they come to a better understanding of their relationship with television as a complex cultural and social phenomenon. Television studies is also "critical" in that it has raised questions about power and agency. Whose interests are served by television's use as an advertising medium? Who has access to television and for what purposes? Television studies is also self-critical. There is a great deal of debate *within* television studies over the field's object of study, the future both of television and television studies, and the relationship of television studies to other fields (particularly media studies, cultural studies, and cinema studies).

It looks like most of the essays in this collection were written within the past ten years. How do they differ from the earlier work in television studies you've outlined?

When it began to take shape in the 1970s and 1980s, television studies was organized in relation to a particular understanding of what its object of study was. That object "television" was in turn a product of the particular technological, institutional, economic, cultural, and social "state" of television *at that time* in those places where television studies was in formation. As we have seen the "state" of television varied considerably from nation to nation, and thus it was to some degree a different "object" of study for scholars working in the UK than for those working in Australia or the US. So although the following generalities hold better for some television cultures than for others, the object of television studies in the 1970s and 1980s tended to be imagined as including the following characteristics:

- Production and distribution of television programming lay in the hands of entities other than the viewer (production companies, broadcasting stations, networks, government agencies).
- There was assumed to be a relative scarcity of channels and programming and hence of viewing options
- Viewing opportunities were limited to and determined by the simultaneous over-air transmission of programming from an originating site to geographically dispersed individual TV sets.
- In some countries (the US in particular) television assumed the dominance of advertiser-driven, commercial entertainment broadcasting with each network seeking the largest possible fraction of the viewing audience at any given time.
- television involved the consequent unavoidability of commercial messages, whose "interruption" of television programs structured the viewing experience.
- In other countries, television meant either a national, public service broadcasting system or competing and limited public service and regulated commercial broadcast services, each expected to provide a wide array of programming of appeal to a relatively wide spectrum of tastes and interests.
- Experientially, television was understood to be a private (as opposed to public) and hence domestic medium.
- Television's normative viewing situation was assumed to be a single television set in the household watched by all members of the family.

But while this new generation of television scholars was busy organizing their own work and their new field around the presuppositions above in the early 1980s, however, another feature of television had to be added to the list:

- Constant, rapid, and unpredictable technological, institutional, and economic change.

There is not space here to outline all of the changes that together would transform "television" in the 1980s and 1990s and, in the process, change the kinds of work being done as television studies, but let me remind you of two. Again at the risk of really annoying non-US readers, I'll simplify this chronology by highlighting the effects of these changes upon US television culture—the culture from which I am watching and writing about TV.

Cable

Originally developed in the late 1940s as a way of delivering broadcast signals from a community antenna through cables to homes in areas too remote from television stations to receive a clear picture, cable television expanded into more and more urban US television markets in the 1960s and 1970s. Cable television continued to be adopted in some areas in order to receive high quality broadcasting signals. But following the FCC's approval of domestic communications satellites in 1973, cable's appeal was based upon more and different programming options not available via over-the-air broadcasting and provided to cable operators via what we would now call "B2B" (business-to-business) satellite transmission. In 1975 Home Box Office (HBO) became the first "television" programmer to deliver its product entirely by satellite—usually to local cable operators for routing to their subscribers.

Because programs carried by cable companies were distributed via satellite and delivered to customers by wires rather than over radio waves, cable operators were not subject to public service, advertising, or program content regulations imposed upon terrestrial broadcasters by the US Federal Communications Commission. The cable industry was further "de-regulated" by the Reagan administration in 1984. The 1980s saw an explosion in both the number and types of cable programming channels. Cable services attempted to attract audiences away from broadcast television by offering program content not allowed on broadcast television: nudity, strong language, etc.; by programming for particular audience segments: teenagers, women, children, African–Americans, evangelical Christians, Hispanics; and by carving out a niche in one particular content area: news, weather, sports, comedy, music, etc.

By 1990, the three commercial broadcast networks (ABC, NBC, CBS), which had dominated American television since its inception as a mass medium, were merely one set of players (albeit large, important players) in a much more diverse and dynamic media environment. Between 1984 and 1992, cable companies spent $15 billion in the US wiring communities for cable—the largest construction project in America since World War II. By 1990 more than half of all US households subscribed to cable, and the number of cable programming channels had increased from 28 in 1980 to 74. In April 2002, for the first time in US television history, Nielsen Media Research found that more television sets were tuned to a cable channel during the "prime-time" hours (8–11 p.m.) than to broadcast television. And in September of that year, the season debut of the HBO series *The Sopranos* marked the first time that a program distributed only via "premium" cable (cable programming services that are paid for separately and in addition to basic cable channels) drew higher ratings than any broadcast network during the same time period—even though fewer than one-third of all television households subscribe to HBO.[16]

For a variety of reasons (government regulation, the cost of laying cable, availability of good quality over-the-air broadcasting signals, competition from Direct To Home (DTH) satellite services, etc.), cable has not had the same impact on television in the UK, continental Europe, or Australia. However, the combined penetration of cable and satellite services into these parts of the world has greatly expanded the number and range of channels delivered into millions of homes and, as a result, the experience of television is also vastly different for the generation of viewers born since 1980 than for those of us who only knew television as terrestrial broadcast television throughout most of our lives.

For those television scholars and teachers interested in the analysis of television programs, cable provoked a reconceptualization of the "texts" of television. For example, the television dramas and situation comedies of the 1960s or 1970s certainly represented textual differences from the autonomous texts of the novel or the Hollywood film, but single episodes of *Cheers* or *L.A. Law* were identifiable and critically graspable as texts—even if they referenced events from prior episodes or left narrative questions unresolved. New cable services, however, did not necessarily organize their output as discrete "programs." Cable News Network (CNN), for example, ran non-stop newscasts, which both recycled material from earlier in the day and updated this material as the day went on. How was the analyst to delimit a part of this "flow" and constitute it as a text to be studied? Network broadcast programming carefully delineated program content and advertising. On some cable services that emerged in the 1980s however, (Home Shopping Network, QVC) the advertisement *was* the program.

This critical quandary also reflected changes in the way that television was being "read" by viewers. The innovation of the remote control as the mediator between the viewer and a growing array of simultaneously available program options (thirty or forty-channel cable systems were common in American cities by 1990) encouraged viewers to "watch" more than one program during the same time period and to organize their viewing experience in terms of scans of the remote control channel selector rather than programs.

Video cassette recorder

The video tape player/recorder (VCR) had been introduced in the US, the UK, Canada, and Australia as a consumer product in the late 1970s, but it did not move out of the technological novelty phase until the early 1980s. Between 1984 and 1987, however, reductions in equipment prices, the emergence of a dominant technical system (VHS), resolution of the legal status of off-air taping in the US (it's ok to do so), and expansion of VCR features (longer tape capacity in particular), combined with greater availability of feature films on video tape for sale and rental, produced a tidal wave of consumer interest. In less than forty-eight months, the VCR went from being an expensive toy owned mainly by technophiles to sitting atop or beside TV sets in most households in all four countries. By 1990, the percentage of households with VCRs ranged from 70-75 percent in the US and Australia to 40-60 percent in the UK and Canada. Estimates of VCR penetration worldwide were as high as 31 percent, or 206 million video households.

In the 1980s the VCR became part of the experience of television in different ways in different countries. In the US, a media environment with a wide and expanding range of broadcast and cable television viewing options, the VCR represented a relatively inexpensive adjunct to existing television services (time-shifting, zipping through commercials, recording and archiving favorite programs) and, with the development of video rental and sales markets, an alternative legal mode of film viewing. Rapid VCR penetration in the US actually helped to push cable penetration and vice versa: more channels to view also meant more programs to tape. It should also be noted that the VCR became the primary vehicle in the US for legally distributing hardcore pornographic films in the 1980s: as the number of "adult" movie theaters plummeted, the number of XXX films produced in the US more than quadrupled. The availability of XXX videos at video rental outlets helped to drive VCR purchases and kept many video rental stores profitable between 1977 and 1984 while mainstream Hollywood studios made up their minds whether or not to embrace this new technology.[17]

In countries with limited terrestrial broadcast viewing options and/or tight government regulation and control of broadcasting, the VCR became a way of expanding the range and number of viewing possibilities—some legal, some illegal. As Tom O'Regan noted as early as 1991, "The inauguration of the VCR also marked the virtual end of central political control over information flows and cultural production in many developing and Eastern bloc countries." The VCR made possible a form of low-tech "pay-TV" that was difficult if not impossible to police by government authorities. The VCR also helped to create a huge market for illegally duplicated commercial films. In 1985, the circulation of pirated video copies of theatrical films made up nearly 100 percent of the video market in Brazil, Colombia, Mexico, and Taiwan.[18]

There is not space here to explore the impact of the VCR on all countries around the world, but it is certainly safe to say that in many countries the VCR not only altered what people watched on their television sets but it also changed how people watched. The combination of "time-shifting" (taping a television program for later viewing) and the remote control meant that programming was no longer viewed in the way it was "meant" to be seen by program producers and distributors. The commercial availability of prerecorded tapes for rental and sale (whether legal or illegal, proscribed on ideological, religious, or intellectual property grounds) along with the recording and swapping of tapes (within families and neighborhoods or across national boundaries) set up a new media distribution channel that circumvented the control of broadcasters and government regulators. New terms had to be devised to describe the new ways people interacted with their television sets: "channel surfing" (jumping quickly from one of dozens of channels to another), "grazing," (sampling bits of programming across channels rather than watching any one program from start to finish). Viewers could "zap" out advertisements and "zip" through portions of a program they wished to skip past.

In the late 1980s, Hollywood began to acknowledge the potential of videotape technology to provide an alternative distribution channel for feature films. By 1990 there were more than 25,000 video rental outlets in the US, taking in more than $8 billion per year. In 1992, retailers sold more than 260 million copies of Hollywood films on videotape, taking in more than the US movie box office. Today a majority of US households own a feature film on videotape, and the average family's tape library includes more than 50 titles. Worldwide, more than one billion prerecorded videotapes are sold each year.

At the beginning of the 1990s, with VCRs in 62 million households and cable television in a majority of homes, the network broadcast television era effectively comes to an end in the US. Although the commercial broadcasting networks among them would continue to garner a majority of viewers throughout the 1990s, they would have to compete with a growing array of non-broadcast programming options. For thirty years, from 1950 until 1980, ABC, NBC, and CBS routinely captured more than 90 percent of the available viewing audience on any given night. By 1993, one third of viewers were watching one of the other thirty channels available on the average home's TV set, and MTV was claiming a US audience of 46 million and a worldwide audience of 77 million regular viewers. By 2000 broadcast network audience share had fallen to 45 percent.

In the mid-1990s the development of pizza-pan-sized receiving dishes made Direct Broadcast Satellite (DBS) services competitive with cable television in the US—providing yet another non-broadcast distribution system for television programming and further expanding the number of channels that could be carried into the home television set. In only eight years (1994–2002), the number of DBS subscribers in the US increased from 70,000 to more than 18 million (about 17 percent of households), and the worldwide audience for DTH (Direct to Home) satellite services is estimated to be more than 80 million.

Any comprehensive discussion of the impact of the VCR and cable on television culture would also need to factor in the "deregulation" of European (and other) broadcasting systems in the 1980s and 1990s, which resulted in the proliferation of broadcast and non-broadcast television channels and programming options. At the end of 2000, there were 36 million DBS subscribers and 240 million cable subscribers worldwide. For some people in some countries, television continues to mean over-the-air broadcasting of a small number of channels. But for hundreds of millions of others, particularly in Europe, the Antipodes, and North America, any definition of television would have to include these features:

- multiple and proliferating channels
- multiple transmission systems (over-the-air, cable, satellite)
- multiple simultaneous viewing options, negotiated through a remote control device
- recording of programs off-air for replay at a later time
- playback of prerecorded material through the television set
- niche or "narrowcast" channels appealing to particular demographic, language, or interest groups
- increased availability of imported programming
- multiple television business models: advertiser-supported, subscription, pay-per-view, rental/ purchase of pre-recorded material, government financed, advertising *as* programming (home shopping channels)
- multiple television sets in the home
- use of the television set for playing video games
- home production of video via camcorders
- streaming of video via broadband internet
- viewing television outside the home (sports bars, waiting rooms, etc.)
- use of video for public surveillance

And to this list we would, again, have to add:

- constant, rapid, and unpredictable technological, institutional, and economic change.

For example, arguably, the VCR era came to an end in 2001, when for the first time sales of films on DVD exceeded those on videotape. Adoption of DVD technology in the late 1990s occurred at an even faster pace than did adoption of VCR technology in the 1980s: between 1997 and 2002, more than 30 million US households purchased DVD players. Increasingly, home computers come equipped with DVD drives, which makes the desktop monitor or laptop screen a functioning video display. Rental of DVDs in the first six months of 2002 increased 116 percent over the same period in 2001. As the *New York Times* put it, most television industry prognosticators believe the VCR will "go the way of the vinyl disk and the dodo bird."[19] Readers in Asia will be saying, "What took you so long?" By 1997 VCR technology already had been supplanted by the CD-based video compact disc (VCD) in China and other countries in the region. Initially marketed for use in karaoke clubs, there are now more than 25 million VCD players in China (it is the most requested wedding present) but only 20 million VCRs.[20] Street vendors and VCD shops offer a wide range of films, including (pirated) copies of Hollywood films not yet out of theatrical release.

Furthermore, although the overall penetration levels are still tiny, digital personal video recorders (PVR) are also supplanting tape-based video recording and playback systems. Storing programming digitally on computer hard drives and linked to cable or satellite program guides, PVRs make it possible to effortlessly record and store up to one hundred hours of programming *and* to easily skip over commercials. Some industry analysts predict that taken together the various modes of "on-demand television" will reach the magic penetration level of 50 percent of all households in the US by 2007 and will provoke a crisis for advertiser-based broadcasting and cable services.[21]

You seem to be saying that (1) what television is depends on where you are; (2) what television "was" when you wrote this is likely to be different from what television "is" by the time I read it; and (3) television studies will always be trying to track down and catch up with its object of study, but it will always be outrun.

I couldn't have put it better myself.

Then if you can't come up with a concise, stable, and universally-applicable definition of television and television studies, where do you suggest I start?

Wherever you are. Start with where you find television in your own life. Make a list of all the things, experiences, knowledge, institutions, phenomena the terms "television" and "television studies" would have to encompass to be comprehensive and usable for your purposes.

You go first.

All right. At this particular time my definition of television would have to include:

- a recently purchased PVR (personal video recorder) with a 40 gig hard drive, which my wife and I regard as the greatest invention of the twentieth century (excepting, perhaps, the heart-lung machine)
- more channels of satellite TV than we can count or watch
- eight remote control devices scattered about the house
- two drawers full of films on videos in our eight-year-old daughter's playroom
- another cabinet full of TV programs on videotape, including 34 episodes of *Mystery Science Theater 3000*
- four operational TV sets, four operational US-format VCRs, one combination VCR/DVD player, one multiformat VCR in our house
- five soon-to-be-obsolete analog camcorder cassettes of home videos, most of our daughter, and the camcorder they were recorded on (which I will sell you for $25 — the camcorder, not the videos)
- a combination TV/VCR that my daughter watches in the back of our minivan when we drive to visit grandparents
- roughly 150 videos stacked in my office, which I use in teaching film and television
- something I write and teach about
- several shelves worth of books about television
- seeing myself on the TV monitor erected atop the entrance of the supermarket we shop at with a sign below it that reads: "CCTV cameras are in use to assure the safety and security of our customers and associates."
- reading about television
- talking about television
- watching *Friends* in a hotel room in Beijing and realizing that the only place I can see *Friends* in China is in a hotel catering to foreigners

- occasionally watching streaming video on my laptop computer and getting tired of doing so real fast
- participating in an internet chat room discussion of recent plot developments in *Guiding Light* (a US daytime soap opera)
- memories of television: not just memories of programs but where and who I was when I saw them, and when and how I watched them. Example: watching the sitcom *Pete and Gladys* with my two sisters on a January evening in 1960 when I was nine years old and my mother coming home from the hospital to tell us our father was dead.
- flicking on the TV set at 11:35 a.m. on January 26, 1986 while I was making a peanut butter and jelly sandwich in my kitchen and watching the Challenger space craft explode at 11:39
- appearing on television a few times
- my daughter's playroom full of plush toys, computer games, board games, and lunchboxes, all of which reference television programs or movies she first saw on videotape
- my Alzheimer's-afflicted stepfather watching the same TV channel for sixteen hours every day

I think I get the idea. Once I've made such a list for myself, then what?

Ironically, the ubiquity of television and its insinuation into so many aspects of our daily lives in so many ways makes "television" almost invisible to many of us and thus makes it difficult to identify as a distinct object of reflection and inquiry. (Can you list every encounter you've had with some form of television over the last twenty-four hours? The last week?) Because it seems to be unproblematically and unremarkably everywhere, it usually doesn't register very much as a separate and distinct phenomenon. Except, of course, when it registers so emphatically that for some minutes or hours it fills our perceptual field, our consciousness, our social lives—as it did for many people on September 11, 2001. Thinking seriously about television: understanding the implications of its presence in our lives, sorting through the multiple and proliferating modes of television, connecting our experience of television with that of people in the same room or in other countries—requires that we make television's presence in our lives visible.

In the 1930s German sociologist Alfred Schutz (1962) suggested that in order to understand social interactions with other people, we first had make "strange" those things that we most take for granted. The essays in this book will encourage you to make television and your relationship with it visible, strange, and, as a result, "remarkable." Reading these essays will also encourage you to think about what, if anything, is central to your experience of television as well as where the borders of television can be seen—those places where television seems to morph into some other realm of experience: cinema, the internet, gaming, software, etc. Or you may be persuaded that this experiential, institutional, technological, aesthetic hybridity *is* constitutive of television today.

What were your goals for this reader?

Our goals in putting together this reader were to:

- Present contemporary work on a wide range of television modes and experiences—from watching broadcast television in the home and renting videos to the use of television in public spaces and intersection of television and other media.
- Present contemporary work that reflects the multidimensional and dynamic nature of television—television as a changing cluster of technologies; complex institutional relationships;

"geographies" of production, circulation, and viewing; set of formal capacities; representational instrument; and aspect of everyday life;

- Present work that speaks to the dynamic nature of television and, in particular, changes that have occurred since 1990.
- Foreground work on television that reflects the intranational, national, regional, transnational, and international character of television in the anglophone world at the beginning of the twenty-first century.
- Produce a volume that would be especially useful as a resource for teaching but that would also acquaint students and scholars from other fields with the scope and diversity of contemporary television studies.
- Speak to a diverse readership by not assuming their familiarity with particular instances of television programming.

Does this last goal mean that you excluded from consideration essays that did presume the reader's knowledge of particular programs or that were extended analyses of a small group of programs?

Yes. Some students and teachers of television will find the absence of extended textual analyses to be a rather glaring omission from a book that presumes to call itself *The Television Studies Reader*. Looking closely and systematically at a particular documentary, advertisement, music video, newscast, cartoon, dramatic program, or the multiple episodes that make up a television series or serial can be very useful in illuminating their stylistic particularities, means of addressing the viewer, deployment of generic conventions, modes of storytelling or documentation, and representation of social groups or current issues in the culture at large, among other things. Such work also shows how theories and methods derived from the analysis of other kinds of texts (films, live performance, novels, discourse) can be brought to bear upon television.

Even at the risk of omitting some very imaginative, and for some teachers, pedagogically useful critical essays, we decided not to include extended textual analyses for several reasons. We did not want to use essays whose value was limited to only those readers who were familiar with the program/s under analysis. The popularity of a program or series in one country does not at all guarantee even its availability in another.

There is also the problem of access to particular television programs for teaching purposes, even within the country where it enjoyed high ratings—a problem that is exacerbated in countries beyond that of the program's initial production and reception. When I teach a course on contemporary American cinema, questions of student access to particular films rarely enter into the decision as to which films to include on the syllabus or which critical essays to assign. The predictable, systematic, and convenient availability of almost any Hollywood film on video, DVD or both within six months of its theatrical release and for an indefinite period on the video store shelves, at internet retailers, or in the university library means that by the time I assign particular analyses or discuss particular films in class every student at least will have had the opportunity to view the film in question multiple times. Although increasingly US television program-rights owners are turning to videotape and DVD as avenues for marketing programs after or during their distribution on broadcast, cable, or satellite TV, there is not nearly the comprehensive, inexpensive (and legal) availability of TV programming on tape even in a market as large as that in the US than is the case with mainstream cinema.

But there are what we might call substantive as well as logistical reasons for encouraging you to find critical analyses of particular programs outside the pages of this reader and/or to undertake your own. Despite the influence of cinema studies on television studies, the academic study of television has been much less focused on the analysis of particular texts (television programs) than has the study of films. In large part, this has been because determining what the "texts" of television are is much more difficult. Ironically, although the video and DVD revolutions have now greatly complicated the normative model of both cinematic textuality and reception, most film studies courses and textbooks continue to assume that feature films are autonomous texts and isolatable viewing experiences. You pay your money at the box office to see a particular screening of a particular film and once the film's closing credits run, that text and the experience of viewing it are over.[22] Very different models of textuality characterize television programming and very different reception situations apply. What constitutes the "text" of an episodic TV series such as *Friends*? One episode? One season? All the episodes ever broadcast? How could you possibly say you had "read" the entire text of TV serials such as *Guiding Light* or *Coronation Street*, when the former has been broadcast almost every weekday since 1952 and the latter every week since 1960? Are the advertisements and network announcements that precede, interrupt, and immediately follow programs shown on commercial television a part of the "text" of those shows? What about the banners that sometimes run at the bottom of the screen while the program is displayed, announcing upcoming programs, news headlines, or links to internet sites? What about "picture-in-picture" features on digital TV sets that allow two programs to be watched at once? If television ever was organized around the continuous, rapt viewing of individual, semi-autonomous programs, that era ended twenty years ago with the innovation of the infrared remote control. Today, program makers and distributors must assume that many viewers watch TV with the remote in their hands and that channel "surfing" or "grazing" among dozens and dozens of simultaneously available viewing options is as much or more the norm than continuous, attentive viewing of a single program.

The more that television programs are made to resemble the autonomous and intently viewed texts of theatrical cinema (editing out or zipping through advertisements, extracting a given program from the scheduling "flow" in which its transmission was initially embedded, etc.), the more that one of the defining features of television texts and viewing is suppressed: what we might call their situatedness. Although the personal video recorder increasingly allows for television viewing to be removed from the flow of scheduled program distribution, for most people television programming is still situated within a chronological flow of programming.

Each program is also situated in the matrix of simultaneous viewing possibilities that can be activated by use of the remote control. Although I have seen plenty of twelve-year-old boys watching movies in this way, it is still the case that most adult megaplex moviegoers don't dash from one screening room to another over a two-hour span. But the family's experience of watching a melodrama or game show is definitely colored by dad's insistence upon switching over to the cricket match or football game during commercials. Which raises another way in which television programming is situated: the television set is usually situated in a social environment that exists for some purpose other than or in addition to watching television. It is situated within particular spaces of the home, each of which provides a different social and physical setting for television viewing: the sitting room, family room, kitchen, bedroom, child's playroom, and (since 1984) the "media room." Furthermore, as several of the essays discuss, outside the domestic realm, television sets are situated in bars, waiting rooms, airport lounges, department stores, and dozens of other spaces.

The meaning of any television program is also shaped by its position (its situatedness) within television schedules and within discourses about television. For example, during the 2002–3 broadcast season in the US, any account of the meanings and pleasures associated with watching the political drama *The West Wing* would have to include the ideological and personal contrasts between the presidential character of Jed Bartlett and the occupant of the "real" White House, the popular and critical success of the show as an instance of American commercial network *broadcast* programming (as distinct from cable), and its position within the NBC schedule (anchoring the Wednesday night prime-time lineup and scheduled in tandem with NBC's equally popular and critically-acclaimed *Law and Order*).

When *The West Wing* was shown in the UK and Australia, however, its situational frames were necessarily different. It was, first of all, a US import. Comparisons were made to other highly-touted US series shown in Australia and the UK. *The Sopranos* and *The West Wing* were frequently discussed together by critics as examples of "quality" US television programming, despite the fact that the former is a product of the very different and competing programming environment of US cable television. Although viewers in Australia and the UK receive far more information about American political institutions and processes than US viewers do about any other country, viewers outside the US could not be expected to "get" all the jokes, political references, and allusions to actual political figures and forces writer/producer Aaron Sorkin wove throughout the series' intricate scripts. In Australia, *The West Wing* was shown on commercial Channel 9, while in the UK it was carried on the advertising-supported, alternative public service venue, Channel 4. Both networks initially scheduled the program in the late evening, which virtually guaranteed that it would not have a huge audience. And, perhaps as a result of this initial scheduling decision, *The West Wing* became what critics called a "cult hit" but not a popular hit in both countries: a show eagerly watched and discussed by a small but devoted audience. It was, as one British critic put it, "more talked about than watched."

The West Wing is by no means unique: the meanings and pleasures to be derived from every program are dependent to some degree upon the "place" the show occupies in the lives of viewers, in the apparatus of television scheduling and marketing, and in the discourses about television. Cinema studies might still be able to assume (although I would challenge this) that for analytical and interpretive purposes, viewing *Titanic* at a theater in Sydney is not consequentially different than viewing it at a theater in Durham, North Carolina, or Durham, England. But it is much harder to ignore the myriad local situational factors that are constitutive of the experience of television.

Why aren't there essays on the history of television? Isn't television history a part of television studies?

This was a tough decision for someone (me) who sometimes masquerades as a cultural historian. We left out historical work on television because we felt its questions and approaches were sufficiently distinct to merit it being the subject of another reader. Also writing on television history has, for the most part, tended to focus on the development of television within a particular nation and to assume that the reader was familiar with the particular set of government policies, corporations, programs, and individuals that constituted the subject matter for that history.

Some of the essays in this book deal with television cultures pretty far removed from my own experience of TV. How are they relevant to my attempt to understand television in my own country?

It is not our attempt here to "cover" the experience of television around the world. With a few exceptions, the essays presented here deal with television as it is known and experienced in North America, the UK and Australia. And, for the most part, the essays are written by scholars who work in these parts of the world. The choice of articles also reflects the experience and biases of the reader's editors, one of whom (take a wild guess which) works in the US, the other in the UK. Similarly, we have selected and organized these essays in relation to the way that television studies is taught in North American, British, and Australian universities.

We hope the essays in this book, taken altogether, will support two complementary strategies for the study of television. Some of the essays will be resources for examining, "making strange," and reflecting upon your own experience of television. They might reveal dimensions of the "television" that you are familiar with but might not have thought very much about: television as a tourist destination, non-broadcast modes of television, television in public spaces, or the regulation of television as a public utility, to give but a few examples. "How," you might ask, "is the television I know situated within my own culture, within my own life, and in relation to other economic and social institutions?" "How are particular instances of television situated with programming schedules, the routines of everyday life, discourses about television?"

Other essays will encourage you to think about the relationship between the television you know and its situation within your own environment, on the one hand, and, on the other hand, television as it is experienced by other people in different environments. Again, we have not attempted to present a comprehensive survey of national television cultures around the world, or even in the English-speaking world. We did, however, want to include essays that highlight the particularity of television in different countries and for different social groups within national television cultures. For example, Brian Larkin's essay on Nigerian video films (See Chapter 23) calls our attention to a use of television technology and institutions (high quality, relatively inexpensive video production equipment; the video cassette as a relatively inexpensive mode of product duplication; retail video rental and sales as a means of marketing a regional or national product that is alternative to the film business and that circumvents control by broadcasters or government regulators; the VCR and television set as widely available technologies of presentation) that has become an important cultural force in Nigeria but that is relatively unknown elsewhere. His essay asks "How did this technology—widely available in other countries—come to be deployed in this particular way in this particular national culture?" And his essay prompts the non-Nigerian reader to ask, "Are there parallels between the Nigerian video film phenomenon and the use of VCR technology in my own country?"

It is worth underscoring the fact that US students reading this book are themselves situated within a large, diverse, but paradoxically insular television culture. Furthermore, as several of the essays in this collection will discuss, some national television cultures are more permeable than others. For example, I agree with Tom O'Regan's claim (see Chapter 4) in his essay that, for the English speaker, Australia is a "good place to watch television." In addition to locally-produced fare, Australia's government-supported channel and three commercial networks all run imported programming from other English-language countries: principally the US, Britain, and Canada. Also, since 1980 Australia's Special Broadcasting Service (SBS) Television channel has operated under a mandate to serve Australia's increasingly multiethnic population and to broadcast non-English-language programming from around the world. Australian broadcast television makes available a greater variety of foreign television programming than any other national television system in the world.

In the US, on the other hand, program diversity comes as a result of the expansion of channel capacity through cable and satellite delivery services. But despite the fact that US cable and satellite services now routinely offer 100 or more channels, and despite the fact that the US has been a multiethnic society for much longer, US television culture is much more insular and closed to foreign-produced programming than is the terrestrial broadcasting sector in Australia—a country with less than one-tenth its population! To be sure, there are pockets of imported program availability: an increasing number of Spanish-language services available on cable and satellite services, some non-English-language broadcasting in large, multi-ethnic cities, and Hong Kong, Bollywood and Latin American videos on the shelves of Asian markets and *tiendas* around the country. But I would be hard pressed to find a single non-English-language television program shown dubbed or subtitled on my 150-channel satellite service tonight, and, except for the British drama and comedy that has been a part of the schedule on US public television for the past twenty-five years or so and on cable channels more recently (A&E, for example), it is hard to think of a single imported program that has made it onto the schedules of primetime commercial network television in the US. One consequence, as O'Regan notes, is that Australian television viewers tend to judge locally-produced programs in relation to their US and British generic counterparts, whereas American viewers tend to know only other domestic programs. Television in the US "*means* US-produced television."

The familiar, "American" face of television shown to US viewers hides its involvement in a complex international television culture—an involvement that television viewers in many other countries are all too aware of, but that remains largely "invisible" to Americans until and unless they experience the television culture of another country. Producing for one of the largest and certainly the richest television market in the world, US program makers have long enjoyed the competitive advantage of being able to recoup the costs of expensively-produced shows in the US market and then to sell these shows in other countries for far less than it would cost to produce similar programming locally. Scott Olson's essay on the "narrative transparency" of Hollywood film and television forms and Timothy Haven's essay on the international marketing of *The Cosby Show* explore different dimensions of this phenomenon. US television viewers are also probably unaware of the international origins of some of their favorite programs. *Big Brother*, for example, originated in Holland, and what US viewers see is one of more than twenty different national versions. Albert Moran's essay (Chapter 16) describes the mechanisms by which television program formats such as *Big Brother, Survivor, Who Wants to Be a Millionaire,* and *Funniest Home Videos* are devised, circulated, and adapted. Jane Roscoe (Chapter 19) discusses how *Big Brother* was "localized" in Australia.

Will some of these essays contain terms I'm not familiar with?

Yes.

Will I need to read some of these essays more than once?

Yes. Most of the essays in this reader were originally published as articles in scholarly journals or chapters in academic books. Thus, some of them assume that their audiences have a general familiarity with television studies, its terminology, and its literature that the reader of this anthology might not (as yet) possess. Part introductions will provide you with an overview of some of the issues and questions that link the individual essays in each section and connect pieces in one section with essays elsewhere in the book. In most cases the meaning of specialized terms becomes apparent in context. Although the overall level of accessibility varies from essay to essay, we have left out work that we feel is too specialized or overly weighted down by theoretical jargon. However, some of these essays will benefit from two readings: before and after you have discussed the essay in class.

What kinds of editorial changes were made to the essays?

We've tried to assure that each previously published essay retains its integrity as a piece of scholarship. In the interest of including as many different essays as possible, we have shortened some essays from their original length. Wherever we've done this, we've indicated the excision by ellipsis points [. . .]. Full citations for the originally-published version of each essay are indicated in the Acknowledgements. In essays that were originally published as book chapters, we have eliminated references to other chapters of that book (ie: "As I discussed in Chapter 7 . . ."). We have also eliminated illustrations that accompanied the texts in their original versions, and have tried to keep editorial interjections to a minimum. They are set apart from the author's original text by the use of brackets: [ ].

The essays are organized into thematic sections or parts. Did you try to find essays to fill the sections or did you choose the essays first and then try to organize them into groups?

For the most part, we chose the essays first according to the criteria listed above and then arranged them into groups. As the logics of the various parts emerged, however, we sometimes felt the need to commission an essay from a scholar particularly well-positioned to write about the issues and questions addressed in that corner of the field of television studies.

Is there more than one way the essays might be arranged into parts?

Yes. This means that an essay in one Part might well take up issues that are also dealt with by an article in another Part. Television studies is such a young field that rigid subdivisional lines have not emerged. Television studies honors the complexity and multi-dimensional nature of the television experience. As a result, an essay on the role of television viewing in everyday life, for example, might well raise issues of gender, race, sexuality, age, scheduling, address, or other features of television. Our hope is that you will put each essay into conversation with the other essays with which it is grouped, and that you will discover ways of broadening that conversation to include concepts, ideas, and insights from essays in the other parts as well.

Suggested final examination essay topic: Create an alternative scheme for organizing the essays in *The Television Studies Reader* and arrange the essays into a new table of contents. Write Part introductions reflecting your own rationale.

Notes

1   Charlotte Brunsdon, "What Is the 'Television' of Television Studies?" *The Television Studies Book* Christine Geraghty and David Lusted (eds), (London: Edward Arnold, 1998), pp. 95–113; Lynn Spigel, "Television Studies for 'Mature' Audiences," *International Journal of Cultural Studies* 3:3 (2000): 407–20.

2   John Corner, *Critical Ideas in Television Studies* (Oxford: Oxford University Press, 1999), p. 4.

3   Charles K. Atkin, John P. Murray, and Oguz B. Nayman, "The Surgeon General's Research Program on Television and Social Behavior: A Review of Empirical Findings," *Journal of Broadcasting* 16:1 (Winter 1971–72): 21–35.

4   Horace Newcomb, "American Television Criticism: 1970–1985," *Critical Studies in Mass Communication* 3: 2 (1986): 217–28.

5   Ernst van den Haag, "Of Happiness and of Despair We Have No Measure," and Dwight MacDonald, "A Theory of Mass Culture," both in *Mass Media and Mass Man*, Alan Casty (ed.) (New York: Holt, Rinehart and Winston, 1968), pp. 5–11, 12–23, respectively. Even the publishers of this anthology weren't quite sure to which field it belonged. The back cover of my paperback copy has "English" printed at the top to guide the befuddled bookseller as to where to shelve it. Obviously, there was no "television studies" section of bookstores in 1968.

6   Lynn Spigel, "The Making of a TV Literate Elite," in *The Television Studies Book*, Christine Geraghty and
     David Lusted, eds, (London: Edward Arnold, 1998), pp. 63–85.
7   To confirm my memory of the extent of what was called "administrative" research, I went back to the issues
     of the *Journal of Broadcasting* that appeared around the time I was entering graduate school. The Winter
     1972–73 issue contained a study of "The Repeat Audience for Movies on TV," which was called by the
     editors "An excellent example of cross-disciplinary research . . . in which an economist makes some research-
     supported suggestions on scheduling of motion pictures seen on television so that audiences for re-runs may
     be maximized." Ryland A. Taylor, "The Repeat Audience for Movies on TV," *Journal of Broadcasting* 17: 1
     (Winter 1972–3): 95–100.
8   Brunsdon, p. 96.
9   John Hartley, "Housing Television: Textual Traditions in TV and Cultural Studies," in *The Television Studies
     Book*, Christine Geraghty and David Lusted, (eds), (London: Edward Arnold, 1998), pp. 33–50; Brunsdon, p.
     96.
10   On the role of the love/hate relationship between cinema studies and television studies in the emergence of
     television studies in the 1970s see John Caughie, "Television Criticism: A Discourse in Search of an Object,"
     Screen 25:4 (July 1984): 109–21; and John Fiske, "Television and Popular Culture: Reflections on British
     and Australian Critical Practice," *Critical Studies in Mass Communication* 3: 2 (1986): 200–16. Fiske sites
     as a key "sign both of the growing status of television criticism and of its dependence on film theory" the
     1976 special issue of the influential film journal *Screen* on the British crime drama, *The Sweeney*.
11   Caughie, p. 115; Fiske, p. 202.
12   Albert Moran, *Moran's Guide to Australian TV Series* (Sydney: Australian Film Television and Radio School,
     1993), p. 13.
13   Graeme Turner, "Studying Television," in *The Australian TV Book*, Graeme Turner and Stuart Cunningham,
     (eds), (Sydney: Allen and Unwin, 2000), pp. 3–12.
14   Paul Attallah, "Canadian Television Exports: Into the Mainstream," in *Peripheral Vision: Patterns in
     Global Television*, John Sinclair, Elizabeth Jacka, and Stuart Cunningham, (eds), (Oxford: Oxford University
     Press, 1996, pp. 161–91.
15   Richard Collins, *Culture, Communication, and National Identity: the Case of Canadian Television* (Toronto:
     University of Toronto Press, 1990), p. 197.
16   Jim Rutenberg, "Cable Thrives, But Broadcast TV Is Hardly Extinct," *New York Times*, September 23,
     2002, p. C1,6.
17   Michael J. Tucker, "Testing the VHS argument: how pivotal is porn in developing the market for CD-ROM?"
     CD-ROM Professional, November 1995 , p. 64.
18   Tom O'Regan, "From Piracy to Sovereignty: International VCR Trends," *Continuum: The Australian Jour-
     nal of Media & Culture* 4: 2 (1991).
19   Rick Lyman, "Revolt in the Den: DVD Sends the VCR Packing to the Attic," *New York Times*, August 26,
     2002, p. A1.
20   http://www.screendigest.com/yp_97–11.htm
21   Brian Morrissey, "The TiVo Effect: Advertisers See Less TV Ad Spending," *Internet Advertising Report*,
     November 25, 2002.
22   I must underscore my own belief that such a model of movie texts and movie reception is not particularly
     useful and does not take into account the way that most films are experienced today.

Bibliography

Atkin, C. K., Murray, J. P. and Nayman, O. B. (1971) "The Surgeon General's Research Program on Television and
     Social Behavior: A Review of Empirical Findings," *Journal of Broadcasting* 16: 1 (Winter 1971–72): 21–35.
Attallah, P. (1996) "Canadian Television Exports: Into the Mainstream," in John Sinclair, Elizabeth Jacka, and
     Stuart Cunningham (eds) *Peripheral Vision: Patterns in Global Television*, Oxford: Oxford University Press:
     161–91.
Brunsdon, C. (1998) "What Is the 'Television' of Television Studies?," in *The Television Studies Book*, Christine
     Geraghty and David Lusted (eds), London: Edward Arnold: 95–113.
Caughie, J. (1984) "Television Criticism: A Discourse in Search of an Object," *Screen* 25: 4 (July 1984): 109–21.
Collins, R. (1990) *Culture, Communication, and National Identity: the Case of Canadian Television*, Toronto:
     University of Toronto Press.
Corner, J. (1999) *Critical Ideas in Television Studies*, Oxford: Oxford University Press.

Fiske, J. (1986) "Television and Popular Culture: Reflections on British and Australian Critical Practice," *Critical Studies in Mass Communication* 3: 2 (1986): 200–216.

Hartley, J. (1998) "Housing Television: Textual Traditions in TV and Cultural Studies," in *The Television Studies Book* Christine Geraghty and David Lusted (eds), London: Edward Arnold: 33–50.

Lyman, R. (2002) "Revolt in the Den: DVD Sends the VCR Packing to the Attic," *New York Times*, August 26, 2002: A1.

MacDonald, D. (1968) "A Theory of Mass Culture," in Alan Casty (ed.) *Mass Media and Mass Man*, New York: Holt, Rinehart and Winston: 12–23.

Moran, A. (1993) *Moran's Guide to Australian TV Series*, Sydney: Australian Film Television and Radio School.

Morrissey, B. (2002) "The TiVo Effect: Advertisers See Less TV Ad Spending," *Internet Advertising Report*, November 25, 2002.

Newcomb, H. (1986) "American Television Criticism: 1970–1985," *Critical Studies in Mass Communication* 3: 2: 217–28.

O'Regan, T. (1991) "From Piracy to Sovereignty: International VCR Trends," *Continuum: The Australian Journal of Media and Culture* 4: 2.

Rutenberg, J. (2002) "Cable Thrives, But Broadcast TV Is Hardly Extinct," *New York Times*, September 23, 2002: C1,6.

Schutz, A. (1962) "The Stranger: An Essay in Social Psychology," in *Collected Papers*, The Hague: Martinus Nijhoff 2: 91–105.

Shayon, R. (1962) The Eighth Art, New York: Holt, Rinehart, and Winston.

Spigel, L. (2000) "Television Studies for 'Mature' Audiences," in *International Journal of Cultural Studies* 3: 3: 407–20.

Spigel, L. (1998) "The Making of a TV Literate Elite," in Christine Geraghty and David Lusted (eds), *The Television Studies Book*, London: Edward Arnold: 63–85.

Taylor, R. A. (1972) "The Repeat Audience for Movies on TV," *Journal of Broadcasting* 17: 1 (Winter 1972–73): 95–100.

Tucker, Michael J. (1995) "Testing the VHS argument: how pivotal is porn in developing the market for CD-ROM?" *CD-ROM Professional*, November 1995: 64.

Turner, G. (1996) "Studying Television," in Graeme Turner and Stuart Cunningham (eds) *The Australian TV Book*, Sydney: Allen and Unwin: 3–12.

van den Haag, E. (1968) "Of Happiness and of Despair We Have No Measure," in Alan Casty (ed.) *Mass Media and Mass Man*, New York: Holt, Rinehart and Winston: 5–11.

PART ONE

Institutions of Television

A SIGNIFICANT AREA OF RESEARCH within television studies has addressed the institutional character of television. From the initial experiments that led to the invention of television in the 1920s through its innovation as an electronic broadcast medium in the 1930s and 1940s, the high costs and organizational complexity involved in the development, manufacture, and operation of the technologies of television production, transmission, and reception required huge and continuing outlays of funds. The combination of the technological complexities of television and the costs associated with using those technologies to broadcast sounds and images to thousands and then millions of individual television sets has meant that wherever and whenever television has been used as a broadcast medium around the world, it has required the resources of institutions rather than individuals.

It is, of course, the case that all media of mass (as opposed to interpersonal) communication involve technology and hence the costs associated with acquiring and using that technology. However, it is hard to think of another mass medium of the twentieth century that has been so expensive and consequently so dependent upon institutions—governments, religious organizations, corporations, etc,—as has television. Even though the cinema in the US and Europe came to be dominated by a few large companies quite early in its history, for decades, any entrepreneur with a car and a few hundred dollars to buy a projector and a few films could become part of the "film business" as an itinerant exhibitor. The cost of silent film cameras and editing equipment was low enough to allow many individual artists and documentarists to become filmmakers and, thus, low enough for important traditions of individual experimental and documentary filmmaking to grow up along side (and in many cases in opposition to) institutionally-based modes of film production, distribution, and exhibition. Even some other electronic media have been more open than television to non-institutional participants. Parallel with the history of institutionally-based radio broadcasting (by corporations, churches, government agencies, etc.) is the history of amateur radio: since the 1920s hundreds of thousands of individuals have built their own radio transmitters and receivers and "broadcast" to other enthusiasts around the world.

It was not until the mid-1970s and the introduction in the consumer market of relatively inexpensive, light-weight, and easy-to-operate video cameras and recorders that "ordinary" individuals were able to "do" television. But even though the camcorder and VCR have allowed individuals to make their own television, those video artists, documentarians, amateur porno-graphers, and home video makers could not become broadcasters as well.[1] The institutional character of television derives not only from the fact that institutional-sized resources have been required to own and operate its technologies, but also because in every country where television technology has been used for broadcasting, the experience of television has been shaped by yet another set of institutional forces: those of government policy and political ideology.

Regardless of its "content," every instance of broadcast television represents the implemen-tation of a set of prior political decisions—decisions that authorize some entity to use the air-waves for its own purposes. Broadcasting relies upon the naturally-occurring phenomenon of radio waves to carry sounds and images from transmission towers to television receiving sets. The radio spectrum is finite, and only a small number of television signals can occupy the same section of the radio band at the same time. So while a theoretically infinite number of book publishers, news-papers, film producers, or theater companies can coexist in any given geographical locale, only a fraction of all the possible or aspiring television broadcasters can operate in a given area. The scarcity of spectrum space means that every broadcast transmission represents not only the government's tacit authorization that this slice of band-width can be used by this particular entity (company, religious group, university, etc.) for this particular purpose, but it also represents the denial of other actual or potential users of that spot on the TV dial for whatever other purposes they might have had in mind.

In many countries, the inextricable link between broadcast television and the state grew out of government policies regarding radio broadcasting laid down in the 1920s, 1930s, and 1940s. Initially, in Great Britain and in other European countries, the national government kept for itself the sole right to use the air waves for first radio and then television broadcasts. Broadcasting, like other public utilities, was to be operated in what the state believed was the public interest. In the US, however, the federal government stepped in to license radio broadcasters in the 1920s only after unregulated competition for band-width and signal strength threatened to turn radio into an unintelligible cacophony of overlapping signals. With a much more restricted notion of the government's appropriate role in the provision of public services, the US government decided not to undertake broadcasting itself, but rather to serve as technical regulator and licensor of organ-izations who would, in turn, agree to serve "the public interest, convenience, and necessity."

By the early 1930s in the US, if very large corporations regarded it as serving the public convenience to link dozens of local radio stations so that millions of people spread out over a vast continent could hear the good news about the whitening power of Dreft laundry detergent, that was regarded by the government as a politically acceptable economic and social use of the valu-able electromagnetic spectrum. So, by the time television was developed as a nationally-marketed domestic technology after World War II, there was no real debate in the US over how the TV portion of the air waves would be used or by whom: TV was an opportunity for the nation to *see* the clothes that Dreft whitened. Yes, some TV band-width was set aside for non-commercial purposes, but political pressure from the now well-entrenched commercial broadcasting industry assured that there would be no strong, national, publicly-financed, non-commerical public service television in the US that might compete with commercial networks.

When laid out in such a blunt and schematic fashion, both the politics and the economics of television as institution might seem to be self-evident, but as scholars working within what has come to be called the political economy strand of television studies have pointed out, these dimensions of commercial television are usually not experienced as such by the viewer. Indeed, they are obscured. The overwhelming tendency of the principal US agency that regulates television, the

Federal Communications Commission, to routinely renew the licenses of established broadcast operations and to allow, in effect, for the "sale" of licenses by one company to another, give both local stations and the commercial networks with which they are affiliated, the appearance of being more or less permanent features of television culture and somehow entitled to their places on the TV dial. More generally, the economic basis of commercial television around the world is obscured by the focus on television programming as the service provided to owners of television sets at no apparent cost to them. In this representation of the economics of television, advertising is the ancillary and incidental matter surrounding and interrupting programming, which viewers are "free" to watch or ignore as they choose. In fact, what commercial television has to "sell" is the aggregate viewership for advertising messages. We, then, are the commodities bought by advertisers and sold by broadcasters.

As some of the essays in this section discuss, there are, of course, other institutional models of television. Cable and satellite services sell their channel packages as subscriptions, some of whose channels adopt the advertiser-based model of broadcasting, and some of which the viewer pays for directly either as premium services or on a pay-per-view basis. But still, the institutional arrangements that are represented by these "new" forms of television and the economic incentives and potential that drive their operation remain largely invisible to viewers. Paying the cable or satellite bill each month is no more likely to prompt a sustained reflection on the inner workings of the television industry or the political system that authorizes it than paying the water bill is to encourage users to perform a monthly chemical analysis of their drinking water.

This casual equation of television and water *as* utilities raises another point that some political economy scholarship has made, either implicitly or explicitly, about the institutional bases of television. Television represents a set of institutional relationships that are *ecological* in their complexity and consequences. This work would insist that the seemingly innocent pleasures of a situation comedy or soap opera cannot be abstracted from the political and economic interests served by its enjoyment, any more than eating a steak can be divorced from an agricultural system that encourages the mass production of animals for consumption, the use of scarce arable land for the production of animal feed, and the use of pesticides, herbicides, and antibiotics to facilitate both.

The economics of commercial television around the world links television to another enormous set of institutional forces: those involved with the production, sale, and marketing of the consumer products and services advertised on television. For those of us in countries where commercial television has dominated television culture for as long as we can recall, the constant interruption of television programming by advertisements is something we take for granted as a feature of television's institutional environment. Political economy scholarship asks us to think about the fact that commercial broadcasting's use of the electromagnetic spectrum—a public utility, after all—to sell people to advertisers pre-empts the use of that resource for purposes that are, arguably, more socially beneficial, and it also enshrines consumption as *the* pre-eminent social value. Buying products advertised on television is presented not only as a way to prevent cavities or to clean dirty clothes. Consumption itself is implicitly touted as a path to individual fulfillment, a means of exercising democratic choice, a necessary feature of (hetero-) sexual desirability, and as a vehicle for assuring the happiness and safety of loved ones.

The term public sphere, adapted by media scholars from the work of German social theorist Jürgen Habermas, will be used by a number of scholars whose essays appear in this section and elsewhere in this collection. It refers to a figurative "space" in the public life of democratic societies, which is not controlled by sitting governments, particular political parties, or other sectarian interests and where issues of concern to the society as a whole might be raised, explored, and rationally debated. Habermas sees coffee houses, debating societies, and newspapers as key institutions in the development of the public sphere in Europe in the eighteenth century. Television scholars have used Habermas's historical arguments and his notion of the public sphere to examine the role of television as a political and social institution at the end of the twentieth century.

Two essays deal specifically with public service broadcasting (what's called "public" television in the US, the BBC in the UK, ABC in Australia, CBC in Canada, etc.) and raise the issue of television's relation to the public sphere. In an essay adapted for this collection from his book on public service broadcasting, Richard Collins argues that European public service broadcasting has been defined and its effectiveness assessed in two different ways: either as the sum total of the ways in which public service broadcasting has functioned in the past (the "ises" definition of public service) or in relation to a set of ideals according to which public service broadcasting might and should function (the "oughts"). In either case, however, it is indisputable that all European public service broadcasting systems have been seriously challenged by the twin forces of globalization and technological transformation of television from a limited number of terrestrial channels to an ever-increasing range of broadcast, cable, and satellite viewing options.

As Collins details, in most countries in Europe, the public service broadcasting ethos has deep and strong roots in the national culture of television. In some cases (the UK for example), public service broadcasting was the first and for some time only form of television available. There and elsewhere even commercial broadcasters were obliged to adhere to certain public service requirements (threshold amounts of cultural, religious, public affairs, news, or children's programming; or service to minority viewing populations, for example) in exchange for access to broadcasting rights.

As Ouellette and Lewis discuss in their essay, the situation in the US is considerably different. Broadcasting in the US meant commercial, advertiser-based broadcasting long before there was an effort to establish a nation-wide system of public service television. Public television emerged as a response to what some saw as the "vast [cultural] wasteland" of commercial television of the 1950s and early 1960s. Rather than trying to appeal to the general public (which would have meant competing against entrenched commercial broadcasting interests), National Educational Television (NET) and then Public Broadcasting Service (PBS) were built upon an attempt to provide white, educated, adult, middle-class viewers with the kind of television they were increasingly unable to find on commercial network or local television: public affairs, opera, nature and historical documentaries, and original drama.

The relationship between public television and the college-educated, professional classes in the US was cemented by the unwillingness of either federal or state governments to provide an adequate and reliable source of funding for public service television. Vested in a loose confederation of dozens of separately operated, geographically dispersed, local, non-commercial stations, public service broadcasting in the US turned to viewer fundraisers and corporate underwriting to make up the difference. In the process, public television in the US came to see and represent itself as culturally more than and socially better than the mere entertainment offered by the commercial networks. Ouellette and Lewis offer a case for public funding of public service television in the US based on a renewed engagement with popular culture and with sources of innovation that freedom from advertisements would afford. Borrowing lessons from the history of European television, they also propose a complementary re-regulation of commercial broadcast television in the public interest.

The complex institutional relationship between the state and television extends well beyond the government's authority to issue broadcast licenses and the authority of designated government agencies to regulate broadcasting, cable, and satellite technologies and programming practices. David Hutchison's essay, drawn from his book on media policy, encourages us to think about the relationship between all forms of mass media, especially television, and the legal frameworks within which they operate. All societies must somehow adjudicate among the interests of individuals, media organizations, the society as a whole, and the state itself. Both the US Constitution and the European Convention on Human Rights protect the individual's right to free expression of opinion, but the same countries that would recognize this protection as fundamental would also acknowledge another individual's right to a fair trial, an individual right to privacy, a protection against defamatory attack, the state's responsibility to protect national security, and society's interest in protecting children from pornography and represented violence. Since becoming the pre-eminent form of mass media in many countries, television has found itself at the center of many such legal conflicts.

Tom O'Regan's essay uses a comparative approach to examine the development of Australian broadcast television's distinctive institutional character. That character has been shaped, he argues, in response to local political, geographic, and cultural forces, but also in relation to the quite different institutional models provided by the US and the UK. Drawn from O'Regan's book on Australian television, this essay provides Australian readers with an institutional overview of that country's television culture. For non-Australian readers, it makes visible a host of fascinating institutional issues, which O'Regan sets in relation to both American and British institutional contexts. For example, he reminds us that the same technological innovation can be deployed to quite different institutional effect. In the US, the development of satellite technology had the effect of reducing the power of the established television networks, as cable operators used this technology to add non-broadcast programming options and, in doing so, to build a competing television delivery system. In Australia, however, this same satellite technology (in conjunction with government policy) strengthened the position of existing commercial and public service broadcasters by enabling them to expand their reach and programming influence nationally.

O'Regan also extends the definition of the institutions of television to include public discourses about television, especially television criticism. Debates over the social and political role of television in the UK and continental Europe have been dominated by questions of how well television serves the public interest and by the frequently conflicting agendas of public service and commercial broadcasters. By contrast, O'Regan points out, critical discourse on television in Australia has had "a less 'civic' and more 'nation-building' character." The rhetorical division in Australian television criticism has been less between public service and commercial broadcasting than between Australian and imported, particularly American, programming. Discussions of television in Australia, then, cannot be understood outside the context of the influence of American and British culture on Australian life more generally.

As Ouellette and Lewis acknowledge in the conclusion to their essay, cable and satellite television delivery services greatly complicate arguments regarding television regulation based upon the scarcity of over-the-air channel capacity. If one of the justifications for public funding of public service broadcasting and for the regulation of commercial broadcasters is to encourage some level of service for minority audiences, might this not be accomplished by market forces if dozens or hundreds of programming providers targeted audience segments based upon race, gender, ethnicity, language, cultural interests or taste? Eileen Meehan and Jackie Byars's essay is based on their long-term study of the first US cable channel to represent itself as "television for women": Lifetime. They examine the complex institutional factors involved in the formation and operation of this attempt to appropriate the rhetoric of liberal feminism for the purposes of advertiser-based commercial cable television.

Note

1   There are exceptions to the institutional monopoly over the use of "broadcast" television technology in a number of countries. Eric Freedman's essay in Part Three (Modes of Television), discusses public access television, for example. Cheap and easy-to-operate video cameras and editing equipment, combined with non-broadcast means of video distribution have also opened up opportunities for individuals and groups to make and circulate television outside of the control of broadcasters and, in some cases, beneath the regulatory control of governmental institutions. See Brian Larkin's essay on the Nigerian video film in Part Four (Making Television).

Chapter 1

RICHARD COLLINS

'ISES' AND 'OUGHTS'
Public service broadcasting in Europe

Preface

THE ORIGINAL TEXT FROM WHICH THIS CHAPTER IS DRAWN, was
first published in 1998 (Collins 1998) and is based on research undertaken in the early 1990s.
What has changed in public service broadcasting (PSB) since then?

First, it's important to note that although PSB has extended beyond its origins in Western
Europe (notably to what Louis Hartz called the new societies created by Europe in its own image
in North and South America, Australasia and Africa) its heartland remains in Western Europe. It's
particularly striking that, in spite of strenuous efforts, public service broadcasting has not yet been
implanted successfully in Central and Eastern Europe. Karel Jakubowicz, of Telewizja Polska,
observed (2002: pp. 6–7) that 'In Central and Eastern Europe . . . many state and public service
broadcasters have already been marginalized and are limping along.' East European PSB is weak
despite Western European states' (and public service broadcasters') efforts to assist countries that
were formerly on the east side of the Iron Curtain in developing a robust civil society with a
strong PSB pillar. Central to these efforts has been the merger of the European Broadcasting
Union and its eastern equivalent, the OIRT (Organisation Internationale de Radio et Télévision),
in 1993. However, PSB has not, it seems, been able to do much more than figure as an ideal to
those working to (re)establish democratic and pluralistic societies east of the Elbe. And in more
than one of the 'new societies' considered by Hartz (e.g., in Canada and New Zealand) PSB has
lost ground.

In its West European heartlands, PSB has enjoyed mixed fortunes. In some countries (e.g.,
Germany and the UK) PSB has maintained a dominant position in the radio and television markets
and has successfully extended its presence onto the world wide web. Some, however, argue that
PSB has secured such successes at the price of a fatal compromise of its programming ideals. Aidan
White the General Secretary of the International Federation of Journalists, for example, has
argued that 'Over the last 20 years many of Europe's public broadcasters have moved in a
decidedly commercial direction. Companies like ARD, ZDF, RAI, TVE, RTP and the BBC[1] have
been seeking to maximise market share and increase their commercial revenues' (White 2002:
p. 12).

Nonetheless, PSB retains its place in the hearts and minds of many European politicians and
viewers and listeners. Its special status has been sanctified by a special public service broadcasting
amendment (the 'Amsterdam Protocol') to the European Treaty and a Resolution and a separate
Recommendation each supporting public service broadcasting by the Council of Europe.[2] However, the special status for public service broadcasting, established in national laws and regulatory

regimes and in pan-European provisions such as these, has not prevented national and European competition authorities from persistently raising concerns about the privileged status of public service broadcasters and their, possibly, anti-competitive behaviour. For example, the UK's main competition regulator, the Director General of Fair Trading John Vickers, referred specifically to the BBC in his speech 'Competition Policy and Broadcasting' of 24 June 2002 and observed, 'Should some broadcaster(s) have special immunity from competition law, perhaps on grounds of having a "public service" remit? Not in my view. It is clear that some socially desirable services need subsidy to be provided. However, the provision of such services should not result in undue distortion of competition on the wider market place' (Vickers 2002: p. 3).

All of these live issues centring on PSB raise questions of definition – what is public service broadcasting? The same question is addressed in the text that follows.

Introduction

'Does public service broadcasting cut such a poor figure? The end of its monopoly and the advent of television from space, enabling satellites to relay a vast quantity of programmes from elsewhere, in multilingual versions, on channels that digital compression has made less scarce–do, in fact suggest that the vocation of national stations must evolve in both public and private sectors' (Bourges 1993: p. 2). Between 1982 and 1992, European public service broadcasting experienced an unprecedentedly comprehensive and intense two-fold regime of change: technological change, in the form of communication satellites, and regulatory change, in the form of the integration of the European Community's (later European Union) television market under the jurisdiction of the European Commission's Competition Directorate. These interdependent forces shifted the European broadcasting paradigm and transformed a long established European regime, based on national broadcasting markets dominated, if not monopolised, by a single national public service broadcaster, into a new, pluralised (and in some areas genuinely competitive) transnational system.

Satellites made it possible for new services to be established and for new services to cross national frontiers. Creation of a single European market in television among the Member States of the European Community (EC) meant that television, hitherto regulated under national (and largely non-commercial) regimes, was henceforth conceived as a service traded within and between EC Member States and subject to EC competition regulation. These changes revealed fissures in, and between, the institutional and ideological definitions of European public service broadcasting and showed that European public service broadcasters did not always agree on what public service broadcasting was.

The introduction of a new information and communication technology, satellite television, in Europe in the early eighties transformed the conditions under which television broadcasting had hitherto been arranged. It provoked widespread debate about the ends and means of broadcasting policy and a recognition that broadcasting policy could no longer be made in the old, largely national, terms. Abolition of spectrum scarcity seemed to delegitimise political intervention in broadcasting markets; no matter that there were, and are, other grounds for intervention in broadcasting markets.[3] And new services were slowly established which eroded the privileged positions enjoyed by national public service broadcasters. Accordingly, the case for the organisation of broadcasting on market lines grew in force and salience – not least because the formidable 'Television without Frontiers' Green Paper (Commission of the European Communities 1984) provided solid arguments for considering television a traded service.

Such arguments were strengthened by the perceived failure of public service broadcasting. New services and new possibilities focused attention on public service broadcasters' performance which was trenchantly criticised for wasteful use of resources, poor matching of programme supply to audience demand, and susceptibility to capture by political and cultural elites, (see, inter alia, Peacock 1986, Keane 1991: pp. 54–7 and Kimmel 1982 passim and Kumar (in MacCabe and Stewart 1986). Indeed, the BBC (British Broadcasting Corporation) itself has acknowledged the force of such criticisms stating: 'For much of its history, the BBC has been part of a high cost industry. ITV (Independent Television) and ILR (Independent Local Radio)[4] as well as the BBC were characterised by entrenched working practices, cumbersome organisation structures, over-staffing and poor industrial relations' (BBC 1992: p. 52).

In contrast, advocates of market principles of organisation claimed that provision of broadcasting services via markets, (even if imperfect markets),[5] better matches offer to demand, (thanks to a signalling system via price which registers the preferences and intensity of preferences of consumers), uses resources more efficiently and is less subject to capture by cultural and political elites than is and was public service broadcasting (see, inter alia, Peacock 1986). Their theoretical case seemed to be empirically vindicated by a substantial shift in viewing in favour of the new commercial services. The combination of technological and regulatory change thus altered the landscape of European broadcasting both empirically, through the establishment of new services, and theoretically, by posing a powerful intellectual and ideological challenge to established public service rationales.

Definitions of public service broadcasting

What then is the 'public service broadcasting' that was threatened? Perhaps we all know what we mean by the term. But what is customarily taken for granted customarily proves troublesome. What one believes a term to mean may not correspond to what others understand by it. Induction and deduction offer possible routes to a definition of public service broadcasting: induction via codification of what public service broadcasting 'is'; deduction via theoretical systematisation of what public service broadcasting 'ought' to be. Characteristically, inductivists have been concerned with the actual historical practice of public service broadcasters whereas deductivists have focused on a theoretical ideal of public service broadcasting. Blumler (1992) provides an inductive, empirical, approach to the question, as do the Broadcasting Research Unit (BRU nd) and some of the cogitations of public service broadcasters themselves (e.g., Perez 1983 and 1983a). Garnham (1990 and 1992), Keane (1991), and other neo-Habermasians[6] offer a deductive, theoretical, approach.

These approaches can be characterised respectively as studies (and defences) of public service broadcasters and of public service broadcasting. The first type of approach has an admirable concreteness but, for good or ill, weds its exponents indissolubly to the practice of actual and existing public service broadcasters the second, for good or ill, emancipates its exponents from the challenging task of defending the historical practice of public service broadcasters but risking idealist invocation of 'oughts' with a tenuous connection to real historical 'ises'.

The 'ises' of public service broadcasting

The modern era has seen the emergence of three distinct forms of state. Monolithic, often absolutist, states, (such as the former Soviet Union or the People's Republic of China), in which the boundaries between a centralised state apparatus, political party and control of economic activity are absent or indistinct. States where government and its apparatus perform a 'nightwatchman' function in respect of the economy and in which political parties and the apparatus of the state, (often a plural apparatus), are clearly differentiated, where economic activity takes place within a framework of law established and guaranteed by political authority, but where political authority (in theory at least) has no direct part in economic activity, (such as the United States of America). And a third, intermediate, form of state, (such as the states of Western Europe), where economic activity is characteristically but not exclusively conducted by the private sector, where political authorities intervene more actively in the economy than is characteristic in the second kind of state but less comprehensively than is characteristic of the first, and where the state apparatus is customarily distinct from political parties. This third, intermediate, type of state customarily has a pluralistic and decentred structure to the state and its apparatus. States such as these often have a rich, and sometimes confusing, plurality of state and para statal structures.

These three types of state have distinctive and characteristic forms of organisation of broadcasting. In the first kind of state, broadcasting is customarily organised as an arm of government, in the second it is customarily located in the private sector (and therefore absent from government and any state sector), and in the third it is part of the state, but part of a decentred and pluralistic structure of political power and authority. European public service broadcasting organisations have been the locus of state institutional power in broadcasting and characteristically separate from government but part of a loose and pluralistic state structure.

European states characteristically established their broadcasting services as national public sector monopolies. Although broadcasting in several European countries (including the UK) was begun by commercial interests, (seeking to create a market for radio receivers), for the most part private interests soon lost their hold on broadcasting. True, in some countries such as Germany (where the Reichs Rundfunk Gesellschaft had significant participation from the private sector) and France (which had a number of commercial stations in the interwar years, including some for foreign listeners transmitted in languages other than French) the private sector retained a presence. But after the Second World War, French broadcasting came to be dominated by a public sector national broadcaster, the ORTF (Office de la Radiodiffusion et Télévision Française), and German broadcasting was reconstructed by the Allied Control Commissions on exclusively public service lines. However, exceptionally, Luxembourg, perennially the black sheep of European broadcasting, maintained a profit making public company delivering advertising financed services (and services which, moreover, were directed to listeners outside Luxembourg). It was subsequently joined by other European states, first the UK and Finland in the 1950s, in permitting commercial services. But, in spite of these exceptions, European television was dominated by national public service monopolies until the 1980s.

The European experience contrasted with that of other developed countries. In the USA broadcasting was commercial. In Australia and Canada and South Africa, for example, public service broadcasting was belatedly established to complement and compete with established commercial services. Europe was thus the heartland of what came to be known as 'public service broadcasting', a distinctive institutional form which characteristically combined three elements: publicly owned not for profit organisation, a monopoly of service provision and a strongly normative programming policy emphasising national and high cultural themes. It is perhaps only from a contemporary perspective – which has a strong anti-statist flavour (it is not only east of the Elbe that the doctrine of 'Perestroika' has come to dominate) – that the organisational form which so many states chose for broadcasting requires to be explained and justified.

Yet justification is required in the context of a dominant official European Community ethos hostile to public enterprise. This hostility derives from the mismatch between a fundamental assumption of Community policy, that competitive markets are normal and normative, and the wealth of long established institutions, including public service broadcasters, which simply do not fit that paradigm. Public sector enterprise is a problem because its methods and institutions do not conform to the norms of competitive markets. Not only do public sector enterprises represent unfair competition but they threaten the normative status of competitive markets and the institutions specific to them. Indeed, a European public service broadcaster in Portugal, RTP (Radiotele-visao Portuguesa) stood accused, under the provisions of the European Treaty, of improper receipt of state aid in the form of public finance for broadcasting. True, it was exonerated but the judgement defined the legitimate boundaries of public finance for broadcasting very narrowly – essentially as permitting only activities that a profit seeking firm would not undertake.[7]

In Europe, as elsewhere, understandings of the term public service broadcasting have been shaped by the memory and past experience of the services that have gone under that name. In Western Europe quite different institutional forms, where broadcasting is closely associated with the state, (and used as an instrument of central state power), to highly regionalised and pluralistic systems, are all known as public service broadcasting. Even in the United Kingdom, where thanks to the international prestige and longevity of the BBC, what comes closest to an internationally accepted normative institutional definition of public service broadcasting is to be found, there is scant consensus on the meaning of 'public service broadcasting'. The most recent official enquiry into broadcasting in the UK, the Committee on Financing the BBC (the Peacock Committee[8]), stated (Peacock 1986: p. 6) that there is no 'simple dictionary definition' of public service broadcasting. Indeed all established terrestrial television channels in the UK, the advertising free BBC, the for profit advertising financed Channel 3 (ITV) and Channel 5, and the not for profit advertising financed Channel 4/S4C,[9] have the status of public service broadcaster.

The Peacock Committee (Peacock 1986: p. 7) cited eight characteristics of public service broadcasting borrowed from a Broadcasting Research Unit (BRU) study (BRU nd). BRU had identified these characteristics in a classically inductive fashion by polling established British broadcasters and commentators. From its respondents' comments it derived eight characteristics of public service broadcasting (see also Keane 1991: p. 117). These are:

- geographic universality – everyone should have access to the same services
- catering for all interests and tastes
- catering for minorities
- catering for national identity and community
- detachment from vested interests and government
- one broadcasting system to be funded directly from the corpus of users
- competition in good programming rather than for numbers
- guidelines to liberate programme makers and not to restrict them.

Other contemporary European notions of public service broadcasting are broadly similar. Two sources, (one academic one professional), provide convenient conspectuses of European views; they are Jay Blumler's 'Television and the Public Interest. Vulnerable Values in West European Broadcasting' (Blumler 1992), and the report of the EBU's Perez Group (Perez 1983) on the nature and role of public service broadcasting.

Blumler defined the most salient characteristics of public service broadcasting as: comprehensive remit, generalised mandates, diversity, pluralism and range, cultural roles, place in politics and non-commercialism (Blumler 1992: pp. 7–14). His formulations are particularly noteworthy for they derive from discussions at a pan-European conference, (of a predominantly academic character), held in Liège in 1990 where the problems of, and policies for, public service broadcasting in eleven European states were discussed.[10] The aim of the conference, titled 'Vulnerable Values in Multichannel Television Systems: What European Policy Makers seek to Protect', was 'to identify the principal values and related programming forms that European policy makers are striving to protect from marketplace pressures' (Blumler 1992: p. 4). As the conference title suggests, public service broadcasting, (and the values it embodied), were perceived to be threatened by recent changes to European broadcasting.

Because of their provenance, Blumler's findings have a general European representativeness and correspond closely to BRU's definitions of public service broadcasting. For example, the 'comprehensive remit', (which Blumler cited as a defining characteristic of public service broadcasting), chiefly refers to range in programming, rather than to the geographical universality of service to which BRU drew attention. Yet, overall, Blumler's formulation is compatible with the principle of universal service as defined by BRU.[11]

Blumler's term, 'generalised mandate', refers to the characateristic delegation of authority to public service broadcasters by political authorities which corresponds to what BRU defined as 'detachment from vested interests and government' which, Blumler argues, has given rise to a distinctive high minded professional broadcasting culture. Blumler's terms 'diversity, pluralism and range' closely correspond to BRU's 'catering for all interests and tastes' and to BRU's 'catering for minorities'. All of these prescriptions are based on a notion of broadcasting as an emancipator of its audience through the provision of diversity, and thus of choice. Blumler contrasted the minoritarian, choice enhancing, ethos of public service broadcasting with what he identified as a majoritarian, choice restricting, ethos of commercial television.[12]

But the other characteristics of public service broadcasting which Blumler identified are less certain vehicles for the emancipation of the audience. His fourth category 'cultural roles' charges broadcasting with responsibility for providing a national cultural cement by disseminating culturally valuable programming. By discharging its cultural role public service broadcasting will, Blumler argues, act as a 'centripetal, societally integrative force' (Blumler 1992: p. 11). Blumler explicitly couples this characteristic of public service broadcasting with the related characteristic of providing programme quality (captured in BRU's list of characteristics as 'good programming') and thereby transposes views Arnold advanced in the latter half of the nineteenth century to a contemporary context. Arnold saw dissemination of the 'best that had been thought and said' (Arnold 1963: p. 6) as a social glue for 'culture is the most resolute enemy of anarchy because of the great hopes and designs for the State which culture teaches us to nourish' (Arnold 1963: p. 204).

Blumler is not, of course, so explicitly authoritarian as Arnold. But, unlike Arnold, he did not recognise the significance of cultural stratification (notably on class and ethnic lines) and that, consequently, there may be scant social consensus on questions of cultural quality. Whereas Arnold explicitly proposed a resolution of the problem of cultural stratification through cultural homogenisation from above, ('sweetness and light' was recommended as a prophylactic against the anarchy Arnold feared and which, in default of effective cultural prophylaxis, he recommended 'the old Roman way . . . flog the rank and file and fling the ring-leaders from the Tarpeian Rock' (Arnold 1963: p. 203), Blumler does not recognise the problem for public service broadcasting posed by cultural difference. For public service broadcasting's cultural mission may divide, rather than integrate, the target community to which its programmes are transmitted.[13]

Public service broadcasting and cultural identity

Public broadcasters had, and have, an intractable problem in that their mandates provide that they should lead, rather than follow, public and popular taste and yet their social productivity (and institutional legitimacy) depends on the degree to which their programmes and services are used and valued by viewers and listeners. In conditions of monopoly this contradiction could not prove troublesome – audiences took what they were given and, in the absence of alternatives, for the most part liked what they were given. But once alternatives were available, the contradiction at the heart of European public service broadcasting became palpably evident as viewers (and listeners) migrated to new commercial alternatives and public broadcasters found themselves skewered on the contradiction of satisfying what Tracey has called the 'public as audience' (Tracey 1992: p. 21) and fulfilling their public and, broadly defined, educational mandate.

The constitutions of many European public service broadcasters explicitly charged broadcasters with a cultural mission, and those public service broadcasters which were not explicitly so charged customarily have long traditions of discharging high cultural responsibilities. The importance of tradition, rather than law, in determining broadcasters' cultural conduct is probably best exemplified in the case of the BBC, but the BBC is far from the only case. In theory, as Shaughnessy and Fuente Cobo state, the BBC enjoys 'complete freedom' (Shaughnessy and Fuente Cobo 1990: p. 88) in programming, and now of the British Terrestrial Broadcasters (BBC, Independent Television or Channel 4) was specifically charged with cultural responsibilities. The BBC and Channel 4 (and, to a somewhat lesser extent, ITV) have also vigorously maintained an extensive commitment to programmes about culture and of high cultural quality.

In Germany too the cultural responsibilities with which public broadcasters have been formally charged are not onerous. For example Bayerischer Rundfunk is enjoined to exercise 'a sense of cultural responsibility' and West Deutscher Rundfunk[14] to take into account 'artistic factors' in the discharge of its responsibilities (Shaughnessy and Fuente Cobo 1990: p. 44). But German public service broadcasters have characteristically given cultural programmes important places in their television schedules and cultural programmes departments have enjoyed prestige and high levels of resources. More important, the production and construction of entertainment dramas (such as feature films, single and series dramas) have been strongly marked by 'high cultural' values–notably by a preeminence of the authorial voice. To be sure there are counter indications; of which 'Schwarzwaldklinik' (Black Forest Clinic) is only the best known. Nor too are 'high culture' values and popularity necessarily antipathetic; witness Edgar Reitz's 'Heimat' (Homeland) (1980–84).

The Austrian public service broadcaster, ORF, (Österreichischer Rundfunk), is charged with the promotion of arts and sciences, to offer a service of high quality and to provide comprehensive information about culture (Shaughnessy and Fuente Cobo 1990: p. 32). And the RAI, (Radiotelevisione Italiana), in Italy, is specifically charged with fostering cultural pluralism and regional and national culture. Moreover the RAI has a general obligation to promote the diffusion of the Italian language and culture abroad (Shaughnessy and Fuente Cobo 1990; pp. 102–3).

Ireland's RTE, (Radio Telefis Eireann), is charged with promoting Irish culture (to 'ensure that programmes reflect the varied elements which make up the culture of the people of the whole island of Ireland, and have special regard for the elements which distinguish that culture') *and* with 'developing public awareness of the values of other countries, especially those which are members of the European Economic Community' (Shaughnessy and Fuente Cobo 1990: pp. 107).

Dutch public broadcasters are subject to extensive cultural mandates (including an obligation to allocate 20 per cent of broadcasting time to cultural items. See discussion in NOS 1990: pp. 4–5 and NOS 1991: pp. 4–5). But the requirements[15] to which broadcasters became subject following promulgation of the 1987 Media Act did not apply before 1987, prior to that date broadcasters were responsible to the Minister of Culture and, moreover, Shaughnessy and Fuente Cobo (1990: p. 123) state that the 1987 Media Law was promulgated to 'reflect the importance the Government attaches to the cultural obligations of public broadcasters'. Like their colleagues elsewhere in Europe, Dutch public service broadcasters have interpreted their formal and informal mandates as both requiring and permitting their discharge of extensive cultural responsibilities.

The Portuguese Broadcasting Act of 1979 mandates RTP to promote and defend the national culture and language, to promote Portuguese culture internationally and to strengthen relations with other nations. Moreover RTP is obliged to 'reflect in its programme schedule the diversity and pluralism of classical works, modern cultural and artistic expression' and to 'offer events and programmes of high quality and diverse content' (Shaughnessy and Fuente Cobo 1990: p. 130).

These broadcasters, (the ARD, IBA, NOS, ORF, RAI, RTE, RTP),[16] have thus all been mandated, either by tradition or by law or both, to discharge a cultural role. Three have also been explicitly charged with promoting their respective national cultures. However, it's important to recognise that components of public service broadcasting's mandate may sometimes be contradictory. Implementation of any particular broadcasting policy may therefore involve choices about the relative priorities to be attached to any individual goal. For example, catering for minorities may be at the expense of catering for national identity and community; efficient use of resources may be hostile to provision of an extensive range of services under diverse ownership and control. Competition provoked reflection, within and outside the ranks of public service broadcasters, on these contradictions and how they should be managed.

The Wangermée and Perez Groups

The Wangermée and Perez Groups, established within the EBU in the early 1980s, to consider the nature and future of European public service broadcasting, produced definitions which chimed closely with those of Blumler and BRU. The Perez Group,[17] which reported in 1983, characterised public service broadcasting as the:

- provision, at a moderate cost, of a service accessible to all
- varied and balanced programming designed to meet the needs of all sections of the public and all age groups
- impartiality in the presentation of news
- good balance between informative and artistic programmes
- predominance of original productions
- enterpreneurial character of public service organisations – employing highly qualified technical staff, more often than not also training them, frequently constituting the country's major employer of performers, and collaborating with national electronic industries in research and development.

(Perez 1983: p. 4)

Perez identified universality and diversity, impartiality and (smacking rather of special pleading) the role of public service broadcasting as a patron and author of original productions and a trainer and educator of professional broadcasters as the defining characteristics of public service broadcasting.

The Wangermée Group, (the parent EBU committee to which the Perez Group reported),[18] also defined public service broadcasting and stated that public service broadcasting should:

- provide in a national community for the intention (sic) of the general public, diversified and balanced programming for all categories of the population, including minorities;
- ensure in particular that the various currents of opinion and thought are present in their programmes;
- ensure an important part of the original production which they broadcast, and in any case be fully in control of it;
- serve the public by the most appropriate technical means;
- to reinvest the main part of the results of their operations in the development of broadcasting.

(AG 551 SPG 2642 June 1984: p. 6)

The two EBU groups emphasised rather different elements in the portfolio of public service broadcasting's attributes. Wangermée's list lacks Perez's insistence on impartiality (and therefore on broadcasters' independence from government). However Wangermée, like Perez, strongly emphasised universality and diversity. There is then, if not complete consensus, a high degree of communality in the content of the lists of attributes of public service broadcasting generated inductively by academics and broadcasters. The core attributes of public service broadcasting identified by BRU, Blumler, Wangermée and Perez were *diversity*, *universality* and *impartiality*.

The 'oughts' of public service broadcasting

A second, deductive, approach to defining public service broadcasting has foregrounded, not the historical practices of public service broadcasting (the post hoc 'ises'), but the role which broadcasting should perform; the 'oughts' of public service broadcasting. From definition of broadcasting's role comes a specification which will, *propter hoc*, tell us how broadcasting 'ought' to be. There are clear merits to such an approach which is more open to innovation and reassessment of the structure and practices of public service broadcasting than is an inductive approach. Moreover, a deductive approach does not readily lend itself (in contrast to an inductive approach) to the fetishisation of the historical practice of particular institutions. Further, a deductive approach has the signal merit of forcing into explicit definition the underlying social visions implicit in different models of how non-market public service broadcasting ought to be. There are at least two such visions, each of which has been ably put forward in the UK. The first, authoritarian, vision may be found in the UK Pilkington Committee's report of 1962 (Pilkington 1962) and the second, libertarian, vision in the writings of British neo-Habermasians, such as Garnham (1990 and 1992), Keane (1991) and Murdock (1990).

The Pilkington Committee put forward a clear vision of public service broadcasting representative both of the established ethos of British public service broadcasting, (rooted in Reith's[19] BBC), and of the broadcasting order which prevailed from its publication in 1962 to 1986 and the next major landmark in British official thinking about broadcasting policy: the Report of the Committee on Financing the BBC: the Peacock Report (Peacock 1986). Pilkington believed that the audience for broadcasting was vulnerable and should be protected. Radio and, in particular, television, (which the Committee judged to be 'the main factor in influencing the values and moral standards of our society' (Pilkington 1962: Para 42), had to be organised so that viewers (and listeners) were protected, not only from the baleful influence of a powerful medium, but also from themselves and their own tastes and desires. 'To give the public what it wants', Pilkington stated, 'seems at first sight unexceptionable' (Pilkington 1962: Para 44). But it is 'patronising and arrogant' (Pilkington 1962: para 48) for giving the audience what it wants is justifiable only if it is assumed that viewers and listeners not only know what they want but also what is good for them. Such a view, Pilington argued, mistakes 'what the public wants . . . for the public interest' (Pilkington 1962: Para 408).[20] It is hard to resist the view that Pilkington's notion of public service was one of Platonic Guardianship. Servants of the public broadcasters, (and regulators), they might be but they were servants who were certainly not expected to take directions from those whom they were appointed to serve. For the masters were considered less competent to govern than were their servants.

The neo-Habermasian defence of public service broadcasting

Neo-Habermasian proponents of public service broadcasting[21] adopt an approach different to Blumler's. They provide not an apologia for the past achievements and established institutions of European public service broadcasting, ('ises'), but in a priori arguments, ('oughts'), for public service broadcasting as its chief institutional guarantor and bearer of a modern public sphere. Their arguments offer potential for institutional innovation, because grounded in 'oughts', and recognise that authoritarian rationales for public service broadcasting, like Pilkington's, are insufficient to stand against the resurgent libertarianism of free market doctrines (see, inter alia, Brittan 1987).

Habermas' ideas were introduced to the English language debate on broadcasting by Nicholas Garnham in 1986 (Garnham 1986 and reprinted in Garnham 1990: pp. 104–14) and were developed by him and others (see, inter alia, Garnham 1990 and 1992, Keane 1991). Although Garnham's 'The Media and the Public Sphere'[22] first appeared in 1986 the term 'public sphere', the core Habermasian concept borrowed by British neo-Habermasians was first used by Garnham in an earlier, very influential, article first published in 1983 (Garnham 1983, reprinted in Garnham 1990: pp. 115–35) titled 'Public Service versus the Market'.[23]

In 'Public Service versus the Market' (Garnham 1990) Garnham argued that market rather than public service mechanisms are inimical to the public interest. For, he claimed, public service principles of organisation are superior 'to the market as a means of providing all citizens, whatever their wealth or geographical location, equal access to a wide range of high-quality entertainment, information and education, and as a means of ensuring that the aim of the programme producer is the satisfaction of a range of audience tastes rather than only those tastes that show the largest profit' (Garnham 1990: p. 120).

The market has, Garnham argues, led to diminished diversity in a reduction in the number of enterprises which control (or at least very strongly influence) the production and circulation of information and culture, and to inequitable relationships between dominant, and metropolitan, enterprises at the expense of subordinate, and peripheral, entities. These market driven inequities and inequalities in turn have sustained pervasive and deep-rooted social inequality and inequity. Moreover, technological change promises, contrary to the libertarian and libratory rhetoric of its advocates, to accelerate these processes of actual and relative deprivation.

Whilst challenging the claims made for the market, Garnham argued that discussion of broadcasting policy had been stultified by a pervasive dualism which opposed the concepts of 'State' and 'Market' (Garnham 1990: p. 106 and Garnham 1984: p. 6). He argued for a third term, the Habermasian notion of a 'public sphere', which offered an escape from dualism and a 'space for a rational and universalistic politics distinct from both the economy and the State' (Garnham 1990: p. 107). But, of course, Garnham's argument was not simply for an abstract third category, distinct from the terms 'state' and 'market', but in favour of what he, and others, (see inter alia Keane 1991), designated the institutional embodiment and guarantor of the modern public sphere – public service broadcasting.

However, whilst Garnham's triad escapes from dualism it is not problem free. For, whilst a third term conceptually mediating between state and market, may be intellectually productive and signify a distinctive ethos in (at least some) broadcasting institutions at (some) moments in history, the notion of the public sphere helps only to a limited extent when concrete questions of broadcasting policy and organisation arise. For how is broadcasting to be funded if not by either the state[24] or the market? Moreover, others have shown that public service broadcasters' actual practice is far from that which would characterise a well functioning public sphere (see inter alia Docker 1991, GUMG 1976, Hjarvard 1991). Indeed, the discontinuity between Habermas' own arguments about broadcasting and the concrete broadcasting context in which he wrote makes the appropriation of Habermas' term, public sphere, for defence of public service broadcasting rather curious.

Habermas' 'Strukturwandel der Öffentlichkeit' (Habermas 1989 [1962]), was written in a society where broadcasting services were provided by perhaps the most perfect form of public service broadcasting yet institutionalised (see, inter alia, Collins and Porter 1981 and Falkenberg 1983). Yet, Habermas asserts quite unequivocally the *necessary* inferiority of audio-visual media to print media for rational understanding and democratic exchange.[25] He stated, (with characteristic opacity):

> Radio, film and television by degrees reduce to a minimum the distance that a reader is forced to maintain toward the printed letter – a distance that required the privacy of the appropriation as much as it made possible the publicity of a rational-critical exchange about what had been read. With the arrival of the new media the form of communication as such has changed; they have had an impact, therefore, more penetrating (in the strict sense of the word) than was ever possible for the press. Under the pressure of the 'Don't talk back!' the conduct of the public assumes a different form. In comparison with printed communications the programs sent by the new media curtail the reactions of their recipients in a peculiar way. They draw the eyes and ears of the public under their spell but at the same time, by taking away its distance, place it under 'tutelage', which is to say they deprive it of the opportunity to say something and to disagree
>
> (Habermas 1989: pp. 170–1)

Habermas developed his notion, the public sphere, in the course of a general critique of contemporary mass society and mass communications and not to defend public service broadcasting (to which he gave scant attention). Like most members of the Frankfurt School, Habermas disdains demotic culture and the mass media's reduction of human experience to, what Marcuse trenchantly described as, 'one dimensionality' and its reification of culture as a commodity (see, inter alia, Marcuse 1972: p. 24). Thus appropriation of the term, public sphere, for a defence of public service broadcasting may appear to have been rather arbitrarily chosen.[26] Not least because, as several commentators have observed, Habermas' category – the public sphere is open to objection and qualification.

Keane (1991: p. 35–6), for example, has argued that Habermas sentimentalised the heroic bourgeois era,[27] an argument which Schudson (1992) has explored in an excellent concrete historical analysis of a US case. And Bauman has cruelly compared Habermas' conception of the public sphere to 'society shaped after the pattern of a sociology seminar, that is, that there are only participants and the one thing that matters is the power of argument' (Bauman 1992: p. 217). Perhaps Nancy Fraser's definition of the category 'public sphere' as a 'conceptual resource' (Fraser 1992: p. 110) rather than a term signifying a strong identity between Habermas' own intellectual system and that of the user best captures the nature of neo-Habermasian proponents of public service broadcasting's debt to Habermas.

So too is the reality of European public service broadcasters' commitment to a public sphere somewhat equivocal. Broadcasters' commitment to informing and educating their public too often led them to serve an audience of their imagination rather than the real audience. Rather than a democratic public sphere, in which the actual experience and interest of a real empirical public was represented, monopolistic European public service broadcasters too often addressed the public experience and interests, the public sphere, of elites. 'Bottom up' public services, which gave voice to a real public, (or, to use Reith's term, publics), and represented a demotic and genuinely democratic public sphere were conspicuous by their absence until competition with commercial services compelled public broadcasters to address the real public rather than that of broadcasters' imagination. Claims for public service broadcasting's success in satisfying audiences' tastes can be reconciled only with difficulty with the dramatic loss of audience share experienced by European public service broadcasters when their monopolies were first challenged by commerical competitors. Recognition of 'the public as audience' (Tracey 1992: p. 21) did not come about spontaneously but as a consequence of competition with commercial broadcasting: that is, through public service broadcasters' presence *in* the market.

Culture and the public sphere

Habermas' etymological discussions in the Strukturwandel provide some useful clues to the Arnoldian character of his conception of culture and to the consequences of advocacy of public service broadcasting based on Habermasian foundations. Habermas' conception of culture is unfortunately reminiscent of the outlook which identified 'Culture [as] the product of the old leisured classes who seek to defend it against new and destructive forces' (Williams 1963: p. 306). Habermas points out that just as 'public' and 'lordly', the public sphere and the state, were irrevocably intertwined, so too were the roots of the cultural elements of a public sphere, a growing 'representative publicness', to be found in the culture of both the nobility and the bourgeoisie (Habermas 1989: p. 9). The culture of Habermas' emergent public sphere was an elite culture (albeit rooted in the tastes and experience of the new as well as the old upper classes); if the 'humanistically cultivated courtier replaced the Christian knight' (Habermas 1989: p. 9) little change is likely to have been apparent to those enjoying membership of neither courtly nor merchant classes. The common man was not the same as the educated man and the culture of the 'public' was not that of the 'mass' and the only way of making it so was (as Matthew Arnold enjoined) by educating common men and women. Habermas follows Kant in proposing that humans are limited by their own incapacities (from which they could be emancipated by others) as well as by duress imposed by others.

But, as Kant stated, in a section of 'What is Enlightenment?' (Kant 1959 [1784]) tellingly cited by Habermas (Habermas 1989: p. 104), 'Enlightenment is man's release from his self-incurred tutelage. Tutelage is man's inability to make use of his understanding without direction from another. Self-incurred is this tutelage when its cause lies not in lack of reason but in lack of resolution and courage to use it without direction from another. Sapere aude! "Have courage to use your own reason!" – that is the motto of enlightenment' (Kant 1959 [1784] p. 85). Emancipation from 'tutelage' is both a social activity in which individuals may learn from others, and thus be freed by them, but also an individual activity in which the individual must release her or himself from a tutelage imposed by others.

Habermas recognised the necessity of a social and collaborative dimension to emancipation and enlightenment. 'Liberation from self-incurred tutelage meant enlightenment. With regard to the individual, this denoted a subjective maxim, namely; to think for oneself . . . enlightenment had to be mediated by the public sphere' (Habermas 1989: p. 104). Here Habermas clearly offers a foothold for proponents of public service broadcasting, (a foothold initially provided by Kant). Citing further from 'What is Enlightenment?' he (and Kant) state 'For any single individual to work himself out of the life under tutelage which has become almost his nature is very difficult' (Habermas 1989: p. 104, Kant 1959 [1784] p. 86). Clearly proponents of public service broadcasting (from Reith, through Pilkington to the neo-Habermasians) have seen public service broadcasting as a mediating institution in the public sphere which assists individuals to work themselves out of what Kant called 'tutelage'.

A statement by Reith captures this Janus faced inheritance very well and aptly characterises the potential of public service broadcasting to be both an instrument of tutelage and a means of emancipation from it. Reith testified to the democratic effect of broadcasting, but defined this democratic effect in terms of an improvement in information flow from above to below. Reith wrote (in a statement where he explicitly compared broadcasting to the Athenian agora) that broadcasting brought 'the personalities of the leading figures to the fireside' (Reith 1949: p. 135) of (those whom elsewhere he called ordinary people) 'mini-men' whom he regretted 'have all got votes' (cited in Boyle 1972: p. 18).[28]

However, in his discussion of tutelage, Habermas did not cite other sections of 'What is Enlightenment?' which are relevant to consideration of the role and purpose of public service broadcasting. Kant also stated, that:

> Laziness and cowardice are the reasons why so great a portion of mankind, after nature has long since discharged them from external direction [. . .], nevertheless remains under lifelong tutelage, and why it is so easy for others to set themselves up as their guardians. It is so easy not to be of age. If I have a book which understands for me, a pastor who has a conscience for me, a physician who decides my diet, and so forth, I need not trouble myself. I need not think, if I can only pay – others will readily undertake the irksome work for me.
>
> (Kant 1959 [1784] p. 85)]

This passage has the authentic, noble, smack of Kant's earnest Prussian pietism about it. It affords little space for fun, diversion or the seductions of being not of age. However it stands as a powerful rationale for benevolent social action to emancipate man from tutelage, (to use Kant's category) and one chosen by European public service broadcasting which, when free of competition, chose to prioritise information and education over entertainment.

The intellectual matrices in which different European public service broadcasting systems were formed have their own national specificities and the influence of their Kantian inheritance is more directly apparent in some than in others. One looks, for example, in vain for a mention of Kant in Reith's writings. Yet in his and his successors' definitions of public service broadcasting there is, surely, an unmistakably Kantian strain. Reith wrote thus of the BBC:

> The BBC had founded a tradition of public service and of devotion to the highest interest of community and nation. There was to hand a mighty instrument to instruct and fashion public opinion; to banish ignorance and misery; to contribute richly and in many ways to the sum total of human wellbeing
>
> (Reith 1949: p. 103)[29]

Reith's successors', (as Directors General of the BBC), statements resonated with similarly Kantian strains (see Curran 1971 cited in Smith 1974: p. 190–1; Haley 1948 cited in Smith 1974: p. 83; Milne cited in Peacock 1986: p. 130). Like Reith's simultaneous endorsement and negation of Kant's emancipatory vision they testify to the contradiction at the centre of public service broadcasting's project. Which emancipates on the terms set by the broadcasting elites and who, like Habermas, have seen popular taste as a problem to be rectified rather than a centre of value. Habermas stated:

> mass culture has earned its rather dubious name precisely by achieving increased sales by adopting to the need for relaxation and entertainment on the part of consumer strata

with relatively little education, rather than through the guidance of an enlarged public toward the appreciation of a culture undamaged in its substance.

(Habermas 1989: p. 165)

It is easy to see popular taste, and the commercial broadcasting which has served it, as embodying Kant's vision of being not of age, of immersion in a 'book which understands for me' and Habermas' attribution of a 'dubious name' to mass culture clearly refers directly to contemporary, for profit, mass media. But we may also see public service broadcasting as embodying Kant's vision of an agency of tutelage. What more clearly than Pilkington's definition of the role of the governors of broadcasting exemplifies Kant's notion of 'a pastor who has a conscience for me, a physician who decides my diet'. Pilkington referred to 'the Governors' and Members[30] concern to represent and secure the public interest in broadcasting. It is for them to judge what the public interest is, and it is for this that they are answerable. They must not do so by assessing the balance of opinion on this or that element of programme content, and then adopting the majority view as their own; for as we have already noted, this would be to mistake 'what the public wants' in the misleading sense implied when the phrase is used as a slogan – for the public interest' (Pilkington 1962: Para 408).

Habermas' formulation 'through the guidance of an enlarged public toward the appreciation of a culture undamaged in its substance', clearly does not refer to a relationship of equals but to a Pilkingtonian guidance of consumers by guardians away from what he calls 'consumption ready' cultural goods to 'serious involvement with culture' (Habermas 1989: p. 166). As Peacock (1986), Kimmel (1982), Bourges (1993) and others have recognised public service broadcasting has paid too little regard to the needs and desires of those whom it has undertaken to enlighten.

Not only were public service broadcasters too little prepared to recognise the importance of demotic entertainment in their programme schedules, (and paid a high price in loss of audience share and legitimacy when confronted with commercial competition which supplied viewers' and listeners' taste for cakes and ale), but so too are proponents of public service broadcasting characteristically slow to recognise that broadcasting is more than a political medium – it is an aesthetic medium too. As Kant stated 'If we attend to the course of conversation in mixed companies consisting not merely of scholars and subtle reasoners but also of business people and women, we notice that besides storytelling and jesting they have another entertainment, namely, arguing' (Kant 1949: p. 250–1 cited in Habermas 1989: p. 106). Curiously, Habermas cites Kant's recognition that human conversation and social experience is animated by storytelling and jesting as well as by argument to appropriate Kant's invocation of argument but Habermas neglects Kant's acknowledgement of storytelling and jesting. European public service broadcasting has similarly given greater salience to argument than to jesting, and consequently has been vulnerable to the influx of competing commercial channels that followed technological and regulatory change in Europe during the 1980s.

Common to the inductivist and deductivist proponents of public service broadcasting is a categorical opposition between public service broadcasting and the market. This opposition is clearly signalled in the title of Garnham's seminal article 'Public Service versus the Market' (Garnham 1983) but Blumler is scarcely less explicit. He proposed a categorical difference between market and public service broadcasting systems. One, he contends, is rooted in a 'standpoint of social ethics' and the other animated solely by the 'capture of audience as market as the prime, normative and pragmatic goal of the broadcasting business' (Blumler 1992: p. 2). It is undoubtedly true that the formula 'capture of audience as market as the prime, normative and pragmatic goal of the broadcasting business' (Blumler 1992: p. 2) justly characterises some contemporary European broadcasters. But it does not accurately represent the outlook of all theorists of (or apologists for) the adoption of market principles as a basis for the organisation of broadcasting. Indeed part of the power of market ideas has been the ethical component which they contain (see, inter alia, Friedman and Friedman 1981). And it is difficult to reconcile many public service broadcasters' intransigent defence of their historical monopolies, their subordination to party political agendas or their own commercial practices with a 'standpoint of ethics'. As 'modernising' public service broadcasters have recognised.

Notes

1   ARD Arbeitsgemeinschaft der Öffentlich-rechtlichen Rundfunkanstalten der Bundesrepublik Deutschland. Germany. ZDF Zweites Deutsches Fernsehen. Germany. RAI Radiotelevisione Italiana. Italy. TVE Television Espanola. Spain. RTP Radiotelevisao Portuguesa. Portugal. BBC British Broadcasting Corporation. UK.

2   See Collins 1998a for discussion of the EU Protocol. The Council of Europe's fourth Ministerial Conference on Mass Media Policy (Prague 7–8 December 1994) promulgated Resolution No. 1 on the Future of Public Service Broadcasting and the Committee of Ministers of the Council of Europe adopted Recommendation R (96) 10 guaranteeing the independence of public service broadcasting. See Jakubowicz 2002.

3   Not least the peculiar economic characteristics of broadcasting, (which mean that the theoretical criteria of well functioning markets can only be satisfied at the expense of significant welfare loss), and which therefore provide solid grounds for intervention in broadcasting markets. Cave (1985) and Garnham (1990: p. 120) have pointed out that spectrum scarcity is not the only rationale for the regulation of broadcasting. Garnham has argued that a range of social, political and cultural public policy goals legitimise intervention and that market arrangements will entrench information poverty and disempower the poor. Both contend that welfare is likely to be maximised through forms of public provision of services.

      Cave, (following Coase), has argued that the public good, non-excludable, character of market failure in broadcasting provides powerful reasons for intervention which are independent of spectrum scarcity and that, moreover, establishment of excludable services will not satisfactorily rectify market failure.
Because one person's consumption of a broadcast signal deprives no other person of the opportunity to consume it broadcasting is considered to be a 'non-rival' good. Moreover, because viewers and listeners cannot be excluded from consuming broadcast signals broadcasting is, unlike most other goods and services, 'non-excludable'. The 'non rival' and 'non excludable' characteristics of broadcasting have meant that, (until recent developments in communication technologies, notably the development of robust and inexpensive systems for encrypting broadcast signals), broadcasting markets were 'failed markets' and that, therefore, political intervention is both necessary and legitimate.

      Cave argued (Cave 1985: p. 26) that excludable services (such as subscription television) will tend to undersupply broadcasts and that even a broadcasting market offering a range of satellite supplied encrypted services will be a failed market in which intervention is required to maximise welfare.

4   For more than eighty years, the BBC has been the UK's flagship public service broadcaster providing radio and television services. ITV was established in 1955 as a commercial, advertising financed, highly regulated television network. ILR, commercial advertising financed, local radio began in 1973.

5   Since all markets are to some degree failed markets, market theorists can argue that even market which is acknowledged to be imperfect may be the 'least worst', even if not the 'first best', basis for the organisation of broadcasting services.

6   Neo-Habermasian refers to the development of ideas advanced by the contemporary German philosopher, Jürgen Habermas, by British commentators on public service broadcasting, of whom Garnham has been most influential.

7   The Peacock Report, properly known as the Report of the Committee on Financing the BBC, was commissioned by the UK government and published in 1986. It is known as the Peacock Report (and the committee which wrote it is known as the Peacock Committee) after Alan (now Sir Alan) Peacock who was the committee chairman.

8   Channel 4 and S4C (the Welsh language television channel serving Wales) were established in 1982 as public service television channels.

9   Austria, Belgium, France, Germany, Italy, the Netherlands, Portugal, Spain, Sweden, Switzerland, the United Kingdom.

10   One of the most interesting features of the proposal to establish a fifth terrestrial television service in the UK is that this service will *not* be universal. Large areas of the UK, including the southern littoral, will not be served. This decision represents an important shift in UK policy priorities, universal service has been subordinated to the goal of making the fullest possible use of the radio spectrum resource.

11   It is worth noting here that the BBC's comedy series *Fawlty Towers*, one of the most vaunted glories of public service broadcasting in the UK of recent years, was brought to German viewers by the commercial channel RTL Plus.

12   Blumler's attribution of a majoritarian ethos and vocation to commercial television and investiture of public service broadcasting with a necessarily minoritarian role overstates an important distinction. For public service broadcasting has often assumed the majoritarian role of nation building, (the Australian Broadcasting Corporation is known not as a public service broadcaster but as a *national* broadcaster), and, per contra, commercial television has offered minoritarian, e.g., speciality, services. But Blumler was right to recognise, (as BRU did not), the incompatibility of a minoritarian, public service, and a majoritarian, nationalist, vocation for broadcasting. These two vocations can be reconciled only in circumstances of monopoly. One reason why European Public Service Broadcasters found the ending of their monopoly so difficult was that they have been compelled to face this fundamental contradiction.

13   Bayerischer Rundfunk and West Deutscher Rundfunk were, and are, major German public service broadcasters.

14   The 1987 Media Act provides that the Minister of Culture sets the levels of programming required of Dutch public broadcasters in each of four categories; education (5%), culture (20%), information (25%) and entertainment (25%).

15   ARD Arbeitsgemeinschaft der Öffentlich-rechtlichen Rundfunkanstalten der Bundersrepublik Deutschland. Germany; IBA Independent Broadcasting Authority. UK; NOS Nederlandse Omroepprogramma Stichting. Netherlands; ORF Österreichisher Rundfunk. Austria; RAI Radiotelevisione Italiana. Italy; RTE Radio Telefis Eireann. Ireland; RTP Radiotelevisao Portuguesa. Portugal.

16   Then of Antenne 2 (a French public service television channel) and later an EBU official heading the Television Programmes Department. The members of the Perez Group were Henri Perez (Antenne 2), Carel Enkelaar (NOS), Michael Johnson (BBC), Hans Kimmel (ZDF), and Muiris MacConghail (RTE).

17   The Perez Group was one of four EBU groups to report to the Wangermée Group: the others were a radio group, (chaired by Manfred Jenke), a legal group and a technical group.

18   John Reith, later Lord Reith, was the first Director General of the BBC and is regarded as the founding father of public service broadcasting in the UK.

19   The Pilkington Committee's arguments deserve to be read in full but a fuller version of the extract cited in the text reads: 'the Governors' and Members' concern is to represent and secure the public interest in broadcasting. It is for them to judge what the public interest is, and it is for this that they are answerable. They must not do so by assessing the balance of opinion on this or that element of programme content, and then adopting the majority view as their own; for as we have already noted, this would be to mistake "what the public wants" in the misleading sense implied when the phrase is used as a slogan – for the public interest. Their task is, as we have said, to be thoroughly aware of public opinion in all its variety, to care about it and to take proper and full account of it. Having done so, they must then identify the public interest in broadcasting, and secure it through control of the executive arm (Pilkington 1962 para. 408).

20   So far as I have been able to discover Habermas' ideas about the public sphere were first introduced to English language readers in 1974 when *New German Critique* published a translation of a brief essay, (an encyclopedia article), by Habermas titled The Public Sphere. Habermas' book *Strukturwandel der Öffentlichkeit* was published in German in 1962. An English translation was published in the UK in 1989. However for our purposes Habermas' impact on broadcasting studies dates from Garnham's essay of 1986 The Media and the Public Sphere which quotes from the seven-page essay first published by *New German Critique*. The customary English language translation, 'public sphere', of one of Habermas' central ideas (Öffentlichkeit) has now become so widely used as to be unchallengeable. However, I prefer 'public forum as a better translation of Habermas' term. Whatever the English term used, Habermas' influential notion refers to a space (whether physical, conceptual or symbolic) where citizens can gather and exchange ideas and information in an unprejudiced way and through collective deliberation and dialogue reach well founded views on matters of public concern.

21   Garnham has published two different essays under the title 'The Media and the Public Sphere' (Garnham 1986 and Garnham 1992). Both have substantial sections in common but each essay contains much material which is absent from the other. This infuriating and confusing choice of title is unlikely to serve the author well. However the intrinsic interest of the arguments posed in the second essay (published in

1992) titled The Media and the Public Sphere is such that those who do not read it, believing that it is simply a reprinted version of the first essay (published in 1986 and reprinted in 1990), will be denied valuable insights and much material for productive reflection.

22 And also in Garnham's editorial (Garnham 1983a) to an issue of the journal *Media Culture and Society* about Critical Theory 'After the Frankfurt School'. Here Garnham stated that 'Central to this whole debate is the concept of the public sphere, which takes the place within the tradition of ideology and hegemony' (Garnham 1983a. p. 3).

23 An answer often given in the UK and other Western European countries is 'Via the licence fee', however licence fees are simply a tax (and a particularly regressive form of taxation) under another name.

24 Habermas qualified his anathematisation of broadcasting by contrasting its development in Western Europe with the mode of development it assumed in the United States. However, to state that 'In Great Britain, France, and Germany these new media were organized into public or semipublic corporations, because otherwise their publicist function could not have been sufficiently protected from the encroachment of their capitalistic ones' (Habermas 1989: p. 188) hardly constitutes a rousing defence of public service broadcasting. Habermas' own work offers a meagre foundation for the neo-Habermasian's use of Habermas in their advocacy of public service broadcasting.

25 However, Habermas does state explicitly that 'Today newspapers and magazines, radio and television are the media of the public sphere' (Habermas 1974: p. 49).

26 As Habermas himself stated, his work 'leaves aside the plebian public sphere' (Habermas 1989: p. xviii).

27 Reith's reflections on broadcasting and democracy read 'Democracy had for years past been a ruling formula in this country and elsewhere. A philosopher's word, its actual as distinct from its theoretical content varied greatly. Further analysis of the theory was not of much avail; what was required was some mode of linking it to real life around; to the world as known to men and women as they were. Now broadcasting had emerged; was it the tempering factor that would give democracy for the first time under modern conditions a real chance of operating as a living force throughout the extended community as long ago it operated in the city state? It must cover more and more of the field of social and cultural life; become more and more valuable as an index to the community's outlook and personality which the statesman was supposed to read. The microphone could achieve where print and the philosophic formulation of doctrine had failed; could familiarise the public with the central organisation that conducted its business and regulated its inner and outer relations. Not the printable scheme of government but its living and doing, the bringing of the personalities of the leading figures to the fireside, which could unite governments and governed in democracy as in dictatorship (Reith 1949: p. 135).

28 It would misrepresent Reith if the pawky selfdeprecation with which he closed his statement were exercised, he ended his statement 'Marvellous. That was the way one had to talk in those days' (Reith 1949: p. 103).

29 That is, those who formed the governing bodies of the BBC (its Board of Governors) and the IBA (Members of its Board).

References

European Community and European Broadcasting Union documents, where not published, are cited using the internal reference numbers of those organisations.

Arnold, M. (1963 [1869]) *Culture and Anarchy*. Cambridge: Cambridge University Press.
Bauman, Z. (1992) *Intimations of Postmodernity*. London: Routledge.
Boyle, A. (1972) *Only the Wind will Listen*. London: Hutchinson.
Bourges, H. (1993) 'The Public Service Channels in France: independence and responsibility'. In *Diffusion*. Summer, pp. 2–6.
BBC (British Broadcasting Corporation) (1992) *Extending Choice: The BBC's Role in the New Broadcasting Age*. London: BBC.
Blumler, J. (1992) *Television and the Public Interest: Vulnerable Values in West European Broadcasting*. London: Sage.
Brittan, S. (1987) 'The Fight for Freedom in Broadcasting'. In *Political Quarterly*, Vol. 58, No. 1, January/March, pp. 3–23.
BRU (Broadcasting Research Unit) (nd c.1985) *The Public Service Idea in British Broadcasting*. London: BRU.
Cave, M. (1985) *Financing British Broadcasting*. In *Lloyds Bank Review*. No. 157. July. pp. 25–35.
Coase, R. (1950) *British Broadcasting: A Study in Monopoly*. London: Longmans Green.

Collins, R. (1998a) 'Public Service and the Media Economy: European Trends in the Late 1990s'. In *Gazette* 60.5. pp. 363–76.
—— (1998) *From Satellite to Single Market: New Communication Technology and European Public Service Television*. London: LSE Books/Routledge.
—— and Porter, V. (1981) *WDR and the Arbeiterfilm: Fassbinder, Ziewer and others*. London: British Film Institute.
Commission of the European Communities (1984) 'Television Without Frontiers'. Green Paper on the establishment of the Common Market for broadcasting especially by statellite and cable. COM (84) 300 final. Luxembourg: Office for Official Publications of the European Communities.
Curran, C. (1971) 'Broadcasting and Society, Speech at the Edinburgh Broadcasting Conference, in Smith (ed.) 1974.
Docker, J. (1991) 'Popular Culture Versus the State'. In *Media Information Australia* No. 59 February pp. 7–26.
Falkenberg, H-G. (1983) 'No Future? A Few Thoughts on Public Broadcasting in the Federal Republic of Germany'. In *Media Culture and Society* Spring 1983, Vol. 5 No. 3/4 July/October pp. 235–45.
Fraser, N. (1992) 'Rethinking the Public Sphere: A Contribution to the Critique of Actually Existing Democracy'. in C. Calhoun (ed.) *Habermas and the Public Sphere*. Cambridge, MA: MIT Press.
Friedman, M. and Friedman, R. (1981) *Free to Choose*. New York: Avon.
Garnham, N. (1983) 'Public Service Versus the Market'. In *Screen* vol. 24 No. 1. pp. 6–27.
—— (1986) 'The Media and the Public Sphere'. In P. Golding *et al* (eds) *Communicating Politics*. Leicester: Leicester University Press.
—— (1990) *Capitalism and Communications*. London: Sage.
—— (1992) 'The Media and the Public Sphere'. In C. Calhoun (ed.) *Habermas and the Public Sphere*. Cambridge, MA, MIT Press.
GUMG (Glasgow University Media Group) (1976) *Bad News*. London: Routledge and Kegan Paul.
Habermas, J. (1974) 'The Public Sphere'. In *New German Critique*. No. 3. Fall. pp. 49–55.
—— (1989 [1962]) *The Structural Transformation of the Public Sphere*. Cambridge: Polity.
Haley, W. (1948) 'The Lewis Fry Memorial Lecture'. Extracts in Smith (ed.) 1974.
Hartz, L. (1964) *The Founding of New Societies: Studies in the History of the United States, Latin America, South Africa, Canada and Australia*. New York: Harcourt Brace and World.
Hjarvard, S. (1991) 'Pan European Television News. Towards a European Political Public Sphere?' Paper at the *Fourth International Television Studies Conference*. London 1991.
Jakubowicz, K. (2002) 'What are the Prospects?' In *Diffusion 2002/3*, pp. 6–9.
Kant, I. (1959 [1784]) 'What is Enlightenment?' In *Foundations of the Metaphysics of Morals*. Trans. and ed. L. W. Beck. Indianapolis: Bobbs-Merrill.
Keane, J. (1991) *The Media and Democracy*. Cambridge: Polity.
Kimmel, H. (1982) 'What is Public Service Broadcasting (PSB) Now and Tomorrow?' Evidence to the Perez Group. ZDF mimeo 6.9. 1982, Mainz.
Kumar, K. (1986) 'Public Service Broadcasting and the Public Interest'. In C. MacCabe and O. Stewart (eds) (1986) *The BBC and Public Service Broadcasting*. Manchester: University of Manchester Press.
Marcuse, H. (1972) [1964]) *One Dimensional Man*. London: Abacus.
Murdock, G. (1990) 'Redrawing the Map of the Communications Industries: Concentration and Ownership in the Era of Privatization'. In M. Ferguson (ed.) *Public Communication: The New Imperatives*. London: Sage.
Negrine, R. and Papathanassopoulos, S. (1990) *The Internationalisation of Television*. London: Pinter.
NOS (Nederlandse Omroep Stichting) (1990) 'Regulations Covering Comprehensive Programming'. In *Hilversummary. Broadcasting News from the Netherlands*. 2: 4–5. Hilversum: NOS.
—— (1991) 'Dutch broadcasting and Culture'. In *Hilversummary. Broadcasting News from the Netherlands*. 2: 4–5. Hilversum: NOS.
Papathanassopoulos, S. (1990) 'Towards European Television: The Case of Europa-TV'. In *Media Information Australia*, No. 56. May pp. 57–63.
Peacock, A. (Chairman) (1986) *Report of the Committee on Financing the BBC*. Cmnd 9824. London: HMSO.
Perez (1983) *Conclusions of the TV Programme Committee's Group of Experts on the Future of Public Service Broadcasting*. (Chairman: H. Perez) Submitted to the Television Programme Committee meeting April 1983. EBU Mimeo.
—— (1983a) *Summary of the Discussions of the Last Meeting of the Perez Group* (Chairman: H. Perez) Geneva 9.12.83. Presented to the 4th Meeting of the Study Group on Public Service Broadcasting, 25–26 January 1984.
Pilkington, H. (Chairman) (1962) Report of the Committee on Broadcasting (1960). Cmnd 1753. London: HMSO

Reith, J. (1949) *Into the Wind*. London: Hodder and Stoughton.

Schudson, M. (1992) 'Was there ever a Public Sphere? If So, When? Reflections on the American Case'. In C. Calhoun (ed.) *Habermas and the Public Sphere*. Cambridge, MA: MIT Press.

Shaughnessy, H. and Fuente Cobo, C. (1990) *The Cultural Obligations of Broadcasting*. Manchester: European Institute for the Media.

Smith, A. (ed.) (1974) *British Broadcasting*. Newton Abbot: David and Charles.

Tracey, M. (1992) 'Our Better Angels. The Condition of Public Service Broadcasting'. In *Media Information Australia*. No. 66 November. pp. 16–27.

Vickers, J. (2002) 'Competition Policy and Broadcasting'. A speech at the IEA conference on the Future of Broadcasting. 24 June 2002. at www.oft.gov.uk/news/speeches/2002/competition+policy+and+broadcasting.htm

White, A. (2002) 'Public Media; Democratic Values'. In *Diffusion 2002/3* pp. 10–13.

Williams, R. (1963) *Culture and Society*. Harmondsworth: Penguin.

Chapter 2

LAURIE OUELLETTE AND JUSTIN LEWIS

MOVING BEYOND THE "VAST WASTELAND"
Cultural policy and television in the United States

IN THE UNITED STATES, there are two basic positions on television and cultural policy. The dominant position, promoted by the television industry and by free-market conservatives, is that television culture is best left in the hands of commerce: if the people want certain types of programming, then the market will provide them. This view can be traced to the free-market ideology that permitted U.S. broadcasting, unlike most European models, to develop as a commercially sponsored, private enterprise.

The second position, promoted mainly by liberal reformers, argues that television must be at least partially protected from the ravages of commercialism, with its drive toward cultural malaise and the lowest common denominator: only through some type of policy intervention can cultural standards be maintained and the public interest be served. This view achieved its peak of legitimacy in the 1960s, when an unsuccessful move to upgrade the quality of commercial television, fueled by Federal Communications Commission (FCC) Chairman Newton Minow's (1961) metaphor of the "vast wasteland" eventually spawned the establishment of a nationalized public broadcasting system (Baughman 1985). With the exception of political economic critiques of media ownership that circulate on the margins of public discourse, these positions dominate public debates about television and cultural policy.

In this article, we suggest that both views are fraught with contradictions. The first, as many critics have observed, overlooks the limitations of the free market (Lewis 1990) and the concentration of cultural resources among an ever smaller number of corporations (Bagdikian 1997; Herman and McChesney 1997). Commercial television favors its more affluent consumers (Meehan 1990) and is wedded to content that pleases advertisers, who typically do not wish to associate products with gritty realities and political controversies (Barnouw 1978). The free-market approach to television culture ultimately is geared toward the maximization of profit and the minimization of financial risk (Streeter 1989, 1997). Thus, it is prone to imitation, blandness, and the perpetual recycling of those genres, themes, and approaches deemed most profitable (Gitlin 1983). We agree that intervention is needed to correct these flaws.

On the other hand, the liberal reformist position, which has been less scrutinized by scholars, is deeply rooted in cultural hierarchies and class biases. The most influential broadcast reform initiatives in the United States have emerged within the liberal intelligentsia and have conflated commercial constraints with the cultural tastes and competencies of the educated middle class. Demands for "better" broadcasting have typically meant infusing popular mediums with superior cultural alternatives deemed enlightening or educational for less privileged citizens (see Ang 1991 and Murdock 1992) for a similar observation about early European public broadcasting).

Popular or mass culture, in contrast, has historically been shunned by reformers. In the United States, in particular, the idea that popularly favored, commercially successful media formats are also worthy of public investment is rarely discussed (Lewis 1990).

There are multiple reasons for this legacy. The first is the intelligentsia's general dislike and mistrust of mass culture, a pattern well documented by cultural studies scholars (e.g., Williams [1958] 1963; Hall and Whannel 1965). Alternatives to commercial mass culture have historically been conceived as high cultural or morally "uplifting," not popular, relaxing, or entertaining. The market's failure to cultivate learning and self-improvement—two core values of American middle-class culture (Rubin 1992)—helped legitimate the slow development of educational broadcasting, for decades the only alternative to commercial broadcasting in the United States. That precedent, in turn, shaped dominant perceptions of public television's legitimate role.

Second is the infusion of cultural hierarchies with liberal pluralist promises. Multicultural rationales for policy intervention in broadcasting have often hinged on an avoidance of what makes television popular, a conflation that codes cultural diversity as an exceptional and educated privilege. The vast majority of the limited public funding for television goes to high cultural, intellectual, or experimental programs that draw highly educated audiences, not to situation comedies, action adventures, social dramas, soap operas, or popular news programs, with the potential to draw large and diverse audiences. Finally, few broadcast reformers have questioned the equation of popular appeal with commercial control. Most have been rather willing to leave mass culture to the market, and this failure has served the commercial television industry, with its economic interest in the advertising sales drawn from popular programming, very well.

Thus, a combination of ideological, cultural, and economic factors have limited the scope of broadcast reform in the United States. Significantly, the most vocal opposition to the resulting class biases has come from conservatives, who have voiced political opposition to publicly funded programming in broader terms that reference cultural hierarchies and inequities. The perpetually contested U.S. public television system, described by the Corporation for Public Broadcasting (1992) as an "oasis" in the vast wasteland of U.S. television culture, is an important case in point. At a time when conservative accusations of cultural elitism and liberal bias in public television are growing louder and more virulent, this article traces the historical basis for class bias and argues that the system's cultural elevation made it vulnerable to marginalization and opportunistic political critique. The article concludes by proposing a more progressive rationale for policy intervention in the television sector, one that engages with the popular while also recognizing the impact of commercialization.

Public broadcasting service (PBS) versus the "vast wasteland"

The U.S. public broadcasting system came of age during the presidency of Lyndon B. Johnson and was passed by Congress in 1967 as an extension of Great Society programs. While officially presented as a vehicle to bring quality, diversity, and public interest goals to all Americans, the service—with the key exception of children's programs—became a channel for the professional middle class (Lyle 1975; Statistical Research 1974; LeRoy 1980). Conceived against the grain of the "vast wasteland," U.S. public television did not solicit public involvement (Rowland 1976, 1986), nor was the service intended to provide widely viewed news and entertainment. The public broadcasting system was created as a noncompetitive, cultural supplement that would present specialized programs to small audiences (Aufderheide 1991). While potentially geared toward the many diverse groups that constitute American society, public television's fragmented schedule was especially suited to people with advanced education and the types of socially approved tastes, habits, dispositions, and intellectual competencies sociologist Pierre Bourdieu

(1984) terms "cultural capital." Despite its outwardly pluralist and democratic mission, PBS addressed itself primarily to the nation's "opinion leaders" (Ouellette 1999).

Because the architects of U.S. public television saw no contradiction between noncommercial goals and the pursuit of private funding to fill the gaps left by inadequate and uncertain tax support (Engelman 1996; Ledbetter 1997), the unquestioned class and cultural hierarchies that underwrote public television's mission were magnified by a reliance on sponsorship, philanthropy, and viewer patronage. Sponsors preferred to underwrite elevated programming (e.g., BBC imports, live cultural performances, news programs geared to opinion leaders) that drew influential and upscale (if small) audiences (Barnouw 1978; Ledbetter 1997). Early audience research conducted by the Corporation for Public Broadcasting was used to sell sponsors a viewing demographic characterized as a highly educated and culturally "selective" group of white-collar professionals (Corporation for Public Broadcasting 1972). Viewer donations also were courted with promises of good taste and social distinction. Demonstrating how upper-class symbolism was played out in such endeavors, one fundraising newsletter proposed:

> The success of the *Forsyte Saga* has inspired a money-raising idea at Channel 2 Boston. A red carpet party (champagne, black tie, expensive tickets) will be thrown in the studio to preview the last episodes. Guests may be invited to come in Forsyte Saga get-up. Hopefully this will appeal to Saga enthusiasts going away on winter vacations or just to those who like to be "in the know."
>
> (National Friends 1970)

The prospect of nurturing popular television within a noncommercial environment was outside the parameters of public television's official programming goals (Kettering Conference 1969; Blakely 1971; Macy 1974). Such a mission would have made PBS potentially competitive with commercial television and would have made it more difficult for bureaucrats to solicit private financial support. But while economic factors are partly culpable for U.S. public television's narrow development (Hoynes 1994; Ledbetter 1997), it was also legitimized by a specific cultural environment. To fully understand the system's particularities, it is helpful to briefly revisit the reform history that predated its arrival.

According to Susan Douglas (1987), many of the class biases that oriented PBS can be traced to the earliest criticisms of commercial radio. As she notes, the intelligentsia of the early 1920s was opposed less to the commercialization of popular culture than to the new medium's "barbaric" cultural output (p. 313). According to Robert McChesney (1994), advertising-sponsored radio was also "appalling" to reformers and to many influential radio listeners of the 1930s, as was the idea of corporations directing public discourse via mass broadcasting. However, as he notes, the reform movement that sought noncommercial channels as a condition of the 1934 Communications Act was plagued by elitist views of how radio should be properly used and by a failure to attract widespread popular support. Since commercial radio was thought, in the words of one reformer, to be already geared to the "moronic mob" who lacked "good taste and intelligence and ambition for culture," some called for an alternative "aimed at and above a frankly upper-middle class" (pp. 95–96). Class-based cultural ideals were rationalized by the tenuous claim that the benefits of such an alternative would trickle down to less privileged radio listeners. As McChesney documents,

> The purpose of non-commercial programming was to provide the cultural uplift that had not been deemed profitable by the commercial broadcasters. This stance left the broadcast reform movement in a precarious position. On one hand, it generated a class-based

populist critique of the corporate domination of the ether on free speech grounds that had the potential to appeal to society's dispossessed elements. On the other hand, its cultural critique was aimed largely at an elite audience and, if anything, it repelled potential support from those who welcomed a significant place for entertainment programming on radio.

(McChesney 1994, p. 67)

Quality television, for Minow (1961) and his supporters, was also conceived as the antithesis of the Westerns, quiz shows, and other popular commercially successful television shows of the 1960s. The medium's vulgar cultural orientation, not its commercial organization, was the issue. The tastes of the intelligentsia, whether televised opera or portentous panel discussions, were again justified as uplifting for the uncultivated mass audience. But as James Baughman (1985) notes, Minow's efforts to improve commercial television were stymied by a failure to attract public support.

The size and composition of Minow's supporters presented difficulties. Those sharing most of his concerns tended to be among the least representative Americans: the well-educated, well-heeled upper-middle-class liberals. Although expert at mobilizing a PTA chapter, they made for a minor constituency, an elite. Absent were members of the working class or racial and ethnic minorities.

(Baughman 1985, p. 170)

According to Baughman (1985), Minow's failures signaled a crack in liberal "idealism about the possibilities of the American system of broadcasting," which "once expected capitalist owners to serve a mass market and a higher mission" (p. 173). When demands for a public alternative (beyond the limited ETV system) emerged in the late 1950s and escalated in the early 1960s, the reform discourse drew on the historical equation of popularity with commercial control, public service with small audiences and cultural privilege (Ouellette 1999). Following the quiz show scandals of 1959, for example, Arthur Schlesinger Jr. (1961), implored the U.S. government to "rescue" television, defining the placement of high culture on television as the priority (p. 149). Conceding that if "horse opera sells more autos than Ed Murrow then the advertiser has to go for horse opera," the editor of *Harper's* magazine called for a public service entity to produce high-quality news, arts, classical music, and theater. As he saw it, the viewer who was not interested could simply turn to a "western on CBS or a song-and-dance number on ABC" (Fischer 1959, pp. 10–14).

Another example was Walter Lippmann's (1959) declaration that there was "something radically wrong with the national policy under which television operates." Writing in his *New York Herald Tribune* column, Lippmann cast commercial television as a "prostitute of merchandising," but his main complaint was the lack of "effective news reporting, good art, and civilized entertainment." The solution, as he saw it, was for the people at "Harvard and Yale and Princeton and Columbia and Dartmouth" to run a public service network that would broadcast" not what was popular but what was good." Presuming the service would not be widely viewed, he rationalized that "it might well attract an audience that made up in influence what it lacked in numbers" (p. 26; Ouellette 1999).

By the late 1960s, the Carnegie Commission and the Ford Foundation had joined influential critics and citizen reform groups in the call for a fully fledged noncommercial public service network (Engelman 1996). Numerous critics have noted that PBS was created without adequate or politically insulated funding, but fewer have examined the dominant cultural assumptions that guided public television. The policy makers who debated the 1967 Public Broadcasting Act drew from, and reproduced, a history of broadcast reform discourse cast in a top-down framework. The promise of bringing "excellence and diversity" to the airwaves thereby was limited by two naturalized assumptions during the hearings. The first was that excellence in broadcasting was incompatible with large numbers. Policy makers equated popular "mass appeal" programming with commercial television and considered it unworthy of public subsidy. The second assumption (although one that was rarely overtly stated) was that the minorities most underserved by commercial television were college-educated viewers seeking sophisticated television alternatives.

Policy makers were unsure of how public television would serve the majority of Americans who did not hold college degrees. This, coupled with the view that commercial television catered all too well to the public's "mass wants," led some to propose cultural connoisseurs as the specialized audiences most needing of greater choices. As one supporter reasoned,

> There are many areas of interest to minority "publics," especially in the fields of art, drama, and music, that cannot be economically profitable. It is these areas that are in need of public support. The Public Broadcasting Act of 1967 can give the total population of these United States a real choice in television viewing . . . The choice will not be the present artificial choice between two or possibly three stations programming similar kinds of entertainment, but the choice between programs of entertainment and programs of cultural worth.
>
> (House Committee 1967, p. 113)

Policy makers and their supporters envisioned quality against the grain of commercial television's popular formats rather than proposing more diversity and innovation within them. This occurred partly because the commercial networks were believed to be adequately serving the mass audience and partly because mass culture was deemed inherently inferior by the policy makers who charted the course for PBS.

Many cited high cultural performances and public affairs programs (which had been deemed poorly rated and thus unprofitable by the commercial networks) as pressing priorities for public television. Since public funding was involved, programming geared to the educated middle class was rationalized as having trickle-down benefits for the less privileged. According to U.S. Secretary of Health, Education, and Welfare and Carnegie commissioner John W. Gardner, public television would expose millions of people to "the best in our cultural tradition" (House Committee 1967, pp. 26–7). Supporters of public television implied that exposure to "better television" would uplift popular taste and improve public morale, aims that according to Tony Bennett (1991, 1992, 1995), also motivated supporters of public museum culture.

The expulsion of popular culture from these priorities constituted a narrow understanding of quality that left commercial television's cultural hegemony intact. Policy makers were especially suspicious of the use of public funds for entertainment purposes, explaining that entertainment was already plentiful on commercial television. Even the more radical (and marginalized) of public television's visionaries accepted this logic. For example, Ford Foundation president McGeorge Bundy's unrealized call for a public network distributed by satellite and funded by commercial broadcasters conflated commercial constraints with cultural hierarchies.

> Commercial television is commerce first, and with the marginal exception it exploits only that part of the promise of television which give the most assurance of the most profit. To the commercial networks, time is money, and they cannot give much of it away. It follows that non-commercial television must do the job that commercial

television cannot do. Walter Lippmann stated the justification for non-commercial educational television in 1959 when he wrote that it should be a network which can be run as a public service, and its criterion not what will be most popular but what is good.

(House Committee 1967, p. 371)

The presumption that better programs, as defined by policy makers, would alone be sufficient to circumvent the "TV problem" surely hindered PBS's ability to become a significant presence in the lives of most Americans. This class bias was partly concealed, during the hearings, by the promise of cultural pluralism. A top-down construction of the mass audience was made opaque by the promise that public television would recast the masses as a plurality of specialized and fragmented audiences. James Killian, head of the Carnegie Commission, envisioned public television as a vehicle for bringing "more choices, more opportunities" to a plethora of viewing publics. "The public television system we visualize is not for the elite," he claimed, but for a "broad cross section" of the American population (House Committee 1967, p. 148). Nonetheless, Gardner revealed the class biases of this liberal pluralist reasoning when he explained why the proposed public television system would not compete for commercial television's customers.

There is an element of competition in the sense that all of our publicly supported cultural efforts, whether they are public libraries or universities or university presses, are in competition with other kinds of activities, but I would say the record would show that this is a very modest kind of competition. This is a competition for a segment of the audience, a rather small segment of the audience.

(House Committee 1967, p. 80)

The presumption that commercial television was for entertaining and selling consumer products, whereas noncommercial television constituted a "whole other world of broadcasting" (House Committee 1967, p. 446) freed commercial broadcasters from their public interest duties in the minds of some policy makers and supporters. Beyond unprofitable cultural programs, public television became the focal point of demands for in-depth news and specialized programming in arts, humanities, sciences, and public affairs. Some even envisioned public television as a way to relieve the commercial "burden" of the Fairness Doctrine. With public television available to do the job, argued one advocate, the commercial broadcaster who "reasoned that he can sell more time if he stays away" from controversial issues altogether would no longer jeopardize the health of American democracy (House Committee 1967, p. 362).

People like who?

While PBS claims to reach a cross section of the U.S. population (Public Broadcasting Service 1995a), audience research has consistently shown that its core adult viewership is small, well-educated, and above average in socioeconomic status (LeRoy 1980; Public Broadcasting Service 1990a, 1990b, 1995b). The cultural aura that surrounds public television, coupled with its programming priorities, has also limited the service's multicultural policy goals. The political turmoil that accompanied PBS's 1969 debut coincided with a secondary focus on serving racial minorities and disenfranchised Americans. These goals were renewed in the 1980s with the creation of the Independent Television Service chartered by the U.S. Congress to serve publics underrepresented by mainstream PBS fare (Aufderheide 1991). What is significant here is that public television's historical avoidance of multiple needs and tastes has been a huge barrier to expanding its benefits beyond the white, educated, middle class (Daressa 1996).

Black news and cultural programs broadcast on PBS during its early years comprised a small percentage of the system's overall schedule (Public Broadcasting Service 1972). The primacy of programming geared to white, college-educated, middle-class viewers was ideologically concealed by the equation of specialized, unserved taste minorities (such as "music lovers" and "news junkies") with racial and ethnic minorities (Public Broadcasting Service 1970). Black programs were difficult to find, and because they did not attract corporate sponsors, they were poorly promoted and prone to funding shortages and cancellation (Ledbetter 1997). Beyond these obstacles, their presence on PBS was a problem. As critics of the era noted, PBS's image as a cultural service for the white intelligentsia was an obstacle in drawing black viewers (Gray 1972).

Shows such as *Black Journal and Soul!* created an Afrocentric television aesthetic, but they were far removed from commercial television's formats. The idea that PBS might also nurture programs such as the "ghetto" sitcoms of the early 1970s in a noncommercial environment—and thus free them from the quest for maximum ratings, advertising pressures, and a tendency to trivialize urban black poverty—was out of the question. Such possibilities subverted the rigid line between popular entertainment and public service.

Children's programming was the key exception to PBS's failure to serve the whole of American society. Programs such as *Sesame Street* blended educational goals with styles and aesthetics that mimicked top-rated commercial programs (Museum of Television and Radio 1994). Because public children's programming was rooted in the great society goal of equality of opportunity, it was compelled to reach a large, multiethnic, cross-class audience. For publicly funded children's programs to become a cultural service for the middle class would have been extremely problematic in light of their much-publicized mission of serving disadvantaged and middle-class children simultaneously. Children's programming is still cited by liberal supporters, such as Vice President Al Gore, as the crowning jewel of PBS (Gore 1995).

What has not been adequately addressed is public television's failure to attract a similarly large and diverse adult audience with enriching programming. We attribute the high "drop-out" rate among adults to several factors. First, the subdued aesthetic that dominates PBS programming is, for many viewers, solemn, intellectual, and dull, a distinction that stems from the service's mission to be wholly different from commercial television. Second, public television's reliance on upscale BBC imports and preference for domestic programming with an aura of intellectual and high-cultural cachet cast PBS as an exclusive niche on the television dial. Even programs that work hard to use popular styles and narratives, such as the 1980s *Eyes on the Prize* series on the civil rights movement, have difficulty escaping this cultural demarcation: it is as if they were being shown at a theater in a neighborhood that was mostly white and upscale, with audiences, in such cases, defined more by the nature of the neighborhood than by the form and content of the programming. Public television also tends to avoid the popular zeitgeist until it carries the dust of respectability, making it less topical and exciting than its commercial counterpart. While PBS would never show baseball, for example, it will show Ken Burn's historical study of the game.

Until these cultural biases are addressed, and a progressive basis for television policy is developed, policies that stray from the free-market approach to television will be perpetually subject to free market and conservative attacks of elitism (Rowland and Tracey 1990). So it was that the Nixon White House moved swiftly and strategically to blunt the growth of public service television in the United States (Stone 1975; Powledge 1972; U.S. National Telecommunications 1979). Nixon framed his politically based criticisms of PBS programming in pseudo-populist terms, casting public television as a bastion of cultural elitism ruled by the liberal Eastern

Establishment. By naming privileged liberals as the beneficiaries of a system paid for by the "silent majority" of taxpayers, Nixon hoped to win support for its marginalization and depoliticization.

Nixon's critique drew from a history of corporate rationalizations. According to McChesney (1994), the corporations that controlled the early radio industry responded to the broadcast reform movement of the 1930s by claiming that most radio listeners did not share the concerns of reformers and critics. The masses preferred popular entertainment over cultural uplift, and they were merely being given what they wanted, said executives. According to William Boddy (1990), commercial broadcasters also defended their profit motives in terms that exposed the class biases of reform efforts: "plain folk" were championed by early television executives; critics who pro- tested network programming were dismissed as "intellectual snobs" (p. 237). By aligning itself with the tastes of the less privileged, the television industry legitimated its cultural power in authoritarian populist terms, the "people" against an arrogant power bloc (Hall 1988).

Nixon's referencing of cultural elitism set the tone for future conservative attacks on public television. In 1995, Newt Gingrich called to "zero out" funding altogether using similar termin- ology. From the Republican Right's perspective, it has been a convenient and effective coupling, one that has gone hand in hand with public television's shrinking public subsidies. While the rhetorical strategies used by conservatives are surely disingenuous, they are not, we have shown, entirely without foundation. If we are not to simply forfeit the notion of popular television to the unregulated free market, we need to rethink the biases that have infused reform initiatives and television policies.

Toward a progressive policy for television

Our aim, here, is to briefly look at some of the issues involved in developing a progressive cultural policy for television in the United States. As we have argued, liberal approaches to this question have historically begun from a class-bound, elitist notion of culture. While Minow's (1961) metaphor may, at times, ring true, the notion of commercial television as a "vast wasteland" invokes an aesthetic in which it is television's popularity—rather than its commercial structure— that is often derided as banal. Our attempt to avoid reproducing hierarchical cultural values is, in some ways, a modest one. It involves beginning with popular forms rather than with preconceived notions of quality or artistic merit.

While our approach emerges from cultural studies, we are aware of the need to tread carefully past a number of ideas that are, in policy terms, blind alleys. There is a tendency within cultural studies to invert traditional notions of culture and thereby to celebrate the popular without exploring the ideological limits of popular commercial culture or to engage in questions of political economy. The approach we are advocating is quite different. In Britain, cultural studies emerged from a critique of Leavisite notions of high culture, the thrust of which was not to turn Leavis upside down, but to question the criteria of cultural distinction, to recognize the importance of the popular, and to engage with it.

The failure of PBS, for all its bright moments, is precisely its tendency to reject the popular rather than build on it. This does not mean falling into the embrace of popular television as it is now defined. For most people, commercial television is popular in the United States not because it is a source of a variety of joys but because it is the only game in town. If we want a cultural policy that will make television more diverse, more innovative, more educational, and in its profound sense more popular, we do not achieve it by abandoning those aspects of television culture that have made it so successful in attracting an audience.

As we have suggested, PBS has engaged with popular forms in its children's programming. It has, in so doing, significantly enriched children's television culture. Had it chosen this course to guide most of its adult programming, PBS would have built its schedule around sitcoms, quiz shows, domestic drama series, soap operas, sports, and other popular forms. What it might have done with these genres is another question, but by including them on only an occasional basis—and often in culturally loaded formats such as *Masterpiece Theater*—PBS made no attempt to cultivate the "vast wasteland"; it simply abandoned it for a more rarefied place unsullied by the assumed vulgarity of mass audiences.

It is hard to underestimate the effect of this abandonment on the climate for media policy. While there are thorough critiques of commercial (rather than public service) media systems (e.g. McChesney 1994; Streeter 1996; Herman and McChesney 1997), constructing the political case for public service television—as with many conspicuous forms of public spending—depends on widespread support from a range of citizens. In its current form, we would argue, PBS works against this political project because it has made the idea of public media, in many people's eyes, neither popular nor entertaining. When public television's constituency consists largely of those who already have more than their share of cultural and economic resources, it is vulnerable to attack (whether those attacks are disingenuous), and rightly so. If a case is to be made for building support for public television in the United States, or for a public service model of commercial television, it needs to serve the interests of a broad range of constituencies.

Such a case should not be a matter of supplementing popular culture with high or middlebrow cultural fare but of building on popular irritations and frustrations with the commercial system and by examining its limits and constraints as a delivery system for entertainment and information. In this context, we shall briefly discuss strategic aspects of the two main arenas for cultural policy: how the system is paid for and how it is regulated.

The case for public funding

The main goal for the public funding of television, we would argue, is to ameliorate the influence of advertising. The critiques of a free-market system based on advertising revenue that emerge from political economy (Kellner 1990; Gerbner, Mowlana, and Schiller 1996; Schiller 1996; Herman and McChesney 1997) suggest that a commercial television system based on advertising revenue is neither free nor, in many instances, responsive to viewer demand. Thus, for example, the gradual increase of time devoted to advertising in the wake of deregulation is in spite of, rather than in response to, viewer preferences. Most people want less commercial interruption, not more (Lewis and Jhally 1998).

The critiques from political economy have tended to focus on the broad ideological constraints of leaving television culture in the hands of large, corporate entities with specific economic interests (Herman 1995). These are palpable, but the limits of commercial television are not merely a function of corporate ownership; the system is constrained by its very structure. This is not simply a matter of requiring channels funded by advertising to continually pursue those audiences sought by advertisers. In the current system, any form of television that does not fit the need for constant interruption by commercial messages is unsuitable for broadcast. Most television genres in the United States are written around commercial breaks every seven or eight minutes, an aesthetic requirement that makes any kind of sustained action, drama, or mood impossible. This also means that for every hour we spend in front of the television set, we are obliged to watch almost fifteen minutes worth of vignettes celebrating the joys of consumption. Television programs may vary, but there is a sense in which commercial television itself is always about the same thing. Health, happiness, freedom, beauty, and human comfort, we are told over and over again, is only achieved through the purchase of commodities.

This point is scarcely trivial, but it is often forgotten, particularly at a time when deregulation and the rapid concentration of ownership in the media industries draws attention away from the system itself and toward the shrinking group of people who control it. Certainly, it matters that Fox is owned by a conservative ideologue such as Rupert Murdoch, or that NBC and Viacom/CBS are both linked to the defense industry (GE and Westing-house) [*CBS* was purchased by Viacom in May 2000] but even if regulation diversified ownership so that media owners were as many or as altruistic and benign as Charles Dickens's good men of industry, the lightly regulated use of television commercials as a source of revenue in itself closes down a range of possibilities. The simple act of taking the commercials out of television is to radically transform it. It frees writers from the massive constraint of writing around advertisements and programmers from only showing the eminently interruptible. No more desperate pleas from local news anchors (keep watching, and we'll tell you if it's going to rain tomorrow), no more time-outs and "two-minute warnings." And television itself, for both children and adults, is free to be about something other than the need to consume. These are significant freedoms, and they apply as much to popular entertainment as they do to PBS's "quality" television. Indeed, we would argue strongly against the notion that it is only those with the "sophisticated" sensibilities of PBS viewers who would appreciate or benefit from fewer commercial interruptions.

Our point here is to simply emphasize the degree to which a broadcasting system is constrained or liberated not only by its organizational structure but also by its revenue source. It is therefore not enough to introduce democratic structures into the management of the public airwaves: unless we place significant limits on the presence of advertising, advertising will place significant limits on television programming. This may be hard to conceive in a country so thoroughly colonized by commercial appeals, where even the postal service has become a marketing system, but the arguments against advertising are economic as well as cultural. As a revenue base for the delivery of television programs, advertising is inefficient and regressive.

There are three ways of paying for television programs: by advertising revenue, through some form of taxation, or by direct payment (e.g., pay-per-view or subscription channels such as HBO). Of these three, it is advertising that costs the consumer most dearly: first, because, like private health insurance, it introduces a middleman and, second, because it requires consumers to pay not only for the production of television programs but also for the production of television commercials (Barwise and Ehrenberg 1984). We thereby are paying for two cultural industries rather than one, both of which expect to make a high rate of profit. Since most television advertising is defensive, the high cost of television advertising is rarely recouped by dramatic increases in sales and passed back to consumers through economies of scale. The cost must therefore be passed on to the consumer, who pays for television at the shopping mall or the supermarket checkout (one of the reasons, for example, why "brand names" are both more enticing and more expensive). It is oddly appropriate, in this sense, that so many check-out aisles are decked with copies of *TV Guide*, a subtle if unintentional moment of honesty in a system that purports to be free.

This, like the sales tax, is a generally regressive way of raising revenue. The same might be said of some systems of raising revenue for public service networks, the notable instance here being the British Broadcasting Corporation, which collects revenue through a license fee on homes with one or more televisions sets. While we would-argue for more progressive forms of revenue generation, the BBC license fee at least has the merit of efficiency, being mainly devoted to the delivery of television programs.

It is, in our view, difficult to argue that television commercials serve the useful function of providing consumers with information in a product-saturated marketplace. Nonetheless, while the information provided by television advertising is largely symbolic, it is not entirely specious to say that consumers derive satisfaction from buying a product because advertising allows them to associate it with being popular, attractive, healthy, or secure (Leiss, Klein, and Jhally 1990). The real test of this argument, however, is to allow "rational consumers" to be able to choose to watch television without, or with less, advertising if they wish, a choice that the current system does not permit.

As we have argued, the freedom to have access to television programs without frequent commercial interruptions is, on its own, a substantive issue about television content. There are two main obstacles to the establishment of popular, publicly funded channels. The first is the political resistance to paying taxes for something that appears to be free. The amount of money involved, however, is not substantial, particularly if one considers its effect on an area of cultural life to which people devote an average of thirty hours a week. The money might be raised by reversing what amounts to the current cultural policy of subsidizing advertising as a tax-exempt activity—one of the many apparently inadvertent ways in which the U.S. government promotes a corporate cultural system (DiMaggio 1993; Miller 1997)—or by revisiting former RCA head David Sarnoff's suggestion (from an era when a public service model was at least taken seriously) that a tax levied on commercial broadcasting might be used to pay for public broadcasting (Kellner 1990).

The more significant obstacle to a popular public television is the power of the commercial channels themselves, a powerful lobbying group that has been extremely successful throughout the history of broadcasting (McChesney 1994), particularly in the past two decades. The 1996 Telecommunications Act, which the National Association of Broadcasters lobbied hard for, pushed commercial broadcasting further away from the idea of a public service model than it has ever been (Aufderheide 1998). Since they would compete for the same audience as popular public channels, commercial broadcasters would clearly see a popular public television system as a threat—as opposed to PBS, which has little impact on its ability to attract an audience but whose existence relieves them, in terms of political pressure, from public service responsibilities. Here, once again, we need to stress that overcoming the power of commercial broadcasting in this regard will only be achieved by a popular campaign with tangible benefits to most television viewers.

In a more general sense, the public funding of television is attractive because it allows us to conceive of a programming rationale based on social or cultural criteria rather than on the insistent monotone of profit maximization. Nonetheless, public systems of broadcasting are vulnerable to other forms of pressure, notably, as the history of PBS illustrates, from governments that ultimately control the flow of revenue. Any policy for public television must therefore involve the creation of systems of long-term funding and separation of control to minimize these risks. This necessitates, for example, developing creative alternatives to a supervisory or management structure overseen by political appointees, such as the FCC. It is also useful to consider what might be achieved by using regulatory structures to impose a public service framework on commercial broadcasters.

The potential of regulation

We have argued that the creation of PBS in the United States deflected a number of the criticisms leveled at commercial broadcasting. PBS, after all, provided a space for the liberal and/or highly educated constituencies pushing for television reform to escape to. Whether public television was the limited reform that stopped a revolution of the whole system, PBS certainly makes it easier for the commercial channels to go about their business unencumbered by public service requirements, while creating the impression that it is commercial rather than public service television that deals with popular culture. As we have suggested, this conflation between the popular and the commercial has been the backdrop for many of the broadcasting debates in the United States since the 1960s.

If we begin policy questions by addressing the limits of commercial broadcasting, we can formulate a series of regulatory principles that might make popular television more creative, innovative, and more able to serve a variety of interests. Even if we do not more than draw on the experience of European broadcasting systems, it is possible to identify a variety of regulatory strategies that might promote creativity, innovation, and diversity.

First, many countries continue to regulate the number and/or frequency of commercials per viewing hour. This lessens creative constraints on schedulers and writers in almost every genre. One reason why soccer has never taken off in the United States, for example, is because despite being one of the most popular games to play in schools, the necessity for showing advertisements every seven or eight minutes means that it simply does not fit well into a schedule in which commercials are not regulated.

Second, this principle might be extended further in relation to children's television. Past experience suggests that requirements on the educational content of children's programming are difficult to police. If networks were required to show children's programming commercial free— and it is hard to see how such an idea could be opposed on any social or educational policy grounds—many of the more pernicious influences on children's programming (i.e., the use of children's programming as commercial vehicles) would diminish.

Third, at present, the regulatory structure governing both network and cable television contains no real provisions for diversity. Thus, it is possible to have 90 percent of cable channels all attempting to appeal to the same four or five lucrative demographic groups. The most plausible way of regulating diversity is to define the terms on which leases are granted to broadcast, whereby the renewal of leases is dependent on the fulfillment of certain criteria: thus, various companies might compete with another for slots designed for various communities of interest (this was the remit for the creation of Britain's Channel 4, for example). While this is not a new idea in the U.S. context (Kellner 1990), the failure of regulators in the past to police their requirements makes it seem so.

There are, of course, considerable obstacles in the way of introducing, or in some cases reintroducing, these kinds of regulatory structures. First, the broadcast industry's power has, since the 1980s, pushed government away from regulation rather than toward it. Second, as DiMaggio (1983) points out, the dominant interpretation of the First Amendment tends to ignore market-based restrictions on speech, saving scrutiny only for government regulation. Third, the proliferation of channels made possible by cable and satellite has complicated television and thereby has complicated any forms of regulation that might be effective.

As we have argued, any strategy for taking on the interests of corporate broadcasters must be based on popular discontent with the existing system. While this is no guarantee of success, change without it is unthinkable. Such a campaign must also challenge the dominant interpretation of the First Amendment, which has the bizarre effect, in this instance, of disabling the power of government to promote freedom of speech while protecting the rights of corporations to limit it. As DiMaggio (1983) argues, government is already deeply involved in the marketplace of ideas through various tax exemptions and educational institutions; it simply prefers to pretend that it is not. This is a matter of introducing cultural policy into political discourse even while it already exists in political practice.

The development of cable systems may have put a great deal of regulatory power in the hands of cable operators such as Time/Warner or TCI, but it has also opened up avenues for challenging this kind of corporate power. First, it has emboldened many communities to challenge their cable operator's choices, thereby introducing notions of democratic accountability into the system that might be developed and extended. It has also made the economic argument for advertising revenue as a source of funding more fragile; not only are many people paying directly for commercial channels, but the existence of successful channels funded mainly by subscription rather than advertising, such as HBO, suggests a willingness to pay for television by other means.

But if we are to envision and strive for a different kind of broadcasting in America, we must move beyond the limits of a public system created in the image of PBS. In its current form, public television, with all its cultural baggage, is more a hindrance than help in efforts to reform television. In short, we need to reclaim the popular from the corporate, ad-based system that has defined it for the past fifty years.

References

Ang, I. 1991. *Desperately Seeking the Audience*. New York: Routledge.
Aufderheide, P. 1991. Public Television and the Public Sphere. *Critical Studies in Mass Communication* 8, 168–83.
—— 1998. *Communications Policy and the Public Interest: The Telecommunications Act of 1996*. New York: Guilford.
Aufderheide, P. *et al.* 1997. *Conglomerates and the Media*. New York: New Press.
Bagdikian, B. 1997. *The Media Monopoly*. Boston: Beacon.
Barnouw, E. 1978. *The Sponsor: Notes on a Modern Potentate*. New York: Oxford University Press.
Barwise T., and A. Ehrenberg. 1984. *Television and Its Audience*. London: London Business School.
Baughman, J. 1985. *Television's Guardians: The FCC and the Politics of Programming, 1958–1967*. Knoxville: University of Tennessee Press.
Bennett, T. 1991. Putting Policy into Cultural Studies. In *Cultural Studies*, edited by L. Grossberg, C. Nelson, and P. Triechler, 23–50. New York: Routledge.
—— 1992. Useful Culture. *Cultural Studies* 6 (3): 395–408.
—— 1995. *The Birth of the Museum*. London: Routledge.
Blakely, R. 1971. *The People's Instrument: A Philosophy of Programming for Public Television*. Washington, DC: Public Affairs Press.
Boddy, W. 1990. *Fifties Television*. Urbana: University of Illinois Press.
Bourdieu, P. 1984. *Distinction: A Social Critique of the Judgment of Taste*. Cambridge, New York: Harvard University Press.
Corporation for Public Broadcasting. 1972. Auction and Underwriting Special. Unpublished report, July. National Public Broadcasting Archives, Hornblake Library, University of Maryland, CPB Collection, Box 53.
—— 1992. *From Wasteland to Oasis: A Quarter Century of Sterling Programming*. Washington, DC: Corporation for Public Broadcasting.
Daressa, L. 1996. Television for a Change: To Help Us Change Ourselves. *Current*, 12 February, 20.
DiMaggio, P. 1983. Cultural Policy Studies: What They Are and Why We Need Them. *Journal of Arts Management and Law* 13 (1): 241–8.
Douglas, S. 1987. *Inventing American Broadcasting, 1899–1922*. Baltimore: Johns Hopkins.
Engelman, R. 1996. *Public Radio and Television in America: A Political History*. Thousand Oaks, CA: Sage.
Fischer, J. 1959. TV and Its Critics. *Harper's* (July): 12–18.
Gerbner, G., H. Mowlana, and H. Schiller. 1996. *Invisible Crisis: What Conglomerate Control of Media Means for America and the World*. Boulder, CO: Westview.
Gitlin, T. 1983. *Inside Primetime*. New York: Pantheon.
Gore, A. 1995. Address on Public Broadcasting before American University. Unpublished speech, Washington, DC, White House, Office of the Press Secretary, 3 March.
Gray, K. G. 1972. Black Journal: An Overview. *Educational Broadcasting Review* 6 (4): 231.
Hall, S. 1988. *The Hard Road to Renewal*. London: Verso.
Hall, S., and P. Whannel. 1965. *The Popular Arts*. New York: Pantheon.
Herman, E. 1995. *Triumph of the Market: Essays on Economics, Politics, and the Media*. Boston: South End.
Herman, E., and R. McChesney. 1997. *The Global Media: The New Missionaries of Corporate Capitalism*. London: Cassell.
House Committee on Interstate and Foreign Commerce. 1967. Public Television Act of 1967: Hearings on H.R. 6736. 90th Congress, 1st session, 11–21 July.
Hoynes, W. 1994. *Public Television for Sale*. Boulder, CO: Westview.
Kellner, D. 1990. *Television and the Crisis of Democracy*. Boulder, CO: Westview.
Kettering Conference on Public Television Programming 1969. Transcript of proceedings, 25–28 June, Wingspread, Wisconsin. National Public Broadcasting Archives, CPB Collection, Box 34.

Ledbetter, J. 1997. *Made Possible by. . . . The Death of Public Broadcasting in the United States*. New York: Verso.

Leiss, W., S. Klein, and S. Jhally. 1990. *Social Communication in Advertising*. New York: Routledge.

LeRoy, D. 1980. Who Watches Public Television? *Journal of Communication* 30 (3): 157–63.

Lewis, J. 1990. *Art, Culture and Enterprise*. London: Routledge.

Lewis, J., and S. Jhally. 1998. The Struggle over Media Literacy. *Journal of Communication* 48 (1): 109–20.

Lippmann, W. 1959. The TV Problem. *New York Herald Tribune*, 27 October, 26.

Lyle, J. 1975. *The People Look at Public Television*. 1974. Washington, DC: Corporation for Public Broadcasting.

Macy, J. W. 1974. *To Irrigate a Wasteland*. Berkeley: University of California Press.

McChesney, R. 1994. *Telecommunications, Mass Media and Democracy: The Battle for Control of U.S. Broadcasting, 1928–1935*. New York: Oxford University Press.

Meehan, E. 1990. Why We Don't Count: The Commodity Audience. In *Logics of Television*, edited by P. Mellencamp, 117–37. Bloomington, IN: Indiana University Press.

Miller, T. 1997. The "Black Eye on the Arts" Takes a Blow· U.S. Cultural Policy In the 1990s. *Culture and Policy* 8 (3): 139–50.

Minow, N. 1961. The Vast Wasteland [Address to the 39th annual convention of the National Association of Broadcasters, Washington, DC, 8 May]. In *Equal Time*, edited by L. Laurent. New York: Anthenum.

Murdock, G. 1992. Citizens, Consumers, and Public Culture. In *Media Cultures: Reappraising Transnational Media*, edited by K. C. Schroder and M. Skovand, 17–41. London: Routledge.

Museum of Television and Radio Seminar Series. 1994. *The Children's Television Workshop 25th Anniversary*.

National Friends of Public Television Newsletter. 1970. 1–2 March. National Public Broadcasting Archives, National Friends of Public Broadcasting Collection, Box 1.

Ouellette, L. 1999. TV Viewing as Good Citizenship? Political Rationality, Enlightened Democracy and PBS. *Cultural Studies* 13 (1): 62–90.

Powledge, F. 1972. *Public Television: A Question of Survival*. Washington, DC: Public Affairs Press.

Public Broadcasting Service. 1970. *A Chance for Better Television*. Opening statement and press release. National Public Broadcasting Archives, Reference Shelf.

—— 1972. *PBS on Record: The Public Broadcasting Service Programming October 1971-October 1972*. Washington, DC: Public Broadcasting Service.

—— 1990a. 1990 Public television member study. PBS Station Independence Program, unpublished report, September.

—— 1990b. 1990 Public Television National Image Survey. PBS Station Independence Program. Unpublished report, September.

—— 1995a. *Facts about PBS*. Alexandria, VA: Public Broadcasting Service.

—— 1995b. National audience report. Unpublished report, Spring.

Rowland, W. D. Jr. 1976. Public Involvement: The Anatomy of a Myth. In *The Future of Public Broadcasting*, edited by D. Cater and M. J. Nyham, 109–40. New York: Praeger.

Rowland, W. D. 1986. Continuing Crisis in Public Broadcasting. *Journal of Broadcasting and Electronic Media* 30 (3): 251–74.

Rowland, W. D., and M. Tracey. 1990. Worldwide Challenges to Public Service Broadcasting. *Journal of Communication* 40 (2): 8–27.

Rubin, J. S. 1992. *The Making of Middlebrow Culture*. Chapel Hill: University of North Carolina Press.

Schiller, H. 1996. *Information Inequality: The Deepening Social Crisis in America*. New York: Routledge.

Schlesinger, A. 1961. Notes on a Cultural Policy. In *Culture for the Millions?* edited by N. Jacobs, 149–53. Princeton, NJ: D. Van Nostrand.

Statistical Research Inc. 1974. Public broadcasting audience analysis. Unpublished report, 31 May, National Public Broadcasting Archives, reference shelf.

Stone, R. 1975. *Nixon and the Politics of Public Television*. New York: Garland.

Streeter, T. 1989. Beyond the Free Market: The Corporate Liberal Character of U.S. Commercial Broadcasting. *Wide Angle* 11 (1): 4–17.

—— 1996. *Selling the Air: A Critique of the Policy of Commercial Broadcasting in the United States*. Chicago: University of Chicago Press.

—— 1997. Blue Skies and Strange Bedfellows: The Discourse of Cable Television. In *The Revolution Wasn't Televised*, edited by L. Spigel and M. Curtin, 221–44. New York: Routledge.

U.S. National Telecommunications and Information Administration. 1979. *Nixon Administration Public Broadcasting Papers 1969–1974*. Washington, DC: National Association of Educational Broadcasters.

Williams, R. [1958] 1963. *Culture and Society, 1780–1950*. New York: Columbia University Press.

Chapter 3

DAVID HUTCHISON

PROTECTING THE CITIZEN, PROTECTING SOCIETY

[. . .]

I N THIS CHAPTER the focus will be on the protection by the state of the citizen and of society as a whole against the media, and also on the protection of the media as they exercise their legitimate functions. [R]ights in practice have to be balanced one against the other. This will never be a simple matter. Even if we are prepared to assert, as for example the American legal theorist, Ronald Dworkin, does, that there is a 'natural right of all men and women to equality of concern and respect',[1] of which legal and political systems are therefore obliged to take account, hard cases will still need to be adjudicated. Although Dworkin himself argues that such adjudications are possible, and correct answers can be found, it is always going to be a fraught process, as the dilemmas which are about to be discussed will illustrate.

The American Bill of Rights, which contains the various amendments to the Constitution, states that 'Congress shall make no law . . . abridging the freedom of speech, or of the press', and other more recent conventions contain similar provisions. The Universal Declaration of Human Rights of 1948 and the European Convention on Human Rights both assert that individuals are entitled to hold what opinions they wish, and to communicate them to others, but both also quickly add that there may be good reasons – 'respect of the rights or reputation of others or for the protection of national security or of public order or of public health or morals' – why these rights may have to be restricted in some circumstances.[2] In adjudicating between competing claims now, instead of the interests of the state being weighed in the balance against the interests of citizens, the rights of individuals will need to be considered vis-à-vis those of other individuals, organizations such as the media, and also perhaps the state. This may well mean that the state is required to protect citizens against itself, which is no easy task. And that is why a properly democratic society has to ensure that the institutions of the state are not simply branches of one overarching monolith, but component parts which have discrete, and on occasion, conflicting functions.

[T]his separation of powers is to be seen most vividly in the USA: not only is the Presidency distinct from the Congress, but the courts also, including the Supreme Court, have a role in upholding the constitution and in enforcing the rights of the citizen against the other agencies of the state, if that becomes necessary, as it did, for example, during the civil rights struggles of the 1950s and 1960s, when decisions of the Supreme Court rendered discriminatory social and educational practices illegal.[3]

Individual rights and the law

All citizens are entitled to redress for defamatory attacks, to a fair trial and to privacy. Such a statement might seem axiomatic, but in practice these entitlements are far from straightforward, nor are they universally accessible.

Defamation occurs when false statements are made about individuals, which damage them in the eyes of their fellow citizens: oral defamation is known as slander, written, libel. Different legal systems have slightly varying definitions but this is the gist of what is involved.[4] And few would wish to argue that erroneous statements about individuals should be circulated without some kind of penalty being imposed on the perpetrators. In Britain the remedy lies in suing those responsible and hoping for substantial damages if the case is won. The difficulty is that legal aid is not available, and the lawyers' fees accumulated during an unsuccessful defamation suit can be ruinous. Arguably that prevents frivolous actions, although it must also discourage people who feel they have a good case, but are unhappy about risking financial nemesis. For the media, libel is a central and ongoing concern, since newspapers and broadcasting organizations, if they are doing their jobs properly, must frequently put into the public realm material which is damaging to the individuals involved. It cannot easily be argued that if such material is a pack of lies there should be no punishment. However if the penalty for libel is very high, there must be a serious risk that the media will hesitate to publish, not simply because there might be a lingering doubt over the veracity of the allegations being made, but because, in the event of a libel suit which is successfully resisted, there might still be substantial legal bills. The situation just described is the one which has pertained in England for a very long time – not in Britain as a whole, it must be stressed, for in Scotland the procedures are different, and the rewards for the successful litigant in practice much lower than is the case south of the border.[5]

Indeed London has become known as the libel capital of the world because of the large damages awards, sometimes of half-a-million pounds or more which have been made against newspapers and on occasion broadcasting organizations.[6] Even although in the mid nineties it became possible for the English Appeal Court to reduce awards, there is still a remarkable contrast in the approaches taken in Britain and in the United States. In 1964 the American Supreme Court ruled that for a libel case against the press instituted by a public official to be successful then the official had to demonstrate 'actual malice', which was defined as 'with knowledge that . . . [the statement] . . . was false or with reckless disregard of whether it was false or not'.[7] While discussion continues as to who exactly can be regarded as a public official, what this decision means in practice is that if a newspaper or broadcasting organization makes allegations of improper conduct against a politician, which turn out to be false, but can argue convincingly that it genuinely believed the accusations to be true, and had not acted recklessly, then it will not find itself paying substantial damages. In the UK that option has not been available (however, an appeal court judgment in mid-1998 has suggested that a limited form of it might become available in the future).

The consequences of this contrast are clear enough. It is often pointed out that 'Watergate' could never have happened in Britain. This does not mean that a scandal similar to the one which enveloped President Nixon in the early 1970s could never occur in the United Kingdom. But the way it was exposed by two *Washington Post* journalists, Bob Woodward and Carl Bernstein, who made allegations about the behaviour of the President and his entourage, which in the initial stages could not have been justified in court, would have been impossible to replicate in Britain: the immediate response of the relevant public officials would have been to send for their lawyers and to sue, with every expectation of success.[8] [. . .]

In the UK, and in other countries, there is legislation which prohibits the dissemination of material designed to stir up racial hatred. In practice the British law has hardly been used against the media, and when it has, it is fringe publications produced by fanatics which have been prosecuted. What the existence of such legislation does, however, is to send a clear signal that freedom of speech does not encompass racial abuse. Again there is a marked contrast with America, where only if it can be shown, for example, that a racially offensive broadcast is likely to produce violence, will the Federal Communications Commission (FCC) take action. In recent years American talk radio 'shock jocks' have hurled abuse at minorities, women, the federal government and the President of the United States with impunity, under the protective umbrella of the First Amendment.[. . .]

If citizens are entitled to redress for defamation and protection against racially motivated abuse, then they are also entitled to a fair trial, and it would therefore seem to follow that from the moment of arrest until the judicial process is completed there should be no publicity which might interfere with that objective. The approaches taken on either side of the Atlantic differ considerably.

In Britain prejudicial reporting before or during a trial consititutes contempt of court, for which the penalities include both fines and imprisonment. The law has been rather slackly interpreted on occasions in England in recent times – for example, after the arrest of the serial murderers, Frederick and Rosemary West, in 1994 the English tabloids ran stories which were openly prejudicial – although it still supposedly holds good.[. . .] In America, on the other hand, after O.J. Simpson was charged with murdering his wife in 1994, there was a barrage of reporting, some of it of the evidence which the prosecution was intending to present during the trial, which meant that the task of finding a jury which had not been affected by this exposure was extremely difficult. The American media would argue that their right to comment and report should not be curtailed in such a situation, and in so doing they draw on a 1941 Supreme Court ruling that only if there is 'a clear and present danger' to the administration of justice should that right be restricted; others might say that the media's freedom in this instance results in the undermining of the citizen's right to a fair trial. In cases involving prominent individuals, such as Simpson or Senator Edward Kennedy's nephew, who was charged and acquitted of rape in 1991, such reporting, as it continues through the actual trial, can turn the judicial process into a melodramatic spectacle, which is then offered as diversion to readers and viewers.[9] [. . .]

One disadvantage of the generally strict approach to contempt of court in Britain takes us back to libel. The publisher and media mogul, Robert Maxwell, drowned in 1991, and it was soon apparent after his death that the man had been a swindler on a massive scale, who had not only broken company law on numerous occasions but had also plundered his employees' pension fund. Maxwell frequently resorted to the courts alleging libel, and won some cases, so it became very clear that his immediate response to accusations of impropriety would be to sue. If a damaging report was printed and Maxwell had then instigated proceedings, any further report which was published before the libel action was completed, would have constituted contempt. Maxwell's trick, on a number of occasions when he utilized this approach, was to delay bringing the full libel case to court, and thus to prevent further discussion of what it is now abundantly clear was thoroughly criminal behaviour which there was a very strong public interest in exposing.[10] [. . .]

It appears then that laws designed to protect individuals against erroneous accusations and to ensure the fairness of the judicial process can be abused by the rich, the powerful and the criminal, and that the media can thus be prevented from carrying out their responsibilities. However, the freedom of the media to publish can lead to harassment of public officials and serious interference with the judicial process. It is arguable that neither the USA nor the UK has found the correct balance in these matters

Privacy

In Britain during the nineties there was much discussion as to whether legislation needed to be introduced in order to protect individuals from unwarranted intrusion into their private lives by the media. Such legislation would be related to [. . .] data protection law but it would in practice be more concerned to safeguard aspects of people's personal behaviour, for example, their sexual and family relationships, rather than say medical or financial information, although there would inevitably be some overlap. Privacy legislation does exist in some countries. For example, in France an individual's personal life is considered sacrosanct and criminal penalties can be imposed on media employees who take or publish unauthorised photographs and information; it is also open to the courts to act to prevent an infringement which is pending. That President Mitterrand had a daughter by a mistress only became general public knowledge in the last year of his life. In Britain – or in America – it is very doubtful if such information would have stayed long in the private realm, for the most intimate details of the personal lives of the famous are published regularly in the tabloid press. In the nineties it has been possible, for example, to read a transcript of a conversation which supposedly took place between the Prince of Wales and his alleged mistress, and the claims from one of the Prince's servants about where and how the heir to the throne and the lady made love. Pictures of a makeshift bed on which a cabinet minister and his mistress had intercourse, together with transcripts of the conversations which allegedly took place between them, have also been printed. Nor do relatively unknown citizens escape: for example, in 1995 one newspaper published an account of sex parties at a caravan park in south-west Scotland complete with photographic illustrations.

All of these stories appeared, the papers concerned averred, in order to meet a clear public interest: after all, the royals are financed by the taxpayers, who are entitled to know what they are up to, and whether their conduct is becoming, cabinet ministers who exhaust themselves in extramarital liaisons are clearly not able to do the job which the electorate pays them to do, and the swingers of Girvan were engaging in unprotected sex, which, in the era of Aids, constitutes a horrifying threat to public health. Despite such protestations of solicitude *pro bono publico*, cases of this sort have given rise to considerable unease, and in the mid nineties the British government toyed with the idea of introducing legislation on privacy. This would have offered a civil remedy, and individuals who felt they had a case would have been able to sue – though they would have been obliged to pay their own legal expenses in the first instance, for no legal aid was to be offered. The government was reluctant to act for a variety of reasons, not least the fact that the British newspaper industry had in 1991 reconstituted the generally discredited Press Council as the Press Complaints Commission (PCC). That body produced a code of practice, which included provisions on privacy, and sought to enforce its application by issuing adjudications against offending publications, which are obliged to print them. [. . .] In Britain the choice was made not to legislate: if the citizen has a right to privacy then that right was to be enforced by self-restraint and self-policing by the press and the broadcasters. However the decision taken by the newly elected Labour government in 1997 to incorporate the European Convention on Human Rights into the UK's legal framework might mean that *de facto* case law develops, as individuals seek enforcement of the general right to privacy contained in that document in the courts. Such an outcome could well force parliament to legislate directly on the matter.

However, as a result of a number of high profile actions brought by celebrities in 2001–02, it became clear that the courts were rather reluctant to become involved in establishing case law, or to award substantial damages where redress was needed, so the Press Complaints Commission currently remains the chief arbitrator in this area.

Similar points can be made about the so-called right of reply, that is the opportunity to correct inaccurate statements in the media about individuals or organizations. This right has statutory backing in some countries, for example France and Germany, but in Britain and North America voluntary systems apply, and where there are bodies concerned to deal with complaints from aggrieved citizens, much of their time is taken up adjudicating on whether opportunities have or have not been afforded to correct factual misrepresentations; no legal remedy is available. [. . .]

The media effects quandary

In the earlier part of the twentieth century much research focused on possible behavioural changes which the media might generate. There was concern that anti-social activity might be learned from the cinema screen or comics, that crime might increase as a consequence of exposure to representations of criminality, that sexual licence might be encouraged through erotically charged imagery. There is still much anxiety about those issues, indeed such anxiety is absolutely central to public discourse about the roles of the media in society, with government officials and groups of citizens frequently arguing that restrictions need to be imposed, particularly on the depiction of violence and sexuality. Researchers, however, are much less certain than their predecessors were about what exactly the media do to behaviour, and on occasion can give the impression that, despite millions of hours and a great deal of money devoted to the task of discovery, they really have little to say which connects with public concerns.[11]

There is not space here to offer an extensive resumé of the debate about media effects but it is impossible to have an intelligent discussion about protection policies in the absence of some engagement with it. The fundamental problem which needs to be addressed is how exactly these supposed effects can be measured. It is one thing to count, for example, the number of viewers attained by a particular television programme, through the use of electronic meters distributed on the basis of well-established sampling techniques, but quite another to assess more intangible aspects of the impact of the media. All of us are subject to a variety of influences as children and adults, from our immediate family, our communities, school, society as a whole and no doubt the media. Nobody would claim that any of these has no impact whatsoever on our attitudes and/or behaviour, but how do we decide how each influence impacts on us at any one time and what its relationship is to the other influences which affect us; the difficulty comes with quantification and measurement.

For example, supposing we wished to ascertain what effect formal education had on young people, one way to find out might be to select at an early age two groups of youngsters roughly similar in terms of intelligence and social background, and to rigorously control their lives for the next five years so that one cohort went through the normal education processes and the other received no formal education whatsoever, and then to consider how they differed at the end of the experiment. Just to suggest such a project is to invite derision, for no civilized society would permit it, although perhaps there might be researchers who would be willing to organize it. A similar point can be made about the impact of television on young people. It might be feasible to devise a scheme whereby one group of children was brought up in exactly the same way as another group, with the single distinction that the first group was never allowed to see a television set, far less any programmes. Another possible experiment might involve controlling the diet of television so that one cohort of, let us say five- to ten-year-olds, was exposed to television programmes high in violence, and the other shown programmes completely free of it. At the end of a given period aggression scores would be measured and compared with those found at the outset. No such research would ever be allowed, but even if some foolish government did authorize it, implementation would involve horrendous practical problems. In the real world we have to rely on laboratory experiments and fieldwork studies, many of which are carried out with the utmost rigour, but which by their very nature can offer only tentative conclusions, and these can be undermined immediately by raising the fairly obvious objections about the artificiality of laboratory settings and the difficulties of isolating one of the many factors which influence behaviour, not to mention the effect on participants of the researchers and interviewers themselves.

Since effects research is inevitably inconclusive, it might be tempting to say that almost nothing of significance can be deduced about the impact of the media on attitudes and behaviour. And some observers have suggested that this is the only rational basis for public policy.

A more common academic response is to argue that we should be less concerned with supposedly measurable effects and more interested in the various ways in which different individuals and groups of individuals 'read' or interpret media messages. There are however very serious difficulties for policy makers if they take this apparently reasonable approach. Even if effects research does not offer definite conclusions, and may never be able to do so, it does not follow that because something cannot be isolated and observed it does not exist. Secondly, there is what might be called the 'common sense perspective'. Many people, who have never opened a book on media effects in their lives, and are unlikely to do so, genuinely believe that, for example, newspapers can have some impact on people's voting behaviour – a perspective which appears to be shared not only by the papers themselves but also by many cabinet ministers – and that exposure to violent videos and films can encourage real violence, particularly if the implication onscreen appears to be that violence is inherently attractive and helps one get what one wants in life.

It is easy for academics to dismiss such perceptions as unscientific. But in a democracy it is not so easy for policy makers in general, and practising politicians in particular. Many of them undoubtedly share with their fellow citizens a series of related, and even contradictory, hunches about these matters. They know, for example, that advertisers spend millions in the belief that it is possible to persuade people to buy particular commodities; while they realize that the effectiveness of advertising derives from our propensity to consume, they are not entirely sure as to what the success of advertising means when it comes to a consideration of more general media effects. They may indeed believe that, on the one hand, the depiction of violence in fictional material could precipitate some of those viewing towards violent acts in life, that it might encourage a very small number of disturbed individuals to do something they might not otherwise have contemplated; it might, on the other hand, have a cathartic effect and thus reduce actual violence, it might have no behavioural effect whatsoever. Again, such depictions might affect our attitudes to real violence by making us believe there is more 'out there' than there actually is, they might in some insidious fashion corrupt us by offering as entertainment spectacles which should horrify and revolt us. They might so disgust us that we come to loathe violence in real life. Perhaps it is the case that repetitive viewing of the sadistic and the brutal – factual and fictional – in some subtle way corrodes our sensibilities, with the result that we lose the capacity to believe in the possibility of creating a civilized and ordered world in which cruelty and horror are, if not eliminated, at least minimized.

The trouble is that politicians, policy makers, – and all of us for that matter – will never be sure about the impact of violent imagery either on behaviour or on attitudes. If that is the case, might there not then be an argument for the exercise of discretion and care? But, it may well be countered, it is important that people are not cocooned from the true nature of the world in which they live, and from a knowledge of the kind of behaviour in which human beings engage. [. . .]

Discussion of what should and should not be shown must inevitably grapple with these issues, and must engage too with the generally perceived need to protect children from experiences which they have difficulty in handling before they reach adulthood.

Sex and violence are often linked in debates about what should be presented in the media, and although there is a crucial distinction to be made between violence, which involves the harming or the destruction of another human being, and sexual activity between – or even among – consenting adults, which is pleasurable and non-destructive, there is an area of overlap which has become a matter of great concern to some observers.[12] Erotic material is designed to stimulate sexual desire, and many people seem perfectly happy that this should be so, although in the Western world the sheer volume of suggestive imagery, aimed at men and women, has reached remarkable levels in the last twenty years.

Pornography is a more difficult area. The distinction between the erotic and the pornographic is not always easy to make, and the multimillion pound sexual publications industry offers examples of both, often side by side. Nonetheless it might be argued that pornography tends to focus on the mechanics of sexual acts in such a way as to exclude any kind of consensual relationship between the participants: much pornography aimed at men is dominated by representations of women displaying their genitals in ways that might seem more appropriate in an anatomy class than in any sexual encounter, and the message appears to be one of eager availability. Some material depicts women being abused, humiliated or even tortured. If we put aside the issue of whether such photographed acts actually took place, rather than being simulated – if the former were the case, it could well be a matter for the criminal law – and assume that the depictions are fictitious, might it be the case that such imagery encourages an aggressive attitude towards women? Might it even encourage acts of indecent assault and rape? We are back with the difficulties, perhaps impossibilities, of measuring specific effects. And even supposing we were absolutely convinced that exposure to such material had no impact whatsoever on actual male behaviour, could we be comfortable with the circulation of representations which suggest that women are easily available, or eager to be violated or humiliated? This is in many ways a much more intractable issue than that of non-sexual violence, for if by some chance we had a more draconian system of censorship of violent imagery than currently obtains in the Western media, it is hard to believe that human happiness would be greatly diminished. However, if serious restrictions on allegedly dangerous pornographic imagery were instituted, it is highly likely that erotic material would be caught up by such measures, and there would be a significant diminution of harmless pleasure.

Policy makers who engage with these questions also have to take account of the rather nebulous concept of public taste. People may well have no wish to watch the depiction of sexual acts in their living rooms, or perhaps even in the cinema, not because the representations are pornographic or because they feel that as viewers they are being harmed, but because they believe sex is a private activity and should be presented with restraint and discretion, particularly on a public medium open to all ages and kinds of viewers, often in mixed family situations. Many parents still find explicit sexuality on television embarrassing if their children are in the room, and so too do many children.

As many viewers are unhappy about explicit sexual depictions, so many resent the use of swearing and profanity on the airwaves, indeed the major British broadcasters frequently assert that they receive far more complaints in this area than about sex or violence. People of religious convictions do not like having their sensibilities frequently assaulted by what they consider to be casual blasphemy, and many of no religious convictions whatsoever are also uneasy about the use of obscenities.

Codes of practice

The responses of policy makers to the general discussion about media effects have been varied, and they shift with perceived alterations in public mood, and pressure from lobby groups and politicians. In an attempt to deal with the difficulties they confront, bodies, such as film censorship boards or broadcasters, draw up codes of practice in order to set out the parameters within which sensitive matters are to be handled. For example, the BBC's guidelines on the depiction of violence in drama state that: 'Programme makers should ask whether the violent incident and the detail shown are essential to the story or whether it has been included simply for its own sake. The use of violence should never be gratuitous'.[13]

[. . .]

The Canadian Broadcast Standards Council, which represents the private sector in that country, returns to the same theme when it declares that 'programming containing gratuitous violence (should) not be telecast'[14]

When it comes to sex, we find comparable provisos:

> For each of us sexual activity happens after moral decisions have been made; its portrayal, therefore, should not be separated from recognition of the moral process. Drama has a part to play in illuminating the darker side of human nature. Sometimes themes and images are explored which may shock. However, we must draw the line well short of anything that might be labelled obscene or pornographic. The test to apply is one of intention and judgement: are we illuminating or demeaning?[15]

[. . .]

In America in the late 1980s the Federal Communications Commission introduced a ban on indecency on the airwaves between the hours of 6 am and midnight, which meant that indecency, though not obscenity, could be transmitted in a six hour 'safe harbor'.[16] In 1996 Congress passed a Telecommunications Act, which made provision for the so called V chip – V for violence – which enables parents to shut out programming they do not wish their children to see; the American legislators felt able to be extremely confident about the impact of violent imagery:

> Studies have shown that children exposed to violent video programming at a young age have a higher tendency for violent and aggressive behavior later in life than children not so exposed, and that children exposed to violent video programming are prone to assume that acts of violence are acceptable behavior.[17]

They were also confident about the impact of the depiction of sexual activity: 'Studies indicate that children are affected by the pervasiveness and casual treatment of sexual material on television, eroding the ability of parents to develop responsible attitudes and behavior in their children'.[18]

While there might be serious doubts about the unambivalent certainty of the American legislators, as far as the various codes of practice quoted from above are concerned, they are all liberal, well intentioned and commonsensical. If they were not, and a huge gap were to open up between, on the one hand, general public opinion as it manifests itself through such surveys as are conducted, the expressed views of politicians, and pressure group activity – three rather different things – and, on the other, the codes themselves, then the legitimacy of the organizations responsible for them would be seriously undermined.

Terrestrial broadcasting is not cinema, or video, nor is it quite the same thing as satellite broadcasting, and the evidence we have suggests that although there has been a marked increase in the last twenty years in explicit sexual representations on British terrestrial television and in swearing and blasphemy, there has been no corresponding increase in the depiction of violence. In the United States mainstream television has tended to be less sexually explicit and more violent than in the UK, which is why the clamour for the introduction of the V chip has been much louder there than in Britain, or for that matter Europe. On both sides of the Atlantic however there has been concern about the increasingly graphic presentation of violence in entertainment movies and videos, and to a lesser extent about explicit sexuality.

In cinema and video there are pre-release control mechanisms available. Censorship/ classification boards, which exist throughout the world on either a voluntary or mandatory basis, often have the power to ban a film. Likewise, cuts can be imposed if particular scenes are considered unacceptable. Finally, films and videos are usually categorized according to the minimum age at which patrons can be admitted to cinemas showing the film in question, or are entitled to purchase or hire the video concerned. There may even be guidance to parents attached to particular classifications. What this kind of approach should mean is that heavily explicit sexual material, for example, would not be seen by minors. While that might be true of cinema exhibition, it is hard to believe that any system could ever be watertight in video rental and retail stores. Even if it were, what is to prevent an adult, if so minded, obtaining such material for minors? Or – a more likely scenario – what is to prevent children covertly viewing material which their parents have obtained for their own use? We are now in a situation where technological change has not made classification itself any more difficult, but the actual enforcement has become problematic. As a consequence, the grading of video tapes tends to be tougher than that of films.

Are there final boundaries?

Where in all of this protective activity are the rights of the citizen to express himself and to 'seek, receive and impart information and ideas of all kinds, regardless of frontiers, either orally in writing or in print, in the form of art, or through any other media of his choice'? But that right, as was noted at the beginning of this chapter, is circumscribed in the succeeding clause of the Declaration from which it comes, where it is accepted that there may be good grounds for such restriction – public order, public health or morals – and film censors in the past have been far from reluctant to act zealously in pursuit of these objectives. Indeed the history of censorship can very easily be presented as an attempt by those in power to prevent the circulation of ideas which are considered dangerous, and to impose ludicrously puritan values on the populace.[19] But the ridiculousness of past decisions need not lead us inevitably to conclude that the entire activity is wrong. What we require to be clear about is what is acceptable in the kinds of societies in which we live, and what is not. There is unlikely to be much disagreement about restrictions on the material which children can see, but real difficulty arises over what adults should be exposed to. Should we assume, for example, that all adults should be allowed to make up their own minds what they think of any film which any producer wishes to put before the public? It has to be said that in practice many film makers prefer a centralized pre-exhibition classification system, whose decisions are generally acceptable, rather than the hazard of not knowing when a criminal or civil action might be raised against them. But that is not an argument of principle so much as of convenience. To return to principle, are there any justifiable limits on the kinds of representation which adults should be free to view? Paedophilia is illegal, and depiction of it for prurient purposes must surely lead to criminal sanctions, but if, for example, there is a market for images of the sexual humiliation of adults, which there clearly appears to be, should it be catered for? If it is to be, in what conditions, and what view should we take of the fact that such depictions may involve the degradation of the participants?

In practice at the moment the final limits are drawn legally, and they vary from society to society. Britain, for example, continues to have fairly strict laws on material which is considered liable to 'deprave and corrupt' those who see it, while many European countries – Holland and Sweden, for example – are tolerant of imagery which would lead to seizure and criminal prosecution in the United Kingdom. Indeed, even although the average American book store sells magazines which depict sexual acts far more graphically than corresponding publications available in similar shops in Britain, European explicitness is generally considered to be greater than what is found in the USA.[20] Fierce controversies on the issue have ensued in America, where as a result of a Supreme Court ruling in 1973, obscenity depends on three criteria being met, that the work is deemed by the average person applying contemporary community standards, to be appealing to prurience, that sexual conduct is presented in a patently offensive fashion and that taken as a whole the work has no artistic or intellectual merit.[21]

[. . .]

It is clear that the law can be of value in providing a forum for discussion of the boundaries beyond which the media should not go as far as the depiction of sexual activity is concerned. However it is of rather less help when it comes to violence and matters of taste, and in these areas regulators have little option but to continue the struggle in their codes of practice and actual decisions to strike a balance between 'freedom' and 'responsibility' on behalf of the citizens with whose protection they are charged.

Summary

As the state may sometimes require to protect itself, so too there are occasions when the individual requires protection against other individuals and against the media. Sometimes this involves the law, and different countries strike different balances in the areas of defamation and contempt of court; some countries legislate in the area of privacy. The debate about the behavioural and attitudinal impact of the media continues, and various codes of practice and regulatory procedures have developed, which deal, among other topics, with sex, violence and taste. The conflict among the rights of individuals, groups, the media and society as a whole has been resolved in contrasting fashion in different societies.

Notes

1 Ronald Dworkin 1977: *Taking Rights Seriously*. London: Duckworth, p. 182.
2 See Rowland Lorimer with Paddy Scannell 1994: *Mass Communication: a comparative introduction*. Manchester: Manchester University Press, chapter three.
3 See for example, R. Divine, T. Breen, G. Fredrickson and R. Williams 1991: *America Past and Present* (third edition). New York: HarperCollins, pp. 869ff.
4 See for example Geoffrey Robertson and Andrew Nicoll, 1992: *Media Law* (third edition). London: Penguin, and Roy L. Moore 1994: *Mass Communication Law and Ethics*. New Jersey: Erblaum, for a comparison of the British and American situations.
5 See B. McKain, A.J. Bonnington and G.A. Watt 1995: *Scots Law for Journalists* (sixth edition). Edinburgh: Green.
6 See Robertson and Nicoll *op. cit.*, pp. 43ff.
7 See Roy L. Moore *op. cit.* and R.L. Weaver and G. Bennett 1993: New York Times Co. v Sullivan: the 'Actual Malice' – standard and editorial decision making. *Media Law and Practice*, 14, 2–16.
8 See Bob Woodward and Carl Bernstein 1974: *All the President's Men*. New York: Simon and Schuster.
9 Roy L. Moore *op. cit.*, p. 97.

10   See Tom Bower 1991: *Maxwell: the outsider*. London: Mandarin.
11   See for example Guy Cumberbatch and Denis Howitt 1989: *A Measure of Uncertainty — the Effects of the Mass Media*. London: Libbey, and Oliver Boyd-Barrett and Chris Newbold 1995: *Approaches to Media: a reader* (section three). London: Arnold.
12   See Catherine Itzin (ed.) 1992: *Pornography: Women, Violence and Civil Liberties*. Oxford: Oxford University Press.
13   BBC 1996: *Producers' Guidelines*. London: BBC, p. 65.
14   Canadian Broadcast Standards Council 1988: *Voluntary Code Regarding Violence in Television Programming*. Ottawa: CBSC, p. 3.
15   Broadcasting Standards Council 1994 *op. cit.*, p. 37.
16   See Roy L. Moore *op. cit.*, p. 254.
17   *US Telecommunications Act* 1996, section 551, a(4).
18   Ibid. section 551, a(6).
19   See for example Tom Dewe Mathews 1994: *Censored*. London: Chatto.
20   See Brian McNair 1996: *Mediated Sex*. London: Hodder.
21   See Roy L. Moore *op. cit.*, p. 525.

Bibliography

Arnold, M. 1932: *Culture and Anarchy*. Cambridge: CUP.
Babe, R. 1989: *Telecommunications in Canada: technology, industry and government*. Toronto: University of Toronto Press.
Barnett, S. and Curry, A. 1994: *The Battle for the BBC*. London: Aurum.
Barker, M. and Petley, J. 1997: *Ill Effects: the media violence debate*. London: Routledge.
—— 1984: *The Video Nasties: freedom and censorship in the media*. London: Pluto.
Barnouw, E. 1966: *A Tower in Babel*. New York: OUP.
—— 1968: *The Golden Web*. New York: OUP.
—— 1970: *The Image Empire*. New York: OUP.
Belsey, A. and Chadwick, R. (eds) 1992: *Ethical Issues in Journalism and the Media*. London: Routledge.
Bentham, J. 1948: *Principles of Morals and Legislation*. Darien, Connecticut: Hafner.
Bolton, R. 1990: *Death on the Rock and other stories*. London: W.H. Allen.
Borden, W. 1995: *Power Plays*. Goteborg: University of Goteborg.
Bower, T. 1991: *Maxwell: the outsider*. London: Mandarin.
Briggs, A. 1961–95: *History of Broadcasting in the United Kingdom*. Oxford: OUP.
Buchan, N. and Sumner, T. (eds) 1989: *Glasnost in Britain*. London: Macmillan.
Busterna, J.C. and Picard, R.G. 1993: *Joint Operating Agreements: the Newspaper Preservation Act and its application*. Norwood: Ablex.
Carey, J. 1992: *The Intellectuals and the Masses*. London: Faber.
Collins, R. 1994: *Broadcasting and A-V Policy in the Single Market*. London: Libbey.
—— and Murroni, C. 1996: *New Media, New Policies*. Cambridge: Polity.
—— and Purnell, J. 1995: *The Future of the BBC: commerce, consumers and governance*. London: Institute for Public Policy Research.
Congdon, T. 1995: *The Cross Media Revolution*. London: Libbey.
Cumberbatch, G. and Howitt, D. 1989: *A Measure of Uncertainty – the Effects of the Mass Media*. London: Libbey.
Curran, J. 1978: Advertising and the Press. In Curran, J. (ed.): *The British Press: a manifesto*. London: Macmillan.
—— 1995: *Policy for the Press*. London: Institute for Public Policy Research.
—— and Seaton, J. 1997: *Power without Responsibility* (5th edition). London: Routledge.
Denton, R.J. (ed.) 1993: *The Media and the Persian Gulf War*. Westport, New Jersey: Praeger.
Desbarats, P. 1990: *Guide to Canadian News Media*. Toronto: Harcourt Brace Jovanovich.
von Dewall, G. 1997: *Press Ethics: regulation and editorial practice*. Düsseldorf: European Institute for the Media.
Dorland, M. (ed.) 1996: *The Cultural Industries in Canada*. Toronto: Lorimer.
Dyson, K. (ed.) 1988: *Broadcasting and New Media Policies in Western Europe*. London: Routledge.
Emery, E. 1972: *The Press and America* (3rd edition). Englewood Cliffs, New Jersey Prentice Hall.
Eysenck, H.J. and Nias, D.K.B. 1978: *Sex, Violence and the Media*. London: Temple Smith.
Evans, H. 1903: *Good Times, Bad Times* London: Weidenfeld and Nicolson.

Featherstone, M. 1995: *Undoing Culture*. London: Sage.
Ferguson, M. (ed.) 1990: *Public Communication: the new imperatives*. London: Sage.
Gauntlett, D. 1995: *Moving Experiences*. London: Libbey.
Garnham, N. 1990: *Capitalism and Communication*. London: Sage.
Glasgow University Media Group 1985: *War and Peace News*. Milton Keynes: Open University.
Habermas, J. 1989: *The Structural Transformation of the Public Sphere*. Cambridge: Polity.
Harvey, S. and Robins, K. (eds) 1993: *The Regions, the Nations and the BBC*. London: British Film Institute.
Hennessy, P. 1990: *Whitehall*. London: Fontana.
Herman, E. and McChesney, R. 1997: *The Global Media*. London: Cassell.
Hirsch, F. and Gordon, D. 1975: *Newspaper Money*. London: Hutchinson.
Hirsch, M. and Petersen, V.G. 1992: Regulation of Media at the European Level. In Siune, K. and Truetzschler, W. (eds) *Dynamics of Media Politics*. London: Sage.
Hoggart, Richard 1958: *The Uses of Literacy*. Harmondsworth: Penguin.
Hood, Stuart 1997: *On Television*. London: Pluto.
Horkheimer, M. and Adorno, T. 1977: The Culture Industry: Enlightenment as Mass Deception. In Curran, J., Gurevitch, M. and Woollacott, J. (eds) *Mass Communication and Society*. London: Arnold.
Hull, W.H.N. and Stewart, A. 1994: *Canadian Television Policy and the BBG 1958–1968*. Edmonton: University of Alberta.
Humphreys, P.H. 1996: *Mass Media and Media Policy in Western Europe*. Manchester: Manchester University Press.
Inglis, F. 1990: *Media Theory: an introduction*. Oxford: Blackwell.
International Institute of Communications 1996: *Media Ownership and Control in the Age of Convergence*. London: IIC.
Ishikawa, S. (ed.) 1996: *Quality Assessment of Television*. Luton: University of Luton Press.
Itzin, C. (ed.) 1992: *Pornography: women, violence and civil liberties*. Oxford: OUP.
Jarvie, I.C. 1992: *Hollywood's Overseas Campaign*. Cambridge: CUP.
Johnson, L. 1979: *The Cultural Critics*. London: Routledge.
Jones, N. 1995: *Soundbites and Spin Doctors*. London: Cassell.
Kaitatzi-Whitlock, S. 1996: Pluralism and Media Concentration in Europe. *European Journal of Communication*, 11, 4.
Keane, J. 1991: *The Media and Democracy*. Cambridge: Polity.
Klapper, J.T. 1960: *The Effects of Mass Communication*. Glencoe, Illinois: Free Press.
Knightley, P. 1982: *The First Casualty*. London: Quartet.
Leavis, F.R. 1930: *Mass Civilisation and Minority Culture*. Cambridge: Minority Press.
Lorimer, R. and Scannell, P. 1994: *Mass Communications: a comparative introduction*. Manchester: Manchester University Press.
Macdonald, D. 1965: *Against the American Grain*. New York: Vintage.
McLoone, M. (ed.) 1996: *Broadcasting in a Divided Community: seventy years of the BBC in Northern Ireland*. Belfast: Queen's University Press.
McNair, B. 1996: *Mediated Sex*. London: Hodder.
McQuail, D. 1992: *Media Performance*. London: Sage.
LeMahieu, D.L. 1988: *A Culture for Democracy*. Oxford: Clarendon.
Maltby, R. 1996: Censorship and Self Regulation. In Nowell-Smith, G. (ed.) *The Oxford History of World Cinema*. Oxford: OUP.
Mathews, T.D. 1994: *Censored*. London: Chatto and Windus.
Mill, J.S. 1910: *Utilitarianism, Liberty and Representative Government*. London: Dent.
Milton, J. 1968: *Areopagitica*. London: University Tutorial Press.
Mitchell, J. and Blumler, J.G. 1994: *Television and the Viewer Interest*. London: Libbey.
Mohammadi, A. (ed.) 1997: *International Communication and Globalisation*. London: Sage.
Moore, R.L. 1994: *Mass Communication Law and Ethics*. New Jersey: Erlbaum.
Morita, A. *et al.* 1987: *Made in Japan*. London: Collins.
Morrison, D. and Tumber, H. 1988: *Journalists at War*. London: Sage.
Murschetz, P. 1997: *State Support for the Press: theory and practice*. Düsseldorf: European Institute for the Media.
Paine, T. 1969: *The Essential Thomas Paine*. Hook, S. (ed.) New York: Signet.
Ponting, C. 1990: *Secrecy in Britain*. Oxford: Blackwell.
Raboy, M. 1990: *Missed Opportunities*. Kingston: McGill/Queen's University Presses.
—— (ed.) 1996 *Public Broadcasting for the 21st Century*. Luton: Libbey.

Robertson, G. and Nicol, A. 1992: *Media Law* (3rd edition). London: Penguin.

Rolston, B. (ed.) 1991: *The Media and Northern Ireland: covering the Troubles*. Basingstoke: Macmillan.

Scannell, P. and Cardiff, D. 1991: *A Social History of British Broadcasting, Volume One*. Oxford: Blackwell.

Schramm, W. *et al.* 1956: *Four Theories of the Press*. Urbana: University of Illinois Press.

Schiller, H. 1976: *Communication and Cultural Domination*. White Plains, New York: M.E. Sharpe.

Seymour-Ure, C. 1996: *British Press and Broadcasting since 1945* (2nd edition). Oxford: Blackwell.

Skogerbo, E. 1997: The Press Subsidy System in Norway. *European Journal of Communication*, 12, 1.

Smith, A. 1976: *The Shadow in the Cave*. London: Quartet.

Smythe, D. 1981: *Dependency Road*. Norwood, New Jersey: Ablex.

Snoddy, R. 1993: *The Good, the Bad and the Unacceptable*. London: Faber.

Storey, J. 1993: *Introductory Guide to Cultural Theory and Popular Culture*. New York: Harvester.

Taylor, C. 1992: *The Malaise of Modernity*. Boston: Harvard University Press.

Thomson, A. 1992: *Smokescreen: the media, the censors and Gulf War*. Tunbridge Wells: Laburnham and Speellmount.

Thompson, J.B. 1995: *The Media and Modernity*. Cambridge: Polity.

Thompson, Kenneth (ed.) 1997: *Media and Cultural Regulation*. London: Sage.

Thompson, Kristin 1985: *Exporting Entertainment: America in the world film market 1907–34*. London: British Film Institute.

de Tocqueville, A. 1968: *Democracy in America*. London: Fontana.

Tomlinson, J. 1991: *Cultural Imperialism*. London: Pinter.

Trevelyan, J. 1973: *What the Censor Saw*. London: Michael Joseph.

Tunstall, J. 1977: *The Media are American*. London: Constable.

—— 1996: *Newspaper Power*. Oxford: Oxford University Press.

—— and Palmer, M. 1991: *Media Moguls*. London: Routledge.

Vincent, A. 1987: *Theories of the State*. Oxford: Blackwell.

Whitehouse, M. 1967: *Cleaning Up TV*. London: Blandford.

Williams, G. 1994: *Britain's Media*. London: Campaign for Press and Broadcasting Freedom.

Williams, R. 1963: *Culture and Society 1780–1950*. Harmondsworth: Penguin.

—— 1974: *Television, Technology and Cultural Form*. London: Fontana.

Wilson, D. (ed.) 1984: *The Secrets File*. London: Heinemann.

Woodward, B. and Bernstein, C. 1974: *All the President's Men*. New York: Simon and Schuster.

Chapter 4

TOM O'REGAN

AUSTRALIA'S TELEVISION CULTURE

O N MANY COUNTS AUSTRALIAN TELEVISION'S characteristic form can scarcely be claimed as its own. By the time television was introduced in 1956 to Sydney and Melbourne, its form had become stabilised as a free, governmentally regulated, broadcast service for a well-defined geographic area. The US had pioneered commercial television, and the British established public service and later mixed broadcasting environments (with the commercial ITV and the BBC). US and British programming models were on hand to instruct Australian program production and have continued to do so to this day. US and British programs also dominated that half of Australian television schedules taken up with imports. Given the minimal Australian contribution to television drama in the 1950s, to feature films until the 1970s feature revival, and to limited episode television drama until the mini-series boom of the 1980s (production of which has greatly declined since), these imports tended to define particular program categories. In the process they have become integral features of the Australian television landscape. Contemporary innovations such as indigenous television were first developed in Canada (Barker 1984; Brisebois 1990). Australian television audiences, in terms of their viewing habits and uptake of television are not markedly different from those in the US and Britain. They tune in and out of programs, advertisements and limited episode serials in similar ways to UK and US audiences (Barwise and Ehrenberg 1988, pp. 5–7) with the percentage of Australian households with the VCR roughly matching US, UK and Canadian figures.[1]

But if television services around the world share many technological and distribution features, these services still need to be tailored to the environmental, social, commercial, cultural and political conditions of the country in question. Television policy, regulation, programs, broadcasting, scheduling, criticism and buying take distinctive national routes. The general transnational form of television represented by the US and the UK became indigenised in Australia. If this ensured there would always be close family resemblances between Australian and US and UK television, it also made Australian television subtly and distinctively different.

To understand Australian television's distinctiveness it will be necessary to look to the use made of the same television technologies, the nature of the public and commercial broadcasting mix, the local trajectories of domestic and imported programming, the relation between television and national culture, the nature and direction of local television criticism, and of the exhibition and distribution networks for television (its market settings, and its regulations controlling television's introduction, viewing area, number of licences, and new television services).

Australia's national broadcasters (ABC and SBS) [Special Broadcasting Service: established in 1980 as a national public broadcaster with a mandate to provide multicultural and multilingual programming.] and its commercial stations are different from their British and US counterparts. Australian television indigenised imported programming concepts, often taking them some distance from their US or British original. It developed its own drama concepts with reference to Australian cultural forms and adjacent US and British programming. Audiences customised and broadcasters framed the imported programming in an Australian informational and cultural context. Similar sorts of television regulation in Australia and the US led to different outcomes. Television technologies like videotape and satellites – were used to different ends. By the same token multicultural and indigenous television evolved their own shapes in SBS-TV and Aboriginal television initiatives.

Given Australia's poly-ethnic society, the geographic dispersal of television markets, and the different television environments across the country, it is important to allow for the internal diversity of the Australian experience of television. Television viewing was different in regional Australia to the metropolitan centres (until 1990–91 most of regional Australia – making up some 30 per cent of the viewing audience – had only one commercial television station and the ABC). It was also different for ethnic groups at some cultural distance from mainstream Australian society. This is shown for instance, in that regional Australian and immigrant groups had a higher uptake of the VCR during the first half of the 1980s than did the rest of the Australian population (Connor Report 1985, p. 405). Such cultural disparities led in the 1980s to regional television equalisation and the 'minorities initiatives' of SBS-TV and Aboriginal television.

Comparing television cultures

Australian television should be regarded as distinct from – not worse or better than – UK and US television. US and Australian commercial television regulations governing ownership and control have mostly borne a distinct family resemblance to each other. Each prohibited ownership above a stipulated number of television station licences until the mid-1980s. In Australia the limit was two stations, in the US a limit of five VHF stations and seven stations overall. Both had localism doctrines encouraging local ownership, programming and control of television stations. Their regulation initially permitted crossmedia ownership of radio, press and television franchises in the one service area and prohibited the ownership of more than one television station in a given market. Subsequently, both regulated against cross-ownership; the US in 1970, Australia in 1986. As part of a deregulationist agenda both moved after 1985 to clear up the glaring anomalies created by the limitation on station ownership rule – which, in the Australian case, saw owning Townsville and Cairns licences treated as equivalent to owning Sydney and Melbourne licences. The US raised the number of station licences permitted to twelve and set a ceiling on the audience share any one group could have at 25 per cent of the nation's population (Head and Sterling 1990, p. 452); Australia adopted an audience share of 60 per cent of the nation's population, scrapped station ownership limitations expressed in numbers of stations, and simultaneously introduced cross-media ownership rules.

Despite these similarities the outcome on the ground was different. Because US networks pioneered television services they retained the control over the television service they had exercised in radio (Barnouw 1975, pp. 22–96). Yet Australia's major radio network, Macquarie, failed to gain the place in television it had expected (McKay 1959). In Australia, newspaper companies – not radio companies – dominated the principal broadcasting markets and benefited from the station licensing process. By 1953 in the US, local television stations were little more than rebroadcasting outfits as networks provided affiliates with 'a reasonably full schedule of sponsored evening programs' (Summers and Harrison 1966, p. 96). The development of coaxial and microwave links was critical to US networking (New York and Chicago were linked in 1949 and East and West coasts were linked in 1951 Summers and Harrison 1966, p. 76). These links enabled the three networks (CBS, NBC and ABC) to reach over 95 per cent of homes with television by the mid-1950s (Head and Sterling 1990, p. 69). By contrast, Australian commercial television networks (Seven, Nine and Ten) did not obtain this audience coverage until the advent of three commercial stations in the major regional Australian markets between 1990 and 1991. It was only then that Australia's commercial networks offered a national schedule simultaneously broadcast around Australia, and something approximating US network affiliation came to Australia. Significant differences remained, as Australia's non-network-owned stations retained control over advertising but now had less control over their schedule than did their US counterparts.

Station independence has been the norm for most of Australian television history. Stations in Australia never surrendered their control over advertising to networks or to advertisers. Networking arrangements between Sydney, Melbourne, Brisbane, and Adelaide (SMBA) were cooperative arrangements between independent stations, with each contributing towards both the purchase and production of programs according to their market size (Walker 1967, pp. 293–4; Moran 1985, p. 22). Such arrangements only started to be formalised in this way during 1963 and 1964 (some seven years after television's introduction). Up until the mid-1980s programs were mostly distributed by transporting film prints and videotapes – sometimes the same copy, sometimes a multiple copy – from station to station, usually by aeroplane (called program bicycling or syndication) for later broadcasting at the convenience of local stations. The use of this more loosely organised and cheaper form of program distribution meant co-axial and microwave linkages were not as critical to the development of television services as they had been in the US. Consequently, they took time to develop (Sydney and Melbourne were not linked until 1962, and it took another eight years to complete the east-west connection to Perth). Like US television, Australian television screened much the same programs nationwide. However it did not schedule them at the same time or on the same day. This only changed in the five major capital cities (Sydney, Melbourne, Brisbane, Adelaide and Perth) during 1988 and 1989 and in most regional television markets between 1990 and 1991.

Characteristically, the US television industry distinguishes between the more loosely organised syndicated programming distribution structure used for repeats and items of regional interest, and the more tightly organised nationally networked daily schedule of programs. The Australian equivalent of this programming mix is the distinction between imported and locally produced programming. Local programs needed to be networked around SMBA [Sydney, Melbourne, Brisbane, Adelaide] to cover immediately a sufficient proportion of production costs for programming to be viable, while imported programs (with their lower purchase costs) did not (they could be profitably sustained through syndication). Because roughly half the schedule was made up of imported programming (mostly US on the commercials, British on the ABC, and European on SBS) Australian television could purchase this half of its programming requirements on a station-by-station basis from US distributors, not the Australian networks. This market structure enabled commercial stations to remain for many years relatively independent from each other. The situation was only reversed with changes in the regulations governing ownership and control, and the advent of satellite program distribution.

In the US, the networks were less tied to the stations than in Australia. Although the US networks – CBS, NBC, and ABC – owned television stations in the most profitable and largest markets, this never amounted to the significant levels of ownership of the system possible in the Australian system. In the US, ownership of five VHF stations amounted to, at most, access to 23 per cent of the total US audience; a figure the three major networks roughly owned each (Reel 1979, p. 43). Even with the 1985 regulatory changes in the US, this situation continued. In Australia there was no real separation between network and stations. Networks were controlled by the Sydney and Melbourne stations because the Australian two station ownership rule in force from 1956 to 1986 permitted two then, after the third commercial station in 1965, three groups to control 43 per cent of the entire Australian viewing audience through controlling licences in Sydney and Melbourne. When total audience reach regulation was developed in 1986 enabling an upper limit of 60 per cent of the viewing audience, this control was further reinforced. The 1986 regulations permitted ownership of two of the three next largest Australian cities – Brisbane, Adelaide, and Perth – in addition to Sydney and Melbourne. It was this extension of ownership which drove US-style national networking and scheduling in Australia in the late 1980s. By contrast, lack of common ownership drove the network-affiliate relations characteristic of US television history.

Even the same hardware led to different outcomes. For instance, US television introduced videotape so that East and West coasts could see the same programs at the same time irrespective of time zones. US television evolved – indeed, was principally sold to advertisers – as a broadcasting medium with identical network program scheduling across the country. In Australia, videotape was one of the factors which enabled stations outside Sydney and Melbourne to remain relatively independent in terms of their identity and their control of program scheduling. It helped them maintain separate profiles before advertisers while broadcasting the same programs. It held back the extensive use of telecommunications infrastructure on a routine basis. The ABC was encouraged to use these telecommunication facilities while the commercials did not make nearly so much use of them. (In similar fashion the ABC was encouraged to restructure its operations around AUSSAT in the mid-1980s.) Not until the late 1970s with the advent of greater commercial television interest in nationally packaged sporting events and current affairs television – notably Australian rules football with *Victorian Football League* (now *Australian Football League*), *World Series Cricket, The Mike Walsh Show* (later *The Midday Show*), and *60 Minutes* – did commercial television make extensive use of telecommunications facilities.

Differences can be also observed with broadcast satellites. In the US, broadcast satellites helped diminish the power of the networks. These enabled local stations to better develop their own news and information structures, conferring upon themselves relative informational independence from network feeds leading to a regionalisation of news broadcasts (Fields 1987, p. 84). With greater station independence from the networks syndication became of greater importance to stations. Additionally, a combination of cable television and satellites launched new television services such as CNN, Home Box Office and the Nashville Network. These new services eroded network shares and hastened the development of a long-awaited fourth broadcast television network (Rupert Murdoch's Fox). In Australia, the satellite justified the extension of the metropolitan television environment of three commercial stations, the ABC and SBS to regional Australia in a process called 'equalisation'. Regional commercial operators – like RTQ 7 in Rockhampton in Queensland, which had been the only commercial station operating in its service area – were forced into network affiliation and turned their stations into relay facilities for network scheduling. The domestic satellite was critical to Australian networks asserting their national dominance. Current affairs feeds were concentrated into centralised operations in Sydney and, to a lesser extent, Melbourne. The era of *A Current Affair, Real Life, Lateline* and *Hinch* had arrived. The importing sources available to commercial television contracted as the independent buying organisation Regional Television Australia folded as a direct consequence of equalisation; the ABC reduced its operations in Brisbane, Adelaide, Perth, and Hobart (BAPH is the industry acronym for these metropolitan centres) and its regional operations (in Rockhampton and Townsville). Unlike in the US, new television services using the satellite (like Pay TV) were held back to permit equalisation. The Hawke government shelved Pay TV in 1983; the moratorium on its provision ended in 1991, with 1992 and 1993 (then) dominated by policy changes but little commercial development (see Cunningham 1992, pp. 104–36).

Australia's mixed public and commercial broadcasting arrangements also differed from those obtaining in Britain. Unlike the BBC, the ABC was cast into a secondary role. The British situation – until the late 1980s – insisted upon the 'equality' of the commercial and public broadcasters. The British regulated commercial broadcasting through a policy of complementarity with, rather than competition to, the BBC, and this helped ensure that public and commercial broadcasters resembled each other. British broadcasting policy did this by restricting the number of commercial licences, doubling the number of BBC channels to two, and creating closely supervised regional monopolies in commercial television. In Australia, the ABC was always competing against two and then three commercial stations in the major population centres. Under these conditions the Australian national broadcaster did not occupy the central position that the BBC did, with government spending on non-commercial television and radio services per capita being less in Australia than in Britain and Canada – Geller put the 1989 figures at Australia $25, the UK $30, and Canada $36, with Australia still spending slightly more than Japan ($18), and five times more than the US ($4.56) (Geller 1990, pp. 115–16, Australian dollars). The Australian arrangement, whereby commercial stations can pick up a product after its ABC screening and achieve greater ratings with it, would be impossible in Britain. Yet this is what happened to *Mother and Son* in 1987. Screened on the ABC, it rated between 14 and 18 in Melbourne; its subsequent Ten Network screening saw it rate in the 20s (ABT 1991a, p. 154). In these circumstances, the ABC developed a characteristic identity crisis. It sought to be competitive with the commercials to justify taxpayer expenditure, but this drew criticism for chasing ratings and therefore aping the commercials. Expected to provide a complementary service, the more it takes this route the more it draws criticism for failing to 'speak to the people of Australia' to justify taxpayer expenditure on such a low rating network. The ABC was always and peculiarly susceptible to 'reform' compared to its British counterpart. By contrast, Australian commercial broadcasting's highly competitive market (initially in SMBA, later in Perth and the regionals), and with powerful media proprietors heading the major television companies (Hall 1976; Chadwick 1989), made commercial television operations, as in the US, more politically 'off limits'.

The commercials also functioned differently in Australia. They adjusted to the ABC's presence; Seven was close to the ABC in many areas (it would successfully show British commercial television programs) and Nine to the commercial and entertainment side, while Ten struggled for an identity. Sometimes it found it to the more commercial side of Nine with *Number 96*, and sometimes to the quality side of Seven with its involvements in the Kennedy Miller mini-series including *The Dismissal, Bangkok Hilton*, and *Bodyline* in the 1980s.

Moreover, the nomenclature was different. The ABC and SBS (after its 1980 introduction) are termed 'national' broadcasters, the stations not primarily government-funded are 'commercial' or 'local' stations. In Britain, the BBC was always the 'public (service)' broadcaster and the commercials 'independent television'. In Australia, the ABC was initially expected to be the national network while the commercials were to be local (commercial) stations, as in radio. Rhetorics of the 'public interest', the 'social good' and the 'state' preoccupied UK debates. In the Australian context, where commercial market segmentation dynamics developed largely outside interventionist government settings, and the public broadcaster adjusted itself to a secondary role, the rhetoric took on a less 'civic' and more 'nation-building' character. Concepts of 'an Australian look', 'Australian content' as nurturing Australian culture, and ideas about the important place of television in national life promoting national identity emerged as central policy reference points. With more television in the UK and Europe, less interventionist governmental regulation there, a diminished – even secondary – role for the public broadcaster, and the sovereignty issue forced by the reality of the European Community, the same 'national' tropes as in Australia are now emerging there to displace rhetorics of the 'public interest' from centre stage.

Television criticism took a particular direction in Australia. Take the television violence controversies in the US and Australia from the late 1950s to the mid-1970s. Because these controversies were associated in Australia with imported product, the *importing* of that product became a political issue in Australia; in the US, the issue was one of influencing Hollywood's generation of product. Controversies over the same programs in Australia carried an additional weight in that Australian kids were not just being affected by violence, they were also being Americanised. Social and educational elites in Australia found themselves supporting Australian production as a quality alternative to exploitative US programming with its ambiguous moral and social values. Quality television meant non-US television drama (British and Australian). This legacy can be seen in programs such as *A Country Practice, Flying Doctors, Bellbird, Certain Women, GP*, and *Homicide*, which treat social problems less sensationally than do some US programs, with their producers priding themselves on their social responsibility. In the US, calls for quality television were calls for the adoption by US producers of British styles of television production in a less advertiser-driven television service (the consequence can be seen in the 'quality' US television of *Mary Tyler Moore, Hill Street Blues* and *Northern Exposure*).

Critiques of the concentration of power in television, and the need for a greater diversity of programming, were associated with different projects in the US and Australia. Before 1976, public critics of the existing structure of the Australian television service called for greater independence of the regulatory agency, better funding of the ABC (to enable it to be an antidote to the commercials), one less commercial television station (in order better to underwrite 'quality' Australian programming), stiffer Australian content rules, and greater public control of commercial networking through the adoption of a British-style Independent Broadcasting Authority structure as a means of achieving economies of scale and reducing network power (McClelland 1974). At the same time in the US, critics were associated with anti-network, locally orientated public television funded by local communities, the limited breaking up of network monopoly of prime time by access rules to redress the imbalance in the relationship between networks, program suppliers and television stations, and support for more, not less television as a means to create program diversity (Baughman 1985, pp. 153–65). Thus similar concerns about media concentration and ameliorating television's perceived social effects in Australia and the US became attached to different programs.

In a similar fashion, 'minorities' issues in the 1980s were handled differently in both countries. Australia created an additional national broadcaster – SBS – to handle ethnic minority issues; while the US left it to the market with additional commercial television operations for Hispanics developing in the SIN network and cable television. There are differences in the public culture of each: Australians do not share the deep hostility to state intervention and institutions of Americans and do not so quickly associate at a public policy level solutions to social problems with market solutions.[2]

Like the French and British, Australian and Canadian lobbyists invoke national and cultural traditions to legitimate local content rules. But no Australian or Canadian content lobbyist entertains the Japanese-French-Anglo ambition of stipulating allowable foreign content on domestic screens; rather they promote levels of local content, proposing such content as a supplement to the international product. Success in Australia and Canada is measured by getting to certain levels of local program capacity and by bringing prices paid for imported (US) programming under control. By contrast the French and British target the entire schedule. They try to create local programming to match and displace program imports. Australian and Canadian responses are thus defensive, the English and French offensive. Notions of protecting the nation's culture are associated with different programs of action. Australian and Canadian responses are developed in a context where international programming and outlooks are firmly present, where local drama production is outward as much as inward looking, and in which policy explicitly provides a framework within which international program imports can develop (often at state expense as in ABC and SBS schedules, or the programs from France's La Sept network on Canadian Cable and Radio Canada).

Comparing Australian with British and US television is part of the rhetoric of television in Australia. This talk is facilitated by Australia's comparative isolation from the humdrum realities of both systems 'American' and 'British' television comes to mean particular aspects of these systems for Australian debates.

Australia's medium-sized television service

Some kinds of television are more famous than others. British and US television constitute 'Television' in ways that Australian, Canadian and Dutch television services do not. Both US and British television have a distinctive form, their television fare is exported widely, and they have come to represent two poles of the televisual experience, public service television and commercial television. Both constitute models to aspire to – and to resist – within other television systems. The British model is one of public service broadcasting alongside carefully regulated commercial broadcasting, managed so as to promote the centrality of a public service broadcasting ethos for both sectors and the separation of broadcasting from the government of the day. In the US context, multi-channel commercial television services operate with few governmentally imposed entry barriers, alongside an under-funded public television service.

However, British and US television are generally unrepresentative of television in that they mostly: create their own product; have limited imports; fill a relatively 'pure' model of public service television and commercial television respectively; have a culturally valued status within the international system (the UK supplying the best 'highbrow' television, the US supplying the best 'popular' programming); and produce programs with high production values by virtue of their market size, their export market potential and the international pre-eminence of the English language.

The less famous Australian, Canadian, and Dutch television services are not at the centre of definitions of television, in that these nations import program concepts and programs (usually drama, documentary and musical entertainment, with imports making up a substantial proportion of their schedules); they do not have extensive or valuable export markets; their local product is not so much critically valued with reference to itself as with reference – often negatively – to 'imports'. When exported, such local programming is rarely as popular or as critically respected internationally as are British and US programs (also available in those same markets). Sometimes program exports may even suffer from problems of 'program' identification; Australian programs often get confused in export with British and US products.

These television services typically fail the 'ideal' represented by US and British television for audiences, lobbyists, policy makers and critics alike. Australian television, for example, fails the public service television ideal in that political intervention rather than 'arm's length' separation from the government of the day dogs the public service broadcaster (Harding 1979), while the operations of the regulatory body and broadcasting policy are prone to political intervention (Armstrong 1974; Chadwick 1989). It fails the commercial television ideal of a relatively unregulated, multichannel television environment with minimal barriers to entry and competition in that there are stricter licensing controls and forms of social regulation through content provisions (McGuinness 1990, p. 22). And it fails the originality test by being so reliant upon British and US television in the form and direction of its program development (Bridges 1991).

Australian television is a medium-sized Western television service operating in the English language. Servicing 17 million people, it is not large enough to support local programming across the schedule as can the huge US and Japanese television markets. Nor is it large enough to support the scale of local production in higher budgeted movie and limited episode serial television as can the large countries of Europe (France, Germany and Italy). Like other medium-sized systems operating in the OECD with populations between 6 and 25 million, Australian television affords imported programming a much more important place than do larger countries. High-rating imported product routinely includes series and serial television in addition to blockbuster films (in French, German, and Italian television, block-busters are the high-rating imported product). Imports rate more consistently than in larger countries and have a greater prime time presence. Because of this the international program trade with Australia is regular and predictable. Television markets like Australia, Canada, Holland, Sweden, and Austria are natural markets for imported programming. Such markets develop long-term arrangements with overseas broadcasters and producers. In Canada, US programming carries a common North American culture; in Austria, Germany's programming is part of the broader German-language cultural area; in Australia, US programming on commercial TV and British programming on the ABC are central to its definition as an Anglophone television service.[. . .]

Because Australia's indigenising dynamics have definite limits owing to its market size, imports routinely occupy both pivotal and filler spaces in prime time (6–10 pm) and off-prime time alike. Yet those imports as a whole tend to attract less significant viewing from audiences than their half of all broadcasting time would suggest. Overall, Australian programs are decidely more popular than the imports although individual US and UK series and movies do attract some of the highest individual ratings. In markets like Australia's, lower cost local production is important. This prioritises 'infotainment', news and current affairs, and sets clearly defined upper limits to local participation in higher budgeted television such as documentary series and one-offs, made-for-TV films, and high-budget limited episode TV serials. Participation in those categories is often dependent in Australia (as in Canada, New Zealand and the Netherlands) upon state subsidies and/or tax concessions.

As with other countries which constitute a minor fragment of the language-speaking group within which they participate, Australian television's import profile centres imported programming. This centring impacts upon the forms of local television, criticism of it and of television generally.

A distinctive television culture?

Sir: I am an American visiting Australia and, although I am charmed by this country and enamoured of the people, there is one facet of life here to which I take great offence. It is in the direct theft in television of American concepts.

I understand the importance of American programming itself to please an audience, but what disgusts me is the adaptation of American televisual ideas without even changing the names. Programs such as *Let's Make a Deal, Family Feud, Australia's Funniest Home Videos*, and several more are plucked directly from the US market.

I was prompted to write this letter on the discovery that Steve Vizard had won a Logie award for most popular personality for his program, *Tonight Live*. This program could not more directly be a copy of its American counterpart, *Late Night with David Letterman*, and it shocks and offends me that Vizard can win awards without acknowledging proper credit to the creators of the concept which has brought him fame.

It seems from the time that I have spent in this country that Australians are quite self-conscious about a belief that they have little artistic culture of their own. The solution to this, I'm afraid, is not to 'borrow' from another culture, but to develop one's own artistic ideas.

James Bridges
18 March 1991, (*Sydney Morning Herald*)

Bridges's complaint is that Australian television is derivative. It is at once too American and (in its inept imitation and concept 'theft') not American enough. Such Australian derivativeness has also been assigned a positive value by some cultural critics. For them Australian cultural production generally – and not simply television – is positively unoriginal in that the Australian 'imitation' disadvantages the standing of the 'original' program or concept (Morris 1988, pp. 241–9).

The cultural derivativeness both positions assume is sustained by the close family resemblance between Australian and US and British social, cultural and political formations. In television this means a likeness in programming, scheduling and production models. The close affinity is further underscored by the significant presence of US and British programs on Australian screens. These conditions encourage a sense amongst audiences, schedulers and program purchasers that the Australian product is to a significant extent interchangeable with US and British products. Not surprisingly then, Australian programs tend to be akin to US and British programs – whether or not imitation was intended by producers or thought to be an issue for viewers.

The program concept purchase arrangements for quiz, sports, variety and current affairs formats that Bridges finds so disturbing are not theft – they are, after all, mostly paid for – but are part of a broader system of commonalities and cultural exchange (which is not simply one way) between the US and Australia. Nor is this exchange even across formats. In infotainment and sporting formats Australian innovation through concept purchase is possible as infotainment programming needs to be localised; the US original simply will not do. American baseball league games are not going to displace test and one-day cricket with Australian participants. Yet such arrangements are more difficult in drama programming because the US and British original has a ready Australian market. Consequently, Australian drama relies on innovation through producers adjusting – and audiences adjusting to – local program and cultural traditions with common international formats evident from contemporaneous US and British imports.

Bridges's contention that the Australian program is a poor copy of a US original and his image of Australians as having no idea that what they were producing was not the 'real article' both assume the standing of the US original and use it as the yardstick against which local programs are to be judged. But local programs – even format remakes – do necessarily redispose the original (just as the original program is itself a combination of previous formats only some of which are US). That Bridges can find Australian programs both too 'American' by their imitation and not 'American' by not striking out on their own suggests an Australian disposing of materials which is sufficiently different for recognition of difference to be noted but sufficiently similar for such difference not always to be recognised as something in its own right and to be valued as such. Australia's television culture continues to provide critics and audiences with many such opportunities to label Australian difference as flaws and misconstrue commonalities in both cultures as evidence of endemic Australian unoriginality.

[. . .]

Though it has not made Australians more (US) American, or more British per se, their exposure to US and British programming over more than three decades has endowed them with a specifically Australian imagining of the US and of Britain. This invention may have little to do with those countries' indigenous realities. The French have a word for their imaginary America created through exposure to US culture: *Americanité*. Australia's imagining of 'America' is, I am sure, similarly fantastic. So, though Australian audiences may share many of the same cultural resources as the Americans and British, it does not follow that they read their programs in the same way, attach the same value to them, or use them for the same purposes. As Riddell described it, 'a weekly injection of *Peyton Place* is not going to turn a Richmond dairy farmer into an Idaho potato grower' (1968, p. 27).

The accusation that Australian television is derivative means only that local programs can be viewed as similar to other US and British programs. Sometimes this similarity is formalised as when program concepts – such as *60 Minutes* – are bought and redisposed for the Australian market.[3] Sometimes it stems from the 'borrowing' and 'redisposing' of pre-existing materials that is characteristic of *all* popular art (Routt 1982). Sometimes it stems from the fact that Australian producers hit upon similar formats and solutions to problems as their US and British counterparts. Australian television drama producers turn to US, British and (since SBS) European programming formats in addition to local ones for inspiration. *Homicide*, for example, owes its existence to both Crawford Productions' and Australian radio's venerable history with police and detective serials, and to the success of *The Untouchables* on Australian television.

At other times, the similarity between Australian and US and British programs resides in the minds of viewers, who often assume, for example, that Australia shamelessly 'borrows' its quiz show formats. Yet the Australian tradition of quiz show production (first on radio, then on television) is longer and more extensive than Britain's, and nearly as long as North America's. And the same can be said for variety. Even the Australian 'outdoors' series and serials owe as much to an Australian popular fiction tradition going back to the nineteenth century as they do to US westerns and British 'period' television.

However, there is a crucial difference. Australian audiences (and critics), when they are disposed to criticise their home-grown product, tend to compare their local output with the US and British output on offer. In this way audiences and critics routinely weigh the Australian production tradition against contemporaneous US and British programs. By contrast, when US audiences (and critics) criticise their programming, they tend to do so with reference only to US product. In this way a US production tradition assimilates new programming into itself. This is because television in the US *means* US-produced television (until recently this has been also the case in Britain). Thus US and British audiences are provided with many more co-ordinates with which to consider their programming (including US television drama remakes from imported concepts) as a seamless continuation of their respective traditions. This close identification of television with the 'home-grown' also helps explain why US and British producers do not normally go outside their respective production traditions to look for new ideas; and why when they do – as with US remakes of British comedy – the result is promoted (and perceived by audiences) as a development of the local production tradition.

[. . .]

Australia is a good place to watch television. It always has been a place from which to watch US and British television programming. Since SBS, it's also been a good place to watch a fair amount of world television. Australian television services are not as parochial and inwardly focused as British, US, and Japanese services. For Australians, locally produced programming gives one more program choice, providing one more vantage point from which to be critical of the programming mix. The import component also explains why Australians are not as serious about their television as are Americans and Britons. How can you be as 'serious' about imported programming whose processes of construction exclude your participation save as an 'audience'? Unlike Britons and Americans, who believe they make the best television in the world (British professionals and critics often smugly phrase theirs 'as the least worst television in the world'), Australians typically labour under few delusions about their product being consistently the 'best'. Indeed there is often a good deal of disrespect for local programs and a tendency to be more generous in estimations of imports. This is because critics of local programs can use imports as a yardstick against which Australian programs fail to measure up in addition to their normal critical tropes.

But there is more to the identification of Australian television's 'Americanness' than the presence in commercial and ABC television's schedules of US product. It is also that Australia (along with Canada and the US) is another imagined 'America'. The promise of Australia is of a latter-day 'America'. Certainly waves of Australian immigrants from Ireland, Croatia, Vietnam, Italy, England and Lebanon (to name a few) saw Australia, Canada and the US as interchangeable destinations. This was as true for my Lebanese relatives who came here in the early 1970s as it was for my Irish ancestors in the nineteenth century.

There were and still are good reasons for this interchangeability of destination. Some are structural. They are predominantly English-speaking 'settler cultures' in which indigenous people were displaced. Each has traditions of dealing with many immigrant ethnicities. Each offers the promise of citizenship rather than guest worker status to immigrants. Each sees its culture as emergent and mixed, producing a new society. None demands as stringently as do the more traditional 'nations' that change be constructed in accordance with 'primordial' national traditions. Each has a version of the 'bush' and the frontier which predisposes each to the 'western' and similar kinds of conceptions of the wilderness and the environment. Each shares common elements in political, legal and constitutional arrangements. And for the immigrant there are – at least in the first generation – likely to be relatives in more than one of these three 'Americas'. When added to the pre-eminent place of the US in international audiovisual trade, these conditions help explain why the US – the major vision of 'America' – should have in Australia and Anglophone Canada its best television export markets.

In addition, Hollywood and British drama provide a point of continuity for migrants. As the major suppliers of international programming within the world system, the US and Britain export to most of the countries from which Australia draws its immigrants. For the migrants who will have already watched Hollywood and British programming, the Australian screening of this programming provides for points of continuity. Given the degree of Australian cultural proximity to the US and Britain, this programming probably assists 'integration' more than is commonly recognised, in that it provides rough maps of Australia, its values, and its institutions.[4] Additionally, SBS-TV's provision of Italian, French, Chinese, and German programs furnish additional forms of continuity for particular ethnic communities not as publicly available in the US.

Australian-made programs are also important to ethnic communities as an informational and entertainment resource. Australian productions provide information about the life of the 'host' culture. They often serve as a reference point in the maintenance and transformation of ethnic identities. For example, parents use Australian programs to instruct their children on the differences between Australian social and cultural practices and those of their ethnic fragment, just as their children use those same programs to negotiate their own relation both to their parent's culture and the broader 'host' culture (see Turnbull 1992, passim).

Television programs help transform ethnicities in a dynamic way facilitating the creation of hybrid identities and cultural formations such as the Australian Croatian and the Australian Italian. Typically, Australian programming as 'host programming' sits beside international programs in a dynamic interrelationship facilitating the self-management by immigrant communities of their mixing into the broader Australian society. This mix has probably aided more than hindered the effective social and cultural integration of ethnic minorities.

Simultaneously different and the same; this is the peculiarity of the television service as it is of debates about it (Routt and Bertrand 1989, p. 4). What is different for some about Australian television is what is the same for others; what is culturally similar is also that program which is dissimilar; one person's original Australian program is another's fake. Simultaneous difference and sameness structure Australian understandings of what is produced and imported. It produces anxiety about lack of originality and the effect on Australians of what is imported; just as it promotes vigorous assertions of originality, identity and Australian competence to produce television to an international standard.

The difference and sameness dynamic also means that the criticism of Australian television does not have to pass through Australian production traditions to authorise itself or to understand that work. Thus, Nick Roddick wrote glowingly of Australian television from the moment he landed in Australia (Roddick 1985). Criticism can simply use the contemporary imported content as the yardstick. This creates a relatively open informational culture. This is a structure for Australian television, and by implication its culture, which requires little previous experience and expertise for participation. If this can be positive in that it is so inclusive, it is also negative in that ignorance about Australia, its television and its production traditions are often structured into Australian television debates and production processes.

Critics and audiences routinely ignore the fact that Australian television is only a medium-sized market and criticise it for failing to measure up to what can be expected of large country television services. But local productions cannot afford the budgets of US and UK television nor easily match the US and UK product at their own game. Local product must instead be differentiated from imports to carve out a market niche for itself in its own domestic market.

[. . .]

From the arguments put in this chapter, Australian television is a particular invention of television in the international television system. This invention has advantages and disadvantages stemming from limitations which are both self-imposed and structural to it as a medium-sized television service operating in the English language, and as a service for a new society formed by the interaction of many settler and indigenous cultures.

Notes

1   In fact, the percentage of Australian households with the VCR tended to be a few percentage points higher than US, UK and Canadian figures over the 1980s.
2   [T]he word American is used to indicate someone or something from the US. Although anyone from the Americas is an American, I felt I had to persist with this admittedly imperialist useage as it was the least misleading option. To use Yanks would be derogatory to (US) Americans; while North American includes Canada and Mexico whose experiences with television – not to mention their respective global position – are at some distance from the US.
3   The US imports concepts too, with the principal British impact upon US television being through concept remakes. Australia is also an exporter of program concepts and television scheduling expertise through both the Grundy organisation and Rupert Murdoch's satellite television involvements in Europe with Australian television formats being most notably used to introduce Sky Channel in the UK.
4   The observations on ethnic communities here are drawn from the ethnographic work of Dona Kolar-Panov for her Murdoch University PhD in progress.

Bibliography

Armstrong, Mark 1974, 'Obstacles to sensible broadcasting regulation', *The Australian Quarterly* vol 46, no. 4, pp. 7–21
Australian Broadcasting Tribunal (ABT) 1991, 'Arts programs on Australian television', *OZ Content* vol. 3, ABT, Sydney, pp. 143–58
Barker, Wayne 1984, *The Inuit broadcasting system: Some possibilities for Australia*, AGPS, Canberra
Barnouw, Erik 1975, *The Tube of Plenty*, Oxford University Press, New York

Barwise, Patrick and Andrew Ehrenberg 1988, *Television and its Audience*, Sage, London

Bridges, James 1991, 'Letter to the Editor', *Sydney Morning Herald*, 18 March

Brisebois, Debbie 1990, 'Whiteout warning: Courtesy of the federal government', Inuit Broadcasting Corporation, Ottawa, October

Chadwick, Paul 1989, *Media mates: Carving up Australia's media*, Macmillan, South Melbourne

Collins, Richard 1990, *Television: Policy and Culture*, Unwin Hyman, London

Connor Report 1985, also known as *Committee of Review of the Special Broadcasting Service, Serving multicultural Australia: The role of broadcasting, Part One*, AGPS, Canberra

Cunningham, Stuart 1992, *Framing culture: Criticism and policy in Australia*, Allen and Unwin, Sydney

Fields, Howard 1987, 'DC crowded as stations elbow in for news feeds', *Film and Radio Times*, 14 September, pp. 51–2, 84

Geller, Henry 1990, 'Broadcast regulation in a changing environment', *TV 2000: Choices and challenges*, ed. Elizabeth Moore, ABT, Sydney, pp. 113–24

Hall, Sandra 1976, *Supertoy*, Sun Books, Melbourne.

—— 1981, *Turning on turning off: Australian television in the eighties*, Cassell, North Ryde

Harding, Richard 1979, *Outside interference: the politics of Australian broadcasting*, Sun Books, Melbourne

Hartley, John 1992, *Tele-ology: Studies in Television*, Routledge, London

Head, Sydney and Christopher Sterling 1990, *Broadcasting in America* 6th Edition, Houghton Mifflin, Boston

McClelland, James 1974, 'The role of federal government in Australia's media', Paper presented to Seminar, 'The Media and Society', Adelaide, 22 February

McGuinness, Padraic 1990, *The media in crisis in Australia*, Schwartz and Wilkinson, Melbourne

McKay, Ian K. 1959, *Macquarie: The story of a network*, privately published

Michaels, Eric 1990a, *Unbecoming: An Aids diary*, EM Press, Sydney

—— 1985, *Images and Industry: Television Drama Production in Australia*, Currency Press, Sydney

Morris, Meaghan, 1988, 'Tooth and claw: Tales of survival and *Crocodile Dundee*', in *The Pirate's fiancée: Feminism, reading and postmodernism*, Verso, London, pp. 241–69

Reel, A. Frank 1979, *The Networks: How they stole the show*, Charles Scribner's Sons, New York

Riddell, Elizabeth 1968, 'Entertainment', in *Ten Years of Television*, ed. Mungo MacCallum, Sun Books, Melbourne, pp. 27–43

Routt, William 1982, *Prolegemena to a theory of popular art*, PhD diss., Committee on Social Thought, University of Chicago

Routt, William and Ina Bertrand 1989, 'The Big Bad Combine: Some aspects of national aspirations and international constraints in the Australian cinema, 1896–1929', in *The Australian Screen*, eds A. Moran and T. O'Regan, Penguin, Ringwood, pp. 3–27

Spigel, Lynn 1990, 'Television in the family circle: The popular reception of a new medium', in *Logics of Television*, ed. Patricia Mellancamp, Indiana University Press, Bloomington, pp. 73–97

Summers, Robert E. and R. Harrison 1966, *Broadcasting and the public*, Wadsworth, Belmont

Turnbull, Susan (1992) 'The media and moral identity: Accounting for media practices in the lives of young women', PhD, La Trobe University

Walker, R.R. 1967, *Communications*, Landsdowne Press, Melbourne

Chapter 5

EILEEN R. MEEHAN AND JACKIE BYARS

TELEFEMINISM
How Lifetime Got Its Groove, 1984–1997

CRITICAL THEORISTS HAVE LONG BEEN INTERESTED in capitalism's ability to co-opt oppositional movements by defusing, appropriating, and absorbing selected elements of those movements (Gitlin 1979, 1983). Liberal feminism—with its emphasis on gaining equality within the capitalist system through equal opportunities for education, employment, and consumption—has been particularly appropriated by advertisers and media makers (Byars 1991; Kaplan 1992; Steeves 1987). In the 1980s, this appropriation tapped a pool of new consumers—middle-class women with white-collar jobs who controlled their disposable income—at a time of economic recession (Bluestone and Harrison 1992; Meehan 1993). However, both "upscale women" and "women in general" were still considered by the advertising and television industries to constitute a small, specialized, and highly limited niche audience well into the 1990s (Bronstein 1994; Byars and Meehan 1994).[1] Our historical case study of the first fourteen years (1984–1997) of the American cable channel Lifetime Television examines how that cable channel became a successful capitalist venture by targeting this niche market through its programming, most notably through Lifetime's original films.

In the United States, both cable and broadcast programming are uplinked from a network or channel's homebase to satellites that distribute the materials to the downlinks of local broadcast stations (for network television) or to the downlinks of the local cable company (for cable channels, which include the networks that are transmitted both via cable and via broadcasting). Approximately 70 percent of U.S. households subscribe to cable, which guarantees advertisers that they are purchasing bona fide consumers: persons with the desire, disposable income, and geographic access that allows them to subscribe to their local cable company. Since the 1980s, local cable companies have been owned by larger firms, the so-called multiple system operators (MSOs), which since the late 1980s, have been expanding into ownership of channels as well as cable systems. This was certainly the case with Viacom, which owned cable systems as well as one-third of Lifetime. All of Lifetime's owners—Viacom, Hearst, and CapCities/ABC—produced or owned programming; CapCities/ABC also owned one of the three major broadcast television networks in the United States. This type of industrial integration focused Lifetime's strategies for acquiring or producing programming on the capabilities of its owners to provide or license such materials. By the mid-1990s, for example, all of Lifetime's original films were produced at least partially by the production arms of one of its parent companies. Before Viacom sold its portion of Lifetime to Hearst and to CapCities/ABC in 1995, that ownership guaranteed Lifetime a place on Viacom's systems, which certainly helped the company rise into and remain on the roster of the top ten cable channels in the United States.

We argue that in Lifetime's programming and corporate practices, two forms of co-optation occurred. The initial form was expressive. Lifetime's original films appropriated and defused the subculture of liberal feminism, particularly its ideals of the strong woman and the egalitarian couple. We suggest that both the appropriation and the defusion are functions, first, of Lifetime's position in the cable industry and the structure of its co-ownership and, second, of internal differences between management teams. The second form of co-optation was institutional as Lifetime legitimated its programming as "women's television" and its male CEO through formal relationships with liberal feminist organizations, particularly the National Organization of Women (NOW) and the MS Foundation. The initial form of co-optation illustrates the media's constant search for subcultural novelty that can be reprocessed to fit work routines, thus producing innovation in commercial culture. In Lifetime's case, this produces telefeminist programming formulae that defuse any basic structural challenges to patriarchy and its institutions. That form of co-optation has been widely recognized among cultural scholars and political economists. The second form, which is much rarer, illustrates the processes whereby a corporation entered into an institutional alliance with liberal organizations within social movements to gain legitimacy. We will argue that such co-optations have the effect of both defusing feminist critiques of capitalism and legitimating the participants by granting them institutional status within each other's spheres of influence.

To do that, we have organized our materials (gleaned from personal interviews,[2] close textual analyses, and institutional analyses) into five periods of the channel's existence: prehistory, 1982 to 1984; emergent, 1984 to January 1993; transitional, February 1993 to January 1995; established, January 1995 to mid-1995; and absorbed, mid-1995 to mid-1997. For each period, we will first briefly sketch Lifetime's economics and programming policies and comment in passing on Lifetime's original programming from the period. In doing this, we will trace how Lifetime organized itself as a niche programmer targeting upscale women as its primary—but not its only—audience, and we will show how the channel has variously defined the term "television for women" through its original films, appropriating liberal feminism and generating a telefeminist formula that changed as Lifetime's management team changed and redefined the channel's target audience. We will contextualize these changes to trace the process of co-optation. We begin by examining Lifetime's precursors, which were created in the early 1980s.

Lifetime's prehistory: 1982 to 1984

Those were the days of the first great expansion in cable channels, and they came as a result of three interacting factors that played out against a weakening economy (Meehan 1984). First, cable achieved the magical penetration rate of 50 percent, which analysts claimed was necessary to be profitable. Second, the A.C. Nielsen Company began reporting ratings for cable channels. Finally, national advertisers began buying more time on cable channels. In March 1982, Hearst and ABC joined together to launch Daytime, a cable service that targeted women and that ran only on weekday afternoons. Most of the programming was based on Hearst's line of magazines for women, and most followed the talk show format. For example, on Daytime's *Cosmo* show, Helen Gurley Brown reprised her editorial role on Hearst's *Cosmopolitan* magazine by leading chats on glamour, diet, and office romance. Working against Daytime were its truncated hours of service and limited carriage by cable services. Put bluntly, neither Hearst nor ABC had the muscle in cable operations to secure widespread distribution.

This was not a problem for Viacom's Cable Health Channel, which debuted in June 1982. As one of the top five MSOs in the cable industry, Viacom simply carried its new channel on its systems. During the week, the channel's programming ran the gamut from diet to exercize, from motherhood to fashion. On Sundays, Viacom carried in-service medical training programs, thus bringing new methods in heart surgery and orthodonture into the living rooms of cable households. All programming accepted advertising, with the medical in-service dominated by pharmaceutical companies.

Ratings for regular programming on Viacom's Cable Health and on Hearst/ABC's Daytime showed a relatively strong (for cable) female viewership distinguished by upscale demographics. While audiences with upscale demographics were increasingly presumed to be the natural target for cable television, the female audience was still seen by advertisers, cable channels, and the trade press as a highly specialized, very narrow niche audience. With Cable Health and Daytime both attracting that niche audience, their owners merged the two channels in 1984 to form Lifetime.

Emergent period: 1984 to January 1993

The new firm reported to a board of directors on which Viacom, Hearst, and ABC were equally represented. That board hired Lifetime's first CEO, Thomas Burchill, and his staff included personnel from the previous operations. In programming, little changed. Many of Lifetime's shows had been carried over from Daytime and Cable Health; Sundays were still devoted to medical programming over which Lifetime's entertainment division exercized no influence. While Lifetime personnel eventually lobbied for control over the Sunday schedule, the channel needed the guaranteed income from medical in-service as Lifetime's executives began to sort out its programming and create its identity. Burchill's team needed to differentiate the channel from its progenitors, to generate a consistent image of the channel for its advertisers, and to provide a coherent "brand name" for its viewers. They began experimenting with syndicated programming, acquiring *Cagney and Lacey* after its cancellation by CBS.

With that acquisition came the first real surge in Lifetime's ratings. *Cagney and Lacey* offered two strong, yet flawed, female protagonists (D'Acci 1994). Although plain spoken and competent, neither protagonist fell into the "man hater" stereotype, and both were resolutely heterosexual. As police detectives, Christine Cagney and Mary Beth Lacey pursued their careers in a workplace dominated by male colleagues and male offenders. Indeed, Cagney and Lacy remained best friends despite differences in class, marital status, and, ultimately, rank. As such, they supported each other through alcohol addiction, breast cancer, department politics, romantic difficulties, and family crises. Thus, the series blended a traditionally female genre (melodrama) with a traditionally male genre (station house drama), while focusing the series on unexpected protagonists— female police officers. By incorporating female characters as representatives of the law, the series also reinforced a patriarchal legal system. During its run on Lifetime, this combination drew both upscale females and upscale males. Here was a formula that seemed to work, especially in prime time.

Having found a formula, Lifetime's problem became finding more series to follow it. In the independent and off-network syndicated markets, Lifetime acquired rights to series featuring tough but tender female cops (*Lady Blue*), physicians (*Kay O'Brien*), and private detectives (*Partners in Crime*). However, given the relative scarcity of female protagonists in syndicated series, Lifetime also sought out "female friendly" shows. Such programs, epitomized by *Spenser for Hire*, had enjoyed a strong female viewership during their network runs despite casts dominated by males, strong identifications with male-oriented genres, and strong male viewership.

Problems in acquisition made it clear to Burchill's team that building a consistent image, brand name, and program schedule would require some origination of programming. This emergent period saw three major initiatives: first, the continuation of a female-identified network show; second, the creation of original series; and third, the launch of made-for-Lifetime movies. We will treat each in turn.

Despite strong female audiences, and perhaps because of weak male audiences, NBC canceled the dramatic series *The Days and Nights of Molly Dodd* after 26 episodes. When it acquired the series,[3] Lifetime launched a major promotional campaign: *Molly Dodd* would be rerun in order of original broadcast, beginning in January of 1989, and new episodes, created especially for Lifetime, would be aired subsequently. Because this was a relatively unusual tactic, *Molly Dodd* attracted considerable attention from the press. However, viewership was not overwhelming and *Molly Dodd* eventually disappeared from Lifetime's schedule. The experiment in reviving a network show failed. Significantly, this particular show was about a woman, her emotions, and her relationships. Unlike *Cagney and Lacey* or *Spenser for Hire*, *Molly Dodd* was watched mainly by women (Wilson 1994).

In the emergent period, Lifetime also experimented with dramatic series. Among the first experiments were an anthology series (*The Hidden Room*) and a detective series (*Veronica Clare*). *The Hidden Room* combined aspects of *The Twilight Zone, Thriller*, and *Alfred Hitchcock Presents*. Its chilling tales of mystery, adventure, and intrigue generally ended with a twist and typically featured a female protagonist. In contrast, *Veronica Clare* had a regular cast of characters organized around the nightclub owned by the title character. Most of the mysteries were solved by the men in the supporting cast with Clare functioning as "the good looking dame" in this softboiled detective series. Neither series was particularly successful in the Nielsen ratings, and neither lasted very long (Johnson 1994; White 1994).

Lifetime's third initiative—original films—proved its most successful. Producing an occasional made-for-Lifetime movie allowed significant flexibility in terms of scheduling, costing, casting, themes, and genres. The original films were promoted as special events that broke into regularly scheduled programming. Following the pattern set by Turner Broadcasting for its original films, Lifetime reran each new film in the evening schedule during the month of its premiere and then rotated it through its afternoon and late-evening slots for movies. Those slots also provided Lifetime's owners (Viacom, Hearst, and CapCities/ABC) with opportunities to recycle old made-for-television or theatrical films from their own libraries.

Initially called "World Premier Movies," the first of Lifetime's original films debuted in July 1990. From then to 1993, seventeen movies (about six a year) were produced for Lifetime. These films included movies from such disparate genres as the thriller, family melodrama, social-problem film, historical drama, historical reenactment, detective film, coming of age film, spy film, and political fantasy film. Yet, a consistent type of protagonist unites them: the romantic crusader. This female crusader was a professional with a career. Strong and relatively altruistic, she was romantically linked in a serious—although often strained—relationship with a man. She was placed in a situation in which she must confront a failure in the system, but always for someone else. She won on her own, even if the victim whom she championed died. Usually, she got romanced along the way, but above all else, she was active and spunky. Most of these films earned ratings in the 2s and 3s, which Lifetime and its advertisers found acceptable although low.

Typical of Lifetime's "World Premier Movies" were *The Good Fight* and *Shame*, which yielded the lowest (1.1) and the highest ratings (5.1), respectively, for the movies made in this period. Brief summaries of these films illuminate the romantic crusader formula and illustrate its defusion of the liberal feminist ideal of the independent woman: the woman whose income, personal identity, and sexual politics allow her to enter relationships as a full, equal, and self-directed partner.

In *The Good Fight*, attorney Grace Craven (Christine Lahti) sued a tobacco company on behalf of a professional baseball player who developed mouth cancer from years of dipping snuff. The athlete contacted her because of his childhood friendship with the two children born to Grace and her exhusband Henry (Terry O'Quinn). The marital subplot, then, added the melodramatic element to a film that already blended the social problem and courtroom drama genres.

Although the two had pursued their legal practices separately, Henry had enjoyed consider-ably greater financial success. He had also remarried and again divorced while Grace remained single. To avoid paying alimony to his second wife, Henry retired. When Grace took on the athlete's case, Henry realized that Grace needed his help, which he provided pro bono. Thus, circumstances allowed them to slowly and unevenly negotiate their relationship. Despite the athlete's death, the reconciled, but not yet reunited, Cravens continued their crusade against the tobacco company. When a mistrial was called, Grace announced her commitment to retry the case—not while in court but while riding in Henry's convertible, with the wind in her hair, as they went home together. Although *The Good Fight* earned only a 1.1 rating, its formula was repeated in the most highly rated Lifetime movie of this period, *Shame*.

In *Shame*, Diana Cadell (Amanda Donohoe) was a disillusioned Los Angeles district attorney who took to the highway to find herself riding a motorcycle given to her by her (never-seen) boyfriend. After a mechanical breakdown in a small town, Cadell befriended a young woman who had grown up on the proverbial wrong side of the tracks. Subsequently, the woman and a female friend were raped by local teenagers from the good side of town. After the rapes, the youths conspired with some townspeople to intimidate the victims and other residents to cover up the rapes. Cadell challenged this reign of terror, triggering a series of violent confrontations that ultimately resulted in the death of her friend. Faced with this tragedy, Cadell succeeded in persuading the second victim to file charges.

In both *The Good Fight* and *Shame*, female lawyers depended on their men to enable the women's careers. This was most obvious with Henry and Grace. Grace's status as mother brought her the baseballer's case, which she lacked experience to handle. Henry's financial independence and legal expertise facilitated her handling of the case and opened the way for their reconciliation. The centrality of the male was less obvious in *Shame*, because the enabling boyfriend was unseen. He provided Cadell with the magical talisman, the motorcycle. Thus, he gave her the means to escape the scene of her disillusionment with the courts; but the motorcycle also transported her to the scene of the crimes, restoring her faith in the courts. Achieving that restoration required that two women be raped and one of them die. From this perspective, both films presented female professionals whose independence and agency was rooted in domestic and/or romantic relation-ships. This defused the threat to traditional gender relationships that was embodied in the ideal of the independent woman, without destroying the female protagonists' ability to struggle against the odds and to win back, in *The Good Fight*, a husband (traditionally the wife's patriarch), and in *Shame*, a faith in the courts (a traditionally patriarchal institution).

Both *The Good Fight* and *Shame* illustrated Lifetime's operational definition of "television for women" during this emergent period. The formula might be codified like this. First, take a strong, active, and heterosexual woman. Second, give her background by referencing a strong, though sometimes strained, interpersonal relationship. Third, place her in a situation where she must confront a failure in the system. Then watch her win on her own. This romantic crusader formula was developed under Burchill's management team, and it changed when Burchill resigned.

Transitional period: February 1993 to February 1995

We see Lifetime, in this period, developing a clearer definition of what it meant to target the niche. That audience, composed of women aged 24 to 44, did not qualify as the youthful audience so often preferred by advertisers; however, their residence in households making more than

$40,000 made them an attractive audience (Bronstein 1994; Streeter and Wahl 1994). In prime time, Lifetime's niche audience was composed of primarily professional, upscale, working women. These women retained some control over their disposable income and were believed to "cocoon" with their male counterparts at home in the evenings.[4] This was a salable audience, actually composed of upscale, heterosexual couples who found Lifetime's romantic crusaders acceptable. A shake up of the executive personnel resulted in an increased consolidation of that vision—for production and for advertisers.

In late 1992, with the channel ranked last of the top six cable networks, Thomas Burchill announced his resignation from Lifetime. Two internal candidates were ready to replace him: Pat Fili, senior vice president of original programming, and Douglas McCormick, executive vice president of sales. While Fili had been intimately connected with the crusader formula, McCormick's only experience in programming was a brief stint at Samuel Goldwyn. In February 1993, Lifetime's board selected McCormick. Fili subsequently joined ABC's daytime programming unit. McCormick quickly assembled his own team, hiring Judy Girard, head of programming at NBC's flagship station in New York, to replace Fili as Executive Vice President for Programming and Production (in July of 1993). Girard instituted a six-month freeze on new projects to review Lifetime's policies on original movies. During this time, she hired Sheri Singer away from Disney to become Lifetime's Vice President for Long Form Programming. In this capacity, Singer headed Lifetime's movie division in Los Angeles.

However, Lifetime could not refuse to air projects commissioned under Burchill and Fili. Part of the rationale was economic: movies unshown would have to be paid for. Part was certainly structural: most made-for-Lifetime movies involved Lifetime's owners, Hearst, CapCities/ABC, and Viacom. Hence, we term this period "transitional" because it marks a policy shift not yet reflected in programming. While Lifetime continued to air films that followed the crusader formula, McCormick's management team freely criticized that formula. Citing low ratings, they argued that the formula did not give women what they wanted. Such films were termed "preachy" rather than "entertaining." Finally, McCormick's team dismissed the films as reflecting the views of a few who had been inside the company rather than reflecting the views of Lifetime's audience. The new films would avoid these errors (personal interviews with Judy Girard, Sheri Singer, and Meredith Wagner on 13–15 January 1994).[5]

In the meantime, the new team was saddled with some completed films and some developing projects that could not be canceled. Among the officially "distasteful" films were two projects that earned the lowest ratings to date: Night Owl (1.4) and Guinevere (0.7, an all-time low) (personal interview with Douglas McCormick on 3 March 1995). In Night Owl, a female protagonist successfully battled a female ghost who lured men to their death via radio broadcasts; thus, the woman regained the trust of her husband. Guinevere retold the legend of King Arthur. In this version, Guinevere abandoned both her female-centered religion and her beloved Lancelot to marry Arthur and ensure his political success. Clearly, both films involved particularly convoluted twists on the crusader formula and had been too far along for the new team to reform.

However, some of the film projects were considered more salvageable. The series of four Spenser for Hire movies illustrated how differences between the two management teams influenced content. In all four Spenser movies, the male detective strongly resembled the hero typical of romance novels: Spenser combined a "spectacular masculinity" with an "extraordinary tenderness and capacity for gentle nurturance" (Radway 1984, p. 74). Spenser nurtured not only his girlfriend, Susan, but most of the women and children who crossed his path. As noted before, the female-friendly Spenser series had done well in syndication on Lifetime. The Burchill team's decision to negotiate the Spenser movies with ABC suggested a more cautious approach to continuing a canceled series than the failed experiment with Molly Dodd. In any case, two of the films were completed and a third was in development when McCormick's team took over. The second and third Spenser films were interesting, then, because of the continuities and differences between the versions of Spenser and Susan proffered by the different management teams.

Although Spenser and Susan's relationship was not a crucial element in the action/adventure television series, that relationship became central in the Lifetime movies. In this way, the Spenser films acquired the strong female presence required by Lifetime's formula and integrated a stable, monogamous romance into the Spenser saga. The infusion of romance into an action/adventure formula was also indicative of what some refer to as the feminization of the public sphere in this period, with the rise of confessional talk shows and increasing targeting of female audiences. The networks were cutting costly drama, such as action/adventure series, and between 1990 and 1994, action/adventure went from 20 percent of network prime time to 1 percent. Lifetime transformed the genre with the first two Spenser films and transformed it even further in the third and fourth films. The depiction of the Spenser–Susan romance, and its participants changed as management teams and their notions of Lifetime's audience changed. An examination of the second and third films makes this clear.

The detective plot of the second film, *Spenser: Pale Kings and Princes*, had Spenser finding a killer, who was also a drug dealer. The detective plot of the third, *Spenser: A Judas Goat*, had Spenser finding an assassin who had targeted the leader of a developing country, while the detective also coped with a manipulative employer. Susan was directly involved in the detective plot of *Pale Kings and Princes*, like the romantic female crusaders of the formula. To be so involved, she abandoned her practice without notice to leave Boston with Spenser. In *A Judas Goat*, when Spenser left Boston, Susan stayed behind, minding her practice. Throughout both films, however, attention continually returned to Spenser and Susan's relationship. As such, the films melded the male-friendly focus on international intrigue and adventure with the female-friendly focus on relationships and nurturing men. For our purposes, the plots were of less interest than changes in the characterization of Spenser, Susan, and their relationship.

In *Pale Kings and Princes*, the couple was presented as young and foolish. Susan, played by a noticeably young actress (Barbara Williams), was flighty and carefree. Her status as a Harvard-trained psychologist operated solely as background for the character. Although Urich had aged, Spenser was frozen in time. The two characters bantered about sex, with Spenser literally jumping into bed with Susan. At one point, Spenser preened before a mirror and declared himself "hunkus Americanus." Similar elements gave the film an air of irony closer to Generation-X viewers than to baby boomers. However, Spenser's ability to nurture remained intact: he not only solved the mystery with ease but also protected the innocent by keeping a teenage boy, his mother, and Susan from being forced to appear in court.

With the advent of McCormick's management team, matters changed. In interviews, Girard identified this change as indicating the shift in tone and focus that McCormick effected. For *A Judas Goat*, Susan was recast and was visibly older, as Wendy Crewson was older than Barbara Williams.[6] Susan's demeanor and costuming were more elegant, suggesting both the socioeconomic background of a Harvard graduate and the income of a successful psychologist. Spenser no longer preened or pretended to be youthful. Their relationship was affectionate and mature, with sexual banter and acrobatics absent. The point was made strongly in a bedroom scene in which Spenser and Susan reclined together, eating popcorn while watching an old movie on television. She sniffed; he handed her a tissue. The Crewson-Urich film presented the lovers as an older, established couple for whom affection and television had replaced sex and banter. In short, Spenser and Susan appeared like the cocooning baby boomers comprising the audience targeted by the McCormick team. Presumably, Lifetime's cocooning thirty- to forty-somethings would see themselves as they watched Spenser and Susan watching television in bed (Feuer 1994).

Clearly, the decision to admit Urich's/Spenser's age and to cast a similarly mature Susan agreed with liberal feminism's rejection of prejudices based on age, particularly those prejudices that presumed older men would only consort with younger women and that older women were asexual. Similarly, the characters' financial independence also paralleled the ideal of the egalitarian couple. Yet, in both incarnations, Spenser and Susan also embody stereotypical dichotomies separating sexuality from tenderness, and aging from sexuality, that the liberal feminist subculture firmly rejected. To the degree that Spenser and Susan were sexually active, both were depicted as youthful and adventurous; however, Susan was irresponsible, and her occupational status was unbelievable. To the degree that the couple was tender, they were depicted as asexual. Spenser remained adventurous while Susan stayed responsibly home to care for her patients. Because it was woven into her actions and dress, Susan's occupational status was believable. These depictions depended on stereotypical linkages and dichotomies: first, for both genders, the linkage of sex and youth versus tenderness and maturity, and second, for females, the linkage of sexualized, adventurous but ignorant youth versus asexual but responsible, learned maturity. The notion that women must choose between their sexuality and a career had long been rejected by liberal feminism. While explicitly drawing on liberal feminism for their material, the films co-opted some of its precepts, defusing the threat of female independence and of fully egalitarian relationships.

Other films produced during the transitional period also embraced romantic couples composed of a strong career woman and her nurturing, profoundly masculine male. While the romantic crusader formula persisted, it was massaged to become more male friendly and more couple oriented. This meant redesigning the generic role played by male leads to incorporate the nurturing male who retained a primal masculinity. These changes illustrated how Lifetime's programming philosophy and target audience changed under McCormick. The focus shifted from programming for a niche audience of upscale women aged 24 to 44 to a niche audience of upscale couples aged 24 to 44. Significantly, this placed Lifetime in a position to take advantage of known biases in the Nielsen sample, which measured cable subscribers and oversampled upscale, dual income, professional couples whose viewing was limited to the single television.[7]

At the same time, McCormick's team launched its signature promotional campaign for Lifetime, using the slogan "Lifetime—television for women." Also, McCormick began building relationships for Lifetime with the MS Foundation and NOW. Lifetime became involved in public service programming on taking our daughters to work during Women's History Month, black women's contribution to American society during Black History Month, breast cancer awareness, and similar concerns that form part of the agenda of liberal feminism. Lifetime also instituted coverage of women's sports, starting with the sponsorship of the first female crew in the America's Cup.[8] Thus, McCormick addressed the difficulty of his position as the male CEO for the women's channel.[9] These linkages, his team's public service programming, and the campaign to "come out" as women's television may seem somewhat ironic given the industrial constraints that fostered the shift to entertaining an audience of upscale couples.[10]

Established period: January 1995 to mid-1995

By January of 1995, McCormick's team had control over all production deals for original films. At this point, Lifetime was moving up, out of sixth place among cable channels according to the Nielsen ratings. Given the Nielsen sample, targeting the evening cocooners had become more explicit and more important to Lifetime, as well as to other cable and broadcast channels. Lifetime remained "television for women" in its promotions. The "World Premiere Movies" were renamed "Original Films" and advertised as "made for you," with the neutral pronoun emphasized.

McCormick's management team considered these movies to be their most explicit expression of the niche for which they programmed and sold to advertisers.

This was made evident in Lifetime's presentation to the TV Critics Association in Los Angeles in January 1995. The team announced that beginning in March, Lifetime would premiere one new "Original" movie every month. The first film in that series was *Choices of the Heart: The Margaret Sanger Story* (starring Dana Delaney and Rod Steiger). The team positioned *Choices* as a strong statement to viewers, advertisers, and critics about Lifetime's ability to produce high-quality films that would attract upscale audiences in droves. A historical drama, *Choices* effectively integrated the nurturing male into the romantic crusader formula. The film portrayed Margaret Sanger (Delaney) as a strong, professional woman whose marriage to Bill Sanger (Henry Czerny) was a nearly perfect romantic relationship and firm friendship. Margaret took on the federal government and its laws forbidding the circulation of information about birth control. These abstractions were embodied in postal inspector Anthony Comstock (Steiger). Throughout her campaign, Bill supported and assisted her, sacrificing his own interests for her altruistic pursuits. The film made clear that Margaret had no interests in controlling her (and Bill's) fertility. Instead, she sought to provide information to poor women so that they could make informed choices about matters of the heart. The point was not the politics nor the practice of birth control, but rather the need to inform poor women.

As Margaret made her own choices to challenge Comstock and the law, so too, Bill decided to support those choices. The drama of the tale thus avoided the sort of parallel story in which Margaret might struggle with both Comstock and Bill. Instead, with Bill behind her and sacrificing for her, Margaret confronted Comstock. Here, the liberal feminist ideal of the egalitarian couple was undermined by the representation of the male as doormat, dominated by a strong-willed woman.

To the TV Critics Association, the Lifetime team pitched *Choices* as embodying Lifetime's new take on films: strong stories, strong emotions, and solid entertainment. Although *Choices* might seem to address a controversial topic, the movie was really about relationships. Similar tactics promoted *Choices* to viewers in Lifetime's announcements of the film's premiere, as well as in materials promoting *Choices* to the MS Foundation, NOW, and other women's organizations. Despite this, *Choices* earned the worst rating (1.8) of any original film aired during this period, perhaps evidence of the rejection by those cocooning couples so sought by Lifetime.

Distinctly more successful in terms of ratings was *Almost Golden: The Jessica Savitch Story* (Sela Ward). In fact, *Almost Golden's* 7.9 rating surpassed the ratings earned by ABC, making *Almost Golden* a benchmark event for Lifetime and for McCormick's team. However, the film departed from both the romantic crusader and the romantic crusader/nurturing male formulae. The film explored how Savitch capitalized on her looks and icy demeanor to secure her career. Her self-interest and self-destructiveness clearly marked her as no crusader for women's rights.

In the film, Savitch clawed her way to the top of the newsreader business but lacked the skills or knowledge of her male colleagues. Cool and collected on air, Savitch threw violent temper tantrums during commercial breaks, only to resume her calm demeanor on cue. The character truly embodied the worst sort of "queen bee" stereotype. At home, Savitch was awash in drugs, alcohol, and exploitative, unnurturing men. But when the effects of her abusive lifestyle slurred her speech on camera, Savitch realized that she had to change. While she sobered up, her network superiors decided to fire her. Shortly afterward, a drug-and-alcohol-free Savitch was killed in a car acccident.

As in the Greek tragedies, Savitch held the seeds of her own destruction: even her realization and positive action could not save her from a tragic fate. The resulting film provided a polysemic account of Savitch. The character could be read as a selfish woman who got what she deserved, a woman whose life was cut short just as she was poised for real success, a victim of her own feminine nature that was naturally unsuited to the stress of the workplace, an exemplar of feminism's distorting influence in the workplace, a victim of institutional sexism that catapulted her into a position that she was not qualified to handle, and so on. Thus, *Almost Golden* invited both feminist and antifeminist readings, and provided a rather troubling twist in Lifetime's continuing redefinition of "television for women," a redefinition that laid bare the corporate nature of "telefeminism."

(Early) absorbed period: mid-1995 to mid-1997

Four events occurred in mid-1995 that changed Lifetime's economic status. First, Viacom sold its third of Lifetime back to Hearst and CapCities/ABC. This freed Lifetime from a supplier that McCormick had characterized as problematic (personal interview with Douglas McCormick on 8 November 1995). Second, with that departure, Lifetime also lost its automatic access to Viacom's many cable systems. However, with Lifetime's status as one of the most viewed cable channels, that shift could not have seemed immediately significant. Third, Time Warner announced the acquisition of Turner Broadcasting Services (TBS). Not only was Time Warner the second largest MSO in the U.S. cable industry but its board of directors included the largest MSO—Telecommunications, Inc. (TCI). Time Warner's acquisition, then, boded well for TBS's ability to get its six channels into cable homes; but perhaps, it boded ill for Lifetime, given most systems' limited number of channels.[11] Last was the event that imbued Lifetime's loss of guaranteed access with significance: Time Warner's closest rival, Disney, announced its acquisition of CapCities/ABC. While Disney controlled vast holdings across the media industries, it neither owned nor had interests in any cable MSO.

During interviews directly after Disney's announcement, McCormick's team expressed excitement at this turn of events. Co-ownership by Disney meant up-front deals with Disney's subsidiaries in television and film production, including Buena Vista Television, Hollywood Pictures, Touchstone Pictures, Touchstone Television, and Miramax Film Corp. In such deals, McCormick's team saw the opportunity to trade funding for influence over scripting and casting. Furthermore, by providing up-front funding, Lifetime would be in a position to request the shooting of alternative versions of scenes inappropriate for Lifetime's niche audience as well as extra material to be seen only in the television version. Already a customer for syndicated Disney series such as *Unsolved Mysteries*, Lifetime could gain a position as a preferred recycler of Disney's television series (personal interviews with Douglas McCormick, Judy Girard, Meredith Wagner, and Brian Donlon on 8–10 November 1995). Vertical integration into Disney, then, promised much for Lifetime, but its implications were not necessarily in Lifetime's favor.

In terms of cable carriage, Disney's acquisition had the immediate effect of prompting a threat from TCI/Time Warner. In 1996, as Lifetime began negotiating its role in the Disney empire, TCI announced that it would drop Lifetime from certain markets, with the implied threat that the channel might be dropped across all TCI systems. This would make way for an allnews channel created by Rupert Murdoch's Fox, Inc., a channel in which TCI was a partner. Neither Disney nor Hearst directly confronted the threat through antitrust complaints or similar avenues of redress. Instead, McCormick placed advertisements in affected markets—such as Newport, Rhode Island, and Eugene, Oregon—alerting viewers to the possibility that TCI might drop Lifetime, the only channel serving women. Women, women's groups, and prominent political figures rallied, calling TCI. Among the politicians criticizing TCI's move were Senator Bill Bradley of New Jersey; Representative Patricia Schroeder of Colorado; Libby Pataki, the wife of New York Governor George Pataki; and Representative Peter DeFazio of Oregon (Carter 1996; e-mail correspondence with Brian Donlon on 24 September 1996). Thus was the struggle engaged as liberal feminists, and their supporters, came to the defense of Lifetime as "television for women." Ironically, this came at a time when Lifetime saw its prime-time audience as women and men drawn from a specific portion of the consumerist caste (upscale couples).

In terms of Lifetime's films of that period, a brief discussion of *Jitters* should indicate the sort of material being generated for this audience. The film turned on the decision of a long-time couple (Evan, a veterinarian, and Rita, a dentist) to get married. Evan (Brian Wimmer) and Rita's mother, Louise (Anne Meara), blithely made assumptions about the wedding, about housing, and about children without discussing them with Rita (Joely Fisher).[12] Rita made efforts to resist, prompting Louise to ask her why she must do everything differently. Finally, as Rita tried on highly traditional wedding gowns, her inability to commit herself to a traditional marriage won out. Although she called off the wedding, Rita admitted that she still loved Evan. He then called off the entire relationship. Louise was distraught, envisioning her daughter a childless spinster. The film climaxed in a scene in a restaurant when Rita, finally understanding Evan's feelings and overcoming her jitters, knelt and asked him for his hand in marriage. They negotiated, and eventually, he agreed. She hyphenated her name; he did not. She wore a slightly nontraditional— but nonetheless white—wedding dress, with flowers in her hair, replacing a veil. And the film ended with their wedding, fading out on the kiss. The point here is that she may have done things differently, but she did the expected, the socially sanctioned. *Jitters* preserved the professional couple in a mature relationship and examined the nature of commitment, as it reinforced hetero-sexual marriage as the norm. Unlike many of the Lifetime films from this period—which ostensibly still focused on issues such as adoption or breast implants, while examining interpersonal relationships—this film entirely erased the need for a social consciousness.

Conclusion: telefeminism and economic contexts

In its first fourteen years on cable, Lifetime responded to changes in ownership, management teams, and industrial conditions by refocusing its definition of target audiences, movie formulae, and programming strategies. Lifetime drew from the subculture of liberal feminism and on the strengths of organizations associated with that subculture to construct its programming, legitimate its CEO, and defend its position on TCI's cable systems. We have sketched the experiments under the Burchill team that formed the basis for Lifetime's programming strategies emphasizing the acquisition of male- and female-friendly, hybrid series as well as the creation of original movies using the romantic crusader formula. Burchill's replacement by McCormick triggered a rethinking of the strategies associated with Burchill and McCormick's rival, Fili. This rethinking focused mainly on original films, which became increasingly tied to notions of pure entertainment that would attract upscale couples watching television together. The parallel between this strategy and the construction of the Nielsen sample has been noted, as has the ratings success of many of the films produced by McCormick's team. The failure of *Choices* was chalked up to its being a costume drama (personal interview with Judy Girard on 8 November 1995), and a vestige of the romantic crusader remained in at least some of Lifetime's films, although often massaged almost beyond recognition. *Almost Golden's* polysemically inverted (and truncated) romantic crusader/nurturing male formula, and *Jitters'* cheerfully affirmed traditional marriages with dual incomes, signaled some hybridization between the Disney version of family values and the liberal feminist ideal of the egalitarian couple.

However, the significance of those three films surely positioned Lifetime vis-à-vis Disney somewhat differently. Lifetime's emphasis on entertainment and upscale couples softened the Burchill team's focus on strong, female protagonists who won on their own. That softening was accompanied by an engagement with liberal feminist organizations, which ultimately allowed McCormick's team to enlist liberal feminists in securing Lifetime's continued presence on TCI systems. Arguing that Lifetime is the sole channel programming for women, liberal feminists and their organizations seem to have mounted an effective defense of Lifetime as "television for women."

That that co-optation worked in such a manner is significant. Lifetime struck on elements of liberal feminist subculture that resonated with upscale women measured in the Nielsen ratings. Pressure from owners, managers, and advertisers to expand Lifetime's audience and to earn higher ratings encouraged a dilution and reworking of those elements to provide a similar resonance with upscale men in the ratings sample. Yet, TCI's threat to Lifetime was successfully rebuffed not by Hearst and Disney but by liberal feminists defending "television for women." This should remind us that co-optation's power rests on its ability to provide something of value to those who have been co-opted. For liberal feminists, their organizations, and Lifetime's viewers, Lifetime provided programming that was less violent, featured more female protagonists, and addressed concerns that American ideology treats as typically female. Clearly, the case study of Lifetime's telefeminist formulae for its original movies has illustrated how the media's constant search for subcultural elements to be reprocessed for profit results in one of capitalism's most powerful tools for adaptation: co-optation.

Notes

1 Lifetime's recognition of the nature of its niche, by the early to mid-1990s, was also indicated by its internet presence, first on America Online and then on its own website (http://www.lifetimetv.com).

2 The authors would like to thank the following employees of Lifetime Television—past and present—for their generous cooperation with this project: Douglas McCormick, Judy Girard, Brian Donlon, Meredith Wagner, Sheri Singer, Bari Carelli, Gwynne McConkee, Joanne Franzese, Vivian Guardino, Jackie Corso, Winnie Atterbury, and Alex Wagner.

3 The acquisition and extension of *Molly Dodd* in July 1988 was the brainchild of Pat Fili, whom Burchill had hired four months earlier. See Joshua Hammer (1991).

4 This term was popularized in The Popcorn Report, a trade-oriented newsletter describing the lifestyles of consumers. By "cocooning," Popcorn meant that consumers were staying home to watch television or videos, often surrounded with take-out containers from moderate-to-expensive take-out restaurants and designer beverages. Cocooning was a change of lifestyle that boded well for advertisers, electronics manufacturers, take-out or home-delivery restaurants, broadcasters, cable casters, video manufacturers, and video rental stores.

5 All used the terms "preachy" and "entertaining"; each used the dichotomy in this manner.

6 Sheri Singer (personal interview on 13 January 1994) claims responsibility for recasting Susan between the second and third films.

7 This was so widely known that it was discussed in the documentary "Can You Trust the Ratings?" as part of the series *Nova* on PBS.

8 The extremely low ratings received by the coverage of the female America's Cup team did not discourage Lifetime's coverage of women's sports. Rather, Life-time turned to less elite, more mainstream sports, such as basketball, running specials on the women's Olympic team and later becoming one of the three networks that air games of the Women's National Basketball Association.

9 McCormick and his management team, in fact, sowed the seeds of his eventual departure through the very tactics that made the cable channel profitable. In February of 1999, when his contract expired, he was replaced as president and CEO by a woman, Carole Black. See Lifetime Online, "About Our CEO" (http://www. lifetimetv.com./site_map/frameset.shtml/index.html).

10 The irony was compounded by reports that McCormick's ascension and Fili's departure were tied to McCormick's "fear that her (Fili's) approach was too feminist" and "that 20 or 25 female programmers soon quit or were pushed out" because of Fili's departure, as Maura Sheehy (1994) claimed. For a typical discussion of a "regular guy" heading the women's network, see Joe Mandese (1993). For a more typical discussion of personnel changes in this period, see Michael Burgi (1993).

11   Turner's six channels are TBS, TNT, TCM, Cartoon Network, CNN-1, and CNN-2. Telecommunications, Inc., and Time Warner also own or participate in numerous channels.

12   Joely Fisher plays Paige, Ellen Morgan's best friend, on ABC's *Ellen*, which is produced by Disney and which is now syndicated by Lifetime.

References

Bluestone, B., and B. Harrison. 1992. *The Deindustrialization of America*. New York: Basic Books.

Bronstein, C. 1994. Mission Accomplished? Profits and Programming at the Network for Women. *Camera Obscura* (special volume on Lifetime: A Cable Network "For Women," edited by J. D'Acci) 33–34: 213–40.

Burgi, M. 1993. Pat Fili Flees to Head ABC Daytime as Brain Drain Continues at Lifetime. *Mediaweek* 31: 4.

Byars, J. 1991. *All That Hollywood Allows*. Chapel Hill: University of North Carolina Press.

—— and E. R. Meehan. 1994. Once in a Lifetime: Constructing the "Working Woman" Through Cable Narrowcasting. *Camera Obscura* (special volume on Lifetime: A Cable Network "For Women," edited by J. D'Acci) 33–34:13–41.

Carter, B. 1996. TCI Plan to Cut Lifetime Angers Women's Groups. *The New York Times*, 14 September, 17, 21.

D'Acci, J. 1994. *Defining Women: Television and the Case of* Cagney and Lacey. Chapel Hill: University of North Carolina Press.

Feuer, J. 1994. Feminism on Lifetime: Yuppie TV for the Nineties. *Camera Obscura* (special volume on Lifetime: A Cable Network "For Women," edited by J. D'Acci) 33–34:133–45.

Gitlin, T. 1979. Prime Time Ideology: The Hegemonic Process in Television Entertainment. *Social Problems* 26 (3): 251–66. Reprinted in *Television: The Critical View*, 4th edn, edited by H. Newcomb, 507–32.

—— 1983. *Inside Prime Time*. New York: Pantheon.

Hammer, J. 1991. The Chance of a Lifetime. *Working Woman* 16: 79–81.

Johnson, E. 1994. Lifetime's Feminine Psychographic Space and the "Mystery Loves Company" Series. *Camera Obscura* (special volume on Lifetime: A Cable Network "For Women," edited by J. D'Acci) 33–34: 43–74.

Kaplan, E. A. 1992. Feminist Criticism and Television. In *Channels of Discourse: Television and Contemporary Criticism, Re-Assembled*, 2d edn, edited by R. Allen. Chapel Hill: University of North Carolina Press.

Mandese, J. 1993. Doug McCormick: Attuned to Women's Issues as Lifetime Chief. *Advertising Age* 64: 34.

Meehan, E. R. 1984. Toward a Third Vision of an Information Society. *Media, Culture & Society* 6 (3): 257–71.

—— 1993. Heads of Households and Ladies of the House: Gender, Genre, and Broadcast Ratings, 1929–1990. In *Ruthless Criticism: New Perspectives in US Communications History*, edited by W.S. Solomon and R.W. McChesney. Minneapolis: University of Minnesota Press.

Radway, J. 1984. *Reading the Romance: Women, Patriarchy, and Popular Literature*. Chapel Hill: University of North Carolina Press.

Sheehy, M. 1994. Whose Lifetime Is It, Anyway? *Working Woman* 19:12.

Steeves, H. L. 1987. Feminist Theories and Media Studies. *Critical Studies in Mass Communication* 4 (2): 95–135.

Streeter, T., and W. Wahl. 1994. Audience Theory and Feminism: Property, Gender, and the Television Audience. *Camera Obscura* (special volume on Lifetime: A Cable Network "For Women," edited by J. D'Acci) 33–34: 243–61.

White, S. 1994. Veronica Clare and the New Film Noir Heroine. *Camera Obscura* (special volume on Lifetime: A Cable Network "For Women," edited by J. D'Acci) 33–34: 77–102.

Wilson, P. 1994. Upscale Feminine Angst: *Molly Dodd*, the Lifetime Cable Network and Gender Marketing. *Camera Obscura* (special volume on Lifetime: A Cable Network "For Women," edited by J. D'Acci) 33–34: 103–32.

PART TWO

Spaces of Television

EACH TIME WE USE THE WORD "television" we actually commemorate one of the signal novelties of this technology: its capacity to allow us to see (-vision) at a distance (tele-). The first startling effect of electronic television technology was no doubt the capturing of the human form by the camera's electron beam and that image's simultaneous, recognizable reconfiguration as black and white dots on a television monitor. But the second set of "oohs" and "aahs" came in response to the human face being captured in one location and then transmitted via radio waves to a television set miles away. Unlike cinema, television allows for the seemingly simultaneous capture *and* reproduction of images. But the innovative "liveness" of the television image has long been exploited through television's spatial capacity: broadcasting those images without wires through space to a theoretically infinite number of spatially dispersed, anonymous, individual receiving sets.

Because broadcasting relies upon radio waves, the space any given signal covers is limited to a few dozen miles (depending on topography) from the transmission site. But even before the advent of television as a popular medium in some countries in the 1950s, the use of long-distance telephone lines had enabled radio programs to be sent and simultaneously received hundreds and thousands of miles beyond the range of their broadcast signals. Television adapted this same technology and innovated new ones to "network" dozens of geographically separated broadcast stations into regional and national systems—rendering the space between production and reception of images in some ways a logistical and experiential irrelevance. The advent in the 1980s of communication satellites for relaying television signals meant that television broadcasts could span continental and transoceanic distances. The spatial, indeed, the geographic relationship between the sender of a television transmission and its eventual receivers became even more attenuated and uncertain.

Thus, although television doesn't *necessarily* entail our seeing events as they occur in some place that we are not, some of our best remembered moments of television frequently do depend upon the seemingly magical capacity of television to collapse distance between the space of a captured event and the space of its viewing. In other words television can seem to put us in two places at once. It is said that the television age began in Great Britain on June 2, 1953, when audiences throughout the country watched as a new queen was crowned in Westminster Abbey (audiences in other parts of the commonwealth had to wait for jet bombers to transport film of the event for local broadcast!). Television broadcasting in Australia began just in time for Victorians who couldn't get tickets to watch the Melbourne Olympics in November 1956. US audiences did not witness the assassination of John F. Kennedy in 1963 on television, but millions *did* see his alleged assassin himself assassinated as he was being transferred to a Dallas, Texas, jail. Millions of people around the world spent December 31, 1999 and January 1, 2000 watching televised images of revelers around the world as a new millennium was greeted in Sydney, New Delhi, Rome, London, and New York.

There are other spatial dimensions of television. The television set itself occupies space in our homes—although the space required for television seems to be both contracting and expanding, from a tiny device that can be worn on the body to a wall-filling display unit. Until the relocation of the primary space for watching movies from the movie theater to the television set in the late 1980s, watching movies was associated with a particular dedicated space. Hence, both "the cinema" and "the movies" have been used to refer both to the thing viewed and to the place where it was shown. Television, on the other hand, transforms the space it occupies—the sitting room, sports bar, doctor's office, airport concourse, department store display window—*into* television space (for more on this, see Anna McCarthy's essay in Part Six: Watching Television). And it thus creates a mobile, dynamic, and contingent social space around it. As the essays in Part Six attest, understanding the nature of those social spaces within which television is experienced has been a major emphasis of television studies for the past twenty years or so.

Unlike radio (at least until stereo came along), but like the cinema, television also represents space. Indeed, it used to be argued that one of the defining differences between the film image and the television image was that the "big screen" was predisposed to represent landscape space, whereas the more limited resolution and smaller screen size of the television image gave it an affinity for the human face and for domestic spaces—hence the western film but the television soap opera, or so the argument went. Whatever the relative representational limits of the television image might still be (if any), as Nick Couldry discusses in his essay in Part Four (Making Television) the weekly, sometimes daily reproduction of intimate spaces on television can give them a greater sense of familiarity than even the spaces of our much more immediate, non-televisual environments.

There are, then, a number of ways in which it might be said that space is an important aspect of our experience of television, and, correspondingly, a number of ways in which the "spaces of television" might be taken up in television scholarship. Most of the essays in this section concern themselves with what we might call a geographic notion of space and its relationship to television. They foreground one of the defining features of television since the early 1990s and also showcase one important strand of television studies that has emerged in relation to it: the linking of myriad local sites of television reception with increasingly transnational networks through which an extraordinary amount and diversity of television programming is regionally or globally circulated.

As the communist regimes of Eastern Europe discovered to their detriment in the late 1980s, satellites do not respect the political boundaries of the nation state. Television broadcasting frequently had been closely regulated by national policies. Access was limited by geographic proximity to the source of production and transmission. But in an age of multiple-channel terrestrial broadcasting and hundred-plus channel cable and satellite systems, the "flow" of television programming across national boundaries has accelerated enormously. Television's transnational character at the beginning of the twenty-first century has encouraged the development of new understandings of, to use the title of the internationally-circulated Australian soap opera, "home" and "away." Through both the use of high-tech satellite and cable technologies and the relatively low-tech VCR, television has become an important vehicle for members of diasporic and exile communities around the world to stay connected with each other and to their "homeland." Television, to use the phrase coined by historian Benedict Anderson, becomes a tool for the construction of nation, not as a geographically bounded and fixed space, but as an "imagined community."

The essays that follow raise a number of key questions of import to both television scholarship and television citizenship alike. What are the implications of the transnational television environment for national and local television cultures around the world? What role does television—in its various and changing technological manifestations—play in the construction, maintenance, and dismantling of local, national, regional, and transnational spaces and identities? How do the meanings and pleasures associated with particular television programs change as they circulate far beyond the cultures in which and for which they were made?

Scott Robert Olson's essay, a chapter from his book provocatively entitled *Hollywood Planet: Global Media and the Competitive Advantage of Narrative Transparency*, concerns the traversal of both geographic and cultural space by media products. How, he asks, can we account for the fact that some but certainly not all media products enjoy popularity across disparate cultures— even cultures whose norms and values are very different from those of the culture within which and for which the product was originally produced? How is it, in other words, that some films and television programs seem to be able to "travel" so well across such vast cultural and geographic space? Furthermore, how do we account in particular for the conspicuous success that US film and television programs have had in appealing to audiences around the world? After surveying the major categories of explanation, he hypothesizes that the trans-cultural popularity of some film and television texts may be explained in part by what he calls their narrative transparency: "the capability of certain texts to seem familiar regardless of their origin, to seem a part of one's own culture, even though they have been crafted elsewhere." The producers of American films and television programs, he argues, have become particularly adept at making and exporting texts that blend easily into a variety of other cultures—texts that encourage the projection of many different local narratives, values, and meanings onto them.

Although, as the title of his book suggests, Olson is concerned primarily with the global circulation of American media, his argument might provoke us to test its applicability to other examples of trans-cultural media circulation and reception: the popularity of Latin American *telenovelas* in Russia or South Korea, the international appeal of certain television formats (*Big Brother*, *The Dating Game*, *Wheel of Fortune*), or the global popularity of Japanese video games and anime, for example. We also might ask what other factors—economic, political, and social – might help explain the "competitive advantage" that Hollywood media enjoy in the world market.

If Olson's argument plays down mediating factors in the global circulation of television culture, John Sinclair's essay strongly reasserts those factors. Building on the notion of the geolinguistic region he formulated with Elizabeth Jacka and Stuart Cunningham in the book *New Patterns in Global Television* Sinclair explores what he calls the "paradigm case" of the regional organization of global cultural and media space: Latin America.[1] As he notes, the Spanish geolinguistic media "region" would include not only the entirety of South America (excepting Portuguese-speaking Brazil) and Central America, but also Spain and the US, whose over 30 million Spanish-speaking residents make it the fifth-largest Spanish-speaking country in the world. He might also have noted that Los Angeles is the fourth-largest Spanish-speaking city in the world!

Sinclair uses the example of the Spanish geolinguistic region to underscore the fact that any particular "local" television culture is the result of multiple spaces being mapped on top of each other. In the case of viewers in South America, "television" means news and other programming produced for a local, metropolitan-defined area; networked sports and entertainment programming addressing a national audience; *telenovelas* "imported" from another country in the region; and with the increasing penetration of cable and satellite services, a variety of "global" Spanish-language channels (CNN, HBO Latino, MTV Español, etc.). Only in Latin America, argues Sinclair, "are audiences in a whole host of nations able to be addressed by virtue of their more or less common linguistic and cultural heritage as a kind of 'imagined community' on a world-regional scale . . . ."

In his essay Colin Sparks takes up what he says may be the most "fashionable" terms in media studies of the 1990s—all of which have spatial connotations: "the global," "the local," and "the public sphere." They are worth interrogating, however, not because they have been in vogue, he says, but because they refer to important features of contemporary media and have a particular salience in light of recent technological, economic, and political developments. As we have discussed elsewhere (the introduction to Part One: Institutions of Television) and as a number of scholars discuss in their own essays in this collection, Jürgen Habermas's notion of the public sphere has been one of the most influential ideas in television studies of the last two decades. Sparks begins by acknowledging that the meaning of the term itself is open to debate as is the accuracy of Habermas's historical analysis of its origins in eighteenth century Europe. Nevertheless, Sparks (like Richard Collins in his essay in Part One) finds the term has value in that it provides a guide for assessing the social and civic performance of specific media systems. Sparks then takes up the "the local" and "the global" as these terms apply to media studies and asks whether there seems to be empirical evidence to support a set of popular hypotheses about the relationship between them in the age of globalization. Sparks asks us to think through what is being meant when these terms are employed and to guard against the overgeneralization that their use seems to encourage.

We include in this section an essay that deals with the use of television among diasporic communities. Examining the use of television in its various forms (broadcast television, satellite services, the sale/rental/lending of video tapes, etc.) by diasporic communities encourages a reconceptualization of the "spaces" of television and a reconsideration of the relationship between ethnically and culturally-bound groups and the political entities that we routinely think of as having a definite spatial dimension—nation, for example.

The title of Stuart Cunningham's piece, "Popular Media as Public 'Sphericules,' " refers to his argument that the nationally-bounded, unitary use of the term "public sphere" does not adequately address the contemporary phenomenon of multiple, fragmented, globally dispersed, minority communities, for which mass media operate as a central part of their public "sphericules." He urges us to think in terms of multiple, dynamic, non-state-based public sphericules existing alongside or in the shadow of national public spheres. "[E]thno-specific global mediatized communities," he argues, "display in microcosm elements we would expect to find in 'the' public sphere."

Cunningham's essay grows out of a larger research project (*Floating Lives: The Media and Asian Diasporas*, co-authored with John Sinclair), which examined the "mediascapes" of Asian diasporic communities, especially in Australia. Australia provides a particularly good place to study the global phenomenon of diasporic mediascapes: with more than 150 ethnic groups, speaking 100 languages living as a part of only 18 million people, Australia is the world's second-largest immigrant nation on a proportional basis. For Cunningham's purposes, diasporic communities are transnational groups of ethnically-bound individuals who live as minorities, typically in western countries. They may share a linguistic and cultural heritage, but they certainly share a sense of cultural and social difference from the majority population of their place of residence as well as personal identities shaped by a strong sense of connection to a literal and symbolic place from which they are now physically and politically distanced. But in calling them diasporic ''com-munities,'' Cunningham would quickly point out that they challenge the idea of geographically-identifiable entities. Although some particularly large diasporic communities are associated with particular urban areas (Chinatown, Little Korea, etc.) and dedicated institutions (temples, clubs, shops), in many other cases there is no critical mass of individuals or families to form such enclaves or sustain such institutions. As a result, diasporic communities are to a significant extent constituted through media and media performance.

Note

1   Sinclair, J., Jacka, E., and Cunningham, S. (eds) (1995) *New Patterns in Global Television: Peripheral Vision*, New York: Oxford University Press.

Chapter 6

SCOTT ROBERT OLSON

HOLLYWOOD PLANET
Global media and the competitive advantage of
narrative transparency

> American mass culture did not even feel like an import . . .
> (Richard Pells 1997, p. 205)

OURS IS BECOMING A HOLLYWOOD PLANET.
Tunstall (1977) proclaimed 20 years ago that "the media are American." Now, Tunstall (1995) is backing off a bit, seeing the possibility for other nations to be successful in the global media marketplace, but if anything, his earlier claim was somewhat timid: It is not that the media are American, but something much broader and more profound. Hollywood has conquered the world.

The evidence is staggering. Seventy-five percent of movie tickets sold in Europe in 1995 were to films made in the United States. This is up 34 per cent from 10 years earlier. Thanks to the proliferation of satellite and cable, 70 per cent of the movies shown on European television were also American ("Hollywood conquers Europe," 1996). Trends in other parts of the world are similar. Hollywood is everywhere, and there seems to be nothing outside of Hollywood so "one question in every mind must be whether the geographical source of an individual's or country's media any longer matters" (Smith, 1995, p. 1). Even media made outside Hollywood have grown to have a Hollywood quality about them.

Swartzenegger, Stallone, Willis, and their coinvestors certainly call attention to this phenomenon by having named their successful restaurant chain Planet Hollywood. In its emphasis on the veneration of movie and television artifacts and the marketing of its brand name (rather than its menu), these restaurants claim to be little microcosms of a global obsession with media. They underestimate their own significance. The world is not a solar system of little Planet Hollywoods, but one Hollywood Planet. Hollywood is not a microcosm but the cosmos.

What does a *Hollywood Planet* mean? The traditional notion of global media, of course, is that if the planet is Hollywood, then a global monoculture—an American one—is taking root. This may be far too simple a conclusion, however. Among media theorists, a consensus is growing that this most fundamental assumption about transnational media is wrong. It may not be true that when the media from one culture are introduced into another, they force indigenous values and beliefs more in line with those that the media portray. The corollary of this assumption, and the source of its power, is that this infusion of nonnative values can be measured. This assumption and its corollary have guided academic research in this area for many years, and yet the results have been disappointing and inconclusive. The major failing of this approach is that it ignores essential work being done in postmodern and literary theory.

Examples of this mistaken approach to global media are easy to find. Kang and Wu (1995) and Kapoor and Kang (1995) are in good company. They wonder why it is that despite their elaborate methodology and attention to detail, they can find no changes in attitudes and beliefs among young people in India and Taiwan in spite of their recent introduction to extensive American television broadcasting. They wonder if they have selected the wrong sample or somehow asked the wrong questions: How could the effect of this new programming be so dramatically missed? In a sense they have asked the wrong question, just not at the level at which they suspect. They do not recognize their paradigm is in fact a theory that does not fit the evidence or that it is time for a new theory.

Why is it, then, that the television programs and movies produced in the United States are so dominant throughout the world, in places culturally similar to the United States as well as places that are vastly different, and so much so that many countries feel it necessary to severely limit their import, but measuring the media often shows that television and movies have little or no effect? American film and television "can be and are exported almost everywhere" (Dennis and Snyder, 1995, p. xii), so why is it that in Japan, for example, where they are voracious consumers of American cultural products, they consume them in a way that is entirely Japanese (Tobin, 1992; Yoshimoto, 1994), and audiences stay Japanese in the process? Indeed, although "the attractions of Western media at first seem overwhelming and transforming . . . people easily swim back to the surface of their lives" (Smith, 1995, p. 4). If the existing theory is wrong, a different theory should replace it by demonstrating more explanatory power with the data that has been gathered.

Perhaps the effect the media brings is of a type that has not been widely considered, one outside the dominant epistemology. Joseph Yusuf Amali Shekwo (1984), late social mobilization official from Abuja, Nigeria, told the story of how his people, the Gbagyi (often called Gwari), watched "Dallas" (CBS TV). He was intrigued by the popularity of this American program in such a different land, and knew that the traditional explanation for it—that people in the developing world were attracted to Western media because they emulated the Western lifestyle (e.g., Lernet, 1977; Schramm, 1964; de Sola Pool, 1977)—was naively incomplete. In talking to Nigerians who watched "Dallas," Shekwo came to the conclusion that although what was on the screen was more or less identical to the program that aired in the United States, they were not really watching the show in the same way that Americans were. Because of the way they watched it, they were watching a different show.

How could this be true? They were bringing to their understanding of American television a completely different set of cognitive assumptions, taxonomies, and background narratives. It became clear to Shekwo that what the Gbagyi saw in "Dallas" was not anything particularly American, but something more personal and more proximate—something indigenous. For example, his analysis revealed that the character of J.R. Ewing, the unscrupulous oil magnate played on the show by Larry Hagman, was perceived by the Gbagyi as having the same specific traits as Gbagwulu, a trickster worm from Gbagyi mythology. In a sense, J.R. acted as an archetypal surrogate for Gbagwulu.

Hardly any Americans and perhaps none of the "Dallas" production staff thought of J.R. in association with Gbagwulu (of whom they were no doubt unaware), so why is it that the Gbagyi make that connection? There are three possibilities. First, through some long forgotten act of diffusion, Gbagwulu has actually affected the evolution of American villain archetypes, just as African American slaves retained traditional African tales by evolving them into Brer Rabbit (Faulkner, 1977), so that J.R. is really a descendant (of sorts) of Gbagwulu. Second, the narrative archetype that J.R. embodies is so sufficiently encompassing that more particular archetypes and characters from other cultures can be projected into him, even if he did not descend from them. Last, there has been a little of both, a mix of diffusion and suffusion. In any case, the "Dallas" that the Gbagyi watched was theirs. There is an important difference, however, between the indigenous tale and "Dallas": The traditional stories existed primarily to satisfy spiritual and social needs; imported media may serve this need, but their raison d'être is commercial, what Schiller (1989) called the market criterion (p. 75).

The J.R.–Gbagwulu story is not an isolated phenomenon. Punjabi Hindu and Sikh families living in Southall, England see in the character of Mrs. Mangel, on the soap opera "Neighbours" (Australian TV) an embodiment of their cultural tradition of *izzat*, which is concerned with preserving honor and name through extensive familial control of social relationships (Gillespie, 1995a). Television watchers in Trinidad see in the soap opera "The Young and the Restless" (CBS TV) a manifestation of a defining national characteristic, *bacchanal* (Miller, 1995). Audiences everywhere see themselves reflected in films such as *The Lion King* (1994) or television shows such as "Walker: Texas Ranger" (CBS TV).

Consider the projective reception of *Titanic* (1997), a film that roared past the small list of films with revenues over $1 billion, earning at least $1.5 billion, and becoming the highest grossing film of all time, even adjusted for inflation. It was a different film to each interpretive community that viewed it. Japanese audiences reported an attraction to the cultural virtue of *gamen*—the ability to remain stoic in the face of adversity (Strom, 1998)—that they saw in the film. The film prompted such grief in Russian audiences that a national contest was devised for audience members to write a new, happy ending (Bohlen, 1998). The Chinese used the film as a challenge to develop the indigenous film industry (Eckholm, 1998). French cultural elites saw their own political consciousness reflected in the film (Riding, 1998). *Titanic* reminded Turkish audiences of their indigenous film *Bandit* (Kinzer, 1998). One Egyptian fan of the film declared to *The New York Times* that "it is not an American movie" (Jehl, 1998, p. AR 29). The Brazilian soap opera "Por Amor" incorporated scenes from *Titanic* (Sims, 1998). In short, *Titanic* was not one film but many depending on the interpretive community that watched it. One reporter covering the phenomenon said simply, "different countries have viewed the phenomenon of *Titanic* in their own ways" (Riding, 1998, p. AR 1).

To put it more theoretically, Jameson (1986) argued that all Third World novels are "national allegories," and Burton-Carvajal (1994) described certain first world cinematic texts as "allegories of colonialism." Given that texts lend themselves to a multiplicity of meanings and that particular readings of a text are privileged primarily through externally coded values and norms, is it possible that consumers in the developing world interpret imported American cinematic and televisual texts as national allegories too? This is a position somewhat consistent with Bhabha's (1994) and other postcolonial work, yet one commonly ignored in the study of media across cultures.

The dominant argument about the effect of global media on culture ignores the subtleties of Bhabha's observations, and instead goes something like this:

Major premise: Indigenous cultures are disappearing.
Minor premise: The reach of electronic media is now global.
Conclusion: The global media cause indigenous cultures to disappear.

This argument has several unexamined assumptions and consequently suffers from a *post hoc ergo propter hoc* fallacy. The following questions need to be asked:

• Are indigenous cultures really disappearing, or is something else happening to them?

- Are the media really causal in the process? If so, are they the primary causal agent that they are assumed to be?
- If they are the primary causal agent, what is the mechanism and effect of that agency?

Perhaps, despite alarms to the contrary, the world is not being melted down into a single, hegemonic, more-or-less American monoculture, even though American cultural products dominate the world. On the one hand, other production and distribution venues are developing (Tunstall, 1995). On the other hand, when one looks closely at the way that texts are read in specific cultures, rather than becoming overwhelmed by the astonishing magnitude of cultural exports alone, a multitude of differences and otherness emerges. György (1995) described the particular case of Ukrainians watching American media and noted that without an American cultural context, they are not watching the same program. Naficy (1996) showed how Iranian audiences made Hollywood films into indigenized hybrids. In both cases, imported media perpetuated rather than extinguished the Other. Despite its attempts, universality does not vanquish particularity (Yoshimoto, 1994), a claim generally borne out by history. Although readers around the world are increasingly gaining access to the same materials to read, they do not have access to the same ways of reading.

It is the thesis of this text that, due to a unique mix of cultural conditions that create a transparency, the United States has a competitive advantage in the creation and global distribution of popular taste. *Transparency* is defined as any textual apparatus that allows audiences to project indigenous values, beliefs, rites, and rituals into imported media or the use of those devices. This transparency effect means that American cultural exports, such as cinema, television, and related merchandise, manifest narrative structures that easily blend into other cultures. Those cultures are able to project their own narratives, values, myths, and meanings into the American iconic media, making those texts resonate with the same meanings they might have if they were indigenous. Transparency allows such narratives to become stealthy, to be foreign myths that surreptitiously act like indigenous ones, Greek gifts to Troy, but with Trojan citizens inside the horse. For better or worse, the transparency phenomenon facilitates the fragmented and incoherent beginnings of postcolonial culture. Hollywood studios have learned to profit from transparency and increasingly exploit it in the production of television programs and feature films.

The design of those media texts is driven, wittingly or unwittingly, by transparency. Consequently, as Smoodin (1994) pointed out, it is not nearly so important to understand what particular texts mean, as to ask " 'who are these meanings available to?' and, related to this, 'how does meaning vary from audience to audience?' " (p. 17). By enabling different readings, by allowing and even encouraging subaltern perspectives, transparent media increase their market share. Paradoxically, however, in earning those additional revenues, they perpetuate indigenous culture in hybrid form.

It also does not mean that transparency is bereft of cultural consequences, that the global media have no effect. They do, but in a manner that differs from dominant assumptions in two ways: The process of cultural change is slower than generally assumed because it involves the accretion of new, transplanted images and consequently memories, and the process is causally the reverse of what is generally assumed—the indigenous culture actively reaches out, haggles (Naficy, 1996), and does not merely absorb in hypodermic, magic-bullet fashion some set of injected cultural values. The readings of a transparent text are indigenous, but the images and sounds are transplanted. Over time, these new images become familiarized, naturalized, and "real," just like those they replace. The result is something new, something interstitial, but not something American or Americanized.

Premises

Five premises lead to the conclusion that something like transparency must be present in the American media and that it can and ought to be observed and categorized. The first premise is that American media exports dominate the world media market. This initial premise stipulates, rather uncontroversially, that American movies and television programs are phenomenally successful internationally by almost any measure. The international market is a huge share of American movie and television profits, and more emphasis is being put by Hollywood into developing foreign markets. In fact, entertainment is the second largest U.S. net export, after aerospace. ("The entertainment industry," 1989; Olson, 1993).

[. . .]

"Dallas" is a good example. As Ang (1985) pointed out, "Dallas" was viewed in 90 countries. With its huge volume and substantial economic significance to both the domestic and international media market, it is clear that the American media industry must be considered the major supplier of world entertainment.

A second premise is that the most common explanations for American media dominance and for the way audiences receive the media are incomplete. Frequently proffered explanations of U.S. television and film success are reducible to three basic perspectives:

1   The materialist explanation that American media dominate by sheer economic hegemony. In this model, the threat of U.S. media is primarily economic because it subverts the development of a domestic production capacity (see Mattelart *et al.*, 1984; Schiller, 1969, 1989, 1995; Tunstall, 1977).
2   The traditional development model, which makes use of Lerner's (1977) want-get ratio (see also Lerner and Schramm, 1969), and which contends that American movies and television are popular because other cultures emulate the American lifestyle presented there. Although for Lerner and Schramm (1969), and other traditionalists, the emulation of U.S. culture was desirable because it led to economic development and modernization, for cultural preservationists, it was undesirable because it subverted, even colonized, indigenous cultures.
3   The reader-response or reception approach theorized by Iser (1980) and Jauss (1982) and applied by Ang (1985) and others. It argues that audiences are capable of active and empowering readings of mass communication.

These three explanations are ultimately unsatisfying in explaining what has facilitated the American media's increasing dominance in world media because they fail to recognize what Bourdieu (1993) called "the objectivity of the subjective." Mattelart *et al.*'s (1984), McChesney's (1998), and Schiller's (1989) critical-materialist explanation was that the expanded presence and international role of multinational corporations and new media technologies that enable rapid and widespread dissemination of information lead to American dominance. Although these are certainly major factors, this explanation does not seem complete. Mustn't the success of the American media exports have something to do with the programs themselves? The materialist explanation is unfinished because it ignores the pleasure that American media certainly bring to many people (see Ang, 1985) or what Barthes (1977) and then Fiske (1987) called *jouissance*. Although it is true that American media are in many ways imperialist and hegemonic, most of the audience chooses to watch them. Governments would not have to regulate to limit their import unless there was sufficient domestic demand to warrant doing so; clearly, American culture "fascinates those very people who suffer most at its hands" (Baudrillard, 1988, p. 77). American media dominance cannot be explained, then, by simple imperialist models, and this approach is guilty of treating a complex human process in purely objective, material terms (see Bourdieu, 1993; Johnson, 1993). In more recent writing, Schiller (1995) recognized the need for incorporating audience behavior into his formulation of U.S. hegemony, describing an international "culture of contentment" whose attitudes and belief shape political and economic behavior (p. 469), a significant modification to his view of substructuration.

The traditional development explanation that the international community emulates America also fails to explain the global popularity of American media. On the one hand, it can scarcely be argued that the American media reflect any real American culture to emulate; "Dallas" or "Baywatch" are not representative of American norms and attitudes. On the other hand, cultures that are enamored with American media may be otherwise indifferent, or even repulsed by, the United States; it is possible to love certain things about American popular culture but be critical of American culture in general [. . .] Traditional development explanations underestimate the ability of persons within a culture to pick and choose and treat a complex human process in purely subjective terms (see Bourdieu, 1993; Johnson, 1993), ignoring the extent to which subjective and objective factors affect each other.[. . .]

The third approach to international media popularity is also incomplete, but encouragingly focuses on audience reception of television and film. Most reader-response criticism and reception theory (Ang, 1985; Bacon-Smith, 1992; Fiske, 1987; Jenkins, 1992) does not systematically look at what viewers themselves are saying. Those scholars generally form the theoretical basis for which later experimental methods must be developed and the need for more studies of lived culture has been recognized (Harms and Dickens, 1996) and, to some extent, addressed.

So political economy, development theory, and reader-response criticism all fail to account for the breadth of American media dissemination. A fourth approach, *cultivation theory*, is less interested in why American media are popular than in how those media are affecting cultures. It has matured into a theory with a set of methodological tools, but this maturity has not produced a complete and convincing portrait of audience interaction with the media.

The basic contention of cultivation theory and its methodological offshoot, *cultivation analysis*, is that the greater the exposure to the same media, the more the culture will become homogenized. Yet, although cultivation analysis has made important contributions to the understanding of media effects, it is as incomplete an understanding as political economy, development theory, and reader-response criticism, and one that is not well-suited to examining the subtleties of how identity is situated within culture or the interstitial nature of subaltern culture.

[. . .]

In its most common manifestation, cultivation analysis assumes, and therefore discovers, that American media will render the world American, even when the evidence for that transformation is merely small effects. Other contemporary research seems to indicate that, although global cultural change is occurring, it is more likely that indigenous cultures will adapt the American media to their own purposes than for them simply to adopt wholesale American cultural values, beliefs, and behaviors. Although cultivation analysis recognizes that cultural differences will occur in response to the media, it maintains that the perspectives of the producers of that media, rather than that of its recipients, will dominate (Morgan, 1990).

To review briefly, the second premise underlying the argument in this text is that existing explanations of American media dominance and reception are incomplete, that the approaches used and conclusions gleaned from materialist-political economy, traditional development theory, reader-response criticism, and cultivation analysis are only stray pieces from a larger puzzle. A corollary to this second premise is that shared meaning across cultures is improbable and unlikely. [. . .]

A third premise is that the media texts themselves must provide at least part of the explanation for their global popularity. It is significant that some American media texts are internationally popular and others are not, a point lost on the materialist explanation of U.S. media dominance. "Dallas" was successfully exported throughout the world, but, despite attempts, "The Tonight Show with Johnny Carson" (NBC TV) was not. This indicates that although at least part of the explanation for the success of any text resides in the culture consuming it, another and perhaps more significant part resides in the text itself. This is particularly true given that certain texts are successful in so many different cultures; if the reason for the popularity of a text is found only in the culture, then why do so many cultures share such an interest in particular texts? Although "Dallas" was successful in Nigeria because of specific cultural attributes of the Gbagyi, Ibo, Fulani, and Hausa, perhaps even more of its success is due to the structure, images, and ideology of the text.

Not all scholars would support such careful analyses of media texts as a potential explanation of their power. One can identify many nontextual causes for the global preeminence of U.S. media: American foreign policy (see Pells, 1997), media pricing structures (which charge an African country 1/10 the price charged a European country for the same television program, e.g.), the accelerating conversion of national broadcasting systems to an advertising model (McChesney, 1997, 1998), the growth in satellite television and access to VCRs, the global spread of the English language (Pells, 1997), and other explanations. Many scholars warn against looking any deeper than these political and economic explanations.

[. . .]

Although media texts alone do not hold the complete answer to their own success, neither does a careful examination of a media text preclude examination of the system that brought it into being. In fact, the purpose of this argument is to examine the interrelation between the text and the system as a means of explaining American media success. [. . .]

A fourth premise is that if the answer is in the text, then that is where one must look. Although this may sound obvious, the text is looked at too infrequently in the analysis of America's role in dominating world culture: Schiller's (1989) study of corporate control of world media, for example, never actually looks at the vehicle of domination, the television and movies themselves, and there are many other studies like it. Yet, if, as Bourdieu (1993) suggested, each work of art is "a manifestation of the field as a whole, in which all the powers of the field, and all the determinisms inherent in its structure and functioning, are concentrated" (p. 37), and if it is true that the best explanation for American media's global success is found in the movies and television programs themselves, then a close examination of them ought to reveal consistent attributes. This does not necessarily mean that all successfully exported programs share the same attributes and are consequently popular for the same reasons; it is possible, for example, that "Dallas" and "Dynasty" (ABC TV), another successfully exported prime-time soap opera, were successful for different reasons and in fact textual analyses reveal this to be the case (Ang, 1985; Gripsrud, 1995). In addition, it should not be assumed that the presence of particular textual properties guarantees export accomplishment. It does seem likely, however, that there is at least a pool of traits from which the American media draw. [. . .]

It is important to remember that a text is not merely the mediated object, but rather the meeting of that artifact and the person who reads it. Consequently, any examination of texts that does not look at audiences is only partially formed. It is surprising how little this is recognized, but it is safe to say that the vast majority of those who theorize about the media do not look at specific audiences engaging with specific texts. [. . .]

Happily, more researchers are now looking at what audiences actually do, applying ethnographic methodologies to the problems of texts. It is from this promising direction that this thesis proceeds. Among the media researchers establishing this method are Bacon-Smith (1992), Gillespie (1995a, 1995b), Jenkins (1992, 1994), Leuthold (1998), Liebes and Katz (1993), Naficy (1996), Waisbord (1998), and Wheeler (1998). Their writing suggests that although responses to media are overwhelmingly local and most media research ignores "the resiliency of local identity and cultural difference" (Wheeler, 1998, p. 359), these observations hold out the potential to extrapolate a theory of how local responses to media originate.

A fifth and final premise is that the international popularity of American media must find its genesis in American culture itself. This is a slightly more contentious premise because the linking of a text to the culture out of which it is born is difficult, problematic, and full of traps; nevertheless, products do seem to bear evidence of the culture that manufactures them (Porter, 1990, 1998). Every text is poured out of three crucibles: the author, the culture, and the technology of its production. The study of the first of these is appropriately called *authorship study* and approaches the text in search of the distinguishing characteristics placed there by the human agent of its creation (see Caughie, 1981), although isolating an individual creator is of course problematic (see Bourdieu, 1993). [. . .]

The easiest way to study the second of these, the cultural crucible, is through genre studies, because genres inculcate what is present across many texts significant to a particular culture, undergirding the authorship of each text. A genre reveals what is ideologically, morally, and narratalogically important to the society that gives birth to it. In every text, there is a tension between genre and author: The genre anchors the text to the culture, insuring it will be meaningful, whereas the author makes certain aspects of it unique. [. . .]

The third crucible in any act of narrative creation is the text itself, particularly its unique technological properties. The book *The Shining* (King, 1978) is not the film *The Shining* (1980). Of course, in addition to the technological differences there are also different authors in conflict here. Stephen King did not direct the film, which was directed by Stanley Kubrick, who is widely regarded by cinema scholars to have a distinctive style. It is the difference in technology that best explains the difference between this book and film, however, because different media have such different properties, not only of transmission, but of audience reception (Ellis, 1992). [. . .]

These three crucibles—author, genre, and technology—give the text its shape. All of them can be linked to culture to one degree or another. The author is the product of a culture and chooses to convey the narrative in a particular language; the genre is a formative part of the culture as well as its product, and if one subscribes to narrative theory, it is the culture (see Coste 1989; also Lakoff, 1987); technology also has cultural causes and effects. With the exception of genre, making these connections is difficult, however. The extent to which personal agency is socially created or the extent to which the technology of High Definition Television (HDTV) can be said to be Japanese or American is not known. This becomes a complex and subtle problem when considering the global media. For example, although the American media may not dominate every television market, in many cases, markets are dominated by locally produced programs that "[copy] the American series" (Tunstall, 1995, p. 8), embodying and replicating an essentially American genre. China is trying to do something like this now by engineering its own version of a Mickey Mouse character ("Mickey Mao," 1996).

Still, given America's unique ability to produce globally ubiquitous programs, there ought to be a connection between its store of textual formulae and the culture that produced it. Porter (1990) observed that certain societies are better at producing certain products; although he only briefly examined the entertainment industry per se, his method applies there as it does to automobiles or microwave ovens. Porter's approach involves analyzing how the four elements of his national competitive advantage diamond are manifest in a particular national industry: These include *factor conditions, demand conditions, supporting industries,* and *strategy, structure, and rivalries.*

Porter's method does not work unless the properties of the product and its market are fairly well-understood. Unfortunately, little scholarship has been done on the textual reasons behind American media hegemony. The few books that even peripherally consider it are rather old. Ang's (1985) *Watching Dallas* is useful but is 10 years out of date; it was criticized for its *ad hoc* methodology, its focus on pleasure instead of meaning, and for considering the case of only one television program in one particular nation state. Schiller's (1989) *Culture, Inc.* shared a deficiency of much of the neo-Marxist literature: Although purporting to examine the American media, it never looked at the films and television programs themselves. Schiller's analysis of the political-economy of the television industry is useful, but it does little to explain the actual mechanism of the media he purports to study because it suffers from Bourdieu's (1993) objectivist fallacy. Perhaps one of the best books on international media use is one of the more recent ones: Liebes and Katz's (1993) *The Export of Meaning*, which situates American television in actual audience behaviors. The current study is in some ways an attempt to theorize on their observations. [. . .]

A few more recent books do a better job of applying contemporary theory to transnational media. Shohat and Stam's (1994) *Unthinking Eurocentrism: Multiculturalism and the Media* is an important study of postcolonial media and provides a good deal of useful data for the study proposed here. Its focus is not, however, primarily on narratology and textual apparatus. Gillespie's (1995b) *Television, Ethnicity, and Cultural Change* is particularly interested in resistant and recombinant readings, but her scope is narrower than the one proposed here. She primarily focused on the use of transnational media by South Asians in London.

Tunstall (1977) updated his seminal *The Media Are American* into a new edition (1994) that included a new foreword. His central argument was that the media themselves embody American-ness, in "the same way that spaghetti bolognese is Italian and cricket is British" (p. 13). Mattelart *et al.* (1984) did extensive work on the political and economic aspects of the international media; their most relevant book for this project is *International Image Markets*, which advocates abandoning the concept of cultural imperialism of the sort Schiller (1989) used in favor of a more complex approach that recognized greater subtlety and interstitial dialectics in the behavior of national markets and industries. They recognized textual reasons—the symbolic dimension—as part of the formula of American success, but, did not focus extensively on the text from an audience-use perspective.

[. . .]

Such a study is urgently necessary because major world treaties like the North American Free Trade Agreement (NAFTA) and the General Agreement on Trade and Tariffs (GATT), not to mention issues of national and cultural sovereignty, hinge on understanding how the American media function in an international context. If American media dominate the world market, existing explanations for this dominance are incomplete, the media texts must provide at least part of the explanation for their own global popularity, looking in the text can elucidate particular general attributes, and these attributes can be traced to the American cultural crucible, then the success of the American entertainment industry can be systematically studied and at least tentatively accounted for using an approach like Porter's (1990). Much of the intercultural, ethnographic, and economic empirical data for such a study has already been collected. What remains to be done is to synthesize that data and suggest what they mean from the standpoint of recent media, semiotic, and cultural studies theory. This is not an easy thing to do because

> no simple answer is possible . . . Very divergent factors, including historical ones, contribute to this, and it seems almost pointless to try to examine the success of *Dallas* without taking into account the wider social context of the postmodernist media culture.
>
> (Ang, 1985, p. 5).

Placing American media in that wider social context is the next step. The primary contention of this work is that the existing data and a close examination of American media texts reveal that the most successfully exported ones are culturally transparent. Prior to offering that argument in detail, however, it is important to pin down the slippery meaning of *transparency*.

Defining transparency

The term *transparency* has been used differently by different media theorists. Baudrillard (1993) meant by it an absence, "disappearance and disembodiment" (p.16), a similar sense to Virilio's (1991) "aesthetics of disappearance," in which small bits of time disappear. Ang (1985) meant by *transparency* something closer to, but not as encompassing as, the usage for this text: For her, it meant the visual media's use of a conventional style that seems natural, that has the "illusion of reality" (p. 41), and consequently, allows viewers to project themselves easily into the narrative. In the context of this analysis, the term *transparency* is used more literally, in its most traditional sense of "appearing through"—not invisible but hypervisible. (In this sense, Baudrillard, 1993, and Ang, 1985, are really talking about opaqueness, something in the text that cannot be seen.) The *transparent* is diaphanous, luminous and lucid, penetrating, and clear, both in its literal sense of enabling something to be seen through and its figurative sense of the understandable manifestation of meaning.

Transparency is the capability of certain texts to seem familiar regardless of their origin, to seem a part of one's own culture, even though they have been crafted elsewhere. The commercial advantage to a movie or television program of this type is that it has the potential to garner a large global market; a film of narrow interest to a particular culture or subculture, a film that would seem inaccessible or incoherent to some segment of the world's population, in short, a film that lacks transparency has much more limited commercial possibilities. Given the tremendous costs of producing a feature film, culture factories like Hollywood increasingly rely on international distribution to make films profitable and have consequently toiled to increase the exportability of their product. Producing films with intercultural appeal is not an easy thing to do even for Hollywood.

Hollywood does not hold a monopoly on the production of transparent texts, and in specific media domains, other culture factories are dominant: Britain is unrivaled in exporting pop music; India and Hong Kong are exceptional exporters of feature films; Brazil excels at producing and distributing soap operas; and Japan controls the computer game market. To some extent, every text has some measure of transparency because external social determinants are necessarily refracted in any process of reading or viewing (Johnson, 1993). Where Hollywood is unrivaled, however, is in the creation of *synergy*—an industry term that means the coordinated marketing of a single concept across manifold media platforms, product merchandising, licensing, spin-offs, and simulated environments. Outside of Hollywood, rare is the sort of strategic commercial coordination behind the simultaneous release of *Jurassic Park* (1993), its affiliated dinosaur toys and human action figures, games (both traditional and computer), the tie-in with a McDonald's promotion, licensed clothing, candy, and television specials about the making of *Jurassic Park*, not to mention the theme park ride. In the end, *Jurassic Park* and its by-products are estimated to be worth over $1 billion worldwide, making it not only one of the biggest films in history, but essentially an industry unto itself. In order for it to have succeeded in communicating with such a large audience across so many different nations and cultures, *Jurassic Park* must possess some level of transparency; such successful global synergy would otherwise be impossible.

Jurassic Park is unique, but it epitomizes a trend in media programming design and distribution. Because American film and television are phenomenally popular throughout much of the world, many countries seek to limit their import. The disagreement between France and the United States over American cultural exports became a major stumbling block to the negotiation of the GATT treaty in 1993 (Cohen, 1993; Moerk and Williams, 1993; Williamson and Dawtrey, 1993). France was understandably sensitive because *Jurassic Park* had outgrossed a domestic production released the same day (Cohen-Solal, 1995). [. . .]

What enables meaningful crosscultural transparency is that audience members, acting in interpretive communities that exchange and reinforce meaning, perceive or read (i.e., actively engage and interpret) the media differently based on their own cognition, culture, and background narratives. This is not a new concept, but has been of interest to media scholars for at least 10 years, often with the "Dallas" television program as the catalytic object. There are several possible explanations for how transparency allows a text to generate different meanings in its audience, but they can be approximately categorized into two theoretical camps: On the one hand, there is negotiation theory, primarily associated with Hall (1980) through his theory of negotiated codes and oppositional decoding; on the other hand, there is polysemy, an approach advocated by de Certeau (1984) and Fiske (1987, 1996). The fundamental distinction between these two approaches is that negotiation is inherently dialectical, presuming two or three meanings, a few inferred and one implied, with the production of a synthesized meaning. *Polysemy*, however, presumes that the text is capable of implying, and the reader capable of inferring, a much broader range of meanings; the process is less like negotiation than like selecting from a smorgasbord.

Hall (1980) argued that every act of communication must go through a process of encoding and decoding in order for it to be transmitted. When this is applied to the mass media, it can be seen that certain interests naturally tend to be encoded in the transmitted text, particularly the interests of advertisers, media conglomerates, and the powerful institutions to which they cater. This is what Hall called the *dominant code*—the code that is intended. The audience most likely decodes media messages using this dominant code, especially if their producers encode them skillfully, and this encourages audience decoders to behave in the prescribed manner, for example, to buy the product advertised. Members of the audience are not limited to this response, however. They may also negotiate their decoding or oppositionally decode. The negotiated code occurs when audience members accept the basic legitimacy of the hegemonic capitalist system that created the message, but nevertheless interpret the message in a manner different from the intended meaning. Oppositional decoding occurs when members of the audience reject not only the message, but also the system that created it and interpret the message in a manner critical of its originator.

Hall's approach to negotiated meaning has been applied to the crosscultural understanding of media and even to "Dallas." Liebes (1988) studied how "Dallas" was perceived by an international audience, accurately concluding that "it cannot be taken for granted that everybody understands the programs in the same way or even that they are understood at all" (p. 277). Meaning of television programs is, for Liebes, constructed within interpretive communities, but all programs seem to permit diverse readings. Ultimately, however, this argument relies on the traditional notion that television programs "infiltrate into the culture" (p. 278), a process contradictory to true transparency and reception theory, where it would be more accurately argued that the culture infiltrates the television programs.

Ang (1985) hinted at polysemy in documenting how "Dallas" was received and interpreted by Dutch viewers. Ang's explanation for their attraction to the program centered on the pleasure this soap opera afforded them, but a pleasure that was generated in different ways. For some, the text was a pleasurable program centered on the pleasure this soap opera afforded them, but a pleasure that was generated in different ways. For some, the text was pleasurable because they enjoyed the costumes and the settings; for others, pleasure came from the twists and turns of the plot; still others got pleasure from projecting themselves into the characters. This led Ang to conclude that "each has his or her own more or less unique relationship to the program" (p. 26). Yet, despite these differences in reading, these viewers had a great deal in common: gender, nationality, and language. The most interesting implication of this was not examined by Ang: if understandings of "Dallas" greatly vary within a culture, then how much must understandings vary between cultures?

Schiller (1989) was critical of Liebes' and Ang's style of audience-response media study. His argument with it had four components:

1   Audience-response theories ignore social factors external to the consciousness of a single audience member but that are nonetheless powerful conditioners of the manner in which they will interpret what they see, factors such as economic class.
2   These theories are unrealistic in their attribution of active, involved, and pluralistic readings of television and movies to an audience that is actually quite passive.
3   Audience-response theories make use of questionable methodology and overly subjective interpretation of data.
4   These theories ignore the massive and monolithic coordination and control that corporations exert over the production and dissemination of media programming.

Consequently, for Schiller (1989), although audiences are capable of diverse readings, they rarely assert this capability because "their capacities are overwhelmed" (p. 156). Schiller's criticisms are apt, but do not necessitate an abandonment of audience-response methodologies. Instead, a modification of these theories is possible so as to take into account social and economic factors. This would constitute an overdue resolution of a serious conflict between the critical and hermeneutic schools of media study.

Ultimately, negotiated meaning theory fails to answer the question that is the primary focus of this text: What is it about the American media that make their programming so adaptable to other cultures? This is not an empirical question, but a semiotic one: It has to do with the structure of the text itself, the images it uses, the type and relationships of the characters and the way in which an individual narrative fits into the overall narrative, parallel and contradictory readings, and consequently the text that must be studied to find answers.

Polysemy is the most persuasive explanation for why American media are so transparent. Fiske (1986, 1987) did not take a truly global perspective on polysemy and did not feel that texts were open to an infinitude of meanings. In an acknowledgment of Hall (1980), he argued that certain meanings are given preferentiality, but texts are nonetheless capable of creating a great many meanings. For Fiske (1987), polysemy is the result of several textual devices, each of which opens the text up to alternative reading. These devices include irony, metaphor, jokes, *contradiction* (by which he meant the resistance of various elements in the text to a tidy resolution), and *excess* (by which he meant *hyperbole*, as in the over-the-top indulgence of wealth on "Dallas" or *semiotic excess*, the presence of too many signs in any text for their meaning to be controlled).

Whereas negotiation is a process of an audience, polysemy is the properties of the text. Another useful term more descriptive of a process resident in the reader or viewer is *eisegesis*—the antonym of exegesis. Whereas in *exegesis* the reader draws meaning out of the text, in *eisegesis*, the reader puts personal meanings into the text. Traditionally, and particularly in the area of Biblical scholarship, eisegesis has been considered an improper method, a fallacy, and a misreading. Yet, eisegesis is clearly consonant with contemporary theories and methods of literary criticism and textual interpretation. Two entire schools of critical interpretation-reception theory (Iser, 1980; Jauss, 1982) and reader-response criticism (Fish, 1980; Tompkins, 1980)—are eisegetic, and Bloom (1975) argued that all reading is actually *misprision*, misreading. Indeed, rather than eisegesis being a fallacy, it seems that denying its role in the production of meaning is the real fallacy. So, the presence in a text of transparency enables polysemy, which enables eisegesis, which gives the text the illusion of indigenous meaning.

[. . .]

Merging polysemy with transparency resolves many of the contradictions and conflicts between the reader-response and critical schools of media study. Polysemy is a middle ground between critical analysis, such as Schiller's (1989), and audience-response analysis, like Ang's (1985), because it recognizes the audience's role in the consumption and understanding of texts, but also acknowledges that this is conditioned by external social factors internalized by each audience member, such as culture, race, class, and gender. Transparency is a further resolution of these two schools of thought, because it acknowledges both the deliberate corporate design and intention that guides the design and production of media programming, but also acknowledges the audience's ability to project meaning into these same programs, to adapt them to indigenous needs, as postcolonial studies (Bhabha, 1994) and other approaches indicate. Each of these functions is compatible with transparency, because each serves a different need of the text: The program designer's need for capital is satisfied by a program that does well internationally, and the emotional needs of the audience find fulfillment in its narrative.

If the polysemy of the American media account for their international success, then another question must be raised: What is it about these movies and television programs that makes them polysemic? This is a complex question, and one with no simple answer [. . .]. Answering it requires examining the media texts themselves.

Meaningful archetypes

Polysemy is not boundless because culture inhibits the possible range of readings. Even those whose acts of interpretation diverge substantially from the norm, such as those diagnosed as schizophrenic, decipher and depict their experiences within culturally bounded linguistic and narrative parameters. Meaning resides in and is conferred by the language and narratives themselves, and consequently, is an inescapable context. The form that meaning takes is relevant to understanding not only how it is conferred, but how related, corollary forms can seem to convey different meaning in different contexts. The most common and time-tested form of meaning is myth, which can be either ancient or modern. The human need for myth has not waned in the face of Enlightenment scientism (Blumenberg, 1985).

Myth is a system of signification that has authority, credibility, and a claim to truth (Lincoln, 1989). In other words, *myth* is a form of speech that is respected and believed, although not necessarily as fact; myth possesses the literary truth of the parable or aphorism, not the documentary truth of a newspaper. For Barthes (1972), myth is *metalanguage*, "a second language, in which one speaks about the first" (p. 115), a level of signification once removed. It is a contention here that polysemic forms act transparently as if they were *mythotypes*, latent archetypal needs that act as the architecture of manifest historical myths, the human longings that encompass and undergird all myths.

Myth and meaning are inextricable. Can meaning resist myth? In other words, is it possible for meaning to be conveyed in language itself, without mythic insinuation or resonance? Not for Barthes (1972).

> Myth is always a language-robbery . . . Is there no meaning which can resist this capture with which form threatens it? In fact, nothing can be safe from myth, myth can develop its second-order schema from any meaning and, as we saw, start from the very lack of meaning. (1972, p. 131)

All communication has at least some mythic component, and the more successful it has been in conveying meaning, the more likely it is that myth has been extensively invoked. Cinematic and televisual language is almost always mythic, although the displacement of the myth can be at different levels of remove; that is to say, its mythology can be latent or manifest.

It is important, then, to understand what myths are and how they function in order to understand international media, not so much because media programs retell national myths, but because they function as myth. It is precisely because humans have such a need for meaning that insures that it is frequently entrusted to the simplest and most accessible narrative forms. For Bettelheim (1977), this form is the fairy tale, which he saw as capable of conveying truths great and deep:

> Through the centuries (if not the millennia) during which, in their retelling, fairy tales became ever more refined, they came to convey at the same time overt and covert meanings—came to speak simultaneously to all levels of the human personality, communicating in a manner which reaches the uneducated mind of the child as well as that of the sophisticated adult. Applying the psychoanalytic model of human personality, fairy tales carry important messages to the conscious, the preconscious, and the unconscious mind, on whatever level each is functioning at the time. (pp. 6–7)

What are the conveyers of fairy tales in the modern age if not television and the movies? This is explicitly so with media aimed at children, which often animate the very tales Bettelheim cited (e.g., Snow White, Goldilocks, Cinderella, Sleeping Beauty, Aladdin, Beauty and the Beast, etc.) and with which so many children, at least in the United States, spend so much time. Given that tales such as these form a child's language, his or her sense of narrative coherence, and his or her general outlook on the condition of society and nature, it is not surprising that, as Bettelheim suggested, they continue to have meaning for adults within the same culture: For the adult these stories are reiterative and reinforcing of what has already been learned and is still believed. Because the most basic function of the media is reinforcement (Klapper, 1960), television and film narratives targeted at adults never stray very far from the fairy tales aimed at children. The farther they stray, the less familiar, less accessible, and less coherent these narratives become. In a sense, myth functions like genre, as Frye (1957) demonstrated; more accurately, genres are rearticulations of basic mythic tropes. The 1998 film *Ever After . . .*, a postmodern retelling of the Cinderella story rated PG-13 in the United States and therefore aimed at teenagers and young adults rather than small children, is just one example.

One of the reasons that myth is so powerful is that it is inclusive; whether it be in the form of allegory, analogy, or fable, the reader senses from myth that it is speaking directly to him or her, that it has something relevant and useful to convey. Barthes (1972) characterized this function of myth from a personal perspective, stating that "it is *I* whom it has come to seek. It is turned towards me, I am subjected to its intentional force, it summons me to receive its expansive ambiguity" (p. 124). This is because myths "tell the truth" (Eliade 1954, p. 46), at least in the sense that truth is understood within a particular context. How could it be otherwise, because it is they who have been seen as the developmental catalyst and benchmark of truth through the ages? As Lincoln (1989) showed, however, this is an elastic truth, as adaptable to progressive or revolutionary agendas as to reactionary ones.

If the meaning found in media programming is comparable to the meaning found in myth, there ought to be a morphology to the media narrative that is analogous to the morphology Propp (1968) delineated for the folk-tale. Propp taxonomized the internal structure of fairy stories—the components, relationships, and motifs out of which they were constructed. Although tales have superficially different settings and characters, for Propp:

> the names of the dramatis personae change (as well as the attributes of each), but neither their actions nor function change. From this we can draw the inference that a tale often attributes identical action to various personages. This makes possible the study of the tale according to the functions of the dramatis personae. (p. 20)

This also made possible Propp's lengthy and detailed articulation of the structure of the archetypal tale, one in which the functions of characters are stable and constant and in which the sequence of functions is limited.

If, as Lincoln (1989) asserted, contemporary culture transmits meaning via the authority, truth, and credibility claims of modern mythologies, then the vehicle for their transmission—the mass media—must possess meanings comparable to that of Bettelheim's (1977) and a morphology comparable to that of Propp's. Media certainly provide the sort of ritualized experience Eliade (1954) saw as essential to the creation of a personal projection into mythic time. This does not mean that myths or media rituals are universal; quite the contrary, it means that myths and rituals are particularized, but grow out of a human need for myth that is essentially the same everywhere. Universal human needs, then, may constitute an underlying structure to the iconic narrative, analogous to the underlying structure that Propp (1968) documented, which could therefore be examined and catalogued. A media morphology would not only be a descriptor of cultural norms and beliefs, but the architecture of narrative exportability—the structure of ubiquity. Such a structure would allow narrative particulars—names and characteristics of the dramatis personae, settings, moral lessons, all traditional and significant to the culture in question—to be projected onto the transparent narrative architecture. The indigenous narrative is merged with the supposedly alien, transparent narrative and J.R. is Gbagwulu because media consumers continue to need the social and psychological satisfactions of mythic storytelling.

[. . .]

Clearly, then, it is not possible to discuss some universality of myth that is encoded in American media and then decoded elsewhere. The world does not share a single myth system, mythologist Joseph Campbell's musings to that effect notwithstanding. Therefore, attempts to explain American media success in terms of mythic displacement are doomed to failure. Something else is going on: The American media do not so much encode myth as become (or function as) myths themselves. They embody something prior to myth that enables them to satisfy the need for myth. Although authorial intention does not define the nature of a literary act, it is clear that some of the leading Hollywood media producers believe they distill, displace, and display mythic archetypes. Steven Spielberg and George Lucas are perhaps the best examples. Their use of mythic displacement ranges narrowly from the overtly manifest to the slightly less manifest, particularly in their work together, which explicitly mine Western mythology (e.g., the Ark of the Covenant in *Raiders of the Lost Ark*, 1981; the Last Supper and Holy Grail legends in *Indiana Jones and the Last Crusade*, 1989). [. . .]

Such deliberate intention is not the only wellspring of mythic displacement, of course. Myth permeates culture almost by definition, so much so that it is inescapable. Lucas and Spielberg do not need to announce the mythic substructure to their work; what choice did they have? Their great accomplishment, and the accomplishment of others like them, resides not in their use of myth per se; myths are culture-specific and are consequently not particularly transferable to other cultures. On the contrary, their global intercultural success can best be attributed to their ability to reduce myth to its prior elements, elements that like those on the periodic table are recombinant and universal. Their success does not lie in regenerating a particular myth, but in transgenerating a new, elemental one. This can best be called a *mythotype* because it transcends any particular myth. Ang (1985) was only half correct when she said that "Dallas" developed "into a modern myth" (p. 2); what also happened was that a modern mythotype developed into "Dallas."

The discussions of media enculturation in Asia, which found the introduction of television to have no effect (Kang and Wu, 1995; Kapoor and Kang, 1995) indicate that existing theory does not describe the relation between American media and their international audiences. Yet, the data seem to confirm perfectly the theory of media transparency: There is an effect to the American media, but it is not to project American values; quite to the contrary, American media are now cleverly designed so as to reinforce existing values. This results in interstitial readings and polyglot cultures, but not monoculture. The media are not so much catalysts as catalyzed. Actual media producers have abandoned the want—get ratio of traditional development theory (Lerner, 1977; Lerner and Schramm, 1969; Pye, 1986; Schramm, 1964). They no longer need to create a market for American products, because they can design products that act as though they are indigenous. Polysemy is built in. All that is ultimately necessary is selling the product and that is better accomplished without having the burden of transforming the culture first. "The Other" has become just another commodity to sell.

This is not to say that the presence of American television has no effect. It does have a very powerful effect, but not in the way often presumed. [. . .] It may initially seem peculiar that the media of one culture can actually reinforce the values and beliefs of another, but not if one considers the possibility that those alien media may contain a narratology and apparatus designed for exactly that purpose.

There is but one Larry Hagman, and only one multichaptered "Dallas" text, but apparently there are many J.R. Ewings. Indeed, "Dallas" represents American cultural hegemony, the export of a particular economic and political perspective, the channeling of money from throughout the world into Hollywood, and the potential seed of cultural change. Yet, these oversimplify: If crude monocultural colonizing tactics were the sum total of what "Dallas" is, it would not be so successful; in essence, there has to be more to "Dallas" than these intentional functions. It must have a corollary potential that allows it to become so widespread, so successful. Without such stealth, it could not bring about a monoculture, nor promote a particular worldview—its audience would not allow it. "Dallas" must have significance in all its contexts. Without the appearance and accessibility of indigenous meaning, it would be of no interest. It would be unintelligible. To convey meaning, it has to be understandable and coherent on local terms, although in hundreds of particular local ways that by their sheer number suggest its creators cannot control or intend them. It must be crossculturally polysemic, enabling hundreds or thousands of eisegeses.

Somehow, Lorimar Productions, the producers of "Dallas," did not need to do extensive research on traditional Gbagyi mythology for J.R. to be Gbagwulu. Somehow, J.R. is not only Gbagwulu, but also Hermes, Brer Rabbit, Winnebago Hare, Prometheus, Coyote, Picaro, Reynard, Circe Loki, Iago, Karagös, Felix Krull, Dakota Spider, and Jacob. Somehow, "Dallas," together with many other Hollywood media creations, is transparent. That transparency forms the tectonic plates of a Hollywood planet.

References

Ang, I. (1985). *Watching Dallas*. London, England: Methuen.

Bacon-Smith, C. (1992). *Enterprising women: Television fandom and the creation of popular myth*. Philadelphia: University of Pennsylvania Press.

Barthes, R. (1972). *Mythologies*. (A. Lavers, Trans.) New York: Hill and Wang.

—— (1977). From work to text. In R. Barthes (ed.), *Image, music, text* (pp. 155–64). New York: Hill and Wang.

Baudrillard, J. (1988), *America* (C. Turner, trans.), New York. Verso.

—— (1993). *The transparency of evil: Essays on extreme phenomena* (J. Benedict, trans.). New York: Verso.

Bettelheim, B. (1977). *The uses of enchantment: The meaning and importance of fairy tales*. New York: Vintage Books.

Bhabha, H. (1994). *The location of culture*. New York: Routledge and Kegan Paul.

Bloom, H. (1975). *A map of misreading*. New York: Oxford University Press.

Blumenberg, H. (1985). *Work on myth*. (R. Wallace, Trans.). Cambridge, MA: MIT Press.

Bohlen, C. (1998, April 26). Why *Titanic* conquered the world: Moscow. *The New York Times*, p. AR 28.

Bourdieu, P. (1993). *The field of cultural production* (R. Johnson, ed.). New York: Columbia University Press.

Burton-Carvajal, J. (1994). "Surprise package": Looking southward with Disney. In E. Smoodin (ed.), *Disney discourse: Producing the Magic Kingdom (pp. 131–47)*. New York: Routledge and Kegan Paul.

Caughie, J. (1981). *Theories of authorship*. New York: Routledge and Kegan Paul.

Cohen, R. (1993, December 8). U.S.-French cultural trade rift now snags a world agreement: Paris talks of film onslaught from Hollywood. *The New York Times*, pp. A1, D2.

Cohen-Solal, A. (1995). Coal miners and dinosaurs. *Media Studies Journal*, 9(4), 125–36.

Coste, D. (1989). *Narrative as communication*. Minneapolis: University of Minnesota Press.

deCerteau, M. (1984). *The practice of everyday life* (S. Rendell, trans.). Berkeley: University of California Press.

Dennis, E., and Snyder, R. (1995). Global views on U.S. media. *Media Studies Journal*, 9(4). xi–xv.

de Sola Pool, I. (1977). Technology and policy in the information age. In D. Lerner and L. Nelson (eds), *Communication research: A half-century appraisal* (pp. 261–79). Honolulu: University Press of Hawaii.

Eckholm, E. (1998, April 26). Why *Titanic* conquered the world: Beijing. *The New York Times*, p. AR 28.

Eliade, M. (1954). *The myth of the eternal return or, cosmos and history*. Princeton, NJ: Princeton University Press.

Ellis, J. (1992). *Visible fictions: Cinema, television, video* (2nd edn). New York: Routledge and Kegan Paul.

Entertainment has become the United States' second-largest export. (1997). *Screen Actor*, 38(6), 4.

The entertainment industry. (1989, December 23). *The Economist*, pp. 3–4.

Faulkner, W. (1977). *The days when the animals talked: Black American folktales and how they came to be*. Chicago: Follett.

Fish, S. (1980). *Is there a text in this class? The authority of interpretive communities*. Cambridge, MA: Harvard University Press.

Fiske, J. (1986). Television: Polysemy and popularity. *Critical Studies in Mass Communication*, 3(4), 391–408.

—— (1987). *Television culture*. New York: Routledge and Kegan Paul.

—— (1996). *Media matters: Everyday culture and political change*. Minneapolis: University of Minnesota Press.

Frye, N. (1957). *Anatomy of criticism: Four essays*. Princeton, NJ: Princeton University Press.

Gillespie, M. (1995a). Sacred serials, devotional viewing, and domestic worship: A case-study in the interpretation of two TV versions of *The Mahabharata* in a Hindu family in West London. In R. Allen (ed.), *Speaking of soap operas . . .* (pp. 354–80). New York: Routledge and Kegan Paul.

Gillespie, M. (1995b). *Television, ethnicity, and cultural change*. New York: Routledge and Kegan Paul.

Gripsrud, J. (1995). *The Dynasty years: Hollywood television and critical media studies*. New York. Routledge and Kegan Paul.

György, P. (1995). Seeing through the media. *Media Studies Journal*, 9(4), 109–17.

Hall, S. (1980). Encoding/decoding. In S. Hall, D. Hobson, A. Lowe, and P. Willis (eds), *Culture, media, language* (pp. 128–138). London, England: Hutchinson.

Harms, J., and Dickens, D. (1996). Postmodern media studies: Analysis or symptom? *Critical Studies in Mass Communication*, 13(3), 210–27.

Iser, W. (1980). *The act of reading: A theory of aesthetic response*. Baltimore: Johns Hopkins University Press.

Jameson, F. (1986, Fall). The Third World novel as national allegory. *Social Text*, 15, 65–8.

Jauss, H. (1982). *Toward an aesthetic of reception* (T. Bahti, trans.). Minneapolis: University of Minnesota Press.

Jehl, D. (1998, April 26). Why *Titanic* conquered the world: Cairo. *The New York Times*, p. AR 29.

Jenkins, H. (1992). *Textual poachers: Television fan and participatory culture*. New York: Routledge and Kegan Paul.

—— (1994). Do you enjoy making the rest of us feel stupid? Alt.tv.twinpeaks, the trickster author, and viewer mastery. In D. Lavery (ed.), *Full of secrets: Critical approaches to Twin Peaks* (pp. 51–69). Detroit, MI: Wayne State University Press.

Johnson, R. (1993) Editor's introduction: Pierre Bourdieu on art, literature, and culture. In P. Bourdieu (ed.), *The field of cultural production* (pp. 1–25). New York: Columbia University Press.

Kang, J. and Wu, Y. (1995, May). *Culture diffusion. The role of U.S. television programs in Taiwan*. Paper presented at the International Communication Association National Conference, Albuquerque, NM.

Kapoor, S. and Kang, J. (1995, May). *Use of American media and adoption of Western cultural values in India*. Paper presented at the International Communication Association National Conference, Albuquerque, NM.

King, S. (1978). *The shining*. New York: Dutton.

Kinzer, S. (1998, April 26). Why *Titanic* conquered the world: Istanbul. *The New York Times*, p. AR 29.

Klapper, J. (1960). *The effects of mass communication*. Glencoe, IL, The Free Press.

Lakoff, G. (1987). *Women, fire, and dangerous things: What categories reveal about the human mind*. Chicago: University of Chicago Press.

Lerner, D. (1977). Communication and development. In D. Lerner and L. Nelson (eds), *Communication research: A half-century appraisal* (pp. 148–66). Honolulu: University Press of Hawaii.

—— & Schramm, W. (1969). *Communication and change in the developing countries*. Honolulu: East West Center Press.

Leuthold, S. (1998). *Indigenous aesthetics: Native art, media, and identity*. Austin: University of Austin Press.

Liebes, T. (1988). Cultural differences in the retelling of television fiction. *Critical Studies in Mass Communication*, 5(4), 277–92.

—— and Katz, E. (1993). *The export of meaning: Cross cultural readings of Dallas*. Cambridge, MA: Polity Press.

Lincoln, B. (1989). *Discourse and the construction of society: Comparative studies of myth, ritual, and classification*. New York: Oxford University Press.

Mattelart, A., Delcourt, D., and Mattelart, M. (1984). *International image markets: In search of an alternative perspective*. (D. Buxton, Trans.), London, England: Comedia.

McChesney, R. (1997). *Corporate media and the threat to democracy*. New York: Seven Stories Press.

—— (1998). The political economy of global media. *Media Development*, 65(4), 3–8.

Mickey Mao (1996, August 3). *The Economist*, p. 32.

Miller, D. (1995). The consumption of soap opera: *The Young and the Restless* and mass consumption in Trinidad. In R. Allen (ed.), *Speaking of soap operas . . .* (pp. 213–33). New York: Routledge and Kegan Paul.

Moerk, C., and Williams, M. (1993, December 20). Moguls swat GATT-flies: Recession and Eurocrats can't nix global ties. *Variety*, p. A1.

Morgan, M. (1990). International cultivation analysis. In N. Signorelli, and M. Morgan (eds), *Cultivation analysis: New directions in media effects research* (pp. 225–47). Newbury Park, CA: Sage.

Naficy, H. (1996). Theorizing "Third-World" film spectatorship. *Wide Angle*, 18(4), 3–26.

Olson, S. (1993). The United States and Canada as a core market: Culture, manufacturing, and industrial strategy. In A. Kozminski and D. Cushman (eds), *Organizational communication and management* (pp. 9–21). Albany: State University of New York Press.

Pells, R. (1997). *Not like us: How Europeans have loved, hated, and transformed American culture since World War II*. New York: Basic Books.

Porter, M. (1990). *The competitive advantage of nations*. New York: The Free Press.

—— (1998). *Competitive strategy: techniques for analysing industries and competitors*. New York: The Free Press.

Propp, V. (1968). *Morphology of the folktale* (2nd edn, rev., L. Wagner, ed., L. Scott, trans.). Austin: University of Texas Press.

Pye, D. (1986). The Western (genre and movies). In B. Grant (ed.), *Film genre reader* (pp. 143–58). Austin: University of Texas Press.

Riding, A. (1998, April 26). Why *Titanic* conquered the world. *The New York Times*, pp. AR 1, 28–9.

Schiller, H. (1969). *Mass communication and American empire*. Boston, MA: Beacon Press.

Schiller, H. (1989). *Culture, Inc., The corporate takeover of public expression*. New York: Oxford University Press.

—— (1995). The context of our work. In K. Nordenstreng and H. Schiller (eds), *Beyond national sovereignty: International communication in the 1990s* (pp. 464–470). Norwood, NJ: Ablex.

Schramm, W. (1964). *Mass media and national development*. Stanford, CA: Stanford University Press.

Shekwo, J. (1984). "Understanding Gbagyi folktales: Premises for targeting salient electronic mass media programs". Unpublished doctoral dissertation, Northwestern University, Evanston, IL.

Shohat, E., and Stam, R. (1994). *Unthinking Eurocentrism: Multiculturalism and the media*. New York: Routledge and Kegan Paul.

Sims, C. (1998), April 26). Why *Titanic* conquered the world: Buenos Aires. *The New York Times*, p. AR 29.

Smith, A. (1995). The natives are restless. *Media Studies Journal*, 9(4), 1–6.

Smoodin, E. (1994). Introduction: How to read Walt Disney. In E. Smoodin (ed.), *Disney discourse. Producing the Magic Kingdom* (pp. 1–20). New York: Routledge and Kegan Paul.

Strom, S. (1998, April 26). Why *Titanic* conquered the world: Tokyo. *The New York Times*, p. AR 28.

Tobin, J. (ed.). (1992). *Remade in Japan: Everyday life and consumer taste in a changing society*. New Haven, CT: Yale University Press.

Tompkins, J. (ed.). (1980). *Reader-response criticism: From formalism to post-structuralism*. Baltimore: Johns Hopkins University Press.

Tunstall, J. (1977). *The media are American: Anglo-American media in the world*. New York: Columbia University Press.

—— (1994). *The media are American: Anglo-American media in the world*. (2nd edn). London, England: Constable.

—— (1995). Are the media still American? *Media studies Journal*, 9(4), 7–16.

Virilio, P. (1991). *The aesthetics of disappearance*. (P. Beitchman, trans.). New York: Semiotext(e).

Waisbord, S. (1998). When the cart of media is before the horse of identity: A critique of technology centered views of globalization. *Communication Research*, 25(4), 377–398.

Wheeler, D. (1998). Global culture or culture clash: New information technologies in the Islamic world—a view from Kuwait. *Communication Research*, 25(4), 359–76.

Williamson, M., and Dawtrey, A. (1993, December 27). Gatt spat wake-up on yank market muscle. *Variety*, 45.

Yoshimoto, M. (1994). Images of empire: Tokyo Disneyland and Japanese cultural imperialism. In Smoodin, E. (ed.), *Disney discourse: Producing the Magic Kingdom* (pp. 181–99). New York: Routledge and Kegan Paul.

Chapter 7

JOHN SINCLAIR

GEOLINGUISTIC REGION AS GLOBAL SPACE
The case of Latin America

IN ORDER TO UNDERSTAND how the globalization of television production and distribution has developed and assumed the ever more intensive and complex forms it has today, it is necessary, though not sufficient, to take language and culture into account as primary "market forces" which enable the major producers and distributors of television programs and services to gain access to markets outside their nations of origin. In this context, it becomes helpful to discard the metaphor of the "worlds" which share a common language in favor of the concept of "geolinguistic region." Such regions have been the initial basis for the globalization of the media, notably in television programs and services. It should be emphasized that a geolinguistic region is defined not necessarily by its geographical contours, but more in a virtual sense, by commonalities of language and culture. Most characteristically, these have have been established by historical relationships of colonization, as is the case with English, Spanish, and Portuguese. However, in the age of international satellites, not only do former colonies counterinvade their erstwhile masters with television entertainment, but geolinguistic regions also come to include perhaps quite small, remote and dispersed pockets of users of particular languages, most often where there have been great diasporic population flows out of their original countries, such as Indians now living in the Gulf States, Britain, and North America, or the unique case of the Spanish-speaking minorities of diverse origin who inhabit the US.

The paradigm case of a geolinguistic region is Spanish, which is the "mother tongue" of some twenty countries in Latin America. The Portuguese situation is different, in that all the speakers of Portuguese in Latin America are in the one country, Brazil. Just as the United States contains about four times as many native speakers of English as does the UK (Crystal, 1997: 30 and 60), Mexico's population of 96 million is more than twice that of Spain, with its 39.7 million, and Brazil has sixteen times as many people as Portugal. Yet as well as Spain, there is one other major Spanish-speaking nation outside of Latin America but in that geolinguistic region to be taken into account, even if it is one in which Spanish is not the dominant language: if we take the current estimate of 26 million people of Hispanic origin living in the US, which is nearly ten per cent of its total population of 265.8 million, the US would be the fifth-largest Spanish-speaking country in the world (*El Estado del Mundo*, 1996: 614–19).

In the geolinguistic regions of Spanish and Portuguese, certain media corporations have arisen which have been able to exploit the massive size of the domestic markets for which they produce as the key to the opening up of foreign markets in other nations that speak the same language. These other countries have provided them with a "natural" constituency for their output, and in spite of the fact that all of them also import English-language television programming and other media products such as films, the crucial fact is that the most popular programs, indeed entire television genres such as the Latin American soap opera or *telenovela* in particular, are in the same language and cultural ambit of the countries which so avidly consume them as imports.

Latin America as postcolonial space

Mil cuatrocientos noventa y dos: 1492 was the year which marks the beginning of "a major extended and ruptural world-historical event . . . the whole process of exploration, conquest, colonisation and imperial hegemonisation" (Hall, 1996: 249). The same year in which Christopher Columbus landed on the islands of Cuba and Hispaniola, and claimed them for the Spanish Crown, saw the beginnings of the creation of the "proto-modern" nation-state of Spain (Galeano, 1973: 22; Williamson, 1992: 61–3). Soon after, an agreement to regulate territorial rivalries with their neighboring kingdom of Portugal, the Treaty of Tordesillas in 1494, established a dividing line between the Spanish- and Portuguese-speaking nations of the Americas just as existed in Iberia (Schwaller, 1987: 69; Bakewell, 1991: 57–80).

While it is not the intention here to provide a potted history of the Iberian nations and their American colonies, it is important to establish the main features of their colonial relationships. In this regard, it is significant to note that, although Latin America is the oldest postcolonial region outside the Mediterranean and its nations have had their independence for the longest period of time, relative to Asia and Africa, it also had the longest period under colonization, for independence did not begin to happen until some 300 years after settlement.

However, the banishment of Spain from Latin America ushered in an era in which other European powers and then the US could set up neocolonial relationships with the new nations through trade and investment. This initial trade with Europe laid the basis for the indebtedness and dependency which have continued to characterize the region. René Chateaubriand, French foreign minister at the time, observed, "In the hour of emancipation the Spanish colonies turned into some sort of British colonies" (quoted in Galeano, 1973: 216), referring to the considerable investments which Britain was able to make throughout the region, once the main barrier to its unconcealed ambitions there had been removed. Yet within a few decades, France also was involved: indeed, Fernand Braudel records that the name "Latin America" was in fact first used by France in 1865, expressly to further its own interests at a time when the French emperor Napoleon III was attempting to establish a European monarchy in Mexico (1993: 427). Thus, although "Latin America" since has been adopted universally as a neutral cultural-linguistic descriptor referring to all those nations which share a "Latin" language, either Spanish or Portuguese, in a region stretching from the US border with Mexico in North America to the tip of continental South America, as a concept it has highly politicized and tendentious origins in European colonial rivalries.

As to the present century, the US government has a long history of direct and indirect interventions; support for client states led by repressive dictatorships and juntas; and "covert operations" and "low intensity conflicts." These tactics have been motivated by a desire to protect the massive private investment by US corporations in Latin America, often denounced as "US imperialism," and its determination to maintain the "security" of the region against whatever forces the US government has perceived to be inimical to those interests. Proceeding with both force and diplomacy (as in the Good Neighbor Policy between the World Wars, or the Alliance for Progress in the 1960s), the US has clearly and consistently asserted its political as well as economic hegemony over the entire region in the postcolonial era (McClintock, 1992: 89–90; Williamson, 1992: 322–7).

Language: "the perfect instrument of empire"

The story is told that when, in 1492, Antonio de Nebrija presented Queen Isabel of Spain with his grammar of Castilian, the first of any modern European language, she asked him what such a work was good for. "Language," replied the scholar, "is the perfect instrument of empire" (Williamson, 1992: 62). Castilian is the language that we now recognize as "Spanish", which became a world language in the process of colonization, but the name serves as a reminder that although Spain was the first nation to have a national language (Klee, 1991: 1), even in Spain itself today, there are several other languages still widely spoken in distinct regions, not to mention a surviving range of native languages and imported linguistic influences in the Americas over which Spanish was imposed.

Relative to the other languages of the Iberian peninsula, Castilian was a "language-of-power" (Klee, 1991: 1), not just as the language of administration for a vast empire, but the language upon which a "national print-language" could become standardized, and so create the "imagined community," the cultural dimension of nationhood, in Benedict Anderson's influential formulation. In fact, Anderson sees the nation-states of the Americas as the first independent nations of their kind (1991: 45–6), models for the postcolonial world. He makes the point that all the new American nations established in the independence era, whether Spanish, Portuguese, or English-speaking, were "creole states," that is, the colonial-born shared the same language and cultural heritage as the metropolis from which they had to free themselves. At least for these creole elites, there was no issue of an alien language, as there would be later with the new nations of the twentieth century in Asia and Africa. The outcome is that, compared to the other postcolonial continents, Latin America exhibits a unique linguistic homogeneity, for the most part at the level of a first language, and at the very least at the level of a lingua franca, a common tongue, amongst native peoples. Even the differences between Spanish and Portuguese are not so great as those which exist between the different languages of most neighboring countries in Asia or Africa. However, this homogeneity is tempered by some heterogeneity which should not be ignored.

English speakers are familiar with sometimes considerable national variations in English, such as between British, American, Australian, and Indian English, and furthermore, with regional variations within a nation, such as English as it is spoken in New York compared to Atlanta or Los Angeles. Such variations can be differences in grammar and vocabulary as well as of pronunciation and accent, some of which might be particularly difficult to understand, or carry a negative status. Just so are there the same kinds of variations in the Spanish-speaking world: the characteristic lisp of Iberian Spanish is not used in the Americas, for example. Similarly, national groups such as Argentinians and Mexicans can be sensitive about each other's accents, in the same way as an American accent might still grate when heard on British or Australian television. Yet, although not all English speakers are exposed to a wide range of variations, by and large English speakers the world over can understand each other. This is one of the factors which makes English the world's principal geolinguistic region, and the basis for its development as a global television market. The point here, however, is that this also has been true for the Spanish- and Portuguese-speaking geolinguistic regions, although the traditional predominance of Latin American companies is now challenged in the age of international satellite transmission and globalization by US-based services transmitted in the region's languages.

In such an era, we have to think of how viewers might relate in different ways to television programming from various sources at distinct levels. For example, at the local level, viewers get the local news and sport in their city or district and at the national level, networked news and entertainment programming produced in and for the national market. There are two transnational levels: the world-regional level, at which *telenovelas* and other entertainment from the major producers in Latin America circulate; and the global, which usually means subscriber services like CNN—all in Spanish or Portuguese, of course. So, viewers in Lima, for example, can enjoy watching a local league sporting match and then the national news, affirming their identities as Limans and Peruvians respectively. However, watching an Argentinian or Mexican *telenovela* reminds them of the similarities they share with neighboring countries in their region (and perhaps also the differences), while flipping over to CBS Telenoticias or a Hollywood film dubbed into Spanish might make them feel more like privileged citizens of the globe.

This is not the place to speculate on whether any of these levels is becoming dominant over the others, as theorists of cultural imperialism and globalization have tended to fear. Rather, the point is that even though viewers in other regions of the world have access to all these levels, including the world-regional, only in Latin America are audiences in a whole host of nations able to be addressed by virtue of their more or less common linguistic and cultural heritage as a kind of "imagined community" on a world-regional scale, a feature of the region which the larger television producers have been well-placed to exploit. Furthermore, we are talking here not just of the geographic region of Central and South America and the Spanish-speaking Caribbean, but of the whole geolinguistic entities created by Iberian colonization: that is, the nations of Spain and Portugal themselves have to be included as part of the region in which their respective languages are spoken.

In the absence of comparative audience studies, it is not possible to say how far viewers, and which kinds of viewers, might be drawn in by the idea of a common Hispanic (Spanish) or Lusitanian (Portuguese) identity, or alternatively, how far the submerged differences between and within the Latin nations might provided counterweight of resistance against being addressed as a member of such as international imagined community (Waisbord, 1996: 24–5). What is clear is that there is a demand for local, national and regional programming, that Latin America has developed its own television programming and genres which are popular at all these levels, and that a small number of producers have been able to seize a strategic advantage out of emphasizing similarity at the expense of difference, and so build themselves hegemonic positions over the commercialization of cultural similarities within their respective geolinguistic regions.

Now that many countries have had almost fifty years of television, it appears that passing through an initial stage of dependence to a maturity of the national market is, if not universal, then certainly a common pattern, of which the Latin American experience is paradigmatic. Crucial in the transition is the growth not just of the audience size, but of domestic program production, the emergent consensus amongst observers being that audiences come to prefer television programming from their own country, and in their own vernacular, or if that is not available, from other countries which are culturally and linguistically similar. Joseph Straubhaar calls this "cultural proximity:" "audiences will tend to prefer that programming which is closest or most proximate to their own culture: national programming if it can be supported by the local economy, regional programming in genres that small countries cannot afford" (1992: 14).

The development of Latin American national markets for television programming bear out this hypothesis, including the pre-eminence of Mexico and Brazil as "net exporters" within the region, to follow Rafael Roncagliolo's (1995) classification. Venezuela and Argentina are "new exporters", with Colombia, Chile, and Peru seeking to join them, but coming from far behind, while the rest of the nations in the region, most of which are the smaller nations of Central America and the Caribbean, are "net importers" (1995, p. 337). However, the last decade has seen rapid growth in the number and variety of channels available, due to the expansion of cable and satellite modes of distribution, which has brought in new service and content providers, including US corporations. Indeed, the age of Westinghouse's CBS Telenoticias and Time-Warner's HBO Olé, and other such special Latin services provided by the major US cable channels, is already moving into a further stage defined by the advent of digital direct-to-home (DTH) satellite delivery. This new "postbroadcast" technology has encouraged the major Latin American producers and distributors to enter strategic alliances with US satellite and cable services. These alliances, with their plans extending to Europe as well as Latin America, mark the beginning of a phase which brings Latin American television into the mainstream of globalization.

The consumption of television is related in the globalization literature to questions of cultural identity. In counterpoint to the evident trend towards cultural homogenization, a trend towards heterogenization is also recognized: "Culture is a multi-layered phenomenon; the product of local, tribal, regional or national dimensions, which is anything but a single national culture" (Richards and French, 1996: 30). Rather too often, however, the "local" becomes a catch-all category set up in contrast to the global, and tends to become equated with the "national" (Sreberny-Mohammadi, 1991). It was argued earlier that we can usefully think of different kinds of television addressing audiences at local, national, world-regional, and global levels. In the debate about globalization, and cultural imperialism before it, there tends to be a static, zero-sum conception of culture, or at least, the assumption that global or other foreign cultural influence carried by the media somehow necessarily drives out the local, national, and regional identities, rather than just adding another level of identification which co-exists with them in any given individual. As Morley and Robins have observed,

> every culture has, in fact, ingested Foreign elements from exogenous sources, with the various elements gradually becoming "naturalised" within it . . . cultural hybridity is, increasingly, the normal state of affairs in the world, and in this context, any attempt to defend the integrity of indigenous or authentic cultures easily slips into the conservative defence of a nostalgic vision of the past.
>
> (Morley and Robins, 1995: 130)

It is in this context that the Latin American theorization of *mestizaje* or hybridity has much to contribute, a perspective in which cultural identity "is not simply an object that is acted upon by external forces, but rather has been rethought as a complex field of action" (Schlesinger and Morris, 1997: 8–9). Although rejecting the concept of postcolonialism as not applicable to Latin America, Nestor García Canclini is also explicit in his rejection of the dichotomies of dominator and dominated, center and periphery, and sender and receiver. This leads to a postmodernist view of identity as deterritorialized and decentered (1997: 23–4). Jesús Martín-Barbero also draws attention to the deterritorialization of identities, in particular, as attributable to international television. He argues that Latin American television production and distribution on a regional basis is deterritorializing to the extent that the local is lost, and that it subsumes the cultural differences between Latin American nations, at the same time as it shapes a commercialized Latin American imaginary (Schlesinger and Morris, 1997: 10–11).

Silvio Waisbord is more agnostic. While accepting Ien Ang's view that subjective identities are "dynamic, conflictive, unstable, and impure" (quoted in Waisbord, 1996: 27), he also argues that "Perhaps the death notices written for national identities were premature" (1998: 389). Apart from this reminder that nation-states are still legitimate and effective units of political, economic, and sociocultural organization in a globalizing world, Waisbord poses the question of identities as an empirical one, a matter of audience research to ascertain "how citizens actively build a sense of national identity beyond the interpellation of authorities and the shared consumption of mass culture." Even if we accept that Latin America is one of the world's eight great "civilizations" (Huntington, 1997), just because Latin American nations share a similar linguistic and cultural heritage does not ensure that pan-Latin American television programming is going to be uniformly accepted and interpreted—a program might have the right language and commercial properties, but the wrong cultural resonance (1997: 24–25). Evidence from regional programming executives suggests that this is indeed the case: programming "must be flexible enough to accommodate quite distinct national market contexts" (Wilkinson, 1995: 207). It follows that the sensitivity of such differences would be heightened in program exchanges between Latin American and Iberian nations.

[. . .]

Convergence and the challenge to geolinguistic monopolies

Like "globalization," one of the great buzz-words of the 1990s is "convergence." The communications satellite, in both symbolic and practical terms, is one of the most significant instances of this epoch-making fusion of broadcasting, telecommunications, and data transmission. Much of the discourse about convergence presents it as a technological phenomenon, but that needs to be kept in perspective: it is not the technologies as such, but the commercial infrastructure sustaining them which is so consequential (McAnany, 1984: 188–9).

That is, as well as at the technological level, convergence is also occurring within the structure of the communication and information industries themselves, as telecommunication companies take up strategic holdings in more entertainment based cultural industries such as subscription television, and enter into joint ventures with national and regional companies to do so. Vertically-integrated structures for content production and distribution formerly were amongst the more distinctive features of the Latin American model of corporate organization, of which Televisa and Globo are the paradigm cases, but now this mode of integration is becoming globalized. As is apparent in the case of both the Murdoch and the Hughes' Galaxy DTH ventures in Latin America, these integrated structures can cross the former divide between hardware or "carriage" (in that case, satellite design, manufacture, and management), and software or "content" (television program production and distribution). This kind of convergence has also transformed the international television business from an import—export trade in programs as products, to a postbroadcast industry which provides not so much particular products but continuous transmission of services, whether delivered via cable or delivered direct to subscribers.

Such immense technological and structural transformation has consequences for how we understand communications theoretically, and this includes the implications for language and culture. Following the Spanish geographer Manuel Castells, Morley and Robins argue that what Harold Innis called the "space-binding" properties of communications media now are redefining space in terms of flows, rather than of places as such, although with key economic and cultural "nerve centers" in the network of flows (1995: 26–9). We can think of geolinguistic regions as prime examples of such virtual restructured spaces, in which new centers have emerged. These include not just Mexico City and Rio de Janeiro, the home bases of Televisa and Globo, but also Miami. More than a strategically-located center for television production and distribution to serve both Americas, Miami has assumed a mythical place in the Latin American "collective imagination" (Monsiváis, 1994: 124), a virtual "capital of Latin America" (Whitefield, 1997).

But while respatialization, understood in this way as a dimension of globalization facilitated by convergence, seems to be overflowing geographical barriers to create global markets, the barriers of language and culture seem more resistant. They have substance as "market forces," or as Collins observes:

Although new communication technologies have reduced the costs of transmitting and distributing information over distance (space binding), distinct information markets remain; here the most important differentiating factors are those of language and culture.

(Collins, 1994: 386)

Thus, while paradigmatic of global respatialization, the transcontinental niches which the Spanish- and Portuguese-speaking television markets have carved out for themselves are also emblematic of the reassertion of linguistic and cultural difference which is taking place in the face of globalization. Even within those geolinguistic regions, there is further linguistic and cultural differentiation. Just as in Asia, where Sony first elaborated its strategy of "global localization," and Murdoch's Star TV tailored its offerings to the major linguistic groups rather than seek a pan-Asian audience, some of the US-based cable channels in Latin America have found it necessary to adapt and differentiate their services to the local market. This is a significant trend because it shows how the drive for global economies of scale, a force towards homogenization, is attenuated by the heterogenising factors of language and culture, although as Morley and Robins note, "the local" is usually not more specific than national, regional, or even pan-regional differences (1995: 117).

The technical properties of the new digital compression on the current generation of satellites not only allow the satellites to transmit many more channels than ever before, whether from the US, Europe, or elsewhere, but facilitate the provision of multiple audio tracks. This means that one image, say a Hollywood film on HBO Olé, or a Discovery channel travelogue, can be made available to cable operators and DTH subscribers dubbed into Spanish or Portuguese, as well as in the original version. Clearly for the Latin American market, the provision of at least dual audio tracks is elemental, but there are now much more culturally-sensitive bases for differentiation, such as musical taste cultures. Viacom's MTV not only has a separate service for Latin America, and within that, one for Brazil, but has created special programming feeds for Mexico at one end of the Spanish-speaking zone, and Argentina at the other. Based in the mythical space of Miami, so as to be seen to be above national partisanship, the core international material is augmented with distinct Mexican and Argentinian segments for those respective feeds. As well as increasing its total subscribers in the region, this strategy has also attracted local advertisers, in addition to the global ones that one expects to find everywhere on MTV (Goldner, 1997). MTV Latin America represents the kind of challenge which Televisa, Globo, and the other major producers and distributors of the region now face on their home ground in the era of convergence.

Thus, the comparative advantage of language difference which the Latin American companies once enjoyed as a kind of natural monopoly is under threat. It is not only the new satellite technologies of digital compression and conditional-access DTH reception which have brought this about: several of the global channels have gained their experience in the US with the potential audience of over 26 million Spanish speakers there, and the move into Latin America represents immense opportunities for them to exploit. At the very least, it is well worth their while to dub programs which have been produced in English. It could even be said that the prospect of the 300 million or more Spanish speakers of Latin America gives US producers an incentive to develop programming for the Latino market in the first instance, with Latin America, and Spain, as aftermarkets.

The development of the CBS Telenoticias news channel from a US domestic to an international service is a good case in point. A CBS executive observes that Latin America is more attractive than Europe for such ventures because the whole region only requires channels in two languages, as against the several languages needed for Europe (Frances and Fernandez, 1997: 38–40). As Mexico City and Rio surrender their traditional monopoly as centers of dubbing from English to Spanish and Portuguese to Los Angeles and Miami (Wilkinson, 1995: 22), US capital flows into new channels: one US investment group has joined with the Cisneros Group "to create a pan-Ibero-American media network" based in Miami (Sutter, 1997/98: 34).

As well as CBS and MTV, there is Turner's CNN, the Time-Warner/Sony venture HBO Olé, Murdoch's Fox Latin America, Spelling's TeleUno, ESPN, Discovery, and other US-based global channels providing satellite and cable services in Spanish and/or Portuguese to Latin America, so it is not surprising that as of 1996, 90 percent of television services (that is, satellite and cable signals rather than programs) imported into the Iberoamerican region were found to be from the US (Media Research and Consultancy Spain, 1997: 14). The same study found that the export of such services from the region mainly (70 percent) came from Televisa and Multivisión in Mexico, especially by virtue of their involvement with the Murdoch Sky and Hughes Galaxy DTH ventures respectively. Even though 90 percent of the services exported from Iberoamerican countries went to other regional nations of the same language (the rest mainly to the Spanish-speaking networks in the US), evidence of the geolinguistic cohesion of the region's trade, it also shows that the US services have been able to cross the language barrier without much movement back in the other direction. This trend is likely to consolidate if, as the study predicts, the trade in services rather than programs soon becomes the major form of audiovisual exchange (1997: 17–18).

Given that the US-based and other global corporations such as Hughes not only have taken over the technological vanguard in the region once held by PanAmSat, but also faced up to the content issue by extending themselves into the provision of services in the regional languages, if postbroadcast services do come to eclipse programs as the core of the television trade, then much of the comparative advantage once enjoyed by the major Latin American companies would be undermined. This will depend greatly on the level of cost of the subscriber services, which at present are such as to keep DTH out of the reach of mass audiences in most Latin American countries. In the medium term, it is likely that the subscriber services will remain the preserve of the more affluent and already more cosmopolitan elites who can pay to receive the global programming, while the mass audiences for broadcast television will continue to form a loyal market for the national and regional producers and distributors (Sinclair, 1999: 166–70).

It has been argued in this paper that the era of cultural imperialism in the 1960s and 1970s, when television program imports from the US reached their high-tide mark, has proven to be just an initial phase of television development. It was overtaken by a phase in which audiences learned to have more appreciation for programs which came to them out of their own language and culture. Beginning in the late 1970s, this has been the era in which Televisa and Globo have exploited their advantages to become the market leaders in their respective geolinguistic regions, but the indications are that this stage also will pass. As McAnany predicted, the fact that a nation can develop a strong cultural industry "may be no guarantee that the threat of external influence will not surface at a later date" (1984: 196). By the same token, the reassertion of US corporate dominance should not be interpreted teleologically, that is, as the always-already inevitable victory of American capitalism, but analytically, as the logic of a cultural industry in which the US has a unique set of advantages able to overcome those of its competitors, ultimately even in their own national and regional markets.

Acknowledgement

This chapter draws substantially from material published in the author's book, *Latin American Television: A Global View*, Oxford University Press, Oxford and New York, 1999.

References

Anderson, B. (1991). *Imagined Communities: Reflections on the Origin and Spread of Nationalism* (2nd edn). London: Verso.

Bakewell, P. (1991). "Colonial Latin America." In J. Knippers Black (ed.), *Latin America: Its Problems and its Promise*, 57–66. Boulder, CO: Westview Press.

Braudel, F. (1993). *A History of Civilizations*. New York: Penguin Books.

Collins, R. (1994). "Trading in culture: the role of language." *Canadian Journal of Communication*, 19, 377–99.

Crystal, D. (1997). *English as a Global Language*. Cambridge: Cambridge University Press.

El Estado del Mundo: Edición 1997. (1996). Madrid: Akal Ediciones.

Frances, G. and Fernandez, R. (1997). "Satellites south of the border." *Via Satellite*, February, 28–42.

Galeano, E. (1973). *Open Veins of Latin America: Five Centuries of the Pillage of a Continent*. New York: Monthly Review Press.

Garcia Canclini, N. (1997). "Hybrid cultures and communicative strategies." *Media Development*, XLIV(1), 22–9.

Goldner, D. (1997). "MTV rocks to Latin beat." *Variety*, May 19–25, 22.

Hall, S. (1996). "When was 'The post-colonial'?: thinking at the limit." In I. Chamber: and L. Curti (eds), *The Post-Colonial Question: Common Skies, Divided Horizons*, 242–60. London: Routledge.

Huntington, S. (1997). "The clash of civilizations?" In Foreign Affairs Agenda (ed.), *The New Shape of World Politics*, 67–91. New York: Norton.

Klee, C. (1991). "Introduction." In C. Klee and L. Ramos-Garcia (eds), *Sociolinguistics of the Spanish-Speaking World*, 1–8. Tempe, AZ: Bilingual Press.

McAnany, E. (1984). "The logic of the cultural industries in Latin America: the television industry in Brazil." In V. Mosco and J. Wasko (eds), *The Critical Communications Review Volume II: Changing Patterns of Communications Control*, 185–208. Norwood, NJ: Ablex.

McClintock, A. (1992). "The angel of progress: pitfalls of the term 'post-colonialism'." *Social Text*, 10(2/3), 84–98.

Media Research and Consultancy Spain (1997). "*La Industria Audiovisual Iberoamericana: Datos de sus Principales Mercados 1997*." Report prepared for the Federación de Asociaciones de Productores Audiovisuales Españoles and Agencia Española de Cooperación Internacional. Madrid.

Monsiváis, C. (1994). "Globalisation means never having to say you're sorry." *Journal of International Communication*, 1(2), 120–4.

Morley, D. and Robins, K. (1995). *Spaces of Identity: Global Media, Electronic Landscapes and Cultural Boundaries*. London: Routledge.

Richards, M. and French, D. (1996). "From global development to global culture?" In D. French and M. Richards (eds), *Contemporary Television: Eastern Perspectives*, 22–48. New Delhi: Sage.

Roncagliolo, R. (1995). "Trade integration and communication networks in Latin America." *Canadian Journal of Communication*, 20(3), 335–42.

Schlesinger, P. and Morris, N. (1997). "Cultural boundaries: identity and communication in Latin America." *Media Development*, XLIV(1), 5–17.

Schwaller, J. (1987). "Discovery and conquest." In J. Hopkins (ed.), *Latin America: Perspectives on a Region*, 57–70. New York: Holmes and Meier.

Sinclair, J. (1999). *Latin American Television: A Global View*. Oxford: Oxford University Press.

Sreberny-Mohammadi, A. (1991). "The global and the local in international communications." In J. Curran and M. Gurevitch (eds), *Mass Media and Society*, 118–38. New York and London: Edward Arnold.

Straubhaar, J. (1992). "Assymetrical interdependence and cultural proximity: a critical review of the international flow of television programs." Paper presented to the conference of the Asociación Latino-americana de Investigadores de la Communicación, São Paulo, August.

Sutter, M. (1997, 1998). "Hicks sets $500 mil Latin fund." *Variety*, December 22–January 4, 34.

Waisbord, S. (1996). "Latin American television and national identities." Paper presented to the conference of the International Communication Association, Chicago, May.

Waisbord, S. (1998). "The ties that still bind: media and national cultures in Latin America." *Canadian Journal of Communication*, 23(2), 381–401.

Williamson, E. (1992). *The Penguin History of Latin America*. London: Penguin Books.

Wilkinson, K. (1995). "When culture, language and communication converge: the Latin American cultural-linguistic television market." PhD dissertation. University of Texas at Austin.

Chapter 8

COLIN SPARKS

THE GLOBAL, THE LOCAL AND THE PUBLIC SPHERE

THE TITLE OF THIS CHAPTER could be mistaken for an amalgam of all that is fashionable in the study of the mass media. On the one hand, the pairing of 'the global and the local' occurs everywhere in books and articles on communication. On the other, 'the public sphere' is the subject of endless debates about democracy and the mass media. Almost the only thing missing in the title is the term 'civil society'.

There are two things to be said about this. The first is that, despite the fact that these terms are fashionable, they nevertheless point to some very important issues about the contemporary role of the mass media. The questions which this title address us to are therefore worth spending time upon and taking seriously. The second is that, perhaps as a condition of their being fashionable, they lack agreed and precise definitions. Very often, it seems as though they are terms that mean just what the particular author wishes them to mean. Consequently, if we are going to have a valuable discussion of these issues, we need start off by being clear as to what is here meant by the terms, and why they are important. It is very unlikely that the usage I adopt here will be the one that magically commands universal support, but at least if I spell it out, readers will know what exactly it is I am talking about.

Consequently, I begin this chapter with a brief account of what I mean by the term 'public sphere,' and why I think that this is a central category for discussions about the mass media. I then look at some of the problems involved in the global/local pairing. Thirdly, I briefly recount the results of some recent work that I have done on the status of the global public sphere. I then look at the local public sphere. In conclusion, I draw out what I believe to be the general implications of my discussion.

[. . .]

The public sphere

Habermas's concept of the public sphere has been one of the most used, and most challenged, ideas in the field of media studies in the last decade. Many contemporary discussions of the relationship between the media and democracy have been conducted in terms of the public sphere. Despite numerous debates, however, the term remains deeply problematic. Part of the problem is that historical investigation has shown that what Habermas called the 'bourgeois public sphere' of eighteenth-century England and France never existed, and what did in fact exist differed systematically from the kind of communicative space that the theory requires, indeed in important respects reality was directly contrary to the claims of theory (Curran, 1991; Schudson,

1992). It has further been argued, I believe convincingly, that Habermas's belief that the development of the modern commercial mass media and of public broadcasters led to a 'refeudalization' of the public sphere in which democratic debate was replaced by displays of corporate power, was wrong in some of its central propositions (le Mahieu, 1988; Scannell, 1989). These media in fact both extended the range of topics open to public debate and opened those debates to wider layers of the population, although it is also true that they acted to limit and constrain that debate, and access to it, in important ways. Finally, I think that few writers would claim that any of the existing media, in any country of the world, actually embody the formal criteria that Habermas specified were characteristic of the public sphere.

It is obviously tempting to ask: 'Why, then, continue to employ this category?' My answer lies in the dual nature of the concept. While its empirical claims do not seem to be sustainable, its normative value remains considerable. The formal requirements for the constitution of a public sphere are, it can be argued, the essential conditions for the conduct of a democratic polity. While we may not expect to find them fully embodied in actual media systems, they remain an aspiration. That does not imply that they are wholly abstract and without practical utility. On the contrary, they provide a guide to media policy. It is the level of policy that provides the mediator between social scientific accounts of what is and philosophical accounts of what is desirable.

It is from this perspective that I wish to highlight three key attributes of Habermas's account of the public sphere. In the formulation which was first translated into English, Habermas gave as defining characteristics of the public sphere that 'access is guaranteed to all citizens' and that they 'confer in an unrestricted fashion' (Habermas, 1974: 14). He went on to say that, if there was a public sphere in contemporary society, this would necessarily be embedded in the mass media. We can use these as norms against which we can measure the performance of actually existing media systems. We can ask: to what extent are they open to all citizens? We can ask: to what extent is debate free and uncensored? We can ask: to what extent are citizens participants in, rather than spectators at, the debate? It seems likely that most media systems do not fully embody those desiderata. Certainly, the one I am most familiar with, that of the UK, falls a long way short on all three axes of measurement. Others, like the USA, do very much better on the axis of freedom and censorship, but perhaps worse on the other two axes. Some European examples, notably Sweden, seem to do much better on all axes; all though are still well short of the ideal. To the extent that we are concerned with policy formation, we can then use the results of such a study to help formulate proposals to improve the functioning of the media in these respects.

There are three other, more general, questions raised by the concept of the public sphere which should be mentioned at this point. The first is to note that the public sphere can be usefully contrasted with the notion of 'public opinion', which is its major competitor for discussing the role of the media in contemporary democracy. The latter sits most comfortably with theories of elite democracy. It is concerned with measuring what the public think, and with understanding how that opinion comes to be formed, not to say manipulated. It produces relatively little space for discussions of the public as the initiators of, and participants in, the formation of their own views. This is a radically different focus from that of the public sphere, which is primarily concerned with the public as the active subject of discussions, and focuses discussion on the mechanisms in the mass media by which this is either encouraged or impeded: public opinion is what is formed as a result of discussion in the public sphere. The theory of the public sphere sits more comfortably with radical theories of democracy which value active and participatory citizens.

The second point to note is that it is an historical limit of the debate about the public sphere that its greatest reach has been that of the state system of modernity. This should hardly be surprising, in that the category, and the problems it proposes to address, are exactly those of the modern, capitalist, state. It shares this limitation with theories of democracy, which have, per-force, been concerned with how the citizens of particular states might exercise greater or lesser degrees of control over their own governments. Categories formed on this basis evidently need to be rethought to confront a situation, like that suggested by theories of globalization, in which the decisive locus of public affairs has shifted beyond the state to the world economy, world institu-tions, and a world polity. Accordingly, there are writers who have argued for the necessity of constructing a global public sphere to allow people to exercise some degree of control over these global political and economic forces that are determining more and more aspects of life (Garnham, 1992; Hjarvard, 1993).

The third point to note is that Habermas argued for the existence of two kinds of public spheres. The first is the familiar, political, public sphere concerned with rational discourse dir-ected to reaching agreement about matters of public policy. The second is the literary public sphere, more concerned with matters of taste and general social behaviour, although, of course, having profound political implications. We are here concerned almost entirely with the first, political, public sphere, although at some points I touch upon the latter. This is largely for reasons of space, and it implies a serious limitation to this study, since it has often been argued that the issues of globalization and localization are most clearly articulated in the contemporary approxi-mation to the literary public sphere (Negus, 1996). The conclusions of this study should be read with that limitation in mind, although I believe that a fuller consideration of the question would in fact demonstrate that the same conclusions held for the literary public sphere as for the narrower political public sphere.

[. . .]

The global and the local

The terms global and local are often, although not invariably, conjoined in discussion, but the relative values of these terms differs widely from theorist to theorist, and there are very many theorists of globalization to choose from. Within this diversity, it is possible to identify three general classes of theorizing that assign different values to the local/global pair. We can consider each in turn, both with regard to their viewpoint on the general terms and their more precise implications for the mass media.

The first of these consists of those theories of globalization that see it as a generalization of existing, and usually Western, trends. The most obvious representative of this current is Giddens, who views globalization as the generalization of modernity. There is certainly a 'local' in this account, but it is that characteristic feature of western modernity, the nation state, that is globalized. 'Local,' here, means 'state:'

> The nation state system has long participated in that reflexivity characteristic of modern-ity as a whole. The very existence of sovereignty should be understood as something that is reflexively monitored. . . . One aspect of the dialectical nature of globalization is the 'push and pull' between tendencies towards centralization inherent in the reflexivity of the systems of states on the one hand and the sovereignty of particular states on the other.
> (Giddens, 1991: 69)

If we attempt to operationalize this (very difficult with Giddens, and something a grand social theorist like him never stoops to) in media terms, it seems to imply the global diffusion of 'modern,' and therefore essentially state-based, mass media. It might reasonably be taken as a view which corresponds closely to that phase of thinking about resistance to media imperialism that spawned New World Information and Communication Order (NWICO) as part of a defence of national sovereignty.

The second group of theories are those that propose a uniform and homogenous process spreading throughout the world. Ritzer, for example, wrote of the process of bureaucratic rationalization he termed 'McDonaldization' that:

> The spread of American and indigenous fast-food throughout much of the world means that there is less and less diversity from one setting to another. The human craving for new and diverse experiences is being limited, if not progressively destroyed, by the national and international spread of fast-food restaurants. The craving for diversity is being replaced by the desire for uniformity and predictability.
>
> (Ritzer, 1993: 138–9)

In this kind of theory, the process of globalization is one which destroys the local, at whatever level it is manifested, and replaces it by a single, standard, and usually US-inspired, society. Translated into media terms, this would suggest that the development of global media means the progressive erosion of local media and their incorporation into, or replacement by, their larger predators. Neither the state, nor any more genuinely local formation, provides the basis for an alternative to this process of homogenization. One specifically media-based articulation of this position is that offered recently by Herman and McChesney (1997), in their analysis of the ways in which very large media companies, operating on an international scale, tend to ensure the dominance of a US-inspired model of advertising-financed media at the expense of a diversity of different national forms.

The third kind of theory proposes a state system under siege. It is attacked by globalization 'from above,' with abstract forces, notably the world market, acting at a level more general than that of the state, and imposing solutions upon the state and its citizens. But it is also attacked 'from below', with other forces relating much more directly to the immediate experience of the population within a more limited scope. Raymond Williams put the issue clearly in an early formulation:

> It is now very apparent, in the development of modern industrial societies, that the nation state, in its classical European forms, is at once too large and too small for the range of real social purposes. It is too large, even in the old nation-states such as Britain, to develop full social identities in their real diversity. . . . At the same time it is obvious that for many purposes . . . the existing nation-states are too small . . . (because of) the trading, monetary and military problems which now show this to be true, and which have so heavily encroached on the supposed 'sovereignty' of the nation-states.
>
> (Williams, 1983: 197–8)

If we attempt to operationalize this view in terms of the mass media, it would seem to suggest that we would observe a simultaneous process of the erosion of the power and influence of the state-based media on the one hand, and a parallel strengthening of both the local and the global media. We would expect to find media organization, and regulatory structures, migrating 'up' to global forms or 'down' to local forms. We would expect the audiences for state-oriented media to decline relative to those for local and for global media.

For the purposes of this chapter, I propose to bracket the first two of these theoretical positions. [. . .] The third position provides a much more fruitful starting point. [. . .]

To say that it provides a useful starting point, however, is not to say that it provides a complete and coherent account of the issues at stake. It is possible to identify two major problems that need exploration. The first concerns what level is being specified when we use the term 'local.' The 'global' might not be very well theorized, but there is a commo-sense usage that is adequate for most purposes: it refers to some level of social, economic, political and cultural organization that is more extensive than that provided by the states that divide the world. The local, on the other hand, can mean widely different things, and the media forms in question can be quite different. Some writers, indeed, have made a postmodern virtue out of this lack of definition: 'I . . . have refrained from burdening (the local) with a definition that might have constricted analysis' (Drilik, 1996: 42).

We, unfortunately, are obliged to constrict our analysis to the public sphere, and so do need to undertake the burden of at least some definitional work. An obvious starting point is the fact that there is social space for a number of different levels below that of the state, and it is not clear exactly which of them is pertinent to the global/local discussion. There is a common distinction between what is often termed the 'regional', meaning some geographically and, possibly, cultur-ally defined unit of large extent, and the more properly 'local' in the sense of the relatively small community of the town, district or urban neighbourhood. In this chapter, I shall provisionally adopt that distinction, although it has two major shortcomings. In the first place, it ignores possible intermediate levels, for example the city, that are an important focus of social life, both in general and in terms of the mass media. In general, I shall assign things like cities to the regional level, for reasons that I hope will become obvious below. Secondly, it is clear that, within both the categor-ies of region and locality, there are major differences in the kinds of phenomena under discussion. [. . .]

Bringing together both the local and the global, it seems reasonable to say that, to the extent that there is a tendency towards globalization which is manifested in and through localization, the old media based on the state system are being eroded, while the global and local media are in the ascendant. The old, imperfect, state-based public spheres are being eroded and new, albeit possibly even more imperfect, global and local public spheres are emerging, particularly around the new forms of the local. The propositions can be reformulated in terms of more or less testable hypotheses:

- the state-based public spheres are eroding as a consequence of globalization
- a global public sphere is emerging and growing relative to the state-based forms
- local public spheres are growing in strength relative to the state-based forms
- this growth is more marked for the new forms of locality than for the old
- the growth of the new local public sphere is articulated with, if not an embodiment of, the tendency towards a global public sphere.

We can therefore move on from the rather arid plateau of theoretical analysis to the lusher pastures of empirical investigation.

A global public sphere?

Most writers in this vein point to the emergence of satellite broadcasting, and global media corporations, as evidence for the fact that we are living in an age in which the necessary media infrastructure for a global public sphere does already exist. If there is indeed a global public sphere coming into being, then we should be able to find concrete television and radio channels, or newspapers and magazines, that embody that sphere. Since I have already written extensively on this, it would be wrong to burden you with the details that are available elsewhere. I therefore present in this section a summary, in which all the evidence cited is to be found, except where specifically noted, in what I discovered when I first went out to look for the global public sphere (Sparks, 1998).

In brief, my conclusion was that there is at present no global public sphere, nor is there any sign of one emerging in the immediate future. In the first place, the belief that the communication satellite is in itself a global, or even supra-national, medium is mistaken on two grounds. The first concerns the regulation and control of satellites. These occupy slots assigned by inter-governmental agreements, and are subject to the regulatory efforts of particular states. The reception of satellite signals, particularly when it is mediated through a Satellite Mater Antenna Television (SMATV) system, is again subject to state-based regulation. It is possible for states to force signals they don't like off particular satellites. The most notorious example is the People's Republic of China (PRC) deal with Murdoch over the objectionably critical BBC news service he carried on the northern beam of Star TV, but there are others like the British government's struggle against pornographic broadcasters, in which state-based regulation (the provisions of the 1990 Broadcasting Act) proved adequate to prevent the offending material being broadcast.

The second reason why it is a mistake to think of satellites as necessarily global communication media has to do with content. There is a tendency to think that the free-to-air model, either state- or advertising-supported, will be the dominant one for future satellite broadcasting, as it has been in the past. There are very strong grounds for thinking that this is not likely to be the case in the future. Various kinds of subscription and pay-per-view systems are already in operation, and these have no necessary connection with the global. In order to view such a service, it is necessary to have a decoder, and the running of that very terrestrial piece of equipment is controlled by a subscription management system. In order to attract audiences, and thus to maximize their revenue, broadcasters are obliged to seek premium content, particular for these services. But rights holders are also keen to maximize their revenue, and therefore characteristically attempt to subdivide the rights to broadcast their material. One of the traditional ways in which markets are divided up is along 'national' lines, and the design of a subscriber management system makes that model replicable in the case of the satellite. It is therefore in the interests of both the broadcasters and the rights holders to continue with the national organization of audiences in the future, subscription-oriented television economy. From this perspective, the cross-border potential of satellite broadcasting is the temporary and accidental product of the undeveloped state of the technology prevailing in the 1980s.

If we shift our attention from technology to social form, and ask what channels there are that might constitute the basis for a global public sphere, we arrive at the conclusion that there is very little evidence for its existence. The obvious candidate for the role of embodiment of the global public sphere is CNN, and this is regularly cited as having transformed viewing habits. There are strong arguments that would say that this is essentially a US, rather than a global, news channel, but let us leave those aside. If we ask how large the audience for this global channel is, both absolutely and relative to the existing state-based broadcasters, we come to the conclusion that it is so small as to be irrelevant from the point of view of constituting a genuine public sphere. Even in the USA, even in 1991, the year of the Gulf War and CNN's finest hour, the channel got an audience rating of 3.7 percent; in more normal years it hovers around 1 percent (Greenberg and Levy, 1997: 139). Outside the USA, the audiences are even smaller. In the UK, in the first quarter of 1998, the ITC reported a viewing share of 0.1 percent for CNN. Everywhere, the terrestrial broadcasters have experienced an erosion of their audiences at the hands of cable and satellite, but it has not been to any significant extent caused by the rise of a global news service taking the viewers for their national products as part of the growth of a global public sphere.

[. . .]

One further important point concerning these media is that they are overwhelmingly in English. While this is the most widely diffused of languages, it is, of course, very far from the mother tongue of the vast majority of the world's population. The ability to use this language to a very high level, or maybe Spanish as an alternative, is thus an extremely restrictive condition on access to whatever kinds of discussions take place in the global media.

These three factors lead me to the conclusion that there is no such thing as a global public sphere at the moment. There are certainly media that are concerned to address issues on a global scale, but their audiences are too small, too rich, and too English-speaking to be considered inclusive. Nor can I detect anything in the dynamics of these media that is likely to make them more accessible in the near future: to the extent that they are profitable operations, they are profitable precisely because they do address an elite, and have little incentive to extend their reach significantly. At the same time, there is little in either the new television or in international newspapers that suggests any serious erosion of the state-based public sphere. This sphere may well be eroding, but I can see no evidence that this is because substantial numbers of citizens are defecting to global forms that correspond more readily to their experience of interaction with social power. It may indeed be the case that more and more significant events in the lives of ordinary people are determined by events over which the state has little or no control, as the current crisis in Indonesia suggests, and which are at least initiated by global factors, but there is no sign that this is what is leading to a crisis for the state-based public On the contrary, I agree with critics of the general 'globalization of the media' thesis that the state remains a significant actor in this realm (Schiller, 1991; Ferguson, 1992). Indeed, I would go rather further: a study of the British case reveals that in important respects the state has, over the last two decades, been increasingly ready to intervene in the working of the mass media (Sparks, 1995). My conclusion is therefore that talk of the erosion of the state-based public sphere from above by forces of globalization is at least premature and, at the present, quite mistaken.

A local public sphere?

The case with the local public sphere is quite different. It is very easy indeed to find examples of the mass media that are either entirely local in their orientation, or at least have a strong local dimension. What is more, these tend to have a substantial concern with issues of public discussion, and to be relatively open to the views and voices of their audiences. These media have many shortcomings and limitations, and vary widely between themselves as to how seriously and extensively they address public issues, but, to a surprisingly large degree, they do sustain a (limited and imperfect) public sphere. But while there may not be much doubt about the existence of a local public sphere, the issue of how this is related to the more general question of the global and the local is much more complex.

To begin with the question of the articulation between global and local, and the extent to which they are interdependent, we can note that one striking feature about these local media, and the local public spheres that they sustain, is that they tend to be relatively independent of the global media operators, as described by Herman and McChesney (1997), for example. Murdoch, to take the paradigmatic example of a global media operator, and one who is most certainly concerned to intervene in public debate, does not appear much interested in local operations, outside of his original patrimony in Australia. In the UK, his newspaper operations are entirely national in scope, as is his satellite service. In the USA, while it is true that Murdoch has owned 'local' papers (e.g. *The New York Post*), he has never tried to build a chain of US newspapers in the manner of Gannett or Knight-Ridder. In television, it is a distinctive feature of what has happened to Fox since Murdoch acquired it that it has tried to become the fourth national TV network:

Murdoch has not concentrated simply on acquiring lucrative stations in particular localities. He nowhere appears to have a strategy of finding local partners and working with them. His alliances are with companies that operate at the state level. There is little evidence, in most of his main theatres of operation, that Murdoch wants to undermine the state from above and below. (Indeed, there is precious little evidence that, despite his public speeches, he wants to undermine even very despotic states from above. Provided he can do business with them, butchers are quite OK.) The famous slogan, attributed to News Corporation as well as to many other companies, of 'Think Global. Act Local' seems to mean, in practice, 'Think Global. Act National.' If the local is articulated with the global, it is in more complex and subtle ways than through direct relationships between the two kinds of media.

Providing evidence relating to the hypotheses that the local public sphere is growing relative to the state-based sphere, and that it is growing faster with regard to the new forms of locality, requires a more extensive discussion. We can begin by considering the printed newspaper press. In many countries the press began locally, and continues up until today to be predominantly local. The USA is the most obvious case, in which there are more than 1,500 daily newspapers, only two of which, *The Wall Street Journal* and *USA Today*, are properly 'national' newspapers in the sense understood elsewhere. In this respect, the UK experience of a daily press dominated by London-based, large-circulation, national newspapers is an unusual and extreme example of the opposite situation. In most countries in Europe, there is a substantial local newspaper press existing alongside a small number of titles that have a wider remit.

The long existence of the local press suggests that it has little to do with any relatively recent shift in the direction of a global/local nexus that is dislocating the state system. [. . .]

That is not to say that the local press is in a state of rude health and posing an increasing challenge to the state-based media. The other points to bear in mind here are that the local press, defined in the old sense, is only local up to a point, and that it is a declining force in society. There has always been a tendency, for powerful economic reasons, for local newspapers to be grouped into ownership chains, and this process has accelerated in recent years, notably in the USA. The development of these chains, and their increasing informatization, implies a 'nationalization' of policy, of managerial personnel, of business arrangements, and so on. Editorial material is another matter. The non-local material in the local press has long been predominantly dependent on press agency supply, for example through AP [Associated Press] and UPI [United Press International] in the USA and the Press Association in the UK, and this suggests that they have a 'global' dimension that stretches back to the last century. [. . .]

We can therefore conclude from a study of the press that, while there is undoubtedly a form of the local public sphere, this is so long-established as not to be considered an aspect of globalization. The main form which this local newspaper press takes is the 'old and local' one. There are some very important examples of a 'new and local' press, but they are, in overall terms, marginal in number and in circulation. The whole sector, however, is decreasingly local in terms of ownership, and at least some aspects of operation, and it is declining, rather than growing, at a rate faster than is its state-oriented cousin.

The case of broadcasting provides additional insights into these problems. There are certainly numerous examples around the world of radio and television broadcasters whose audience is defined by areas or groupings much less inclusive than those of states, although, by its nature, television in particular, tends to construct the 'local' much more broadly than does the press. With this medium, we are mostly concerned with the regional level that we discussed above. Once again, there is very strong evidence, at least from Europe, that news and current affairs are the strongest aspect of the local and regional broadcasters (see Jankowski *et al.*, 1992). We can therefore say that there is evidence that there is something of a local and regional public sphere in broadcasting, albeit subject to many limitations. What is more, in most of Europe, although not the USA, these local broadcasters are a relatively new development, produced by political and economic action during the last two decades (Hollander, 1992: 9). We seem to have here evidence for a process which might constitute the local dimension of a global/local nexus.

This plethora of local or regional broadcasters, however, conceals a very considerable paradox. As is very well-known, the economics of broadcasting, both in radio and in television, lead in the direction of networking. According to the logic of economics, there should be a very rapid process of consolidation into one or a few chains of broadcasters with the whole territory and population of the state at their disposal. That this has not been the case has primarily been due to regulation. The Federal Communications Commission (FCC) in the USA has always had very strict rules as to the number of stations that any one company can own, and these have survived, albeit in weakened form, in the recent deregulatory Federal Communications Act. Elsewhere, there are similar attempts to prevent the erosion of local interests. In other words, the continued existence and health of the local in broadcasting has been predicated on action by the existing state machines. This action has been under constant threat from the forces of commerce, and where the regulatory regime has been relaxed, for example in the UK, there has been a sharp trend towards the consolidation of ownership and operation into fewer, more centralized hands (Porter and Combe, 1998). These same pressures appear to be operating with a similar force in other circumstances, for example Denmark (Jauert and Prehn, 1997).

The second point to note is that the most successful attempts to construct local and regional broadcasting seem to have been those that rely on the most strongly marked of the old regions. The greater the degree of regional difference, particularly in language, the easier it seems to be to construct a viable broadcaster. The trend towards the regionalization of broadcasting was very marked in the 1970s and 1980s, but there seems to have been a general retreat since then.

[. . .]

The problem of financing broadcasting is even more acute for local groups. It seems to be a problem that has haunted many of the efforts in Europe over the last decade, and undoubtedly lies behind much of the pressure to produce networks out of stations set up for specifically local purposes. If we examine the broadcasting of 'new and local' groups, we can certainly find examples of radio broadcasting   London Greek Radio, for example – which are representations of some of these collectivities. Here the factors that permit a local broadcaster are similar to those that permit local broadcasting based on the old localities: available spectrum and the existence of an advertising market able to sustain a limited amount of production. Television, on the other hand, is much more problematic. The costs of producing genuinely local programming are so high that such broadcasters tend to be dependent upon state-based institutions. In some cases, for example in terms of British news and current affairs television that represents new localisms, this is mediated through the existing state-based broadcaster. In the case of Amsterdam, subsidy from the local state seems to have been crucial (Gooskens, 1992). In other cases, the relationship to the state structure does have more of a global dimension, since it is a broadcaster based in another state that provides programming. [. . .]

Overall, then, the analysis of the local public sphere certainly suggests that there are examples (albeit imperfect and limited ones) of this category in the contemporary world. They do not appear to be obviously linked with global media companies. With regard to the newspaper press, the majority of these local forms have existed for a long time and relate primarily to the old forms of locality, based on physical proximity. There are some newspapers which represent new forms of locality, but these are very much the minority. The local public sphere, as articulated in the printed press, is eroding rather than growing, and aspects of its localism are declining in favour of state-wide organization. In the case of broadcasting, there are indeed local public spheres in radio, and to some extent in television. The strongest of these are in the old forms of regional organization. Those in the new regions seem to be stagnating if not declining. Even some of these successful old regional forms of television are dependent upon subsidy from the state. The forms of television appropriate to the new localities do exist, although they are few in number, and they are not generally economically self-sufficient. Subsidy from the state is an important condition for the viability of many of them. It seems reasonable to say that the local public sphere does indeed exist, but that there is little evidence that it is growing, disproportionately linked to new forms of localization, or articulated closely with the process of globalization.

Conclusions

None of the hypotheses regarding the global and the local that we suggested might be tested seem to be supported by the evidence we have reviewed here. On the contrary, the evidence directly contradicts them.

[. . .]

If all that was at stake was an issue of theoretical clarity, we could stop there. The fashionable formulations are wrong. But there is more at stake than just having the right ideas. Theory is important, but so too is practical action. The issues which we have been discussing, and which most theorists of globalization tend to mis-recognize or exaggerate, are important practical questions. There is no doubt that the international money markets, and in their wake the International Monetary Fund (IMF), have an enormous importance to people's lives in Indonesia, Korea, Thailand, Russia and Brazil today, and perhaps elsewhere tomorrow. There is no doubt that the populations of many advanced countries are ethnically very diverse. There is no doubt that the democratic system in the USA, and to a lesser extent elsewhere, is experiencing some kind of a malaise, if not a fully-fledged crisis. These issues have implications for our understanding of the public sphere, whether global, state-based or local. Mis-recognizing the issues at stake as some kind of vaguely formulated process of globalization in fact disables us not only from understanding the real dynamics of the situation but also from developing any policies that could make it easier for people to exercise their democratic rights. I want, in closing, to develop three issues that seem to me possible extrapolations that one could draw from the analysis I have sketched here.

First, there are real forces, beyond the direct control of even the most powerful of states (i.e. the USA), that affect, directly or indirectly, the life experience of all the world's population. It would be an extension of democracy, although not an antidote to the destructive effects of global capitalism, if these forces were placed under the same kinds of surveillance and control as are many states. To take an example, the IMF does not publish the details of its policies. The best that one can obtain are press releases and reports of speeches. What the IMF does matters, both to the people to whom it does things and to those whose money it risks when doing it. There can be no serious discussion of the role of the IMF without access to the information it is acting upon and the agreements that it is reaching. Simply assuming that a global public sphere is coming into being obscures the need for real pressure to bring the doings of the IMF into the public sphere, even to make its policies transparent, let alone to subject it to democratic control. To the extent that these globalizing forces gain in strength and impact, so the need for an open and accessible global public sphere will become all the more urgent. Left to themselves, there is no chance that the existing fora for global debate will evolve towards inclusive public spheres. To produce a public sphere on a global basis will require a sustained and conscious effort.

Second, the state is not withering away as a result of a siege from above and below. It is true that the scope for activity of even the most powerful of states is circumscribed by global forces. It is true that neo-liberal policies have meant that many of the social-services functions of the state, and many of the industries it ran, are being privatized. What is left, however, is still the essential 'special bodies of armed men with prisons etc. at their disposal,' which show no signs of disappearing. At the same time, the state remains the most powerful of social actors, and many states are subject to some democratic controls. The function of the state-oriented public sphere remains crucial. It is today under threat, for example because of the fragmentation of broadcasting consequent on the end of channel scarcity. Defending and extending that public sphere remains a central democratic task.

Third, the 'old' local and regional public spheres are in varying states of health, and some need assistance to survive. On the other hand, many of the 'new' public spheres are in a very uncertain state, particularly with respect to their ability to represent the lived contemporary experience of the diverse groups whose homes are in the great metropolises of the developed world. There are, for example, around 275 languages spoken in London, more than 190 first languages spoken in London schools. In inner London, more than 40 percent of children speak a language other than English at home. More than 30 percent of those who speak another language at home are not fluent in English. In my daughter's class of six year olds, there are half a dozen or so languages spoken at home. Admittedly, London is the most cosmopolitan city in the world, today more so, apparently, even than New York, but I think that the reality of complex and diverse ethnoscapes will be generally recognized, albeit in less extreme forms. It goes without saying from the point of view that values a public sphere, that all of these children, when they become adults, and their parents as of today, have the same democratic right to enter into the public sphere as I do. The notion that an elite of confidently bilingual 'community leaders' could fully represent these diverse populations does not fit easily into a theory of democratic involvement. What is more, the impact of new technologies of communication, the famous 500 channels that we hear so much about, means that it is technically possible to realize that right. But that, of course, is not what is happening. The 500 channels are going to be used to give us NVOD (Near Video On Demand) and sport. There are two obstacles to realizing the desirable state of an inclusive local public sphere which could embrace all of these new groups. The first is regulatory: the imposition of the obligation to carry such material as a condition of a franchise. The second is economic: the provision of the same kind of subsidy that enables Welsh speakers to enjoy a developed public sphere for other language defined groups like speakers of Bengali, Turkish, Cantonese, and so on. Whether either of these objectives could be realized or not is an open question: I am not in the short term optimistic. But the point is that, in order to realize either of them, it would be necessary that the existing state be forced to take action. Very far from replacing the state, the new localities need the state in order to represent themselves.

I hope that I have shown that 'getting it right' with regard to the global, the local and the public sphere is more than just a matter of the correct formulations. How we understand these complex developments in the world, and in the public sphere, has a direct bearing on the kinds of policies that are appropriate to extend democratic debate and involvement.

References

Curran, J. (1991). 'Rethinking the media as a public sphere'. In P. Dahlgren and C. Sparks (eds), *Communication and Citizenship*, 38–42. London: Routledge.

Drilik, A. (1996). 'The global in the local'. In R. Wilson and W. Dissanayake (eds), *Global/Local: Cultural Production and the Transnational Imaginary*, 21–45. London: Duke University Press.

Ferguson, M. (1992). 'The mythology about globalization'. *European Journal of Communication*, 7(1), 69–93.

Garnham, N. (1992). 'The media and the public sphere'. In C. Calhoun (ed.), *Habermas and the Public Sphere*, 359–76. Cambridge, MA: MIT Press.

Giddens, A. (1991). *The Consequenes of Modernity*. Stanford, CA: The Stanford University Press.

Gooskens, I. (1992). 'Experimenting with minority television in Amsterdam'. In N. Jankowski, O. Prehn and J. Stappers (eds), *The People's Voice: Local Radio and Television in Europe*, 225–34. London: John Libbey.

Greenberg, B. and Levy, M. (1997). 'Television in the changing communication environment: Audience and content trends in US television'. *Studies in Broadcasting*, 33, 131–74.

Habermas, J. (1974). 'The public sphere: An encyclopaedia article'. *New German Critique*, 3(1), 14–21.

Herman, E. and McChesney, R. (1997). *The Global Media: The New Missionaries of the Global Capitalism*. London: Cassell.

Hjarvard, S. (1993). 'Pan-European television news: Towards a European political public sphere?' In P. Drummond, R. Patterson and J. Willis (eds), *National Identity and Europe*, 71–94. London: British Film Institute.

Hollander, E. (1992). 'The emergence of small scale media'. In N. Jankowski, O. Prehn and J. Stappers (eds), *The People's Voice: Local Radio and Television in Europe*, 7–15. London: John Libbey.

Jankowski, N., Prehn, O. and Stappers, J. (eds) (1992). *The People's Voice: Local Radio and Television in Europe*. London: John Libbey.

Jauert, P. and Prehn, O. (1997). 'Local Television and Local News'. *Communications*, 22, 31–56.

Le Mahieu, D. (1988). *A Culture for Democracy*. Oxford: Clarendon Press.

Moragas Spà, M. de and Garitaonandía, C. (eds) (1995). *Television in the Regions, Nationalities and Small Countries of Europe*. London: John Libbey.

Negus, K. (1996). 'Globalization and the music of the public spheres'. In S. Braman and A. Sreberny-Mohammadi (eds), *Globalization, Communication and Transnational Civil Society*, 179–96. Cresskill, NJ: Hampton Press.

Porter, V. and Combe, C. (1998). 'The restructuring of UK independent television, 1993–1997'. Paper presented to the conference 'Media Beyond 2000,' April 16–17, London.

Ritzer, G. (1993). *The McDonaldization of Society*. London: Pine Forge Press.

Scannell, P. (1989). 'Public service broadcasting and modern public life'. *Media, Culture and Society*, 11(2), 135–66.

Schiller, H. (1991). 'Not yet the post-imperialist era'. *Critical Studies in Mass Communication*, 8(1), 13–28.

Schudson, M. (1992). 'Was there ever a public sphere?' In C. Calhoun (ed.), *Habermas and the Public Sphere*, 146. Cambridge, MA: The MIT Press.

Sparks, C. (1998). 'Is there a global public sphere?' In D. Tussu (ed.), *Electronic Empires*, 108–24. London: Arnold.

—— (1995). 'The survival of the state in British broadcasting'. *Journal of Communication*, 45(4), 140–59.

Williams, R. (1983). *Towards 2000*. London: Penguin.

Chapter 9

STUART CUNNINGHAM

POPULAR MEDIA AS PUBLIC 'SPHERICULES' FOR DIASPORIC COMMUNITIES

THE RESEARCH TEAM THAT AUTHORED *Floating Lives: The Media and Asian Diasporas* (Cunningham and Sinclair, 2000) mapped the mediascapes of Asian diasporic communities against the background of the theoretical and policy territory of understanding media use in contemporary, culturally plural societies. In this article, I will take further than *Floating Lives* the nature of the public spheres activated around diasporic media as a specific form of public communication, by engaging with public sphere debates and assessing the contribution that the research conducted for *Floating Lives* might make to those debates.

The public sphere, in its classic sense advanced in the work of Jürgen Habermas (1989 [1962]), is a space of open debate standing against the state as a special subset of civil society in which the logic of 'democratic equivalence' is cultivated. The concept has been used regularly in the fields of media, cultural and communications studies to theorize the media's articulation between the state and civil society. Indeed, Nicholas Garnham claimed in the mid-1990s that the public sphere had replaced the concept of hegemony as the central motivating idea in media and cultural studies (Garnham, 1995). This is certainly an overstatement, but it is equally certain that, almost 40 years since Habermas first published his public sphere argument, and almost 30 years since it was first published in outline in English (Habermas, 1974), the debate continues strongly over how progressive elements of civil societies are constructed and how media support, inhibit or, indeed, are coterminous with such self-determining public communication.

The debate is marked out at either end of the spectrum by those, on the one hand, for whom the contemporary western public sphere has been tarnished or even fatally compromised by the encroachment of particularly commercial media and communications (for example, Schiller, 1989). On the other hand, there are those for whom the media have become the main, if not the only, vehicle for whatever can be held to exist of the public sphere in such societies. Such 'media-centric' theorists in these fields can hold that the media actually *envelop* the public sphere:

> The 'mediasphere' is the whole universe of media . . . in all languages in all countries. It therefore completely encloses and contains as a differentiated part of itself the (Habermasian) public sphere (or the many public spheres), and it is itself contained by the much larger semiosphere . . . which is the whole universe of sense-making by whatever means, including speech . . . it is clear that television is a crucial site of the mediasphere and a crucial mediator between general cultural sense-making systems (the semiosphere) and specialist components of social sense-making like the public sphere. Hence its implied opposite, the private sphere, but as a 'Russian doll' enclosed within a larger mediasphere,

itself enclosed within the semiosphere. And within 'the' public sphere, there may equally be found, Russian-doll style, further counter-cultural, oppositional or minoritarian public spheres.

(Hartley, 1999: 217–18)

Hartley's topography has the virtue of clarity, scope and heuristic utility, even while it remains provocatively media-centric. This is mostly due to Hartley's commitment to the strictly textual provenance of public communication, and to his greater interest in Lotman's notion of the semiosphere than Habermas' modernist understanding that the public sphere stands outside and even against its 'mediatization'.

I will complicate that topography by suggesting that minoritarian public spheres are rarely subsets of classic nationally bound public spheres but are none the less vibrant, globalized but very specific spaces of self- and community-making and identity (see, for example, Husband, 1998). I agree with Hartley, however, in his iconoclastic insistence that the commercial realm must be factored into the debate more centrally and positively than it has been to date. Diasporic media entrepreneurs and producers are mostly uninterested in or wary of the state, in part because the copyright status of much of their production is dubious.

I will also stress another neglected aspect of the public sphere debate developed by Jim McGuigan (1998: 92) – the 'affective' as much as 'effective' dimension of public communication, which allows for an adequate grasp of entertainment in a debate dominated by ratiocinative and informational activity. McGuigan speaks of a 'rather softer' conception of the public sphere than is found in the work of Habermas and others (1998: 98) and develops these ideas around the significance of affective popular politics expressed through media mobilization of western responses to poverty and aid campaigns. Underdeveloped, though, and tantalisingly so, is the role played by the entertainment content of the media in the formation and reproduction of public communication (McGuigan, 1998: 98, quoting Garnham, 1992: 274). This is the domain on which such strongly opposed writers as McGuigan and Hartley might begin to at least share an object of study.

Todd Gitlin has posed the question as to whether we can continue to speak of the ideal of *the* public sphere as an increasingly complex, polyethnic, communications-saturated series of societies develop around the world. Rather, what might be emerging are numerous public 'sphericules': 'does it not look as though the public sphere, in falling, has shattered into a scatter of globules, like mercury?' (Gitlin, 1998: 173). Gitlin's answer is the deeply pessimistic one of seeing the future as the irretrievable loss of elements of a modernist public commonality.

The spatial metaphor of fragmentation, of dissolution, of the centre not holding, assumes that there is a singular nation-state to anchor it. Thinking of public sphericules as constituted beyond the singular nation-state, as *global narrowcasting of polity and culture*, assists in restoring them to a place – not necessarily counter-hegemonic but certainly culturally plural and dynamically contending with western forms for recognition – of undeniable importance for contemporary, culturally plural societies and any media, cultural and communication studies claiming similar contemporaneity.

There are now several claims for such public sphericules. One can speak of a feminist public sphere and international public sphericules constituted around environmental or human rights issues. They may take the form of 'subaltern counterpublics', as Nancy Fraser (1992) calls them, or they may be termed taste cultures, such as those formed around gay style (which doesn't of course exclude them from acting as 'counterpublics'). As John Hartley and Allen McKee put it in *The Indigenous Public Sphere* (2000: 3), these are possibly peculiar examples of public spheres because they are not predicated on any nation that a public sphere usually expresses – they are the 'civil societies' of nations without borders, without state institutions and without citizens. These authors go on to suggest that such public spheres might stand as a model for developments in late modern culture generally, with do-it-yourself citizenship based on culture, identity and voluntary belonging rather than based on rights derived from, and obligations to, a state.

My present argument is in part a contribution to the elaboration of just such a project. However, there are still undeniably relations of dominance, and 'mainstreams' and 'peripheries'; the metaphor is not simply a series of sphericules, overlapping to a greater or lesser extent. Although this latter explanatory model goes some distance in explaining the complexity of overlapping taste cultures, identity formations, social commitments and specialist understandings that constitute the horizon of many if not most citizens/consumers in post-industrial societies, there are broad consensuses and agenda-setting capabilities that cannot be gainsaid in enthusiasm for embracing *tout court* a 'capillary' model of power. The key, as Hartley and McKee identify, is the degree of control over the meanings created about and within the sphericule (2000: 3, 7) and by which this control is exercised.

In contrast to Gitlin, then, I argue that ethno-specific global mediatized communities display in microcosm elements we would expect to find in 'the' public sphere. Such activities may constitute valid and indeed dynamic counter-examples to a discourse of decline and fragmentation, while taking full account of contemporary vectors of communication in a globalizing, commercializing and pluralizing world.

Ongoing public sphere debates in the field, then, continue to be structured around dualisms which are arguably less aids than inhibitors of analysis: dualisms such as public-private, information-entertainment, cognition-affect or emotion, public versus commercial culture and – the 'master' dualism – public sphere in the singular or plural. What follows is no pretence at a Hegelian *Aufhebung* (transcendence) catching up these dualisms in a grand synthesis, but rather a contribution to a more positive account of the operations of media-based public communication – in this case, ethno-specific diasporic sphericules – which place a different slant on highly generalized debates about globalization, commercialization and the fate of public communication in these contexts.

The ethno-specific mediatized sphericule

First, they are indeed 'sphericules'; that is, they are social fragments that do not have critical mass. Nevertheless, they share many of the characteristics of the classically conceived public sphere – they provide a central site for public communication in globally dispersed communities, stage communal difference and discord productively, and work to articulate insider ethno-specific identities – which are by definition 'multi-national', even global – to the wider 'host' environments.

The audience research for *Floating Lives* was conducted in communities in Australia. Although Australia is, in proportional terms, the world's second-largest immigrant nation next to Israel, the relatively low numbers of any individual group (at present, more than 150 ethnic groups speaking over 100 different languages) has meant that a critical mass of a few dominant Non-English Speaking Background (NESB) groupings has not made the impact that Hispanic peoples, for example, have made in the United States. No one non-Anglo Celt ethnic group has, therefore, reached 'critical mass' in terms of being able to operate significantly as a self contained community in the nation. For this reason, Australia offers a useful laboratory for testing notions of diasporic communities that need to be 'de-essentialized', adapted to conditions where ethnicities and sub-ethnicities jostle in ways that would have been unlikely or impossible in their respective homeland settings or where long and sustained patterns of immigration have produced a critical mass of singular ethnicities.

Sinclair *et al.*'s (2000) study of the Chinese in *Floating Lives* posits that the sources, socio-economic backgrounds and circumstances of Chinese immigrant arrivals in Australia have been much more diverse than those of Chinese communities in the other great contemporary immigrant-receiving countries such as the United States, Canada, Britain and New Zealand, or earlier immigrant-receiving countries in Southeast Asia, South America, Europe and Africa. To make sense of 'the' Chinese community is to break it down into a series of complex and often interrelated sub-groupings based on geographical origin – mainland (PRC), Southeast Asia (Indonesia, Malaysia and Singapore), Taiwan, Indochina (Vietnam, Laos, Cambodia), Hong Kong – together with overlapping language and dialect use.

Similarly, Cunningham and Nguyen's (2000) Vietnamese study shows that there are significant differences among quite a small population along axes of generation, ethnicity, region of the home country, education and class, and recency of arrival and conditions under which arrival took place. And for the Fiji Indians in Manas Ray's work (2000), if it was legislated racial discrimination that compelled them to leave Fiji, in Australia they find themselves 'othered' by, and othering, the mainland Indian groupings who contest the authenticity of Fiji Indian claims to rootedness in Indian popular culture.

The formats for diasporic popular media owe much to their inscription within such 'narrow-cast' cultural spaces and share many significant attributes: karaoke, with its performative, communal and de-aestheticized performative and communal space (Wong, 1994); the Vietnamese variety music video and 'Paris/Sydney/Toronto by Night' live show formats; and the typical 'modular' Bollywood film and accompanying live and playback music culture.

Against the locus of examination of the 'diasporic imagination' as one of aesthetically transgressive hybridity produced out of a presumed 'ontological condition' occupied by the migrant subject, these are not necessarily aesthetically transgressive or politically progressive texts. Their politics cannot be read off their textual forms, but must be grasped in the use to which they are put in the communities. In *Floating Lives* we see these uses as centring on popular culture debates – where communities contend around the politics, identity formations and tensions of hybrid popular forms emerging to serve the diasporas.

Much diasporic cultural expression is a struggle for survival, identity and assertion, and it can be a struggle as much enforced by the necessities of coming to terms with the dominant culture as it is freely assumed. And the results may not be pretty. The instability of cultural maintenance and negotiation can lead, at one extreme, to being locked into a time warp with the fetishized homeland – as it once might have been but no longer is or can be; and, at the other, to assimilation to the dominant host culture and a loss of place in one's originary culture. It can involve insistent reactionary politics and extreme overcommercialization (Naficy [1993: 71] cites a situation in 1987 when Iranian television in Los Angeles was scheduling more than 40 minutes advertising an hour) because of the need to fund expensive forms of media for a narrowcast audience; and textual material of excoriating tragedy (the [fictional] self-immolation and [actual] atrocity scenarios played out in some, respectively, Iranian and Croatian videos), as recounted by Naficy and by Kolar-Panov (1997).

Second, there is explanatory pay-off in pursuing the specificity of the ethno-specific public sphericule in comparison with other emergent public spheres. Like the classic Habermasian bourgeois public sphere of the café society of eighteenth- and nineteenth-century France and Britain, they are constituted as elements of civil society. However, our understanding of civil society is formulated out of its dualistic relationship to formal apparatuses of political and juridical power. Ethno-specific sphericules constitute themselves as potentially global civil societies that intersect with state apparatuses at various points (immigration law, multicultural public policy and, for the irredentist and the exilic, against the regimes that control homeland societies). It follows that ethno-specific public sphericules are not congruent with international taste cultures borne by a homogenizing global media culture. For diasporic groupings *were* parts of states, nations and polities and much of the diasporic polity is about the process of remembering, positioning and, by no means least, constructing business opportunities around these pre-diasporic states and/or nations.

It is out of these realities that the assumption grows that ethnic minoritarian publics contribute to the further fragmentation of the majoritarian public sphere, breaking the 'social compact' that subsumes nation and ethnicity within the state; a process that has been foundational for the modern nation state. Irredentist politics and 'long-distance' nationalism, where the prime allegiance continues to be to an often-defunct state or regime, are deemed non-progressive by most commentators – classically captured by Susan Sontag in her celebrated essays on the Cubans in Florida. However, a focus on the popular culture of diasporas and its place in the construction of public sphericules complicates these assumptions, as it shows that a variety of voices contend for recognition and influence in the micro-polity, and great generational renewal can arise from the vibrancy of such popular culture.

Sophisticated cosmopolitanism and successful international business dealing sit alongside long-distance nationalism – the diasporic subject is typically a citizen of a western country, who is not stateless and is not seeking the recognition of a separate national status in their 'new' country, like the prototypal instances in the European context such as the Basques, the Scots or the Welsh. These sphericules are definitively transnational, even global in their constitution but are not the same as emerging transnational polities and cultures of global corporate culture, world-spanning non-governmental organizations and international bodies of governments.

Perhaps the most consistent relation, or non-relation, that diasporic media have with the various states into which they are introduced concerns issues of piracy. This gives another layer to the notion of civil cultures standing against the state, where 'public' is irreducible to 'official' culture. Indeed, given that significant amounts of the cultural production exist in a paralegal penumbra of copyright breach and piracy, there is a strong desire on the part of the entrepreneurs who disseminate such products to keep their distance from organs of the state. It is apparent that routinized piracy makes of much diasporic media a 'shadow system', as Kolar-Panov (1997: 31) dubs such minority video circuits as they are perceived from outside. They operate 'in parallel' to the majoritarian system, with few industry linkages.

Third, they reconfigure essentialist notions of community and reflex anti-commercialism. These sphericules are communities in a sense that goes beyond the bland homogeneous arcadia that the term community usually connotes. On the one hand, the ethno-specific community assumes an importance that is greater by far than the term usually implies in mainstream parlance, as the community *constitutes* the markets and audiences for the media services – there is almost no cross-over or recognition outside the specific community in most cases of diasporic cultural production. The 'community' therefore becomes an economic calculus, not only a multi-cultural demographic instance. The community is to an important extent constituted *through* media (see Hartley and McKee, 2000: 84) in so far as media performance is one of the main reasons to meet together, and there is very little else available as a mediator of information and entertainment. These media and their entrepreneurs and audiences work within a de-essentialized community and its differences as a condition of their practice and engagement.

Diasporic media are largely commercially driven media but are not fully fledged markets. They are largely constituted in and through a commercial culture but this is not the globalizing, homogenizing commercialism that has been posed by neo-Marxist political economists as threatening cultural pluralism, authenticity and agency at the local level. With notable exceptions such as global Chinese popular cultural forms such as cantopop and Hong Kong cinema, which has experienced significant cross-over into both dominant and other emerging contemporary cultural formations, and the Indian popular Bhangra music and Bollywood cinema which is still more singularly based in Indian homeland and diasporic audiences, this is small business commercialism that deals with the practical specificities of cultural difference at the local level as an absolute precondition of business viability.

The spaces for ethno-specific public communication are, fourth, mediacentric, and this affords new configurations of the information-entertainment dualism. Given the at times extreme marginalization of many diasporic groupings in public space and their lack of representation within leaderships of influence and persuasion in the dominant forums of the host country, ethno-specific media become, by default, the main organs of communication outside of certain circumscribed and defined social spaces, such as the Chinatowns, Koreatowns, the little Saigons, the churches and temples, or the local video, spice and herb parlours.

The ethno-specific sphericule is mediacentric but, unlike the way that mediacentricity can give rise to functionalist thinking (media are the cement that forms and gives identity to the community), it should be thought of rather as 'staging' difference and dissension in ways that the community *itself* can manage. There are severe constraints on public political discourse among, for example, refugee-based communities such as the Vietnamese. The 'compulsive memorialisation' (Thomas, 1999: 149) of the pre-communist past of Vietnam and the compulsory anti-communism of the leadership of the Vietnamese community are internalized as unsavoury to mainstream society. As part of the pressure to be the perfect citizen in the host society (Hage, 1998: 10), there is considerable self-censorship in the expression of public critical opinion. This filtering of political partisanship for external consumption is also turned back on itself in the community, with attempts by members of the community to have the rigorous anti-communist refugee stance softened (by the mid-1990s, only 30 per cent of the Vietnamese community in Australia were originally refugees) met with harsh rebuke. In this situation, Vietnamese entertainment formats, discussed below, operate to create a space where political and cultural identities can be processed in a self-determining way, where voices other than the official, but constitutive of community sentiment, can speak.

Mediacentricity also means, in this context, a constant blurring of the information-entertainment distinction, giving rise to a positive sense of a 'tabloidized' sphericule wherein McGuigan's *a*ffective as well as *e*ffective communication takes on another meaning. The information-entertainment distinction – usually maintained in the abundance of available media in dominant cultures – is blurred in the diasporic setting. As there is typically such a small diet of ethno-specific media available to these communities, they are mined deeply for social cues (including fashion, language use and so on), personal gossip, public information as well as singing along to the song or following the fictional narrative. Within this concentrated and contracted informational and libidinal economy, 'contemporary popular media as guides to choice, or guides to the attitudes that inform choices' (Hartley, 1999: 143) take on a thoroughly continuous and central role in information and entertainment for creating a negotiated *habitus*.

The Vietnamese

The Vietnamese are by far the largest refugee community in Australia. For most, 'home' is a denigrated category while 'the regime' continues in power, and so media networks, especially music video, operate to connect the dispersed exilic Vietnamese communities. As Cunningham and Nguyen (2000) argue in our chapter in *Floating Lives*, there are obviously other media in play (community newspapers, Hong Kong film and video products) but music video carries especial significance and allows a focus on the affective dimension of public communication. Small business entrepreneurs produce low-budget music videos mostly out of southern California (but also Paris), which are taken up within the fan circuits of the United States, Australia, Canada, France and elsewhere. The internal cultural conflicts in the communities centre on the felt need to maintain pre-revolutionary Vietnamese heritage and traditions; find a negotiated place in a more mainstreamed culture; or engage in the formation of distinct hybrid identities around the appropriation of dominant western popular cultural forms. These three cultural positions or stances are dynamic and mutable, but the main debates are constructed around them, and are played out principally within variety music video formats.

Although by no means exhausting the media diet of the Vietnamese diaspora, live variety shows and music videos are undeniably unique to it, as audio-visual media made specifically by and for the diaspora. These media forms bear many similarities to the commercial and variety-based cultural production of Iranian television in Los Angeles studied by Naficy in his benchmark *The Making of Exile Cultures* (1993), not least because Vietnamese variety show and music video production is also centred on the Los Angeles conurbation. The Vietnamese grouped there are not as numerous or as rich as Naficy's Iranians and so have not developed the business infrastructure to support the range and depth of media activity recounted by Naficy. The business infrastructure of Vietnamese audiovisual production is structured around a small number of small businesses operating on very low margins.

To be exilic means not, or at least not 'officially', being able to draw on the contemporary cultural production of the home country. Indeed, it means actively denying its existence in a dialectical process of mutual disauthentification (Carruthers, forthcoming). The Vietnam government proposes that the *Viet Kieu* (the appellation for Vietnamese overseas which carries a pejorative connotation) are fatally westernised. Ironically, the diasporic population makes a similar counter-charge against the regime, proposing that the homeland population has lost its moral integrity through the wholesale compulsory adoption of an alien western ideology – Marxism-Leninism.

Together, the dispersed geography and the demography of a small series of communities frame the conditions for 'global narrowcasting' – that is, ethnically specific cultural production for widely dispersed population fragments centripetally organized around their disavowed state of origin. This makes the media, and the media use, of the Vietnamese diaspora fundamentally different from those of the Indian or Chinese diasporas. The last revolve around massive cinema and television production centres in the 'home' countries that enjoy international cachet. By contrast, the fact that the media uses of the Vietnamese diaspora are globally oriented but commercially marginal ensures that they flourish outside the purview of state and major commercial vectors of subvention and trade.

These conditions also determine the small business character of the production companies. These small enterprises run at low margins and are constantly undercut by piracy and copying of their video products. They have clustered around the only Vietnamese population base that offers critical mass and is geographically adjacent to the much larger ECI (entertainment-communications-information) complex in Southern California. There is evidence of internal migration within the diaspora from the rest of the United States, Canada and France to Southern California to take advantage of the largest overseas Vietnamese population concentration and the world's major ECI complex.

During the course of the 20 and more years since the fall of Saigon and the establishing of the diaspora through flight and migration, a substantial amount of music video material has been produced. Thuy Nga Productions, by far the largest and most successful company, organizes major live shows in the United States and franchises appearance schedules for its high-profile performers at shows around the global diaspora. It has produced more than 60 two- to three-hour videotapes since the early 1980s, as well as a constant flow of CDs, audio-cassettes and karaoke discs, in addition to documentary specials and re-releases of classic Vietnamese movies. The other companies, between them, have also produced hundreds of hours of variety music video.

Virtually every overseas Vietnamese household views this music video material, most regularly attends the live variety performances on which the video material is based, and a significant proportion have developed comprehensive home libraries. The popularity of this material is exemplary, cutting across the several axes of difference in the community: ethnicity, age, gender, recentness of arrival, educational level, refugee or immigrant status, and home region. It is also widely available in pirated form in Vietnam itself, as the economic and cultural 'thaw' that has proceeded since the government's so-called Doi Moi policies of greater openness has resulted in extensive penetration of the homeland by this most international of Vietnamese forms of expression. As the only popular culture produced by and specifically for the Vietnamese diaspora, these texts attract an emotive investment in the overseas communities which is as deep as it is varied. The social text that surrounds, indeed engulfs, these productions is intense, multi-layered and makes its address across differences of generation, gender, ethnicity, class and education levels and recentness of arrival.

The key point linking attention to the textual dynamics of the music videos and media use in the communities is that each style cannot exist without the others, because of the marginal size of the audience base. From the point of view of *business* logic, each style cannot exist without the others. Thus, at the level of both the individual show/video and company outputs as a whole, the organizational structure of the shows and videos reflects the heterogeneity required to maximize the audience within a strictly narrowcast range. This is a programming philosophy congruent with 'broadcasting' to a globally spread, narrowcast demographic: 'the variety show form has been a mainstay of overseas Vietnamese anti-communist culture from the mid seventies onwards' (Carruthers, forthcoming).

In any given live show or video production, the musical styles might range from precolonial traditionalism to French colonial era high modernist classicism, to crooners adapting Vietnamese folksongs to the Sinatra era and to bilingual cover versions of *Grease* or Madonna. Stringing this concatenation of taste cultures together are comperes, typically well-known political and cultural figures in their own right, who perform a rhetorical unifying function:

> Audience members are constantly recouped via the show's diegesis, and the anchoring role of the comperes and their commentaries, into an overarching conception of shared overseas Vietnamese identity. This is centred on the appeal to . . . core cultural values, common tradition, linguistic unity and an anti-communist homeland politics.
>
> (Carruthers, forthcoming)

Within this overall political trajectory, however, there are major differences to be managed. The stances evidenced in the video and live material range on a continuum from 'pure' heritage maintenance and ideological monitoring; to mainstream cultural negotiation; through to assertive hybridity. Most performers and productions seek to situate themselves within the mainstream of cultural negotiation between Vietnamese and western traditions. However, at one end of the continuum there are strong attempts both to keep the original folkloric music traditions alive and to keep the integrity of the originary anti-communist stance foundational to the diaspora, through very public criticism of any lapse from that stance. At the other end, Vietnamese-American youth culture is exploring the limits of hybrid identities through the radical intermixing of musical styles.

The Fiji Indians

In a remarkably short time, essentially since the coups of the late 1980s which pushed thousands of Fiji Indians out of Fiji and into diaspora around the Pacific Rim in cities such as Vancouver, Auckland and Sydney, the community in Sydney has fashioned a vibrant popular culture based on consumption and celebration of Hindi filmdom and its associated music, dance and fashion cultures. It is an especial irony that a people 'extracted' from mainland Indian polity and culture a century or more ago – for whom the relationship with the world of Hindi film is a purely imaginary one – should embrace and appropriate such a culture with far greater strength than those enjoying a much more recent connection to the 'homeland'.

Manas Ray's analysis of the Fiji Indian public sphericule in *Floating Lives* (2000) is structured around a comparison with the expatriate Bengalis. The two groups are contrasted on a caste, class and cultural consumption basis, and Ray stresses that, given that there is no critical mass of sub-enthnicities within the Indian diaspora in Australia, cultural difference is definitional. The Bengalis are seen as locked into their history as bearers of the Indian project of modernity which they assumed centrally under the British Raj. The once-unassailed centrality that the educated, Hindu Bengali gentry, the *bradralok*, had in the political and civic institutions of India has been challenged in the decades since independence by the subaltern classes:

> It is from this Bengal that the *bradralok* flees, either to relatively prosperous parts of India or, if possible, abroad – to the affluent west, taking with them the dream of a nation that they were once so passionate about and the cultural baggage which had expressed that dream.
>
> (Ray, 2000: 142–3)

The Bengali diaspora, argues Ray, frames its cultural life around the high culture of the past, which has become a 'fossilized' taste culture (2000: 143).

In startling contrast to the Fiji Indian community, which is by far the highest consumer of Hindi films, for the Indian Bengalis, Indian-sourced film and video is of little interest and is even the subject of active disparagement. The literature and other high cultural forms, which once had 'organic links to the independence movement and to early post-independence hardship and hope', have fossilized into a predictable and ageing taste culture that is remarkably similar whether the Bengali community is in Philadelphia, Boston, London, Düsseldorf, Dubai or Sydney (Ray, 2000: 143). The issues of inter-generational deficit as the young turn to western youth culture are evident.

The politics of popular culture are fought out across the communal fractions and across the generations. The inter-communal discord between mainland Indians and Fiji Indians, which are neither new nor restricted only to Australia – where many mainland Indians continue to exhibit deeply entrenched casteist attitudes and Fiji Indians often characterized mainland Indians with the same kind of negativity they were wont to use for ethnic Fijians – are often played out around media and film culture. There are elements of fully blown popular culture debates being played out. At the time of a particularly vitriolic controversy in 1997, the editor of the mainland *Indian Post* argued that while the Fiji Indians are 'good Hindus' and 'they are the people who spend', their 'westernised ways' and 'excessive attachment to filmy culture' bring disrepute to the Indian community as a whole (Dello, 1997). The resolution to these kinds of issues is often found in the commercial reality that Fiji Indians are the main consumers of the products and services advertised in mainland Indian shops!

Despite virtual slavery in the extraction period and uprootedness in the contemporary period, the affective dimension of the Fiji Indian public sphericule is deeply rooted in Hindu belief and folklore. The central text of Hinduism, 'The Ramayan', thus was used to heal the wounds of indenture and provide a cultural and moral texture in the new settlement. A strong emotional identification to the Ramayan and other expressions of the Bhakti movement – a constrained cultural environment, continued degradation at the hands of the racist white regime, a disdain for the culture of the ethnic Fijians, a less hard-pressed post-indenture life and, finally, a deep-rooted need of a dynamic, discursive site for the imaginative reconstruction of motherland – were all factors which, together, ensured the popularity of Hindi films once they started reaching the shores of Fiji. This was because Hindi film deployed the Ramayan extensively, providing the right pragmatices for 'continual mythification' of home (Ray, 2000: 156).

As a result, second-generation Fiji Indians in their twice-displaced settings of Sydney, Auckland or Vancouver have developed a cultural platform that, although not counter-hegemonic, is markedly different from their western host cultures. In contrast, 'the emphasis of the first generation Indian Bengali diaspora on aestheticised cultural forms of the past offers to [the] second generation very little in terms of a home country popular youth culture with which they can identify' (Ray, 2000: 145).

References

Carruthers, Ashley (forthcoming) 'National Identity, Diasporic Anxiety and Music Video Culture in Vietnam', in Yao Souchou (ed.) *House of Glass: Culture, Modernity and the State in Southeast Asia*. Singapore: Institute of Southeast Asian Studies.

Cunningham, Stuart and John Sinclair (eds) (2000) *Floating Lives: The Media and Asian Diasporas*, pp. 91–135. St Lucia: University of Queensland Press (and Boulder, CO: Rowman & Littlefield, 2001).

Cunningham, Stuart and Tina Nguyen (2000) 'Popular Media of the Vietnamese Diaspora', in Stuart Cunningham and John Sinclair (eds) *Floating Lives: The Media and Asian Diasporas*. St Lucia: University of Queensland Press (and Boulder, CO: Rowman & Littlefield, 2001).

Dello, Sanjay (1997) Interview with Manas Ray, Sydney, May.

Fraser, Nancy (1992) 'Rethinking the Public Sphere: A Contribution to the Critique of Actually Existing Democracy', in C. Calhoun (ed.) *Habermas and the Public Sphere*, pp. 109–42. Cambridge, MA: MIT Press.

Garnham, Nicholas (1992) 'The Media and the Public Sphere', in C. Calhoun (ed.) *Habermas and the Public Sphere*, pp. 359–76. Cambridge, MA: MIT Press.

—— (1995) 'The Media and Narratives of the Intellectual', *Media, Culture and Society* 17(3): 359–84.

Gitlin, T. (1998) 'Public Sphere or Public Sphericules?', in T. Liebes and J. Curran (eds) *Media, Ritual and Identity*, pp. 175–202. London: Routledge.

Habermas, J. (1974) 'The Public Sphere', *New German Critique* 1(3): 49–55.

—— (1989[1962]) *The Structural Transformation of the Public Sphere: An Inquiry in a Category of Bourgeois Society*. Cambridge: Polity Press.

Hage, Ghassan (1998) *White Nation: Fantasies of White Supremacy in a Multicultural Society*. Annandale: Pluto Press; and West Wickham: Comerford and Miller.

Hartley, John (1999) *Uses of Television*. London: Routledge.

—— and Allen McKee (2000) *The Indigenous Public Sphere*. Oxford: Oxford University Press.

Husband, Charles (1998) 'Differentiated Citizenship and the Multi-ethnic Public Sphere', *Journal of International Communication* 5(1/2): 134–48.

Kolar-Panov, D. (1997) *Video, War and the Diasporic Imagination*. London: Routledge.

McGuigan, Jim (1998) 'What Price the Public Sphere?', in Daya Kishan Thussu (ed.) *Electronic Empires: Global Media and Local Resistance*, pp. 91–107. London: Arnold.

Naficy, Hamid (1993) *The Making of Exile Cultures: Iranian Television in Los Angeles*. Minneapolis: University of Minnesota Press.

Ray, Manas (2000) 'Bollywood Down Under: Fiji Indian Cultural History and Popular Assertion', in Stuart Cunningham and John Sinclair (eds) *Floating Lives: The Media and Asian Diasporas*, pp. 136–84. St Lucia: University of Queensland Press (and Boulder, CO: Rowman & Littlefield, 2001).

Schiller, H. (1989) *Culture Inc.: The Corporate Takeover of Public Expression*, New York: Oxford University Press.

Sinclair, John, Audrey Yue, Gay Hawkins, Kee Pookong and Josephine Fox (2000) 'Chinese Cosmopolitanism and Media Use', in Stuart Cunningham and John Sinclair (eds) *Floating Lives: The Media and Asian Diasporas*, pp. 35–90. St Lucia: University of Queensland Press (and Boulder, CO: Rowman & Littlefield, 2001).

Thomas, Mandy (1999) *Dreams in the Shadows: Vietnamese-Australian Lives in Transition*. St Leonards: Allen & Unwin.

Wong, Deborah (1994) ' "I Want the Microphone": Mass Mediation and Agency in Asian-American Popular Music', *TDR (The Drama Review)* 38(3): 152–67.

PART THREE

Modes of Television

AS WE ARE USING THE TERM, "modes of television" speaks to the fact that there are multiple, changing technologies of television, multiple ways these technologies have been and may be used, and multiple ways they have been experienced by viewers. For most people in the English speaking world for most of the history of television, television has been synonymous with broadcast television. But the term "modes of television" also reflects the fact that television's technologies have been and can be used for purposes other than broadcasting. As the non-broadcast uses of television technology multiply with technological innovation, and as cable and satellite connections replace roof-top antennae, terrestrial broadcasting is losing its position as the default "mode" of television for many people.

Although some cable and satellite channels still rely upon the programming forms and scheduling strategies of terrestrial broadcasting, others have innovated entirely different programming and scheduling logics. CNN Headline News, BBC World, Sky News, the Weather Channel, MTV, and a host of home shopping channels, for example, have built their schedules around single programming forms: the headline newscast, the weather report, the music video, the infomercial. The variety of modes of production, distribution, use, and experience of television has further expanded in the 1990s. There are many more video cameras being used today for surveillance than in the production of sitcoms, and many more cameras being used to record vacation experiences and family gatherings than in the production of soap operas or news programs. The issues raised by the proliferation of non-broadcast modes of television are taken up in other sections as well. For example, you might want to look at Brian Larkin's essay on the Nigerian video film in Part Four: Making Television and essays by Jon Dovey and Arild Fetveit on camcorders and surveillance videos in Part Seven: Transforming Television.

The term modes of television also reflects the variety of ways in which these multiple, diverse technological applications are experienced in everyday life. It is worth comparing cinema and television in this respect. Cinema also involves multiple technologies, which can be and have been deployed in a variety of ways for a variety of purposes over the last century or so. And yet, courses in cinema studies and the textbooks and anthologies that accompany them tend to limit their discussion to the one "modality" of cinema, if you will, that we most commonly associate with the movies: theatrical feature films shown in movie theaters.[1] In part, this focus on the feature film as the principal mode of cinema and the movie theater as the principal site of reception are themselves products of cinema studies' aesthetic orientation: the more a given film can be seen as possessing some of the qualities of an art work, the more central it is likely to be to the project of cinema studies.

But the much more narrow modal focus of cinema studies also reflects the fact that over the past twenty years or so, the ways most of us experienced cinema as a set of technologies were contracting while the ways that we experienced "television" expanded. Home video technology completely replaced home *movie* technology in the 1980s. Many college and university courses in filmmaking became courses in video production around the same time and as a result of the same consumer video revolution. By the early 1990s, more people in the US were watching video tapes of Hollywood films on their television sets than were paying to see them in theaters. Even within the movie theater, the range of cinematic experiences we expect to have there has greatly narrowed since the advent of broadcast television. In the 1930s and 1940s, going to the movies meant seeing cartoons, newsreels, comic shorts, *and* a ninety-minute fictional, feature film. Today no one goes to the movies to catch up on the week's news. Going to the movies means going to see the feature film. To be sure, our expectations of what we will see in the movie theater varies according to the genre of film we are led to expect (by advertising, reviews, word-of-mouth, etc.). Going to see a slasher film is not the same experience as going to see a romantic comedy. But those experiences are less different from each other than, say, watching a sitcom at home and then seeing yourself on a store surveillance monitor when you go out for beer and nachos later the same day—or even watching a sitcom and later watching the evening news on the same channel.

In cinema studies the critical concept of genre has been used to discuss the balance that Hollywood cinema attempted to maintain between similarity and difference. The Hollywood "dream factory" system of film production depended upon a high degree of standardization in product output. This standardization also produced a broad understanding among audiences as to what constituted the experience of moviegoing. Regardless of the film's title, director, stars, or the movie theater in which it would be shown, audiences came to expect all Hollywood films to share certain basic traits: they would all be of roughly the same length; they would all be fictional; and they would all be narratives whose plots would be brought to closure by the time the film itself came to an end.

But in order to bring the audience back next week to see another film, each Hollywood film had to be unique in some respects, but not so different that the audience felt that their cinema-going experience had slipped into another modality. By organizing the production of Hollywood films around sets of conventions—of setting, subject matter, plot, and/or characterization—Hollywood created a structure of generic similarity within which each film could be a "different" moviegoing experience. An establishing shot of a lone cowboy riding his horse across the vast expanse of the American western desert was sufficient to signal to the film's audience that the film experience they were about to share was one that they and the producers of the film understood to be a "western." One of the primary sources of pleasure in watching any film western is to see how the familiar conventions of the genre will be deployed differently in that particular retelling of the "western" story.

Genre has also been a useful concept in the critical analysis of broadcast television. But even when applied to this single mode of television, the term genre must reflect broadcast television's much wider range of programming forms. Broadcast television innovated its own versions of the cinematic western, melodrama, police drama, and sci fi film, among other generic adaptations. But very early on in its history, broadcast television also innovated programming forms (some of them drawn from radio and, initially at least, all of them live) for which there were no direct cinematic correlatives, among them the game show, televised sporting events, live coverage of news events, the talk show, the variety show, and the soap opera.

The application of genre theory to broadcast television must somehow accommodate the fact that the differences between a game show and a sitcom go well beyond the typical differences between Hollywood film genres. The sitcom typically takes place in a fictional setting drawn from the world outside of television and features characters who inhabit that world. Its goal is to make us laugh in part by having funny things happen to characters whom we know to be fictional constructs. The world of the game show, on the other hand, exists entirely within the world of television. It has hosts and contestants but no characters. We are encouraged to laugh at the recurrent but ultimately inconsequential misfortunes of sitcom characters, but our interest in the game show depends, in part at least, upon our knowledge that the contestants are not fictional characters but "real" people and that their fortunes or misfortunes within the show might have a bearing on their lives beyond it.

In this example, it can also be seen that while Hollywood films make no claim for truthfulness, a number of television genres rely upon their "realseemingness" as the basis for their appeals and effect. What we might call the referential capacities of television will be taken up in a number of essays throughout this collection and will be couched in a number of different terms—liveness and indexicality, among them. We raise the issue here to point out that viewers make generic distinctions between those types of programs that we are to regard as merely fictional and those we are supposed to take as in some ways and to some degree making a claim upon belief: a category that would not only include news, documentary, and current affairs programming but game shows, talk shows, infomercials, and various forms of "reality" programs. Furthermore, as discussed in essays as diverse as Margaret Morse's on TV news, Eric Freedman's on the autobiographical mode of public access television, and Jon Dovey's and Arild Fetveit's on camcorders and surveillance video, some modes of television, particularly non-institutional and non-broadcast modes, are seen as having a special quality of "realseemingness" about them.

Hollywood film genres were also attempts to mobilize the interests of particular audience segments: melodramas were designed to appeal especially to women, westerns to men. Some forms of television programming go much further in attempting to address the presumed interests of discrete audience groups. Since their inception as radio dramas in the 1920s, US soap operas have been targeted overwhelmingly at young adult women. We speak of "children's TV" as a general programming form that includes a number of different genres: cartoons, live-action comedies and dramas, wildlife and nature documentaries, etc.—all of which are linked by their being addressed primarily (though certainly not exclusively) to audiences of *non*-adults.

In the broadcasting era of television, when a few terrestrial broadcasters competed against each other for the largest available audience of television viewers, generic diversity was one scheduling strategy for appealing to different audience groups at different times of days, as well as a way of differentiating programs on offer by one channel in relation to other viewing options on other channels at the same time. Because the economics of commercial, terrestrial broadcasting encouraged regular, habitual viewing, genres emerged to encourage viewers to tune in "the same time tomorrow" or "the same time next week." Thus television genres took advantage of the "always thereness" of television and its insinuation into the daily and weekly cycles of everyday life. Unlike the moviegoing experience, which presumes that there is no continuing narrative, theme, or characters linking our visit to the movie theater this week with our experience there the week before, much of our experience of broadcast television is of programming forms comprised of multiple, regularly-occurring episodes. One of the most distinctive of broadcast television's programming forms, the open-ended soap opera, is predicated upon the impossibility of any given episode ever being capable of bringing the show's narrative to resolution.

The applicability of genre approaches developed in film and literary studies to broadcast television forms the point of departure for Jason Mittell's essay. Rather than attempting to draw generic distinctions from an analysis of individual television programs (or "texts," as he will call them), he proposes that we conceive of television genres as discursive practices. In other words, he suggests, our understanding of what a game show or sitcom is derives not only from the conventions present in a given show itself (host and contestants, luck and skill, laugh-track, the living room set, etc.) but also from how that show is positioned, referred to, marketed, and responded to as well—in short, through the discourses about it.

Thus, someone interested in the meanings, appeals and pleasures of *Big Brother* might look at the ways in which that particular show was positioned in relation to other instances of television and other genres of television across a range of sources (television industry trade press, advertisements, press reports, critical commentary, websites, and even *Big Brother* parodies) in addition to studying the program itself. How, we might ask, does discourse (talk, in the most general sense of the word) about it draw upon, relate it to, distinguish it from the game show? The documentary? The surveillance tape? The soap opera? How does discourse about *Big Brother* in newspapers, on other TV programs, in ads, on internet sites shape our relationship with its contestants/characters/personalities and condition our satisfaction or frustration at its conclusion?

Until the development and industrial adoption of videotape in the 1960s, broadcast television was assumed to mean *live* television: that is to say, events were displayed on the television screen simultaneously with their occurrence in front of the television camera.[2] Liveness, along with television's smaller image size and its location within the home, were regarded as the defining attributes of the new medium and the qualities that distinguished the experience of television from the experience of cinema. Jérôme Bourdon argues in his essay that liveness became marginalized in much of the theoretical and critical writing about television in the 1980s and 1990s as attention shifted to the ways in which the images and sounds of television are or might be manipulated, particularly in the age of digital recording and editing and computer enhancement (see John Caldwell's essay in Part Four, for example). Bourdon argues, however, that what he calls the possibility of live broadcasting remains an important resource for television institutions around the world and remains a fundamental feature of the viewer's experience of television. In short, he argues that liveness continues to be a distinguishable and defining mode of the experience of television. Certainly, as we'll see, the issue of television's connection with some notion of the "real" re-emerges in recent scholarship on non-broadcast modes of television (home videos, surveillance video, etc.).

By placing the phenomenon of liveness back at the center of his discussion of television, Bourdon asks us to think about what we and what television producers understand by that term and what difference it makes that a moment of television or an entire program is represented as or received as "live." Just as Jason Mittell sees genre as a category constructed as much by discourses about television as by the qualities of the television text itself, Bourdon argues that liveness is a belief in the status of what we see on the screen that is produced not only by cues we get from the image itself but also by what we are *told* about it by the discourse surrounding it (by newscasters, by "live" written at the bottom of the screen, by promos for the show, etc.).

Acknowledging that there are types and degrees of liveness in our experience of and expectations about television, he sees the post-broadcasting era of television as one still very much reliant upon the possibility of liveness.

Four of the essays in this section examine different genres of broadcast television. Derek Paget's essay, drawn from his book on the subject, explores the conventions of what is sometimes called the "dramadoc" in the UK and the "docudrama" in the US, Australia, Canada, and New Zealand. Regardless of the name by which it is represented, audiences know this genre of dramatic television to lie at the intersection of history and enacted fiction. Although the form varies from country to country, Paget argues that it relies upon similar conventions to make a claim upon our belief in the non-fictional status of the show's historical context, setting, and (at least some) characters: authoritative voice-over narration, captions ("Sydney, 1938"), and documentary footage, among them. At the same time, we expect to see actors impersonating famous historical figures, narratives structured according to the conventions of fictional drama, and imagined intimate dialogue that was written by a scriptwriter rather than transcribed from the public record. In short, this genre draws together what would seem to be contradictory capacities of television: to show us what "really" happens in the world and to construct emotionally-engaging fictional worlds. Paget teases out the strategies used by practitioners of this genre to bring these two tendencies together in a single moment of television.

If the docudrama has emerged as the way that broadcast television reformulates history, news is the generic term we use to stand for the way that it, in Margaret Morse's words, puts "the world as an object into words and images. . . ." Morse argues that American television news's claims of democratizing knowledge about the world and of carrying on print journalism's traditions of objectivity are belied by its very format. This format—with its sincere, wise anchor presiding over a coterie of less prominent reporters "in the field," who in turn select, organize, and interpret the images, sounds, and voices produced by news events themselves—greatly limits what anyone who is not an anchor or reporter can actually say about the events that touch upon their lives. Reduced to a sound bite or a fleeting image, the people who are most affected by the events that make up the news are denied the opportunity to challenge the reporter's interpretation or agenda or even to determine the length or context of their own remarks. Morse explores the nature and implications of what we might call the "American" news format (although its influence is felt in television systems around the world) through an extended analysis of US television news coverage of the Romanian revolution in 1989.

John Corner's essay, "Adworlds," acknowledges the presence of the television commercial in the daily experience of hundreds of millions of viewers around the world. Indeed, as he points out, the expansion of channel capacity and the commercialization of previously state-operated systems of broadcasting in the 1990s together have had the effect of extending advertiser-based television "to societies in which it was previously either marginal or non-existent, while in those societies where it has an established place it has often become even more culturally pervasive and representatively subtle." The economic logic of commercial television—whereby the availability of viewers to watch advertisements is "sold" to advertisers by broadcasters, and whereby we "agree" to accept advertisements as an unremarkable facet of our television viewing experience—places the commercial at the center of television's institutional arrangements and singles it out, as Corner puts it, as an "extraordinary form of television." Not surprisingly, then, the study of advertising has occupied television scholars for a long time.

Soap operas or television serials are, arguably, the most popular and successful form of drama in the history of world television. Regardless of their subject matter, country of production, or duration, serials are linked by their distinctive narrative structure: the drawing out of multiple storylines across multiple episodes and the consequent engagement of the viewer with the world of the serial over a period of months, years, or decades. Robert Allen's essay, adapted from the introduction to an anthology of international scholarship on television serials, discusses the two basic types of serial television drama: the "open" serial, which is designed to continue indefinitely (*EastEnders, Neighbours*, US daytime soap operas) and the "closed" serial familiar to Latin American audiences as *telenovelas*, which is designed eventually to end. It also discusses the transnational circulation of serials, as Mexican and Brazilian *telenovelas* are exported to dozens of countries worldwide and Australian soaps become fixtures on UK television. Is the international success of television serials, we might ask, a function of their "narrative transparency" (as Scott Olson might argue in his essay in Part Two: Spaces of Television) or to a combination of other factors?

Albert Moran discusses another way in which television is circulated between national television systems, through a category of television programming that in some ways complicates both the notion of the television genre and of the television text: the television format. As noted above, Margaret Morse uses the term "format" to describe the way in which our experience of the news is structured by the newscast's particular and hierarchical arrangement of space (the set), time (the organization and arrangement of segments), images and voices. The format of US network daily newscasts then becomes distinguishable from other "news" formats: "tabloid" news shows, confessional talk shows, and alternative non-fiction documentaries, for example. As Moran discusses in his essay, format is also used within the television industry to describe a particular arrangement of generic elements from which individual episodes of television programming can be derived and which may be adapted to take into account local conditions or requirements. In the case of a game show, a format might consist of a package of elements: a description of the game's rules and participants, blueprints for set design, computer software (including particular graphics and sounds), music (theme song and occasional music), and even sample questions and answers. Not only is any given episode of the show an activation of these format elements, the format itself can be "sold" to television producers in other markets or in other countries.

The international market in television formats has exploded in recent years, as cable and satellite systems have drastically increased channel capacity and hence the need for programming to fill channel schedules. *Big Brother, Survivor, Wheel of Fortune, Funniest Home Videos, Who Wants to be a Millionaire?, Most Wanted, Family Feud, Sale of the Century*, and the *Idols — Pop Idol* (UK), *American Idol* (US), *South African Idol* (South Africa) — are but a few of the format-generated programs running in a number of national television markets.

The international circulation of program formats raises a number of interesting questions about the international circulation of culture more generally. What, exactly, is being circulated? What in cultural terms is being "exported" and what "imported"? What difference does it make that the soap opera about separated twins who (unknowingly) fall in love with each other as adults, which is produced in Germany as *Verbotene Liebe*, in Greece as *Apagoreymeni Agapi*, in Indonesia as *Belahan Hati*, and in Sweden as *Skilda Världar*, is generated from a format that originated as a 1970s Australian serial entitled *Sons and Daughters* and is now being licensed by an Australian company (Grundy) that is a subsidiary of the largest television production company in Europe (FremantleMedia), 90 percent of which is in turn owned by the German-based multinational media conglomerate Bertlesmann AG?

Notes

1 To be fair, it should be pointed out here that film scholars and film courses have also examined other cinematic forms: the experimental film, the documentary, the amateur film, and the educational film, among them. However, the literature on these other forms would make up a rather short shelf in the library of cinema scholarship compared with the number of works devoted to the fictional feature film.

2 The exception to this generalization is the broadcasting of films and programs recorded on motion picture film.

Chapter 10

JASON MITTELL

A CULTURAL APPROACH TO TELEVISION GENRE THEORY

EVERY ASPECT OF TELEVISION EXHIBITS a reliance on genre. Most texts have some generic identity, fitting into well-entrenched generic categories or incorporating genre mixing (as in "dramedies," such as *Ally McBeal*, or blends, such as *Make Me Laugh*, a comedy / game show). Industries rely on genres in producing programs, as well as in other central practices such as self-definition (channels such as ESPN or Cartoon Network) and scheduling (locating genres within time slots, as in daytime soap operas). Audiences use genres to organize fan practices (generically determined organizations, conferences, and Websites), personal preferences, and everyday conversations and viewing practices. Likewise, academics use generic distinctions to delineate research projects and to organize special topic courses, while journalistic critics locate programs within common frameworks. Even video stores and *TV Guide* reveal that genre is the primary way to classify television's vast array of textual options. But despite this virtual omnipresence of genre within TV, little theoretical research has explained the role of genres specifically in the context of television.

A number of factors explain this lack of theoretical exploration. Some scholars may view the vast body of genre theory produced within literary and film studies as sufficient, able to explain genre in any medium. Much literary and film genre theory, however, does not account for some of the industry and audience practices unique to television, as well as for the mixture of fictional and nonfictional programming that constitutes the lineup on nearly every TV channel. Importing genre theories into television studies without significant revision creates many difficulties when accounting for the specifics of the medium.

The greatest obstacle to the development of television-specific genre theory stems from the assumptions of traditional approaches. Most genre theory has focused on issues that may seem outdated to some media scholars. Formal and aesthetic approaches to texts or structuralist theories of generic meanings, for example, may seem incompatible with contemporary methods. In particular, the central questions motivating many media scholars today—how do television programs fit into historically specific systems of cultural power and politics—appear distant from those that typify genre theory.[1] Thus, a return to genre theory might imply theoretical backtracking, either to structuralism, aesthetics, or ritual theories, all of which take a back seat to current cultural studies paradigms within television studies. Even the most comprehensive discussion of television genre theory, Jane Feuer's essay in *Channels of Discourse*, ultimately concludes that genre analysis does not work as well as a paradigm for television as it has for film or literature.[2] So what's a media scholar to do?

The answers so far have not been fully satisfying. Many television genre scholars seem content to take genres at face value, using the labels that are culturally commonplace without giving much consideration to the meanings or usefulness of those labels. Television scholars who do "stop to smell the theory" have been quick to employ film and literary theories, often (though not always) with brief disclaimers in which they note the flaws inherent in these paradigms, while adding the now-ubiquitous phrase "more work in this area is needed." This essay is a first step toward undertaking "more work in this area." It proposes an alternative approach that better accounts for the cultural operations of television genre than traditional approaches. This theoretical offering is admittedly brief and does not put this theory into detailed practice, which is the ultimate goal.[3] Despite these caveats, this essay may at least put the topic of television genre theory more squarely on the academic agenda and provide some ideas for further discussion.

[. . .]

Traditional genre analysis and the textualist assumption

Media scholars have traditionally looked at genre as a component of the text, using a variety of guiding questions and theoretical paradigms. One tradition poses *questions of definition*, looking to identify the core elements that constitute a given genre by examining texts so as to delimit the formal mechanisms constituting the essence of that genre.[4] Another approach, probably the most common in media studies, raises *questions of interpretation* by exploring the textual meanings of genres and situating them within larger social contexts.[5] Within this approach, a number of specific theoretical orientations have emerged—ritual, ideological, structuralist, psychoanalytic, and cultural studies, to list some central (and potentially overlapping) paradigms.[6] A third (and less developed) form of genre analysis poses *questions of history* to emphasize the evolutionary dynamics of genres. Here the central issue is how changing cultural circumstances bring about generic shifts.[7]

Despite this variety of methods and paradigms, most examples of genre analysis consider genre primarily as a textual attribute. We might characterize this central notion as the "textualist assumption," a position that takes many forms. Some scholars (more common in literary theory) make explicit claims that genre is an intrinsic property of texts.[8] Media scholars more frequently *imply* that genre is a component of a text through a number of practices—situating a genre within larger discussions of texts (as opposed to industries, audiences, or culture),[9] mapping an internal/external distinction onto texts versus "other factors,"[10] or methodologically examining a genre primarily through textual analysis.[11] This textualist assumption seems to have contributed to the decline in genre analysis; as cultural media scholars have moved away from textual analysis, genre has been left behind with topics like narrative and style as perceived relics of extinct methodologies.

So what is wrong with the textualist assumption? Aren't genres just categories of texts? Certainly genres do categorize texts. We might consider that genres categorize industrial practices (such as the self-definition of the Sci-Fi Channel) or audience members (such as sci-fi fans), but in these instances the textual category precedes the industry's and the audiences' use of the term—science-fiction programs are the implied unifying factor within both the industry and the audience categories. This is not to suggest that genres are not primarily categories of texts, but there is a crucial difference between conceiving of genre as a textual *category* and treating it as a *component* of a text, a distinction most genre studies elide.

The members of any given category do not create, define, or constitute the category itself. A category primarily links discrete elements together under a label for cultural convenience. Although the members of a given category may all possess some inherent trait that binds them together, there is nothing intrinsic about the category itself. [. . .]

We do not generally differentiate between shows that take place in Boston and those that take place in Chicago, but we do differentiate between programs set in hospitals and those set in police stations. Texts have many different components, but only some are used to define their generic properties. As many genre scholars have noted, there are no uniform criteria for genre delimitation—some are defined by setting (westerns), some by actions (crime shows), some by audience effect (comedy), and some by narrative form (mysteries).[12] This diversity of attributes suggests that there is nothing internal mandating how texts should be generically categorized. In fact, some scholars have pointed to instances where the same text became "regenrified" as cultural contexts shifted.[13] If the same text is open enough to be categorized under various genres, then it follows that it is problematic to look for generic definitions solely within the confines of the text.

Genres are not found within one isolated text; *Wheel of Fortune* is not a genre in and of itself but a member of the generic category "game show." Genres emerge only from the intertextual relations between multiple texts, resulting in a common category. But how do these texts interrelate to form a genre? Texts cannot interact on their own; they come together only through cultural practices such as production and reception. Audiences link programs together all the time ("This show is just a clone of that one"), as do industrial personnel ("Imagine *Friends* meets *The X-Files*"). Texts themselves do not actively link together without this cultural activity. Even when one text explicitly references another (as in the case of allusions, parodies, spin-offs, and crossovers), these instances become activated only through processes of production or reception. If we watch *The Jeffersons* without knowing that it was spun off from *All in the Family*—as surely many audience members have—then we cannot usefully claim that intertextuality is relevant or active at that moment of reception. Thus, if genre is dependent on *intertextuality*, it cannot be an *inherently textual* component.

[. . .]

Genres are *not* intrinsic to texts; they are constituted by the processes that some scholars have labeled "external" elements, such as industrial and audience practices. But we cannot simply replace an intrinsic textual approach to genre with an extrinsic contextual theory. The dualities between text and context, internal and external, are artificial and arbitrary.[14] We need to look beyond the text as the locus for genre and instead locate genres within the complex interrelations among texts, industries, audiences, and historical contexts.[15] The boundaries between texts and the cultural practices that constitute them (primarily production and reception) are too shifting and fluid to be reified. Texts exist only through their production and reception, so we cannot make the boundary between texts and their material cultural contexts absolute. Genres transect these boundaries, with production, distribution, promotion, and reception practices all working to categorize media texts into genres. Emphasizing the boundaries between elements "internal" and "external" to genres only obscures how genres transect these fluid borders.

[. . .]

Discursive practices and generic clusters

Decentering the text within genre analysis might cause some methodological hesitation. If genres are components of texts, there is a clear site of analysis on which to focus our critical attention. But if genres are not properties of texts, where exactly might we find and analyze them? While there are certainly many theoretical approaches that we might adopt to explain how a category becomes culturally salient, it is more useful to conceive of genres as *discursive practices*. By regarding genres as a property and function of discourse, we are able to examine the ways in which various forms of communication work to constitute generic definitions and meanings.

This discursive approach emerges out of contemporary poststructuralist theories, as genre seems to fit perfectly into the account of discursive formations offered by Michel Foucault.[16] For Foucault, discursive formations are historically specific systems of thought, conceptual categories that work to define cultural experiences within larger systems of power. He notes that discursive formations do not emerge from a centralized structure or from a single site of power but are built bottom up from disparate micro-instances. Even though discursive formations are often marked by discontinuities and irregularities, they follow an overall regularity and fit into a specific cultural context's larger "regime of truth." Discursive formations often appear to be "natural" or internal properties of beings, such as humans or texts, but they are actually culturally constituted and mutable. Like Foucault's notion of the "author function" of discourses, we can approach genre as a function of discourse that is neither intrinsic nor essential to texts.[17] All of these features of discursive formations hold for genres as well, as will be argued below.

To examine generic discourses, we should analyze the contextualized generic practices that circulate around and through texts. We might look at what audiences and industries say about genres, what terms and definitions circulate around any given instance of a genre, and how specific cultural concepts are linked to particular genres. These discursive practices can be broken down into three basic types by how they work to constitute genres: *definition* (for instance, "this show is a sitcom because it has a laugh track"), *interpretation* ("sitcoms reflect and reinforce the status quo"), and *evaluation* ("sitcoms are better entertainment than soap operas").[18] These discursive uterances may seem to reflect on an already established genre, but they are themselves constitutive of that genre; they are the practices that define genres, delimit their meanings, and posit their cultural value. If genres are formed through intertextual relationships between texts, then the discursive enunciations that link texts become the site and material for genre analysis.

This discursive approach offers a new framework by which to examine media texts—instead of examining texts as bounded and stable objects of analysis, texts should be viewed as sites of discursive practice. A discursive approach to genre necessitates that we decenter the text as the primary site of genre but not to the extent that we ignore texts completely; media texts still function as important locales of generic discourses and they must be examined on a par with other sites, such as audience and industrial practices. Television programs explicitly cite generic categories, and advertising, promotions, parodies, and intertextual references within shows are all vital sites of generic discursive practice. In decentering the text from genre analysis, we cannot jettison the text as a site of discursive generic operation; rather, we should simply acknowledge that an isolated text does not define a genre on its own.

Generic discourses are best examined and mapped in their surface enunciations, rather than interpreted and "read into" like media texts. We should not attempt to interpret generic discourses by suggesting what statements "really mean" or express beneath the surface. Instead, we should focus on the breadth of discursive enunciations around any given instance, mapping out as many articulations of genre as possible and situating them within larger cultural contexts and relations of power. For example, to examine the quiz show genre, we should look beyond singular sites such as texts or production practices. Instead, we should gather as many diverse enunciations of the genre from the widest possible range of sources, including corporate documents, press reviews and commentaries, trade journal accounts, parodies, regulatory policies, audience practices, production manuals, other media representations, advertisements, and the texts themselves. Linking together these numerous discourses will begin to suggest more large-scale patterns of generic definitions, meanings, and hierarchies, but we should arrive at these macro-features through an analysis of micro-instances. Although discontinuities and ruptures among definitions, meanings, and values will certainly emerge, generic discourses point toward larger regularities that provide the appearance of stability and coherence in a genre.

Our goal in analyzing generic discourses is not to arrive at the "proper" definition, interpretation, or evaluation of a genre, but to explore the material ways in which genres are culturally defined, interpreted, and evaluated. Shifting our focus away from projects that attempt to provide the ultimate definition or interpretation will enable us to look at the ways in which these definitions, interpretations, and evaluations are part of the larger cultural operations of genre. Instead of guiding questions, such as "What does a given genre mean?" or "How can we define a genre?" we might look at widespread cultural practices of genre interpretation and definition, leading to questions such as "What does a given genre mean for a specific community?" or "How is a genre's definition strategically articulated by socially situated groups?" This approach requires much more specific and detailed research into a genre at a given historical instance, suggesting that sweeping accounts of a genre are probably partial and incomplete. This is not to say that genres do not have largescale diachronic and cross-media histories; larger trends are valid objects of study, but the abstract and generalized mode of media history most common to generic historiography tends to efface specific instances in the name of macro-patterns. We can begin to build a more satisfying macro-account of a genre's history from the bottom up, by collecting micro-instances of generic discourses in historically specific moments and examining the resulting large-scale patterns and trajectories. This bottom-up approach reflects how genres actually form and evolve—out of the specific cultural practices of industries and audiences, not out of macro-structures.

Since genre discourses do not stem solely from a central source—be it industrial or ideological—we need to look at genre history as a fluid and active process, not as a teleological tale of textual rise and fall. Thus, instead of typical questions of definition or interpretation, we should foreground *questions of cultural process* in our attempts to analyze media genres. A number of scholars have proposed the notion of genre as a discursive process, although it has only recently been explored as a more fully realized approach.[19] The key work in this area is Rick Altman's recent book *Film/Genre*. Although Altman provides many compelling and convincing arguments for a process-based approach to genre—points that are congruent with my approach—he finally argues for augmenting his influential textualist semantic/syntactic theory of genre with a consideration of the pragmatic aspects of genre as well. This structuralist textual tradition is not easily compatible with his poststructuralist revision of generic processes and pragmatics. Despite Altman's foregrounding of cultural processes, textual structure still remains central to his approach, making it difficult to provide an account of how genre categories operate outside the bounds of the text.

We should examine the cultural processes of generic discourses before examining the texts that have been traditionally viewed as identical to the genre itself. Specifically, genre theory should account for how generic processes operate within cultural contexts, how industry and audience practices constitute genres, and how genres can be both fluid over time yet fairly coherent at any given moment. We should also examine the specificities of the medium; Altman convincingly argues that the film industry promotes multiple genres around any single movie to maximize audience appeals. Even though we may find similar trends in television, we cannot simply import such an argument into a distinct medium with vitally different industrial imperatives and audience practices. We should carefully adapt the theoretical advances offered within film studies to the particularities of television genres, as well as develop specific insights from the detailed analysis of television genres. This approach synthesizes previous accounts of generic processes so as to offer a model specifically for the study of television genres, while presenting theoretical notions that might be useful in the study of other media as well.

Approaching genres as discursive formations enables us to balance notions of genres as both active processes and stable formations. Although genres are constantly in flux and under definitional negotiation, generic terms are still salient enough that most people would agree on a common working definition for any genre. Even if we cannot provide an essential definition of a genre's core identity, we all still know a sitcom when we see one. Discourse theory offers a model for such stability in flux—genres work as *discursive clusters*, and certain definitions and meanings come together at any given time to suggest a coherent and clear genre. But these clusters are contingent and transitory, shifting over time and taking on new meanings and definitions in different contexts. In addition, these clusters are hollow. They are formed from the outside. Although the gathering and linking of meanings create the appearance of a generic core, this centre is as contingent and fluid as more "fringe" discourses. At any given moment, a genre might appear quite stable, static, and bounded; however that same genre might operate differently in another historical or cultural context. Using this approach to generic clusters, we can see how genres are simultaneously fluid and static, active processes and stable products. Thus, genre historiography should provide a genealogy of discursive shifts and rearticulations to account for a genre's evolution and redefinition, not just a chronology of changing textual examples.

Another central facet to this approach is that the generic discourses within a given cluster are *not* solely media texts. The discourses that constitute a generic cluster are the enunciations and practices that *locate* a text within a genre (including textual discourses as well). In the case of quiz shows, for example, it is not the individual programs that constitute the genre but the production and reception discourses that articulate programs together and situate them within the genre. The texts themselves are certainly brought into the genre and are components of the cluster, but they cannot be seen separately from the ways industries and audiences (broadly conceived) position them within or in relation to the genre. Thus, *Win Ben Stein's Money* should not be examined as a textual example (or a counterexample) of a quiz show but as a site of generic discourse in which competing (and harmonious) voices and practices work to position the text in relation to the genre.

Needless to say, this cultural approach to genre is of a somewhat different order than the traditional methods of genre analysis. The three typical approaches to genres outlined above—definitional, interpretive, and historical—all engage in *textual generic criticism*; they look at genre texts to uncover and identify definitions, meanings, and changes. Other approaches, such as psychological examinations of generic pleasures, also begin with the text in order to analyze the larger operations of the genre.[20] While we might accept all of these methodological options in the name of theoretical pluralism, we must recognize that if we conceive of genres as cultural categories, then most typical approaches do not actually analyze *genres* per se. Rather, they use generic categories to delimit their textual projects but do not engage in the level of categorical analysis that an account of genre necessitates. It is "putting the cart before the horse" to analyze the texts of a given genre in the name of analyzing the genre itself; instead, we must explore the categorical operation of a genre before looking closely at its component texts if we want to understand the genre in cultural practice.[21] Once we chart out how genres are culturally constituted, defined, interpreted, and evaluated, we might look to other methods to analyze common textual forms, psychological pleasures, or structuring principles, but we should first understand how genres operate culturally to utilize the assumed generic terms that delineate such a study.

[. . .]

Conclusion: Five principles of cultural genre analysis.

[. . .] The goal of studying media genres is not to make broad assertions about the genre as a whole but to understand how genres work within specific instances and how they fit into larger systems of cultural power. This new approach can better our understanding of how media are imbricated within their contexts of production and reception and how media work to constitute our vision of the world. In conclusion, five core points need to be highlighted:

Genre analyses should account for the particular attributes of the medium

We cannot simply superimpose genre definitions from film or literature onto television. Certainly, medium distinctions are becoming increasingly blurred with the rise of technologies such as home video and integrated digital media, and we cannot regard "medium" as an absolute fixed category (any more than genre). But film genre processes cannot account for many specific television practices; indeed, television's constant integration of fiction and nonfiction, narrative and nonnarrative, especially confounds the dependence on narrative structure typical of most film genre criticism. Similarly, film has few equivalents to genre-defined channels or genre-delimited scheduling practices. These are commonplace in television, especially today.[22] Audience practices of genre consumption and identification also seem to be different for television, featuring more active practices of fan involvement with ongoing series, especially serials.[23] [. . .]

Genre studies should negotiate between specificity and generality

Obviously, genre is a categorical concept and therefore somewhat transcends specific instances. But traditional genre analysis has tended to avoid detailed specificities in lieu of sweeping generalizations. A more nuanced approach can account for this tension more effectively. There are two general directions from which to approach any genre analysis. One way might start with a genre and analyze one specific element of it. That would mean focusing on a historic turning point (like the quiz show scandals), isolating a core social issue (like representations of minorities on sitcoms), or tracing a genre's origins (like the prehistory of music videos). By narrowing the focus to a specific aspect of a genre's definition, meaning, history, or cultural value, we avoid the problems of overgeneralization that have been typical of more traditional genre studies, as well as acknowledge that genres are too multifaceted and broad to be understood in their totality.

Another way to approach genre analysis would be to start with a specific media case study and analyze how genre processes operate within this specific instance. [. . .] Such projects might isolate a variety of starting points—an industrial formation (like the Cartoon Network), audience practices (like science fiction fan conventions), a textual instance (like genre parody in *The Simpsons*), a policy decision (like educational programming mandates), or a moment in social history (like the coverage of civil rights struggles in news and documentaries). Each of these topics may serve as the nexus point of analysis, but we cannot let them dictate the methodological terrain of the entire study. Just because we start with a textual case to motivate our study, we must still examine how genres transcend textual boundaries and operate within audience and industry practices. [. . .]

Genre histories should be written using discursive genealogies

Genre histories have traditionally chronicled generic texts, often using both definitional and interpretive approaches. To understand genres as cultural categories, we need different methods; generic discourses are not deep repositories of hidden meanings, formal structures, or subtextual insights. Rather, we should follow the model of Foucauldian genealogy, emphasizing breadth over depth and collecting as many discursive instances surrounding a given instance of generic process as we can.[24] [. . .]

Genres should be understood in cultural practice

As noted above, genres are cultural processes that are best examined in specific historical instances. But one important aspect of genre studies builds upon literary critic Tzvetan Todorov's distinction between historical genres—those that are found in cultural practice—and theoretical genres—those that form ideal categories for scholars.[25] Theoretical genres can be useful for positing links among texts and practices that were not previously operative, positing new categories that might later be taken up as more widespread genres (such as *film noir*).[26] [. . .]

Genres should be situated within larger systems of cultural hierarchies and power relations

The goal of most cultural media scholarship is not to understand the media in and of themselves, but rather to look at the workings of media as a component of social contexts and power relations. One of the reasons that genre studies have been generally absent within cultural approaches to the media is that genre has traditionally been conceived as a formal textual element and thus not conducive to the study of mediated politics. Even when scholars do approach genre by foregrounding cultural power relations, such as in the traditions of ideological and structuralist criticism, they tend to analyze genres at a level of abstraction ill suited to understanding the specifics of cultural practice. By looking at genre as a contextual discursive process, we can situate genres within larger regimes of power and better understand their cultural operation. Since genres are systems of categorization and differentiation, linking genre distinctions to other systems of difference can point to the workings of cultural power.

How these links might play out are limitless. Although there is certainly a strong tradition connecting genre analysis and gender differences, for instance, we can broaden this approach to include other axes of identity differentiation as well, such as race, age, sexuality, class, and nationality. We might also look at how genre differences are imbricated within hierarchies of cultural value, both among genres and within one specific genre. Drawing upon the influential studies of cultural distinctions by Pierre Bourdieu, we could map a genre like the talk show onto larger distinctions such as aesthetic value, audience identity, codes of realism, and hierarchies of taste.[27] This analysis would produce a spectrum of generic conventions and assumptions (such as "tabloid" versus "hard" news) that are explicitly tied to greater systems of cultural power and differentiation. This approach to genre distinction avoids the tradition of text-centred analysis, accounting for the ways in which cultural agents articulate genre differentiation as constitutive of genre definitions, meanings, and values. Using this mode of examination, cultural media scholars could turn to genre analysis without abandoning their larger political projects.

Not only does this approach *enable* us to deal with cultural politics, it *requires* that we situate genre within power relations. Just as Foucault asserts that discourses are always processes of power, genres are also constituted by power relations. Genres are not neutral categories but are situated within larger systems of power and thus come "fully loaded" with political implications. This is not to suggest that we limit our genre analyses to cases in which cultural politics are obviously foregrounded. Instead, we should look for the political implications and effects of genre distinctions in seemingly "nonpolitical" case studies as well. If we accept that genres are constituted by cultural discourses, we need to acknowledge that those enunciations are always situated within larger systems of power and that the political can never be effaced from these generic processes. [. . .]

This overall approach to television genre analysis—examining genres as clusters of discursive processes running through texts, audiences, and industries via specific cultural practices—places genre analysis back onto the agenda of critical media studies. The traditional scholarly practices of analyzing generic texts will not—and should not—simply disappear. Much has been gained by all of those prior methodological and theoretical approaches, ranging from more careful formal understanding of horror narratives to critiques of the structures underlying the typical western film. Nonetheless, we need to question the "given" in these approaches—that there is an already established generic category that can serve as the foundation for genre analysis. By first examining genres as cultural categories, unpacking the processes of definition, interpretation, and evaluation that constitute these categories in our everyday experiences with media, we can arrive at a clearer and more comprehensive understanding of how genres work to shape our media experiences, how media work to shape our social realities, and how generic categories can then be used to ground our study of media texts.

Notes

1   This is not true for all approaches to genre. [. . .]
2   Jane Feuer, "Genre Study and Television," in Robert C. Allen, ed., *Channels of Discourse, Reassembled* (Chapel Hill: University of North Carolina Press, 1992), 138–60, 157. [. . .]
3   I trace out the major trends in genre theory and consider some of the more subtle nuances and theoretical implications of this approach and offer a number of case studies to put my theory into practice in Jason Mittel, "Television Genres: From Cop Shows to Cartoons in American Culture" (New York: Routledge, forthcoming).
4   For one of the few definition-based analyses of television genres (in conjunction with film), see Steve Neale and Frank Krutnik, *Popular Film and Television Comedy* (New York: Routledge, 1990); for a paradigmatic example of this approach within film studies, see Noël Carroll, *The Philosophy of Horror or Paradoxes of the Heart* (New York: Routledge, 1990).
5   For a range of typical interpretive accounts of television genres, see John Dennington and John Tulloch, "Cops, Consensus and Ideology." *Screen Education* 20 (1976): 37–46: E. Ann Kaplan, *Rocking around the Clock: Music Television, Postmodernism, and Consumer Culture* (New York: Methuen, 1987); David Mare, *Comic Visions: Television Comedy and American Culture*, 2nd edn (London: Blackwell Press, 1997); Laura Stempel Mumford. *Love and Ideology in the Afternoon: Soap Opera, Women, and Television Genre* (Bloomington: Indiana University Press, 1995); and Horace Newcomb, *TV: The Most Popular Art* (Garden City, N.Y.: Anchor Press, 1974). For more influential film examples, see Will Wright, *Sixguns and Society: A Structural Study of the Western* (Berkeley: University of California Press, 1975); Thomas Schatz, *Hollywood Genres: Formulas, Filmmaking, and the Studio System* (Philadelphia: Temple University Press, 1981); and John G. Cawelti, *The Six-Gun Mystique*, 2nd edn (Bowling Green, Ohio: Bowling Green State University Popular Press, 1984).
6   Note that some of these critical schools do not examine texts solely for meanings. [. . .]
7   A paradigmatic historical genre analysis is Feuer's account of the sitcom. A more satisfying and complex historical account of a film genre is Rick Altman, *The American Film Musical* (Bloomington: Indiana University Press, 1987), although Altman refutes a number of his positions in his more recent work in genre theory, Rick Altman, *Film/Genre* (London: British Film Institute, 1999).
8   Literary scholar E. D. Hirsch offers a theory of one correct "intrinsic genre" corresponding to the author's intended meaning: E. D. Hirsch, Jr. *Validity in Interpretation* (New Haven: Yale University Press, 1967).
9   For one typical example, see Graeme Turner, *Film as Social Practice*, 2nd edn (New York: Routledge, 1993), 85–93. [. . .]
10 Feuer specifically divides her analysis between media developments that are "internal to the genre"— namely textual form and content—and those that are external, such as cultural and industrial changes. While this division may seem useful, this false internal/external binary leads us away from how genres operate within cultural contexts. [. . .]
11 This mode of analysis is typical of nearly all the approaches to genre described above.
12 Altman suggests that traditionally genres have been viewed as equal to the corpus that they seem to identify and that this corpus is defined by a common structure and topic. [. . .]
13 See Steve Neale, "Questions of Genre," in Barry Keith Grant, ed., *Film Genre Reader II* (Austin: University of Texas Press, 1995), 159–83, for his discussion of *The Great Train Robbery's* reclassification from crime film into western, drawing on Charles Musser's research. [. . .]
14 For a provocative debate on the boundaries of the text, see John Fiske's "Moments of Television: Neither the Text Nor the Audience," in Ellen Seiter *et al.*, eds, *Remote Control: Television, Audiences, and Cultural Power* (New York: Routledge, 1989), 56–78, and Charlotte Brunsdon's "Text and Audience," also in Seiter *et al.*, *Remote Control*, 116–29.
15 This approach to media studies—examining the integrated relationships among industry, audience, text,

and context—is drawn from Julie D'Acci, *Defining Women: Television and the Case of "Cagney & Lacey"* (Chapel Hill: University of North Carolina Press, 1994); see also Stuart Hall, "Encoding, Decoding," in Simon During, ed., *The Cultural Studies Reader* (New York: Routledge, 1993), 90–103, and Richard Johnson, "What Is Cultural Studies Anyway?" *Social Text* 16 (1987): 38–80.

16   For his most central accounts of discourse, see Michel Foucault, *The Order of Things: An Archeology of the Human Sciences* (New York: Vintage Books, 1970); Michel Foucault, *The Archeology of Knowledge and the Discourse on Language*, trans. A. M. Sheridan Smith (New York: Pantheon Books, 1972); Michel Foucault, *The History of Sexuality: An Introduction*, vol. 1, trans. Robert Hurley (New York: Vintage Books, 1978); and Michel Foucault, *Power/Knowledge: Selected Interviews and Other Writings, 1972–1977*, ed. Colin Gordon (New York: Pantheon Books, 1980).

17   James Naremore, *More than Night. Film Noir in Its Contexts* (Berkeley: University of California Press, 1998) offers a similar link between Foucauldian theory and media genres in theorizing his "history of the idea" of *film noir*.

18   There are obvious (if misleading) links among the three modes of discursive practice for genres (definition, interpretation, and evaluation) and the three models of genre theory proffered at the beginning of this essay (definition, interpretation, and history). I do not mean to equate these trios. [. . .]

19   See Neale, "Questions of Genre"; Robert C. Allen, "Bursting Bubbles: 'Soap Opera,' Audience, and the Limits of Genre," in Seiter *et al.*, *Remote Control*, 44–55; Tony Bennett, *Outside Literature* (New York: Routledge, 1990); and Ralph Cohen, "History and Genre," *New Literary History* 17, no. 2 (1986): 203–18.

20   Psychological approaches primarily refer to either psychoanalytic or cognitive accounts of the pleasure derived from genres. For examples of psychoanalytic approaches, see Robin Wood, "Return of the Repressed," in Barry K. Grant, ed., *Planks of Reason: Essays on the Horror Film* (Metuchen, N.J.: Scarecrow Press, 1984), 164–200; Margaret Tarratt, "Monsters from the Id," in Grant, *Film Genre Reader II*, 330–49; and Kaplan, *Rocking around the Clock*. For examples of cognitive approaches to genre, see Carroll, *The Philosophy of Horror*, esp. chap. 4; Torben Grodal, *Moving Pictures: A New Theory of Film Genres, Feelings, and Cognition* (Oxford: Oxford University Press, 1997); and Noël Carroll, "Film, Emotion, and Genre," in Carl Plantinga and Greg M. Smith, eds, *Passionate Views: Film, Cognition, and Emotion* (Baltimore: Johns Hopkins University Press, 1999), 21–47.

21   This argument (and most appropriate cliché) is made most clearly in Tudor, "Genre," 10.

22   Similar film practices include differentiating movie bills in the 1930s and 1940s into separate newsreel, animation, "A" feature, and "B" feature slots, genre-defined theaters (such as art houses or porn theaters), and generically delimited film festivals or screenings. Yet film genre analysis mostly ignores these issues. Any attempt to draw parallels between these practices and television scheduling and channel delineation would need to be rethought significantly.

23   Exceptions include film series, such as *Star Wars*, but certainly television serials are far more common.

24   Note that in arguing for "breadth" over "depth," I am not calling for studying a genre broadly. Rather, the breadth must encompass the widest range of discourses and sites of genre operation as possible, all focused on a specific historical instance framing the genre study.

25   Tzvetan Todorov, *The Fantastic: A Structural Approach to a Literary Genre*, trans. Richard Howard (Ithaca: Cornell University Press, 1975), 13–14.

26   Theoretical genre creation has been less common in television studies than in cinema studies.

27   See Pierre Bourdieu, *Distinction: A Social Critique of the Judgement of Taste*, trans. Richard Nice (Cambridge: Harvard University Press, 1984), and *The Field of Cultural Production: Essays on Art and Literature*, trans. Randal Johnson (New York: Columbia University Press, 1993). I map out the talk-show genre onto other cultural hierarchies in Mittel, *Television Genres*.

Bibliography

Allen, R.C. (1989) 'Bursting bubbles: "Soap Opera," Audiences and the Limits of Genre', in E. Seiter, *et al.* (eds) *Remote Control: Television, Audiences and Cultural Power*, New York: Routledge.
Altman, R. (1987) *The American Film Musical*, Bloomington: Indiana University Press.
—— (1999) *Film/Genre*, London: British Film Institute.
Anderson, C. (1994) *Michael Jackson Unauthorized*, New York: Simon & Schuster.
Bennett, T. (1990) *Outside Literature*, New York: Routledge.
Bourdieu, P. (1984) *Distinction: a Social Critique of Taste*, R. Nice (trans.), Cambridge: Cambridge University Press.

—— (1993) *The Field of Cultural Production: Essays on Art and Literature*, R. Johnson (trans.), New York: Columbia University Press.

Brunsdon, C. (1989) "Text and Audience," in E. Seiter *et al.* (eds) *Remote Control: Television, Audiences and Cultural Power*, New York: Routledge.

Carroll, N. (1990) *The Philosophy of Horror or Paradoxes of the Heart*, New York: Routledge.

—— (1999) "Film, Emotion and Genre," in C. Plantinga and G.M. Smith (eds) *Passionate Views: Film, Cognition and Emotion*, Baltimore: John Hopkins University Press.

Cohen, R. (1986) "History and Genre," *New Literary History* 17 (2): 203–18.

D'Acci, J. (1994) *Defining Women: Television and the Case of Cagney & Lacey*, Chapel Hill: University of North Carolina Press.

Dennington, J. and Tulloch, J. (1976) "Cops, Consensus and Ideology," *Screen Education* 20: 37–46.

Feuer, J. (1992) "Genre Study and Television," in R.C. Allen (ed.) *Channels of Discourse, Reassembled*, Chapel Hill: University of North Carolina Press.

Fishelov, D. (1993) *Metaphors of Genre. The Role of Analogies in Genre Theory*, University Park: Pennsylvania State University Press.

Fiske, J. (1989) "Moments of Television: Neither the Text Nor the Audience," in E. Seiter *et al.* (eds) *Remote Control: Television, Audiences and Cultural Power*, New York: Routledge.

Foucault, M. (1970) *The Order of Things: An Archaeology of the Human Sciences*, New York: Vintage Books.

—— (1972) *The Archaeology of Knowledge and the Discourse of Language*, A.M. Sheridan Smith (trans.), New York: Pantheon Books.

—— (1978) *The History of Sexuality: An Introduction (Vol I)*, R. Hurley (trans.), New York: Vintage Books.

Gold, R. (1982) "Labels Limit Videos on Black Artists," *Variety* 15 December 73+

Grodel, T. (1997) *Moving pictures: A New Theory of Film Genres, feelings, and Cognition*, Oxford: Oxford University Press.

Hall, S. (1993) "Encoding, Decoding," in S. During (ed.) *The Cultural Studies Reader*, New York: Routledge.

Hirsch, E.D. (1967) *Validity in Interpretation*, New Haven: Yale University Press.

Johnson, R. (1987) "What is Cultural Studies Anyway?," *Social Text* 16:38–80.

Kaplan, E.A. (1987) *Rocking Around the Clock: Music Television, Postmodernism, and Consumer Culture*, New York: Methuen.

Marc, D. (1997) *Comic Vision: Television Comedy and American Culture*, 2nd edn, London: Blackwell Press.

Mittel, Jason (Forthcoming) *Television Genres: From Cop Shows to Cartoons in American Culture*, New York: Routledge.

Naremore, J. (1998) *More Than Night: Film Noir in its Contexts*, Berkeley: University of California Press.

Neale, S. (1995) "Questions of Genre," in B.K. Grant (ed.) *Film Genre Reader II*, Austin: University of Texas Press.

Neale, S. and Krutnik, F. (1990) *Popular Film and Television Comedy*, New York: Routledge.

Newcomb, H. (1974) *TV: The Most Popular Art*, Garden City NY: Anchor Press.

Schatz, T. (1981), *Hollywood Genres: Formulas, Filmmaking, and the Studio System*, Philadelphia: Temple University Press.

Stempel Mumford, L. (1995) *Love and Ideology in the Afternoon: Soap Opera, Women and Television Genre*, Bloomington: Indiana University Press.

Taraborelli, R. (1991) *Michael Jackson: The Magic and the Madness*, New York: Birch Lane Press.

Tarratt, M. (1995) "Monsters From the Id," in B.K. Grant (ed.) *Film Genre Reader II*, Austin: University of Texas Press.

Todorov, T. (1975) *The Fantastic: A Structural Approach to a Literary Genre*, R. Howard (trans.), Ithaca: Cornell University Press.

Tudor, A. (1995) 'Genre', in B.K. Grant (edn) *Film Genre Reader II*, Austin: University of Texas Press.

Turner, G. (1993) *Film As Social Practice*, 2nd ed., New York: Routledge.

Vande Berg, L., Wenner, L.A. and Gronbeck, B.E. (1998) *Critical Approaches to Television*, Boston: Houghton Mifflin.

Wood, R. (1984) "Return of the Repressed," in B.K. Grant (ed.) *Planks of Reason: Essays on the Horror Film*, Metuchen NJ: Scarecrow Press.

Wright, W. (1975) *Sixguns and Society: A Structural Study of the Western*, Berkeley: University of California Press.

Chapter 11

JÉRÔME BOURDON

LIVE TELEVISION IS STILL ALIVE
On television as an unfulfilled promise

TO BEGIN WITH, let us pose the thesis that this article will uphold throughout: television remains deeply influenced by the possibility of live broadcasting, this despite the fact that, from a historical point of view, the golden age of live broadcasting (the 1950s in the USA and Western Europe) has long been over. If we can talk of a 'language' of television, or, more modestly, of a semantic specificity of the medium, it lies in this possibility, not always accomplished, but at least virtually present in many programmes or sequences of television. This claim is both semiotic and sociological: we will try to understand why a technical possibility, translated into specific codes, remains a fundamental part of viewers' expectations.

In television theories, the current academic trend is to reduce the importance of live broadcasting (Corner, 1997), arguing that the evolution towards 'narrowcasting' and 'fragmented broadcasting' calls for the end of global analyses of television. I propose, however, that it is still relevant to talk about 'television' as a unified medium. Granted, most of the examples of programmes in the following article are taken from general audience and national channels in various national contexts, be they public or private. However, despite the already dated prophecies on the advent of 'narrowcasting' or 'fragmented television', let us note that general audience channels still draw most of the audiences worldwide. I will, in addition, make the claim that much of what happens on cable and satellite channels is still related to 'liveness', as many themed channels emphasize their ability to broadcast live alongside general audience channels which continue doing so.

Let us remind the reader of how the word 'live' (or its translation in French 'direct', Italian 'diretta', German 'direkt') has been used, and is still being used (or alluded to) in programme titles. This is a very widespread feature of television, both old and modern, which can be confirmed by different national histories (e.g. Baget Herms, 1993; Bourdon, 1990; Briggs, 1979; Grasso, 1992). In the USA, from *Saturday Night Live* and *Primetime Live*, the word 'live' has never disappeared from the names of talk or variety shows. In France, *En direct de* (live from) was the name for a series of programmes in the 1950s – 'from' actually referred to a variety of hard-to-reach or strange locations (from an aircraft carrier, from a sink hole, etc.). Here, television wanted to exhibit its technical capacities. In the 1980s, on the second French channel, star-host and anchorwoman Christine Ockrent fronted a show simply called *Direct*. In Israel, where the talk show is a major primetime genre, the word 'live' proliferates. For three years, the second (and leading) channel has been broadcasting, three times a week a programme called *Live with Dan Shilon Interviewing*. Finally, much of what has been called in the 1980s 'reality programming' in the United States, 'television verità' in Italy, and 'reality-shows' in France actually consists of live programming: most shows conforming to this so-called 'new' genre use the live spectacle of ordinary viewers telling us about their pains and problems, with the help of the ever-present host (*Eurodience* 1990).

Beyond the historical fact that live broadcasting has declined between the 1950s and the 1960s (simply because game-shows, not to mention drama, moved from live broadcasting to film or tape), the use of live broadcasting as an explicit and important resource has not disappeared from television. Television reminds us that it links us live to something to a specific place ('live from'), to a specific person ('live with'). A fully fledged history of live broadcasting would probably discover other interesting examples of the use of live broadcasting, beyond the permanence of the rhetoric of live broadcasting. A good example is Vianello's (1986) analysis of live television in the context of the 'power politics' of the networks in the American television system. However, my point here is that this history presents a fundamental, socio-semiotic unity.

'Liveness' in television theories

Many theories of television have – and continue to be – centred on 'liveness', first, as part of a professional ideology. In its early days, when professionals started debating the specificity of television (notably in comparison with the cinema), they related it to three characteristics, namely screen size, domestic reception and, finally and most notably, 'liveness'. This last characterization of television has evoked lyrical texts. Live broadcasting has been exalted as a way to conquer time and distance, to have vast groups of people commune in a new experience. Historical research (see, for the United States, Vianello, 1986) reminds us of the place of liveness in professional ideologies, most clearly among television engineers and technicians but also among critics. At a talk presented by the French director of programmes in 1955, television was presented, as was typical of the time, as 'the possibility at last given to mankind to defeat, through the image, the limitations of time and space' (Bourdon, 1986: 49).

Even though 'liveness' was a professional theory, with a strong emphasis on ideological notions such as 'authenticity' and 'truth', it was adapted by academic theory in various countries. Books and treatises about the aesthetics of live television were written during the 1950s and the 1960s. However, these theories seem to have become unfashionable. Most recently, a vigorous attack against theories of live broadcasting as central to television has been launched by J.T. Caldwell (1995). Studying American television, he diagnoses a mutation which he calls 'televisuality': under the effects of competition, of the economic crisis which it has caused, mass television (the major networks) has started stressing its stylistic performances, the quality of its authors and 'signatures' and its ability to process pictures through digital packaging. This televisual regime, which he terms 'exhibitionist', also corresponds to a technical and industrial mutation. In this context, live television is seen as quite secondary, and the ideology is rather one of television as an opaque medium.

Despite the quality of his argument, Caldwell omits two major points. First, stylistic exhibitionism has not erased genres which systematically use live broadcasting as a resource. These genres stress 'liveness' through a quite traditional series of indices, such as the direct address to the viewer, and editing as a sign of continuity of the action. These indices will be reviewed in detail later in this article. Second, refined stylistic treatment is more a major mutation of television than a strategy of American networks at a given point of their history and in given genres. World television, both national and local stations, still resorts massively to live broadcasting in traditional genres.

Furthermore, emphasizing the capacity to broadcast live can operate together with stylistic refinement, as we have seen during the Barcelona Olympics: the most refined digital effects are not incompatible with the fact that this image, however reprocessed and manipulated, is a 'live' image. And this is reinforced by the capacity of the image, at any time, to stop being processed (slow motion, divided screen) and to fill the whole screen. I suggest that these manipulations show the intervention of the televisual enunciator (that is, the channel and its various delegates, hosts and commentators) in the live event, rather than the disappearance of the live event itself into the televisual representation. Furthermore, all this processing does not affect (or very rarely does so), the acoustic data so fundamental in television yet perennially forgotten by theorists and professionals alike: the voice. Television is always an audiovision (Chion, 1994).

[. . .]

Four types of television: fully live, continuity, edited, fiction

At this point, let us propose a division of television texts not so much into genres, in the traditional sense, as in terms of types, where live television is more or less achieved. Two qualifications: these types do not necessarily correspond to complete programmes; they might concern sequences within programmes. And again: live really is not only about the technical performance, but also about the spectatorial belief – these, as we have seen, do not completely overlap.

This distinction, incidentally, is present in the technical vocabulary of many television stations. French television once classified its programmes as 'vrai direct' (truly live), versus 'direct différé' (recorded-live television), or 'faux direct' (falsely live). At the level of spectatorial beliefs, we will oppose 'fully live', where the spectator has the full sense of experiencing a life event, and 'continuity television', where the spectator only partly has this feeling. Our third type is 'edited television'. All television is edited (directors of live programmes actually talk of 'live editing' – 'montage en direct'). However, in this article, I will use the expression only for programmes that are edited after shooting (in the editing room) and are not fictional, which have been shot 'in real life'. Our fourth type is fiction, played by actors, and edited – as far from live broadcasting as one can think, since it presupposes a high degree of previous elaboration. Some fictional genres actually retain proximity with liveness, but more on that later. Of course, live television is also elaborated, and we are aware of that. But that elaboration is supposed to serve an ongoing event, to give us a chance to see not so much the work of television as such but the workings of the world (albeit the television studio) in its most interesting aspects.

Fully live versus continuity

Fully live television is best exemplified by major media events when television cannot possibly not be live: these major media events have been theorized by Dayan and Katz (1992) who have described them as 'windows' or 'holes' in the usual routine programming. At these moments, television seems to be completely at the service of the event, even if it might have contributed to its organization. In such cases, the paratext (Genette, 1997) also works at full capacity. It is not only from the screen where the Pope is walking (Poland, 1979), where Sadat arrives in Jerusalem (Israel, 1977) that you can be sure the event is a live event. It is also because, weeks before, you have been told the event is about to occur. The world around you can be visibly affected by the passion surrounding the event. The city is deserted, everybody is watching, you have been told by the radio not to drive around the airport or the stadium where the event is taking place.

In our daily life as viewers, we experience less the regime of 'fully live' than that of 'continuity'. We are in a televised world where a lot looks (and sounds) live but is not necessarily so. We infer liveness from the text and also from assumptions about specific genres (news is more likely to be live than variety shows, major weekly prime-time variety shows are more likely to be live than daily daytime game shows). Of course, the word 'live' might be chromakeyed on the screen (as during the news, in many cases, or in the titles of programmes). However, some programmes are live without claiming their liveness in such a way. Moreover, if television claims to be live, it never claims not to be live (or on very specific occasions, as will be analysed later). Thus, a rich, ambiguous land is created for the viewers' inferential work.

Suppose, however, the viewer has just subscribed to cable and turns on their set to discover a new channel. Is it live? The answer might come from textual indices: a host looks at us straight in the eyes, in the flat lighting of the video, and starts stammering, then apologizes. We tend to think routinely, that we are seeing a live programme. Our knowledge of programming might also help. If you turn on your television at 8 pm in France, at 9 pm in Spain, this is the hour of the newscast. If you turn on your set at 10 pm in the same countries (too late for the main news, too early for the late night news), you are left with two alternatives: a newsflash, which indicates a major event has occurred, or a documentary or a report on the news, which uses live television as archive footage. If this latter inference is the right one, then the familiar face of the host will soon be replaced by another familiar face, or covered by a voice-over, which will tell you how to interpret these images.

Sequence-guarantors of live continuity: the direct address (the look to the camera)

Using the example of news, I have been driven to treat 'live broadcasting' and the 'look to the camera' of the newscaster as nearly equivalent. Before referring to programmes as whole, we should try to consider the basic segments, or sequences of television, inasmuch as they help us to identify one of our four types: liveness, continuity, editing, fiction. Let us talk, following many authors, of the 'direct address', to define the sequence where a person looks straight at the camera (as if at the viewers) and addresses the viewers, using the appropriate deixis [proof of 'liveness']. The most evident part of this deixis is of course the personal pronouns 'I' (the host) and 'you' (the viewers at home). One should add that the word 'live' might be used here ('we are coming to you live'), and interpreted as a specifically televisual deictic: it refers not only to the moment when the speaker is talking (even if the sequence was recorded), but to that moment inasmuch as it is the same moment for the speaker and for the addresses (the viewers at home). 'I am talking to you live' is the televisual version of 'I am talking to you now'.

Even though Umberto Eco has written that it is one of the characteristics of the 'neo-television' of the 1980s, which he claims stresses contact with the viewers (Eco, 1990), the 'direct address' has been important from the first days of television. We should carefully distinguish two phenomena: the systematic exploitation of television stardom (which characterized competitive commercial television systems), and the presence of a group of familiar mediators, of television figures, which is a common feature of television. From the early experiences of live television, programmers have 'naturally' resorted to television mediators, who looked and talked at the camera.

Where do we find the 'direct address', the look to the camera of the 'I and you together'? In a very systematic manner, in the opening and closing sequences of continuity television programmes, when the host greets us, enumerates the list of his guests, and gives us an appointment for next week (or for many weeks to come). There are variations according to genres, but the basic pattern is present in newscasts (be it reduced to a simple 'good day' and 'good bye'), in talk shows, in game shows, in variety shows, or in political debates.

The look to the camera is present in another type of sequence, one which I call 'addressed actuality'. The mediator still addresses us, but tells a story in the third person, of what has happened. He uses deictics like 'yesterday' and 'today', but the viewers are no longer referred to in the discourse. There is still some sense of live television, but less than in the direct address. In another case, the mediator looks at us, but eliminates references to the deixis of the present. He tells us a story of the past. This sequence I call the 'addressed history'. The story might be told in the present tense, but the tense is used always with the value of a preterite: it describes the succession of events in the past, without any relation to the time when the story is told. Such was the regime of shows where a narrator (usually a famous mediator) would tell stories of the past (James Mason in English, Alain Decaux in French). This type of show seems no longer to be popular on television. Was it a live programme? Again, at the textual level, there are some indications to the contrary. Verbally, we are detached from the time of the actual telling of the story. Visually, there might be some carefully edited sequences to illustrate the narrator's story. At the level of production, in the case of the French programme, we know that it was initially broadcast live, then later moved to tape.

Continuity television: the part of the voice

As we can see, our television types are not necessarily related to entire shows. In effect, the types of television are realized more or less in specific sequences of unequal duration. We want to try to break the flow of television into constitutive sequences (bearing in mind we cannot completely escape the notion of flow, to which we will return later). Of course, these sequences are related to one another by specific traits, which we might call 'suprasequential' (to paraphrase the 'supra-segmental' used in linguistics). As the reader might have noticed, we consider the voice and its relation to images as a key criterion for classifying basic sequences of television. The voice, and sound in general, are continuously neglected in many analyses of television and film, with notable exceptions (Scannell, 1991; Chion, 1994). Chion, one of the most interesting analysts of sound in film, goes as far as to claim that television is nothing but 'illustrated radio'. This is extreme. I will follow him when he affirms that television, although a visual medium, is a 'vococentric' medium, a medium where the voice orients the viewers decisively in certain directions of interpretation. The voice governs television. But then, there are different kinds of voice.

Again, we have to distinguish between technology and belief. We analyse television from an ideal viewer's point of view. Let us consider three situations. First, the viewer perceives the voice as 'voice-over'. It has been added to the film at the time of editing. The voice is slow, which often creates the effect of a text being read. In that case, I will speak, after Michel Chion (1994), of 'acousmatic voice'. The acousmatic voice, which has no physical identity, can be opposed to the voices which belong to the films, which are all visualized, or, at least, visualizable. They do not generate the effect of a text read, of a prepared story, but of more spontaneous (or less formal) interventions. As opposed to the acousmatic voice, visual and visualizable voices belong together. One can always switch from a visualizable voice to a visualized voice, and conversely (a journalist commenting on his film is now on camera and addresses us). But the acousmatic voice has to remain off screen, at least for the duration of the documentary concerned.

I have tried to avoid using technical terms (like voice-over, voice-off camera), because my point of view is not technical. Let us come back to the example of synchronized play-back. When the singer was singing his song 'live', for most viewers it was a visual voice. Some knew it was sound over simulated synchronization (we might call it 'pseudo-visualized voice'). Another case: in a documentary, relevant sounds are added to pictures of a crowd. Again, we can speak of 'pseudo-visualized sounds': in most cases, the viewers will actually perceive such sounds as recorded at the time the film was shot, as belonging to the pro-filmic, to the 'world-being-televised'. While, in the case of acousmatic sounds, the sound's source belongs to the television institution, operating 'from above' on the world-being-televised.

Let us return to continuity television. As far as sound is concerned, continuity television precludes acousmatism: all sounds are either visualized or visualizable. In the studios of game shows, variety shows and talk shows, this is obviously the case of the voices of guests and mediators – journalists and hosts – belonging to the institution. However, some people might be very far from the set, while their voices will still be visualizable. In some shows, people are requested to phone from home. Their vocies are visualizable (even though sometimes the screen, as a technological synecdoche for the individual speaking, presents a close-up of the phone), even though we might never see them. We know who they are, they have a social identity. They are people interacting in front of us, in the world-being-televised. A more subtle case is the one of sound-only news reports. The newscaster tells us we are about to hear a report by a certain correspondent; then we hear the correspondent's voice, usually with a photograph of her/his face, over the background of a map of the country where the events reported are taking place, and from where the correspondent is calling (or has called?). Sometimes the voice is recorded, sometimes it is live (and the word 'live' might be chromakeyed). If it is recorded, the newscaster is actually listening 'with us' to a tape, not to a human being. My contention here is that, phenomenologically, the whole apparatus of television is working to create the illusion of a voice that is both visualized and live.

The case of music is partly similar. Music is an interesting case. Music, as Nattiez (1975) has written, has something fictional to it. Temporally oriented, charged with emotion, it is accepted (even as acousmatic music) by viewers of fiction. In continuity television, there is very little music. The bulk is visualized music in variety shows, or in some talk shows. There is very little music which is not visualized, and only visualizable. A good example is provided by the game show 'Countdown' (originally a French format called 'Des Chiffres et des Lettres'). When the candidates are searching for the solution of the problem, there is a light, musak-type background music. This is visualized music in the sense that it is played in the studio, live to the candidates and to us together. It is unobstrusive, for the same reason that there is very little non-visualized music in continuity television. Music would take on a life of its own, be perceived as acousmatic, and definitely ruin the impression/illusion of liveness.

Continuity programmes cannot easily be divided into sequences on the basis of the work done by the apparatus of television, precisely because it aims at transparency. Editing, in particular, is supposed to be fluid, and switches between cameras should not create the impression of abrupt, unexplained switches between places and periods, as in a documentary or a fiction film. The voice, again, and, more precisely, the verbal, is the main criterion to analyse the flow of continuity television. Continuity television should be analysed with tools derived from conversational analysis, as initiated by Sacks et al. (1974). Television talk has its own rules of turntaking. The analysis should start with a major distinction, between routing turns (questions, requests, evaluations) and routed turns. The first belong, most of the time, to mediators: they have the privilege of routing and of addressing the viewers. Routed turns belong to guests, who are requested to respond to routing in an appropriate manner. A mediator talking can move from different types of turns, starting with a direct address to a viewer, and moving to a series of routing turns.

The voice in fully live or continuity television is visualizable, even if we do not see the speaker for a long period of time. The best example is the voice of the sports commentator, in the sequence we will call 'involved commentary'. This sequence has specific phonetic features, besides its specific vocabulary. On radio, even in a language you do not know, you might identify the commentary of live sports, by its rhythm and prosody. If you know the language, the use of tenses, the variety of the deixis (personal pronouns, adverbs of time and place) are striking. Of course, the voice of a live commentary can be recorded and broadcast later with the pictures to create the illusion of live television. This is especially the case for sports events which take place with a time lag. In France, some events of the Atlanta Olympics were broadcast in such a way, even though viewers were told before the broadcast that the events were not actually live. Less honestly, the French first channel TF1 broadcast a football match a few hours after the event, with the live commentary recorded, trying to beat the channel which had exclusive live broadcasting rights by acting as if nothing had happened. Another kind of involved commentary, less passionate than sports, can be heard during any sort of live event, from a major media event to more ritual live events, like the annual Bastille Day parade in France.

Be it for media events or for sports events, viewers can hear a voice without actually seeing the face of the speaker for long stretches of time. Why then claim that such a voice is visualizable? The commentator has a name, which is given in the credits, he has a face in many other programmes, especially in sports magazines, or in the coverage of television by the press. Most viewers know this face and can actually visualize a familiar personality when they hear the commentary. During the match or the event itself, it is not unusual to see, during the intermission, commentators with their headphones on their heads. This is not only a question of identifying the mediators. For the institution, the sequence where we see the commentators of the event is a way of guaranteeing the spectator that the commentators are actually commentating on the event, that they are part of the event, and not, like us, in front of their screen. No matter what the quality of the commentary, the commentator has to be a live witness. When, as for the Barcelona Olympics, it was reported that some journalists had been commenting from their hotel rooms, this was perceived as a professional failure and a breach of confidence.

Edited (and non-fictional) television: documentaries and news reports

In this article I have opposed continuity television to edited television: that is, to the programmes in which the after-the-event editing (not live editing) can be perceived and is perceived by all viewers. The editing is perceived at several levels. Visually, the shots connect unrelated times. Acousmatic music is also typical of edited television (fiction and non-fiction alike). Acousmatic voice, however, is a very specific case: it is the privilege of edited, non-fictional television. Edited non-fictional television is only represented by a small number of genres: documentaries, news reports, credits, advertising, music videos, propaganda (especially, in democracies. election programmes). Let us start with documentaries and news reports. They share many features, except for their relations with news and their length (the news report is brief, and has become shorter since its birth, while the documentary can be long). Furthermore, the documentary offers a good example of the evolution towards what is sometimes called 'thematic television', i.e. genres as channels.

News reports, but also documentaries (despite their ancestry in the cinema newsreels and cinema documentaries) are affected by their being television genres. A news report is, as Vianello (1986) has observed, something of a paradox: it is central to a genre which puts high value on being broadcast live, the news. Yet, most news reports are made of edited visual material – they are, at least visually, not live. The case of the voice in news reports is complex. The reporter's commentary is mostly live, but sometimes recorded. Sometimes, a short report is delivered live by the anchor (this practice has become extremely frequent in the short news flashes of non-stop news channels). Within the news report, American television was the first to introduce 'the stake out': the reporter addresses his commentary to the camera, from the place of the 'action', opposite the Presidential Palace or the Court where the trial is taking place (Hartley, 1982). The voice is visualized. The 'stake out', following the professional term, actually is the sequence I have already called addressed actuality. There is a question of who the reporter is talking to: the gaze is somewhat ambiguous, while the verbal indications (especially the use of the name of the anchor to signal the end of the 'stake out') seems to indicate he is talking to the anchor. Finally, we have the case, which we have already discussed, where news reports are often reduced to a voice added to the photograph of the correspondent.

With news programmes in general, especially before American professional practices started being imported, the 'voice-on news' has long been dominant. Let us refer to 'voice-on news' as the story delivered by a reporter off camera. The voice is visualizable: the name of the reporter is given in the credits, and many viewers have actually seen him on the screen. The story is edited, therefore the images are not live, but the voice can be live (it always was in the early days of the newscast). In short, a report within the news borrows some of the conventions of liveness, even though most of the time at least part of it is not live.

More surprisingly, the documentary, a genre born as an elaborated discourse on the world, not linked to news (Jacobs, 1971), has been submitted to the pressure of liveness when becoming a television genre, as has already been noted. Corner (1996: 2) writes that the documentary, having started as a 'cinematic essay', now mostly has the form of an 'expanded reportage'. The most obvious sign of this is the frequent occurrence of direct address. Many television documentaries, especially documentary series, include a mediator who addresses the viewers at regular intervals. Of course, these 'direct addresses' are usually not recorded in the studio. They might be shot 'on location' in places connected to the theme of the documentary. The viewer probably never assumes them to be live. And yet, the 'here and now' of the mediator's living gaze is here, an indelible indicator of 'presentness'.

The direct address is also quite frequently used before the documentary. A personality, usually a celebrity of some kind, is there to 'launch' it (as if it did not have enough energy of its own). In 1998, the long and very successful (and controversial) documentary series *Tkouma*, produced by Israeli television on the occasion of the country's fiftieth anniversary, was launched in such a way by famous public personalities. Again, the documentary might be about the past, but the 'launching sequences' show us a mediator using the present tense for proposing that we see something, tonight (to sit with him in the studio, maybe, and to watch together – therefore perhaps transforming all living rooms into one huge communal television studio).

Documentary, like news reports, can be easily divided into specific sequences. In documentaries, apart from the 'direct address', we find basically three different types of sequences: 'scenes', 'interview excerpts' and 'acousmatic commentaries' (or documentary voice-overs). Formally speaking, a scene is identical to a sequence from a fiction film: the characters 'play their own role', do not seem to pay attention to the camera (or, more exactly, studiedly do not pay attention to it). In television documentaries, scenes are rare, most likely because of their fundamental ambiguity. If we turn on our television set and discover a scene, it might take a little time for us to decide if we are dealing with fiction or with non-fiction. This ambiguity usually is quickly resolved. First, the style of shooting suggests either a documentary or a certain type of fiction that borrows from the conventions of documentary and news reports. Second, we quickly realize we have no major character, no plot, but only bits of 'real life'. Here is a major difference from the documentary tradition of the cinema: scenes are central, and were from the very start (what is *Nanook of the North* 'Robert Flaherty, 1922' but a succession of scenes?). Major documentary directors (Frederick Wiseman, Raymond Depardon) are famous precisely for using mostly or only 'scenes' of real life.

The same documentary directors exclude what is the staple of television documentaries: the interview excerpts and the acousmatic commentaries. The interview excerpts (with or without the interviewer's questions) are somewhat similar to the 'interventions' of continuity television.

However, they belong to a different temporality. The editing suggests someone engaged in recollecting a variety of encounters and presenting them to us. The interviewer might very well be, when there is just one, the documentary 'anchor', the one in charge of the direct address (even though he does not always do all the interviews). Interview excerpts (from documentaries but also from news reports) can be divided according to the category of interviewee, elite and vox pop following a division I have suggested (1982) independently from, but similarly to Hartley (1982). Elite interviews are named and might have a chance to have their voices turned into a voice-over, illustrated by some images (especially in documentary and current affairs programmes, where there is more time for the editing than in news reports). Vox pops, anonymous interviewees, are not named, are sometimes presented as groups (a series of brief interviews with similar questions, or group interviewing) and have much less chance to enjoy the political privilege of having their voices turned into voice-overs.

The most typical sequence of some documentaries, absent from news reports, is the acousmatic commentary. It is specific because the voice is a visual. The voice is less involved in talking to us than in 'speaking a text', with a grammar which is not that of spoken, improvised language. The credits might actually state: commentary read or given by, in cases where a famous actor has hired out his voice. That slow and static voice has some pretelevisual ancestors, between teaching and preaching. We could compare it to the voice of an invisible priest at the back of a temple. It is a voice of authority, which dominates the picture, in the name of a carefully prepared and recorded text. The question of the authority of the voice is central to television: be it in involved commentary, or in voice-over news, the absence of the speaker goes along with a sense that the voice knows, that it is there to explain, continually, the event or the story to us. The acousmatic voice still is, in all cases I have been able to observe, a male voice, sometimes called the 'voice of God', as Corner (1996: 29) has reminded us. Even more than for the direct address, the politics of the voice on television is heavily gendered.

Edited television: advertising, music videos, credits, propaganda

These four sequences seem to have little in common. We might well start with the credits, which have a lot to teach us about edited television in general. At the start, as in film, credits were musical sequences. As television became richer, and more competitive, credits have changed, using more images and increasingly complex editing. Credits have many functions, far beyond the naming of those who are given credit. They signal a recurrence: the same familiar programme is coming back to us. They vary according to genres, and also to location. Opening credits which try to draw us into the programme, use the whole gamut of visual and sound resources. Conversely, for many continuity and live programmes, the closing credits are often rolled over the silent set, where the viewer can see the host and guests, the newscaster and the interviewee, still talking. Just like advertising, credit sequences are a major place for trying out and experimenting with new techniques, such as digital effects and computer graphics.

Advertising and music videos are more complicated than credits. The regime of belief they establish stands somewhere between fiction and nonfiction. They are often built as little fictions, with a story sometimes related to the song for music videos. At the same time, the viewer is reminded that it is only a song: images of a story are interspersed with that of the band playing, or of the singer singing. In advertising, we are reminded that this is only an advertisement: the product is there, after all, to contradict the idea of an autonomous story. Not all advertisements are built as fictions. Many resort to a celebrity addressing the audience to promote the product.

Music videos might be interpreted as a complex generic configuration. Before they emerged, there had been filmed singers in variety shows or in musicals, always addressing the audience while singing. They established the power of the song as a popular, semi-fictional genre. The singer both tells a story and represents, through gestures and attitudes, the story for us. What is new about the music video is the way the story is represented. Beyond a basic continuity (of the music, and, to a lesser extent, of the singer's face), there is an extreme discontinuity of the editing (with, however, an often cyclic use of the same series of shots in different locations). This discontinuity seems to embody the power of the singer to become someone else through the music, and to create one or several new worlds through his songs. We could define the music video as a rhetorical game between sound continuity and visual disruption, which has created its own conventions: the viewer expects the disruptions in editing, according to certain rules, but first and foremost we have the presence of the singer. This modern form is easily combined with the archaism of continuity television. The same disjoined singer is also interviewed in a studio, or on MTV, within the traditional conventions of continuity shooting (save for the odd camera angles, which have also created their own conventions).

The voice, the verbal

Whether acousmatic or visualized, almost all television voices have something in common: they are at the service of verbal language that is clearly understandable, whether in sports commentaries, in variety shows or in news. Even more than in the movies, there is not only 'vococentrism' but 'verbocentrism' (Chion, 1994). The technology of the microphone and the work of television mediators (hosts and journalists) are to a large extent used mostly to convert voices into clear language. The 'in-between' situation, so frequent in real life, where voices are clearly saying something, but something we do not completely understand, is banished from television, and largely from films, with, again, some major exceptions (Jean-Luc Godard being one).

In continuity television, a certain dose of confusion can be tolerated, but within certain (evolving) conventions. First of all, the moments of confusion are limited. After a row, the host has to show he is in control again. Second, the confusion belongs to a certain sub-genre, the talk-shows of tabloid television. In the 1980s, the American *Geraldo*, the French *Droit de Réponse* (Right to Reply), the Israeli *Popolitika* (Here is Politics), were debates where noisy rows were part of the expectations of viewers, but within certain limits. Each has one or more famous episodes where it went beyond its own limits, and had to fall back within the borders of the 'acceptable scandal' that is part of their substantial definition as a genre.

Television voices are always clear. But there is more: television is always talking. That is a convention which might be stronger than the social and moral conventions of *what* can be said: *something* has to be said. On television, almost everything can be said, as long as television keeps on talking clearly. News journalists are often said to be desperate when they have no pictures to illustrate a major event. But the need for words is as pressing as the need for images. Silent images are rare. Silent looks are even less frequent. This is probably an interesting zone which is rarely transgressed. What is a silent look, instantly directed at your own eyes? It is heavily charged, either positively (seduction), but mostly negatively (aggression, madness), as Barthes (1980: 175) has noted. The doubt cannot be easily dissipated. We cannot interrogate the figure on the screen, and react as we would do in real life, simply turning away or responding aggressively: 'why are you looking at me like that?' The silent look brings us back to the absence of the characters on the screen, and then to the fact that there is no event, no fact, only a flow of pictures. Television has to use the voice to bring about a phenomenological presence as completely as it can.

Fiction, seriality, live television

Finally, although fiction (at least in today's television) is no longer live, and sometimes only shot live (some sitcoms), it is influenced by the context of television. Let us start with famous television actors: beyond the fictional story on the screen, viewers can often follow, through television itself and other media, the real-life story off the screen. Behind the character, the actor is always there, much more than in the cinema. Some actors find this worrying. Others use it. Peter Falk *is* Columbo. In France, the actor Roger Hanin *is* the policeman Navarro (the character he has embodied for years in a famous crime series). The use of the name sometimes oscillates between the real-life name and the character's name. In comparison with the movies, the suspension of disbelief is not quite the same. We might watch a story, but we also watch Peter Falk playing Columbo, knowing he will come back next week.

This process of actors being actors more than characters culminates in sitcoms. As much as it is a fiction story, we watch a theatrical representation being broadcast, aware of the presence of the audience (live audience or simulated audience through recorded laughter). The actors often play with a specific detachment, sometimes criticized as bad acting. In a famous French sitcom, the bad acting has interestingly been analysed as offering a chance for young viewers to identify more with the actor and less with the character. More precisely, it is as aspiring actors and stars that viewers can think of themselves as having more chance to participate, some day, in this kind of fiction than in fully fledged fiction (Pasquier, 1999). This hypothesis could be generalized in relation to many sitcoms and soap operas. The stereotyped or simplified way of acting, the heavy coverage of the real-life character by the media between the episodes, and the very duration of the series create a sense of real-life temporality, sometimes lasting for years, very specific to television. [. . .] Some viewers can actually view the whole flow of television as nothing but a life-long serial about the life of television celebrities.

Finally, television fiction can be affected by the phenomenon of liveness in another way. Watching television live is also watching non-recorded television. It is well known that viewers mostly record movies and series. The case of soap operas and sitcoms might be different: they might be recorded, but viewers who want to keep up with the series, especially if they share it with other viewers, might prefer to watch it live or with only a small delay. Watching fiction live may help us to become part of a specific interpretive community, and, beyond, of a national audience.

[. . .]

Live television as historical fulfilment

Why is it that the possibility of live broadcasting has remained so important, whereas the percentage of fully live television is actually small on general audience television? I do not believe in an essentialist view of technologies, nor am I a technological determinist. Rather, I think that liveness should be interpreted as a development within media history as a whole. Media technological history at least partly reflects an effort to reduce the gap between events and media users. It is intimately linked to a history of communication as speed, where we experience the rhythm of printing presses, the use of the telegraph by press agencies, the transmission of photographs, the circulation of films (by plane), then the circulation of video signals through transmission and satellite. Live broadcasting, in this context, is the quintessence of 'news', whose 'discovery' has been a major break in the history of the press, if it has not marked the birth of the modern press altogether (Schudson, 1978)

Why such pressure? I certainly do not want to privilege either a critical explanation, from the top down (the media economy has created a need for consumers), or a populist explanation, from the bottom up (liveness is a natural need for the modern citizen). Rather, there has been a mutual adjustment between technique, society and economy. From the top, major institutions have all used news, then radio and television liveness, to create a connection between the masses and events (thereby reinforcing mass sentiments). At the base, the need to connect oneself, with others, to the world's events, is central to the development of the modern nation, as Anderson has noted (1991). [. . .]

This historical perspective may possibly lead to an explanation as to why most prophecies of the death of mass television have been repeatedly belied by historical evolution. Broadcasting has not yet been defeated by narrowcasting, particularly not by the ultimate form of narrowcasting, the VCR, which is supposed to give one a chance to free oneself completely from the constraints of scheduling. However, as is well known, the VCR remains subject to the programme schedule. The only exception is in the case of big immigrant communities who live in countries where they have no television channels in their own language, and resort massively to video consumption. However, most people still watch more broadcast (or even cable and satellite) television than video. Furthermore, video recording itself is used not to detach oneself completely from the channels' schedules, but only for slightly delayed viewing of some specific programmes one is not free to watch on a specific evening. This explains why audience measurement systems can actually include part of the VCR viewing of a specific programme in their statistics, as in the UK where this is called timeshift viewing.

The taste for 'live broadcasting' (in the sense of 'non-VCR' viewing) can be related to the need to know others are watching at the same time. Furthermore, watching television 'live', even though one is dealing with the broadcasting of recorded programmes, offers a guarantee that, at any given time, the flow can be interrupted by a special newsflash. Thus, even when we are completely engrossed in a major fiction film, we are not completely cut off from world events. This possibility has been noted by theoreticians of liveness, notably by Mellencamp (1990). An example: on the evening of Itzhak Rabin's assassination (November 1995), the French second channel was broadcasting a variety show, recorded as if live, a typical example of what I have called continuity television. At the time when the event was discoverd, the show was not interrupted. However, the information was chromakeyed at the bottom of the screen, which created a strange sensation: what looked live was not really live. A tragedy was taking place, and the show's participants kept talking happily. Of course, viewers particularly interested in the event could have always changed to CNN, LCI (the French non-stop news channel) or to radio.

The promise of liveness in contemporary television

Most of the aforementioned examples have been taken from general audience and national channels. Let us now qualify my initial claim that liveness will not disappear with the 'new television'. Obviously, the multiplicity of channels and the increased competition and 'choice' they entail have some implications for liveness. The most talked-about aspect of this transformation is the emergence of 'global news'. CNN and BBC World, even though they broadcast some magazines, promise the viewers regular news bulletins and instant interruption in case of the occurrence of a newsworthy event: they can be included in the long history of the rhetorics of live television. One cannot be certain that these transformations are about globalization, or mostly about globalization. In countries which have the capital, and when the cable market has matured long enough, producers create a national news channel, which is more successful than the

Anglo-Saxon or American model. Non-stop news channels are now broadcasting in France, Germany and Italy; many are planned in other countries.

The real change that CNN heralds is also related to a different relationship with the nation, with television as a national enunciator. In the 1960s, it was the BBC (in the UK) or the ORTF (in France), which used the promise of live broadcasting. In the 1990s, it is international (and, increasingly, national) non-stop news channels. But, above the channels, there is a meta-enunciator: the national or private cable company marketing its services to the viewers. A non-stop news channel is always an important part of the promise of this meta-enunciator. Thus, Paris-Cable promises to Parisian viewers a 'bouquet' of channels, including both CNN and LCI. Non-stop news channels might not be the ones with the biggest audience shares, but they have another privilege. Studying remote control switching patterns might well show us that viewers 'check up on' the news channels regularly. If such a pattern is confirmed, live broadcasting might not be disappearing – rather, it would be entering a new chapter in its history.

Note

This article was published in a shorter version in French in *Réseaux* 81: 61–78, 1997. It has its remote origins in a thesis written under the direction of Christian Metz, who was not only a fine theorist but the best of pedagogues.

References

Anderson, B. (1991) *Imagined Communities: Reflections on the Origin and Spread of Nationalism*. London and New York: Verso. (Orig. pub. 1983.)

Baget Herms, J.M. (1993) *Historia de la Televisión en España (1956–1975)*. Barcelona: Feed-Back Ediciones.

Barthes, R. (1980) *La chambre claire: Note sur la photographie*. Paris: Gallimard.

Bourdon, J. (1982) 'Histories de grèves', pp. 162–88 in J.N. Jeanneney and M. Sauvage (eds) *Télévision, nouvelle mémoire: Les magazines de grand reportage*. Paris: Seuil.

—— (1986) 'Techniques de production et genres télévisuels', pp. 43–80 in *Histoire des programmes de radiotélévision: Actes de la journée d'études du 24 février 1986*. Paris: Radio-France.

—— (1990) *Histoire de la télévision sous de Gaulle*. Paris: Anthropos.

Briggs, A. (1979) *A History of Broadcasting in the United Kingdom, Vol 4: Sound and Vision*. Oxford: Oxford University Press.

Caldwell, J.T. (1995) *Televisuality: Style, Crisis and Authority in American Television*. New Brunswick, NJ: Rutgers University Press.

Chion, M. (1994) *Audiovision: Sound in Film*. New York: Columbia University Press. (Orig. pub. 1990.)

Corner, J. (1996) *The Art of Record: A Critical Introduction to Documentary*. Manchester and New York: Manchester University Press.

—— (1997) 'Television in Theory', *Media, Culture and Society* 19(2): 247–62.

Dayan, D. and E. Katz (1992) *Media Events, the Live Broadcasting of History*. New York: Harvard University Press.

Eco, U. (1990) 'A Guide to Neo-Television in the Nineties', pp. 245–55 in Z. Barański and R. Lumley (eds) *Culture and Conflict in Post-War Italy*. London: Macmillan.

Eurodience 46 (1990) *Reality-Shows: Television's New Frontier?* Paris: Institut National de L'Audiovisuel.

Genette, G. (1997) *Paratexts*. Cambridge: Cambridge University Press. (Orig. pub. 1987.)

Grasso, A. (1992) *Storia della television italiana*. Milano: Garzanti.

Hartley, J. (1982) *Understanding News*. London Methuen.

Jacobs, L. (1971) *The Documentary Tradition*. New York: Norton.

Mellencamp, P. (1990) 'TV Time and Catastrophe: Or Beyond the Principle of Television', pp. 240–66 in P. Mellencamp (ed.) *Logics of Television: Essays in Cultural Criticism*. Bloomington: Indiana University Press.

Nattiez, J.J. (1975) *Fondements d'une sémiologie de la musique*. Paris: Union Générale d'Editions.

Pasquier, D. (1999) *La Culture des sentiments. L'Expérience télévisuelle des adolescents*. Paris: Editions de la Maison des sciences de l'homme.

Sacks, H., Schegloff E. and Jefferson G. (1974) 'A Simplest Systematics for the Organization of Turn Taking in Conversation', *Languages* 50–4: 696–735.
Scannell, P. (ed.) (1991) *Broadcast Talk*. London: Sage.
Schudson, M. (1978) *Discovering the News*. New York: Basic Books.
Vianello, R. (1986) 'The Power Politics of "Live" Television', *Journal of Film and Video* 37(3): 26–40.

Chapter 12

DEREK PAGET

CODES AND CONVENTIONS OF DRAMADOC AND DOCUDRAMA

THE 'SIAMESE TWIN' term dramadoc/docudrama not only highlights the differences between British and American practice over the second half of the twentieth century but also reflects the fact that the separate terms have now become almost interchangeable in English-speaking cultures. Where American culture dominates, usage favours 'docudrama', and this term is used often in British writing on the form; 'dramadoc', however, is rarely used in American writing.[1] Whichever term is used, the principal codes and conventions of the form are now common to both traditions. In general, it is codes and conventions to which people in a media-literate environment respond and which they recognise prior to categorisation. I hope the reader will cross-check what I say about this against their own experience of dramadoc/docudrama. [. . .]

Dramadoc/docudrama has almost always set out to do one or more of the following:

(a) to re-tell events from national or international histories, either reviewing or celebrating these events;
(b) to re-present the careers of significant national or international figures, for similar purposes as (a);
(c) to portray issues of concern to national or international communities in order to provoke discussion about them.

Increasingly in recent times it has also aimed

(d) to focus on 'ordinary citizens' who have been thrust into the news because of some special experience.

And finally, almost as a by-product of all this, it has

(e) provoked questions about its form.

The last feature is an indicator of a 'coming of age' for dramadoc/ docudrama in particular and for the media in general.

Questions about 'referentiality' and 'representation' (see Corner 1996: 42–3) probe the extent of the documentary coding in a programme. The moral (and legal) justification for having actors depict real-life events is often debated, especially when a dramadoc/ docudrama is controversial (as in the case of the 1992 Granada docudrama *Hostages*). Controversy about dramadoc/

docudrama is like the issue of portraying violence in the media: everybody has a view (even if they have not seen a particular programme). Some commentators will always hold that the inherent representational dangers of dramadoc/docudrama (especially of misleading a gullible public) far outweigh any informational advantages claimed. Drama coding increases debate about what John Corner calls the 'manipulation' issue.

The dramadoc/docudrama, then, contains material that is usually already familiar to its audience (or, if not familiar, accepted by it as already widely known). Trails before programmes, print media advertising and captions/voiceovers in transmission highlight this familiarity for promotional purposes. Closeness in time to contemporary historical events helps, because the audience's memory of events that are still recent will not need much refreshing prior to their representation. *Hostages* followed up a major news story with which people throughout the Western world would have been (relatively) familiar in 1992–93. The structure of the current affairs story (kidnap, incarceration, torture, 'ransom', possible escape/release) was arguably already in the minds of the audience when the programme was first transmitted. The original treatment written by Executive Producer Alasdair Palmer counted on just this factor. Its first sentence reads: 'This is the story of how five men reacted to being kidnapped, chained to the floor, beaten, and held under the constant threat of death.'

Failing the presence in the story of well-known names and events, the dramadoc/docudrama links specific events to a more general set of historical events. An historical 'macro-story' is thus hooked on to a lesser-known 'micro-story' (especially in pretransmission publicity). Granada's 1993 *Fighting for Gemma* thus took its place in the history of television programmes investigating the long-term effects of the nuclear fuel industry on the environment and on public health. The real life and real death of little Gemma D'Arcy acted as a metonymic device through which the dangers of nuclear power could be debated publicly. Even though it was located within a narrowly British frame of reference, this debate is part of the culture of all nuclear fuel-using nations.

[. . .]

Captions

The first key convention of the form is direct reference to such real-life events, usually by means of opening, closing and linking *captions*.[2] Nowadays programmes are generally topped and tailed by them, and as often as not they use white lettering on a black screen or the device of the news agency teleprinter clattering out the latest news. There is a verbal equivalent: the sepulchral *voiceover* telling an audience that 'The Events You Are About To Witness Are True' (such voices habitually capitalise words); but this device is seen as rather old-fashioned, and mixtures of still and rolling captions are usually preferred (see below for other functions of the voiceover). *Hostages and Fighting for Gemma* provide good examples of the use of captions.

The *caption* used in the pre-credits sequence of *Hostages* is typical of a contextualising device connecting the film to its real-life referent. The very first film frame seen by the viewer contains white lettering centred on a black background. Music in a classical style builds and we see/read:

> Between 1984 and 1992 more than fifty
> Western citizens were held hostage in Beirut.
> This film dramatises incidents which illustrate
> what happened to some of them.

Thus the first, contextualising, caption gives us time, place, indications about character (a focus on

'Western citizens') and the beginning of a disclaimer (dramatisation that 'illustrates'). The visual and aural values are emphatically 'high concept' (see Edgerton 1991).

After about five seconds the caption starts to roll and the black background lightens to reveal the dawn scene of a bay with a town (Beirut) left of frame and in the middle distance. The frame is carefully composed and the scene is both imposing and peacful, an impression reinforced by the string-dominated music. The rolling captions extend both the disclaimer and the description of the 'illustration' proposed by the programme:

> Dialogue has been created based upon publicly
> available material, interviews with former hostages,
> their friends and relatives, diplomats and
> politicians from the United States, Europe and
> the Middle East.
> No endorsement has been sought or received
> from anyone depicted.
> To compress six years into two hours, chronology
> has been changed and some events have been
> amalgamated. The names of minor characters
> have also been altered.

Opening caption material often incorporates this kind of disclaimer, acknowledging (as per television regulations) the partial nature of versions of events offered in dramatisation. Such lengthy statements would be unthinkable in 'documentary' and unnecessary in 'drama'. The disclaimer in *Hostages* was especially important in view of the pre-transmission, published objections of the real hostages. Such captioning is regarded with almost talismanic reverence by the Granada team and is part of the tradition pioneered by *World in Action* in the 1970s. It has several purposes: it places the film historically; it sets the scene dramatically; it argues a representational case; it protects against legal action.

[. . .]

Voiceovers

The *voiceover* is another convention that dramadoc/docudrama shares with documentary more than drama. Either it takes the form in which a voice reads out a visible caption, or it is direct-address narration by an actor from the drama, a news anchor commentator, or even a real person involved in the pro-filmic events depicted. As the aural equivalent of the visual caption, the device has been used in the past to convey facts and information, but today it tends to function as part of the dramatic *mise-en-scène*. In *Hostages* the voices of news reporters are used in the opening sequence, for example, to contextualise the conflict in Beirut (see next section).

The term diegesis is useful here. Developed by film theory, it refers to the method of narration employed in a film and is used to mark the degree to which necessary information is conveyed to an audience from within the world of the film story. In the realist film information mostly comes 'diegetically'. The audience receives it from the words of characters, from the *mise-en-scène* (or 'what is seen in the frame' of the individual shot) or from what the camera picks out for its attention (in terms of depth of focus, angle of vision, etc.). In dramadoc/docudrama both the caption and the 'authoritative' voiceover are 'non-diegetic' – they come from outside the story world. Their function is threefold: to start us off with the necessary prior knowledge of the non-story world; to help the story take temporal and locational leaps as the narrative unfolds; and to project us back into the real (non-story) world at the end of the film. Dramadoc/docudrama has a higher level of information to convey (as has documentary) and there is little choice but to mediate it non-diegetically from time to time.

Documentary material

Use in the film of actual *documentary material* is an important and distinctive convention by which both information and authentication are achieved. Drawn from the same archives as those which supply news, current affairs and documentary programmes, such material authenticates a programme at the documentary level and connects it visibly to its documentary claims. At a dramatic level in contemporary dramadoc/docudrama it rarely disrupts the narrative flow as it provides vital contextualisation. Like captions, documentary material frequently sets the scene in time and place for the unfolding drama.

After the opening captions in *Hostages* the film cuts to a montage of contemporary newsreel footage with voiceover commentaries. They establish clearly the nature of the conflict in Lebanon. The peace of the tranquil dawn-over-the-ocean opening shot is shattered in a very specific way by the documentary footage. Rocket launchers, for example, fire right to left of frame (in film terms, towards the peaceful seaside town of the opening frames). The first voice we hear says: 'Lebanon is not the scene of one war but many . . .' in the tones of a front-line television reporter. News footage/commentary is then intercut with the credits for the film, the voices of Western newsreaders fading in and out with the visual material. The scene is thereby set in two ways: we see literal scene-setting in the form of landscapes and places and we hear metaphorical (and historical) scene-setting in the form of facts and information about the Lebanese conflict. The joint visual/discursive mode is distinctive in the balance that is effected between the pictures seen and the words heard; the codes are principally documentary.

The *Hostages* newsreel footage and its accompanying voiceover, however, are tricky: they partly function as a non-diegetic caption, but they are 'semi-diegetic' – both in and out of the story world. So, although the footage is there to inform us directly about the historical situation in the Lebanon between 1984 and 1992 and to 'set the scene' (as a caption might), it is also used seamlessly within the dramatic action in order to progress the drama naturalistically. The technique that achieves this result is a montaging of the documentary with the drama. The first drama scenes in the opening section of *Hostages* are intercut with the documentary news material in a rhythmical balance that, additionally, includes actor-credit information.

Credit sequences in today's television drama are always multilayered and designed to maximise the viewer's interest. In *Hostages* we see first Jay O. Sanders (as Terry Anderson), then Josef Sommer (Tom Sutherland) being snatched from the streets of Beirut by Hezbollah kidnap squads. These dramatised scenes are confirmed by (simulated) news voiceovers that identify the victims. In the first scene proper we see John McCarthy (played by Colin Firth) making just such a news report about Brian Keenan being taken hostage. In three neat dramatic steps we are presented with the four main players in the drama, the historical sequence of their abduction and the general context of the war in Lebanon.

That we are in the realm of drama on these occasions is obvious from the deliberate contrast in quality of the film stocks and shooting styles. The documentary footage reads as news – it has all the rough-and-ready hallmarks of being shot in natural light and under pressure (simple set-ups, lens flarings, occasional lack of focus, camera shake, arbitrary framing). Whereas its quality as image is affected by being copied from archive sources, the drama footage is quite the opposite. Here we have multiple camera set-ups and self-conscious framings as well as the smooth transitions of continuity editing. There are establishing shots of bombed-out streets; there is clear point-of-view identification of kidnappers and kidnapped through close-ups and eyeline matches.

Dramatic depth is achieved in sequences such as that in which Anderson is metonymically mal-treated (his glasses are knocked to the ground and shattered). Sutherland's point-of-view of the back of the limousine that will carry him into captivity has clarity of framing and focusing, but camera wobble conveys the naturalism of Sutherland's struggle against his captors while simultaneously alluding to the documentary values of the earlier newsreel footage.

In the dramadoc/docudrama these are supporting rather than opposing camera rhetorics, but drama is prioritised; in the last example the camera shake of documentary is simulated. That which is forced on the news camera operator in the field (and which we saw in the montage of Beirut) is affected for dramatic purposes. Like the experienced speaker who uses the debating trick of putting facts and figures alongside an entertaining anecdote, the dramadoc/docudrama uses the continuous experience of viewing to fold two quite different techniques into one. The codes and conventions are mixed as a result of the development of the form, so that within such a sequence as this they can scarcely be separated.

In the first scene proper of *Hostages* the programme-makers connect the simulated event with the news and quasi-news material we have just been watching. The drama thus draws additional credibility from the documentary that has 'set the scene'. A (fictional) news crew is shown in an establishing shot (Firth/McCarthy at centre of the frame). Firth/McCarthy gives us information about Keenan (whom we have yet to see) while the camera closes in on him. The camera finishes up in medium close-up on Firth/McCarthy's face. Around him the 'news crew' become part of the *mise-en-scène* establishing him as journalist-in-the-field.

Jill Morrell comments on this scene:

It was weird seeing other people play us, but it all fell into perspective in the opening few minutes when John had been curiously transformed from producer to reporter. We all burst out laughing; it was simply incorrect.

(McCarthy and Morrell, 1994: 616)

It is certainly possible to read the scene as 'McCarthy the television reporter' doing a piece to camera. In a way he *is* – in the television dramadoc for which we are his audience. The producer of *Hostages*, Sita Williams pointed out, however, that the camera set-up foregrounds the Worldwide Television News (WTN) sound-recordist's microphone and that there is no camera in sight – personnel wander about in a way that would not be possible for any piece to camera. Acknowledging that it was possible to misread the scene as depicting a television crew, she refuted the idea that this had been deliberate and also rejected the accusation that McCarthy's work in Beirut did not include reporting. McCarthy describes his work as acting bureau chief for WTN as: 'co-ordinat[ing] the activities of the camera crews and liais[ing] with London on the details of their coverage and the best means of shipping the cassettes', but Williams was adamant that occasional reporting could and did occur. McCarthy himself corroborates this, writing in *Some Other Rainbow* about conducting interviews, accompanying the crews as they went about their work and filing a report on Keenan's kidnapping (McCarthy and Morrell, 1994: 31–8).

This section of *Hostages* usefully illustrates the kind of slippage that is always likely to occur when documentary becomes dramadoc/docudrama. Disputes tend to take place at the (dramatic) edges of the (documentary) truth claims. This is why the form is hedged with disclaimers from makers and denials from participants, all of which can create doubt in viewers. The elisions declared in the captions to *Hostages*, although manifestly necessary for the two-hour drama, will always tend to work against the claims of authenticity. For the viewer the very suspension of disbelief necessary to accept the drama reinforces disbelief at any subsequent consideration of the documentary.

In the form in which it is currently presented in the English-speaking world documentary is increasingly used rhetorically and diegetically. For example, archive news footage is used several times in *Hostages* and its primary function continues to be the authentication we saw in the opening sequence. But additional dramatic points are usually made in today's practice. In *Fighting for Gemma* the nuclear past is held up for our attention in Scene 54 of the script, in which Martyn Day's legal team view some 1950s newsreel footage about Windscale, the nuclear plant that became Sellafield. Yorkshire Television's 1983 documentary *Windscale – The Nuclear Laundry*, which first exposed the problems associated with Sellafield's reprocessing plant, is also used in the film. This has several functions: documentarily, it helps the audience understand the 'backstory' of nuclear power; dramatically, it enables the audience to share the legal team's learning curve on the issue.

The mix of archive/library material and acted reconstruction in the early part of *Hostages* amounts to a *simulation of documentary material*, so closely do the two intercut. Increasingly, this is used to develop character in the narrative, producing dialogue between figures in the drama who sometimes exist at different levels of representation. For example. President Reagan appears so often in *Hostages* that his documentary image becomes a character (a highly suitable role, perhaps, for the Hollywood President). First seen calling the Arabs 'barbarians' in the pre-credits sequence, he 'participates' directly in a scene depicting Terry Anderson's Christmas 1988 video message. The recorded message is a faithful 'note for note' copy of Anderson's actual video, so this part of the sequence is demonstrably a simulation. But whereas the scenes of the making of the video in Beirut, its transmission on US television and its reception in the home of his campaigning sister Peggy Say (Kathy Bates) are wholly acted, they are intercut with Reagan's documentary reaction at a White House press conference. With the actor Charlton Heston also in shot, Reagan gives his response to Anderson's video: 'I don't think that was Terry speaking. I think that was . . . I think he had a script – that was given to him. When I was given a script, I always read the lines!' The sycophantic laughter that follows this shaft of wit, in which Heston joins enthusiastically, underscores the film's theme of official muddle-headedness and collusion in keeping the hostages imprisoned for so long. A president-actor performing to camera does not get you out of a Beirut jail.

What I am calling 'simulated documentary material' – both faked footage and the device of editing together documentary and acted footage to create dialogue – is not unusual. In *Fighting for Gemma* the cutting together of footage from a Granada *Update* regional magazine programme and David Threlfall's performance as Martyn Day enables a 'virtual documentary' of Day's original dialogue with representatives of BNFL to take place. This device brings the dramadoc close to American docudrama practice. In the 1988 TV docudrama *Shoot-down* (about the downing of Korean Airlines flight KAL 007 by Russian planes in 1983) Angela Lansbury (playing the mother of a victim) similarly 'participated' in an edition of the syndicated American talk show *Donahue*. The same technique was used whereby an actor's simulation replaces a real individual's side of a conversation, which is edited-out.

This is something of a 'high-concept' technique, however. The 'Long Island Lolita' trilogy, by contrast, is packed with stereotypical simulated press conferences and journalistic ambushes of the protagonists.[3] Broadcast and print journalists did indeed pursue the real protagonists in 1992, eagerly signing them up as soon as they could. In the docudramas they are portrayed as a kind of 'Rent-a-Media-Mob'; they jostle each other, thrusting microphones and cameras forward, but the babble of questions always quietens quickly so that the story can be advanced when the audience hears a key question. 'Low-concept' docudrama offers the conventions of news reportage purely as a narrative aid, confident that its audience is sufficiently used to the codes and conventions of news reporting itself to be able to transpose them enough to 'read' the drama.

Conventions aim increasingly to knit together the documentary and the drama rhetorically, from within the parameters of film realism. News hounding of Amy Fisher *et al.* is recreated to preserve the visual values of the made-for-TV movie. High-concept programmes are more likely to incorporate poor-quality but 'dramatic' original news footage and devices to signal their presence. A 'channel-zapping' visual/aural blip in *Hostages*, for example, helps the regular switches between archive and re-creation. When we surf the channels with our remote controls we not only interrupt individual programmes, we discover – indeed make – connections between different television genres. The snow-and-static of the connective frame 'sutures' the polished frames of the drama to a documentary footage authenticated partly by its poor quality (a camera operator under fire will be unlikely to study the finer points of framing and focus).[4] Reagan's comment on Anderson's performance is thus simultaneously within the drama (and is itself 'dramatic') and without the drama (as a documentary image). Anderson's sister Peggy Say comments in the drama as she watches her brother: '[the State Department] will say he was forced to read that.' A visual blip later Reagan does just that documentarily, and the dramadoc/docudrama narrative sequence is complete.

The channel zapping convention is a direct acknowledgement of the continuum of mediations available in the world of television. All mediations, from news to cartoons, are necessarily conventionalised, and the device is 'knowing' in the sense that it expects the audience to be media-literate enough to be able to see both with and through it. The device also betrays an anxiety: interrupting the dramatic diegesis is to be avoided at all costs, therefore documentary must function actively within the drama – or not at all.

Drama conventions

Most of the other conventions of dramadoc/docudrama lie in the realm of *realist drama*. Modern practice in filmed television drama involves multiple camera set-ups on realistic sets or actual locations, 'key lighting', sound recorded for maximum clarity of narrative flow, continuity editing (minimising the interruptions to the narrative flow) and non-diegetic music dubbed in during post-production to influence mood. For performers the avoidance of direct address to camera is linked to believable behaviours that are reproducible to order and filmed out of sequence with the narrative. Documentary makes its presence felt in the research contribution to the *mise-en-scène*, in the unwritten rules of casting (where a broad resemblance to the real-world original is an advantage) and in the favouring of a 'low-key' acting style.

The modern thrust towards simulation and re-enactment, where actors cast for resemblance perform in patiently recreated interiors, has one anomaly: the simulation of exterior scenes is often much more of an approximation. Alasdair Palmer did obtain some footage of Beirut for *Hostages*, but most of the location filming was, rather paradoxically, done in Israel.[5] [. . .] There is a routineness in the exchanges of real and fake at this level that is rarely mentioned (because it is accepted by most audiences as a matter of course).

However, exceptions do occur. The town councillors of St Bees, a seaside resort in Cumbria, objected both to Granada and to their local MP, William Whitelaw, about a scene in *Fighting for Gemma*. They alleged that the scene in question showed tests for radiation levels being made on a beach that was recognisable as theirs. As a result, suspicions about its radioactivity would harm tourism. Such claims are perfectly understandable at a simple level of representation. The drama's establishment of place used the beach metonymically – it stood for 'beaches tested for radiation' – but the councillors read the scene documentarily against the intentions of the film makers. In fact, in reception terms the recognition of somewhere one knows in a film drama is always more likely to cause alienation from the drama, puncturing the suspension of disbelief, than to cause concern about what might be being said about that particular place. This intrusion of the (unintended)

documentary into the drama is irritating for the programme maker, but comes with the representational territory.

In the matter of *casting*, the convention for well-known public stories is to go for the 'lookalike' performer, then to use the considerable skills of costume and make-up departments to
enhance the resemblance. Actors are chosen who resemble their real historical counterparts
sufficiently for an audience to accept the simulated identity with no significant interruption to the
suspension of disbelief necessary to enjoy realist drama. In *Hostages* there is such 'sufficient
resemblance' between, say, the actor Jay O. Sanders and Terry Anderson and between Colin Firth
and John McCarthy. In less well-known stories, such as *Fighting for Gemma*, this convention is not
quite so urgent, but there is always some awareness that, in publicity at least, there may be
advantages in being able to put the performer and the real person side by side without too much
dissimilarity being evident. If anything, and inevitably, performers are usually slightly more
glamorous than their real-life originals.

The conventions (referred to in the *Hostages* caption above) of *telescoping events* and creating
composite and fictional characters deserve mention, since they point up the structural nature of
drama's meeting with documentary in the dramadoc/docudrama. 'Compositing', or folding a
number of real-world individuals into one dramatic unit, is done principally for dynamic purposes.
If necessary, a totally fictional character can be invented. Whichever route is chosen, the scripting
action is taken to progress the story at the necessary rate within the requirements of the slot in the
schedule for which the programme is intended. Without these devices the story could become
clogged with detail that might well be of interest documentarily but is regarded as extraneous
dramatically and much feared by makers of dramadoc/docudrama. [. . .] Documentary detail can
only be justified while it continues to 'serve the narrative'. The most obvious compositing in
Hostages is in the presentation of the hostage protagonists' dramatic antagonists – their Arab
captors and the politicians/diplomats. The latter are the real villains of the piece, and the film's
composites are actually stereotypes. In structural terms they have such limited functions to play –
because they are at the margins of the experience being depicted – that they can only be
stereotypes. By contrast, the Arab guards, although recognisably stereotyped, are treated with
some sympathy.[6]

Moments of *inherent dramatic tension* and/or *dramatic irony* within actual situations are actively
sought and highlighted in treatments. In Alasdair Palmer's original treatment of the hostages'
story, for example, the relationship between Keenan and McCarthy is a dramatic key:

> If McCarthy saved Keenan from self-destructive rage, Keenan put steel into McCarthy's
> soul, and helped him to the strength he needed not to be scythed into submission by the
> guards and the dirt and degradation of his situation.

The moment when McCarthy and Keenan eventually meet is a dramatic climax in Part 1:

> Without explanation, they are suddenly hurled, both naked and blind-folded, into the
> same pitch dark room. They say nothing for some time. Then McCarthy gradually slips
> down his blindfold, sees the stinking hirsute Keenan and says: 'Fuck me, it's Tom [*sic*]
> Gunn!' He then has to explain to Keenan who Tom Gunn is.[7]

Although the convention in the credit sequence to *Hostages* told us directly who was representing whom, we are denied a sight of Ciaran Hinds as Keenan until this 'Treasure Island'
moment. In the drama's emotional trajectory of hope and despair the dramatic impact of the
relationship between the central characters must be maximised. The separation of the two at the

end of Part 1 provides a televisual equivalent of a theatrical 'curtain line' as Keenan tries to convince himself: 'He'll be back. They'll not kill him. Just a few questions. He'll be back in a minute.' Structurally, the conventions of the modern dramadoc/docudrama are arranged around the dramatic, not the documentary, dynamic. [. . .]

Editing out

The fear of losing an audience's attention determines to some extent what factual material stays in and what is edited out, since such material is sometimes excessive in relation to the dynamic of the drama. *Editing out* is thus a vital feature of the organisation of dramadoc/docudrama, and it is unavoidable when plots are driven naturalistically. It is no wonder that veteran docudrama maker Leslie Woodhead takes the view that 'the most effective programmes satisfy almost Aristotelian rules of dramatic construction'. In his experience, 'the Aristotelian shape is an instinctive human impulse for narrative order rather than a planned strategy'. Sita Williams put it this way: 'One thing you have to do with dramadoc is not simplify but rationalise and structure in a more definite pattern than actually happens in reality.' To rationalise and shape in dramatic terms means to edit out in documentary terms.

One of the reasons for the failure of *Hostages* was the large number of characters. The cramming in of hostages, their helpers, their captors and their governmental representatives crowded the narrative. Keenan's sisters. Jill Morrell and Anderson's sister Peggy Say are all underdeveloped within the drama. Sita Williams now admits that the women were 'undersold', yet feels that 'being properly ruthless' would have improved the film as drama:

> we should probably have dropped them altogether. In dramadoc you filter out the number of characters so that the ideas and the issues are open through a limited number of characters whom the audience get to know and relate to.

But because the functions of the characters in the film duplicated their real-life roles (helpers to the heroes/hostages in the battle with the diplomats) the women could not be edited out completely.

Even so, it is difficult in this genre to resist the sheer randomness inherent in the detail of real events: in *Fighting for Gemma* there is a lawyer called Martyn Day and a scientist called Philip Day. These two protagonists are not related. No dramatist, however dedicated to realism, would write such a coincidence into their play for fear that the audience would ask the irrelevant question, 'Are they related?' In 1990, a Yorkshire TV dramadoc *Shoot to Kill* treated the events of the John Stalker inquiry into the Royal Ulster Constabulary's alleged policy of that name. Its writer Michael Eaton noted that all the main participants were called 'John' and that this 'problem' for the writer could only happen in a form of drama compelled to some extent to stick to known facts.[8]

The dramatic narrative of the contemporary dramadoc/docudrama may be primarily one of character and relationships, but the documentary narrative is of events in the public domain in which certain personalities feature irreducibly. Perhaps the salient point about the mixed form is that it is more likely to present a relationship between individuals and institutions than mainstream television drama, even if they are now being mediated via 'dialogueing' between documentary image and drama. [. . .]

The extra-textual

As sport on television features pre- and post-match analysis and discussion, so the dramadoc/docudrama is often preceded and followed by interview and discussion programmes. Sometimes they are intended to ensure balance and are part of the codes of practice [of dramadoc/docudrama]. They are *extra-textual* events in themselves; Jane Feuer calls them 'nonstory materials' (1995: 35). The turbulence that results from screening a version of an anterior reality cannot be accommodated without further television talk (for this is what such programmes inevitably contain). This is another convention of the form. In a similar way documentary theatre performances often trail in their wake foyer displays of documentary material and extensive programme notes (sometimes containing facsimile documents).[9] The extra-textual includes continuity announcements, talk-show appearances, discussion programmes, even newspaper campaigns (both for and against). They are as much a feature of the modern dramadoc/docudrama as the captions of their opening and closing sequences.

As part of pre-publicity in the USA Tom Sutherland met his impersonator Josef Sommer on ABC's *Good Morning America* (16 February 1993) in front of an audience of nearly five million people. In contrast to this publicity-driven exercise, BBC2's arts magazine programme *The Late Show* offered a polarised debate (between those in favour of the form and those against) on the night of the British transmission of *Hostages*. The level of the debate was signalled by its framing question (asked by presenter Sarah Dunant) – 'Is *Hostages* exploration of fact or exploitation through fiction?' – and by a news clip of Brian Keenan expressing the view that Granada's film was not helping the hostages to find 'a new bond of trust with the world'.

Alasdair Palmer was then called upon to defend the film against three 'opposers' (four, if you count Dunant herself) and two familiar charges: that *Hostages* was underdeveloped dramatically; and that its authority as fact was fatally undermined by the limitations of its form and the absence of approval of the hostages themselves. This is a 'bad documentary/bad drama' line; *Hostages* stood condemned as bad on both counts. The issues rehearsed included: individual privacy versus public interest, 'copyright' on personal experience, impartiality in broadcasters, and public trust in the inherent 'decency' of broadcasters.[10]

Another kind of extra-textual vehicle frequently found is the advertising of support systems for victims and those similarly traumatised. Following the screening of Granada's 1996 *Hillsborough* a continuity announcement talked through some on-screen 'helpline' numbers: 'If you are distressed by this programme a helpline is now open [Hillsborough helpline] . . . or if you have been affected by the loss of a child and would like to talk to someone [child death helpline].' On regional television the next morning, discussion programmes further examined the continuing trauma of the 1989 football stadium disaster and the notion of police culpability raised both in the campaign of the Hillsborough parents' group and in the film itself. [. . .] [T]he support mechanisms around *Hillsborough* carried the film forward on a tide of sympathy that culminated in a television award in 1997. [. . .] The extra-textual phenomenon can therefore be supportive of, and not antagonistic towards, the dramadoc/docudrama.[11]

Definitions[12]

In the dramadoc/docudrama, documentary's promise of privileged access to information is added to drama's promise of understanding through 'second-order' experience. The camera accesses two different kinds of reality – a record of external events (which still constitutes the basis of the documentary's appeal) and a simulated reality of acted events. The promise of the camera (its documentary offer to show events to an audience distant in place and time as though that audience were present) is extended, but only as a defining paradox. The camera's promise cannot be fully delivered in actuality since there are places either where it cannot go or where it has missed its chance of going. In the dramadoc/docudrama those things which the camera has missed (because its ubiquity is a convenient fiction rather than an actual fact) or which it can't get at (because 'the actual participants are dead or dutifully dumb', in Granada executive Ian McBride's words) can still be shown – but only up to a point and at a price. Audiences who accept the extension of the camera's documentary showing do so increasingly within the context of dramatic suspension of disbelief. There is also, perhaps, a general cultural need to believe the camera's universal access to be more than just mythically true. All this guarantees the codes and conventions of dramadoc/docudrama as we watch. Following the moment of reception, the form's bid for belief is as often *dis*abled by these factors as it is *en*abled. It is dramadoc/docudrama's cultural role to be believed and then disbelieved, so to speak.

The establishment of broad conventions permits provisional definition to take place at this point. It is often the case in the arts that definition lags behind practice. But the difficulties peculiar to the docudrama/dramadoc have often been focused on the question of definition – as if clear categorisation would somehow solve everything. The purpose of such definition has too often been to hold back a tide of journalistic unease about the form.[13] Attempting for the moment to ignore unease about the ethics of the form (but acknowledging that this will need to be discussed), my definitions of the four key terms are as follows:

1   *Drama-documentary* uses the sequence of events from a real historical occurrence or situation and the identities of the protagonists to underpin a film script intended to provoke debate about the significance of the events/occurrence. The resultant film usually follows a cinematic narrative structure and employs the standard naturalist/realist performance techniques of screen drama. If documentary material is directly presented at all, it is used in a way calculated to minimise disruption to the realist narrative.

2   *Documentary drama* uses an invented sequence of events and fictional protagonists to illustrate the salient features of real historical occurrences or situations. The film script may or may not conform to a classic narrative structure; if it does not, documentary elements may be presented non-naturalistically and may actively disrupt the narrative. But 'documentary' in this form is just as likely to refer to style as to content (and to be about the 'look' and 'sound' of documentary proper), in which case the structures of film naturalism once more obtain.

3   *Faction* uses a real-world template of events and characters to create the basic structure of a fiction. Factions rely on their audiences to connect with the 'out-of-story' factual template in reception and do little within the film to effect this connection. Film naturalism is, almost inevitably, the staple dramatic means of representation.

4   *Dramadoc* and *docudrama* are contemporary shortened terms that describe television programmes that mainly follow the drama-documentary methodology. The two words are now used virtually interchangeably (thereby partly denying thirty years of practice).

I want to use these definitions experimentally in an analysis of the form that is simultaneously specific (to instances of practice) and general (in terms, especially, of the history of fact-fiction mixed forms of broadcasting within institutions).

[. . .]

Accepting convention

Dramadoc/docudrama's particular set of representational codes and conventions appeals to belief just like any other kind of convention in representation, and the appeal to belief is anchored in a distinctively twentieth-century faith in images – especially moving ones. We accept what we see according to our previous knowledge and experience. To the degree that we have been persuaded by the documentary and convinced by the drama in previous manifestations of the form, our knowledge and experience encourage us to think that we will enjoy further exposure to such representations.

Conventions of any kind are, as Richard Sparkes has said, 'the condition on which the bargain of the suspension of disbelief is struck with the audience' (1992: 147). There is pleasure to be found in any set of conventions that are well understood and widely shared (but not yet ridiculed or despised). If, however, the conventions become out of date or difficult to give credence to, or if they have been trumped in some way by new forms, significant change must occur otherwise a form will disappear. Conventions are always subject to a kind of 'Emperor's New Clothes' test, through which the majority of people will decline to question what they see most of the time. Indeed, the acceptance of mediated forms in general depends on this. But the fable of the emperor's new clothes is also salutary because it is important in another way to question what has been naturalised by convention. This is, of course, the very point of the fable: the unsophisticated child is so much more usefully critical than the sophisticated but sycophantic adult who cravenly kowtows to the emperor's vainglorious fantasy of importance.

The rise of television to prominence in the 1950s makes those years its primal decade – the time of emergence for generic conventions of all kinds. It was only gradually that these conventions began to be questioned, both inside and outside the television industry, and to be changed. In the formative historical period of television, as John Corner has written.

> A primary factor in the formation of generic styles was the search for the distinctively 'televisual', which perhaps worked from cinematic, theatrical, radio, newspaper or music-hall precedents, but which then reshaped the material in ways which used the medium to the best possible advantage. (1991: 13)

The generic conventions of drama-documentary and of documentary drama are quintessentially televisual.[14]

It is easy to see why the dramadoc/docudrama is likely to continue to have a place in broadcasting. In this form the camera's ability to go anywhere and see anything is both borrowed from documentary on behalf of the drama and extended by the drama on behalf of documentary. They go together to increase the camera's truth claim by denying its actual deficiency (it was not there in fact, but we can pretend it was in fiction). Our gaze as audience is disembodied; we are in the 'there-but-not-there' realm of the record at the same time as we inhabit the 'I-am-there' identificatory realm of the drama. In both cases the hidden corporeal presence behind the camera lens in real time is composed of a several-bodied film crew, but in television time (i.e. when we watch) there is only ever 'us alone' as we wrestle with the demands of evidence and belief. People sometimes want to ratify emotionally what they may already have understood intellectually. The camera's promise of complete seeing can only ever achieve completion if our emotions are stirred dramatically as well as our understanding increased intellectually.

The codes and conventions used in dramadoc/docudrama have been principally dependent on the changing nature of television drama. The direct influence of documentary has been less marked. Although there have been times when broadcasting institutions have tried to make programmes of this type a more permanent feature, they are usually made either by documentary or drama departments or by units of production formed especially to investigate something when there is no other way to tell it. The claim of 'no other way to tell it' is, pre-eminently, what makes dramadoc/docudrama such a controversial and disputed form[15] [. . .]. The least remarked thing that any controversy in the arts does is to measure the degree of our willingness to accept conventions. [. . .]

Notes

1   The only example I have found is in Feuer (1995: 41, note 2): 'recent drama documentary films such as *Silkwood* (1983).' On an American Internet search mechanism, 'the Electric Library', tapping in the word 'docudrama' (6 October 1997) yielded nineteen recent references: the word 'dramadoc' yielded none.

2   See also Derek Paget, 'Disclaimers, denials and direct address: Captioning in Docudrama', in John Izod and Richard Kilborn with Matthew Hibberd (eds), *From Grierson to the Docu-soap: Breaking the Boundaries*, University of Luton Press, 2000, pp. 197–208.

3   The 'Long Island Lolita Trilogy' was the name given to three docudramas based on a tabloid news story about an attempted murder in New York. The major networks all got involved, ABC making *The Amy Fisher Story* and NBC making *Lethal Lolita* (both 1992), while CBS broadcast *Casualties of Love* in 1993. See Alan Rosenthal, *Writing Docudrama: Dramatizing Reality for Film and TV*, Focal Press, 1995, pp. 19–20.

4   The theoretical term 'suture' usefully draws attention to the way the literal 'stitching together' of film frames by editing almost always guarantees a smooth narrative flow. See Hayward (1996: 371–9).

5   Sita Williams tells an instructive anecdote about this strange situation: the Israeli crew removed Marlboro cigarette packets from the Arab captors' table at one point, believing that these men would not buy a product made by 'the Great Satan'. In fact, this detail had been very carefully researched.

6   Both Keenan and McCarthy present much bleaker pictures of their guards in their memoirs.

7   This is very 'accurate' in terms of the published memoirs – see McCarthy and Morrell (1994: 101) and Keenan (1992a: 91) – apart from the mistake in the name of Robert Louis Stevenson's character (Ben, not 'Tom', Gunn); Palmer was possibly thinking of the poet Thom Gunn.

8   Michael Eaton was speaking at the 'Reality Time' conference, April 1996.

9   One celebrated American example was Donald Freed's 1970 play *Inquest*, which even had displays outside the theatre (see D. Freed, *Inquest*, New York, Hill and Wang, 1970: 17).

10 The 'opposers' were Peter Kosminsky, himself a maker of drama-documentaries, Roger Bolton, maker of such documentaries as Thames TV's *Death on the Rock*, and Mark Lawson, who was at that time television critic for the *Independent*.

11 Eventually there was a judicial review of the case and a private prosecution in 2000, brought by the Hillsborough Family Support Group.

12 Two major books on docudrama have appeared since *No Other Way To Tell It* was published in 1998; both will be found useful on definitions. See: Alan Rosenthal (ed.), *Why Docudrama?: Fact-Fiction on Film and TV*, Southern Illinois University Press, 1999; Steven N. Lipkin, *Real Emotional Logic: Film and Television Docudrama as Persuasive Practice*, Southern Illinois University Press, 2002.

13 Lynne Truss's remark (8 July 1996) in her *Times* review of *Killing Me Softly* (a dramadoc about Sara Thornton, a woman jailed for killing her husband and released after a campaign) is representative: 'With docudrama, two types of reality fight it out, and neither wins.'

14 Commentators from Caryl Doncaster in 1956 to David Edgar in 1981 have made this point; the drama-doc/docudrama (like the talk show, the sitcom, the soap opera and the news broadcast) is a televisual form; there is nothing quite like it in other media.

15 The phrase 'no other way to tell it' was originally Leslie Woodhead's. See the text of his Guardian/BFI lecture of 1981 in Rosenthal, 1999, pp. 101–10.

References

Corner, J. (ed.) (1991). *Popular Television in Britain: Studies in Cultural History*. London, British Film Institute.

—— (1996), *The Art of Record: A Critical Introduction to Documentary*, Manchester and New York, Manchester University Press.

Edgerton, G. (1991), 'High concept, small screen: reperceiving the industrial and stylistic origins of the American made-for-TV movie', *Journal of Popular Film and Television*, 19:3, 114–27.

Feuer, J. (1995), *Seeing Through the Eighties: Television and Reaganism*, London, British Film Institute.

Garnham, N. (1972), 'TV documentary and ideology', *Screen* 13:2, 109–15.

Hayward, S. (1996), *Key Concepts in Cinema Studies*, London and New York, Routledge.

McCarthy, J. and J. Morrell (1994), *Some Other Rainbow*, London, Corgi Books.

Sparkes, R. (1992), *Television and the Drama of Crime: Moral Tales and the Place of Crime in Public Life*, Milton Keynes, Open University Press.

Chapter 13

MARGARET MORSE

NEWS AS PERFORMANCE
The image as event

The drama of duration: the untelling of a dictatorship. [The Filipinos] watched the whole 50 minutes, the little family tyrant, repeating, obsessing . . . holding on for . . . the moments the Americans would cover . . . they were watching a dead man, and every second was savored. TV had been reversed and now power flowed upstream. A dictator under surveillance, television stripping the emperor bare. A whole nation watched a machine hand out its own justice, as spectacle toppled before the wrath of the real.

(Steve Fagin, *The Machine that Killed Bad People*, 1990)

THE YOUNG NEWS PRESENTERS in the Video Workshop of the Roŝka Refugee Camp in Slovenia in 1993 found that, "People had a particular model in their heads of what television was. It was in the minds of these people. So we had to make the news *look* like the news—what people were used to seeing. It was then that it became credible." The news in question consisted of reports of social unrest and armed conflict from around the globe (not just Bosnia), bootlegged off satellite from Radio Sarajevo, CNN, and Sky television and used as raw material to be integrated into a new narrative, edited by Bosnian refugees for Bosnian refugees. In the process of learning how to simulate the news, the refugees or "stowaways" found that it "was all one big manipulation." One of the two presenters sitting at the news desk in Chris Marker's documentary *Prime Time in the Camps* can't help breaking up as an ordinary person, or rather, a refugee, a "zero," performing an exalted role on the other side of the television screen.

However much the camp video succeeded in mimicking the format of the news, the refugees' project was different in instructive ways from American-style news productions, with their sharp role divisions and hierarchical structure. In the Video Workshop of Roŝka everyone was involved in capturing, sorting, editing, and performing the news: "We are all in the same situation and on an even footing. On both sides—those who film and those who talk." When the camp news producers/presenters found different interpretations of events in their sources, they simply juxtaposed them for the viewer to compare and evaluate her- or himself.

In another room in Camp Roŝka, refugees were invited to speak to the camera at length. Their willingness to participate and to pour out their hearts was not because these people were deprived of images of themselves: "Video has become part of daily life. In the room, the family explained that . . . even their departure [as refugees from Bosnia] has been filmed and they promise to bring the cassette." Their hunger was rather to be able to tell their own stories of what was now lost to someone who would listen and then to hold onto those stories in the flow of time. "These room stories show a huge need to communicate and, at the same time, an understanding that they are recording their memory." On the other hand, the ordinary person invited to tell his or her story to an American reporter will find that it is raw material for processing into a sound bite, a "cartoon bubble" of prepackaged thought that, according to Daniel Hallin's analysis, was an average of 4.2 seconds long in 1988, as compared to the 8.9 seconds granted to the elite of experts 1994, p. 137). Admittedly, the camp "room" stories were not designed to become news *per se*, but to satisfy other needs for the *intersubjectivity* that is the foundation of the sociality and civility most sorely missed by refugees. However, those needs—to be recognized, to communicate, and to remember—belong to people everywhere. It is appropriate to ask how they are or are not being satisfied every day in American society as well as during upheavals and crises in distant places.

Of course, a format is freely displaceable—anyone, even a "zero," can pose as a "television news anchor" and use the "look" if not the production values of the waning form of American news on television to tell quite different stories. Yet this normative format is a product of history that exacts its own price on the democratic values so closely associated with the news.

Formatting power: news that looks like the news

In research over the last fifteen years on the news, as well as other discursive formats and genres of American television employing the format of direct address by television personas to viewers— talk shows, commercials, sports, how-to's, logos, title and introductory sequences—I have concluded that disparities in power are marked into the format of the news, in stark contradiction to what has been called "television democracy." The American network news format is a very restrictive rather than inclusive discursive type with a monologic structure that both legitimates and severely limits the subjects produced by the news. While still drawing on the values and ethos of objectivity that evolved in print journalism (i.e., the referential fallacy), television news depends on a personality system employing virtual direct address to the viewer (that is, on the enunciative fallacy) in a "here" and "now" that is composed of what are actually highly processed and symbolic images. This format of news delivery cloaks what is, after all, an impersonal transmission with the impression of discourse across a desk with the quasisubjects or personalities in the machine. Far from confronting us with social reality, instrumental and impersonal relations are given their most disguised and utopian expression by simulating the paramount reality of speaking subjects exchanging conversation in a shared space and time. This is not at all to impugn the motives, integrity, or the journalistic methods of any particular news personnel, but rather to seek to identify large historical trends and to interpret their meaning. The resort to such charismatic and primary forms in the news suggests also that it is part of a larger cultural shift of dominance away from the disengaged forms of realism, literacy, and objectivity which have been dominant in Western culture since the age of industrialization.[1]

Full subjectivity in American television is reserved for representatives of television (i.e., talk show hosts, news anchors), the spokespersons of corporate sponsors and advertisers, and, under special circumstances, the president and a few other representatives of government and the armed forces. In a position of frontality in what simulates a first-order space shared with us, beyond the glass, the anchor speaks to us virtually as if fully engaged with us as viewers. The anchor is also the reference point for the division of the virtual realm inside the news image into planes that are arranged hierarchically nearer to or farther from the anchor. These planes sink in and out of visibility and audibility depending on transitional graphics and sounds and the anchor's words and gestures such as the gaze shift, the head "toss," and the chair swivel. Thus, the news anchor also acts as shifter between stories and levels within the news, as well as between television and the viewer.

The effect of American news conventions is to extremely constrain, if not actually deny members of the public the opportunity to speak as subjects, to shift the agenda under discussion, or to govern the length or context of a statement. The one-way structure and hierarchial conventions of television are ill-equipped to satisfy the desire of ordinary persons to "be someone," and to be recognized or to speak as subjects about the things that give meaning and structure to life in common.

In contrast, dialogue demands that we take the other seriously, that we take responsibility for our statements and their consequences in the world, and most of all, that we are prepared to change our beliefs or at least our demands in response to the other. However, the viewer's influence on television discourse consists largely of the power to switch channels or turn the power off. (Interactivity that does not serve inter-subjectivity does not remedy this fundamental powerlessness.)

Yet why should anyone expect television to satisfy the need for intersubjectivity or substantive discourse? Though television de facto is a quasipublic realm, it is not a fundamentally democratic institution. Despite the catch phrase of "television democracy," the power of consumers to collectively influence television ratings must be strongly distinguished from voting (Meehan 1990), just as popular entertainment meets other needs than does public discourse. Rather television is corporate and commercial and its programming dominated by entertainment designed to attract advertising through high ratings. There are admirable exceptions to this generalization, for instance, on public broadcasting, public access channels or the cable channel CSPAN; however, these forums are not really public in the sense that they can afford to display oppositional values or to air social conflict for very long. Even political candidates are forced to address the public largely in the form of commercial advertising.

The great divide

Perversely enough, the very barrier of the screen that anchors and hosts are empowered to overlook or disavow in order to virtually address the viewer is, according to Dan Hallin, actually a great divide between television and the public, at least on American television:

> [Television journalism] presents the interpretation of political events as belonging to a sphere that includes the journalists themselves and other political élities, but does not include the audience. This message is implicit in the treatment of the television screen as an impenetrable barrier. In Italy, political thinking is assumed to take place on both sides of the screen, which represents only a line between those who have current information and those who don't yet have it. In the United States politics takes place only behind the screen, and members of the public can become a part of it only to the extent that they are represented there by journalists.
>
> (Hallin 1994, p. 129)

Hallin concludes that "journalists need to move from conceiving their role in terms of mediating between political authorities and the mass public, to thinking of it also as a task of opening up political discussion in civil society, to use the term popular in the new democracies in Eastern Europe" (1994, p. 176).

Beyond the screen between television and the public, there is another divide or "wall within" the news which segregates members of the public from news personalities. "Sound bites" emanate purely from that other space about which the news is reporting and consist of very brief snatches of, for instance, comments made in interview, or a bit of ambient sound and speech from victims at a disaster site. Since the news is about putting the world as an object into words and images, sound bites provide that essential bit of authenticity that becomes all the more necessary in television news that is saturated with its own personalities. Sound bites are also at the bottom of the discursive hierarchy of the news, at two, three, or four degrees' remove from the anchor. Like the inhabitants of story space in the novel or film or behind the fourth wall in a dramatic presentation, the on-screen public in the news must pretend to be unaware of the camera and to address their responses to the second-degree narrator, the reporter. In other words, the counterpart of the fiction that the anchor in the image *can* address the television audience directly is the fiction that members of the public in the image *cannot*. Instead, members of the public are mediated by television itself as the only full subject.

The brevity of audiovisual material generated at the scene of an event and by people speaking for themselves rewrites history in a number of ways. First and foremost, all discourse in the world becomes raw material for the news institution's own performance. One egregious example of this occurred on CNN on December 27, 1989, in an aftermath-of-revolution story on the advent of free speech in Romania:

> "Now everyone wants to talk," said the reporter in a stand up. "Hold on a minute. Here's someone who wants to talk to you." The video image cuts to a man looking directly at the camera, saying it was his first time on Western television and he had some words for Americans. Cut to a woman in 3/4 view saying, "I can die with a smile on my lips." Cut to a man saying, "I could before speak only to friends and family between four walls. I am asking the American people for information, foreign press accounts (fading out as the voice over of the reporter begins), educational materials."

Note the significance of the Romanians' shift from virtual address to American viewers into the conventional eyes-averted interview: we see a public being taught its place according to the conventions of power and position in news discourse. We see *that* members of the Romanian public speak, but hear next to nothing of what they say. The contradiction between conventional television practice and free speech is opened up in this typical and quite professional news story.

Between first-order (virtual) television discourse and the bottom level inhabited by the public, there are inflected and part-subjectivities. In my "Talk, Talk, Talk" (Morse 1985a), I identified these intermediate levels as the speech of anchors and other news presenters among themselves, the second-degree narration of reporters and interviewers in the field, as well as the partial subjectivity of experts in three-quarter face. Persons on a monitor in the news set are held at a one-degree ontological remove from the anchor's physical space. Multiple interviewees can even appear in different monitors anywhere on the set and conduct a second-order virtual conversation among themselves.

Perhaps the most appropriate metaphor for the news stack of discursive levels that results is the *zoom* or shifting focus of a lens, that in moving from the macro through telescopic lens reveals utterly different worlds of reference that have in common their link to the anchor. Another contemporary metaphor is the computer desktop with a stack of hypercards that can be shuffled by strings of association . . . In any case, this multilayered space is hierarchically arranged around the anchor, who relates the news "personally," albeit virtually, to the viewer.

[. . .]

Anchor appeal

[. . .] The credibility assigned to the news format (as I discuss at length in "The Television News Personality and Credibility", (1985b) is a function of its engaged and subjective mode of presentation, exemplified by "the display of news personnel" and "the visual coverage of events" (Comstock cited in Morse, 1985b, p. 55). Note that the anchor is a special kind of star supported by subdued sartorial and acting codes that convey "sincerity." Sincerity is the unification of social role and personal belief, as well as the unification of the speaking subject and the subject in the sentence that our own twentieth-century cultural experience tells us is *imaginary*. The news as institution, however, does not admit this disparity (which, to use Lionel Trilling's terms, would mean being "authentic" rather than "sincere"). It posits instead a subject who embodies "a shared viewer fantasy, a collective need" (Powers 1977, p. 2) for what has come to be, according to former CBS President Richard Wald, "the traditional sense of what an anchorman is: in effect, the all-wise, all-seeing mouth, that person who knows everything and will tell it to you. That person never really existed" (quoted in Barrett 1978, p. 22). However, that person may be constructed, even in the face of healthy skepticism, in order to maintain cohesive cultural fictions. Cronkite said recently he wanted to respond to people who tell him, "I believe every word you say" with "You're not supposed to" (James). In the language of disavowal or the "I know it's just TV news," the "but nevertheless" was at its strongest when television was newer, more centralized, and yet to be challenged by cable, satellites, and the Internet. As Caryn James writes, "As Cronkite talked to middle America, he came to stand for middle America, but such authority is not possible or even desirable today."

While the local news anchor team of mixed race and gender allude to a diverse community, since the early 1980s the network anchors have been three almost interchangeable "tall, white, Anglo-Saxon Protestants with dark hair coiffed very carefully, thin faces with an intelligent look."[2] Of course, network television news is actually performed by an entourage of news professionals, as well as by the TV producer and crew, and the on-screen network anchor or team (or in television terms, the "talent") is merely the most visible representative of this speaking collective subject. Interestingly, the part of the news consisting of "tell stories" was called "the magic" by Walter Cronkite, anchor of the "CBS Evening News" from 1962 to 1981. Indeed, it is the speaking subject or anchor as "talking head" that is the link between the message or utterance and the enunciation of the news, performing the "magic" of binding so many elements and cultural institutions together to form a coherent "reality."

For the anchor represents not merely the news *per se*, or a particular network or corporate conglomerate that owns the network, or television as institution, or the public interest; rather, he represents the complex nexus of all of them. In this way, the network anchor position is a "symbolic representation of the institutional order as an integrated totality" (Berger and Luckmann 1967, p. 76), an institutional role on a par with that of the president or of a Supreme Court justice, although the role originates in corporate practices rather than political or judicial processes. [. . .]

An unscheduled presidential address interrupting regular programming (and, of course, without ads) conventionally signals the power of the office and an extraordinary situation. The then President Bush's address and quasideclaration of war ("The Liberation of Kuwait has Begun," January 16, 1991) suspended commercial imperatives on television, in favor of the martial imperatives. Subsequent analysis of polling data shows that a significant gap in public opinion against and in support of war remained that was simply suspended for a time, in a bandwagon effect of patriotic fervor (Mueller 1994, p. 138–9). The flurry of discussion that began in the crisis mode quickly abated; dissent was discredited and downplayed. The computer graphics had long been prepared to roll; the experts from Brookings and the retired generals were on the network and cable payrolls. But the militarization of television went deeper. Instead of sound bites from "real" people, that is, troops or civilians, weapons such as the Stealth were personalized as hometown heroes and military spokespersons became television hosts with the power to make the press into secretaries for oral dictation. Reporters in the field were sent into the desert without an uplink. Even the president had to defend his supreme anchor position against the wild popularity General Schwarzkopf had garnered as the chief anchor of war reporting.

    [. . .]

    Since there are few other organs for inclusive and substantial discourse on social and cultural values in American life, the responsibility for interpreting the world and posing a political course of action and a social agenda falls on a very limited number of public personas, including such news personalities and the presidency[3] (Relatively more personas in entertainment enact our dreams and nightmares and are rewarded to varying degrees with money and unrelenting public fascination.) The rest of us are the voice on the phone on the shopping channel, an inhabitant on the floor of a talk show, or are trapped in a sound bite that, as Dan Hallin's research shows, grows shorter by the year. Our restrictive discursive system not only drastically reduces the number and kind of subjects who can speak for themselves to a wider public, it also might explain why, despite hundreds of hours of news and talk per week on American television, television as a cultural form seems to have said little about "what's really happening in this country."

Tabloids

The hierarchical model of the news has been challenged by even more engaged and somewhat less hierarchical formats in daytime talk shows that feature an on-screen audience of "real people." The audiences act as a kind of jury that evaluates onstage discourse and often pronounces judgment on the guests, other ordinary or "real" people who represent some aspect of socially controversial behavior. Daytime talk show guests are usually singled out by means of a low dais or stage, signifying their slightly different plane of performance and their availability as objects for scrutiny by the crowd. The home viewer may be positioned variously as a voyeur, a member of the audience, or may share collusive glances with the host. The talk show host acts as mediator between realms of the dais or stage, studio audience, and television viewer.[4]

    The subject matter of daytime talk shows is controversial but with few exceptions, trivial. Elaine Scarry, writing in the critical context of the deliberations that preceded the Gulf War's announcement (not declaration), pronounced talk shows on the crisis with Iraq a spectacle of communication that lacks substance. Rather than functioning as public discourse or as a genuine populism, the burgeoning numbers of talk shows "perform a kind of *mimesis of deliberation*," that infantilizes and marginalizes the American population (Scarry 1993, p. 59). Thus the issues we see debated on television talk shows are not the grave matters for which we are responsible, but private affairs which are not a public concern. We are asked to authorize only what entails little to no risk or sacrifice on our part.

    Contemporary daytime talk show discourse on television is not organized around the slow payoff of working through an issue or controversy inclusively and over the long term. Instead a kind of discursive virginity is preferred, in which something is disclosed or done or someone is confronted, preferably for the first time, live. Far from allowing truth to surface, such a perform-ance elicited by the camera is designed to create a spectacle that might otherwise never have happened or might never have been such an exaggerated, or on occasion, deceitful way to provoke the emotional reaction of the parties involved. Then the participants are left on their own to sort out the aftermath of this intervention in their lives. In extreme instances, the ambush and shock tactics of talk shows have resulted in actual mayhem, injury on the show or, subsequently, murder.[5]

Considering how potentially humiliating the situations on the dais in daytime talk and evening dating shows can be, why are "real people" so willing and eager to participate in them? Presuming they have some rights and must give permission, why do even malefactors on police "reality programming" allow themselves—without pixellated faces—to be frisked spread-eagled by police? Perhaps even a minor role of being bad on television is good, a kind of confirmation that, yes, one has lived and even mattered in the social drama; the largely thwarted desire to speak and be recognized and to know and be known is such a powerful motivating force in ordinary social life that any context serves better than oblivion.

Tabloid news magazines use exaggerated techniques of virtual address to the viewer, but they are less concerned with "real people" than with featuring celebrity interviews and gossip. Hallin regards the tabloids as a "deeply problematic development for culture," threatening to divide the news even further into knowledge for an elite and reports for the poor and less educated that appeal to irrationality, fear, and personal threats. However, it could be argued that the tabloids, with their relentless, even persecutory attention to the personal lives of celebrities, may be a perverse manifestation of the hunger for a discourse on changing social values. Is the obsession of American media with quirky areas of celebrities' personal lives and fates so consuming because prurient interest in this pantheon of stars is so extraordinary or because it is a displaced discourse on larger social values, albeit stripped of political significance and personal responsibility? Television tabloids and talk shows are pleasurable and titillating forums that do challenge social conventions and probably do appeal to the profound mysteries of human desire—without, however, plumbing them.

The weakness of a public sphere in the United States has long been recognized and criticized in different ways by social critics, philosophers, and scholars; and, it could be said to be endemic to a system where democratic access is almost universally subordinated to the commercial exchange-value of discourse. Television discourse is with few exceptions a function of the market value of time sold to advertisers and sponsors, a crippling limitation on public and civic life, now largely conducted in the media and on the Internet rather than the piazza or public square. Fewer yet are the forms (such as the archaic and rarefied town meeting) in which members of the public are invited to air their differences with each other. The discourses that could bind disparate social groups together, build empathy, and convey a sense of responsibility for society as a whole are feeble on television, and in vast areas of society they do not figure at all. Rather than addressing the obstacles to achieving a fair and free society, representations of the good life in advertising and entertainment have become the "cultural glue" of the American dream, with little attention to the hope or dignity needed to achieve it. The mood of dissatisfaction and disillusionment with politics, government, and social engagement of all kinds in large sectors of the population suggests that this "glue" is losing its grip.

The lack of public discourse also makes any exposure of tales and images of victimization on television into a dilemma. If television viewers sense that watching images of horror from all over the globe entails a kind of moral responsibility, no wonder they are said to fear the "CNN syndrome" (that is, emotional anguish at the sight of the images of victims of atrocity or disaster on television, leading to short-term international attention to those victims whose plight was most recently aired) and to suffer from moral, sympathy, or donor fatigue in what seems an amorphous and overwhelming task of living up to our image as "the world's only remaining superpower." While we caught glimpses on television of the victims of what Daniel Schorr called a "living room holocaust" in Bosnia (in his PBS radio commentaries), there was very little public discussion on what meaning the ethnic conflicts in the former Yugoslavia might have for Americans, what values were at stake, and what moral as well as mortal risks were involved in the ultimate intervention of the United States and NATO in them. The domestic American response was long in a state of near paralysis, lacking the direction and conviction, if not consensus, that such a public (not merely a grudging congressional) airing could have given it. The problem has often been identified as one of leadership, though it appears to be more fundamentally institutional. Bosnia is only the most recent of the great ruptures in the post-Cold War world in which Americans appear to drift. Not quite knowing who we as a people are, or, more accurately, how we perform ourselves, either in our own domestic eyes or abroad, we don't know what is worth our sacrifice.

"The turning"

While discourse as conversation and even public speech is usually characterized by the reversibility of "I" and "you," discourse simulated on television is presented as if it were direct and permeable, when it is actually one-way and irreversible. Or rather, it just seems that way. Depending on the extremity of the circumstances, the tables will turn—subject becomes object—and the valence of power and fame can shift from plus to minus in a matter of seconds. The electronic spectacle that makes or breaks celebrity is equally capable of sanctioning or undermining the dictatorial power of a Marcos or Ceauşescu in a matter of hours. Extreme situations also highlight the potential for twists and reversals in what can never be a simple or straightforward speech-act.

In 1989, the historical shift the Germans call "die Wende" or *the turning* took place, "a staggering news story . . . the crumbling of communism as the sole official truth in the nations of Eastern Europe and now even in the Soviet Union. There will not be many bigger stories this century, if ever" (Du Brow 1990). Unlike the "velvet revolution" that seemed to fold into Western socioeconomic expectations without resistance, the Romanian revolution and atrocities in Bosnia signaled that despite "winning the Cold War," "the turning" wouldn't go smoothly—even for Americans.

The favorite U.S. television icon of the end of the Soviet or Evil Empire is the Berlin Wall chipped at by thousands, eventually falling bloodlessly like the walls of Jericho. Yet, in a way, the Wall might as well have been a photographic negative or a left/right mirror inversion of America, for it reflected the projections of not-self against which a sense of Americanness was constituted. Communism had been our major stabilizing and unifying force, the justification for a belief system that has framed and hierarchized American values, deciding the allocation of resources and damping down the acceptable degree of public dissent since the end of World War II (see Hallin 1994). Now that dark mirror was broken after more than four and a half decades of military potlatch—that is, the destruction of economic resources for deterrent display or, as President Reagan put it, "spending them [that is, the Soviets] into the ground." The end of it all seemed suddenly as dreaded as it was desired. "Winning" the Cold War paradoxically shook American confidence and its sense of mission[6] Even its sense of time would have to change from that of a constant state of emergency. (The alternative is not a nostalgic view of an intact America uncontaminated by government and illegal immigration.)

Is anything more uncanny than to lose a prime foundation of one's identity—the orientation "East" and "West"? In such a situation, an air of unreality or tentativeness hovers over recent events. The narrative of reform or revolution in Eastern Europe did more than any other news story, including stories about domestic issues of a staggering deficit or social and environmental ills, to allow awareness of the inadequacies of the American media-political superstructure to surface, however briefly. Though Gorbachev cried "uncle" first, the long-term toll of the Cold War on our own economy and social fabric had become very conspicuous by 1989. A growing sense of the failure of "television democracy" was expressed (largely in the print media),[7] at the same time that television and other high technology were considered at least partly responsible for freeing Eastern Europe, namely the heroic "revolution in a box," extolled by Ted Koppel [host of ABC "Nightline"]. These two strands of media self-criticism—a self-questioning mode and a celebratory mode—also influenced the tone of American press and television coverage of Eastern Europe.

American televisual coverage of the Romanian Revolution reveals as much about Americans and our public sphere as about the events in Romania in 1989. It is instructive to compare American coverage to the "televisual events" on Romanian television. In a "televisual event" the image on screen and acts in physical space interact with and change one another. On such occasions, televisual hierarchies can fall apart. The televisual events in Romania were presented "live" and in duration, not in the "real time" that simulates duration of American television. Processed and compressed, computer-generated, and packaged images and stories control the flow of time and are "live" only by virtue of their simultaneity of transmission and reception. The heterogeneous temporalities channeled into simultaneous strands of "flow" on television may simulate the *duration* of time unfolding, but do not open into the unknown, nor do they accumulate or invite knowledge or favor reflection. The news is rather an effort repeated daily from zero and delivered in packages moving at an ever-faster pace. Banishing duration from the American form of the news—with the exception of disasters, wars, crises, trials, hearings, and the like—has economic rationality and strategic advantages in the deployment of power as spectacle.

When a *media event*—a ceremony in real space staged for televisual transmission (Dayan and Katz)[8]—is disrupted or gets out of control, it can become one or more *televisual events*, often marked in the flow of images on-screen by such things as wobbling and mobile framing, freeze-frames, masking, and "snow." The revolution, the uprising, and, in the light of subsequently compiled evidence, the coup d'état[9] in Romania commenced during a media event on December 21, 1989, televised from the square in Bucharest in front of party headquarters. [. . .] Speaking directly, albeit virtually, to his nation-state as the all-powerful Father, Ceauşescu suddenly shifted from subject to pathetic object of terror under the electronic gaze of the camera. Some people in the crowd, a compulsory assembly frozen below the dais under a claque of Securitate, were enraged by rumors of a massacre in Timisoara. Apparently willing to risk imprisonment or death, they had begun to shout down Ceauşescu's address to television. The state television camera began to shake as it caught the shift of terror from the space under the gaze of absolute power to the frozen body and impotent voice of an old man, who didn't at all resemble the "Genius of the Carpathians" on huge banners below. As one of those later inside a car honking in celebration exclaimed, "To think that it was just an idiot we were afraid of. People had to die to get rid of him!" Suddenly, "snow" interrupted the image transmission for three minutes, but left the sounds of catcalls and a patriotic song on the screen. Stock footage of crowds waving giant banners was quickly substituted for the emptying square. Then television transmission ceased for a while. In untransmitted footage of the moments following Ceauşescu's humiliation, Ceauşescu can be heard continually shouting "Hallo! Hallo!" as if this lapse of image were a simple interruption in television transmission that could be restored if only the power came on again. Ceauşescu's visible loss of power—marked by loss of television signal—created the vacuum in which subsequent events could occur. Many of those events were captured via camcorder, while still others remained unrecorded conspiratorial moments, the content of which can only be surmised.

In this case, "the turning" was expressed in the perceptible shift of power from the screen to the physical space in the public square beyond the frame. According to Geert Lovink, "What was special about the Romanian tele-revolution is that the cameras faithfully rendered the dynamics and rhythm of the events, and that for a few days they were not following any orders from above" (Lovink 1993, p. 59). Thus, shifts of power were all the more clearly marked in manipulations of the image stream, including instances when cameras (televisual and camcorder) actually turned around and sought out events out of curiosity and without agenda or supervision. The following sections will compare "the turning" or reversal of power as it occurred in Romania with the Romanian Revolution on American network news, CNN, and "Nightline" coverage, plus a camcorder record compiled by Harun Farocki and Andrei Ujica's documentary *Videogramme einer Revolution*.

Romanian televisual events

[. . .]

The televisual event that made viewers into on-screen protagonists of the revolution occurred on December 22, the morning after Ceauşescu's debacle and after Ceauşescu had escaped from Bucharest by helicopter from the Central Committee Building under siege. Part of the crowd heading toward the state television station in Bucharest met the poet Mircea Dinescu, newly liberated from house arrest, and put him on their lead tank. The crowd entered the studio and formed a memorable image of collective subjectivity at and behind a table in the tiny and somewhat antiquated television studio. "What one sees here is a nation packaged into a compact-image, where ethnic groups are being put together in a brotherly way. Everybody gets his pick here: young and old; man and woman; and not only for the Romanians, but for the whole world" (Lovink 1993, 60). Dinescu, after being passionately introduced, proceeded to speak a blessing from amidst a tableau of people on the screen: "God has turned his face toward Romania again"—in effect televisually declaring the end of Ceauşescu's government (Cullen 1990, p. 104). (Later, behind the scenes in the Farocki-Ujica documentary, he says, "I hope things will turn out all right.") After he spoke, others in the tableau of people around him on-screen took turns speaking. This example of power grasped from the bottom up was an opportunity seized for autonomous and creative public discourse, though speech from the tableau of a crowd on-screen to the television audience remained one-way. Furthermore, the position seized was an unstable inversion of Ceauşescu's speaking subjecthood and the speeches uttered there were as likely to be based on lies and deceit as on shattering emotional release and vulnerability.

The National Salvation Front used the tableau in the television studio to establish its legitimacy operationally, essentially allowing it to govern by issuing directives that called the army to the aid of the populace, declared solidarity with the people, warned against poisoned water, and gave orders deploying troops and provisions. It is hard to imagine a more direct convergence of the television as a stage and social reality into one virtual whole—not to ignore the staging that was going on behind the scenes.

After the December uprising appeared to have been hijacked, crowds began again to gather in front of the television station in Bucharest, demanding that their protests against continued communist control (and for an independent Romanian television) be shown on Romanian television. In response, a monitor was set up outside showing the crowd on television to the crowd, in another doubling effect. Perhaps the drive for agents in "real" space to see their own images, to see and be themselves, or better yet, to see their desire confirmed, is underestimated wherever television is understood as "representation." There was a glimpse of success in fulfilling the crowd's demand for self-confirmation; a utopian vision of self-determination was realized, if only on the screen and without immediate consequences for social change. Later, many Romanians reportedly played cassettes of the Romanian television of those days in December over and over, again and again until utter disillusionment set in.

[   ]

Ironically, later in June 1990 the very same performative use of television that constituted the revolution served newly elected President Iliescu to brutalize protest into submission and to rewrite the significance of this act, in a procedure reminiscent of Chinese publicity after the massacre at Tiananmen Square. Such rewriting is another kind of performative act and a televisual event.

The American Romanian revolution

The Romanian revolution in the country in which it occurred was not the event as it was reported in national news and CNN in the United States. In Romania and much of Eastern Europe, the events in the state television studio and on the streets unfolded on screens almost without interruption—except for significant lapses in transmission or "snow." American viewers saw the surreal spectacle just before Christmas of a crowd of half a million people in the streets, tank warfare and house-to-house fighting, bodies wounded and dead, and cries of grief, that appeared on various national and satellite-cable networks. However, reviewing many hours of archival recordings of American television confirms that Romanian television was almost never discussed in American programs about Romania, nor was it retransmitted at length. Nor did the "universal hallmark of the revolution," the tableau of the crowd in the television studio, have the significance in the United States that it held elsewhere in Eastern or Western Europe.

The network news, even Ted Koppel's half-hour of analysis on ABC, "Nightline," is the antithesis of duration, a model of brevity and immediacy, focused on telling stories, and hearing from experts in the immediate present, and hence not a tool for analysis of long-term trends or indepth investigation of issues.[10] Although there are different registers and a wide disparity in the degree of news condensation and "processing" in network news, CNN, PBS's "MacNeil-Lehrer NewsHour" (now "The NewsHour with Jim Lehrer"), and Ted Koppel's "Nightline," in each case, discourse in the world of events is compressed rather than allowed to unfold. (The only exception might be CSPAN.)[11] However, it is important to remember that truth does not reside in any particular pace or editing strategy.

Reports of a crackdown in Romania began on network news on December 18, followed on the 19th by interviews with dissident Romanians, conducted in a "terrorized" mode—disguising voices and using black silhouettes on screen.[12] Though coverage in the U.S. was typical of each news institution's presentational style, and the news stories, even on the networks, were slightly longer than usual, footage from Romania was offered typically in brief sound bites. It was, however, as part of "the reform movement in Eastern Europe," the most heavily covered news story of 1989 in the United States (Center for Media and Public Affairs 1990).

"Nightline" and "television democracy"

In his earlier 1989 ABC special, "Revolution in a Box," "Nightline" host Ted Koppel had expressed faith in television democracy, referring to popular access to technological means of capturing, storing, and distributing images—the camcorder, the VCR, the portable satellite dish, and the computer, technologies that he appears to regard as social change in and of themselves:

> Television used to be the exclusive province of government and enormously wealthy corporations. They decided what you would see and when. Not any more. Television is falling into the hands of the people. The technology is becoming more affordable and accessible. They haven't mastered it yet, but they will. A form of television democracy is sweeping the world, and like other forms of democracy that preceded it, its consequences are likely to be beyond our imagination.
>
> I am Ted Koppel. Good Night.

Koppel was not anticipating anything as low-tech as the takeover of the Romanian state television station in Bucharest. Indeed, his "Nightline" report on Romania in April 1990 ignored the series of televisual events with very real political consequences discussed above in favor of focusing almost entirely on power at the top: the fall of the Ceaușescus—their opulent lifestyle, their escape, capture, trial, and execution, all set to ominous underscoring. (Koppel's program on Tiananmen Square has been criticized on similar grounds.) "Nightline"'s research team gathered amazing footage of the fate of the Ceaușescus supplied by camcorders operating seemingly everywhere, supplementing "Nightline"'s own footage of the regime's secret listening posts in underground tunnels and behind double walls. Of course, the documentary report featured Koppel as narrator and editorial commentator throughout and submitted all its documentation to extensive editing and electronic manipulation. [. . .]

While, by his own reckoning, approximately 60 percent of Koppel's Romania program in April consisted of roving camcorder footage, it was framed by Koppel's very strong presence and his project of debunking both the revolution and Ceaușescu's apparatus of terror as a sham. And despite Koppel's belief in the camcorder as "television democracy," he himself has framed the issue of video footage made by "real people" on the news largely in terms of its tenuous reality-status. "The same technology that can be used to reveal truth can be used to conceal it, to confuse reality. . . . Manipulation or altering reality is now within the budget of almost any political group in the world."

Why is such amateur footage of disasters, uprisings, riots, and hostage situations used as the sign of the real so often discussed as potential fraud? Why is what on one hand seems so real—the finality of death or the spontaneously "live"—greeted with such uneasiness and disbelief? Perhaps the most superficial explanation is that the expansion of nonprofessional access to television is a threat to any notion of reality or truth in a single and authoritative sense. The sense of mastering and being actually above world events conveyed by the American news media is set at risk. [. . .]

Camcorders in the hands of the general public enlarge the capacity for real-time recording, as well as the possibility of continuous surveillance of a society from below without pause, always. The advantage of surveillance from below is not in its greater reality or truth, but in its multiplicity—provided it is disseminated in a way that allows discourse to unfold. Media "democracy" as a private camcorder culture of oppositional video not only in Poland and Czechoslovakia but in the American gay subculture, in Chile, or the West Bank can be a force that eludes not only state but corporate control and transcends national boundaries as well as professional protocols. Consider, however, that camcorder footage is almost never allowed anything more than a sound bite presence in conventional formats on American television.

[. . .]

Camcorder events à Farocki and Ujica

Harun Farocki and Andrei Ujica's documentary on the Romanian Revolution, *Videogramme einer Revolution*, is a concordance of camcorder footage, reconstructing the same events from multiple vantage points in counterpoint to what was happening on official Romanian television. The footage in question was available in archives because it was no longer a fresh and thus valuable commodity. Perhaps because many of the camcordists in question were television and governmental workers, we also have astonishing access to what is going on behind the scenes.[13] The documentary's approach honors its sources with lengthy shots in chronological sequence and few voice-overs. Shots are allowed to implicitly comment on each other. Long, one-shot sequences with an utter lack of photogenia are embraced.

The opening segment of the documentary offers a prime example of camera-induced performance. A wounded young woman is seen on a gurney moaning in pain in Timisoara, Romania on the same day as Ceauşescu's failed media event—December 21, 1989. Told (citing the translation in subtitles) "Speak to the camera, you'll be on TV," a mask appears and a podium-style speech is elicited as she speaks lucidly and directly to the camcorder without pause for over three minutes, concluding, "in the name of the Co-op, I wish to join the great revolution, the youth of Timisoara and Bucharest. We want a better life, freedom for young people, bread to eat and happiness." Her speech is so eloquent throughout, it has the flavor of something preprepared or canned, yet it is spoken by someone wounded and in pain—hardly a media event. Seeing her performance in its entirety from the gurney is the only way to fully appreciate the effort involved. Instead, the performance points to the other side of the image, the camera in an *offscreen* space of enunciation that teaches us to ask, who elicited this performance and where were they situated? That is, we consider the station point of the photographer also as a metaphor of social position and vested interest.

[. . .]

Videogrramme documents duplicity in events behind the scenes and on television with strategic contrasts. At one point in the Bucharest TV station, something is held up as a symbol of the revolution that proves to be a lipstick; later, in a tearful Christmas celebration, another symbol of the revolution, a little red heart, is held up by one of the people in the tableau on screen. There is also a fairly humorous discussion about whose helicopters have been shot down in confusion—supposedly by Libyan terrorists, though we hear men behind the scenes exclaiming, "What terrorists?! The helicopters could only be yours [the army's] or mine [the Securitate's]!"

[. . .]

Meanwhile, shooting seemingly at random continued in the streets for days after the outcome of it all was quite decided. Somehow the snipers fighting the revolution were never active on the scene when the camcorders or news cameras arrived. Again, *Videogramme* teaches us to ask about vectors reaching beyond the field of view on screen: who is shooting at whom and why? There is a particularly funny sequence of outtakes of an American reporter on the scene of what purports to be a gun battle. Every time he begins his "crouch-down" report, the soldiers around him start to shoot, clearly performing for the camera, but drowning him out in the process. In commentary about the shooting, a voice-over informs us that "later there was talk of combat units from the military intelligence service which in simulated skirmishes had to feign an armed opponent in order to assist the army to victory on the side of the revolution."

However, the documentary also offers moving performances of testimony: the last shot is an address to a crowd and the camera that suggests that despite the futility and sorrow of the uprising, the speaker had learned something about privation and its effects:

I just wanted to add, the dictator, the criminal we saw today on TV is dead. He lied to us so much that we hated someone if he earned 300 more lei. His children had millions in the bank. He forced us to do without . . . "our land needs every dollar" . . . and all the time the money was shared among the party. We had no fun. The lights went out at 6 pm. We grew up hating minorities. And the Hungarians and the Germans are our friends; we've lived together for ages. And now our children have died . . . and many of us have died.

[. . .]

Cyberculture in context: The process and "working through"

Remembering how "the process" functions on CNN, John Ellis has hypothesized that television as a whole works in a similar way that he calls "working through" ("Television as Working Through" 48). Drawing on Pierre Sorlin's suggestion that in the face of the often inadequate and totally contingent image material of the news, documentaries, soap operas, and television fiction are all involved in a metaphorical "steadying of the image" (Sorlin, cited in Ellis 1996), Ellis proposes television to be a vast "forum for interpretations" (p. 71).[14] Events that are "radically incomplete," yet that "demand explanation" or "incite curiosity, revulsion and the usually frustrated or passing desire for action," are submitted to a "process of repression that psychoanalysis describes: a process that does not eradicate but places them elsewhere" [in what might be called the Symbolic order], "a process necessary for civilized life to remain possible" (p.53). Beginning with the news as "wild footage from a wild world" and passing through various genres—chat or talk shows, soap opera, documentary, sport, and narrative forms, in a progression of increasing narrative closure— television "comes to terms" with the flood of information that would otherwise overwhelm us. Ellis stresses the openness of this process, in which no material is ever entirely explained or resolved, just "continually worried over until it is exhausted" (p. 48). [. . .]

While Ellis cautions that the process is not like sausage making, his notion of working through does rest upon a nature/culture contrast in which the news is raw material for civilization, as if news were the first footfall into jungle or desert. It also implicitly considers the news in terms of representation, not presentation. However, Ellis would probably agree that the raw material of the news is already "culture," that is, already full of many voices telling stories which news conventions effectively silence. "The news" is not a found object, but a cultural product and its reality is the social reality that we perform and call forth together.

While I question assumptions in the progression from news to narrative, Sorlind and Ellis's fundamental point about the repetition on television of similar material in genre after genre can be illustrated with numerous examples. Take, for instance, the justice system as it passes through transmission of the actual "live" trial and the recorded trial with commentary, to the reenactment of an actual trial by actors to "People's Court" (a television surrogate court that "actually" decides cases) and "The Judge" (offering dramatic reenactment of legal cases), to docudramas and fictional court cases on "Perry Mason," "L.A. Law," and "Murder One." The enforcement of the law takes shape in camcorder footage, "live" and recorded transmissions, reenactments and simulations in, for instance, "Cops" (direct documentary), "Top Cops" (reenactments), and "America's Most Wanted" (reenactment and audience interaction as a surrogate justice system allied with actual police departments). The proposed airing of state executions is the limit condition of what appears to be an incipient parallel system of justice with its own televisual codes that operates in a virtual space between police squad cars and helicopters, the courts/television studios, and our living rooms. This mix of simulated and actual justice is not only ontologically confused with real consequences, it could gradually change the law itself in ways that are more televisual and directly "interactive." As part of a surrogate justice system, viewers have gradually been asked to become both judge and jury (in the court of public opinion) by watching television. "Working through" then takes ontologically diverse forms that reach beyond the television set and into the built environment. [. . .]

Notes

1   Max Weber developed this religious concept for sociology. Richard Dyer, in his section on "charisma" in *Stars*, discusses Weber's concept of charisma as one means of legitimation of political order (1979, pp. 34–7).

2 'You know it's Tom, Dan, and Peter . . . Sometimes I think they're all the same guy. They must move from studio to studio." Reese Schoenfeld, speaking on PBS in 1984.

3 Hallin (1994) finds that journalism's responsibility as "the major institution outside of the state which performs the function of providing political interpretation and critique" accounts for its conventions of representation, including a greater tendency to frame and interpret, the use of narrative structures, and extensive use of visual images and their integration into the semantic structure of the story (pp. 124–5).

4 There are at least three established formats for television talk—night, day, and the political or public service interview or roundtable—that are inflected in myriad ways. For a description of the classic "Tonight" show format with Johnny Carson see Morse 1985a.

5 The best-known instances include the shooting to death of the "blunt" talk radio host Alan Berg at the curb of his Denver home in 1984, the breaking of Geraldo's nose on his television show in 1988, and the murder of Scott Amedure three days after the disclosure of his secret love on the March 6, 1995, taping of *Jenny Jones* by Jonathan T. Schmitz, the "humiliated" object of his affection. See Freeman 1995.

6 "While there was a strong sense that the Soviet Union had probably lost the cold war, few [of the American public interviewed] were willing to say the United States had won." In a series of interviews with the public, the opinion, "We're just not a superpower anymore," uncovered apprehension "as if the fading of the Communist threat only illuminated other perils, especially the specter of sharpened economic competition with the Germans and the Japanese" (Schmidt 1990, p. 1).

7 Du Brow's critique of television news finds it good on the breaking story, but "increasingly shallow and trivial . . . combining to create an audience that is turned off by lengthy discussion and depth," and conditioned by "the new priorities of TV news—drama, extreme brevity, instant gratification, anything to prevent the viewer from zapping." Another critic, Michael Oreskes, wrote:

> Television was originally viewed as a democratizing force. It did help break down party machines and let candidates speak directly to the electorate. Now another result is becoming clear. . . . As America's democratic visions and values seem to triumph around the world, an unhappy consensus has emerged at home that domestic politics has become so shallow, mean and even meaningless that it is failing to produce the ideas and leadership needed to guide the United States in a rapidly changing world. . . . Instead of responding to changes in the world, the officials elected to lead the nation say they live each day in fear of the four horsemen of modern politics: televised attacks by their opponents, intense personal scrutiny by the press, cynicism on the part of the public and the need to raise huge sums to buy television time to combat the attacks, scrutiny and cynicism.
>
> (Oreskes 1990, 1, 16)

See also Oreskes, 1990b on "the swamp of photo opportunities and sound bites."

On the other hand, Christopher S. Wren's book *The End of the Line*, among others, stresses the subversion of Eastern regimes by the technological revolution in the West, and "the photocopier, video-cassette recorder, computer, and satellite dish."

8 Elihu Katz and Daniel Dayan see live media events on television as symbolic performances designed to celebrate the common identity of the audience. While disparaged as "pseudo-events" in Daniel Boorstein's *The Image: A Guide to Pseudo-Events in America*, the raison d'être of televised ceremonial occasions is to issue declaratives bringing forth alliances, proclamations of faith, and statements of conviction sanctioned by social position. Performative speech as a form of action that brings forth new conditions in the world can and does take place without television; however, its power to bring forth and celebrate the common identity of the audience can be effectively multiplied into the millions by means of spectacle masquerading as participation. Furthermore, the institution of television itself seems to supply the legitimacy that performative speech acts, according to J. L. Austin, require. Television seen as a discourse is not a medium or a message, but is there in and of itself to constitute or more often to ratify a particular kind of reality.

9 Since every conjuncture resulting in social change is overdetermined, all three are appropriate at different times, in relation to different protagonists.

10 "At some lost moment in our history, journalism became identified with, defined by, breaking news, the news flash, the news bulletin. When that happened, our understanding of journalism as a democratic social practice was impossibly narrowed and our habits, of reading, of attention, of interpretation were impaired. Journalists came to think of themselves as being in the news business, where their greatest achievements were defined as being first rather than best, with uncovering the unknown rather than clarifying and interpreting the known" (James W. Carey in Manoff and Schudson 1986: p. 195).

11   CSPAN is a cable channel that transmits speeches largely from legislative bodies, now including British Parliament, and free speech from the public via telephone. A use in crisis of duration on the networks would be Senate hearings, such as the Army-McCarthy hearings, Watergate, the Bork nomination to the Supreme Court, and Iran-Contra hearings, forums that notably brought down McCarthy, Nixon, and Bork, and made a hero of Oliver North. While the hearings occurred at significant junctures in the creation and maintenance of faith in national leaders, I would argue that televising these hearings in total allowed a play of discourse with unforeseeable consequences to take its course. In other words, discourse unfolding in duration in the validating institution of television acts as a kind of fate, distributing not so much justice as popularity and belief.

12   This masked discourse also marked reports on the June violence, after the evacuation of the main square, when Romanians refused to be seen on camera and reporters spoke for them. One miner could be seen blocking off the television lens with his hand in WNN coverage that appeared on all networks and CNN, comparable to segregationist hands that blocked the camera lens during the civil rights movement in the early 1960s in the U.S.

13   The unofficial VHS format camcorders in question were not amateur, but rather the private tools of professionals from film and television studios for making money on the side. The documentarists selected material on the first five days of the revolution from December 21, 1989, choosing from about 120 hours of live coverage archived in the Culture Ministry of Romania (see Lovink 1993, pp. 59–60). The untransmitted footage of Ceausescu's failed media event was included in this documentary.

14   Compare Newcomb and Hirsch (1994).

References

Allen, Jeanne. "The Social Matrix of Television: Invention in the United States." In E. Ann Kaplan, ed., *Regarding Television*, 109–19.

Barrett, Marvin (1978) *Rich News, Poor News*. New York: Crowell.

Barthes, Roland (1972) *Mythologies*. Trans. Annette Lavers. New York: Hill.

Berger, Peter, and Thomas Luckmann (1967) *The Social Construction of Reality*. New York: Anchor-Doubleday.

Boorstein, Daniel (1977) *The Image: A Guide to Pseudo-Events in America*. New York: Atheneum.

Carey, James W. "Why and How? The Dark Continent of American Journalism." In Manoff and Schudson 195–96.

Carey, John, and Pat O'Hara (1995) "Interactive Television." In d'Agostino and Tafler 219–34.

Carman, John (1997) "NBC Learns ABCs of News." *San Francisco Chronicle* 23 Jan. 1997: E1, 9.

Center for Media and Public Affairs (1990) "Drawing Back the Iron Curtain: TV News Coverage of Eastern Europe in 1989." *Media Monitor* 4, no. 3 (1990): 1.

Cullen, Robert (1990) "Report from Romania." *The New Yorker* 2 Apr. 1990: 94–112.

d'Agostino, Peter, and David Tafler (eds) (1995) *Transmission: Toward a Post-Television Culture*. Thousand Oaks, Calif.: Sage, 1995.

Dayan, Daniel, and Elihu Katz (1992) *Media Events: The Live Broadcasting of History*. Cambridge: Harvard University Press.

Doane, Mary Ann. "Information, Crisis, Catastrophe." In Mellencamp, *Logics* 222–29.

Du Brow, Rick (1990) "TV News Too Trivial to See the Big Picture." *Los Angeles Times* 10 Feb. 1990: F1, 6.

Dyer, Richard (1979) *Stars*. London: British Film Institute.

Ellis, John (1996) "Television as Working Through." In the series *Media Knowledge and the Role of Television*. Ed. Jostein Gripsrud. *Rhetoric – Knowledge – Mediation Working Paper 2*, 47–73. Bergen: University of Bergen.

—— (1982) *Visible Fictions: Cinema, Television, Video*. London: Routledge and Kegan Paul.

Freeman, Michael (1995) "Murder by television? 'Jenny'-related shooting has raised concern over talk-show content." *Mediaweek* 20 (Mar. 1995): 9–10.

Hallin, Daniel (1994) *We Keep America On Top of the World: Television Journalism and the Public Sphere*. London and New York: Routledge, 1994.

—— "Where? Cartography. Community and the Cold War." In Manoff and Schudson 109–145.

James, Caryn (1997) "Looking Back on the Oracle as Everyman." *New York Times* 5 January 1997: H37.

Jeffords, Susan and Rabinovitz, Lauren (1994) *Seeing Through the Media: The Persian Gulf War*. New Brunswick, NJ: Rutgers University Press.

Kaplan, Ann, E. (ed.) (1983) *Regarding Television—Critical Approaches: An Anthology*, American Film Institute Monograph Series, vol. 2, Fredrick, MD: University Publications of America.

Longworth, R. C. (1990) "Access to TV revolutionizes Eastern Europe." *San Francisco Chronicle* 7 Jan. 1990: A12.

Lovink, Geert (1993) "Aesthetics of the Video Document: The Romanian Tele-revolution according to Farocki and Ujica." *N5M* (1993): 59–60.

Manoff, Robert and Schudson, Michael (1986) *Reading the News*. New York: Pantheon Books.

Marin, Louis (1988) *Portrait of the King*. Minneapolis: University of Minnesota Press.

Meehan, Eileen (1990) "Why We Don't Count: The Commodity Audience." In Mellencamp, *Logics* 117–37.

Mellencamp, P. (ed.) (1990) *Logics of Television: Essays in Cultural Criticism*. Bloomington: Indiana University Press.

Morse, Margaret (1985a) "Talk, Talk, Talk: The Space of Discourse in TV News, Sportscasts, Talk Shows & Advertising." *Screen* 26, no. 2 (March–Apr. 1985): 1–11.

—— (1985b) "The Television News Personality and Credibility: Reflections on the News in Transition." *Working Paper No. 5* (Fall 1985). Center for Twentieth Century Studies, University of Wisconsin; in *Studies in Entertainment: Critical Approaches to Mass Culture*, 55–79. Ed. Tania Modleski. Bloomington: Indiana University Press, 1986.

Mueller, John (1994) *Policy and Opinion in the Gulf War*. Chicago: University of Chicago.

Multimediale 3. Karlsruhe: Zentrum für Kunst und Medientechnologie, 1993.

Newcomb, Horace, and Paul M. Hirsch (1994) "Television as a Cultural Forum." In *Television: The Critical View*, 5th edn, 503–15. Ed. Horace Newcomb. New York, Oxford: Oxford UP.

Oreskes, Michael (1990a) "America's Politics Loses Way as Its Vision Changes World." *New York Times* 18 Mar. 1990: 1, 16.

—— (1990b) "Political Failures Are Creating a New Constituency for Change: Rules on Television Ads and Fund Raising Sought." *New York Times* 21 Mar. 1990: 1.

Powers, Ron (1977) *The Newscasters*. New York: St. Martin's P, 1977.

Rath, Claus-Dieter (1985) "The Invisible Network: Television as an Institution in Everyday Life." In *Television in Transition: Papers from the First International Television Studies Conference*, 199–204. Ed. Phillip Drummond and Richard Paterson. London: British Film Institute.

Rosenberg, Howard (1991) "Title." "The Media and the Gulf: A Closer Look". Proceedings of a Conference at the Graduate School of Journalism, UC Berkeley. 3–4 May 1991. Berkeley: University College Berkeley.

Scarry, Elaine (1993) "Watching and Authorizing the Gulf War." In *Media Spectacles*, 57–73. Ed. Marjorie Garber, Jann Matlock, and Rebecca L. Walkowitz. London and New York: Routledge.

Schmidt, William E. (1990) "In U.S., Timid Hope on a New World." *New York Times* 11 Mar. 1990: 1.

Tafler, David (1995) "Boundaries and Frontiers: Interactivity and Participant Experience—Building New Models and Formats." In d'Agostino and Tafler 235–67.

Terry, Don (1992) "Decades of Rage Created Crucible of Violence." *New York Times* 3 May 1992: 1, 17.

Trilling, Lionel (1980) *Sincerity and Authenticity*. Cambridge: Harvard UP, 1972. Rpt. New York: Harcourt Brace Jovanovich.

White, Mimi. "Site Unseen: An Analysis of CNN's War in the Gulf." In Jeffords and Rabinovitz 121–141.

Willemen, Paul (1994) *Looks and Frictions: Essays in Cultural Studies and Film Theory*. Bloomington: Indiana University Press.

Wren, Christopher S. (1990) *The End of the Line: The Failure of Communism in the Soviet Union and China*. New York: Simon and Schuster.

Chapter 14

JOHN CORNER

ADWORLDS

IDEAS ABOUT ADVERTISING have been at the centre of international media theory and media research for a long time. While the anxieties about political mediation, news and documentary have been grounded in a sense of the 'proper' public role for television in these areas, anxieties about advertising have often been grounded in a belief in its essential impropriety. In many commentaries, advertising has, indeed, been positioned as the quintessentially 'anti-public' form, a kind of anti-news designed to mislead rather than inform and to promote selfish emotion over civic reason.[1] Its nature, both as an economic and a representational practice, has thus been viewed pathologically, and much effort has been put into devising means either to regulate and reduce its influence or to develop the possibility of a media system (and an economy) which could manage without it. Yet, despite this tradition of critical concern (variously reflected in the political and public sphere as well as in academic analysis), advertising has increasingly become assimilated into everyday life as a basic constituent of late modernity. In recent years it has become much more international, extending to societies in which it was previously either marginal or non-existent, while in those societies where it has an established place it has often become even more culturally pervasive and representationally subtle.[2]

One consequence of this move towards advertising as economically and culturally *normal* has been the emergence of a revised perspective on it within media theory. Such a perspective keeps up its connections with the earlier tradition of criticism but modifies this with newer, more accommodating, tones. For as well as it now being very hard to think *counterfactually* against the sheer penetration of advertising into social and cultural experience, the newer aesthetics which advertising has adopted have often had a depictive energy and social resonance which has prompted analytic interest more immediately than dismissal.

I want to examine some features of television advertising, paying attention to aspects both of the established critical debate about its forms and consequences and to revised versions of this. My principal concern will be with the character of the communication itself, rather than the nature of advertising as an industry. Despite this tightening of focus, however, I hope that a concern with television advertising form can be made to connect with those more general questions about the relationship between advertising and society. Having first looked at the way in which advertising is placed within the aesthetics of television, sometimes initiating and sometimes reflecting changes elsewhere, I shall look at the distinctive way in which questions of aesthetics are linked to questions of 'influence' in advertising. Finally, some of the different and quite often conflicting evaluations which have recently been made of advertising's social consequence will be explored. Given the rapid turnover in television commercials and the now broad, international familiarity of their different types, I have not referred extensively to specific examples in my commentary, preferring to let readers test my points against their own viewing experience.

Advertising and television aesthetics

The 'commercial' is one of the most *intensive* deployments of television form. This is a combination of the extremely tight time constraints placed upon it and the need to develop within these constraints the significatory definition and power to 'get the message across' in a manner which will exercise some form of persuasion upon the viewer. Such intensity and such an explicit commitment to influence marks commercials out as an *extraordinary* form of television, but the basic devices which they use to engage and to 'woo' the viewer frequently draw on television's communicative *ordinariness*, its routine (by turns, dramatic, personalised, serious, comic, relaxed, hectic) kinds of representation. In this sense, then, commercials often work as a kind of *essential television*, using the generic system of broader television culture, with its grouped conventions of speech and image, and working their elements up into a range of 'micro-formats', where they appear transformed but nevertheless recognisable (often, in recent advertising, constructed as the subject of pastiche and parody). There are also strong indications of a movement the other way too, in which forms of mainstream television (for example, travel programmes, music shows, youth magazines) have reworked their look and their sounds so as to incorporate developments in television commercials. There has even been a shift in some television drama towards certain styles of lighting, ways of using settings or composing a shot and a manner of acting which have been seen by some critics as showing the influence of 'commercials' culture'. Cinema has also been an important source of ideas for the television commercial, offering its own distinctive generic range and visual styles. Many commercials are produced for both cinema and television screening (albeit in different versions). The number of cinema directors now also doing commercials work indicates that stylistic influences are partly the direct consequence of professional toing and froing.

The *contexts* in which television ads often appear, a 'break' in programming consisting of a sequence of commercials, clearly exerts an outer level of influence on their character and their potential for giving pleasure. As an interruption in programming these breaks are both welcome (a chance to make coffee, see to something in the house) and unwelcome (a blocking of continuity in the enjoyment of the programme). The way in which these two conflicting aspects of the setting in which ads occur affects the disposition of viewers towards them, especially in the context of multi-channel availability, is certainly worthy of further study.[3] However, the internationalisation of advertising-financed television has made such breaks a routine part of the modern viewing experience in many countries (the early use of the term 'natural break' by television companies was an attempt to anticipate this).[4]

The television commercial: Basic communicative elements

Clearly, advertising on television is communicatively different from advertising in other media. In poster and newspaper advertising, for instance, the advertisement is *static*, though, of course, it may well imply narrative action. The temporal element involved in the interpretative work performed upon it (connecting with basic questions about the nature of the product and its attractiveness as well as with the appeal of the ad itself) is very much determined by the viewer, by how long they wish to engage with the images and words. There may be external constraints on this time (e.g. posters at busy traffic intersections, designed to be seen briefly but regularly) and constraints imposed by routine (e.g. the daily browse through a newspaper, moving through the pages and returning to some for more detailed attention, in accordance with established habit). In television advertising, however, the temporal dimension is very much part of the advert's communicative structure and this regulates the interpretative time available to the viewer. In the making of advertisements, such a regulation of interpretative time allows, of course, for the possibility of the increased comprehension and pleasure consequent on *repetition*. It has also, increasingly, to make allowance for the possibility of the advert's status as a *video item*. Whilst, theoretically, this allows the viewer to rerun the ad at their leisure, giving it extra attention, it is much more likely to result in it being fast-forwarded so as to receive hardly any attention at all.

A number of studies of advertising have developed analytical accounts of its semiological character without due regard to the differences between media in which advertisements occur and to how these differences might bear on advertising's cultural consequences. For instance, Leiss *et al.* (1986) develop a very useful historical survey of advertising imagery, together with a typology of advertising structure, by focusing primarily on newspaper and magazine ads. Williamson's influential account (1978) of the ideological character of advertising imagery draws exclusively upon examples from magazines. Pateman's highly original attempt (1983) both to offer a critique of previous, semiotic, approaches and to develop an analysis grounded in linguistic ideas concerns itself, too, with examples from posters and newspapers. His conceptualisation of advertising as a certain kind of communicative act (following Searle's notion of the 'speech act') and his analytic vocabulary for discussing this are related exclusively to printed forms.

There are many things about advertising which can, and should, be addressed at a cross-media level, but a prerequisite for this general commentary is a recognition of the variety of distinctive media which advertising now uses. For television, this would involve attention to three basic communicative features not present in poster or newspaper formats – speech, action and music.

Speech

Speech gives to the television ad both a regulatory and a dramatic facility. The male voice-over pronouncing in sonorous tones upon the special qualities of the product is a cliché of television advertising, now much parodied both in television and in radio formats. But with the more 'serious' types of product (medication, for instance, or educational materials) or where it is assumed that a 'straight pitch' will work best, the direct address mode is still employed in a manner derivative of news or documentary practice – an authoritative presentation, strong in immediacy values, of 'news about the product'. Direct address, either in voice over or in-shot, allows a number of communicative functions, amongst which are:

(1) product identification (as in the emphatic and perhaps repeated use of the brand name)
(2) product description (key characteristics and use of product stated)
(3) product affirmation (evaluative claims as to product quality made).

These three functions can all work to *personalise* the address of the ad, situating it as social communication in a way which does not occur in print forms. This factor may be used strategic-ally, as for instance in the use of a professional male middle-class voice to sell car security devices, or the use of a young woman's voice to sell a diet drink. Sometimes, rather than a subliminal appeal, a 'neutral' connotation is sought. In other ads, the use of pronunciation and accent is such as to project the social identity and/or character type of the speaker for the viewers' conscious recognition. The social relations of direct address speech on television make it possible for the speaker to adopt a conversational register and to assume a relationship of familiarity with the viewer. Clearly, the direct address speech of advertising is routinely used not only for the delivery of 'hard' product information but also for the 'soft' task of establishing sociable relations.

Speech also clearly serves the need of television advertising to offer dramatic representations. In the typical dialogue of the commercial, the dramatic requirements of the speech are in combination with the requirement for product promotion. 'Realist' portrayal often gives way, in dramatic exchange, to an emphasis on product quality and the repetition of the product name (sometimes requiring a marked shift from dramatic, indirect address to 'individual' or 'choral' forms of direct address).

Action

The possibility of showing action takes television advertising into areas of product representation simply not available in static depiction, however ingeniously this is organised. We can identify four main consequences of kinetic representation.

Dramatic

The potential of the television ad as micro-drama has provided modern societies with one of the most intensively developed promotional forms. Dramatic structure, even in so brief a format as the commercial, allows for a degree of 'character' development, with important consequences for the strength of viewer identification and for any personalising strategy – for example, that organised around a celebrity – which is used. It also allows for a much stronger representation of *sociality*, since the product can be set within the dynamics of social action, 'caught up' within the warmth, adventure or sensuality of social *processes* rather than 'located' within social *spaces* as in a photographic depiction (though one must not underestimate the power of viewer imagination here). The comic dimension of advertising is, of course, greatly increased by dramatic depiction, which allows generic imitation of both film and television comedy as well as the development of distinctive, 'condensed' formats of its own. The idea that ads have become another media 'product', whose relationship to the product which they promote is actually becoming less determinative than their own entertainment value for audiences, is very much premised on the relatively independent status which micro-dramas, both comic and serious, can achieve for themselves in audience estimation. Although recent ads have become a good deal less obvious in the ways in which products are placed within their scenarios, the micro-dramas of the commercial still typically close, if not with an old-style 'pack shot', then by using a strong (often 'frozen') image of the product in context.

Demonstrative

Another function of kinetic depiction is that it allows the product to be seen in *action*. For many products, this 'functional' level of representation is inappropriate but for others the appeal of demonstration can be considerable, even where objectivity is not expected (e.g. the perfect surface of the scratched table after the application of polish, the braking power of the car on the airport runway test). The most traditional type of demonstration ads actually set themselves up as tests for viewer witnessing (e.g. blindfolded housewives testing margarine; two attempts at cleaning the bath, one with the advertised cleaner) but, again, any rationally demonstrative function is now usually mixed with elements both of the self-consciously theatrical and the comic.

Symbolic

Symbolism, in the sense of a non-literal significance being generated by (and attributed to) words and images, is a key element of nearly all advertising communication. The classic analysis of its presence is perhaps that by Roland Barthes. In his essay 'The Rhetoric of the Image' (1977)

Barthes uses the term 'connotation' and 'myth' to engage with this level of associational (often metaphoric) meaning, providing a case study which has become a major influence on subsequent academic commentary. A frequent assumption in such work is that the 'symbolic' level is in fact a 'hidden' level of textual meaning in the sense that it is not consciously registered by viewers even while it is being generated by them from the text. It has therefore been regarded by many analysts as the level at which advertising power is most operative and most in need of critique (this is in contrast to the 'literal' levels of speech and image, where questions of misdescription, fraudulent claims, misleading illustration, etc. have provided a traditional point of address for consumer groups and regulatory bodies). I shall return to this point later in the context of conflicting arguments about influence.

The extension of overall symbolic field provided by the use of moving images and by speech allows advertising to deploy a rich aesthetics of movement and process. In early commercials the links with static forms of symbolic display were stronger, a matter of technical limitation as well as of imaginative convention. Commercials can either be developed on a base of realist depiction (e.g. the 'scene from domestic life'; the comic sketch) or else developed directly within either continuous nonrealist narrative (e.g. a fantasy scenario) or in mixed, semi- or non-realist and perhaps non-representational formats (the montage sequence; the abstract employment of sound and colour). In this latter area, developments in music video production have been a significant influence. There has recently been a marked increase in the number of adverts using non-representational shapes, colourings, sounds and movements. This provides an articulation of symbolic meaning which appears to have links with other shifts in contemporary cultural form, including these in the visual styles of magazines and computer games.[5]

Depictive

'Depictive' is an awkward term in this context, but I use it here to indicate the possibilities for *camera movement* which follow from the use of the television medium. That is to say, not the way in which the camera can represent action taking place in front of it but the way in which the use of zooms, pans, glides, tilts, tracking shots and so on can construct an ad within an aesthetic altogether different from that of the static image. This aesthetic clearly connects with all three of the above 'action' functions – dramatic, demonstrative and symbolic – but it also has a powerful use as a way of organising apprehension of the product spatially and temporally. We can think of the example of a car, notionally static within the frame of the shot. The camera will control our perceptions, organising them into a rhythm of shifts – part to whole; the low-angle 'journey' around the front; the zoom on to the wheel hubs; the marking out, through controlled perception both of product beauty and product power. This method of providing enhanced perception of a product's physical being – its 'thingness', replete with potential for use and for pleasure – is employed extensively in television advertising, with wide variations in the pacing and styles of disclosure.

The depictive scope of ads has been considerably increased recently by the use of computer graphic simulation and modelling. This has allowed perspectives, perceptual movements and 'transformation' scenes of a kind either difficult or impossible to achieve in relation to real objects and it has thereby enhanced the possibilities for visual pleasure.

Music (and sounds)

The function of music in commercials is more fundamental than it might appear to be. It may seem merely 'additional'. In many commercials cast in the dramatic mode, the music provides the primary indication of mood, very quickly establishing the 'correct' way of reading character and action. In commercials cast in other modes, music is often similarly important in establishing moods and in providing a strong reinforcement of product identity (the 'jingle' is, of course, a traditional form for the projection of brand). Given the brief and intensive character of many commercials, music is not only a *thematic* factor however, but also very importantly an agency of syntax and punctuation, serving to link together the various parts of a commercial, giving movement within shot and movements between shot an overall structural appropriateness and bringing the whole assembly to a strong conclusion.[6] Whether or not singing is used, music allows an element of *repetition* within the form of the ad. This frequently supports linguistic repetition, though it should not be confused with it, as the consequences of musical repetition for the aesthetic of the commercial are far more comprehensive. Clearly, not only does the use of music allow commercials a broader range of cultural cross-referencing (the use of pop music and rock music being particularly important here) but it also allows the sociality of commercials to be projected more effectively, emphasising 'togetherness', 'happiness' and forms of 'fun' as well as a range of more dramatically themed emotional states.

Sounds and noises are also included in many commercials. At one level, they are necessary to support action, whether dramatic or otherwise, as indicated above. But they also frequently exceed this literalist function. They are deployed as mechanisms of heightened realism, for instance, in order to develop a stronger sense of product identity (e.g. the crunch of breakfast cereals, the fizz of an opened can of lager). In some commercials, their use is designed to underscore non-realist actions associated with the product (the cartoon-like repertoire associated with speed, sudden stops, collisions, jumps, etc.). Almost always, they are woven into a soundtrack of voices and music to give the commercial a firmer and more memorable structure, to punctuate it more attractively and add to its overall vivacity.

Genre and the television commercial

Many commentaries on advertising have offered a basic typology of the television commercial, identifying the principal kinds of communicative strategy. Among the more perennial of these are the 'testimonial ad', in which a celebrity of some kind endorses a product; the 'scientific-rational ad', in which the qualities of the product are 'proved' by some form of ostensibly objective testing, variously visualised in the commercial itself; the 'animation ad', in which the product or product name is represented within an abstract or cartoon format; and the 'slice of life' ad in which the product appears, or is mentioned within, a micro-drama of everyday life, presented within some version of realism. There are many variants and combinations even within this basic selection. For example, in detergent advertising the use of an 'ordinary housewife', either alone or in combination with a (male) presenter, has been used as a key testimonial form. This kind of ad has also frequently employed elements of the 'scientific-rational', insofar as it has 'shown the difference' between washes using the product and those using other brands. Two other broad kinds of ad which have been around for a long time but which have recently become more dominant are the 'comedy ad' and the 'fantasy ad'. In many contemporary comedy ads the humorous entertainment of the viewer is frequently undertaken in a way which may appear subversive in relation to the product itself (not merely to competing products). In advertising for all types of goods, there has been a movement away from the emphatic sincerity of earlier kinds of 'hard sell' commercials towards the more relaxed, oblique and ironic significations of product quality offered by comedy. As I have indicated, the parodying of 'serious' formats has been a feature of many new-style humorous commercials whilst the parodying of earlier advertising is also widespread in current British commercials, along with the use of elements from a broad range of television entertainment. A fashion for using archive footage (old black and white movies particularly) and intercutting this with newly shot material has been one of the most notable recent developments in comic commercials, though its force of novelty is quickly expended. Together with the broad tendency towards parody, this kind of mix is often cited as an example of just how 'postmodern' in sensibility advertising culture has now become.[7]

An equal, if not greater, amount of innovative effort has gone into the subgenre of the 'fantasy ad'. Fantasy (like comedy in this respect) has been a traditional component of television commercials, whose interest in generating viewer/consumer desires has obviously required a discourse able to stimulate notions of the ultimate, the ideal and the perfect and to place the *attainable* in a strategic relationship with the *unattainable* (as we shall see later, getting this 'trick' right is central to the efficiency of much advertising). What is new about fantasy in advertising is its degree of self-consciousness and of elaboration. In many recent commercials (I draw on viewing experiences in the United States, Britain, Sweden and Australia but imagine the tendency to be fully international) 'fantasy' is overtly signalled by the presence of an overt symbolism of location, of shot composition, and of action and speech. Here, one source of influence from the late 1980s has been the new science fiction cinema (for instance, 1982's *Bladerunner* or 1987's *Robocop*), where advanced cybernetics meets urban dystopia. Within some treatments, the level of directness and emphasis on fantasy desires has the effect of tipping such projections into the comic or ironic, often thereby giving them a social acceptability and enjoyableness which they might lack if taken 'straight'.

[. . .]

I now want to explore matters of form a little more by using the subheadings of 'knowledge' and 'pleasure'. These, I hope, will allow me to get further analytic purchase on the kind of communicative and aesthetic work going on in television commercials.

Knowledge and pleasure in the television commercial

It is very hard to imagine a television commercial having any effect at all (that is to say either a 'good' one as seen by the advertiser or a 'bad' one as seen by critics of advertising) without some kind of 'knowledge' being generated in the viewer. I will leave aside for the moment the question of whether such knowledge is consciously held or not. It is also very hard to see how commercials can hope routinely to win the minimum level of attention necessary for their effectiveness if they do not set out to give pleasure to the viewer in some way, visually or verbally, through humour, parody, excitement, sexual appeal and so on.

The knowledge generated by commercials inevitably concerns information about product identity, product use and product qualities. That is to say, however minimalist their style, all ads indicate *what* is being marketed. In many cases, the *kind* of thing it is may be redundant information, given the presumed consumer awareness of the viewer, but some statement about quality is nearly always present. Even the methods of representing established brands, whose manufacturers may feel able to rely simply on pre-existing assumptions about 'quality', involve a degree of quality projection. The very simplicity and restraint of these ads are designed to work as a textual marker of quality. They show the ad to be more active in its *implicit* promotional work than its explicit discourse would suggest.

Of course, the taking of knowledge from ads is almost invariably done in a way which recognises their distinctiveness as a mode of *persuasive* communication and recognises, too, the sorts of communicative moves they are likely to make (including the use of selectively positive information, the use of exaggeration and the linking of the product, with varying degrees of directness, to established forms of 'goodness'). This interpretative fact about ads, that they are typically read within the cultural 'rules' for reading them, is sometimes forgotten by academic analysts, who have shown a tendency to regard them as texts to be related to culture-in-general directly, rather than via the mediations of such 'rules'. Here, it is interesting to note an erroneous assumption often made by students of advertising (particularly in school and media studies classes) about the 'promise of ads'. This assumption focuses on that which is put into the ad to lend a product desirability (say, an attractive woman sitting in a sophisticated-looking restaurant, clearly somewhere in Europe; a well-built, handsome man using an aftershave) and regards this as indicating a promise to the viewer along the lines, 'If you buy this product then you will be (more) like this person'. Whatever the psychological mechanisms by which a displacement, or an act of 'value transfer', is achieved between certain non-product features of the commercial and the product itself, this very rarely amounts to a proposition which could become an element of viewers' conscious reasoning ('Yes, I would love to look like that and do that kind of thing, so I'll buy that perfume right away'). The response is much more likely to be one which, interpreting within the 'rules', finds aspects of the product's depiction either thematically or formally attractive and desirable but continues to register the radical implausibility of any major *personal transformation* occurring as a result of purchase. Such a response is not likely to view the ad as fraudulent in its depiction, since it may regard the implausibility of personal change of this kind as just too widely accepted for people to be vulnerable to deceptive appeals. The 'rules' therefore permit ads to connect their products to 'goodness' in a number of ways without a promise being seen to be made.[8]

This is to move from an emphasis on knowledge to one on pleasure and to see ads, particularly perhaps those of contemporary television, as a kind of 'cultural game' played across knowledge/pleasure with the general acquiescence of the viewer. Advertisers have become extremely adept at making sure that they do not break the rules, particularly not their selective codification in the regulations governing television advertising practice (in which context, to be seen to be making a substantive promise to consumers which the product was unable to fulfil would be to risk a legal penalty). In a useful account (developed in the form of a classical dialogue) of how advertising messages work, John Thompson (1990) has suggested that the basic model is a 'rational core', which is read by viewers as giving 'knowledge of the product' and to which legal constraints on product description in merchandising apply, and a 'decorative periphery', to which viewers attribute little or no knowledge function at all, instead regarding this as a legitimate attempt by the advertiser to please them and to 'win them over'. This latter area is not the subject of marketing and consumer legislation but, instead, has to conform to a broader set of laws and 'public taste codes' concerning public representation through image and speech. For certain types of potentially harmful products such as alcohol and tobacco, the codes may be explicit and combined with restrictive legislation.

Thompson's distinction is a useful one in breaking with the more simplistic approaches to the 'advertising message' (hidden or otherwise) but the disjunction of 'core' and 'periphery' seems to me to be unhelpfully abrupt when applied to the textual organisation of most contemporary ads. The terminology also cannot help but attribute a representational primacy to the rational, although Thompson recognises that current tendencies in advertising are often productive of a minimalist, quite notional, 'core' and an extravagantly developed 'periphery'. My own view is that the interarticulation of the propositional and the entertaining, of that which can be seen as a quality of the product and that which is there merely to sell it, is more a matter of movement across levels of interpreted significance within the *reading* of the ad as a whole, rather than a function of two distinct and detachable communicative schemes at work within it. Nevertheless, Thompson's rejection of the idea of unified signification, which either 'influences' the viewer or doesn't, is cogently worked through and it may be that his core/periphery model was devised primarily in relation to static adverts (posters and magazine display) where its binarism might prove less awkward than with the dynamic form of the television commercial. It is also true that many static adverts give far more time to detailed (printed) product information than could prudently be included in a commercial's voice-over or captioned text. For certain products, new hi-fi accessories or new models of car for example, it is sometimes the case that potential buyers require this level of 'technical' information about 'product performance' before making a decision about purchase. In such cases, the television advertisement can only act as a point of *attraction*, projecting product identity and value with sufficient force to push potential buyers on to the next stage of seeking printed information either in newspaper and magazine ads or through specialist publicity produced by the manufacturers themselves.

For other products, of course, such an emphasis on subsequent information seeking will not be necessary, since purchasing decisions will not be based on product performance to anything like the same extent. However, nearly all television adverts form part of a more comprehensive marketing strategy for a particular product. In this strategy, not only ads in other media, but also marketing campaigns in shops, mail-shot leaflets and perhaps a whole range of other promotional devices, will be employed. The television ad is usually regarded as being in the vanguard of the campaign. If it does its pleasure-knowledge job effectively, the other elements are means of support, amplification and extension. If it doesn't, then the product is not likely to achieve the minimum level of public visibility necessary for it to 'take off' on the market.

Mechanisms of influence

I remarked above that the basic method by which many ads work to create positive evaluations of their product is through a process of *value transfer*. This term, sometimes to be found in advertising training manuals, is perhaps too mechanistic to capture adequately the complexity, and the degree of unpredictability, involved in the actual business of generating 'good feelings' around products, but it has the merit of clarity and pointedness. By locating the product in the context of what are, in one way or another, positive situations, people, events, other goods, etc., a generalised positive feeling is produced which then becomes attached to the product. Value transfer can also seek to work through form alone, setting up a pleasure in colours, sounds, shapes and movements which then becomes the object of transfer.

As I have noted, where 'realist' scenarios of good living are involved, it is certainly not a part of advertising strategy to persuade the viewer that by buying the product they will actually gain an entrance to this world. However, it may well be part of the strategy to encourage them to play around with the idea of themselves in such a setting, to stimulate a daydream around this *im*possibility. Within such a circumstance, the product does not become the *agency of transformation* but a kind of *fantasy aid*. The viewer's recognition of the impossibility of a significant shift in personal circumstances goes along with an enjoyment of the reverie (and the possibility of positive consequences for the product's image). This is particularly the case with goods which are self-consciously marketed as *personal products* (bath salts, perfumes, aftershave lotions, soaps, cosmetics, shampoos, etc), in relation to which self-conscious fantasy about the 'improved self' is culturally conventionalised (a matter of everyday talk among friends and the subject of comic narratives in different media). I suggested that no purchaser is likely to feel cheated by an ad of this kind when the product does not act as an agency of real change.

In assessing the general relationship between product values and broader cultural values and the way in which the latter are deployed to determine and project the former, it is worth registering how talk about 'advertising influence' frequently collapses together two rather different lines of potential power, selling power and cultural power.

Selling power

Ads are designed to sell goods and one very clear criterion of their success (maybe not so clear to measure *conclusively* but clear enough as a general guide) is their ability to increase sales. To do this, they must do two things. They must establish a brand name in the minds of viewers, so that the existence of the product becomes widely known and available to memory at subsequent moments of purchase (particularly so in the case of routinely purchased items of modest price, where 'giving X a try' is feasible). They must also, in most cases, provide the viewer/consumer with some reasons as to *why* they should make the purchase. With a completely new product this will require the projection of novel qualities and functions. In the far more typical case of a branded item in competition with many others, the distinct advantages available from *this* brand need clear articulation, which may or may not require implicit reference to other, 'lesser' brands.[9] As we have seen, in order to carry out both these communicative tasks, advertisers have recourse to two broad areas of evaluative discourse. Although the separation between these becomes at times purely notional, we can call these an *intensive discourse*, in which features of product design and performance are the subject of affirmation, and an *extensive discourse*, in which the product is situated within a whole range of much broader, cultural values. In this way, the product is projected both as a 'tool' (in the sense that a perfume is a 'tool' for personal enhancement) and as an object with a specific cultural resonance. Some advertisers regard this latter area of product projection as the 'value added' factor, giving the product (via mechanisms of value transfer) that degree of extra definition and/or attractiveness which makes all the difference to the selling power of the ad.

Critical anxieties about selling power have typically taken the form of a suspicion that viewers/consumers are somehow under an unacceptable level of communicational coercion from ads to buy things which they do not really need and which they do not really want. In an extension of this, some viewers/consumers are seen as living within an advertising-induced regime of purchasing aspirations which they have not the money to fulfil.[10] Although anything like adequate documentation of the real needs and wants being 'falsified' here is rarely provided (see Marcuse [1972] for a classic piece of question-begging on 'false needs'), the belief that unwarranted constraint on rational consumer choice is a primary function of advertising discourse remains a strong one. It is, understandably, frequently linked to theories about a *subconscious* level of advertising effect, one which therefore is exerted 'below' the level of the viewer's awareness. Such a view may also see impositions of this kind, not as the localised 'bad practice' of a particular industry, but as something which is perfectly functional for the larger socio-economic system. That is to say, capitalism requires excessive consumption in order to maintain profits, and one way (perhaps the only way) in which excessive consumption can be maintained is by persuading people to buy things in a quantity and of a kind which it is unlikely that a rational consideration of requirement alone would suggest was sensible. Advertising, from this point of view, is demonstrably a form of anti-public, anti-rational activity, and may be judged as generally illegitimate without recourse to specific arguments about its effectiveness.

Cultural power

Cultural power in the form of strategically organised cultural resonance, including the evocation of various types of 'goodness' and 'badness' from images and words, is an important dimension of advertising's selling effectiveness. However, the cultural power of advertising has been regarded by many writers to reach well beyond that which is self-consciously deployed by the advertisers in order to sell the product. It has widely been seen as having a deep and general connection with the basic classification and value system of social life, such that advertising reproduces and sustains the larger pattern of values, prejudices, anxieties and desires. This pattern is formed within terms broadly established by the dominant social and economic groups. Usually, this is much more than a theory about how advertising 'reflects' existing social prejudice, thereby inhibiting social change. Indeed, some accounts place the emphasis on the *constitutive* function of advertising's cultural character and regard this function as one frequently carried out in a deliberately *non*-reflective way. Here, it is precisely the combination of the *gap* between existing social realities and advertising, on the one hand, and the *influence* of advertising on cultural values on the other, which is the focus of anxiety. Children are often viewed as being particularly vulnerable to the broader cultural 'lessons' which advertising teaches.

The devices by which 'selling power' works usually involve a kind of *centripetal* energy, in which desirable aspects in the broader culture come to be focused on or around the product itself. Advertising has become strategically adept at picking up on, or in some cases prefiguring, cultural trends in order to carry out this 'culturalisation' of the product. Some of the most revealing studies of advertising in this respect are those of 'repositioning' campaigns, in which a product which broadly remains the same is 'moved' in its cultural associations. So, for instance, the glucose drink 'Lucozade', long associated with convalescence and the sick bed, was given a successful new image by being associated with sport and leading sports personalities. In shifting the connotations from those of illness to those of super-fitness, the advertisers were able to provide the drink with new connotations and a new 'use' (energy replenishment for the already healthy).[11]

In contrast, whatever 'cultural power' advertising possesses is generated by a *centrifugal* process. This is one in which the associations generated around the product work to sustain the desirability (or perhaps just the normality) of certain features of personal and social life. In the strongest versions of how 'cultural power' operates, advertising not only reinforces existing patterns of value but works to initiate new ones (for instance, around certain kinds of leisure product). I noted that one of the problems with seeing the 'selling power' of ads as illegitimately coercive is that of establishing the 'true judgements' people would make about their product needs if they were not the addressees of advertising. One of the problems with viewing the 'cultural power' of ads as an effective determinant of social value is that of situating the influence of ads within the context of other cultural influences, including those coming from other uses of media and from a range of formal and informal types of experiential setting (e.g. home, school, work, environment, leisure interest). It is the belief that advertising does indeed work in a 'dispersed' way to encourage certain values and beliefs, as well as in a 'concentrated' way to sell goods, that has generated so much controversy about advertising as a communicative practice. Although anxiety about 'selling power' remains a primary concern with consumer groups, it is forms of 'cultural power' which have, internationally, been at the centre of recent debate about advertising, particularly advertising on television.[12]

Arguments about influence

The pursuit of arguments about advertising's cultural power has produced a vast literature of empirical research, textual analysis and commentary. At least as much has been written here as on the question of advertising's more limited (though still disputed) ability to sell products to consumers. Arguments both about the dangerous scale of such influence and, conversely, about its relative marginality, have had recourse to close analysis of advertising forms themselves. It is fair to say, however, that within the tradition of cultural critique, attention to advertising's images and words has played a greater role than either direct examination of the industry itself or, indeed, investigation of those who are deemed to be vulnerable before its powers – the television-watching and product-buying public. The shortage of work of this latter kind, on advertising audiences, is perhaps largely a result of the way in which the critical tradition in mass media research has only recently emerged from a phase where focus on textual forms was the dominant approach. In this phase, to some extent a consequence of the considerable influence exerted by structuralist and other linguistic paradigms on the human sciences, texts were regarded as bearers of ideological (and therefore mostly 'hidden') meanings which were open to relatively secure analysis through the concepts and methods of semiotics.[13] The re-evaluation of semiotics as a research tool now suggests problems with the 'scientific' levels of analysis which some of its advocates once propounded, as well as more general problems of social explanation.[14] Meanwhile, the more general and substantive question of 'ideological reproduction' (the various deployment of meanings in the maintenance of power relationships) has undergone revision too, making it much more an open question as to just how, and in what ways, the practical consciousness of media audience is affected by what they see, hear and read. It is interesting to note here just how *frequently* the example of advertising was used within media studies employing semiotic analysis and theories of ideological reproduction. It is not hard to see why this should be. Constructed out of some of the most innovative devices of cultural technology for imaging and symbolising self and society, and constructed precisely to reproduce and develop a central function of the capitalist social system, commodity consumption for profit, advertising often exerted a strong (and strongly political) pull on the analysis of mass communication. This resulted in many questions about it being asked repeatedly and some questions about it hardly being asked at all. [The original essay includes two sections looking at 'advertising as art and as pornography', those have been omitted here.]

[. . .]

Television advertising: a 'revised' aesthetics and a 'revised' debate[15]

Advertising has been with us for a long time, and even television advertising now has a history (in many countries, one well worthy of further scholarly attention). However, there is an emerging view that both the advertising and its relation to other aspects of culture and social life are now undergoing considerable revision. Advertising is being seen to be more complex and diversified as a phenomenon at the same time as it has clearly become more extensive. In a comprehensive survey of recent trends in promotionalism, Andrew Wernick (1990) has pointed to the way in which advertising activities of one kind or another constitute a chain of interdependent promotional images and terms binding politics to sport to television programmes to toys to entertainment 'celebrities' and so on. This 'chaining' of promotional discourses – a phenomenon which has to be viewed as a radical departure from the idea of self-contained promotional acts, each with its own separate 'influence' – Wernick describes as constituting a 'vortex of publicity'. His own assessment views this as pathological. Insofar as it is an assessment grounded in his sense of the pervasiveness of promotional forms, the negative judgement is convincing. However, insofar as it concerns questions about the kind of impact these forms are currently having on contemporary consciousness, then once again, the pessimism is not adequately supported by evidence of actually sustained cultural damage. Nor is there sufficient real argument supporting the claim.

In a way which recalls Booth (1982), the entire case about the cultural effectiveness of advertising tends to go by default. A textual reading indicates the kinds of cultural value informing most ads (to a large extent, the observations made here are unexceptionable) and then this whole set of symbolised values is made over into audience consciousness. I have suggested that the formalism of this kind of approach is not acceptable as grounding for *sociological* propositions about advertising's consequences. It has become just too familiar a move to proceed directly from a detailed analysis of signification to a comprehensive judgement of cultural effect. Even if, finally, the evidence of empirical research both on advertising practice and on audience interpretation does not seem to require much modification of these judgements (which I doubt), it is still a requirement for cultural analysts to address extra-textual factors and data. Wernick usefully draws our attention to recent changes in promotional form but we are presented with little to convince us why we should agree with his assessment of their cultural significance.

But if a revised perspective on the study of advertising is suggested by the continuing untenability of many critical ideas about 'cultural badness', it is also required by changes in the nature of advertising itself. The Navas' (1990) point about the level of autonomy which ads now enjoy warrants further exploration but so, too, does their suggestion that advertising (in many countries recently hit by recession and a subsequent cutback in corporate 'adspend') is not at all confident about how effective it is or about what directions might best sustain it as an industry.

In Britain, one sign of this uncertainty has perhaps been the shift towards the kind of aesthetic density which the Navas point to as part of their argument about ads as art. Here, cross-cultural allusions, the 'recycling' and 'periodising' of earlier styles, the cultivation of indirectness, enigma and irony, seem to suggest a giving up on the *referentiality* of conventional 'value transfer' as ads compete for audience attention and some level of memorability in the increasingly busy audio-visual space within which everyday life is lived. In this space, novelty and cleverness are at a high premium, driven by the rapid rate at which ideas become used up and require renewal in response to changes in style and taste elsewhere. The way in which ads are forced by this relentless opportunism into being nervously parasitic upon other forms as well as an influence themselves, needs more attention than it gets.[16]

Another indication of a certain instability in the industry has been the emergence in Britain of a self-consciously 'socially responsible' advertising, particularly associated with the newer agencies in London. In this approach, conventional stereotypes are either undercut or replaced by emphatically non-stereotypical representations. For instance, in one recent television commercial for a photographic firm, images of mentally disabled people were used to bring attention to the way in which photography can be a force for social understanding and social empathy. Of course, this particular approach can only work effectively with certain products and a cynical view might see it as just another way of riding shifts in general public concern in order to benefit the product (just another device of 'value transfer'). However, it is at a considerable remove from those banal projections of power, success and family joy which Booth took as the focus for his critique. Whilst it seems clear that most advertising is by its very nature committed to the maximisation of private profit and therefore fits awkwardly with any attempt to promote public values which are not instrumental to that end, this does preclude shifts in advertising discourse which align it more closely, if only partially, with non-commodified values and forms of social relationship. However, in the context of recent international shifts and tendencies (see Mattelart, 1991) any general optimism might seem misplaced.

Television advertising will remain an important focus for media analysis. Its iconography, narrative formats, use of character types and shifting pattern of themes and values will continue to be of technical interest in respect of developments in media discourse and of cultural interest insofar as they are indicative of broader aesthetic, ethical and social factors. But this indicative quality cannot be read either as directly expressive (advertising reflecting the culturally normative) or as directly constitutive (advertising shaping the culturally normative). As Michael Schudson has pointed out in his splendidly sceptical study of advertising power, 'the consumer culture is sustained most of all not by manufactured images but by the goods themselves as they are used and valued in social groups' (Schudson, 1993, p. 248). Unfortunately, far too much work in media analysis has been reluctant to move much beyond the clues (rich and suggestive though these are) provided by the advertising text. This has not helped to refine our sense of either the 'selling power' or the 'cultural power' of advertising and it has led to a situation in which the professional journals of the advertising industry frequently contain more valuable indications on these matters than the academic literature. A perspective is needed which seeks critical dialogue with the professional discourses themselves as well as with consumers.

Moreover, as a result of the analytic focus on the role of advertising as ideological reproduction, the industrial power of advertising, its massive underpinning of public communication systems in many countries, has tended to be marginalised as an issue in academic teaching and research. The two are related, of course, in that it is advertisers' belief that 'messages' about desirable life style in relation to commodity use are actually getting across which justifies their huge contribution to the budgets of the media industries. However, it seems to me that the more pressing requirement in many countries is to develop a public policy on media funding which guards against the overextension of advertising into the central system of public information. This, not primarily because of the bad effects of the ads themselves, but because of the kind of skew introduced into the routine management of such systems as a result of excessive corporate control. The experiences of old 'Eastern Europe' will be instructive here, as they shift from one kind of explicit control to a less obvious and less direct set of imperatives. To give an example of the kind of initiative which needs more attention, some kind of levy on advertising, which required advertisers to fund short periods of network airtime (together with associated production costs) for public use as 'access slots' might be attempted, despite the problems of administering this adequately.

The scale and reach of the television commercial in modern societies certainly provides everyday life with a steady, continuous stream of messages about 'good things' and about how these are tied to possession. They image and imagine a personal and social life lived almost exclusively as a happy consumer. With very few exceptions, they do this without any reference whatsoever to disease, poverty, unemployment or the global conditions which lie beyond the glow of the high street shop window. In registering this, we must certainly reckon with their impact on contemporary consciousness. But we must also reckon with the ways in which contemporary consciousness has 'learned to live' with advertising, not altogether in ways of its own devising but by no means altogether in the ways advertising projects for its own consumption either.

Notes

1 Packard (1957) is the classic text on psycho-social risk. Dyer (1982), with a strongly negative assessment of cultural consequences, has been an influential textbook in British media studies. Booth (1982) develops an American anti-advertising case, discussed later, whilst more recently Haineault and Roy (1993) criticises the effect of advertising on the unconscious, drawing on the French experience.

2 Mattelart (1991) reviews developments in Western Europe and then globally. Schudson (1992) examines the implications in Eastern Europe whilst being primarily concerned with the United States.

3   Agencies themselves have commissioned research into the changing conditions of reception, including video recorder use.
4   Williams (1970) is scathing about the manner in which this was institutionalised in Britain.
5   Such links in French culture are analysed in Guyot (1992).
6   A musicological and social analysis of the function of music in advertising is developed in Klempe (1993)
7   Lee (1993) reviews the arguments about how current advertising culture is linked to economic and cultural shifts in Western societies.
8   A similar point is made by John Thompson (1990). In teaching advertising together to first-year, first-term undergraduates we were confronted with an interesting range of assumptions about how advertisements work and about their 'effects'.
9   Davidson (1991) draws on his own agency experience to discuss 'branding' strategies, including methods of 'value addition'.
10 Dyer (1982) suggests both possibilities, in line with a large critical literature in the United States and Britain.
11 This is described fully in a 'case study' contained in Broadbent (1984, pp. 141–54).
12 The forms of racism and sexism which advertising or particular advertisements might serve to promote is a frequent focus not only of academic but also of journalistic commentary.
13 Williamson (1978) is perhaps the most cited text here.
14 A sustained critique of the application of structuralism to advertisements is Francis (1986). Given its range of examples and its clarity, it deserves to be more widely known.
15 The most comprehensive and lucid account of the 'revised' view of advertising is Schudson (1993), cited briefly later. It is interesting that this concludes on a note of measured ambivalence rather than a positive assessment. Curran (1990) is an important essay on the more general tendency towards a 'revisionism' in media research.
16 These kinds of changes in the industry are discussed in Davidson (1991).

References

Barthes, R. (1977) 'The rhetoric of the image.' In *Image-Music-Text*. London: Fontana.
Booth, W.C. (1982) 'The Company We Keep', *Daedalus*. III.4 1982.
Broadbent, S. (1984) *The Leo Burnett Book of advertising*. London: Business Books Ltd.
Curran, J. (1990) 'The New Revisionism in Mass Communication Research: A Reappraisal', *European Journal of Communication* **5**, 135–64.
Davidson, M. (1991) *The consumerist manifesto*. London: Routledge.
Dyer, G. (1982) *Advertising as communication*. London: Methuen.
Francis, D. (1986) 'Advertising and Structuralism: The Myth of Formality'. *International Journal of Advertising*, 5 197–214.
Guyot, J. (1992) *L'Ecran publicitaire*. Paris: Editions L'Harmattan.
Haineault, D.L. and Roy, J.-Y. (1993) *Unconscious for sale: advertising, psychoanalysis and the public*. Minneapolis: University of Minnesota Press.
Klempe, H. (1993) 'Music, Text and Image in Commercials for Coca-Cola' in J. Corner and J. Hawthorn (eds) (1993) *Communication Studies* (Fourth Edition). London: Edward Arnold.
Lee, M. (1993) *Consumer culture reborn*. London: Routledge.
Leiss, W., Kline, S. and Jhally, S. (1986) *Social communication in advertising*. London: Methuen.
Marcuse, H. (1972) *One dimensional man*. London: Paladin.
Mattelart, A. (1991) *Advertising international*. (tr. Michael Chanan), London: Routledge.
McGuigan, J. (1992) *Cultural populism*. London: Routledge.
Mellancamp, P. (ed.) (1990) *Logics of television*. London: British Film Institute.
Nava, M. and Nava, O. (1990) 'Discriminating or Duped? Young People as Consumers of Advertising/Art', *Magazine of Cultural Studies*, **1**, pp. 15–21.
Packard, V. (1957) *The hidden persuaders*. New York: D. McKay.
Pateman, T. (1983) 'How is Understanding an Advertisement Possible' in P. Walton and H. Davis (eds) *Language, image, media*. Oxford: Blackwell, pp. 187–204.
Schudson, M. (1993) *Advertising: the uneasy persuasion*. (Second edition), London: Routledge.
Thompson, J.O. (1990) 'Advertising's Rationality' in M. Alvarado and J. Thompson (eds) *The media reader*. London: British Film Institute. 208–12.

Wernick, A. (1990) *Promotional culture*. London: Sage.

Williams, R. (1970) 'ITV'S Domestic Romance', *The Listener*, 30 July. Reprinted in O'Connor, A. (ed.) (1989) *Raymond Williams on television*. London: Routledge. 109–12.

Williamson, J. (1978) *Decoding advertisements*. London: Marion Boyars.

Chapter 15

ROBERT C. ALLEN

MAKING SENSE OF SOAPS

WHETHER CALLED SOAP OPERAS, soaps, telenovelas, *teleromans*, or, as my mother calls them, simply "my stories," television serials together constitute one of the most popular and resilient forms of storytelling ever devised. In some television cultures (Russia, China, Italy, Germany), serials are relatively new phenomena. In others (the US, Great Britain, Australia, and several countries of Latin America), they have been staples of broadcast programming since the early days of radio. Some serials eventually end (if only after hundreds of episodes). Others, even after a half-century of continuous unfolding, are no closer to their characters living "happily ever after" than when the first episode was broadcast.

Whether set in a middle-class American suburb, a Welsh village, nineteenth-century Rio, or the sacred time and place of Hindu myth, television serials are linked—in the way they are constructed, broadcast and watched—by their distinctive serial narrational structure. A serial narrative is not merely a narrative that has been segmented, but one whose segmentation produces an interruption in the reading, listening, or viewing process. Furthermore, that interruption is controlled by the producer or distributor of the narrative, not by the reader. In other words, the producer of the narrative determines not only how and when the narration of the story stops and starts, but also how and when the reader's engagement with the text stops and starts.

The serialization of narrative long predates the broadcast soap opera. Indeed, the rise of the literary serial narrative in the eighteenth century marks a crucial turning-point in the development of both literature and publishing. By the 1850s serialization had become a standard means of publishing novels in Europe and America. Most of Dickens's readers during his lifetime read his works as magazine serials not published books. One of the key institutional roles of the serial form has been to exploit new technologies of narrative production and distribution. Serialized novels in the nineteenth century helped build consumer demand for mass circulation newspapers and magazines, which had themselves been made possible by the development of high-speed presses. Serial comic strips facilitated the exploitation of high-speed color printing around the turn of the century. Movie serials helped to build a regular audience for the cinema in the 1910s.

Serial narrative was also crucial to the development of national broadcasting systems in a number of countries, and no more so than in the US. Devised around 1930 as one of a number of programming strategies to lure women to daytime radio and advertisers to program sponsorship, within only a few years soap operas proved to be one of the most effective broadcasting advertising vehicles ever devised. By 1940, the sixty-four serials broadcast on network radio constituted 92 percent of all sponsored programs during daytime hours. The ten highest-rated daytime programs were all serials. In 1948, of the thirty top-rated daytime radio programs, all but five were serials.[1] Serials have dominated daytime television schedules in the US since the 1950s. Several serials have run continuously for more than thirty years, and one, *Guiding Light*, has been seen or heard (with a short gap in the 1940s) since 1937, making it the longest story ever told.

Although the fashion for prime-time serials in the US has waxed and waned since the astonishing success of *Peyton Place* in the mid-1960s and the global popularity of *Dallas* and *Dynasty* in the 1980s, daytime serials remain important to broadcasters today. Sustained and loyal viewership among women between the ages of 18 and 35 provides the basis for soap opera's continuing profitability for US network broadcasters.

The contemporary popularity of serials in the US is overshadowed by what popular journalists have taken to describing as outbreaks of "soapmania" in other parts of the world. The most popular and talked about television program in China in 1991 was *Kewang (Yearnings* or *Expectations)*, which was, according to the *Washington Post*, "the biggest hit on television in Chinese history." Telenovelas constitute half of the total output of Televisa, Mexico's largest communications company, and in 1991 one Televisa serial was watched by 70 percent of the population with access to television. Most Latin American television systems broadcast a dozen or more telenovelas each weekday, and they consistently produce higher viewership than any other form of programming—domestic or imported. In Brazil, choice prime-time slots are reserved for serials, which can be expected to attract an audience of up to 40 million viewers.[2]

One of the most striking demonstrations of the popularity of serial television was the seventy-two part weekly serialization of the Hindu religious epic *Ramayan* broadcast in India in 1987–1988 and regularly watched by an audience of 80 to 100 million people. Broadcast on Sunday mornings, the popularity of the *Ramayan* prompted students at a number of schools to demonstrate against the scheduling of examinations on Sunday mornings and provoked the destruction of an electrical substation when a power failure interrupted a *Ramayan* broadcast. Three thousand sanitation workers in Amritsar responded to the news of the serial's imminent end by going out on strike. As the city braced for a cholera epidemic, business leaders threatened to close their doors unless agreement could be reached with the Ministry of Information and Broadcasting for the serial to be extended. It was.

Although American serials are distributed widely around the world, they are eclipsed by the astounding global circulation of serials made in other cultures. Mexico's Televisa exports its serials to fifty-nine countries, including the US. A Televisa serial was the most popular program in Korea in 1991, and in 1992 another became the most popular dramatic series in the history of Russian television. Serials are one of Australia's most important media exports, and British serials have been sold to nearly twenty countries. But the prize for the world's most successful exporter of serial drama goes to Brazil's TV-Globo, the world's fourth largest television corporation. TV-Globo serials have been seen in more than 100 countries.

Why do they say such terrible things about soap operas?

No other form of television fiction has attracted more viewers in more countries more regularly over a longer period of time than has the serial. Given this fact, it is ironic that, until recently, serials largely have been ignored in the "serious" literature on television and typically have been regarded with dismissive disdain in the popular press. Elsewhere I have argued that in the United States, this paradox is primarily a function of the status of soap operas as a gendered form of narrative and its resistance to being read according to the protocols of more closed narrative forms. Especially when compared to high-brow forms of fiction or drama, the soap opera seemed to critics to be the very epitome of the low. As early as 1940, one American commentator called radio soap operas "serialized drool."[3] Serials have been regarded as some form of trash by critics and commentators virtually everywhere their popularity has prompted public comment: as waste-of-time women's trash (US daytime soaps); glitzy, tasteless trash (*Dallas* and *Dynasty*); glitzy, tasteless, American cultural-imperialist trash (*Dallas* in France); badly-produced trash (Mexican serials); adolescent trash (*Neighbours*); adolescent, colonial revenge trash (*Neighbours* in Britain); etc., etc.

In the US the very term *soap opera* marks out the serial's ironic relationship both with high art and the dirt soap is bought to eliminate. The "soap" in soap opera alludes to the use of the serial form from its earliest days to the present as an advertising vehicle for laundry detergents and household cleaning products. The "opera" in soap opera signals a travesty: the highest of dramatic art forms is made to describe the lowest. (Similarly, western movies were called "horse operas" in the 1930s).

As a "soap opera" the serial is a drama about two kinds of dirt. In calling his study of the British serial *EastEnders, Public Secrets*, David Buckingham points to the tendency of serials to be "about" trash: they seem to revel in the concealment (to other characters and initially to the viewer) and revelation (to some other characters and to the viewer) of the dirty little secrets of characters' lives.[4] One of the most common ways for a serial character to demonstrate his or her villainy is to obtain and threaten to disseminate some "dirt" about another character: his mistaken parentage, her previous lover, his extramarital liaison, her child given up for adoption.

In the US and in other countries where serials function within commercial broadcasting systems to attract female viewers there is another dirty drama going on in the commercials that interrupt the narration of the serial. Characters in the soap opera commercial have, quite literally, dirty secrets: dirty laundry, dirty floors, dirty toilets, dirty bodies, dirty appliances, dirty children, dirty homes—which require the cleansing only this particular brand and type of soap can offer. Not coincidentally, it is female characters who are associated with dirt in the commercials. According to the commercials' logic, it is their inadequacy in controlling dirt that creates a problem, and it is their responsibility to eliminate the home's sources of fifth.

Wherever they are shown, the act of watching serials seems to generate another kind of dirt: the dirty discourse of gossip. Perhaps more than any other form of television, serials encourage viewers to extend the pleasure of watching to the pleasures of talking about what they watch. Dorothy Hobson has documented the pleasures viewers take in gossiping about serials: what has happened, what might happen, what consequences whatever happens might have on the intricately patterned set of relationships that constitute any serial's social world.[5]

Like the trash generated by consumer capitalism, the serial has been associated with the masses and mass culture. For cultural critics such as Dwight MacDonald and Ernest van den Haag in the 1950s the spectator was being diverted from "serious" art by mass-produced, predigested works of mass culture, anonymously manufactured and distributed in bulk. The sheer quantity of mass culture was drowning real art, they argued, while its easy pleasures stupefied the spectator and rendered him or her incapable of aesthetic discrimination. MacDonald even singles out radio serials as a prime example of mass-produced mass culture that threatened to inundate authentic culture "by its sheer pervasiveness, its brutal, overwhelming *quantity*."[6] Thus, condemned for its ubiquity and written off as the unfortunate consequence of programming for the least common denominator of audience taste, the soap opera's very popularity has served as an obstacle to its serious scrutiny. With a few notable exceptions, the television critic writing in magazines and newspapers has shown about as much interest in writing about soap operas as the restaurant critic has in writing about McDonald's—and for much the same reason: they are both regarded as "junk."

Soap operas in media and cultural studies

Given the antipathy of most literary critics to mass culture in general, television more specifically (with the exception of anthology drama in the "Golden Age" of television in the early 1950s), and soap operas in particular, it is hardly surprising that it was not until the 1980s that soap operas began to be taken seriously as texts. To be sure, social scientists had subjected television soap operas to quantitative "content analysis" in order to compare the construction of some aspects of social reality in the world of the soap opera with their bases in "real life." Such studies assume that fictional texts are (and are understood by their readers to be) direct reflections of objective social reality and further assume that the features of that reality fastened upon in the study (occupational and sex roles, communication patterns, causes of death and disease, etc.) function within the text in the same ways they do outside of it. In general, content analysis tells us little about the way soap operas work as texts, generate meanings, and allow pleasures for their viewers because its procedures deny the soap opera any status as a complex fictional text.

Within this historical context, then, Tania Modleski's discussion of American daytime soap operas in her dissertation and book, *Loving With a Vengeance* (1982), was important for several reasons.[7] Demonstrating the usefulness of applying the methods of post-structuralist criticism to serials, Modleski situates soap operas and their study squarely within the context of feminist theory. She argues that soap operas, along with several other forms of popular culture, position their female "readers" quite differently than more male-oriented texts and make possible quite different pleasures and meanings. This is not to say that Modleski celebrates soap operas as feminist or progressive texts; indeed, she sees their formal structure and thematic concerns meshing all too neatly with the domestic demands placed upon women within patriarchal capitalism. Denied the omnipotent reading position to be found in more closed narrative forms, soap opera viewers are asked to relate to the diegetic families of their serials as they are expected to do to their own. They must exercise patience and tolerance in the face of unending tribulation, wresting pleasure from consolation and sympathy rather than from any expectation of final resolution. The narrative structure of soap operas—cutting in the middle of conversations from one plot line to another, interrupting constantly with commercial messages— mimics the rhythms of the mother/reader's domestic life.

Although Modleski's approach is textual rather than ethnographic, it also points to the importance of understanding soap operas and other forms of popular culture within the contexts of their reception and use. That concern for the reader or viewer also underlies my own study of American daytime soap operas, which appeared a few years later (*Speaking of Soap Operas*, 1985). In it I address the paradox of the soap opera's cultural status in the US: on the one hand, the soap opera is the most successful broadcast advertising vehicle ever devised; on the other, it is among the most disdained forms of popular culture of the last half century. At the crux of this paradox, I argue, lies the "gendered" nature of the soap opera's appeals and popularity. Soaps are both highly valued (by advertisers and broadcasters) and dismissed (by critics) as a "woman's" form.

Furthermore, soap operas operate according to very different narrative and dramatic principles than more closed narrative forms: they are predicated upon the impossibility of their ever ending. Hence, the critic attempting to "read" an episode of a soap opera comes to a story already years in the telling, and one that will be unaltered by anything occurring in that episode. Put in semiotic terminology, US daytime soap operas trade an investment in syntagmatic determinacy (the eventual direction of the overall plot line) for one in paradigmatic complexity (how any particular event affects the complex network of character relationships). The long-term, loyal viewer of the soap opera is rewarded by the text in that her knowledge of the large and complex community of characters and their histories enables her to produce subtle and nuanced readings, whereas a single episode of any given soap opera, viewed out of context by a textually-naive critic, appears to be so much pointless talk among undistinguishable characters about events of maddeningly indeterminable significance.

The early 1980s also saw the first important critical work on British soap operas. The BFI monograph of *Coronation Street* (1981) and Dorothy Hobson's book on *Crossroads* (1982)[8] mark the inclusion of the serial form as an object of inquiry on the agenda of the emerging field of cultural studies. As any British television viewer knows, since 1960 semi-weekly episodes of Granada Television's *Coronation Street* have chronicled the lives of the residents of its eponymous working-class neighborhood set in a fictional northern city. The working-class milieu of *Coronation Street* and, since 1985, its chief rival in the ratings, the BBC serial *EastEnders*, has made class a central issue in critical analyses of British serials and set them apart from both American daytime and prime-time serials. The nature of class, the constitution and character of the working class, and the academic study of both were foundational issues for British cultural studies, in part because they figured so prominently in the work of such key figures as Richard Hoggart, Raymond Williams, E. P. Thompson, and Stuart Hall. Because *Coronation Street* emerges from the same cultural moment as Hoggart's influential study of working-class culture, *The Uses of Literacy* (1958)[9] and in the wake of the Angry Young (Working-Class) Man movement in British literature, theater, and cinema, it is a privileged and sustained instance of popular culture's engagement with questions of class and, as such, a convenient springboard for Richard Dyer, Terry Lovell, Christine Geraghty, and the other contributors to address the more general theoretical and methodological questions it gives rise to.

Ironically—given the contemporaneous struggles in the US to admit the critical study of soap operas to the academic agenda—*Coronation Street* was of scholarly interest to Dyer and his co-contributors because it enjoyed substantial scholarly sympathy and critical acclaim, albeit in spite of its status as "soap opera." The same definitely cannot be said of the object of Dorothy Hobson's 1982 book, *Crossroads: The Drama of a Soap Opera*. If *Coronation Street* was marked in the early 1980s as a program that transcended the conventions of its genre, *Crossroads* was frequently singled out by critics and broadcast regulators as the most egregious example of soap opera—and, by extension, commercial television—at its technical and aesthetic worst. As is frequently the case when such charges are made about soap operas, the only people who disagreed (or could not have cared less) were the millions of devoted viewers who watched each week: in the early 1980s, *Crossroads* was battling *Coronation Street* for supremacy in the weekly ratings.

Hobson's book contributed importantly to the early critical literature on soap operas in several ways, although its influence was felt much more and more immediately in Britain than in the US: with *Crossroads* not shown on American television, her book was not widely distributed in the US. Based on research for her dissertation at the Centre for Contemporary Cultural Studies at the University of Birmingham, Hobson's published account is organized around a pivotal moment in the diegetic, institutional, and reception history of the serial: after seventeen years as its central female character, Meg Mortimer was to be written out of the show and the contract of the actor playing her, Noele Gordon, not renewed. This decision became the subject of enormous controversy in the popular press and prompted thousands of angry letters from Meg's fans. Meg's demise provided Hobson with an opportunity to examine the meaning of *Crossroads* for the company that produced it; the writers, producers, cast, and crew that made it; the press that covered it as "news"; and the audience that watched and read about it.

Methodologically, what distinguishes Hobson's study is what might be called its ethnographic orientation. Hobson is not concerned with *Crossroads* as text but how—as production challenge, enacted script, subject of public discourse, or viewing experience—it takes on meaning for the various groups that encounter it in any of its varied manifestations. Her role, then, is not so much critic as observer and commentator on the observations of those whom she interviews about *Crossroads*.[10] Hobson's account of the audience for *Crossroads* replaces the American functionalist model of viewer/text interaction with one that foregrounds the production of meanings and pleasures. Furthermore, she argues that those meanings and pleasures cannot be "read off" the text in isolation but rather are deeply embedded in the social contexts of its viewing. Thus, they vary from viewer to viewer: *Crossroads* is a different experience for the young mother who feeds her child while she watches than for the widowed grandmother who views alone. Hobson's finding of the diversity of meanings and pleasures connected with watching *Crossroads* also suggests that they may be quite different than those assumed by its producers, writers, actors, or sponsors.

The investigation of the pleasures of soap opera viewing and their relationship to both genre conventions and the gendered nature of the serial audience also forms the focus of *Watching "Dallas": Soap Opera and the Melodramatic Imagination*, Ien Ang's study of the reception of *Dallas* in Holland. Published in Dutch the same year as Hobson's work (1982) and translated into English in 1985, *Watching "Dallas"* is the first book-length work to examine the cross-cultural reception of serials.[11] Based on forty-two letters from *Dallas* viewers solicited in a Dutch woman's magazine, *Watching "Dallas"* is not so much a study of the audience for soap operas as it is an extended essay on relationships among gender, genre, and ideology generated by a "symptomatic" reading of viewer discourse on *Dallas* at a time when the show's popularity was a controversial issue in Holland.

Like Hobson and Modleski, whose work she acknowledges, Ang is concerned with the pleasures associated with soap opera viewing, particularly the pleasures available to female viewers (all but three of her respondents were female). However, Ang also investigates the ironic pleasure some viewers seem to take in hating *Dallas* or in disliking the values they see it representing so much that they enjoy watching the show in order to condemn and ridicule it. Ang relates this pleasure in displeasure to both an implicit critique of mass culture and to concerns about the influence of American popular culture on Dutch life.

More than any work to that point, *Watching "Dallas"* foregrounds the complex and sometimes contradictory nature of the pleasures watching soap operas produces for some of its viewers. Many of the letters expressing considerable enjoyment of the act of watching *Dallas* also confess to finding some aspects of the program politically problematic, implausible, silly, insulting, or excessive. Serials, Ang suggests, engage their viewers along a number of different axes, and deriving enjoyment from the viewing experience would seem to depend upon the negotiation of multiple tensions. For example, being a regular serial viewer involves resolving or at least accommodating the tension between recognizing the soap opera world as fictional construct and accepting its "as-if-it-were-real" character. As both Hobson and Ang demonstrate, female soap opera viewers—frequently charged in the popular press with an inability to distinguish soap opera fiction from "real life"—move easily and knowledgably in their discourse about soaps between pleasure in soaps' status as fabricated products of the show business industry and the different kinds of pleasure to be derived from involvement with soap characters as if they were (but still knowing they are not) people.

Sparked in part by these and other early critical investigations of serials, the late 1980s and early 1990s . . . witnessed a burgeoning of work on the form around the world among scholars operating within what might be called "media studies" or "cultural studies" academic paradigms. Critical work on soap operas also expanded as theories of media derived from structuralism and post-structuralism supplanted or at least were allowed to coexist with more empiricist models in academic curricula. Studies of serial audiences benefited from the increased interest in ethnography among media scholars in the wake of David Morley's *Nationwide* monograph (1981) and his *Family Television* (1986), as well as John Fiske's celebration of such studies in his work. David

Buckingham's *Public Secrets: EastEnders and Its Audience* (1987) certainly reflects this interest as well as a concern to link institution, text, and audience in the study of serials.[12]

The other major locus of critical work on serials in the 1980s and early 1990s was Latin America, particularly Brazil. As Maria Teresa Quiroz has noted, although serials have been a part of Latin American broadcasting since the 1940s, they have attracted the serious attention of critics and scholars only recently.[13] Interest in the Latin American television serial, the telenovela, has been prompted not only by the enormous contemporary popularity of the form from Mexico to Chile, but also by the rise of Brazil, Mexico, and Venezuela as major serial exporters both within and outside of Latin America. Brazil's TV Globo sells telenovelas to more than 100 countries around the world; serials produced by Mexico's Televisa have been number one hits in Korea and Russia; and Venezuelan serials have engendered "novelamania" in Spain.

Scholars of Latin American serials, such as Ondina Leal, Tomas Lopez-Pumarejo, Michèle and Armand Mattelart, Jesús Martín-Barbero, Renato Ortiz, Nora Mazziotti, Monica Rector, and others[14] have seen telenovelas as well as imported US serials as opportunities to explore questions of national identity, cultural authenticity, the relationship between television and everyday life, and the gaps between serials' representation of social reality and that experienced by serial viewers. But more than anything else, the telenovela has been discussed in terms of its relationship to modernity: the economic, cultural, and psychic reorganization of society around the demands of consumer capitalism. Modernity has certainly been an important issue to scholars in Europe and North America, but principally as a historical phenomenon and in relation to its epochal successor, postmodernity. For scholars of Latin America, however, the project of modernity is of current not just historical interest. Television has been seen as an important instrument of modernity in Latin America—supplanting premodern modes of experience, suppressing linguistic and cultural differences, addressing the viewer as consumer, and offering a window onto a high-tech, secular, market-driven world into which the viewer is somehow expected to fit. Jesús Martín-Barbero, along with Mattelart and Mattelart, views telenovelas as a mixture of modern and more traditional modes of storytelling and reception. The attenuation of the story over a period of weeks and months evokes the slow, cyclical rhythms of the seasons and family life. But within each daily episode, the viewer encounters the frenetic pace and fragmentation both of contemporary television style and of modernity itself.

Soaps go global

The development of cable and satellite technologies in the 1980s expanded the delivery capacity of many national television systems. At the same time and in response to some of the same forces, governments across Europe began to shift from a public-service model of broadcast policy to a "mixed" or entirely commercial model. The expansion of channel capacity and the growth of the commercial broadcasting sector combined to produce the need to build new audiences for television and to find relatively low-cost sources of entertainment programming. Importing serials from other countries became an attractive programming option for several reasons. In addition to being internally self-promoting—each episode is implicitly an advertisement for the next—serials also advertise and promote the medium through which they are delivered to consumers. In order to realize any pleasure from their engagement with serials, the viewer must "stay tuned." Given the number of hours of programming they represent and the size of audience they can attract, imported serials are relatively inexpensive (US$4,000 to US$8,000 per episode in Greece or Spain, for example)—especially when compared to the cost of locally produced dramatic programming.

For decades it has been axiomatic that the international circulation of television programming occurs from north to south and from west to east: that is to say, US and, to a lesser degree,

European program producers maintain their hegemony over the global television market by selling their programs at a low cost to foreign broadcasters, particularly to broadcasters in Latin America, Asia, and Africa. They can do so because their production costs have been recovered in the far larger and richer domestic market. Thus prices for foreign sales can be kept at a level low enough to discourage domestic drama production elsewhere but still high enough to be profitable to the producer.

Interestingly, however, it was not US producers who benefited most from the increased demand for serial programming in the 1980s, although a few US companies scored spectacular successes in the early part of the decade with such shows as *Dallas, Dynasty*, and *Falcon Crest*. Rather, Latin American producers, particularly Brazil's TV-Globo and Mexico's Televisa, moved aggressively into the international arena, both benefiting from their near-monopoly domestic positions. TV-Globo, which in 1991 captured 60 percent of the Brazilian television advertising market, began exporting telenovelas to Europe in 1975. Within a decade, its annual profits on foreign telenovela sales to nearly 100 countries had risen to US$20 million.

A further instance of the "flow" of television programming from south to north, periphery to center, is the export of Australian serials, particularly Grundy Television's *Neighbours*. Originally produced for Australia's Seven Network in 1985, it was cancelled after seven months, then picked up by the competing Network Ten. A surprise hit on its new network, *Neighbours* was launched on commercial television in Great Britain in November 1986, becoming the first serial there to be "stripped:" shown each weekday. Its success in the UK was even more surprising than its ratings-topping popularity in Australia. Grundy Television claims that the *Neighbours* cast is the first of any television series to have traveled to Britain at the request of the royal family for a Royal Command Performance. *Neighbours* has now been seen in some twenty-five countries around the world, from Bulgaria to Zambia.

Ironically, producers of US daytime serials are now in the position of taking lessons from their Latin American and antipodean competitors, as they turn to the export market to offset domestic declines in viewership and revenue. Although they continue to be profitable, the future of US daytime soap operas is perhaps more uncertain than at any time since the genre made its successful transition from radio to television in the early 1950s. Total network viewership, both prime-time and daytime, is steadily falling, as more viewers have access to dozens of channels.

For the four major commercial networks, dispersed viewership across an increasingly fragmented market means lower ratings, reduced total advertising revenue, reduced advertising rates, and, with program production or licensing costs not declining, reduced profit margins, especially for daytime. Although soap operas have gained in some audience segments over the past ten years —men and adolescents especially—these are not groups traditionally targeted by the companies whose advertising has sustained the genre for a half century. Total viewership among the most valuable segment of the soap opera audience—women between the ages of 18 and 35—has declined since 1980 as more women have entered the paid workforce and as women at home defect to other programming alternatives.

The penetration of the VCR into the American market over the same period (currently over 90 percent of US homes have a VCR) has had a curious impact on soap opera viewership. Although soap operas are one of the genres most "time-shifted", soap opera viewing on videotape does not figure into audience ratings data, and even if it did, advertisers would discount such viewership, believing (probably accurately) that most viewers "zip" through the frequent commercial messages.

As they scramble to staunch the flow of audience to cable, satellite, and independent stations, the networks have turned to programming forms that require minimal start-up investment and carry low production budgets: game and talk shows. Both these genres represent serious competition for soap operas.

As cable systems enlarged their channel capacity and new cable programming services began to target specific audience segments ("narrow casting," as opposed to the commercial networks' traditional strategy of "broadcasting"), some predicted that cable programmers would turn to the soap opera as a way of attracting and maintaining viewership. This vision of different soap operas for every audience segment has, for the most part, not come to pass. Most cable programmers have not commissioned new soap operas for several reasons. First, even though production costs are still far less than dramatic programming shot on film, the weekly budget for an hour-long soap opera exceeds US$500,000. Although soap audiences can be extraordinarily loyal, viewership and viewer loyalty can take years to build. For cable programmers attempting to program for a tiny sliver of the available audience, with advertising revenues a fraction of those for the commercial networks, and, consequently, with minuscule programming budgets, buying network series reruns from syndicators and developing new programs within cheaper genres (talk shows, game shows, and "reality" programs) seems a better risk than starting new soap operas.

The crowning irony, of course, would be the conquest of the US market by Latin American serials. Although this has not yet occurred, Latin American serials have become staples in one segment of the US television market. Telenovelas have become mainstays of Spanish-language cable, satellite, and broadcast channels, now available throughout the US. However, because they are not subtitled in English and since most Americans living north of the southern rim of the country do not speak Spanish, the impact of Latin American serials on US television is greatly circumscribed.

From its beginnings in the late 1940s, US commercial network television has been informally closed to foreign programming. With a huge domestic television production infrastructure, the world's richest consumer market to absorb high production costs, and program suppliers able to offer programming to the networks for less than their actual cost of production (because of lucrative syndication, foreign, and other ancillary rights accruing to a series with a successful network run), there was no incentive to seek alternative, offshore sources of programming. Furthermore, using wonderfully circular logic, the networks reasoned that since there was no tradition of watching programs dubbed or subtitled, or even programs with different English accents on network television, audiences would not tolerate such programs. Thus, the only national broadcasting service that has relied heavily upon imported programming has been public television, which has provided a venue for British drama, documentary, situation comedy, and, with the importation of *EastEnders* from the BBC, serials. But PBS is a distinctly minority service, attracting on average about 3 percent of the available primetime viewing audience.

Open and closed serials

The term "serial" draws our attention to the one feature *Kewang, Coronation Street, Guiding Light, Dallas, Ramayan, Los Ricos Lloran Tambien*, and even the programs that make up *Masterpiece Theatre* all share—their seriality. True serialization—the organization of narrative and narration around the enforced and regular suspension of both textual display and reading activity—produces a very different mode of reader engagement and reader pleasure than we experience with non-serials. As literary theorist Wolfgang Iser has noted, the act of reading any narrative involves traversing textual terrain over time, as the reader moves from one word, sentence, paragraph, and chapter to the next. Or, in the case of cinematic or televisual narratives, from one shot, scene, sequence, or episode to the next. As readers or viewers we take up what he calls a "wandering viewpoint" within the text as we move through it, looking back upon the textual terrain already covered (what Iser calls retention) and anticipating on that basis what might lie around the next textual corner (protension). Both processes occur in the gaps between words, sentences, and chapters (or shots, scenes, and sequences)—those necessary textual silences where we as readers/viewers are called upon to connect the words, sounds and/or images of the text to form a coherent narrative world.[15]

The serial, then, is a form of narrative organized around institutionally-imposed gaps in the text. The nature and extent of those gaps are as important to the reading process as the textual "material" they interrupt. Each episode ends with some degree of narrative indeterminacy: a plot question that will not be answered until the next episode. In the US, where daytime serials are broadcast Monday through Friday, the greatest indeterminacy is left with the viewer at the end of the Friday episode, encouraging her, as the announcer's voice used to say, to "tune in again next time" on Monday. These gaps leave plenty of time for viewers to discuss with each other both the possible meanings of what has happened thus far as well as what might happen next. Thus, regardless of the cultural context of their production and reception, regardless of their plot or themes, television serials around the world seem more than any other form of programming to provoke talk about them among their viewers. Indeed Christine Geraghty sees this as their defining quality:

> Soap operas . . . can now be defined not purely by daytime scheduling or even by a clear appeal to a female audience but by the presence of stories which engage an audience in such a way that they become the subject for public interest and interrogation.[16]

Non-serial popular narratives tend to be organized around a single protagonist or small group of protagonists and to be teleological: there is a single moment of narrative closure (obviously involving the protagonist) toward which their plots move and in relation to which reader satisfaction is presumed to operate. The classic example of this type of narrative is the murder mystery, in which the revelation of the murderer at the end of the story absolutely determines the movement of the plot. By contrast, the serial spreads its narrative energy among a number of plots and a community of characters, and, what is even more important, sets these plots and characters in complex, dynamic, and unpredictable relationship with each other. Because serials cut between scenes enacting separate plot lines, the viewer is prompted to ask not only "Where is each of these plot lines going?," but also "What might be the relationship between different plot lines?"

It is at this point that we need to distinguish between two fundamentally different, but frequently conflated, forms of television serial: what I call "open" and "closed" serials. US daytime, British, and Australian serials are open narrative forms. That is to say they are the only forms of narrative (with the possible exception of comic strips) predicated upon the impossibility of ultimate closure. No one sits down to watch an episode of one of these programs with the expectation that this episode might be the one in which all individual and community problems will be solved and everyone will live happily ever after.

In a sense, these serials trade narrative closure for paradigmatic complexity. Just as there is no ultimate moment of resolution, there is no central, indispensable character in open serials to whose fate viewer interest is indissolubly linked. Instead, there is a changing community of characters who move in and out of viewer attention and interest. Any one of them might die, move to another city, or lapse into an irreversible coma without affecting the overall world of the serial. Indeed, I would argue that it is the very possibility of a central character's demise—something that is not a feature of episodic series television—that helps to fuel viewer interest in the serial.

US daytime soap operas are "open" in another sense as well. Events in a daytime soap are less determinant and irreversible than they are in other forms of narrative, and identity, indeed ontology itself, is more mutable. For example, generally, when a character dies in a fictional narrative (assuming we are not reading a gothic horror tale or piece of science fiction) we expect that character to stay dead. In soap operas, it is not unusual to witness the resurrection of a character assumed to be but not actually dead, even after the passage of years of intervening story. I remember one character on a now cancelled soap opera called *The Edge of Night* who was presumed drowned in a boating accident in the Caribbean literally for five years before she returned. It turned out she had been rescued by a passing French yacht and discovered to be suffering from amnesia. She was taken to Paris where she lived for five years before recovering her memory and returning to her husband and family in the States.

Another distinguishing feature of open serials, particularly US daytime serials, is their large community of interrelated characters. More than half of all US daytime serial episodes are one hour in length and all are broadcast five days each week. As a result, it is not uncommon for the cast of a daytime soap to include more than thirty regularly-appearing characters—not counting a dozen or more others who have moved away, lapsed into comas, been incarcerated or otherwise institutionalized, or are presumed dead. Furthermore, the audience comes to know some of these characters quite literally over the course of decades of viewing. In the nearly forty years that actress Charita Bauer played the role of Bert Bauer on *The Guiding Light*, her character evolved from young bride to great-grandmother. Viewers of *Coronation Street* have followed events in the life of character Ken Barlow since he was introduced in the show's first episode in December 1960. Thus, the community of soap opera characters shares with the loyal viewer a sense of its collective and individual history, which, in some cases, has unfolded over decades both of story-telling and viewing: the viewer who began watching *The Guiding Light* in 1951 as a young mother caring for infants might herself now watch with her grandchildren. Truth to tell, writers seldom draw upon their characters' or viewers' specific knowledge of story events from decades past, although some viewers are quick to chastise writers when they inadvertently violate that shared history.

The size of the open serial community, the complexity of its character relationships, and the fact that these characters possess both histories and memories all combine to create an almost infinite set of potential connections among characters and plots events. The revelation of hidden parentage—a plot device common, so far as I can determine, to television serials around the world —is emblematic of this feature of serials, in which to whom someone is or might be related is frequently more important than anything that character might do.

The open serial's emphasis on relationships among characters also helps to explain a frequently commented upon feature of open serials: their redundancy within a given episode. Such a program might devote most of an episode to relating a single piece of narrative information—the revealing of parentage, let's say. One character overhears someone telling someone else, who then tells another character, who telephones yet another with the news, etc., etc. This reiteration does nothing to advance the plot, and the uninitiated viewer might well regard it as redundant. However, to the experienced viewer, who tells whom is just as important as what is being related: each retelling affects relations among the community of characters.

It is not uncommon to hear people who don't watch open serials complain that "nothing ever happens" in them. "Why bother watching every day or even every week," they puzzle, "when you can keep up with the plot by watching an episode a month." This complaint is grounded in two fundamental qualities of open serial narrative, but it also reveals an equally fundamental misunderstanding of how these narratives function and the nature of the pleasures they might generate. It is true that no story event will push the open serial narrative any closer to ultimate closure. It is also true that, compared to other types of popular narrative, the emphasis in soap operas is on talk rather than action. But, as we have seen, events in open serials take on meaning for viewers not so much in relation to their place in a syntagmatic chain but rather in terms of the changes in the paradigmatic structure of the community those events might provoke: if, after twenty years, Jason's father is revealed to be Ralph, then Jason must call off his engagement to Jennifer who is now revealed to be his half-sister, and he must come to terms with the fact that Jeremy, his nemesis, is also his half-brother! But, because he is not a regular viewer, the soap opera critic is ignorant of this complex paradigmatic structure and its history. Soap operas are to him merely so much syntagmatically inconsequential talk. To him, little changes from year to year in the soap opera community; to the competent viewer, however, each episode is loaded with important adjustments or possible alterations to that world.

The centrality of paradigmatic structure in the open serial thus helps to account for the emphasis on talk over action as well as for the typical settings in which this talk occurs, and, in the case of US daytime soaps, at least, the kinds of occupations soap opera characters are given. Open serials tend to be organized around locations where characters regularly have occasion to meet: restaurants, hospitals, nightclubs, doctors' offices, lawyers' offices, corporate headquarters, etc. And characters are given occupations that depend on "talk": doctors, nurses, lawyers, entrepreneurs, police officers, entertainers, etc. US daytime soap operas are middle- to upper middle-class in their social settings, and working-class characters seldom figure prominently in plot lines. British soaps, on the other hand, tend to represent working-class social worlds. Still, their key settings are places where characters come to talk: the most important location in both _Coronation Street_ and _EastEnders_ is the local pub.[17] These locations and occupations also facilitate the introduction of new characters, who enter the story as hospital patients, newly assigned doctors or nurses, bar patrons, crime victims, criminals, etc., in the case of US daytime soaps, and newly arrived residents of "the street" or Albert Square, in the case of _Coronation Street_ and _EastEnders_. Conversely, US daytime and British soaps, typically do not give characters occupations that are non-social, solitary, or non-verbal: farmers, factory workers, computer programmers, night-watchmen, or lighthouse keepers.

The absence of a final moment of narrative closure also indefinitely postpones any moment of final ideological or moral closure in the open serial. Open serial writers and producers can raise any number of potentially controversial and contentious social issues without having to make any ideological commitment to them. The viewer is not looking for a moral to the story in the same way he or she is in a closed narrative, even a closed serial. This is not to say that open serials are not ideological constructs, but it is ultimately not in their interest (or that of their producers or sponsors) to be seen to take sides on any particular issue or to appear to be overtly didactic. _Brookside_ creator Phil Redmond has said that his serial

> remains, always has and always will remain, neutral with no particular view or axe to grind. The characters within the programme can be as extreme in their views as the story, characterization or reality demands—although the programme itself must not be seen to take any particular viewpoint.[18]

At the center of this normative space are those values, attitudes, and behaviors implicitly or explicitly believed by producers to be held by the core group of intended viewers: in the case of US daytime serials, middle-class women between the ages of 18 and 35. These norms form, for the most part, the unarticulated givens of the serial social structure. However, in their continuing efforts to keep storylines "current" and interesting to viewers, writers frequently introduce plot lines dealing with controversial social or moral issues. The narrative structure of open serials enables these plot lines and the implicit values they carry to be tried out and allows their fates to be influenced (if not determined) by viewer response. If viewers lose interest in a given plot line or find it offensive, it and the character(s) to which it is attached can be dispensed with or the character can be divested of it (drug use, prostitution, radical political views, etc.). Another strategy for dealing with aberrant values is to attach them to a character on the margins of the serial's core value systems and thus keep them at the edge of the serial's normative territory.

Indeed, the open serial frequently provides a more politically acceptable venue for the airing of controversial issues than more determinant forms of television drama. The first successful television serial in the Republic of Ireland was *The Riordans*, which ran from 1965 to 1978. This story of family life in a rural community dealt with a wide range of highly charged social issues: the living conditions of farmworkers, sexuality and the use of contraceptives, alcohol and tranquilizer addiction, and the role of the church in Irish society. That it was able to do so on government-controlled television, in a society where the majority, as late as 1986, opposed divorce, and under the ever vigilant gaze of the Catholic Church, was a direct consequence of its open serial form. It could raise these issues without taking a perceptible stand or proffering solutions.

But it is important to note that the nature of the paradigmatic structures of US daytime and other examples of open serials themselves carry implicit ideological valences. For example, there are three basic types of relationships among characters in a US daytime soap. One might be related to another character through kinship (as a mother, father, brother, sister, uncle, cousin, etc.), through romance (husband, wife, lover, former lover, potential lover, secret admirer, etc.), or through social bond (employer, co-worker, friend, neighbor, enemy, etc.). White, heterosexual characters move easily among these three categories: a neighbor becomes a lover and is later revealed to be a father as well, the possibility of romance developing among colleagues is ever-present, and even criminals and their victims become romantically involved. However African-American, gay, and lesbian characters are consigned to much more restricted positions in this paradigmatic matrix, more because of the underlying ideological values of that structure than any direct consequence of biology or sexual orientation. Although there have been homosexual characters in soap operas, they have in the main been treated like contentious social issues: introduced from outside the community as a part of a specific and limited story line and, after a while, disposed of without lasting impact upon the community. The presence of more than a token gay character among the paradigmatically embedded central characters of a soap opera would call into question the very structure of that community. Similarly, with interracial hetero-sexual romance still problematic for the normative world of the US soap opera, black characters are relegated to "second-class" citizenship on soap operas: because they are less likely to be actual or potential romantic partners for white characters and thus not likely to be revealed as their parents, brothers, or children, black characters operate largely among their own tiny subcommunities and appear in the larger community only as co-workers, neighbors, friends or acquaintances.

Unlike the open serial, the Latin American telenovela and other forms of closed serial are designed to end and their narratives to close—although this closure might not be achieved until after several months or 200 episodes. It has been said that the narrative trajectory of the Brazilian telenovela, which usually is broadcast nightly for four to six months, can be divided into three stages. The initial episodes introduce a variety of characters and open up a number of plot lines. In the next twenty or thirty episodes two or three major themes emerge, central characters are defined in greater detail, and plot lines are further complicated. The final third of the telenovela is devoted to bringing the major plot lines to some form of resolution.

To Nico Vink, closure represents a key difference between Brazilian and North American serials. The teleological thrust of the telenovela privileges the final episodes institutionally, textually, and in terms of audience expectation and satisfaction. The ending of a telenovela is heavily promoted, and, in the case of particularly popular telenovelas, becomes the subject of anticipatory public and private discourse: "how will everything work out?" "Who will win and who will lose?" "Who will live and who will die?" Two endings were shot for *Roque Santeiro*, a telenovela broadcast in 1985. The nature of each was publicized as the serial approached its final revelatory episode and a public opinion poll taken to determine which the audience preferred. Both commentators and ordinary viewers (through letters to newspapers) attempted to see in each ending a meaning that extended well beyond the narrowly textual. One critic saw one ending as transforming the serial into an allegory for the socio-political situation in Brazil. A viewer responded by published letter that the alternative ending provided moral closure for the world of the text in compensation for the lack of it in the real world. "Everyone knows," she wrote, "that in reality the powerful never go to prison. Just for that reason at least a [tele]novela should offer this satisfaction."[19]

As the public discourse surrounding the ending of *Roque Santeiro* suggests, closed serials also offer viewers an opportunity after closure to look back upon the completed text and impose upon it some kind of moral or ideological order. In this sense, closed serials are inherently melodramatic in nature. To use Peter Brooks's phrase, melodramas are narratives of the "moral occult."[20] They offer us worlds in which the unthinking decision, the chance encounter, the accidental occurrence, the meaningless tragedy all seem connected to some deeper but obscure pattern of significance, some hidden moral order. Each twist of the plot implicitly prompts us to ask "what does this mean?" "Why is this happening?" The melodrama defers providing any answers until the end, when the outline of the operative moral or ideological universe comes into view through the way in which resolution and closure are imposed upon the narrative. The attenuation of the narrative in closed serials combined with the privileging of closure—both within the text and in intertextual discourse—invites the viewer to supply or discern a moral to the story.

The open serial's lack of closure enables it to accommodate a wide range of interpretations among its viewers. Indeed, the elaborate discourse about serials—generated by viewers as they watch, among viewers on a work break or on the playground, and in the pages of magazines devoted to serials—reflects the process that occurs within each viewer as she or he comes to terms with the serial text. Because of the gaps created by its serial structure, even the closed serial, for a time at least, opens up issues, values, and meanings that the text itself cannot immediately close off.

The serial form and its various manifestations on television systems around the world clearly engage viewers in ways and on a scale that is perhaps unprecedented in the history of storytelling. To attribute this phenomenon either to the hypnotic power of the media or the mental inadequacies of soap opera viewers (both of which have been proposed in the past) accounts neither for the meanings or the pleasures they generate.

Notes

1 Robert C. Allen, *Speaking of Soap Operas* (Chapel Hill, NC: University of North Carolina Press, 1985), pp. 114–22.
2 See, among other testimonials to the popularity of serials, Matt Moffett, "All the World Sobs Over Mexican Soaps," *Wall Street Journal* (January 9, 1992), p. 1; and Everett M. Rogers and Livia Antola, "Telenovelas: A Latin American Success Story," *Journal of Communication* 35 (4) (1985).
3 Allen, *Speaking of Soap Operas*, pp. 8–29.
4 David Buckingham, *Public Secrets: EastEnders and its Audience* (London: BFI, 1987).
5 Dorothy Hobson, "Soap Operas at Work," in Ellen Seiter, Hans Borchers, Gabriele Kreutzner, and Eva-Maria Warth (eds), *Remote Control: Television, Audiences, and Cultural Power* (London: Routledge, 1989), pp. 150–67.
6 Dwight MacDonald, "A Theory of Mass Culture," *Diogenes* 3 (summer 1953), pp. 10–17.
7 An article on soap operas taken from her dissertation was published in 1979. See "The Search for

Tomorrow in Today's Soap Operas," *Film Quarterly* (fall 1979). See also her *Loving With a Vengeance* (Hamden, Conn.: Archon Books, 1982).

8   Richard Dyer, Christine Geraghty, Marion Jordan, Terry Lovell, Richard Patterson, and John Stewart, *Coronation Street* (London: BFI, 1981); Dorothy Hobson, *Crossroads: The Drama of a Soap Opera* (London: Methuen, 1982).

9   Richard Hoggart, *The Uses of Literacy* (London: Penguin, 1958).

10   Hobson's insistence on examining *Crossroads* as the result of a dynamic set of institutional practices and a different but equally complex set of reading (viewing) practices can also be seen in one of the first scholarly books on Australian serials: John Tulloch and Albert Moran's *A Country Practice: "Quality Soap"* (Sydney: Currency Press, 1986). They speak of the meaning of the serial they investigate (*A Country Practice*) arising from its "performance," not just by actors but by all those involved in its production, distribution, and reception.

11   Ien Ang, *Watching "Dallas" : Soap Opera and the Melodramatic Imagination*, trans. by Della Couling (London: Methuen, 1982).

12   See, in particular, Fiske's *Television Culture* (London: Methuen, 1987). David Morley, *The "Nationwide" Audience* (London: BFI, 1980); Buckingham, *Public Secrets*.

13   Maria Teresa Quiroz, "La Telenovela peruana: antecedentes y situacion actual," in Nora Mazziotti (ed.), *El espectaculo de las pasion: Las telenovelas latinoamericanas* (Buenos Aires: Ediciones Colihue, 1992), pp. 111–32.

14   See Monica Rector, "A televisao e a telenovela," *Cultura* 5 (18), pp. 112–17; Ondina Leal, *A novela das oito* (Petropolis: Vozes, 1985); Tomas Lopez-Pumarejo, *Aproximacion a la telenovela* (Madrid: Catedra, 1987); Michèle and Armand Mattelart, *The Carnival of Images: Brazilian Television Fiction* (New York: Bergin & Garvey, 1990); Jesús Martín-Barbero, "Communicacion, pueblo y cultura en el tiempo de las transnacionales," in M. de Moragas (ed.) *Sociologia de la comunicacion de masas* (Barcelona: Gustavo Gili, 1985); Renato Ortiz, Silvia Hebera, Simões Borell, José Mário, and Ortiz Ramos, *Telenovela: historia e producao* (São Paulo: Editorio Brasiliense, 1988); Nora Mazziotti (ed.), *El espectaculo de las pasion: Las telenovelas latinoamericanas* (Buenos Aires: Ediciones Colihue, 1992).

15   Wolfgang Iser, *The Act of Reading: A Theory of Aesthetic Response* (Baltimore, Md.: Johns Hopkins University Press, 1978).

16   Christine Geraghty, *Women and Soap Opera: A Study of Prime Time Soaps* (London: Polity, 1991), p. 4.

17   The late (and, by some, lamented) British serial *Crossroads* used a motel for the same purpose. An exception to the above—sure to be noted by British readers—is Channel Four's *Brookside*, which debuted in 1982. Creator Phil Redmond quite consciously rejected the idea of centering the serial around a pub, feeling that British social life in the 1980s no longer revolved around pubs. Instead he set *Brookside* in an eponymous suburban cul-de-sac, where, as in *Neighbours* three years later, character interaction could develop among its residents. See *Phil Redmond's Brookside: The Official Companion* (Weidenfeld & Nicolson, 1987).

18   *Phil Redmond's Brookside*, p. 7.

19   Nico Vink, *The Telenovela and Emancipation: A Study on Television and Social Change in Brazil* (Amsterdam: Royal Tropical Institute, 1988), p. 179.

20   See Peter Brooks, *The Melodramatic Imagination: Balzac, Henry James, Melodrama, and the Mode of Excess* (New York: Columbia University Press, 1985).

References

Allen, R.C. (1985) *Speaking of Soap Operas*, Chapel Hill: University of North Carolina Press.

Ang, I. (1982) *Watching "Dallas": Soap Opera and the Melodramatic Imagination*, D. Couling (trans.), London: Methuen.

Brooks, P. (1985) *The Melodramatic Imagination: Balzac, Henry James, Melodrama, and the Mode of Excess*, New York: Columbia University Press.

Buckingham, D. (1987) *Public Secrets: Eastenders and its Audience*, London: British Film Institute.

Dyer, R. *et al.* (1981) *Coronation Street*, London: British Film Institute.

Fiske, J. (1987) *Television Culture*, London: Methuen.

Geraghty, C. (1991) *Women and Soap Opera: A Study of Prime Time Soaps*, London: Polity.

Hobson, D. (1982) *Crossroads: The Drama of a Soap Opera*, London: Methuen.

—— (1989) "Soap Operas at Work," in E. Seiter *et al.* (eds) *Remote Control: Television, Audiences and Cultural Power*, London: Routledge.

Hoggart, R. (1958) *The Uses of Literacy*, London: Penguin.

Iser, W. (1978) *The Act of Reading: A Theory of Aesthetic Response*, Baltimore: Johns Hopkins University Press.

Leale, O. (1985) *A Novela das Oito*, Petropolis: Vozes.

Lopez-Pumarejo, T. (1987) *Aproximacion a la Telenovela*, Madrid: Catedra.

MacDonald, D. (1953) "A Theory of Mass Communication," *Diogenes* 3: 10–17.

Martín-Barbero, J. (1985) "Communication, Pueblo y Cultura en el Tiempo de las Transnacionales," in M. de Moragas (ed.) *Sociologica de la Communicacion de Masas*, Barcelona: Gustavo Gili.

Mattelart, M. and A. (1990) *The Carnival of Images: Brazilian Television Fiction*, New York: Bergin & Garvey.

Modleskei, T. (1979) "The Search for Tomorrow in Today's Soap Operas," *Film Quarterly*.

Moffett, M. (1992) "All the World Sobs Over Mexican Soaps," *Wall Street Journal* 9 January: 1.

—— (1982) *Loving With a Vengeance*, Hamden, CI.: Archon Books.

Morely, D. (1980) *The "Nationwide" Audience*, London: British Film Institute.

Ortiz, R. *et al.* (1988) *Telenovela: Historia e Producao*, Sao Paulo. Editorio Brasiliense.

Quiroz, M.T. (1992) "La Telenovela Peruana: Antecedentes y Situacion Actual," in N. Mazziotti (ed.) *El Espectaculo de las Pasion: Las Telenovelas Latino-Americanas*, Buenos Aires: Ediciones Colihue.

Rogers, E.M. and Antola, L. (1985) "Telenovelas: A Latin American Success Story," *Journal of Communication* 35 (4).

Tulloch, J. and Moran, A. (1986) *A Country Practice: "Quality Soap"*, Sydney: Currency Press.

Vink, N. (1988) *The Telenovela and Emancipation: A Study on Television and Social Change in Brazil*, Amsterdam: Royal Tropical Institute.

Chapter 16

ALBERT MORAN

THE PIE AND THE CRUST
Television program formats

What is a format?

HOW THEN DO WE DEFINE A FORMAT? The term had its origin in the printing industry where it is a particular page size in a book. My word processor's thesaurus lists 13 different synonyms for the term, ranging from 'blueprint', through 'pattern' and 'design', to 'model' and 'shape'. However, where these terms suggest an aesthetic dimension in designating an object that can be copied, the term format in the phrase – television format – carries a particular industrial set of implications. In radio first and then in television, the term has been intimately linked to the principal of serial program production. A format can be used as the basis of a new program, the program manifesting itself as a series of episodes, the episodes being sufficiently similar to seem like instalments of the same program and sufficiently distinct to seem like different episodes. Similarly, behind industrial/legal moves to protect formats, lies a complementary notion that formats are generative or organisational. Thus, from one point of view, a television format is that set of invariable elements in a program out of which the variable elements of an individual episode are produced. Equally, a format can be seen as a means of organising individual episodes. Van Manin quotes a television producer who offers a more colloquial summary of this latter point: 'The "crust" is the same from week to week but the filling changes'.

Several elements constitute a format (Dawley 1994). From an industrial perspective, television programs can be divided into two types: those to do with 'reality' programs, such as news, talk and game shows; and those to do with drama, including situation comedy. In turn, van Manen identifies a series of material components of each of these types. A game show's elements, for example, include a written description of the game and its rules, a list of catch-phrases used in the program, information on how prizes are to be assembled, copies of artwork and decor designs and blueprints, and software for computer graphics. In the case of situation comedies and drama series, the concept will typically include an outline of the narrative situation of the series, perhaps with projected story-lines, together with a detailed outline of the characters. In addition, the package may also contain further elements useful in subsequent productions such as computer software, scripts and footage. The software may facilitate the production of graphics and program titles; the filmed footage can be included in both a program such as a game show and in an anthology-type program such as *Funniest Home Videos*; while the scripts can be used directly in a new version of a program, can be modified or adapted to a new setting, performers or production circumstances, or may simply be available as background material.

There are two other elements that may be in a format package and although they are not formally a part of a format, nevertheless their inclusion signifies the actual nature of the exchange taking place under the name of the licensing of a format. The first element is the Bible – a compilation of information about the scheduling, target audience, ratings and audience demographics of the program for its broadcast in its original national territory. Needless to say, it is only programs that have been successful in gathering large audiences in one territory that will be attractive for licensing purposes in other territories. The second element is a consultancy service provided by the company owning the format. The consultancy will generally take the form of a senior producer from the original production overseeing and advising the early production of the adaptation.

At this point, by way of illustration, we can briefly examine a television format package that has recently become available for licensing.

Room 101 was a light entertainment series broadcast on BBC2 in the UK in 1994. The program was described as a chat-based comedy show that each week featured a celebrity guest star. Subsequently, in 1995, the program was formatted, an operation whereby the precise production elements and their organisation, including the steps of production, were documented in a booklet known as the Format Guide, itself part of BBC Programme Format and Production Kits series ('The cost-effective way to originate your own successful series'). Like a cooking recipe, the Guide identifies both the ingredients and the sequence and manner of their combination that will produce an adaptation of *Room 101*. The booklet, prepared by the BBC, includes general notes on the host, the guest, the 'rules' of the show, the set and the individuals that constitute the production team. A second section deals with the organisation of time in the production process and includes descriptions of how an episode is researched, how choices are finalised, scripting, timetabling the studio day. Yet another part of the Guide deals with the budget and an audience profile based on audience research on the UK production. Finally the package also contains a sample post-production script based on a UK episode together with detailed studio and set plans. A note on the cover of the Guide indicates further elements of the overall package: the Format, whose rights are jointly owned by an independent production company, Hat Trick, and the BBC; Consultancy ('Advice and guidance throughout the production process'); Design ('Studio plans and set design'); and, Video Cassette ('BBC programmes for reference and inspiration'). The front page summarises the benefits of the package, most especially the format:

> Repeat the winning formula – Create your own successful series of *Room 101* with BBC World Wide Television's format package. Minimise the risks – formats offer tried and tested creative ideas for reliable quality programming. Grasp the essentials – each package contains many elements you need to make an individual series tailor-made to your own particular requirements.

However, the analogy between a television program format and a cooking recipe breaks down when we consider the legal and industrial dimensions of television program formats. For if part of a format package consists of a list of ingredients and an outline of how these are to be combined, this act of documentation carries its own industrial and legal significance. Many of the elements already described exist as intellectual properties so that formatting involves not only the documenting of constituent features of a format but also involves obtaining legal clearance for their use in format adaptations. In other words, as well as having an aesthetic component, television program formats also have an important legal dimension.

The legal context

Adopting a broad historical perspective, we can suggest that, coincident with the international television industry's elaboration of the elements of the format has been the attempt to secure legal protection for the creator and owner of a format. This has been sought through three legal instruments − copyright, breach of confidence and passing-off (Mummery 1966a, 1966b; Lane and Bridge 1990). Copyright appears to be the most important of the three: certainly, it is the first area to which van Manen attends in his legal handbook on formats and it is the one that receives most attention (pp. 25–68). Van Manen cites a number of cases of legal action in countries such as the Netherlands, France, Germany and the US which were based on the perceived copyright infringement of television program formats. However, what is revealing is the fact that all these actions were lost, a view that has been corroborated several times. (cf. Fuller 1993a) To paraphrase van Manen:

> The extent or magnitude of protection by the copyright act is not large: a new production can be created by changing characters or other elements in a format; the combination of the elements may be protected by copyright but such protection exists in limited degree for the individual elements; excessive imitations can be fought with the Copyright Act but the imitator who makes some minimal changes is likely to succeed. Often the strength of the format lies in the idea which forms the basis of the format and it is this which has been shown to be least protected. In any case, there are doubts as to whether program formats can be copyrighted.
>
> (1994 pp. 25–6, paraphrase by van Canon/Moran)

This point has been reinforced by other writers (Rubinstein 1957; Burnett 1988; Kean 1991; 1957). For present purposes, it can be underlined by a brief examination of two cases where legal action was initiated on the grounds of copyright infringement. The first occurred in the US and concerned the situation comedy, *The Cosby Show*, which starred popular black comedian Bill Cosby. The matter began in 1980 when Hwesu Murray, following preliminary discussions with an NBC official, submitted short written proposals for five new shows to the network (Levine 1989). One of these was a situation comedy, *Father's Day*, which concerned a black middle-class family where the father was a lawyer. At NBC's request, Murray expanded several of these proposals. *Father's Day* subsequently grew to two pages and included the casting suggestion that actor Bill Cosby play the lead role. Late that year, NBC returned the material and indicated that it was not interested in the proposal.

In 1984, NBC aired *The Cosby Show*, a situation comedy about an upper-middle-class family where the father is a doctor and the wife is a lawyer. The series starred Bill Cosby. Murray took legal action against NBC and the packaging company that produced the series for the network. The grounds included infringement on the format of *Father's Day* and breach of implied contract. In 1987, the defendants moved successfully in a district court in New York to have the complaint dismissed on the grounds that Murray's 'ideas' (format) lacked sufficient novelty to sustain a misappropriation action. An appeal in the following year upheld this decision.

There are various anomalies in the case, most especially in the court's decision that have been discussed elsewhere (Levine 1989 pp. 139–51). For our purposes though, it is worth noting two features of the case. The first is the fact that since the US Copyright Act of 1976, the US Copyright Office has recognised television program formats as copyrightable (Libbert 1968; Fine 1988). Nevertheless, the court in this case decided that the format for *Father's Day* was not sufficiently novel as to attract legal protection. The second detail is the fact that the format existed only as a series of verbal ideas communicated by Murray to NBC and as a two page written outline. Van Manen makes the general point that the more concrete a format is the more chance it has of attracting copyright protection (1994 pp. 69–71). The third feature is a set of specific facts associated with the case. The original format for *Father's Day* existed only as a written outline and not in the form of a finished program which might have been tendered as evidence. In addition, the circumstance that the alleged offence occurred in the same country where the original had been developed meant that legal action also occurred there.

The second case concerns a much more concrete format that was imitated in another national territory so that initial court action, following the Berne Convention, occurred in the country where the alleged infringement took place. In 1978, Hughie Green, who created, produced and compered the long running British television talent game show, *Opportunity Knocks*, was contacted by the British Inland Revenue for an account of royalty payments for a version of his program being produced by the Broadcasting Corporation of New Zealand. Green had never been approached by the BCNZ for permission to use his format nor had the Corporation offered him payment for its use. On checking the unauthorised version of the format being produced by BCNZ, Green found that it imitated all the important aspects of his format with the obvious exception of not using him as the host. Negotiations between the parties broke down and Green sued in the New Zealand courts on the grounds of passing off and copyright infringement. The action failed. Subsequently he decided to appeal the decision. Because New Zealand is a member of the British Commonwealth, the appeal was heard at the Privy Council in London. In 1980, the latter upheld the New Zealand decision on the basis that the format of *Opportunity Knocks* had little or no dramatic value and therefore no copyright could exist (Lane and Bright 1990; Lane 1992). In turn, that decision has led to debate about whether the new UK Broadcasting Act needed amendment (Lane and Bright 1990a, 1990b; Lane 1992; Martino and Miskin 1991; Smith 1991).

These two cases – the *Father's Day / The Bill Cosby Show* and *Opportunity Knocks* – highlight the uncertainty concerning copyright protection of television formats. In addition, the two plagiarised formats had no more legal protection under the other two grounds of breach of confidence and passing off. Not surprisingly, van Manen's legal handbook on formats urges producers to include in their contracts every possible means of legal protection in the area of intellectual property, including patent law, brand names and trade marks, a call that is echoed elsewhere. (van Manen 1994 pp. 69–121; Battersby and Grimes 1986; Freedman and Harris 1990; Kurtz 1990) In other words, a closer examination of the legal context of television program formats discloses that finally they may have little protection in law. That does not however prevent an elaborate legal machinery playing its part in the international format business. Formats are registered for copyright purposes, format libraries are bought and sold, licence fees are paid, legal threats are continually made and court actions launched. In fact, for the most part, format owners, producers and others behave as though formats have solid legal protection. If we turn to an examination of the industrial context of program format adaptation, then it becomes clear as to why the arena needs to appear as though it is ordered and bound by legal rules rather than chaotic.

The industrial context

In a real sense, to ask the question 'What is a format?' is to ask the wrong kind of question. Such a question implies that a format has some core or essence. As our discussion has suggested, 'format' is a loose term that covers a range of items that may be included in a format licensing agreement. The term has meaning not so much because of what it is, but rather because of what it permits or facilitates. The format is a technology of exchange in the television industry which has meaning not because of a principle but because of a function or effect. A relevant analogy is with another regulatory function in the broadcasting industry, namely the system of program ratings. Television program ratings have often been criticised both for errors in their calculation and on the grounds that they are not accurate indicators of how audiences actually listen to radio or watch television. In fact though, such criticisms are beside the point. For finally the function of ratings is more important than their accuracy. Ratings are a mechanism of exchange between broadcasters and advertisers where what is exchanged is the 'audience'. Ratings 'work' not because they are valid indicators of what real viewers do when they watch television but because they quantify an object that broadcasters can sell to advertisers, namely a market (Ang 1991).

Similarly, the concept of a television format is meaningful in the television industry because it helps to organise and regulate the exchange of program ideas between program producers. In the past, before the formalisation of the format, the exchange of such ideas was improvised and *ad hoc*. Plagiarism – borrowing of ideas without sanction or payment – was rife. In particular, program producers from European countries such as the Netherlands, from Australia and from South America regularly adapted program ideas from US radio and later television. Early payments for the use of program ideas were *ad hoc* and more in the nature of a courtesy to the original producer or owner. Brunt, for example, notes that the BBC in 1951 paid Goodson-Todman, the US devisors of the radio game show *What's My Line?*, a total of 25 guineas an episode for the use of the format (Brunt 1985 p. 28). Clearly with the cost of development of a format (if indeed it might be said to have a cost – the cost of devising a format being amortised in a program's original production), a licence fee had to be set according to what a licensee could pay. While the originator was anxious to extract as much payment as possible, there was also a *de facto* ceiling on the level of payment; an exorbitant licensing fee for the use of a format can lead to borrowing without payment. By the late 1970s, as part of a larger formalisation of the exchange of program ideas, a regular licence fee system seems to have emerged in the international television industry (Mason 1996). In turn, this formalisation seems to have helped stimulate international trade in formats in the 1980s and the 1990s.

However, the expansion of the format market in this period can also be linked to other, more salient factors. The period has seen a dramatic change in national television systems in many parts of the world with de-regulation, privatisation and the advent of new distribution technologies. This has led to a multiplication of television channels available within national boundaries. The increase in channel choice, in turn, has the potential to fragment television audiences and, as a consequence, the ever-present industry imperative to try to ensure audience popularity for new programs is exacerbated. Obviously, the import of low-cost, foreign programs is one way to fill the expanded number of time slots in the new television environment. However, such a strategy does not necessarily ensure good ratings and, ultimately, does not expand or even guarantee existing advertising revenues. In surveying the particular significance of formats from the point of view of national television producers and broadcasters, we can note constraints relating to pro-gram imports on the one hand and national program productions on the other. In other words, why do countries such as Germany and France produce their own versions of a television program such as *Wheel of Fortune* when other countries such as the Philippines and Columbia prefer the more economical option of importing the US version? The answer is a mixed one. For some producers and broadcasters in some national territories, the overwhelming consideration will be financial and the US version will be imported and screened. However such a version will always be 'foreign': American-English will not be the language of the national population and the program may have to be subtitled or dubbed; the version will feature American contestants and host; the game in this version will draw on cultural knowledges and abilities most available to Americans; prizes will be in the form of goods and services deemed desirable by Americans but not necessar-ily by other national populations. However, financial considerations have also to be reckoned against ratings success. A locally-produced version of *Wheel* will be more expensive than the imported version but, with local contestants, host, questions and references, prizes and so on, is likely to have more national appeal and is therefore likely to achieve better ratings. Certainly that seems to be borne out by some long term studies of the process of import-substitution of television programs. As a UK-based market analyst put it:

> . . . there is an interesting counter-phenomenon occurring, which is the increasing domestic level of demand in peak time in television schedules. So, for example, American dominance of key terrestrial broadcasters around the world is dropping. In the peak 6 pm to 11 pm slots, it is very difficult now to get a major American series to work on the main channels here – BBC1 or the ITV Network. So big hit, syndicated shows like *The X Files, Emergency Room* and *NYPD Blue* are actually working as cults here on Channel 4 and BBC2 with a half or even a third of the audience reach that they would get in comparable markets. What we notice around the EC is this domestication of prime time means that there is some local vitality in those markets. I do believe that, long term, the domestication issue will spread. There is a classic S curve at work here. When a new channel enters the market, whether by cable or satellite subscriptions or advertising, it has very little earnings. It is therefore in a position where it has to import low-cost programming. I helped the launch of a satellite channel in the UK called *UK Living*. It was targeted to women. And the buy-ins were 95 per cent. But it was already noticeable on this minor channel that in any 15 minute day part it had only 30,000 viewers (although its cumulative audience for the week is high) that the domestic element – a couple of hours of chat and life style which we originated – were already very popular. Within 18 months . . . (this program) . . . had been extended to three hours. The second thing that has occurred is that a couple of American shows have been licensed to be re-made with British components. So you can already see the domestication of this minor channel. We have predicted that within five years over 50 per cent of its prime time content will be original, although, in many cases, it will have been licensed from American formats.'

> (Stiles 1995)

If there is a general commercial logic at work that leads to a preference for the more expensive domestically-produced program over the lower cost imported program, then the same logic will tend to favour a format-adaptation over an original concept. An original concept is exactly that; it is untried, untested and therefore offers a broadcaster little in the way of insurance against possible ratings failure. Even if a broadcaster commissions a development, there is no guarantee that the would-be program will survive the trialling process and will go into production. And even if it does, the producer and broadcaster have no security that the program will be a popular success. Formats, on the other hand, are almost invariably based on programs which were a popular success in another national territory. In other words, formats come equipped to survive the trialling process of being tried and tested. The ratings Bible is a kind of guarantee that the format is a successful one: an adaptation of the format is therefore likely to repeat the program's original success. In addition, a video episode of the program from the other territory, recorded off-air, can be offered as an equivalent of a pilot episode for the new series (D'Alesandro 1997). Thus, for example, Reg Grundy Productions contracted to produce an American version of the game show, *Sale of the Century*, for the NBC Network on the basis of an episode of the Australian version. This kind of practice represents a significant cost saving and will help offset part of the licence fee for a format adaptation. In other words, there are significant savings in the area of program development to be achieved through using a format from another territory rather than developing an original concept. Of course, previous success does not absolutely guarantee future success. Adaptations frequently fail with audiences. However the point is that the format-adaptation offers some insurance and security to broadcasters and, in an industry so beset with uncertainty, such a promise is worth having.

Of course, there still remains the question: why pay a licence fee for using the format, why not simply borrow the program idea without paying a fee? The answer is reasonably obvious. Unauthorised infringement may lead to costly legal action. Paying a licence fee is, therefore, a means of offsetting the cost of defending the action. In addition, the unlicensed use of a format will damage a producer's business reputation and may lead other format owners in the future not to deal with that producer. However, as the *Father's Day / The Cosby Show* and the *Opportunity Knocks* cases demonstrate, borrowings without payment continue to take place (cf. Fuller 1993; Driscoll 1994). Thus, the capacity of format owners to protect formats would seem to be directly related to their commercial strength and ability to bring legal pressure on others. The more positive reason, though, why licence fees are paid is because it appears to give access to the format's previous success in another national territory.

However – and this is an important point – in licensing a format, a producer is allowed a good deal of flexibility so far as the choice and arrangement of elements in the adaptation is concerned. There is a recognition that the original set of ingredients and their organisation may have to be varied to fit production resources, channel image, buyer preference and so on. The original formula does not have to be slavishly imitated but rather serves as a general framework or guide within which it is possible to introduce various changes to the original formula. In other words there is variation within repetition. Thus, for example, . . . the German-originated game show format *Mann O Mann* was adapted for an Italian version: the title was changed to *Beato Tra Le Donne*; the set, decor and costumes were varied; the number of contestants increased, and the program was elongated from an original length of about 55 minutes per episode to 140 minutes per episode. And indeed in the case of drama adaptations, the new version may move a considerable distance away from the original with new characters, situations and storylines, new settings, and new sounds. Thus, for example, the BBC's *EastEnders* is set in a working class part of London, the characters who have British names, such as Pete and Kath Beale, speak English with Cockney and other accents. An adaptation of that program's format, *Het Oude Noorden* (The Old North), produced by IDtv in the Netherlands, is, by contrast, set in Rotterdam and the characters, who have mostly Dutch names such as Jozefien Otteveanger and Ismael en Van Ozcan, and speak Dutch with regional accents, including that of Freisland.

Significantly, under standard format licensing agreement, the variations to a television format developed through these types of adaptation become a further part of the format with ownership vested in the original owner. Clearly, under this type of permitted variation, there is no veneration of originality; rather, the format is seen as a loose and expanding set of program possibilities. There is, on the part of the owner, the overriding imperative to gain maximum commercial advantage from everything generated from the initial set of elements. In turn, the new elements introduced as variations in the adaptation will be equally as available as the original should a further adaptation of the program be required. Thus, for example, a South American version of *Man O Man*, prepared for broadcasters in Argentina, Uruguay and Paraguay in 1996/7, drew as much on the Italian version of the format, *Beato tra le donne*, as it did on the German original. This flexibility contained in format adaptation underlines an important general point. Among the few media researchers who have noticed the phenomenon of television format adaptation, there is a tendency to assume that adaptations are a mechanical repetition of the initial format (cf Strover 1994; Lull 1995; Sinclair 1996). Such accounts tend to assume that formats are invariably those of game shows, a genre that is held in low critical esteem, such that adaptation is no more than a simple repetition of the ingredients in the original version of the program. Aside from a High Culture snobbery around notions of originality, this line ignores the extent to which an adaptation of a format for a particular national territory will involve considerable amounts of skill and experience in adapting, varying, amending, improvising, creating and so on using the initial format as a source. In other words, the process of nationalising a television program format is undoubtedly a more subtle and complex process than some commentary would have one believe. After all, as has already been suggested, a television format is actually a regulatory mechanism in the international television industry. The written concept of a particular format may be brief indeed so that a producer, in adapting such a concept for a particular national territory, may have the task ahead of her or him.

Finally, we should note that besides commercial considerations, national television producers and broadcasters have to consider the political implications of importing a program or adapting a format. It was noticed above, for example, that some countries import the US version of *Wheel of Fortune* while others produce their own versions under licence. Aside from cultural considerations, program imports have little in the way of a domestic financial spin-off. A national adaptation of a format, on the other hand, provides employment in the national territory and may lead to international sales of the adaptation. It will also provoke fewer complaints and less unrest among production workers, cultural critics and politicians than will imports or co-productions. And aside from employment arguments, there are also cultural arguments in favour of what is nationally produced. Here one runs into an interesting situation in that there appears to be a general reluctance on the part of national cultural critics and policy makers to make any distinction between programs wholly originated in the national territory and those that are adaptations of international formats. In practice, these two different kinds of program are regarded by media regulators and governments alike as domestic or national. Such a classification has not been the outcome of debate or enquiry: indeed, there is a general policy vacuum surrounding this aspect of format adaptation. While the classification may seem like an obvious and sensible response to the situation – after all, audiences make no distinction between the two types – nevertheless what is interesting is the lack of political debate, the fact that television program format adaptation usually does not appear on the political or cultural agenda. And yet, there are often relevant precedents and policies at work in related areas. Thus, for example, the regulation of Australian content in commercial television has never involved a consideration of the national origins of a program that is locally produced. Quite the contrary. Programs that are Australian adaptations of overseas programs are equated with programs that are based on locally derived ideas, both qualifying as Australian (Moran 1985). On the other hand, what constitutes Australian content so far as government support for Australian film production is concerned has often been more closely defined. In 1983 the Federal Minister for Home Affairs issued guidelines for film producers on the criteria that should be taken into consideration in deciding on the Australian content of a project for tax-relief purposes. The guidelines specified that the source of the script be Australian. They went on:

> . . . where the source is non-Australian, the scriptwriter would be expected to be Australian and the subject-matter should be demonstrated to be in accordance with the above criteria (viz. the 'concept of a film can be expected not to be alien to the Australian multi-cultural experience'). *'Australianised' versions of foreign scripts would not normally be acceptable.*
>
> (Quoted in Dermody and Jacka 1987 pp. 149–150; my emphasis)

The argument then is that 'formats' are a relatively recent development in the international television industry that has led to both a formalisation and a regulation of the movement of program ideas from one place to another. A format is a cultural technology which governs the flow of program ideas across time and space. The elaboration of what is being transferred together with its embedding in a legal framework has been a powerful means both of codifying and stimulating trade in this area. By turning to an examination of the role played by program formats in international television, we can strengthen this argument about the relational meaning of formats.

References

Ang, I. 1991, *Desperately Seeking the Audience*, London and New York: Routledge.

Battersby, G.J. and C.W. Grimes 1986, 'Merchandising revisited', *The Trademark Reporter*, Vol. 76, pp. 271–314.

BBC Worldwide Television 1994, *Formats*, London: BBC Enterprises Limited.

Brunt, R. 1985, 'What's My Line?', in L. Masterman (ed.), *Television Mythologies*, London: Comedia.

Burnett, M. 1988, 'The protection of ideas for radio', *EBU Review*, Vol.39, No. 1, pp. 32–39.

D'Alesandro, K.C. 1997, 'Pilot programs', in Newcomb, *Encyclopedia*, pp. 1258–9.

Dawley, H. 1994, 'What's in a format?', *Television Business International*, November, pp. 24–6.

Dermody, S. and Jacka, E. 1987, *The Screening of Australia Volume 1: Anatomy of a Film Industry*, Sydney: Currency Press.

Driscoll, G. 1994, 'Here's an idea I stole earlier', *Evening Standard*, (UK) 21 September, p. 56.

Fine, F.L. 1988, 'A case for the Federal Protection of Television Formats: Teasing the limits of "expression" ', *Pacific Law Journal*, Vol. 17, pp. 49–75.

Freedman, R.I. and R.C. Harris 1990, 'Game show contracts: Winners and losers', *Entertainment Law Review*, pp. 209–14.

Fuller, C. 1993, 'Copycat riot', *TV World*, January, p.15.

Kean, C. 1991, 'Ideas in need of protection', *Television*, October, pp. 20–1.

Kurtz, L.A. 1990, 'The rocky road to character protection', *Entertainment Law Review*, Vol. 1, pp.63–7.

Lane, S. 1992, 'Format rights in television shows: Law and the legislative process', *Statute Law Review*, pp. 24–49.

Lane, S. and R.M. Bridge 1990a, 'The protection of formats under English law – part II', *Entertainment Law Review*, pp. 131–42.

Lane, S. and R.M. Bridge 1990b. 'The protection of formats under English law – part I' *Entertainment Law Review*, pp. 96–102.

Levine, D.A. 1989, 'The Cosby Show: Just Another Sitcom?' *Loyola Entertainment Law Journal*, Vol.9, pp.137–51.

Lull, J. 1995, *Media, Communication, Culture: A Global Approach*, Cambridge: Polity Press.

Martino, T. and C. Miskin 1991, 'Format rights: The price is not right', *Entertainment Law Review*, pp. 31–2.

Mason, B. 1996, Interview with Albert Moran, Sydney.

Moran, A. 1985, *Image and Industry: Australian Television Drama Production*, Sydney: Currency Press.

Mummery, J. 1966a, 'The protection of ideas – I', *The New Law Journal*, 27 October, pp. 1455–6.

Mummery, J. 1966b 'The protection of ideas – II', *The New Law Journal*, 3 November, pp. 1481–2.

Rubinstein, S. 1957, 'Copyright in the past and in the present', *Revue Internationale du droit d'auteur*, n.XV, pp.75–107.

Sinclair, J. 1996, 'Mexico, Brazil and the Latin World', in J. Sinclair, E. Jacka and S. Cunningham, (eds.), *New Patterns in Global Television: Peripheral Visions*, New York: Oxford University Press, pp.35–66.

Smith, P. 1991, 'Format rights: Opportunity knocks', *Entertainment Law Review*, pp.63–5.

Stiles, P. 1995, Interview with Albert Moran, London.

Strover, S. 1994, 'Institutional adjustment to trade: The case of US-European coproductions', paper delivered at the *Turbulent Europe* conference London, July.

van Manen, J. 1994, *Televisie formats: en-iden nar Nederlands recht*, Amsterdam: Otto Cranwinckle Uitgever.

PART FOUR

Making Television

HOW MUCH DO WE AS VIEWERS know about the processes by which various forms of television are made? What and how much do the various genres and modes of television reveal (or claim to reveal) about themselves as the products of institutional, technical, economic, aesthetic, ethical, and social processes? How important is it that we, as both viewers and students of television, know something about how television is made?

As any parent of a small child can tell you, understanding television's images and sounds (at some level of intelligibility) and deriving pleasure from the experience of watching some kinds of television are not at all dependent upon the viewer's knowing anything about how, why, or by whom those images and sounds were produced. Adult viewers who have never been inside a television studio, read a script, or seen a television camera can talk quite eloquently about the narrative or dramatic complexities of their favorite programs.

In fact, some genres of television work very hard to hide any marks of their having been "made" by anyone. In his essay in Part Two (Spaces of Television), Scott Olson talks about the narrative "transparency" of Hollywood film and television drama. By this he means "the capability of certain texts to seem familiar regardless of their origin, to seem a part of one's own culture, even though they have been crafted elsewhere." The transparency of storytelling, characterization, and subject matter characteristic of the US-made television programming Olson discusses is produced with the help of a corresponding and reinforcing stylistic transparency, which television adapted from the conventions of Hollywood film production. Hollywood conventions of acting, camera work, composition, editing, and sound reproduction render the production process itself invisible to the viewer. These conventions work together to create a seamless and believable world on the other side of the film or television screen that seems to exist independently of its having been captured for our benefit. Film theorists call this the "reality effect" and the stylistic conventions that produce it those of the classical Hollywood narrative cinema.

Our awareness of the process by which broadcast television is made and delivered to our living rooms is also obscured by the fact that there is no human agency involved in the presentation of its sounds and images on our television sets. We speak of the film industry as being made up of three branches: production (the process of making the film), distribution (the process of duplicating and circulating the film to theaters), and exhibition (the presentation of the film in movie theaters). Broadcast television certainly has a production sector, which secures funding to make programming; obtains the technological, human, and physical resources required; organizes and executes the process by which sounds and images are captured; and edits material together into the final product. In the era of live television, production occurred at the same time as transmission, so that broadcasters were also usually producers of television. But as John Ellis discusses in his essay, today television production might be undertaken by companies or organizations quite separate (institutionally and physically) from the entity responsible for *distributing* programming: broadcasters, cable or satellite channels, video tape/DVD rental/sales outlets, etc.

But regardless of "who" made the program and regardless of the means by which it arrives on our television screens, there is no television counterpart to the exhibition sector of the film industry—no place in most countries separate from our homes that is dedicated to "presenting" television and no cadre of people (theater managers, box office workers, popcorn poppers, projectionists, ushers) who form the last human links of a chain connecting the production process with our experience of its products. Instead, television programs seem to hurl *themselves* through the ether and project *themselves* into our homes and lives. Young children will often look into or behind the television set to see if there's anyone back there making the pictures, voices, and music appear. Magic, then, not human agency, is the first logic we associate with the television production, and it sometimes seems as if television is quite content to sustain this belief into our collective adulthood!

By the same token, however, John Ellis points out that in other respects television is extraordinarily reflexive about its own production processes. "Virtually everyone knows its jargon and production secrets . . .," he writes. "Could we say the same about plastics, waste disposal or even education? Indeed, such is the self-reflexivity of TV and the extent of reflection on TV in other media that many have rushed to see it as the 'post-modern' medium par excellence." Far from hiding the technologies and human labor responsible for their making, some forms of television seem to be exhibitionists in this regard. Newscasts (from local stations in the US to the BBC World Service) now make the "newsroom" (or parts of it at least) the broadcast set, and viewers have become accustomed to seeing television cameras and floor crew in establishing shots and figures in the background talking on telephones or watching display monitors while the newsreader or anchor speaks to us from the foreground. One primetime news magazine program in the US used to end with an overhead shot of the broadcast control room as we overheard the director's voice saying to his crew "Good job, everyone."

Even forms of television that usually conceal their production processes from audience view have capitalized on our interest in and knowledge of what goes on "behind the scenes": rather than being erased as worthless (and expensive!) production mistakes, flubbed lines of dialogue, giggle-fits, and collapsing scenery are recycled as material for "blooper" compilations. Television programs, magazines, and newspaper articles routinely "expose" what the world of television production is *really* like in their stories about star salary negotiations, network programming decisions, and censorship battles between producers and network executives.

But television's selective reflexiveness about the circumstances of its own production and its seeming eagerness to expose the artifice that lies just beyond camera range are themselves carefully calculated *representations* of the production process. Their aim is not to provide viewers with a systematic, comprehensive account of the imperatives, goals, logics, costs, and implications of the production processes upon which various forms of television are based, but rather to present partial, self-promotional glimpses of what they would like us to see. You can look at broadcast, cable, and satellite television programming forms across a range of national systems and find in operation two seemingly contradictory strategies for representing the production process. One strategy is to hide the production process as much as possible; the other is to show it off.

This apparent contradiction is, we think, related to another that is inherent in television. On the one hand television presents itself as offering immediate, apparently unmediated visual and auditory access to the world in front of its cameras and microphones. Unique among mass media, the technologies of television seem to be able to extend our own sense of sight and hearing into distant spaces and capture what we *would* see and hear *there*. We can all think of moments of television when the technological and production apparatus seem to disappear from our experience of television, as we are encouraged to immerse ourselves in the images and sounds being televised.

At other times it suits television's institutional purposes to emphasize the expensive and complicated technologies, elaborate facilities, and professional expertise that are required in order for television to have the *effect* of offering us this immediate and seemingly transparent window on the world or of offering us a representation of the complexities of the world that only the technological and institutional sophistication of television can provide. Election night broadcasts, for example, almost always foreground the production processes of television and the technologies that are employed to move us instantaneously from one precinct or constituency to another or to allow us to see victor and loser on the same screen at the same time. Here's all the stuff it takes, these programs suggest, for television to allow you to "see" the election occur better than you could see it if you were "there!"

John Ellis's essay, specially prepared for this collection, takes the reader through the five stages of the broadcast television production process—from securing financing for a production idea to marketing the finished product. His account underscores two defining qualities of the making of broadcast television in any television-producing country (Ellis is using the term "broadcast" to include over-the-air as well as cable and satellite television): what might be called its collective or corporate mode of organization and its reliance upon routine and standardization. Although it is technically possible for a single person (and, these days, a not very technically adept person, at that) to "make" a television program (think Garth and Wayne in *Wayne's World*), in practice television production for broadcast purposes involves a host of individuals—as the credits at the end of any program attest. In some ways the more that the production process itself is rendered invisible, the more people that are required to make the marks of production disappear! Some programs appear to bear the imprint of a single individual, but more than likely that person's apparent "authorship" of the program or series derives much more from his or her visibility in front of the camera than from any determinative role he or she played behind it.

As Ellis notes, television production adapted a particular mode of social organization from the making of feature films, which, in turn, is based upon the factory system of manufacturing: a division of labor among workers, separation of design functions from execution (the lighting director is not involved in the writing of the script and need not even know what the narrative is about), and a clear hierarchy of responsibilities and authority. The economics of commercial television around the world favor the production of multiple episodes of a given program, across which some elements remain constant (in the case of dramatic programs: the central cast members, recurrent settings, duration, etc.). These continuing elements create a framework within which each episode's narrative can differ from week to week. They also help to standardize the production process and make many production tasks into repeatable routines.

Set against the routines of US broadcast television production, John Caldwell sees the emergence in the 1980s of a new "stylistic exhibitionism," which he calls "televisuality." Caldwell argues that a generational transition occurs in US television production at the same time that a host of new technologies allows television directors, lighting directors, editors, directors of photography, and other key creative personnel to explore "the formal potential of the television image, and especially the question of what can be done within the constraints and confines of the limited television frame." Drawing upon industry discourse about its own production practices, Caldwell discusses the stylistic and in some cases theoretical self-consciousness with which practitioners approach their work in both series television and commercials. What both their practices and discourse reveal, he argues, is a fascination with the status of television's visual image *as* an image.

One of the most prominent international programming and hence production trends of the late 1990s was what might be called "reality" television: formats that, on the one hand, distinguished themselves from fictional dramas by being grounded in some way in an externally-existing reality and, on the other, clearly departed from traditional news and documentary formats. Such program formats as *Survivor, Pop Idol* and *Big Brother* blurred categorical and production boundaries between drama and documentary, game show and soap opera. The very popularity of some of these new formats in some countries provoked television critics to see them as harbingers of a new generation of "cheap and dumb" television productions that would supplant more traditional (and, in their estimation, socially useful) dramatic and documentary forms. In her essay, Jane Roscoe takes *Big Brother* as an emblematic instance of the trend toward reality television and argues that it commands the attention of television scholars as an important new development in both television programming and television production. Her assessment of the importance of reality television was echoed by US broadcasting executives in early 2003. The chief executive officer of one network claimed that the success of the genre had fundamentally changed the logics of broadcast production and scheduling. Roscoe argues that the production of such docusoaps and reality gameshows takes advantage of the "convergence" of information and communication technologies (internet, broadcasting, print media, telephony, radio) and provides opportunities for viewer interaction that older television formats do not. Roscoe focuses on the first season of the Australian version of *Big Brother*, broadcast in 2001. As she notes, with more than 170 staff producing and editing 96 hours of video material each day for twelve weeks, *Big Brother* was the most elaborate production in the history of Australian television.

We might have placed Sonia Livingstone and Peter Lunt's essay on audience discussion programs in one of several parts of this collection. The audience discussion program (*Oprah, Jerry Springer, Kilroy*, etc.) does represent an important television programming form in a number of countries, and Livingstone and Lunt's discussion of it very much relates to other essays in Part Three (Modes of Television). Neither would their essay have been out of place (so to speak) in Part Two (Spaces of Television), given their focus on the distinctive and revealing nature of the social space created in the genre. The space of the audience discussion program is, they argue, a marginal or liminal space, which contains "the potential for both the reproduction of existing beliefs, representations and practices and the transformation of traditional social forms through the construction of a public sphere which mediates between established power . . . and everyday experience."

We chose to include it in this section, however, because it helps to expand and perhaps challenge our understanding of "who" makes television. As Livingstone and Lunt argue, the audience discussion program form is an "anti-genre," which works by complicating a number of oppositions normally used to talk about television programs, including "text/audience, production/ reception, sender/receiver, interpersonal/mass communication." For decades, various genres of broadcast television have represented the viewing audience through the device of the studio audience. Their "spontaneous" response to the performance presented for "them" reinforced the unique capacity of television to present a "live" performance to millions of people at once, while, at the same time, it collapsed the distance between production and reception by making it appear that the two occurred in the same space. The audience discussion program further elaborates and complicates the dynamic among television performer, audience, and viewer by multiplying the categories of participants in the production process: hosts; guests (usually drawn from people not associated with television production); experts; guests' family members/friends/enemies in the studio audience; other members of the studio audience who interact with all of the above; etc. This essay and Jane Roscoe's on *Big Brother* in Australia underscore the degree to which and the ways in which some forms of broadcast television work to involve the audience, the "public," the viewer in the production process and, in doing so, to make television production appear to be participatory and interactive.

Nick Couldry's essay on the *Coronation Street* experience, the centerpiece of Granada Television's studio tour in Manchester (UK), also links issues of television production to those of the spaces of television. Here Granada Television has made the standing exterior set of Britain's longest-running soap opera *Coronation Street* into a tourist attraction. Organized around life on its eponymous urban, working-class street in Northern England, *Coronation Street* has been a fixture of commercial broadcast television in Britain since 1960, and, in the process, tens of millions of viewers in the UK, Canada, Australia, New Zealand, and other countries have become intimately familiar with its painstakingly reproduced shops, pub, front doors, stoops, and mailboxes. Open to the (paying) public, the Street as tourist destination becomes "a place which condenses memory, a place with 'aura,' a 'ritual place,' even a place of 'pilgrimage'. It embodies a connection between the visitors' history of watching the programme and their brief 'time on the Street.' "

Couldry's essay encourages us to think about where and how television is "made" and how these various processes of making television are linked. At one level, a trip to the set of *Coronation Street* is an opportunity to see "where" the show is made and to compare the experience of seeing the Street with your own eyes to the way in which it is experienced on the television screen. Because *Coronation Street*'s appeal is based in part at least on its rootedness in a social and cultural world that exists outside the show itself (the world of urban, working-class life in the north of England), seeing the Street is also an opportunity to see how the latter is "made" into the former—how, in other words, the Street works as an exercise in social and visual representation. But as a cultural process the "making" of *Coronation Street* does not only occur on the set of the Street or in the (physically separate) studios of Granada Television. It also occurs as a part of the process of watching the show—in this case a process that can extend over multiple decades. The experience of walking down the Street, then, links two different time frames and two different but intertwined processes of cultural production: the "here and now" of the Street tour is linked with all the "theres and thens" of the show's viewing, while the process by which the television *program* is produced is linked with the process by which that program's meanings and pleasures are produced through viewing and memory.

Eric Freedman's essay addresses a mode of television operating very much at a local level: public access or community access television. In the introduction to Part One (Institutions of Television), we pointed out that historically the cost of owning and operating television technology has greatly restricted its use, while the finite capacity of the electromagnetic spectrum has limited access to the television airwaves to those who controlled the small number of channels able to broadcast in any given locality. These two factors have combined to suppress non-institutional modes of television production and circumvent access to broadcasting by small groups and individuals.

There are, of course, significant exceptions. Eric Freedman's essay discusses public access television and its relation to the community television movement in the US, which, as he puts it, "aspired to use TV as a means of communication and empowerment without interference from professional middlemen such as journalists, directors, producers and corporate officers." The development and marketing of relatively light-weight, hand-held, portable, and easy-to-use video recording equipment in the late 1960s made it possible for the first time for one or two people without extensive training in television production to "make" television and to do so outside a television studio.

This technological innovation caught the attention of artists (video artist Nam June Paik is said to have bought the first Sony "Portapak" video recorder shipped to the US from Japan in 1965) and of the counter-culture "community" in the US and Canada, who saw the potential of non-institutional television as an instrument of community organization and social change. Michael Shamberg's influential 1971 book, *Guerilla Television*, argued that "video" might become a grassroots, community-based alternative to institutionalized "television."[1]

At the same time, many cities were negotiating contracts with cable companies for the right to provide cable television service in those localities. In some cities (New York was an important early example), municipal authorities required the cable companies to set aside channels for educational, governmental, and public use, and to use a portion of their subscription revenue to equip and staff elementary production facilities. The movement to use cable television systems as a means of opening up "television" to "the public" received an enormous boost when in 1971 and 1972, respectively, the Canadian government and the US Federal Communications Commission required cable operators to set aside channels and make available production facilities for public use.

The legal and regulatory status of public access television has been subject to challenge and legislative change over the past thirty years, but today 2,000 public access cable channels operate in the US, and in 1997 some 8,000 individuals and 2,000 organizations produced programming at 235 public access channels in Canada. The German "Open Channels" initiative, begun in 1986, operates in 90 cities, and 30 Swedish cities provide some form of public access television. The Global Village Community Access Television website (www.openchannel.se) provides links to public access sites in 20 countries. The advent of digital video means that a community access television production "studio" can now be operated with consumer-grade video cameras and laptop-based video editing software. Although cable television systems remain the primary distribution mechanism for public access television in most countries, other avenues are also possible, including low-power UHF terrestrial broadcasting, digital broadcasting, and, of course, the internet.

The very local orientation of public access television, its ephemeral nature, and the variety of uses to which this mode has been put in thousands of communities over the thirty years of its history together make it very difficult to assess its overall impact. *Wayne's World*'s parody of US public access TV notwithstanding, Freedman argues that, at the very least, public access has addressed the needs of marginalized or ignored local special-interest audiences and has developed programming forms that challenge television's institutional norms. Focusing on a public access show targeting the gay community in West Hollywood, he explores the ways in which some genres of public access television raise interesting questions about the relationship between different modes of television (in this case, between home video and "broadcast" television), performance and celebrity, autobiography and community. We might also ask how public access television draws upon what Bourdon discusses in his essay as the "possibility" of liveness for its power and appeal.

Brian Larkin's essay on Nigerian video films examines a mode of television production made possible by the recent advent of relatively inexpensive and easy-to-operate video production equipment combined with the widespread availability of the VCR as a means of circulating indigenously-produced video dramas. As he notes, historically, Nigerian television audiences have had limited broadcast viewing options, and the range of films available in movie theaters was restricted to Hollywood fare and other imported films from India and Hong Kong. The oil boom in Nigeria in the 1970s and 1980s coincided with the introduction of the VCR as a piece of consumer media technology around the world. In Nigeria the effects of the VCR revolution have been significant and long-lasting. The circulation of pirated copies of imported movies and television programming resulted in a "massive expansion of program choice for the average Nigerian viewer." At the same time, the corresponding revolution in video production technology opened up new opportunities for indigenous production and carved out a new space for a Nigerian media culture that operated independently from state-controlled broadcast television, on the one hand, and from the commercial cinema, on the other.

Larkin provides an overview of the cultural, social, aesthetic, and economic contexts within which one type of Nigerian video film has emerged: those made in the Hausa-speaking region of northern Nigeria. These feature-film-length melodramas frequently draw upon popular local literary genres for their source material, Hollywood and Bollywood cinema for elements of style, local theater groups for their acting talent, and the personnel of state television stations for their technical and creative personnel. Larkin also situates the extraordinary flowering of this distinctive form of television production within the more general rise of "small media": relatively cheap, readily available and accessible forms of electronic technology (audio and video cassettes, fax machines, photocopiers, computers) that can serve as the basis for alternative forms of media production. Small media forms do not require massive investment in equipment or physical plant and often circulate outside more institutionally-controlled channels of distribution. A low cost of production (sometimes as little as US$4,000) and a correspondingly low break-even point (as few as 10,000 cassettes sold for between US$2–3 each) have created a flourishing video production sector in Nigeria, with more than 600 feature-length tapes released each year.

Note

1   Michael Shamberg, *Guerilla Television* (New York: Henry Holt, 1971). Unfortunately, this book is now out of print.

Chapter 17

JOHN ELLIS

TELEVISION PRODUCTION

T ELEVISION'S LANGUAGE is evolving at great speed, and the medium reflects upon itself to a considerable degree. This self-reflexivity ensures that even casual viewers can remain fluent in their understandings. Popular understanding of how TV is produced is necessary if viewers are to know the status of what they are being shown, not so that they can go out and make TV themselves. They need to identify what is live and what is recreation, what is fiction or fact. They have to distinguish between contemporary or archive footage. They need to distinguish between the different levels of factuality claimed by particular footage: literal truth or the statement of a particular point of view. They will come to a judgement about whether an interviewee is telling the truth or whether they have been 'exploited'. They need to make correct generic identifications and to measure a particular programme against generic models.

Modern TV audiences already have an understanding of TV production, at least in the developed world. TV's reflexivity is extraordinary, ranging from the bloopers of the stars to the instant recycling and commentary upon the latest piece of startling news footage. Mix in the commentaries on TV in related media, radio DJs chatting about last night's 'must see' show or newspaper gossip and revelation, and you have a medium which is exceptional in the way that its production processes are open to the world. Virtually everyone knows its jargon and production secrets; could we say the same about plastics, waste disposal or even education? Indeed, such is the self-reflexivity of TV and the extent of reflection on TV in other media that many have rushed to see it as the 'post-modern' medium par excellence.

This is to miss the point. The only reason why television is reflected upon, why its production processes have become common knowledge, is the universality of the medium which has gained the currency of everyday life itself. To ensure significance in the developed world today, any new phenomenon has to touch and be touched by television. That is, it must be touched by the dominant form that television takes in modern society: the form of broadcast television pro-grammes supplied into people's homes. Other uses exist, from the seemingly automatic forms of surveillance cameras to the highly wrought forms of video art, and all have their own organisations of production. Yet so powerful is the dominant form that the term 'television' is virtually synonymous with its broadcast form, especially if we see 'broadcast' as including all scheduled, linear services, including cable and satellite services.

Programme product circulates relatively freely within this constellation of channels, and production processes are similar. US cable shows like HBO's *Six Feet Under* appear on free-to-air broadcast channels in other countries (e.g. Channel 4 in the UK) with advertising breaks. In commodity terms they are no different from other programmes on those channels. To produce a series for HBO rather than the networks in the USA does not involve a fundamentally different production process, except in the important respect that there is a greater degree of editorial freedom, which is partly the result of a degree of flexibility in terms of the size of series runs, budget level and so on. Hence this article will use the term 'broadcaster' to cover a wide range of organisations interested in obtaining TV programmes for broadcasting over networks to a substantial domestic customer base, be that through free-to-air distribution or through subscription.

Broadcast television defined as scheduled linear services for a domestic audience is a universal given in the first world. Self-reflexivity is the by-product of this universality. Self-reflexivity in television is the equivalent of word play and jokes in language, a constant attempt by speakers to assert their control and creativity within the vast and universal system of language. But there is a crucial difference here. In language, all listeners can become speakers, even if the power relations in particular circumstances might radically restrict what they can say. But, up to now at least, those who receive television have little or no possibility of becoming producers of television utterances. So the general understanding of television remains partial. It does not take viewers very far in understanding the routinised aspects of television; the cultures that produce its particular forms; or its attempts to regulate supply and demand. Television's backstage is less glamorous than it might seem from television's own representations of itself.

Routine

Television production has become routinised because television watching has become such a central part of everyday life. Television can mount special events, but the overwhelming quantity of television consists of series and established formats, and indeed that is what all but the most old-fashioned of commentators expect of it. The routines provide security, both for the industry and for its audiences. As more channels appear, the routinised aspects become more rather than less marked. The early years of television in the middle of the twentieth century, sometimes referred to nostalgically as a 'Golden Age', saw what appears now to be a remarkable number of single plays or films (in series with titles like the *Philco Television Playhouse*, *Armchair Theatre*, *Wednesday Play*, *Comedy Playhouse*). This early period lasted into the 1970s in Europe, with the production of short-lived but much loved series (*Fawlty Towers* for instance). Who now would waste such ideas on a single outing, except, of course, those who are producing high-profile events, high-end drama or 'TV movies'? It is no longer possible for single episodes or short runs of more routine TV production to win a place in a marketplace already crowded with excellent and/or loved material. Television is a victim of its own ubiquity. Its principal means of giving currency to its own new productions is to establish them as a fragment of the everyday realities of their audiences. So television becomes routinised even at the point of creativity.

Routinisation has its advantages for producers. It brings considerable certainties and efficiencies to the production process, which is fraught with risk and creative wastage. It means that each production is made within a framework of common understandings. Each genre has its normal ways of doing things: 'gameshow' means a studio-made event with an audience, celebrity presenter and contestants. It means a ritualistic process with its own catch-phrases. It also means a long series and a relatively brash visual and aural style. Imagine trying to explain all of that to a broadcaster before you can say what makes your format different; imagine having to define the genre for the technicians, the designer, the presenter, the gag writers. Specific formats are difficult enough to work out and define in any case, however simple they may look on screen.

Some degree of standardisation is necessary in any industry but there are few global standards in production for broadcast television. Cultural specificity and the need to adapt successful formats for local conditions have long been crucial aspects of the industry. The makers of the successful US gameshow *Wheel of Fortune* were able to roll it out into many different countries. But they did not only try to sell the original shows they made for US television. They also licensed the format to broadcasters and/or production companies in Germany and France, etc. to make local versions of the format, with local presenters and contestants, local gags and prizes appropriate to the market.[1] They also allowed local production companies to alter the running time and even budget level and production values to suit national broadcasting conditions.

Standardisation

Considerable standardisation does exist in broadcast television, but it is different in different nations and regions. A crucial part of the skill of a producer is to know those standards, and a skilled producer can 'read' the probable level of the production budget just by looking at a TV programme produced in their own market.[2] This informal standardisation is often reflected in the 'guide prices' that are issued by broadcasters when they put a slot or format out to tender in the production community. The price is only a starting point for negotiation on the chosen project, but to tell a producer that a drama will cost 'x' per episode rather than '2x' is to send powerful messages about the expected nature of the product. Running time is another significant method of standardisation. Broadcast TV has standardised into slots of 30 minute units, with very rare exceptions. A producer or director claiming that their project has a 'natural duration' of 11 minutes per episode is undertaking a form of commercial suicide, unless they are addressing a broadcaster with a particular need. Such needs can include material for a magazine format designed to fit a 30- or 60-minute slot, a larger entity like the 'open plan' children's TV sequences, or to fit the gaps left in the slot structure by a feature film.

The pattern of slots based on 30 minutes is practically universal in scheduled broadcast TV: it provides the basic building block of the schedule. But the precise duration of the programmes that fit those slots varies according to the practices of different broadcasting markets. The US network primetime slot is around 44 minutes; the UK commercial network slot is around 51 minutes; for the BBC it is more like 56 minutes. The difference is the permitted level of commercials (and in the case of the BBC, the lack of commercials). Hence drama series made for the BBC have to be cut for US transmission, except on channels like PBS which carry no commercials. In the UK, it sometimes creates space for short items; sometimes a schedule of two US products back-to-back; sometimes a plethora of trailers for forthcoming shows. Co-productions are sometimes hampered by this lack of standardisation: the BBC wildlife series *The Blue Planet* and the *Life of Mammals* were made in co-production with Discovery Channel. In order to make the episodes up to an hour-slot for BBC transmission, an extra segment was added to the end of each show, detailing the intricate and ground-breaking production methods behind some of the spectacular sequences. A new level of reflexivity was added to the programmes.

Production standardisation is therefore a feature of each production context rather than a universal. Within each production context, it underpins the organisation of production, enabling workers within the production community to move easily between projects for the wide range of outlets within the national broadcasting market. It enables crews to come to a common understanding quickly about the scope and ambition of the project they are working on; it enables broadcasters and producers to have meaningful conversations about creative ideas. Finally, it enables production work to become more collectivised, leading to developments such as team scriptwriting. To become a key production worker within a particular market, it is essential to acquire a sense of its underlying culture of standardisation.

Division of labour

Television production has a factory nature, and as in many modern factories, most of the workers are hired on a casualised basis, to complete a job or project. When compared to the feature film industry, much work in television is standardised, repetitive and anonymous at most levels. But it still depends upon the creativity of the people who work within it. This creative process is organised into different levels. Writing an episode of a soap is different from devising the series as a whole. But the people who devised the soap, who created it originally, came up with a format, a blueprint, and not hundreds of finished episodes. They will have written sample scripts, and will usually be heavily involved in the scripts for individual episodes for the early years. But what the devisers have created is a virtuality, a potential imagining of a programme which has to be shared if it is to come into being. This more collective basis of television production is difficult to reconcile with traditional views of authorship, even as applied to feature filmmaking. It depends upon a known division of labour, a hierarchy of creative responsibilities, and a sharing of creative activity. These are the result of product standardisation.

Organisation of production

It is convenient to divide TV production into five phases: finance, pre-production, shooting, post-production and marketing. From the point of view of any one programme, they appear to be a natural sequence: first you find the money, then you plan and shoot, then you edit, and then you distribute the finished product to an audience. However, each stage makes assumptions about the others. Changes at one point have profound consequences at another. For instance, in 1994 the BBC made the marketing decision that it should show more trailers as on-screen promotion of future programmes. Every programme, regardless of length, had to be shortened by one minute. Not much of a problem for a 60-minute drama, but more of a problem for my series called *French Cooking in Ten Minutes*, which lost 10 per cent of each programme a week before it went into the studio.

Production in each broadcast market (normally a national broadcast market) has a particular national character resulting from both its internal evolution and the impact of foreign practices upon it. Production organisations generally take three forms: the vertically integrated producing broadcaster, independent production and forms of co-production.

Vertical integration

In the early days of live TV, especially in Europe, it was natural for broadcasting and the production of programming to be contained within the same organisations. Programmes were made and broadcast from the company's own studios. The only alternative was to produce work on film for broadcast later, and the costs of this were prohibitive until a substantial viewership had been created. Nevertheless, the live studio model of production continued to dominate many genres, and vertical integration continued to be a logical way of organising broadcasting.[3] As the medium evolved, live studio production became a relatively specialised part of television production. Many broadcasters continued to produce a substantial amount of their own programmes, but as a result of the gradual increase in production values since the 1970s, almost all broadcasters have had to look beyond their own resources in a systematic way.[4]

This has created a fundamental cultural shift within the organisation of vertically integrated companies, often referred to by the term used within the BBC, 'producer choice'. Essentially, the process is one of adaptation of a large vertically integrated company to the demands of full-cost budgeting, where everything is costed in terms of money rather than a mixture of money (paid to outside companies) and resource time (allocated by the vertically integrated broadcaster). The BBC came to this process relatively late, and because of its size and its cultural position as a primary definer of 'public service broadcasting' for many smaller markets (e.g. the Scandinavian nations), the process has been the subject of several academic studies.[5] The vertically integrated broadcaster has most of the equipment and studio space necessary to make its own productions. So the process of production was most conveniently planned by allocating resources by time: so many days in the studio; so many hours editing; a crew of a given size for a given number of days; a director for a specified number of days. This simplified internal resource allocation and gave producers a clear indication of what they had to work with. A separate cash budget was then drawn up for the money to be spent beyond the confines of the vertically integrated broadcaster: be it on talent (actors, writers, freelance workers) or materials (sets, lunches, archive material, car hire, costumes, etc.).

This model had many advantages; but knowing how much a programme cost was not one of them, as there was no charging structure for the internal resources. Over time, therefore, it becomes difficult for a vertically integrated broadcasting organisation to know how efficient it is compared to other production organisations. It becomes difficult to put a price on its own products; and impossible to compare costs with production companies working in a full-cost way, paying to buy or hire everything from other companies. The process of moving to a full-cost production model is difficult, as it implies that the resources allocated to producers would need to have a price put upon them, and a price that would enable the organisation to plan its own maintenance and renewal of those resources. The BBC, under the Director General John Birt, adopted an aggressive version of this process which sought to price all activities internally, and after a time allowed staff producers to spend their budgets on resources chosen at will from within and beyond the BBC.[6] This created an internal market, exposed to competition from external companies of very different natures, and therefore tended to erode the central back-up services (library, press clippings service, pronunciation unit, etc.), which create the economies of scale that are characteristic of an efficient large organisation.[7] However flawed the implementation of this process, the principle was essential: in the long term, a vertically integrated broadcasting organisation has to be able to compare its own operations with those of other companies in the same field. This is a prerequisite of the necessary level of production standardisation within a particular production culture. As a direct result of the process, vertically integrated broadcasters were able to reduce their 'plant' and equipment costs and cut the number of fulltime employees. In doing this, they were participating in a widespread trend in modern industries towards the use of skilled freelance labour and the outsourcing of aspects of production to independent companies.

Independent production

Independent production takes place when a broadcaster contracts with a separate company to provide it with programmes. It therefore takes many forms. An independent can simply be an outside company that provides ideas and talent but uses studios and other facilities owned by a vertically integrated broadcaster. Or it can be a totally separate company that proposes an idea, has it accepted, finds or even provides all or part of the finance, makes the programmes and simply delivers them to a broadcaster at the end of the process. Independent producers sometimes sell all the rights in their programmes to the broadcasters financing them (the model that still prevails in the UK at the time of writing); or sometimes keep specified rights to sell the programmes to other broadcasters in the same or in foreign markets. Independent producers sometimes own their own production resources; sometimes hire them from other specialist companies. Independents sometimes have their own talent under contract (actors, directors, etc.); sometimes hire them in on a project-by-project basis. There is only one thing that defines an independent producer: it is a company with no access of its own to a broadcast channel on which to show its products. An independent production company therefore has to make a contract with a broadcaster for this access, and therefore has to seek commissions for programmes from broadcasters. Even this definition is clouded in some markets, where broadcasters take a direct investment stake in independent production companies.

Co-production

Co-production involves the co-operation between companies on a specified project. Co-production usually takes place when one broadcaster cannot afford to produce something on its own, so has to seek financial or other contributions from other parties or may simply wish to share the costs and hence the risks associated with programme production. Co-productions often involve arrangements between programming producers or between producers and broadcasters, but may also involve banks or other investment organisations; commercial organisations, political or charitable organisations with a message to promote; or even the independent production company itself. In all cases the old maxim of 'nothing is for nothing' will operate. Where a broadcaster from another national market is involved, there may well be issues of cultural specificity or different running times or other issues of product standardisation to be resolved, as with the examples of *The Blue Planet* and *The Life of Mammals* above. Where outside finance is involved, the programmes will tend to be produced to maximise potential revenue both from the sale of the programmes and from spin-off products. Where organisations with a particular message are concerned, their motivation is at least clear and known from the outset.

Production organisation

Production is organised differently in each of the major genres of TV. Situation comedies and series fiction (also known as drama) may appear to be similar in that they show fictional characters in a variety of narrativised incidents leading to a conclusion. However, their styles of production can be very different.

An established sitcom like *Frasier* has a standard pattern. There is a large writing team, consisting of a number of paired writers. For each episode, a pair will be delegated to write a first draft as part of the overall series planning. This will have planned the narrative arc of development for the characters during the series; the general themes of particular episodes; and any episodes with unusual set requirements (holiday locations etc.). The show is heavily dependent on a small number of standard sets: Frasier's main apartment room being the chief one, along with the radio station, Café Nervosa, Niles's apartment and the other rooms of Frasier's apartment (kitchen, bedroom). A normal episode will be allowed an additional special set, the requirements for which will have been planned in advance. Each Monday during production the pair delegated to the week's episode read their draft, and it is discussed by the writing team as a whole. Rewrites of specific scenes are allocated to other writers. On Tuesday these are brought together into a composite script which is again read through by the writers and given to a writer whose specific job is polishing: adding business and smoothing through the flow of gags. On Thursday the cast read through the script for the first time with the writers. If it works, the show is taped in the studio on Friday. If urgent rewrites are required, the taping is put off until Saturday. And on Monday they start over again, usually for 26 weeks a year. It is normal for sitcoms to be scripted by more than one person or even a team in the UK and Europe, and to follow something of this pattern. However the degree of rewriting habitual in the US is unheard of in the UK. In the USA, team writing of drama series has also become a common practice, though it is rare elsewhere. In episodic series fiction like *NYPD Blue* or *ER* the activity of assembling a script is more complex because of the multiple story lines involved. European drama, prime-time soaps apart, is more often the work of a single writer and is planned in shorter seasons.

The shooting of sitcoms and drama differs markedly. Most sitcoms are made like *Frasier*, shot in studio sets with multiple cameras in front of an audience. TV drama never has an audience at its shoots, and – with the important exception of daytime soaps – moved out of the confines of the studio during the 1960s to adopt a much more filmic method of production centring on single camera shooting. The shooting of a 30-minute sitcom can be done in the space of about three hours. Thirty minutes of drama shot with a single camera would normally take six days, though tight finance, careful planning and routinisation (enabling the use of multiple cameras) can reduce this time substantially, as is the case with soaps. As production differs so markedly for different genres in different markets, any general statement about the nature of production has to be taken with caution. However, it is possible to distinguish between five broad stages.

Stages of production 1: Finance

TV production involves spending other people's money, and usually a lot of it. For example, the Australian first series of *Big Brother* cost approximately 16 million Australian dollars (approximately US $9 million) – see the article by Jane Roscoe in Part Four. Unsurprisingly, those people like to have a say in what is produced, so the activity of financing a production often determines its most intimate details. In addition, there are few agencies outside the television or media business that are interested in investing in speculative TV production because of the nature of television finance. Purely speculative production (that is, producers spending money without a pre-arranged outlet) tends to take place for the cinema rather than for television. There are a number of reasons for this, besides the most obvious one that cinema is more glamorous.

The first reason is that television companies make expensively but buy cheaply. Broadcasters are prepared to pay more for programmes they commission than they are for ready-made material. There are two very different price scales for programmes depending on whether the broadcaster is involved in commissioning and/or making them themselves, or is buying them as completed programmes. A broadcaster might well commission a documentary costing £50,000 (approximately US $75,000) on the basis of little more than an idea and the director's track record. However, the same documentary offered for sale as a finished item by the same director would be purchased for, at best, £10,000 (approximately US $15,000). It all seems rather odd, as there would seem to be less risk involved in buying something that is already finished.

There are several reasons for this. The most important is that when a broadcaster pays for the production of a programme, they will own it (or a substantial share in it) as a commodity. The rights in the programme can then be sold over and over again to different broadcasters as well as to other outlets like video and DVD. However, programmes are rarely simply sold from one market to another for reasons of cultural specificity or the different nature of product standardisation in different markets. A broadcaster may, for example, use a particular known voice for documentary commentaries, so will wish to add this voice. They may well wish to rewrite the commentary to suit local conditions, both for range of references and for overall tone. So the advantages of having a finished programme often have to be measured against the advantages of exclusivity (of being the first to show the completed programme) and creativity (of having 'an input', meaning telling the director to do certain things, and of being able to cater for cultural specificities). With increasing competition between channels, the issue of 'creating a unified look' or of branding has become increasingly important, permeating the look of individual programmes to a remarkable extent. Hence broadcasters tend to want to control such aspects of the production, and so put a premium on controlling the production process through investment in it. Purely speculative television production is therefore a difficult option for investors, outside areas such as children's programming where the brand is often the character or the toy which will become more valuable as a result of the TV programme. Where a producer is selling limited rights to a broadcaster (e.g. the right to show the programme three times over one year), or where broadcasters from different countries are involved, the producer may well end up making different versions of the same programme, complicating both shooting and post-production.

For both parties, the broadcaster's knowledge of scheduling, of how the programme will 'fit' into a slot in a sequence of programmes remains crucial, even for drama series. In addition, the television market place is full of programmes being offered for sale by broadcasters and program producers from other, usually international, markets, all of whom participate in the same financial model. In the case of smaller territories, the purchase of large amounts of foreign-produced material at low cost is what makes possible the provision of a broadcast service extending for hours and hours.

The second reason for the lack of speculative production in television is that the industry has a long history of vertical integration, of single companies undertaking both production and broadcasting. TV's early history as a live medium, where shooting and transmission were one activity, meant that it was natural for them to be contained in the same organisation. The one market that saw an early division of the two activities was the USA. The existence of four time zones made it desirable to record the nation's peak evening entertainment for delayed transmission to other time zones. In the USA also regulation produced a situation in which local broadcasters were separate from the emerging national distribution networks and contracted to take all or part of their output from them, but tended to reschedule some of it for their own reasons. In the smaller territories of Europe, single national broadcasters emerged like the BBC in Britain or RAI in Italy. Subsequent developments in Britain tended to be variants on the broadcaster-as-producer model until the introduction of Channel 4 in 1982, which introduced the model of commissioning productions from independent producers. This model was widely adopted elsewhere during the subsequent decade.

The complexities of US television finance

Production finance in the USA had organised itself along a radically different model. American television began with separation between networks and stations, providing a secondary domestic market. So producers could sell their productions once to a network and then over again to local television stations. This 'syndication' market opened up in the 1950s, enabling producers to sell filmed series, game shows and sitcoms to local stations to fill the endless hours of daytime and early evening TV which the network did not provide. Syndication provided material as well for those not infrequent spaces in the schedule that arose when stations affiliated to the network refused what the network offered, not least because they wanted to keep all that slot's advertising revenue for themselves. The equivalent in European broadcasting emerged only with the arrival of multiple cable and satellite broadcasters in the late 1980s. Even then, European terrestrial broadcasters, usually the principal or only financiers of production, tended to hold on to the right to reshow programmes they had financed, rather than allowing producers to retain them. This was because they typically provided all of the production costs, whereas production for the American networks had long since been on a shared risk model: the network provided a proportion of the costs and the producer had to find the rest.

American TV production finance became as complex as feature film finance as long ago as the late 1950s. American networks would commission – and usually finance – pilots for series. On the basis of the pilots, successful programmes were commissioned as series. The broadcaster would pay a proportion of the costs to secure a number of showings of each episode over a delimited period of time. The producer would then raise the rest of the money, aiming for the lucrative income from successful shows with 100 or more episodes, which could then 'go into syndication'. Although such successes represented only a small fraction of all the shows broadcast on network television, the aggregate size of all the local markets in the US meant that a 'hit' show could generate hundreds of millions of dollars for its rights holder. Often, therefore, the non-network finance would come from distribution companies skilled in selling to the syndication market, and interested in the income from sales to TV stations outside the USA. These distributors are large enough to be able to spread their bets across a wide range of projects in the hopes that enough will go to syndication. This model of production worked well for long runs of filmed fiction and sitcoms, which is perhaps why these forms seem to dominate in the USA.

Other models emerged as well. Sometimes straightforward sponsorship by advertisers would cover the difference between production costs and what the network would pay. Soap operas are so called because soap companies like Procter & Gamble originally produced the shows themselves. More recently, barter has been popular for cheaper studio-based programming such as talk shows, cookery or cinema review programmes. Network TV will pay the full production cost of such programmes, but in the syndication market the producer will split the income for the advertising breaks, selling half to national advertisers to cover production costs and generate a profit, and leave half for the local station to fill.

Such are the complexities of the US market. Other production markets have not yet arrived at such a system, but as the number of channels and the weight of independent productions both increase, such models will begin to become more typical. Both systems still involve one crucial phase for almost all successful productions of any size: the involvement of a substantial broadcaster from the beginning of the project. Nowadays this can be a subscription channel like HBO rather than a free-to-air advertising-supported network like NBC, CBS, ABC, Fox, WB or UPN, but it is crucial to have a contract with a major broadcasting company that will bring the production to viewers and seal its reputation.

Commissioning

The activity of obtaining a production contract from a broadcaster is often called deal-making by producers and commissioning or ordering by broadcasters. The two are conflated within vertically integrated companies, and considerable tension exists when independent suppliers compete with broadcasters' own production units for commissions. In either case, the process has a number of steps, some of which can be skipped depending on the producer's confidence in their idea or their degree of contractual intimacy with the financiers.

What comes first are ideas and needs, but it is not necessarily the case that producers have ideas and broadcasters have needs. Producers can come up with ideas, but they also identify 'gaps in the market' or seek to exploit talent with which they 'have a relationship'. Broadcasters identify problems with their output and seek ideas for dealing with them, sometimes defining them very tightly. But they also cast around for the talent of the future and for the coming ideas, looking for the faces and genres that are coming into fashion. They are aware that they are in an ideas business and often generate their own. Producers looking for finance for ideas will often research the output of channels to find the most suitable place for their ideas or scheduling weaknesses which their ideas can address. Sometimes producers will generate investment for projects before approaching broadcasters in order to make the proposal seem attractive or even viable. Audience viewing figures and more general market research are therefore habitually used at this point as a crucial tool in developing ideas. Ideas may sometimes be abstract at their moment of conception, but from there on they have to assume very concrete forms.

Once a need encounters an idea, a deal can be negotiated. The deal is essentially a blueprint for production. It specifies the who, what, how, when and where as well as the how much. Typical deals between separate organisations (producers, broadcasters, other financiers) will cover the following kinds of issues:

- the eventual look of the programmes produced, specifying cast and senior crew, length of shooting time, what technologies will be used, delivery dates, lengths of programmes, etc.
- the ownership of rights in the programme, which are often of limited duration (e.g. terrestrial broadcast rights for five years), limited in territory (e.g. USA and Canada only), and even limited in number (e.g. three runs over five years). Rights then revert to the production company or are passed on to other investors.
- Who has the right to control aspects of the content of the programmes, and at what point this right can be exercised. This includes issues such as the right to re-edit for particular purposes or the specification of different versions for different purposes to be delivered by the original producer (e.g. a specific European version to be longer than the US version, and to include material specifically addressed to the European market).
- The way that the finance is structured: who will pay what when, and what happens if they don't.

There are many parties to most deals. Even the simplest, involving a programme 100 per cent financed by a broadcaster envisaged for a single broadcast, will require a number of parties on the broadcaster's side, from scheduling to consulting the interests of other departments.

Stages of production 2: Pre-production

Pre-production is all about planning and anticipation. This is expressed in two formats: the budget, which anticipates spending, and the schedule, which anticipates the use of resources over time. These both rely on further plans. For documentary planning will typically be the result of a period of research; for drama, a period of scriptwriting. Even as writing and research are taking place, the idea that was agreed with the broadcaster is analysed into its component parts, and each is brought into line in an overall plan and budget. An outline budget will have been drawn up during the negotiation of the finance. In pre-production a detailed budget will be developed which allocates resources to the various departments and phases of production: so much for the cast, so much for archive footage, so much for music, so much for editing, so much for digital effects, etc. A budget will be set initially within broad outlines of the prices that can reasonably be expected from an up-to-date knowledge of the market. As pre-production continues, as scripts and/or research become more definite, these prices are progressively negotiated according to the detailed expectations of the production planning and the actual circumstances and quoted prices of suppliers. The precise outcome is only known, however, once the production is concluded. All the time that the production is active, the budget will be revised according to the actual, rather than predicted, expenditure.

The budget is refined as the detailed planning of the production continues. A documentary idea is researched to refine its details, find the most appropriate interviewees or (increasingly in contemporary documentaries) real people who can perform being themselves. Drama scripts are broken down into lists of locations and which scenes are to be shot in them. Locations are found and booked for the estimated number of days that it will take to shoot those scenes. Casts are found for the roles that were not specified for named stars in the contract. A schedule emerges from the process, whose precise form is dictated by a network of other commitments (dates of star availability, limitations of locations, etc.), all geared to the contracted delivery date agreed with the broadcaster and other financiers. The larger the production (a 26-part drama series for example), the more complex the process. As part of the planning of the detailed schedule, prices for services are negotiated within overall guidelines of the budget. So there is a constant interaction between the two planning mechanisms: the schedule and the budget.

Pre-production is also a period of contract negotiation and writing. The detailed terms of the contract with financiers may still be in negotiation; certainly it is the period for negotiation of the terms under which the production company engages artists and technicians. It is also the period in which the underlying intellectual property rights ("copyright") in the production are contracted. Components such as the scripts, the original story, the music, the archive footage and so on all exist as separate artistic works and are protected by copyright. Copyright law differs in different countries. Production companies have to buy all or part of those rights. The different rights in a piece of music, for instance, involve the simple right to incorporate the music in the programme (and that can be further limited to specific territories only) to a major or even exclusive interest in selling the music through other media such as CDs, radio sales, etc. Music copyright is also divided into the copyright for the composition and the copyright for the performance. So the situation can quickly become complex because many copyrights ('underlying rights') are incorporated into even relatively simple programmes. This web of copyright is essentially another aspect of planning and anticipation. Copyright negotiations are usually governed by 'what if?' (as in 'what if the programme is really successful?'; 'what if it is sold to a US network?', etc.).

Where extensive use of computer generated imagery is to be used, pre-production is also a period of image design and planning, particularly where images are to be shot to be combined into composites in post-production.[8] Particularly important in television is the planning of the graphic style of a programme format, integrating everything from sets to title sequences, name captions and spin-off merchandise. Even modest productions now design a logo and an overall style as perhaps their prime means of differentiation in a crowded market. So it is important to see pre-production also as a phase of publicity. In a fast-moving market, the more publicity a programme can receive, the better.

Stages of production 3: The shoot

Shooting, the creation and collection of images and sounds, takes many forms in television. Both film and video are used for different purposes. Considerable changes have taken place in the technologies available, and this has had visible effects on the kinds of programmes produced. The industry is also making increasing use of various forms of computer generated imagery and digital effects.[9] Some genres use the specifically televisual form of the multiple-camera studio shoot, particularly game shows, daytime talk shows and sitcoms.

Studio production is intensive and involves a major division of labour. The director is physically separate from the action on the studio floor, and is mainly concerned with the 'instant editing' of the material from a number of cameras. Except in the case of live transmissions, this creates a master tape that can be trimmed and tightened later, especially when a subsidiary tape is made of a camera feed that is not being used in the live assembly. This is now a standard practice. The director is usually supported by a team who communicate through talkback with presenters and with the floor manager who is responsible for managing the activity in the studio space during recording. The television studio is now a familiar feature of the self-reflexivity of the medium, and representations of it tend to emphasise its artificiality and the degree to which physical separation determines control over the finished product. For those who work within it however, studio practice is highly routinised and relatively inflexible, though not without its moments of tension. The multi-camera studio format is also adapted to location work, particularly in sport broadcasting where the liveness of the sport event is crucial. In these circumstances, the apparatus of the studio gallery or control room, as it is called in the USA, is contained within an outside broadcast ('OB') truck, receiving the input from cameras stationed for the best possible points of view compatible with basic editing conventions (football and baseball are shot from one side of the field, for example).

Studio production brings all the elements of the programme together into one space and time, ensuring a contemporaneous and spontaneous atmosphere to the programme, which is a significant aspect of the genres that most use it. Other forms of shooting are more spread out over time, and imply a greater role for post-production. The technologies for both non-studio shooting and post-production have transformed fundamentally since broadcast television became a cultural commonplace. Television relied on celluloid film for the production of any recorded and post-edited material until the introduction of video tape around the beginning of the 1960s – almost a quarter of a century after the first regular broadcast TV services. Film remained the preferred medium for larger budget production and is still used for much higher budget drama today. There are many reasons for this. Until digital technologies evened out the differences, film provided a superior image quality. In shooting conditions it can deal with a wider range of light levels within one shot, and is regarded as having a less 'flat' and 'bright' image quality. Film has historically seemed a more stable storage medium than tape, and its superior image quality meant that production on film could be more easily transferred to new formats like widescreen or digital storage. So the decision about shooting on film or tape has usually been linked to the planned quality and durability of the programmes.

Videotape, however, has advantages, especially in documentary situations where tape reels and cassettes have a larger capacity than film magazines. A filmed interview on 16mm had to break off every 10–12 minutes to change the roll of film in the camera magazine; tape formats with a running time of an hour are commonplace. Until the introduction of cassette-based formats like Betacam in the mid-1980s, however, film technology was significantly lighter, more compact and more trustworthy in difficult conditions than tape. Betacam enabled high-quality location video shooting using two person crews similar to 16mm film crews. With the development of the camcorder in the mid 1990s, tape became significantly lighter and usable by single operators, often directors. This led to a revolution in documentary film-making, allowing longer and more reactive shooting periods and a more conversational and confessional style of interviewing.[10]

In general, the technological aspects of shooting have simplified during the history of television. Fewer individuals are required and processes have become more automated. However, the human or 'front of camera' aspects of shooting have become more complicated. In fiction, there is a marked tendency to higher production values, with broadcast series like *ER* or *NYPD Blue* having distinctly filmic characteristics: complex sets, showy camera work, deep shots with plenty of background action.[11] In documentary, it has become more difficult to negotiate the permissions to shoot as companies and ordinary individuals alike have become more used to the processes of television. Media awareness training is now a commonplace for large corporations and political campaigns; suspicion of television is also a deep rooted public attitude.

Stages of production 4: Post-production

In post-production, images and sounds are processed into the final programme form. In addition to the assemblage of images and sound from the shoot phase, post-production involves the creation and addition of material, such as commentaries, music and animation effects. This is an area of increasing sophistication, especially when a major amount of graphic design is involved. The demands of scheduling slots mean that programme durations have to be finely calculated, and the differing demands of broadcasters described above lead to a considerable activity of revision (or 'reversioning') of material to fit their formats and cultural demands.

All of this has been considerably helped by a technological revolution: the move from linear to non-linear editing. This has revolutionised the look and the internal pacing of programmes. Studio shot material is now routinely edited to sharpen its timing and to insert more complex visual information. Studio shows from the late 1980s, before the general use of non-linear editing, now seem archaic in their pacing and construction. Documentary and factual programming have seen an increasingly fast pace of shot transition and a sophistication in sound construction.

Non-linear is the term normally used for digital editing, using computer-based programmes such as AVID. Versions of these are now available for home PC use, and the key to the revolution is the increase in affordable computer memory. Video images are complex and require gigabytes of storage space, especially if all the information recorded on the tape is to be retained ('compression' refers to a process of averaging out image information to reduce the space it takes up). Tape is still used as a shooting medium in most circumstances because it is able to store large amounts of electronic data and is relatively robust. Some cameras have been developed using hard drives, but it is expected that tape will be eliminated as a shooting medium only when solid state cameras are developed which store information on chips. Before the introduction of multi-gigabyte hard drives, tape was used for editing as well. Computerised editing consisted of the precise copying of video material from one source tape to a master tape, one shot at a time in linear order, inserting effects by using an inline mixer.

Linear editing has a number of weaknesses. Any mistake involving a wrong shot length (omitted or unwanted material for example) means that the whole programme has to be reassembled on the master tape from that point on. Tape to tape editing involves a loss of image quality each time a transfer takes place ('generation loss'). So there are problems with the simple expedient of copying the rest of the programme to another tape, inserting the missing material, and then recopying the wanted rest of the programme to the master. The image quality of the end section has gone through two generations, so will be of inferior image quality. Three generations were deemed acceptable in most industrial contexts, so if the initial edit had involved a couple of generations, then the repair job would become more complex. The problem of generation loss was also a major constraint on the generation of special effects such as layered images and complex graphics. Non-linear editing has made these constraints a thing of the past.

Non-linear editing can take place at different levels of image quality depending on how much the image and sound information is compressed. So normal video editing practice is still to use higher rate of compression to make the initial edit choices and to assemble the programme in what is called an offline edit. The online edit then follows this template at the minimum level of compression. This process is dictated simply by expense: there is no point in tying up expensive equipment for long periods on one project during the period of assembly. An offline edit is usually calculated in days or weeks; an online in hours. This reflects a division of resources and labour from the practices of tape editing, where low-quality assemblies on VHS or similar formats enabled editors and directors to make creative decisions ('try things out') without the pressure of costs implied by an online edit.

Film editing follows a similar pattern, in which positive print material of rushes is assembled by the editor, and the finished cut is then sent to specialists who cut the negative material according to its guidance. Film editing was often preferred to linear tape because of its greater flexibility, but the non-linear revolution has largely replaced traditional editing on celluloid even within the feature film business. Non-linear editing also enables a level of sound post-production that was difficult to attain with linear tape, so that many productions now involve considerable work of sound design and a separate stage of sound mixing after the images have been assembled in their final form. Non-linear editing has also enabled the creation of new kinds of job in the industry, such as the sound designer or the colourist, as well as eliminating others such as the assistant editor.

Post-production also involves considerable administrative work. The final accounts are produced, and in productions that are going badly, this often involves an attempt to reduce the costs of post-production. Paperwork is produced in large quantities, describing the programmes as commodities in various ways: everything from the transcripts of dialogue needed for subtitling and translation, to detailed descriptions of the origins of all the footage used and any copyright restrictions, to contracts with key personnel and even publicity material.

Stages of production 5: Marketing

Marketing is an integral part of broadcast production. During pre-production and shooting various kinds of publicity material are prepared: plot synopses, stills, interviews with leading actors, etc. Post-production involves the production of trailers and other promotional material from the shot footage. Sometimes this is the responsibility of the production company; sometimes it is undertaken by broadcasters themselves. There is a particular challenge to marketing a show on broadcast television: there is a very short span of time (usually only a week or two) to publicise the one-time transmission of a show or an episode of a show at a given time on a given date. In the competitive television market, channels are spending increasing amounts of on-screen time and production resources in producing on-screen promotional material for forthcoming shows, to the extent of shooting expensive material simply for this purpose.

Marketing also involves attempting to control media coverage. The horizontal integration of media companies has greatly affected the marketing of TV programmes. The Disney Channel, for example, routinely cross-promotes TV programmes, Disney-produced or distributed movies, computer games, theme parks, toys, etc. The News Corporation in Britain uses its newspapers (the *Sun* and *The Times*) to promote programmes and events on its BskyB satellite channels. Marketing has also been extended to the web, with banners at the bottom of the screen driving viewers to programme-linked websites and, conversely, websites set up especially to promote a new show or serve as a vehicle for fan interaction. Marketing is not always a matter of spreading information, however. In 1985, the BBC decided that the launch of its new primetime soap *Eastenders* was to be shrouded in secrecy, with no press access to contracted actors and no advance leaking of the plot. Even now that the series is well established, the feeding of information to the press is still tightly controlled, so that the information that an actor is leaving the cast will trigger speculation about the way in which this will be managed in script terms, enhancing public interest in the series. Elsewhere, gossip about the cast and their views on the characters they play are provided to magazines aimed at the core sections of the audience, primarily pre-teen and early teen audiences.

Such are the marketing activities involved in production for broadcast television. There is, however, a lot more to television than broadcasting, and a lot more to production for broadcasting than just programmes and ancillary material. The rest of this chapter outlines some of the major aspects of television beyond the cultural dominance of broadcast programming.

Beyond broadcast

Broadcasting as defined here is a culturally dominant way of using television technology. Other forms exist which dwarf broadcasting in terms of their economic importance in production terms. Some, like the use of surveillance cameras in public spaces, involve little in terms of production activity until crucial images require enhancement for detection purposes. Others, currently represent relatively small areas of activity, but are the harbingers of a trend: the application of television technologies to everyday commercial activities.

This section will deal briefly with four areas: the production of commercials for television; the use of television in corporate communication; video art and the realtively new domain of personal production.

Commercials

Much television production outside of the broadcasting industry itself is concentrated in advertising. Indeed, advertising pays for much of the production activity of the broadcasting industry as well. Spot advertising underpins much of the current broadcasting industry, yet broadcasting is simply one way of reaching consumers, and, increasingly, it is seen as a relatively ineffective means of doing so. When a major brand like Heinz decides to shift resources out of television advertising into other forms of influencing consumers, the whole broadcast industry indulges in a bout of severe anxiety. Broadcasting, though culturally important, is a relatively minor industrial activity. As a British investment adviser once put it: 'they're terribly nice people to deal with, but you could buy the whole industry out of the retained profits of ICI'.[12]

Many of the concerns of commissioning practice and editorial niceties that I have described simply do not exist for advertising, so advertising production should be considered as a separate form of production, as it is in the audio-visual industries. The genesis of a commercial is very different from that of a television programme: the concern is the message and the brand, the impact in the market. Creative decisions are guided by these concerns and are made by more disparate groups of people than is commonly the case in broadcasting. They will involve campaign directors as well as film directors; market researchers as well as programme researchers; clients as well as creatives. Advertising involves a number of different functions, any or all of which can be found within one corporation. The first is the client, the company with a product to sell that has already been the subject of considerable consumer research and consequent conceptualisation. Second is the agency that conceptualises the advertisement (the concept). Third is the production house that produces the physical objects, advertisements, which often exist in related forms across a number of different media. Fourth is the organisation that buys the display space for the advertisement, the spot in the advertising break or the programme sponsorship deal. The common conception of the 'advertising agency' is of a company that undertakes all these functions for a client, including a considerable amount of the initial market research and product conceptualisation. The situation is often far more fluid, with large corporations taking various functions 'in house' or seeking to control the budgetary aspects of the physical production of commercials by imposing their own production controllers on separate production companies.

Production is dominated by a perfectionism that is rare in broadcasting. Since every frame of an advertisement will be seen dozens of times by an average viewer, every implication of every image has to be teased out. Every frame of a high-budget advertisement is meticulously pre-planned, and will freely borrow techniques from the film industry including the lavish use of computer generated imagery. The production cost per minute of the average advertising break will be many times that of the broadcast programming that separates one break from another. Yet there also exist commercials whose skimpy production costs seem entirely out of keeping with the cost of putting them on air.

One of the great points of tension within television production is the relationship with the advertising industry. Spot advertising was devised as the simplest means of separating the interests of the corporations using broadcast TV for advertising from those of the corporations making money from broadcasting itself. So two separate but inseparable interests have been at work within broadcasting since the start. Even the early BBC, whose public service remit rigorously excluded advertising, had agonised discussion about how to deal with brand names that were in common circulation ('Hoover' for vacuum cleaner etc.), and what details they should give of commercial gramophone records that they played. In the movement away from the dominance of network television and the fragmentation of the television audience across dozens if not hundreds of channels, spot advertising has become less effective. Instead, sponsorship has increased, seeking to associate commodities with programmes on the basis of a connection between their brands. The confectionery company Cadbury's sponsors ITV's long-running soap *Coronation Street* with the legend 'brought to you in association with Cadbury's Drinking Chocolate', linking a familiar and comfortable programme with a product that hopes to produce the same feelings in its consumers. The spot commercial, however, has found a multitude of other outlets. Public display television monitors can be found at railway stations, gas/petrol stations, supermarkets, planes, in short they are in all the waiting areas that are part of modern existence. Video images in motion pass across them, and given the nature of the spaces involved, sound can often not accompany them. Many kinds of spot commercial are ideal for this visual form of display.

Corporate communication

Global corporations rely on television to create a corporate culture with a sense of common purpose, using it in several distinct ways. Management uses television as a means of direct and charismatic communication, and television training is a key part of the skills of a senior manager. Live feeds of important addresses from senior managers are the most effective means of communication at times of crisis or celebration. The preparation for the launch of a new product involves high budget productions communicating the virtues of new products in ways that are distinct from the presentation of that product to customers. With the increasing complexity of the modern workplace, video is used routinely to provide instructional material detailing workaday processes. As workplaces become screen-based rather than paper-based, this kind of visual instructional material will increase in importance and complexity. Some of these forms draw upon broadcasting, if only to enhance their cultural status. Corporate communications will often use television faces or voices as presenters, and sometimes use real or imitated TV formats to get their message across.

Corporate communication will grow as television becomes a more usual means of spreading information. Already corporate websites use video quite routinely, and the building industry increasingly uses video 'walk-throughs' of planned buildings to secure permissions and to make advance sales. Estate agency/realtor businesses use video material of homes for sale as a means of aiding customer selection.

Video art

Artists have used video since the late 1960s, when Sony introduced the Portapak, using an open reel to reel tape rather than a cassette (cassettes were introduced in 1973). Video provided artists with the ability to capture time and process much more easily than did film, enabling collaborative work with performers. Artists like Bill Viola also worked with the physical nature of the image display itself, placing monitors under water (a recurrent theme in his work) or on their sides which suddenly made them look surprisingly tall and narrow. Video art often plays with the incongruity of this domestic form within the gallery setting, with artists like Gillian Wearing taking the television interview relationship into areas unexplored by broadcasting. Her first major work was *Signs that say what you want them to say and not Signs that say what someone else wants you to say* (1992–93) in which she photographed random passers-by holding statements that they had written down spontaneously. In one image a smartly-dressed young businessman with a mild expression holds up a sign saying simply, 'I'm desperate'. Television technology presents interesting challenges for the workings of the art market, with digital technology eroding the uniqueness of the artistic work even further than still photography. Wearing's solution is ingenious: she sells a limited number of tapes, each with a playback machine and monitor. These together constitute the artwork. Others have used television to create webcam events, merging broadcasting with artistic concerns with time, process, biography and exhibitionism to create a new category of artistic experience.

Personal production

The most fundamental change in television within the recent past has been in the availability of digital production tools for the ordinary domestic consumer. Digital camcorders can be combined with editing software on domestic PCs to provide an effective production route. Dissemination can take place through websites as well as video cassettes. The real significance lies in the increase in audio-visual communication that it enables. Video communication can replace written communication where appropriate. Personal production also provides growth in audio-visual literacy to the general population, which feeds back very quickly into production for broadcasting and for advertising. The result is not a democratisation of broadcasting so much as the introduction of the audio-visual into person-to-person communication. Broadcast television may well be the cultural dominant at the moment, but in production terms it is already a specialised area, and it will become an exceptional model of production as new forms proliferate.

Notes

1   See article in this collection by Albert Moran.
2   See Pierre Bourdieu. *The Field of Cultural Production*. Cambridge: Polity Press; New York: Columbia University Press 1993.
3   The term 'vertical integration' is derived from business studies, where it refers to a single company operating or controlling all phases of the production of a particular product. The term works well when applied to the development of broadcasting outside the USA, but in the USA the period of actual vertical integration of commercial broadcasting was really quite brief. The commercial networks were forbidden from becoming vertically integrated by the 'syn/fin' (syndication and finance) rules drawn up by regulatory body the FCC. They were strictly limited in the number of TV stations that they could own, and so relied on deals with independent stations and chains of stations in order to construct a network. This meant that drama and comedy programming was made on film and by independent production companies, mainly in Los Angeles, from very early in the 1950s, as Christopher Anderson details in his excellent *Hollywood TV: The Studio System in the Fifties* (University of Texas Press 1994). Thus, since the 1960s through the 1980s, the three commercial networks in the States were able to exercise oligopoly power not through vertical integration but through their networked distribution of programming. Now that the syn/fin rules are no more, the networks have more power in production, but in a radically altered market.
4   See John T. Caldwell, *Televisuality*, Rutgers University Press, 1995
5   See for instance Victoria Wegg-Prosser 'The BBC and Producer Choice: a Study of Public Service

Broadcasting and Managerial Change' *Wide Angle*, Vol. 20 no. 2 pp. 150–63; Georgina Born, 'Television research and the sociology of culture', *Screen* no. 41, vol. 3 2000 and Georgina Born and Tony Prosser, 'Culture, citizenship and consumerism: The BBC's fair trading obligations and public service broadcasting', *The Modern Law Review* no. 64, vol 5. 2001.

6   Other UK broadcasters also did this (the ITV companies) but much less drastically, not least because they were more used to using external production facilities.

7   Colleges have libraries for the same reason, so that individual students and staff do not have to buy copies of the same book. The producer choice system at its worst meant that it was cheaper for a production to buy books or CDs than to borrow them centrally.

8   As, for example, in the cinema film *The Matrix*.

9   See Caldwell op.cit.

10   See Stella Bruzzi *New Documentary: an Introduction*, Routledge, 2000 and Brian Winston *Lies, Damn Lies and Documentaries* British film Institute, 2000.

11   See Jeremy Butler 'VR in the ER: ER's use of e-media' in *Screen*, Winter 2001 vol. 42 no. 4 pp 313–31.

12   ICI, Imperial Chemical Industries, was a large conglomerate producing products ranging from industrial chemicals and consumer products. It has since been demerged into several separate companies which deal with more specific markets.

Bibliography

Anderson, C. (1994) *Hollywood TV: The Studio System in the Fifties*, Texas: University of Texas Press.

Bourdieu, P. (1993) *The Field of Cultural Production: Essays on Art and Literature*, Cambridge: Polity Press.

Born, G. (2000) 'Television Research and the Sociology of Culture', *Screen*, 41, 4: 404–24.

—— and Prosser, T. (2001) 'Culture, Citizenship and Consumerism: The BBC's Fair Trading Obligations and Public Service Broadcasting', *The Modern Law Review*, 64, 5: 657–87.

Bruzzi, S. (2000) *New Documentary: A Critical Introduction*, London: BFI Publishing.

Butler, J. (2001) 'VR in the ER: ER's Use of E-media', in *Screen* 142, 4: 313–31.

Caldwell, J. (1995) *Televisuality: Style, Crisis and Authority in American Television*, New Brunswick, NJ: Rutgers University Press.

Wegg-Prosser, V. (1998) 'The BBC and Producer Choice: a Study of Public Service Broadcasting and Managerial Change', *Wide Angle*, 20, 2: 150–63.

Winston, B. (2000) *Lies, Damn Lies and Documentaries*, London: BFI Publishing.

Chapter 18

JOHN THORNTON CALDWELL

MODES OF PRODUCTION
The televisual apparatus

> These radio news pictures projected from magic lantern slides onto the screens of the best picture theatres in the cities . . . [mean that] no newspaper can possibly put news events before the public as quickly as the theater can with radio news pictures.
>
> (Technical proposal for theatrical television, *SMPE Journal*, May 1923[1])

> Although some parts of the program technic may parallel the technics of the stage, motion pictures and sound broadcasting, it will be distinct from any of these. In effect, a new art form must be created.
>
> (Modernist aesthetic espoused by RCA engineer R. R. Beal, 1937[2])

TELEVISION ENGINEERS HAVE OFTEN acted as closet artists. From the very beginning, developers of production technology have seldom shied away from offering aesthetic theorizations about their new and constantly developing technologies. Even a cursory survey of the technical literature from the 1920s and 1930s shows that television might have ended up radically different from the form that we now know. Engineers hawked various visions of the artform: as a cinematic type of theatrical television, as a facsimile system, as radio photographs that produced paper prints, as a visual newswire, and as a video phone.[3] From the perspective of the 1990s, these early and alternative technical proposals, along with alternative economic proposals—like pay per view and a system of programming subsidized by TV set license fees—all seem incredibly forward-thinking. Each prototype, after all, now plays an important part in the contemporary multinational, multimedia environment. Yet, by 1950, each prototype had been written off as a failure.

This shepherding and attrition of technological and artistic prototypes suggest two things. First, media technologies are not easily dichotomized as either deterministic (forces that effect change) or symptomatic (phenomena that reflect cultural needs and ideologies), as Raymond Williams suggests.[4] As the above epigraphs indicate, prewar RCA and Society for Motion Picture Engineers (SMPE) aestheticians actively broached and bartered different aesthetic models in a give-and-take process of negotiation with stockholders, with government regulators and with the supposed needs and tastes of the American people. William Boddy has shown incisively how government sanctioned monopolistic practice in the post war era was a clear incursion into technological development—an exclusionary process of control that benefitted specific business interests.[5] To the deterministic-symptomatic model, then, one must also then add a third axis: the interventionist. History shows that mass-cultural processes are not always as subtle as some cultural studies suggest, nor are they always as ambiguous and contradictory as ideological criticism implies. Explicit aesthetic and theoretical discourses—as well as overt interventions of power—have always accompanied new media technologies and will continue to do so. Political and economic interests have never been queasy about publicly flexing corporate muscle to control paradigm shifts. These manifest tendencies in television's mode of production had an effect on televisual style as well.

[. . .] I want to examine here some of the industrial conditions behind the emergence of televisuality. A consideration of the televisual mode of production—its production technology, methods, personnel, and organizational form—shows that the excessive looks of primetime television in the 1980s were not just illustrations of a stylistic or postmodernist sensibility, but were rather indications of substantive changes within the televisual industry and its production apparatus. To understand these changes, it is important to look at several key televisual technologies, their affect on production practice, and two major influences on televisual programming: the film-style look and the style-obsessed world of primetime commercial advertising.

[. . .]

Televisual technologies

Simply looking at television's flow of ads, shows, and promos on any given night reveals the importance and consciousness of the televisual mode of production and its technologies. If many primetime shows now use all of their available "bells and whistles," then ads and music videos actually make production equipment a crucial part of their dramatic action as well. When director David Fincher, for example, used the new Raybeam, a lighting grid with thirty 1 Ks on a recent Nike commercial, he liked the polished high-tech look so much that he included it as a prop in the background. From then on he had to re-rent the light as a prop to insure continuity among the other spots in the entire Nike television campaign.[6] The production tool became a fetishized toy in the hip urban world that Nike fantasized for its audience.

But new production tools not only influenced what was seen by viewers within television images, they also had a profound influence on how those images were constructed, altered, and displayed. It is important to see the emergence of stylistic exhibitionism in the 1980s alongside the growing popularity of six new technical devices in the televisual production world: the video-assist, motion control, electronic nonlinear editing, digital effects, T-grain film stocks, and the Rank-Cintel. The development and availability of digital video effects, for example has always promised (or threatened) to replace conventional production methods—a potential celebrated both by techno-futurists and production executives looking to save money in primetime by getting rid of real (and expensive) locations and sets.[7] [. . .] Before considering the broader implications of these televisual technologies, however, a closer look at their importance in primetime production discourse is needed.

Video-assist

If one observes a film-based shoot for television today, one frequently confronts a production spectacle notably different from the way things used to be done. It is not uncommon today to see production personnel clustered around a glowing video monitor, entranced by the electronic image rather than by the actors or the action in front of the film camera. The video-assist makes possible this radical shift of the production group's gaze. In the old days, the nature of the image was really the business of only one or two people on a telefilm shoot: the director of photography and the camera operator. Although ultimately responsible for the show, the director was more concerned with acting and could only engage with the image as it was being shot, through the vague visual approximation offered by a neck-strung director's finder. Reinforcing the invisible nature of the television image during the shoot was the fact that the director and crew had to wait for projection of the film dailies—work-prints made from the camera original negative—which came back from the lab well after the day's shoot was over. As with feature filmmaking, sometimes the results were acceptable, sometimes they were not. For many years, television's 35mm Mitchell cameras did not even have reflex viewing. Camera people were forced to develop complicated "rack-over" systems to shift the camera away from the lens to enable the operator to frame a shot. This shift allowed the camera people to predict what the camera was seeing. Later, "reflex-viewing" on Panavision cameras allowed the operators to see the action exactly as it was being shot, but no one else at the time, including the director of photography, had any *certainty* about whether the shot worked, that is, whether it was exposed or framed correctly. The image was always in some ways a mystery, one that revealed its secrets only after a return journey from the lab's dark, chemical soup. This invisibility lent itself well to the mystique of the cinematographer's difficult craft and to the cult of professionalism.

With the introduction and availability of fiber optics, however, there was but a short and logical leap to the video-assist. Tiny fiber optics were tapped into the reflex view finder, fed out into a video pick-up device (a tiny video camera), and electronically fed to a monitor on the set. This device, then, allowed one and all on the set simultaneous and critical access to the once-mysterious camera image. What occasionally results from its use is a kind of team visualization, where every one of the key creative personnel has access to the composed image. This device, of course, saves money: a lot of takes never need to be printed, because flaws in acting or blocking become immediately apparent as the shot is being made or when videotape recorded from the video-assist is played back between takes. Yet the *displacement of the production gaze from the proprietary mysterium of the cinematographer*, to the public consumption of the entire crew makes everyone an expert on the image. The video-assist allows extreme precision during a setup, and saves money, but it can also be the bane of image makers when gaffers, actors, grips, and other "experts" offer suggestions about better ways to compose the image. Construction of the televised image before video-assist was based primarily on verbal commands between key personnel and mathematical calculations made by the cinematographer and his assistant(s). The video-assist, by contrast, allows everyone on the set to be highly conscious and concerned about visual quality. For better or worse, now everyone seems to be a master of the image.

Motion control

Another type of equipment that complements the video-assist, in both the *dispersal and intensification of the image*, is motion control. I include in this category not just the computer-controlled units that automatically program cameras to perform and reduplicate complicated camera moves, but also the Steadicam, Camrail, robotic-controlled studio cameras, and much less cybernetic devices like jib arms and motorized cranes. All of these devices are alike in one important way: they physically *take the camera away from the camera operator's eyes and move it through space in very fluid ways*. The resulting effect can be eerily nonhuman, as with the Steadicam—a body-mounted camera harness governed by a gyroscopic control that minimizes jerkiness and vibration. By taking out even the sensation of human steps when the operator moves, the camera eye seems to float through space with a mind of its own. [. . .]

Everybody seems to want disembodied camera fluidity, not just feature film-makers. The jib arm, a less sophisticated leverlike extension that mounts and pivots on the head of a tripod or dolly, also takes the camera eye far away from the operator's head. With video-assisted monitoring, television shots can now start far above a cameraperson's eye level and sweep laterally, vertically, or diagonally through a shot even as the camera rolls. Periscopic lenses on jib- or dolly-mounted cameras allow television cinematographers to shift from sweeping renditions of exterior action to snaking arterial moves through microscopic spaces as well. Programmed, computerized control of these moves allows directors to repeat identically the same complicated shots for one or one hundred-takes, all without the inevitable flaws and subtle differences that a human operator brings. [. . .] As well as being stylish, then, television's robotic and autonomous eyes also have dire labor implications. Even the extensive and highly stratified camera crews in primetime production stand back and watch as a single composite operator (cameraman/DP/ assistant cinematographer/grip) coaxes the Steadicam eye through its dramatic flight-like apparitions.

This family of motion-control devices all do one thing for the television image: they automate an inherently omniscient point of view and subjectivize it around a technological rather than human center. If anything reflects the ontological death of photographic realism in television, it is surely this gang of new and automated motion-control devices. The ideological effect of this basic televisual apparatus is one of airless and high-tech artifice. The televisual image no longer seems to be anchored by the comforting, human eye-level view of the pedestal-mounted camera, but floats like the eye of a cyborg.

Electronic and nonlinear editing: "Thirty-two levels of undo"

If video-assist and motion control effected stylistic consciousness and disembodied fluidity *within the frame*, then a third group of technologies—electronic editing—helped shatter the *sequential and temporal* straitjacket necessitated by conventional forms of editing. Electronic editing of videotape has been pervasive since the early 1970s, first as control-track editing, and then as frame-accurate SMPTE (Society for Motion Picture and Television Engineers) "time-code" editing.[8] From the start, many telefilm producers despised these options. While video editing was acceptable for short network news stories, it proved impractical for longer forms, since video editing allowed no flexibility for change, modification, or revision once a succession of shots was laid down. [. . .] Editing film, on the other hand, might be slower, but it allowed for numerous editorial reworkings. [. . .]

In the face of this uneven industrial reception by the primetime producers, major video equipment manufacturers—masters in the 1970s and 1980s of a high-tech industrial world obsessed with research and development—announced ever more highly sophisticated videotape editing systems. By 1993 even Sony's industrial and low-end broadcast editing systems had become proficient at loading up the television image with multiple simultaneous images and slow motion. Sony boasted that their "BVE-2000 editor connects to as many as 12 VTRs, controlling up to 6 in any one edit."[9] This was the very kind of extreme visual facility that telefilm editors failed to find in the earlier variants of videotape editing. [. . .]

The resistance to cutting on tape by the major telefilm producers began to loosen in the mid and late 1980s, with the development of newer random-access memory electronic editing systems, like Lucasfilm's Editdroid, the EMC2, the Montage Picture Processor, and the CMX-6000. All promised primetime program producers the ability to do film-style editing for television. The technological breakthrough that made this possible, was the increasing cost effectiveness and memory-storage power of newer recording media: electronic video discs and greatly expanded computer hard drives. As alternatives to videotape-based recording or editing, films or tapes were loaded into a computer's RAM, video discs or hard drives and any part of the original source material could be called up at any time within a microsecond. [. . .]

At first, the claim to fame of this editing equipment was its ability to show your producer or client ten different completed versions of the same scene or program during the same screening session. The broader implications, however, also became clear: *nothing visual was set in stone*. Again, the majors at Universal and Warners were willing to consider the technology, not just because they wanted to ape the flashy style of MTV, but because it promised serious production economies.[. . .] By 1993, one of the newest and least expensive nonlinear systems—the Mac-base Avid—received the kind of acclaim that indicated its new and extensive popularity. Avid was awarded an Emmy for technical accomplishment by the Academy of Television Arts and Sciences. Nonlinear Avids were, after all, being utilized everywhere: in New York-based commercial post-production houses, in music videos, in primetime program production. The reason? The trades boasted about its ability to provide limitless reworkings. "The bottom line is that this system gives me enormous creative freedom. I can edit unlimited versions and save them all. The Avid has *thirty-two levels of undo* and that completely frees up the editor to *experiment*."[10] Even mainstream television people in Los Angeles, then, saw and valued the dramatic experimental potential of the new systems. Forget orthodox editing wisdom, the whole point for editors now frequently is to demonstrate how far one can push the editing syntax on a project or scene, and how many stylistic variations one can showcase. After all, with nonlinear, there is no risk. Nothing is stylistically set in stone. Nonlinear encouraged, or fed, the televisual appetite for stylistic volatility and infinite formal permutations.

The two other crucial televisual technologies—the Rank-Cintel telecine and new high-speed film stocks—are best understood within the broader context of two emergent obsessions in 1980s television: the film-style look and primetime commercial advertising.

Playing with limits

Self-conscious primetime practice

> Lighting for features, lighting for television, the light is identical.
> (George Spiro Dibie, president, American Society of Lighting Directors[11])

> On television, you can't be Vittorio Storaro. But what you can do is like music.
> (Oliver Wood, director of photography, *Miami Vice*[12])

One of the central working concerns in television production in the 1980s concerned the formal potential of the television image, and especially the question of what can be done within the constraints and confines of the limited television frame. Consider the diametrically opposed views outlined above. Some DPs saw in primetime Bertolucciesque cinematic potential; others, melodic sensitivity. TV was inherently like film; TV and film were antithetical. Such contradictory answers—about what television can and cannot do, and what it can do best—abounded, but the question became more and more pervasive in the working and marketing discourse of the industry. Academic high theory, on the other hand, was working from two very different and problematic assumptions: first, that producers-practitioners could not be aware of the deep structure or ideological implications of their work, and second, that producers-practitioners used aesthetic criteria that were incomplete or naive. Evidence for this bias is found in the widespread penchant that high theory has for inventing its own frameworks, aesthetic categories, and critical terminology.

Even a limited examination of recent literature from the industry, however, shows that these assumptions and write-offs of the industry are misguided. Not only is television currently stylish, but it can be stylish in an extremely self-conscious and analytical way. While high theory was speculating on television as a distracting verbal-aural phenomenon, something very different was happening within the producing industry. There, in producer story sessions, in conversations between DPs and gaffers on sets, and among editors in postproduction suites, an awareness was growing of television as a style-driven phenomenon heavily dependent upon the visual.

Since the systematic approach to visual style is very much on the minds of some practitioners, and evident in the practice of many others, it is worth examining how media producers conceptualize this visuality. Two areas of industrial debate—film-style programming and videographic programming—correspond roughly to a major generic programming division in television. That is, the division mirrors an institutional split between primetime dramatic and comedy series on the one hand—producer-dominant genres that use *film* pervasively—and the other extensive array of director-editor-dominant program forms and genres that are heavily dependent upon extensive *electronic* postproduction. [. . .]

The film look

The issue of image superiority in the film versus video debate and questions about the merits of film-style production methods for television have received much attention in the 1980s and 1990s. Landmark work in this area was produced by Harry Matthias and Richard Patterson, and other works have followed[13] I am not interested so much in the technical aspects of this debate as in the ways that practitioners interpret and explain the film look in television. To understand this kind of discourse, however, it is important to survey some of the technical issues that have become central for those television production people that make heavy use of film technology. A discussion of more fully electronic variants of televisuality will follow.

New film stocks

Predictions to the contrary, film origination in television has not been replaced by video imaging. Far from it, film origination has thrived and prospered in two major areas of television: (1) primetime programming (episodic shows, movies for television, and miniseries), and (2) commercial advertising for television. [. . .] Even as the aesthetic and formal possibilities offered by film increased, the popularity of shooting television on film stock also increased. Film-tape manufacturers argued that certain TV scripts in fact call for quality "production values that are more appropriate for film," especially any genre requiring "fantasy" rather than "immediacy."[14]

Not only did shows shot on film dominate television in the late 1980s, the quality of the film stocks allowed for a kind of visual sophistication impossible during the zero-degree telefilm years of the 1960s and 1970s.[15] In the early 1980s first Fuji, then Eastman, and then Agfa all introduced new lines of film negative stock with dramatic improvements in both sensitivity to light and graininess. Chemically engineered around new and less visible T-grain silver halide particles in the emulsion, the new stocks could be used in extremely low-light situations, could be easily "push processed" one or two stops, had more saturated color rendition, and provided a greater range of contrast and tonality within a single image than any of the earlier stocks. [. . .]

By 1990, Eastman provided a vast menu of professional negative stocks for telefilm producers, from grainless, color-saturated daylight stocks to nighttime stocks that could be pushed to 1000 ASA or higher. These were overwhelming options for television cinematographers trained in the 1960s and early 1970s. A period when one or two stocks were typically available and when high-speed negative was defined as a mere 64 ASA. Film stocks, therefore, had a direct impact on the ability of producers and cinematographers to marshal variant visual looks. The reasons were not just photochemical, however. With the increased use of computer technology—for design, engineering, and quality control of new emulsions during the 1980s and 1990s—film stock companies like Agfa, Eastman, and Fuji were now able to make potentially limitless numbers of stocks. [. . .] Extreme international competition by Fuji and Agfa have changed the way that both business and engineering is done in the industry. But the facility with engineering endless photographic looks is not just an economic consequence, it is also an outgrowth of interaction between computerized emulsion engineering and the publicized stylistic needs of a new generation of primetime and feature cinematographers.

By 1991, filter manufacturer Tiffen had created a host of designer-color filters: "grape, chocolate and tropic blue—all available in three densities, and all available in half-color and graduated to half-clear."[16] Not only did the new film stocks have a direct impact on camera mobility, low-light sensitivity, and photographic tonality, they also allowed *a new level of visual detail in front of the camera*. Televisual sets and locations got visually denser and more complicated after Ridley Scott's *Blade Runner* and Chiat Day's Macintosh television spots in 1984, even as the ability to render such images by new film stocks—and higher resolution color television monitors at home—improved. In addition, the whole optical film industry was revolutionized by the improved resolution and chrominance abilities of television. Far from the days when prime-time DPs were locked into the polar world of filters limited mostly to color and density corrections between tungsten light and daylight, the new filters and stocks were designed to render both wild variations and subtle nuances of color within a single image. When industrial players like Tiffen baptize their new "grape" glass as a "designer filter," the association is complete. The designer televisuality of Michael Mann's *Miami Vice* is matched by the designer optics of Tiffen's lense-mounted glass. When television cameramen now ask for more coral rather than simply more orange, the televisual revolution symbolically betrays its technical as well as producerly roots.

Rank-Cintel

The desire to infuse video with a visual style more typical of film was enabled by one technical development as much as by any other. In 1977, the first Rank-Cintel "flying spot scanner" was installed in the United States. Several generations of design improvements followed, and other companies marketed their own versions of the chip-based film-to-video transfer machines. Higher quality images could be rendered on videotape, since the Rank-Cintel was able to reproduce and take advantage of film's unique look and "incredible dynamic range."[17] Practitioners boasted that the Rank meant that "film provides an ability to record as much as a 400:1 range of brightness which is the difference between the brightest and darkest elements in any scene. This allows a talented cinematographer to use light to paint very subtle details which establish mood and setting."[18] Consider the not so subtle conceptual transformation that takes place here, from a purely technical description of contrast to an aesthetic theorization. Mere television transfer technique is redefined in terms of painting and cinematography. This simple verbal deduction undercuts the way that television image technology has traditionally been defined: as amorphous, low-resolution, flat, and crudely contrasty.

Television's marked shift toward using film negative was based in part on the promise that Rank-type transfer units could reduce electronic noise in the picture, while at the same time maintaining details in the darkest shadow areas of the television image. Rank-Cintel now offers producers a menu of various and distinctive looks depending on the type of film format being transferred: original camera negative, interpositive, dupe negative, or low-contrast projection prints all demand different setups and parameters on the Rank-Cintel. Each variety of stock affords the producer a different visual look. [. . .]

Transfer technology in the 1980s, then, did not just make the image *better* visually, it actually multiplied the various visual looks of television into discrete codes that could be tied to specific program ends. [. . .] Transfer technology, then, helped codify the look of television even before the artisans of postproduction were fully involved in a given program.

Once these two technical conditions existed in television (origination in film and transfer via flying spot scanner), pressures to change production aesthetics itself would intensify. Achieving the so-called film-look in shooting style became a production cliché in the 1980s. Originally, film-style video simply referred to the shift from three-camera live in-studio TV to remote single-camera shooting that became popular in the late 1970s. Electronic news gathering (ENG) changed to electronic field production (EFP) for more discriminating producer-practitioners. But this early shift in the way that video shoots in the field were organized—to ENG and EFP—was mostly logistical, since it had as much to do with camera and recorder placement as anything else. It was not until the 1980s that a more intensive change began to occur within the visual frame itself.

Improvements in lighting developed alongside EFP, and a subsequent shift to charged-couple devices (CCD) in cameras (rather than conventional tubes) afforded producers greater subtlety in visualizing their images.[19] It is, obviously, unlikely that technical changes alone intensified the image in television. Formal changes in genre and narrative greatly impacted the rise of televisuality. Industrywide though, there was an increased interest in transforming television images into complex, subtle, and malleable graphic fields. It is likely, given this shift, that formal and narrational changes provided the ideational resource required by an industrial transformation of this scale.[20] MTV and *Miami Vice* certainly were landmark programming developments that changed the way that television looked.[21] These changes have been discussed in detail elsewhere, so I will merely reiterate that distinctive programming forms and shows like these provided the conceptual framework—that is, the audience expectation and the cultural capital—needed to effect a shift in the televisual discourse. If film origination and Rank-Cintel transfers provided, in Brian Winston's terms, the "technical competence" needed for a change in the television industry, then the new highly stylized shows like *Miami Vice* and *Crime Stories* and MTV provided the ideational requirement for industry changes in the 1980s.[22] By the time feature-film director Barry Levinson was showcased on network television in 1993, the importance of televisual transfer technology was clear. Each episode of Levinson's *Homicide* opened with stitched-together footage shot on a primitive, spring-wound cast-off 16mm Bolex camera and feature-style images shot on 35mm. This mixing and matching of emulsion and format types, and the manipulation of colored filtered effects and black-and-white stock, were all possible because Rank-style transfers provided extreme options for stylistic control and reworking, even after the primetime footage was in the can.[23]

Program Individuation

While new stocks and transfer technologies reinforced and enabled one influential televisual ideal—film-style video—programming practice, acting, and promotional considerations encouraged a second industrial mythology: program individuation. [. . .]

It is commonly understood in industry parlance today that each show should have its own "look."[24] Even relatively traditional-looking and visually restrained shows like *Cagney and Lacey* postured an identifiable visual stance. The show's DP [Director of Photography] explains how taking over the show also meant taking over the burden of its established look. "They wanted a more visual look, and to me that meant they wanted more contrast."[25] After choosing a film stock that gave them this contrast, the company also intentionally used long lenses in "over half of the shots" in the 1986–1987 season in order "to flatten space."[26] In addition to the practical effect of making downtown L.A. look like New York, both devices (long lenses and contrasty stock) helped to *stylistically individuate* the show. In competition with other primetime shows, this artificially constructed sense of place and geography was merely part of the overall effect that resulted from the show's distinctive stylization.

But shows like *Cagney and Lacey* only hint at the increased role that visual style played in other dramas. In the network dramatic series *Covington Cross*, the DP waxed eloquent about the historicity of their "flamboyant" signature style: "Smoke is the key element, because at that time, smoke was the source of energy for everything. At night, everything [in the show] looks as if it is lit by firelight, candlelight, or flambeaus. I'm using a quarter-fog filter on almost everything." He goes on to justify this excessive use of flammable and incendiary devices based on the assumption of an inherent physical need in television. In "TV where you have a smaller image, you need to go in stronger to create an atmosphere. I am also trying to light with a fair bit of contrast. People have always said you mustn't be too contrasty for TV."[27] In one fell swoop, then, this primetime cameraperson throws out the traditional view of the medium in its entirety. Precisely because the TV screen is smaller than that of film, *producers need stronger stylization*, not the weakened style that academic theorists have dichotomized.

Consider in addition the following breakthrough claim from the production of CBS's *Beauty and the Beast*: "We're very proud of *Beauty and the Beast* because the cinematography is really very important to it. The producers feel strongly enough about it to give the director of photography a credit at the beginning of the show rather than at the end—and *Beauty* is the only episodic TV show that does it that way."[28] Note that the programming breakthrough here is described as the process by which the shooter is given an unusual amount of creative power and a visible position in the credits along with other "above-the-line" personnel and talent. Not only was the show excessively stylish, but it was self-conscious about that trait. The show's unique style was centered around the heavy use of smoke, colored gels, Rembrandt lighting, fog- and halo-effect filters.[29] Writers for the show have discussed the unusually low ratio of total script pages to program running time.[30] With *Beauty and the Beast*, scripts frequently involved twenty to thirty pages of dialogue, rather than the forty to sixty pages typical of hour-long dramas. This sheer reduction in script verbiage challenges the most conventional wisdom about television style. When comparing their quality to highly visual film scripts, for instance, one frequently writes-off the quality of TV scripts as being too wordy, too explicit, or too expository. In worst case situations, television scripts can have dialogue that reads more like a director's cues, with overly explicit and redundant dialogue that repeats obvious visual information. In worst case scenarios, one actor may announce to another, "I think we should go to the door" rather than simply going to the door. In television, many producers have typically depended on the word to carry the story. Rationales for this verbal privilege are frequently based on the argument that television's low resolution image is unable *by itself* to communicate essential narrative detail.

This orthodox wisdom about the centrality of verbiage and exposition in television scriptwriting now appears to be changing. Shows like *Beauty and the Beast* not only minimize talkiness, they also let an expressive visual style dominate the viewing experience. The fact that the producers of the show hired a poetry consultant as a member of the production staff suggests that even the nature of the script's written word has changed.[31] Script verbiage here is consciously addressed in a poetic and lyrical manner, rather than solely as an expository or action-oriented mode. This kind of shift suggests that even mainstream television can aim to gain viewership and win Emmys by foregrounding embellishment and expressive visuality. This stylization is not latent or subjugated by story either, as it would be in a classical context. Rather, the producers champion their visual style and iconographic accomplishment directly to viewers.

Masquerade

If some recent programs work by selectively intensifying their mise-en-scène around an identifiable look others depend upon a third televisual mythology: a more eclectic and selective use of visual codes better termed "masquerade." That is, whereas *Beauty and the Beast* was known for specific photographic effects (saturated colors, directional lighting, smoke), other shows promote themselves by playing off or parodying cinematic styles. Film history itself becomes a playing field for many of today's television stylists. The award-winning and widely viewed series *Moonlighting* and *thirtysomething* on ABC were among the most visible of these network exercises in television and film history. Both shows toyed with numerous and eclectic visual styles in ironic and self-conscious ways. The knowing display of style became, for *Moonlighting*, an integral part of its performance. Viewers came to expect style references, and they got them in the various presentational guises that *Moonlighting* took on. Moonlighting did film noir; did MTV: did Orson Welles–Greg Toland deep focus; did Capra screwball comedy. In the later seasons of the series, the dramatic content of an individual episode was frequently tied to a specific visual style. What looked at first like aesthetic eclecticism though, became, through its presentational facility and range, a sign of connoisseurship. The boast is not just that such shows can do this or that visual style, but that they can cycle through a range of visual styles with virtuosity.

[. . .]

Moonlighting was not unique in this respect. In fact, many shows by the late 1980s had consciously utilized various methods of retrostyling and the explicit adoption and performance of visual style. By 1989, an episode of the sitcom *Day by Day* literally transformed itself into an episode of the 1960s *The Brady Bunch*. Five minutes into the contemporary program, a corresponding rupture in style occurred. Studio quality state-of-the-art sitcom video gave way to 16mm film origination, even flatter studio lighting, identifiable film grain, and poor camera registration. [. . .]

These increasingly common practices suggest several things. First, primetime audiences by the late 1980s could apparently appreciate and *decode* self-conscious displays of cinematic and televisual form. Second, many shows now began to work not by simply making their mise-en-scène more excessive, but by making their *presentational demeanor* more excessive and sophisticated. In a sense, shows like those mentioned above positioned themselves as *impresarios* of style and aesthetic awareness. Masquerade shows revel in marshaling and displaying aesthetic systems, not just at making images more visual, which they also do. By doing this, by standing back from and acknowledging the form itself, the producers promote the television image as an image-commodity. If televisuality is about signs of excess, then its semiotic abundance comes not just from the frame that DPs and gaffers argue about, but also from the very broad cultural and pictorial traditions that practitioners can now bring to bear in producing shows.[32] For this reason, one cannot simply talk about televisuality's two-dimensional signs. One must shift from a compositional discourse to a pictorial and cultural one in order to understand televisuality's excesses. By manipulating pictorial sign systems, whether from film history or pop culture, television boasts to the viewer that it is a master performer of visuality, a master of stylistic masquerade.

In the past, television genres were defined by the fact that their narrative formulas were fundamentally static and repetitive, while only their situations changed from week to week.[33] Style was even more static than formula given the fact that style frequently came as part of the development package—it was dictated by the facilities and soundstages that housed the productions. This *static formula-dynamic situation* concept rang true of television in the 1960s and 1970s. Now, however, in many program and nonprogram forms, the stylistic and presentational aspects are the very elements that change on a weekly basis, while characterization becomes the medium's static and repetitive given from episode to episode. With *China Beach, thirtysomething, The Wonder*

Years, Quantum Leap, Northern Exposure, and, yes, even less prestigious shows like *McGyver*, the viewer is now encouraged to speculate before each episode about what the program might *aesthetically transform itself into this week:* documentary, dreamstate, oral history, music video, homage to Hollywood, or expressionist fantasy.

Electronic cinematography

[. . .] The new mythology of film-style video, with its emphasis on visuality, has permeated non-primetime and video-origination programming as well. Even if producers do not have the resources to light and shoot television shows on film, many simply make their videos more cinematic and stylish by electronic means. The low-budgeted syndicated police show *The Street*—emblematic of the newly popularized genre, "reality programming"—was shot on video in urban locations and at night. At a frantic pace that enabled the crew to cover 125 script pages in five days, this show could in no way be described as prestige primetime telefilm material. Given this frenzied production schedule, the producers claimed, ironically, that they shot with a film aesthetic in order to achieve a "TV feel." Director of photography Rob Draper was hailed for treating "the camera as 'another film emulsion.' Ignoring the factory specified 125 ASA, Draper runs the Sony BVP-5 video camera at 800 ASA, and at +9dB. This results in a grainy feeling with electronic noise. Combining this technique with a spare-like lighting style gives the show its film look and documentary TV feel."[34] Although the producers argue that this gives them "a realistic look" for the show, what they actually get is an image far from illusionistic. In fact, by electronically boosting video gain (+9dB) to compensate for low-light actually only succeeds in filling the image with snowy electronic noise, or electronic grain.

The assumption here, then, is that viewers decipher noisy and low-resolution video images as both realistic and as somehow cinematic. Realism depends apparently on graphic opacity, rather than on representational illusionism. Far from clear or highly resolved, these images are forcibly videoized and degraded through the imposition of noise, but are somehow read as real nevertheless. So much for André Bazin's ontology of realism, a theory that constructed realism around a mode of visual and transparent replication, not around the graphic muddiness fabricated by this kind of television.[35] The frequent use of electronic degradation in "reality shows" does suggest that viewers can discriminate among the various presentational styles: from the film history masquerades choreographed in film-origination to the *ontological* obsessions of electronic origination. Both modes, the cinematic and videographic, are authorized by the narrative and generic assumptions of specific shows. In the case of *The Street*, all "film style" turns out to mean is minimal or nonexistent lighting, not elaborate motion-picture production value. Electronic noise, then, is considered as much a televisual code as are high-resolution transfers of richly toned film negative with their *absence* of grain. Each distinct look is tied to a specific referent, and shows are individuated by using either code. So powerful was the mythology of cinema's visual prowess, that even video noise could be conceptually retrofitted by television as a badge of stylistic distinction.

Commercial advertising

Madison Avenue—defined and fueled by stylization—influenced the emergence of televisual exhibitionism as much as the family of cinematic mythologies: the film look, program individuation, and masquerade. If American television had an avant-garde in the 1980s it was surely primetime television commercial production. Commercial spots continue to be the most dynamic sites for visual experimentation on television. Packed into tiny temporal slugs of thirty and sixty seconds, advertising spots were probably the first type of programming to exploit the discursive and emotive power of hyperactive and excessive visual style. Standard production wisdom says that a spot should focus on one major message in its short duration.[36] Given the limited potential for verbal discourse in short spots, then, nonverbal mechanisms are much more important in triggering the needed emotional appeals that drive home the spot's intended message to the viewer.

Well before MTV, in the late 1960s and 1970s, commercial spots learned the advantages of engaging viewers through the lower-sensory channels, through sight, sound, and tactility. Over several decades primetime advertising mastered a process in which the viewer is simultaneously flooded by a range of sensory signs. Visual style became visually excessive and temporally hyperactive on network television, one might argue, because ads must fight for the attention of distracted viewers during breaks from the program. Ad sequences with shot durations of one second or less now frequent both network and cable television. Ad cinematography, on the other hand, is frequently defined by its heavy use of designer filters (especially grads, diffusion, and colored effects). Primetime spots are, to use industry parlance, excessively "lensed." Cutting in contemporary commercial practice makes classic Soviet montage look lethargic. Since television really is about advertising, about selling viewers to advertisers, it is important to survey at least some of the favored televisual manifestations found in commercial spots during this period.

Digital compositing

The clean European design and controlled studio product photography of an earlier period gave way in the early 1980s to ads that pushed television and its resolution to their limits. Producers sought to make video look like film, and talented newcomers left music video production for commercial advertising and program production. In the process, stylishness became a requisite for productions and products that sought memorability. The new commercial style infiltrated network programs as well. Title sequences in many programs began adapting the new frenetic visual style from spots. Even the segues to ads within programs became less overt as a result. A direct influence of MTV style showed in the *Saturday Night Live* title sequence of the 1986 season. Layer after layer of live-action imagery was artificially composited together. When broadcast, *SNL* cast members and digitized New York landmarks unscrolled past viewers on the screen. In this heightened performance of technical wizardry and hipness, no static frames were visible; and no shots existed in any traditional sense of the word. Instead, a realistically photographed, but graphically dense and continuous scroll unwound for viewers. The weeks that followed *SNL*'s use of the digital scroll saw widespread use of the mode by advertisers, who profited from the new and highly stylized visual effect.

Coca-Cola used the same effect to promote its newly announced product Cherry Coke. Significantly, they hired the Emmy-winning co-originator of the *Saturday Night Live* intro, John Kraus, to work on their piece as director of photography. While the final effect in both instances was dependent mostly upon the digital graphics capabilities of the new Charlex system and graphic Paintbox, the footage was all shot on high-end video. According to DP Kraus, the key to the success of the spot and intro was the use of a complicated film-style lighting scheme.[37] The lighting design aimed for directionality, 3-D modeling, and a complex and shifting color scheme tied to specific objects or persons in the unfolding graphic scroll. All light was to be motivated in someway in order to fight the flatness and artificiality associated with most video effects. In addition, each of the multiple visual components and icons, filmed individually, was given a specific visual code or look. "We lit Marilyn [Monroe] with hard edge, 1950s light and matched up two shots of her with and without her coat. When a werewolf who pops out of a movie screen, turns into a handsome man after sipping Cherry Coke, and then turns up later on a rooftop with a lovely woman, we kept him in black and white to make that connection. We lit his date in a very rich light to convey glamour."[38] All of these "actions" actually happened only in the electronic ether. Cinematography here was essentially a process of *collecting* individual elements and fabricating virtual worlds through imagined light sources. Filmic and televisual composition, then, depends heavily upon electronic postproduction. Compositing demands and rewards directors who can skillfully choose from a wide range of specific visual lighting codes and styles. A style is no longer construed in a classical sense as a unifying formal element. Instead, in this type of compositing practice, styles are more like codified cards that are collected, layered, juxtaposed, and played with in a process of electronic postproduction. The frameless, digital environment that resulted in the *SNL* opening and Coke spots stands apart from the television image theorized in traditional media analysis. The penchant for visual density and the self-conscious orchestration of stylistic and lighting codes—evident in *SNL*/Coca-Cola's Emmy-winning compositing "break-through"—began to permeate the industry on other fronts as well.

The anti-ad

Whereas new videographic methods like digital compositing demanded of directors facility and skill in manipulating style codes—that is, the director needed to collect and combine a *lot* of imagery for a short amount of screen time—other commercial production practices foregrounded the issue of televisual style in a very different way. Visually aggressive "anti-ads" also became industry trendsetters in the 1980s. Consider the following industry explanation of the origins and aesthetic methods of the anti-ads: "Directors had been playing with Super-8/16mm black-and-white film for years, and these tools entered the commercial mainstream, as in Paula Grief and Peter Kagan's 'Revolution' for Nike. Down and dirty film techniques made $200,000 spots look like home movies. Gritty was chic."[39] A self-conscious revolution had started, then, in and with the Nike ads. The "revolution" was not, however, based on high production values nor did it emphasize verbal messages. The visual stuff of the image itself—emulsion grain, flash-frames, scratches, in short *the very elements that decades of production had sought to hide or disavow*—became in the emergence of televisuality part of the content itself. The down-and-dirty physical image that defined the Nike ad campaign was repeated numerous times with other corporate campaigns in the months that followed. What was it, one is led to ask, about raw footage and acts of physical aggression against the image that inspired producers and attracted consumers? The great irony of this trend and the many anti-ad campaigns that followed, was economic. Commercial spot production budgets, which had only recently ascended to the quarter-million dollar range, now found themselves facing crude, and ostensibly inexpensive, forms of image degradation. Super-8 footage, amateur-looking but street smart, gave to the emerging televisual repertoire a new and influential code—a kind of "televisual povera."[40] What was being sold to American consumers of the 1980s was the street: the edgy urban environment, a raw and racially peopled existence that was as alien to Reagan's image of America as it was to the classical styles of earlier advertising. What was being sold, then, was an attitude, an ambience, and an image of America that was street smart, young, and raw.

An allied sensibility infused the Levi's 501 ad campaign produced by Foote, Cone, and Belding.[41] With the Levi's spots, the film stock and format were larger than Nike's super-8, and the distinctive look was colorized blue rather than black and white, but the visual codes were the same. Jerky handheld camera work, long lenses, and extremely abrupt cuts focused on hip Caucasian adolescents termed by the admen "urban cowboys." The message was really just a mood and a lifestyle. Levi's ideal buyer fantasized about hiply slumming it on the streets. No verbal discourse even survived in these spots. The "anti-ad" Levi's 501 campaign, like other high-end commercial productions during the period, was selling a specific lifestyle and attitude, not just a product.[42] The images and sounds were stylized but self-consciously fleeting and ambient. In the evolution of advertising, the verbal strata—along with the physical product itself—was no longer even a requisite part of commercial spots.

The documercial

Clio award- winning director Joe Pytka solidified spontaneity into a systematic visual code for use in what he coined "documercials"—a strategy that attempted to counter Madison Avenue's own flash with "authenticity." Visually confusing, aggressive, but thematically open ads by Pytka followed for the Wang business computer corporation. John Nathan invoked the same documercial codes for AT&T in its campaign. In Nathan's acclaimed "Washroom" spot for AT&T an executive panics when he discovers that the huge phone system he bought for his company is suddenly obsolete. " 'You don't think they'll fire me?' he asks a colleague, who suppresses his gloat. The film is grainy, the lighting funereal. The camera whizpans between the two young men, desperately trying to record the conversation, a blur of paranoia, a career literally in the toilet".[43] Apparitions, paranoia, whippans to marked corporate men. These were advertising's hallmarked displays of authenticity and angst. Commercial director Nathan lauds his own innovations. "Now we're getting at what people are really saying and thinking." Thinking? Hyperactive camerawork, film grain, and visual and editorial desperation seem more related to fleeting sensation and apparition than they do to thought. Nevertheless, the director's hyped interpretation is important, for it shows that a systematic process was going on in the evolution of commercial production style to *find apt visual codes* for cultural preoccupations; to create and codify visual signifiers for the viewer—of thought, sensation, desperation.

In Pytka's commercial productions for Wang computers, the style is no less obscure and is intentionally disorienting. The viewer is never allowed, for instance, to see the whole picture or whole scene. In one spot, the camera is locked down on the back of a man's head. The concealed subject is talking to a vague, anthropomorphic shape that is pacing back and forth in the background. In another spot, two men listen to a speaker phone, but the viewer never sees their entire bodies. which are continuously and aggressively cropped. In a third spot, two shapes walk down a long hallway toward the camera and are entirely out of focus. These standing and shifting blurs of light and shadow finally dissolve to an all white logo, and the graphic message: "Call Wang."

What then, do these new and influential anti-approaches to television production style, found in both programs and nonprogram broadcast materials, have in common? Consider their formal operations. *The Street* added video and electronic noise to the image. Nike added extreme emulsion grain and contrast. Levi added jerky and disorienting camera work and unnatural colors. The producers of AT&T spots added washed-out funereal lighting and whip-pans. The *Washroom* spots for Wang used impossibly shallow depth of field and constantly obstructed the viewer's line of sight. These formal tactics have one general stylistic principle in common. They all take otherwise state-of-the-art imaging systems and *degenerate* them through technical and stylistic flaws. Levinson flawed his primetime show *Homicide* in the same way.

This kind of active and pervasive self-destruction and *flawing of the image* does not produce, in any conventional sense, a realism based on illusion. One might argue from this practice that the image-flawing trend belies my thesis that there has been an increased stylization in the television image. But this criticism only makes sense if visuality is defined by degrees of optical resolution. In fact, televisuality is not dependent upon higher and higher resolution. Instead, imagistic and stylistic violations continually draw attention to the television screen and to the *status of its image* as an image. Strategies of image annihilation are far removed from the goals of classical media image making, precisely because they work to show-off such actions as stylistic marks and stylistic accomplishments. There really is no argument that these types of spots and codes were received as visual codes either. The industry press interpreted the trend immediately. One advertising producer, Stockler, explained the growing sense that such ads were over-kill and trendy: "Handheld died when it began, critics said. Some work went beyond cinema verité, to video obscurité: Product was mystifyingly submerged."[44]

Stylistic fashions come and go, but it is worth considering the reasons that producers and agencies opted for self-annihilating visual tactics. Nathan explains that "the cliché-ridden vision of what goes on in the world—the domain of the TV commercial *until now*—has begun to pale and is perceived to be irrelevant to consumers."[45] Production people, then, counter the critique of the industry as clichéd by arguing that *their* cutting-edge methods and preoccupation with style are both relevant and interpretable to consumer-viewers. The image-destructive style perpetuated by anti-ads and documercials should really be seen, then, as a counter move, as a strategy to regain viewers. Production tendencies, even apparent antistylistic techniques, were hardened into marketable and reproducible displays that more accurately signified the thought and sensibility of America's changing consumers. Although the commercial advertising industry pretends to be a paragon of dynamic change and innovation, it also is a process that immediately hardens stylistic practice into an assembly-line succession of variant looks. Once made public, Madison Avenue's issuance of codes can then be taken over by other agencies, for different products and for different genres.

[. . .]

This dizzying array of poses suggests that advertising brings to television not just a range of styles but an obsessive ritual and appetite for stylistic differentiation. *Advertising teaches television* in more ways than one: it is a hungry proving ground for new televisual production technologies; it is a leaky cache of creative personnel that denarrativizes television; it is an omnipresent aesthetic farm-system for primetime. Advertising's budgets, however, are far from minor league. In contrast to primetime's per-minute production costs, advertising budgets dwarf television's financial commitment. Advertising production, that is, gets more stylistic "bang for the buck" than primetime or off-prime programming. For this reason, commercial spot production also underscores and reinforces one of the driving mythologies behind televisual exhibitionism: the idea that overproduction and stylistic excess provide industrial leverage and corporate marks of distinction. *The televisual mode of production, then, is really an ad industry-proven mode of over-production.*

[. . .]

Notes

1   C. F. Jenkins, "Radio Photographs, Radio Movies, and Radio Vision," *Journal of Society of Motion Picture Engineers* (May 1923), 81.
2   R. R. Beal, "RCA Developments in Television," *Journal of Society of Motion Picture Engineers* (August 1937), 143.
3   A good and accessible source for this early technical literature is Jeffrey Friedman, ed., *Milestones in Motion Picture and Television Technology: The SMPTE 75th Anniversary Collection* (White Plains, NY: Society of Motion Pictures and Technical Engineers, 1991), especially 97–233. The word "television" was later added to the professional organization's prewar name, SMPE.
4   Raymond Williams, *Television, Technology and Cultural Form* (New York: Schocken Books, 1974).
5   William Boddy, *Fifties Television* (Urbana: University of Illinois Press, 1990), especially chapter 1.
6   From comments by Ray Peschke, quoted in *Film and Video* (November 1991), 74.
7   "Episodic Television has always had to narrow its scope because of lack of money, but digital technology can open up all kinds of possibilities," states Hal Harrison, vice president of postproduction, Viacom. Stalter, "Working in the New Post Environment," 100.

8   SMPTE time-code editing refers to an electronic timing and identification scheme standardized by the Society for Motion Picture and Television Engineers. This time-code system laid down a stream of digital audio blips onto an existing audio or address track on the recorded videotape stock. Once done, each video frame had now been assigned an identifying address that any standardized editing controller could find and cut on automatically. Frame accuracy in editing was but one of the advantages of this system.

9   Sony, direct-mail advertising insert, included as a promotional insert in *Video Systems* (June 1993), 16–17.

10   Iain Blair, "*Needful Things*: Producer Jack Cummins, Director Fraser Heston and Cinematographer Tony Westman Bring Their production of the Stephen King Novel to the Pacific Northwest," *Film and Video* (April 1993), 99.

11   Quote from "Small Screen Shooters: Four Distinguished Cinematographers Discuss the Craft of Shooting Film for Episodic Television," *Millimeter* (April 1988), 143.

12   Ibid., 142.

13   See especially Harry Matthias and Richard Patterson, *Electronic Cinematography: Achieving Photographic Control Over the Video Image* (Belmont, Calif.: Wadsworth, 1985), and Anton Wilson, *Anton Wilson's Cinema Workshop* (Los Angeles: American Society of Cinematographers, 1983), 243–297. Other books that examine both technical and aesthetic issues in the film versus video image discourse include David Viera, *Lighting for Film and Electronic Cinematography* (Belmont, Calif.: Wadsworth, 1993), and the introductory text, Larry Ward, *Electronic Moviemaking* (Belmont, Calif.: Wadsworth, 1990).

14   Quote of Eastman kodak executive from "Electronic Imagery," *American Cinematographer* (June 1987), 89.

15   I am, of course, comparing only the quality of *color* film stocks between the two periods. Some of the 35mm black-and-white negative stocks used in the 1950s, while much slower in light sensitivity than many modern color stocks, could achieve the kind of rich tonality impossible for any color stock to render, if lit properly. But this comparison is a bit like comparing apples and oranges.

16   Ad for Tiffen filters, *Film and Video* (November 1991), 71.

17   From Richard Schafer, "Choice of Transfers: Film to Tape," *American Cinematographer* (September 1986), 97.

18   Ibid., 97.

19   In practical terms CCDs replaced vacuum tubes in cameras with rectangular chips that were comprised of grids of light-sensitive microscopic materials. This field of points corresponded roughly to the pixels that make up the grid on a computer screen. The more points or pixels in a grid, the higher the visual resolution.

20   It is also likely that this transformation—this intensive reinvestment in primetime production—may be related to the slowly atrophying number of feature films that were being produced each year during the early 1980s. The availability of both ideational and labor surpluses in Hollywood during this period might partly explain the renewed focus on primetime production practice in the 1980s. The complexities of this relationship between feature film and primetime are, of course, beyond the scope of this book.

21   For an in-depth analysis of the ideology of MTV's visual style, see E. Ann Kaplan, *Rocking Around the Clock*, Todd Gitlin gives an excellent feel for the visual look and demeanor of *Miami Vice* in *Watching Television*.

22   Brian Winston, *Misunderstanding Media* (London: Routlege, Kegan Paul, 1986), discussed and applied to video in Roy Armes, *On Video* (New York: Routledge, Chapman and Hall), 206–8.

23   *Film and Video* (May 1993), 112–14.

24   Gone are the days when one might describe TV's sound stage, high-key look as a zero-degree television style. The term is from Roland Barthes, *Writing Degree Zero* (New York: Hill and Wang, 1953).

25   Quote from Ed Plante, in Bob Fisher, "Cagney and Lacey: The New York Look in L.A.," *American Cinematographer* (January 1987), 88.

26   Ibid., 88.

27   Alan Hume, DP, *Covington Cross*, quoted in Ober, "Cover Story: Teamwork on Covington Cross," 3.

28   From Stevan Larner, ASC, in "Beauty and the Beast: God Bless the Child," *American Cinematographer* (April 1989), 71. The producer goes on: "It's a very creative show and any input is greatly appreciated."

29   Ibid., 71.

30   Eric Estrin and Michael Berlin in conversations with the author, California State University, Long Beach, California, March 1990.

31   Ibid.

32   While many of the newer craftspeople and cinematographers have now actually had aesthetic and film historical training in university film schools, even middle-aged and older DPs who immigrate to prime-time from feature filmmaking bring with them a tradition that values interdisciplinary research and

aesthetic sensitivity to cultural image making. For one of the best single sources that betrays the DP's not uncommon interest in art, art history, still photography, design, and architecture, see Dennis Shaefer and Larry Salvato, *Masters of Light* (Berkeley: University of California Press, 1986). Of course, even if a contemporary television DP had never been to film school or mastered the art historical sensitivity of his ASC brethren (a consciousness seldom limited to an awareness of Rembrandt lighting), he or she would have to have been amnesiatic for the past decade to be ignorant of the design and art historical consciousness that has pervaded commercials and print advertising.

33 Horace Newcomb uses this tension between the static formula and the need for some generic change as a partial basis for his proposal that continuity is one of the chief aspects of a television aesthetic in Newcomb, *Television: The Most Popular Art* (New York: Anchor, 1974). Thomas Schatz does a similar thing in *Hollywood Genres: Formulas, Film-making and the Studio System* (New York: Random House, 1981).

34 From David Heuring, "The Street: Shooting Video with an Eye to Film," *American Cinematographer* (June 1988), 73.

35 André Bazin, "An Ontology of the Photographic Image," *What Is Cinema?*, trans. Hugh Gray (Berkeley: University of California Press, 1967), 9–16. What has changed obviously, is the conventionality and cultural form of realism. That is, audiences and makers alike now can read degraded electronic realism, because they understand, to some degree, that the look results from technologies very different from those that produce photographic realism.

36 Robert Hilliard quotes S.J. Paul of *Television/Radio Age* as describing the temporal pressure in which "a mood is created . . . and a sales point is made," that is, a singular objective for both mood and point. Robert L. Hilliard, *Writing for Television and Radio* (Belmont, Calif.: Wadsworth, 1981), 41.

37 This information is from an article on the spots by Brooke Sheffield Comer, "Music Video That Looks like Film," *American Cinematographer* (September 1986).

38 Ibid., 95.

39 From Bruce Stockler, "Seducing Reality: Documentaries Mix Truth and Fashion," *Millimeter* (May 1988), 48.

40 I am taking the word "povera," or poverty, to describe this genre of televisuality, from the continental European tradition that described conceptual and environmental art of the 1960s and early 1970s as "art povera." In short, this low-tech, hand-made anti-art was seen during the period as an extreme form of aesthetic and cultural radicality. The radical intent of art povera is ironic given the product oriented aims of the Nike Corporation.

41 Stockler, 49.

42 Ads have always sold the sizzle rather than the steak, the sensation rather than the product. Within this tradition, however, Levi's anti-ads are worth noting for the *degree* to which they avoid both descriptions of the product and also representations of the product. Anti-ads are far removed aesthetically from the product shot aesthetic that glamorized goods in print and broadcast during the preceding two decades. Levi's anti-ads left one with crude apparitions and fragments of activities on the street, not sensations of the product. In advertising's ongoing tactic of sensory surrogacy, the sensory connection to the product in the anti-ad became more tenuous and open than ever.

43 Stockler, 48.

44 Ibid., 47.

45 Ibid., 47 (italics mine).

Bibliography

Allen, S. (1990) "Lighting for Television: Faster Filmstocks Are Changing the Ways that Cinematographers Approach Their Work," *Film and Video*, June: 47.

Barthes, R. (1953) *Writing Degree Zero*, New York: Hill and Wang.

Bazin, A. (1967) *What is Cinema?*, H. Gray (trans.), Berkeley: University of California Press.

Beal, R.R. (1937) "RCA Developments in Television," *Journal of Society of Motion Picture Engineers*, August: 143.

Beardsley, M. and Wimsatt, W.K. (1987) "The Intentionalist Fallacy" in M. Weitz (ed.) *Problems in Aesthetics*, New York: Macmillan.

Blair, I. (1993) "Needful Things . . ." *Film and Video* April: 99.

Boddy, W. (1990) *Fifties Television*, Urbana: University of Illinois Press.

Bordwell, D. Staiger, J. and Thompson, K. (1985) *The Classical Hollywood Style: Film Style and the Mode of Production to 1960*, New York: Columbia University Press.

Finnerman, G.P. (1989) "Here's Looking at You Kid," *American Cinematographer* April: 70–1.

Fisher, B. (1987) "Cagney and Lacey: The New York Look in LA," *American Cinematographer* January: 88.

Friedman, J. (ed.) (1991) *Milestones in Motion Picture and Television Technology: The SMPTE 75th Anniversary Collection*, White Plains, NY: Society of Motion Pictures and Technical Engineers.

Gans, H. (1974) *Popular Culture and High Culture: An Analysis and Evaluation of Taste*, New York: Basic Books.

Gradus, B. (1981) *Directing the Television Commercial*, Los Angeles: Directors Guild of America.

Heuring, D. (1988) "The Street: Shooting Video with an Eye to Film," *American Cinematographer* June: 73.

Hilliard, R. (1981) *Writing for Television and Radio*, Belmont, CA.: Wadsworth.

Jameson, F. (1983) "Postmodernism and Consumer Society" in H. Foster (ed.) *The Anti-Aesthetic*, Port Townsend, WA.: Bay Press.

Jenkins, C.F. (1923) "Radio Photographs, Radio Movies, and Radio Vision," *Journal of Society of Motion Picture Engineers*, May: 81.

Larner, S. (1989) "Beauty and the Beast: God Bless the Child," *American Cinematographer* April: 71.

Matthias, H. and Patterson, R. (1985) *Electronic Cinematography: Achieving Photographic Control Over the Video Image*, Belmont, CA.: Wadsworth.

Newcomb, H. (1974) *Television: The Most Popular Art*, New York: Anchor.

Ober, J. (1992–93) "Cover Story: Team Work on Covington Cross," *In Camera*, Eastman Kodak, Spring: 4.

Oblowitz, M. (1989) "Close-ups," *Millimeter* February: 196.

Schafer, R. (1986) "Choice of Transfers: Film to Tape," *American Cinematographer* September: 97.

Schatz, T. (1981) *Hollywood Genres: Formulas, Filmmaking and the Studio System*, New York: Random House.

Shaefer, D. and Salvato, L. (1986) *Masters of Light*, Berkeley: University of California Press.

Sheffield Comer, B. (1986) "Music Video That Looks Like Film," *American Cinematographer* September.

Stalter, K. (1993) "Working in the New Post Environment," *Film and Video* April: 100.

Stockler, B. (1988) "Seducing Reality: Documentaries Mix Truth and Fashion," *Millimeter* May: 48.

Viera, D. (1993) *Lighting for Film and Electronic Cinematography*, Belmont, CA.: Wadsworth.

Ward, L. (1990) *Electronic Moviemaking*, Belmont, CA.: Wadsworth.

Williams, R. (1974) *Television, Technology and Cultural Form*, New York: Schocken Books.

Wilson, A. (1983) *Anton Wilson's Cinema Workshop*, Los Angeles: American Society of Cinematographers.

Winston, B. (1986) *Misunderstanding Media*, London: Routledge.

Chapter 19

JANE ROSCOE

BIG BROTHER AUSTRALIA

Performing the 'real' twenty-four-seven

BOTH LOCALLY AND INTERNATIONALLY, primetime television has changed considerably in the past 10 years. There has been a general shift away from drama, long-running serials and current affairs shows, towards more factually-based light entertainment programming (Brunsdon *et al.*, 2001; Mapplebeck, 1998). These shifts are widely regarded by conservative as well as left-liberal media commentators as symptoms of changes within media culture, popular culture and in the relationship between the media and the public sphere. Conscripted into narratives of decline, these changes are held to reflect an impoverishment of public discourses, to herald the onset of tabloidization or, specifically, to demonstrate the reduction of popular factual entertainment (commonly referred to as reality TV) to the sensational and voyeuristic (See Kilborn, 1994; Dovey, 2000; Hill, 2000).

There is a tendency to use the term 'tabloidization' rather liberally (and incorrectly), applying it beyond its original usage in relation to newspapers, to a range of television programmes including talk shows and docusoaps (Langer, 1998; Lumby, 1999; Turner, 1999). Discussions that describe popular factual entertainment programmes in such a way tend to lump them all together as 'cheap and dumb', while providing little in the way of specific analysis. In the deluge of commentary, little attention is paid to the differences between programmes (for example between *Big Brother* and *Survivor*), and scant consideration of why local and international audiences might engage with these forms. Accordingly, little attention is given to understanding their significance to broader changes taking place in contemporary television production.

Debate cannot be moved along if an idealized, consolidated formation of *Big Brother* is simply conscripted onto an already formed position, as an exemplary text put into the service of a highly political argument. In stepping aside from this tradition, I want to provide a more specific analysis of *Big Brother* which addresses issues of production through interviews with the programme-makers, as well as considering the textual strategies employed, and the various forms of engagement offered to audiences.

Such an analysis can be the starting point for a very different conversation about popular factual entertainment. The starting point for this analysis is an understanding of *Big Brother* as a hybrid format that is both innovative and engaging, and as such warrants serious critical attention. Such programmes are not cheap alternatives to proper documentary or to drama, but rather a response to changes in international broadcasting contexts in which it is increasingly difficult to fund drama productions, and where traditional documentary formats have found it increasingly difficult to capture audience attention (Kilborn and Izod, 1997). They can also be understood as a more general response to what Dovey (2000) describes as a shift towards first person media, and to what Corner (2000) describes as a post-documentary culture.

Many of these new formats (such as docusoaps and reality gameshows) blur the conventional boundaries between fact and fiction, drama and documentary and between the audience and the text. They defy categorization and are continually stretching and testing the limits of their formats (Corner, 1996, 2000). As we shall see, they make the most of media convergence and span a number of media platforms (telephone, internet, print media, radio and television). Importantly, they provide a central role for the viewer with real opportunities for interactivity. *Big Brother Australia* is a good example of these new television formats, and can be used to discuss some of those broader changes in media and popular cultures.

Big Brother 'down-under'

The *Big Brother* format, developed by Endemol Entertainment in the Netherlands, has proved to be an international success. Having been sold to countries all over the world it has achieved dream ratings in every country bar Sweden and the US. In the UK, 70 per cent of the population claimed to have watched at least one episode of the show, and over 10 million viewers tuned in to watch the final eviction (Hill, in press).

The joint venture in Australia between Southern Star and Endemol has allowed Southern Star to move from drama production into factual and light entertainment programming, and has given Endemol an opportunity to test the Australian market. While *Big Brother* has a standard format, in Australia this basic model has been extended and developed by the incorporation of a number of technical and textual innovations, as well as reflecting the local context. Here the house and the production facilities are located at the Dreamworld theme park on the Gold Coast in Queensland. The house and production buildings are permanent, allowing further *Big Brother* productions to take place here, as well as creating for Dreamworld the opportunity to broadcast their own productions. The decision to join forces with Dreamworld was based on more than a need for initial investments. It also provided an opportunity to manage and harness the public interest in the show by staging events in which the public could participate – in particular, the live eviction shows on Sunday evenings.[1]

The show is huge, with over 170 staff managing material from 25 cameras (7 with remote 'hot head' control, 4 infrared, and 5 full broadcast quality cameras, all in widescreen format) and 36 microphones (12 contestant radio microphones and 20 fixed microphones located around the house and garden). This produces 96 hours of video material a day (into which the audio is fed) which is managed through 2 streams (A and B), recorded and mixed separately. This raw material then forms the basis of the daily shows, the Thursday *Big Brother Uncut, The Saturday Show* and the *Live Eviction Show* as well as feeding the live streams on the web. The production is the largest and most expensive 12-week shoot to hit Australia (Ward, 2001) and, estimated to cost between A$13–16 million, it is far from 'cheap TV'. This is serious television.

A national thing

Big Brother is an international format, and to a certain extent will be the same no matter what its geographical location. However, there are a number of ways in which *Big Brother* performs its Australian-ness and speaks to its local Australian audience. According to Tim Clucas, the network executive in charge of the programme: 'we wanted this to be a real Aussie house, that means relaxed lifestyle, sunshine, backyard pool, backyard BBQ, a real Aussie *Big Brother*'.[2] As a result, the house is very different from some of the overseas versions which have used a compound/

prison-like environment; cheaply made with few home comforts. (The second series of the show in the UK, however, is marked by the changes made to the house; it no longer looks like a prison after its 'Changing Rooms' makeover.) Getting together around the pool and the 'barbie' are central signifiers of a relaxed Australian lifestyle and this is captured in the design and furnishing of the house. The house had to reflect the local, then, but also be a non-issue in the sense that once you take the house out of the equation, the audience is free to focus on the people and their relationships.

It is not only the house and its location on the Gold Coast that expresses a certain conceptualization of Australian national identity; the housemates and their behaviours seem also to express certain ideas about what it is to be Australian. There is a great emphasis in the house on fitness and outdoor activities. The very first morning in the house, Johnny, a personal fitness trainer, conducted a yoga and exercise class. Each morning Johnny can be seen jogging around the garden with at least one other member of the household. Jemma has made weights by filling empty milk cartons with soil, and Christina (the ballerina) can be seen using the fitness balls each morning to do her abdominal exercises and so on. In fact, all of the housemates (except Sarah-Marie) engage in morning exercise rituals and see keeping fit as a top priority.[3] Ben and Blair present other versions of Australian masculinity. They belong to the 'good bloke country' (see Sherborne, 2000), where the men all call each other mate, drink plenty of beer and obsess about football. They like to joke around, but have some ground rules (as Blair noted before the arrival of two intruders, 'it's like when a new player joins the footy team, they have to prove themselves').

The challenges are mostly taken straight from overseas versions with a few notable exceptions; for example, it is possible to do more outdoor challenges because of the weather, and the pool allows for some inventive tasks such as synchronized swimming. While the challenges may not necessarily reflect any national characteristics, Dave English, one of the producers, has noted a cultural difference in terms of how the houseguests respond to and participate in the tasks. Elsewhere, the challenges have played an important role in generating some of the emotional drama and conflict; the tasks have either led to squabbles and recriminations, or have allowed the participants to develop stronger emotional bonds. But apart from lessening the everyday boredom for the Australian housemates, the challenges did not seem to be having the expected effect on the group dynamics. English responds to this by saying:

> It's a cultural thing. . . . They don't seem to give a bugger whether they fail or lose. They seem quite willing to put up with a loss of 50 percent of their money. They say, yeah, its tough but it's only six days and then there'll be another one which we might win, so it doesn't seem to have the bonding or separating effect in this group anyway near as much as it did anywhere else. The proof of that is that they failed the circus thing, but they had a great time doing it. Some of them studiously worked at it individually, but not because anyone else was pressuring them, and they didn't feel they had to do it to not let the team down. It was internally generated. And then when they lost the thing they all cheered and went on having their party, and genuinely didn't give a bugger.[4]

Social experiment or human zoo?

There has been much public discussion around the idea of the programme as both a social experiment and a human zoo. In fact, Tim Clucas describes it in such ways: 'It is a social experiment in many ways, an experiment that every psych lecturer in the world would love to be able to conduct if they had the money.'[5] Psychologists are central to the show and have in many regards given credibility to it as some sort of experiment. Psychologists were central to the selection process, conducting both psychological tests and counselling sessions to weed out those who may not be able to cope. At the website you can access the psychological profiles of the housemates, as well as their vital statistics and star signs (which suggests there are limits to psychology). We are told that Sarah-Marie is a Leo and her psychometric test revealed her to be 'adept at adapting to change'; Jemma is a Capricorn and 'good at de-dramatizing stressful events, as well as good at adapting to change' and so on.

The psychologists continue to play an important role on a day-to-day basis, providing counselling to the housemates whenever they request it. These sessions, conducted in the Diary Room, are filmed but none of this material ever makes it to the television or website. Housemates are assured of confidentiality, and contractually are allowed some privacy in their very public life in the house.

The Saturday Show and *Thursday Uncut* often feature psychologists who provide a framework through which the behaviours of the housemates can be understood, and a motivation for the edited packages of footage. For example in an episode of the uncut show, Dr Cindy Pan provided an analysis of the sexual activities of the house, and provided a psychological framework through which to make sense of the relationship between Christina and Peter. In using psychological terminology, the expert guides the viewer towards a certain type of understanding. For the moment then, the relationship was not a piece of gossip, but an object of scientific interest to be studied and analysed, serving to legitimate both the show and our viewing of somewhat private material.

While the ratings for the show can tell us very little about why and how people are interacting or engaging with *Big Brother* there has been some speculation as to why the show seems to be attracting a large number of older professional women. One suggestion made by programme-makers is that the show provides a site in which the psychological and emotional are fore-grounded, enjoyed and deliberated over. Further, this is the sort of gossip that professional women either do not have time for, or do not have access to, hence their interest in the show.[6] There are some striking similarities here with earlier discussions of soap opera as a women's genre and the importance of gossip to the enjoyment of the form (Ang, 1985). Perhaps it is more useful to talk about this in terms of what Corner (1999: 95) describes as the pleasures of 'para-sociality': the pleasures we can derive from talking about and listening to those discussions of feeling and experiences. While initial ratings may suggest this as gendered, such pleasures are not necessarily confined to women viewers.

While such elements may support the '*Big Brother*-as-psychological inquiry' position, some involved with the production are more cautious about such claims: '[I]t has those elements and I think that's part of its intrigue . . . and many of its redeeming features come from those things, but it's not principally why it's there'.[7]

In the face of criticism about the voyeurism or salacious tendencies of the show, however, it is obvious why the programme-makers would be so keen to promote this pseudo-scientific construction.

There has also been much popular commentary on the idea that the house is a human zoo. Such comments seem to be of little concern to Clucas, who responds: 'and as for a zoo, yeah, there are lots of people who slow down at traffic accidents as well, and this is very similar to that'.[8] Anyone who has been able to visit the house and take a tour through the camera runs (which the crew often refer to as 'the rat runs' – another reference to psychological experiments) will attest to the appropriateness of the term 'human zoo'. As you walk through the darkened corridors, you are reminded of the nocturnal houses of zoos. Everything is very quiet and the fairy lights that mark the route out contribute to the artificiality of the place. These corridors house the five cameras that track along the one-way mirrors, all other cameras are static and inside the house.

Pulling the curtains apart just enough to see in (too much light would alert the houseguests to the location of the cameras) the house, and the housemates are revealed.

As in the nocturnal houses, the housemates are displayed in a simulated 'natural environment'. The layout of the house, the furniture and appliances all suggest 'normality', while at the same time, the wall of mirrors, the bright lighting (outside as well as inside) and the lack of any personal effects remind us of the constructed nature of this site. Just as in the zoo we gaze in wonder at the animals and behaviours, so too, looking into the house we are amazed by seeing them 'in the flesh'.

All about looking

Many commentators have been quick to describe the show as voyeuristic, assuming that is the only way to understand the relationship between the houseguests and the audience. As noted earlier, such debates tend to limit discussions as to the variety of relationships constructed between the audience and the text through their insistence on the exploitative or sensationalist aspects. The house, like the zoo, is a public site in which gazing and looking is not furtive or secretive, but conscious and legitimate. Those inside the house know they are being watched (it is the very premise of the show) and the cameras are not hidden. There is no attempt to pretend that the camera is not there (as in observational documentary, or nature documentary). On the contrary, the show is constructed around the explicit acknowledgement of the cameras. When asked why she wanted to be in the house, Andy exclaimed: 'I like people looking at me.' The housemates are performing for the cameras, for each other and for the television audience. We are all invited to gaze, and to continue gazing. (Interestingly, there has also been much discussion amongst the housemates about *not wanting to be watched*. In one weekday episode, a row broke out between Peter, Blair and Jemma. Jemma has refused to shower naked because she does not want the public to see her in that way. While Peter and Blair responded to her by saying that they were supposed to be acting naturally as they would in their 'real' lives, she responded by saying that it *wasn't real life, but television*.)

Voyeurism is not necessarily the most useful or appropriate way to describe the relation between the audience and the housemates. Perhaps it is more a performance of exhibitionism and a satisfaction of scopophiliac tendencies. While viewing *Big Brother* may not necessarily be about sexual pleasures, it does offer the pleasure (so central to documentary) of watching events unfold before our eyes, coupled with a sense that the housemates are arranging the play themselves without a script. The fact that the show exists in real time further contributes to this experience of watching a live event unfold. There is also the possibility of gaining pleasure from looking at people who are a bit like us. These are real and ordinary people, not professional actors, and there are therefore possibilities for identification. This in part would explain the reason Sarah-Marie has been such a popular housemate; people describe her as 'real' and 'ordinary', just like us. *Big Brother*, like the docusoaps before it, has taken the mundane aspects of life that are usually excluded from our television screens and placed them at the centre of the show.

There are pleasures in seeing such mundane domestic elements on screen that cannot be described as voyeuristic. However, if voyeurism is an inappropriate means of understanding the relationship between the programme and the audience, it may still be appropriate to describe the relationship between the housemates and those looking in through the corridors that surround the house. You are aware that the housemates cannot see you as you peer through the windows, but the experience of thinking that you see them looking back is unnerving and uncomfortable. The feeling of being caught watching (which feels like shame) is a physical sensation so strong as to override any rational understanding of the situation.

The 'living soap'

Rather than describe *Big Brother* as a reality gameshow, the programme-makers prefer to call it a 'real-life soap':

> When I started someone said to me, well, really it's a soapie where the actors get to write the script as they go along, and that is so close to the truth. So, instead of the director directing it, they run the agenda and we simply make every facility available to cover what it is they do. From that I was able to get a much clearer idea of what was expected of me as a producer of it.[9]

Big Brother draws on the kind of docusoap primarily concerned with personal and emotional issues, in effect the smaller dramas of everyday life (Bethell, 1999). *Big Brother* is constructed around the housemates, their personalities, interactions with each other and how they cope out of their normal environment. The similarities between *Big Brother* and soap opera are reflected in the production processes. Executive Producer Peter Abbott says:

> The other significant thing we have done is to try and emulate the pace and the grammar of the soap opera much more than anyone else has done. We are using voice over to truncate, we're editing to truncate. The classic format [of *Big Brother*] is four scenes . . . and when you are sitting in the cutting room and you are thinking about sending this out at 7 pm tonight, you just know it won't work. So within the first week we were rapidly evolving into a different show and cutting much shorter segments. . . .

This process is further explained by Dave English, one of the producers:

> Roughly speaking there are four breaks, five segments, each with maybe two-three stories in each, so you're talking about 12–15 brief story lines per episode. They vary day-to-day, but each run for about two-three minutes. So that's really what is culled down out of the 24 hours.[10]

Structurally, then, the show has a strong relationship to soap opera and it references this far more than say, observational documentary or the gameshow. Like the soap opera, there is much repetition: at the beginning of each nightly episode there are synopses, and at the end, tomorrow's episode is previewed. It is a familiar format, as Peter Abbott notes:

> I think the audience is ready for it because they have a literacy in the grammar of soap operas, which means you can come into the scene two-thirds of the way as long as you know what the plot line is. [The classic format] is not for this time-slot, not for this competitive environment.[11]

The producers are very clear about this being a constructed event, rather than 'real life'. From 96 hours of footage, material has to be pieced together of a standard suitable for a primetime slot. The soap opera provides a structural framework in which to present the material, and provides the audience with a way into the show. But as Dave English noted earlier, this is a soap in which the participants themselves write the script. No matter how constructed the event, or how closely it conforms to the structure and narrative of the soap opera, there is always a potential element of unpredictability in the show. This is perhaps best highlighted in a discussion of the casting of the show.

Casting the show

Casting for the show started before Christmas 2000 when a call for interest was made in various media across Australia. Over 10,000 people initially applied, from which 1,000 were asked to make a tape about their lives and to complete an application form which detailed their likes and dislikes. These were then screened into 'yes' and 'no' piles to reduce the number to 400. These 400 were seen as 'possibles', and a team of four (headed by Executive Producer, Peter Abbott) sat down and watched all the tapes. They selected 120 to come to the day-long auditions. The auditions involved various group activities, designed by the psychologists, developed to reveal the individuals' characteristics and coping strategies. A drama consultant also designed a number of role-play activities for participants. They eventually interviewed 90 people, and from that contracted 40 to potentially take part in the show.

In casting the show, the producers were looking for a group of people who would be able to cope with the pressures of being locked away for up to three months, able to deal with the cameras on them 24 hours a day, and psychologically complex enough to be of interest (to themselves and the audience) for that amount of time. Casting for a non-fiction show, no matter how constructed that show, is a very different process from casting a drama, as Peter Abbott explained:

> It is quite the reverse from casting a drama. In a drama you have very defined characters and how they relate, and because you are employing actors, the actors will be how the character bible works, and the script will be that way. In this case it was working backwards putting together real people who have all those dimensions that you can imagine about them and putting those together and asking does that make an interesting cast?

He goes on to say:

> I saw it intuitively as casting a dinner party, or a weekend away with a group of friends. There were a lot of preconceptions in the press, 'they must be looking for conflict', about how 'they must be looking for mad people'. . . . No, because you wouldn't do that at a dinner party, you would never invite someone to a dinner party just because they were going to cause trouble all the time. You might invite somebody to be provocative, but you would have to assume that the party was still going to be a pleasant experience for everybody. . . . It was a failure in the American *Big Brother* that they cast too much for conflict and there was no sense of group.[12]

All about performance (and being famous)

> All life is but a rehearsal for television.
>
> (Quentin Crisp, quoted in Kilborn, 2000: 118)

Big Brother is a show that is constructed around performance. With 25 cameras and 36 microphones there is literally nowhere to hide. Those who go into the house know that they are there to perform – for each other, and for the audience watching at home either on the internet or television. There are clearly different levels of performance, as participants are playing a number of different and often contradictory roles. Within the house each has to play the role of 'housemate' which requires them to be a team player and to bond with the group. Housemates have to be liked by the group to enhance their chances of avoiding being nominated for eviction. At the same time, they have to play as a gameshow contestant; after all, there is a prize and there can only be one winner. While the housemates tend to play down this aspect of the show, it is still a key part of the experience. Gameshow contestants are expected to do anything to win, which might include cheating, lying and other deceptions. While the cameras might pick up such activities, each housemate has to keep such activities hidden from the other houseguests. However, as well as managing their images within the house, the housemates also have to perform for the audience who can, potentially, see everything they do.

There are a number of different levels of performance taking place, not just in terms of individuals, but across the formats of the different shows. The weekday evening shows tend to foreground what might be called the performance of the everyday. Here, we as viewers join in the game of normality – the narratives are constructed around the simulation of the everyday: mealtimes, washing, general emotional ups and downs, deciding on the shopping list and so forth. Here, we might also begin to glimpse some of those contradictions in the roles played by each participant. For example, quite early on in the series, it became clear that Johnny was seen to be the caring and sharing type by the housemates themselves. However, viewers who knew who he had voted for and what he said in the diary room perceived him to be more of an 'operator' – more of a contestant – than the other participants.

Big Brother is also about being famous. For some of the houseguests it is a motive for their participation; Andy said she wanted 'money and fame' out of her *Big Brother* experience. For others, fame comes with the experience. As Jemma arrived at the house to be greeted by hundreds of onlookers all screaming and waving, she shouted that she 'felt like a rock star'. As the show progressed there were a number of discussions amongst the housemates about how they imagine their lives will have been changed by the experience of being on the show.

Developing a fan base

Big Brother has created an active fan base as well as an audience for the show. The show has rated well with Channel Ten's target audience; in the first five weeks they have managed to secure (and retain) over 50 per cent of the 19–39 year olds. However, it is not just that people are watching, but they are participating in a number of ways across the various media platforms.

There are three important ways in which *Big Brother* has allowed for participation on behalf of the audience: through the site at Dreamworld, through Big Brother Online, and through telephone voting. These activities and sites are central to the creation of a fan base. Here I am drawing on the work of Jenkins (1992) and Abercrombie and Longhurst (1998), who see fans as active in their appropriation of texts, critical in their understandings of them, and, importantly, also as a producer rather than a consumer of texts.

The location of the house, production facilities and the studio at Dreamworld allows for a number of different spin-off events and experiences. It brings together entertainment and education, via the location set within the theme park, and is certainly unique in terms of the worldwide *Big Brother* productions. For the fan of the show there are opportunities to go behind the scenes and find out more about how the show is put together. Visitors to the *Big Brother* exhibit are able to view the control room, although they cannot look into the actual house. They can visit a mock-up diary room and have their photograph taken, and share a confession or two (which may be used in a future Saturday or Sunday show) as well as watching live feeds from the house on the giant screens in the auditorium. For the fan visitor it is a chance to engage in what Couldry (2000: 69) calls a 'shared fiction', that is the shared experience of being there. Couldry suggests that this experience is not always about memories or nostalgia, but is an 'anticipated act of commemoration' (2000: 77), an experience to be remembered in the future when watching the show.

Being on-site can enhance the viewing experience and enjoyment of the show because it allows access to the production processes that are so often hidden. Seeing the banks of TV screens in the control room gives a sense of how much material there is, and how little makes the 7pm show. It erodes the usual distinction between viewer and producer by allowing the visitor access to knowledges that are specialized and usually reserved for those working in the industry.

In every *Big Brother* there is always a crowd to greet the week's evictees, but in Australia, the crowd is managed and regulated in quite a specific way. One of the reasons why locating the house at Dreamworld was so attractive was the possibility of using the large auditorium to turn the eviction show into a live event. It has proved to be popular, with the A$20 tickets selling fast each week. The eviction show has evolved into a forum in which a whole range of fan activities can be performed. The live audience are there to be seen, both by the evictee on arrival in the auditorium, but also by the audience at home. They are encouraged to dress-up as their favourite housemate, conscious that a prize of a A$20,000 entertainment package awaits the best-dressed fan of the series. Sarah-Marie's fans dress in her trademark pyjamas with bunny ears (and often false breasts!) and perform the 'bum-dance' on request from the host, Gretel. Christian's fans often turn up in tutus with signs saying 'Christina Ballerina'. By the time the evictee has reached the auditorium at the end of the show, the crowd has been primed to roar with excitement. For the evictee, it is the first time they will experience 'fame', and their arrival on stage is not unlike the appearance of a pop star at a concert. The fans cheer, the evictee waves and thanks them for being there. What the show does very successfully is to turn the experience of being an audience into an active participation, where the viewer is as much a producer of the text as a consumer of it. This is continued with the use of the website.

The website is a central component of the event that is *Big Brother* and it provides the audience with a range of activities that allow them to construct different relationships with the text and other viewers. 'We never intended to be just a support site for the TV show. It's actually about something extra. . . . More depth is what we like to think. Also, it's a direct interface to viewers and users'.[13] The *Big Brother* website is extensive with activities ranging from the live streams (four cameras and one audio track), through to daily updates on the activities in the house, an archive of all previous stories, chat rooms, open forums, an uncut section, background information on all of the participants, the house and show as well as various shopping sites. You can also vote online (as well as download the theme tune for your mobile phone). Traditional notions of authorship and audience fail to convey the new and diverse ways in which users interact with this material, both consuming and producing these texts.

This highlights an aspect of the programme which is often missed by the media commentators, the kind of literacies it takes for granted. As a media event, *Big Brother* assumes its audience to be highly media-literate. It is assumed that viewers know the show is constructed for television, that they are able to engage with it as a hybrid format, and that they are able to acknowledge it as a performance of the real. There are many moments of self-reflexivity built into the event, from the behind the scenes studio tours, through to the insider gossip on the Saturday show, and the on-screen discussions between the housemates about their experiences of being in front of the cameras 24 hours a day. There has even been a task in which the housemates have had to make a short film. There has been an increasing amount of discussion in the house about how they imagine they are being represented, and some understanding of the processes through which they have become the driving force of the constructed narratives. When housemates leave the house they are often asked to reflect on the experience of being part of a TV show, and to reveal the perceived gap between their 'real' selves and their representations. On balance, they seem better informed than most experimental subjects.

Big Brother: the future of television?

Big Brother in Australia is an example of the new fact-fiction hybrid formats that are changing the face of contemporary television. It owes as much to drama (especially soap opera) as it does to the fly-on-the-wall observational documentary, and the gameshow. It treats its audience as knowing, and gives them a central role in the construction of the narrative of the house. It problematizes boundaries between public and private, and between notions of consumers and producers. As a media event it has successfully developed across various media platforms, and through its association with a theme park has created a new forum for audiences. In this way, it must be seen as a precursor to fully interactive TV and a prototype for future media events, as well as both a symptom of, and a response to, changes in fictional and factual programming in global TV. These changes are not unique to Australia, but detailed analysis of the local can help us to understand the broader significance of such forms. In doing so, we open up the debate about popular factual entertainment programming to move beyond the simplistic political commentary that currently pervades the public sphere.

Acknowledgements

I would like to thank all my interviewees for their time and assistance, especially Tim Clucas and Peter Abbott who gave me access to *Big Brother*.

Notes

1   Interview with Tim Clucas, Head of Factual Programming at Channel Ten, 22 May 2001.
2   Interview with Tim Clucas, Head of Factual Programming at Channel Ten, 22 May 2001.
3   Sarah-Marie is also the only housemate who is overweight, yet she is the housemate who seems to be most comfortable with her body, and least conscious of the cameras. In this way, she represents an alternative to the stereotypical bodies on display within the house. She flaunts her curves and roundness, frequently displaying her breasts to the housemates and the cameras, and has become famous for her 'bum-dance'. Over time, even Sarah-Marie seems to have succumbed to the requirement of the idealized female form of slimness and moderation. After discussions with Jemma and Johnny (who each represent what might be thought of as idealized feminine and masculine bodies) she has conceded that she would like to lose her 'love-handles', but she refused to start an exercise regime until she leaves the house.
4   Interview with David English, Producer, 22 May 2001.
5   Interview with Tim Clucas, Head of Factual Programming at Channel Ten, 22 May 2001.
6   Both Dave English and Tim Clucas alluded to this in their interviews.
7   Interview with Peter Abbott, Executive Producer, Southern Star Endemol, 9 June 2001.
8   Interview with Tim Clucas, Head of Factual Programming at Channel Ten, 22 May 2001.
9   Interview with David English, Producer, 22 May 2001.
10 Interview with David English, Producer, 22 May 2001.
11 Interview with Peter Abbott, Executive Producer, Southern Star Endemol, 9 June 2001.
12 Interview with Peter Abbott, Executive Producer, Southern Star Endemol, 9 June 2001.
13 Interview with Louise O'Donnell, Executive Producer of BBOnline, 22 May 2001.

References

Abercrombie, N. and B. Longhurst (1998) *Audiences*. London: Sage.
Ang, I. (1985) *Watching Dallas: Soap Opera and the Melodramatic Imagination*. London: Routledge.

Bethell, A. (1999) 'A Job, Some Stars and a Big Row', *BFI Mediawatch 99, Sight and Sound* 9(3): 34–5.

Brundson, C., C. Johnson, R. Moseley and H. Wheatley (2001) 'Factual Entertainment on British Television: The Midlands Research Group's 8–9 Project', *European Journal of Cultural Studies* 4(1): 29–63.

Corner, J. (1996) *The Art of Record.* Manchester: Manchester University Press.

Corner, J. (1999) *Critical Ideas in Television Studies.* Oxford: Oxford University Press.

Corner, J. (2000) 'Documentary in a Post-Documentary Culture? A Note on Forms and their Functions', *European Science Foundation 'Changing Media – Changing Europe'* Programme. Team One (Citizenship and Consumerism): Working Paper No. 1.

Couldry, N. (2000) *The Place of Media Power.* London: Routledge.

Dovey, J. (2000) *Freakshow.* London: Pluto Press.

Hill, A. (2000) 'Fearful and Safe: Audience Response to British Reality Programming' in J. Izod, R. Kilborn and M. Hibberd *From Grierson To The Docu-Soap*, pp. 131–44. Luton: University of Luton Press.

Hill, A. (in press) '*Big Brother*: The Real Audience', *Television and New Media*.

Jenkins, H. (1992) *Textual Poachers: Television Fans and Participatory Culture.* London: Routledge.

Kilborn, R. (1994) 'How Real Can You Get? Recent Developments in 'Reality' Television', *European Journal of Communication* 9(4): 421–39.

Kilborn, R. (2000) 'The Docusoap: A Critical Reassessment', in J. Izod, R. Kilborn and M. Hibberd *From Grierson to the Docusoap: Breaking the Boundaries*, pp. 111–20. Luton: Luton University Press.

Kilborn, R. and J. Izod (1997) *An Introduction to Television Documentary.* Manchester: Manchester University Press.

Langer, J. (1998) *Tabloid Television: Popular Journalism and the 'Other' News.* London: Routledge.

Lumby, C. (1999) *Gotcha: Life in a Tabloid World.* Sydney: Allen and Unwin.

Mapplebeck, V. (1998) 'The Mad, the Bad, and the Sad', *DOX* 16: 8–9.

Sherborne, C. (2000) 'Eddie McGuire Inc', *The Eye*, 20 April-1 May, pp. 31–5.

Turner, G. (1999) 'Tabloidisation, Journalism and the Possibility of Critique', *International Journal of Cultural Studies* 2(1): 59–76.

Ward, S. (2001) 'Producing Reality Television: *Big Brother*', *QPIX Newsletter* (June): 12–14.

Chapter 20

SONIA LIVINGSTONE AND PETER LUNT

STUDIO DISCUSSIONS

Introduction

AUDIENCE DISCUSSION PROGRAMMES can be understood as part of social space, as places where people congregate for public discussion, even as a 'forum'. What kind of space is the audience discussion programme and what are its social implications for participants and for public discussion more broadly? Any space has an internal set of rules, roles and procedures and is constituted through the particular accomplishments of the actors. Furthermore, social spaces are also embedded in, and so constitutive of, the wider community. Their boundaries may vary in permeability over space and time: some spaces are genuinely public and offer open access to anyone, others are closed to all but a few. Some spaces are heavily rule-governed and restrict opportunities according to criteria of status or power, while others are more open to negotiation and flexibility. The constitution of a particular space, with particular rules of access and opportunity, also affects the meanings of other spaces.

Different societies may be characterized by the presence or absence of certain kinds of spaces, with implications for the understanding of citizenship, or the public, in these different societies. For the bourgeois public sphere, the space must offer equal access and equal opportunities to participants, and to the extent that it does not, it has been refeudalized: according to Habermas (1989) there is no space for the development and expression of critical consensus in contemporary society.

In this chapter, we consider audience discussion programmes as social space. For participants, we ask what kind of experience it is to appear on television. For viewers, we explore the idea of watching television as parasocial interaction – viewing 'as if' it were face-to-face interaction with the characteristics of primary social experience, asking whether the viewer is involved in the constitution of the audience discussion programme as an imaginary community and possibly as a public sphere. But, however far one takes these arguments, audience discussion programmes remain mediated spaces, subject to institutional control and management by the mass media.

Audience discussion programmes as conversation

At the centre of audience discussion programmes are conversations between ordinary people and representatives of established power. The public sphere depends on these conversations being genuine rather than manipulated, with rights of access and opportunity being institutionally protected rather than undermined, and resulting in critical rather than false consensus. Interestingly, both face-to-face conversation and television can be unfavourably compared with print media in that their speed and intimacy prioritizes trust and credibility over critical thought (Petty and Cacioppo, 1981; Ptau, 1990).

How can we analyse the conversations that occur on television? Schudson (1978) outlines five criteria for the American conversation ideal: continuous feedback between two people in a face-to-face setting; multichannel communication (hear, see, touch); spontaneous (and thus unique) utterances; each person is both sender and receiver of messages; norms of conversation are egalitarian (both follow same rules). Avery and McCain (1982) argue that these criteria are not met by 'conversation' on the mass media, even in talk shows and call-ins. Callers may be cut off and humiliated, they avoid calling shows where they disagree with the host's perspective, they lack visual information, and so forth.

However, while participation programmes fall short of these conversational ideals, so too, frequently do face-to-face conversations. There is a danger of idealizing everyday conversation and comparing that idealization to the realities of mass-communicated communication. In everyday conversation, feedback is not continuous but problematic, subject to misinterpretation, especially when more than two people are involved. A telephone conversation, which lacks both touch and vision, is generally regarded as real conversation, while television discussions provide both sound and vision. While on one level, all interactions are spontaneous and unique, conversations are highly rule-governed, frequently repetitive, and commonly used to repeat handed-down or unoriginal ideas (i.e. common sense).

In many conversations, the roles of sender and receiver may be unbalanced – it's hard to be the sender when talking to a 'gossip'. More subtly, textual theories of communication challenge the roles of sender and receiver, for senders take into account the anticipated responses of receivers, even on television, and receivers may make creative and diverse interpretations of messages sent. In practice, interpersonal and mass communication interact: the receiver of a television message may be the sender in the living room who then alters the interpretations of other receivers who may then in turn shout back at the television or turn it off. Finally, the ideal that sender and receiver should be bound by the same interactional rules – who can interrupt, or make jokes, or disagree – does not occur in many face-to-face conversations. Conversations where participants are differentiated by gender, generation, status, or power, all place different demands on the participants, who speak with different voices reflecting a variety of subject positions.

The experience of appearing on audience discussion programmes

Let us begin our analysis of audience discussion programmes as social space by exploring the experience of ordinary people on these programmes. People are sometimes confused about the experience of appearing on television; after all there are few cultural representations with which to frame their experience. Not all participants are naive and overwhelmed:

> I've done quite a lot of public speaking of one description or another so I think I managed to get the point across. I don't think I made very good studio audience material because I talk too fast, but I think I made the point that I wanted to make.
>
> (Tony, studio audience)

Tony is aware of the skills required, but is mainly concerned with making his point in public. Although 'British people are becoming less and less nervous about what they say on television' (John Stapleton, host of *The Time, The Place*, speaking on TV Weekly, ITV, 19 November 1992), some still experience difficulties:

> I chickened out really. It was towards the end of the show when I bubbled up enough to think 'yeah, I ought to say something, this is ridiculous,' but it was literally within the last

five minutes of the show and I put my hand up to speak as he was coming down but I deliberately didn't look at him so he didn't pick me which was a bit stupid so I chickened out basically. I was too scared basically, the sweat was pouring out of me.

(James, studio audience)

Some studio audience members appear on the programmes not intending to speak: 'I automatically assumed that I wouldn't be speaking, so I didn't really think about the topic at all' (Ruth). Others try to find a way into the discussion and may not manage what the experts also acknowledge to be the difficult task of timing one's intervention, catching the host's eye, getting a microphone, speaking to the point, not being cut off or interrupted, and so forth. The lay participants are given some encouragement and instructions about the rules before the programme:

Mike Scott said 'we like a lively debate, please don't be too polite, it makes good television if people are actually a bit rude and forget their British reserve and actually just push in, talk on top of each other, so please don't be typically Brits, don't be reserved, if you feel strongly then please speak up'.

(Alice, studio audience)

Kilroy said 'just relax, and just say what you want,' and he said he apologized in advance that if he pushed anyone by trying to get round the studio don't take it personally, 'if I try to sit down beside you and shove the microphone across you don't get offended'. He said 'if you've got a point to make just say it and hopefully I'll hear you and come running round,' and he said 'just speak freely and try to join in as much as you want'.

(Margaret, studio audience)

The floor manager had said about carrying on the conversation, making sure that we didn't trip him over, making sure that we didn't shout over anybody else, put our hands up and were nice and polite about the way we carried out the discussion. I think he said something about swearing, that we shouldn't swear too much because the audience wouldn't like it. He was trying to portray the idea that he was facilitating a discussion amongst the audience and that he wanted us to address points to each other rather than to him.

(Martin, studio audience)

We asked people what they gained from participating in a studio-audience discussion. They differed in whether they felt the interaction to be genuine:

I think if I hadn't already known a number of 'media people' I would have learnt something about what media is about and how artificial the whole thing is but I knew that these shows are rigged and I knew the way the audiences were set out and this sort of thing so I think personally I didn't learn very much.

(Tony, studio audience)

I'm glad I had a chance to say it, because even if it doesn't make any difference to the litter problem at least I've vented my spleen and I feel I've done something, I've got my anger and frustration out on television and who knows it might do some good in the long term.

(Alice, studio audience)

Margaret did not go with a particular aim in mind, rather she was just making up the numbers but things still worked out in such a way that she made a contribution:

> It just happened it was really apt with my particular situation at the time, and I had a lot to get off my chest in a way. And so, it just happened at the beginning they were talking about marriage, and I didn't feel quite that what I had to say would be relevant, and then it just happened that there was an opportunity where what I had to say was fitting and part of it.

For Margaret it was not a matter of changing the world but of gaining social support for herself, which she felt to be successful. For some, the occasion was too nerve racking for any contribution.

> Every time I went to say something or . . . I didn't even muster up enough courage because every time I went to say something my heart would have gone bump, bump . . . I started getting very nervous, so I didn't actually, I felt 'oh no, it's too much stress to actually say something,' because I was very aware that I was on camera.
>
> (Ruth, studio audience)

Participation is clearly an emotional experience:

> I leant forward and just made a comment because he was sitting right next to him and it couldn't be avoided and then he came and sort of sat round next to me and we had this conversation for maybe three or four interchanges and I just felt really angry, I was almost shaking with anger from what he'd said because he was talking about morals and ethics and young people and being incredibly patronising and didn't know what he was talking about and he obviously wanted to be sensational so I can remember sitting there and thinking 'how can I look threatening?' so I sat there and went '. . .', like that.
>
> (Martin, studio audience)

For James, *Donahue*'s topic of toyboys was experienced through his feelings about his parents' divorce:

> I have personally had my family break up over, not over a toyboy as it goes, but over affairs and things like that which I wasn't too happy about. But then if somebody had come along and said 'do you think people should be able to work at a marriage they can't stand and live together in a hostile environment for even longer?' I'd obviously turn round and say 'no, it's silly,' the idea of making two people who can't stand each other live together is absurd, guaranteed to lead to violence and animosity so it was that sort of outlook which I didn't have at that time and nobody on that panel really offered that, otherwise I would have perhaps thought about it a bit more after the show, it was all sort of running round the bedroom having a good laugh sort of thing and that we should all live with people and have a good time.

Self-disclosure on television

Nonviewers of discussion programmes are often concerned with the invasion of privacy which may result from expressing personal revelations and emotions in a public place. However, viewers were unconcerned: they felt all topics were legitimate, and focused more on the value of personal expression for the public sphere and for heightening the sense of involvement and authenticity. Viewers are more concerned that studio audience participants were representative, so that valid conclusions could be drawn from their contributions. Nonviewers interpret the programmes as offering isolated accounts of personal experience in the context of a chaotic chorus. For viewers, the programme is experienced as an integrated whole so that from the retelling of a series of personal stories, significant results may emerge – the construction of public opinion, the expression of the repressed or culturally invisible, the valorization of lay experience, etc.

The issue of public self-disclosure is complex. One can distinguish between revealing consensually defined 'personal' facts or taboos about oneself (concerning sex, relationships, illness, money) from revealing facts which, for whatever idiosyncratic reason, are emotionally difficult to say. The difficulties – and the thrills – audiences may experience on hearing self-disclosure by others may result either from hearing taboo issues aired in public, which even though readily volunteered by the speaker may be difficult for the hearer, or from hearing facts which the speaker finds emotionally difficult to express. Self-disclosure may thus arouse emotions in the hearer or may make the hearer bear witness to emotions in the speaker.

Reflections on participation

Reflecting on their participation after appearing on television, studio audience members differed in whether they felt the conversation to have been genuine. For some, the end of the programme was by no means the end of the experience:

> So we went back in the lift down to the reception area and they had orange, wine, peanuts, light stuff. But people were talking about it. Because by the end of the programme, more people were wanting to join in. In fact the whole programme came to life, so people were still on a bit of a high and still wanted to talk about it, and pick up on some of the comments they'd heard other people make. And so I heard a couple of people say 'ah, you've gone through a bit, I went through a similar thing' or, you know, I made a couple of comments to people like 'that's really good the comment you made'. It wasn't as though the programme finished therefore the discussion finished – it continued.
>
> (Margaret, studio audience)

Others felt that the constraints of the genre prevented spontaneous interaction:

> I felt that we were placed there a few minutes before, we hadn't really had time to settle in to the surroundings, to even discuss or talk to people beforehand. I felt as though I knew no-one there. And so it wasn't like a real discussion, because no ice was broken, so to speak. Even the way it's set out you have the seats facing cameras, every one is facing forward. To talk to someone you have to look over the other side of the audience, it's not like any other situation we're usually in really. Whenever we're discussing something you're sitting opposite someone and you're in a much more informal situation.
>
> (Ruth, studio audience)

It felt very artificial to me, I don't usually have conversations with someone sitting in front of me with their back to me. Apart from anything else it gives you a very strange, peculiar kind of experience.

(Martin, studio audience)

As 'we didn't have any introduction to anyone' and 'we'd had very little information about what they wanted us to do' (Martin, studio audience), participants were playing by unknown rules. Nonetheless, this meant that both experts and lay people entered the discussion without advance planning of their contribution beyond possibly a general sense of the main point(s), resulting in a sense of involvement in a real conversation where their contribution emerges spontaneously out of the discussion:

You had more of a sense of real conversation, real interchange and I thought therefore that it was probably serving an educational function . . . There was no barracking, there was a sense of a real attempt of arguing with each other. I thought Kilroy induced that quite deliberately and also quite successfully so in a sense he switched the conversation around but he'd try on the whole to keep things going, he got people to make points that were germane to what was under discussion so it was very much more like putting business structure into what could actually have been a bar room brawl but actually became a bar room conversation. Not totally dissimilar to the sort of conversations that do from time to time take place in bars, but with more structure and slightly more discipline. Very much less artificial than from having politicians talking and I thought that politicians actually began to behave slightly differently in that atmosphere.

(Expert 5, academic in government)

Participants do not always stay involved: 'after that I felt "oh right, great, I've had my say" and I switch off then, I thought "right, let everybody else get on with it" ' (Martin, studio audience), but of course this can also be true for face-to-face interaction.

This level of spontaneity attests to the informal character of the audience discussion programme as social situation. It is a place where people go to become involved in a personal conversation in a public space, where self-disclosure and argument intertwine in a tournament that privileges a private voice for a brief time. Corner identifies the 'radical revelatory' consequences of the documentary, where viewers are 'put in touch with one another by revealing infrastructural relations of interdependence' (Corner, 1986: x). To the extent that a conversation is generated in the studio, this radical revelatory aspect is surely all the more powerful in the audience discussion programme, where ordinary people are put in touch with each other in a direct, immediate and spontaneous manner.

Parasocial interaction

In parasocial interaction (Horton and Wohl, 1956), the audience has the experience of face-to-face communication when watching television. This 'intimacy at a distance' is such that people count television characters, especially television personas such as talk show hosts, amongst their friends and family: '*Oprah* viewers, for example, feel quite comfortable greeting their favorite host with comments on her current hairstyle, clothing or weight' (Cerulo *et al.* 1992: 120). The informal, ritualized and interactive style of talk show hosts encourages this – a conversational style of speech, a direct gaze at the camera, giving the audience an apparent role in an 'interaction' (M. Levy, 1982). The audience know what to expect, they have a role to play, and as neighbourhood ties are reduced, 'parasocial' interactions become an increasing source of intimate bonds:

> The para-social relationship develops over time and is based in part on a history of 'shared' experiences . . . the daily 'visit' of the newscaster is valued by the viewer, perhaps because the news persona, like a friend, brings gossip.
>
> (Ibid: 180)

The rapid technological changes in electronic media (fax, car-phone, cable and satellite television) challenge us to characterize primary social relationships in terms of their functions for the individual rather than their institutional forms, in part an artefact of particular technological forms. Primary social groups must be defined not only in terms of their psychological functions but also in terms of social space and social relations. Recent institutional and technological changes in the mass media may, it is argued, enable them to play a more positive role in constituting social relations rather than being a mass of isolated individuals:

> Technological and cultural developments in the structure of the mass media – developments fully implemented during the 1980s – have drastically changed the nature of a mass communication. These changes have enabled the mass media to become a new source of primary group affiliations . . . that provide social members with a sense of identity and purpose, strong and enduring emotional bonds, and a source of immediate social control.
>
> (Cerulo *et al.* 1992: 109)

Audience discussion programmes may substitute for coffee mornings, chats with friends or gossip and, 'with regular viewing, combined with the call-in capability of such shows, the common interests and opinions of both host and audience members become crystallized. As a result, people become identified on the basis of their talk-show affiliations' (ibid.: 115–16).

Imaginary places

There is a sense in which the social world is transformed as social relations are removed from public occasions and institutions and placed in the private living rooms of viewers. The informal organization of the social world is transformed from a 'real' to an 'imagined' community (Anderson, 1991) and community involvement changes from public participation to private consumption. In *No Sense of Place*, Meyrowitz (1985) suggests that 'the evolution of media has decreased the significance of physical presence in the experience of people and events' (ibid: vii). Mass communication collapses space and time such that we can witness events which are distant from us or which would previously have taken time to communicate and the traditional barriers and spaces of social life – both public and domestic – have been penetrated by the broadcast media: 'The family home is now a less bounded and unique environment because of family members' access and accessibility to other places and other people through radio, television, and telephone' (Meyrowitz, 1985: vii).

The decoupling of space and time in modern mediated communication (Giddens, 1985) also detaches psychological experiences from specific contexts and locations, breaking down traditional social structures and relations. Social space is no longer constituted through physical settings but rather through imaginary communities which mix physical and mediated situations and, consequently, mix interpersonal and mass mediated communication. While traditional social structures were enshrined in different communicative contexts for people from alternative social groups, generations and genders, this mapping of the social onto different locales has been blurred particularly by the broadcast media.

For example, Meyrowitz draws on Goffman's (1981) concern with overhearing by multiple audiences to note that adopting mass mediated forms of communication disturbs our ability to communicate strategically to different audiences. Children have access to 'adult' conversation, men may listen to women's issues discussed on 'women's programmes', politicians cannot say one thing to one constituency and something else to another. In the audience discussion programme, a media event occurs which would not have occurred in any other space-time dimension and so the space created is unlike any other. It is inconceivable that the meetings we see daily on audience discussion programmes would have occurred spontaneously during the course of unmediated social interaction.

Following Alexander's (1990) analysis of the role of inconsistencies in social progress, we suggest that one consequence of these new media events (Dayan et al., 1985) is that the media do not establish shared meanings so much as make visible inconsistencies in meaning across particular locations or material conditions. For example, through accounts of ordinary people's experiences, audience discussion programmes express inconsistencies in current social arrangements, showing how existing institutional categories fail to accommodate lay concerns. The expression of such inconsistencies is part of the dialectic relationship between institutionally encoded meanings and everyday experience – representing not the legitimation crisis but a moment in the unfolding relationship between theory and practice.

Social space

The physical limits of the human body place a set of spatial and temporal constraints on the social construction of place and on the social actions possible within it (Giddens, 1985; Hägerstrand, 1967).

> Time-geography is concerned with the infrastructural constraints that shape the routines of day-to-day life, and shares with structuration theory an emphasis upon the significance of the practical character of daily activities, in circumstances where individuals are co-present with one another, for the constitution of social conduct.
>
> (Giddens, 1985: 269)

Hägerstrand shows how the trajectories of individual actors over different time periods intersect in 'time-space maps'. Thus in audience discussion programmes we see that the participants are each on very different paths and they have to influence the joint accomplishment of the social occasion as best they can to fit in with their plans. Consistent with notions of the oppositional public sphere (Fraser, 1990), participants with different life projects negotiate the relationship between their interests and those of others. Whatever the outcome, participants then return to their own life projects (Giddens, 1985, 1991).

The studio discussion has characteristics both of proximate forms of communication, based on all members being co-present in the same locale and engaged in traditional face-to-face communication, and of new, distanced forms of communication across locales through the transmission of the discussion to a mass audience. The space is defined by the relations established between different categories of participant – home and studio audience, expert and laity, host and guest. Giddens appropriates Goffman's (1959) distinction between front and back (or public and private), together with that of disclosure and enclosure (the covering up or open display of information), to analyse the boundaries used to organize social spaces.

In audience discussion programmes, the space is partly organized so as to manage and integrate the disclosure of personal experience and official analysis, getting people together who in the unmediated playing out of social life would never talk to each other. In what other public space could a mother living in bed-and-breakfast accommodation talk to a member of government? Where else could a patient with a grievance discuss it with a representative of the British Medical Association?

The programmes are ostensibly constructed as the 'front', 'where the action is', the place where the laity can publicly express grievances and bring officials to account, where interest groups can contest the definition of social problems, and where official bodies can publicly display the positive aspects of their organizations. This management of disclosure controls public and official access to information and expression. By such outrageous juxtaposition of representatives of established power and the laity the media offer themselves as both a forum for contemporary society and as an implicit critique of existing social arrangements.

However, as in any television programme, the view presented to the viewer hides the mechanisms of production. The viewer gets a partial view of the space in which the discussion takes place. The 'front' that the viewer sees disguises the 'back' which contains all the means of production of the image. Here the front/back distinction maps onto the space as perceived by the viewer and the space as part of the media institution, limiting what is disclosed to the viewer. Disclosure/enclosure is also mediated through time: there are various activities before and after filming, some of which take place in ante-rooms and some of which take place 'off camera': switching on the cameras transforms the space into a public sphere visible to all.

The space created by this genre is also constituted through its relations with other genres and other spaces. In the audience discussion programme, we have a bounded region of access. As ordinary people and representatives of established power demand access, the media make available a backwater, a trivial and unimportant realm of television. People can now be said to have a say in the production of television but that say is strictly bounded and therefore contained from spreading and polluting the rest of the broadcast media. Thus the managed show of participation is partly achieved by locating participation in a particular region of television. The programmes are liminal spaces through which citizens pass, form temporary coalitions and then return to their social identities.

Analysing the space created by the programmes requires us to consider these programmes both as regions of television and as constituting a locale of their own with regional division within the programme. Multiple comparisons of front/back and disclosure/enclosure are possible when analysing occasions that have 'traditional' authenticity in terms of the product (a conversation, a critical discussion) but which are constructed and disseminated in a very 'modern' way (with distributed and shifting locales, with communication at a distance).

Thus the programmes are both locale and region, front and back, private and public, disclosing and enclosing, communicated through co-presence and through distance. They exemplify what Harvey (1989) terms 'time-space compression', a central characteristic of the organization of social space in postmodern or late-capitalist society. Just as the problems of mass production (Fordism) and Keynesian economics demanded the speeding up of turnover time and a relaxation of economic regulation, so too is the media under similar pressure. Audience discussion programmes suit this change: they are cheap to produce and respond quickly to changes in current affairs. They represent the postmodern version of public debate, claiming the advantages of broader participation and relevance but vulnerable to the criticisms of being fleeting and superficial. [. . .]

Any attempt to explicate unambiguously the political and social functions of the genre of audience discussion programmes must be doomed. [. . .] We have emphasized the multiple levels of influence in the production, accomplishment and transmission of audience discussion programmes and in their relation to social structure. [. . .] We have examined the audience discussion in terms of social space, arguing that the relations between studio space and the living room or between front and back are complex, as are the rules which organize interactions within and across these spaces.

[. . .]

References

Alexander, J. C. (1990) Analytic debates: understanding the relative autonomy of culture. In J. C. Alexander and S. Seidman (eds), *Culture and society: Contemporary debates*. Cambridge: Cambridge University Press.

Anderson, B. (1991) *Imagined communities: Reflections on the origin and spread of nationalism*. London: Verso.

Avery, R. K. and McCain, T. A. (1982) Interpersonal and mediated encounters: a reorientation to the mass communication process. In G. Gumpert and R. Cathcart (eds), *Inter/Media: Interpersonal communication in a media world* (Second edn). New York: Oxford University Press.

Cerulo, K. A., Ruane, J. M. and Chayko, M. (1992) Technological ties that bind: media-generated primary groups. *Communications research*, *19*, 109–29.

Corner, J. (ed.) (1986) Preface to *Documentary and the mass media*. London: Edward Arnold.

Dayan, D., Katz, E. and Kerns, P. (1985) Armchair pilgrimages: the trips of John Paul II and their television public: an anthropological view. In M. Gurevitch and M. R. Levy (eds), *Mass communication review yearbook*, 5. Beverly Hills, Cal.: Sage.

Fraser, N. (1990) Rethinking the public sphere: a contribution to the critique of actually existing democracy. *Social text*, *25/26*, 56–80.

Giddens, A. (1985) Time, space and regionalisation. In D. Gregory and J. Urry (eds), *Social relations and spacial structures*, Basingstoke: Macmillan.

—— (1991) *Modernity and self-identity: Self and society in the late modern age*. Cambridge: Polity Press.

Goffman, E. (1959) *The presentation of self in everyday life*. Harmondsworth: Penguin.

—— (1981) *Forms of talk*. Oxford: Blackwell.

Habermas, J. (1989) *The structural transformation of the public sphere: An inquiry into a category of bourgeois society*. T. Burger with F. Lawrence (Trans.). Cambridge, Mass.: The MIT Press.

Hägerstrand, T. (1967) *Innovation diffusion as a spatial process*. Chicago: University of Chicago Press.

Harvey, D. (1989) *The condition of postmodernity*. Oxford: Blackwell.

Horton, D. and Wohl, R. R. (1956) Mass communication and para-social interaction. *Psychiatry*, *19*, 215–29.

Levy, M. R. (1982) Watching TV news as para-social interaction. In G. Gumpert and R. Cathcart (eds), *Inter/Media: Interpersonal communication in a media world* (Second edn) New York: Oxford.

Meyrowitz, J. (1985) *No sense of place: The impact of electronic media on social behavior*. New York: Oxford University Press.

Petty, R. E. and Cacioppo, J. T. (1981) *Attitudes and persuasion: Classic and contemporary approaches*. Iowa: W. C. Brown Co.

Pfau, M. (1990) A channel approach to television influence. *Journal of broadcasting and electronic media*, *34(2)*, 195–214.

Schudson, M. (1978) The ideal of conversation in the mass media. *Communication research*, *5(3)*, 320–9.

Chapter 21

NICK COULDRY

MEDIA PILGRIMS
On the set of *Coronation Street*

THE 1980s AND 1990s HAVE SEEN a massive proliferation of tourist and heritage sites in Britain and many other countries. An important, but little-studied, aspect of that expansion has been media tourist sites. At one end of the spectrum are the highly commericialised, organised sites with museum-like displays and theme park entertainment. Best known are Disney–MGM and MCA's Universal Studios in the USA. Disney–MGM alone receives in the order of 25,000 visitors daily (Fjellman, 1992: 445). [. . .] At the other end of the spectrum are the many locations in Britain and elsewhere, which are not fully commercial leisure sites (entry is free), but are visited simply because they have been sites of media production, especially filming. In the past ten years in Britain, it is these smaller, less commercial sites which have expanded fastest. [. . .]

Granada Studios Tour (GST), which opened in July 1988 on a site next to Granada Television's Manchester studios, falls somewhere between these two extremes. On the one hand, it is now a fully developed commercial theme park, but on a much smaller scale than the main US sites. Operated by a separate subsidiary of Granada Group PLC, it represents an investment of approximately £25 million (Disney–MGM by contrast cost more than $500 million); GST has received over four million visitors since it opened, with up to 4,500 visitors a day during the peak summer season (source: interview with Helen Jackson, Operations Manager of GST, September 1996). It markets itself as 'Europe's Biggest Film and Television Day Out'. It is a significant site, but still small compared with Disney-MGM's turnover. On the other hand, a major part of GST's attraction has always been one particular location: the external set (built in 1982) currently used in filming *Coronation Street*, Britain's longest-running television soap. This programme is produced by Granada Television.

GST's original focus was exclusively television, and certain television attractions have remained since 1988: (1) the external *Coronation Street* set; (2) 'Telestars' (where you can 'appear' in a *Coronation Street* episode via Chromakey superimposition techniques); (3) a tour of television 'backstage' areas (mock-up dressing-rooms, make-up rooms, special effects demonstrations, a set of 10 Downing Street, and so on); and (4) two other large-scale sets ('Sherlock Holmes' Baker Street' and 'The House of Commons', both from Granada television series). As the marketing emphasis has switched to more general media themes, other attractions have been added: a sound effects show, the 'Motionmaster' show with moving seats, and various film-related rides. [. . .]

To complete the context, I must say something about the programme *Coronation Street* itself. As Britain's longest-running television soap (it opened in 1960), it has acquired an iconic status, at least in Britain; it is exported also to countries with large expatriate British communities, such as

Canada and New Zealand. It was the first British television soap to establish itself as representing an image of 'ordinary' British working-class life in north-west England. It was not until the 1980s that other British soaps emerged with comparable influence and close regional associations, such as the BBC's *Eastenders* (based on working-class east London), and Channel Four's *Brookside* (based on working-class Liverpool). [. . .]

The external set of *Coronation Street* is GST's principal attraction for many, perhaps most, of its visitors, and there is something paradoxical about it. People pay to visit a location they have already watched free on television for years; part of the pleasure is not seeing something different, but confirming that the set is the same as something already seen.

As we will see, the set undoubtedly has the 'power of place' in Dolores Hayden's (1995) phrase,[1] and yet it seems poorly qualified to satisfy her definition of the term (ibid.: 9): 'the power of ordinary urban landscapes to nurture citizens' public memory, to encompass shared time in the form of shared territory'. The Street set is only an image of an 'ordinary urban landscape' (no one has ever lived or died there); at most it is a focus of British television's dispersed 'electronic network' (Rath, 1985: 200). The Street set's 'power of place' rests not on public history in the usual sense, but on shared fiction. It is a place which condenses memory, a place with 'aura', a 'ritual place', even a place of 'pilgrimage'. It embodies a connection between visitors' history of watching the programme and their brief 'time on the Street'.[2]

What do people do on the set of *Coronation Street*? They walk down it: people sometimes summed up their visit in this phrase. But, since many spend an hour or more on the set, there must be more to the visit than that. People take photographs and are photographed at points of interest – outside the Rovers Return pub, the shops, the houses – but that too is over quickly. Almost everyone spends time testing the boundaries of the set's illusion: looking through the houses' letter boxes or windows, pressing doorbells and knocking on doors; looking round the houses' backs (the 'old' houses have paved yards backing onto an alley, the 'new' houses have gardens). People compare the details of the set with their previous image of the Street. Some of the set's details, in fact, are aimed at visitors, not the television audience: for example, the 'for sale' notices in the newsagent's window. There is a lot of laughter, especially when the set is crowded. It's enjoyable to pretend, for a moment, that you live on the Street, posing with door knocker in hand or calling up to one of the characters. The visit is an elaborate form of performance[3] and exploration.

Many visitors will already have visited GST before. Even if returnees are a distinct subset of visitors, the fact that people return to GST *at all* needs to be explained. Chris Rojek has written of 'the sense of anticlimax that often accompanies the visit' to contemporary tourist sites: 'we see it; but have we not seen it before in countless artifacts, images, dramatic treatments, and other reproductions?' (1993: 196). That risk is all the greater at GST: everyone has seen the Street countless times on television. As one young couple put it: '[Woman:] You see it every night on TV, so there's not all that much difference apart from size. [Man] To say you've actually been there, that's probably part of it.' Not only, however, were such comments rare, but, even for this couple, 'to say you've actually been there' was not trivial; it had significance, even if not a personal one. Perhaps visiting the Street set is significant precisely *because* it is the place you routinely watch. As one man put it: '[CS] is the part [of GST] that we seem to enjoy most because it's something you see every week on television.' We need to unravel the implications of this apparently simple statement.

Most people I interviewed were positive about their visit to GST. There was, of course, a wide spectrum of engagement. People may visit out of interest: to see 'what goes on', 'how it all works', finding it 'educational'. There is the pleasure of participating in the fiction, seeing '*Coronation Street* come to life'. But the visit may also involve considerable emotional investment for both men and women: 'for years, I've always wanted to come' (woman); 'I've just been desperate to see it for years now' (woman); it may be 'a dream come true' (Michael), 'a lifelong dream' (woman). For John, the intensity of going to the Street was 'like being on a drug'. Peter spoke of the 'adrenalin' rush when he visited the Street: 'Just feel so excited when you go on to the actual Street (. . .) don't know what it was (. . .) it was a bit of adrenalin I think, it seems strange, I know, but that's what happened every time I went.'

Some people said they found it difficult to believe that they were actually there, on the set (six cases). Underlying all these reactions is the sense that it is significant to 'be there': it is an 'experience' marked off from the 'ordinary' (a defining feature of the 'tourist gaze': Urry, 1990). As one man put it: 'I want to see the place (. . .) where this thing is, you know. It's an absolute experience, isn't it, a magnificent experience, isn't it, to come to this place.' Being on the Street set, then, is intrinsically significant.

[. . .]

Memory

Since *Coronation Street* is Britain's longest-running television soap, GST is an obvious example of television-related nostalgia. It can easily be fitted into the general growth of 'heritage' and 'nostalgia' tourism. [. . .] But GST can also, and perhaps surprisingly, tell us interesting things about the construction of social memory. The issue of how the media themselves are remembered has been largely neglected in wider social theory. My argument, however, is that GST (in particular, the Street set) functions as a material form for commemorating the practice of viewing television.

Following Maurice Halbwachs' (1992) [1924] fundamental insight that memory (both individual and social) requires a framework or *cadre* – a shared material and social context – in which to be reproduced, and following Paul Connerton's (1989) analysis of how rituals actually produce social memory through acts of repetition, we can see the Street set as a 'mnemonic system' (ibid.: 87), that takes effect through visitors' actions on the set. What does this mnemonic system commemorate? Obviously not the existence of the programme (this is 'commemorated' every time people watch) but rather the programme's past history and visitors' own past practice of viewing. The set, I suggest, provides an ordered space – a 'framework' (in Halbwachs' term) – in which memories of viewing can be organised, shared and thereby reproduced. Because of GST's commercialism, this commemorative function is easily overlooked. This feature of the Street set parallels a distinctive feature of the programme itself. For nearly forty years, *Coronation Street* has offered a continuous fictional reality, operating in parallel to viewers' lives. For some, it may serve as a mnemonic system for events in their own life. John, for example, expressed this powerfully:

> . . . for 36 years it has survived and that is incredible (. . .) And the thing about it is, and this sounds really silly, but I've grown up with it, I've actually experienced things in my life, and when I think back (. . .) to certain episodes, I can relate them to things in my life, and when I think, well, oh yes, when Patricia Phoenix was in it, I was working at such and such a place and we went on such a trip, or when Ena Sharples [did] whatever, I can remember I was living in such and such. And I can relate it (. . .) to my family and what they were doing at the time . . . so that nostalgia is fantastic, and you can't change that.

For such visitors at least, visiting the set has a temporal depth connected not just with the programme's history but with their own lives.

But how specifically does the set work as a memory-frame? First, visiting the Street involves mapping your sense of the Street's geography from years of watching onto the set's actual geography. Some found this easy, others wanted a map or name plates to confirm who 'lived' where. Either way, the process of working things out has a commemorative function. It takes many forms: for example, people's comments or jokes about details of houses and props [. . .], or their questions to guides or each other about the set's history. Second, visiting the Street set can remind people of specific episodes from the programme's past. Such memories are stimulated by many aspects of GST: the show of video clips from old episodes called 'The Coronation Street Experience'; the photographs of past scenes dotted around the site;[4] the costumes and props from the programme shown on the Backstage Tour [. . .]; and the shops full of souvenirs branded with Street characters. In recent years, the commercial exploitation of nostaliga for *Coronation Street* has increased markedly (through videos of old episodes, the recycling of old episodes on cable and satellite channels). But there can be a more personal aspect as well. Some people supply their own vivid memories of past episodes as they walk on the Street. Barbara, for example:

> I couldn't believe that I was actually on the spot of the 1983 showdown that rocked the nation, between Ken, Mike and Deirdre (. . .) I then carried on walking and approached the spot where Ena and Elsie bickered for all those years and even nearly came to blows in one episode that I now enjoy watching on video.

For Barbara, the Street set was a place with a precise history. It might seem paradoxical to consider television, let alone the set of a television programme, from the point of view of commemoration: television is, after all, stereotypically the ephemeral medium. But a programme comprising nearly forty years of storytelling involving a large proportion of the British population surely requires some mechanism of commemoration. As Christine Geraghty (1981: 18) pointed out, programmes such as soaps are constrained in how much of their 'accumulated past' they can 'remember' in their storylines. Against this background of generalised forgetting, the act of visiting the Street set is hardly trivial.

Being on the set, however, does not only reproduce memories of the programme. Being there is itself inherently memorable, transforming future watching of the programme. Take, for example, the apparently banal things people do on the Street set to connect up with the outside, non-fictional world: posting cards in the Street pillar-box or using the telephone box (both of them functioning!). When people described these acts, they often referred to an *anticipated* act of commemoration, to occur when they watched the programme again or when the card was received: 'I even rang my mum from the phonebox on the end of the Street *just so that I could say* I'd been in it *every time it came on the TV*.' (Barbara [added emphasis]). [. . .] Writing or making a call is something you do on the Street which others can later vouch for as evidence that you were once there. Indeed *anything* you do in relation to the set is something you will be able to recall when you watch the programme: 'The first thing I saw was the telephone box from which I phoned home to say, I was on *Coronation Street*. Now every time the Street comes on I say [to myself] you made a call from that box' (Michael). [. . .]

Doing something on the set of *Coronation Street* is 'inherently memorable' in precisely the sense that Michael Billig (1992) has analysed in relation to people's meetings with British royalty. Such meetings are memorable not simply because of their content, but because they are guaranteed to be retellable: they are joined to a frame of reference (royalty) whose continuity is itself assumed to be guaranteed (ibid.: 220–23). Similarly, the programme's continuous frame of reference makes everything you do on its set inherently memorable, and this is reinforced by each subsequent viewing: 'For us [the visit to GST] was just a wonderful experience, something we will remember for the rest of our lives. Every time we see the titles come up on the program we live it all again' (Susan, letter). Such 'inherent memorability' is a feature of situations where the normal hierarchy between sites of discourse (Stallybrass and White, 1986) is suspended. The link with a place or person whose significance everyone knows is automatically retellable, and that fact creates a connection significant in itself. Establishing such a link can be seen, adapting de Certeau (1984), as a 'tactical' use of the programme's 'strategic' storytelling frame which ensures that your own actions in relation to the programme are memorable (de Certeau in fact does not consider the possibility of interacting, as here, with the space of television production itself). For once, that frame yields a story that you can report in the *first* person. As Debbie put it: 'It's not just somewhere on telly now, it's actually somewhere I've been, I've actually stood there.'

Being on the Street

The basis for the Street set's significance seems very simple: it is the place where the programme's filming goes on, the actual place you have watched from your home over the years. There is, of course, also an important fantasy element to being on the Street, the feeling that you are in the place where the cast are filmed: it was 'quite magical really, to actually believe that you're there on the spot where . . . the stars walk along' (a comment by Barbara echoed in other interviews). But this imaginative connection with the programme's fictional frame depends on fact: the fact that the set *is* the place of external filming. What are the implications of this?

The Street's significance as the place where filming in fact goes on was marked routinely in people's language. To be on the Street set was to be on the 'actual Street', to 'be there' at the place where 'programmes are actually made'. Its houses are the 'real' places of filming, not mere 'studio sets' or 'mock-ups'. This was a principal reason why people went to the Street set: 'I just wanted to see where it was done' (Julie); 'good to see the actual street where the show is filmed' (letter). [. . .]

Visiting the Street set may even involve an element of dislocation. If television 'constantly invokes . . . an unmediated experience that is forever absent, just beyond a hand reaching for the television dial' (Anderson, 1994: 82–3), then collapsing this distance may be puzzling: 'it's really weird though walking on it, because you watch it on TV and then you're thinking, well, people actually walk down this Street filming' (as one woman put it). [. . .] For some people, the significance of 'being there' – on the Street set – goes beyond what they can rationally explain. For John, there was a sense, almost, of privilege:

> I know that's silly because literally millions of people go a year now, and millions of people have seen it, but I felt that I was the only one, I felt I was there and I'd seen it for so long, and . . . it was like a dream come true, really.

A Canadian woman, originally from India, visiting during a holiday in Europe, put it this way:

> It's hard to express what I felt when I walked up to the Street to actually feel I was there, I mean I think that's going to stay with me for ever. Because it was such a wonderful feeling, it just left me speechless, you know, I just wanted to stand there. Why does it matter so much 'just to stand there', to be able to show others you have been there?

Why does it matter so much 'just to stand there', to be able to show others you have been there?

[. . .]

People's preferences for seeing the real Street' (the 'original') are also interestingly at odds with Walter Benjamin's famous thesis (1968) on the loss of aura in the age of mechanical reproduction. What people who reject the Blackpool 'Experience' hope to obtain at GST is precisely an 'aura' — not the aura of something outside the mechanical reproduction of filming, but *the aura of the place and process of filming itself*: using Benjamin's phrase, 'its unique existence at the place where it happens to be' (ibid.: 220). As Debbie put it in relation to the Street set, 'people never appreciate it, unless they're there'.

John's language suggests that this aura, for him, is more than some general notion of 'being there' inherent in any media site, but rather a quality precisely tied to the set's material history. Benjamin defined 'authenticity' in just this way: 'the essence of all that is transmissible from [the object's] beginning, ranging from its substantive duration to its testimony to the history which it has experienced' (ibid.: 221). Compare that with John's explanation of why the Street set is better than a mere studio set:

> I have seen studios (. . .) but nothing to compare with the Street (. . .) When you're sitting in the studio, you do see (. . .) the unreality, but on the Street (. . .) it's a real street, albeit there's nothing behind the door as such. But you're still there, it's still real (. . .) There was a funny thought that went through my mind, that it had been raining (. . .) And I actually looked down and thought, this is real because there's real rain, it sounded so stupid. And I stood in a puddle and I thought, Oh Crikey! Yeah, this is real, it's not covered over, it's always outdoors . . . the actors go out in all weather (. . .) it's real rain and it's real cobbles and it's real dirt [laughs] (. . .) You don't expect a set to be that real.

The rain is significant in part, I suggest, because in a small way it is 'a testimony to the history' which the set 'has experienced' (Benjamin); it is a token of the set's authenticity and John's authentic experience of it, his definitive access to its 'aura'

The Street set as ritual place

Here is how Michael described being on the Street set:

> From the moment I put my foot on the Street I feel like a star. I start my walk down the Street starting from the 'Rovers Return' to the 'corner shop'. I look through *all* the windows and through *all* the letter boxes. I touch the stone cladding of number 9. I feel so so very happy and trouble free when I walk down the Street (. . .) I just can't believe it. Every time I walk down the Street I get that same wonderful happy feeling (. . .) It [GST] is the best thing and most wonderful thing I have ever done. [original emphasis]

There is a palpable sense of ritual here. Again, rather than dismiss it as eccentric, I want to contextualise it in terms of what is perhaps the Street set's most fundamental attraction: its status as 'ritual place'. [. . .]

We return here to the basic question: what (for all visitors, not just devoted fans) does being on the Street set involve? Being on the Street involves a comparison between what you have watched over the years and the set itself. This is, on the face of it, a banal comparison (seeing if the Street 'is actually like it is on telly', as one visitor put it), but its dimensions are worth considering. First, you are linking things in two different *time-frames*, the years during which you have watched the Street and the time now when you walk onto the set: 'for me, it was amazing because I've seen it on the TV for so many years now (. . .) For me it was brilliant to finally see everything' (woman); 'it was weird to walk down the road that I had seen on television since I was about three as it was really familiar and unfamiliar at the same time' (Sarah, letter). It is the bringing together of two separate time-frames (the time of your regular watching over the years, the time of your visit now) that allows a sense of completion: 'to finally see everything'. This sense of completion is so vivid in John's account that it is worth quoting at greater length. Immediately before he went on the Street set he had seen the video selection called 'The Coronation Street Experience'. After-wards, a curtain was pulled, revealing a wall which is partly transparent, and the Street behind:

> I shall never forget the first time that I saw the 'Street'. At the end of the tour the public is guided to a 'Coronation Street Experience' which consists of a slowly revolving platform which moves around and shows the sights and sounds of past events in the Street. As the last one fades and the revolving stage stops, you are faced with a brick wall. This slowly moves away to reveal, for the first time, the actual set of the Street outside. (letter)

Here the transition between the time-frames of long-term watching and present visit is repro-duced exactly in the transition from the final video image of the Street to the sight of the Street set itself. Barbara's account was similar:

> You went in a room where they showed you a video of sort of past episodes, and then they drew the curtain back. You'd watched it on the telly and then it was actually there. And then you set off and then you walked along it.

The feeling of walking into the space of the screen is vivid, and this 'freedom' is clearly a designed effect of sites such as GST (Rojek, 1993; Davis, 1996). It works, however, partly because it reproduces in miniature the transition between time-frames that being on the Street itself involves. That is why, for Barbara, there was 'no point of actually going on the Street and then doing the video'.[5]

Second, being on the Street involves comparing the results of two different *activities*, two ways of looking, for which sometimes people used different words. 'Watching' the Street on television – at least without new developments in interactive television – you are constrained in how you can look at the set: you are limited by camera-angles, and so on. 'Seeing' the Street set allows you to look at its details in your own time and from any angle, and then put the whole thing back together:

> I wanted (. . .) really to try and put the whole thing together myself. You know, from not just watching it on the square box at home, but to actually see it. (woman)

> I spent quite a bit of time there [on the set] and then after lunch I went back there and took a small turn [. . .] you know standing back and seeing it and picturing it in my mind as to how it appears on TV. (woman)

Seeing what the set is actually like is an active process of finding out, qualitatively different from watching television.

There is also a third, *spatial* dimension to the comparison. 'Watching' the Street is something we do in the home, whereas 'seeing' the Street set can only be done in GST's public space. Being on the set therefore connects two normally separate sites of discourse: the home and the site of media production. All these dimensions (time, activity, and space) are combined in Julie's comment:

It was nice to see. An experience that you (. . .) actually sit in your living room and you're actually watching that place, but now you're actually standing in that place, and you can say (. . .) I've actually been there, and it felt good.

'Being there' involves connecting your everyday practice of private viewing with the public place where the programme is actually filmed.

This connection of different times, places, and activities is neither neutral nor trivial:

It's magic, it's a great feeling, sitting at home when you watch telly and say *I was there!* To think you could do that. (woman)

Just nice to know that you've seen [it], when you watch telly, that you've actually been and seen it for yourself. (woman)

As we saw earlier, this connection is revived when you watch the programme in future:

I mean, we were *unbearable* when we first came home, because as soon as it came on, [we said] We were there! [Glenys laughing]. And that's where we stood! [. . . 4 pages] Every time we see it, we think, [whispers] Oh we've been there! [Glenys laughs] And it's still, it's still there, Oh, we've been there. It's really good, you know. (Susan)

Because the connection made by 'being there' is intrinsically significant in this way, the most basic acts of occupying space on the Street are significant in themselves: 'to actually stand in the Street is lovely' (woman); 'just walking up and down something you see regularly in front of your eyes' (man). It is enough that you are 'there'.

I want to suggest that what underlies the Street set's 'power of place' – the force of the connection it embodies – is the way it formalises and spatialises the symbolic hierarchy of the media frame. The work of the anthropologist Jonathan Smith (1987) is helpful in making precise this apparently abstract point. Smith has drawn on Durkheim (1981) and Levi-Strauss's (1995) theories of symbolic classification to develop an original account of ritual place. The key points of his argument for my purpose are as follows. 'Ritual' is 'a mode of paying attention . . . a process for marking interest' (ibid.: 103) rather than a particular type of content. 'Place', in turn, is 'a fundamental component of ritual: place directs attention' (ibid.), and it performs this function, again not because of any particular content, but 'rather as *social position* within a hierarchical system' (ibid.: 45, added emphasis). 'Ritual' he argues:

relies for its power on the fact that it is concerned with quite ordinary activities placed within an extraordinary setting . . . Ritual is a relationship of difference between 'nows' – the now of everyday life and the now of ritual place; the simultaneity, but not the coexistence, of 'here' and 'there'. Here (in the world) blood is a major source of impurity; there (in ritual space) blood removes impurity. Here (in the world) water is the central agent by which impurity is transmitted; there (in ritual space) washing with water carries away impurity. Neither the blood nor the water has changed; what has changed is their location. This absolute discrepancy invites thought, but cannot be thought away.

(ibid.: 109–10)

On the Street set, analogously, people do ordinary things: walking up and down, looking in shop windows, and so on. But they do them in an extraordinary setting: the frame of the Street set.

Indeed, the whole process of being on the Street, as just argued, brings out connections – and differences – between the 'ordinary' process of television viewing (the 'now' of everyday viewing) and the 'extraordinary' moment of the visit (the 'now' of being on the 'actual Street'). The two situations remain of course separate, and the difference 'cannot be thought away': it is a difference within a symbolic hierarchy. The set is not any space, any street, but the 'actual Street' that you and everyone else have been watching all those years from your home. It is, in this precise sense, a ritual place, where two 'worlds' are connected.

It is time to return to John's discussion, quoted earlier, of the rain on the set. If we apply to it the notion of the street set as ritual place – as a ritual 'frame' (in Mary Douglas' [1984] sense) that symbolically connects two hierarchically ordered places and temporalities – its meaning becomes still clearer. There is a parallelism between John's 'world' (the viewer who is temporarily a visitor) and the media's 'world': 'you're still there, it's still real', 'actors go out . . . you can walk'. For a moment the two 'worlds' intersect. There is rain in both 'worlds' (the rain which fell on the set before John came, the rain still there when he is there) and of course it is the same rain. The rain, in other words, is what *articulates* these two 'worlds', normally segregated from each other. The rain embodies the connection, and the difference, that makes the Street set a ritual place.[6]

Once we understand the Street set as a ritual place, then otherwise puzzling aspects of people's accounts become clearer. First, the importance some people attached to the set being clean: they doubted whether it was the real place of filming because parts of it were dirty. I asked Barbara about the graffiti around the backs of the set which I knew annoyed some guides. She quoted her friend's reaction: ' "I don't know how they can do it (. . .) this is the *Coronation Street*, how can they write on the fences?".' Second, there is some people's sense that entering the Street set is like crossing a boundary: a 'limen' or threshold in van Gennep's (1960) sense. We saw earlier how John and Barbara described their entry onto the set. Susan mentioned how she and Glenys deferred walking onto the set until the last moment:

> We delayed going down the Street, we really did [Glenys laughs] (. . . one page) I stepped out of the [souvenir] shop, actually onto the Street . . . I was clutching on [to Glenys] . . . [Glenys laughs] I went, Ooh! [highpitched] We're here. We're here. I went, Ooh God! It's a mad woman.

Also interesting are remarks on the small differences between people's image of the Street from television and the physical space of the set. One difference people recounted to me months after their visits was the small gap between the Rovers Return and the start of the terraced houses. Here is Julie:

> I tell you one thing that I have never noticed, that I did notice, that there's an alleyway. You've got the Rovers Return and then there's the alleyway and *then* there's the houses. Now I never noticed that before until I went to the Street (. . .) that was another thing that amazed me. (cf. John)

The importance given to this apparently trivial difference exemplifies the 'parcelling out' which Levi-Strauss regards as typical of all ritual: a process which 'makes infinite distinctions and ascribes discriminatory values to the slightest shade of difference' (1981: 672–5, quoted in Smith, 1987: 111). At GST the 'ritual' lies in elaborating the differences between Street set and television image of the Street, which condense the underlying difference between the 'media world' and the 'ordinary world' of watching.

This reinforces the sense that journeys to GST are, effectively, 'pilgrimages'. GST is a pilgrimage point in the sense that it is a central, symbolically significant place which focuses the attention of a whole territory, the dispersed 'territory' of the 'electronic network' (Rath, 1985: 200). It is a place where 'special' time can be spent apart from the time of 'ordinary' life (cf. Turner, 1974), time that is special simply because spent within 'media space': 'your time on the Street'. What is affirmed by going there is not necessarily values associated with *Coronation Street* the programme, or even with the act of watching it. What is affirmed, more fundamentally, are the values condensed in the symbolic hierarchy of the media frame itself: its symbolic division of the social world into two.

Notes

1 Cf. Bill Bryson's comment in his popular English travel diary: '[it was] a profoundly thrilling experience to walk up and down this famous street' (1996: 229).
2 In GST's exhibition of video clips from the programme, a former cast member is scripted to say: 'I hope you enjoy your time on the Street as much as I did mine'.
3 On media-related performativity, see Abercrombie and Longhurst (1998: 78–96), Chaney (1994: 170–71, 197).
4 Recalled by some visitors not as incidental background, but as 'memorabilia' (Julie), 'a history of the Street' (Susan).
5 When John first visited the Street set you could *only* enter from the video room: it constituted the end of the 'tour'. Later, to John's dismay, you could approach the Street from any angle, without seeing the video footage first.
6 Admittedly, Smith's account of the ritual water/wine and my own (and John's) account of the rain on the set place the emphasis differently. The first emphasises the *change* in status which a ritual location has on the water/wine, while the second concentrates on the rain on the set and emphasises that it is *both* ordinary and (since on the set) special. This is simply to focus on different moments in structurally similar processes.

References

Abercrombie, Nicholas and Longhurst, Brian (1998) *Audiences: A Sociological Theory of Performance and Imagination*, London: Sage.
Anderson, Christopher (1994) 'Disneyland' in Horace Newcomb (ed.) *Television: The Critical View* 5th edition, New York: Oxford University Press.
Benjamin, Walter (1968) 'The Work of Art in the Age of Mechanical Reproduction' in *Illuminations* tr. H. Zolm, New York: Schocken Books.
Bilig, Michael (1992) *Talking of the Royal Family*, London: Routledge.
Bryson, Bill (1996) *Notes From a Small Island*, London: Black Swan.
Buckingham, David (1993) *Children Talking Television: The Making of Television Literacy*, London: The Falmer Press.
Chaney, David (1994) *The Cultural Turn: Scene-Setting Essays in Contemporary Cultural History*, London: Routledge.
Connerton, Paul (1989) *How Societies Remember*, Cambridge: Cambridge University Press.
Couldry, Nick (1998a) 'The View from Inside the Simulacrum: Visitors' Tales from the Set of *Coronation Street*', *Leisure Studies*, 17(2): 94–107.
—— (1998b) 'Sites of Power, Journeys of Discovery: Place and Power in the Hierarchy of the Media Frame', unpublished PhD dissertation, University of London.
Davis, Susan (1996) 'The Theme Park: Global Industry and Cultural Form', *Media, Culture and Society*, 18(3): 399–422.
de Certeau, Michel (1984) *The Practice of Everyday Life* tr. S. Rendall, Berkeley: University of California Press.
Douglas, Mary (1984) [o.p. 1966] *Purity and Danger: An Analysis of Concepts of Pollution and Taboo*, London: Ark Paperbacks.
Durkheim, Emile (1995) [o.p. 1912] *The Elementary Forms of Religious Life* tr. K. Fields, Glencoe: Free Press.
Dyer, Richard, Geraghty, Christine, Jordan, Marion, Lovell, Terry, Paterson, Richard and Stewart, John (1981) *Coronation Street*, London: British Film Institute.

Eco, Umberto (1986) *Faith in Fakes*, London: Secker and Warburg.

Fjellman, Stephen (1992) *Vinyl Leaves: Walt Disney World and America*, Boulder: Westview Press.

Geraghty, Christine (1981) 'The Continuous Serial – A Definition' in Richard Dyer, Christine Geraghty, Marion Jordan, Terry Lovell, Richard Paterson and John Stewart *Coronation Street*, London: British Film Institute.

—— (1991) *Women and Soap Opera: A Study of Prime-Time Soaps*, Cambridge: Polity Press.

Halbwachs, Maurice (1992) [o.p. 1924] *On Collective Memory* tr. L. Coser, Chicago: University of Chicago Press.

Hayden, Dolores (1995) *The Power of Place: Urban Landscapes as Public History*, Cambridge, Mass.: The MIT Press.

Levi-Strauss, Claude (1981) *The Naked Man* tr. J. and D. Weightman, London: Jonathan Cape.

Maffesoli, Michel (1996) *The Time of the Tribes: The Decline of Individualism in Mass Society* tr. D. Smith, London. Sage.

Project on Disney, The (1995) *Inside the Mouse: Work and Play at Disney World*, Durham and London: Duke University Press.

Rath, Claus-Dieter (1985) 'The Invisible Network: Television as an Institution in Everyday Life' in Philip Drummond and Richard Paterson (eds) *Television in Transition*, London: British Film Institute.

Rojck, Chris (1993) *Ways of Escape: Modern Transformations in Leisure and Travel*, London: Macmillan.

Sallnow, Michael (1981) 'Communitas Reconsidered: The Sociology of Andean Pilgrimage', *Man* (N.S.), 16: 163–82.

—— (1987) *Pilgrims of the Andes. Regional Cults in Cusco*, Washington DC: Smithsonian Press.

Shields, Rob (1991) *Places on the Margin: Alternative Geographies of Modernity*, London: Routledge.

Smith, Jonathan Z. (1987) *To Take Place: Toward Theory in Ritual*, Chicago: University of Chicago Press.

Stallybrass, Peter and White, Allon (1986) *The Politics and Poetics of Transgression*, London: Methuen.

Turner, Victor (1974) *Dramas, Fields and Metaphors: Symbolic Action in Human Society*, Ithaca and London: Cornell University Press.

—— and Turner, Edith (1978) *Image and Pilgrimage in Christian Culture: Anthropological Perspectives*, Oxford: Basil Blackwell.

Urry, John (1990) *The Tourist Gaze: Leisure and Travel in Contemporary Societies*, London: Sage.

van Gennep, Arnold (1960) [o.p. 1908] *The Rites of Passage* tr. M. Vizedom and G. Caffee, London: Routledge & Kegan Paul.

Willis, Paul (1990) *Common Culture: Symbolic Work and Play in the Everyday Cultures of the Young*, Milton Keynes: Open University Press.

Chapter 22

ERIC FREEDMAN

PUBLIC ACCESS/PRIVATE CONFESSION
Home video as (queer) community television

MY INITIAL GOAL IN WRITING about public access cable television was to validate the many programs I felt had been overlooked in previous critical and historical work on access, and to claim the shows that I watched in my own home as essential ingredients in the mix of community activism. What is the role of the psychic, the healer, or the guru in the field of localized production and the sphere of more general excursions in community-based production?

Public access programming on cable television emerged as a new form of journalism and of noncommercial television in the United States in the late 1960s and early 1970s. At issue during this period was the reservation of cable television channels for noncommercial use (a struggle over media access that had centered on the AM radio spectrum in the 1930s and the broadcast television spectrum in the 1950s). These cable TV channels, conceived as free of charge and available on a nondiscriminatory basis, were meant to provide programming controlled by the general public and public institutions rather than by the cable operator. A Federal Communications Commission mandate laid out the general contours for not only public access but also educational and government access provisions. "Public access" itself was construed to mean that the cable company should not only make available airtime but also make available equipment. As an ideally democratic arrangement, literally anybody could produce programming and use channel space on a first-come, first-served basis, with a freedom of speech and action subject only to standard obscenity and libel laws. In some cases, a local organization was set up to manage the access system (oftentimes a nonprofit city government entity), while in others, the cable operator itself assumed these duties. The drive for access stations was part of a larger community television movement, which aspired to use TV as a means of communication and empowerment without interference from professional middlemen such as journalists, directors, producers, and corporate officers. Such a drive, however, would only be fully realized in cable access production if access personnel could link technical training to a critique of the institutional imperatives of broadcasting for their prospective community producers.

Access programming, like the other forms of independent media production which preceded it (and run concurrent with it), is invested in the dissemination of information in a variety of generic forms. In that this information is still being disseminated along a marginal distributive pathway, current access programs have an affinity to guerrilla television from the 1960s and 1970s. Yet, this is the only link to guerrilla activity for many recent programs; at the level of form and/or content, many of them are not inherently political. Some programs use the stylistic vocabulary of guerrilla television, while their content is actually divorced from the politics of guerrilla activity. For this reason, it is problematic to speak of all contemporary access programming as being political. When the program is subversive in its content but does not use the stylistic vocabulary of alternative media production (choosing instead to replicate the codes of commercial television), it is equally problematic to speak of the program as being political. Nonetheless, much of contemporary access work hints at the various limits of commercial fare, and opens up the possibility for thinking differently about the television industry.

Media activism takes a variety of forms. Its most obvious manifestation, guerrilla video practice, is linked to issues of visibility; at a time when consciousness raising was a vital part of collective media production, showing that people could produce (demonstrating what the technology could do), and being out on the streets producing, was just as important as what was being produced. As articulated by Michael Shamberg in his 1971 book *Guerrilla Television*, my use of the word "guerrilla" does not refer simply to tactics of physical subversion (pirate broadcasting and the like) but more importantly to the construction of alternative support systems for the manufacture and distribution of information. Indeed, much of contemporary cable access practice is best understood using this latter definition of guerrilla activity; although the work is not necessarily produced on the streets (activity is commonly housed in the studio), notions of visibility are still vital. People from a variety of backgrounds have come to their cable centers, some with histories in street activism (political activism) and some without.

What these two models of guerrilla activity share is their dependence upon the formation of a communal identity among respective media makers, all of whom must be united toward a common goal of shared resistance. Yet, this identity is not carved out in the execution of one project or in the formation of one collective; rather, it exists in the liminal spaces between projects and collectives or between users at disparate facilities.[1] Although not all access producers may think of themselves as engaging in acts of resistance, or for that matter of having a shared communal identity with other access producers (although I would argue that all access producers are part of a community, to the extent that they are obligated to abide by the operating procedures of a particular facility and, in following policy, are taking into consideration the needs of their colleagues), it is my intent here to articulate the various communal identities attached to access producers, productions, and products (the middle term referring to the producerly act, as distinct from its end result—the program).

The products of public access cable television production have not changed much since the 1970s, although many of the boundaries between program types have been breached (a boundary-blurring that is found in commercial programming as well). In his 1975 assessment of cablecast programs from 1971 to 1973 on the Teleprompter Manhattan cable system, Alan Wurtzel identified a fixed number of program categories (eleven in all) and found that the largest percentage of programming was either entertainment, informational, or instructional.[2] In her study of programming on New York City's Teleprompter Channels C and D—a survey of shows from November to December 1972—Pamela Doty found that the most common program format was the "talking head" show.[3] The shows identified by Doty were put on by various public organizations (such as the Harlem Better Business Bureau and The Society for the Prevention of Drug Addiction), and all seem to be talk shows, devoted to disseminating information by those people with expertise in the group's area of interest.[4] According to Doty, the second most common format on public access was the videotape of a real event (anything not specifically staged for television), such as a block party, a press conference, a demonstration, or even a birthday party.[5] Talk shows and real-event videotapes made up about 95 percent of all public access television programming in Doty's study. Among the other 5 percent were the "video visit" and the man-in-the-street interview.[6]

It is clear that even in its infancy, public access provided a valuable forum for presenting material that was, for a variety of reasons, unavailable to the television audience via traditional broadcast stations. For the most part, this programming was designed for special-interest audiences, produced by local community groups, and featured local talent; and in most cases, the programming was directed at residents in a particular neighborhood. Facilities for live programming were not available at the time, so news programming was minimal, and call-in shows were nonexistent.

Rather than simply quantify contemporary public access formats, here I want to explore the ideological residues attached to one particular form of production, that of the "video visit." Doty's analysis leaves the quantitative realm only to speculate about the relative boredom produced by each of her objects of study, while Wurtzel's quantification of the contents of access never leads back to his initial desire to understand whether public access is actually being used in the service of communal identities.

Many public access producers have turned to their local access centers as a way of breaking into commercial television and are using access either as an inexpensive testing ground for mapping out their ideas before pitching them to commercial production houses and/or networks or to simply promote themselves in their efforts to be discovered (as TV personalities) by commercial agents and/or producers. Yet, the access producer's interest in self is not always connected to commercial (or self-gratifying) pursuits. While many producers title their programs after themselves, and many local access bulletin boards literally read like phonebooks (lists of surnames), some starring producers use their shows not to promote themselves but to promote their communities. What Doty refers to as the "video visit" is the kind of program that perhaps contributes the most toward developing the local community spirit that the earliest proponents of public access tried to encourage. At bottom, community spirit rests on personal acquaintance and feelings of mutual involvement among neighbors; for many citizens, participating in community affairs and joining civic groups is only a secondary pursuit.

The individualistic performances of the video visit are distinct from shows that simply rely on the host's star power. These diaristic video "house-calls" play an important role in mapping an imagined community (of producers and viewers). Such semi-autobiographical shows are not simply centered on the host—the host as producer, the host as the star who can secure the best acts—but more significantly, in the broadest sense, they are about the host. The programs work to define the host's own subjectivity, and in doing so, they are more than private confessionals given a public airing; these tapes are site-specific interventions that have just as much to say about the communities in which they are produced and aired, as they do about the individual host/producer. It could be argued that network airing of home videos say as much about culture in general as their access counterparts, but access shows can in very concrete ways speak to the socioeconomic determinations of broadcasting, while network programs work on every level to conceal the same determinations.

The idea of democratic video as taken up by corporate television (in programs such as *America's Funniest Home Videos*) is quite different from that espoused by access producers working on the margins. William Boddy notes that while many U.S. independent video makers working in the early years of the medium based their optimistic views of the new mass media on the theories of Bertolt Brecht (*Radio as an Apparatus of Communication*), Walter Benjamin (*The Work of Art in the Age of Mechanical Reproduction*) and Hans Magnus Enzensberger (*Constituents of a Theory of the Media*), what they culled from these texts was the impropriety of the imbalance between the number of transmitters and the number of receivers of electronic media (the former outnumbered by the latter).[7] Oversimplifying the equation, many artists sought to simply invert this ratio, ignoring what Brecht, Benjamin, and Enzensberger had formulated as the inherent "tension between the social formation and communications technology."[8] Indeed, the networks have since capitalized on this tension, developing a whole new genre of programming for the acting out of "active citizenship," programs that subsist by soliciting material from their viewers. Shows such as *America's Funniest Home Videos* and *MTV News Unfiltered*, among others, invite viewers to send in their prerecorded tapes and in so doing seem to speak to universal access; yet, these gestures only reinforce the divide between the professional and the amateur production, both in style and in content. The viewer's tape relies on the sponsored program to give it meaning (subjugated to the logic of the host program's narrative) and invites a visual comparison between it and the professionally produced show, the interstitial material and the commercial.

This analysis examines the unique parameters of home modes that are narrowcast in the spaces of public access and considers the significance of "liveness" in a commercial-free environment. This essay reads the ideological resonances of select public access cable television production methods and positions the resulting access work in relation to commercial television. The purpose here is to consider whether local access producers can activate a communal identity that is otherwise unrealized by network broadcasting, as well as to reveal the multiple communities that may be signified in access work.

Redefining the limits of field production and broadcast distribution through visual and narrative excess, access shows that are performative invoke an aspect of liveness, commonly figured as the unpredictable scenario of an on-the-street interview, or the traveling host who drops in on guests unexpectedly. The particular subject of this analysis is *The Paul Kent Show*, which follows the host, Paul Kent, into the homes and haunts of a number of friends and celebrities in West Hollywood. The most popular of Paul's visits are those with local gay porn stars, programs that apparently reveal both Paul's private desires as well as those of his guests (with Paul encouraging his guests to strip down before each show's end).

Distinct from a live event program (such as a tape of a rally or parade), Kent's show is exemplary of a mode that involves a unique form of interaction between host and (potential) subject; the parameters are largely unspecified, and the coverage is more performance-based (literally involving the host's body) than reportage. What is relayed is not information but the results of a predefined situation in which the character/host is willing to give up a degree of control (under the constant, albeit constructed, threat of the show's "live" cancellation during midbroadcast).

As a form of video vérité, this work has a structured structurelessness; it is work of a perpetual nature, without a literal narrative arc. As such, it works as autobiography, replicating subjectivity and merging the lived context with the apparatus of production. Kent frequently addresses the camera, talking his viewer through each visit and making sarcastic asides about both himself and his guests. Kent's crew is minimal (typically just a camera operator), and the events are apparently unrehearsed. Each episode is largely a conversation without direction. Kent begins each program from the confines of his apartment, addressing his audience before leaving to find his guest (as the show unfolds, the audience becomes voyeur rather than participant, as the conversation shifts from one between Kent and his viewer to one between Kent and his guest). Kent is uniquely responsive to his viewers, as one show's introduction suggests:

> Hi everybody. My name is Paul Kent and this is *The Paul Kent Show*. And thank you for watching again, and again, and again. Or if you haven't, please continue watching again, and again, and again, so that you'll be part of my audience. I have to have an audience to stay on the air. The audience that has been watching has informed me that they like the shows about the young guys that are in turmoil rather than the shows that are about successful gay men who belong to organizations and are uplifting the community. You guys are really into drama. So I have to give you the shows that you like.

While Kent does not really need to worry about his ratings, he nevertheless is invested in providing audience members with what they want (solicited either by fan mail or phone calls).

Autobiography is signified here in performativity: the cult of the individual and his or her play in an environment. This work is not evidence in and of itself of a structured resistance to a mainstream system (of commercial television); it does not evoke a blocking of narrative codes; a rupture, a movement through narrative to a space governed by antinarrative. The work does not bother with revision, with shaping experience around the argumentative edit; as an extension of earlier vérité practices, the mechanisms of production and distribution are distinct, while the resonance of vérité codes and aesthetics have themselves been radically redefined by private and public discourse.

Stylistically aligned with a home mode, this work is nevertheless more interested in forward movement (psychical development, emerging subjectivity) than in nostalgia. More importantly, the work reads like a violation of public space, as it resonates (formally) like a home mode not designed for public exhibition (because home modes need a narrative context or frame to be publicly consumed), and represents a literal violation of domestic space; yet, it is inherently linked to social space, returning to the public eye via public access (a destination admitted in its dialogic address).

Drawing from Emile Benveniste's and Roman Jakobson's distinction between utterance and enunciation, the true locus of autobiography is not the past as re-created in autobiography but rather the re-creation of that past in the present unfolding of the autobiographical act. The self-referential gesture is the central and determining event in the transaction of autobiographical reference.[9] Kent is indeed uttering and enunciating; the latter is evidenced in the repertoire of tasks required to conceive, shoot, and edit. This is not a confession (as we as viewers can read the movement from "I" to "you"), nor is it an essay (the speaking subject may be the subject of the statement, but this is not arrived at in an explicit coming to consciousness or an act of analysis, such as the edit).

Nonetheless, the private speech of the individual engaged in the autobiographical act is derived from a public discourse structured by code and convention, the unwitting imitation of contemporary common narrative forms. In this case, however, Kent's reflexive cheap media aesthetic foregrounds the contemporary lingua franca of verisimilitude: "I have to do these extreme close-ups in front of the fireplace because you probably think I have a beautiful apartment and I don't."

Public access programs are products of a particular community, physical signifiers of a particular community (both in their content and by virtue of their very existence), and potential tools for extending the boundaries of a particular community. Community, apart from representing shared physical space (geography), can more abstractly represent shared psychical space. As a mode of address, many gay and lesbian public access programs pitch themselves to a gay and lesbian community: a group of individuals with a shared value system, a commonality assumed to be intrinsic to occupying a shared "space" at the margins (being marginal), a shared sensibility at the level of same-sex desire (a way of speaking to a particular margin), or even a shared "reading" strategy. Yet, the generic grammar of television prevents certain programs from acting out, and acting queerly (outside of the limits of the text), while narrative itself can be an insidious form of regulation. My use of the term "text" refers both to the individual show and the larger frame of television.

West Hollywood Channel 36 is a city access center funded by franchise fees; Channel 36 is a center run by the city of West Hollywood (under the jurisdiction of city government) rather than by the multiple system operator (Century Communications).[10] Other cities around Los Angeles such as Santa Monica and Eagle Rock have active public access production facilities; however, both of these cities rely on their cable companies to manage and operate access production and programming.

The general mission of West Hollywood Public Access (WHPA) is to facilitate communication within the community by providing members of the West Hollywood community access to cable television via the Public Access Channel 36. Public access is available to community members for training on access facilities to produce programming for the access channel; public access is also available for community members to submit programs in their possession that they would like to see on the access channel. WHPA falls under the Public Information Office/Cable Television division of the City Manager's office, department of the City of West Hollywood. It is run by the public access coordinator under the supervision of the city's public information officer. Producers are categorized as either resident users (those with permanent residency in West Hollywood) or non-resident users; the latter must be affiliated with a West Hollywood-based organization that has a resident user on file.

WHPA is one of the more active sites of queer access production (though not all of the programming aired on the channel is queer, and West Hollywood itself is not simply a population of gays and lesbians; and the producer demographics at WHPA reflect the general community's demographics). It is a useful arena to discuss the intersection of community politics and media production at a structural level, considering the birth of the area, the integral nature of city politics, the economic infrastructure of the area, perceived cultural needs, producer demographics, and the demographics of the population as a whole. These, of course, are many of the same arenas that connect with the emergence of access centers across the country, so a study of any one access center (such as Channel 36) can also reveal some useful generalities about the birth of access, the history of access production, and the significant role that access itself can play in defining a community.

Populated by members of our local community, although commonly people we do not know, the public access channels of local cable television are littered with shows that we may personally have no interest in. Regardless, these programs are a fundamental part of a local politics. They are programs produced by, for (in the interests of), and starring members of a local community: community in a physical sense referring to individuals residing in a particular geographic radius. Interviewing a diverse array of personalities that live and work in West Hollywood, including porn stars and homeless drug users, Kent is not simply giving voice to alternative representations (because most residents of West Hollywood are acquainted with at least the types of characters that Kent features) but, more significantly, personalizing these representations, not allowing them to exist as universal signifiers (or stereotypes). Kent paints a portrait of the West Hollywood community by videotaping individuals in rather mundane moments. The community, as Kent's show leads the viewer to believe, is more appropriately depicted as a series of personal and private moments, rather than more collective and public ones (such as rallies or parades). To this end, Kent displays his technical conceits to his viewers, in a manner that moves beyond the tactics of demystification employed by such groups as Paper Tiger, and fully explicates his process and implicates his audience in the act of production.[11] Kent identifies himself as one of many producers of meaning; when he grounds his aesthetic concerns in guilt (apologizing for the mess in his apartment), he displaces himself from the privileged position of author.

In one episode, Kent invites a young homeless man back to his apartment. The act is functional; it brings an otherwise transient man to a localizable space and inevitably positions the man as a subject for Kent's half-hour episode. At the same time, the functionality of Kent's gesture is complicated by its conflicted public and private status. The public dimension of Kent's interview is the dialogic process by which Kent clearly positions the man as a social type, though complexly so; the man is homeless, addicted to drugs, and hustling, and Kent's interview reveals that he has been alienated from his family and is perhaps only gay for pay (his sexual orientation is never clearly fixed in the interview). The private dimension of Kent's interview is visual, evoked in elements of performance and style; by using the term "private," I am suggesting that particular aspects of performance and style reveal Kent's individual desire. Certainly, in that it is visualized and broadcast, Kent performs his desire for public consumption. The episode is shot with a single camera, and divided into segments. Each segment is shot as a single uninterrupted take with minimal reframing and there are no transitions (such as cutaways) between segments. This leads to radical breaks in continuity; the audience is presented with a jump cut each time that Kent and his subject are revealed in a new location during successive segments. Kent begins the interview in his living room from behind the camera, posing his questions from offscreen while operating the camera. In the next segment, Kent has framed himself with his subject, and they are conversing in front of the camera while still seated in Kent's living room. In this segment, Kent physically prompts his guest by gesturing to him and by occasionally putting his arm around him. Kent's subject is in a drug-induced haze, and Kent tries to steer his conversation and draw him out; he attempts to pull together his guest's fragmented stream of consciousness mutterings. In the third segment, Kent has moved with his subject to the bedroom; as they converse, the man lies on his stomach with his shirt off while Kent sits up in bed next to him, stroking his back. In the fourth segment, Kent once again speaks to his subject from behind the camera but has relocated to the bathroom; Kent continues the interview while the man takes a bath, and the conversation fluctuates between the immediate (they talk about how dirty the man is) and the general.

What is the status of Kent's program as autobiography, and more generally, how does autobiography signify on public access? In the case of Kent's work, as autobiography, it consists of a unified identity of author, narrator, and subject; in this case, authorship is linked to his status as producer and oftentimes camera operator. Although Kent's show moves from an exploration of self to an exploration of other, disjoining author/narrator from subject in the particular, he nevertheless fuses himself with his subject (to the extent that the subject speaks of/to Paul Kent's desire). It is this fusion of subject as self and subject as other that is the appeal to community.

The autobiographical act in Kent's show is of a community speaking to and about itself; access can be a signifier of a local identity and a local community. As a reader, a fellow producer of access in West Hollywood, or a member of a West Hollywood community, this text works as a collective autobiography, of a community writing itself. Yet, when displaced from its site of origin, the status of the work as collective autobiography is difficult to perceive. As a communal form of production, the work is dependent upon Kent's residing in a particular place; his resident status in West Hollywood gives him access to the production equipment, the facility, and channel time. At the same time, the existence of the facility itself speaks to the collectivity of citizens working with city officials to secure funding for the facility, a willingness of the community to turn over franchise fees to the creation and operation of the facility. The work functions as collective autobiography when it is read in its local frame (the West Hollywood home). Although the work's literal narrative is a continual present, it nevertheless speaks of a history of legislative action in the City of West Hollywood. The subject of the work is West Hollywood—a site, a geographic locus, a community—and the author of the work is indeed one and the same (to the extent that Kent's program speaks to a larger authorial voice, that of the city that has made it possible for him to speak through video).[12] In this manner, access activates a particular inflection of autobiography that mass-produced, distributed, or specifically broadcast acts cannot, and it embodies a potential for self-referentiality that is greater than in any commercial text. The liberatory/democratizing discourse of access is thus not that it simply allows more people to speak but that it implicitly allows people to speak about the ability to speak, to the extent that it refers back to the basic socioeconomic conditions that have made their speech possible.

Local productions that serve to center particular queer personalities do little to contribute to forging a communal identity. The most liberatory local shows rework commercial media processes toward democratic ends (activating program content and/or program form) and in some way speak to the host's identity as a community member (de-centering the host). Yet, it is often difficult to understand how locally produced programs activate (or fail to activate) the signification of a local community and its politics; when local shows are divorced from their indigenous sites of production, distribution, and exhibition, their use value is quite hard to assess. Any consideration of local programming should not subject its objects of study to the same strictures used to evaluate nationally inflected productions; it is quite limiting to ask that public access speak only to a national politic that is itself expressly popular and oftentimes benignly democratic.

At the same time, the ideological underpinnings of any national network and any local show need to be examined in light of actual production strategies. The national text is limited in its radicalism, in its ability to speak of uniquely inflected local politics, if it is forged from traditional televisual formats. Likewise, even the most local show is limited if it embraces a conservative aesthetic. Rather than simply generalizing about how both the national and the local show operate, it is important to ground any reading in a study of form. The national show seems less likely to be radical in its aesthetic, for aesthetic radicalism seems at odds with broadcast ability. But the local show is not inherently more radical in its aesthetic.

Formal analysis needs to be reattached to a reading of ideology. How does aesthetic verisimilitude (the relation of the access text to the network text) inhibit any program's ability to effectively speak to, for, and about a community? The battle invoked in the identity politics of the text (as producers choose among formal strategies, to produce television or countertelevision) is quite similar to that invoked in identity politics at large. Community as it applies to gay and lesbian subjects mobilizes and radicalizes both sameness and difference, but more importantly, one form of sameness and difference: sameness within and difference without. To formulate an inherent unity, the idea(l) of community masks differences within and samenesses without. What must also be examined are the reasons for the call to community. A notion of community forged in deference to nostalgia is disempowering, because it ignores the particulars of current social and economic formations; one is blinded by (or blind to) history, so to speak. Indeed, differences are what the concept of community is intended to overcome, as Linda Singer notes,

> Whether through appeal to a myth of common origins in God or to the natural order, to preestablished harmonies, human nature, or social contracts—to name but a few of the apparati nominated for this function—the effect of these hegemonic formations of community has been to solidify a logic of sameness with respect to that which it also collects, while concealing or mystifying the mechanisms by which this effect is produced.[13]

What notions of community as shared resistance conceal are possible forms of colonization from within, while the call to "community standards" is itself an authorizing force of exclusion. As gay and lesbian access producers seek inclusion in the mainstream, their programs risk losing their political vitality. The degree to which any program can speak to *a* gay and lesbian community should be questioned, because the identity of a national community of gays and lesbian is itself suspect. The cry for equal representation is a dangerous one indeed. As gay and lesbian programming pushes to the mainstream and goes national (forever losing its queerness), localism is left at the margins, while alternative representational strategies are either never articulated or, once articulated, are replaced by convention (or simply become conventional). My ideal vision is one of national marginality, of local countertelevision efforts that add up to a nation of counter-programming but do not constitute a national movement; yet, this seems unlikely

The drive toward differentiation is matched by the drive toward sameness, and these drives can be addressed at the level of form as well as content, with the former attached to the production of the television text and the latter attached to the production of identity. The need to differentiate a queer identity is balanced by the need to find a shared vocabulary to express that identity, to locate a community of a shared sensibility; in the best case scenario, the imagined community manifests itself as an actual viewing community (the program's assumed demographic), and readily definable production techniques (techniques that are not invisible but can be easily read by a viewer) promote a bond between producer, player and viewer.

The need to differentiate the access program from network television fare is often balanced by a desire for sameness; the difference that is made manifest in a program's content (the representation of, for instance, the queer body) often is not carried into the program's form. When a program mirrors the format or genre of the network text or tries for verisimilitude at the level of "polish" (using a seamless technique and demonstrating a level of skill and surface—which refers to more than shooting on a high-grade format—that can be equated with standards of professionalism), its producers are obviously not interested in an immediate visual differentiation of their product from network fare, although the program may ultimately read differently if only because it depicts something else. In this case, where content may be at odds with the network text but form is not, the disruptive effect of difference has been partly erased and the punitive rhetoric of difference perhaps internalized. In the case in which both form and content of the access text mirror the network text, difference may be erased altogether. Finally, in the case in which both form and content of the access text are distinct from the network text, there seems to be a demand for the recognition of difference. In each of these three scenarios, however, there are two superseding discourses. The first is that of the network text, against which difference ultimately becomes meaningful; if the access text is constantly compared to the network text, the network text is centered and as such is defining the margins (or appropriating them, erasing difference and consequently deradicalizing the access text; such was the effect when guerrilla news-gathering techniques were adopted as the network standard for electronic news gathering in the early 1970s). The second discourse is what Singer identifies as the totalizing discourse associated with hegemonic forms of authority; although this discourse encompasses the network text itself, it is much larger, referring to the voice that has the power (through language) to activate the use of the term "community."[14] It is the degree to which the access producer gives up this voice, by not speaking or simply not producing, that ultimately determines what is articulated across the spaces of access. Even the most commercial access text (one that replicates the form and content of the network text) can be read as resistant if its meaning is not deduced by or for the prevailing hegemony.[15] The ability to speak differently about access, appealing to any of a number of communal identities, is the ultimate sign of empowerment.

The utopic visions of television, cable, and video born in the 1970s have undergone significant revision in subsequent decades, reflecting changes in the media landscape and responding to significant political struggles in which media policy and regulation seem unavoidably attached to broader social issues. The catalogue of work created by queers includes tapes about civil rights, human rights, and identity politics: tapes that simultaneously play on community identity and self-empowerment. Yet, these images are not always explicitly activist; in the 1990s, the on-the-street demonstration appears less frequently than the studio variety show. Nonetheless, there are shared frames of reference through which one must consider all contemporary queer access work, frames that include the history of the gay and lesbian movement, the queering of movement rhetoric, and the AIDS crisis, but just as important, the history of the hardware (television, video, and cable) and the battle waged over public access itself.

Notes

1   A liminal state is one defined by its transiency in time and space, in this instance referencing the degree to which consciousness is situated between arenas, in flux and in motion rather than static or situated in a fixed position, identity, moment, location, or group.

2   Alan Wurtzel, "Public-Access Cable TV: Programming," *Journal of Communication* 25, no. 3 (Summer 1975): 16.

3   Here, style (the head shot) assumes the status of genre, and content is erased altogether.

4   Pamela Doty, "Public-Access Cable TV: Who Cares?" *Journal of Communication* 25, no. 3 (Summer 1975): 34.

5   Ibid., 36.

6   Ibid., 38.

7   Brecht, with the cry "For innovations, against renovation!" suggests that the new media (in this case radio) may be used to restructure the social order but only if its use value is reconsidered; even then, the notion of a social order that must "surrender" suggests a conflict between the individual and the state. Enzensberger calls for everyone to become a manipulator (of the media) but warns of the dangers of disguised social control (by, in particular, bourgeois culture). Finally, Benjamin asserts the positive social potential of the new media (in this case film) in a utopic stance on the political utility of mass media (a position that must be understood within the context of fascism). See: Bertolt Brecht, "The Radio as an Apparatus of Communication," in *Brecht on Theatre: The Developments of an Aesthetic*, translated and edited by John Willett (New York: Hill and Wang, 1964) 51–3. Walter Benjamin, "The Work of Art in the Age of Mechanical Reproduction," in *Illuminations*, translated by Harry Zohn (New York: Schocken Books, 1969) 217–51. Hans Magnus Enzensberger, "Constituents of a Theory of the Media," in *The Consciousness Industry: On Literature, Politics and the Media*, translated by Stuart Hood (New York: The Seabury Press, 1974) 95–128.

8   William Boddy, "Alternative Television in the United States," *Screen* 31, no. 1 (Spring 1990): 101.

9   This conception of autobiography is based on the work of Philippe Lejeune and a discussion of Lejeune's work authored by Paul John Eakin. See: Philippe Lejeune, *On Autobiography*, edited by Paul John Eakin (Minneapolis: University of Minnesota Press, 1989). Emile Benveniste's work on the nature of communication and the act of utterance and his consideration of subjectivity in language are among his significant contributions to general linguistics; while Roman Jakobson's application of structuralism to the study of linguistics provided the theoretical groundwork for the delineation of the distinctive features in phonology. See, for instance: Emile Benveniste, *Problems in General Linguistics*, translated by Mary Elizabeth Meek (Coral Gables, Florida: University of Miami Press, 1971). Roman Jakobson and Morris Halle, *Fundamentals of Language* (The Hague, The Netherlands: Mouton and Co., 1956).

10 The cable franchise agreement for the City of West Hollywood expired in January 2000; renewal negotiations are currently under way between the City of West Hollywood and Adelphia, the new owner of Century Cable.

11 The Paper Tiger Television Collective formed in 1981 to produce cable programming for the public access channel in New York City. Its earliest programs featured media critics performing close readings of various tools (newspapers, tabloids, television shows) of the communications industry. Paper Tiger assumed the structure of an open-ended collective of volunteer staff members who assisted producers of specific episodes.

12 Ironically, the City of West Hollywood is considering removing Kent's show from the access lineup, following a viewer report that one episode of the program contained obscene footage from a gay porn video.

13 Linda Singer, "Recalling a Community at Loose Ends," in *Community at Loose Ends*, ed. Miami Theory Collective (Minneapolis: University of Minnesota Press, 1991), 124.

14 Ibid., 125.

15 The concept of hegemony emerges from classical Marxism and is developed in the work of Antonio Gramsci. The term refers to the exertion of authority by particular social groups over other subordinate groups; the resulting power structure is arrived at through the winning (and the subsequent internalization) of consent rather than through coercion. The dominant ideology, reflective of the ruling class and its ruling ideas, is naturalized, it is never brought into question and remains seemingly unattached to a particular interest group. See: Antonio Gramsci, *Selections from the Prison Notebooks of Antonio Gramsci*, translated and edited by Quintin Hoare and Geoffrey Nowell Smith (New York: International Publishers: 1971).

Bibliography

Benjamin, W. (1969) *Illuminations*, H. Zohn (trans.), New York: Schocken Books.

Benveniste, E. (1971) *Problems in General Linguistics*, M. E. Meek (trans.), Coral Gables, Florida: University of Miami Press.

Boddy, W. (1990) "Alternative Television in the United States," *Screen* 31(1): 101.

Doty, P. (1975) "Public-Access Cable TV: Who Cares?," *Journal of Communication* 25 (3):34.

Eakin, P. J. (1989) *On Autobiography*, Minneapolis: University of Minnesota Press.

Enzensberger, H. M. (1974) *The Consciousness Industry: On Literature, Politics and the Media*, S. Hood (trans.), New York: The Seabury Press.

Hoare, Q. and Nowell Smith, G. (trans. and eds) (1971) *Selections from the Prison Notebooks of Antonio Gramsci*, New York: International Publishers.

Jakobson, R. and Halle, M. (1956) *Fundamentals of Language*, The Hague: Mouton and Co.

Singer, L. (1991) "Recalling a Community at Loose Ends," in Miami Theory Collective (eds) *Community at Loose Ends*, Minneapolis: University of Minnesota Press: 124.

Willett, J. (ed.) (1964) *Brecht on Theatre: the Developments of an Aesthetic*, New York: Hill and Wang.

Wurtzel, A. (1975) 'Public-Access Cable TV: Programming', *Journal of Communication* 25 (3): 16.

Chapter 23

BRIAN LARKIN

HAUSA DRAMAS AND THE RISE OF VIDEO CULTURE IN NIGERIA

This is a demo tape. If you have bought or rented this movie call 1-800-NO COPIES. All calls confidential.

Copyright message found on many Hollywood videos on sale in Nigeria

IT USED TO BE THAT VIEWERS IN NIGERIA could watch only what the government provided for them on one or two television channels, or could go to the cinema where they were restricted to the few films imported from the United States, Hong Kong, and India.[1] In the last two decades the emergence of video technology has transformed all that for the Nigerian middle classes, making available a massive range of the world's media products to those who can afford them. Video culture has thoroughly altered the landscape of Nigerian media, but it is only within the past few years that Nigerians have begun to use the technology to produce their own works. The making of Nigerian videos in Yoruba, Igbo, Hausa, and English constitutes one of the most vibrant sectors of Nigerian media production, based firmly on a grassroots popular audience. Often ignored because the "industry" is younger and less sophisticated than its Igbo and Yoruba counterparts, Hausa video dramas are nevertheless rapidly spreading all over northern Nigeria, creating their own publics, their own fans, and generating their own critics.

Video dramas are a new genre of fictional drama made specifically for video consumption. Textual analysis of these new forms and genres of Hausa videomaking is an important area for future research; this essay offers only some preliminary insights on that score. Instead, I will be concerned primarily with situating the rise of Hausa video (and by extension all Nigerian video) within the wider sociology of what I describe as a cassette or video *culture*.[2] The context is double: at the macro level, the economic and social conditions that underlie the rise of video as a technology and video dramas as an aesthetic form, and at the micro level, the local social, religious, and cultural values in northern Nigeria that mediate the ways video as a technology is accepted and that shape the creation of media publics. Video culture, then, refers to the articulation of transnational economic and technological flows and the cultural forms they have generated within the particular social context of Hausa culture.

By moving between these macro and micro levels I wish to emphasize that the rise of Nigerian videos, while seemingly a local phenomenon, is part of a worldwide change in the political economy of contemporary media. In Nigeria video culture represents a fundamental shift in the structure and style of media production. Most important, the rise of video culture signifies the emergence of a new kind of public sphere in Nigeria, one that is based on the privatization of media production and consumption. Earlier periods in Nigerian political history were associated with different kinds of media technologies, based on particular forms of economic organization, which created varying kinds of communicative spaces. The rise of video (and to a lesser extent, cable and satellite) embodies new kinds of media funding and control and creates new configurations of audiences. Video culture is constituted by a simultaneous burgeoning of cultural production at the global *and* the local levels.

What has been eroded in this moment of the global and the local is the position of the national. In both colonial times and the first decades of independence the state played a huge role in the sponsorship and regulation of media production and reception. But the contemporary video culture operates largely outside state control. The World Bank's insistence on privatization as a precondition for financial aid has combined with the savage economic effects of its Structural Adjustment Program to decimate the funding, authority, and morale of older state-based mass media such as television and radio. For almost the first time in Nigerian history the social importance of electronic mass media, the publics they create, the social worlds they make meaningful to Nigerian audiences, the spaces of political and religious communication they foster, are being formed in arenas outside state intervention. These are the wider sociological changes that have shaped video production in Nigeria and that give context to the reception of any particular video drama.

The public sphere of Nigerian media

In arguing that video technology has facilitated the emergence of a new public sphere in Nigeria, I am drawing on the concept of public sphere developed by the critical social theorist Jürgen Habermas (1962). Habermas defines the public sphere as a new arena of public communication and debate that emerged in the late seventeenth and early eighteenth centuries. He claims that the interaction between new technologies of mass communication, such as the newspaper and print technology, and a developing market economy combined to create bourgeois self-consciousness and an arena in which the middle class could critically debate the conduct of the state. I find Habermas's work theoretically attractive because he lays emphasis on the ability of media to create new communicative spaces, and grounds his analysis of these spaces in a historically informed account of political, economic, and social relations. Most of all, Habermas provides a theoretical way to move between the economic conditions of media existence and the ways those media gain symbolic significance.

While the limitations of Habermas's utopian concept of a critical rational arena of debate are well observed, I still find his insistence on embedding analyses of media within particular legal, moral, and political economic formations fruitful. Electronic media were introduced to colonial Africa as part of the universalizing (Western) discourses of technology and modernity. Like other colonial technologies, such as the railway or the factory, media brought about new ways of being in the world, creating new modes of perception and association and new ways of experiencing time and distance. These technologies are embedded in relations of production that embody particular types of social relations. Cinema, for instance, introduced an alienated mode of popular culture based around commodity exchange, one that brings a disparate group of people together in a way that is structured by formal and informal categories of censorship. Television, by contrast, is situated largely in the domestic arena. Here the social and the institutional collide as the structures of financing and political regulation create new modes of public and private interaction. As media constitute new social relations they bring about the need for regulation intended to organize and limit their effects. It is in the dance between the media's legal and political conditions of existence and their often unintended consequences that the social significance of media lies.

The contemporary public sphere of privatized video culture in Nigeria can best be understood by contrast with earlier periods in Nigerian media history. This history can be broken down into three discrete moments: the colonial era, the time of early independence up until the oil boom, and the post-oil boom period. Each of these periods is associated with specific media technologies and particular structures of economic organization, political control, and popular spectatorship. Each new period is mapped onto the older one—not replacing it, but affecting its importance and social significance.

Colonial media

Cinema and radio dominated the colonial public sphere of Nigerian media. Both were large, capital-intensive industries that were heavily regulated by the colonial government. [. . .] The mobile cinemas of the Colonial Film Unit (CFU) (*majigi* in Hausa) shared with radio the aim of advancing the needs of the modernizing colonial state. Designed to inculcate popular support for the empire as well as to promote British-defined colonial development, funding for the CFU and radio was largely dependent on how well it was seen to meet those aims.

[. . .]

Commercial and colonial cinema and radio were extremely influential in creating new communicative arenas in Nigeria. They opened up Nigerian popular culture to the global influences of foreign media, from Hollywood to Indian films, and made these media an everyday part of Nigerian life. Where commercial cinema was largely restricted to urban areas, the traveling cinema vans of the CFU and the wide range of radio waves increased the involvement of rural areas in the new media world. Both cinema and radio, however, depended on huge state or corporate capital investment. [. . .] The consequence of this was that colonial programming of both radio and cinema was top down, driven more by the paternalist developmental aims of the state than by the interests of the wider population.

Television and the postcolony

The formation of regional television networks during the era of independence dominated the second public sphere of media in Nigeria. While these networks were initiated during the dying moments of colonization, they marked the pride and self-confidence of the independent Nigerian state.[3] [. . .] Like colonial cinema and radio, television was a mass medium dominated by the needs and aims of government, but now it was the Nigerian regional governments rather than the British Empire. As in the period before it, the capital-intensive character of television offered little room for grassroots intervention. Viewer feedback was important to the production of entertainment programs, but politically the independence of television was quickly eroded (if it ever really existed) and stations were often used as publicity machines for regional heads of government at the expense of political and ethnic opponents.[4]

Television and media in the postcolony were transformed by the oil boom of the 1970s and early 1980s. The oil boom transformed the Nigerian economy, destroying the dominance of traditional agricultural exports (cocoa, peanuts, and palm oil) and tying the nation's fate to the fortunes of a single commodity: oil. The importance of the oil boom to Nigerian media cannot be overstated. As well as redefining the urban landscape of Nigeria by encouraging mass migration, the boom internationalized the consumption habits of the bourgeoisie, creating the basic economic and symbolic conditions for a much greater penetration of electronic media into Nigerian daily life.

One consequence of the oil boom was the redefinition of Nigerian television. The boom represented the ultimate moment of the second period of Nigerian media (as well as the beginning of the third)—a moment of large economic investment and supreme cultural self-confidence for Nigerian television. Massive investment was lavished on the federal Nigerian Television Authority (nationalized in 1976) and later, in the early eighties, oil money provided the funds for the creation of state television networks such as City Television Kano.[5] The huge national self-confidence during this time combined with a growing international awareness of the negative effects of cultural imperialism[6] to make media programming an issue of national concern. The fight against cultural imperialism privileged the national state as the defender of indigenous values and the patron of media. The state organized and paid for a new generation of federal and individual-state media professionals, on both technical and management sides, to go abroad to Britain and the United States for training. On their return they were supported in creating a stream of innovative programming that marked a flowering of Nigerian media production.

Video culture and the commodification of media

The oil boom also set in motion the creation of a radically new public sphere of media. This period is defined by the privatization and diversification of media access in Nigeria. For the first time in Nigerian history the state has a shrinking role in the production and circulation of electronic media. This is the most distinctive feature of the contemporary public sphere, one with far-reaching consequences for the political and grassroots use of media technologies. With the World Bank looking over its shoulder, the Nigerian state has moved toward relinquishing government monopoly over television and radio programming. While the strength of government commitment to privatization remains to be seen, a consequence of the destruction of the Nigerian economy is that the older mass media technologies of cinema, radio, and television have lost much of their dynamism and prestige. In their wake have come a range of new technologies, such as video, cable, and satellite, which operate largely outside government hands. While cable and satellite are still restricted to the rich, the availability of video has extended access to this programming to the middle class and even poor Nigerians.[7]

[. . .]

In Nigeria the rise of privatized media at the expense of state-controlled media is most obvious in the massive use of cassettes, the technology most associated with the contemporary Nigerian public sphere. While privatization has resulted globally in the intensification of corporate control over large-scale media production, the presence of cassettes has facilitated the rise of new communicative spaces and created possibilities for local media production. This has happened in two ways. First, widespread piracy has enabled the global flow of films and programs, resulting in a massive expansion of program choice for the average Nigerian viewer. Second, cassette technology has opened up spaces for local media production, from video dramas to religious preaching and local music.

Instead of centralizing and homogenizing media production, cassette technologies create a dispersed and diverse system of production that has profoundly affected the dominance of older mass media such as cinema and state-run television. Where these older mass media were characterized by mass production, large-scale industrial output, and organized exhibition, newer media are more fragmented and diverse, appealing to different audiences and based on more privatized modes of consumption. This diversification and privatization has proved more resilient in the era when Structural Adjustment has undermined the funding and morale of older state-based media. In the same period, despite continuing economic hardship for the Nigerian people, video culture has proliferated so much that today it is the most vibrant sector of Nigerian media. Contemporary video culture has created a distinctly new media era, which interacts with older forms of mass media and popular culture but is different in its economic organization and social relations.

Nigerian video and the rise of small media

Video- and audiocassettes make up part of what has been referred to by media scholars as "small media" (Sreberny-Mohammadi and Mohammadi 1994). Small media refers to technologies such as video- and audiocassettes, photocopiers, faxes, and computers, which differ from the older "big" mass media of cinema and television and radio stations.[8] Unlike state television networks, which require massive financial investment, or the corporate production of cinema, small media are more decentralized in their ownership. This makes them more like unofficial forms of popular culture, from rumors to jokes and mimicry, in that they create cultural and political spaces of communication that are outside of the control of the state and corporations. Sreberny-Mohammadi and Mohammadi argue that this makes small media suited for the articulation of oppositional and subversive points of view, and that this process is especially effective in nations where access to government-controlled mass media is restricted. Perhaps the most famous example of this oppositional use of small media came during the Iranian revolution when followers of the Ayatollah Khomeini used cassettes as one of the principal means to spread his ideas among the Iranian people.[9] But there are many other examples of the unofficial use of small media. In India, politicians whose access to mass media is restricted have been taping campaign videos of themselves and sending them to areas where they are not able to travel. Religious cassettes have also been one of the major ways that the groups opposed to the Fahd royal family in Saudi Arabia have been able to disseminate their teachings and build up the charisma of key opposition leaders.

Video- and audiocassettes are perhaps the quintessential small media. As vinyl records disappear, compact discs remain out of the reach of most of the world's poor, and film is increasingly impossible to finance in developing nations, cassettes have emerged as the dominant technology outside the West. Light, durable, easily reproduced and, in the case of audiocassettes, powerable by batteries (important in areas where electricity supply is periodic), cassettes offer the advantages of cheap production costs along with incredible ease of reproduction and consumption. Peter Manuel has discussed this at length in his exemplary book, *Cassette Culture* (1994), where he details the transformation of the Indian music industry after the arrival of cassette technology in the 1970s. The emergence of cassettes, he argues, resulted in a decentralization and democratization of the music industry, breaking apart the dominance of multinational oligopolies. In the mid-1970s music from Indian films, nearly all produced by large corporations, accounted for 90 percent of the market share of Indian music. The rise of cassettes provoked the recording of a huge range of regional, devotional, and secular music genres, so much so that film music now makes up only 40 percent of Indian musical production. What Manuel's example demonstrates is that particular technologies can have far-reaching social and economic effects; cassettes facilitate diverse kinds of regional and cultural production that were extremely difficult under older forms of mass media.

This production is both heightened and threatened by the complicated problem of piracy. In the Nigerian case, cassettes, aided by widespread piracy, have enormously increased the range of media available. While television stations are still required by law to limit the amount of foreign programming, no such controls on video watching are possible. Piracy is now central to the circulation of media flows within the Third World. Many video entrepreneurs see themselves as latterday Robin Hoods, robbing the wealthy media conglomerates so that the world's poor can have access to programs that are otherwise beyond their means. Certainly the United States, which is the nation most affected by copyright infringement because of the dominance of its media and computer industries, has made copyright violation a matter of national industrial policy, especially in relations with China. On a lesser scale, however, piracy can also paralyze indigenous film and video industries. Haynes and Okome (2000) chart the economic problems that video piracy causes for directors of Yoruba films. Ekpo (1991) argues that a strong film culture is impossible in Nigeria until the problem of copyright infringement is dealt with, and piracy remains a key problem for the development of the new video industry.[10]

Videos in Nigeria

In Nigeria, cassettes have become a part of everyday life. The sounds of tapes playing Indian songs in tailor shops or echoing from buses, the broadcasts of religious praises from the minarets of mosques, or the sight of bicycle vendors selling cassettes next to cinemas or at busy intersections are a familiar part of the northern Nigerian landscape. Cassette recording and duplication is often a highly organized affair. In Kano, for instance, the traditional market Kofar Wambai, known for the sale of thread for embroidery, has also become famous for the hundreds of small businesses duplicating and disseminating all kinds of audiotapes, from religious teachings to Indian music and Hausa singers. All these businesses are linked under the umbrella of the Kano State Cassette Sellers and Recording Co-operative Society. Video shops have similarly become a ubiquitous part of Nigerian urban life, offering customers a range of the world's media, from religious preachers like Jimmy Swaggart to popular Indian film stars like Sanjay Dutt and Salman Khan. And of course, growing in prominence and confidence is the burgeoning indigenous video industry, making fictional dramas of past and present Hausa life.

The unofficial political use of small media is well known in Nigeria and reminds one that the entertainment drama is only one of the many possible uses of cassette technology. Followers of the radical Islamic leader Ibrahim El-Zakzaky have long used cassettes to disseminate the teachings of their leader while he is denied access to the government mass media of radio and television.[11] (For a discussion of the importance of media in northern Nigerian Islam see Larkin 1998.) Both Christians and Muslims have given the religious use of audio- and videocassettes increasingly important roles in religious proselytizing. Because they allow for the possibility of political communication outside government censorship, cassettes are also implicated in the intensification of ethnic and religious conflict. The spread of video recordings of religious preachers such as the Christian evangelist Reinhard Bonnke or the Muslim Ahmad Deedat from South Africa has been cited as contributing to religious conflicts between Muslims and Christians (especially in Kaduna in 1987 and Kano in 1991). Both these preachers represent the global flow of religious ideas into Nigeria facilitated by new media technologies.

Small media have been used in diverse other ways in different contexts to produce alternative spheres of religious, political, and cultural communication. One of the reasons for the popularity of Sudanese music in the north, for instance, is that Hausa Muslims buy cassettes in order to help them learn Arabic. *Mallams* (religious teachers and healers) in the north have been known to use cassettes of Qur'anic recitation imported from Saudia Arabia in order to help in cases of possession (Casey 1997). The emergent and ephemeral nature of small media means that much research remains to be done in this area, especially as these technologies become more central to the Nigerian media landscape.

Cinema versus video: The social spaces of media in northern Nigeria

To summarize my argument so far, the contemporary production and reception of media in Nigeria forms a new kind of public sphere. The emergence of Hausa (or Igbo or Yoruba) video dramas is not an independent invention but relies on a profound change in the organization, control, and production of media in Nigeria. To understand the sociological significance of video dramas it is necessary to situate them within this larger theoretical context, but this can only explain one aspect of the public sphere of video culture. To complete the picture it is necessary to examine the local-level processes whereby communication technologies are mediated within local social and religious norms. What are the social consequences of media technologies? How does the shift in the public sphere of media production affect the everyday ways that northern Nigerians watch and interpret particular films, videos, or TV programs? In this section I explore these basic questions by examining the social and aesthetic spaces created by cinema and contrasting them with those generated by video to highlight the particularities of each technology.

My thoughts in this section have been shaped by my research on the significance of Indian films within Hausa culture (see "Indian Films and Nigerian Lovers," 1997). I am interested in how the transnational circulation of Indian films offers Hausa viewers an imaginative space where they might consider alternatives to both Western modernity and Hausa tradition. As part of this research it was necessary to examine the social situations within which media were exhibited. For instance, the same film might be projected in a cinema, broadcast on television, or played on a VCR, but the social relations that surround those viewing events vary according to the social meanings that accompany the technologies. In northern Nigeria, who gets to watch cinema as opposed to television or video differs widely according to class, gender, ethnicity, and sometimes religious belief. Understanding the interaction between technologies and local cultural values is central to coming to terms with the meanings media create.

Cinema in northern Nigeria occupies a distinct moral position that regulates who attends it. The first cinemas appeared in the colonial period and were immediately associated with British colonialists and southern Christian Nigerians, leading to questions about their Islamic acceptability for Hausa Muslims. Adding to this problem was the traditional Islamic prohibition on the creation of images, which raised the fundamental issue of whether the practice of viewing itself was un-Islamic. The early Hausa names for cinema, such as *majigi* (derived from magic) and *dodon bango* (evil spirits on the wall) betray the linguistic traces of these controversies. From the beginning, then, cinema had a disreputable, un-Islamic air about it (see Larkin forthcoming).

When cinema was first established in the city of Kano, it was located outside the *birni*, the traditional Muslim center of Kano, in the modern area of Sabon Gari (new town). The result was that in the minds of many Hausa, cinema became associated with the moral depravity that characterized the reputation of Sabon Gari. It became part of what was known as *bariki* culture, associated with other illicit activities such as drinking alcohol, male and female prostitution, and pagan religious practices. This negative conception of the cinema as a social space still continues today, and the result is that cinema in northern Nigeria is an overwhelmingly lower-class, male activity. The few women who do frequent cinemas (less than 15 percent of the audience) are seen as prostitutes, and many men attend because of the presence of sexual desire both on and off the screen. Cinema has become for many Hausa a condensed sexual space, an arena of pleasure and desire that has many negative connotations. Even today, many Hausa youths refuse to attend cinema on religious principle, and Hausa men cease attending as they grow older and more respectable. One friend strikingly illustrated this continuing ambivalent attitude toward cinema when he remarked to me that when he was young his parents warned him that if he went to the cinema more than seven times he would go to hell.

These social and religious values articulate with the signifying properties of media technologies to regulate the ways that media create relations of spectatorship—the basic way in which people watch and understand media. Take the watching of Indian films at the cinema, for instance. The cinema is based around a disparate group of people who come together for a few hours and then disperse. This relative anonymity is heightened by the fact that audience members sit in the dark, their identities merged with that of the larger crowd. The combination of this relative anonymity with the (im)moral sense of cinema in urban Hausaland can result in a loosening of social control. This is why cinema is associated with other illicit activities, from shouting sexual comments to actresses on screen to fumbled sexual encounters and the smoking of marijuana.

As a consequence of the negative moral associations around cinematic space, Hausa women have largely been denied access to this arena of popular culture. The still common Islamic practice of *kulle* (female seclusion) restricts urban women from freely leaving the home during daylight hours, and women are especially restrained from frequenting mixed-sex spaces such as the cinema. Not surprisingly, this strict form of segregation has major implications for the social composition of media audiences. By contrast, both television and video are domestic technologies, located (for the most part)[12] in the familial household, and are especially important for women in a society where women are expected to remain within the home. The emergence of television and then video revolutionized the participation of women in the wider public sphere of media in northern Nigeria. Perhaps this is most obvious in the fact that before the 1970s the audience for Indian films was largely restricted to male cinemagoers, yet the popularity of Indian films on television and video has been so great that nowadays many in northern Nigeria refer to Indian films as "women's films." Television and video have created what is in effect a privatized female public sphere. It is private in the sense that it gives women in seclusion access to media, making available to them what has previously been denied in a male-centered public world. It is public because television enabled the coming together of a new common public of female viewers based, among other things, on the common knowledges, tensions, and pleasures of media genres. Today, young Hausa women who incorporate aspects of Indian films within local popular culture by wearing jewelry or head scarves associated with Indian actresses are participating in the cultural worlds made available to them through the rise of contemporary electronic media.

Local contexts of media exhibition and reception not only regulate who has access to particular technologies, but can affect the experience of spectatorship itself. Watching the image of the Indian actress Sridevi dancing across a twenty-foot-high cinema screen in an arena with thousands of other men, many whistling and shouting sexual comments, is a visceral experience. This sensuality is only heightened by the sexual availability of *karuwai* (prostitutes) wandering from row to row, bantering with the men who are calling out to them. Compare this experience with watching the same film on video or television. Here the technology is situated in the domestic arena. Instead of a giant colorful image, Sridevi now performs on the tiny screen of a home television, her image fractured by crackly reception or the poor quality of pirated videos. Instead of the relative anonymity of the cinema, in the domestic space everyone is well known to each other, occupying defined social places, and the young men who frequent the cinema may now be sitting in the presence of their mothers and sisters with the everyday chores of family life going on around them. The sensual charge of the image takes on different ramifications because of the different social contexts that surround distinct media technologies and, as a result, the individual experience of film watching can be highly variable.

Hausa videos

The recent production of Hausa videos did not arrive ex nihilo, but developed out of older forms of popular culture. *Wasan Kwaikwayo*, or drama, has a long tradition in Hausa society and continues to be popular. The Kano State History and Culture Bureau alone has over 130 drama clubs registered. Some of these clubs date back to the initiatives of early pioneers of Hausa nationalism, such as the Maitama Sule Drama Club, founded by the 'Dan Masanin Kano, Maitama Sule.[13] Video production depends heavily on the experience and training of these drama clubs, and some clubs, such as Tumbin Giwa (full name: Kungiyar Wasan Kwaikwayo ta Tumbin Giwa), have themselves gone into the production of videos. (Tumbin Giwa is responsible for the highly popular period drama *Gimbya Fatima*, parts one, two, and three.) Other clubs hire out their actors to independent producers, but in both cases much of the raw talent for video dramas derives from these established forms of popular culture. Another important resource of new videomakers comes from the recent rise of popular Hausa fiction. *Soyayya* (love) authors have been intimately associated with Hausa videomaking as writers, directors, actors, and producers, and a number of videos are adaptations of previously published novels. Adamu Mohammed's *Kwabon Masoyi*, Ado Ahmad's *In da so da k'auna*, and Bala Anas's *Tsuntsu Mai Wayo* are all examples.

Hausa videos also rely heavily on the technical expertise of producers and camera operators who come from years of experience at federal and state television stations. These technical staff have often left television stations such as City Television Kano (CTV), and have set up their own private production companies. Bashir Mud'i, the cameraman on a number of the most popular Hausa videos (among them *In da so da k'auna, Tsuntsu Mai Wayo*, and *Gimbya Fatima*), left CTV to work at Fine Tunes Nigeria. This is one of a number of small-scale independent companies that constitute the technical backbone of the new video production. The staff at Fine Tunes provide a range of technical services. They hire out their labor (as writers, cameramen, directors, and editors) to independent producers and also produce their own videos. These may be fictional dramas, biographies of eminent citizens, or commercial films for local businesses. MTS Productions, which produced the video *Gidan Haya*, is another such company that, like Fine Tunes, hopes to make business out of the federal government's initiative to privatize broadcasting.

The fact that actors and talent for Hausa videos are based in drama clubs while technical expertise comes from independent producers means that videomaking is a collective endeavor. The typical Hausa video starts life either as an adaptation of a popular Hausa novel or as a new production by one of the drama clubs. Once the script is written, the cameraman and director are hired from an outside company. Unlike in the south, there is, as yet, little capital investment in videos, and consequently the role of the producer is less important. Hausa producers are less likely to be independent businessmen looking to invest in an industry and more likely to be the people who have written the drama and who are committed to the realization of their work.

After the video is completed, videomakers often try to recuperate their expenses by arranging screenings at cinema halls all over the north before releasing the video for general sale. Ado Ahmad, producer and director of *In da so da k'auna*, explained that the aim of this is to try to lessen financial liability, given the widespread nature of video piracy; he personally took the first part of his video to cinema halls from Sokoto to Maiduguri to Zaria. As Ahmad's experience suggests, the pattern for the distribution of Hausa videos is likely to determine whether this new form of media can establish long-term profitability. As of yet, there is no standard for either production or distribution. Tumbin Giwa relied on sales of videos through video shops for its profits. Ahmad first exhibited through cinema halls, then sold individual shops the rights to duplicate and sell his tapes. Bala Anas, another popular videomaker and author, copied the southern model of selling video shops prerecorded cassettes, each with their own video cover. This latter attempt requires a great deal more capital investment, but the production of individual covers makes it much easier to identify pirated copies.

Hausa videos are a perfect example of the efflorescence of local media production made possible by the advent of video culture. Already the number of videos produced eclipses the small number of Hausa films made over the last forty years. Unlike many of those films, the videos do not rely on state patronage, but depend solely on the market of Hausa viewers, making the videos one of the first truly popular forms of Hausa electronic media. The new video industry has raided older mass-media industries such as television for their technical expertise and the waxing of videomaking represents the waning of influence, morale, and funding of these state-based media.

Whereas television was designed to provide a Nigerian (regional) alternative to the influx of global media, Hausa videos often borrow from other film and video genres and remain outside local or national regulation.

The videos themselves reference the global-local interactions that make up the wider video culture. Videos such as *In da so da k'auna* and *Gimbya Fatima* run advertisements for Hausa video stores like the Kano shop Alhaji Musa Mai Caset. In the commercial for his shop, which is intercut at intervals during the video drama itself, Alhaji Musa lists the range of global and local media products on offer on video, from war films to Indian films, documentaries of the pilgrimage to Mecca, recordings of the Islamic preacher Ahmed Deedat, Hausa videos, and audio recordings of famous Hausa singers such as Mamman Shata and 'Dan Kwairo. These global media provide raw material that is often intertextually reworked within Hausa videos themselves. One of the clearest examples of this is the influence of Indian films on Hausa videos.

Like Indian films, Hausa videos depict a world of melodrama and romance, often situated among the wealthy elite classes of Nigerian society.[14] This makes them different from television dramas that are more geared toward humor and social commentary (Furniss 1996). Both Hausa and Indian popular narratives share a concern for the conflicts that arise over the tension between arranged marriages and love marriages. Like contemporary Indian films, Hausa videos often critique the erosion of cultural values associated with Western materialism, while at the same time visually reveling in the spectacle of consumer goods and lifestyles that materialism brings about. Above all else, the popular nature of Hausa videos has led to a concentration on themes of romance and thus a close engagement with the styles of love present in Indian films—by far the most important visual medium dealing with the theme of love.[15]

All cultural borrowings involve acts of reinvention and reappropriation. Indian films, which were once derided by Indian critics for imitating Hollywood, are now recognized to be based on a worldview and emotional context very different from Western films (Thomas 1995). When directors do borrow from a particular Hollywood film, they know that in order for it to be acceptable to a local Indian audience there must be considerable changes in both form and content. The same is true of African popular culture, which has long been involved in acts of creative creolization where cultural influences from the West, the Islamic world, and Asia have been incorporated into African expressive traditions and their representational power subordinated to an African aesthetic.[16] Hausa *bandiri* singers, who take songs from popular Indian films but change the words to sing praises of the Prophet Mohammed, are an example of this intertextual recoding. Bori adepts who are possessed by spirits dressed as European soldiers or Kano school-girls who, when possessed by unknown spirits, start dancing like actresses from Indian films,[17] also illustrate the bricolage of African expressive traditions. Hausa videos sit firmly within this tradition. They borrow influences from many sources—Igbo novels, Igbo and Yoruba videos, romance books and magazines—but rework and transform these influences so that the final product makes sense within local Hausa cultural and religious values.

[. . .]

Conclusion

The success of Hausa videos is generating a growing body of fans and also a number of critics. Many of the same accusations that are made against the soyayya books are also made against Hausa videos. These are that they focus too much on romance rather than on the real issues facing Hausa people, and that they corrupt Hausa romance by dramatizing ideas that come from elsewhere—often Indian films. *Gimbya Fatima* was criticized by many for its scenes of the two main lovers walking unchaperoned in the garden of Fatima's father. In another scene Fatima sneaks out of her room at night to visit her sleeping lover, who passionately declares his love for her. While many feel that these practices run contrary to Hausa culture, the videos have also proved to be hugely popular, and it seems likely that the new communicative space opened by Hausa videos will generate its own critical discourse.

Most Nigerian videos are made outside state intervention and thus outside the state media mandate for moral uplift and social renewal. Nigerian videos represent the privatization of media production, and the commodification of the technology is mimicked in the content of the videos themselves. Here the aesthetic form mirrors Nigerian global-local interactions as the international hotels, the transnational businessmen using cellular phones, the commodification of kinship [. . .] or politics (*Glamour Girls*), create the spectacle from which much of the pleasure of the text derives. The parade of fashions, the constant cutaways to home furnishings and consumer goods, the ubiquitous parties where the elite and corrupt mingle, combine to display the commodified world from which video culture emerges.[18]

Video culture has expanded the private realm in Nigeria and highlights the ambivalent role of the Nigerian state—still omnipresent but receding in its power. Electronic mass media emerged in particular formations. These are the outcome of economic and juridico-political regulations intended to delimit what media may be, and local social and aesthetic relations that determine how these technologies are made to have meaning. Once introduced, media often follow their own unruly trajectory. They provide resources to be manipulated in potentially uncontrollable ways. Even now Nigerian video production takes place in the midst of a lively debate about its success and its potentially negative effects. Nigerian video films borrow from state media and from the transnational flows of Indian and American films, Nigerian romance magazines, folkore and rumors, but can be reduced to none of them. As the economic and technological order of the world shifts, so does the media landscape within Nigeria. The rise of video culture is emblematic of that shift and is part of a new era in Nigerian media production.

Notes

1   Research for this article was funded by the Wenner-Gren Foundation for Anthropological Research and a research grant from New York University. The article could not have been written without the help and support of many of the young, creative talents of the Hausa video world. I especially thank producer and author Ado Ahmad, director Aminu Hassan Yakasai, author and actor Adamu Mohammed, and camera operator Bashir Mud'i, who collectively introduced me to the world of Hausa videos. Organizations such as the Kano State Cassette Sellers Recording and Co-operative Society were informative and helpful. My research in Nigeria was entirely dependent on the institutional support of the Kano State History and Culture Bureau and Arewa House Centre for Historical Documentation in Kaduna. My gratitude for their logistical and intellectual help runs deep. I benefited from discussions with the independent video production houses such as MTS Productions and (especially) Fine Tune Nigeria productions. I thank 'yan toxics for watching many videos with me and for so much help I cannot begin to list it here. The article has benefited from the reading and comments of Meg McLagan and Antonio Rossi and from the careful editorial work of Jonathan Haynes.

2   I adapt this term from Manuel's concept of cassette culture, discussed more fully below.

3   To give one example, the Western Nigeria Television Service, established in 1959, was the first television service not only in Nigeria, but in Africa as a whole. The nationalist leader Chief Awolowo established the station as a direct challenge to British colonial control of the instruments of mass communication. In 1958, in protest against the constitutional debate on the eve of Nigeria's independence, Awolowo staged a walkout from the Federal House of Parliament. When his actions were condemned by the colonial government over the federal radio service, Awolowo demanded a right of reply and was refused. In response he initiated the creation of the first African television station, in order to secure a means of communication independent of colonial authority. Given the lack of possible television viewers, this was a highly symbolic act, establishing the Nigerianization of the means of electronic communication. For an account see Ariyo 1977.

4　This tendency was only exacerbated by the bitter divisions of the civil war, and resulted in the take-over of regional television stations by the Federal Government in 1976 (Ariyo 1977).

5　For those unfamiliar with Nigerian history it is necessary to explain briefly the difference between federal, regional, and state broadcasting networks. Under British rule, Nigeria was divided into three regions, North, East, and West, and this tripartite structure was carried over into the early independence period. The first television networks were divided between the regional system, each region having its own station, and a federal network. As a consequence of the civil war, Nigeria's three regions were divided into twelve different states. In 1976 the old regional networks were taken over by the federal government to create a single federal system (justified in the name of national unity). Local state agitation, however, meant that by the early eighties individual states were again allowed to create their own broadcasting networks. Currently broadcasting in Nigeria is still split between the federal National Television Authority (NTA) and local networks based in individual states, which have now been joined by privately owned stations.

6　The commitment to fighting against cultural imperialism has been fundamental for both Nigerian media makers and academics, though of course this does not prevent the Nigerian federal government or the individual state governments from using media for their own political ends. For discussions of media and cultural imperialism in Nigeria see MacBride 1980, Nwuneli 1986, and Uche 1989.

7　Individual ownership of video cassette recorders is, of course, a middle-class phenomenon, but the rise of small video parlors and traveling video entrepreneurs (see note 12) means that even poor Nigerians can have some access to this new technology. Moreover, while ownership of satellite dishes is restricted to the rich, its programming is given much greater social range as it is taped and circulated on video or television. Nigerian news broadcasting uses images from CNN. In this way the importance of CNN extends beyond the relatively few satellite owners to the mass public watching NTA or television stations run by the various states.

8　Small media may also refer to nonelectronic forms of media production such as stickers and slogans that decorate taxis, buses, and motorbikes in Nigeria, or the art on the side of Nigerian trucks. On taxi slogans see Lawuyi 1988. On taxi art see Pritchett 1979.

9　In the years leading up to the Iranian revolution, the shah-dominated government used increasingly authoritarian means to control the mass media of television and radio and limit the spread of antigovernment ideas. Sreberny-Mohammadi and Mohammadi (1994) point out that this repressive control was countered by Islamic activists using the small media of photocopying and cassettes to spread antigovernment, pro-Islamic ideas. The teachings of the Ayatollah Khomeini were played over the phone from Paris to Tehran, where they were recorded, duplicated on cassettes, and sold at mosques and through street vendors. The distribution of Khomeini's teachings on cassette was crucial to the mobilization of revolutionary action.

10　Interview with producer Ado Ahmad, June 1995. See also the interview with Amaka Igwe in the *Guardian on Sunday*, 30 March 1997: B8. For the problem of video piracy see also Okhaku 1992.

11　The political consequence of radical religious media was made obvious when El-Zakzaky was arrested in September 1996 for (according to the police) producing and presenting illegal radio broadcasts.

12　In northern Nigeria, as in many other parts of the developing world, video parlors also function as mini-cinemas. These semiprivate, semipublic spaces, often located in houses where one room is used for small-scale public exhibition, extend the social range of video access to the poor, who cannot afford televisions and videos. Entrepreneurs also visit rural areas taking a television, video, and generator, screening Indian and Hong Kong films and Hausa videos for rural audiences.

13　Sule himself pioneered the production of Hausa entertainment dramas for radio.

14　The notable exception to this is *Gimbya Fatima I–III*, which showcases traditional Hausa customs.

15　Romance is the most popular genre of all Nigerian videos (and Ghanaian videos, too) and, of course, has a long history in Nigeria from the famous Igbo market pamphlets of the 1940s, '50s, and '60s (see Obiechina 1971a) to contemporary Hausa soyayya books (Larkin 1997) and romance magazines such as *Hints*.

16　Studies of creative creolization date back to T. O. Ranger's classic text on the Beni dance in East Africa (1975).

17　See Cascy 1997 for a discussion of the recent phenomenon of mass possession of Kano schoolgirls.

18　This spectacle is not simply a celebration of commodification because, as any viewer of Lagos videos knows, much of the pleasure derives from an aesthetic of outrage. In these videos the narrative is driven by a series of moral shocks where cultural norms are outrageously violated. This creates an emotional engagement based on outrage and combines the spectacle of materialism with the moral critique of the behavior it produces.

References

Ariyo, Michael Egbon (1977) "The Origin and Development of Television Broadcasting in Nigeria: An Inquiry into Television Development in a Non-Industrialized Nation." Ph.D. disseration, University of Wisconsin, Madison.

Casey, Connerley (1997) "Medicines for Madness: Suffering, Disability, and the Identification of Enemies in Northern Nigeria." Ph.D. dissertation, University of California, Los Angeles, 1997.

Ekpo, Moses F. (1991) "The Implications of the Nigerian Copyright Law for a Virile Film Policy in Nigeria." In *Operative Principles of the Film Industry: Towards a Film Policy for Nigeria*, ed. Hyginus Ek-wuazi and Yakubu Nasidi, 37–45. Jos: Nigerian Film Corporation.

Furniss, Graham (1996) *Poetry, Prose, and Popular Culture in Hausa*. Edinburgh: Edinburgh University Press, for the International Africa Institute, London.

Habermas, Jürgen (1962) *The Structural Transformation of the Public Sphere: An Inquiry into a Category of Bourgeois Society*. Reprint, Cambridge: MIT Press, 1994.

Haynes, Jonathan and Onookome Okome (2000) "Evolving Popular Media: Nigerian Video Films." In *Nigerian Video Films*, ed. Jonathan Haynes, 51–88. Athens, Ohio: Ohio University Press.

Larkin, Brian (1997) "Indian Films and Nigerian Lovers: Media and the Creation of Parallel Modernities." *Africa* 67.3: 406–40.

—— (1998) "Uncertain Consequences: The Social and Religious Life of Media in Northern Nigeria." Ph.D. dissertation, New York University, 1998.

—— (forthcoming) "The Social Space of Media: Cinema and the Production of Moral Space in Northern Nigeria." *Visual Anthropology Review*.

Lawuyi, Tunde (1988) "The World of the Yoruba Taxi Driver: An Interpretative Approach to Vehicle Slogans." *Africa* 58.1: 1–13.

Macbride, Sean (1980) *Many Voices, One World Communication Today and Tomorrow*. Ibadan: Ibadan University Press.

Manuel, Peter (1993) *Cassette Culture: Popular Music and Technology in North India*. Chicago: University of Chicago Press.

Nwuneli, Onuora E., ed. (1986) *Mass Communication in Nigeria: A Book of Readings*. Enugu: Fourth Dimension.

Obiechina, Emmanuel (1971) *An African Popular Literature: A Study of Onitsha Market Pamphlets*. Cambridge: Cambridge University Press.

Okhaku, Marcellinus (1992) "Towards a National Film Policy: The Case of Video Piracy." In *Operative Principles of the Film Industry: Towards a Film Policy for Nigeria*, ed. Hyginus Ekwuazi and Yakubu Nasidi, 272–87. Jos: Nigerian Film Corporation.

Okome, Onookome 1991 "The Rise of the Folkloric Cinema in Nigeria." Ph.D. thesis, University of Ibadan.

Pritchett, J. (1979) "Nigerian Truck Art." *African Arts* 12.2: 27–31.

Ranger, Terence (1975) *Dance and Society in Eastern Africa, 1890–1970: The Beni Ngoma*. London: Heinemann.

Sreberny-Mohammadi, Annabelle, and Ali Mohammadi (1994) *Small Media, Big Revolution: Communication, Culture, and the Iranian Revolution*. Minneapolis: University of Minneapolis Press.

Thomas, Rosie (1995) "Melodrama and the Negotiation of Morality in Mainstream Indian Film." In *Consuming Modernity: Public Culture in a South Asian World*, (eds) Carol Breckenridge and Arjun Appadurai, 157–82. Minneapolis: University of Minneapolis Press.

Uche, Luke Uka (1989) *Mass Media, People and Politics in Nigeria*. New Delhi: Concert.

Uchegbu, Benjamin (1978) "The Nature of Colonialist Anti-Nationalist Propaganda in British Africa: The Case of the Colonial Film Censorship in Nigeria 1945–48." Ph.D. dissertation, New York University, 1978.

PART FIVE

Social Representation on Television

I N HER ESSAY IN THIS PART, Julie D'Acci reminds us that any discussion of the ways in which television represents society might start by asking what is meant by the term "representation." The temptation, she says, is to regard the social world as being a fixed, independently-existing reality, which television then reflects, distorts, or reproduces. And, indeed, some mass communication researchers have attempted to assess television's capacity to represent society by measuring its representations of particular social groups (women or ethnic and racial minorities, for example) against empirically-verifiable features of those groups (percentage of women working outside the home, proportions of ethnic groups employed in various professional capacities, etc.). Such studies almost invariably are used to demonstrate that television's representation of society is "unrealistic" in particular respects.

However, the essays in this section work from a different and more complicated understanding of all three terms: "society," "television," and "representation." Although there is far from unanimity among scholars as to the meanings of these terms, television studies generally speaking would underscore the *constructedness* of both society and of the representation of social worlds in various modes and genres of television. Rather than regarding the social worlds we live in as simply and unproblematically "there," D'Acci asks:

> What if . . . reality really is construed by humans, really is humanly constructed? What if, furthermore, different human societies train (even inadvertently) their humans to perceive and interpret reality in particular ways? And what if this humanly produced social reality passes in most societies for natural reality, the common sense understanding about the world, the truth? And what if the constant generation of *representations* of this social reality enforces over and over again the notion that this human, social construction is really the real thing?

To further elaborate the premises upon which these essays are based: what if we accept that our social worlds are always already mediated by the meanings, norms, and values that we attach to various elements of those worlds *before* any particular instance of television gets around to representing them? And, to make things even more complicated, what if we accept that the process by which we attach meanings, norms, and values to our social worlds has itself been influenced by our experience as television viewers? In other words, what if we acknowledge television's role in constructing the social reality that gets re-represented on television? And finally (before you get up to take something for that headache) what if we factor into our thinking the realization that the process by which social meanings, norms, and values are formed within and outside of television is not only dynamic but also operates at a number of levels: conscious and unconscious, the articulated and the taken-for-granted, rational and emotional?

To simply see television as a funhouse mirror, reflecting back at us a recognizable but distorted social world populated by people richer, prettier, thinner, whiter, and funnier than ourselves and the people we encounter in our "real" lives is to greatly oversimplify and underestimate television's role in the representation of the social world. Television not only represents social groups; it also helps to construct and maintain the norms and values through which society is ordered.

For example, in the 1970s and 1980s, many US daytime soap operas added African-American characters to their social worlds. In some ways the roles these characters played were indistinguishable from those of the white characters on the shows: they were doctors, nurses, lawyers, detectives, friends, co-workers, fathers, and mothers. Racial difference was usually not written into their plotlines in an overt fashion. But because interracial heterosexual romance and marriage were thought by the shows' producers and sponsors to be values and norms unacceptable to their core viewing audience, the relationships African-American characters could have with white characters was greatly circumscribed. Heterosexual romance lies at the heart (so to speak) of the soap opera's normative universe, and many plot developments involve the working out of past, present, future, realized, thwarted, celebrated, and hidden love affairs and their emotional, biological, moral, and social consequences. Disqualified as actual, past, or potential romantic partners of white characters, African-Americans were consigned to an invisibly bounded yet very much *represented* relational ghetto and second-class social and narrative citizenship.

Studying social representations on television means examining not just depictions of women and men but representations of femininity and masculinity, not just images of people of other races but constructions of racial otherness, and not just the presence of gay characters in sitcoms but how sexuality and desire are manifested throughout television's modes and genres. In trying to understand the importance of television's capacity to represent society, we would want to look beyond particular representations to consider the ubiquity of television in many societies and the reach of its images into our everyday lives. As political economy scholars have done, we would want viewers and students of television to be reminded that commercial television's social representations are not in the service of furthering human understanding but to provide a social context for the consumption of consumer goods, both on television and in the world of the viewer. We would also want to underscore the fundamental asymmetry of power relations involved in representing anything on broadcast television: relatively speaking, a very few people are in positions to decide what will be represented and how to millions of others not in positions to respond through the same medium and with the same force.

We would also want to view issues of social representation within the context of television's role as a profoundly modern and modernizing force. Theorists of modernity have argued that individual identity itself is not only constructed but an endless work in progress. In traditional societies and in the pre-modern era in the west, individuals occupied more or less fixed places within rigid social structures. No one had to be told to "get a life": you lived the life you were given and then you died. Our understanding of the self in modern societies and in the modern age is quite different. For the modern self, achieving personal happiness before death rather than fulfilling a preordained role in a fixed social order becomes the whole point of individual human existence. The course of one's life, although still constrained by forces beyond the control of the individual, is regarded as being independent to some degree of those forces and as the result of individual choice and behavior. We become authors of our own lives, the protagonists of our own life stories, or at least we would argue with anyone who would claim that we are not.

The process by which the modern self is formed and constantly reformed is characterized by what social theorist Anthony Giddens calls reflexivity. By that he means that the process of self-construction occurs as we monitor and respond to the social world around us. Our sense of self and other is not fixed and given but dynamic and shaped by incessant gauging of our own feelings, beliefs, appearance, values, and goals in relation to those of others. As Giddens puts it, "The self today is for everyone a reflexive project—a more or less continuous interrogation of past, present and future. It is a project carried on amid a profusion of reflexive resources: therapy and self-help manuals of all kinds, television programmes, and magazine articles."[1]

Giddens also uses the term *disembedding* to talk about several of the characteristic features of our relationship with the modern social world. In traditional societies and pre-modern times, both time and space were firmly grounded in the local. "Now" intrinsically meant "here and now." One of the hallmarks of modernity is its disembedding of both time and space from the local. As technologies for the measurement and regulation of both time and space emerged (portable clocks, standardized calendars, maps, sextants, etc.) time and space became abstracted from any given place and made applicable to any other place in the world. Knowledge in traditional societies is also deeply embedded in local belief systems and personal experience: the power of a traditional healer extends only as far as the community who believes in his or her abilities. With modernity, knowledge becomes abstracted from personal experience and the local and becomes portable through systems of expertise. We routinely entrust our health and safety to people we've never met (airline pilots, doctors, engineers) not because we trust *them* but because we trust the system of expertise they represent.

The term disembedding also applies to the general processes of identity formation and the development and revision of norms, values, and systems of belief in the modern age. In traditional societies and in the pre-modern era, all individuals were enmeshed in a tightly-bound system of social relations, which gave institutions (the church, the crown, the family) enormous power over their lives and beliefs. Modernity involves the gradual historical loosening of these social bonds and the consequent radical decline in power of these extra-individual sources of authority and legitimation: in other words, the individual becomes disembedded from the social structure that once defined him/her and limited his/her ability to choose. The process by which one "gets a life" and orders that life in relation to the larger social world has become increasingly independent from the institutions that would constrain those processes *and* from the power of any institution to validate the life choices one makes.

What does all this have to do with television and with the ways it represents society? In the first place, it should be clear that all mass media have facilitated the disembedding of time and space by abstracting words, ideas, images, and sounds from the local and allowing them to be reproduced and circulated. Television's capacities to reorder the experience of time and space are particularly radical. Secondly, television helps to disembed our experience of the social world from the realm of direct personal experience. In contrast to the limited number of individuals we interact with in the course of our everyday lives in the communities where we live and work, television presents us with a multitude of individuals whom we "know" or might get to know only because they appear on television. Television brings into our homes opportunities for numerous vicarious social encounters every day and leaves it to us to figure out what status those encounters might have in our own lives.

To be sure, feature films also offer us representations of social groups and enactments of social encounters, but our experience of movies in movie theaters is removed from the world outside and is delimited by its one-time evocation of a social world we know at some level to be fictional. Television requires that we shift abruptly from the apprehension of social representations that we know to be fictional constructs (sitcoms, drama) to others that are represented as belonging to some real social world outside of television (political figures, the actors who play fictional characters) to yet others whose status is purposely blurred (celebrities endorsing products in infomercials, for example).

As a system of social representation television must be viewed in relation to its technological capacity for what we might call "realseemingnessness." In the introduction to Part Three (Modes of Television), we noted that a number of different modes and genres of television play upon the power of television to deliver to millions of homes at once a seemingly faithful reproduction of that which is placed in front of the television camera. Sports, news, documentaries, cooking shows, advertisements, talk shows, home videos, surveillance tapes, infomercials, game shows, "reality" formats (*Big Brother*, *Survivor*, etc.) all make a claim upon our belief, to some degree and in some ways. Furthermore, as a number of essays in this collection point out, television has the capacity to mimic interpersonal modes of social engagement. As Margaret Morse notes in her essay on the direct address format of US television newscasts (Part Three), "This format of news delivery cloaks what is, after all, an impersonal transmission with the impression of discourse across a desk. . . ." In other words, television's extraordinary capacity to disembed time and space from any particular place and moment is routinely used to simulate the social dynamics of the "here" and "now," the "you" and "me."

Television exploits our quintessentially modern reliance upon experts to guide us in the unending process of "discovering" who we are and of setting and adjusting norms, assigning values, and forming systems of belief. Various genres of television routinely confer expert status upon those who inhabit their social worlds—from the news anchor, whose reading of "the news" must mean that he knows more than we do, to the hosts of advice and DIY shows. Sometimes participation in television itself seems to be sufficient grounds for claiming expertise. Some years ago, an American soap opera actor became a commercial spokesman for a particular brand of children's cough syrup. "I'm not a doctor," he announced at the beginning of each ad, "but I play one on television."

But even when figures on television are not set up explicitly as experts, television nonetheless serves what John Hartley will call (in his essay in Part Six: Watching Television) a teaching function, and one that is directly related to its power as a means of social representation and to the reflexive project of identity construction. As Hartley puts it, television teaches "different segments of the population how others look, live, speak, behave, relate, dispute, dance, sing, vote, decide, tolerate, complain; television is a major source of 'people-watching' for comparison and possible emulation." He uses the term "Do-It-Yourself" citizenship to refer to the process of identity formation facilitated by television.

Julie D'Acci's essay, prepared especially for this reader, considers not only how television represents gender but how issues of gender representation on television have been and might be taken up in television studies. As she points out, early studies of television's representation of gender focused almost exclusively on the representation of *women* on television. This was understandable given women's importance as members of the commercial television audience and of the use of heterosexual desirability to sell consumer products on television. More recently, however, television studies has broadened its notion of gender representation as the field of gender studies itself has challenged the very premises upon which distinctions between "male" and "female" have been based. D'Acci discusses how these changes in theories of gender have influenced studies of television's representation of both. She also proposes an approach to the study of television and gender that moves well beyond analysis of the "roles" played by men and women in particular television programs. Drawing upon insights from both cultural studies and gender studies, her approach would stress the need to examine gender in relation to four "spheres" of television: production, programming, reception, and social/historical context.

As D'Acci notes, one of the most significant changes in the concept of gender in recent years has been the explosion of the simple binary "man/woman" as the basis for understanding sexual difference. "Woman" can no longer be posed as the categorical and complementary opposite of "man," with each serving as the assumed object of the other's sexual desire. Together gender and sexuality form the basis for a continuum of biological and cultural orientations, not a simple and fixed dualism. Ron Becker examines the sudden and continuing "visibility" of fictional gay characters in American commercial television programs since the mid-1990s, and places the dramatic increase of openly-gay characters within the context of both social change and of economic changes to commercial television in the 1990s. He argues that the representation of gays on American broadcast television is directly tied to the need of terrestrial broadcasting networks to hang on to a "quality" audience of affluent, sophisticated, highly-educated adult consumers — an audience increasingly being lured away by cable and satellite channels. As a result, gay characters must be assimilable within fictional social worlds that appeal to up-scale *straight* audiences. Becker reflects upon the implications of the diverse gay, lesbian, and bisexual community being represented *as* socially and economically secure for an audience *of* affluent viewers and of inhabiting fictional social worlds "nearly always devoid of serious discrimination and hate crimes. . . ."

Becker's essay might be read in tandem with Victoria Johnson's article on "heartland" values in the neo-network era of American television. Together the two essays highlight the seemingly contradictory strategies employed by different terrestrial broadcasters in the 1990s as they all struggled to adapt to the new technological and economic landscape of US television. The two pieces also point out the inextricable link between the presumed or projected social norms and values of the audience sought by broadcasters and the representational strategies employed in programs they might be lured to watch. Johnson's essay concerns an institutional "synergy" that emerged in the late 1990s between the American commercial network CBS and a new cable channel. PAX, launched in 1998, promoted itself as a cable channel built around religious, "family-oriented" programming — a significant portion of which had originally been broadcast by CBS. Both CBS and PAX, argues Johnson, eschewed the urban, sophisticated audiences Becker sees being targeted by shows with gay characters, and instead positioned themselves in relation to an imagined audience of "real, God-fearing Americans who have otherwise been 'forgotten' by America's 'elite' popular culture producers." The programming strategies pursued by CBS and PAX, redefine the nation in terms of a mythical "heartland," geographically associated with the small-towns of the Midwest and culturally imagined as the repository of "real" American values: home, the nuclear family, and a Christian conception of the divine.

David Morley's essay also takes up broadcasting's role in the construction of what he calls the "national family," and addresses specifically the question of "who feels included or excluded from symbolic membership of the nation." Focusing principally on broadcasting in the UK, Morley surveys the work of a number of scholars who have examined the ways in which television works to transform the involuntary geographic circumstances of an individual's birth into the basis for allegiance to a collective history and set of national symbols. Morley returns to the concept of the public sphere to discuss television's role in the construction and maintenance of a sense of nation and citizenship. If, he argues, national media now largely constitute the public sphere in many countries, then "whoever is excluded from those media is in effect excluded from the symbolic culture of the nation." He ends with a discussion of mobile, migrant social groups, who are not contained by the notion of nation—groups excluded from or marginalized within the public spheres of their host countries.[2] This discussion might lead us to other essays in this collection that also address the relationship among television, nationhood, and diasporic communities (e.g. Stuart Cunningham's essay on "public sphericules" in Part Two).

Timothy Havens's essay is one of the few in this collection that is devoted to a single instance of television programming: the American sitcom *The Cosby Show*. (The reasons for our editorial bias against including detailed analyses of single television shows are laid out in the general introduction.) However, Havens makes a good case for singling out this particular program for an extended analysis. Conceived by African-American comedian Bill Cosby in 1984, *The Cosby Show* was a stylistically traditional situation comedy. Its singularity derived from its being "about" an upper-middle-class African-American couple and their five children. *The Cosby Show* was the highest rated show on American television from 1985 to 1988 and remained among the top twenty shows for eight years. It continued to be broadcast by local television stations, following its network run, generating a record $600 million in syndication revenues. However, the focus of Havens's essay is on the international circulation of the show, which, in his words "set the representational and marketing standards that continue to determine what types of African-American shows get produced, and where those shows are sold." *The Cosby Show* enjoyed extraordinary popularity in non-US markets for ten years (1985–95), finding ratings success in diverse television cultures from the Philippines and Australia to Lebanon and Norway. Havens examines the institutional context of *The Cosby Show*'s international success before discussing the reception of the show's representation of race and nationality in other countries.

Notes

1   Anthony Giddens, *The Transformation of Intimacy: Sexuality, Love and Eroticism in Modern Societies* (Stanford: Stanford UP, 1992), p. 30.
2   The notion of the "public sphere" and its use in television scholarship are discussed in the introduction to Part One. See also the essay by Collins in that section, as well as those by Sparks and Cunningham in the Part Two section.

Chapter 24

JULIE D'ACCI

TELEVISION, REPRESENTATION AND GENDER

IF I ASKED PEOPLE THE WORLD OVER to tell me what immediately sprang to mind when they heard the phrase "television and gender representations" I would undoubtedly be deluged with wildly different responses. Different because different cultures and countries and different people within them conceive of these terms in widely divergent ways; different also because right now the terms themselves are in tremendous flux. But I would also surely get a flood of similar responses, because these three terms have come to achieve a kind of common-sense understanding in many areas of the globe. It is in the spaces among these similarities and differences surrounding gender, television and representations, among the persistence of particular meanings and the struggles over new ones, that I want to situate this essay. I could plunge in with an exploration of any of the three terms, but because this book is devoted to television, let me begin there.[1]

Television

It is clear that television not only means different things but has different functions and uses in societies all over the world. From the perspective of a cultural critic working within a Cultural Studies perspective in the United States, I have come to understand TV and analyze it in some very specific ways. On a most general level, I conceive of it as a technology, and as a social, economic, cultural, and ideological institution. As a technology (and at a most rudimentary level), I see it as producing electronic images and sounds; as a social institution, as producing viewers and citizens; as an economic institution (in some societies), as producing consumers; as a cultural institution, as producing programs and schedules; and as an ideological institution, as producing norms and rules that tell viewers what's okay and what's not in any given society. In other words, television's electronic sounds and images, its programs and its regular schedules of news, commercials, announcements, and so forth, gather viewers (often for many hours every week) and give them a sense of who and what they are, where they are, and when (morning, late-night, holiday seasons, for instance), if they are safe or in danger (from threatening weather, hostile attacks, economic recessions, and so forth), and how they ought to feel and be. Television's schedule, its information, and its stories, therefore, have active roles in shaping the ways TV viewers think about themselves and feel about themselves and their worlds, including how they think and feel about themselves as gendered human beings.

As a cultural institution that produces programming (or more basically televised content), TV continuously represents gender to its viewers. It also, of course, represents race, ethnicity, age, class, sexuality, nationality, religion—all of the categories that humans and their social institutions have developed in order to classify and regulate the chaos of their universe. While this particular essay focuses on television and gender, other essays of its kind could focus (and have focused) on the other categories (also called markers, axes, identities, and social representations) listed above. We can see, in fact, from the articles collected in this volume that many scholars the world over have turned their attention, from many different points of view, to the analysis of TV and these (among other) various dimensions.

Even though we may come to agree that TV is a technology and a social, economic, cultural, and ideological institution, it exists as such within a whole range of different relationships to the countries in which it is produced and/or consumed, and to the economic, religious, and ideological frameworks of those countries. Television's infrastructure and programming, for example, may be controlled and shaped by national governments, private corporations, religious entities, or local communities (to name some arrangements), and the various beliefs and interests—including those pertaining to gender—that impel and motivate them. But as is abundantly clear the world over, television is also in the throes of radical change, transmogrifying into digital signals, and satellite, cable and Internet delivery systems; becoming more interactive and in some countries (such as the US) more oriented to niche programming; and holding out, in these changes, the promise (however tenuous) of more viewer negotiations over gender representations (and all representations for that matter), as well as more alternatives to conventional depictions of gender and the other social categories.

Representation

If television is a term with multiple meanings and is currently caught up in revolutionary changes (many the result of technological and geopolitical shifts), "representation" too has many meanings and is itself undergoing conceptual transformations. Recently, a number of philosophical and theoretical debates, as well as scientific advances (in, for example, the field of physics) have revolved around the notion of representation and its presumed correlate, reality.

As a term, "representation" has typically been defined as referring to signs, symbols, images, portrayals, depictions, likenesses, and substitutions; and we have tended to think of representation as the primary function that television performs. "Television representation," therefore, conjures up notions of one thing standing in for something else; and we typically contrast this representation to reality, believing, for example, that the electronic image of a man on the TV screen is a portrayal, a substitute, or a reproduction of a flesh and blood man out there in the world of empirical reality. But, as much recent writing has argued, it may not be as simple as that.[2]

Recognizing that there are raging debates about this issue, with radically different positions espoused, let me take a particular stance and ask: What if the *truth* of nature, the world, the universe, *reality*, is fundamentally unknowable by human beings? What if it is the human being that imposes order and categories on the world within the limits of human perceptual capabilities (eyes, ears, brain and so forth)? What if reality is truly a swirl of molecules (or some other unknown substances or non-substances), and if we were able to perceive differently we would see it, hear it, feel it in a totally different way than we do with our human senses and brains? What if nature actually does present some repeated patterns, some similarities and differences (amidst the wildness), but what if nonetheless we, as human beings, are still fundamentally bound by our own limited ways of processing, interpreting, making meaning out of them? What if, in other words, reality really is construed by humans, really is humanly constructed? What if, furthermore, different human societies train (even inadvertently) their humans to perceive and interpret reality in particular ways? And what if this humanly produced social reality passes in most societies for natural reality, the common sense understanding about the world, the truth? And what if the constant generation of *representations* of this social reality enforces over and over again the notion that this human, social construction is really the real thing?

It is in the spirit of these questions that we may speak (among many other things) of representations as human constructs and as social representations. Speaking of them as human constructs emphasizes that representations are produced by the human brain and other human perceptual systems. It emphasizes that representations are mediations—that is, they are formed in the human mind and are human interpretations of some exterior realm. Speaking of representations in this way also emphasizes that they are distinct from reality, a step (at least) removed from it. Representations in this sense are also spoken of as "social representations" to underscore the fact that they don't spring up in isolated human minds, but rather they come into being, exist, and do their work in the social realm (in groups of human minds and bodies), in the realm of particular, empirical, human societies.

To take a gender-related example, in many societies a boy, at a particular point in his life, may start to dress like the men in his family or region or country. He may then represent to himself and to those around him something like young manhood or masculinity. He may start to talk and move and adopt the behaviors of the men around him, again representing masculinity. Pretty soon, these representations come to seem to him (as they have before to those around him) natural. He's a boy who is becoming a man and this is how men are, this is how they represent a masculinity that's out there in nature. The point, of course, that needs to be made here (and will be discussed more later) is that there is no real manhood out there in nature of which this enactment is a re-presentation. The representation, the social construction, has come to stand in for an imaginary original reality.

Whereas representations such as the one involving this boy are referred to by some as *social* representations, other representations such as those involving the spheres of television, film, · literature, art, and so forth, often get referred to as *cultural* representations, representations that exist and do their work in the cultural realm—the realm of language, art, entertainment; the realm specific to ideas, thoughts, and the mind. In making this distinction some people have intended to imply that the difference between cultural representations and social representations is a fundamental one, with cultural representations usually serving to shore up, buttress, or reinforce the more primary and more important social representations. (More important because, within the terms of this distinction, social representations may be thought to be more directly connected to the material existence of the empirical human body, and more directly connected to actual societies and their various economies).

The notion of nation may serve here as an example of a cultural representation, because in many ways, nation is a representation that primarily derives from what have traditionally been called cultural spheres. We read about nations (our own and others') in newspapers, magazines, and books; we see a nation's boundaries and its geographical relationship to the rest of the world on maps and atlases; we learn about the culture, politics, and symbols of nations from television— Prime Minister Tony Blair argues his case before British Parliament, the British royal family is profiled in a documentary, the Beatles are mobbed by British teens in a TV retrospective. Or we see that Pakistan is comprised of three major ethnic groups (Punjabi, Sindhi, and Pashtun), that tensions with India are ongoing over the disputed state of Kashmir, that President General Pervez Musharraf seeks to present a picture of a strong and unified country. Some Pakistani and English citizens may come to see the "imagined communities" portrayed on TV as commensurate with their own notions of their nations, in the same ways that many of us have come to imagine our own and other nations based on what we've watched on TV, read in newspapers, or seen on maps. The main point to be made here is that we don't really see nations out there in our everyday social reality. We derive a sense of them from our exposure to various cultural representations, often over the course of our lifetimes. We then come to see our everyday social (and national) worlds through the lens of these cultural representations. But it is completely clear that these cultural representations have the same power and effects as what I described earlier as social representations.

It is, then, a contention of this essay that the distinction between the social and the cultural (although often useful for the purposes of analysis) is too arbitrary and too artificial to be ultimately sustained. One of the main points I want to argue is that television representations of gender (like television representations of nation and other categories) indeed have very profound effects on very real human bodies, societies, and economies. For example, most of us come to have at least an inkling of what the normative ideal of a woman or man from our own nation is supposed to look like, behave like, think like, and feel like. And this inkling is absolutely tied up with the rules of the gender and nationality game that govern the societies in which we live, and which we, in one way or another, come to live by (or not).

To tie some of these remarks about representation even more tightly to television, it may be useful to ponder for a moment the often heard truisms that "television holds a mirror up to nature" or "television reflects society." It is probably clear already that my position on television and representation does not support these metaphors. Although it seems natural for us to think about TV in these terms and hard to extricate ourselves completely from their grip, it may be productive now to pry them apart, to consolidate some of the points we've already covered, and to look toward a couple of new ones. First, TV can't hold a mirror up to "nature" because, as I've already suggested, nature is not simply waiting out there to be reflected, it is not simply knowable, it is already humanly and socially constructed. Second, TV can't even hold a mirror up to (or reflect) society's or the human being's version of nature (or reality or society) because TV *itself*, for a whole range of reasons, is utterly selective about what it chooses to represent and how. The reasons it is selective have everything to do with the countries or regions in which it is produced and the types of institutional arrangements (government, public, community, commercial, religious, local, and so forth) that fund or support it. In the commercial US system, for instance, it is possible to trace direct relationships between television representations and television's economic imperatives.

For example, with regard to one aspect of gender, US television in its early history (1950s–1970s when US TV was dominated by three commercial networks), repeatedly produced representations of young, white, middle-class, heterosexual, conventionally attractive (according to US standards), domesticated women, as the norm of femininity. One of the obvious reasons it did this was to attract the largest possible audience of young upscale mothers who would then go out and buy the home and beauty-related products advertised on screen. Another reason (which also continues to this day) is that particular representations of femininity (and masculinity) have long been used by commercial culture to associate heterosexual desirability with consumer products and consumerism in general—to encourage consumption by linking it to images of idealized objects of heterosexual desire. But we can see from this example that, in its earliest years, US TV didn't even hold up a mirror to the social representations of femininity in the country in which it was produced—many US women were not middle class, white, young, or heterosexual. Perhaps it could be said, using the words of advertising historian Roland Marchand, that what TV held up was a distortional fun-house mirror to society.[3] But actually it was even worse than that, because US television's "mirror" was selective not only in the sense of distorting what was there for the sake of its own economic exigencies, it was selective in the sense of largely ignoring (particularly in those early years) whole segments of the society that it purportedly reflected. For most of its early history, US TV rarely depicted the people of color, the poor, the citizens with handicaps, the lesbians, and so forth that also constituted the category of US femininity. But television's selective, distorted, and constrained representations of femininity came, for many years and for many people, to constitute the truth or reality of femininity, what femininity out there in the world of the US was actually about. It came, moreover, to figure as a *universal* ideal of femininity for many in the (myopic) United States because US television was after all simply reflecting all reality, mirroring nature, in another of its defining metaphors, simply being a "window on the world."

However, as US TV has changed dramatically since the mid-1980s (with the break-up of three network hegemony, the proliferation of cable and satellite services, the marketing to niche audiences, the competition from the more adventurous cable channels, the more daring forays of the older three networks in the face of cable's competition, and so forth), the representations of femininity have changed in a number of ways. For example, a special on HBO (Home Box Office, a premium and costly cable channel) called *Queens of Comedy*, featured a large black comedienne named Monique who is ruthless in her overt critique of conventional white femininity; and the network program, *Ellen*, featured a lesbian character and an out lesbian star. It cannot be denied that these new venues and practices are offering up representations that complicate the more conventional ones; and they also hold out the hope of more and more alternative representations. Nonetheless, we are constantly reminded when looking at US TV (and TV from many other nations, for that matter) that *particular* ideals of beauty and femininity are still held up as the norms against which these other more innovative manifestations are positioned. And this is the tension in which some television and its representations of gender are currently caught.

Gender

Gender, like representation, has been the topic of much theoretical and scientific debate in the past thirty years and its meanings are also hotly contested. It has, over the years, been defined as the social and cultural meanings or representations assigned to biologically sexed bodies; with the terms "masculine" and "feminine" usually referring to socially and culturally-produced gender, and "male" and "female" referring to biologically-produced sex (with "man" and "woman" floating in between, but often closer to the social/cultural side). When we look at the writing that has grappled with television and gender representations, we notice that some of it, particularly in the earlier days of the research (in the 1970s and early 1980s), studied the depictions of male and female fictional characters or personalities (such as news people), and perpetuated (inadvertently, perhaps) the binary divisions of gender into the hard and fast categories of male/female, masculinity/femininity.[4] We see, however, that a good deal of later work approached television representations of gender in many broader ways.[5] The binaries of male/female, masculinity/femininity, and the conventional ways of thinking about and enacting gender that they legislate, perpetuate, and underwrite are nonetheless hard to dislodge.

In the last few years, a number of scholarly articles and books, including Judith Butler's, *Gender Trouble* and *Bodies that Matter*, have taken on the task of breaking the binaries, of shaking up the conventional notions and definitions of gender, and have argued, in Butler's words, that "the sexes" are not "unproblematically binary in their morphology and constitution;" and further that if, "the immutable character of sex is contested, perhaps this construct called 'sex' is as culturally constructed as gender; indeed, perhaps it was always already gender. . . ."[6] Butler here makes reference to the fact (alluded to above) that over the past few decades, the term gender has been used to designate the social and cultural construction of sex; and the term sex has been used to designate the seemingly obvious and uncontested biological difference between males and females. She argues explicitly that not only gender but sex itself is a social and cultural construction, that the binaries male/female (as well as the binaries masculine/feminine) do not hold.

Butler and others, for one thing, can point to enormous ranges of hormone distributions in individuals we typically call male and female, ranges of secondary sex characteristics such as facial and body hair and muscle mass; more instances of sexual dimorphism (babies born with both penises and vaginas) than we realize, more instances of transgenderism—individuals with one sex organ who feel like members of the other gender, and so forth. There are enough actual instances, in other words, to call into question the binary division of two sexes, and, given what seems to be incontrovertible evidence of a wide range and breadth of gender manifestations, surely enough evidence to call the division of two genders into question. In this respect (and in addition to a range of other arguments), Butler advocates a radical reconception of both gender and sex as cultural constructions, as performances, enactments, iterations of regulatory norms that *make bodies matter* according to laws of human history rather than those of nature.[7]

Without going into the details of the argument here, and without saying much more about culture and biology, nurture and nature, or some combinations thereof, it is important to recognize that work like Butler's has made the investigations of gender and its television-based representations an ever more pressing pursuit, and has expanded the boundaries of gender's definition and potential power. And even though people still want to argue that hormones or genes are the primary (and sometimes sole) determinants of behavior, of gender, or of sexuality, there is, I contend, no way of finally settling this question. The closest, it seems, we can come to adjudicating the debate is to say that *both* biology and nurture, both nature and social construction figure in the formation of what we call gender (and sex). How, in lieu of raising a control group of children in hermetically sealed environments (and even that, of course, wouldn't yield incontrovertible findings), could we ever prove that one side or other of the debate is right?

Having said all of this, it is still crushingly clear that even though on an intellectual, and perhaps even an ethical, level many people believe in gender as a continuum rather than gender as two binaries, it is also extraordinarily hard to actually live out those beliefs. Whether one is involved in raising children, forging new ways of enacting gender, or simply negotiating the affairs of an ordinary day, one is continually confronted with the regulatory norms of gender (with the written and unwritten rules) and what it means or could mean to transgress them. For example, some, but not many, people are comfortable encouraging their children to be as fluid with gender as possible, or are comfortable letting their sexually dimorphic babies forego surgery. The consequences, for many, however, seem far too great; and the courage of those who break the binaries should never be ignored or underestimated.

This, of course, brings us squarely up against the question of why. Why is the maintenance of these gender norms deemed so crucial? Why does the blurring or the crossing of the gender binary cause such discomfort, indeed such panic? Why does it promote such atrocities? Why were two cross-dressing US adolescent males (Deon Davis and Wilbur Thomas) killed (as have other cross-dressing and transgendered teens been killed) in August 2002? Something as devastatingly charged as this thing called gender is obviously in need of a great deal more thought and study.

Studying television and representations of gender

As we will see more below, television scholars have moved the study of gender well beyond examining the depictions of male and female characters. But early research on gender and television had its beginnings in the worldwide second-wave feminist movements, and initially (primarily in the early 1970s) focused on representations of femininity—images of female characters or personalities in television fiction or news programs.[8] Such was the case because feminism was initially bent on illuminating the egregious inequalities caused by worldwide gender systems in constructing woman as the subservient category to man in the gender binary. This research and writing on images of women on television was soon criticized for being too atomistic, that is, for plucking the women characters in fictional programs out of their contexts and neglecting, for example, the ways in which women were portrayed in the overall narrative; and, furthermore, for focusing on particular limited dimensions of the characters, such as their professional statuses (were women portrayed as physicians or as housewives, etc.?) or their personality traits (were they active or passive, etc.?).[9]

Soon also, and spurred mainly by the work of women of color, it was made apparent that to study gender in isolation was to replicate what the category itself excludes or represses—the myriad other social representations (or identities) upon which and against which notions of gender are produced—identities involving race, ethnicity, class, age, sexuality, nationality, and religion, for example. It became apparent that future work on the representations of gender would have to take into account the ways the categories masculinity and femininity depended on such exclusions and repressions, the ways, for example, that normative femininity on early United States television was not only represented as white, middle-class, young, maternal, heterosexual and American, but was utterly dependent on the excluded categories of black, ethnic, working-class, old, non-maternal, lesbian, and non-American as its repressed others. It became clear, in other words, that scholars could not continue to speak of the category gender without recognizing its dependence on its formative exclusions.[10]

Research and writing on representations of masculinity soon followed the initial work on femininity. Here scholars sought to stress that even though femininity was the devalued term of the masculinity/femininity binary, masculinity's representation was also severely constrained and circumscribed in its conventional deployment. In the words of John Fiske in *Television Culture*, "Masculinity is a paradox of power and discipline. The privilege of authority is bought by the discipline of duty and service."[11] Fiske and other scholars wanted to drive home the point that masculinity was not the unmarked term of the gender binary, that is, not a natural un-socialized manifestation of gender, but was, in fact, just as thoroughly constructed as femininity. They were trying to stress that although femininity may be more readily understood as a constructed category (because of its association with things like make-up, hairstyles, clothing, body standards, plastic surgery, particular ways of moving and talking—artifice of all kinds), masculinity (which is often seen as just plain natural in, for example, its rugged outdoorsy unkemptness) was equally socially constructed. Masculinity, in other words, was shown to be a marked category in the same way that whiteness (which seems to some Americans completely free of marking—pure, plain, normal, and natural) has been shown to be as wrapped up in ethnicity as blackness, Native American, Latino American, Asian American, and so forth.[12]

Soon, writing on what some refer to as non-normative sexualities, and some call queerness, including gayness, lesbianism, bisexuality, and transgenderism, followed the initial research on femininity and television. This writing illuminated, among many other things, how the conventional binary of masculinity/femininity worked to limit the depiction of multiple sexualities and genders on television; and to enforce the notion that the two categories in the conventional binary were universally accepted and have clear inviolable boundaries. To the contrary, as Alexander Doty demonstrated in *Making Things Perfectly Queer*, television representations of masculinity and femininity could be interpreted by scholars and by everyday TV viewers for all the queerness they actually mobilize but that society and culture works so hard to repress and contain. For Doty (following Judith Butler and Sue Ellen Case), queerness:

is something that is ultimately beyond gender—it is an attitude, a way of responding, that begins in a place not concerned with, or limited by, notions of a binary opposition of male and female or the homo versus hetero paradigm usually articulated as an extension of this gender binarism.

If we looked at television with new eyes, we could see, for example, all the repressed homoeroticism in traditional TV depictions of men police teams or of women's friendship. In Doty's words, we could see the queerness contained within what we thought were obvious examples of heterosexual women and heterosexual men in relationships of just plain friendship. We could, as Doty does, interpret the US program *Laverne and Shirley* (a show about two hetero-sexual women friends) as a lesbian or a queer program.[13]

In other words, we could try to unleash the multiplicities in gender that are bound up in the conventional binaries of male/female, masculinity/femininity, man/woman. We could try to see gender (and sexuality) as a continuum (of multiple genders and sexualities), with innumerable possibilities for individuals and for relationships.[14]

Also in the history of studying representations of gender on television, scholars began to argue that TV needed to be studied for its representations of gender that were not confined to characters or TV personalities alone. They argued that we needed to study gender as it was manifested in, or at least associated with, whole genres—talk shows, soap operas, melodramas, soft news could be seen as feminine; sports, hard news, financial facts and figures reporting could be seen as masculine, and so forth. Others argued that we needed to see gender as it was manifested in and associated with particular narrative structures—open-ended serials could be seen as more feminine, whereas closed narratives (ones that achieved final resolution) could be seen as more masculine. Yet others believed that television itself manifested or was associated with the feminine because it was domestic, passive, and generally oriented to consumption rather than production. As might be imagined, these arguments continue to be debated in the overall field, with different scholars taking various and conflicting positions.[15]

All in all, and as I think we have seen, the study of the relationships between gender and television from a Cultural Studies position brings us squarely up against some tricky imperatives. On the one hand, we face the importance of demonstrating exactly how the conventional mascu-line/feminine binary gets produced and reproduced by television, and of demonstrating exactly how the representation of variations in terms of gender get tamped down. Similarly we face the importance of championing new, alternative representations of gender (the multiple representa-tions of gender that are actually lived in the social sphere, representations that may foster new and unimagined possibilities, and representations that might hasten the demise of the gender category altogether). But on the other hand, we face the importance of not replicating (even inadvertently) the gender binary while we demonstrate its cultural construction, or while we fight against the injustices it fosters. Similarly, we face the importance of not underestimating the ways the conventional gender binary structures most people's everyday lives even as we speak out against the atrocities committed in its service. And finally, we face the importance of recognizing the need for groups forged within the terms of the binary's inequalities (women's movements, for example), at the same time as we try to break the binary apart.

An integrated approach to the study of television representations of gender

Let me now advocate a particular approach to the study of television representations of gender, an approach that many scholars working in a Cultural Studies tradition have used in one way or another, and an approach that I believe greatly aids research and analysis. In other places I have used the phrase, the "integrated approach" to the study of television to refer to this approach, one that conceives of its field of study as involving four interrelated sites or spheres: television production, television reception, television programming (or overall content), and television's social/historical context. The approach is solidly based in Cultural Studies, and draws on Stuart

Hall's *encoding/decoding* model (1980), Richard Johnson's *circuit of production, circulation, and consumption of cultural products* (1986), and the Open University's *circuit of culture* (1997/99). I have elaborated my own take on this model in an article called "Cultural Studies, Television Studies, and the Crisis in the Humanities."[16] The point I want to make here is that each of these four sites (not simply programming) is involved in generating or constructing representations of gender, and each needs to be examined and analyzed for the ways it does so. This is not to say that every individual study of gender and television needs to include an investigation of each of the four sites—it would be virtually impossible to do this. It is simply to say that the specific activities of each site and the potential interactions among them should be considered when conceiving a particular research project involving television and gender, when posing the questions that impel the research, and when drawing the final conclusions. In any actual study, an investigation into one or two of the sites may virtually eclipse the others.

As I think we have seen, when we think of gender representations and television, we may initially tend to think of the ways men and women are represented in programs (news, commercials, fictional forms, and so forth) and how those representations constitute the norms up against which actual people enact, or do not enact, culturally legitimated femininity and masculinity. We will return to a discussion of programming shortly, but at this point we have to remember a few things: (1) Representations of gender are continually constructed and very much operative not only in the site of programming but in the other three sites as well. (2) Representations of gender (even when one is focusing on the site of programming) should not simply be equated with TV depictions of male/female or masculine/feminine characters or personalities. As mentioned above, we have to look at the position of characters in plots, at narrative structures as a whole, at genres, at the overall television enterprise, among potentially many other things. (3) Representations of the conventional binaries of male/female, masculinity/femininity, man/woman need to be studied not only for how they get constructed, reproduced, and enforced, but also for how they already are and can continue to be broken apart. (4) Representations and constructions of gender variations need to be studied as much as representations of conventional masculinity and femininity; and we need to figure out how to forge ahead with such studies without minimizing the repressive and oftentimes horrific power that accompanies the enforcement of the conventional binary.

Let me turn to US television for some general examples, but let me add that each national television system may be analyzed along similar lines. Let me also say that even though I will be using a commercial system to provide examples, public service systems could equally be mined for the many illustrations of the "integrated approach" they would provide. Finally, let me also say that my following remarks on the four sites are only meant to suggest a few of the ways this approach may be put into action when examining any individual site or the numerous interactions among them.

Production

If we turn to the site of *production* and US television, for example, we find that there are a number of levels on which gender is constructed and needs much more investigation. First, at the general structural level of the corporate capitalist enterprise, the way gender is imagined and represented in the mind's eye of the television industry, has everything to do with the historical distribution of jobs, money, and power—with the functioning of the industry as an economic and social sector. This, of course, has everything to do with the ways in which the binary male/female has structured US society and specifically the ways it has structured the distribution of jobs in the news and entertainment industries, where jobs have been distributed primarily (but not always) according to traditional gender lines. For much of its early history, the television industry, for example, directed women to such professions as "continuity girls" (the people responsible for the continuity from shot to shot—is the actor's hair parted on the same side in every shot of the scene, is the glass of bourbon at a consistent level from shot to shot, is the actress wearing the same shoes in every shot of the scene, and so forth). This assertion does not mean to imply that individual women in early US TV could not or did not hold jobs in the upper echelons of the industry (soap opera creator/writers, Irna Phillips and Agnes Nixon, come to mind, as do Lucille Ball, and producer, writer, actress, Gertrude Berg). It is simply to point out the inequities in the television workplace that have structured the sphere of production. Today, the barriers to women in many areas of TV production, although by no means as rigid as in earlier years, are nonetheless still in evidence. The action group, Women in Film, founded by women working in the film and television industries in the 1970s and still active today, sprang up to specifically combat the discrimination these conditions perpetuate.

Such conditions, moreover, have countless repercussions for not only the division of labor and wages but for what actually ends up on the home screen as well. More scholarly attention needs to be paid here because the issue is an enormously complex one. But as we have seen, the gender binary has structured many people's notions about what is and should be associated with masculinity and what with femininity. To turn for a moment to an example from British television, research indicates that in the sphere of factual entertainment, more women have become involved in key stages of production (filming, directing, editing, producing), especially in independent production. However, they have typically been associated with "reality TV" and have come under criticism for "feminizing" documentary practices—for focusing on everyday life, gossip, and so forth. What we see here, then, is an example of the complexities involving gender in this situation. The women from the outset may have been assigned to reality TV because for some in the television institution, that may be the genre most immediately and traditionally associated with females (soft rather than hard news). Also, the women's own culturally-constructed femininity may, in fact, have influenced the ways they grappled with the news material (zeroing in on the personal, the private, rather than the public, details of life). But, furthermore, the television they produced was received by the wider professional community in conventional gender-based ways (others in television production judged the women's work as too "feminine" and as working to "feminize" television documentary).[17]

Conversely, the point has been made in the US that even if women are a fundamental part of a production team, their presence in and of itself cannot have a large effect on changing what actually gets produced in the heavily routinized and constrained commercial system. The women, this argument runs, necessarily become swallowed up by the commercial exigencies of industrial practices and don't have the leeway to introduce much change.[18] From yet another point of view, criticisms of Lifetime Television demonstrate the ways that one of the US cable channels dedicated specifically to programming for women (and employing a number of women), produces very conflicted representations of femininity, representations that draw on some of the most egregious dimensions of the conventional binary.[19] Each of these criticisms is illuminating and each needs to be more fully pursued. None, however, may be viewed as the definitive analysis of the situation. It is difficult, for example, to predict what would happen on the level of programming if large numbers of women and men with critical views and analyses of the conventional gender binary were part of the television work force.

The work of some scholars on race and television representations, however, may point us in the right direction. Herman Gray's writing on the US program *Frank's Place*, for example, demonstrates the influence of black producers and writers (who had well-developed critiques of white society and white television culture) on the production of innovative and complex representations of blackness on the program. Crystal Zook's study, chronicling the appearance of black writers at FOX entertainment television in the late 1980s and 1990s, does the same. Zook additionally underscores the dearth of black women writers who she feels (because of their formulated critiques of white society and gender) could have and would have introduced significant differences with regard to both representations of race and gender onto the home-screens.[20]

Within US TV production, gender is also produced at the level of the overall production process—in the myriad imperatives that directly govern the construction of audiences and programs. A majority of these imperatives are tightly tied up with conventional gender, such as the ways the industry has consistently fashioned its market and programs according to gender: the ways it has developed formulaic programs that it thinks and hopes will appeal to conventionally-produced and identified males and females; and the ways it has divided its programming and scheduling according to the formulaic genres and times of day that it thinks will draw large numbers of respective male and female viewers (for example, sports on weekends to attract men, soaps during weekdays to attract women and so forth).

Target audience analyses may also illuminate not only how conventional gender representations get produced but also how variations regarding gender and sexuality make it onto television. For example, Ron Becker's work on the spate of gay-themed television programs in the 1990s demonstrates the ways that both new representations of gender and sexuality were introduced to US home screens, attracting gay, lesbian, and bi-sexual audiences along the way; but also how these representations were used to attract and shore up a particular segment of the mainstream heterosexual audience.[21]

The sphere of production needs also to be studied for the other ways that differences with regard to gender and sexuality may be seen to function. Sean Griffin's work on Disney, for example, examines gay professionals who work at Disney, gay-inflected films and programs, and gay interpretations by audience members. Although this study is directed more specifically toward the film industry, it points the way to other such studies for television.[22]

Only these few specific instances with regard to studying the site of TV production and gender can be suggested here. But the key point is that the sphere of production (whether it is commercial, public, community, religious, cable access, or state-controlled) needs to be rigorously examined for all the ways it depends upon conventional gender demarcations for its functioning and its production of audiences and programs; and consequently for how it contributes to, draws on, and circulates particular representations and conceptions of gender as opposed to others. It must also be studied, however, for the ways it may produce variations, differences, and innovations in the representations of gender and sexuality.

Reception

The sphere of reception is replete with its own gender dimensions that need intensive examination. They involve, first, the overall institution of viewing—the social and environmental factors that comprise viewing situations and revolve around gender, such as traditional family hierarchies and the venue of home viewing documented in the work of David Morley, Ann Gray and others. Likewise conventional gender roles and their enactments in out-of-home public venues such as bars, community centers, and so forth also call for further investigation. Anna McCarthy's work on television in public places is particularly instructive in relation to these.[23]

Reception also involves the gender dimensions of the actual viewer/program interactions. How, for example, do meaning, pleasure, and other forms of affect actually get produced? How exactly do audience members absorb, reject, or negotiate the norms of gender offered up by programs? How and why do particular groups (teenagers, for example) choose programs based on conventional gender designations? How do audiences use cultural representations to rally for changes in conventional social assumptions about gender? How do fans become avidly identified with programming in gender-based ways? How do gay, lesbian, bisexual, and transgendered viewers interpret the gender-based dimensions of particular programs in different ways than the programs were intended? How do particular women's audiences (and so forth) do the same? How do shows with a marked difference of subject matter and dramatic innovations in the portrayal of sexualities and gender (such as US Showtime's and British Channel 4's *Queer as Folk*, for instance) forge their own new situations of viewing as well as new relationships between viewers and programs?[24]

It must, furthermore, be remembered when talking about reception, that scholars have debated over TV's role in shaping our identities. On the one hand, scholars have argued that because of television's continual shifts in point of view, in genres, in subject matter; because of its overall structure of fragmentation and distraction, it may indeed contribute to the construction of human beings that are not structured as solidly within the terms of conventional binaries, including the binary of gender. According to this argument, television may, in fact, be contributing to the formation of new types of human beings—ones less forged by all the conventional binaries (male/female, white/black, rich/poor, young/old, etc.), simply because TV viewers, in a variety of global systems, are continuously bombarded with all sorts of different points of view, modes of address, enactments of gender, race, nation and so forth.[25] On the other hand, other scholars have continued to argue that TV works to construct a generic feminized viewer, a passive, consumption-oriented, domesticated being—a consumer rather than a citizen. And although the conventional binary-based import of these designations is not lost on the proponents of this position, it is one that we must be careful to interrogate more completely than we have to date.

Programming

If we turn to the sphere of programming itself, we recognize the complexity of gender representations in actual television fare. First let me make clear that I am using the term programming here to refer to all televised content, including commercials, voice-overs, channel announcements, promos, written slogans, weather reports, and so forth, everything that we see or hear on the screen. Needless to say, each of these facets needs to be studied more from the point of view of gender.

When we turn to examine the fictional programs in this sphere, we see, as the feminist critics in the late 1970s and 1980s came to see, that gender cannot be analyzed in isolated images alone, but must be seen as it is produced in all of its specificity, in and through all the formal dimensions of television. We see that gender is represented in the unfolding of the narrative, in the genre, and in each of the techniques such as camera work (close ups and soft focus, for example); editing (romantic dissolves, for example); sound (authoritative speech or voice overs, for example); and mise en scene (which includes lighting, makeup, costumes, sets, props, and the way the characters move, and might, for example, generate a figure of typical "macho" dimensions—a large white body, toting a gun, and jumping over roof tops).

We also see, when examining this sphere, and as discussed before, the ways some forms and genres of television, not to mention television itself, have been considered gendered. Especially given the fact that recent writing on television points to the gendered nature of the medium itself (as well as the viewers it produces) this contention too needs a lot more investigation,

Social / historical context

Finally, the social and historical context is the major sphere that demarcates the ways general social events, movements, beliefs, and changes, produce or represent particular notions about gender in and for the society at-large. Here, for example, we see how, among many other things, social movements such as the women's movements, the gay and civil rights movements, and the fundamentalist religious movements, introduced different and conflicting representations of gender into US society during the last half of the twentieth century, representations that influenced the television industry, its programming, and reception, and in turn further influenced the social/ historical context. We also see here how philosophical and theoretical debates may have a real influence on the ways in which gender, among other categories is actually conceived and lived.

It is in social and cultural institutions like television that specific representations of gender get generated day in and day out and circulated as tacit and not so tacit norms to millions of viewers the world over (based, of course, on the different beliefs and interests that undergird both the norms and the shaping of the television programs). And it is for this reason that gender, representation, and television need to be thought together and examined ever more fully for their specific interrelations in all television systems throughout the world.

Notes

1 Thanks to Bobby Allen, Annette Hill and Ron Becker for their astute comments on earlier drafts of this essay.
2 See Stuart Hall, ed., *Representation*, London: Sage and the Open University, 1997, for a synopsis of these issues.
3 Roland Marchand, *Advertising the American Dream*, Berkeley: University of California Press, 1985, p. xvii.
4 For some examples see Gaye Tuchman, Arlene Kaplan Daniels, and James Benet, eds, *Hearth and Home: Images of Women in the Mass Media*, New York: Oxford University Press, 1978; Matilda Butler and William Paisley, *Women and the Mass Media*, New York: Human Sciences Press, 1980; Diana M. Meehan, *Ladies of the Evening: Women Characters of Prime-Time Television*, New York: Scarecrow Press, 1983. Most of this early research came from a liberal or sociological feminist perspective and was published before the rash of socialist, materialist, and poststructuralist feminist writing that interrogated the masculine/feminine binaries.
5 For overviews of this literature see Charlotte Brunsdon, Julie D'Acci, Lynn Spigel, eds, *Feminist Television Criticism*, London: Oxford University Press, 1997; Laura Stempel Mumford, "Feminist Theory and Television Studies," in Christine Geraghty and David Lusted, eds, *The Television Studies Book*, London: Edward Arnold, 1998; Lisbet Van Zoonen, *Feminist Media Studies*, London: Sage, 1994.
6 Judith Butler, *Gender Trouble*, New York: Routledge, 1990, p. 6 and 7; Judith Butler, *Bodies That Matter*, New York: Routledge, 1993.
7 Judith Butler, *Gender Trouble*, New York: Routledge, 1990; Judith Butler, *Bodies That Matter*, New York: Routledge, 1993. See also Elizabeth Grosz's *Space, Time and Perversion*, New York, Routledge, 1995.
8 See notes 4 and 5 above.
9 Diane Waldman, "There's More to a Positive Image than Meets the Eye," in Patricia Erens, ed., *Issues in Feminist Film Criticism*, Bloomington: Indiana University Press, 1990, pp. 13–18. Newer work began to focus on the place of women characters in overall narrative structures, on genres, and on broader questions of gender and representation. See Charlotte Brunsdon, "*Crossroads*: Notes on a Soap Opera," *Screen*, 22/4, 1981, pp. 32–7; Tania Modleski, *Loving with a Vengeance: Mass Produced Fantasies for Women*, Hamden CT.: Shoestring Press, 1982; Serafina Bathrick, The Mary Tyler Moore Show: Women at Home and at Work, in Jane Feuer, Paul Kerr, and Tise Vahimagi, *MTM: "Quality Television*," London: British Film Institute, 1984, pp. 91–131; Robert C. Allen, *Speaking of Soap Operas*, Chapel Hill: University of North Carolina Press, 1985; Helen Baehr and Gillian Dyer, eds, *Boxed In: Women and Television*, London: Pandora, 1987; Lorraine Gamman and Margaret Marshment, *The Female Gaze*, London: The Women's Press, 1988; E. Deidre Pribram, ed., *Female Spectators: Looking at Film and Television*, London: Verso, 1988; Lynn Spigel and Densie Mann, eds, *Private Screenings*, Minneapolis: University of Minnesota Press, 1992.

10   See Michele Wallace, *Invisibility Blues: From Pop to Theory*, London: Verso, 1990; Jacqueline Bobo and Ellen Seiter, "Black Feminism and Media Criticism: *The Women of Brewster Place*," *Screen*, 32/3. 1991, 286–302; bell hooks, *Black Looks: Race and Representation*, Boston: South End Press, 1992; Toni Morrison, *Playing in the Dark: Whiteness and the Literary Imagination*, Cambridge, MA: Harvard University Press, 1992, Gail Dines and Jean M. Humez, *Gender, Race and Class in Media*, Thousand Oaks, CA: Sage, 1995; Sasha Torres, ed., *Living Color: Race and Television in the United States*, Durham and London: Duke University Press, 1998. For gender representations and class considerations see Andrea L. Press, *Women Watching Television*, Philadelphia: University of Pennsylvania Press, 1991.

11   John Fiske, *Television Culture*, London and New York: Methuen, 1987, p. 208.

12   See John Fiske, *Television Culture*, London and New York: Methuen, 1987; Constance Penley and Sharon Willis, eds, *Male Trouble*, Minneapolis: University of Minnesota Press, 1993; Maurice Berger, Brian Wallis, and Simon Watson, eds, *Constructing Masculinity*, New York: Routledge, 1995; Mark Simpson, *Male Impersonators: Men Performing Masculinity*: New York, Routledge, 1994.

13   Alexander Doty, *Making Things Perfectly Queer*, Minneapolis: University of Minnesota, 1993, pp. xv and 39–62.

14   As television began to portray more diversity regarding gender and sexuality, more scholars focused on gay and lesbian representations. For some examples see Hilary Hinds, "Fruitful Investigations: The Case of the Successful Lesbian Text," in Sally Munt, ed., *New Lesbian Criticism*, New York: Columbia University Press, pp. 153–72; Rosanne Kennedy, "The Gorgeous Lesbian in LA Law: The Present Absence?" in Diane Hamer and Belinda Budge, eds, *The Good, the Bad, and the Gorgeous*, London: Pandora Press, 1994, pp. 132–41 (both articles also reprinted in Brunsdon, D'Acci and Spigel, eds, *Feminist Television Criticism*, London: Oxford University Press, 1997).

15   Andreas Huyssen, "Mass Culture as Woman: Modernism's Other," in *After the Great Divide: Modernism, Mass Culture, Postmodernism*, Bloomington: Indiana University Press, 1986, pp. 44–62. Lynne Joyrich, "All that Television Allows: TV Melodrama, Postmodernism and Consumer Culture," *Camera Obscura* 16, 1988, pp. 129–54. John Fiske, *Television Culture*, London and New York: Methuen, 1987; Lynne Joyrich, *Re-Viewing Reception: Television, Gender, and Postmodern Culture*, Bloomington: Indiana University Press, 1996.

16   Stuart Hall, "Encoding/Decoding," in Stuart Hall, Dorothy Hobson, Andrew Lowe, and Paul Willis, eds, *Culture, Media, Language* (London: Hutchinson, 1980). The essay had previously circulated as a Centre for Contemporary Cultural Studies stenciled paper (in a longer form) as "Encoding and Decoding in Television Discourse." See also Stuart Hall, Ian Angus, Jon Cruz, James Der Derian, Sut Jhally, Justin Lewis, and Cathy Schwichtenberg, "Reflections upon the Encoding/Decoding Model: An Interview with Stuart Hall," in Jon Cruz and Justin Lewis, eds, *Viewing, Reading, Listening: Audiences and Cultural Reception* (Boulder, Colorado: Westview Press, 1994) pp. 253–74. Richard Johnson, "What Is Cultural Studies Anyway?" *Social Text*, 16, Winter 1986/7, pp. 38–80. Julie D'Acci, "Cultural Studies, Television Studies and the Crisis in the Humanities," in *The Persistence of Television*, Lynn Spigel and Jan Olsen eds, Duke University Press, forthcoming. Julie D'Acci, "Television Genres" in the *International Encyclopedia of Social and Behavioral Sciences*, Oxford: Elsevier Science Ltd., 2002, pp. 15574–8.

17   See Dover, C. J. (2001) British documentary television production: tradition, change and "crisis" within a practitioner community. Unpublished thesis: Goldsmiths College, University of London.

18   Hollywood producer, writer and network executive, Barbara Corday, personal conversation, 1996, University of Southern California.

19   Special issue on Lifetime Television, ed. Julie D'Acci, *Camera Obscura*, 33–4, 1994–95.

20   Herman Gray, *Watching Race: Television and the Struggle for "Blackness,"* Minneapolis: University of Minnesota Press, 1995; Kristal Brent Zook, *Color by FOX: The Fox Network and the Revolution in Black Television*, New York: Oxford University Press, 1999.

21   Ronald Becker, "Prime Time Television in the Gay Nineties: Network Television, Quality Audiences and Gay Politics," *Velvet Light Trap*, Fall 1998, pp. 36–47.

22   Sean Griffin, *Tinker Belles and Evil Queens: The Walt Disney Company from the Inside Out*, New York, New York University Press, 1999.

23   Morley, David, *Family Television: Cultural Power and Domestic Leisure*, London: Comedia, 1986; Gray, Ann, *Video Playtime: The Gendering of a Leisure Technology*, London: Routledge, 1992; McCarthy, Anna, *Ambient Television: Visual Culture and Public Space*, Durham: NC Duke University Press, 2001.

24   In the UK, *Queer as Folk* (shown on Channel 4) raised quite a stir in the British tabloids. See Annette Hill and Katarina Thomson's work for the British Social Attitudes Survey detailing how the British press used the program as a marker for extreme gender representations, Hill, Annette and Thomson, Katarina (2001) "Sex and the Media: a Shifting Landscape" in R. Jowell, J. Curtice, A. Park, K. Thomson, L. Jarvis,

C. Bromley, N. Stratford, eds, *British Social Attitudes the 17th Report: Focusing on Diversity*, London: Sage: 71–99.

25 See E. Ann Kaplan, *Rocking Around the Clock: Music Television, Postmodernism, and Consumer Culture*, London: Methuen, 1987; Jim Collins, "Television and Postmodernism," in Robert C. Allen, ed., *Channels of Discourse Reassembled*, second edition, pp. 327–53.

Bibliography

Allen, R. C. (1985) *Speaking of Soap Operas*, Chapel Hill: University of North Carolina Press.

Baehr, H. and Dyer, G. (eds) (1987) *Boxed In: Women and Television*, London: Pandora.

Bathrick, S. (1984) "The Mary Tyler Moore Show: Women at Home and at Work", in Jane Feuer, Paul Kerr, and Tise Vahimagi, *MTM: "Quality Television"*, London: British Film Institute: pp. 91–131.

Becker, R. (1998) "Prime Time Television in the Gay Nineties: Network Television, Quality, Audiences and Gay Politics", *Velvet Light Trap*, Fall, pp. 36–47.

Bobo, J., and Seiter, E. (1991) "Black Feminism and Media Criticism: *The Women of Brewster Place,*" *Screen*, 32/3: pp. 286–302.

Brunsdon, C. "*Crossroads*: Notes on a Soap Opera", *Screen*, 22/4: pp. 32–37.

—— D'Acci, J. and Spigel, L. (eds) (1997) *Feminist Television Criticism*, London: Oxford University Press.

Butler, J. (1990) *Gender Trouble*, New York: Routledge.

—— (1993) *Bodies That Matter*, New York: Routledge.

Butler, M. and Paisley, W. (1983) *Women and the Mass Media*, New York: Human Sciences Press.

Collins, J. (1992) "Television and Postmodernism", in Robert C. Allen (ed.) *Channels of Discourse Reassembled* (2nd edn), London: Routledge: pp. 327–53.

D'Acci, J. (2002) "Television Genres", in the *International Encyclopedia of Social and Behavioral Sciences*, Oxford: Elsevier Science Ltd: pp. 15574–8.

—— (forthcoming) "Cultural Studies, Television Studies and the Crisis in the Humanities," in Lynn Spigel and Jan Olsen (eds) *The Persistence of Television*, Durham, NC: Duke University Press.

Deidre Pribram, E. (ed.) (1988) *Female Spectators: Looking at Film and Television*, London: Verso.

Dines, G. and Humez, J. M. (1995) *Gender, Race and Class in Media*, Thousand Oaks, CA: Sage.

Doty, A. (1993) *Making Things Perfectly Queer*, Minneapolis: University of Minnesota.

Dover, C. J. (2001) "British Documentary Television Production: Tradition, Change and 'Crisis' Within a Practitioner Community", Unpublished Thesis: Goldsmiths College, University of London.

Fiske, F. (1987) *Television Culture*, London and New York: Methuen.

Gamman, L. and Marshment, M. (1988) *The Female Gaze*, London: The Women's Press.

Gray, A. (1992) *Video Playtime: The Gendering of a Leisure Technology*, London: Routledge.

Gray, H. (1995) *Watching Race: Television and the Struggle for "Blackness"*, Minneapolis: University of Minnesota Press.

Griffin, S. (1999) *Tinker Belles and Evil Queens: The Walt Disney Company from the Inside Out*, New York, New York University Press.

Grosz, E. (1995) *Space, Time and Perversion*, New York, Routledge.

Hall, S. *et al.* (1994) "Reflections upon the Encoding/Decoding Model: An Interview with Stuart Hall," in Jon Cruz and Justin Lewis (eds) *Viewing, Reading, Listening: Audiences and Cultural Reception*, Boulder, Colorado: Westview Press: pp. 253–74.

—— (1980) "Encoding/Decoding," in Stuart Hall, Dorothy Hobson, Andrew Lowe, and Paul Willis (eds) *Culture, Media, Language*, London: Hutchinson.

—— (ed.) (1997) *Representation*, London: Sage and the Open University.

Hill, A., and Thomson, K. (2001) "Sex and the Media: a Shifting Landscape," in R. Jowell, J. Curtice, A. Park, K. Thomson, L. Jarvis, C. Bromley, N. Stratford (eds) *British Social Attitudes the 17th Report: Focusing on Diversity*, London: Sage: 71–99.

Hinds, H. (1990) "Fruitful Investigations: The Case of the Successful Lesbian Text," in Sally Munt (ed.) *New Lesbian Criticism*, New York: Columbia University Press: pp. 153–72.

hooks, b. (1992) *Black Looks: Race and Representation*, Boston: South End Press.

Huyssen, A. (1986) "Mass Culture as Woman: Modernism's Other", in *After the Great Divide: Modernism, Mass Culture, Postmodernism*, Bloomington: Indiana University Press: 44–62.

Johnson, R. (1986) "What Is Cultural Studies Anyway?", *Social Text*, 16, Winter 1986/7, pp. 38–80.

Joyrich, L. (1988) "All that Television Allows: TV Melodrama, Postmodernism and Consumer Culture", *Camera Obscura* 16: 129–54.

—— (1996) *Re-Viewing Reception: Television, Gender, and Postmodern Culture*, Bloomington: Indiana University Press.

Kaplan, E. A. (1987) *Rocking Around the Clock: Music Television, Postmodernism, and Consumer Culture*, London: Methuen.

Kennedy, R. (1994) "The Gorgeous Lesbian in LA Law: The Present Absence?", in Diane Hamer and Belinda Budge (eds) *The Good, the Bad, and the Gorgeous*, London: Pandora Press: pp. 132–41.

McCarthy, A. (2001) *Ambient Television: Visual Culture and Public Space*, Durham NC: Duke University Press.

Marchand, R. (1985) *Advertising the American Dream*, Berkeley: University of California Press.

Meehan, D. M. (1980) *Ladies of the Evening: Women Characters of Prime-Time Television*, New York: Scarecrow Press.

Modleski, T. (1982) *Loving with a Vengeance: Mass Produced Fantasies for Women*, Hamden CT.: Shoestring Press.

Morley, D. (1986) *Family Television: Cultural Power and Domestic Leisure*, London: Comedia.

Morrison, T. (1992) *Playing in the Dark: Whiteness and the Literary Imagination*, Cambridge, MA: Harvard University Press.

Press, A.L. (1991) *Women Watching Television*, Philadelphia: University of Pennsylvania Press.

Spigel, L. and Mann, D. (eds) (1992) *Private Screenings*, Minneapolis: University of Minnesota Press.

Stempel Mumford, L. (1998) "Feminist Theory and Television Studies", in Christine Geraghty and David Lusted (eds) *The Television Studies Book*, London: Edward Arnold.

Torres, S. (ed.) (1998) *Living Color: Race and Television in the United States*, Durham and London: Duke University Press.

Tuchman, G., Daniels, A. K. and Benet, J. (eds) (1978) *Hearth and Home: Images of Women in the Mass Media*, New York: Oxford University Press.

Van Zoonen, L. (1994) *Feminist Media Studies*, London: Sage.

Waldman, D. (1990) "There's More to a Positive Image than Meets the Eye," in Patricia Erens (ed.) *Issues in Feminist Film Criticism*, Bloomington: Indiana University Press: pp. 13–18.

Wallace, M. (1990) *Invisibility Blues: From Pop to Theory*, London: Verso.

Zook, K. B. (1999) *Color by FOX: The Fox Network and the Revolution in Black Television*, New York: Oxford University Press.

Chapter 25

RON BECKER

PRIME-TIME TELEVISION IN THE GAY NINETIES
Network television, quality audiences, and gay politics

IN 1994, *Entertainment Weekly* dubbed the decade "the Gay 90s."[1] A look at the period's prime-time network-television programming seems to prove the announcement prophetic. Throughout its first four decades, television virtually denied the existence of homosexuality. The families, workplaces, and communities of most network programming were exclusively heterosexual. As recently as the early 1990s, in fact, even the most astute television viewers could likely spot only a handful of openly gay, lesbian, and bisexual characters in an entire year of network television. After only a few television seasons, however, gay-themed episodes and references to homosexuality were everywhere. By the 1995–96 season, for example, even the relatively casual viewer might have spotted several openly gay characters in just one night. At least two dozen openly gay, lesbian, and bisexual recurring characters have been featured on over twenty shows, including *Roseanne, In the Pursuit of Happiness, Mad about You, Spin City, Chicago Hope, Melrose Place, N.Y.P.D. Blue, My So-Called Life, Fired Up, The Crew, Profiler*, and *High Society*. Hit shows such as *Wings, Veronica's Closet, Suddenly Susan, Grace under Fire, Dr. Quinn—Medicine Woman, Beverly Hills 90210, Coach, Cosby, Homicide: Life on the Street, Murphy Brown, ER, The Nanny*, and *Law & Order*, as well as short-lived programs like *Hudson Street* and *The Faculty*, all had specific episodes focused on gay topics and many others riddled with gay references and jokes. In addition to the dramatic increase of openly gay and lesbian characters, a good number of avowedly straight characters have been mistaken (or not) as being gay or lesbian, including just about every male cast member on *Friends, The Single Guy, Frasier*, and *Seinfeld*. The expansion of gay and lesbian issues on prime-time television reached a new level with the April 1997 coming-out episode of *Ellen*. Gay-themed television, it seems, is the programming trend of the nineties.

In this essay I explore a major force behind this recent trend, namely, network desire to target a quality audience in the increasingly competitive era of nineties narrowcasting. The recent representations of gays and lesbians certainly exist within wider social contexts. The gays-in-the-military debate, the Clinton presidency, anti-gay legislation battles, lesbian chic, and openly gay and lesbian celebrities are only a few of the multiple and interwoven factors at play behind television's fascination with homosexuality. Yet such cultural and political impulses interact with the structures, constraints, and imperatives of network television. Here, I focus specifically on industry conceptions of its quality audience and argue that network executives have incorporated gay and lesbian material into their prime-time lineups in order to attact an audience of "sophisticated," upscale, college-educated and liberally minded adults.[2] For the networks, this programming strategy also has the advantage of targeting a distinct segment of that demographic group, namely, middle- and upper-class gays and lesbians. While examining the relationship between the industry's conception of its audiences and the recent deluge of prime-time homosexuality helps explain some of the forces at play behind one of the decade's dominant programming trends, it also leads to a consideration of the serious consequences at stake for gay politics.[3]

The audience is crucial to the business of television. As the commodity sold by networks to advertisers, it constitutes the economic raison d'être of the industry. Yet, as many critics point out, the television audience doesn't simply exist out there for network executives to find; it isn't, as Ien Ang asserts, "an ontological given."[4] Instead, networks use tools such as ratings and marketing research to produce a specific understanding of its audience. Although influenced by the social conditions in which real viewers live, industry conceptions of the television audience are also shaped by the economic imperatives of an advertiser-based medium. Consequently, for the American television industry, at least, the audience is a collection of consumers, known by their demographic profiles—consumers which the industry tries to attract through specific programming.

While the industry sees the television audience as a commodity to be drawn in, packaged, and sold, critics have encouraged us to see television audiences from alternative perspectives. Feminist media scholars have looked at the lived social experiences of female viewers and at the role television viewership plays in the construction of women's gendered identities. Similarly, many involved in the gay and lesbian civil rights struggle have seen the television audience as a collection of political constituents that can be mobilized not to buy consumer products but rather to participate in supporting gay rights, a perspective that is especially important as gay and lesbian characters and gay-themed material become increasingly prevalent on network television. Work on television audiences, however, must also analyze how industry conceptions of its audience help influence the ways socially situated viewers engage with television. Integrated approaches to media studies, most notably Julie D'Acci's examination of *Cagney & Lacey* and the struggles among producers, networks executives, writers, and viewers to define notions of femininity through the program, have begun to explore these relationships, yet more work needs to be done.[5] Consequently, this article focuses on the economic imperatives behind television's use of gay material and begins to examine the subsequent tensions that develop between industry notions of consumers and a gay civil rights notion of politicized citizens.

Targeting a quality audience in the nineties

As an industry, network television has always been driven by selling viewers to sponsors, and although anxious to claim possession of the mass audience, especially in prime time, the networks have, at least since the 1970s, consistently been interested in the appeal of their programs to certain demographic groups. The so-called quality audience, broadly comprised of upscale adults, age eighteen to forty-nine (those assumed to be the most active consumers with the most disposable income), has been the underlying target demographic of all three networks for several decades.[6] Research, however, has shown that highly educated and upscale viewers tend to watch less television than their lower-income counterparts and that those who do watch are increasingly switching to cable channels.[7] Consequently, networks have been forced to work particularly hard in order to attract these hard-to-reach viewers. Although the industry maintains an idea of a broad audience of upscale adults, in practice the networks have had to work from a narrow and fluid conception of the quality audience. Reacting to changes in social and cultural contexts, the networks have continually updated their notion of this most prized audience segment and have repeatedly developed new programming strategies to target those specific viewers. In the early

1970s, CBS, concerned with the revenue of its urban-centered owned-and-operated stations, used *All in the Family* and *Mary Tyler Moore* to attract a distinctly urban demographic. In the 1980s, as cable television and changes in women's employment patterns forced them to reassess their audiences and programming strategies, the networks used shows like *Cagney & Lacey*, *Kate and Allie*, and *Designing Women* to target a quality audience of upscale working women.

In the 1990s, the networks, adapting to both industrial and social changes, have once again updated both their profile of the quality audience and their programming strategies. The increasing pressure from intense competition has forced the networks to target even narrower audience segments and to court them more aggressively with programming geared to their specific interests. Between 1984 and 1996, the big three networks' [ABC, CBS, NBC] audience share dropped from 73.9 to 50.5 percent.[8] At the same time, Generation X-ers, with tastes and attitudes shaped by record levels of college enrollment, the AIDS epidemic, Reaganomics, and childhoods saturated with cable television and marked by high divorce rates, have come of age. Believed to be critical individualists and cynical libertarians with seen-it-all attitudes, these latest members of the eighteen-to-thirty-four demographic have forced many companies to rethink their conception of the adult market. Consequently, in the mid-1990s, the quality demographic that has become the most widely sought after isn't simply upscale adults but, more specifically, "hip," "sophisticated," urban-minded, white, college-educated, upscale eighteen to forty-nine year olds with liberal attitudes, disposable income, and a distinctively edgy and ironic sensibility, a group basically comprised of segments of the aging yet still socially progressive and upwardly mobile baby boomers and the youthful twenty- and thirty-somethings that follow in their wake.[9] While the industry hasn't yet found a name for the members of this new psychographic market, I will dub them slumpies: socially liberal, urban-minded professionals. As networks work to cultivate the slumpy audience, prime-time schedules have seen a slew of programs featuring what network executives believe the world of this audience looks like—a world that, in many cases, includes gays and lesbians.

NBC is the network that has targeted this specific quality audience most forcefully. In the early nineties, NBC was a weak third in the ratings. ABC, on the other hand, was the top-rated network in prime time, its success partially built on strong family sitcoms like *Full House, Grace under Fire, Home Improvement*, and *Family Matters*. Working within the broadcasting industry's twenty-year-old, de facto Family Hour policy, ABC scheduled shows with kid appeal during the early evening hours. Scheduling executives hoped to attract children who in turn would bring the parents—the network's real target audience—as the family watched TV together. While shows with strong kid appeal helped ABC capture first place in 1994, NBC gained enormous ground by abandoning the family-hour strategy and blatantly going after eighteen to forty-nine year olds, especially the young, hip, urban, professional segment.[10] Shows like *Friends, Seinfeld, Frasier*, and *Mad about You* successfully apealed to the new quality audience.

NBC's new strategy was encouraged by a perceived change in viewing practices among the industry's audience. Ted Harbert, president of ABC Entertainment, explains, "Seventy percent of households now have more than one TV set. . . . You now have parents putting their kids in one room to watch their show and they can go in the other room and watch a more adult show designed for them."[11] Unconcerned with kid appeal, NBC was able to target its key adult demographic more efficiently by placing sitcoms filled with so-called adult situations and themes throughout its entire prime-time lineup, not just after 9 P.M. Advertisers, glad to reach these highly prized consumers, rushed to spend their dollars at the rejuvenated NBC.

By the 1995–96 season, the other networks eagerly followed NBC's lead, resulting in a noticeable trend in programming. More shows targeted to the perceived interests of a hip, cosmopolitan, professional, adult audience appeared throughout prime time. ABC dropped family sitcoms like *Full House*, moved shows considered to have more adult appeal such as *Roseanne* and *Ellen* to earlier time slots, and added *The Naked Truth* and *Murder One*. CBS, which had long targeted a slightly older and perhaps more rural and conservative audience of twenty-five to fifty-four year olds with *Murder She Wrote*, *In the Heat of the Night*, and *Evening Shade*, joined the trend with *Central Park West, Almost Perfect*, and *Can't Hurry Love*—shows clearly targeted at a younger, more urbanminded demographic. Similarly, Fox picked up shows like *The Crew, Partners*, and *Ned and Stacey*. Meanwhile, NBC placed *Caroline in the City, The Single Guy*, and *In the Pursuit of Happiness* on a schedule already heavy with similar programs.

As new shows have flooded the fall schedule, prime time has been filled with programs about the lives of childless, often single, almost exclusively urban, white, upscale twenty and thirty year olds. Characters usually live in big city apartments and work as often directionless yet still well-off professionals whose lives revolve around the trials of urban living, dating, and sex. Frequently displaced, of course, are the standard family sitcom preoccupations with suburban living, child rearing, and marriage. This preoccupation with the slumpy audience ignores the interests of viewers both younger and older than the target market; rural, conservative, and working-class adults; and many minority audiences. Conversely, such programming likely appeals to a segment of the lucrative upscale eighteen to forty-nine market once unserved by the family-hour strategy—specifically, adults without children.

Many of these programs have also been populated with significant numbers of openly gay and lesbian characters and filled with numerous gay references. With children as well as older and more conservative viewers increasingly out of the loop, writers, producers, and networks have been able to take greater risks with what was previously risqué material. In 1990, for example, a great deal of controversy surrounded an episode of ABC's *thirtysomething* in which two gay characters appeared in bed together. Even after ABC forced producers to edit out a same-sex kiss, numerous advertisers pulled their sponsorship. The network lost $1.5 million in revenue and refused to air the episode in summer reruns. Four years later, a similar controversy started to brew around a proposed lesbian kiss on *Roseanne*. The kiss remained, however, and the program was a ratings smash for ABC. Seemingly a quick learner, NBC consciously used gay and lesbian material as part of its strategy to rise from its third-place ratings slump and attract its quality audience. In a 1994 episode of *Frasier*, Frasier Crane, in a classic sitcom series of misunderstandings, ends up on a date with his new gay boss. The show was such a big hit that NBC reran the episode in the November sweeps period accompanied by a large promotional campaign.[12] A year later, during the November 1995 sweeps, NBC promoted its Thursday night sitcom lineup with a gimmick called "Star-Crossed Thursday" in which characters from each program made guest appearances on one of the other shows. The evening lineup was also linked by the repeated appearance of gay material. *Caroline in the City*'s Lea Thompson assumes *Friends*' Joey and Chandler are a gay couple. On *The Single Guy*, Jonathan stays with his gay neighbors and goes on a date with *Friends*' Ross, while on *Seinfeld*, Elaine's armoire is stolen by two apparently gay thugs.[13] Both NBC's characters and its audience are caught up in a world in which gays and lesbians clearly belong.

As all four networks work to reach the same target audience, incorporating gay and lesbian characters and plot lines may be a shrewd business decision. When the key demographic is one that prides itself on being politically progressive in general or gay friendly in particular, including a gay neighbor, a lesbian sister, or some queer plot twist is not only possible but also lucrative for those networks and producers anxious to differentiate their product in a saturated market of *Friends* and *Seinfeld* imitators. Network executives appear convinced that this new quality audience of white, urban sophisticates is not only comfortable with but is even drawn to programming featuring gay material. With such a perspective, bringing controversial issues from current headlines can give a show the politically correct and in-the-know quality helpful in attracting a hard-to-reach audience uninspired by warm-hearted family sitcoms and other standard network fare. Thus, while Roseanne goes to a gay bar to show how "cool" she really is on an episode of the ABC sitcom, network executives hope that viewers from its target audience will tune in to prove how "hip" they are.

The desire to reach the quality audience was most certainly a factor in Disney/ABC's decision to allow Degeneres and her writers to out Ellen Morgan in an April 1997 episode that may well mark the climax for gay and lesbian characters on prime time. When it first appeared as *These Friends of Mine* in 1994, the program was clearly seen as ABC's attempt to compete with NBC for the slumpy audience. As one critic pointed out, "It was *Seinfeld* with women."[14] Observers, however, have argued that the program never gained an identity of its own; it was always "following trends but never setting them (first it was a female *Seinfeld*, then a *Friends* clone)."[15] Throughout its short history, producers dramatically retooled the show in an attempt to attract the socially liberal, urban-minded, white, adult audience. In the 1995–96 season, for example, producers decided to highlight the program's Los Angeles setting to exploit further the possibilities of its big-city surroundings.[16] That same season saw the increased importance of two gay characters, Peter and Barrett, whose sendup of traditional gay stereotypes tested the audience's hipness and progressive politics.

Opening the closet door for the lead character was a logical step in revamping the program. As the immense media attention and high ratings generated by the coming-out story illustrate, a gay Ellen Morgan certainly distinguished the show not only from family sitcoms like *Step by Step* and *Home Improvement* but also from clones like *Caroline in the City* or *Suddenly Susan*. At the time many observers argued the move might give the show the much-needed "identity" required to attract the target demographics. Paraphrasing a high-ranking studio executive, one media observer claimed that "commercially, making Ellen Morgan a lesbian would give *Ellen* an edginess that might bring back its sophisticated *Seinfeld*-type viewers."[17] Even the immense backlash by Christian conservatives—a reaction that would most definitely have scared any network away from a coming out story just a few years ago—may actually have worked in *Ellen* and ABC's favor; watching a new "controversial" Ellen and thus thwarting the extreme conservative agenda of a Pat Robertson or Donald Wildmon may have offered liberally minded, "sophisticated" viewers that "edginess" in which they seem to find so much pleasure.

Targeting the gay and lesbian audience in the nineties

While networks and producers have used gay and lesbian material to attract an audience of urbane and upscale adults, the recent programming trend could also be particularly effective at appealing to a highly lucrative segment of that quality audience, specifically, upscale gay and lesbian viewers.[18] As network audience shares decrease and the imperatives of narrowcasting intensify in the nineties, it would be poor business for the networks not to look to gay and lesbian viewers as a profitable market. Narrowcasting often encourages a network to discover markets currently being underserved by other outlets. In this case, television programming's ubiquitous heterosexuality has turned away many in the gay and lesbian community. At the same time, the dissolution of television's so-called mass audience and the segmentation of viewership have reduced the risk networks face by airing gay material. While still somewhat fearful of controversy, the networks are under less pressure to please all viewers. Consequently, if Christian conservatives, demographically more rural and southern, aren't part of a network's target audience, including gay and lesbian material becomes less hazardous. While many sponsors appear more cautious than the networks, the dynamics of niche marketing work in similar ways for them. Thus, the danger of offending certain viewers/consumers by sponsoring a controversial program featuring gay material could be outweighed by the benefits of reaching a prime target market.

Ultimately, however, both networks and sponsors will only target gays and lesbians if they think doing so would be worth their while. In the last five years, economic and social changes, self-serving promotion on the part of a new gay press and marketing firms, and coverage in the business press have worked together to focus more and more of the business world's attention on what gay men and lesbians do with their money. In the process, they have constructed the gay community as not only a viable but also an important market in the highly competitive business world of the 1990s. In April 1994, for example, over 150 consumer products companies paid up to $1,500 each to put up booths at the Meadowlands Convention Center in Secaucus, New Jersey, in what was billed as the First National Gay and Lesbian Business Expo. The event, according to *New York Times* advertising columnist Stuart Elliott, was yet one more "indication of one of the least expected business trends of the 1990's: the growing efforts by many mainstream marketers to reach consumers who are homosexuals."[19]

Similar economic changes that have led network television to alter its programming policies have led businesses in general to change how they sell their products to consumers. Ray Mulryan, a partner in the Mulryan/Nash advertising agency, explains that in the 1990s "the mass market just doesn't exist. . . . If you want to reach America, you've got to identify them by group—and then you have to talk to them."[20] Faced with greater competition, then, more companies have had to specialize their sales pitches to appeal to ever narrower groups. Stuart Elliott asserts such economic incentives have led mainstream companies to look to new markets previously ignored: "The need to attract dollars from consumers has become so overwhelming that they're willing to target messages to consumers that they might not have been willing to talk to in previous years."[21] As the 1994 expo illustrates, one such segment is the gay and lesbian community.

Although economic incentives have led many companies to turn to niche markets, other forces are at play to convince them that the gay and lesbian community is a commercially viable niche. A political and social shift that has taken place in the 1990s concerning the position of gays and lesbians has opened the door for advertisers to openly target gay dollars. In the late 1970s and early 1980s numerous companies began pitching campaigns to the gay market. With the emergence of AIDS in the mid-1980s and the social stigma generated around the gay community, however, advertisers retreated.[22] By the early 1990s, companies like Johnnie Walker and K Mart gradually made guarded overtures to gay consumers with ambiguous ads.[23] Nevertheless, in 1990, one media analyst was still warning retailers to "be careful with niche segmentation, so you don't offend some old customers who . . . might think, 'That's where the gays shop.' "[24] Yet as one observer pointed out four years later, such caution "was pre-Clinton, -gays-in-the-military, -Colorado-legislation headlines."[25] By the 1992 election, presidential candidate Clinton actually hired an advertising and PR firm specializing in reaching the gay and lesbian community to help him get the gay vote. As news coverage after the election reframed gay men and women, moving them closer to the mainstream, more and more advertisers have decided to follow Clinton's example and have turned to the gay market.

If a new social context made the gay market viable, the emergence of new gay magazines, advertising agencies, and research firms made it attractive. Traditionally comprised of local magazines produced on newsprint, focused on covering politics, and supported by locally gay-owned business and explicit sex ads, the gay and lesbian press saw a dramatic change in 1992. National magazines like *Out, Genre, Deneuve,* and *10 Percent* debuted on glossy paper and were filled with trendy layouts, full-color photos, and articles from nationally recognized writers. Faced with the new competition, the nation's oldest national magazine, *The Advocate*, followed suit, getting rid of its sexually explicit personals section and moving to glossy print. All these magazines needed to attract mainstream, national advertisers willing to pay the writers, designers, printing fees, and circulation overhead of a nationwide periodical.[26] Consequently, these magazines rapidly began touting the attractive demographics of their readership, trying to convince Madison Avenue and its clients that buying space in their magazines was a smart investment.

The magazines quickly turned to research firms like Overlooked Opinions and advertising agencies like Mulryan/Nash and aka Communications, all of which specialized in promoting the gay and lesbian community, to provide the sterling demographics needed to woo national companies. A widely reported study by Overlooked Opinions claimed that America's estimated 18 million gay and lesbians were spending over $500 billion annually.[27] Profiles of gay and lesbian consumers were almost always compared to data for average Americans. Data compiled by aka Communications from research by Simmons Market Research, the U.S. Census Bureau, and Overlooked Opinions claimed that 40 percent of lesbians and 47 percent of gay men hold managerial jobs compared with 15 percent and 31 percent nationwide. Twenty-seven per cent of gay people are frequent fliers compared to a national average of 2 percent, while 66 percent are overseas travelers compared to 14 percent nationwide.[28] According to a report by Mulryan/Nash, "61 percent of gay people have a four-year college degree, as opposed to 18 percent of average Americans. . . . 43 percent of gay people work out in a gym as opposed to 8 percent of average Americans. . . . 64 percent of gay people drink sparkling water as opposed to 17 percent of Americans."[29] Other surveys claim that a typical gay male couple earns $51,600 a year, while the average straight couple earns only $37,900. The average lesbian couple reportedly earns $42,800.[30] According to aka Communications, 18 percent of gay households have incomes over $100,000.[31] Not only do gay men and lesbians have all this income, these reports suggest, they also tend not to have children. Without the worries of braces, college tuition, and medical bills, gay men and women's disposable income is even greater.

As if such stellar statistics weren't enough to convince blue-chip firms, many reports claim that gays and lesbians are amazingly loyal to businesses that openly court their patronage. According to a poll of its readers, *The Blade*, a Washington, D.C., gay weekly, found that 80 percent of its readers claimed to be loyal to *Blade* advertisers, and 70 percent said they would change their shopping habits if a retailer advertised in the paper.[32] According to *American Demographics*,

> gay men and lesbians show their gratitude to marketers who have the courage to serve them. In return for what they see as acceptance and respect, gay consumers will go out of their way to patronize these companies. Furthermore, they will actively spread the word through an amazingly efficient network that circulates not only through word of mouth, but through 200 electronic bulletin boards.[33]

Finally, other reported but less tangible qualities of the gay community make it a particularly important demographic segment. According to the report by Mulryan/Nash, because of their prominent position in the fields of fashion, design, media, and the arts, gay men and lesbians "occupy a special sphere of influence and shape national consumer tastes. Gay men have been credited with popularizing blow-dryers, painter's pants, the gentrification of urban neighborhoods, disco music, Absolut Vodka, Levi's 501 jeans, Doc Marten boots, and Santa Fe home-style furnishings."[34] What better target market could a profit-hungry company want?

Madison Avenue and its clients seem to be convinced. When Hirman Walker & Sons were marketing its Tuaca liqueur, according to Laurie Acosta, group product manager, they wanted to reach young, hip consumers, "and by definition, that includes the gay and lesbian market."[35] BMG Records and RCA Victor have begun selling gaytargeted classical compilations like "Out Music" and "Out Classics," and Atlantic Records has established a department dedicated to marketing music to gay audiences. Articles inform banks, booksellers, radio stations, travel agents, and retail stores on the importance of tapping into the gay and lesbian demographic. In addition to the traditional ads from entertainment, clothing, and liquor companies, gay magazines are being filled with full-page ads selling everything from Apple computers, Naya spring water, and Xerox copiers to Continental Airlines, Swatch watches, and MCI long distance. The gay press has even been able to tap into the lucrative automotive market; Saab and Subaru have both placed print ads in gay periodicals. A number of data lists of people assumed to be gay or lesbian—lists compiled from magazine subscriptions, gay credit card holders, single-ticket buyers for plays like *Jeffrey*, and even lists of AIDS organization donors—are sold to companies interested in direct mailing.[36] IKEA, a Sweden-based furniture company, produced a now-famous television ad featuring a gay male couple shopping for a dining table. The thirty-second spot aired in a number of big city markets.

When asked why their companies are targeting gays and lesbians, the responses of company spokespeople dramatically illustrate how widely accepted and influential the demographic picture of the gay market has become. C. J. Wray, a marketing vice-president, believes, "It's a market that has money." Virgin Atlantic Airlines' ad executive asserts, "They're an audience that we believe will give us a great return on our advertising investment." Benetton's director of communication claims that "anyone who would pass over this market without giving it thorough analytical treatment is remiss and probably guilty of knee-jerk discrimination. . . . Ultimately it comes down to not minding the shop." Linda Sawyer, executive vice-president for a New York ad agency, best sums up the attitude of many companies in the mid-1990s: "Now including gays seems safe— and smart."[37]

While more and more companies are openly reaching out to gay and lesbian consumers, network executives have never admitted to targeting gay and lesbian viewers.[38] Yet with the extensive attention paid to the statistical profiles of gays and lesbians, it is hard to believe that the demographic-obsessed marketing, advertising, and programming executives at work behind the networks have remained unaware of and unaffected by the numbers.[39] In 1993, just as the trend of gay programming began, *Mediaweck*, a major trade journal, cited the same demographic figures, quoted the same gay-owned advertising firms, and included the same targeting-the-gay-market-is-smart-business advice circulating in other business magazines.[40] Reportedly loyal, highly educated, and affluent with disposable incomes greater than the national average, gay men and women represent the perfect market for networks eager to deliver a quality audience to advertisers. In many ways, the reported demographics of gays and lesbians are strikingly similar to those of the upscale, hip, urban, white, college-educated, liberal audience networks that advertisers are so anxious to reach; in fact, they seem even better.

The construction and promotion of the gay and lesbian market, I argue, does play a role in the recent explosion of gay material on prime time. It certainly is possible that some producers and network executives consciously try to create programming that would particularly appeal to gay and lesbian viewers. More frequently, however, the highly attractive demographic profile of the gay and lesbian market enables networks to push television's conventions and use gay material in order to aggressively target their broader quality audience, an audience that apparently finds a gay twist with their television appealing. When such a strategy has the advantage of appealing to an audience that is as lucrative as gays and lesbians appear to be, it is much easier to risk offending more conservative viewers whose demographics aren't as attractive and who aren't part of the target audience.

For their part, some advertisers are also warming up to the presence of gay material on the shows they sponsor. While once presenting a rather unified front against any overt images of homosexuality, some sponsors are increasingly willing to break rank. While a home goods company like Procter & Gamble may be very hesitant to risk offending Christian conservatives by linking themselves too closely to gay issues, hightech computer firms like Apple and IBM, whose target audiences are very different, can take more risks. Although some companies pulled out of the coming-out episode of *Ellen*, for example, many more were glad to take their place and to pay premium prices to do so. Of Volkswagen of America, Inc.'s decision to buy time on the episode, Tony Fouladpour, company spokesperson, explained, "It's about advertising our products to a target audience of drivers, which matches the viewers of *Ellen* and which would include many different life styles."[41] Rebecca Patto, senior vice-president at E-Trade Group, an on-line broker-age firm that aired spots during the show in New York and San Francisco, felt the program would reach its desired audience· "We really appeal to people who think for themselves."[42]

Such comments are certainly far less overt in acknowledging a desire to target gay and lesbian consumers. Marketers and sponsors, even those highly interested in reaching gays and lesbians, realize that network television is different from marketing strategies like direct mail or print ads. Television's cultural importance is certainly greater, and, despite the increasing impact of narrow-casting, TV is still seen by many as a mass medium designed to serve the interests of a national audience. Nevertheless, such comments do echo those from companies and ad agencies which claim that targeting gays and lesbians is smart business and suggest that at least some sponsors have realized that television, even prime-time television, may be useful in reaching a niche market of gay men and lesbians.

Conclusions

In the 1990s, gay men and women have had an increasingly visible role in the world of prime-time television. But just how have gay characters and issues been presented? Used as textual selling points, gay and lesbian characters and their lives have often mirrored both the demographic profile of the urban, upscale, white, and adult quality audience networks seek and the demographic profiles of the gay community created in the marketing press. *Frasier's* gay boss, for example, is an upwardly mobile radio station manager who moved to Seattle from London after a messy breakup that included a dispute over opera recordings. Paul's sister on *Mad about You* and her obstetrician partner are upscale professional Manhattanites who become romantically involved while on a ski weekend. *Spin City* is somewhat unusual in that it offers one of the few African American gay characters on prime time, yet Carter's race is less important to his characterization than his sexual identity, and his background as a political activist is repeatedly downplayed in story lines that focus on the lives of young professionals working in the New York mayor's office. And although *Ellen's* Peter and Barrett aren't decidedly professional, they live and work in the decidedly urban world of Los Angles and trendy Hollywood.[43]

Many observers, including some from the gay and lesbian community, have wholeheartedly praised the recent programming trend. Loren Jarvier, a spokesperson for GLAAD, asserts, "It's great because television is finally saying. 'We're not a sideshow. We're just like you. We're your friends and your family. We go to school with you.' "[44] Paul Witt, co-creator of *Soap* and WB Television's *Muscle*, agrees: "You're beginning to see openly gay characters portrayed just like everyone else, who don't embody stereotypes."[45] The problem, of course, as with nearly all television representations, is that they do embody stereotypes. Instead of images of nelly queens or motorcycle dykes, we are presented with images of white, affluent, trend-setting, Perrier-drinking, frequent-flier using, Ph.D.-holding consumer citizens with more income to spend than they know what to do with. For many, such a stereotype is equally frightening.

The gay characters featured on shows like *Friends, Ellen*, and *Murder One* and the highly touted statistical profiles featured in *Fortune, Mediaweek*, and the *New York Times* work together to construct a specific view of the gay and lesbian community. Television's representations are imbricated within the economic imperatives of major production companies and networks anxious to attract a quality audience to sell to advertisers. Driven by similar economic forces, national gay and lesbian magazines and ad firms devoted to marketing to the gay community—institutions for which profit, not gay liberation, is the bottom line—have generated and promoted much of the market research. Consequently, the results of reader surveys done by the gay press are often conflated with profiles for the entire community, and the gay men and lesbians who can't afford to buy the magazines or don't identify with the images of gay life presented in them are increasingly excluded from the mainstream's understanding of what it means to be gay or lesbian in the nineties, an understanding reinforced by television's recent prime-time representations. The results of broader surveys based on random samples are similarly skewed. Because of homophobia, gay men and women, particularly gay teens, older gay men and women, and those in less urban areas and with less financial security, are far less likely to identify themselves as gay or lesbian and are consequently ignored. Finally, both television representations and market researchers exclude the significant numbers of bisexual men and women.[46] While helping to construct an industry knowledge of gays and lesbians as a consumer audience, such sampling biases also result in a demographic picture that badly misrepresents the gay community.

The exclusion of a range of gay and bisexual men and women from both prime-time television and statistical profiles has serious consequences for gay politics and underscores the conflict between industrial conceptions that commodify individuals as an audience of consumers and politicized notions that try to mobilize people into a social movement. While appearing to have economic clout can translate into real political progress, it is not the same as actually having real economic power.[47] In fact, misleading data touting the size of the gay pocketbook has worked against gay civil rights struggles in states like Oregon and Colorado where antigay advocates used the statistics to discredit the assertion that gays and lesbians were socially oppressed. Effaced from market reports and most television programs, of course, are the real lived experiences of thousands of gay and bisexual people who do face economic discrimination every day. The economic oppression faced by lesbians and gay people of color is even more egregiously erased. The conflation of the gay, lesbian, and bisexual community with a specific quality audience of gays and lesbians moves the entire debate to the realm of consumption, disregards all notions of wider social oppression, and threatens to fracture the gay community along axes of class, gender, race, and sexual identity even more than it currently is.[48] Such problems are exacerbated when such incomplete images of gay and lesbian experience are targeted at a quality audience of liberal television viewers, both straight and gay, who may feel that by watching "sophisticated" programs with gay and lesbian characters or gay-themed programs they are somehow supporting the struggle for gay rights.[49] But when that world is nearly always devoid of serious discrimination and hate crimes, as is true of most television programming, little change and thus little effort on the part of viewers is called for.[50]

Thus, while marking a significant change in the representation of gays and lesbians on television, the recent deluge of gay material in prime/time calls as much for caution as for celebration. Situated within the specific industrial forces driving television, images of gays and lesbians have consistently been constructed with a highly straight, white, affluent audience in mind. We must also be wary of constructing a progress narrative for gay and lesbian visibility on television. Just because there are more images doesn't mean they are inherently better, and even the few advances made can quickly be lost. In the 1997–98 season of *Ellen*, for example, gay and lesbian material and characters became significantly more than just window dressing as week after week the show tried to deal humorously and directly with gay and lesbian experiences. While the program's scripts were inconsistent (a problem the sitcom had always faced), the audience's ambivalence to the new *Ellen* and ABC's tepid promotion and eventual cancellation of it may indicate a limit to just how gay prime-time television in the 1990s can get; network executives and the audience may allow the closet door to open just so far. As industrial situations and network motivation change, programming trends come and go. As with all programming, shows using "edgy" gay material to attract a quality audience are situated within the innovation-imitation-saturation cycle that drives primetime television.[51] The same imperative to reach a new audience in new ways that helped propel gay material onto dozens of shows could also lead to its demise.[52]

While economic forces are clearly at work behind the recent spate of gay content on prime time, this examination has been only the first step in understanding the reasons behind and impact of this programming trend. Television is not only a profit-generating industry. It is also a site of cultural negotiation, and as the struggle for gay and lesbian rights has heated up in the 1990s, television has become one important front along which that battle has been played out. For both the gay and lesbian community and those studying television, it is important to understand the complex interaction among industrial forces, social movements, cultural conflict, and political aims.

Notes

1 *Entertainment Weekly* 8 September 1995: cover.
2 I don't want to suggest that the recent outbreak of gay and lesbian material is limited to network prime-time programming. HBO's *The Larry Sanders Show*, MTV's *The Real World*, NBC's *Saturday Night Live*, ABC's *All My Children*, the Discovery Channel's *Interior Motives*, and the syndicated hit *Xena*, for example, all reflect the growing importance of gay material across the television landscape. However, I have chosen to focus on network prime-time television because these hours still represent the peak viewing period where most advertising revenue is at stake.
3 Throughout the paper I will use the term gay and lesbian to refer to the characters and issues represented on television and to the community/market described by a variety of magazines and marketing firms. The selection of such terms is not meant to deny the presence of bisexual men and women in the gay community and political movement but to best reflect the images and discourses constructed in these texts. The consequences such images and discourses hold for the community they describe/construct are explored below.
4 Ien Ang, *Desperately Seeking the Audience* (London: Routledge, 1991) 3. Also see Thomas Streeter and Wendy Wahl, "Audience Theory and Feminism: Property, Gender, and the Television Audience," *Camera Obscura* 33–4 (1994–95): 243–6.
5 Julie D'Acci, *Defining Women: Television and the Case of Cagney & Lacey* (Chapel Hill: U of North Carolina P, 1994).
6 For work on quality audiences, see D'Acci; Eileen R. Meehan, "Why We Don't Count: The Commodity Audience," *Logics of Television: Essays in Cultural Criticism*, ed. Patricia Mellencamp (Bloomington: Indiana UP, 1990) 117–37; Jackie Byars and Eileen R. Meehan, "Once in a Lifetime: Constructing 'The Working Woman' through Cable Narrowcasting," *Camera Obscura* 33–4 (1994–95): 13–41; Pamela Wilson, "Upscale Feminist Angst: Molly Dodd, the Lifetime Cable Network and Gender Marketing," *Camera Obscura* 33–4 (1994–95): 103–30: Jane Feuer, Paul Kerr, and Tise Vahimagi, eds, *MTM: "Quality Television"* (London: British Film Institute, 1984); Todd Gitlin, *Inside Prime Time* (New York: Pantheon, 1983) 203–20.
7 Xiaoming Hoa, "Television Viewing among American Adults in the 1990s," *Journal of Broadcasting and Electronic Media* Summer 1994: 353–60; Byars and Meehan 21–2.
8 Keith Marder, "Cable Television Gaining Fast on Big 3 Networks," *State Journal Register* 10 October 1996: 25.
9 The adjective "hip" is certainly far from precise. Nevertheless, I use it here because marketers, network executives, and media observers employ it so frequently. They find it useful, I feel, because, in the nineties, it serves as a safe way to refer to a somewhat socially liberal audience with a cynical, urban-minded sensibility. The term "rural" seems to function in similar ways to refer to an audience of conservative and even Christian viewers.
10 Rick DuBrow, "Television; Networking, 90s Style," *Los Angeles Times* 9 April 1995: Calendar 6.
11 DuBrow.

12   Rex Poindexter, "Laughing Matters," *The Advocate* 13 December 1994: 56–8.

13   Not only does the evening lineup reflect a consistent interest in presenting gay material, the ability of each character to seamlessly move from the diagetic world of his/her hip, Manhattan neighborhood to that of the next show indicates the interchangeable qualities that have resulted from a unified goal of attracting the quality audience. Further, NBC's use of gay material to promote its shows is more recently evident in its fall 1997 promo for the premier of *Working*. The oft-run commercial featured a joke in which Fred Savage's new boss offers him an attractive male secretary as a perk for a new job.

14   Jefferson Graham, "Ellen Happy with Women at Helm/Finding Fun with Female Point of View," *USA Weekend* 19 December 1995: D3.

15   Bruce Fretts, "This Week," *Entertainment Weekly* 25 October 1996: 102.

16   Promotional material from ABC illustrates this shift and indicates the show's relationship to *Friends*. Describing Ellen Morgan, for example, they say she is a "thirty-something urbanite . . . striving to find her niche in L.A." John Carmody, "The TV Column," *Washington Post* 16 September 1996: D6.

17   Gail Shister, "Gay Producers, Actors Urge *Ellen* to Come Out," *Wisconsin State Journal* 18 September 1996: 7D.

18   In the early seventies, urban-centered programming like *All in the Family* and *The Jeffersons* attracted not only the white urban audience CBS so badly wanted but also the increasingly prosperous black middle class. Further, for work examining issues surrounding targeting gays and lesbians in other industries, see Danae Clark, "Commodity Lesbianism," *The Lesbian and Gay Studies Reader*, ed. Henry Abelove, Michele Asina Bardale, and David M. Halperin (New York: Routledge, 1993) 186–201; Gregory Woods, "We're Here, We're Queer and We're Not Going Catalogue Shopping," *A Queer Romance: Lesbians, Gay Men and Popular Culture*, ed. Paul Burston and Colin Richardson (London: Routledge, 1995) 147–63; Eve M. Kahn, "The Glass Closet," *Print* September–October 1994: 21–32.

19   Stuart Elliott, "This Weekend a Business Expo Will Show the Breadth of Interest in Gay Consumer," *New York Times* 14 April 1994: D-18.

20   Jeffrey Scott, "Media Talk; Formerly Standoffish Advertisers Openly Courting Gay Consumers," *Atlanta Journal and Constitution* 5 April 1994: B-3.

21   Charles Feldman, "Advertising Aimed at Gay Community Surges," CNN 7 October 1992: Transcript #200–1.

22   Feldman.

23   See Paul Colford, "The Scotch Ad That's Got 'Em Buzzing," *Newsday* February 1989: 11–2; and Bernice Kanner, "Normally Gay," *New York* 4 April 1994: 24.

24   Kara Swisher, "Gay Spending Power Draws More Attention," *Washington Post* 18 June 1990: F1.

25   Kanner 24.

26   See Rodger Streitmatter, *Unspeakable: The Rise of the Gay and Lesbian Press in America* (Boston: Faber and Faber, 1995) 308–37; Daniel Harris, *The Rise and Fall of Gay Culture* (New York: Hyperion, 1997) 64–85.

27   See Diane Cyr, "The Emerging Gay Market," *Catalogue Age* November 1993: 112.

28   Kathy Kalafut, "Alternative Demos: Profile on Aka Communications Inc.," *Mediaweek* 14 September 1992: 32.

29   Sarah Schulman, "Gay Marketeers," *The Progressive* July 1995: 28.

30   Streitmatter 314.

31   Teresa Carson, "Agencies Push Gay Market Ads to Banks," *American Banker* 21 May 1992: 6.

32   Swisher F1.

33   Hazel Kahan and David Mulryan, "Out of the Closet," *American Demographics* May 1995: 46–7. In this lengthy article, the writers declare the "gay and lesbian market [to be] an untapped goldmine" and basically provide a guidebook for marketers who want to get started examining the gay community.

34   Schulman 28.

35   Cyndee Miller, " 'The Ultimate Taboo,' Slowly but Surely, Companies Overcome Reluctance to Target the Lesbian Market," *Marketing News TM* 14 August 1995: 1. Miller uses the term "hip, young consumer" to introduce the quote from Laurie Acosta.

36   Gary Levin, "List-Generating Hot—To Direct Mail's Delight," *Advertising Age* 30 May 1994: S-1+.

37   Gary Levin, "Mainstream's Domino Effect: Liquor, Fragrance, Clothing Advertisers Ease into Gay Magazines," *Advertising Age* 18 January 1993: 30; Martha Moore, "Courting the Gay Market—Advertisers: It's Business, Not Politics," *USA Today* 23 April 1993: B1; Susan Reda, "Marketing to Gays & Lesbians: The Last Taboo," *Stores* September 1994: 19; Kanner 24.

38   Most network explanations for the recent spate of gay and lesbian characters claim that the trend is simply mirroring social reality. Marc Cherry, executive producer of *The Crew*, for example, asserts, "Gay people

are now more than ever becoming a part of American life . . . You can't deny the existence of gay people throughout the country. They should be represented." John Carman, "Gay Characters Get a Life on TV," *San Francisco Chronicle* 17 August 1995: E1. Such comments efface the hard-nosed economics behind television programming and reflect the power of a long-lasting discursive construction of television as a medium meant to serve the public interest.

39   One brief article in *Advertising Age* illustrates the kind of information executives must be aware of. The factoid gives the top ten rated shows in $60,000-plus households. *Roseanne*, which had recently included two openly gay/lesbian recurring characters, was, despite its decidedly blue-collar tenor, the number one rated show in that lucrative demographic, gaining 13 percent over the previous season. Reading this kind of industry information may be leading executives to put two and 60,000 together. "Hey, Big Spender," *Advertising Age* 15 March 1993: 29.

40   Mark Hudis, "Gays Back in Prime Time," *Mediaweek* 13 December 1993: 14. Also see David W. Dunlap, "Gay Images, Once Kept Out Are Out Big Time," *New York Times* 21 January 1996: 1–29.

41   Dana Canedy, "As the Main Character in *Ellen* Comes Out. Some Companies See an Opportunity; Others Steer Clear." *New York Times* 30 April 1997: D8.

42   Canedy. The E-Trade Group may also be motivated to sponsor a lesbian Ellen Morgan by demographic statistics which claim disproportionately high on-line computer use in the gay community. Forty-eight percent of *Out* magazine readers, for example, subscribe to an on-line computer service compared to a national average of 11 percent. See Michael Wilke, "Wired Lesbian/Gays Lure Marketers," *Advertising Age* 11 December 1995: 33.

43   The representation of gay and lesbian characters on prime time is certainly not entirely homogeneous. *Cosby* included an episode with elderly gay men that were African American and Asian American. *My So-Called Life* featured a Hispanic gay teen. And both *Roseanne* and *Grace under Fire* have featured a variety of gay, lesbian, and bisexual characters who live and work in midsize midwestern towns. Nevertheless, these examples mark the exception to the rule. In most shows, gay material is part of a world defined by the white, urbane, upscale people populating it.

44   Tom Hopkins, "Gays on TV," *Dayton Daily News* 20 August 1995: 1C.

45   Susan Karlin, "TV Discovers Gay Characters," *Electronic Media* 13 February 1995: 6.

46   Lee Badgett from the University of Maryland, for example, has done research that indicates gay men make less, nearly one third less, than their straight male counterparts. See M. V. Lee Badgett, "Beyond Biased Samples: Challenging the Myths on the Economic Status of Lesbians and Gay Men," *Homo Economics: Capitalism, Community, and Lesbian and Gay Life*, ed. Amy Gluckman and Betsy Reed (New York: Routledge, 1997) 73–86. Also see Urvashi Vaid, *Virtrual Equality: The Mainstreaming of Gay and Lesbian Liberation* (New York: Anchor, 1995) 249–59.

47   While many companies have been anxious to take advantage of gay economic power and actively court it, others have faced the consequences of offending the gay community. In 1990, Woodies, a local retail chain in Washington, D.C., was the target of a gay boycott when it refused to give the partner of a gay employee the same family discount as straight employees. As the gay community quickly organized its clout, Woodies examined the situation and decided to concede. Besides granting the discount, the company also agreed to include nondiscrimination based on sexual orientation in its employment policy, add sensitivity training on homophobia for all employees and managers, and engage in public advocacy for legislation that would extend spousal benefits to gay partners. Joseph Culver, vice-president for personnel at Woodies' parent company, states, "We found there was an articulate and financially important gay and lesbian community in Washington." Illustrating what impact such economic muscle flexing can have. Culver claims, "the incident gave us all an awareness in the organization that some of our thinking was archaic and needed to change." Woodies' decision influenced the nine-store Garfinkel's chain to follow suit. George Kelly, president and chairman, states, "We looked at what went on with Woodies and thought it was the right thing to do, considering the realities of today. We did it for business reasons too, since I have seen surveys that show that the gay community is one that shops and spends money way beyond the necessities." Swisher F1.

48   For further discussion, see Amy Gluckman and Betsy Reed. "The Gay Marketing Moment," *Homo Economics: Capitalism, Community, and Gay and Lesbian Life*, ed. Amy Gluckman and Betsy Reed (New York: Routledge, 1997) 3–10. While the vast majority of prime-time programs contribute to the problem, *Reseanne* has done more than any show to actually overcome such fractures. Besides including gay men and lesbians within a decidedly blue-collar context, they also work to construct alliances among gays, lesbians, African Americans, and working-class whites. More work needs to be done analyzing the different ways gays and lesbians are presented on specific programs and in different genres.

49   Network television's use of gay characters as a tool to attract a quality audience of straight consumers in the nineties resembles the strategy of some assimilationist gay politics which tries to win social and political acceptance by marginalizing the more unconventional elements of the gay community in an attempt to appeal to straight Americans. More work needs to be done to explore the relationship between the industrial forces at play behind mass media images of gay life and the political and social forces behind certain political aims. Particularly salient, it seems, is the relationship between identity politics and consumer marketing. Since both marketers and some political activists are concerned with constructing definitions of the gay community and what it means to be gay or lesbian, the two endeavors can easily become intertwined. As Gregory Woods points out, "Considering that one of capitalism's principal means of inveigling individuals into the cycle of production and consumption is the commercialisation of identity, one has to recognise that there is a seamless logic to the process by which, within a capitalist economy, identity politics likewise become commercialised and commodified" (160).

50   A relatively common story line in the nineties involves a show's central characters discovering an acquaintance is gay or lesbian. While certain characters have some problems dealing with it, the show's most sympathetic characters quickly take the stance that (to paraphrase Jerry Seinfield and George Costanza) "there's not anything wrong with it." In fact, a character's problem with someone else's sexuality is often set up as the problem. By the end of the show, the specter of homophobia is usually stamped out; at least the audience is told to believe that the gay character is okay.

   Suddenly Susan, Grace under Fire, Coach, Hudson Street, Dr. Quinn—Medicine Woman, Mad about You, Wings, Cosby, Murphy Brown, and Beverly Hills 90210 all have had such episodes. Further, in a number of other shows, a character's homosexuality is virtually a nonissue within the program's diagetic world (e.g., Seinfeld, Chicago Hope, Fired Up, Suddenly Susan, Relativity, Style & Substance).

51   In his analysis of television documentary in the 1960s, Michael Curtain offers an extended discussion of that genre's saturation cycle. See Michael Curtain, Redeeming the Wasteland (New Brunswick: Rutgers UP, 1995).

52   After a disastrous 1995–96 season in which it wholeheartedly copied NBC and ABC, CBS, for example, returned to targeting a decidedly older, less urban, and more conservative audience with its "Welcome Home" campaign and a lineup of shows like Touched by an Angel, Walker, Texas Ranger, Promised Land, and Cosby. Nevertheless, gay-themed television seemed to sustain its viability in the 1997–98 season. NBC's Veronica's Closet and Homocide: Life on the Streets, for example, have included gay material as significant plot elements. Yet even CBS's Cosby had an episode in which the title character played baseball with an over-fifty gay men's group, attended a gay line-dancing party, and was assumed to be gay by almost everyone, including his wife.

Bibliography

Ang, I. (1991) Desperately Seeking the Audience, London: Routledge.

Badgett, L.M.V. (1997) "Beyond Biased Samples: Challenging the Myths on the Economic Status of Lesbians and Gay Men," in A. Gluckman and B. Reed (eds) Homo Economics: Capitalism, Community, and Lesbian and Gay Life, New York: Routledge.

Byars, J. and Meehan, E.R. (1994–95) "Once in a Lifetime: Constructing 'The Working Woman' through Cable Narrowcasting," Camera Obscura 33–34: 13–41.

Candy, D. (1997) "As the Main Character in Ellen Comes Out, Some Companies See an Opportunity, Others Steer Clear," New York Times 30 April: D8.

Carman, J. (1995) "Gay Characters Get a Life on TV," San Francisco Journal 17 August: E1.

Carson, T. (1992) "Agencies Push Gay Market Ads to Banks," American Banker 21 May: 6.

Clark, D. (1993) "Commodity Lesbianism," H. Abelove, M.A. Bardale and D.M. Halperin (eds) The Lesbian and Gay Studies Reader, New York: Routledge.

Colford, P. (1989) "The Scotch Ad That's Got 'Em Buzzing", Newsday, February: II-2.

Curtain, M. (1995) Redeeming the Wasteland. New Brunswick: Rutgers University Press.

Cyr, D. (1993) "The Emerging Gay Market", Catalogue Age November: 112.

D'Acci, J. (1994) Defining Women: Television and the Case of Cagney & Lacey, Chapel Hill: University of North Carolina Press.

DuBrow, R. (1995) "Television: Networking, 90s Style," Los Angeles Times, 9 April: Calender 6

Dunlap, D.W. (1996) "Gay Images, Once Kept Out Are Big Time," New York Times 21 January: I.29

Elliot, S. (1994) "This Weekend a Business Expo Will Show the Breadth of Interest in Gay Consumer," New York Times 14 April: D18.

Feuer, J., Kerr, P. and Vahimagi, T. (eds) (1984) *MTM: "Quality Television*," London: British Film Institute.

Fretts, B. (1996) "This Week," *Entertainment Weekly* 25 October: 102.

Gitlin, T. (1983) *Inside Prime Time*, New York: Pantheon.

Graham, J. (1995) "Ellen Happy with Women at Helm/Finding Fun with Female Point of View," *USA Weekend* 19 December: D3.

Harris, D. (1997) *The Rise and Fall of Gay Culture*, New York: Hyperion.

Hopkins, T. (1995) "Gays on TV," *Dayton Daily News* 20 August: 1C.

Hudis, M. (1993) "Gays Back in Prime Time," *Mediaweek* 13 December: 14.

Kahan, H. and Mulryan, D. (1995) "Out of the Closet," *American Demographics* May: 46–7.

Kahn, E.M. (1994) "The Glass Closet," *Print* September–October: 21–32.

Kalafut, K. (1992) "Alternative Demos: Profile on Aka Communications Inc.," *Mediaweek* 14 September: 32.

Kanner, B. (1994) "Normally Gay," *New York* 4 April: 24.

Karlin, S. (1995) "TV Discovers Gay Characters," *Electronic Media* 13 February: 6.

Levin, G. (1993) "Mainstream's Domino Effect: Liquor, Fragrance, Clothing Advertisers Ease into Gay Magazines," *Advertising Age* 18 January: 30.

—— (1994) "List-Generating hot – To Direct Mail's Delight," *Advertising Age* 30 May: S–1+.

Marder, K. (1996) "Cable Television Gaining Fast on Big 3 Networks," *State Journal Register* 10 October: 25.

Meehan, E.R. (1990) "Why We Don't Count: The Commodity Audience," P. Mellencamp (ed.) *Logics of Television: Essays in Cultural Criticism*, Bloomington: Indiana University Press.

Miller, C. (1995) " 'The Ultimate Taboo,' Slowly but Surely, Companies Overcome Reluctance to Target the Lesbian Market," *Marketing News TM* 14 August: 1.

Moore, M. (1993) "Courting the Gay Market – Advertisers: It's Business, Not Politics," *USA Today* 23 April: B1.

Poindexter, R. (1994) "Laughing Matters," *The Advocate* 13 December: 56–8.

Reda, S. (1994) "Marketing to Gays & Lesbians: The Last Taboo," *Stores* September: 19.

Schulman, S. (1995) "Gay Marketeers," *The Progressive* July: 28.

Scott, J. (1994) "Media Talk; Formerly Standoffish Advertisers Openly Courting Gay Consumers," *Atlanta Journal and Constitution*, 5 April: B3.

Shister, G. (1996) "Gay Producers, Actors Urge Ellen to Come Out," *Wisconsin State Journal* 18 September: 7D.

Streeter, T. and Wahl, W. (1994–95) "Audience Theory and Feminism: Property, Gender and the Television Audience," *Camera Obscura* 33–34: 243–6.

Streitmatter, R. (1995) *Unspeakable: The Rise of the Gay and Lesbian Press in America*, Boston: Faber and Faber.

Swisher, K. (1990) "Gay Spending Power Draws More Attention," *Washington Post* 18 June: F1.

Vaid, U. (1995) *Virtual Equality: The Mainstreaming of Gay and Lesbian Liberation*, New York: Anchor.

Woods, G. (1995) "We're Here, We're Queer and We're Not Going Catalogue Shopping," P. Burston and C. Richardson (eds) *A Queer Romance: Lesbians, Gay Men and Popular Culture*, London: Routledge.

Wilke, M. (1995) "Wired Lesbian/Gays Lure Marketers," *Advertising Age* 11 December: 33.

Wilson, P. (1994–95) "Upscale Feminist Angst: Molly Dodd, the Lifetime Cable Network and Gender Marketing," *Camera Obscura* 33–34: 103–30

Xiaoming, H. (1994) "Television Viewing Among American Adults in the 1990s," *Journal of Broadcasting & Electronic Media* Summer: 353–60.

Chapter 26

VICTORIA E. JOHNSON

WELCOME HOME?
CBS, PAX-TV, and "heartland" values in a neo-network era

I N T H E S U M M E R O F 1996 American television broadcast network CBS launched a new marketing campaign and new prime-time programming slate. The network appealed to its audience with the promotional line. "The Address Is CBS—Welcome Home!" Concurrently, the series that anchored CBS's prime-time lineup included the Dick Van Dyke vehicle *Diagnosis Murder*, the Martha Williamson-produced, religious-themed *Touched by an Angel* and its spin-off, *Promised Land*, and the pastoral frontier melodrama *Dr. Quinn, Medicine Woman*. The network proceeded to bill Saturday night as "America's Night of Television" (featuring *Dr. Quinn* and the traditional law-and-order action show *Walker, Texas Ranger*) while Sunday night was promoted as "America's Night at the Movies" (currently featuring *Touched by an Angel* followed by family films such as *Tuesdays with Morrie* or *Beyond the Prairie: The True Story of Laura Ingalls Wilder*).

In 1998 PAX-TV was launched by West Palm Beach media magnate and professed born-again Christian Lowell White "Bud" Paxson to feature programming that "project[s] a 'God flavor' " (Green 1988, 20). In its first year. PAX's prime-time lineup, in its entirety, was composed of programs that originally (and, in some cases, concurrently) ran on CBS. Chief among these was Williamson's *Touched by an Angel*. As the year 2000 begins, CBS maintains its "Welcome Home" promotion and is the most watched network in television by both black and white Americans. In its second full season, PAX is making a profit and has been recognized, officially, as Nielsen's seventh network.

The following analysis proposes that CBS's call for Americans to come "home" and PAX's raison d'être—that "talking about God is a good thing and can make you money" (Green 1988)—simultaneously are counter-intuitive to the strategies and practices of their TV competitors while also exceptionally "synergistic" and complementary to one another. Both networks share strikingly similar business strategies, branding appeals, the same flagship programs produced by Martha Williamson, and a shared definition of their target audience and relationship to that audience. The networks' cooperative business dealings have allowed them not only to succeed but to thrive. And yet this study was provoked specifically because CBS's and PAX's successes seem so unexpected within the contemporary media environment. Though it boasts the broadest audience in the television industry, for decades CBS has been the butt of jokes for this same reason. Its mass, multigeneration, unhip demographics (featuring the most rural and oldest skewing audience in television, with a median viewer age of 52.2) seem literally behind the times compared to its competitors' niche, sponsor-friendly demographics. Equally, PAX's programming's insistence " 'that God loves you, that God knows what he's doing, and that God wants to be part of your life' " (Sharkey 1996, 20) immediately made it the target of industry experts who decried the possibility that a broadcast network (rather than an already "niche"-defined cable channel) could exist if completely dependent on explicitly religious "family-oriented programming."

CBS's and PAX's institutional identities are premised on the profitability of three concepts that, they argue, are held dear by their "not-so-chic viewers" (Brown 1998, 91), "real" Americans with core, traditional values: home, the nuclear family, and belief in God. According to CBS's and PAX's promotional rhetoric and programming appeals, these concepts are consciously avoided by their competition, which instead caters to boutique audiences, profiting from targeting specific sets of viewers and responding quickly to the latest trends. CBS and PAX thus argue that they are the last true, populist, democratic American broadcasters whose mission is to serve a core audience of real, God-fearing Americans who have otherwise been "forgotten" by America's "elite" popular culture producers.

Specifically CBS, PAX, and Martha Williamson (who produces much of the two networks' most successful programs) imagine their audience to be made up of midwesterners—"Heartland" Americans. This audience is presumed to be necessarily God-fearing and more "real" than their media-producing and consuming counterparts on either coast. According to Williamson, part of her task as a producer is to *revalue* a middle America that has been forgotten and critically disdained. *Touched by an Angel* thus "remembers the flyovers, that huge bulk of folks who live between the two coasts that most network executives have little in touch with" (Sharkey 1996, 22). Williamson's viewers thus occupy the vast land between the two coasts (though the ratings suggest a large number of coastal/major market viewers as well), where, she argues, " 'there are a lot more people in this country who believe in God than the guys in Hollywood and New York want to believe' " (Stein 1997, 75). By staking their institutional identity—their network "brand"—on Williamson's programs. CBS and PAX thus purport to put God and the true, core Heartland America back on the national stage during prime time.

The typical response to CBS's and PAX's recent successes has been to dismiss them with a healthy dose of critical disdain. With programming featuring angels that never earn industry honors (but annually take home trophies from grocery store or mass mail mounted awards shows such as the TV Guide Awards or the People's Choice Awards) and with audiences "overpopulated" by senior citizens and rural midwesterners unattractive to sponsors, CBS and PAX are generally regarded as entirely too déclassé to merit much discussion. And yet this is precisely the type of disrespect upon which both networks and their programming have staked their considerable success: as the only media outlets that speak for the post-1960s "silent majority," those presumed to occupy a figurative and literal, ideological and geographical, affective, tangible, devout American middle.

Rather than disregard these networks, their programs, and their audiences as aberrant successes, "dull and devoid of content" (Beam 1998, F1.1), instead we might ask, in what ways are CBS's and PAX's strategies and audiences responsive to as well as constitutive of larger social, cultural, and political forces in sharp contention over what it means to be "American" as we enter the twenty-first century? What national desires or communal longing do programs such as *Touched by an Angel* make visible? In an era in which network television, ritually, has been written off as obsolete, how do we begin to explain the sweeping success with which CBS and PAX remade and invented themselves, respectively, as contemporarily engaged representatives of tradition, champions of "the people" versus "the industry," "the God-fearing" versus "the nonbelievers," and the midwestern "Heartland" home versus the urban coasts?

The ideal, core America: Middleness is next to godliness?

CBS's and PAX's identity and audience address are thus grounded in the presumption that the contemporary American cultural landscape is, in the main, a traumatic one. CBS and PAX thus position themselves as *alternative* sites within the channel spectrum that displace trauma by reinstating a *mainstream*, traditional, family-friendly universe. These networks rhetorically identify their mission as the *redemption* of the American media landscape through the *revaluation* of the culture of the middle—a Heartland America imagined to be:

> linked with the rural aspects of regional life and hence with the 'past' and with a kind of cultural nostalgia for 'old folkways, values, and celebrations,' which it is [the networks'] privilege to rediscover and indeed celebrate, against all other 'modern' tendencies which are fast obliterating these cultural differences.
>
> (Brunsdon and Morley 1978, 80, 82)

This is an America wherein "proper citizenship has become progressively more private, more sexual and familial, and more concerned with personal morality" (Berlant 1997, 177), where systemic flaws or injustices are reconciled on an intimate basis as good individuals triumph over bad ones on the terrain of God's Heartland. In this presumed, shared, "commonsense" norm, middle America becomes a preferred place—the core, authentically American locus of genuine affect and of the presence of divinity. Here, the "human world" of traditionally forged attachments to God, family, and small-town community is valued most. Thus, CBS and PAX are positioned as modern technological sites that restore to American national life a localized place for refuge and restoration—the mythic American Pastoral, site of time-bound values of expressed belief in God, pioneering self-sufficiency, "knowable" community, and heterosexual/nuclear-familial ideals. Television, they propose, can revivify and, further, sanctify the nation-at-large by transporting audience members—regardless of their actual location—to an electronic "home" and Heartland that ritualize fantastic connection with an ideal (and divine) locale.

This imagined Heartland stands in as the secular and ecumenical realization of an America redeemed: the edenic middle landscape, site of the nation's humanity and divinity—literally, its heart and soul. From the mid- to late 1990s, accompanied by a relatively unprecedented midwestern economic boom as major corporations up-rooted from coastal hubs to relocate on the plains of Iowa and South Dakota (Cook 1997, 2245), a new version of media buzz about the region and its unshakable mystique as a land of "simple," tradition-bound, God-fearing people began to be noticeable. In April 1995, for example, *TV Guide* published a feature story called "TV Heads for the Heartland" in response to what author Jacquelyn Mitchard identified as a growing trend toward "a whole new America" outside of the fast-paced media hubs of New York and Los Angeles featured in CBS's prime-time series programming. While the article vaguely defines the geographic location of the Heartland as the rural small towns of the American "midcountry" (i.e., anything nonurban and not coastal), it is much more specific when it outlines the qualities and values presumed to inhere in this place and, therefore, explain the Heartland's "contemporary chic" for the American viewing public.

In opposition to the classic centers of television's attention "on either coast," the Heartland is "comfy," "safe," "secure," and "hardy." It is, above all, the site of "strong tradition and family values" where people live "solid lives . . . on commonsense foundations." Everyday life in the televised Heartland is characterized by premodern, Rockwellian American ideals of local continuity, family, a clear Protestant work ethic, and a corresponding staunch religious faith. Distanced from the "world of things" for the priority of the "human" world of church, family, and face-to-face community, the Heartland is triumphantly mundane. In the frenzy of the modern era, it represents a sanctified last refuge—"a spatial place, outside of and independent of the destructiveness of [modern American] society . . . the middle landscape, the zone of peace and harmony" (Carey and Quirk 1970, 421). The *TV Guide* article concludes, thereby, that even though ideals of Heartland life are largely imaginary, they are central to the national common sense—they represent the core values and pioneering spirit upon which America itself was presumably founded. Therefore, most Americans "want to feel they are part of [a Heartland] hometown, even if that's not where they're really from" (Mitchard 1995, 28–30).

The author thus argues that there is an identifiable trend in larger U.S. culture, as now seen on TV, that considers all Americans who value ideals of face-to-face community, safety, security, tradition, and solid nuclear "family values" to be "Heartlanders," regardless of their actual, lived, day-to-day mappable location. Solid, commonsensical Americans thus identify with the Heartland in spirit but also, it is implied, harbor an innate, indigenous desire to ally with this uniquely U.S. *place*—to take up residence *in* the "middle-landscape" home of unchanging, classic American ideals. Certain televised sites, it is claimed, are uniquely capable of allowing such "resettlement" on a weekly basis.

The American middle, so imagined, caters to a "desire to return to a localized reality" (Starobinski 1966, 102), to "[reaffirm] identities bruised by recent turmoil . . . the dislocations" following the 1960s (Lowenthal 1985, 13). Fundamentally, CBS and PAX tap into a suspicion or anxiety that a core American identity has been lost, "some direct, sincere, or 'folk' quality" that can be reclaimed via televisual address that, nightly, renews Heartlander connections "with the *gemeinschaftliche* worlds of extended family, local neighborhood, and organic community" (Lears 1994, 386, 384):

> *Gemeinschaft* is a type [of] social solidarity based on intimate bonds of sentiment, a common sense of place (social as well as physical), and a common sense of purpose . . . [a] high degree of face-to-face interaction in a common locality among people who have generally had common experiences. The sense of social norms is strong and individual deviation is relatively rare. There is a high degree of social consensus and behaviour is governed by strong but usually informal institution such as the family and peer group.
>
> (Krutnik 1997, quoting Tonnies 87)

The Midwest thus stands in as the icon of the *gemeinschaftliche* community (as pitted against the *gesellschaftliche* form of social organization exemplified by the urban, coastal hubs), where traditional morality and mainstream virtues still flourish, where "people [go] to church and [give] the time of day to strangers" (Mason 2000, 31). CBS's and PAX's roles as *redemptive* televisual sites that, nightly, move the traditional home, faith in God, and middle-American virtues from the cultural periphery to the center are informed by a nostalgic vision of a pastoral American that has been presaged by the new conservatism from the close of the 1960s to the present. . . .

[. . .]

Where this ethic of the middle has had the most success as a coherent political force has been in the realm of religion. In the contestations over the constitution of real, core, true American identity in the 1990s, perhaps no interests were more coherently successful than religious leaders on the right who argued, coincident with the Reagan administration and beyond, that being "proud to be an American" implied a whole set of belief systems and iconicity that was shared by "authentic" Americans and disdained by those who, proponents argued, would rather continue the social "divisions" that ostensibly emerged out of the 1960s. Across the 1990s, conservative religion's rhetoric consistently was "mainstreamed" in political initiatives that, particularly, isolated the media as a site of great "sin" via the triumph of private (corporate/financial) interest over public service and commonsense, bedrock American values. Arguably, the ultimate success of the religious right has been the co-optation of and contribution to its more mainstream-friendly rhetoric by neoliberal platforms à la Tipper Gore and even the child-and-family focus now espoused by Hilary Clinton or in President Clinton's Hollywood summit on violence in the media.

That is, the rhetoric positing family values, morality, and traditionalism as iconic of *religious* fealty which served to bolster the strength of the political right through the 1990s is now invoked in secular and ecumenical terms by the political left as well in its attempts to ally its interests with a centrist politics of the middle. The implication is that the ideological values of a larger cultural politics of the middle presumed to inhere in the American *geographic* middle are, in the vast majority, upheld by Heartland residents in their everyday lives. Geographic emplacement in the Heartland is thus presumed analogous to conservative political entrenchment in the American middle.

In fact, the power of the rhetoric of the new conservatism—as evidenced in popular contemporary television—is this entrenched *middleness between* easy identification with the American political "right" or "left." The power of the middle (ideologically/politically and geographically), in fact, is its foundational American iconicity: "true" Americans do not ally with "extremes"; "real" Americans are presumed to gravitate toward a healthily neutral middle ground wherein the family and self are the basic self-reliant units by whom decisions are made on a case-by-case rather than party-line basis. The political strength of popular artifacts of the "middle"—evidenced by CBS's and PAX's branding, programming, and audience address—is, therefore, their very apoliticalness. Cumulatively, they imagine an apolitical nation as the ideal America. The apolitical America is, here, a sanctified America.

"I know that my redeemer lives": The "classic" and "anti-network" network

In his plenary address to the Society for Cinema Studies conference in 1999, Michael Curtin argued that, beginning in approximately 1980, American television entered a "neo-network era" (Curtin 1999). This has been an era characterized by " 'economic restructuring . . . [that] socially reorganizes space and time, reformulates economic roles, and *revalues cultures of production and consumption*' " (emphasis mine; Curtin . . . quoting Zukin 1991, 29). In a multimediated, global context frequently theorized to be hostile to conventional national broadcast networks, CBS and PAX have achieved striking success as neonetworks by reconfiguring themselves as throwbacks to a time prior to this era.

Explicitly, CBS has referred to itself as the last "true broadcaster" from television's classic period (i.e., precable competition), while PAX trumpets its contrariness as an "anti-network network" (Braxton and Hall F2). Specifically, CBS and PAX both claim that their business practices and intended audience are structurally counter to those of their competitors. Rather than follow the economic and programming logic of narrowcasting to a niche audience of focused demographic range, both CBS and PAX are explicitly *broad*casters catering to a multigeneration family audience that is, in their vision, ideally middle American. Both networks emphasize the fact that, unlike cable channels, they are available to viewers across the country via off-air reception. Thus, CBS and PAX suggest that they are in the business of "public service" rather than simple crass commercialism. Their "family-friendly" programming is delivered "free" of charge and represents a democratic "choice" by which viewers can "vote" with their remotes (against the competitors' arguably non-family-friendly fare). This rhetoric bolsters both networks' arguments that their audiences occupy—or at least palpably desire—an ethereal rather than overtly commodified Heartland home, prioritizing affect and face-to-face interaction while still remaining "connected" to the contemporary realities of multimediated society and consumerism.

CBS and PAX have thus embraced the neo-network era in the service of tradition, "revaluing" the culture of the imagined American middle. They promote themselves as the lone, dependable "homes" of the "family hour's" reclamation; they explicitly claim to reinstitute the Heartland and Heartlander values to cultural prominence or to move the American periphery back to the center of cultural production; and they claim to be the only truly democratic, populist, and authentically responsive sites within the contemporary TV landscape. While programs with ostensibly populist, Heartland appeals have existed throughout the history of American network television, in the late 1990s, wherein recognizable network branding has become essential to corporate survival, it is critical that CBS and PAX have claimed the Heartland as definitive of their *institutional* identity as well as characteristic of their flagship programs.[1] CBS and PAX thus posit the compatibility of cultural values and beliefs from the imagined, idealized American past—as located in the nation's vast middle—with the most contemporary forms of media address and interactivity (on television as well as in the form of World Wide Web sites) (Lipsitz 1989, 98). These strategies and their apparent success with audiences, while initially seeming contrary to contemporary paradigms for media success, are, in fact, synchronous with the paradox that "globalization seems also to have led to a strengthening of 'local' allegiances and identities *within* nation-states" (Hall 1996, 354).

[. . .]

With an off-air coverage range of 76 percent of Nielsen households, PAX is the largest owned and operated network of stations in the country and has been officially designated the seventh network (Halonen 1999). On basic cable, PAX now has a greater coverage range than Lifetime, Turner Network Television, or USA Network (Higgins 1998, 6). In total, PAX stations reach all but 15 percent of the American TV-viewing population. PAX's rapid success has been staked largely on recently upheld must-carry rules that require cable companies to carry all local broadcast channels, including the almost eighty low-power UHF stations that make up the backbone of the PAX chain.

"Bud" Paxson calls PAX an "anti-network network." Whereas usually start-up networks "counterprogram with . . . sex and violence" and riskier fare to grab attention, PAX programs propose and embrace overt, devout evangelical spirituality, imagine insular, shared community, explicitly reference the pioneering, frontier past, and, weekly, exemplify blissful unawareness of urban life and urban populations (Schneider 1998, 31). Significantly here, PAX-TV's start-up was marred by an uproar over its promotions in major news and industry trade papers which condemned the major networks for "promoting 'alternative lifestyles,' " a phrase understood, typically, to refer to gay and lesbian populations. Perhaps only adding fuel to the fire, PAX president and CEO Jeff Sagansky (formerly president of CBS Entertainment) responded to the criticism by arguing that while " 'PAX-Net wouldn't shy away from featuring gay characters in its programming . . . we are not here to promote a gay lifestyle' " (Schneider 1998, 31). Indeed, exemplary of its ethic of "middleness," PAX-TV argues that it does not "promote" conservative religious views either, in spite of the fact that most early press surrounding PAX-TV referred to it as a "Christian network." Paxson maintains only that PAX offers a *universally* desired American safe-space, a "national family network" that represents a nondenominational yet spiritually uplifting "haven for alienated viewers." Invoking the same rhetoric of all-American alternatives, universal common sense, and democratic choice used by CBS, Paxson claims: "Our desire at PAX is to provide people with the opportunity to choose programs that will reinforce family values . . . an alternative we believe the majority of the American public both wants and needs. . . . PAX is not a Christian network. It's a network that will use drama about life to strengthen family values while letting people know that God loves them" (Paxson 1998, 110, 162, 164)[. . .]

If PAX-TV's God-and-family-values-friendly programming is one key to its "anti-network" identity, its business practices and institutional structure are equally counter to the industry at large: the bulk of PAX stations are low-power, UHF outlets; each station is evacuated of most personnel, and none has a news division or carries local news. Essentially, each PAX station serves as a pure distribution point for national programming. Also counter to other networks, including CBS, the majority of PAX-TV's advertising sales are local and regional rather than national. In prime time, particularly, this raises the cost per point to an immensely profitable level, which allows PAX to endure and prosper in spite of relatively low ratings. Further, Barney Rosenzweig, formerly a successful producer with the CBS of the 1980s (e.g. *Cagney and Lacey*), recently voiced his opinion that PAX, playing by opposite rules than other broadcasters, offered him artistic redemption—a chance to return to a position of veneration as a classic entrepreneur and self-made businessman whom the industry at large no longer respected. Rosenzweig expressed a sense of betrayal as an "auteur" who had been displaced by the industry he helped to make. However, now a disciple of PAX, he argues that its "outsider" status in relation to other media outlets positions it as a *redeemer*, revaluing Rosenzweig and allowing cultural inroads that would otherwise be closed to him and to his program's audience:

> Rosenzweig maintains he wouldn't trade his situation for "ER's" ratings if it meant working under the rules that govern the TV business, where a few behemoths produce and control practically every program that makes it onto the screen. . . . For producers like Rosenzweig, the landscape fundamentally shifted in the mid-1990s, . . . [leading to] a flurry of mergers, which has for the most part forced producers into relationships with networks or the studios that own them if they want to get on the air.
>
> (Lowry 1999)

A now prominent and successful network, PAX thus gets portrayed as looking in from outside the "TV business" itself, a Main Street mom-and-pop operation that looks out for the little guy and allows artists with a humanistic vision to flourish.

[. . .]

Revaluing the heartland: God and the intimate politics of *Touched by an Angel*

Fundamentally, in the late 1990s, both CBS's and PAX's institutional identities were built on the success of programs created and produced by Martha Williamson in conjunction with CBS Productions. Most significantly, her *Touched by an Angel* cemented CBS's role as the number one television-viewing destination across America on Sunday nights, while the same program became the weeknightly anchor around which PAX-TV has built its entire prime-time lineup. While other networks depend on a single producer's products to market a uniquely cutting-edge, aesthetically, and thematically hip institutional identity, PAX and CBS trumpet Williamson's work as the epitome of old-fashioned "not-so-chic" programs that speak directly to the residual, populist American middle in the language of "the people."[2] According to Andy Hill, president of CBS Productions, *Touched by an Angel*'s power is that it is a touchstone of stability, comfort, and humanity in an otherwise confusing world:

Right now as a country, we look at a world that in many ways is more frightening and more pessimistic than any of us expected to be living in . . . This show really is about at least part of the solution, which is *people looking to themselves* for answers and quite frankly having a belief in something more than today, and money and power.

(Sharkey 1996, 20)

Indeed, according to fan mail, a good part of viewer loyalty to the program is based on its unfailing weekly structure wherein family and/or community are reconstituted and redeemed through "God's love." *Angel* provides a site that, weekly on CBS and nightly on PAX, helps its viewers " 'place [themselves] in a confusing world' " (Torres 1989, 90). In each episode someone facing a time of crisis must regain or adopt faith in God and arrive at a decision with the help but never the express direction of one of two angels and/or the angel of death. Each program concludes with the same message ("God loves you") and the same visual trope (a dove taking flight). The series' predictability, in this respect, reinforces CBS's and PAX's encouragement to their viewers that, in an ever-more-transient global society, their audiences turn toward self, God, and "home"—toward emplaced and intimate ways of apprehending the world and of solving problems therein.

Angel thus epitomizes CBS's and PAX's promotional rhetoric that they have the power to "rehumanize" and sanctify prime time by revaluing core, traditional, middle-American values of religion, home, family, and shared, knowable community.[3] Williamson has made this ethic of redemption and rehumanization explicit in discussions of *Angel*'s overwhelming success. In an era of "faxing and modeming and on-lining and Fedexing and down-loading," she believes that *Angel* offers rare respite: the renewal of premodern grassroots connections. Says the producer: "You can tell anyone anything anywhere in a matter of seconds now. But it still takes the same amount of time that it always did to get to know someone, to mend a broken heart, to give birth to a child, to grieve the loss of a friend" (Williamson and Sheets 1997, 23).

Counterintuitive to and yet temporally concurrent with television's modern, mobile, cultural appeals, *Angel* succeeds, it is argued, because it presents itself to its audience as a touchstone of sanctity, stability, and knowable community. According to one viewer and contributor to PAX-TV's *Touched by an Angel* discussion group, " 'every single episode is a learning experience as well as a sanity check. . . . a place where you can go [with] no violence/no language barriers . . . a place where you are ALWAYS told of one thing . . . GOD LOVES YOU' " ("Angel Lohay").

Further, however, Williamson argues that of critical, distinctive importance to her programs' sense of community is their explicit attention to place, to Heartland locales and attendant regional values within U.S. culture. In her series' settings (almost exclusively bound in their locations from week to week by the borders of the American Midwest, Great Plains, and rural South), Williamson strives to put Heartland culture back at center stage within television programming. Thus, unlike "hip hits" such as *ER* and *Friends*, Williamson argues that *Angel* purposefully addresses the American middle in an explicitly populist, authentically "real" voice resonant with emotion and explicitly spiritual content. Williamson perceives her audience to thus be not just figuratively midwestern but literally middle American at its core.

"The people" Williamson speaks to are thus pitted against "the industry" that alienates them. In this context, *Touched by an Angel* is believed to have beaten the television odds because, while "usually a hit show starts from the outside, from the coasts and works its way in [*Touched by an Angel* and *Promised Land*] both . . . started in the breadbasket and worked their way out" (Rice 1997, 26). Still, rather than imagine her audience as a boutique demographic with a shared interest in religion, Williamson concurs with CBS and PAX (and the ratings would seem to support) that *Angel* is speaking a "universal" rather than a particularized language. The Heartland is, thus, representative of a shared *national* common sense wherein, it is presumed, anyone who values family, home, community, and optimistic narrative will, necessarily, ally with the spiritual, explicitly localized, middle-American message of each week's/night's program.

And yet *Angel* is undeniably, overtly a religious program. It specifically holds out the promise each week that good individuals, redeemed in their faith, can, one by one, case by case, add up to a good country, redeemed of its (post-1960s) sins and obviated of the need for ongoing systemic or institutional intervention or change. Every problem can (and, ultimately, must) be resolved between the self and God, in the intimate and religious/miraculous realm. The "solution" and "belief" *Touched by an Angel* ritually offers its fans is a vicarious redemption, via their acceptance that "God is love" and that individual choices make one's place in the world.

The intimate politics (and yet paradoxically potentially *cynical*, considering the weekly *deus ex machina* conceit) of Williamson's hit have opened it up to criticism from both the right and the left, arguing that it is both rampantly conservative and entirely too left-wing, too "politically correct," particularly for its frequent discussion of race relations and for its positive portrayal of homosexual characters (Shalit 1998, 31). Williamson, echoing Bud Paxson above, has countered such criticisms by arguing that "religious" does not necessarily mean "political." She instead embraces an ecumenical and populist logic, arguing that her characters simply respond to and act upon the "truth" in each individual situation:

> "Unfortunately religion has become so politicized in our society," she says, "but I think I'm like most people in the world who have a level of faith, but who don't necessarily associate that with a political point of view, liberal or conservative, and I love the opportunity to explore faith without encouraging people to take a stand for anything other than *what's right*."
>
> (Sharkey 1996, 20, emphasis mine)

And what's most "right" to Williamson—and synchronous with CBS and PAX, her programming homes—is her focus on the redemption of the Heartland. Her weekly goal is to affirm her audience as " 'the salt of the Earth' " and to acknowledge that " 'what they believe matters,' " and, unlike other media venues, *Touched by an Angel* knows that this audience is " 'not [to] be made fun of' " (Lowry, *et al.* 1997, 8).

According to Williamson herself, *Touched by an Angel* will likely never be perceived as a critical favorite of media "experts" because of its "emotional chordplucking." Yet these same features—the conventionally derided characteristics of melodrama—give *Angel* its argued authenticity and larger cultural resonance. The otherwise "forgotten" or "underserved" American TV audience—the "real" people who are loyal fans of the show—"recognize its sincerity, and they respond with deeply personal" commitment to the program's success, expressed via volumes of mail, fan organizations and activity, and so on (Williamson and Sheets 1997, 22).

True Stories of real Americans? Populism and the Gospel according to TV

There are four key themes that inform CBS's, PAX's, and Williamson's programs' address to "the people": each imagines its audience as a national community with universally shared values, values that are "localized"/emblematic of "Home" in the traditional American Heartland; each positions itself as symbolic of American democracy, "free" of charge to viewers who now may "vote" for wholesome family "alternatives" to an otherwise alienating cultural milieu; each is explicitly populist in its address to an audience of "real" Americans living everyday lives in the nation's middle landscape (if only in their hearts); and, finally, each encourages the audience's engagement with the network flow and/or program itself, from market support of particular sponsors to letter-writing campaigns, urging viewers that every individual has the power to move traditional Heartland values to the modern American cultural center. While these networks and programs have assumed the task of redeeming an undervalued culture within the United States, each also calls out to loyal viewers to actively do their part to revalue the devout American middle. These shared appeals to "real" folks and "authentic," evangelical American interests extend to the networks' programs' casts and crews. In the case of *Touched by an Angel*, for instance, every public appearance of the cast prompts a narrative recounting of each actor's *autobiographical* connection to the characters they play on the show and, just as significantly, to their status, in spite of their institutional success, as "outsiders" in relation to the industry. (They are each, after all, professed "believers" both in angels and in God.)

As regards network branding strategies, the PAX-TV viewer is immediately struck by the network's use of *Touched by an Angel* as the cornerstone of its identity. The network's titling and promotional graphic motifs are blatantly and unapologetically "borrowed" by PAX from *Angel* to brand the network. For example, a voice strikingly similar to Roma Downey's (one of the three stars of *Touched by an Angel*) intones in promos that "you're watching PAX-TV. Share it with someone you love." The dove—a symbol that opens and closes every episode of *Touched by an Angel* as well as forms part of its main title design—is used by PAX in its network identification logo (perched on the "X") and in program bumpers that urge viewers to "watch for the sign of the dove" as their guide for where to land on the TV dial.

While the dove logo and Downey-esque voice-overs link a very popular and successful program in viewers' minds and/as definitive of PAX itself, the network also makes explicit appeals to "all-American" patriotism in its network promotions, logos, and graphics. There are two network identification bumpers used by PAX. One features a wispy, cloudy, heavenly blue sky against which translucent block letters spelling "PAX" stand as a dove perches on top of them. Typically accompanying this bumper is the above voice-over or the message "You're Watching PAX-TV: A Friend of the Family." The second network identification features "PAX" in alternating red, white, and blue block letters. [. . .] This red, white, and blue PAX with dove motif is also a featured graphic on the network's official website (at http://www.paxtv.com/). This "trad-itional," patriotic mode of address featured on the "new" communication site of the Web points to a conscious effort by the network to define media technology as a site of cultural preservation or reclamation. PAX's Website thus suggests that new technology can serve the interests of tradition, particularly as it posits an electronic community "for the family" and a forum to chat with like-minded folks from all over the nation.

[. . .]

The site features frequently updated "spotlights" on show cast members, emphasizing their humble nature, their natural alliance with the interests of PAX-TV, and their "outsider" relation to other media forums. [. . .] The site also actively encourages PAX's audience to directly interact by expressing opinions about each of the shows via chat groups which may be entered for free, without registration. The PAX-Calendar allows clubs from all over the country to post their activities and events to be shared with the PAX community. Finally, the PAX Website appeals to a "family" audience as a "family-friendly" site by offering exhaustive synopses of each program being aired on PAX that day (so parents can screen in advance, though, ostensibly, there could be nothing in the schedule that *would* offend) and by providing its own "Internet access filtering technology," PAXWAY. Billed by Paxson Communications as "A National 'Clean' Internet Access Kit for Families," PAXWAY "functions as a gateway to the Internet where parents can have full control over what their under-aged children may not view on the internet . . . to establish a 99.45% safe environment."

Touched by an Angel's official Website, while much glossier than PAX's, addresses its audience in a similar fashion (at http://www.touched.com). It encourages viewer activism or, explicitly, newer participation as members of the *Touched by an Angel* "team": from promoting that fans contact "our top advertisers" to voice their thanks (all but three of whom are headquartered in the "Heartland"), to offering opportunities for viewers to contact the show's producer and cast directly, to providing links to Websites for organizations such as Christian Solidarity International and other groups whose interests directly tie in to those addressed in episodes of *Angel*. Finally, the site offers links to the most current news updates about the show with which fans will connect (including a real-time audio/video clip of Roma Downey's acceptance of the Favorite TV Actress award at the 1999 TV Guide Awards) and to the TBAA Store.

Of course, *Touched by an Angel*'s creators and creative talent assume that the majority of their audience is reached directly through television programming itself. [. . .] *Angel* has additionally addressed its audience's presumed shared interest in the "real," "authentic," populist appeals of the series in two specials titled *True Stories of Touched by an Angel* (aired originally on CBS, then syndicated on PAX). These specials allow loyal fans to go behind the scenes of the show's weekly production in Salt Lake City, Utah, and to "meet" the cast, crew, writers, and producers. They thus unveil the artifice of television production while also asserting the exceptional authenticity, responsiveness, and accessibility of the program's narratives and the explicit commitment to these ideals of its cast and crew as "just plain folks" whose task it is to bring the viewers' "own" stories to life.

True Stories foregrounds the fact that *Angel* is grassroots TV, created at a conscious remove from "the industry." It is overtly allied with "real people" from Utah and around the country, outside of the "extremes" of the urban centers of either coast. Thus Williamson (and CBS and PAX, by extension) is able to ground her argument that the program speaks directly to the Heartland in explicitly populist, authentically "real" voices. To add to this "outsider" status, according to cast interviews featured in these specials and consistent with other forms of series publicity, none of the featured actors (Roma Downey, Della Reese, John Dye) actually lives in Los Angeles, favoring homes in and around Salt Lake City. In apparent connection and imagined conversation with their community of fans, the actors are purported to read the multitude of letters they receive each week. Most significantly, however, each cast member professes to have an autobiographical connection to her or his series role. The implication, therefore, is that character and actor are, indeed, merged; that this is not a job, it is "real life." Roma Downey, for instance, emphasizes that, like her character, the angel Monica, she too grew up an orphan. Della Reese, who plays the angel Tess, is an ordained minister in everyday life. John Dye, who plays Andrew, the angel of death, argues that the cast and crew consider themselves to be "family" rather than coworkers.

Finally, the *True Stories* specials visit the "real-life" inspirations for and nonprofessional participants in several episodes of the series. They also discuss the ways that viewers have been inspired (as revealed through their correspondence) to some kind of activism following a screening of *Touched by an Angel*. Former guest stars (from Bill Cosby and Carol Burnett to Edward James Olmos and Cloris Leachman) then contribute their own autobiographical musings on the roles they played on the series (again, equalizing "celebrity" and "everyday" folk). Finally, viewers themselves are interviewed and directly relate their own real-life experiences to those enacted on the show (from a woman in Florida who is the survivor of rape, to residents of a juvenile detention center who appeared as extras in an *Angel* episode).

Yet it is this same homey, responsive, populist ethic for which Williamson's programs and the networks that feature them typically have been met with critical revulsion, in spite of the shows' broad based popularity (or, in part, because of it). In presuming to revalue, redeem, speak to and for a "forgotten" and "underserved" Heartland family audience, these networks and programs are perceived to tread perilously close to an Agnew-esque critique of their competitors, while they position their viewers as a "silent majority" for the next millennium. With striking consistency, popular and trade-press critics of Williamson's programs, for example, displace discussions of the series' narrative characteristics onto the politics inherent in the programs' and their fans' *geographic* identity—its fixed emplacement, rooted in a traditional, old, rural, presumed conservative mindset.

[. . .]

To an undeniable extent there is a consistency with which Williamson's programs, CBS's appeals to "America's" audience, and PAX's "God-flavored" address critically have been singled out as "right-wing" in their assumptions, their contrariness, and their loyal, square audience followings. [. . .] And yet, considering that Williamson's programs have also been vilified for being too left-leaning. I would propose that the larger cultural threat, of which such address is presumed a dialogic part, has more to do with what Herman Gray has called America's inexorable "press toward the imaginary middle,"[4] a triumphantly mundane America marked by an "inoffensive" sameness, the "middle" wherein America is publicly imagined and held in esteem as an *apolitical*, sentimental space wherein "the notion of a public life . . . has been made to seem ridiculous and even dangerous to the nation."

"Middle America" as the localized national vision of America is thus a nation-space in which ideals of citizenship are, increasingly, read through screens of emplaced "voluntarism" whereby "intentional individual goodwill" (in *Angel*, the personal acceptance of God's love and family values) is substituted "for the nation-state's commitment to fostering democracy" (or to institutional changes to a flawed system; Berlant 1997, 5, 7). This is the vision of an America made up of *individuals* paradoxically self-sufficient (in their traditional, pioneering, bootstrap ethic) and yet ultimately dependent on divine intervention for their salvation.

Arguably, the critical consistency with which these programs and networks are met as the "low," politically retrograde other within, respectively, the TV schedule and the contemporary media landscape too easily excises them from critical discourse about television that would prefer to embrace emergent technologies and developments rather than examine the protracted success of residual expressions within or definitions of the medium, its purpose, and its national voice. It also too simply plays into the stereotype that there is a coastal "media elite" out to savage television programs that "the people" actually watch.[5]

[. . .]

[T]he figure of the American Heartland as a nationally redemptive space seems likely to remain important to both networks' address and to popular network programming, as well as to the imagination of the nation at large. The myth of a sanctified place of refuge within American geography and culture is perhaps the most powerful of identity fantasies because of its foundational status for a nation based on the principles that the frontier was edenic and that the middle landscape's balance between industry and nature could be our salvation on earth. Al Gore's campaign for the presidency [in 1992] capitalized on this myth by transplanting from the overtly "politicized" and "cynical" eastern urban culture of "the Beltway" back to his Tennessee home in the "Heartland." And yet, more commonly, most invocations of the "Heartland" are inflected with nostalgia and loss rather than with plenitude and gain. [C]overage of the Columbine High School shootings in Colorado, for instance, explicitly argued that Littleton *had been* (in a time prior to the shooting) exemplary of the American Heartland—"a sanctuary . . . [at] the nation's geographic and emotional center . . . [a] pristine . . . spiritual wellspring of the American dream" (Mohringer 1999, A1). Ostensibly, the "loss" of Littleton's Heartland status—violated by violence unimaginable outside of "urban" centers—can now only be recaptured for its residents through nostalgic, televised travels such as are provided by *Touched by an Angel*. Thus, particularly in times of perceived cultural threat of a nation and global culture outstripping "human" perception, the Heartland provides a mythical touchstone of redeeming godliness, goodness, groundedness, and common sense to which a desirous public discourse repeatedly returns.

Notes

1 For example, past programs with a similar address and presumed audience include series such as *Grand Ol' Opry Time* (ABC, 1955–56), *Ozark Jubilee* (ABC, 1955–61), *The Andy Griffith Show* (CBS, 1960–68), *The Waltons* (CBS, 1972–81), *Highway to Heaven* (NBC, 1984–88), among others.
2 I'm thinking here, for example, of Chris Carter's affiliation with FOX, of David E. Kelley's and Steven Bochco's alliances with ABC or John Wells's or Dick Wolf's productions for NBC, and so on.
3 This rhetoric promoting CBS's and PAX's missions to "rehumanize" television in the service of traditional values is striking on the networks' part, considering that just over twenty years ago this was the same rationale used to promote cable TV's liberating distinctiveness from overair networking. Cable is now perceived to be—and actively discussed by CBS and PAX as—the greatest competitive threat to "classic" TV networks. See Streeter for a thorough discussion of this discourse as regards cable TV.
4 As quoted in Marlon Riggs's *Color Adjustment* (California Newsreel, 1992).
5 Brian Lowry of the *Los Angeles Times* has recently pointed out this critical tendency in the case of HBO's *The Sopranos*, wherein "its place in the spotlight has as much to do with who's watching the show as how many. The TV press and those who work in the entertainment industry simply adore the show, heightening the sense within those circles that the series is an explosive cultural phenomenon," whereas almost three times as many viewers each week make *Touched by an Angel* "appointment" television.

References

Beam, Alex. (1998) "Just the Ticket if Your Heart's in the Heartland." *Boston Globe* 12 August: F1.
Berlant, Lauren. (1997) *The Queen of America Goes to Washington City: Essays on Sex and Citizenship*. Durham: Duke UP.
Brown, Sara. (1998) "Bud Paxson's Coverage Crusade." *Broadcasting and Cable* 19 January: 91.
Brunsdon, Charlotte, and David Morley. (1978) *Everyday Television: Nationwide*. London: British Film Institute.
Carey, James, and John W. Quirk. (1970) "The Mythos of the Electronic Revolution." *American Scholar* 39: 219–41, 395–424.
Carson, Tom. (1997) "God's Countryman." *Village Voice* 15 July.
Cook, Rhodes. (1997) "America's Heartland: Neither One Mind nor One Heart." *Congressional Quarterly Weekly Report* 20 September: 2243–49.
Costello, Victoria. "We're Not in Mayberry Anymore." http://www/paxtv.com/column/.
Curtin, Michael. (1999) "Unraveling the Network Nation: Spatial Logics of Media History." *Plenary Address Delivered to the Society for Cinema Studies Annual Conference*.
Gerstenzang, James. (1992) "Quayle Stands by *Murphy Brown* View." *Los Angeles Times* 22 May: A1.
Gliatto, Tom. (1996) "*Touched by an Angel*." *People Weekly* 26 February.
Green, Linda Murray. (1998) "Will New Christian TV Network Beat the Odds?" *Christianity Today* 27 April: 20.
Grossberg, Larry. (1992) *We Gotta Get out of This Place: Popular Conservatism and Postmodern Culture*. New York: Routledge.
Hall, Stuart. (1993) "Culture, Community, Nation." *Cultural Studies* December: 349–63.
Halonen, Doug. (1999) "Let the Duopolies Begin." *Electronic Media* 9 August.
Higgins, John M., and Sara Brown. (1998) "Paxson Renders unto TCI." *Broadcasting and Cable* 4 May.
Krutnik, Frank. (1997) "Something More than Night: Tales of the Noir City." *The Cinematic City*. Ed. David B. Clarke. New York: Routledge.
Lears, T. J. Jackson. (1994) *Fables of Abundance*. New York: HarperCollins.
Lipsitz, George. (1989) "The Meaning of Memory: Family, Class, and Ethnicity in Early Network Television Programs." *Camera Obscura* 16 January.
Lowenthal, David. (1985) *The Past Is a Foreign Country*. New York: Cambridge UR.

Lowry, Brian. (1999) "Rosenzweig, an Old Pro in a New Game." *Los Angeles Times* 30 November.

—— (2000) "*Sopranos* Is Big—But Not Really that Big." *Los Angeles Times* 21 January.

—— Jane Hall, and Greg Braxton. (1997) "There's a Moral to This." *Los Angeles Times* 21 September.

Mason, Bobbi Ann. (2000) "Fallout: Paducah's Secret Nuclear Disaster." *New Yorker* 10 January: 30–36.

Mitchard, Jacqueline. (1998) "TV Heads for the Heartland." *TV Guide* 8–14 April.

Moehringer, J. R. (1999) "Shooting Strikes at Heart of U.S." *Los Angeles Times* 29 April: A1, 4.

"Net Households Surf the Web, ABC, NBC, and Cable." (1999) *Myers Report* 9 August: 1.

Patton, Cindy. (1995) "Refiguring Social Space." *Social Postmodernism: Beyond Identity Politics*. Ed. Linda Nicholson and Steven Seidman. Cambridge: Cambridge UP.

Paxson, Lowell, with Gary Templeton. (1998) *Threading the Needle: The Pax Net Story*. New York: HarperBusiness.

Rice, Lynette. (1997) "Heaven Can't Wait." *Broadcasting and Cable* 24 Feb.

Schneider, Michael. (1999) "Changing Tides: CBS No. 1 among African Americans." *Electronic Media* 1 February.

—— (1998) "Paxson Learns Politically Correct Lesson." *Electronic Media* 27 July.

Shalit, Ruth. (1998) "Quality Wings: Angels on Television. Angels in America." *New Republic* 20 and 27 July: 24–31.

Sharkey, Betsy. (1996) "Riding the Wings of *Angel*." *Mediaweek* 20 May.

Starobinski, Jean. (1966) "The Idea of Nostalgia." *Diogenes* Summer: 81–103.

Stein, Joel. (1997) "The God Squad." *Time* 22 September.

Streeter, Tom. (1997) "Blue Skies and Strange Bedfellows: The Discourse of Cable Television." *The Revolution Wasn't Televised: Sixties Television and Social Conflict*. Ed. Lynn Spigel and Michael Curtin. New York: Routledge.

Theriot, Nancy. (1990) *Nostalgia on the Right: Historical Roots of the Idealized Family*. Cambridge: Political Research Associates.

Torres, Sasha. (1989) "Melodrama, Masculinity, and the Family: *thirtysomething* as Therapy." *Camera Obscura* January.

"Viacom to Buy CBS for $36 Billion." *Broadcasting and Cable* 8 Sept. 1999.

Williamson, Martha, and Robin Sheets. (1997) *Touched by an Angel*. Grand Rapids: Zondervan Publishing House.

Zukin, Sharon. (1991) *Landscapes of Power*. Berkeley: U of California P.

Chapter 27

DAVID MORLEY

BROADCASTING AND THE CONSTRUCTION OF THE NATIONAL FAMILY

The mediated nation as symbolic home

IN RAISING QUESTIONS about how the mediated public sphere constructed by the institutions of national broadcasting functions as a symbolic home for the nation's members, I shall attempt to move beyond the narrowly rationalist modality in which discussions of the public sphere have predominantly been cast. My focus will be on the question of who feels included in or excluded from symbolic membership of the nation, and how they participate in the idea of the nation as represented in its mediated culture. The original public service model of broadcasting was figured as one in which 'all the citizens of a nation can talk to each other like a family sitting and chatting around the domestic hearth'.[1] Ominously, from the point of view of the inclusiveness or otherwise of that model family in the UK, the daughter of the BBC's first Director General, Lord Reith, reported in her biographical memoir of her father that 'he just could not accept the otherness of members of his family'. As we shall see later, Lord Reith's domestic problems in this respect have uneasy echoes at the macro level of the national audience.[2] In this respect, heritage, as Mike Phillips observes, 'is a fence which marks out the boundaries of exclusion'.[3] The principal form of symbolic articulation, in this respect, concerns the relation of the family home to the image of the National Family. It was King George V who declared that 'The foundations of the national glory are set in the homes of the people', but it was the mass newspaper, the *Daily Mail*, which subsequently adapted this statement as the credo of that central Institution of British Life, the Ideal Home Exhibition.[4]

The role of the media in articulating the dispersed members of the nation to the centres of symbolic power is crucial here. The question is through what kinds of mechanisms this effect is achieved. In this connection Daniel Dayan and Elihu Katz make the analogy between religious processions, in which the image of a saint is paraded through a physical neighbourhood, and media events in which the same 'sacred' image is transmitted simultaneously into households throughout the land. In both cases public values 'penetrate the private world of the residence, with the world of the house being integrated into the metaphor of public life'.[5] This sense of interpenetration of the sacred into the realm of the household is perhaps nowhere given clearer expression than in the example of the royal Christmas broadcast in the UK. Thus, when Lord Reith finally persuaded King George V to 'make a national moral impression' by addressing the media and Empire in a Christmas message in 1932, the King's words were 'I speak now from my home and my heart to all of you. To men and women so cut off by snows, the desert or the sea that only voices out of the air can reach. To all, to each, I wish a Happy Christmas. God bless you!'[6] Here we see one aspect of the crucial role of broadcasting in forging a link between the dispersed and disparate listeners and the symbolic heartland of national life, and of its role in promoting a sense of communal identity within its audience, at both regional and national levels.

In parallel with Paddy Scannell's analysis of the role of the BBC in the construction of a sense of national unity in the UK, Lofgren offers a convincing account of the role of broadcasting in the construction of a sense of national identity in other European countries in the twentieth century.[7] Lofgren's central concern is with the question of how people have come to feel at home in the nation and with the educative role of broadcast media in the everyday process of what he calls the 'cultural thickening' of the nation state. Lofgren calls this the 'micro-physics of learning to belong to the nation-as-home, through which the nation-state makes itself visible and tangible . . . in the lives of its citizens'.[8] In this analysis these media are seen to supply 'the fragments of cultural memory' that compose 'the invisible information structure' which constitutes a person's sense of their homeland as a virtual community.[9] In Sweden, Lofgren observes that by the 1930s, national radio had constructed a new *Gemeinschaft* of listeners tied together by the contents and myths of national radio broadcasting. This synchronised experience of radio came to provide a stable national frame of understanding for local events and topics, in an educative process which turned the nation into something resembling a vast schoolroom. This broadcast national rhetoric took many forms – not least ritual ones, such as familiarising people with the national anthem and inscribing it at key moments in their own domestic practices. Even the weather was nationalised and its national limits clearly demarcated, so that 'in the daily shipping forecast, the names of the coastal observation posts of Sweden were read like a magic chant, as outposts encircling the nation'.[10]

In a similar vein, in his introduction to the catalogue of Mark Power's photographic project on *The Shipping Forecast* in the UK, David Chandler notes that while the information on weather conditions at sea around the UK is plainly of practical use only to seafarers, the size of the listenership of BBC radio's shipping forecast (broadcast four times a day since 1926) and the affection in which the broadcast is held by many who never go to sea, indicates that 'its mesmeric voice and timeless rhythms are buried deep in the public consciousness . . . For those of us safely ashore, its messages from "out there" [and] its warnings from a dangerous peripheral world of extremes and uncertainty are reassuring'.[11] Nikos Papastergiadis has argued that 'the symbols and narratives of the nation can only resonate if they are admitted to the chamber of the home'.[12] Radio often achieves, as Chandler notes, exactly this kind of intimacy. His argument is that if the shipping forecast enhances our sense of comfort in being safe at home, this is also a matter of national belonging in the profoundest sense:

> The shipping forecast is both national narrative and symbol; for seventy years it has given reports on an unstable, volatile 'exterior' against which the ideas of 'home' and 'nation' as places of safety, order and even divine protection are reinforced. In those brief moments, when its alien language of the sea interrupts the day, the forecast offers to complete the enveloping circle and rekindle a picture of Britain glowing with a sense of wholeness and unity.[13]

National broadcasting can thus create a sense of unity – and of corresponding boundaries around the nation; it can link the peripheral to the centre; turn previously exclusive social events into mass experiences; and, above all, it penetrates the domestic sphere, linking the national public into the private lives of its citizens, through the creation of both sacred and quotidian moments of national communion. Not that this process is always smooth and without tension or resistance. Lofgren notes that, historically, what was at stake here was both the nationalisation of the domestic and the domestication of the national, so that 'the radio turned the sitting room into a public room, the voices from the ether spoke from the capital and united us with our rulers, but also with all other radio listeners around the country'.[14] Nonetheless, this socialisation of the private sphere, in the service of the 'civilisation of the peripheries' of the nation, could also give rise to resentment. As one Swedish listener recalls, 'when the radio was on, the room wasn't really ours, the sonorous voices with their Stockholm [accents] . . . pushed our own thick [regional] voices into a corner where we commented in whispers on the cocksure statements from the radio'.[15]

In her analysis of national fantasy and the construction of the landscape of national icon-ography, Lauren Berlant traces the processes through which a common national character is produced. As she puts it, through the accident of birth within a particular set of geographical and political boundaries, the individual is transformed into the subject of a collectively held history and learns to value a particular set of symbols as intrinsic to the nation and its terrain. In this process, the nation's 'traditional icons, its metaphors, its heroes, its rituals and narratives provide an alphabet for collective consciousness or national subjectivity; through the National Symbolic the historical nation aspires to achieve the inevitability of the status of national law, a birth-right'.[16] Berlant's central point, for our purposes, concerns the ways in which desire and affect are harnessed to political life in the cultural forms of the National Symbolic. For her, it is both through the mediated circulation of images and narratives and through geographical perambulation to symbolic monuments and sites that national culture becomes local and rooted in the public forms of everyday life. In line with Martin-Barbero's analysis of the role of cultural institutions in converting the (potentially distant) realm of the national into the quotidian, Eley and Suny remark that 'we are "national" when we vote, watch the six o'clock news, follow the national sport, and observe (while barely noticing) the repeated iconograph-ies of landscape, history and citation in the movies'.[17] Moreover, in the construction of this national symbolism, the national is often figured in the powerful imagery of the familial. Thus, in her analysis of the figuring of national space through familial and domestic imagery, Anne McLintock notes that:

> The term nation derives from natio: to be born – we speak of nations as 'motherlands' and 'fatherlands'. Foreigners 'adopt' countries that are not their native homes and are nationalised in the 'national family'. We talk of the 'family of nations' of 'homelands' and 'native' lands. In Britain, immigration matters are dealt with at the Home Office; in the United States the president and his wife are called the First family.[18]

Participatory models of the media: from ideology to sociability

In his analysis of the socialising function of broadcasting, Scannell argues that radio and television 'brought into being a culture in common to whole populations and a shared life of a quite new kind'.[19] In an extension of this argument Stuart Hall argues that the BBC did not in any way simply reflect the make-up of a pre-existing nation, but rather was 'an instrument, an apparatus, a "machine" through which the nation was constituted. It produced the nation which it addressed: it constituted its audience by the ways in which it represented them.'[20] In his recent work, Scannell has done much to extend and further develop his earlier influential analysis of the role of broadcast scheduling in the temporal structuring of public experience.[21] Ultimately, he links this structuring to Braudel's concept of the *longue dureé* of historical time, as opposed to the *histoire évenémentielle* of the everyday world of events – in relation to which, as Braudel puts it, the 'newspaper offers us all the mediocre accidents of everyday life'.[22] For Scannell, the important contrast is between the flux of the ever changing contents of the media (and of that daily life itself, on which the media report) and the relatively unchanging nature of the stable structures which contain and frame these events. The issue is then how these basic structures themselves are continually reproduced over time.

One of broadcasting's principal achievements lies in the way it links the 'biography' of an occasion or event with the 'geography of situation' of its audiences.[23] The broadcast schedules become so much a part of the audience's everyday domestic routines that change to them can be the occasion of some personal distress for audience members – as witnessed by the comments earlier on the importance of the shipping forecast for many UK radio listeners, and by the outcry of protest that has attended recent changes to the long-established schedules of BBC Radio 4. In order to achieve this degree of intimacy with their audiences, Scannell argues, broadcasters have had to take responsibility for understanding the nature of their audience's domestic circumstances and have had to learn to produce their materials in forms fitted to the circumstances of their audiences' lives and concerns. If the development of broadcasting had involved the 'socialisation of the private sphere' it has, correspondingly, also involved what David Cardiff had described as the 'domestication of public utterance'.[24]

For Scannell, broadcasting is not simply involved in ordinary life but (at least in part) constitutive of it. He follows Harvey Sacks' argument that being an 'ordinary person' involves, among other things, a certain amount of daily television viewing, which is performed, at least in part, so as to be 'among those who have seen' in Claus Dieter Rath's terms.[25] To this extent, anyone who is unable (e.g. some categories of prisoners who have been deprived of the privilege of television viewing as punishment for some misdemeanour) or unwilling (some eccentrics) to do this may well be deemed not to attain full membership of the culture. Cultural citizenship, it transpires, entails responsibilities (to have seen crucial television broadcasts) as well as entitlements. Rather than conceiving of cultural citizenship as a simple binary in/out mechanism, we might do better to think of it as a graduated incline, in which fuller membership depends, among other things, on particular types and amounts of media consumption. However, for Scannell, it is, above all, the temporality of broadcasting which is the key to its understanding. On the one hand, this is the production for the audience community of a patterned temporal regularity at a calendical level, as broadcasting marks (and helps construct) the annual regular festivals and occasions of the culture's yearly, seasonal and weekly cycles. On the other hand, it also involves the continual reproduction of the temporal structure of everyday life at a quotidian level, or as Scannell puts it, the production of a sense of 'dailiness' which 'retemporises time', in 'an endless . . . narrative of days and their dailiness . . . attending to the present moment and producing it as the moment it is . . . "time to get up" . . . or whatever . . . orienting . . . [the audience] to the day today'.[26]

James Carey observes that Benedict Anderson's analysis was decisive in offering us a model of the nation as a sociological organism that moves calendically through a homogeneous time – which is not simply historical time, but media time.[27] This social community is effectively united by the production of a shared sense of reality, which is materially inscribed in the dailiness of the newspaper or media broadcast. In a similar vein Rath argues that the broadcasting of a live media event:

> guarantees our being in time, or being up to date . . . live television thereby functions as an apparatus of synchronisation . . . from the angle of the viewer, the apparently empty time of his or her everyday life is transformed into 'full' time – time filled by public or publicised . . . 'significant' events . . . the viewer becomes part of the social fabric . . . The viewer's life becomes a story . . . [and] the individual . . . appears as part of a symbolic structure.[28]

In all this, the news of the public world of the centres of economic power and political control is woven into the fabric of our ordinary days, as broadcasting articulates the spheres of private and public life for its audiences.

In relation to these issues I am very much in sympathy with much of Scannell's approach. I have argued elsewhere for the need to complement the analysis of the vertical dimension of media power with a corresponding analysis of the horizontal dimension of the media's ritual functions, in organising its audience's participation in various forms of collective life.[29] The difficulty is that, for Scannell, it seems that it is not so much a question of developing any such complementary, or multi-dimensional model of analysis but, rather more simply (especially in his 'Public service broadcasting and modern life') of entirely replacing the vertical dimension of analysis with the horizontal and of 'correcting' cultural studies' (apparent) errors, in focusing, so much as it has done, on the media's ideological role and on the politics of representation. That is, for Scannell, an approach which 'systematically misunderstands and misrecognises its object', and he argues that broadcasting is not to be understood as any

> form of social control . . . cultural standardisation or ideological misrepresentation . . . [but] as a public good that has unobtrusively contributed to the democratisation of everyday life most notably through its promotion of a 'communicative ethos' of more inclusive and extensive forms of sociability among its audiences.[30]

While the rather shrill tone of denunciation employed in this attack on cultural studies is somewhat muted in Scannell's later work, the realm of power and politics is still simply set aside there, in favour of a phenomenological analysis of the media's contribution to the production of 'ordinary *unpolitical* daily life'.[31] Thus, Scannell explains that the starting point and clear focus for his approach is what he calls 'the sociable dimension of radio and television broadcasting as its basic communicative ethos'.[32] If this was all there was to it, while I might personally feel unable to share Scannell's desire to simply set aside the vocabulary of power and politics, I could nonetheless applaud the elegance of many of his analyses of the dynamics of the programme forms and genres he studies. However, even on his own terms, and focusing exclusively on the question of broadcasting's role in the inculcation of sociability, there is a major difficulty with Scannell's Panglossian approach. Sociability is simply not the indivisible Good which Scannell assumes it to be. By the very way (and to the very extent that) a programme signals to members of some groups that it is designed for them and functions as an effective invitation to their participation in social life, it will necessarily signal to members of other groups that it is not for them and, indeed, that they are not among the invitees to its particular forum of sociability. Only a programme constructed within the terms of some form of cultural Esperanto could hope to appeal equally to all, without favour or division. Sociability, by definition, can only ever be produced in some particular cultural (and linguistic) form – and only those with access to the relevant forms of cultural capital will feel interpellated by and at home within the particular form of sociability offered by a given programme.

On some occasions this might be a matter of gender or of generation, on others a matter of class. Thus, Suzanne Moore reports the views of Anthony Smith, an influential figure in the world of British broadcasting, who confessed himself unable to watch daytime television talk shows, featuring ordinary people such as those hosted by Oprah, Jerry Springer or, in the UK, Vanessa Feltz. The ostensible reason for Smith's unease, it seemed, was his (somewhat patrician) concern that the people on these shows were being exploited, notwithstanding their own willingness (and indeed, enthusiasm) to appear on the shows (presumably from Smith's point of view, they were suffering from some form of false consciousness, in this respect). However, one could take the view that the problem was rather that the form of sociability offered by these shows just failed to fit with the cultural predilections of someone of Smith's background. To him, the shows' invitation to this particular form of sociability clearly seems either grotesque or offensive.

Moore concludes ironically that perhaps from the point of view of those such as Anthony Smith, it 'would be better if ordinary people were banned from our screens altogether and then we could just convince ourselves that the world really is (exclusively) populated by articulate, rational, middle class types'. As for the question of why people volunteer to appear on these shows, Moore points to the simple but powerful capacity of the media to offer these participants some form of recognition, however perverse, of their existence. As she notes,

> ordinary people enjoy appearing on television enormously, even if they come across as mad, bad or sad. They video themselves with pride. Why? Because somehow appearing on television feels more real to them than their real lives. Rightly or wrongly, it is a vindication, a validation that they are somebody.[33]

As an answer to the potentially puzzling question as to why people are often eager to appear on talk shows, given how humiliating the situations on such shows can be, Margaret Morse similarly offers an explanation in terms of television's ability to confer confirmation on whoever appears on its screen. As she puts it,

> perhaps even a minor role of being bad on television is good, a kind of confirmation that, yes, one has lived or even mattered in the social drama; the largely thwarted desire to speak and to be recognised and to know and be known is such a powerful motivating force in ordinary social life that any context serves better than oblivion.[34]

However, Moore's point goes further. If Smith is offended by (and/or feels excluded from) this kind of representation of working-class life and culture, there are others who are correspondingly offended by or excluded from the forms of sociability offered by the kinds of programming which someone like Smith probably regards as 'normal' and with which he feels more 'at home'. Thus Moore herself notes that she has never been able to listen, without unease, to Radio 4, as the 'relentless middlebrowness' of its population, she says, 'makes me want to join Class War'.[35] The question is always which forms of sociability feel foreign to whom. Any one form of sociability must have its constitutive outside, some necessary field of exclusions by which the collective identity of those whom it interpellates successfully is defined.

The question of the necessary limits of sociability can also sometimes take a starker form, in relation to the politics of representation of which Scannell is so dismissive. Thus, in his analysis of what he describes as broadcasting's role in the production of 'the merely sociable', he argues that 'public displays of sociability on radio and television . . . provide models of appropriate behaviour . . . [and] affirm that interaction with and between strangers can be not merely non-threatening but positively enjoyable and relaxing'.[36] The difficulty here is perhaps best captured to referring to Alec Hargreaves' work on the representation of immigrants on French television.[37] The whole force of Hargreaves' analysis is that, on the whole, immigrants only get to appear on French television in genres associated with problems and conflict, such as news and current affairs. Correspondingly, they are largely excluded from what Hargreaves calls the spaces or genres of conviviality, such as game shows, quiz shows and the like.[38] By the same token, of course, those who do not see themselves represented in such shows can hardly be expected to be effectively interpellated by them or to feel much of an identification with the culture that they represent. In France, at least, it seems, there are limits to how strange a stranger can be, if broadcasting is still to offer the kind of positive model of interaction which Scannell unproblematically assumes it to do for all, as a matter of course. But broadcasting only does that within the limits of normality – and it is precisely the question of how those limits are reproduced, reconstructed (or transformed) over time that is precluded by Scannell's dismissal of politics.

Beyond the singular public sphere?

My discussion of the work of Scannell, and the joint work of Dayan and Katz has thus far not questioned one of the major premises on which much of their work is based – that there indeed is a public sphere, in the singular, and that it is a Good Thing. As indicated above, I have high regard for some aspects of the contributions made by these scholars to our understanding of how mediated public spheres work, especially in relation to their role in the articulation and synchronisation of the public and the private. However, underlying all this work are certain premises derived from the authors' appropriation of a Habermasian model of the public which do stand in need of interrogation. Thus, for example, I would argue that, despite Scannell's attempts to distance himself from Habermas, his own model of the role of broadcasting in the construction of an undifferentiated sense of sociability replicates, if in a different form, one of the most problematic features of Habermas' model.[39]

The basic narrative of Habermas' work on the public sphere can be argued to represent a 'tragic rise and fall myth' in which that sphere is seen to have arisen in reaction to the limits of an old aristocratic culture but then to have been corrupted by the artificialities of our contemporary mediatised world. In this model the contemporary media function as a corrupting influence on the supposedly 'pristine state of rational openness in which citizens once communicated transparently'.[40] To this extent Habermas' work has been recruited into a kind of conventional wisdom, as Paolo Carpignano et al. describe it, in which public life is seen as having been corrupted by a process of commodification, resulting in a 'form of communication increasingly based on emotionally charged images rather than on rational discourse, such that political discourse has been degraded to the level of entertainment and cultural consumerism has been substituted for democratic participation'.[41] In this narrative, as Bruce Robbins notes, the media are held to have corrupted the habits of self-reliant critical thought, which are taken to be the foundation of democracy. However, there is a substantial problem with the nostalgic model of the Good Old Days of nineteenth-century liberalism, from which the 'Fall of Public Man' (in Richard Sennett's phrase) is calibrated. There may be good reasons to suggest that the 'mythic town square in the sky' in which the sovereign and omnicompetent citizens of liberal democracy were imagined to have conducted their business was, in reality, a 'phantasmagoria: an agora (public forum, assembly) that is only a phantasm'.[42] Similarly, Jacques Derrida argues that public opinion, while being constantly cited or ventriloquised by politicians, pollsters and others, is in effect a spectre which is never actually present in any particular place and is best understood perhaps as 'the silhouette of a phantom'.[43]

The central problem with this phantasmagoria, Robbins argues, is best revealed by posing the simple question of for whom the public sphere is supposed to have previously operated more democratically than it does now. As he puts it,

> Was it ever open to the scrutiny and participation, let alone under the control, of the majority? Was there ever a time when intellectuals were really authorised to speak to the people as a whole about the(ir) interests . . . If so, where were the workers, the women, the lesbians, the gay men, the African-Americans?[44]

The appropriate response, according to Robbins, is to try to get away from the unhappy lament for some lone, lost, idealised single public and to accept that 'no sites are inherently or eternally public'. Instead, we must pay attention to 'the actual multiplicity of distinct and overlapping public discourses [and] public spheres that already exist . . . in diverse forms . . . [as] a multitudinous presence among the conditions of postmodern life', but which are actually screened from view by the idealisation of the single public sphere of the Habermasian tradition.[45] We must recognise the constitutive exclusions on which the definition of the classical public sphere was based – not least those which, as Rosalyn Deutsche among others has argued, in effect defined it as a masculine gendered sphere.[46] We need to pay attention to the role of a variety of alternative public spheres and counterpublics based on divisions of ethnicity, 'race', generation, region, religion or class.[47] As we shall see later, we shall also need to abandon the Habermasian assumption that the public sphere is necessarily (or intrinsically) national in scope and address the issues raised by the existence of cross-cutting transnational and diasporic public spheres. In the end the issue is also one of creating public spheres which are open to the expression of agonistic difference as the core of the democratic process.[48]

The masculine public

Nancy Fraser rightly argues that not only does Habermas' account idealise the liberal public sphere, but that it is because he fails to examine other non-liberal, non-bourgeois, competing public spheres – what she calls subaltern counterpublics – that he ends up idealising the uninterrogated class- and gender-based assumptions of the claim that the bourgeois public ever fully represented the public in the singular. In the first place, Fraser argues, the bourgeois republican public sphere rested on and was constituted by a set of masculinist assumption in its very definition of the topics and modes of rational debate appropriate to that sphere, despite its rhetoric of accessibility and openness. As she observes, the network of philanthropic, civic and professional clubs and associations that constituted the basis of the liberal public sphere in Europe was far from accessible to everyone by virtue of these exclusions and was, in effect, 'the arena, the training ground and eventually the power base of a stratum of bourgeois men'.[49] Conversely, in her analysis of contemporary cultural politics in Egypt, Lila Abu-Lughod argues that television has had a profoundly democratising effect in so far as it gives access to 'stories of other worlds' to women, the young and the rural illiterates as well as to urban men. Echoing Meyrowitz, Abu-Lughod argues that television's central importance is that it 'brings a variety of vivid experiences of the non-local into the most local of situations, the home'. Thus, she notes, when someone like the Nobel prize-winning author Naguib Mahfouz laments the decline of the traditional public sphere, in the form of the Cairo coffee house, where people would go to listen to storytellers, he 'forgets that this older form of entertainment, with the imaginary non-local worlds it conjured up, was only available to men'.[50]

Fraser argues that Habermas and his followers ignore not only the existence of competing and alternative public spheres but also the evidence that relations between them and the bourgeois public were relations of power and conflict, in which the representatives of the bourgeois sphere combated the critiques of its exclusionary nature and blocked demands for wider social participation, as much as they combated absolutism and traditional authority. From Fraser's point of view, these exclusions were always constitutive of the bourgeois conception of the public sphere, so that we need to see it not so much as a utopian ideal which happens not yet to have achieved its full realisation, but as 'a masculinist ideological notion that functioned to legitimate an emergent form of class rule'.[51] For Iris Marion Young, the effective exclusion of women from the universalist model of the public sphere, far from being accidental, follows directly from the equation of masculinity with the (unmarked, invisible) category of the normal (or the rational) and of women, by contrast with the particular, the self-interested or the merely private. The civic public is identified with the general interest or the impartial viewpoint of Reason, as expressed, equally ideally, by a self which has 'no particular history, is a member of no communities . . . [and] has no body'.[52] This means that, given the equation of the realm of femininity with the spheres of desire, affectivity and the body (by opposition to which Reason is constituted) this civic public is a masculine one by definition, from which femininity is excluded as a matter of principle. As Michael Warner notes in his commentary on Pier Paolo Pasolini's observation (made shortly before his murder) that 'tolerance is always and purely nominal', the bourgeois public sphere has, from the outset, always been structured by a logic of abstraction which systematically privileges the normalised (unmarked or disincorporated) male white middle-class heterosexual body.[53] At the same time, this discourse exercises a minoritising logic of domination, in which to be particular (and thus visible) is always to be something less than fully public, whether the particular minority concerned is tolerated or condemned.

In her critique of Habermas' public sphere theory, Joke Hermes also points to the gender-blindness of the dominant models, which unproblematically equate citizenship with masculinity as the unmarked norm, against which femininity is defined by its defects. To this extent, Hermes argues, what has been called the 'Public Knowledge' project in media studies is badly compromised by its masculinist premises – which can be traced back to its equation of femininity with the negative characteristics of 'passivity, emotionalism, irrationality, gullibility, consumerism . . . all those things . . . that . . . clash with honest politics and upright citizenship and . . . can be characterised as deviations from the male norm'.[54] At a more concrete level, Fraser observes that the rhetoric of the public sphere has traditionally functioned to exclude issues of concern to many women from public debate by casting them as personal matters, beyond the realm of public, political debate. As she notes, a viable conception of the public sphere would necessitate the inclusion of all the issues and interests such as these which are labelled private and treated as ipso facto inadmissible by bourgeois masculinist ideology. In this connection we might usefully return to consider the role of the television talk show as a particular form of public sphere.

Drawing on Masciorotte's work on *The Oprah Winfrey Show*, Hermes argues that such shows represent the embodiment of a distinctively feminine perspective in popular discourse which is disruptive of conventional standards of rational discussion in the public sphere. Hermes thus argues that such shows, with their 'participatory chaos and spectacular emotionalism . . . multiple points of view, rather than arguments pro or contra, deferring solutions or closure', represent a significant feminisation of the previously unrecognised masculinism of the culture of citizenship.[55] Certainly, Oprah Winfrey herself has been quoted as claiming that 'we do programme these shows to empower women', and Masciorotte claims that 'talk shows afford women the political gesture of overcoming their alienation through talking about their particular experience as women in society'.[56] In relation to their formal characteristics, Livingstone reports that women viewers among their audiences are less likely than men to find such talk shows problematically chaotic in their presentation, and also less likely than male viewers to side with the experts, against the perspective of the ordinary people on the shows.[57] As we have seen earlier, these shows tend to be perceived by many commentators as representing a regrettable bowdlerisation of properly informed public debate. However, historically, these shows were also the arena in which many social problems, which had been traditionally designated as merely 'women's issues' (such as domestic violence and eating disorders, for example), were first given public voice. To this extent, such shows can be seen to have performed a valuable function as a feminised counterpublic. This is not to suggest that 'subaltern counterpublics are always necessarily virtuous'. As Fraser observes, some are explicitly anti-democratic and anti-egalitarian, and it is easy to think of examples of talk shows that mobilise explicitly reactionary forms of public opinion. Nonetheless, whatever liberals may think of the views expressed on such shows, they are, Fraser argues, properly part of our public life – 'parallel discursive arenas, where members of subordinated social groups invent and circulate counter-discourses, so as to formulate oppositional interpretations of their identities, interests and needs'.[58]

Against the criticisms made by many liberal commentators of the television talk show's supposedly exploitative nature and its reduction of rational discussion to the mere spectacle of dramatic conflict, Carpignano et al. argue that the talk show represents an important structural transformation of the conventional divisions between the producers and consumers of culture, and between the expert, or professional authority, and the lay audience. To this extent, they claim, these shows represent a 'contested space in which new discursive practices are developed in contrast to the traditional modes of political and ideological representation'.[59] In so far as these shows provide 'a forum for the disenfranchised . . . who are not represented in the current know-ledge-based community culture', they function as empowering contexts for minority and margin-alised discourses. The central thrust of their argument is that in previous eras and in other genres, the public has only tended to appear on television anonymously – as the audible public of a sit-com soundtrack; as the visible but inarticulate and de-individualised public of televised sports events; as 'real people' in unusual (and normally humorous) situations, on shows such as Candid Camera; or as ventriloquised vox pop representations of public opinion in news and documentary program-ming. Only in the talk show does 'the public gain full recognition . . . in . . . the role of protagonist', where the show is not simply put on for the public, but is 'constructed around the audience . . . [with] the camera . . . as the instrument of the viewers' presence . . . and the public . . . literally centre-stage'.[60] This is a quite new form of mediated public sphere which, if fractious and sensationalist, nonetheless allows previously disenfranchised sections of the population to be the public stars of their own show.

By contrast to the enthusiasm of Carpignano et al., Sonia Livingstone and Peter Lunt, on the basis of their empirical investigation of participants in and viewers of UK television talk shows, seem ultimately to be equivocal about their role. While they recognise that such shows give voice to ordinary people, they point out that this is not necessarily to be equated with giving them power over 'real decision-making and power relations' and may, indeed (to return to the terms of Habermas' original critique) perhaps amount to no more than 'the illusion of participation' in public affairs. After all, they observe, their participation only occurs in a heavily managed forum in what, in the end, remains 'a bounded region of access . . . in a particular region of television', which is, they argue, ultimately 'a backwater, a trivial and unimportant realm'.[61] However, despite such scepticism, one can argue that the rise of the talk show, with its carnivalesque and dialogic qualities, in which a wide range of voices clamours for expression (based on the authority of their own lived experience, challenging the monophonic authority of the experts who would claim to speak in their names), has rather to be seen as part of the long-term process in which the voices of those who were historically drowned out by the patriarchal and imperialist metanarratives of modernism are finally allowed to speak in public.[62] Of course, beyond this there remains the further question of the relations of power which set the terms within which these voices are represented, or allowed to represent themselves.

The need for a variety of counterpublics is premised on the recognition that public spheres themselves are not spaces of zero-degree culture, equally hospitable to any form of cultural expression. To return to my earlier critique of Scannell's over-simplistic model of the media, as producing some indivisible form of sociability, equally inviting and accessible to all, we have to recognise that public media necessarily function as 'culturally specific rhetorical lenses that filter and alter the utterances they frame; they can accommodate some expressive models and not others'.[63] To this extent, an egalitarian multicultural society depends on the creation and maintenance of a plurality of public arenas in which a wide range of groups, with a diverse range of values and rhetorics, can effectively participate.

The whiteness of the public sphere[64]

If the national media constitute the public sphere which is most central in the mediation of the nation-state to the general public, then whatever is excluded from those media is in effect excluded from the symbolic culture of the nation. When the culture of that public sphere (and thus of the nation) is in effect 'racialised' by the naturalisation of one (largely unmarked and undeclared) form of ethnicity, then only some citizens of the nation find it a homely and welcoming place. The imagined community is, in fact, usually constructed in the language of some particular ethnos, membership of which then effectively becomes a prerequisite for the enjoyment of a political citizenship within the nation-state. On this argument, the Englishness of the public sphere in the UK is its most crucial characteristic. For George Orwell, the English are most quintessentially so in the diversity of their everyday leisure activities at home:

> We are a nation of flower-lovers, but also a nation of stamp-collectors, pigeon fanciers, amateur carpenters, coupon snippers, darts-players, crossword-puzzle fans. All the culture that is most truly native centres round things which even when they are communal are not official – the pub, the football match, the back garden, the fireside and the 'nice cup of tea'. The liberty of the individual is still believed in, almost as in the nineteenth century, but this has nothing to do with economic liberty, the right to exploit others for profit. It is the liberty to have a home of your own, to do what you like in your spare time, to choose your own amusements instead of having them chosen for you from above.[65]

But this is not a merely domestic issue. The public sphere of national broadcast culture is the place where Englishness is then articulated and reflected back to the domestic audience in its own leisure time. Much of popular television is given over precisely to reflecting back to the audience an image of the nation as comprised of a vast range of individualities, eccentrics, hobbies, local and regional traditions – out of whose very differences the unity of the nation is secured symbolically. As Brunsdon and I have argued in our retrospective comments on our earlier analysis of the television magazine *Nationwide*'s presentation of ordinary life, what that programme can actually be seen to have been primarily engaged in was 'the construction of a particular type of white lower middle class national (ethnic) identity as Englishness'.[66] As we have seen, in Scannell's argument, the broadcast schedule is assumed to construct a domesticated public life in common for the whole population, allowing them to then feel at home in this mediated public sphere. In his insightful analysis of the transcript of the *Harry Hopeful* radio show in Britain in the mid-1930s, Scannell observes that in the voice of an elderly member of the public who appears on the programme, 'Miss Lomas', what he hears above all is an expression of 'a rootedness in time and place, a secure achieved identity'. However, one could suggest that what Scannell actually hears (although he fails to register it) is precisely an expression of a secure ethnic identity, which he shares with the speaker and which is so taken-for-granted as to be invisible. However, its invisibility (or – better, in the context – inaudibility) should not be mistaken for its absence.[67] Once we recognise Englishness itself as an ethnicity, we see that not everyone can feel at home in the public sphere, in an easy, naturalised way, as opposed to feeling particularised and, at best, tolerated (as others) within it. Indeed, one could argue that it is precisely through the orchestration of the vernacular forms of English ethnicity that broadcasting has embedded itself in the ordinary lives of the population and thus domesticated a particular ethnic version of the nation.[68]

Conventionally, only minorities have been understood to possess or inhabit ethnicities (which can be tolerated so long as they are confined to the private sphere of family and community) whereas the dominant/majority culture is presented as if it were universal (or modern, by contrast to the 'traditional' ways of ethnic peoples). Once ethnicity has thus been confined to the private sphere, which is where it is seen to be reproduced, the political realm can then be presented as if it were not simply white, but colourless, or ethnically neutral.[69] As Catherine Hall has argued, 'the recognition that Englishness is an ethnicity, just like any other, demands a decentring of the English imagination. For ethnicities have been constructed as belonging to "others", not to the norm, which is English.'[70] The difficulty in this matter is exactly the same as that involved in recognising 'whiteness' as a particular (rather than the absence of) colour. As Richard Dyer argues, whiteness when universalised disappears:

> in the realm of categories, black is always marked as a colour . . . and is always particular-
> ising; whereas white is not anything really, not an identity, not a particularising quality
> because it is everything – white is no colour because it is all colours. This property of
> whiteness, to be everything and nothing, is the source of its representational power.[71]

Scannell's celebration of broadcasting as a public good, 'a culture in common to whole populations'[72] which needs to be defended against the fragmenting forces of deregulation, simply fails to recognise that this public culture itself is already an ethnic culture and has a colour which is only common to some of the citizens of the nation which it supposedly reflects, and which it attempts to address. As Yasmin Alibhai-Brown has remarked, the most influential programmes on British television and radio still remain predominantly white.[73]

White broadcasting in the UK

> If you flick through the national channels for ten minutes, everything is White, White, White.[74]

In his research on the development of debates about 'race' and ethnicity in British broadcasting, Arun Kundnani has traced the ways in which, from the Annan Committee's deliberations in 1977 on the need for broadcasting to better reflect the pluralism of British culture, so as to serve minority groups' 'special needs' (including those of ethnic minorities), through to the enshrine- ment of multiculturalism within the brief of Channel Four, when it was established in the early 1980s, the media have been seen by black critics as orchestrating a largely white perspective which is out of step with the UK's development as a multicultural society.[75] By the time that Channel Four was launched, in the wake of the riots in black areas of many British cities in 1981, the connection between debates about the racialisation of geographical space and the racialisation of the airwaves had become much more apparent. As Kundnani observes, if we understand the media as layers of public space that extend and connect with geographical space, then the demands for better, fuller and more varied representation of black and Asian peoples on and in the British media have to be seen as continuous with the parallel demands for less discriminatory policing of public and private space.[76] Kundnani argues that what we need, in this respect, is a 'history of broadcasting that parallels the history of space, understood in terms of movement . . . ghettoisation, policing of boundaries, mobility out of boundaries and consolidation within them'.[77]

Certainly the Home Secretary at the time of the riots in the UK in 1981, William Whitelaw, understood the connection between real and symbolic geographies only too well. If the price of keeping black people off the streets of Brixton and Toxteth after the 1981 riots was their greater visibility on the screens of the nation (or at least, on some of those screens, at marginal times, on Channel Four) this was evidently a price he was happy to pay.[78] Thus Angela Barry notes that if the images of the black teenage rioter 'slotted easily into the spaces formerly occupied by the mugger and the . . . immigrant', their appearance on British television screens in the early 1980s nonetheless ran in parallel with a sudden increase in the number of black faces making more respectable television appearances. As she puts it,

> in that same year, in those same organisations, a curious thing happened – Moira Stewart began to read prime time news; *Nationwide* seized upon a black female presenter, Maggie Nelson; on ITV, Trevor McDonald became more visible. The BBC introduced *Ebony*, a programme for Afro-Caribbean viewers.[79]

As Paul Gilroy noted at the time, 'the storm which swept through Britain's inner cities in July 1981' was also 'the wind which blew black television onto our screens'.[80]

The question then also arises as to whether a greater presence of minorities (of all types) in the (singular) public sphere is a sufficient remedy to our existing difficulties, or whether we might be better advised to consider the various ways in which (and the sites on which) a variety of alternative, independent or oppositional public spheres might be created in a genuinely multicultural society.[81] For some people Channel Four in the UK was seen, at its inception, as the potential institutional site of such an alternative public sphere, though many have had their hopes disappointed by the channel's subsequent performance overall, notwithstanding its occasional brave forays into difficult territory.[82] In 1999 the channel's Chief Executive, Michael Jackson, declared that the channel no longer wished to be seen as 'a minority channel for minority audiences', as he felt that British culture had now 'moved on', to the point where concerns of ethnically (or sexually) defined minorities were now so much more a part of mainstream culture that a strategy of ghetto broadcasting was anachronistic. The difficulty, from the point of view of Jackson's critics such as Clive Jones, Chief Executive of Carlton Communication, is that, in the end, honourable exceptions notwithstanding, 'television is still White Anglo-Saxon, Britain is not'.[83]

In this connection the recent report on ethnic minority views of British television by Annabelle Sreberny concluded that television is still lagging behind current social developments by failing to reflect the multicultural nature of the country.[84] One substantial criticism that emerges in that report is that still today, on the whole, British television fiction offers only a limited and stereotyped representation of characters from ethnic minorities, so that they still carry the 'burden of representation' of portraying social problems, rather than being presented as rounded persons, as white actors more commonly are. In their earlier report on black minority viewers' responses to British television, Sreberny and her colleague Karen Ross similarly reported that a significant number of African-Caribbeans preferred imported American programming to British, because 'American programmes more routinely use the principle of integrated casting, so characters are not always acting their skin'.[85] Similarly, the migrant Asian community which Gillespie studied in the mid-1980s felt ill-served by the broadcasting media, and for that reason had a particular interest in video, cable and satellite media.[86] In the same vein, the father in one middle-class British Asian family in Moores' study in the early 1990s much prefers Sky television news to that of the BBC – precisely because of the non-Britishness of the newsreaders' mode of address on Sky. As he puts it, with the BBC, you always feel as though the structure of society is there – the authority. Their newsreaders speak just like schoolmasters . . . 'telling' the kids. I think Sky News has more of a North American approach. It's more relaxed. They treat you like equals and don't take the audience for a bunch of small kids.[87]

In this case, his preference for Sky is produced by his dis-identification with the BBC, precisely in so far as he sees the latter as the embodiment of the white British Establishment and its values.[88]

Despite the recent mainstream success of the *Goodness Gracious Me* series on BBC 2, featuring a British Asian cast, the majority of the UK's Asian population still feels largely excluded from British television. In this context it is perhaps not surprising that, according to a survey of British viewers conducted by the Independent Television Commission in 1994, both Asian and Afro-Caribbean households were more likely than British viewers in general to subscribe to satellite or cable television stations.[89] That report concluded that members of ethnic minorities were considerably less satisfied than the general population with the programme services provided on terrestrial television. They were much more likely to regard those channels as biased against their interests and to regard cable and satellite programming as preferable, overall, to that on terrestrial channels (specifically among Asian households, targeted channels such as Zee TV, Asianet and now B4U – Bollywood For You; and among African-Caribbean households, channels such as BET International).

The study of ethnic minority views of British broadcasting conducted by James Halloran *et al.* in 1995 also reported considerable dissatisfaction. One respondent felt that 'Television is not doing well for us [Gujeratis] – not enough programmes for the Asian community'; another said that 'the Asian community is not getting value for money from any channel'; another that 'there is not much for ethnic minorities in television', that 'there is nothing – they only know about Diwali, and that only on the news for a few minutes'; yet another that 'TV doesn't really portray us' (Bengali-speakers).[90] These findings were confirmed by Sreberny and Ross' study in the same year, where one of their respondents said, 'as it is today the BBC are not providing anything for us, so why pay [the licence fee]? If I could opt out I'd do it today.'[91] As another respondent put it, 'I feel cheated. They're asking for £90 a year and you just watch "mainstream" [white] stuff all the time – or you pay more to get cable and see the American stuff – it's much better for ethnic minorities.' The key issue was that respondents felt that 'American cable has channels dedicated to black programmes. You can see the difference in quality, with situations that black people can relate to.'[92] At its simplest, from this point of view, as an Asian viewer put it in Sreberny's later study, 'on Asianet, on cable, they have more realistic images'.[93]

A Bangladeshi group in Burnley interviewed by Sreberny and Ross similarly expressed strong preference for cable and satellite services. In their view, as 'these new cable companies have got Asian programmes, the BBC will have to catch up . . . Compared with cable the BBC is forty years behind'. As one of them puts it, 'I've got to spend £15 a month to see my favourite programmes because the BBC aren't up to it'. Another explains that 'since it's been installed, everybody is subscribing to cable and that's . . . £15 or £30 a month' but, as he said, 'that's for thirty channels to choose from, including Asianet'.[94] In the light of these comments Sreberny and Ross concluded that

instead of complaining, or simply switching off, many black minority viewers are registering their protest silently by subscribing to new cable and satellite services . . . The success of these alternative media bears eloquent testimony to the consummate dissatisfaction that many black minorities feel with terrestrial television.[95]

Four years later, at the time of Sreberny's repeat study, 36 per cent of the ethnic minority viewers in her sample had subscribed to either cable or satellite services – certainly a higher figure than for the UK population overall.[96] In that 1999 study, Sreberny quotes the same refrain of complaint heard over the years: 'We pay for Zee TV and cable TV because we want more of our programmes – for the money . . . they [the BBC] aren't giving us enough.' To this extent many ethnic minority groups clearly continue to feel that they need satellite and cable services because they are ill-serviced by terrestrial television – a situation, as we shall see later, with ready parallels in other countries.[97]

New public spheres also arise and are sustained in different ways, in particular local circumstances, and often involve a recombination of the physical and virtual geographies of community. Black and Asian pirate radio stations in London are frequently structured around the active participation of listening groups, via phoned-in dedications, and 'shout-outs' to their local 'crews' and 'massives'. These practices are perhaps best understood as a ritualistic process of continuous re-confirmation of a virtual community of listeners, through the recitation of their names and of their familiar local landmarks and symbols. Through this process, the listeners are granted (and grant each other) recognition as members of this virtual community, which is overlaid on the geographical space of their lives. As one listener to a London pirate radio station put it,

> It's so down to earth. You hear people that sound like you on the radio, which is unbelievable and [you can] relate to that. [You] know the DJs aren't changing their voice to sound more 'street'. If you know a station's coming out of your area, you feel close to it and want to support it.[98]

In a similar spirit, in relation to these questions of recognition, Trevor Phillips explains that, as the producer of the television show *Black on Black*, his decision to use a visible studio audience was informed by the simple but striking fact that he had

> never seen a television programme in this country which brought together a lot of black people in the studio . . . People in this country are afraid of seeing a lot of black people together. They think we're going to riot, or eat somebody, or something.

As he explains, his purpose in opting for the 'actual visual representation of our community' was to 'give the viewer a sense of solidarity with a community'.[99]

Towards a multi-ethnic public sphere?

As Negt and Kluge remark in their criticisms of the class structure of the public sphere, the claim that it represents the totality of society as an equal, if not homogenous, community cannot be sustained precisely because of its own mechanisms of exclusion. One can not simply bracket status differentials based on ethnicity, class or gender and proceed as if they did not exist. These factors naturally continue to have very real effects – which are all the harder to deal with if their status is not recognised. The problem with attempting to integrate a multi-ethnic society through a single public sphere is that the 'idea of the public as universal and the concomitant identification of particularity with privacy makes homogeneity a requirement of public participation'.[100] To this extent, the dominant group is enabled to monopolise the public sphere in the name of seemingly universal values. The idea that citizens must somehow transcend their particularities in order to participate in the public sphere is, Charles Husband argues, a myth: 'the public sphere that seeks to articulate the public opinion of such a citizenry is already partial and inadequate'. His conclusion is that we must rather 'theorise and realise a politics of citizenship which recognises and empowers difference' – through a variety of particular and differentiated public spheres in the plural.[101]

The difficulty with the conventional view of citizenship is that the idea of the 'same for all' is often translated, in practice, into the requirement that all citizens should be the same. As Young puts it, 'we must develop participatory democratic theory not on the assumption of an undifferentiated humanity, but rather on the assumption that there are group differences and that some groups are actually or potentially oppressed or disadvantaged'.[102] Her argument is that there is a democratic virtue in explicitly recognising difference within a universal formal citizenship. Thus, in his extension of Young's argument towards the specific case of multicultural citizenship, Steven Castles argues for the 'rejection of the conception of all citizens as equal individuals and its replacement by a recognition of all citizens as having equal rights as individuals and different needs and wants as members of groups with specific characteristics and social situations'.[103] It is through a perspective based on premises such as those that we shall perhaps also be best able to arrive at an adequate analysis of the public sphere and of the media's role in it.

Transnational and diasporic public spheres

Thus far, we have considered the limitations of conventional accounts of the public sphere as the national symbolic home from the point of view of those groups whose concerns are not effectively addressed and who do not feel at home within it. However, we must now turn to the question of the extent to which, given the undermining of the nation state by the processes of globalisation, we must also consider the extent to which public spheres are themselves, for many people, transnational in form, as contemporary media enable migrants to sustain up-to-the-minute links with events in their homelands.[104] To attend to the divisions and complexities within the public sphere of any one (imagined) national community is nowadays in itself quite insufficient. Societies all over the world increasingly tend to include a variety of migrant and mobile populations, for whom the public spheres of the host nation in which they geographically reside are far from being the only source of interpellations and identifications. As Dayan puts it, in many places the local has itself become cosmopolitan and 'the masses are no longer confined to the local. They are themselves in motion: they are made of tourists, of television watchers, of *Gastarbeiter*.'[105]

To make these points is not necessarily to fall into some historically naive or uncritical vision in which mediated processes of globalisation are assumed to have entirely swept away national cultures. In this respect, James Curran makes cogent criticisms of the presumption that global television is undermining national cohesion and political participation in some unstoppable process. In broad historical terms, as he observes, television's post-war defeat of cinema (and thus of Hollywood, which had come to dominate world cinema) in terms of overall popularity 'represented a dramatic shift towards the restabilisation of *national* media systems'.[106] Indeed, television, radio and the press are, in most places, still (and despite globalising tendencies) in many respects national media, based on nationally generated content and, where such material is available, majority audiences often prefer it to imported products. However, the difficulty, as we have seen, is that alongside the majority community in many nations, there exist a variety of minorities who often do not feel themselves to be effectively addressed by the discourses of the national media. The members of these diasporic communities are often spread over the geographical territories of various different nation-states, and are typically exposed to a wide range of potential discourses of identity – between which they must choose – or alternate, in different circumstances and on different occasions. As Khaching Tölölyan puts it:

Diasporas have played a major role on both sides of the prolonged struggles between Israelis and Palestinians, as well as in supporting Armenians, Croatians and Chechens in their conflicts. Through television, faxes and electronic mail, the commitments of diasporas are reinvigorated and sometimes polarised by constant contact with their former homes; 'former' no longer means what it did.[107]

Minority and immigrant groups cannot be satisfactorily treated as marginal exceptions to a simple norm of sedentarism. These 'travelling cultures', disassociated from direct territorial inscription, require new models and methods of analysis which focus on the communication networks that sustain them.[108] These networks, which link personal, individual choices to grander, diasporic narratives of identity, are often sustained through a complex mixture of physical mobility (pilgrimages, back and forth travelling, family visits) and symbolic communications through a variety of 'small media' such as exchanges of letters, phone-calls, photographs, and videos.[109] One index of this is the way in which districts of cities with substantial immigrant populations in the UK now tend to feature a plethora of high-street call-centres, offering discount rates for phone calls to the many places that count as home for their residents. Similarly, in Margolis' study of migrants living in 'little Brazil' in New York, it is reported that

> 95 per cent of the immigrants in [the] sample call Brazil on a regular basis . . . they spend sizeable sums on long distance calls; most spend between $85 to $150 a month, while quite a few (sheepishly) admit their bills regularly come to $200 a month or more.[110]

As Roger Rouse observes in his study of Mexican migration patterns referred to earlier,

> Today, Aguilillans find that their most important kin and friends are as likely to be living hundreds or thousands of miles away as immediately around them. More significantly, growing access to the telephone has been particularly significant, allowing people not just to keep in touch periodically, but to contribute to decision-making and participate in familial events from considerable distance.

As Clifford notes in his commentary on Rouse's work, immigrants such as these often establish transregional identities 'maintained through travel and telephone circuits that do not stake everything on an increasingly risky future in a single nation'.[111] Such immigrants often improvise what Aihwa Ong has called forms of flexible citizenship, deterritorialised in relation to any one particular country but highly localised in relation to the places (often in different countries) where the members of their family network live.[112]

In our analysis of all this we must certainly attempt to avoid falling into any kind of romanticisation of mobility *per se*. Nor indeed, in the words of Pheng Cheah's critique of Clifford and Bhabha, should we 'endow cosmopolitan mobility with a normative dimension' which uncritically valorises the often painful nature of diasporic existence, as if it were some kind of state of cultural grace.[113] However, and despite these cautions, it is also true that any analysis of the role of the media in the construction of contemporary cultural identities which assumes the existence of a unified and sedentary population occupying a unitary public sphere, within the secure boundaries of a given geographical territory, is unlikely to be adequate in understanding significant aspects of our contemporary situation.

[. . .]

Notes

1   J. Keane, *The Media and Democracy*, Cambridge, Polity Press, 1991, p. 164.
2   Marista Leishman, *Dictionary of Scottish Biography*, Irvine, Carrick Media, 1999, quoted in the *Guardian*, 5 March 1999; cf. what Richard Sennett called the regressive fantasy or 'wish that diversity and ineradic-able differences should not exist in the home, for the sake of social order'; R. Sennett, *The Uses of Disorder*, London, Faber, 1996, p. 65.
3   M. Phillips, 'Heritage foundations', *New Times*, November, 1999. For my own earlier comments on who feels excluded by or alienated from the world of television current affairs, see my 'Finding out about the world from television news: some difficulties', in J. Gripsrud (ed.), *Television and Common Knowledge*, London, Routledge, 1999.
4   cf. Deborah Ryan, *The Daily Mail Ideal Home Exhibition*, London, University of East London, 1995.
5   Da Matta, quoted in D. Dayan and E. Katz, *Media Events*, Cambridge, Mass., Harvard University Press, 1992, p. 128.
6   Quoted in Dayan and Katz, op. cit., p. 129.
7   P. Scannell, *Radio, Television, and Modern Life*, Oxford, Blackwell, 1996; Orvar Lofgren, 'The nation as home or motel? Metaphors of media and belonging', unpublished paper, Department of European Ethnology, University of Lund, 1995.
8   Lofgren, op. cit., 1995, p. 12; cf. Jesus Martin-Barbero, *Communication, Culture and Hegemony*, London, Sage, 1993, on the role of the media in the construction of a quotidian sense of national life.
9   Coupland, quoted in Lofgren, op. cit., p. 14.
10   Lofgren, op. cit., p. 20.
11   David Chandler, 'Postcards from the edge', in Mark Power, *The Shipping Forecast*, London, Zelda Cheatle Press, 1996, p. i.
12   N. Papastergiadis, *Dialogues in the Diasporas*, London, Rivers Oram Press, 1998, p. 4.
13   Chandler, op. cit., 1996, p. ii.
14   Ambjörnsson, drawing on reminiscences of Swedish radio-listening in the 1940s, quoted in O. Lofgren, 'The nation as home or motel?', p. 26.
15   ibid., p. 27.
16   Berlant, quoted in G. Eley and R. Griger Suny, 'Introduction' to their edited collection *Becoming National*, Oxford, Oxford University Press, 1996, p. 30; see also Lauren Berlant, *Anatomy of a National Fantasy*, Chicago, Chicago University Press, 1991, p. 20.
17   Eley and Suny, op. cit., p. 29.
18   A. McLintock, *Imperial Leather*, London, Routledge, 1995, p. 357.
19   P. Scannell, 'Public service broadcasting and modern life', *Media, Culture and Society*, 1989, vol. 11(2), p. 138.
20   S. Hall, 'Which public, whose service?', in W. Stevenson (ed.), *All our Futures, the Changing Role and Purpose of the BBC*, London, British Film Institute, 1993, p. 32.
21   Scannell, 1996, op. cit.; P. Scannell, 'Radio Times', in P. Drummond and R. Paterson (eds), *Television and its Audience*, London, British Film Institute, 1988.
22   Braudel, quoted in P. Scannell, *Radio, Television and Modern Life*, Oxford, Blackwell, 1996, p. 175.
23   J. Meyrowitz, *No Sense of Place*, Oxford, Oxford University Press, 1985, p. 6.
24   Quoted in P. Scannell, 'Public service broadcasting and modern life', *Media, Culture and Society*, 1989, vol. 11(2), p. 148.
25   H. Sacks, *Lectures on Conversation*, Oxford, Blackwell, 1992; C.D. Rath, 'The invisible network', in P. Drummond and R. Paterson (eds), *Television in Transition*, London, British Film Institute, 1985.
26   Scannell, *Radio, Television and Modern Life*, op. cit., pp. 5 and 149.
27   J. Carey, 'Political ritual television', in T. Liebes and J. Curran (eds), *Media, Ritual and Identity*, London, Routledge, 1998; B. Anderson, *Imagined Communities*, London, Verso, 1983.
28   C.D. Rath, 'Live television and its audiences', in E. Seiter, H. Borschers, G. Kreutzner and E.M. Warth (eds), *Remote Control*, London, Routledge, 1989, pp. 82–3.
29   cf. D. Morley, *Television, Audiences and Cultural Studies*, London, Routledge, 1992.
30   Scannell, 'Public service broadcasting and modern life', op. cit., pp. 158 and 136.
31   Scannell, *Radio, Television and Modern Life*, op. cit., p. 4; original emphasis.
32   ibid., p. 4.
33   S. Moores, 'Don't criticise VictimVision', *Independent*, 8 May 1998. In the same vein, in his comments on his work recording the songs of the American poor for the Library of Congress in the 1930s, Alan

Lomax observed how very much the mere fact of having their songs tape-recorded mattered to the singers that he worked with – see the Notes to the CD *The Alan Lomax Collection*, Rounder Records, 1997.

34   M. Morse, *Virtualities*, Bloomington, Indiana University Press, 1998, p. 46.

35   S. Moores, 'Don't criticise VictimVision', *Independent*, 8 May 1998; as its name implies, 'Class War' is a fundamentalist Marxist organisation in the UK.

36   P. Scannell, 'The merely sociable', University of Westminster, unpublished paper, 1990, p. 20.

37   A. Hargreaves and A. Perotti, 'The representation on French television of immigrants and ethnic minorities', *New Community*, 1993, vol. 19(2). For a detailed discussion of Hargreaves' work, see Chapter 7.

38   For a comparable analysis of the relative visibility of ethnic minorities on British television, see G. Cumberbatch and S. Woods, *Ethnic Minorities on Television*, London, Independent Television Commission, 1996. See also the later section of this chapter on the 'whiteness' of the public sphere.

39   Or 'reasonableness' – cf. Scannell, 'Public service broadcasting and modern life', op. cit., p. 160.

40   Dana Polan, 'The public's fear; or, Media as Monster in Habermas, Negt and Kluge', in B. Robbins (ed.), *The Phantom Public Sphere*, Minneapolis, Minnesota University Press, 1993, p. 36.

41   P. Carpignano, R. Anderson and W. DiFazio, 'Chatter in the Age of Electronic Reproduction' in Robbins (ed.), *The Phantom Public Sphere*, op. cit., p. 93. One of the best-known critiques of Habermas is that by Oskar Negt and Alexander Kluge, who address the question of the limits of Habermasian model and explore the possibilities for the construction of an oppositional, proletarian public sphere in their *Public Sphere and Experience*, Minneapolis, University of Minnesota Press, 1994. Negt and Kluge correctly observe that the bourgeois public sphere was always much more penetrated by the interests of capital than Habermas ever acknowledges. However, there are significant difficulties with their approach, as Polan notes. In the first place there is their romanticisation of the production process and their neglect of the sphere of consumption as an active process. Second, their own perspective is in some ways even bleaker than that of Habermas in their 'image of a contemporary world infiltrated by media at every level'; Polan, op. cit., p. 39.

42   Robbins, 'Introduction', to Robbins (ed.), *The Phantom Public Sphere*, op. cit., pp. viii–ix.

43   Derrida, quoted in Thomas Keenan, 'Windows: of vulnerability', in Robbins (ed.), op. cit., p. 135.

44   Robbins, op. cit., p. viii.

45   Robbins, op. cit., pp. xv and iii.

46   cf. R. Deutsche, 'Men in space', *Artforum*, February, 1990.

47   Thus, to take one historical example, Miriam Hansen suggests that early silent cinema functioned as a kind of proletarian counter-public sphere, in so far as it 'provided a social space, a place apart from the domestic and work spheres, where people of a similar background and status could find company'; Hansen, quoted in Robbins, op. cit., p. xviii.

48   cf. Chantal Mouffe quoted later on this point – see Chapter 8 on 'Community life and communitarianism', p. 190.

49   N. Fraser, 'Rethinking the public sphere', in Robbins (ed.), op. cit., p. 6.

50   L. Abu-Lughod, 'The objects of soap opera: Egyptian TV and the cultural politics of modernity', in D. Miller (ed.), *Worlds Apart*, London, Routledge, 1995, p. 191; J. Meyrowitz, *No Sense of Place*, Oxford, Oxford University Press, 1985.

51   Fraser, op. cit., p. 8.

52   Iris Marion Young, 'Impartiality and the civic public', in S. Benhabib and D. Cornell (eds), *Feminism as Critique*, Minneapolis, University of Minnesota Press, 1987, pp. 59–60.

53   M. Warner, 'The mass public and the mass subject', in Robbins (ed.), op. cit., p. 240.

54   Joke Hermes, 'Gender and media studies: no woman, no cry', in J. Corner, P. Schlesinger and R. Silverstone (eds), *International Media Research*, London, Routledge, 1997, p. 73. On the 'Public Knowledge' project see J. Corner, 'Meaning, genre and context: the problematics of public knowledge', in J. Curran and M. Gurevitch (eds), *Mass Media and Society*, London, Edward Arnold, 1991. I have also addressed the question of 'the gender of the real' in my essay 'To boldly go: the "third generation" of reception studies', in P. Alasuutari (ed.), *Rethinking the Media Audience*, London, Sage, 1999.

55   Hermes, op. cit., p. 87; G.-J. Masciorotte, 'C'mon girl: Oprah Winfrey and the discourse of feminine talk', *Discourse*, 1991, no. 11.

56   Winfrey, quoted in S. Livingstone and P. Lunt, *Talk on Television*, London, Routledge 1994, p. 13; Masciorotte, op. cit., p. 90.

57   S. Livingstone, 'Watching talk', *Media, Culture and Society*, 1994, vol. 16.

58 Fraser, op. cit., pp. 14 and 15.

59 Carpignano *et al.*, op. cit., p. 96.

60 Carpignano *et al.*, op. cit., pp. 109–11.

61 Livingstone and Lunt, op. cit., p. 172.

62 cf. Angela McRobbie, 'Postmodernism and popular culture', *Journal of Communication Inquiry*, 1986, vol. 10(2).

63 Fraser, op. cit., p. 17.

64 In the following section I draw heavily on materials originally collated by my ex-PhD student, Arun Kundnani. I thank him both for access to these materials and for his helpful comments on this chapter. For his later, published, work, see his article 'Where do you want to go today? The rise of information capital', in *Race and Class*, 1998/99, vol. 40(2/3), and his 'Stumbling on: race, class and England', *Race and Class*, Spring 2000, vol. 41(4).

65 G. Orwell, *Inside the Whale and Other Essays*, Harmondsworth, Penguin, 1957, p. 66.

66 D. Morley and C. Brunsdon, 'Introduction' to *The Nationwide Television Studies*, London, Routledge, 1999, p. 12. For the contemporary televisual manifestation of this 'heritage of the oridinary' in the UK, see daytime shows such as the highly successful *This Morning* and its presenters 'Richard and Judy'.

67 cf. P. Scannell, *Radio, Television and Modern Life*, op. cit., p. 37; I am grateful to my colleague, Bill Schwarz for drawing this example to my attention.

68 As Homi Bhabha describes it, in this process 'the scraps, patches and rags of daily life must be repeatedly turned into the signs of a national culture, while the very act of the narrative performance interpellates a growing circle of national subjects'; H. Bhabha, in H. Bhabha (ed.), *Nation and Narration*, London, Routledge, 1990, p. 297.

69 cf. T. Modood, 'The end of a hegemony: from political blackness to ethnic pluralism', paper to Commission for Racial Equality Policy seminar, London, 1995; cf. also Errol Lawrence, 'In the abundance of water the fool is thirsty', in CCCS (ed.) *The Empire Strikes Back*, London, Hutchinson, 1982.

70 C. Hall, *White Male and Middle Class*, Cambridge, Polity Press, 1992, p. 205.

71 R. Dyer, 'White', *Screen*, 1998, vol. 29(4), p. 45.

72 P. Scannell, 'Public service broadcasting and modern public life', in P. Scannell, P. Schlesinger and C. Sparks (eds), *Culture and Power*, London, Sage, 1992, p. 138.

73 Y. Alibhai-Brown, 'Whose Beeb is it anyway?', *Global Thinking: Foreign Policy Centre Newsletter*, London, September, 1999.

74 A. Sreberny, *Include Me In: Rethinking Ethnicity on Television*, London, Broadcasting Standards Council, 1999, p. 27.

75 A. Kundnani, 'Scheduling the nation', unpublished paper, Department of Media and Communications, Goldsmith College, 1995.

76 cf. campaigns about the misuse of the police's 'stop and search' powers – which because of their racist application mean that the physical public sphere is not in fact equally available to all; likewise, campaigning over policing practices which do not extend respect for the privacy of the domestic space to Asians and blacks. On this, see A. Hurtado, 'Relating to privilege: seduction and rejection in the subordination of white women and women of colour', *Signs: Journal of Women in Culture and Society*, 1989, vol. 14(4).

77 Kundani, op. cit., p. 19.

78 cf. Whitelaw's comments, quoted in Lawrence, op. cit., p. 52. On the debates surrounding the establishment of Channel Four, see S. Blanchard and D. Morley (eds), *What's This Channel Fo(u)r?*, London, Comedia, 1982.

79 A. Barry, 'Black mythologies – the representation of black people on British television', in J. Twitchin (ed.), *The Black and White Media Book*; London, Trentham Books, 1988, p. 9.

80 P. Gilroy, 'Channel Four – bridgehead or Bantustan?' in *Screen*, 1982, vol. 24(4), p. 39. On the visibility of blacks on television in the USA after the riots there in the late 1960s, see A. Bodgrokhozy, 'Is this what you mean by color TV?', in L. Spigel and D. Mann (eds), *Private Screenings*, Minneapolis, University of Minnesota Press, 1992; cf. H. Gray, *Watching Race*, Minneapolis, University of Minnesota Press, 1995; see also Chapter 7 on the visibility of immigrants in French cities and on French television.

81 Clearly, the danger here is that such 'alternative' public spheres might be established in such a way that a central (and implicitly white) public sphere might thus remain intact, untransformed, as the privileged space of authentic national citizenship – cf. Kundnani, 2000, op. cit.

82 For the debates surrounding the launch of the channel, see S. Blanchard and D. Morley (eds), *What's This Channel Fo(u)r?*, London, Comedia, 1982.

83   cf. Janine Gibson, 'Jackson's vision for Channel 4', *Guardian*, 10 June 1999; Ed Shelton, 'Breaking out of the ghetto', *Broadcast*, 21 May 1999.

84   Sreberny, op. cit.

85   A. Sreberny-Mohammadi and K. Ross, *Black Minority Viewers and Television*, Leicester, Centre for Mass Communication Research, 1995, p. 11.

86   M. Gillespie, *Television, Ethnicity and Cultural Change*, London, Routledge, 1995.

87   Respondent quoted in S. Moores, 'Satellite television as a cultural sign', *Media, Culture and Society*, 1993b, vol. 15(4), p. 635.

88   cf. D. Hebdige, 'Towards a cartography of taste', in his *Hiding in the Light*, London, Comedia, 1988, and K. Worpole, *Dockers and Detectives*, London, Verso, 1983, for the same kind of dis-identification with the dominant national culture on the part of some white working-class consumers.

89   G. Cumberbatch and S. Woods, *Ethnic Minorities on Television*, London, Independent Television Commission, op. cit. *Television: Ethnic Minorities' Views*, Independent Television Commission, London, 1994.

90   J. Halloran, A. Bhatt and P. Gray, *Ethnic Minorities and Television*, Leicester, Centre for Mass Communications Research, 1995, p. 23.

91   Sreberny and Ross, op. cit., p. 51.

92   ibid., p. 54.

93   Sreberny, op. cit., p. 42.

94   Sreberny and Ross, op. cit., p. 50.

95   ibid., p. 53.

96   Sreberny, op. cit., p. 16.

97   ibid., p. 42. See Chapters 6 and 7 for parallels in the USA and in Europe.

98   Alex Spillius, 'Pirate Telegraph', *Guardian*, 28 January 1995.

99   Phillips, quoted in J. Pines (ed.), *Black and White in Colour: Black People in British Television since 1936*, London, British Film Institute, 1992, pp. 149–50. The argument returns to this focus on the 'whiteness' of the public sphere in Chapter 7.

100   I.M. Young, 'Polity and group difference', *Ethics*, 1989, vol. 99(2), p. 257.

101   cf. C. Husband, 'The multi-ethnic public sphere', paper to European Film and Television Studies Conference, London, 1994, p. 6.

102   Young, 'Polity and group difference', op. cit., p. 261.

103   S. Castles, 'Democracy and multicultural citizenship', paper to Aliens to Citizens Conference, Vienna, November 1993, quoted in Husband, op. cit., p. 11. In his commentary on the Macpherson Report into the murder of Stephen Lawrence in London, Arun Kundnani notes that the report rightly rejected the police claims that their policy of treating all crimes and suspects in the same way exonerated them from the charge of racism. On the contrary, as Macpherson concluded, it was the police force's 'colour blind' approach which had led them to fail to recognise that they were investigating a racist murder – cf. Kundnani, 'Stumbling on', op. cit.

104   To take one example, as Kristin Koptivich observes, Korean Americans can rent last week's news broadcasts by Korean networks in many Korean-run corner stores in North American cities. cf. Kristin Koptivich, 'Third Worlding at home', in A. Gupta and J. Ferguson (eds), *Culture, Power, Place*, Durham, Duke University Press, 1997, p. 245.

105   D. Dayan, 'Media and diasporas', in J. Gripsrud (ed.), *TV and Common Knowledge*, London, Routledge, 1999, p. 19; cf. A. Appadurai, *Modernity at Large*, Minneapolis, University of Minnesota Press, 1996, p. 4, on the conjunction of 'moving images and deterritorialised viewers'.

106   J. Curran, 'The crisis of public communication', in T. Liebes and J. Curran (eds), op. cit., p. 180.

107   Khaching Tölölyan, quoted in S. Huntingdon, *The Clash of Civilisations*, New York, Simon and Schuster, 1996, p. 274; cf. Gerd Baumann's work on the fluidity of appeals to ethnically distinct identities and on accommodations to dominant national discourses among immigrant groups in the UK in his *Contesting Culture*, Cambridge, Cambridge University Press, 1996, discussed later.

108   J. Clifford, 'Travelling cultures', in his *Routes*, Cambridge, Mass., Harvard University Press, 1997.

109   cf. Dayan, 'Medias and diasporas', op. cit.; cf. Dona Kolar-Panov, *Video, War and the Diasporic Imagination*, London, Routledge, 1997, on the role of video-letters in particular.

110   M.L. Margolis, *Little Brazil*, Princeton, New Jersey, Princeton University Press, 1994, p. 193, quoted in U. Hannerz, *Transnational Connections*, London, Routledge, 1996, p. 177.

111   Roger Rouse, 'Mexican migration and the social space of postmodernism', *Diaspora*, 1991, vol. 1(1), p. 13; Clifford, 'Travelling cultures', op. cit., p. 256.

112   Aihwa Ong, 'On the edge of empires: flexible citizenship among Chinese in diaspora', *Positions*, 1993, vol. 1(3), quoted in Clifford, 'Travelling cultures', op. cit., p. 257.
113   P. Cheah, 'Given culture', in P. Cheah and B. Robbins (eds), *Cosmopolitics*, Minneapolis, University of Minnesota Press, 1998, p. 296; cf. Chapter 10 below for a more detailed discussion of this point.

Bibliography

Abu-Lughod, L. (1985) 'The Objects of Soap Opera: Egyptian TV and the Cultural Politics of Modernity', in D. Miller (ed.) *Worlds Apart*, London: Routledge.
Alibhai-Brown, Y. (1999) 'Whose Beeb is it Anyway?', *Global Thinking: Foreign Policy Centre Newsletter*, September, London.
Anderson, B (1983) *Imagined Communities*, London: Verso.
Appadurai, A. (1996) *Modernity at Large*, Minneapolis: University of Minnesota.
Barry, A. (1988) 'Black Mythologies – The Representation of Black people on British Television', in J. Twitchin (ed.) *The Black and White Media Book*, London: Trentham Books.
Baumann, G. (1996) *Contesting Culture*, Cambridge: Cambridge University Press.
Berlant, L. (1991) *Anatomy of a National Fantasy*, Chicago: Chicago University Press.
Bhaba, H. (ed.) (1990) *Nation and Narration*, London: Routledge.
Blanchard, S. and Morley, D. (eds) (1982) *What's This Channel Fo(u)r?*, London: Comedia.
Bodgrokhozy, A. (1992) 'Is This What You Mean By Colour TV?', in L. Spigel and D. Mann (eds) *Private Screenings*, Minneapolis: University of Minnesota Press.
Carey, J. (1998) 'Political Ritual Television', in T. Liebes and J. Curran (eds) *Media, Ritual and Identity*, London: Routledge.
Carpignano, P., Anderson, R. and DiFazio, W. (1993) 'Chatter in the Age of Electronic Reproduction', in B. Robbins (ed.) *The Phantom Public Sphere*, Minneapolis: Minnesota University Press.
Chandler, D. (1996) 'Postcards From the Edge', in M. Power (ed.) *The Shipping Forecast*, London: Zelda Cheatle Press.
Cheah, P. (1998) 'Given Culture', in P. Cheah and B. Robbins (eds) *Cosmopolitics*, Minneapolis: Minnesota University Press.
Clifford, J. (1997) *Routes*, Cambridge MA: Harvard University Press.
Corner, J. (1991) 'Meaning, Genre and Context: the Problematics of Public Knowledge', in J. Curran and M. Gurevitch (eds) *Mass Media and Society*, London: Edward Arnold.
Cumberbatch, G. and Woods, S. (1996) *Ethnic Minorities on Television*, London: Independent Television Commission.
Curran, J. (1998) 'The Crisis in Public Communication', in T. Liebes and J. Curran (eds) *Media, Ritual and Identity*, London: Routledge.
Dayan, D. (1999) 'Media and Diasporas', in J. Gripsrud (ed.) *TV and Common Knowledge*, London: Routledge.
Dayan, D. and Katz, E. (1992) *Media Events*, Cambridge MA: Harvard University Press.
Deutsche, R. (1990) 'Men in Space', *Artforum*, February.
Dyer, R. (1998) 'White', *Screen* 29 (4)
Eley, G. and Griger Suny, R. (eds) *Becoming National*, Oxford: Oxford University Press.
Fraser, N. (1993) 'Rethinking the Public Sphere', in B. Robbins (ed.) *The Phantom Public Sphere*, Minneapolis: Minnesota University Press.
Gibson, J. (1999) 'Jackson's Vision for Channel 4', *Guardian* 10 June.
Gillespie, M. (1995) *Television, Ethnicity and Cultural Change*, London: Routledge.
Gilroy, P. (1982) 'Channel Four – Bridgehead or Bantustan?', *Screen* 24 (4): 39.
Gray, H. (1995) *Watching Race*, Minneapolis: Minnesota University Press.
Hall, C. (1992) *White Male and Middle Class*, Cambridge: Polity Press.
Hall, S. (1993) 'Which Public, Whose Service?' in W. Stevenson (ed.) *All Our Futures, the Changing Role and Purpose of the BBC*, London: British Film Institute.
Halloran, J., Bhatt, A. and Gray, P. (1995) *Ethnic Minorities and Television*, Leicester: Centre for Mass Communication Research.
Hannerz, U. (1996) *Transnational Connections*, London: Routledge.
Hargreaves, A and Perotti, A. (1993) 'The Representation on French Television of Immigrants and Ethnic Minorities', *New Community* 19 (2).
Hebdige, D. (1988) *Hiding in the Light*, London: Comedia.

Hermes, J. (1997) 'Gender and Media Studies: No Woman, No Cry', in J. Corner, P. Schlesinger and R. Silverstone (eds) *International Media Research*, London: Routledge.

Huntingdon, S. (1996) *The Clash of Civilisations*, New York: Simon and Schuster.

Hurtado, A. (1989) 'Relating to Privilege: Seduction and Rejection in the Subordination of White Women and Women of Colour', *Signs: Journal of Women in Culture and Society* 14 (4).

Keane, J. (1991) *The Media and Democracy*, Cambridge: Polity Press.

Keenan, T. (1993) 'Windows: of Vulnerability', in B. Robbins (ed.) *The Phantom Public Sphere*, Minneapolis: Minnesota University Press.

Kolar-Panov, D. (1997) *Video, War and the Diasporic Imagination*, London: Routledge.

Koptivich, K. (1997) 'Third Worlding at Home', in A. Gupta and J. Ferguson (eds) *Culture, Power, Place*, Durham, NC: Duke University Press.

Lawrence, E. (1982) 'In the Abundance of water, the Fool is Thirsty', in CCCS (ed.) *The Empire Strikes Back*, London: Hutchinson.

Leishman, M. (1999) *Dictionary of Scottish Biography*, Irvine: Carrick Media.

Livingstone, S. (1994) 'Watching Talk', *Media, Culture & Society*, 16.

Livingstone, S. and Lunt, P. (1994) *Talk on Television*, London: Routledge.

Lofgren, O. (1995) 'The Nation as Home or Motel? Metaphors of Media and Belonging', unpublished paper, University of Lund.

McLintock, A. (1995) *Imperial Leather*, London: Routledge.

McRobbie, A. (1986) 'Postmodernism and Popular Culture', *Journal of Communication Inquiry* 10 (2).

Margolis, M.L. (1994) *Little Brazil*, Princeton NJ: Princeton University Press.

Martin-Barbero, J. (1993) *Communication, Culture and Hegemony*, London: Sage.

Masciorotte, G-J. (1991) 'C'mon Girl: Oprah Winfrey and the Discourse of Feminine Talk', *Discourse* 11.

Meyrowitz, J. (1985) *No Sense of Place*, Oxford: Oxford University Press.

Moores, S. (1993) 'Satellite Television as Cultural Sign', *Media, Culture & Society* 15 (4): 635

—— (1998) 'Don't Criticise VictimVision', *Independent* 8 May.

Morley, D. (1992) *Television, Audiences and Cultural Studies*, London: Routledge.

—— (1999) 'Finding Out About the World From Television News', in J. Gripsrud (ed.) *Television and Common Knowledge*, London: Routledge.

—— (1999) 'To Boldy Go: The "Third Generation" of Reception Studies', in P. Alasuutari (ed.) *Rethinking the Media Audience*, London: Sage.

Morley, D. and Brunsdon, C. (1999) *The Nationwide Television Studies*, London: Routledge.

Morse, M. (1998) *Virtualities*, Bloomington: Indiana University Press.

Negt, O. and Kluge, A. (1994) *Public Sphere and Experience*, Minneapolis: Minnesota University Press.

Ong, A. (1993) 'On the Edge of Empires: Flexible Citizenship Among Chinese in Diaspora', *Positions* 1 (3).

Orwell, G. (1957) *Inside the Whale and Other Essays*, Harmondsworth: Penguin Papastergiadis, N. (1998) *Dialogues in the Diasporas*, London: Oram Press.

Phillips, M. (1999) 'Heritage Foundations', *New Times* November.

Pines, J. (ed.) *Black and White in Colour: Black People in British Television Since 1936*, London: British Film Institute.

Polan, D. (1993) 'The Public's Fear; Or, Media as Monster in Habermas, Negt and Kluge', in B. Robbins (ed.) *The Phantom Public Sphere*, Minneapolis: Minnesota University Press.

Rath, C.D. (1985) 'The Invisible Network', in P. Drummond and R. Paterson (eds) *Television and its Audience*, London: British Film Institute.

—— (1989) 'Live Television and its Audiences', in E. Seiter, H. Borschers, G. Kreutzner and E.M. Warth (eds) *Remote Control*, London: Routledge.

Rouse, R. (1991) 'Mexican Migration and the Social Space of Postmodernism', *Diaspora* 1 (1).

Sacks, H. (1992) *Lectures on Conversation*. Oxford: Blackwell.

Scannell, P. (1988) 'Radio Times', in P. Drummond and R. Paterson (eds) *Television and its Audience*, London: British Film Institute.

—— (1989) 'Public Service Broadcasting and Modern Life', *Media, Culture & Society* 11 (2): 138

—— (1992) 'Public Service Broadcasting and Modern Public Life', in P. Scannell, P. Schlesinger and C. Sparks (eds) *Culture and Power*, London: Sage.

—— (1996) *Radio, Television, and Modern Life*, Oxford: Blackwell.

Shelton, F. (1993) 'Breaking Out of the Ghetto', *Broadcast* 21 May.

Spillius, A. (1995) 'Pirate Telegraph', *Guradian* 28 January

Sreberny, A. (1999) *Include Me In: Rethinking Ethnicity on Television*, London: Broadcasting Standards Council.

Sreberny-Mohammadi, A. and Ross, K. (1995) *Black Minority Viewers and Television*, Leicester: Centre for Mass Communication Research.

Warner, M. (1993) 'The Mass Public and the Mass Subject', in B. Robbins (ed.) *The Phantom Public Sphere*, Minneapolis: Minnesota University Press.

Worpole, K. (1983) *Dockers and Detectives*, London: Verso.

—— (1992) *Towns for People*, Milton Keynes: Open University Press.

Young, I.M. (1987) 'Impartiality and the Civil Public', in S. Benhabib and D. Cornell (eds) *Feminism as Critique*, Minneapolis: University of Minnesota Press.

—— (1989) 'Polity and Group Difference', *Ethics* 99 (2)

Chapter 28

TIMOTHY HAVENS

'THE BIGGEST SHOW IN THE WORLD'
Race and the global popularity of *The Cosby Show*

Introduction

THE COSBY SHOW CHANGED THE FACE of American television and set a new
standard for representing African American families in non-stereotyped roles. It rewrote the
book on syndication when Viacom required stations to bid for the privilege of airing the show
(Heuton, 1990), and it fuelled the networks' efforts to have the FCC's financial-syndication rules
repealed to allow NBC to share in the show's $600 million syndication revenues (Andrews, 1992).
The Cosby Show also profoundly altered international television syndication, proving the international marketability of the now staple comedy format, establishing Viacom as a major distributor during a time of global deregulation, and drawing dedicated audiences as only *Dallas* and
Dynasty previously had. While many scholars have addressed the show's domestic popularity
(Boyd, 1997; Downing, 1988; Gray, 1995; Press, 1991; Taylor, 1989), its international acceptance
remains a virtual mystery.[1]

Recently, the world has witnessed a dramatic increase in the export of middle-class African
American situation comedies which are directly linked to *The Cosby Show*'s success. This article
investigates the various economic, textual and audience practices that led to the show's international success, and that continue to make middle-class African American sitcoms lucrative
international fare. In an era of increased interdependence of television markets, where shows must
exhibit international appeal 'before anything moves forward' (Schapiro, 1991: 29) in domestic
production, *The Cosby Show* set the representational and marketing standards that continue to
determine what types of African American shows get produced, and where those shows are sold.
While the international syndication industry learned many lessons from *The Cosby Show*, including
the global appeal of domestic sitcoms, this article suggests that deeper revelations regarding the
importance of televisual representations of race in global programming remain unrecognized.

Race in international communication

Matters of race have figured prominently in discussions of international media flows and consumption practices. Race is seen as a transnational identity that can bind together audiences across
national lines. Given 'the dual tendency toward globalization and localization of image spaces'
(Robins, 1989: 156) in international television, homogeneous national identities are increasingly
ineffective for drawing audiences. Instead, audiences coalesce around various transnational identities such as gender, ethnicity and race. Scholars of international television, however, have shown
only passing interest in investigating how racial identities and televisual representations of race

interact on a transnational level. Morley and Robins (1989), for instance, argue that the push to create a common market for European-produced television has resulted in a downplaying of ethnic differences and an exclusion of racial minorities from official definitions of European identity. Ultimately, however, their discussion only 'touches on the questions of race and ethnicity' (1989: 224) and their main interest lies in arguing for a politics of identity articulation that centres on domestic media practices.

This tendency to 'touch' upon race is common in scholarship regarding international communication, but few writers give their full attention to the ways that racialized representations circulate and are consumed worldwide. Ross (1996) has investigated the history of black images in the USA and the UK, as well as the cross-fertilization between these two nations. She argues convincingly that black images have been severely limited in Anglo audiovisual culture, despite the long-fought, creative practices of many black cultural workers. Her concern in the final chapters is that the volume and inexpensiveness of Western popular culture on the world market will strangle oppositional minority voices. While her apprehensions are appropriate, we must be careful not to homogenize all forms of popular culture. As Stuart Hall has written, 'Black popular culture is a contradictory space . . . a sight of strategic contestation' within Western popular culture. It enables 'the surfacing, inside the mixed and contradictory modes even of some mainstream popular culture, of elements of a discourse that is different' (Hall, 1996: 470).

Ross's (1996) adoption of an outmoded cultural imperialism thesis (see Tomlinson, 1991) causes her to ignore the subversive potential in popular culture. In South Africa, for instance, *The Cosby Show* was so incendiary that a Member of Parliament publicly criticized the show for its 'ANC messages' (BBC, 1988). As the current study demonstrates, audiences around the world do find important pleasures in *The Cosby Show*'s dignified representations of an African American family. Their pleasures cannot be explained solely by the cheapness and ubiquity of US programming.

Contrary to Ross's (1996) argument, Gillespie (1995) has found that imported popular culture can be integral to the creation of new ethnic identities. Through extensive ethnographic research, she demonstrates how Punjabi youth living in London use domestic and imported audiovisual culture to understand their identities in relation to the family, the nation, the neighbourhood, the diaspora and the world. In their talk about the Australian soap opera *Neighbours*, for instance, these viewers work out their relationships to local gossip culture, parents and white British society. However, her analysis is not centrally concerned with the appeal of individual artefacts like *The Cosby Show*, which somehow speak to variously situated audiences. Neither is she interested in the economic imperatives that drive most cross-cultural media exchanges. What she offers for the current study is compelling evidence that imported programming can have important intersections with audiences' understandings of social identities like ethnicity.

Jones (1988) provides an important corollary to Gillespie's (1995) work in his ethnography of white British fans of Afro-Caribbean music. Jones accounts for the industrial, textual and audience practices that explain this popularity. He demonstrates how Afro-Caribbean music, especially reggae, was intentionally altered and packaged by the music industry to appeal to white youth. However, he also accounts for audiences' continual reappropriation of these musical forms and the subversive potential that inheres in the most commercialized forms, which can provide important utopic ideals and an entree into Afro-Caribbean culture and counter-economies. These working-class white youths exhibit a sometimes deep affinity with black British politics and culture on the basis of shared economic disadvantage.

Like Gillespie (1995), Jones (1988) is interested in micro-analyses of macro-social processes, which causes him to concentrate on one neighbourhood. This article, on the other hand, aims at comparing audiences across local particulars. While Gillespie shows that extranational television culture can help articulate ethnic identities and Jones demonstrates how economic and textual practices must operate together in international exchanges of popular culture, we still need to understand how 'race' can signify transnationally in order to begin our investigation of the roles that race played in *The Cosby Show*'s international success.

Gilroy (1993) addresses the problem of imagining race transnationally when he attempts to theorize the appeal of black popular music within the African diaspora and beyond. According to Gilroy, black music displays an antimodern aesthetic and politics which links contemporary struggles with past racial horrors and resonates with people of colour across the globe. In this sense, black music has acted as a transnational discourse of blackness throughout modernity, connecting otherwise disparate audiences by referencing shared historical and contemporary circumstances. Music has a history of political and social importance in black communities that traces from slave-era spirituals to contemporary hip-hop clubs.

Gilroy's (1993) concentration on the performative and textual aspects of black popular music is appropriate given his subject, but popular black television images, especially humorous images, hold a far more ambivalent position in black culture (Gray, 1995; Riggs, 1991). In the USA and Western Europe, white-controlled popular culture has for centuries ridiculed blacks through caricature (Pieterse, 1992). This situation has begun to change lately, as black Americans and Britons have gained some control of television imagery and become a lucrative audience segment (see Gray, 1995). Still, television situation comedies like *The Cosby Show* trace their lineage to *Amos 'N' Andy* and minstrel shows. Their consumption occurs in radically different contexts than black popular music and they offer unique representations of blackness which must be understood as a distinct transnational discourse of blackness.

Nonetheless, Gilroy (1993) provides a useful model for our investigation. He is able to specify the structures of feeling that bind together a diasporic audience and how popular culture expresses and constitutes those binds. His ideas are consonant with Goldberg's (1993) discussion of 'race' as a discursive formation. Goldberg argues that race is 'almost, but not quite, empty in its own connotative capacity, able to signify not so much in itself but by adopting and extending naturalized form to prevailing conceptions of social group formation at different times' (1993: 80). In this formulation, race is not reducible to such things as class differences. Instead, it naturalizes those differences. Race also carries 'the sedimentary traces of past significations' (1993: 81), so that skin colour connotes a host of contemporary and historical ideas like class affiliation, citizenship and colonial violence. The question for this investigation, then, is how *The Cosby Show*'s representations of blackness organize and activate certain transnational 'social group formations'.

Two main groupings emerge in this study as salient for understanding the transnational dimensions of racialized televisual discourse. First, many black and non-white postcolonial viewers express an affinity with *The Cosby Show* because of a shared history of racial-colonial exploitation and contemporary class oppressions that derive from that history (see Spivak, 1990 and Marable, 1983). These affinities extend beyond mere economic conditions to include similar histories of imperial exploitation and terror, including Western efforts at cultural genocide. These diverse audiences express admiration for *The Cosby Show* because it avoids conventional black stereotypes while retaining distinctly black cultural references like jazz.

Second, regional identity or affinity resonates with race in several ways. Originally articulated as comparable to race, regional identity gave the impression that racial differences were as natural and inevitable as geographical differences: Asians lived in Asia, Latinos in Latin American, blacks in Africa, and so on (Goldberg, 1993: 186). But centuries of forced and voluntary migration have destabilized these orderly categories. Regional identity today also implies formal political, economic, linguistic and historical ties. Most notably for our investigation, nations in the same region often share television industrial structures, technical standards and programming (O'Regan,

1992). Viewers' comments confirm that they experience regional identity as increasingly distinct from racial identity, although the two often overlap, as suggested by Morley and Robins' (1989) discussion of whiteness and European identity cited above.

The Cosby Show's international star

The Cosby Show's international popularity began in the Fall of 1985 and continued until 1995. During this period, the show ranked in the top ten in such diverse markets as the Philippines, Australia, Lebanon and Norway. The only regions where the show was not a marked success were Central and South America, although many of these television markets did import the show for a period of time. In the Caribbean, *The Cosby Show* experienced its greatest and earliest popularity outside the USA. Many countries in this region depend on the USA to provide large tracts of their programming schedules, and some simply re-transmit US signals via satellite. It is not uncommon for a popular US show to be popular in the Caribbean at the same time, and *The Cosby Show* is a prime example of this tendency. Broadcast throughout the region during its network prime-time run, the show 'was as popular in the Caribbean . . . as it [was] in the United States' (Payne, 1994: 233), and audience surveys show that Caribbean viewers enjoyed the show more than any other viewers outside the USA (Fuller, 1992).

At first glance, the show's popularity in the Caribbean seems to suggest that *The Cosby Show* was most popular in countries with predominantly black audiences. However, non-white audiences in the Middle East and Asia also responded favourably to the show. In Lebanon, for instance, the show was the rated number one in 1988 (Raschka, 1988), while in the Philippines, Indonesia and Hong Kong, the show appeared frequently in the top ten between 1986 and 1989. Prior to 1987, the show was exported predominantly to non-European countries, with the exception of the Scandinavian countries. Significant differences in export policies, programming needs and market size played an important role in keeping the show out of Europe during the first two years of its export. The reasons for success or failure of the show are nicely exemplified if we compare the fate of *The Cosby Show* in the UK and South Africa.

Both the UK and South Africa have large white, English-speaking populations who made up the main audience for *The Cosby Show*. Language transfer was not a concern in these countries. Both countries also have a large non-white population, but there the similarities end. In South Africa, the show was popular with black audiences, while in the UK it was not. The UK has well-established broadcasting networks that produce original programming, while the South African Broadcasting Company (SABC) had been on the air little more than a decade when *The Cosby Show* aired (Nixon, 1994), and had recently upgraded to three channels (Mufson, 1986). As a result of the upgrade, much of SABC's programming came from the USA and the UK during the mid- and late 1980s.

In the UK, *The Cosby Show* was aired from 1985 through the mid-1990s on Channel Four, which was generally regarded as the nation's upscale television channel. The show attracted only a 'cult following' of between 2 and 3 million viewers (Griffin, 1990). By comparison, the first episode of the UK comedy *One Foot in the Grave* drew 14.75 million viewers on the mainstream BBC1 channel (*The Independent*, 1992). Because of the show's lacklustre ratings, Channel Four paid the paltry sum of £10,000–15,000 per episode (Henry, 1986), while its US counterparts sometimes paid close to half a million dollars (Ziegler, 1988) per episode. The series was targeted at, and mostly watched by upscale white audiences, or 'ABs' as they are designated by the industry, whereas non-white audiences tended to find programming geared toward them on Independent Television (ITV). Among ABs, the show performed well for Channel Four, securing its continued, if unremarkable run for nearly ten years (Henry, 1986). Despite the show's lack of popularity among non-white audiences, those black Britons who did watch the show rated it exceptionally highly (Fuller, 1992).

Likewise, in South Africa, *The Cosby Show* was 'the most popular show among Whites' (Mufson, 1986: 17) in 1990, but black South Africans also responded very positively to the show (Fuller, 1992; Mufson, 1986). The show was carried on SABC TV4, a newly introduced channel aimed at a general audience, unlike TV1, TV2, and TV3, which were targeted toward specific racial and ethnic groups. Ranked consistently number one, *The Cosby Show* generated very different responses from black audience members than it did among some whites. A black grocer explained that, 'Cosby is a big doctor, he is consulted, he has authority, and he receives full respect due to him. This is the kind of thing we blacks want here in South Africa' (Mufson, 1986: 17). On the other hand, one white fan expressed his belief that African Americans' 'first world' values make them fundamentally different from black South Africans. He argued that white South Africans could identify with the Huxtable family because they shared the values that black South Africans lacked (Fuller, 1992: 114). For blacks, then, *The Cosby Show* could serve to expose the fallacy of black South African inferiority, while for whites it could encourage that fallacy.

The contrast between the UK and South Africa makes clear many points that are relevant to our discussion. First, we can see that numerous factors influenced the decision to import *The Cosby Show* and the popularity of the show. Among the more prominent are the state of the television industry, the channel on which it was broadcast, and the racial-political climate of the period. In the UK, racial and ethnic minorities could find locally produced shows geared toward them, and *The Cosby Show* could not fill the void it did among black South Africans. Still, race was not a non-issue in the popularity of the show in the UK. In fact, the marketing director for Viacom UK, Martha Burke-Hennessy, suggested that white Britons resisted *The Cosby Show* because the family was black (Henry, 1986).

The political economic context for *The Cosby Show*

As suggested by these examples, investigating the ways that race played into the international popularity of *The Cosby Show* is complex work. It involves the multiple articulations and dislocations between the show's racialized representations and the audiences' understandings of race, both in their own countries and beyond national borders. I will turn shortly to consider the ways that we can begin to untangle these webs of social identity, but first we need to understand how more 'formal' political and economic forces affected the show's export. In this way, we will more clearly see how race did and did not influence the international popularity of the show.

The international distribution rights for *The Cosby Show* were held by Viacom International, Inc. (later Viacom, Inc.) from 1984 until December 1994. International syndication never had the kinds of direct effects on Viacom's bottom line that its domestic distribution did, bringing in $100 million at most in total revenues (Flanigan, 1987). Instead, the show's international sales provided the company with a strong presence on the international television programming scene at a time of widespread global deregulation of television systems and increased programming needs due to technological changes.

Viacom had been looking for a lucrative syndication property for its domestic and international operations for years before it landed *The Cosby Show*. While the company still owned the rights to many popular 1970s CBS series that it had acquired when it was initially spun off from CBS in 1971, those series were rapidly ageing by the early 1980s, and audiences were evaporating (Richter, 1985). The company had expected that 'the benefits to be derived from its [syndication] agreement with CBS would diminish' (Securities and Exchange Commission [SEC], 1987) over the years, as their reruns became less and less marketable. Prior to *The Cosby Show*, however, the company had not yet found properties that could 'offset . . . potential adverse effects from such anticipated diminution over time of the benefits to be derived from the CBS Agreement' (SEC, 1987). Its best earlier efforts had won the rights to such forgettable series as *Dear Detective* and *The Lazarus Syndrome* (Richter, 1985).

Viacom also owned cable companies, television stations, radio stations and cable channels, but it saw programming as the key to its future success and the future of the television business. In 1983, when Carsey-Werner Productions ran into problems financing the initial episodes of the high-budget *Cosby Show*, Viacom provided necessary funding in exchange for exclusive, worldwide syndication rights to the series (Richter, 1985). When the series skyrocketed to number one in the network ratings, consistently attracting more than 50 percent of the US audience (Henry, 1986), Viacom had a hot property on its hands, but it could not begin to syndicate the show until the 1988–9 season because of its agreement with Carsey-Werner (Richter, 1985). Although the company did start receiving profits from syndication sales as early as autumn 1987 (SEC, 1987), there were three years during which it held the rights to the most popular show in US television, had invested significant funds for those rights, and was unable to realize a profit. One of the main impetuses behind Viacom's drive to sell *The Cosby Show* internationally was its desire to generate some income from such a popular and expensive show.

Precise dollar amounts earned from marketing the show internationally are not available in Viacom's public records, but it is obvious that Viacom's international strategy did produce immediate results. Following the company's acquisition of rights to *The Cosby Show* in 1984, total foreign exports jumped markedly: between 1983 and 1984, exports posted a modest 1.7 percent gain; the following year, total exports dropped 5.8 percent; and from 1986 until the end of the decade, exports increased between 12.2 and 29.3 percent each year (SEC, 1987, 1991; Viacom, 1985). While we cannot attribute all of this increase to *The Cosby Show*, it was one of the company's most profitable properties in the late 1980s, and contributed a significant portion of the growth in exports.[2]

Deregulation and technological innovations also played a large role in the global success of *The Cosby Show*. Prior to 1985, global politics had been rocked by numerous charges of gross inequality by the Movement of Non-Aligned Nations. Among these charges were critiques of the imbalance in the ownership of communications systems and unequal flows of global media, especially news, that came to be known as the New World Information and Communication Order (NWICO) debate. Although this debate raged for several years, gaining significant momentum in 1980 when UNESCO's MacBride Commission report called for a more equitable balance of trade and larger number of communication channels, NWICO was effectively short-circuited in 1985 when the USA and UK withdrew from UNESCO. After these withdrawals, UNESCO abandoned NWICO and concentrated its efforts on building infrastructure, avoiding the more controversial topic of global media flows (see Herman and McChesney, 1997).

For Viacom, the end of the NWICO debate coincided nicely with its global offering of *The Cosby Show*. Only a few years earlier, government-owned communications systems around the globe might have made an example of the series. After NWICO, however, many countries were trying to regain US favour. Moreover, the USA had begun 'aggressive global pro-market policies' (Herman and McChesney, 1997: 23) in the 1980s under Reagan in an attempt to get non-Western nations to open up their markets to US goods. A worldwide era of deregulation was under way, which opened more and more national television systems to competition and commercialization, again increasing the number of export channels that Viacom could exploit in its marketing efforts. As the company's 1987 SEC 10-K filing boasts, 'A substantial portion of [foreign distribution] revenues is derived from countries that have import quotas and other restrictions which limit the number of foreign programs and films exhibited in such countries.' Among the nations that began importing the series in 1985, the majority fall into this category of less developed, predominantly non-white nations whose media had recently been commercialized, including Lebanon, (Raschka, 1988), South Africa (Mufson, 1986), Malaysia, Malta and Singapore in 1985 (Fuller, 1992).

The introduction of satellite television greatly increased the speed of commercialization and deregulation around the world. In fact, the NWICO debate had its roots in concerns that satellite technology would allow Western media companies to broadcast into nations with strict regulations (Herman and McChesney, 1997). Because of satellite technology, television systems around the world became more commercialized and began to offer more channels. Along with the increase in channels and broadcasting hours came demand for programming. Viacom was poised to fill the gaps with *The Cosby Show*, as it is cheaper to purchase programming from a distributor than it is to produce original programming (Hoskins *et al.*, 1997).

Beyond deregulation and satellite technology, the unpopularity of the sitcom genre on the international television market at the time, and the subsequent bargain price of the show also affected its success. The price made the show attractive to less wealthy broadcasters. The main reason for the price was a conventional belief in international television programming that 'American comedy had little appeal to an international market' (Huff, 1996: 52). Comedy was seen as a culturally specific phenomenon that could not cross national borders, let alone linguistic borders. Based on previous successes with *Dallas, Dynasty* and *Kojak*, most international television trade at the time consisted of drama and action-adventure shows. As one international television executive explained, 'Car goes down the street, car makes the wrong turn, car blows up . . . everybody understands that' (Schapiro, 1991: 29). Although *The Cosby Show* was dirt cheap in comparison with US prices, it was also an unlikely success. Wealthier European channels were more likely to spend their money on more expensive, but proved formats.

Viacom's lack of confidence in *The Cosby Show*'s exportability comes across plainly if we look at the way Viacom marketed itself and the series in *TV World*, an international television trade journal, in 1985 and 1986. The first Viacom ad to feature *The Cosby Show* for international television buyers appeared in the February 1985 issue. It pictures four shows, *Me and Mom, Star Games, Peter the Great* and *The Cosby Show*, the only sitcom in the line-up. Mention of *The Cosby Show* is buried at the end of the second paragraph of copy, and it is featured for its 'critical acclaim' instead of its humour. Obviously, the company is emphasizing its drama programming in the ad, a fact reinforced by an August 1985 ad for *Peter the Great* which claims that 'The world turns to Viacom for great drama'. Viacom did not see *The Cosby Show* as a significant international property at this time.

One year later, however, in February 1986, Viacom took out a full page ad for the show, suggesting that 'The biggest show in America *is* the biggest show in the world'. The hyperbole of this claim becomes apparent if one reads further; the ad only announces that 'this highly celebrated series is available worldwide', and does not claim that the show is popular around the world. Still, it is apparent that Viacom thought the show would attract enough international buyers to warrant a full-page to itself, unlike a year earlier.

The success of the show in Europe accounts for Viacom's evolving marketing strategy. The company thought little of its sales to less developed industries and did not fully recognize the potential of *The Cosby Show* until it succeeded in Europe. By November 1986, we find an ad announcing boldly in 60-point font that Bill Cosby is 'The World's Newest Superpower'. Minor yet significant copy changes have been made to the February 1986 ad. The February copy reads, 'And now, this highly-celebrated series is available worldwide', while the November copy reads, 'And now, this high-celebrated series *has transcended* language and culture' (emphasis added). While the show had transcended Lebanese language and Malaysian cultural barriers a year earlier, it seems that Viacom was unaware of the show's ability to amuse across different cultures'

(Patterson, 1995) until the show had succeeded in the more fickle – and lucrative – European markets. Of course, it is not surprising that Viacom was most interested in exporting to Europe, even while it was willing to strike deals with any broadcaster interested in the show. Because of the greater penetration of television sets, the degree of commercialization, and the massively larger economies of Europe in general, *The Cosby Show* drew much better profits in Europe and established potentially advantageous future relationships for the company.

Finally, the differential success of the show also derived from the way that buyers viewed the show's performance in other countries in their region. For instance, Middle Eastern buyers could look to the success of the show in Israel and Lebanon and think that the show might do well in their home markets. In Europe, the show's marginal performance in England and its failure in Belgium (*Broadcast*, 1988) made other buyers wary of spending too much money for it. In short, a snowball effect took over in each region, and helped speed or slow the spread of the show.

The political economy of the world television market in the mid- and late 1980s helps to explain a large part of *The Cosby Show*'s popularity. Many developing nations had recently opened their television networks to competition due to increased satellite broadcasting and pressure from the USA and other Western nations, resulting in a huge increase in broadcasting hours around the world. US distributors were well-suited to fill those hours because their programming was so much cheaper than original programming. Because Viacom had the rights to *The Cosby Show*, but no hopes of recouping its original investment in the show for several years, the company began to sell the show worldwide. Much to the company's astonishment, the show became as popular overseas as it was in the USA, contradicting conventional industry wisdom that the sitcom format was too culturally specific for international television trade.

The Cosby Show, blackness and international audiences

While our analysis so far has shown why a sitcom might have been aired in several countries around this time, it cannot explain why this specific show became such a hit, and not one of the other 135 sitcoms that Viacom licensed. The answer to this question lies in textual and audience practices. In many areas of the world, audiences are accustomed to and even prefer Western popular culture, and we might suspect that *The Cosby Show* appealed to international audiences simply because it was the most popular US show at the time. While this assumption is surely accurate, it neglects the importance of race in US popular culture. Western popular culture has long enlisted black culture, performers and bodies in order to build a mass white audience (Hilmes, 1993; Lott, 1993; Pieterse, 1992; Roediger, 1991; Rogin, 1996). The recent explosion of African American images in US television and advertising (Boyd, 1997; Gray, 1995) at a time when these products are expected to appeal to disparate international audiences should cause us to ask whether we are witnessing a similar strategy.

If we compare the export patterns of *Family Ties*, *The Cosby Show*'s 'white obverse' (Taylor, 1989: 163) and perennial challenger in the US ratings, we can see that race is an important element in *The Cosby Show*'s success. *Family Ties* consistently ranked close to *The Cosby Show* in many European markets, Australia and New Zealand, although *The Cosby Show* attracted far greater non-European audiences than *Family Ties*. Each of these shows offers a comparable ideology of the American Dream, where material comfort allows family members to avoid the drudgery of daily work and concentrate on their individual and collective growth surrounded by love and humour. Why, then, did *The Cosby Show* outpace *Family Ties* so dramatically on the world scene? Aesthetic considerations like better writing or better acting may explain some of the difference, but compared with the general ruck of US sitcoms, *Family Ties* and *The Cosby Show* seem more similar than different. *Family Ties'* syndicator, Paramount Television, was as interested in developing its international distribution wing as *The Cosby Show*'s syndicator Viacom. Race is perhaps the only salient difference between these two shows that might account for their differential export patterns and international success. Anecdotal comments from audience members, which will be explored more fully later, show how important the Huxtables' blackness was for their enjoyment of the show.

As mentioned above, two main aspects of race as a discourse affected *The Cosby Show*'s unprecedented success: the audiences' experiences of race, and the racialized representations of the show. Many scholars have written about *The Cosby Show*'s representation of blackness. I do not want to rehearse all of those arguments here, but I will offer an overview of a few prominent insights on the subject that bear directly on the international exportability of the show.

Jhally and Lewis (1992), in their study of white and black audiences for *The Cosby Show*, argue that the show portrays blackness in a limited, post-Civil Rights light, shorn of the economic hardship and exclusion that so often comprises part of what it means to be black in the USA. The authors criticize the show on this account, claiming that class is a necessary component of race, and that *The Cosby Show* leaves white audiences with the impression that all economic barriers for African Americans have been removed through affirmative action, while it placates black audiences by portraying a respectable, non-stereotyped African American family. Regardless of the political implications, it is surely true that *The Cosby Show* tends to avoid addressing specifically American problems by side-stepping issues of economic hardship. In this way, the show is more suited to international audiences, who might find American problems distancing and difficult to identify with.

The Cosby Show, in fact, avoided most overtly political issues, focusing instead on stories of personal and familial growth and adjustment, all the while enacting an 'insistent recuperation of African American social equality (and competence) through the trope of the stable and unified black family' (Gray, 1995: 80). The blackness represented on the show was subdued and dignified, and came across in such things as Blues and R&B music, African American portraiture art that hung on the living room walls, references to Civil Rights and Anti-Apartheid leaders, and the 'Abolish Apartheid' sticker on son Theo's bedroom door (Downing, 1988: 61–2). The show cautiously avoided conventional black stereotypes and inner-city settings, instead marking its characters' blackness through these references to African American high culture. However, by avoiding much of the 'loud' humour that most African American sitcoms employ, where blackness becomes 'an object of derision and fascination' (Gray, 1995: 81), *The Cosby Show* also denied an integral part of black humour, especially working-class black humour.[3] The political work affected by the series lies in its controlled celebration of certain aspects of African American culture; it is a predominantly cultural politics.

The political issues that did surface on the show were not flash-in-the-pan popular topics that interest a sitcom like *Murphy Brown*, but long-standing political concerns like education and Civil Rights. We might, therefore, expect some international audiences to be familiar with these issues. Even if we understand *The Cosby Show*'s familial harmony as a 'retreat into fundamentalist principles of family, whose rigidity suggests not so much the relaxed confidence born of stability as the fear of total disintegration from within or invasion from without' (Taylor, 1989: 165), the show avoids American cultural specificity by limiting its references to the outside world and concentrating on the nuclear family.

Despite its focus on domestic life, the show does make reference to diversity within African American communities and black communities worldwide. As Downing (1988) notes, gender differences and struggles provide one of the main themes in *The Cosby Show*. The show portrays sibling rivalries that appeal to children, parenting problems for parents and the romantic relationship between Cliff and Claire for couples. Many audience members around the world can identify with one or several of these themes. The presence on the show of the internationally recognized Civil Rights and Anti-Apartheid movements also gestures at a transnational black community, bound by similar political goals. Finally, we see 'aspects of international culture [which] are part of the Huxtables' taken-for-granted world' (Downing, 1988: 62) in the travels of various family members and in incidental characters, such as Theo's math teacher who is Portuguese. Over the course of its run, *The Cosby Show* makes clear that these characters' lives stretch beyond the borders of the USA.

The Cosby Show's representation of blackness was uncommon for US television, but the show did retain an abundance of physical humour which is typical of traditional black humour. In one episode, for instance, all of the family members perform a lip-synch pantomime of Ray Charles and the Raelette's 'Night Time Is the Right Time' for the Huxtables' grandparents (Downing, 1988). Bill Cosby, like most black comedians, delivers his lines 'with recognizable expressions and gestures, which, in themselves, are a source of humour' (Watkins, 1994: 41). For international television, the use of physical humour facilitates the show's export: it transfers to different cultures and languages much more readily than verbal humour. Audiences for *The Cosby Show* obviously responded to the show's representations of blackness, and their comments about the show give us important insights into how they see their own racial identities intersecting with the Huxtables'. I draw these comments from published audience interviews and newspaper feature accounts that include interviews with non-US audiences for the show, and reanalyse them with an eye toward their articulations of race, class and regional identity.

Non-white audiences appreciated *The Cosby Show*'s portrayal of dignified blackness. Black audiences worldwide reported similar feelings of pride from watching the show and knowing others in the world were watching it. Compare the following statements made by an American, a Caribbean and a South African respondent:

> I like this show because it depicts black people in a positive way, I think he's [Cosby] good. It's good to see that blacks can be professionals.
>
> > (Jhally and Lewis, 1992: 81) (USA)

> Black people in this show are not isolated, no fun is made of Blackness, and the characters are shown as leading wholesome moral lives.
>
> > (Payne, 1994: 235) (Barbados)

> The show makes me proud of being black.
>
> > (Fuller, 1992: 111) (South Africa)

The pride these respondents feel issues in part from the fact that white audiences are watching, and that the show breaks with traditional portrayals of blacks. Each of the statements indicates an understanding that images of blacks in white popular culture have long been derisive, and expresses pride that, finally, blacks are being positively portrayed. These viewers believe that blacks throughout the West share a history and a common political goal of challenging the representations of blackness in Western popular culture. Their racial identity stretches beyond the borders of the nation-state, and must be understood as a transnational phenomenon (see Gilroy, 1993).

The Cosby Show also offered black viewers solace to help them through their daily struggles. As one black South African fan explained:

> [T]he Cosby Show . . . is saying, 'Come on, you white guys [in South Africa], the blacks are not so bad as you make them out to be. Look at us, we are having a good life and

normal problems here in America. Give those guys down there a chance. Let's change for the better and live together, not apart'.

(Fuller, 1992: 114)

As Downing (1988: 70) explains, the upper-middle-class setting of the show, 'is not simply a matter of blanking out the ugly realities of continuing oppression, but also of offering some sense of resolution to the grinding realities of racial tension and mistrust in the United States'. This audience member's comment reinforces this view, but extends its insights beyond the USA.

Perhaps unsurprisingly, many black viewers identified with the Huxtables, but non-black audiences also derived pride and solace from *The Cosby Show*'s representations of blackness. One Lebanese viewer, a Shiite Muslim and father, explained that 'American blacks are a little like us. They have big families' (Raschka, 1988: 16). Other viewers commented that the Huxtables '[come] across as successful and smart, without having sold out to white culture' (1988: 16). Here, we can see viewers identifying across racial lines. They recognize similar cultural traits, as well as the problems that many people of colour face in achieving material success while maintaining their cultural integrity (see Fanon, 1967). These remarks also point to an understanding of shared economic oppression. The respect that the Lebanese viewers give the Huxtables because of their material achievement suggests that such achievement is difficult and anomalous. Finally, we can see the racial dimensions of this shared class oppression in the identification of 'white culture' as threatening. The comment references contemporary and historical economic exclusions based upon skin colour.

Even as these discourses of class bind together people of different races and ethnicities, the discourse of regional identity can frustrate a shared racial discourse. Some male Barbadian viewers objected to Cliff's lack of authority in the family and claimed that the show taught Caribbean boys to be 'desperate to appease women' (Payne, 1994: 285). Other viewers complained about the show's detrimental influence on Caribbean values, behaviours and youth styles (Payne, 1994). Given the proximity of the Caribbean to the USA and the general dominance of US programming on Caribbean channels, a desire to maintain a distinction between black Caribbeans and Americans is not surprising. This situation offers further evidence that viewers understand international television through the twin discourses of racial and regional identity. Political and historical relations between nations and communities worldwide determine which of these identities is operative for which viewers.

Non-black viewers who reject a racial identification with the Huxtables may still identify with them through a discourse of regional identity. One white South African viewer, for instance, explained why he identifies with the African American Huxtables:

The greatest divide between black and white in this country is not the colour of one's skin but the first- and third-world values and attitudes displayed by the different race groups. . . . Therefore, we do not see the Cosby show as being about black people but we see it as a very entertaining sit-com displaying beliefs and values we can associate with.

(Fuller, 1992: 114)

This viewer asserts a regional Western identity, or First-World values as he puts it, which links him with the Huxtables across racial lines. Curiously, this bond does not extend to blacks who share the same national identity as the writer. We see, then, that this viewer's understanding of race in his own country depends upon experiences of extra-national identities, complicating any strictly national definitions of race. In this instance, regional identity is predominantly imagined as a class identity which includes all Westerners regardless of race.

Finally, white viewers in South Africa and elsewhere who did not identify with the Huxtables often displayed a voyeuristic fascination with the family's blackness. A Swedish journalist explainst that 'the fact that they are black also plays in [to her enjoyment of the show]. It makes it a little special. They are so much more attractive than white people' (Fuller, 1992: 107). This seemingly complimentary statement about black people belies a cliched vision of blacks as exotic Others. Likewise, a white South African viewer commented, 'You'd be surprised what that man [Cosby] has meant to the Afrikaner The Afrikaner doesn't mix with black men. The television brings the black man's quality right into his living room' (Mutson, 1986: 17). We can imagine a less enlightened viewer, perhaps one who is not speaking to an American journalist, saying that the show 'brings black men into his living room'. Both statements illustrate that *The Cosby Show* allows these viewers to experience blackness voyeuristically through the non-threatening confines of the sitcom genre. While audiences cannot 'simply laugh at these characters' (Gray, 1995: 81) they can still consume their blackness as an entertaining commodity and little else.

Conclusion: reframing blackness

The purpose of this article has been to demonstrate through an analysis of *The Cosby Show*'s international circulation some of the ways in which televisual representations of race operate as a transnational discourse of social identity.[4] While much of *The Cosby Show*'s success owes to the timing of its international syndication, which coincided with global deregulation and increased satellite presence, these factors cannot explain why the show became so popular with audiences, nor why it was more successful than its white counterpart, *Family Ties*. To answer these questions, we need to look instead at the twin discourses of race and region.

As we have seen, audiences make a distinction between racial identity and regional identity, although the one often impinges on the other. Among some Caribbeans whom we might expect to identify racially with the Huxtables, we observe instead distancing based upon regional distinctions. On the other hand, a white South African claims to identify with the Huxtables across racial lines based on a shared regional identity. These examples suggest that regional identity, like racial identity, is multidimensional. For the Caribbeans, it relates to historical differences, contemporary economic and cultural relations and an urban-rural dichotomy. For the South African, it refers to class distinctions. While regional identity is distinct from racial identity, the two concepts also overlap. Hence, the white South African's view on regional identity determines his view of black South Africans. Likewise, as noted above, Morley and Robbins' (1989) study shows that a European regional identity is being constructed from a racially specific culture and history. Given the growth in regional cultural exchanges, especially in audiovisual culture (O'Regan, 1992), and the importance of regional economies in the global market, regional identities are becoming increasingly prevalent. Although Gilroy (1993) shows how these identities can be liberating for people in the black Atlantic diaspora, comments from viewers of *The Cosby Show* show how regional identities can also be as insular and xenophobic as national or racial identities.

The interdependence of racial and regional identities should cause us to question any simple explanations about the global appeal of 'Western' shows. Part of *The Cosby Show*'s appeal to non-white audiences was its representation of cultural integrity in the midst of material plenty. These Western middle-class values are all the more powerful when shown as available to, and non-threatening for, audiences of different races and nationalities. *The Cosby Show* offered viewers the comfort of seeing characters with whom they identified enjoy the spoils of Western capitalism for a change. Integral to their enjoyment was the show's representation of a dignified blackness, which broke with centuries of popular Western images of blacks. Apparently, skin colour signifies a certain class identity to international audiences, and *The Cosby Show*'s unconventional image of dark skin in upper-middle-class surroundings seems to have had broad global appeal.

While the consequences of *The Cosby Show*'s export seem to have been positive for many audiences, not all of the influences were laudable. Because the show 'celebrates the virtues of upper-middle-class existence as the most desirable way of life' (Downing, 1988: 67), it promotes the nuclear family as the primary social unit on a worldwide scale. As Miller (1992) has noted in his studies of Caribbean culture, this 'global discourse of the domestic' is often a throwback to colonial ideals of respectability. Here, the nuclear family operates as a safe harbour in an otherwise stormy world, where efforts to shore up the family structure are more important than efforts to change society, and an undue amount of responsibility for maintaining this domestic sphere falls on women. Again, the Huxtables' blackness plays an integral role in disseminating the 'universality' of this particular family unit.

Television programmers at home and abroad learned a similar lesson from *The Cosby Show*: that a rich African American family could draw audiences across racial lines. While the cultural-economic climate surrounding *The Cosby Show*'s distribution was unique, middle- and upper-middle-class African American sitcoms like *A Different World, The Fresh Prince of Bel-Air, Family Matters* and *Moesha*, which followed in the wake of *The Cosby Show*, have achieved significant international success. These more recent shows, however, have primarily capitalized on the position of African American youth styles in global youth culture (see Boyd, 1997 and Gray, 1995), and their distribution has focused heavily on European markets (Schapiro, 1991).

This myopic concentration on Europe in spite of lucrative markets elsewhere, has caused 'black street styles and black bodies [to become] the universal signifiers of modernity and "difference"' (Hall, 1995: 15). Different routes of cultural exchange that would allow for different representations were activated and opened by *The Cosby Show*. However, these routes have since remained largely untravelled by US sitcoms. Nonetheless, the show provides evidence of a willingness among formerly colonized people to engage with representations of racial and regional differences that hold the potential to reshape international television distribution.

Notes

1   Only two scholarly investigations of *The Cosby Show*'s international distribution have been published: Linda Fuller (1992) surveyed audiences in several countries to determine their level of enjoyment of the show, and Monica Payne (1994) interviewed Barbadian men and women regarding their opinions of *The Cosby Show*'s representation of an ideal black family.

2   While some of these profits owe to Viacom's part-ownership of MTV-Europe, that channel did not begin operations until the summer of 1988.

3   Dating back to the days of slavery in the USA, African Americans have 'fostered a dual mode of behavior and expression [including humour] – one for whites and another for themselves' (Watkins, 1994: 32). In the realm of humour, this duality surfaces when 'African-Americans [become] the arbiters of a reversed joke in which others' assumptions of their ignorance [become] the source of humor' (Watkins, 1994: 33). The social and political implications of this self-mocking humour are debatable, and have led to sometimes vehement disagreements within and among African American communities.

4   A more exhaustive audience study would likely have found that gender and age differences are also common global divisions through which race and region signify.

References

Andrews, E.L. (1992) 'Studios Get a Reprieve In Battle Over Reruns', *The New York Times* 8 December: D2.
BBC (1988) 'S African MP Says "Cosby Show" Conveying ANC "Message" ', *BBC Summary of World Broadcasts* 3 June: 4B.

Boyd, T. (1997) *Am I Black Enough for You? Popular Culture from the 'Hood and Beyond*. Bloomington and Indianapolis: Indiana University Press.

Broadcast (1988) 'French Network M6 Has Bought Six Years – 124 Episodes – of *The Cosby Show*' 22 April: 20.

Downing, J. (1988) ' "The Cosby Show" and American Racial Discourse', pp. 46–73 in G. Smitherman-Donaldson and T.A. Van Dijk (eds) *Discourse and Discrimination*. Detroit, MI: Wayne State University Press.

Fanon, F. (1967) *Black Skin, White Masks*, trans. C. Markham. New York: Grove Press.

Flanigan, J. (1987) 'The American Dream Is Best Export US Has', *Los Angeles Times* 9 September: Sec. 4, 1.

Fuller, L. (1992) *The Cosby Show: Audiences, Impact, and Implications*. Westport, CT: Greenwood Press.

Gillespie, M. (1995) *Television, Ethnicity and Cultural Change*. London: Routledge.

Gilroy, P. (1993) *The Black Atlantic: Modernity and Double-Consciousness*. Cambridge, MA: Harvard University Press.

Goldberg, D.T. (1993) *Racist Culture: Philosophy and the Politics of Meaning*. Cambridge: Blackwell.

Gray, H. (1995) *Watching Race: Television and the Struggle for 'Blackness'*. Minneapolis and London: University of Minnesota Press.

Griffin, S. (1990) 'Errors of Comedy', *Broadcast* 11 May: 17.

Hall, S. (1995) 'Black and White Television', pp. 13–28 in J. Givanni (ed.) *Remote Control: Dilemmas of Black Intervention in British Film and TV*. London: British Film Institute.

Hall, S. (1996) 'What Is This "Black" in Black Popular Culture?', pp. 465–75 in D. Morley and K. Chen (eds) *Stuart Hall: Critical Dialogues in Cultural Studies*. London and New York: Routledge.

Henry, G. (1986) 'Why Is It that a Show Which Pulls a Massive 51 Per Cent Following in its Home Country Can Only Muster a Measly Three Million Viewers Here?', *Televisual* 21 April: 33–4.

Herman, E. and R. McChesney (1997) *The Global Media: The New Missionaries of Global Capitalism*. London and Washington: Cassell.

Heuton, C. (1990) 'An Enviable Situation: The Format Once Declared Dead Now Rules Syndication', *Channels* 17 December: 36–8.

Hilmes, M. (1993) 'Invisible Men: *Amos 'n' Andy* and the Roots of Broadcast Discourse', *Critical Studies in Mass Communication* 10(4): 301–21.

Hoskins, C., S. McFadyen and A. Finn (1997) *Global Television and Film: An Introduction to the Economics of the Business*. New York: Oxford University Press.

Huff, R. (1996) 'Sharing the Joke', *Television Business International* October: 52.

Jhally, S. and J. Lewis (1992) *Enlightened Racism: The Cosby Show, Audiences. and the Myth of the American Dream*. San Francisco, CA: Westview Press.

Jones, S. (1988) *Black Culture, White Youth: The Reggae Tradition from JA to UK*. London: Macmillan.

Lott, E. (1993) *Love and Theft: Blackface Minstrelsy and the American Working Class*. New York and Oxford: Oxford University Press.

Marable, M. (1983) *How Capitalism Underdeveloped Black America: Problems in Race, Political Economy and Society*. Boston, MA: South End Press.

Miller, D. (1992) 'The Young and the Restless in Trinidad: A Case of the Local and the Global in Mass Consumption', pp. 163–82 in R. Silverstone and E. Hirsch (eds) *Consuming Technologies: Media and Information in Domestic Spaces*. London and New York: Routledge.

Morley, D. and K. Robins (1989) 'Spaces of Identity: Communications Technologies and the Reconfiguration of Europe', *Screen* 30: 10–35.

Mufson, S. (1986) 'The "Cosby Plan" for South Africa', *Wall Street Journal* 30 July: Section 1, 17.

Nixon, R. (1994) *Homelands, Harlem and Hollywood: South African Culture and the World Beyond*. New York and London: Routledge.

O'Regan, T. (1992) 'The International, the Regional, and the Local: Hollywood's New & Declining Audience', pp. 75–98 in E. Jacka (ed.) *Continental Shift: Globalisation and Culture*. Double Bay, Australia: Local Consumption Publications.

Patterson, R. (1995) 'Chapter Four, Entertainment and Drama', in A. Smith (ed.) *Television: An International History*. Oxford: Oxford University Press.

Payne, M. (1994) 'The "Ideal" Black Family? A Caribbean View of *The Cosby Show*', *Journal of Black Studies* 25: 231–49.

Pieterse, J. (1992) *White on Black: Images of Africa and Blacks in Western Popular Culture*. New Haven, CT and London: Yale University Press.

Press, A. (1991) *Women Watching Television: Gender, Class, and Generation in the American Television Experience*. Philadelphia: University of Pennsylvania Press.

Raschka, M. (1988) 'Hold Your Fire, It's "Cosby" Time: TV Show's Popularity Cuts Across All Factions in Beirut', *Chicago Tribune* 19 June: C16.

Richter, P. (1985) 'Viacom Quietly Becomes Major Force in TV', *Los Angeles Times* 22 September: Sec. 5, 1.

Riggs, M. (1991) *Colour Adjustment*, videocassette. San Francisco, CA: California Newsreel.

Robins, K. (1989) 'Reimagined Communities: European Image Space, Beyond Fordism', *Cultural Studies* 3: 145–65.

Roediger, D. (1991) *The Wages of Whiteness: Race and the Making of the American Working Class*. London and New York: Verso.

Rogin, M. (1996) *Blackface, White Noise: Jewish Immigrants in the Hollywood Melting Pot*. Berkeley: University of California Press.

Ross, K. (1996) *Black and White Media: Black Images in Popular Film and Television*. Cambridge: Polity Press.

Schapiro, M. (1991) 'Lust-Greed-Sex-Power: Translatable Anywhere', *The New York Times* 2 June: Section 2, 29.

Securities and Exchange Commission (1987) Viacom, Inc. 10-K Filing 31 December.

Securities and Exchange Commission (1991) Viacom, Inc. 10-K Filing 31 December.

Spivak, G. (1990) *The Post-Colonial Critic: Interviews, Strategies, Dialogues*. New York and London: Routledge.

Taylor, E. (1989) *Prime Time Families in Postwar America*. Berkeley: University of California Press.

The Independent (1992) 'Television/Statistics' 13 February: 36.

Tomlinson, J. (1991) *Cultural Imperialism*. Baltimore, MD: The Johns Hopkins University Press.

Viacom (1985) *Annual Report*.

Watkins, M. (1994) *On the Real Side: Laughing, Lying, and Signifying, the Underground Tradition of African-American Humour that Transformed American Culture, from Slavery to Richard Pryor*. New York: Simon & Schuster.

Ziegler, P. (1988) 'The $600-Million Man: Will a Record Syndication Gamble on "Cosby Show" Re-runs Pay off?', *Los Angeles Times* 2 October: 4.

PART SIX

Watching Television

A S WAS POINTED OUT in the general introduction, a significant strand of television studies over the past twenty years or so has been concerned with the nature and meanings of "watching television." This work has been referred to variously as the "new" audience studies, reception studies, and ethnographic studies. If forced to choose, we would probably opt for reception studies for a couple of reasons. Reception suggests a process that extends well beyond and begins before the literal act of viewing television. Reception entails viewing and listening to television (raptly, casually, intermittently, or accidentally), but also talking about what we have seen/are about to see, being addressed as a viewer by television's programs and scheduling practices (late afternoon for kids; late night for adults), and encountering television through other media as well (articles about television programs in the press, official or fan-sponsored websites). Because of television's primary (though certainly not exclusive) place within the home, reception studies have attempted to situate television viewing within the rhythms and routines of everyday domestic life.

The study of reception also suggests a different focus and larger goal than the study of the audience. Broadcasters, ratings services, and advertisers have long been interested in determining the size and demographic constitution of the audience for a particular television program. And, again as was discussed in the general introduction, an older tradition of mass communication research attempted to identify the behavioral and attitudinal effects upon particular audiences of television viewing. Reception studies are concerned with the popularity of programs and programming forms, but they are interested in far more than merely the number or kinds of people who watch. Rather they ask how do people understand, make pleasurable, and use the television that they watch?

Reception studies do not dismiss the unequal power relationships involved in the encounter between viewer and television—the term reception still connotes a relationship in which viewers "receive" that which is "sent" by those in a position to control the sounds and images that appear on the screen. Indeed, one of the major debates circulating around reception studies in television has been over the latitude that viewers have in shaping the experience of television to suit their own purposes. But regardless how any given reception study would weigh the balance of power between the interests of viewers and the interests of institutions, it would certainly see the engagement of television by viewers as much more complex and varied than the term "effects" could possibly encompass.

Reception also suggests some things about the nature of our "membership" in the television audience. Although Matt Hills's article will discuss an extreme, especially intense mode of audience identification between cult-TV fans and the programs to which they are devoted, people are not reducible to television viewers. Furthermore, being a part of the audience for a particular program does not preclude our being a part of the audience for many other, different programs, nor our engagement with other media forms. Television constantly has to recruit us *as* audience members. We are encouraged not only to watch a given program, but also in the process to see ourselves as belonging to an imaginary social group linked by our willingness to "become" part of the audience for a given program or a given cable network ("must-see TV"). As a result, reception studies are concerned with the ways that television addresses us as viewers in addition to the ways that we understand ourselves in that role. The essays chosen for inclusion in this section address different aspects of reception and together underscore the complexities of the seemingly simple phrase "watching television."

Television studies' interest in the audience and in issues of reception in the 1980s prompted a search for a conceptual and methodological basis for studying what turned out to be the surprisingly complex and varied phenomenon that occurred whenever someone "watched" television. Ellen Seiter's essay, reproduced from her book, *Television and New Media Audiences*, recounts the emergence of a significant strand of audience or reception research within television studies in the 1980s. For our purposes she very helpfully surveys the theoretical contexts out of which that work emerged and thus eliminates the necessity of our rehearsing that discussion here. In other words, you might want to read her piece first.

She begins that essay by reviewing the kinds of questions asked by what she calls qualitative audience research, chief among them perhaps "How can we study the way viewers interpret television programmes in routinely occurring settings, such as the home or the school?" The approach many television scholars found most amenable to this task derived from the general principles and methods of ethnographic anthropology. The goal of ethnography, as practiced by cultural anthropologists is, as Seiter puts it, "to produce a holistic description of a culture" through extended observation and descriptive writing. As applied to the study of television viewing, ethnography served more as an overall intellectual guide than a generally followed set of prescriptions for data collection or interpretation. Seiter discusses some of the most important expressions of ethnographic audience research in television studies and carefully teases out the difficult methodological and conceptual issues that such studies raise. Not least among these is the relationship between the investigator and the "subjects" whose television viewing is the object of his or her research.

The essay on children's taste in television programming by Hannah Davies, David Buckingham, and Peter Kelley grows directly out of the tradition of reception studies launched in the UK in the early 1980s, which Seiter discusses in her essay. Their essay addresses a rather glaring gap in the television studies literature on reception: despite the fact that children make up a significant segment of the audience for broadcast television in most countries around the world, most reception studies assume that the audience for television is an adult audience. Thus our understanding of how "people" watch television, the meanings and pleasures that might be derived from watching, and the social contexts of viewing are all predicated upon a model of the viewer *as* adult. As was discussed in the general introduction, as early as the late 1960s the child viewer of television was being subjected to enormous scientific scrutiny in the US, but these studies were focused on a single dimension of children's relationship with television: the behavioral and attitudinal effects of viewing represented violence—and were conducted within a research paradigm that inhibited rather than encouraged a holistic understanding of the reception of television among children.

Rather than ask what television does *to* children, Davies, Buckingham, and Kelley ask: how do children "perceive *themselves* as an audience" for television? They use several research strategies in an attempt to elicit from two groups of British school children (one group aged 10–11; the other aged 6–7) a sense of what they see as the differences between programming "for children" and programming "for adults." This piece of research is useful not only for the insights it offers into children's understanding of themselves as audience, but also for its discussion of the implications of the authors' research design and methods. They note, for example, that the opposition adult/child that structured their thinking about the relationship between children and television programming was not necessarily one that the children in their samples were comfortable with.

Just as our assumptions about television reception frequently presume an adult viewer, they also frequently presume that the default-mode site of reception is the home. Anna McCarthy's essay suggests that the focus on television as a domestic appliance and television viewing as occurring in the private spaces of the home may have obscured the role of television in our lives outside the home. She asks us to think about the quite different dynamics of television viewing in the variety of public spaces where television vies for our attention. She is especially interested here in the provision of television in those spaces outside the home where we wait: to travel (airports), to be served as consumers (dentists' offices, automobile dealerships), to gain access to public services (emergency rooms, employment offices). Watching television takes on a different character in such spaces, even if the programs shown are those we could watch at home. As McCarthy argues, watching the program that we and others might regard as a waste of time at home somehow is legitimized by becoming a part of the experience of involuntary waiting in public. Furthermore, an entire sector of the television industry has emerged to provide television sets and programs exclusively for those situations in which we are confined to waiting rooms of one type or another and forced to wait: CNN Airport Network, for example, is now as much a part of the experience of American airports as overpriced food and boarding delays.

One focus of recent work in television and cultural studies has been fan cultures: television viewers who are intensely engaged with particular television programs, performers, and/or genres, and whose "reception" practices extend well beyond merely watching television. Matt Hills's essay, prepared especially for this collection, examines television programs that become the objects of such intense fan devotion and the production, marketing, reception, communicative, and discursive practices that together constitute "cult TV." Hills takes us through the ways in which cult TV might be defined: as particular television texts, as produced through discourse about particular texts, or as a set of fan practices in relation to particular television texts. How we define cult TV is not just a narrow definitional issue, he argues, but has methodological and, indeed, political implications. For example, if cult TV is *merely* a matter of the qualities of particular television texts (certain character types, certain storylines, certain settings, certain stylistic features), then this suggests that cult TV involves the calculated manufacture of television programs *as* cult TV, and that cult TV fans are dupes of the industry. Furthermore, it begs the question of why every program that shares those qualities doesn't become an instance of cult TV. Hills argues that the cult TV phenomenon is most productively viewed as a complex interaction among television programming forms, discourses about them, and fan practices.

We also include in this part a chapter from John Hartley's recent book, *The Uses of Television*. As with a number of the more theoretical essays we've included in this collection, Hartley's essay on television and cultural citizenship resonates with themes from several different parts.

It proposes a very different notion of citizenship than is entailed in other essays that address television's role in the public sphere (see essays by Collins in Part One: Institutions of Television, Sparks and Cunningham in Part Two: Spaces of Television, and Morley in Part Five: Social Representations on Television). Hartley suggests that we reimagine television's relationship with the viewer as one between teacher and the various "addressees" constituted by its multiple discourses: student (of television, first of all), consumer, and citizen.

Television "teaches" two new forms of citizenship: cultural and "do-it-yourself" or DIY citizenship, which do not supplant but are mapped over older understandings of the relationship between the individual and the social and political order. Since the eighteenth century, western democracies have gradually enshrined three types of citizenship and their accompanying constellations of rights: civic (basic individual rights of expression, ownership of property, etc.), political (the right to participate in the political process), and social (the right to basic education and welfare benefits). But not all citizens have shared equally in these rights, and the extension of full citizenship beyond the European, white, adult males to whom they were first applied has been uneven. It is among those groups on the margins of traditional understandings of citizenship (colonized groups, minority racial, ethnic, or religious groups) that, says Hartley, a fourth form of citizenship has most clearly arisen: cultural or identity citizenship. Cultural citizenship entails the "right" to be different, to identify oneself with a larger group based not only on race, ethnicity, or territoriality, but also upon cultural choices and social practices. Cultural citizenship, then, does not necessarily line up neatly with traditional notions of citizenship based upon national identity and held in place by traditional social and political institutions (the legal system, representative politics, etc.). The great fear of early theorists of the mass media was that radio and television would replace the active, individual participant in interpersonal communication with the undifferentiated and passive mass audience. But, Hartley argues, rather than turning the audience into a "mass of infantilized consumers," television and other mass media have helped to "produce an endless succession of ever more weird and wonderful, actual and virtual cultural identities, each one carefully differentiated from the one next door."

Chapter 29

ELLEN SEITER

QUALITATIVE AUDIENCE RESEARCH

LOOKING AT MEDIA in the context of everyday life presents many research problems. How can we study the way viewers interpret television programmes in routinely occurring settings, such as the home or the school? What is the best way to get people to talk about the meanings they derive from television programmes when they may be unaccustomed to interpreting TV material explicitly? How can we study what goes on when people consume media, when so much media consumption takes place in private, and in the domestic sphere, in the context of intimate relationships? How can we study conversation about the media, short of trailing a person throughout the day? How does the researcher herself influence, inhibit, and change the ways people will talk about the media? The media overlap with many dimensions of social life, such as gender roles in the family, political beliefs, social networks of kin and friendship, routines of the clock at home, work, and school, allocation of household resources, and the organization of the workplace. How do we draw the line in our data collection between audience research and the study of society, the family, the community? Should we draw such a line? These are some of the problems facing researchers interested in using qualitative methods to study media audiences.

In this [chapter] I wish to argue for the usefulness of ethnographic methods in studying television viewing and computer use. The dozen studies that I will review in this chapter share a use of semi-structured and open-ended interviews. Most commonly used is a procedure of interviews, often with groups of subjects, where the interviewer follows an outline of interview topics and questions, but allows informants to raise topics not included on the list. Still, considerable variation exists from study to study in terms of contact time, the role of the interviewer, the adherence to questions written out in advance, the settings for the interviews, the use of group interviews, and the means of contacting subjects.

I begin, then, with a consideration of ethnographic method, the anthropological tradition in which its research procedures were developed, and the difficulties in translating this model to the study of media in contemporary social life. I compare the tradition of US mass communication research based on a media effects or uses and gratifications paradigm with audience studies influenced by a cultural studies paradigm. Next, I discuss examples of two kinds of study: one is based on Stuart Hall's encoding–decoding model and focuses on viewer interpretations of specific television programmes; the other is based more broadly on the domestic contexts of media consumption and the way these are structured by family relationships. The next section takes up the influence of Pierre Bourdieu's concepts of cultural capital and aesthetic dispositions on the field of television studies and on my own research. Finally, I discuss the importance of theories of language to audience research, and the importance of self-reflexivity about the researcher's role in shaping the interview process and the 'othering' of research subjects.

Ethnographic method

Ethnographic method is a distinctive research process developed within anthropology and sociology involving extended periods of participant observation and emphasizing descriptive writing of both field notes and the final ethnography. Ethnography's goal is to produce a holistic description of a culture. As anthropologists George Marcus and Michael Fischer describe it: 'Ethnography is a research process in which the anthropologist closely observes, records, and engages in the daily life of another culture – an experience labeled as the fieldwork method – and then writes accounts of this culture, emphasizing descriptive detail' (1986: 18). Very few media audience studies, even those using ethnographic or qualitative methods, have measured up to the normative standards of ethnography proper. Most of the time, 'ethnographic' has been used very loosely to indicate any research that uses qualitative interviewing techniques. Many of the most influential audience research projects, such as David Morley's study of lower-middle-class London families (1986), Janice Radway's work on middle-aged readers of paperback romances (1984), Ien Ang's analysis of letters from *Dallas* fans (1985), Ann Gray's study of video cassette recorder use (1987, 1992), and Elihu Katz and Tamar Liebes's cross-cultural study of focus groups discussing *Dallas* (Liebes 1990), were not designated ethnography by the original authors, but were labelled ethnographic in secondary accounts. While ethnographies are based on long-term and in-depth fieldwork, most audience research has been based on brief periods of contact, in some cases less than one hour, with the informants. Also, while ethnographic methods have traditionally been used to study culture as a whole, media researchers study only one aspect of a culture – such as television – when using this method, and attempt to relate it to social identity (Seiter *et al.* 1989: 227).

Some media research does meet the requirements of ethnography, including Marie Gillespie's study of Punjabi youth in Southall, England (1995), Camille Bacon-Smith's account of US *Star Trek* fans (1992), and Angela McRobbie's study of teenage girls at a Birmingham youth club (1991). The difference between these studies and other audience research is that they involved extended contact time over a period of years, and a combination of methods, including quantitative ones. As Gillespie puts it, ethnographic fieldwork 'is characterised by a multiplicity of data-gathering strategies, in a variety of contexts, drawing upon the experiences of a wide range of people over a long period of time' (1995: 60). [. . .]

Mass communications vs. cultural studies

Central to the renewed interest in qualitative research on media audiences have been questions of how specific audiences make meanings in their engagement with media in the context of everyday life, an emphasis on audience activity rather than passivity, and an interest in why the media are pleasurable. This move stems in part from the increased agency attributed to the media consumer in uses and gratifications research, a paradigm that succeeded in altering the way media effects were discussed before the 1960s in US mass communications research. As communications scholar Carl Bybee characterized the effects tradition: 'The history of mass communication effects research in the United States is the history of a relentless, empirical search, first for direct, powerful short-term attitudinal effects, and later for the intervening variables which could be regarded as either facilitative or obstructive of those effects' (1987: 195). The uses and gratifications research represented a shift to a more optimistic and less harmful characterization of the relationship between media and audiences, emphasizing active engagement and the ways the media could be employed by individuals to satisfy needs and accomplish personal goals. According to Bybee, uses and gratifications research does not represent a dramatic break from the traditional effects perspective, as it kept intact 'its conservative bias regarding the process by which political power is distributed in society' (1987: 194). The shift from the effects model to uses and gratifications is only an evolution at both the systems and individual levels, as the focus of attention changed from the communicator to the audience. What was left behind was essentially an untenable stimulus-response conception of the media effects process. What was carried along was essentially a limited conception of the media effects process, a lack of explicit social theoretical referents for the interpretation of individual level results, and a consumerist frame of reference (1987: 196).

The other influence on audience research has been British cultural studies. The twin influences of the uses and gratifications model and British cultural studies are not easily distinguished in a single piece of research, and often scholars such as David Morley recognize both paradigms as influential on their work. Cultural studies brought to audience research the emphasis on processes of decoding cultural texts, and theories derived from semiotics (Eco 1976) and reader-response literature (Iser 1978). The British cultural studies tradition grew out of ethnographic research carried out at the Centre for Contemporary Cultural Studies (CCCS) in the 1970s at the University of Birmingham, and captured a more nuanced sense of the complexity of television as a text, as well as a conception of audience activity that was informed by Marxist theories of ideology – which brought explicit questions about social power to the research, distinguishing it markedly from the uses and gratifications perspective. The uses and gratifications model is based on a pluralist conception of society – in which there is something for everyone in the media forms on offer – and a functionalist sociological model – focusing on the explanation of social stability. Uses and gratifications research thus lacks a concern with the power relationships that determine both audiences and forms of media production, while the cultural studies model has tried explicitly to address the question of social power on a number of fronts.

The borrowing of ethnographic research methods from anthropology was motivated by a critique of experimental and survey audience research in the mass communications tradition. The critique associated with 'critical communications scholars' addressed research procedures, theoretical underpinnings (especially behaviourism), and institutional influences (such as the preference for quantitative findings). Such research failed to address important questions of reception and audience activity. The charges were that mass communications audience researchers were wedded to methodologies that restricted them to questions answerable through quantitative methods. In particular, there had been too much emphasis on observable behaviours, rather than structures of meaning. This emphasis on quantifiable phenomena locked mass communications researchers into a cycle of number-crunching. Funding agencies increasingly demanded statistical results. Such administrative research thus followed the norms of market research, where sponsors require clear-cut findings.

Mass communications researchers avoided studying the media in context, preferring instead sanitized, controllable situations (laboratory, telephone interviews), producing data that was irrelevant to everyday life. Often researchers remained ignorant of the media forms they studied and handled media content awkwardly, if at all. Finally, mass communications research lacked a theoretical perspective on language as discourse. This led to a preference for reducing answers to easily codified categories or taking subjects' answers at face value. Similarly, content was reduced to verbal summaries of observable events on screen.

The research that I will describe in this chapter represented a departure from these norms, and bears the influence of ethnographic method. First of all, the new audience studies differ methodologically from quantitative research in that their projects tend to proceed without a clear-cut hypothesis, and investigate multiple research questions interpretively. My research deviates, then, from the scientific model widely adapted by US social scientists (even those working in the uses and gratifications tradition) – with the exception of anthropologists – in the twentieth century. Sample sizes tend to be much smaller than those required for survey research, nearly always involving fewer than one hundred research subjects, in some cases fewer than thirty. Thus, statistical generalizability is sacrificed; the model for such research is the case study, rather than the survey.

In many of the television audience studies I will describe here, quantification is avoided, or relegated to an appendix. Instead, extensive quotation of informants is presented. There is as much interest in the thoughts and feelings of audience members as in their behaviour. Typically, the research requires the establishment of rapport between the researcher and the subject. This may range from conducting interviews in a friendly, open manner to establishing personal friendships with informants.

Traditional social scientists have faulted this work for lack of generalizability, bias, political axe-grinding, failure to employ multiple methods, and a casual and sloppy approach to data collection. Some of this new research was carried out by scholars trained in the humanities, often by European rather than US academics, or by those trained in disciplines influenced by recent European theory (such as semiotics and psychoanalysis), especially literary criticism, textual analysis, and film theory. The CCCS, under Stuart Hall's guidance, was a crucial influence on the development of this work. Like much of the research conducted at the centre, these researchers' work was rooted in Marxist and feminist theory, and questions of class and gender have therefore been central. By contrast, audience researchers in the mass communications tradition have been trained in social science disciplines, especially social psychology, or in journalism (Delia 1987). In the mass communications tradition, especially in the USA, there has been less emphasis on theoretical developments. James Curran, in criticizing the 'new revisionism' in qualitative audience research, has expressed understandable irritation with the failure of some researchers to recognize when they are revisiting questions that have been debated since the 1950s, without reference to any work done before 1970 (Curran 1996: 264–7). Thus the conflict between so-called 'ethnographic' audience researchers and mass communications researchers involves a generation gap, a disciplinary split, and a continental divide.

Encoding/decoding

A good way to see the differences between a US mass communications perspective on audiences, and a European media studies approach, is in Hall's influential encoding–decoding model and its application in David Morley and Charlotte Brunsdon's work on the news magazine programme *Nationwide*. The centrality of ideology, the variability of interpretation of television, and the complex variables in viewers' interpretations form the core of the theory.

David Morley's first study followed a detailed analysis with Charlotte Brunsdon of *Nationwide*, which was published as *Everyday Television: 'Nationwide'* (Brunsdon and Morley 1978). In the second project, published as *The 'Nationwide' Audience* (Morley 1980), Morley

> explored how that programme material was interpreted by individuals from different social backgrounds, with a view to establishing the role of cultural frameworks in deter-mining individual interpretations of the programmes in question . . . [and] some of the relations between socio-demographic factors (such as age, sex, race, class) and differen-tial interpretation of the same programme material.
>
> (1992: 75)

The *Nationwide* study was an attempt to elucidate the encoding–decoding model, adapted from Frank Parkins's work. Discussions of the project frequently neglect the close textual analysis that preceded the audience study. It is crucial, however, to the project's conception, that the research was designed first to elaborate the encoding of the programme before exploring the variety of decodings.

The encoding–decoding model was an attempt to get away from a linear sender–message–receiver model of mass communication. It posits three distinctive types of interpretations or decodings. The *dominant reading* is performed by viewers who accept the programme and its genre completely. These viewers would agree with the dominant ideology (the preferred reading) of the programme without formulating any objections in their minds. Such a viewer uses ideology to explain her own life and behaviour, and her social experiences. In a *negotiated reading*, the viewer inflects his interpretation on the basis of a particular social experience. The viewer may enjoy a 'pick and choose' relationship to the genre, ignoring more disagreeable sections and concentrating on those more to taste. Another way to think of this is in terms of 'shifting' the text slightly to fit individual interests. Here, the media consumer is mainly in line with dominant ideology, but needs to adjust certain aspects to fit her local situation. She might ignore some parts of the show, while focusing on others, providing explanations of events portrayed that suit her own worldview, not all of which may be as strongly 'there' as others. The most radical viewing position is that of an *oppositional reading* – in which the viewer goes against the preferred reading. This type of reading is characterized by annoyance rather than pleasure – as when the reader, recognizing the political motivation of a news programme, says, 'There they go, up to their old tricks again!' (Fiske 1992: 292–8).

The encoding–decoding model insists on the struggle involved in gaining people's agreement with ideology; both because television is complex in how it tells stories, and because how people read television will necessarily be based on their own experiences – what kind of jobs they have, where they live, their educational backgrounds, memberships in unions or political parties, as well as gender, ethnicity, sexual orientation, and class.

For the audience project, Morley gathered focus groups of adult education students who viewed a tape of the programme and then participated in a discussion. While some of the decodings were predictable, given the class position of his subjects, Morley concluded that a more complex model was necessary to determine the ways that social position might predispose TV viewers to make certain types of ideological reading. Contradictory in nature are the responses which individuals may make to different types of programme: audience members may read one programme subversively, another according to a dominant reading; or they may read the same material differently depending on the context. A single individual would not read all of the media the same way: some shows might be laughed off, while others are despised; still other shows might be found to be very absorbing. Interpretations or decodings will also vary. [. . .]

Decoding fiction

Another study influenced by the encoding–decoding model was Sut Jhally and Justin Lewis's audience research on *The Cosby Show*. The study was funded in part by Bill and Camille Cosby and was widely publicized in the USA. The design called for focused interviews in which a single episode of the show would be shown and discussed by people who were already familiar with the show. The sample consisted of fifty-three small friendship or family groups, roughly divided between white and African-American residents, and between middle-class and working-class groups. All were residents of a small New England city.

The study, published in 1992 as the book *Enlightened Racism*, incudes a content analysis of the episode, of *The Cosby Show* as a series, and of the history of representations of black and of working-class characters on US television. The ambitions of the study go far beyond the encoding – decoding model – which makes the study a useful polemic, but also limits its interest in terms of audience study. The preface sets out the scope of the book:

This book deals with issues of immense political importance. It addresses two critical aspects of our contemporary culture: how our most ubiquitous cultural form, television, influences the way we think; and how American society thinks about race in the post-Civil Rights era. We chose to study audience reactions to *The Cosby Show* because of its position in relation to these two issues.

(Jhally and Lewis 1992: xv)

In guiding the discussions, trained interviewers showed the programme and then solicited feelings about the characters and descriptions of the plot's episode, in which conflict ensues after Claire discovers her son Theo reading a 'girlie' magazine. Interviewers investigated viewers' decodings only superficially, as in determining whether most respondents liked and admired the characters, and whether they found the situations true to life. Instead, questions about the television programme served as a pretext for getting at larger social attitudes. Even when responses did not suggest attitudes towards class and race, these were pursued by the interviewer:

These innocuous questions often succeeded in opening up the discussion by giving respondents the opportunity to remark on attitudes toward class, race, or gender, attitudes the interviewer could then explore. If respondents were less forthcoming, the interviewer could ask them to comment on these topics – for example, 'How would you feel if the Huxtable family were white?' and 'Would the show be as good if the Huxtables were a blue-collar family?' Because the initial responses to these questions were sometimes ambiguous, guarded, or even misleading, the answers were carefully explored in the ensuing discussion.

(Jhally and Lewis 1992: 11)

Jhally and Lewis claim that their initial findings suggested optimism about the ability of whites to accept black characters – even to love and admire them on television.

The interviewees might have suspected the interviewers of false pretences, as questions about *The Cosby Show* turned increasingly to discussions of race relations in the USA. As the interviewers probed attitudes towards race, they received rather depressing answers: the majority of white respondents enjoyed *The Cosby Show* because the characters were neither too black nor too working class, and – even worse – that the show served as a sort of argument against affirmative action. Thus, *Cosby* is implicated in the defence of Reaganomics, the dismantling of affirmative action, and the widening class divide. In the end, they conclude that *Cosby* has an insidious effect on white Americans:

For many white respondents in our study, the Huxtables' achievement of the American dream leads them to a world where race no longer matters. This attitude enables white viewers to combine an impeccably liberal attitude toward race with a deep-rooted suspicion of black people.

They are, on the one hand, able to welcome a black family into their homes; they can feel an empathy with them and identify with their problems and experiences. They will, at the same time, distinguish between the Huxtables and most other black people, and their welcome is clearly only extended as far as the Huxtables.

(1992: 110)

For black viewers, *Cosby* is pernicious, not because it encourages racist attitudes, as it does with the white viewers, but because it forces African Americans to accept the television industry's position that normalcy means upper-middle-class status, and that a positive portrayal of Blacks necessitates their belonging to a socio-economic stratum that the majority of black viewers cannot hope to attain.

Jhally and Lewis's study, then, successfully publicized an argument about the class background of television characters that has been made most notably by George Lipsitz (1990) – that US television has abandoned dramas about working-class characters and, instead, populates its programmes with upper-middle-class professionals, presenting a demographic picture drastically skewed from that of the real population of the USA. *Enlightened Racism* also introduces an important and too often overlooked discussion of the intersection of class and race identities. But the study's empirical findings are troubling on a number of points. Gender is almost completely erased from its major findings. This seems highly problematic in a study dealing with a genre – the domestic comedy – that turns so centrally around gender conflicts, and an episode theme – magazine pornography – that seems to insist on such a reading. While differences between men and women are rarely highlighted in the interviews, stark oppositions between whites and blacks emerge in terms of attitudes. For the white respondents, the interview situation itself seemed a sort of set-up: to say good things about *Cosby* – perhaps even in the spirit of seeming enlightened, liberal – led one down the road to apologism for an entire decade's political failings – including the retrenchment of the welfare state (H. Gray 1993). This may be a cause of one of the problems that was encountered in conducting the *Cosby* interviews: Lewis notes that analysis of the interviews was difficult because of the 'cautious and evasive' responses on the topic of race. The *Cosby* study calls attention to the ways that informants may be cognizant of the interviewers' wish to categorize them in ideological terms, and may wish to resist these efforts. There is also the question of whether domestic viewing of entertainment programmes can be reducible to ideological position. In another book discussing this research, *The Ideological Octopus* (1991), Justin Lewis described the viewers they interviewed to be lacking in critical discourses about television, but this may speak more to the flaws in the adequacy of the decoding model, and to the superficiality of what respondents feel permitted to say in a focus group, as it does to the degree of racism in the United States.

In some ways, the *Cosby* study tells us little about television itself, since the researchers were eager to move beyond the subtleties of audience interpretation to get to the more important, overarching theme of racism. The danger in such a design is that television is used as a mere pretext for conversation and insufficient attention is given to the complexities of television form. Thus the television programme may be reduced to a series of 'messages' (as in the traditional effects paradigms) and themes – aspects of programming that are clearly only a small part of the experience of television viewing and could easily be ignored or rejected by viewers.

On the other hand, as a study of racism, *Enlightened Racism* offers no information about the connection between words and actions, about the different background of the respondents' lives in terms of their interactions with people of different races. Instead, a highly reified picture of whites emerges that bears little feel for the necessarily lived contradictions of race and class relations in the contemporary USA. Indeed, the picture that emerges is one of a dominant ideological discourse holding total sway over television viewers – something quite other than the adoption of Gramsci's theory of hegemony originally proposed by Hall in the encoding–decoding model.

[. . .]

The encoding–decoding model seems to work better for news and nonfiction programmes than it does for entertainment programmes, where it is much more difficult to identify a single message, or even a set of propositions with which audience members could agree or disagree. Drawing conclusions from his *Nationwide* study – and these would apply to fiction programming as well – Morley has astutely recommended 'dropping the assumption that we are principally dealing with the overtly political dimension of communications' and, instead, 'dealing more with the relevance/irrelevance and comprehension/incomprehension dimensions of decoding rather than being directly concerned with the acceptance or rejection of substantive ideological themes or propositions' (Morley 1992: 127). To some extent this agenda is implicit in the move towards studying the contexts of television reception, especially in domestic space. In the following section I turn to three influential studies of media consumption that are based on the study of the domestic sphere rather than specific texts.

Feminist studies of domestic contexts

As feminist scholars have frequently argued, nuclear families are places where gender roles are produced, played out, and challenged. Three of the foundational works in audience studies that take up this argument are Janice Radway's *Reading the Romance* (1984), David Morley's *Family Television* (1986), and Ann Gray's *Video Playtime* (1992). These projects established the significance for media studies of the feminist tenet that the home is perceived as a place of leisure for men and a place of work for women, and media consumption is inextricably linked to gender roles.

In *Reading the Romance*, Radway relied on a key informant, who worked at a bookstore, recommended paperback books to many customers, and published a newsletter discussing the best romances on the market. This key informant put Radway in touch with other women, to whom she gave a survey questionnaire (thus, employing some quantitative analysis in the book) and invited to focus-group interviews.

In some ways, Radway's study borrowed from the 'uses and gratifications' tradition of media research by asking what place these books have in the lives of her informants. Unlike uses and gratifications research, however, the question of textual interpretation – both Radway's own and that of her informants – is at the centre of the study. Radway's book captures many contradictions inherent in the act of women's reading, by sorting out the differing tendencies in the readers' motivations, in the ideology of the texts themselves, and in the use of reading as a strategy to secure leisure time. The prestige of reading as an activity was used by these women to justify the leisure time required to read books and their own release from housekeeping and childcare chores. Radway mounts a subtle argument that women use these deeply conservative books, in which heterosexual romance provides the ultimate meaning to women's lives, to liberate themselves from the conditions of patriarchal marriage. Radway also frames her study of romance novels with an analysis of the publishing industry, and the place of the genre and its women readers in the economics of bookstores and marketing. In this respect, the study exemplifies a strategy that has been only rarely followed (see Shattuc 1997) of combining political economic research with audience research.

In *Family Television*, Morley found that the behaviours of television usage were inextricably linked to family hierarchies and gender roles. Morley had set out to 'produce a more developed conceptual model of viewing behavior in the context of family leisure' (1986: 17). He interviewed eighteen white families in South London: each family consisted of two parents, two or more children, and had a television and VCR in the home. (Informants were located by a market research firm.) Morley argued that television audiences need to be studied in the natural settings in which most media are consumed, and so he elected to study television at home, among family members.

Morley found distinctively different viewing styles reported by men and women, and a great deal of conflict between them concerning the TV. Husbands charged that their wives and daughters talk too much while the TV is on; wives complained that their husbands talk too little. The men Morley interviewed tended to adopt a style of intense, cinema-style viewing; the women were more distracted, tending to do chores at the same time as watching TV – unless they were alone in the house. Morley organized the gender-related themes in the interview material into the following categories: power and control over programme choice; viewing style; planned and unplanned viewing; amounts of viewing; television-related talk; use of video; solo viewing and guilty pleasures; programme type preference (Morley 1986: 146).

Morley found that men watched more television, planned their viewing more, and tended to control what others in the household watched. Women viewed less, often deferred to other family members in the selection of programmes, and enjoyed watching soap operas and melodramas, especially when they were alone. Morley found that his subjects seemed already to like those 'gender genres' designed for them. Women voiced a taste for soaps and movies; men preferred crime shows and sports. Morley's interviews were conducted *en famille*. Using Pierre Bourdieu's notion of cultural capital, he suggests that men were under-reporting their fictional viewing and over-reporting their viewing of news and documentary, based in part on their perception of the differential evaluations of these kinds of television in the system of social distinctions. Women seemed to feel freer to admit that they watched and liked TV.

In *Video Playtime*, Ann Gray reports on interviews with thirty women from predominantly working-class backgrounds who were contacted through a video rental library. Gray focused on a series of interrelated topics: the incorporation of the VCR into the domestic sphere, the gendered division of labour and leisure in terms of use of and attitudes towards the VCR, and preferences for particular genres of video. All the women in Gray's sample had children at home and had husbands who were the household's primary wage-earner.

Gray found that many women reported that the home was a difficult place for them to relax. The women she interviewed rarely took breaks from domestic chores, which lessened their enjoyment of the VCR. Gray explains that the husbands' greater involvement with the VCR was the result of 'a combination of masculine address of VCR advertising, the relative freedom of male leisure time in the home, and male economic power' (1992: 243). For husbands and children, then, the greater freedom from domestic chores made them more likely to watch videos, rent them, plan ahead for recording and time-shifting, and become adept at operating the machine.

Some of the women expressed resentment towards television and video as a deterrent to engaging in more appealing forms of leisure activities, such as going out, and as a barrier to family communication and intimacy. In an interesting research design borrowed from Cynthia Cockburn, Gray asked her subjects to identify various parts of the VCR controls as 'pink' or 'blue', based on whether they would be more likely to be used by male or female members of the family. The timer switch was always blue, with women depending on their husbands and children to operate it, and the remote control device tended to fall into the hands of the male partner or male child. Only the play, rewind, and record functions were 'lilac', being used equally by male and female family members. Gray insisted that the issue of competence in operating a VCR is inextricably linked to domestic labour.

Gray found more differences among women in her sample in the area of preferences for videos to rent and television material. She divided her sample into two groups: 'Early School Leavers' and 'Later School Leavers and Graduates'. She found starker gender differences in the second group, who tended to evaluate negatively a taste for romance, melodrama, and trash TV. Following Morley, Gray found that her subjects correlated feminine tastes with adjectives such as 'soft, soppy, fantasy, silly, fictional'. They correlated masculine tastes with such words as 'hard, tough, real, serious, and factual'. The more highly educated women in her group tended to share preferences with their partners: 'These women claimed to have similar preferences in programmes and films to their partners and the majority of them were keen to distance themselves from soap opera, particularly American products . . . and to align themselves with "quality" products' (1992: 160). Gray suggests that Bourdieu's work – which I review in the next section – can be used to explain the tendency for these educated women to have achieved 'an aesthetic disposition', which included a distanced objectivity with regard to television products, and, in particular, a distaste for soap operas, and a concern for their ill effects.

Ien Ang and Joke Hermes have criticized these studies for offering essentialist renderings of gender. They have argued that 'an individual's gendered subjectivity is constantly in the process of reproduction and transformation. Gender does not simply predetermine media consumption and use' (Ang 1996: 116). The portraits of domestic life constructed by Morley, Radway, and Gray seem very much at odds with the kind of formulation Ang postulates when she writes: 'Gender identity, in short, is both multiple and partial, ambiguous and incoherent, permanently in process of being articulated, disarticulated and rearticulated' (1996: 125). From this perspective, the families in *Family Television* represent a feminist nightmare: father holds the remote control and imposes his programmes on everyone else; mother desperately, guiltily, sneaks time to watch a weepie. There is a conflict, then, within media studies between theoretical frameworks, modes of doing research, and methods. Radway, Morley, and Gray's works construct their notions of subjectivity through empirical studies of media use by adults with children living in nuclear families – a group that is perhaps more fully engaged in the social reproduction of gender on a daily basis than are single adults. Their research is based on reports of behaviours, interviews, and discussions of everyday practices (a kind of data that is likely to reflect many commonsense notions of gender difference) – a subject defined through a materialist approach to audience research. Ang and Hermes construct media subjectivity through postmodern *theories* of ethnography, through theoretical discussions informed by Michel Foucault, Jacques Lacan, Judith Butler, and others – based at times in textual analysis, but rarely in empirical field research – and argue that gender is constructed as contradictory and shifting.

The problem of gender essentialism in these studies is as much methodological as it is theoretical: more intensive ethnographic methods might have uncovered more contradictory and shifting positions among Morley, Gray, and Radway's informants; Radway and Morley have advocated such methodologies in subsequent work. To some extent, the question of whether the discussion of gender in these studies was mechanical and essentialist is an empirical one. More research needs to be carried out in the field to note the degree to which traditional gendered roles in the family are flexible, shifting, and multiple. [. . .]

Bourdieu on television

Pierre Bourdieu's work, with its emphasis on the differential distribution of cultural tastes and on the embeddedness of tastes in the habitus, the material – and domestic – structures of everyday life, has exerted a major influence on television studies since the publication of *Distinction* in English in 1984. Bourdieu's empirical research and his theories of the role of aesthetic distinctions in the construction of social hierarchies have resonated with questions about television audiences, the importance of the domestic sphere as a site for the inculcation of tastes and a place of aesthetic consumption, and the accentuated awareness of the variability of interpretations of aesthetic texts. *Distinction* has helped scholars conceptualize television in relation to other cultural forms, and to force them to think about the relationship between tastes for particular kinds of television genre and class position. Bourdieu's best-known argument is that 'art and cultural consumption are predisposed, consciously and deliberately or not to fulfill a social function of legitimating social differences' (1984: 7).

In *Distinction* and other work, Bourdieu has had little of a theoretical nature to say about television (more recently he has published a diatribe about the impoverished nature of television programming as compared to academic discourse, and its detrimental impact on democracy. see Eakin 1997). Yet Bourdieu has proved useful to television scholars because he pays particular attention to forms of culture stigmatized by intellectuals and the bourgeoisie: forms considered vulgar rather than refined, emotional rather than mental/intellectual, expressive rather than aesthetically distanced. Of course, such concerns match rather well with most popular television genres, especially sensationalistic forms: talk shows, soap operas, sports, wrestling, ground ideas about the ambiguous social status of television as a cultural form that is at once widely accessible and widely deprecated.

Bourdieu focused attention on the role of education and the influence of 'cultural capital' on taste, the selection and valorization of certain cultural forms. In his introduction, he formulates this in the widely quoted statement 'Taste classifies, and it classifies the classifier' (1984: 7). These distinctions are used to legitimate the privileges of those with more education and more money, who envision themselves as superior to those whose tastes differ from their own. Bourdieu emphasizes that these distinctions are just as present in the selection of novels to read or pictures to hang on the wall of one's home as they are in choices of food or hairstyle. His account focuses on the relationship among types of goods, and argues that the meaning of any given commodity (such as a television programme) derives from its similarities to and differences from other commodities in society (live performances of opera or ballet; football games). Increasingly, society requires consumers to understand and manipulate complex meanings and connotations attached to consumer goods and commodified cultural forms, so that they may choose to make the right impressions – and so that they may avoid mistakes. This can involve complex negotiations in the linking of cultural forms to social status. Emulation involves a double movement: imitation of those richer, and differentiation from those poorer or less 'refined'.

To a large extent, the attention to strategies of decoding texts in audience studies has been an excavation of forms of cultural capital unrecognized by prior forms of communications research – thus contributing to the sense of television as a complex and even fascinating media form with its own codes. In one of the earliest examples, Charlotte Brunsdon pointed out that:

> Just as a Godard film requires the possession of certain forms of cultural capital on the part of its audience for it to 'make sense' – an extra textual familiarity with certain artistic linguistic, political and cinematic discourses – so too does . . . soap opera . . . the narrative strategies and concerns . . . call on the traditionally feminine competencies associated with the responsibility for 'managing' the sphere of personal life.
>
> (Brunsdon 1983: 80)

This kind of argument led to observations by Robert Allen, Dorothy Hobson, Tania Modleski, Andrea Press, and Seiter *et al*, that members of the audience who despised soap opera, often were simply lacking in the cultural capital required to read the text adequately – and that the low status of soap opera audiences could best be explained as a result of a social structure which routinely placed working-class and feminine forms at the bottom.

The concept of cultural capital has been widely appropriated throughout television studies. Bourdieu has described his project 'to grasp capital . . . in all of its different forms, and to uncover the laws that regulate their conversion from one into another' (Bourdieu and Wacquant 1992: 118). Four different forms of capital were identified by Bourdieu: economic, cultural, social, and symbolic. Economic capital includes financial resources of various kinds, and encompasses the bases for most traditional definitions of class, such as by income level. Cultural capital adds to this an embodied state of tastes, preferences, and knowledge, ranging from educational credentials, to preferences in music, to embodiments of femininity. Social capital consists of networks, connections, group memberships, familial relationships: 'Social capital is the sum of the resources, actual or virtual, that accrue to an individual or a group by virtue of possessing a durable network of more or less institutionalized relationship of mutual acquaintance and recognition' (Bourdieu and Wacquant 1992: 119). Finally, symbolic capital is the form achieved when the economic, cultural, and social capital are recognized as legitimate and institutionalized.

Individuals could accumulate large stores of cultural capital in relation to television – for example, knowledge of twenty-five years of a soap opera's history, the names of actors, gossip about the stars, or by watching the evening news every night for decades. This cultural capital could be used in the currency of friendship or polite conversation with neighbours or family members, but unless it can be converted to symbolic capital (to get a job as a TV studies professor, or to land a job at a television network), it has not been translated or exchanged for symbolic capital.

It would be fair to summarize the influence of Bourdieu on television studies by saying that there has been considerable attention to cultural capital, and some attention to social capital in ethnographic audience studies tracing TV as a part of social relationships, but very little attention to, or indeed cognizance of, symbolic capital in relation to these. As Beverley Skeggs explains:

> Symbolic capital is powerful capital: it brings power with it. If one's cultural capital is delegitimated then it cannot be traded as an asset; it cannot be capitalized upon (although it may retain significance and meaning to the individual) and its power is limited . . . Most representations of working-class people contribute to devaluing and delegitimating their already meagre capitals, putting further blocks on tradability, denying any conversion into symbolic capital.
>
> (1997: 11)

The celebration of forms of cultural capital involved in the appreciation of television programmes, a tendency perhaps best exemplified by the work of John Fiske and Henry Jenkins is a position that Bourdieu himself explicitly opposed. Bourdieu is adamant about the necessity of a means of translating cultural capital into social capital for any material rewards to accrue to an individual. Clearly, only a small group of professionals (academics and media producers, usually backed by forms of middle-class education and credentials) can 'convert' the cultural capital of knowledge about television into social capital. Even when researchers identify themselves as fans (Hobson, Jenkins, Bacon-Smith), there is a considerable difference in cultural capital between interviewers and informants. Brunsdon has pointed out that such work has avoided confronting questions about the quality of the media itself:

> Only the inheritors of legitimate culture, researching other people's pleasures, pleasures they may well share, can afford to keep quiet about the good and bad of television. They – we – through years of training have access to a very wide range of cultural production. Watching television *and* reading books about postmodernism is different from watching television and reading tabloid newspapers, even if everybody concerned watched the same television.
>
> (Brunsdon 1990: 69)

Brunsdon argues that too often, by validating the pleasures of television viewing, scholars fail to make any demands for different, even better forms the audience might want.

Here, Brunsdon is in keeping with the spirit of Bourdieu's work, which finds any celebration of the popular bankrupt and warns that: 'To act as if one had only to reject in discourse the dichotomy of high culture and popular culture that exists in reality to make it vanish is to believe in magic . . . What must be changed are the conditions that make this hierarchy exist, both in reality and in minds' (Bourdieu and Wacquant 1992: 84). Like Brunsdon, Bourdieu has insisted that the intellectual's peculiar place in the system of social distinctions – a set of predispositions that make him a poor (or, rather, an inevitably interested) party in discourses about television. Thus, Bourdieu has perhaps inspired one of the recurring critiques of some audience research of the 1970s and 1980s. For example, Jostein Gripsrud comments that, too often, audience researchers have adopted a 'pro-television' position and failed to recognize their position as 'double access' audiences: 'Intellectuals now have access to both high and low culture, they are "double access" audiences; the majority of "ordinary people" have only access to "low" or popular culture. Our double access is a class privilege, a benefit of education, from which we cannot escape' (1995: 125). Audiences who have been denied access to more elite forms of culture tend to rely heavily on television as a media form, but are vulnerable to recognizing a judgement from above of television as trash, as a waste of time. Forms of apology or guilt about television viewing by heavy viewers can be viewed as a symptom of 'symbolic violence', which Bourdieu defines as 'the *violence which is exercised upon a social agent with his or her complicity*' (Bourdieu and Wacquant 1992: 167; emphasis in original). Bourdieu sees the failure to recognize symbolic violence as a chronic failing of sociological researchers, a blindspot in the goal of reflexive sociology: 'Intellectuals are often among those in the least favorable position to discover or to become aware of symbolic violence, especially that wielded by the school system, given that they have been subjected to it more intensively than the average person and that they continue to contribute to its exercise' (Bourdieu and Wacquant 1992: 170). Critics of Bourdieu have suggested that his model is functionalist, overly pessimistic and deterministic, and puts forward the dominant ideology as an all-powerful and universally accepted standard. John Hall explains one aspect of this critique when he points out that Bourdieu assumes that everyone recognizes the legitimacy of distinctions handed down 'from above': 'To describe any one social group's calculus as the effective one is to confer legitimacy to a calculus that, as Bourdieu recognizes, remains in play with others . . .' (Hall 1992: 279).

Another important limitation of Bourdieu's work involves the ways in which it universalizes the quite specific social hierarchy of French society. Clearly, much adaptation is needed of Bourdieu's model to British and probably still more to US culture. Sociologists Michèle Lamont and Annette Lareau have predicted that American legitimate culture is 'less related to knowledge of the Western humanist culture, is more technically oriented (with an emphasis on scientific or computer information) and more materialistic' (1988: 66). They suggest that purchasable – rather than culturally acquired – signals of legitimate culture may be more acceptable and may be granted more weight – in Bourdieu's terms, more easily converted to symbolic capital – in the United States than in France.

Bourdieu's greatest value to television audience research may be his enthusiasm about the practice of empirical sociology, his urgent calls that such field research must complement theoretical work on the sociology of culture. Thus, the move outwards to the audience is in line with his notions of reflexive sociology, a form of research which practises, at best, 'the inclusion of a theory of intellectual practice as an integral component and necessary condition of a critical theory of society . . .' (Bourdieu and Wacquant 1992: 173).

Speaking subjects

Bourdieu's research has often been based on large-scale survey research. It has been open to the same criticism as that lodged at traditional media effects research, in that its use of research procedures do not do justice to the increasing theoretical sophistication about language that informs so much Marxist, postmodernist, and poststructuralist theory. Speech is the primary form through which researchers gain access to information about media audiences. This fact links audience studies with theories about language and subjectivity that have brought about dramatic reappraisals in the humanities and social sciences.

Much of the ethnographic research on audiences is grounded in theories of subjectivity, based in part on the work of Louis Althusser and Jacques Lacan. In this theoretical tradition, subjectivity is a term for consciousness, and 'subject' replaces terms such as individual, person, citizen. The term subject connotes a certain degree of passivity, implying one who is subjected to something (namely ideology and unconscious processes) rather than a free individual acting upon the world (a conception more in line with uses and gratifications research). Some audience researchers have stressed the multiplicity of subjectivities. This position implies a political understanding of differently defined and created identities, such as gender, class, race, ethnicity, sexual orientation; and of the unconscious as well as the conscious mind. The stress here is on the international and unintentional nature of the subject's speech and way of making sense of the world. Language cannot be treated as a perfect match with the intentions of the speaker, nor as a realist system of representation, a transparent, immediately comprehensible vehicle for communication.

In the poststructuralist view, language is theorized as a kind of prison. Language is not a free, open form that expresses us perfectly; rather, it pre-exists us as individuals, and all our utterances are trapped within structured, conventional, ideological systems of language — or discourse. In its current usage, the term discourse carries the implication for speech governed by social, material, and historical forces, which disallow certain other things. Many being said or even thought, while forcing us to say certain other things. Many scholars use it in Foucault's sense to refer to a set of complex, multilayered texts that determine and limit what can be said or known about certain subjects and therefore serve particular interests in the power structure of society [Foucault 1980]. Discourse is not 'free speech'. It is not a perfect expression of the speaker's intentions. Indeed, we cannot think of communicative intentions as predating the constraints of language at all.

The methodological implications of this theoretical work are that what people say when talking about the media cannot be taken at face value. We cannot assume that what subjects say in an interview reflects individual, idiosyncratic views, or that what is spoken is all there is to be said on the subject. First, our subjects may not have access to all that might be going on with their media consumption, because of the role of the unconscious. Second, media tastes do not simply reflect identity, but are actually constitutive of it. Therefore, one of the things we would expect to hear from subjects is the reiteration of certain prior existing discourses on the self, society, politics, and gender.

A somewhat different perspective on the problems of language in qualitative research is offered by ethnomethodologists and conversation analysts, who focus on the ways in which speech events construct and affirm reality for speakers. Their work suggests the importance of looking at the conventions of speech and the commonplace understandings of what is happening that are operative in interview situations. Ethnomethodology would call attention to how researcher and subject 'do interviews' and at the tacit procedures that rule the situation. Ethnomethodology focuses on such speech situations and practices as 'contingent ongoing accomplishments of organized artful practices of everyday life' (Garfinkel 1976: 11). According to Lindlof, conversation analysis is a branch of ethnomethodology that focuses on 'such features of ordinary talk as the way conversations open, the order in which speaking turns occur, the sequencing of utterances, the repairing of problems, reflexive expressions about the talk, and in general, the manner in which spontaneous conversation displays the appearance of a polished performance' (1995: 39). This phenomenological work has so far been less influential on the development of media audience research than have theories of discourse and subjectivity, but it deserves serious consideration by audience researchers.

David Buckingham has usefully summarized the issues as they relate to talk about television concerns:

Clearly, individual users of language have no option but to select from among the available linguistic resources, which are already structured in particular ways. Language therefore cannot be seen as merely a neutral vehicle for 'attitudes' or 'beliefs', or a product of mental entities or processes. At the same time, subjects use language to construct versions of social reality: to a large extent, what people talk about is constructed in the process of talk itself. These versions of reality are consequential, in the sense that they perform specific social functions or purposes. In these respects, then, language is both constructed and constructive.

(1991: 229–30)

At its worst, audience research simply ignored these theoretical developments and fell back on a realist treatment of language, analysing transcription of speech as a pure and direct expression of the mind of the subject. At its best, this research accepts that 'the audience' is ultimately unknowable in some totalizing way, yet strives for a research design that maximizes an awareness of the researchers' own role in moulding what is said and how it gets said. There is considerable difference of opinion as to how much contact is necessary before a group of informants feels comfortable enough to act and speak naturally in the presence of a researcher. Lull (1988), who takes a realist view of language and whose work fits into the US uses and gratifications paradigm, reports that families quickly felt at ease and behaved normally, despite the observer's presence. Others – and I would place myself in this camp – consider the impact of the researcher's presence to be a continuing and strongly influential factor in shaping the interaction, and limiting what is said. [. . .]

Most work on audiences has relied exclusively on verbal transcripts, usually quoted without description of the context in which a statement was made. Dependence on a printed transcript results in a tremendous loss of information in terms of the non-verbal communications that accompany speech, such as eye movements, facial expressions, hand gestures, and head and body movements, as well as tone of voice, rate of speech, loudness or softness, etc. One of the best exceptions to this is the book *Children and Television* by Bob Hodge and David Tripp (1986). The authors collected data by videotaping and audiotaping children while they discussed particular cartoons. Careful attention was paid to non-verbal communication. This is an especially rich method of study for children's language, where vocabulary may be limited but communications are very rich in terms of non-verbal and phatic elements. It is also especially important to look at the power differential between the adult interviewer, who has authority over the children, and the children.

Hodge and Tripp's transcript of the group interview tells one story; the videotape tells another. Hodge and Tripp's discussion benefits from a very finely tuned sense of how the social situation produces what can be said about the cartoon being studied. Similarly, in David Buckingham's interviews with children, he found that:

they perceive the [interview] context as one in which a relatively 'critical' response is at least appropriate, and possibly even required. The 'critical' discourse serves a dual purpose: it enables the children to present themselves as 'adult', for the benefit of each other and myself; and it provides a means of refuting what they might suspect adults (including me) to believe about the influence of television upon them.

(1993: 231)

Hodge and Tripp pay careful attention to how the children's inflections, their use of rising and falling tones, and 'babyish' voices to communicate non-seriousness, significantly shape the meaning of their speech. Throughout the group interviews, boys and girls interact with each other, and individual children become leaders within the groups. In analysing videotapes and transcripts of these discussions, it became apparent that in many instances boys silenced girls, adults silenced children, and interviewers silenced subjects – through non-verbal censure of some remarks (glances, laughs, grimaces), by wording questions and responses in certain ways, or by failures to comprehend each other's terms.

Hodge and Tripp's analysis represents a type of methodology that is very rich in complexity, but – unfortunately – very time-consuming, requiring as it does a careful study of the videotape and notation of all of the children's actions. All kinds of prohibitions exist on the ways that children will discuss television with adults because of status differences, and children's knowledge about adult disapproval of popular culture. Hodge and Tripp accept that researchers simply will not discover everything that children think about TV, but careful attention to non-verbal as well as verbal clues gives many clues to the ways that the contexts of research produce certain forms of speech from children. Children present a particularly obvious case of the importance of non-verbal communications, but researchers dealing with adults need to be similarly aware of the powerful communicative role of the non-verbal in interview and conversational situations.

Ethnography's other

The origin of ethnography is rooted in colonialism. Historically, ethnographies have been written by Europeans and Americans documenting their experiences among people living in Africa, Asia, or Native American cultures. James Clifford and others have mounted a critical challenge to traditional ethnography's implicit insistence on scholarly experience as an unproblematic source and ultimate guarantee of knowledge about a specific culture or cultural process. Clifford has rejected 'colonial representations' as 'discourses that portray the cultural reality of other peoples without placing their own reality into jeopardy' (1983: 128).

Do audience studies also construct a sort of colonial representation? Is there an 'Other' who is the subject of audience ethnography? Most audience research exists in an ambiguous relationship of alterity to the culture: when researchers investigate media use are they venturing into 'foreign' lands or not? Valerie Walkerdine has stressed the ways that fantasies of the 'Other' play a major, if usually unwritten role in social science research, and that, for mass media research, class has been one of the most important structuring differences between researcher and researched. Walkerdine's case studies of families analyse the interplay between video watching and casual conversation. She includes, to a much greater degree than other researchers, or than would be acceptable according to the conventions of most social scientific writing, autobiographical material as well as an analysis of the way her own family background compels her to 'read' the family interactions in certain ways. Walkerdine seeks to avoid 'exoticizing' the Other through this approach. She is harshly critical of the representation of the audience in most social science:

> The audience for popular entertainment, for example, is often presented as sick (voyeuristic, scopophilic) or as trapped within a given subjectivity (whether defined by the social categories of class, race and gender or by a universalized oedipal scenario). What is disavowed in such approaches is the complex relation of 'intellectuals' to 'the masses': 'our' project of analyzing 'them' is itself one of the regulative practices which produce *our* subjectivity as well as theirs. We are each Other's – but not on equal terms. Our fantasy investment often seems to consist in believing that we can 'make them see' or that we can see or speak *for* them. If we do assume that, then we continue to dismiss fantasy and the Imaginary as snares and delusions. We fail to acknowledge how the insistent demand to see through Ideology collides in the process of intellectualizing bodily and other pleasures.
> (Walkerdine 1990: 199–200)

Many studies have focused on women from working-class or middle-class backgrounds (Radway 1984; Morley 1986; A. Gray 1987; Seiter *et al*. 1989; Press 1991). In this work the projection onto the audience as an Other primarily involves class issues, although there is often a strong component of identification and even solidarity between the feminist researcher and her informants.

Most US and UK audience research has involved white researchers and white informants, although the researcher frequently apologizes for the lack of diversity in the sample. As Jacqueline Bobo and I have argued elsewhere, the homogeneity of the samples does not occur accidentally: white researchers have not been alert to the self-selection at work here (Bobo and Seiter 1991: 290–2). People of colour may not have sufficient trust in or comfort with white researchers to participate in audience research. The tendency for qualitative interviews to be carried out in people's homes may also dissuade some from participation. The strain of caring for children and working long hours, sometimes at multiple jobs, will mean that many more impoverished informants will simply not have the time to be interviewed.

Bobo's study of the reception of the film version of *The Color Purple* among African-American women is an important exception to the all-white sample. In Bobo's focus groups, African-American women reported how much they valued being interviewed by an African-American researcher. In a follow-up interview, Bobo mentions to the group that her research has been criticized as representing an atypical sample because her subjects were so articulate:

> Once again, the women displayed a shrewdness about their status in society and about the way black women are viewed by others. One of the women wondered if the critics knew that a person could be intelligent but not necessarily well educated . . . Still another commented that many people react with surprise when they hear black people speak sensibly because, too often, that is not what is allowed to be presented in a public forum. She then asked a rhetorical question toward which the other women responded with spirited agreement: 'Don't you think we would have come off sounding stupid if someone other than another black person was doing research on us?'.
>
> (1995: 132)

Bobo's discussion is an important example of the way that media audiences may be critical of the ways they are characterized by researchers. Bobo's research design, returning to the focus group to discuss her 'findings' and their reception by an academic audience, allowed her to include such criticisms in her discussion. One of the continuing struggles within audience research is to expand the diversity of the researchers and the informants and to heighten self-reflexivity about the impact of racism on our knowledge production; the perception of various methods by groups; and the politics of exploitation of research subjects by researchers. As it stands, we know much more about white, middle-class audiences in the UK and the USA than about any other groups. Media audience researchers are academics with specific social, class, and cultural backgrounds, who frequently leave their normal places of work and residence to seek out 'the field' and learn about groups with social and cultural backgrounds different from their own. These differences are of a lesser magnitude than those between first world/third world ethnographers, but they are present none the less. [. . .]

References

Allen, R.C. (1985) *Speaking of Soap Operas*, Chapel Hill: University of North Carolina Press.
—— (1989) 'Bursting Bubbles: "Soap Opera", Audiences and the Limits of Genre', in E. Seiter *et al*., *Remote Control*, 16–43.
Ang, I. (1985) *Watching Dallas: Soap Opera and the Melodramatic Imagination*, London: Routledge.
—— (1996) *Living Room Wars: Rethinking Media Audiences for a Postmodern World*, London: Routledge.

Bacon-Smith, C. (1992) *Enterprising Women: TV Fandom and the Creation of Popular Myth*, Philadelphia: University of Pennsylvania Press.

Bobo, J. (1995) *Black Women as Cultural Readers*, New York: Columbia University Press.

Bobo, J. and Seiter, E. (1991) 'Black Feminism and Media Criticism: *The Women of Brewster Place*', *Screen* 32/3: 286–302.

Bourdieu, P. (1984) *Distinction: A Social Critique of the Judgment of Taste*, trans. R. Nice, Cambridge, MA: Harvard University Press.

Bourdieu, P. and Wacquant, L.J.D. (1992) *An Invitation to Reflexive Sociology*, Chicago, IL: University of Chicago Press.

Brown, K.M. (1994) 'Fundamentalism and the Control of Women', in J.S. Hawley (ed.), *Fundamentalism and Gender*, New York: Oxford University Press, 175–201.

Brunsdon, C. (1983) '*Crossroads*: Notes on a Soap Opera', in E.A. Kaplan (ed.), *Regarding Television*, 76–83.

—— (1989) 'Text and Audience', in E. Seiter *et al.*, *Remote Control*, 96–115.

—— (1990) 'Problems with Quality', *Screen* 31/1: 67–90.

Brunsdon, C. and Morley, D. (1978) *Everyday Television: 'Nationwide'*, London: British Film Institute.

Buckingham, D. (1991) 'What Are Words Worth?: Interpreting Children's Talk about Television', *Cultural Studies* 5/2: 228–45.

—— (1996) *Moving Images: Children's Emotional Responses to Television*, Manchester: Manchester University Press.

Bybee, C.R. (1987) 'Uses and Gratifications Research and the Study of Social Change', in D.L. Paletz (ed.), *Political Communications Research: Approaches, Studies, Assessment*, Norwood, NJ: Ablex.

Clifford, J. (1983) 'On Ethnographic Authority', *Representations* 1/2: 118–46.

Curran, J. (1996) 'The New Revisionism in Mass Communication Research: a Reappraisal', in J. Curran, D. Morley and V. Walkerdine (eds), *Cultural Studies and Communications*, London: Edward Arnold, 256–78.

Delia, J. (1987) 'Communication Research: A History', in C.R. Berger and S.H. Chaffee (eds), *Handbook of Communication Science*, Newbury Park, CA: Sage, 20–98.

Eakin, E. (1997) 'Bourdieu Unplugged', *Lingua Franca*, August: 22–23.

Eco, U. (1976) *Theory of Semiotics*, Bloomington: Indiana University Press.

Garfinkel, H. (1976) *Studies in Ethnomethodology*, Englewood Cliffs, NJ: Prentice-Hall.

Gillespie, M. (1995) *Television, Ethnicity and Cultural Change*, London and New York: Routledge.

Gray, A. (1987) 'Behind Closed Doors: Video Recorders in the Home', in H. Baehr and G. Dyer (eds), *Boxed In: Women and Television*, New York: Pandora, 38–54.

—— (1992) *Video Playtime: The Gendering of a Leisure Technology*, London and New York: Routledge.

Gray, H. (1993) 'The Endless Slide of Difference', *Critical Studies in Mass Communication* 10: 190–7.

Gripsrud, J. (1995) *The Dynasty Years: Hollywood Television and Critical Media Studies*, London: Routledge.

Hall, J.R. (1992) 'The Capital(s) of Cultures: A Nonholistic Approach to Status Situations, Class, Gender, and Ethnicity', in M. Lamont and M. Fournier (eds), *Cultivating Differences*, Chicago: University of Chicago Press, 257–88.

Hodge, B. and Tripp, D. (1986) *Children and Television: A Semiotic Approach*, Palo Alto: Stanford University Press.

Iser, W. (1978) *The Act of Reading: A Theory of Aesthetic Response*, Baltimore, MD: Johns Hopkins Press.

Jhally, S. and Lewis, J. (1992) *Enlightened Racism: 'The Cosby Show', Audiences, and the Myth of the American Dream*, Boulder, CO: Westview Press.

Lamont, M. and Lareau, A. (1988) 'Cultural Capital: Allusions and Glissandos in Recent Theoretical Developments', *Sociological Theory* 6: 163.

Lewis, L. (ed.) (1992) *The Adoring Audience: Fan Culture and Popular Media*, London and New York: Routledge.

Lindlof, T.R. (1995) *Qualitative Communication Research Methods*, Thousand Oaks, CA: Sage Publications.

Lipsitz, G. (1990) *Time Passages: Collective Memory and American Popular Culture*, Minneapolis: University of Minnesota Press.

Lull, J. (ed.) (1988) *World Families Watch Television*, Newbury Park, CA, Sage.

Marcus, G.E. and Fischer, M.J. (1986) *Anthropology as Cultural Critique*, Chicago: University of Chicago Press.

McRobbie, A. (1991) *Feminism and Youth Culture: From 'Jackie' to 'Just Seventeen'*, Boston: Unwin Hyman.

Morley, D. (1980) *The 'Nationwide' Audience*, London: British Film Institute.

—— (1986) *Family Television*, London: Comedia/Routledge.

—— (1992) *Television, Audiences and Cultural Studies*, London: Routledge.

Press, A. (1991) *Women Watching Television*, Philadelphia: University of Pennsylvania.

Seiter, E., Borchers, H., Kreutzner, G. and Warth, E. (eds) (1989) *Remote Control: Television, Audiences and Cultural Power*, London: Routledge.

Shattuc, J. (1997) *The Talking Cure: TV Talk Shows and Women*, New York: Routledge.

Skeggs, B. (1997) *Formations of Class and Gender: Becoming Respectable*, London: Sage.

Walkerdine, V. (1990) *School Girl Fictions*, London and New York: Verso.

Chapter 30

HANNAH DAVIES, DAVID BUCKINGHAM AND PETER KELLEY

IN THE WORST POSSIBLE TASTE
Children, television and cultural value

STEVE: (aged 6): I love *Animal Hospital*. It's my best programme.
CHARLIE: Did you watch the monkey one?
STEVE: Yeah, that was so funny. It started itching other monkey's bums and they started spitting down on people's heads.

DEBATES ABOUT CHILDREN and television have largely been preoccupied with the potential impact of 'harmful' material. Such debates implicitly define children as a special audience, with distinctive characteristics and needs. Children, it is argued, are in need of protection, not just from commercial exploitation or ideological manipulation, but also from the consequences of their own vulnerability and ignorance.

One of the implicit concerns in these debates is with the question of children's *taste*. It seems to be assumed that, left to their own devices, children will choose to watch material that is not only morally damaging but also inherently lacking in cultural value. Dietary metaphors are common here: children, it is often asserted, will opt for chips and chocolate bars in preference to the nourishing cultural food that adults consistently tell them is good for them. Children's 'natural' taste, it is argued, is for vulgarity and sensationalism, rather than restraint and subtlety; for simplistic stereotypes rather than complex, rounded characters; and it is led by the baser physical instincts rather than the higher sensibilities of the intellect. Children and 'good taste' are, it would seem, fundamentally incompatible.

In this article, we investigate some of these assumptions using data arising from a broader research project about children's television culture. The project used a multi-disciplinary approach to consider changing assumptions about children's characteristics and needs as an audience. Thus, we looked at the implications for children of broader economic and institutional changes in the media environment; at the ways in which broadcasters, regulators and policy-makers define the child audience; and at how children are directly and indirectly addressed and constructed as an audience by the television schedules, and by the formal strategies of specific programmes. Against this background, we were also interested in how children defined *themselves* as an audience – in the kinds of programmes they identified as being uniquely or primarily 'for children', and their reasons for these judgements. As we shall indicate, these different definitions of children's characteristics as an audience necessarily invoke broader assumptions about the meaning of childhood itself.

Children's television/adults' television

Historically, the main focus of public concern in this area has been on the effects of material that is aimed at *adults*, rather than on programmes aimed specifically at children. In 1996, for example, a British market research report revealing that children's preferences are for 'adult' sitcoms and soap operas resulted in outraged headlines about 'the scandal of the "view as you like" generation'.[1] In fact, this story is far from news. Right from the beginnings of television, children have always preferred to watch programmes that were not specifically made for them (Abrams, 1956).

A closer look at the ratings, however, reveals a more interesting story than simply that of children watching 'unsuitable' material or 'growing up too fast'. To be sure, children's programmes are rarely among the top rating shows for children; and there is a good deal of overlap, with the same popular sitcoms and soap operas featuring on both adults' and children's charts. Nevertheless, many of the most popular programmes with children are not especially popular with adults, and vice versa. Our analysis of the ratings for 1995, for example, found that some entertainment-based 'adult' programmes, which were peripheral in the general chart, were consistently in the top 20 for children; while some more serious home-produced dramas, which featured in the general top 20, were absent from the children's chart (Buckingham et al., 1999). To some degree, of course, these differences can be explained through scheduling and availability to view: some of the most popular programmes with adults run after the 9 p.m. watershed, while the most popular 'adult' programmes among children are often screened in the early evenings, especially at weekends. Nevertheless, this kind of comparison should lead us to question any easy opposition between 'children's' and 'adults' programmes.

Clearly, these categories are much more relative — and indeed, more value-laden — than straightforward institutional definitions would seem to imply. Just as sociologists of childhood have increasingly questioned the unitary category 'children', we should acknowledge that what it means to be 'adult' is also heterogeneous and negotiated. Obviously, there are different kinds of grown-ups — in traditional socioeconomic terms such as class and education, but also in terms of lifestyle and culture. Similarly, 'adult' television — that is, television not made specifically for children — offers different kinds of grown-up subject positions, from that of the serious, intelligent citizen who watches a news magazine like *Newsnight* to the ironic, playful viewer of the salacious *Eurotrash* (who might, as often as not, be the same person).

Nevertheless, when we look at the kinds of 'adult' programmes that children watch in their millions, there seem to be particular features and conventions that they have in common, such as action, humour and narrative simplicity. So to what extent can we talk about an *aesthetic* dimension to children's preferences — or indeed a distinctive 'children's taste culture'?

Falling standards

If much of this debate continues to focus on 'adult' programmes, the impact of deregulation and commercialization has given rise to new concerns about the nature and content of *children's* television. Here again, the issue of children's taste is often an underlying — and frequently unacknowledged — concern.

For example, Stephen Kline's (1993) critique of the commercialization of children's culture repeatedly invokes what it assumes are shared assumptions about cultural value. Kline looks back wistfully to the golden age of classic children's literature. These stories, he argues, 'took on the ability to enthrall and delight the child as 'writers joyfully undertook experiments that charted new courses for the literate imagination' (1993: 81). Through the development of popular literature and comic books and thence to television, Kline traces a steady cultural decline, resulting from the 'homogenising' and 'levelling' influence of the mass market. While the Victorians are unstintingly praised for their 'rich emotional texture' and their 'unfettered imagination', contemporary television is condemned for lacking their 'psychological depth', 'exuberance' and 'innocence'. Cartoons in particular are condemned as universally 'formulaic', 'predictable', 'inane' and 'banal': by virtue of their 'truncated characterisation', their 'stylised narratives' and their 'stultified animation', they are judged to be unable 'to deal adequately with feelings and experience' (1993: 313–14).

The problem with these kinds of judgements is not just that the key terms themselves remain undefined, but that the *evidence* that might exemplify and support them is simply taken for granted. It is easy to condemn *The Care Bears* and *My Little Pony*, as Kline (1993: 261) does, for lacking 'the wit, individuality and subtle humour of A.A. Milne's eternal characters', not least when very few of one's readers will ever have seen such programmes. If there is any doubt, a few silly quotations taken out of context will easily do the trick. Such assertions are seen as self-evidently true, and as somehow neutral. In the process, the *social* basis for such judgements of taste is simply evacuated.

As Ellen Seiter (1993) suggests, social class is certainly one dimension here. As in a great deal of Marxist cultural critique, Kline paradoxically takes the position of the 'old' bourgeoisie in his attack on the new ruling ethos. He implicitly judges *The Care Bears* by the criteria one might use to evaluate the relative claims of *Middlemarch* and *The Mill on the Floss*: depth of character, complexity and moral seriousness are seen as 'eternal' qualities whose value is self-evident. As Seiter suggests, such distinctions between 'quality' children's television and 'trash', or between 'educational' and 'non-educational' toys, could well be seen as a reflection of what she calls the 'smug self-satisfaction of educated middle-class people'.[2]

Yet this debate also raises questions about what it might mean for *adults* to pass judgements on *children's* media culture (see Buckingham, 1995a). The problem here is partly to do with the implicit assumptions about the audience that are at stake – and in particular, the notion that adults should be in a position to define what children *need*, irrespective of what they appear to *want*. Why is it that children positively prefer the 'crude' to the 'complex'? Why do they actively seek out 'one-dimensional' characters and 'predictable' narratives, rather than those which possess 'rich emotional texture'? Might there not in fact be very good reasons for these choices? Yet the problem here is not only to do with audiences: it is also to do with the criteria that are being applied in making such aesthetic judgements. Could it be that the value of such apparently 'inane' and 'stultified' productions might need to be judged according to *different* aesthetic criteria, *irrespective* of whether or not they are popular with audiences? And if so, how (and by whom) are those criteria to be identified?

Interpreting taste

To raise the question of taste in this context is inevitably to invoke the work of Pierre Bourdieu (1979). As Bourdieu amply demonstrates, aesthetic judgements cannot be divorced from social relations: distinctions of taste are a means of displaying and sustaining distinctions of class and social power. The preferences and judgements of those who have the power to ascribe cultural value become the apotheosis of 'good taste'; and in this way, the maintenance of aesthetic hierarchies becomes a means of perpetuating social inequalities.

While his argument about the social basis of taste has been widely accepted, Bourdieu's analysis has also been criticized for its deterministic analysis of social class, and for its neglect of other factors such as gender. Furthermore, it has been argued, Bourdieu implicitly sees the hierarchy of taste from the perspective of the dominant classes, failing to take account of the subordinated classes who may not recognize it, or indeed actively refuse to accept it (Frow, 1995; Mander, 1987; Robbins, 1991; Schiach, 1993).

Despite Bourdieu's (1998) denunciation of the medium, discussion of taste in relation to television also rather complicates neat distinctions between 'high' and 'low' culture. Television can obviously offer traditional high culture (opera) as well as low culture (game shows) and many points in between. Indeed, some have argued that it is precisely because of this blending that it has helped to break down traditional distinctions between elite and popular culture (Hartley, 1992).

In this respect, the relationship between taste, aesthetics and social power in the case of television is more complex than such essentialist distinctions allow. There is more heterogeneity both in the cultural objects that are consumed and within the audiences that consume them. Furthermore, for certain groups within the dominant class – particularly those characterized by Gouldner (1979) as the 'new class of intellectuals' or the 'knowledge professionals' – preferences for the low or the popular can themselves be a form of cultural capital. And of course it is precisely these kinds of people who are making popular television programmes.

The white, urban 'knowledge class' seeking to appropriate certain versions of ethnic culture; the gentrification of football as a kind of working-class tourism; or the application of 'camp' as a way of flirting with definitions of sexual difference (Simpson, 1994) – these and many similar phenomena reflect the evolution of new taste cultures that both reflect and serve to construct new social positionings that are not simply tied to fixed class distinctions.

Before cool

To what extent can *generational* differences be interpreted in these terms? Thus far, much of the debate on this issue in cultural studies has centred on the category of 'youth'. As Simon Frith (1998) has noted, the idea of 'hip' or 'cool' is both symbolically and empirically tied up with youth and change. For the 'knowledge professionals', to be youthful, or (more importantly) to *know* about what is youthful, provides a key source of cultural capital which can be traded on the employment market (Peretti, 1998). In this analysis, 'youth' becomes a symbolic construct that is to some extent divorced from biological age. Youth is a pattern of consumption rather than a demographic category: you don't have to be young to go to rave clubs, wear Nike trainers or listen to drum and bass (although undeniably it helps). When Tony Blair [Prime Minister] talks about Britain as a 'young country', or when media advertisers, schedulers and producers chase the elusive 16–25-year-olds, 'youth' is being defined as the ultimate desirable quality, far removed from the actual experiences of unemployed young Britons on government training schemes.

Where do children, and children's tastes, fit into this matrix? For some market researchers and media producers, children seem to be perceived as a kind of 'pre-youth', a taste avant-garde, symbolically at the cutting edge of cultural innovation. What children like today will be what is cool and hip tomorrow. Youth, it could be argued, is getting younger every day. Within the discourse of the children's cable channel Nickelodeon, for example, children are constructed as 'sovereign consumers': sophisticated and difficult to reach, they know their own minds and they are not afraid to speak them (Buckingham *et al.*, 1999). However, as with youth, this new symbolic construction of children – as innovative, smart, street-wise and hip – can obscure the actual experiences of children themselves.

Here again, if we examine the kinds of 'adult' programmes that children watch and like, and the reasons they give for liking them, the picture is more complicated. Their tastes are quite distinctive, but not necessarily 'cool' or 'fashionable': they prefer *Gladiators* to *Inspector Morse*, but they also like the mass market music of *Top of the Pops* rather than the more youth-oriented *TFI*

Friday. Children are choosing to identify with and to occupy *some* 'adult' subject positions rather than others, while at the same time avowedly retaining aspects of 'childishness'.

In the remainder of this article, we intend to explore these questions about children's taste via an analysis of extracts from discussions with children themselves. As we shall indicate, the socially performative nature of the kind of focus group discussions we undertook highlights quite acutely the social uses of judgements of taste (Buckingham, 1993). Like those of adults, children's expressions of their tastes and preferences are self-evidently social acts: they are one of the means whereby children lay claim to – and attribute meaning to – their preferred social identities. This is not, of course, to imply that they are free to select from an infinite variety of subject positions as and when they choose. We need to recognize children's agency in constructing and defining their own tastes and identities; but we need to avoid the sentimental view of children as necessarily 'media-literate active viewers'.

As we shall indicate, children's judgements about the cultural value of television articulate power relations, both within the peer group and in terms of the wider social groupings to which these children belong. Proclaiming one's own tastes, and thereby defining oneself as more or less 'mature', represents a form of 'identity work', in a context in which being a 'child' is effectively to be seen as vulnerable and powerless. Such statements clearly cannot be taken at face value, as evidence of what children 'really' think or believe. On the coutrary, it is through such negotiations and performances that the *meanings* of 'childhood' are constructed and defined.

Talking taste

The data presented in this article are drawn from a larger study of changing views of the child audience for television.[3] In addition to looking at how the television industry defines and constructs the child audience – through practices such as programme production, scheduling and research – we wanted to understand how children perceived *themselves* as an audience (cf. Buckingham, 1994). We decided to focus this aspect of our research around one key question: how do children define what makes a programme either 'for children' or 'for adults'?

We took this question to two classes of children in a socially and ethnically mixed inner-London primary school. Year 6 – the top year of primary school – was selected because of its transitional position. At the age of 10 or 11, these were the most senior or 'grown-up' children in the institution, looking towards secondary school, where they would be the least grown-up (cf. de Block, 1998). We chose to compare this with a Year 2 class of 6–7-year-olds, whose position as 'children' we expected to be more secure and less problematic. In total, we had contact with each class for two mornings a week over the length of the term; and we were therefore present in the school for four days out of five every week. Though our research was not intended to be ethnographic, we did become a regular feature of the classroom routine.

We began with a series of relatively open-ended discussions about the children's likes and dislikes in television.[4] These were followed by two more focused activities. The first was a sorting exercise, in which the children were invited to categorize a broad assortment of programme titles (provided on cards) in terms of whether they were 'for children' or 'for adults' – although in practice, of course, many groups chose to have more than these two categories. The second exercise was a more complicated scheduling simulation, in which the children were given a similarly broad selection of programme cards and asked to fit them into five programme slots on a weekday afternoon and on a Saturday evening. These activities thus attempted to tap into the children's understanding of how childhood and adulthood are constructed within television schedules, and how far they challenged these definitions of space and time.

Throughout each of these activities, the children were invited to comment and reflect on their choices and decisions. They were also permitted to make changes as the discussion progressed. The activities were thus intended to facilitate discussion, rather than to accurately reflect children's viewing tastes or habits; and it is these discussions, rather than the 'results' (that is, the choices themselves) that we primarily focus on here.[5]

What makes a children's programme?

In effect, our research activities deliberately set up the opposition child-adult and asked the children to negotiate it. For various reasons, they found this very difficult. New categories emerged such as 'in between' or 'for everyone'. The older children in particular were uneasy about defining their favourite programmes as 'children's'; while some of the younger ones constructed the category 'babies' to differentiate their tastes from those of their younger siblings. In this respect, the process of classifying programmes explicitly served as a means of social self-definition. For example, when a group of 6-year-old boys collapsed into laughter at the mention of *Teletubbies*, they were clearly distancing themselves from the younger audience for whom the programme is designed – and from the girls in their class who had appropriated its 'cuter' aspects. Similarly, when a group of girls covered their ears every time football was mentioned, they were self-consciously constructing their own girlishness by rejecting the male world of football. In this respect, our activity effectively dramatized Bourdieu's (1979) famous statement: 'classification classifies the classifier'.

In the children's explorations of what makes a programme 'for children', a number of quite predictable factors emerged. Perhaps unsurprisingly, the strongest arguments were negative ones. Programmes featuring sex, violence and 'swearing' were singled out by both age groups as being particularly 'grown-up'. Likewise, children's programmes were predominantly defined in terms of absences – that is, in terms of what they do *not* include. By contrast, the most persuasive and insistent reason given for a programme being 'for children' was simply that they watched and enjoyed it. This definition had an unarguable logic; and it also allowed for more flexibility than a purely institutional definition based on the schedule or on what actually appears on children's channels. Yet in these terms, many of the programmes that they liked and wanted to talk about were actually 'adults' programmes.

In the process of these activities and discussions, a set of loose oppositions emerged that were used by the sample to explain the differences between children's and adults' programmes. We have interpreted these oppositions as follows:

parents	children
grannies	teenagers
old-fashioned	cool
boring	funny
talk	action

These categories are broadly related to each other, with those on the right being associated with each other in opposition to those on the left. While we acknowledge that this kind of schema ignores the fluidity and the contradictions that this kind of discussion inevitably produces, it does provide a useful way of identifying how our sample defined the distinctiveness of children's taste.

Broadly speaking, the children argued for their preferences by emphasizing the criteria on the right of our schema and disavowing those on the left. Of course there were disagreements within groups about *which* programmes they preferred, but the *reasons* put forward for liking or disliking a programme were generally within this broad paradigm. For example, one group of girls disagreed about the long-running soap opera *Coronation Street*: two rejected it on the grounds that it was 'boring' and 'for grannies', while one defended it on the grounds that it had 'good stories' and that it was 'funny'. Despite the differences between them, there was considerable agreement about the basic *grounds* for judgement.

As we have noted, the most obvious criterion for selecting a programme as being 'for children' was that of personal preference (I like it, so it must be for children). Such expressions of preference often involved contrasting their own personal taste with that of parents, most notice-ably in relation to news or current affairs programmes. However, this opposition between parents and children was often expressed in quite complex ways. In some cases, the children made a clear distinction between 'parents' in the abstract and their *own* parent(s). While parents in general were seen to like 'boring stuff' such as *The News*, talk about their own family lives often involved anecdotes about their parents watching and enjoying the same kinds of programmes that they liked. Two 6-year-old boys, for example, referred to the comedy *Mr Bean* in this way:

DANIEL: My mum likes watching it and she's nearly 29.
PAUL: My dad loves it, my dad laughs at it!

In the everyday reality of these children's lives, then, the viewing preferences of the 'grown-ups' (parents) are not independent of the tastes of their children, nor do they necessarily correspond to what are seen as adult norms.

To a large extent, this could be regarded as simply a consequence of the routines and structures of family life: people (parents included) do not always choose what they watch, and they may decide to watch programmes together for the experience of companionship rather than because they actually prefer them. In this sense, the opposition between parent and child is not necessarily fixed and stable.

Aspirational tastes

This parent/child distinction had greater currency among the younger children, who were gener-ally more inclined to accept their dependence on parental and adult authority. The 10-year-olds, looking forward to adolescence and secondary school, tended to make more nuanced distinctions *within* the category of 'childhood'. On the brink of becoming teenagers themselves, they associ-ated particular programmes or types of programmes with this age group. These choices were clearly informed by a broader sense of a 'teen' lifestyle, to which many of them aspired, even though they didn't see themselves as teenagers quite yet. Being a teenager was seen to offer a degree of autonomy and control over their lives which was just around the corner. Thus, they recognized that programmes like the sitcoms *Sister Sister* or *Sabrina the Teenage Witch* might feature teenage characters, but they were quite clearly claimed as programmes for people like them. Unlike older people, however, it was felt that teenagers – the actual bearers of this projected future identity – might also share some of their own tastes:

INTERVIEWER: Do you think it [*Sister Sister*] is a programme for teenagers?
ALL: No.
INTERVIEWER: Why is that? Aren't the characters sixteen?
SHARON: Yes, but they're the sort of age where, you know, we can understand . . .
ANNIE: I think teenagers can like it as well.

Certain lifestyle options were consistently associated with this slightly older age group. Teenagers, it would seem, have social and emotional lives, characterized by boyfriends, girlfriends, fashion and music. During our group interviews, conversations around these subjects were frequent and unsolicited. These conversations clearly had a social, performative role and were used partly as a way of articulating their own (heterosexual) gender positions (for a fuller discussion, see Kelley et al., 1999). However, the identity of the teenager was not only differentiated through sexual and romantic knowledge; it was also about having greater access to the public world. In our scheduling exercise, when groups of older children were asked about what they would watch on a mid-week afternoon, discussion would frequently move on to other things that they did or would like to do at that time – playing football in the park, or 'hanging about' with friends. Spending more time out of the house was also something that they looked forward to and associated with being a teenager.

However, looking forward to being teenage was not at all the same thing as wanting to be grown-up. Certain programmes that were seen as the kinds of things that teenagers would like were enjoyed because of their almost 'childish' silliness and rebellion against adult authority. For example, one boy singled out the character George Dawes in the quiz show *Shooting Stars* as a particular reason for liking this programme, because he was a grown man dressed as a baby:

INTERVIEWER: What's so funny about him?
SIMON: He's a baby and he plays the drums with his hand up and he says 'silly git' and everyone laughs on the show.

The juxtaposition between babyishness and adult humour and swearing is clearly a source of enjoyment to this boy. In cases like this, enthusiasm for the 'childish' and silly aspects of comedy were also combined with a sense of exclusivity. In discussion, it was important for certain children to show that they could 'get' the joke, in order to demonstrate that they were grown-up and sophisticated.

In a sense, then, these were clearly *aspirational* preferences. As Liesbeth de Block (1998) notes, comedies like *Friends* and *Men Behaving Badly* seem to be particularly popular with children in this age group, partly because they allow them to rehearse a kind of adulthood that is independent, autonomous and self-sufficient (living in your own flat with your friends, having control over your own space and time) while at the same time allowing irresponsibility, irreverence and immaturity (watching lots of television, getting into trouble with more 'responsible' grown-ups). Yet, unlike characters in more serious adult soaps or dramas, the male characters in these comedies are not portrayed (or indeed perceived by children) as particularly mature. As de Block suggests, their appeal rests largely on the fact that they are men behaving like boys. Such programmes thus offer children a version of 'adulthood' that combines elements of autonomy and freedom with irreverence and irresponsibility.

It was these qualities, as much as the music or the clothes the characters wore, that defined such programmes as inherently 'cool', as opposed to 'old-fashioned'. As one 10-year-old boy – Luke – with a particular self-esteem problem explained: 'I have to admit this, but I'm quite – I'm not a cool guy. I don't watch *Friends*.' In this aspirational world of 'cool', there seems to be an almost narcissistic relationship between reader and text. It is partly that the qualities of the programme are seen to transfer across to the individuals who watch it; but also that one's existing qualities are somehow necessarily reflected in what one chooses to watch in the first place. In Luke's account, classification very definitely classifies the classifier.

How uncool can you get?

If the cultural identity labelled 'teenage' is characterized by fun, rebellion and sex, it was neces-sary for a contrasting identity to be constructed – as something that was none of these things, and indeed was actively opposed to them. This category was identified by several groups of girls in particular as that of 'grannies'. Given the highly gendered nature of this classification, it is interesting that it was more clearly formulated by the girls. The identity of the granny was defined as boring, old fashioned and censorious:

> INTERVIEWER: Why do you think it [the quiz show *Countdown*] is so boring?
> ANNIE: Because it's full of all these words that you have to make.
> INTERVIEWER: Who do you think would like those kinds of programmes?
> JULIA: Grannies.
> ANNIE: Yeah, grannies!

Likewise, 'grannies' or (more charitably) 'people in their sixties' were also seen as the least appropriate audience for the children's own favourite shows. This renouncement of old age was also used as a strategy in arguments about programmes. In a mixed group, one girl expressed a preference for the sitcom *Frasier*, only to be put down by one of the boys with the withering comment: 'What, old people living in a flat? That's not funny.'

In this way, certain types of adults and adult viewing are very explicitly rejected. Being old and female, it would seem, is the ultimate cultural stigma. Of course, this expression of cultural taste is not unrelated to questions of social power and status, not least as defined by the media themselves: when younger women are valued for their physical desirability, older women are frequently invisible – and, when they are represented at all, often serve as the butt of young people's humour. This might go some way to explaining why it was the girls rather than the boys who were so hostile to 'grannies' and all that they were seen to represent.

You've got to laugh

In response to our somewhat earnest questions about why a programme was chosen or preferred, the most common answer across both age groups was simply that it was 'funny'. Like most audiences, our sample enjoy television that makes them laugh, as one 6-year-old girl related when talking about [British comedy series] *Mr Bean*:

> INTERVIEWER: What makes it a children's programme?
> TONI: Because I like it, because it's funny and I like funny things.

On one level, this kind of explanation is so obvious as to be banal. However, it is important to understand its significance a little more fully. In fact, comedy is one of the areas in which children's tastes are frequently seen to differ fundamentally from those of adults. Children's humour is often (revealingly) dismissed as 'puerile' or 'infantile'. Indeed, in our experience, the children's programmes that are the hardest for adults to watch are the highly stereotyped, slapstick comedies like the BBC's *Chucklevision* and *To Me, To You* – programmes that make *Mr Bean* look like Jane Austen. Such programmes are often highly successful in the ratings.

As we have noted, contemporary critics of children's television tend to adopt a conservative notion of cultural value. Such critics do not deny that children's television can and should be entertaining; but what gives children's television value is not the fun stuff (the cartoons and comedies) but the factual programmes, the literary adaptations and the 'socially relevant' contemporary drama. In this rather sanctimonious context, very few critics seem prepared to stand up for children's right to just 'have a laugh' – although, it should be noted, programme-makers certainly have.

While children's expressions of enthusiasm for comedy are, on one level, simply an assertion of 'personal' pleasure, there are also social functions in talking about what makes them laugh. Different kinds of comedy had different kinds of value in this respect. Programmes like *Mr Bean* or the camcorder show *You've Been Framed* are primarily physical, slapstick humour, although the children's accounts of them focused particularly on the subversive or 'carnivalesque' element of adults behaving like children and making fools of themselves. On the other hand, programmes such as *Shooting Stars* were valued for different reasons. Central to their appeal for the older children was the idea that in 'getting the joke' they were gaining access to an exclusive world of irony and media-references inaccessible to younger children:

ANDREW: *Friends* is – it's not a little kids thing. Like *Shooting Stars* is a show for older
               people.
JAMES: Little kids don't have the patience to watch them.
ANDREW: Yeah, someone younger won't find *Friends* or *Shooting Stars* funny.

For James and Andrew, the 'older people' identified here are implicitly people like them.

Talking about these kinds of programmes seemed to be more important for the boys in the group – which may reflect an aspirational identification with the men who tend to dominate these shows. In several of these programmes, the humour often involves a characteristically male form of banter and one-upmanship. To some extent, being seen to be 'in on the joke' was more important than actually finding it funny. As one 10-year-old boy explained in relation to *Shooting Stars* and other such shows: 'You see them maybe once and sometimes you don't get the jokes, but you still laugh because you know it's meant to be funny. . . . But you don't really know why' (David).

Laughing with the big boys, as it were, has the most social and cultural currency: this is what you *should* find funny. For one particular 10-year-old boy – who saw himself as a taste leader in the class – this became apparent when he discussed the US sitcom *Sabrina the Teenage Witch*. As a less sophisticated, more girl-oriented show, he almost apologized for liking it:

INTERVIEWER: So what's good about *Sabrina*?
JAMES: It's just good.
ALAN: I have to admit, it's not the kind of thing you'd think is good. But it's good,
               it's funny.

Particular kinds of comedy, then, clearly have a social function, which is again associated with being more sophisticated and 'teenage'. To this extent, talking about comedy is a serious business: it can be used to mark out social status and knowledge as well as simply expressing pleasure.

If what is 'funny' was seen to be particularly appropriate for children, then what is 'boring' (and hence lacking in pleasure) was consistently equated with adults – and particularly with 'grannies'. For this group of 6-year-old girls, being boring is a defining characteristic of adult programmes:

INTERVIEWER: So what makes it [*The News*] a grown-ups programme?
TONI: It's boring.

INTERVIEWER:	So does that mean that grown-ups are boring?
RUTH:	Yes, because they like the news.
TONI:	I hate the news.
INTERVIEWER:	Why do you think grown-ups like the news?
TONI:	Because they want to know what's happening?
INTERVIEWER:	And aren't you interested?
TONI:	No!

News as a genre is inherently and essentially defined as adult. A group of 6-year-old boys, for example, saw no clear difference between [The BBC's] *The Six o'clock News* and *Newsround*, despite *Newsround*'s very clear institutional status as children's television:

INTERVIEWER:	What about *The Six o'clock News*, is that for grown-ups?
FRED:	Yeah, sort of.
JACK:	That's like *Newsround*, isn't it?
INTERVIEWER:	Do you think there's any difference between them?
JACK:	No, they're the same.
MICHAEL:	Yes, it's just that one's on later.

Here again, the criteria that were used to define a particular programme as 'boring' – and hence to proclaim one's dislike of it – were quite diverse; but the association between what was 'boring' and what was identified with 'adults' was very consistent. Thus, for a group of 10-year-old girls, *Shooting Stars* – which was a preferred programme among their male peers – is defined as boring, in part because it is associated with one of their parents:

SHARON:	My dad would laugh at *Shooting Stars* . . . sometimes I think it's really boring.
INTERVIEWER:	Is there anything in particular about the programme that makes it for grown-ups?
SHARON:	It's boring. And it's–
JULIA:	They laugh about stupid, dumb things.

Being boring – while it means different things for different children – is thus a cardinal signifier of a lack of cultural value. In contrast, being funny (and 'getting the joke') is seen to convey value on these children as individuals as well as on the programmes that they consume. In the process, the cultural hierarchy that elevates seriousness and civic responsibility is effectively inverted.

Cut to the action

For the younger children in particular, one of the characteristics that was seen to make television boring was *talking*. Needless to say, perhaps, this resistance to talk extended to our research activities: sorting out programme titles on cards could be perceived as an acceptable game, but having to rationalize their choices in response to our questions was something that many of the children resisted. Talk is seen as the antithesis of action. As one of the younger boys explained:

| INTERVIEWER: | Why aren't soaps for children, then? |
| ANDREW: | Well, it's just that there are lots of conversations in them Nothing happens, no funny things. |

This opposition between talk and action was also a key dimension of responses to news, as these 6-years-olds indicated:

GEOFF: And I watched this really, really boring one [*Newsround*]. All it was really – you didn't see any pictures at all – all you heard was talking, talking, talking.
LAURA: [*News*] is boring for children because it's got no acting in it.

As in this instance, television talk is generally *adult* talk. Even children's news programmes like *Newsround* rarely feature children talking in their own right, whether as presenters or as participants in news events (Buckingham, 1997).

In contrast, programmes claimed as children's programmes would often be talked about in terms of their physicality and visceral appeal. The game show *Gladiators* was described in these terms by children in both age groups:

INTERVIEWER: What do you like about *Gladiators*?
TONI: Well, they do activities and stuff.
RUTH: And they wear –
ROBYN: – bright clothes and stuff.
TONI: I'm going to be a Gladiator when I grow up.

(6-year olds)

MARK: I like to see how they, I just like the activities they have. I don't really care about the people, I just want to see how they do in the activities.

(10-year-old)

Typically, talking was associated with fact, while action was associated with stories or performing. However, this distinction was not necessarily the same as that between fiction and non-fiction. Programmes such as *Gladiators* or *Wildlife on One* are non-fiction, but because of their visceral and dramatic content, they were associated by these children with fictional action programmes like *Hercules* or *Xena Warrior Princess*. This preference for action, event and spectacle also underlines the popularity in ratings terms of programmes featuring sport – particularly football – and the National Lottery draw. Whether human, animal or environmental, action – often expressed through 'violence' – is a key criterion in determining these children's television tastes, for both boys and girls. Children, it would seem, like to see things happen.

Conclusion

On one level, children clearly do have distinctive tastes in television. Allowing for other social differences, they seem to enjoy things that adults don't, and vice versa. And even where they watch the same programmes as adults, they often appear to be enjoying them for different reasons.

Psychologists would seek to explain these differences by recourse to notions of development. Thus, children's apparent liking for what we as adults judge to be simplistic narratives, stereotyped characters and crude humour would be seen as evidence of their cognitive and emotional limitations. More charitably perhaps, such tastes could be seen as a developmental *necessity* at a given stage: children, it might be argued, need to see the world in simple binary terms before they can learn to understand its full complexity. While outwardly quite different, psychoanalytic explanations would be inclined to take a similar form. Scatological and sexual humour, for example, would be seen as a necessary stage in the sublimation of the id and the development of the mature ego.

Such analyses have some truth, but they are unavoidably normative – both in terms of *texts* and in terms of *audiences*. Truly 'mature' viewers simply would not get excited by *Gladiators* or *Xena Warrior Princess*; they would not be amused by *Mr Bean* or the silly behaviour on *Shooting Stars*; and they would simply refuse to watch *You've Been Framed* or game shows like *Blind Date*. On the contrary, their television diet would consist solely of *Newsnight*, serious dramas like *Inspector Morse* and perhaps the occasional glimpse of [soap opera like] *Coronation Street*. Such normative judgements are, to be sure, partly about social class and gender; but they are also frequently defined and expressed in terms of *age*.

The reality, as we have suggested, is rather different. As 'adults' – albeit of different generations – the authors of this article will confess to enjoying *Shooting Stars, The Simpsons, Blind Date* and *Top of the Pops* – although we would also confess to drawing the line at *Mr Bean*, not to mention *Chucklevision*. Viewing such programmes is partly a professional necessity, but it is also something that we consciously choose to do in our 'real lives', insofar as we have any. This is not to say that we do not also watch 'adult' programmes like *Newsnight* or *Inspector Morse* – although again we would probably draw the line at [knowledge quiz shows like] *Countdown*. The point is that, as adults, we have multiple tastes – and multiple subjectivities.

More to the point, these tastes are also socially defined. As we have attempted to show in this article, children's assertions of their own tastes necessarily entail a form of 'identity work' – a positioning of the self in terms of publicly available discourses and categories. The labels 'child' and 'adult' are categories of this kind: they are defined relative to each other (and to other age-defined categories such as 'teenagers' and 'grannies'), and as such they are necessarily flexible and open to dispute. Definitions of what is 'childish' or 'adult' – 'mature' or 'immature' – are therefore subject to a constant process of negotiation.

Like the practice of film classification, which publicly defines maturity in terms of age categories, social hierarchies of taste thus provide a scale against which children can calibrate their own maturity and hence make claims about their identity. This is, as we have shown, partly a form of *aspiration* – although for the children we have studied, this is a matter of aspiration towards a 'teenage' identity rather than a fully 'adult' one. Yet it can also be a matter of *subversion* – a celebration of 'childish things' that self-consciously challenge or mock adult norms of respectability, restraint and 'good taste'.

This subversive option has also become increasingly popular for many adults (or at least young adults) in recent years. Just as some older children appear to want to 'buy in' to adulthood, so some adults want to do the reverse. The cult status of the BBC's pre-school series *Teletubbies* among twenty-something clubbers; the camp nostalgia associated with 'retro' children's TV of the 1970s, currently being revived on cable channels; the child-like anarchy and game-playing of Chris Evans's *Big Breakfast* and *TFI Friday*; and the crossover success with adults of children's hosts like Zoe Ball – all these phenomena point to the growing appeal (and indeed the commodification) of 'childishness' as a kind of style accessory. Childhood, it would seem, isn't just for children any more.

Some academics and media commentators appear to be particularly disturbed by what they perceive as this infantilization – or 'paedocratisation' – of the television audience (Hartley, 1987; Preston, 1996). Television, they argue, increasingly addresses the adult audience as emotional, excitable and wanting to be pleasured – characteristics more usually attributed to children. Yet there is a kind of puritanism about this argument. One could interpret this phenomenon more positively, as a necessary process of recovering 'child-like' pleasures – in silly noises and games, in anarchy and absurdity – for which irony provides a convenient alibi. This kind of nostalgia for past pleasures could be seen to reflect the ambivalent status of television as a kind of 'transitional object', which plays a significant role in young people's growth towards adulthood.[6]

Yet to pose this argument in such terms – as a matter of 'infantilization' or alternatively of 'getting in touch with one's inner child' – is to resort to psychologistic interpretations. By contrast, we would argue that this elevation of an apparently 'child-like' anarchy and irresponsibility as the ultimate in cool is a *social* and *political* act on the part of adults. The 'immaturity' of some of these programmes is also a front for a kind of machismo; their self-regarding enthusiasm for celebrity sanctions a barely concealed contempt for the apparent inadequacies of their audience. Without being merely nostalgic, one could see such programmes as a kind of retreat from the public spaces which were partly colonized by more threatening forms of youth culture in previous decades.

Above all, it should be emphasized that this exchange is far from equal. When adults – or at least particular kinds of adults – seek to appropriate children's culture, they inevitably select the aspects that have resonance for their own lives. In the process, there may be a risk of forgetting the material inequalities between children and adults, and the way in which children's autonomy is currently being undermined in the era of educational testing, curfews and enforced homework quotas. When children laugh at the incompetent child-like adult in *Mr Bean* or the spectacle of adults humiliating themselves in *You've Been Framed*, it is partly because these programmes speak to their sense of their own powerlessness. In contrast, when adults revel in the *faux* children's television of shows like *TFI Friday*, the irresponsibility invoked there is a conscious choice. Adults, it would seem, can *choose* to be childish. Children cannot.

Notes

1 *Daily Mail* (20 June 1996).
2 For a fuller discussion, see Buckingham (1995b).
3 'Children's Media Culture: Education, Entertainment and the Public Sphere', based at the Institute of Education, University of London, and funded by the Economic and Social Research Council UK (award no. 1.126251026). Further material from this research is presented in Buckingham *et al.* (1999).
4 Space precludes a more detailed discussion of the research methodology. For accounts of similar studies, see Buckingham (1993) and Robinson (1997). These discussions and activities took place outside the classroom, in the library or a teacher's office. The groups were taped and the tapes were transcribed. Groups were selected on the basis of existing friendship groups and seating arrangements in the classroom. Each child in both classes was interviewed at least twice.
5 Further interpretations of this data, focusing on different issues, can be found in Kelley *et al.* (1999) and Davies *et al.* (1999).
6 We owe this argument to Mica Nava, in a presentation at the Institute of Education in February 1998. The notion of television as a transitional object is drawn in turn from the work of Roger Silverstone (1994).

References

Abrams, M. (1956) 'Child Audiences for Television in Great Britain', *Journalism Quarterly* 33(1): 35–41.
Bourdieu, P. (1979) *Distinction: A Social Critique of the Judgment of Taste*. London: Routledge & Kegan Paul.
—— (1998) *On Television and Journalism*. London: Pluto Press.
Buckingham, D. (1993) *Children Talking Television: The Making of Television Literacy*. London: Falmer.
—— (1994) 'Television and the Definition of Childhood', in B. Mayall (ed.) *Children's Childhoods: Observed and Experienced*. London: Falmer.
—— (1995a) 'On the Impossibility of Children's Television: The Case of Timmy Mallet', in C. Bazalgette and D. Buckingham (eds) *In Front of the Children: Screen Entertainment and Young Audiences*, pp. 47–61. London: British Film Institute.
—— (1995b) 'The Commercialisation of Childhood? The Place of the Market in Children's Media Culture', *Changing English* 2(2): 17–41.

—— (1997) 'The Making of Citizens: Pedagogy and Address in Children's Television News', *Journal of Educational Media* 23(2–5): 119–39.

—— H. Davies, K. Jones and P. Kelley (1999) *Children's Television in Britain: History, Discourse and Policy*. London: British Film Institute.

Davies, H., D. Buckingham and P. Kelley (1999) 'Kids' Time: Childhood, Television and the Regulation of Time'. *Journal of Educational Media* 24(1): 25–42.

De Block, L. (1998) 'From Childhood Pleasures To Adult Identities', *English and Media Magazine* 38: 24–9.

Frith, S. (1998) 'Is Youth the Future?', paper delivered at Institute of Education, London University, March.

Frow, J. (1995) *Cultural Studies and Cultural Value*. Oxford: Oxford University Press.

Gouldner, A. (1979) *The Future of Intellectuals and the Rise of the New Class*. New York: Seabury Press.

Hartley, J. (1987) 'Impossible Fictions: Television Audiences, Paedocracy, Pleasure', *Textual Practice* 1(2): 121–38.

—— (1992) *Teleology*. London: Routledge.

Kelley, P., D. Buckingham and H. Davies (1999) 'Talking Dirty: Children, Sexual Knowledge and Television', *Childhood* 6(2): 241–2.

Kline, S. (1993) *Out of the Garden: Toys and Children's Culture in the Age of TV Marketing*. London: Verso.

Mander, M. (1987) 'Bourdieu, the Sociology of Culture and Cultural Studies: A Critique', *European Journal of Communication* 2(4): 427–53.

Peretti, J. (1998) 'Middle Youth Ate My Culture', *Modern Review* 5 (March): 14–19.

Preston, P. (1996) 'Watch Out, Sex and Violence Are About', *The Guardian* (13 Dec.): 19.

Robbins, D. (1991) *The Work of Pierre Bourdieu*. Milton Keynes: Open University Press.

Robinson, M. (1997) *Children Reading Print and Television*. London: Falmer.

Schiach, M. (1993) ' "Cultural Studies" and the Work of Pierre Bourdieu', *French Cultural Studies* 4(3/12): 213–23.

Seiter, E. (1993) *Sold Separately: Parents and Children in Consumer Culture*. New Brunswick, NJ: Rutgers University Press.

Silverstone, R. (1994) *Television and Everyday Life*. London: Routledge.

Simpson, M. (1994) *Male Impersonators: Men Performing Masculinity*. London: Routledge.

Chapter 31

ANNA McCARTHY

TELEVISION WHILE YOU WAIT

Waiting casts one's life into a little dungeon of time.
(*William James*)

AS THE EMERGENCE OF CORPORATE ENTITIES like the CNN Airport Network and the Commuter Channel indicates, one of television's central institutional tasks in spaces outside the home is to accompany—and, in the case of place-based media, commodify—the act of waiting. This foregrounds the centrality of time, and environmental rhythms, in the processes through which television and TV images interweave with the habitual atmospheres of social space. Many critics have pointed out that the passage of time in home life is measured through the repetitive, segmented structure of the TV schedule, intertwining viewing with other domestic habits and practices.[1] Questions of when, and for how long, we watch TV at home are also questions about how the relationship between time of work and time of leisure in domestic space is demarcated. Marking the familial division of labor in temporal terms, TV plays a crucial role in the (highly gendered) relations of power within the home.[2] Similarly, site-specific relations of time and space shape televisual places outside the home as well. The temporal structures of TV programming interweave with, and sometimes warp, the patterns of time, duration, and repetition in different ways from place to place. The duration of a program or sports game can set a time frame for socializing in a bar or specify times to avoid going there. In the shopping mall the Food Court Entertainment Network aspires to make time spent eating less a retreat from shopping than a "productive" form of consumer leisure—the viewing of commercials.

Now these small-scale processes of time coexist with rather more large-scale temporal mediations, too. Time-based TV processes like live transmission serve to link places—particular homes, particular regions—together in spectacular ways. The technoideology of liveness situates the home within the fictional simultaneity of the nation as an "imagined community," even when the image in question is not literally "live."[3] Such myths of national participation through liveness are not confined to the home screen by any means. Popular representations of live media events often seem to rely heavily on shots of crowds gathering to watch TV *outside* the home, in bars, restaurants, and store windows—think of key scenes in movies like *The Truman Show*, *Quiz Show*, *It's Always Fair Weather*, and *It Could Happen to You*. Live broadcast reception in public places, such Hollywood moments imply, is a metaphor for the nation's collective interest. This idea recurs in the journalistic practice of gauging public opinion of large-scale media events, including sports, by surveying the diverse collectivities of strangers and acquaintances who gather in public locales equipped with TV sets. Such moments of group engagement with live spectacle, guaranteeing the "realness" of public reactions, can constitute a potent image of national *communitas* in journalistic narratives. However, liveness is a temporal ideology of television that can acquire a specific cultural and symbolic resonance in certain public sites and cultural contexts. As a mode of festive viewing it has become closely associated with one particular place—the bar, where sports spectatorship allows fans a sense of virtual copresence on national and international scales. And indeed, these site-specific experiences of television liveness in places like the tavern can politicize the act of spectatorship along class lines.

This chapter asks how TV sets regulate the flow and experience of time in public spaces. As a temporal stricture of TV, liveness is associated with crisis; it interrupts. But here I am concerned with a related, though opposed, organization of televisual time, namely, forms of *deadness*: routine, boredom, and repetition, the unremarkable, taken-for-granted continuousness of the TV schedule. These are the temporal modes against which the shock of live broadcasting is often defined.[4] Outside the home as well as within it the rhythms of reception produced by the cycles and patterns of broadcasting overlap with the rhythms of social life, although not necessarily in the same ways.[5] Certain temporal effects are *limited* to the public screen and its often site-specific programming because they mesh with the flow of time associated with particular institutions. Just as the social organization of time is structured differently from place to place, so too are the ways in which television blurs distinctions between time of work and time of leisure in various locations. As I will suggest, television shapes time flexibly and adaptively, in consort with other institutional and personal elements, and according to site-specific cultural norms and protocols.[6] Moving between very different kinds of space—from the physician's waiting room to Planet Hollywood, a tourist-oriented "theme restaurant"—I analyze in words and images the consistent presence and invisible conventions of TV time in public places of waiting.

To be sure, the waiting area is not the only place where we use TV sets to pass time. Default, time-passing viewing is an activity we can pursue anywhere—we while away hours at home with TV, as much if not more than we find ourselves watching TV while we wait in the bank lobby or the lounge of the auto-parts store. But waiting areas are particular kinds of places, and the TV sets installed in public zones of transit, work, and service—places where waiting often predominates over other activities—become meshed with the features of their environments in particular ways. There is something very distinctive in the fact that waiting rooms are often serialized environments. When we travel, or when we visit places like hospitals, we are often moved from one waiting area to another. It is a testament to the mobility of the spectator in contemporary life that the screens in such places can, on occasion, track the action of a sporting event for passengers moving from one transit waiting area, one airport bar or snack area, to the next. In Tokyo, where many places of transit are equipped with monitors for watching sumo wrestling, this phenomenon is a routine part of municipal life. In the United States a similarly serial address to the spectator moving at jet speed emanates from the monitors of the CNN Airport Network at the gate. As a promotional mailing tells its potential advertisers and subscriber airlines, the network is a service "designed . . . to keep passengers informed while travelling."[7]

This CNN brochure also listed a number of other passenger benefits that offer a useful index of how site-specific media corporations envision the screen's environmental effects on the spectator. According to this mailing, a "passenger research study" had also discovered the network's ability "to make waiting time more productive, to shorten perceived waiting time, to entertain, to alleviate boredom, to reduce stress caused by delays and travel hassles." This is an image of television as a time-warping companion within the waiting area, an environmental distraction that somehow changes the overall affective experience of being there. Yet these "effects" are surely not so easily measured. Even under the rigid quality-control guidelines of corporations like Turner, TV's environmental address is always embedded in other kinds of noise, within other forms of interaction, and modified by additional site-specific factors like, for example, the particular position the screen occupies within the room. Its relation to the space is different depending on whether it blurts its cycles of news above one's head or sits silently in the corner, an incongruously mobile and brightly colored square set against the beige sameness of an institutional décor. If different waiting environments have distinctive features, then any attempt to understand the role of the television screen within them must isolate these features. We must ask how the presence of the screen shapes the experience of waiting as an activity—one often contained within other activities (going to the doctor, traveling)—and pay close attention to the workings of power that are set in motion in places where people, for whatever reason, are required to wait. For waiting is something we generally take for granted, rarely stopping to pay much attention to the specifics of the relationships it establishes in space.

So what, exactly, is at stake in the commodification of an activity so routine, so unmarked, as waiting? Although it is a banal and omnipresent facet of everyday life, waiting is a surprisingly complicated form of human (in)action. In *Queuing and Waiting*, perhaps the most famous study of waiting as a particular set of social relations, sociologist Barry Schwartz approaches waiting as a temporal modality that materializes larger power structures; as he puts it, modern society might easily be divided into two classes: those who have to wait and those who don't.[8] Yet, as he also points out, waiting is most often treated in institutional practices as a purely instrumental problem in the flow of goods and services; environments designed for waiting materialize a set of ergonomic directives and compromises that are more reflective of ideas about efficiency than comfort or habitability.[9] Waiting areas are not places where we dwell; they are places we occupy temporarily, on the way to somewhere else. However, for many people—women, the poor, and others who occupy particularly disadvantaged positions within systems of social administration—the long wait is a time-consuming and inevitable requirement of basic access to goods and services in modern life. Because of this sense of instrumentality and passage, the experience of waiting is associated with low-intensity affects like boredom, which, precisely because of their apparent simplicity, remain inscrutable and inaccessible to others.[10] The vagueness of boredom, waiting, and other "moods and feelings that resist analysis" makes waiting an emblematic instance of the unmarked universality of everyday experience that can all too easily slip through the conceptual nets that surround it.[11]

At the same time, however, waiting is a form of experience that necessarily anticipates change in, and even *destruction* of, predictable temporal flow. After all, although it might be described as a state of inactivity, waiting—along with the queues and traffic jams it engenders—is a situation we often find ourselves in at times of urgency, emergency, and crisis.[12] It would be wrong, therefore, to associate waiting solely with passivity and implicate television in this passivity, despite the fact that it is a medium persistently associated with passivity in certain kinds of cultural criticism. Such prefabricated interpretations neglect the possibility that television might also make the waiting room a place where one wants to remain—making it more like a place of dwelling and attachment. (I can recall waiting situations in which I've found myself hoping that my name would not be called before the end of the TV program onscreen.)[13] If the presence of a screen in a public space is a clue, on entering, that delayed access is a normal, natural, and inevitable fact of social life therein, then it is also a license for the waiting person to indulge in a little TV-viewing. Often associated with *wasting* time, watching television is a way of passing time suddenly *legitimized* when it takes place in waiting environments.

This possibility for multiple relations between TV and waiting means that, rather than insist categorically that television has one dominant effect on waiting spaces, it is wiser to approach the screen's role as highly indicative of the temporal tensions that define the act of waiting—tensions between the here and now and the anticipated future, between boredom and the expectation of its release. My goal in the following is to trace such tensions in the particular discourses and practices associated with television and the act of waiting in a few carefully chosen sites—focusing some-times on TV screens that are placed within waiting rooms per se and TV screens in multiuse environments that serve to designate a space of waiting. I must note, however, that the most immediate obstacle to this task is the fact that waiting rooms are anonymous spaces not meant for dwelling—it is hard to register their distinctive features in light of their overwhelmingly func-tional and institutionalized design. [. . .] The conventions of televisual waiting [. . .] are so familiar as to be invisible to the observer. [. . .] Who has not spent some time waiting in the presence of the cluttered, shell-like console of an older model TV set [. . .] We begin, then, in a small doctor's waiting room in a suburban area of the northeastern United States, moving from this space to others in order to chart the spatial dialectics that crystallize around the presence of the TV screen.

This TV set is located in a general practitioner's office, housed in what was recognizably once a residence, although the space has been remodeled and rendered "institutional" through the addition of a number of functional and decorative elements: drop ceilings, fluorescent lights, framed pastel-toned posters, magazines, no-smoking signs, pamphlets, coat pegs, and more vinyl-cushioned chairs than would ever be found in a real living room. The placement of the screen here provides good material documentation of the space's transformation from domestic living room to institutional waiting room. Located in the most visible spot in the room, the screen has been bleached of all signifiers of domesticity; like many TVS in waiting rooms, it is surrounded by booklets and brochures stacked almost to the ceiling. Its display of a local news broadcast sits at the center of a large informational matrix, a densely packed area of pamphlets, health-education materials, and commercial forms of publicity from drug company literature to credit card applica-tions. This positioning makes the console an instrument of public address rather than private entertainment; to look in its direction is to be reminded, simultaneously, of the medical orienta-tion of the space and of the availability of alternative, and perhaps more health-related, texts with which to spend time waiting.

Through its physical alignment with information, the screen attaches specific meanings to the passage of time and the act of waiting in this space. As part of a syntagm of information dissemination composed of magazines and other paraeducational print matter, it links the activity of passing time to the enduring, institutional goals of education and information Michel Foucault defined in the final chapter of *Discipline and Punish* as a central function of clinical space. Historic-ally, institutional spaces like hospitals and almshouses anchored networks of information dissemin-ation that, in teaching habits of self-discipline and monitoring, enjoined the production of what Foucault calls the "great carceral continuum" of modern society.[14] [. . .]

In medical settings where patients await procedures that have larger social, emotional, or epidemiological consequences (e.g., HIV testing and pregnancy testing), the video screen serves as an outreach tool, targeting particular populations by screening tapes that may—depending on the context—advocate behavior modification (videos that depict safe sex and needle-cleaning pro-cedures), present legally mandated information leading to informed consent (available "choices" for pregnant teens), or explain complex internal physiological events (the mechanisms by which HIV infects cells).[15]

Television's normative alignment with information and self-discipline in the waiting room, whether through its position within a general informational matrix or as a more aggressive outreach tool in patient education, is reflected on an institutional level in medical professional concerns about what patients do with the time they spend in health-care settings. A 1998 article in the journal *Medical Economics* reports that certain physicians are dismayed by the fact that their waiting patients watch "soap-opera couples in heat, and often bizarre day-time talkshow fare (e.g., left-handed vegetarian transvestites baring their souls)."[16] The article extols the virtues of informational television as an alternative way to pass the time in medical contexts: "patient education is the bright side of television in the waiting room . . . By taking an active, creative approach towards television instead of just abandoning it, you can turn the small screen into a practice builder" (141). Surveying physicians, the article notes the widespread phenomenon of waiting-room screens tuned to informational and educational cable channels or to health-related videocassettes to keep patients occupied. It also suggests that doctors might use the TV set to promote their practices, citing the example of a New Orleans urologist who "transform[ed] the waiting-room television into a marketing tool by producing—and starring in—simple videotaped programs" (141).

Like many articles about on-site television, this report emphasizes the importance of minimizing the intrusiveness of the screen through low audio and strategic placement in "a corner or alcove where it won't dominate the waiting room; you don't want to force it on someone who'd rather read a magazine" (141). However, it contradicts its own plea for moderation in its praise for the rather more intrusive presence of the CNN-produced Accent Health Network (AH)—a package of health-related programming, presumably modeled after Whittle's now defunct "Special Reports" network, distributed via laser disc to high-volume physicians' offices. This once local system of on-site TV programming in Florida went national when it signed a production agreement with Turner Private Networks in 1997, subsequently becoming the national standard of health-related television.[17] In 1998 AH could be seen in six thousand health-care facilities nationwide. Its forty-four-minute roster of health-related programming is interspersed with eighteen minutes of advertising designed for each particular office's medical focus (OB-GYN, pediatricians, or general practitioners). Although all place-based TV networks offer us a chance to explore the power relations that emerge around the rise of televisual waiting as a corporate strategy, AH is a particularly interesting case study because the relationship among broadcasting, advertising, and medicine is fraught with long-standing tensions, from policy debates over false medical advertising to current concerns over the "commercialization" of medicine and the American Medical Association. Compared to, say, the Airport Network, AH's presence in spaces of waiting is weighted with a high degree of ethical negotiation.[18]

To explore how AH construes the phenomenon of televisual waiting, I made several visits to a facility in which it was installed: an ambulatory care center attached to an urban hospital in the northeast United States with a large array of office suites devoted to general and specialized medicine. [. . .] I spent my time in this place photographing the screens, observing interactions that occurred around them, and tracking the amount of time people seemed to be waiting.[19] Serving Medicaid clients, members of several different managed care "networks," and, presumably, some percentage of the fortunate few who still have freestanding health insurance, this facility is populated by a large, highly diverse patient base. Patients and staff move constantly among the suites on each floor—from the office of a specialist to the radiology department to the examining table of a "primary care" physician—with much waiting, in the patient's case, along the way. In each suite a video monitor, nestled in its beige casing and occasionally supplemented with magazines "borrowed" from American Airlines (perhaps by one of the staff), helps pass the time between consultations.

Like all place-based media, AH appears to equate location and identity and to attempt an alteration in the itinerary of the viewer on that particular day. A 1990 audience study performed by Lifetime Medical Television, a physician TV network owned by cable's Lifetime Television, claimed—not surprisingly given Lifetime's demographic—that the majority of the medical waiting-room population is female.[20] Informational advertising on AH suggested a similar demographic target. The prevalence of ads for cough syrup and children's over-the-counter medications suggests that AH commercial programming also, undoubtedly, drew on another market research "fact" discovered by Life-time, namely, that women in medical waiting rooms (especially women in the waiting rooms of pediatricians) are likely to visit the pharmacy after their visit.[21]

Knowing this, it was very difficult to conduct this on-site research at first. I could not get past the initial dismay at seeing all of my worst fears about exploitation through advertising confirmed. As the slogan "information for healthy living" plastered to the screen's housing indicates, the network promotes itself as a source of information to peruse as one whiles away one's time, although the information it offers—often presented as trivia quizzes and recipes—seems to equate health education and the promotion of consumption. I gritted my teeth as I sat through commercial testimonies for brand-name health and lifestyle products of questionable therapeutic value in room after room. The sense that the onscreen advertising is a personalized address is reinforced by a bright, first-person, laser-printed sign affixed to the console in each waiting room, inviting the viewer to interact more closely with AH's news and advertisements: "Can't hear me? Turn me up!" (The opposite invitation would be unthinkable: "Am I too loud? Turn me off!")

If the sociological axiom that "the distribution of waiting time coincides with the distribution of power" is correct, then AccentHealth presents us with a persuasive corollary, namely, that these differential power relations are reflected in the question of who has the option to not watch television and which persons are able to isolate themselves from television advertising in a waiting environment—not the staff and certainly not the patients.[22] Freedom from television advertising is apparently a prerogative of the doctors alone. Yet although such an assertion tells us a great deal about the way power is organized within the waiting room, it would be a mistake to assume from this that the people who must sit and wait with the TV screen are passive "dupes" of this process. My righteous indignation at the hegemonic practices of AH was tempered, after a while, by the realization that the people waiting for their appointments approached the screen's promotional conceits with a healthy skepticism. Because there was little to do other than watch TV, people tended to observe me with interest as I photographed. When they saw that my subject was the screen, they would often communicate—verbally or with a wry expression and a shake of the head—their amusement at the irritatingly cheery discourse emanating from the screen. The only thing that really seemed to make waiting patients sit up and take notice of the screen was the sudden realization that they were watching a particular piece of trivia or news segment for the second or even third time. At that moment, knowing I was paying attention to the screen (I think I may have been misrecognized, in some cases, as a representative of either the hospital or AH or perhaps both), a patient might sigh in frustration and look in my direction with a weary expression. One woman held up three fingers as she did so, implying, I think, that this was her third viewing. In light of this obvious annoyance, it is intolerably ironic to note that the network promotes itself to physicians by suggesting that the presence of AH can ameliorate the increasingly inevitable long wait patients must endure: one physician's testimony claims that patients "really like it. . . . Some even take notes. Best of all, they don't complain about their wait as much."[23]

This kind of proposition about television's relation to waiting—the idea that it transforms the experience by providing an edifying distraction—ignores the possibility that the program's perpetual cycle introduces a jarring sense of conflicting temporalities into the waiting room. This temporal dissonance seems far more specifically *televisual* than AH's ability to distract the waiting patient, a job that magazines and pamphlets had been doing all along. Indeed, the network's cyclical, rhythmic programming can be seen as a compressed and speeded up analog of the cyclical returns and repetitions that make up the broadcast day or week. A bubble of machine-like, unvarying time, it foregrounds the structure of access, duration, and delay in the waiting environment, *heightening*, rather than diminishing, awareness of the duration of the wait for those who sit in its presence.

As an alternative to the ideological image of the TV screen as a soothing palliative, I would suggest that AH's articulation of a parallel, although asymmetrical, temporality in the waiting room might best be understood in the context of other, diffuse social anxieties, specifically, those articulated around the kinds of rupture in access to information, goods, and services that constitute *crisis* in modernity.[24] As Schwartz proposes, waiting is an activity that plays an indicative role in social conflict. Detailing the range of norms and challenges to normativity that define the social relations of waiting, he characterizes the everyday phenomenon of the queue as a masked arena of economic exchange and social contest. The long wait thus calls attention to the potential for disrupting flows of supply and demand and exposes the structural fault lines in modern forms of economic exchange, welfare, and leisure.[25] The photographs of New York photographer Anna Norris document these fault lines, showing how the walls of welfare waiting rooms today are plastered with posters telling the waiting person that "your time on welfare is running out" or simply that "the clock is ticking." Such exhortations further infuse the act of waiting with the temporal urgency of impending crisis.

Although situations of waiting and live television coverage of natural and technological catastrophes seem like antithetical entities, both are haunted by the specter of social breakdown and economic disorder, exposing the fragile artifice of the capitalist system as a whole.[26] The congruity is perhaps not so surprising, given that—as several critics have noted—the habitual regularity of the TV schedule and the irregularity of the "live" televised catastrophe are not separate televisual phenomena but rather intertwined modes of temporal demarcation, dependent on each other for their ideological effects. Interruption, in other words, is not outside the regular mechanisms of televisual discourse; it is a genre of TV programming. In Mary Anne Doane's words, interruption is "crucial to television because it . . . corroborates television's access to the momentary, the discontinuous, the real." The potentially radical dialectic of banality and shock produced—as Walter Benjamin has most famously argued—in a spectrum of modern systems of representation and social exchange is, she notes, the deepest cultural meaning of catastrophe coverage's role in broadcast television.[27]

One could argue, initially, that AH disarms the dialectics of shock—if a large-scale catastrophe were to happen while I wait for my doctor's appointment, I might only find out on leaving the building. Isolating televisual routine from televisual interruption and instantaneity, AH can be seen as the final evacuation of the cultural specter of crisis that Doane sees haunting network TV, replacing unpredictability with the semipermanent and endlessly repeating technology of the laser disc. From this perspective TV's ideological image as a news technology of urgency and immediacy recedes in favor of the image of television as the ultimate ossification of habit; AH's comforting bedside manner reassures the viewer that nothing will interrupt its flow.

However, there is one obstacle to such an interpretation: the fact that the chipper commercial address of AH is entering the medical environment at a moment when, in fact, there actually *is* a crisis going on—a crisis in health care, not only health insurance but basic access—and it seems as if there is not much one can do about it. Rather than evacuating crisis from the experience of waiting, AH marks its existence. It calls attention to the probabilistic "just-in-time" economy of scale that leads many facilities to double book and overschedule rooms. For managed care "clients" the wait in the physical premises of the medical facility is often merely the end point of a far longer waiting period. In many companies one must pass the dual gatekeeping examination of the primary care physician and the managed care corporation's case managers before seeing a specialist.[28] Given this advanced institutional network of waiting, I suggest that crisis is still attached to the television screen. But it is not through the spectacular, interruptive iterations of shock that punctuate the boring flow, qualities of the network broadcasting Doane describes. Rather, it is through the resolute, unchanging banality of programming cycles unable to adjust to the cycles of the health care institutions in which they play. It is apparently easier for a place-based network to synchronize its programming with high-volume aviation networks moving millions of people across the globe every day than with health care "networks" on the ground.

To combat this problem, Accent Health now provides its programming solely to doctors' offices that have an average waiting time of under an hour.[29] It also recently entered into a partnership to develop a broadband satellite communications network, on which it now plans to deliver its programming. This network will help Accent Health consolidate profits from the doctor's office as a space of medical communication; the company plans to use it as the basis for a subscription two-way clinical messaging service. If implemented as planned, the Internet-based system will be used by doctors to communicate with consultants, labs, hospitals, and health agencies.[30]

Though it was unadopted, it is worth noting the network's initial response to its timing problems, formulated before these corporate acquisitions took place. It was an attempt to make the medical waiting room TV more integrated with the rhythms of the space while also—as I will explain—bringing the network in line with wider conventions of televisual waiting. In 1998, according to the company president, plans were underway to extend the length of programming significantly: "By the end of 1999, we hope to lengthen the program to *two hours*."[31] Given the significant increase in production costs that come with adding news and other live-action program forms (especially in light of the research requirements, and legal restrictions on content, that all medical marketing faces), the new material added in 1999 would likely have consisted of the kinds of trivia texts—quizzes, recipe substitutions, and "did-you-know" segments—that already make up a large proportion of the programming on AH. Yet although this change would have made AH's program duration correspond more closely to the rhythms and routines of its environment, it would undoubtedly have led to a different kind of relationship between screen and space; in audio terms, for instance, the introduction of more text-based programming would replace the intrusive direct address of the network's "news and views" segments with the kind of benign contemporary Muzak associated with soft-core porn videos or the local forecasts on the Weather Channel. This no doubt explains why the network ultimately sought other solutions.

But this should not obscure the fact that such low-bandwidth, minimal-affect televisual address, closer to signage than broadcasting, is becoming more and more prevalent in television, via the numerous text-based cable channels that air in the wired home, as well as via programs designed for public spaces. Textual screens bearing advertising, trivia questions, top-ten lists, pop cultural quizzes, and other small bits of light information can be found in many sites that fit the latter category: on the (recently bankrupt) Commuter Channel TV screens in regional rail stations, on the Food Court Entertainment Network screens in the shopping mall, and in travel hubs where the screens of Bloomberg TV (a financial network) barrage the passerby with a frenetic, overloaded "info-aesthetic". Affectively and economically, trivia of this kind are an ideally flexible kind of content for site-specific TV networks, easily adapted to the larger purposes of a space. They are cheap to produce, requiring nothing more complicated than an electronic character generator, and the minimal cognitive and emotional investments they solicit are easily integrated into the comings and goings of public space.

Yet the fact that broadcast television can contain similar "teaser" questions (posed, for example, just before entertainment news programs break for commercials) calls our attention to the fact that trivia, despite the pejorative connotations of the term, have a recognized commercial value. Regardless of their program context or spatial location, these routine and unremarkable deployments of the hermeneutic code have a key structural role in the flow economy of television, working to direct attention toward a commercial address during a period of waiting. This possibility is borne out in numerous places of televisual waiting. An obvious example is illustrated by the gift shop at Planet Hollywood, where fan-oriented trivia questions on the in-house network—like the tutelary quiz of Accent Health—work to reinforce the institutional identity of the space (here, the consumer-leisure environment of the theme restaurant gift shop).

The use of TV in this Planet Hollywood waiting area demonstrates how the mode of address, and physical location, of trivia screens in waiting areas work to position the waiting person as a particular kind of consuming subject. The informal slang of the title "Merch shop" addresses the Planet Hollywood customer as a knowing consumer, well aware of the store's commercial purpose. The trivia quiz on the screen tests one's "inside" knowledge of the movie business, asking the waiting spectator to name the actor originally cast as Indiana Jones.[32] It curries the favor of those who have waited in line by extending the thematic conceit of the restaurant's overall environment: that its diner is a movie fan, presumably a member of a group, perhaps even interested in showing off his/her knowledge to others. The questions recall those one sees projected on the movie theater screen (along with advertisements) before the previews—questions themselves clearly intended to distract from the experience of waiting by facilitating social interaction while promoting consumption. This *textual* contiguity with conventions of theater space is one of several ways Planet Hollywood reinforces its market image as an experiential and thematic crossover (born out of larger industrial convergences) between dining and moviegoing. Its "theme," indeed, might be described as the assertion of a metaphorical relationship between restaurant space and movie space—the set, the theater, the home of the star. Indeed, television seems to serve as a means of disguising the deficits and limits of the comparison—without video imagery, the "eatertainment" feel of Planet Hollywood would be severely improverished.[33] Moreover, although the TV screens liberally deployed for scenographic purposes in high-volume, large-party locations like Planet Hollywood may help to secure the spectacle of eatertainment, their spatial function is the rather more prosaic task of accompanying the inevitable wait in such locations. In places like theme parks, where lines for rides can last over an hour, the very existence of a queue can generate revenue, providing the kind of captive audience for television advertising that is highly valued in the economy of the place-based media industry.[34]

This commercial function is not, however, the only purpose of televisual waiting in themed commercial environments. The presence of the screen can also serve a variety of disciplinary agendas, demonstrating the institutional conception of TV as a highly flexible instrument for the management of the public and its time. Consider, for example, a video-saturated midtown Manhattan theme restaurant called Television City (now defunct). The restaurant was located across the street from NBC's Rockefeller Center, where television shows like *The Today Show* and *The Rosie O'Donnell Show* are staged. Its location near TV tapings, a popular entertainment option for both tourists and metro-area people in certain U.S. cities, was undoubtedly the motivation for the restaurant's theme (it was originally conceived as a mock TV studio).[35] Television City was a place to grab a meal after attending one of these tapings—one might describe it as a budget version of dinner and a Broadway show. However, the comparison between seeing a TV show being taped and eating in Television City is perhaps a little too apt; in the entry area the presence of a velvet rope (the premier signifier of exclusivity in New York nightlife) marked the fact that one had to stand in line to get into the restaurant. And waiting, along with being herded in a group, are prominent components of the experience of participating in a live studio audience. On the day I went to see a taping of *Sally*, the Sally Jessy Rafael show, I and the other members of the audience waited more than ninety minutes in a bleak, barracks-like room with a pay phone and an automatic coffee vending machine. Tape after tape of the Jerry Springer show (with commercials) played on the screen. Like the audience line in the studio, the line at Television City linked TV spectatorship with the "dead time" of waiting, as if the mere presence of TV monitors authorized the treatment of the consumer-diner as a member of a mass. At Television City, the TV screen also performed tasks of behavioral management with a closed-circuit camera. The restaurant's lobby featured a matrix of multiple TV monitors in a wooden frame, near which stood a mannequin dressed in clothes bearing The restaurant's logo—a color-bars image. These monitors and the mannequin demarcated the entry to the restaurant's gift shop, located, as in Planet Hollywood, on the way to and from the dining area. On Television City's waiting area screens, however, unlike those at Planet Hollywood, the waiting diner did not see in-house TV programming nor trivia questions but rather the hidden camera image of herself and the others waiting in line.

Putting the closed-circuit image of the queue on the screen, making it a spectacle, seems to serve two distinct purposes within this context. One can read it, on the one hand, as an attempt to distract attention from the length of the wait by making waiting people part of the scenography of the space, in this case by positioning them as "stars" on the screen. Along with the velvet rope, the fashion merchandise, and the close proximity of "real" TV production studios across the street, the hidden camera participated in the space's iconography of stardom, narcissism, and national celebrity. On the other hand, though, the display of closed-circuit imagery at the entryway to the gift shop offered a subtle alert very similar to the message conveyed by the surveillant images that are often prominently displayed at the entrances of retail spaces: when you enter here, you will be on TV. In combining these two signifying functions, the televisual waiting area at Television City offered a solution to some long-standing problems in the evolution of point-of-purchase display within commercial space—not only the enduring retail anxieties historically associated with self-service, as a practice that might easily translate into theft, but also the contradiction between the need to control traffic flow through the space, on the one hand, and to arrest and focus the consumer's attention on the other. This closed-circuit apparatus at the entry to the gift shop did both. As in the other sites of televisual waiting explored here, the placement of TV sets was far from random or accidental; rather, it articulated particular meanings for the act of waiting within the larger temporal rhythms and spatial flows of its environment.

To think so deeply about television as an apparatus of waiting, and the waiting spectator as a subject position deeply imbricated in the social organization of public space, invites consideration of the possibility that waiting is an affective state bound up, on a deeper level, with television viewing in general. If TV, as Paddy Scannell argues, blurs the distinctions between work and leisure, then this ambiguity can make the completion of routine tasks and activities more tolerable, at home as well as in places where we work, places where we are often waiting to leave.[36] The prevalence of TV sets in work spaces calls attention to the fact that work is an activity often suffused with a feeling of waiting for time to pass—something signified in the references to time in the titles of films about the experience of the corporate work space: *Nine to Five* or *Clockwatchers*. On a speculative level this opens up a space for asking, How much is the experience of waiting built into the format of TV programming and images in general—waiting for an upcoming program, a better music video, the resumption of a narrative interrupted by commercials? In other words, is waiting a "deep structure" of television spectatorship regardless of where we watch TV? This structural possibility is certainly suggested in theories of TV viewing like Scannell's, which draw on orthodox Marxist analyses of the functional position of leisure in capitalist relations of production to suggest that TV viewing is, at base, a way of managing the passage of time from one workday to the next.[37]

This proposition can help us understand spectatorship as a commodity experience within the temporal organization of capitalism, although it certainly does not exhaust the analytic possibilities in this area. It offers one way of explaining screen-based places like the growing genre of the mediatized eatery—that caters to the working lives of urban single professionals by providing magazines, television, video, and the Internet as accompaniments to solitary dining.[38] Such places, it could be argued, combat anxieties about time spent eating as a kind of wasted time, similar to waiting in its low-affect vagueness. They make eating a labor from which we must be distracted by news programming, or topical reading, or Web browsing, or all three. Moreover, given the pervasiveness of cultural obsessions with eating and diet, one could compare the discursive task performed by the video screens of the mediatized restaurant to that of the video screens in commercial aircraft. Both help to transform a space potentially fraught with anxiety into nothing more scary than a waiting room. This is an explicit rationale behind certain uses of television out of the home. One Beverly Hills dentist who offers his patients a headset and movies like *Die Hard* and *Braveheart* while he drills makes precisely this claim: "watching television relieves a tremendous amount of anxiety for them."[39] The warding off of difficult bodily sensations is certainly the logic that underlies health-club TV networks. Such networks often broadcast the sound over separate AM frequencies for exercisers with portable radios, allowing one to retreat from the there and then of the gym to another audio zone.

But although such general equations of spectatorship and waiting may access the reasons why some of us like to watch TV while we eat or fly or visit the dentist, I am wary of explanations that package themselves as master tropes for "decoding" televisual space. Specifically, they are of little use for exploring the differences between spaces and the variety of spatial and temporal relations of screen and place that are clearly observable on the microlevel. They lead us instead back toward the heuristically exhausted idea of television as the absence of space and the eradication of spatial difference or, more simply—as the health-club TV example might seem to suggest—"escapism." This perspective can be very narrowing. It makes it difficult to see how places that offer customers a chance to use TV to pass the time while eating might do so in very different ways, serving quite distinct social or economic purposes.

Compare, for example, two quite different places that offer television while-you-eat. The first, the Video Diner, located in the Manhattan hinterlands of the busy West Side Highway, has little in common with the experience of televisual eating in news-oriented spaces like the News Bar. Both offer a dining experience suffused with televisual entertainment, but in each the television screen's relationship to its environment and its viewing—or nonviewing—subjects goes beyond the equation of viewing and waiting. The Video Diner screens, located in private booths, help create miniature "homes" that make the space seem like an oasis of privacy, an escape and retreat from the pace and crowd of city life. Many lunchtime "regulars" (a number of whom work at the nearby Saatchi and Saatchi advertising agency) watch a movie in small portions, day after day, much as they might read a few pages of a book on the train on the way to work or to home.[40] In the News Bar, on the other hand, televisual eating means an aesthetic of "information overload," produced through the multiple video screens that add a fashionable, futuristic sensibility of media bombardment to what would otherwise be a rather unassuming coffee shop in an area of the city already overpopulated with coffee shops. Although waiting is certainly part of the experience of television viewing in such spaces, to understand it as the basic, underlying condition of the viewing process is to ignore the distinctive uses marked out very visibly in its physical position within its location.

The fact that the difference between these two places, the Video Diner and the News Bar, is clearly annotated in the physical positions of the TV screens within them is also a reminder of how important it is to look for these tangible, material conventions of the screen as an object, to engage in "eye-level" readings of televisual places, in order to understand TV's presence in the visual culture of public space. [. . .]

Notes

1   For discussions of television's temporal effects see, for example, Modleski, Search for Tomorrow 12–21; Browne, "Political Economy"; Scannell, "Radio Times"; Williams, *Television*, Spigel, *Make Room for TV*; and Morley, *Family Television*.

2   See Spigel, *Make Room for TV* 74–5.

3   On the construction of the nation in print media as a fiction of copresence and simultaneity see Benedict Anderson, *Imagined Communities: Reflections on the Origin and Spread of Nationalism* (London: Verso, 1983). Key critical and theoretical discussions of liveness may be found in Feuer, Concept of Live Television; Dayan and Katz, *Media Events*; Mellencamp, "TV Time"; and Mary Ann Doane, "Information, Crisis, Catastrophe"; Monika Elsner, Thomas Muller, and Peter M. Spangenberg, "The Early History of German Television: The Slow Development of a Fast Form," *Historical Journal of Film, Television, and Radio* 10, no. 2 (1990): 193–218; Sasha Torres, "King TV," in *Living Color: Race and Television in the United States*, ed. Sasha Torres (Durham, N.C.: Duke University Press, 1999); Zelizer, "Home to Public Forum," 69–79; John Caldwell, *Televisuality: Style, Crisis, and Authority in American Television* (New Brunswick, N.J.: Rutgers University Press, 1994); Williams, "History in a Flash," 292–312. On issues of live TV broadcasting and public space see McCarthy, " 'Like an Earthquake.' "

4   Doane, "Information, Crisis, Catastrophe," 233.

5   See, e.g., Dafna Lemish, "The Rules of Viewing Television in Public Places," *Journal of Broadcasting* 26, no. 4 (1982): 758–81.

6   On the institutional and interpersonal sociology of time see Eviatar Zerubavel, *Hidden Rhythms: Schedules and Calendars in Social Life* (Chicago: University of Chicago Press, 1981); Clay, *Real Places*; Kevin Lynch, *What Time Is This Place?* (Cambridge, Mass.: MIT Press, 1972).

7   CNN Airport Network, "Working for Passengers," Promotional materials, 1994.

8   Barry Schwartz, *Queuing and Waiting: Studies in the Organization of Access and Delay* (Chicago: University of Chicago Press, 1975), 3.

9   Roy P. Fairfield, "Humanizing the Waiting Space," *Humanist* 37, no. 4 (1977): 43.

10   As Adam Philips notes, boredom is rarely discussed in psychoanalysis because psychoanalytic theory "tends to equate significance with intensity and so has rarely found a place, in theory, for all those less vehement, vaguer, often more subtle feelings and moves that most of our lives consist of." Adam Philips, *On Kissing, Tickling, and Being Bored: Psychoanalytic Essays on the Unexamined Life* (Cambridge, Mass.: Harvard University Press, 1993), 68.

11   Ibid., 78.

12   See Vincent Crapanzano, *Waiting: The Whites of South Africa* (New York: Random House, 1985), 44.

13   On the waiting room as a space of dwelling for homeless and mentally ill persons see Greg Lee Carter, "The Interactions between the Staff and the 'Denizens' of a Social Security Waiting Room: An Observational Analysis," *Sociological Viewpoints* 4, no. 1 (1988): 1–16.

14   Michel Foucault, *Discipline and Punish*, trans. Alan Sheridan (New York: Vintage Books, 1979), 293–308. Although he is working with quite different theoretical and empirical materials than Foucault, urbanist Charles B. Goodsells elaborates on the relations among waiting, architecture, and disciplinary operations of the state in "Welfare Waiting Rooms," *Urban Life* 12, no. 4 (January 1984): 467–77. The idea of the waiting room as self-improvement center is certainly apparent in the waiting room of Celebration Health, the hospital serving Walt Disney's model community in Florida, which gives patients pagers and directs them to "specially designed education or fitness centers" while they wait for their appointments. See Robert Lowes, "Is Your Waiting Room a Practice Builder—or a Holding Pen?" *Medical Economics*, July 13, 1998, 132. On contemporary pedagogical practices in the waiting room see "Kaiser Expands Program to Expose Children to Books," *Medical Industry Today*, September 15, 1997, n.p.

15   See Cindy Patton's *Fatal Advice: How Safe-Sex Education Went Wrong* (Durham, N.C.: Duke University Press, 1996) for a discussion of the links between HIV prevention videos and surveillance, and of activist-produced videos designed to counter such tendencies. For an example of the public health perspective on clinic video screenings see L. O'Donnell *et al.*, "The Effectiveness of Video-Based Interventions in Promoting Condom Acquisition among STD Clinic Patients," *Sexually Transmitted Diseases* 22, no. 2 (1995): 97–103.

16   "TV in the Waiting Room: There's More to Watch than Soap Operas," *Medical Economics*, July 13, 1998, 140.

17   Networks for medical settings arrived on the scene, along with many other highly targeted cable and satellite channels, in the early 1980s. See John Brecher. "Keeping the Patient in Stitches," *Newsweek*, August 1, 1983, 65.

18   "Advertising in the Doc's Office," *Phillips Business Information: Healthcare PR & Marketing News* 6, no. 2 (1997). For a discussion of the ethical questions of waiting-room TV see Hochschild, "Taken Hostage," 25.

19   It is a testament to the anonymous public qualities of the space that not once was my presence questioned

by the staff present in the reception area, despite the fact that I carried a camera and spent in one instance more than ninety minutes in one waiting room. Being a "participant observer" in an anonymous public setting is an interesting form of social experience. My research was conducted largely in silence, although on every occasion I left the building feeling as if I had had a great many interactions with other waiting people. However, these interactions were largely nonverbal, involving smiles, gestures, and other expressive ways of forging a sense of commonality within a place. For a detailed description of the sociological characteristics of public space see Erving Goffman, *Relations in Public: Microstudies of the Public Order* (New York: Harper and Row, 1972); Lofland, *World of Strangers*.

20   Moore, "What the Doctor Ordered," 303.

21   Ibid.

22   Schwartz, *Queuing and Waiting*, 14, 16.

23   "TV in the Waiting Room," 140.

24   See Jürgen Habermas, *Legitimation Crisis* (Boston: Beacon Press, 1975); James R. O'Connor, *The Fiscal Crisis of the State* (New York: St. Martin's Press, 1973).

25   Schwartz, *Queuing and Waiting*, 16 Schwartz's hypothesis is borne out in the spatial contexts of welfare reform in the late 1990s.

26   Doane, "Information, Crisis, Catastrophe," 237. See also Mellencamp, "TV Time."

27   Doane, "Information, Crisis, Catastrophe," 238. For more on Benjamin's theory of shock see pt. 1 of Hansen, *Babel and Babylon*.

28   In 1997 a trade publication reported that "a national poll of 1,014 Americans found that about half spend 20 minutes or more in the waiting room." *Hospitals and Health Networks*, September 5, 1997, 26. It should be noted, however, that statistical data on waiting time are somewhat conflicting; moreover, such information is often proprietary, as research on this issue is conducted primarily by health-care organizations themselves. During one ninety-minutes site visit I observed numerous people whose wait exceeded the entire duration of my time there. Now this kind of duration was due in part to the fact that the city was in the midst of a flu epidemic. However, the fact that waiting time could be dramatically increased during the relatively minor crisis of a seasonal, predictable epidemic does indicate a definite shortcoming in this "just in time" model. According to one source, HMOS are moving away from this model by hiring consultants to redesign waiting rooms. See Laura Billings, "Ladies in Waiting," *American Health for Women*, April 1998, 104.

29   This subscription information is provided on the company's website: http://www. accenthealth.com/subscribe

30   Mike Stobbe, "Health TV Company Announces Merger," *Tampa Tribune*, October 27, 1999, Business and Finance section, 1.

31   "TV in the Waiting Room," 141. According to this article, network officials claim that repetitiveness leads 4 percent of subscribing practices to remove the network each year.

32   Tom Selleck.

33   Prior to the installation of this satellite-based in-house TV system, Planet Hollywood TV screens played videotapes of movies. Jeff Jensen, "New TV Net Set for Planet Hollywood Restaurant Chain," *Advertising Age*, July 13, 1998, 18.

34   As Robert Pittman, CEO of the Six Flags park explained in *Advertising Age*, "This is the ultimate zap-proof TV. . . . No one can change the volume, no one can change the channel and they can't go to the bathroom because they'd lose their place in line." Quoted in Scott Donaton, "Six Flags Woos Nat'l Advertisers," *Advertising Age*, January 11, 1993, 13.

35   Cheryl Ursin. "Theme Restaurants Play to Diners' Appetite for Fun," *Restaurants USA*, August 1996, 25.

36   Scannell, "Radio Times."

37   Ibid., 28.

38   The link between reading and eating is particularly strong in the fast-food industry. A study by the McDonald's corporation found that 75 percent of customers read the menu board *after* ordering. An increased awareness of their customers' tendencies to look for things to read while eating is leading fast-food chains to incorporate more and more printed material in the designs of their tray liners and napkins. See Underhill, *Why We Buy*, 66–7.

39   Paul Farhi, "TV Channels Its Energy All Over Town," *Washington Post*, May 5, 1997, A1.

40   David Glynos, Interview with the author, 1998. David Glynos is the owner and manager of the Video Diner.

Bibliography

Anderson, Benedict. (1983) *Imagined Communities: Reflections on the Origin and Spread of Nationalism*. London: Verso.

—— "Study What People Do, Not What They Say." *Marketing News*, January 6, 1992, 7.

Billings, Laura. (1998) "Ladies in Waiting." *American Health for Women*, April, 104.

Brecher, John. (1983) "Keeping the Patient in Stitches." *Newsweek*, August 1, 65.

Browne, Nick. (1987) "The Political Economy of the Television (Super) Text." In *Television: The Critical View*, ed. Horace Newcomb. 4th edn New York: Oxford.

Caldwell, John. (1994) *Televisuality: Style, Crisis, and Authority in American Television*. New Brunswick, N.J.: Rutgers University Press.

Carter, Greg Lee. (1988) "The Interactions between the Staff and the 'Denizens' of a Social Security Waiting Room: An Observational Analysis." *Sociological Viewpoints* 4, no. 1: 1–16.

Clay, Grady. (1994) *Real Places: An Unconventional Guide to America's Generic Landscape*. Chicago: University of Chicago Press.

Crapanzano, Vincent. (1985) *Waiting: The Whites of South Africa*. New York: Random House.

Dayan, Daniel, and Elihu Katz. (1992) *Media Events: The Live Broadcasting of History*. Cambridge, Mass.: Harvard University Press.

Doane, Mary Ann. (1990) "Information, Crisis, Catastrophe." In *Logics of Television*, ed. Patricia Mellencamp. Bloomington: Indiana University Press.

Donaton, Scott. (1993) "Flaws Ax Checkout Channel." *Advertising Age*, February 22, 3.

—— "Six Flags Woos Nat'l Advertiser." *Advertising Age*, January 11, 13.

Elsner, Monika, Thomas Muller, and Peter-M. Spangenberg. (1990) "The Early History of German Television: The Slow Development of a Fast Form." *Historical Journal of Film, Television, and Radio* 10, no. 2: 193–218.

Fairfield, Roy P. (1977) "Humanizing the Waiting Space." *Humanist* 37, no. 4: 43.

Farhi, Paul. (1997) "TV Channels Its Energy All Over Town." *Washington Post*, May 5, A1.

Feuer, Jane. (1983) "The Concept of Live Television: Ontology as Ideology." In *Regarding Television: Critical Approaches—An Anthology*, ed. E. Ann Kaplan. Frederick, Md.: AFI/University Publications of America.

Foucault, Michel. (1979) *Discipline and Punish*. Trans. Alan Sheridan. New York: Vintage Books.

Glynos, David. (1998) Interview by author. New York, N.Y. February.

Goffman, Erving. (1972) *Relations in Public: Microstudies of the Public Order*. New York: Harper and Row.

Goodsells, Charles B. (1984) "Welfare Waiting Room." *Urban Life* 12, no. 4: 467–77.

Habermas, Jürgen. (1975) *Legitimation Crisis*. Boston: Beacon Press.

Hansen, Miriam. (1991) *Babel and Babylon: Spectatorship in American Silent Film*. Cambridge, Mass.: Harvard University Press.

Hochschild, Adam. (1996) "Taken Hostage at the Airport." *New York Times*, October 26, 25.

Jensen, Jeff. (1998) "New TV Net Set for Planet Hollywood Restaurant Chain." *Advertising Age*, July 13, 18.

Lemish, Dafna. (1982) "The Rules of Viewing Television in Public Places," *Journal of Broadcasting* 26, no. 4: 758–781.

Lofland, Lyn H. (1973) *A World of Strangers: Order and Action in Urban Public Space*. New York: Basic Books.

Lowes, Robert. (1998) "Is Your Waiting Room a Practice Builder—or a Holding Pen?" *Medical Economics*, July 13, 132.

Lynch, Kevin. (1972) *What Time Is This Place?* Cambridge, Mass.: MIT Press.

McCarthy, Anna. (1999) " 'Like an Earthquake': Theater Television, Boxing, and the Black Public Sphere." *Quarterly Review of Film and Video* 16, nos. 3/4: 307–23.

Mellencamp, Patricia. (1990) "TV Time and Catastrophe: Beyond the Pleasure Principle of Television." In *Logics of Television*, ed. Patricia Mellencamp, 242–66. Bloomington: Indiana University Press.

Modleski, Tania. (1979) "The Search for Tomorrow in Today's Soap Operas." *Film Quarterly* 33, no. 1: 12–21.

Moore, David J. (1990) "Just What the Doctor Ordered." In *Electronic Media and Technologies IX: Ratings at a Crossroads*. New York: Advertising Research Foundation.

Morley, David. (1990) *Family Television: Cultural Power and Domestic Leisure*. New York: Routledge.

O'Connor, James R. (1973) *The Fiscal Crisis of the State*. New York: St. Martin's Press.

O'Donnell, L., *et al*. (1995) "The Effectiveness of Video-Based Interventions in Promoting Condom Acquisition among STD Clinic Patients." *Sexually Transmitted Diseases* 22, no. 2: 97–103.

Patton, Cindy. (1996) *Fatal Advice: How Safe-Sex Education Went Wrong*. Durham, N.C.: Duke University Press.

Philips, Adam. (1993) *On Kissing, Tickling, and Being Bored: Psychoanalytic Essays on the Unexamined Life*. Cambridge, Mass.: Harvard University Press.

Scannell, Paddy. (1988) "Radio Times." In *Television and Its Audience*, ed. Philip Drummond and Rob Paterson, 135–66. London: British Film Institute.

Schwartz, Barry. (1975) *Queuing and Waiting: Studies in the Organization of Access and Delay*. Chicago: University of Chicago Press.

Spigel, Lynn. (1992) *Make Room for TV: Television and the Family Ideal in Postwar America*. Chicago: University of Chicago Press.

Torres, Sasha. (1999) "King TV." In *Living Color: Race and Television in the United States*, ed. Sasha Torres. Durham, N.C.: Duke University Press.

Underhill, Paco. (1999) *Why We Buy: The Science of Shopping*. New York: Simon and Schuster.

Ursin, Cheryl. (1996) "Theme Restaurants Play to Diners' Appetite for Fun." *Restaurants USA*, August, 25.

Williams, Mark. (1999) " 'History in a Flash: Notes on the Myth of TV 'Liveness.' " In *Collecting Visible Evidence*, ed. Jane Gaines and Michael Renov, 292–312. Minneapolis: University of Minnesota Press.

Williams, Raymond. (1975) *Television: Technology and Cultural Form*. New York: Schocken Books.

Zelizer, Barbie. (1991) "From Home to Public Forum: Media Events and the Public Sphere." *Journal of Film and Video* 43, nos. 1/2: 69–79.

Zerubavel, Eviatar. (1981) *Hidden Rhythms: Schedules and Calendars in Social Life*. Chicago: University of Chicago Press.

Chapter 32

MATT HILLS

DEFINING CULT TV
Texts, inter-texts and fan audiences

IN THIS CHAPTER I want to consider a term that is used in TV industries and by audiences, but which until recently has received relatively little scholarly attention: cult TV (see Reeves, Rodgers and Epstein 1996; Hills 2002; Jones and Pearson forthcoming). Considering how TV Studies might approach cult television and its fans, I will begin by outlining three competing definitions of cult TV: I'll then move on to develop these definitions. The three major definitions of cult TV that I will discuss correspond broadly to different levels in a three-part model of text/inter-text /audience:

Definition I: Cult TV can be defined through textual analysis, and depends on texts

This means analysing what qualities are shared by cult TV programmes. If we emphasise this argument over points II and III then we are suggesting that cult TV can be self-consciously designed by media producers. This argument also implies that cult TV is best thought of as a group of texts, often hailing from the genres of science fiction, fantasy, and horror. This definition would lead to questions such as 'why are certain types of TV programmes more likely to become cults?' and 'what textual and narrative forms/structures are shared by cult TV texts?'

Definition II: Cult TV can be defined through an analysis of secondary texts or inter-texts, and depends on these inter-texts

Secondary texts have been defined by John Fiske in the following terms:

> [S]econdary texts, such as criticism or publicity, work to promote the circulation of selected meanings of the primary text . . . Secondary texts play a significant role in influencing which of television's meanings may be activated in any one reading. Television's pervasiveness in our culture is not due simply to the fact that so much of it is broadcast . . . but because it pervades so much of the rest of our cultural life – newspapers, magazines . . .
>
> (1991:117 and 118)

Fiske illustrates the work of secondary texts, or 'inter-texts' as they are called, by analysing 'the role played by journalistic writing about television' (1991: 118). In terms of cult TV, this could mean examining newspaper coverage, as well as commercially available fan magazines within which certain programmes are described as cults. For example, programmes such as *Angel*, *Buffy the Vampire Slayer*, *Charmed*, *Doctor Who*, *Enterprise*, *Farscape*, *Quantum Leap*, *Roswell*, *Xena: Warrior Princess* and literally many, many more are discussed in the UK cult TV Guide *Cult Times* (a monthly magazine reaching issue 86, November 2002, at the time of writing; see also the website http://www.visimag.com/culttimes/). What might be counted as cult TV has also been written about journalistically in books such as *Cult TV: The Essential Critical Guide* (Lewis and Stempel 1993). Obviously, a vast range of inter-texts could be analysed, but in this piece I will focus only on commercial fan magazines and on what might be described as 'coffee-table' or reference books.

This definition is basically tautological ('cult TV is what is labelled cult TV in journalistic coverage or publicity') but it is nevertheless very important. Rather than arriving at an analytical definition, which is what definition I above tries to do, this position analyses how the term 'cult' circulates through media culture. If we emphasise this argument over points I and III then we are basically saying that cult TV is not predominantly a matter of programmes themselves or audiences; rather, it is constructed through inter-textuality, that is, through secondary texts that activate the meanings and associations of 'cult' for audiences by attaching this label to certain programmes. This definition would lead to questions such as 'which TV shows are dubbed as cults in publicity? Through what criteria?'

Definition III: Cult TV can be defined through an analysis of fan practices, and depends on fan activities

This would mean considering what loyal, dedicated fans of cult TV do to express and indicate their fandom, suggesting that cult status arises, ultimately, through an audience's passion for a TV show. This type of argument positions cult TV as a 'grassroots' phenomenon, assuming that it is created by fans rather than by media producers. Such a view emphasises and celebrates fan audience power, claiming that cult TV can be neither made nor promoted as such by the media industry, but instead hinges vitally on audience take-up and devotion. This definition leads to research questions such as 'what activities do fans of cult TV engage in?', and 'how do fan activities produce cult status?'

Although it may be tempting to side with models of media power and conclude that cult status is constructed as such by producers (depending on qualities in the text), or to side with a more romantic version of cult status as somehow created by fans, I would argue that these single-focus approaches are overly simplistic. Such definitions, where theorists side either with texts or audiences, have haunted academic work on cult film (see, for example, chapters by Timothy Corrigan and Bruce Kawin in the 1991 volume, *The Cult Film Experience*). TV Studies should endeavour to avoid such a producer/audience or text/audience stand-off, attempting more adequate definitions of cult TV. In order to take a step in this direction, I'll now consider each of my three definitions of cult TV in more detail.

Expanding Definition I: Cult TV as depending on texts

Let's look again at defining cult TV as texts. Is it plausible to say that cult TV programmes tend to share certain qualities? Perhaps, but if so these will necessarily occur at quite an abstract level. Comparing a 1960s cult TV show to a 1990s one, for example contrasting *The Prisoner* with *Buffy the Vampire Slayer*, we are hardly likely to conclude that these shows are aesthetically or thematically similar given their very different production, media institutional and historical contexts. And yet both can be thought of as cult TV if we draw in passing on our tautological definition of cult TV as depending on inter-texts (I will say more about this borrowing below), and argue that secondary inter-texts, such as *Cult Times* magazine, discuss these two shows as examples of cult TV.

Following the definition of cult TV as texts, we could then argue that cult TV is characterised by a number of shared textual attributes; it constructs immensely detailed, often fantastic, narrative worlds which we as viewers can never fully encounter, since much of this detail operates like a set of clues or hints to a consistent narrative world which transcends what we learn about onscreen. Elsewhere I have described this as a kind of 'hyperdiegesis' (adapting the term 'diegesis', which means the represented narrative world), suggesting that cult texts can be distinguished by their extended, expansive narrative worlds (Hills 2002: 137).

The fantastic nature of these hyperdiegetic worlds is also significant, as it provides each textual world with distinctive and characteristic rules for its operation; in the 'Buffyverse' wishes can lead us into scenarios akin to the 'parallel dimensions' of science fiction, and vampires are a kind of demon; in the narrative world of *Doctor Who*, the character of the Doctor is a Time Lord who can regenerate into different bodies; in *Star Trek* we are introduced to many different races, Vulcans, Klingons, Romulans and so on, who are important as the enemies or allies of the Federation. As Sara Gwenllian Jones has observed in an article entitled 'The sex lives of cult television characters':

> [T]he overwhelming majority of those series that evolve substantial creative fan cultures [Definition III of cult TV, that is cult TV as depending on fans; see below – MH] belongs to the fantastic genres of science fiction, fantasy and horror. Their fictional geographies are alien, haunted, or mythologized landscapes visually inscribed as strange and mysterious: they are full of night and strange beings (*The X-Files, Buffy the Vampire Slayer, Angel, Beauty and the Beast*); they have a wild and verdant beauty (*XWP, Hercules*); they are home to alien civilisations (*Star Trek, Farscape, Babylon 5*).
>
> (Jones 2002: 85)

Science fiction/fantasy/horror varieties of cult TV often render the fantastic diegetically commonplace by virtue of defining and developing fantastic beings and worlds over a lengthy period of time and in great amounts of detail. The fantastic thus takes on a quality of everydayness by virtue of its repetition, familiarity and narrative iteration. This transformation from exotic or extraordinary into homely/ordinary is, I would argue, one of the key ways that cult TV appeals to its audience over time. For example, Buffy is no longer such an affront to our expectations of what a vampire slayer should look or be like; for audiences who have followed the programme, she simply is Buffy, complete with a long character history and an arc of character development.

Cult TV's hyperdiegesis therefore works serially, by reiteration and by accumulation of detail, to make fantastic worlds appear normal within a format and narrative structure. But in order to keep alive a sense of fantastic disruption – in other words, to stop the narrative worlds of cult TV shows from becoming entirely familiar to their audiences – cult texts must play with their own established rules and norms. Cult TV texts therefore offer a delicate balancing act between establishing detailed narrative continuity which can be trusted and appreciated by audiences, and breaking with or altering this continuity in order to preserve audience interest.

It is such a balancing act that, arguably, has led to the interest cult TV shows have displayed in temporarily re-working their usual formats, such as the *Buffy* musical episode 'Once More, With Feeling', (season 6, episode 7), an episode focused around a minor, geeky character called Jonathan ('Superstar', season 4, episode 17), or an episode where Buffy has never existed and

Sunnydale is overrun by vampires ('The Wish', season 3, episode 9). *Star Trek: Deep Space Nine* episodes have also worked in this way, entering a 'mirror universe' where characters are strangely different ('Through the Looking Glass', season 3, episode 19, and 'Shattered Mirror', season 4, episode 19). Such disruptions, diegetically explained by magic in *Buffy* and fictional technoscience in *Star Trek*, allow seriality to be suspended in specific ways; characters and character relationships can be temporarily redefined without affecting the standard seriality of the shows concerned. Of course, it could be argued that this continuity-making and continuity-breaking 'balance' is simply a function of genre or format, and hence that it has no special relationship to cult TV. My point here would be that cult TV, unlike most realist soap operas, or indeed much contemporary serial and 'quality' drama on TV, does not only accrue a kind of 'series memory'. Given its emphasis on fantasy and the fantastic, cult TV can also play diegetically with its own narrative rules and norms without necessarily breaking the frame, slipping into parody, camp, or producing overtly displayed markers of reflexivity. Cult TV expects its audience to know the many details of its hyperdiegesis, and so offers narrative pleasures for this 'ideal' audience by periodically varying hyperdiegetic details.

Cult TV also repeatedly represents particularly close, though usually non-sexualised, character relationships. Sara Gwenllian Jones has related this textual attribute of cult TV to its emphasis on the fantastic, noting that:

> Because active heterosexuality must continually be reined in if it is not to effect a collapse of the exotic-fantastic into suburban domesticity, protagonists' primary relationships usually fall into one of two categories:
>
> (1) Primary relationships between a male and female character, which signal a mutual sexual attraction that is never fully realized (Mulder and Scully, Picard and Crusher, Aeryn Sun and Crichton) or which cannot progress beyond romance (Buffy and Angel, Catherine and Vincent).
> (2) Primary relationships between characters of the same sex (Kirk and Spock, Hercules and Iolus, Xena and Gabrielle). (Jones 2002:88–9)

In addition to these types of primary relationships, cult TV also characteristically depicts trusting relationships within a close-knit community, for example, the officers of the USS Enterprise in various *Star Treks*, the Scooby Gang in *Buffy*, the crew of the Liberator/Scorpio in *Blake's Seven*, the Doctor and his various companions in *Doctor Who*, and so on. Once again, this textual quality of representing a trusting, communal ensemble of characters can be found far beyond cult TV; soaps feature relatively fixed, ensemble casts bound together in communities or families. However, these qualities appear to be distinctively combined with the fantastic aspects of hyperdiegesis and character identity in cult TV. Here, relationships are often bound together through shared knowledge of the fantastic (various crews of the Enterprise learning about alien races), as well as through the acceptance of characters' extraordinary status (the Scooby Gang supporting Buffy's role as slayer). Where soaps allow characters to develop in and through 'suburban domesticity', this option is typically denied to cult TV characters, as it would threaten characters' extraordinariness or alienness. Despite approaching a human-demon wedding, *Buffy the Vampire Slayer* eventually rejected this scenario and returned its demon character, Anya, to her former, less humanised and less domesticated self.

A further textual attribute of cult TV, arising out of its serialised focus on lead characters within fantastic narrative worlds, is a tendency towards what has been called 'endlessly deferred narrative' (Hills 2002; 134–5). This means that cult TV programmes often fail to resolve their major, driving narrative questions, these questions thus remaining open, and narrative closure being indefinitely deferred.

This type of narrative structure, possibly the most distinctive feature of cult TV, is not the same as the openness characteristic of many other serial narratives. Many soap operas (British primetime soaps and US daytime soaps) lack narrative closure, for instance, although telenovelas do achieve closure after lengthy, serialised runs of episodes. Given that the majority of US and UK soaps lack narrative closure, we might therefore expect many overlaps between soap forms and cult TV forms, and perhaps it is not coincidental that both types of programmes attract dedicated fans (an issue I will return to when I discuss the definition of cult TV as depending on fans in more detail). However, soap narrative is typically multi-stranded, and occasional narrative resolutions correspond to one narrative thread among many, leaving the overall narrative world in process, as it were. By contrast, cult TV programmes usually focus upon a defining narrative enigma or puzzle that is bound up with their creation of fantastic narrative worlds. Such questions include: who is propelling Sam through time in *Quantum Leap*? Who is the Prisoner in *The Prisoner*? Who is the Doctor in *Doctor Who*? What is the nature of the apparent alien invasion plan in *The X-Files* and how does it involve Mulder and Scully? How can the Hellmouth be combated in *Buffy*, and can Buffy find ordinary love while fulfilling her extraordinary duty? Such questions are built into each programme's format and its narrative universe, and their resolution would therefore correspond either to a collapse of the format, or to a major (and risky) reinvention of the show concerned. Soaps, on the other hand, do not generally have narrative enigmas definitionally built into their formats, and no single ongoing narrative question has the capacity to collapse a soap format. Soap narrative is open not by virtue of being endlessly deferred in the way that cult TV is — soap narratives do reach end points — but rather by virtue of being multiple and multi-focused.

Following the definition of cult TV as depending on texts, then, we can argue that cult TV is identifiable as a set of texts which share qualities of fantastic hyperdiegesis, representations of close but non-sexualised character relationships and communities, and a form of endlessly deferred narrative based on narrative enigmas that are central to each programme's character-based and fantasy-based format.

However, there is a major difficulty with this type of definition. And it is captured in the move that I made earlier, when I referred in passing to Definition II ('cult texts can be defined through secondary texts or inter-texts'). The problem with defining cult TV textually is a variation of the 'genre problem' famously analysed in film studies by Andrew Tudor (1976: 121). Tudor raised the question of how it is possible to textually analyse genre films without first implicitly identifying one's chosen films as belonging to the very genre under analysis. If the qualities of a genre are assumed to emerge through close analysis of texts, then the question supposedly being explored has in fact already been answered by the analyst, since s/he has already chosen specific texts as examples for analysis. This difficulty recurs in textual analysis of cult TV. How can we analyse cult TV to discover textual similarities and shared forms without deciding in advance what counts as cult TV? If we have to surreptitiously or implicitly define 'cult' status prior to our textual analysis, then the idea of cult TV as depending on texts must lean on a further notion of cult status, just as here I referred to 'cult TV as depending on inter-texts' (Definition II) in order to back up my choice of texts. This suggests that although Definition I, textual analysis, may be useful in terms of exploring how cult texts share attributes and are not generically random, it appears to be logically subordinated to Definition II (cult TV as depending on inter-texts) or Definition III (cult TV as depending on fans), relying on one or other of these rival definitions for its operation. And so it is to the next definition — cult TV status emerging through secondary inter-texts — that I will now turn.

Expanding Definition II: Cult as depending on inter-texts

Considered as a series of inter-texts, what particular meanings does 'cult' status as a term seek to activate in its primary texts? The scenario that John Fiske discusses in terms of soap fans and their fan magazine inter-texts is one where soap magazines play:

> with the boundary between the representation and the real . . . playing with the viewer's reading position as it switches between involvement and detachment . . . The nature of TV as representation is never lost sight of despite the deliberate denial. These secondary texts are equally concerned to celebrate the hard work and the professionalism of the actors and actresses. They frequently take the reader on to the set to show how the program is made.
>
> (Fiske 1991: 121)

Fiske's examples appear to be commercially available fan magazines, although he describes them as 'fanzines' (1991: 119), a term that is usually applied to non-professional, non-commercial fan-produced magazines or " 'zines". In Fiske's analysis, soap fan magazines produce meanings that playfully blur together the real (actors) and the fictional (the characters they play) while also focusing on the soaps' constructedness and value to fans (actors and actresses are praised for being highly professional). Are these sorts of meanings activated in commercially available fan magazines dealing with cult TV? Although actors and actresses are important in these secondary texts, there are certain repeated features that suggest cult TV is inter-textually activated in specific ways.

For instance, UK-based magazines like *Cult Times, Doctor Who Magazine, Dreamwatch, SFX, Starburst* and *TV Zone* all feature news columns in their opening pages. News can cover plot summaries and reviews of US cult TV as yet unbroadcast in the UK. For example, *SFX* includes a 'spoiler zone' section that has to be torn open if the fan reader wishes to discover what is inside. This section cannot be read by accident! News will also tend to cover advance information on cult programmes prior to their broadcast, as in the following from *Cult Times*, 83:

> Details about *Deep Down*, the season premiere of *Angel* Season Four, are beginning to surface. While it might be expected the first scene would focus on either the plights of Angel or Cordelia, according to Ain't It Cool news the opening situation is set on 28th October 1985 at Thorpe's Academy in Wisconsin.
>
> (no author credited 2002:4)

Other news in this issue included reports that Anthony Stewart Head would appear in ten episodes of *Buffy the Vampire Slayer* Season Seven, according to 'the South Florida Sun-Sentinel' (no author credited 2002:4); stories covering new *Enterprise* episodes; an industrial/financial assessment of *Buffy*'s move from the WB network to UPN, and coverage of a mooted *Quantum Leap* TV Movie. Rather than activating certain meanings in the primary texts, then, this emphasis on timely news activates, or rather seeks to activate, a specific relationship between reader and primary text. Such news assumes that readers will wish to know specific types of detail about their favoured shows ahead of transmission, such as appearances by particular characters, opening scenes, and developments in character relationships as well as continuity points.

Cult Times' industrial assessment of *Buffy*'s move to UPN, however, does not deal with narrative developments or the making of the programme (whereas Fiske's soap magazines focused on character or on discourses of professional acting). Instead, it focuses squarely on the economics of cult TV, and the institutional context within which cult TV is produced. The report, headed 'The Cost of Living Again', states:

> UPN, having paid Fox $2.3 million per episode for Season Six, with a 2% hike for Season Seven, did see expanded ratings but also increased network losses . . . Overall ratings . . . increased by 19% in the key 18–34 age demographic . . . However, *Buffy* advertising revenue averaged only around $55,000 for a 30-second spot, suggesting that on paper the deal created losses of up to $20m for the network. However, the network's increased profile . . . may have been an influencing factor in . . . [*Buffy's*] survival, at least in the short-term.

> (no author credited 2002:6)

Also dealing with the soured relationship between *Buffy* producers Fox and its original network home, WB, this article presents a highly TV-industry-literate take on whether *Buffy's* continuation may be threatened by its move between US networks. Again, this secondary inter-text activates key meanings around the primary text rather than seeking to control readings of it. The relationship between reader and text that is called upon here is not only that of TV-literacy; it is also TV literacy directed towards ascertaining whether *Buffy* will endure. This suggests that fan readers are not only interested in how their favoured shows will develop narratively, but also whether industry economics or institutional factors might disrupt or disallow any such development.

Commercial fan magazines such as *Cult Times* offer no explicit logic for counting certain texts as cult TV. Although *The West Wing* is referred to at the close of the *Buffy* Fox/WB/UPN report, this brief mention appears on the basis that a similar network move may also happen to this other show, and not seemingly because *The West Wing* is counted as cult TV. It may be the case, however, that *The West Wing* is considered relevant to *Cult Times* readers because it is an example of 'quality' TV drama; hence its being mentioned could once again function as a general activation of 'TV literacy'. Without an explicit criteria for cult inclusion or qualification, *Cult Times* is free to combine contemporary TV programmes such as *Buffy* with programmes from the 1950s and 1960s like *The Twilight Zone*, 1970s shows such as *The Bionic Woman*, and late 1980s/early 1990s cult TV like *Star Trek: The Next Generation*. If its selection of what counts as cult TV seems to range across periods of TV history, also combining US and UK programming, *Cult Times* does not lack a sense of history. Significantly, issue 83's news pages are accompanied by a sidebar article headed 'What Was On In . . . August 1967' (Pixley and Rogers 2002: 6). This disrupts the paradigm of the news pages, implying that the magazine and its readers are not only focused on timeliness and on TV now, but that they also possess a sense of cult TV as historically important, and as tied up with its historical context. A powerful interest in contemporary TV is therefore implied by these news pages, but qualified and disrupted by *Cult Times'* simultaneous, if rather more marginal, focus on TV 25 years ago. A similar play with TV as contemporary and TV as historical occurs in SFX where mocked-up covers of non-existent historical issues of the magazine itself are presented for the knowing reader's amusement (no author credited, 'The Issues That Time Forgot: 1979', *SFX*, 98, 2002: 130).

Cult Times also includes TV listings pages, targeted at readers wanting to know what cult TV is on terrestrial, cable, and satellite TV each month in the UK. These listings, again offered without any criteria for what makes it into the magazine and what doesn't, are interesting because although credits are given for episodes of old, repeated TV series and for UK first-run episodes, in both cases cast lists are provided along with writer and director credits only (2002: 40–67).

Whom do fan magazines regard as being the creative force behind cult TV shows? Only writers and directors? Evidently not; elsewhere in *Cult Times*, 83 it is apparent that executive producers are inter-textually activated as a source of authored cult TV, given that the executive producer of *Charmed*, Brad Kern, is interviewed at length (Eramo 2002: 30–34). However, the fact that TV series production teams are reduced to a writer and a director in the listings section indicates that, given pressures of space, the magazine focuses on those creative roles that have been most conventionally linked to markers of quality and authorship. By as it were 'pre-reading' cult TV as being about executive producers, writers and directors, *Cult Times* repeatedly interprets cult TV as authored (this being one marker of cult as 'quality' TV), alongside focusing on actors and actresses.

Certain tensions recur through such commercial fan magazines. While often promoting themselves through cover images of young and typically female stars, these magazines indicate in their marginal details that they are interested in cult TV as authored and thus 'quality' TV (even if this attribution may not be shared by other publicity and secondary texts circulating in media culture). And while offering news pages that emphasise the importance of timely knowledge of up-to-the-minute TV, even in advance of US and UK transmission, such magazines – again in their more marginal and playful details – imply an interest in cult TV as TV history. These tensions are not the blurring of real/fictional that Fiske found in soap opera fan magazines. They could be described, rather, as the blurring of discourses of youth-lifestyle-consumerism (right now what's new, and who's hot) and connoisseurship (what was valuable in TV of the past, and how can we consider cult TV as 'quality', authored TV). As Fiske puts it: "secondary texts are no more univocal than the primary ones" (1991: 121). That this specific tension is written into secondary inter-texts circulating commercially around cult TV should not surprise us. This indicates that cult TV is activated inter-textually both as a form of 'anti-mainstream' distinction, where cult status is about finding quality in unexpected places and revaluing otherwise devalued/popular texts, and also as a brand of 'mainstream' consumerism, with commercially-available episode guides and coffee-table books forming a significant inter-text for many shows activated as 'cult'.

Other secondary texts, or inter-texts, such as *Cult TV: The Essential Critical Guide* (Lewis and Stempel 1993) seek to journalistically map the field of cult TV. This secondary textuality is useful because, of necessity, it makes clear its criteria for counting TV programmes as 'cult'. Lewis and Stempel offer four different definitions of cult TV, swerving between defining cult TV through audience activities, media-institutional contexts, and textual attributes. For example, their first definition is squarely audience-based, cult TV being 'objects of special devotion' (1993: 8).

Lewis and Stempel's next definition appears at first glance to be fan-audience based: '. . . did the series give birth to merchandizing, a fan club, a fanzine, conventions or a secret language?' However, there is no sense in which a TV programme requires a fan audience to 'spawn merchandising', this being the decision of those in the media industry. And a TV programme may inspire merchandising long prior to the formation of its first 'fan club'. Are we to then conclude that only a rigidly socially-organised fandom can indicate cult status, and that any form of non-organised or nascent fandom disqualifies a programme from being a cult? If pursued to its illogical end, this would mean that a TV programme could be non-cult one day and cult the next, by virtue of its fan club having been ratified.

Lewis and Stempel's third definition veers towards making textual attributes the defining feature of cult status: 'is every much-loved and much-repeated programme cult? No. We sought something a little extra from a series . . . something unusual, or adventurous, and preferably kitsch' (1993: 8). If this is so, then the difference between cult and non-cult does not, after all, lie with cult TV being 'a special object of devotion', thus rather contradicting Lewis and Stempel's first point. Instead, they use very loose textual criteria to distinguish cult TV: 'unusual adventurous . . . kitsch.' These qualities are comparative; cult TV is thus defined against what it is supposedly not: it is not ordinary, run-of-the-mill TV; it is not bland and low-risk TV, since it challenges gender representations, say; it is excessive in its aesthetic mode of representation, being again differentiated from 'mainstream' or realist TV drama. Such a definition asserts the value of cult TV, marking it out as somehow ahead of its time. This version of cult TV as 'quality' TV does not draw on the 'cult-TV-as-authored' discourse of *Cult Times*, but instead draws on a notion of innovation rather than authorship.

The last definition offered up by Lewis and Stempel (1993: 8) is perhaps most interesting, since it explicitly states that cult status can only be decided over time: 'cult TV often succeeds only after a troubled start. First the TV executives, then the audiences are slow to catch on'. This is akin to the notion of the 'sleeper hit' in film parlance: sleepers, like this version of cult TV, are not great commercial successes at first. They are set apart from the mainstream by virtue of initial commercial failure, and are adopted by audiences who perceive otherwise unseen value in them. This account of cult TV is therefore a condensation of various discourses: cult as anti-mainstream, cult as being adopted by distinctive, elevated and discerning fan audiences, cult as emerging over time, and cult as textually innovative or unusual.

I have analysed this inter-text, *Cult TV: The Essential Critical Guide*, at length because I want to point out that its definitions are contradictory, moving between cult-as-textually-defined (my Definition I) and cult-as-audience-defined (my Definition III). What is interesting about secondary texts or inter-texts circulating around cult TV, then, is that either they seem to offer no criteria for what is and isn't cult, or they offer extremely muddled and incoherent criteria that are, in fact, dependent on competing definitions. Secondary texts therefore lead us to the fan audience for cult TV, since by leaving criteria for cult status absent, as does *Cult Times* magazine, they refer us to implied fan practices. And where cult criteria are made explicit, these too often refer us to fan devotion or activity. It is therefore to the fan-based definition of cult TV that I will now turn.

Expanding Definition III: Cult TV as depending on fan audiences

Being a fan of cult TV doesn't mean just displaying subjective enthusiasm or a 'special devotion'. It also means, at the very least, being able to attempt to account for and defend one's fan passions; being able to analyse and critically appreciate one's favoured text; and attempting to ward off negative portrayals of fan cultures. All of these activities indicate, as Jostein Gripsrud notes, that 'proper fandom exists when an enthusiasm for some cultural object or other takes on . . . a totalizing, defining role in people's lifestyles and identities. The term "cult" is also related to such instances' (Grisprud 2002: 119). It is precisely because cult TV is centrally important to cult fans' 'lifestyles and identities' that such fans are so keen to legitimate, defend and analyse their own consumption of cult TV. It is worth noting that this does not imply that cult fans will always 'resist' processes of commercialism, or always define themselves against 'consumers'.

Having already observed in my discussion of Definition I that cult texts possess many similarities with soap operas, is it also the case that soap fans share many qualities with fans of cult TV? I want to return briefly to this soap/cult comparison before discussing cult fan audiences in more detail.

Soap fans were the first type of fan to be studied by TV scholars, and seminal books on the subject were written by Ien Ang (*Watching Dallas*, 1985) and Dorothy Hobson (*Crossroads: The Drama of a Soap Opera*, 1982). More recent work on soap fans has also been influential within fan studies (e.g. C. Lee Harrington and Denise Bielby's *Soap Fans*, 1995). This body of work has emphasised the activities and subcultures of soap fans, indicating that fans of cult TV are, in many ways, akin to fans of soaps. However, there are some key differences that I want to point out here. As I will go on to argue in a moment, fans of cult TV have played a part in generically re-organising TV programmes into the category of 'cult'. By contrast, soap fans are linked to a genre of TV programming that is clearly industry-defined. This is not to contrast 'active' fans of cult TV with 'passive' soap fans; soap fans are also a highly active, participatory audience.

A further difference between soap fans and cult TV fans depends on the scheduling and form of the two types of programming. US 'prime-time' soaps that run in seasons, often ending with dramatic end-of-season finales, are probably the closest soap relation to much contemporary US cult TV, which also typically runs in seasons of 24 episodes and often features end-of-season cliff-hangers. This type of seriality seems to support fan practices such as intense speculation over plot (especially across the summer break). But it also allows temporal gaps in real life and narrative gaps in the fiction that support or provoke the creation of fan fiction (fan-fic). Other forms of soap scheduling, such as twice/thrice weekly soaps that have no prospect of narrative suspension over the summer, or the daily transmission of daytime soaps, draw fan-viewers into very intense, routine engagements with the text, but leave relatively little time in real life for the creation of fan fiction. The plot has always moved on by the next day, or within a few days, partly defusing or rendering redundant an interest in writing about the characters. Fan-talk is the more significant mode of engagement here, rather than fan fiction. This type of soap also leaves less in the way of narrative gaps that fan-viewers may weave fan fiction around, since the form is one that constantly moves on to new narrative puzzles rather than being based around a format-defining and endlessly deferred narrative question, as cult TV often is.

It might be supposed that soap fans are predominantly female while cult TV fans are pre-dominantly male, but any gender divide here is by no means conclusive. For example, many cult TV fandoms are predominantly or significantly female (see, for example, Bacon-Smith 1992). Differences between soap and cult TV fans are not, therefore, inevitably ones of gender. And given that both fan cultures have been feminised in the past by hostile stereotypes of 'the fan' (see Jensen 1992; Jenkins 1992), these active fan cultures have much to gain from seeking common ground in terms of combating negative perceptions of fandom. Having said this, and given my arguments above as to the distinctiveness of fans of soap and cult TV, in this chapter I will continue to focus specifically on the activities of fans of cult TV rather than producing a more general account of 'TV fans'.

So, returning to the fan-based definition of cult status, how do fans transform certain TV programmes into cults? Fans arguably create cult status in a number of ways. First, fans organise TV programmes into an 'intertextual network' that is not recognisable as an industry-led, generic grouping:

> I want to focus on media fandom [which does not include soap fans here – MH] as a discursive logic that knits together interests across textual and generic boundaries. While some fans remain exclusively committed to a single show or star, many others use individual series as points of entry into a broader fan community, linking to an intertex-tual network composed of many programs, films, books, comics and other popular materials. Fans often find it difficult to discuss single programs except through references and comparisons to this broader network.
>
> (Jenkins 1992: 40)

Second, fans self-consciously use the term 'cult' to describe these networks of texts as distinctive ('telefantasy' is another term that is often used for this grouping of shows as well as 'cult'). For example, Alex Geairns, contributor to short-lived *Infinity* magazine and an organiser of the annual UK 'Cult TV Festival' (http://www.festival.culttv.net/activities.html) claims to have coined the term 'Cult TV' in 1985!

It was at Wolverhampton University (or 'Polytechnic' as it was then) that CULT TV first came into being. There was no term at that time for the realm of television with fan followings that covered a multitude of genres. Staring at the contents of his bookcase, Alex J. Geairns noticed Danny Peary's seminal book *Cult Movies*. That was when it clicked. No more the TV umbrella with no name – it would be CULT TV. Weekly meetings began in October of this year.

(http://www.festival.culttv.net/history.html)

Third, fans of what is termed cult TV have organised themselves socially into 'Appreciation Societies'. This can happen long after the initial broadcast of a TV programme, indicating that a TV show may inspire a fan following over time, and can gradually become a cult rather than necessarily being cult TV on its initial transmission. *The Prisoner* Appreciation Society, Six of One, was founded in 1976, for example, despite the fact that this programme first aired in 1967 (http://www.sixofone.org.uk/). Similarly, although *Doctor Who* began on the BBC in 1963, its own Appreciation Society (DWAS) was also officially formed in 1976 (http://dwas.drwho.org/).

As well as joining Appreciation Societies, fans of cult TV gather for conventions, where they can share their interests. Again, this creates a sense of communal fan distinctiveness, working to knit together and sustain a fan culture since conventions can become annual events, held in fixed geographical locations, or even the same hotel year after year. Appreciation Societies and conventions both give fandom a spectacular visibility, meaning that it can be stereotyped and represented in media coverage. Although fan activities are not the same thing as texts and inter-texts, they can be represented inter-textually in journalistic coverage of cult TV and even textually within cult TV programmes (see Larbalestier 2002).

Fans also produce commentaries, fan fiction, episode guides and production histories that all work to sustain the distinctiveness of fandom as a community that reads the "intertextual network" of cult TV shows in a characteristic way. Fans are able to produce such detailed analyses and knowledgeable fictions thanks to the fact that they re-view much-loved TV shows again and again, amassing vast amounts of knowledge about these programmes, in terms of their narrative worlds, characters and production details.

Finally, fans of cult TV create a market for memorabilia, merchandise and props that relates to their much-loved TV shows, even long after the cancellation and mass-merchandizing of these shows.

Most of these fan activities are carried out both online and in real life: fans can gather together in virtual spaces as well as in hotel function rooms; they can post interpretations, episode guides and fictions online as well as than publishing them in fanzines; join Appreciation Societies or check their web pages; and check prices of fan memorabilia on ebay.com as well as attending auctions.

Although I would not want to exaggerate the impact of the Internet on the formation of new cult shows, by making it easier for fans to contact other like-minded devotees, the web increases the possibility of small-scale organised fandoms emerging around a wider variety of TV shows. As Kirsten Pullen has noted, 'the Internet may have begun to mainstream fandom' (2000: 60), and if so, it has achieved this by opening 'up the boundaries of fandom, allowing more people to participate in fan culture, and designating more television programmes . . . as worthy of fan activity' (2000: 55). Henry Jenkins has similarly argued that as 'fandom diversifies, it moves from cult status towards the cultural mainstream, with more Internet users engaged in some form of fan activity' (2002: 161).

These accounts of online fandom imply that the Internet affects the generation of cult status by rendering fandom and its practices less distinctively 'anti-mainstream' and less subcultural (the term 'subcultural' implies a localised set of norms and practices within a community, such as goths dressing in a certain way, or fans of cult TV interpreting and following TV shows in a distinctive way). Thus, internet-enabled fan practices will no longer be set apart from broader cultural norms, practices and processes. This technological 'impact' is, however, open to various interpretations. The Internet may well allow fans of already-established cult TV, who interpret this through reading protocols and via massive amounts of fan knowledge, to simply carry on going about their subcultural business. Having easy access to such fan discussion groups will not magic-ally allow new fans to participate meaningfully or be welcomed into these online communities if they lack the knowledge and interpretative competencies that distinguish long-time fans of cult TV. Furthermore, given that fans of cult TV have created an 'intertextual network' of cult texts, there is no reason to suppose that the Web will destabilise or alter these fans' criteria for inclusion as a cult text. These arguments imply that it is unlikely that the fan creation of cult status will, in fact, be significantly affected by the Internet. More TV shows may have small-scale, dedicated online fan followings, yes, but these diverse shows are unlikely to be linked into the existent 'intertextual network' of cult TV or telefantasy.

According to the definition of cult status as depending on fans, then, cult TV emerged at a specific historical moment as fan audiences organised themselves into communities – forming Appreciation Societies from the 1970s on – and generically re-organised TV texts through the category of 'cult' status, this label being used at least from the 1980s onwards, if not earlier. This definition of cult status is immensely useful because it appears to explain textual similarities between cult TV programmes (these are links made and recognised by fans) as well as the role of inter-texts (identifications of cult status at this level can also be viewed as a reflection of the fans' reading protocol that groups texts together in a cult 'intertextual network').

Although it may seem that all roads lead to 'cult = fan audience', and that this is the most plausible and persuasive of the three definitions of cult status being explored here, this definition also has a number of problems. Attributing cult status purely to fan activity ignores the fact that even if fans initially created the term 'cult TV', and a grouping of cult texts, any such term and textual grouping are open to later co-optation and tactical use by media producers. As soon as fans become spectacularly visible through their organisation into Appreciation Societies, they become one possible target market among others. Cults might therefore be constructed by media produ-cers sensitive to what fans count as cult TV and to how they read cult TV.

Building on such an understanding, how would one go about designing a cult show? A good start would be to use key production personnel who have worked in the past on shows included in fans' 'intertextual network' of cult shows. One might also cast a mixture of unknown actors/actresses as well as one or two that have appeared in previous cult shows; publicise your new show as having an executive producer/writer/director who can be cast as a TV author or who has been linked to previous cult shows; base the show around a science-fiction/fantasy/horror premise, but one that has the potential to become familiar to fans, either through catch-phrases, repeated types of scenes, or character types; imply a broader narrative world than that shown on screen; base part of your show's format around a mystery or narrative puzzle that will never be answered; include representations of community within your show; feature characters who are narratively blocked from consummating their love or attraction; or include elements, characters or scenarios that will attract fan audiences interested in other, previous cult shows.

If cult TV has indeed been co-opted by producers trying to target fans as a niche audience, then isn't cult TV now best thought of as a commercial niche product rather than a fan-led redefinition of TV shows? Shows like *Babylon 5*, *Buffy the Vampire Slayer*, *Dark Skies*, *Millennium*, *Roswell*, *VR5*, *Wild Palms*, and even *The X-Files*, as well as the various *Star Trek* franchises following on from the original, can all be thought of as attempts to court a fan audience that already exists for

cult TV. Such a situation is very different to what might be termed 'first-wave' cult TV, characterised by programmes like *Doctor Who* in the UK and *Star Trek* in the US.

Reeves, Rodgers and Epstein (1996) have put forward an argument akin to this. They suggest
that cult TV began in the US as an accident produced via audience engagement and intensified
through the repeat runs of syndication. This type of cult TV, characterised by the original *Star Trek*,
appeared within a TV industry and economic framework that were based on the pursuit of mass
audiences. *Star Trek*, for these authors, became 'a full-fledged cult by the mid-1970s' (1996: 28)
despite having been first broadcast in the US in 1966. Although Reeves, Rodgers and Epstein do
not indicate whether *Star Trek* was commonly (or even rarely) self-consciously described as 'cult
TV' by its mid-1970s US fans, this narrative of cult emergence does match up historically with the
emergence of cult TV in the UK. Here, shows like *Doctor Who* – first broadcast in the UK in 1963
– began to generate organised fandoms by the mid-1970s, even if in the UK the term 'cult' was
not widely used until the 1980s. While *Star Trek* relied on syndication to sustain a fan following,
Doctor Who arrived at this position by virtue of continuing on the BBC from 1963 (it was only
cancelled, in fact, in 1989).

In effect, Reeves, Rodgers and Epstein suggest that 1990s US cult TV has moved on from its
1970s predecessors, splitting into three distinct types of cult show. These shows are not defined
through textual analysis, but in relation to their media-institutional contexts and their targeting of
non-mass, niche audiences. This introduces an important aspect that has been largely absent from
the definitions of cult TV explored here so far: namely, historical shifts in the media industry as
this moves from broadcasters' pursuit of mass audiences to narrowcasters' (satellite/cable) or
new networks' pursuit of fragmented, differentiated audience demographics and niches.

The three categories of cult show identified by Reeves, Rodgers and Epstein are:

(1) The type of cult that follows in the tradition of *Star Trek*, being a primetime show that fails to
    attract a sufficiently large mass audience but which does attract a substantial minority of 'avid
    fans' (1996: 26). *Twin Peaks* is offered as an example of this type (1996: 31).
(2) The type of cult that first appears on cable or in 'fringe timeslots' rather than primetime, and
    which represents 'a category of cult programming . . . never intended to reach a mass audience'
    (1996: 31). *Mystery Science Theater 3000* and *Beavis & Butthead* are given as examples of this.
(3) The type of cult that exists institutionally between 'the network prime-time model and the
    cable/fringe/syndication market' (1996: 31). These shows are typically designed and pursued
    by the new networks in the US like Fox, the WB and UPN, and are intended to occupy a middle
    ground between high-ratings primetime shows and small-but-dedicated-niche-audience shows.
    The X-Files is given as an example of this type of cult TV, but we could add *Buffy the Vampire Slayer*
    and possibly even *Enterprise* to this trend. Such shows do not achieve very large audience shares
    by US primetime standards, but neither do they only appeal to a very small minority of
    dedicated fans. Instead these shows achieve a kind of 'cult crossover' status, both inspiring
    creative fan cultures and winning substantial audiences outside fandom, usually in the desirable
    18–35 demographic.

Partly following Reeves, Rodgers and Epstein (1996), we can conclude by observing that of the
three definitions of cult TV offered and explored in this chapter – cult-as-text, cult-as-inter-text,
and cult-as-audience – each underplays the importance of media-institutional contexts that have
given rise, either by accident or latterly by design, to cult TV. Each definition investigated here also
underplays the dynamics of cult TV, whereby audience-led definitions can be taken up by producers, and where cult status can therefore be commodified and commercialised rather than being a
purely 'grassroots' phenomenon.

Defining cult TV as being either text-based, inter-textually activated, or audience-led, forces what is actually a dynamic process of emergence into a conceptual straitjacket. Cult shows become so over time, through audience routines and repeated viewings, as well as through organised fandoms, reading protocols, textual forms, the situated agency of media producers, and media-institutional contexts such as syndication or prolonged seriality. Perhaps, rather than having to choose between text-based, inter-text-based or audience-based definitions of cult status, what we need is an approach that recognises how cult texts, their producers, and their fans are all insti-tutionally located. This would mean investigating how cult status is generated by texts placed within the institutional contexts of US and UK media industries, by producers placed within the institutional contexts of production companies and professional bodies, and by fans placed within the institutional contexts of organised and online fan communities. Such an institutional emphasis would move us away from the 'heroic individuals' version of cult status, where TV 'authors' such as Chris Carter (*The X-Files*, *Millennium*), Patrick McGoohan (*The Prisoner*), Gene Roddenberry (*Star Trek*), Joss Whedon (*Buffy the Vampire Slayer*, *Angel*), and others, are promoted inter-textually, in fan cultures, and by professionals, as the source of cult texts' distinctiveness. Such an approach would also lead us away from celebrating cult texts for their supposed uniqueness, analysing and defining cult TV as a part of broader patterns within changing TV industries.

References

Ang, Ien (1985) *Watching Dallas: Soap Opera and the Melodramatic Imagination*, Methuen: London.
Bacon-Smith, Camille (1992) *Enterprising Women: Television Fandom and the Creation of Popular Myth*, University of Pennsylvania Press: Philadelphia.
Bassom, David (2000) 'Buffy, Angel and Me', Joss Whedon Interview Part II in *Buffy the Vampire Slayer Magazine*, Issue 12 September 2000: 6–9.
Corrigan, Timothy (1991) 'Film and the Culture of Cult' in J.P. Telotte (ed.) *The Cult Film Experience: Beyond All Reason*, University of Texas Press: Austin, pp. 26–37.
Cult Times (2002) (Number 83, August), Visual Imagination Ltd.: London.
Eramo, Steven (2002) 'The Brad Boy of Charmed' in *Cult Times* (Number 83, August 2002), Visual Imagin-ation Ltd., London: pp. 30–34.
Fiske, John (1991) [1987] *Television Culture*, Methuen: London.
Gripsrud, Jostein (2002) 'Fans, Viewers and Television Theory' in Philippe Le Guern (ed.) *Les Cultes Média-tiques*, Presses Universitaires De Rennes: Rennes.
Harrington, C. Lee, and Bielby, Denise (1995) *Soap Fans: Pursuing Pleasure and Making Meaning in Everyday Life*, Temple University Press: Philadelphia.
Hills, Matt (2002) *Fan Cultures*, Routledge: London and New York.
Hobson, Dorothy (1982) *Crossroads: The Drama of a Soap Opera*, Methuen: London.
Jenkins, Henry (1992) *Textual Poachers: Television Fans and Participatory Culture*, Routledge: London and New York.
—— (2002) 'Interactive Audiences?' in Dan Harries (ed.) *The New Media Book*, British Film Institute: London, pp. 157–170.
Jensen, Joli (1992) 'Fandom as Pathology: The Consequences of Characterization' in Lisa A. Lewis (ed.) *The Adoring Audience: Fan Culture and Popular Media*, Routledge: London and New York, pp. 9–29.
Jones, Sara Gwenllian (2002) 'The sex lives of cult television characters' in *Screen* Vol. 43 No. 1: 79–90.
—— and Pearson, Roberta E. (forthcoming) *Essays on Cult TV*, University of Minnesota Press: Minneapolis.
Kawin, Bruce (1991) 'After Midnight' in J.P. Telotte (ed.) *The Cult Film Experience: Beyond All Reason*, University of Texas Press: Austin, pp. 18–25.
Larbalestier, Justine (2002) '*Buffy*'s Mary Sue Is Jonathan: *Buffy* Acknowledges the Fans' in Rhonda V. Wilcox and David Lavery (eds) *Fighting the Forces: What's At Stake in Buffy the Vampire Slayer*, Rowman and Littlefield: Maryland, pp. 227–38.
Lewis, Jon E. and Stempel, Penny (1993) *Cult TV: The Essential Critical Guide*, Pavilion Books: London.
No author credited (2002) 'The Issues That Time Forgot: 1979' in *SFX*, Number 98, December), Future Publishing. London, p. 130.

Pixley, Andrew and Rogers, Julie (2002) 'What was On In . . . August '67' in *Cult Times*, No. 83, p. 6.

Pullen, Kirsten (2000) ''I-love-Xena.com: Creating Online Fan Communities' in David Gauntlett (ed.) *web.studies*, Arnold, London, pp. 52–61.

Reeves, Jimmie, Rodgers, Mark C. and Epstein, Michael (1996) 'Rewriting Popularity: The Cult Files' in David Lavery, Angela Hague and Marla Cartwright (eds) *Deny All Knowledge: Reading the X-Files*, Faber and Faber: London, pp. 22–35.

Tudor, Andrew (1976) 'Genre and Critical Methodology' in Bill Nichols (ed.) *Movies and Methods* University of California Press, Berkeley, pp. 118–26.

Tulloch, John and Jenkins, Henry (1995) *Science Fiction Audiences: Watching Doctor Who and Star Trek*, Routledge: London and New York.

Websites

'Cult TV-A Short History', http://www.festival.culttv.net/history.html

Cult TV Festival, http://www.festival.culttv.net/activities.html

Cult Times magazine, http://www.visimag.com/culttimes/

Doctor Who Appreciation Society, http://dwas.drwho.org

Six of One, *The Prisoner* Appreciation Society, http://www.sixofone.org.uk/

Chapter 33

JOHN HARTLEY

DEMOCRATAINMENT

My whole trick is to keep the tune well out in front. If I play Tchaikovsky I play his melodies and skip his spiritual struggles. Naturally I condense. I have to know just how many notes my audience will stand for. If there's time left over I fill in with a lot of runs up and down the keyboard.

(Liberace, quoted from *Jazz Monthly*, in Hall and Whannel, 1964: 70)

Love, not quite requited

[. . .] **WHAT IS THE USE OF TELEVISION** at the turn of the millennial century, when it is a well-established medium? With the development of new communications technologies and semiotic systems, from non-broadcast television by video, cable, satellite and digital systems, to the newer virtual and interactive computer-and telecommunications-based technologies, it seems that interest in television as such has declined, at least among marketeers and policy-pundits, whose attention seems entirely fixed on newness. But television in its 'classic' broadcast form is still culturally, if not technologically, pre-eminent. Once the promoters of newness have passed on to new excitements, television is still there – just as its own predecessors, cinema, the press and books are thriving despite television's own much-feared expansion. Among audiences, publics and consumers in all known countries, it is television programming and television culture, not new technology as such, that attract attention. So much of the rhetoric of promotion for new technologies has to do with business expansion, national self-aggrandisement and individual emancipation that their 'functions' for the communities who eventually take them up is forgotten. A question for television as a cultural and historical fact of the last half century, then: what was that all about?

In this context, the argument of this chapter is quite simple. Television is used, both in its original 'mass' broadcast form, and now in its emergent subscriber-choice forms, to teach two new forms of citizenship, which I am calling **'cultural'** and **'do-it-yourself' or DIY citizenship** respectively. I've argued that as a 'transmodern' medium television shares many of its teaching characteristics with pre-modern 'media', especially the European medieval church, and it takes its own cultural place in the 'institutional' setting of talk and the family, which I would designate as essentially pre-modern in its everyday conduct; more anthropological than industrial certainly. In such a setting, during the second half of the twentieth century, television has reached and sustained a position as the foremost medium for cross-demographic communication. Meanwhile, a largely successful campaign has been mounted by government regulators and professional broadcasters alike to stop it becoming directly political in this usage. So its impact for its unprecedentedly large but politically unfocused audiences has been cultural and personal rather than political in the formal sense. However, I argue that exactly these cultural and personal usages have themselves contributed to new forms of citizenship, thereby becoming political in unexpected ways.

If television is a transmodern teacher, the question of what it teaches has eventually to be addressed. But this is not just a matter of describing the content of its 'lessons'. Certainly it teaches general knowledge and facts about the world, and about the day to day conduct of public and private affairs. As Richard Hoggart suggested in 1960 it also teaches 'the amelioration of manners' (meaning the manners of the age rather than table manners); teaching different segments of the population how others look, live, speak, behave, relate, dispute, dance, sing, vote, decide, tolerate, complain; television is a major source of 'people-watching' for comparison and possible emulation. And no doubt television teaches various ethical, ideological and moral precepts, prejudices and perspectives too. But if the television medium as a whole – as a cultural-historical phenomenon – can be characterized as a teacher, then it ought to be possible to identify a similarly general addressee to whom its teaching is directed.

What 'addressee' does the teaching discourse of television call into being? Traditional schooling calls into being the student addressee; one who is self-motivated by a perceived lack of some knowledge or skill to subject themselves to the regime of schooling, including its forms of collective organization and discipline, teaching practices, subject-taxonomies, assessment methods, certification and cultural expectations. By contrast, the 'addressee' of advertising is the consumer; one who is chatted up by the advertising text, which performs all manner of flirty, attention-attracting tricks in the full knowledge that the 'addressee' of advertising has made no prior commitment, expressed no lack and is not self-motivated to see things the same way as this or any advertisement, but who may be entertained, intrigued or informed by what is shown and said, sufficiently to maintain awareness of, interest in and sympathy for a particular brand or product, based on the addressee's 'literacy' in the ways and wiles of advertising, itself built up over a long period, and requiring some degree of mutual trust between advertising and its addressee in order for the system to work at all. Whether the elaborate display of commercial courtship sparks a response powerful enough in the consumer-addressee to result in a consummation (a purchase . . . ; a marriage . . .) is by no means a foregone conclusion, as both parties perfectly well know.

These two extremes of 'addressee' – one purposeful, institutional and regimented, the other based on the rhetoric of declarations of (unrequited) love – show that the 'addressee' of television in general, the audience, may vary, since television addresses its viewers in a variety of ways, ranging from the 'love-object' of advertising to an addressee-position much closer to that of the traditional student in certain types of 'public service' factual and educational programming, for instance. But television in general is neither potential lover nor formal schoolteacher (nor is it, as some critics have long feared, a scandalous mixture of these) – the addressee of television teaching is neither student nor consumer but the audience.

Having called this entertainment-seeking, voluntary (uncommitted, fickle) addressee into being, television 'teaches' it, first of all, to continue to watch television, for example by providing narrative and dramatic genres that promote reconsumption (serials, series, news, weather, sport), and by using semiotic devices at every level from dialogue to plot, characterization to casting, language to location, that might help to carry viewers through, continuing from the heyday of the nineteenth-century novel the famous Wilkie Collins school of good tale-telling – 'make 'em laugh, make 'em cry, make 'em wait'. The 'literacy' of the television viewer in watching television is the first priority of television teaching. Such literacy may be understood as very basic, but it may also become quite sophisiticated, especially over a lifetime of viewing, or where individuals become fans for particular shows, stars or series, and it has the unplanned outcome of promoting relations *among* television audiences, not just between the addresser and addressee. Indeed, investigations into fan cultures have been at pains to point out how active, astute and 'literate' such viewers are, frequently knowing more about a given television show or genre than the best-funded academic or commercial researcher, and investing considerable resources – both of self and money – into conducting a relationship with the show, other fans and the outside world based on their television-literacy. They attend conferences, produce and consume fanzines and websites, buy the clothes, collect the gadgets, live the life (see Jenkins, 1992; Tulloch and Jenkins, 1995; Miller, 1997).

Of course not everyone who watches television goes to such lengths about every or any show, but it is impossible to watch television in a settled context (i.e. in a given country) for long without beginning to participate in an intersubjective conversation with all the anonymous others of that context about the fashions and celebrities of the season, the politics and insider gossip of the production process, the ups and downs of the ratings, the joys and horrors of the great shows and the not-so-great, and the vast, rolling, cumulative oral 'archive' of common knowledge that is both mined and made by television. So 'how to watch television' is a lesson in cultural (intersubjective) as well as media literacy from the start – from the first lessons in repetition (*Tellytubbies*), in generic recognition and media-allusiveness (*Sesame Street*), to full-scale self-reflexive homilies in the micro-politics of everyday life in TV-Land (*The Simpsons*). Television promotes reconsumption of its own forms by teaching lessons in cultural literacy, and within this context it promotes among its 'subjects' – the audience – both 'identity' (sameness with others in TV-Land) and 'choice' (difference within an intersubjective field). It is my contention that what arises from long-tutoring in this non-purposeful cultural-personal semiosis is a new episode in the historical development of modern citizenship (but see also Ellis, 1982; Ang, 1996; and Hartley, 1987 for a previous debate about the implications of seeing the television viewer as what Ellis called the 'normal citizen')

Citizens of media

Does television teach citizenship? How does it? How should it? Once again, the issue is not television itself (as a social institution or on-screen discourse), but the relations among the populations it serves: how these populations can be known, reached, taught; turned into citizens. In previous work I have suggested that citizenship is profoundly *mediated* in the modern/postmodern period – we are all 'citizens of media' (Hartley, 1996: Chapter 3) in the sense that participation in public decision-making is primarily conducted through media (and that this has been true since at least the French Revolution). Traditional political theory sees citizenship as something prior to, separate from and if anything damaged by media relations. But in the modern/postmodern period, citizenship needs to be seen in historical rather than categorical terms; it is an evolving and cumulative concept adapting to changes in western development. As new philosophical, political and industrial conditions became established through the period of the eighteenth to the twentieth centuries, so new rights and claims came to be associated with citizenship. And because development for different social groups was uneven, so citizenship rights varied for different populations; rights tended to be claimed first by urban adult white men who might at first have enjoyed citizenship rights unheard of (if not undreamed of) by colonized and 'ethnic' populations, women, children or people of various 'minorities' from gypsies/ Romanies to gays and lesbians. Nevertheless, the promulgation of rights, freedoms and responsibilities associated with citizenship among one group set up an inevitable standard or yardstick for others, promoting a logic of equivalence by which those whose rights were denied or unrecognized might move forward in their own particular struggles (see Enzensberger, 1970; Laclau and Mouffe,

1985; Hartley, 1996). Hence, at any one time, there may be different forms of citizenship in existence even within the same population. It may need to be stressed here that this 'historical model' of developing citizenship recognizes that there is continuing struggle both to attain and to maintain existing levels of citizenship – this is not a 'treacle-flow' view of history (a slow tide, inevitably rolling forward, outward), but a history of uneven development; one step forward, but sometimes two steps back or, for some, no step at all.

Television has an important bearing on this historically complex and 'mottled' situation, because it is no respecter of differences among its audiences; it *gathers populations* which may otherwise display few connections among themselves and positions them as its audience 'indifferently', according to all viewers the same 'rights' and promoting among them a sense of common identity *as* television audiences. At one and the same time, then, people can experience political differences based on territory, ethnicity, law and heritage between one another, but also, simultaneously and conversely, they can enjoy undiffereniated 'identity' with others based on television audiencehood. While television promotes loyalty among its audiences, and tries to 'subject' each and every viewer to its 'regime of viewing', it does not (on pain of regulatory intervention by the 'secular branch' of government) interfere with people's existing political rights and citizenship. Much of the anxiety about television's social impact rests on the riskiness of this situation – television is seen by some viewers and many governments as a usurper of their own rights and privileges, but at the same time television enjoys unparalleled success in turning actual populations into its 'subjects'.

It seems to me that what has in fact been occurring over the fifty-odd years that television has become established as the world's number-one entertainment resource and leisure-time pursuit is that a new form of citizenship has overlain the older, existing forms. In the long-term perspective of history, this new form of citizenship may be seen not as a competitor with traditional 'political' forms, but a successor, covering and further embedding previous forms certainly, but cumulatively, not supplanting them. However, as it has evolved and spread, observers have frequently taken fright at the apparent *removal* of hard-won civic rights and their *replacement* with 'media citizenship'. My own view is that citizens of media remain citizens of modernity, and the rights struggled for since the Enlightenment are not threatened but further extended in the so-called 'post-modern' environments of media, virtuality and semiotic self-determination.

What's new is that with television, the potential community of 'media citizens' has now run to several billions of people around the world. Populations have been gathered, and cross-demographic communication established with them, beyond the reach of secular states and nations – the television audience has truly become the 'laity' of a new supernational community, exceeding the scope but not the ambition of the medieval Catholic church, overlaying traditional citizenship with something new. Television corporations are the new ecclesiastical bureaucracies, vying with mere governments for the hearts and souls of the laity, ostensibly tending to non-secular needs but actually in constant dialogue with the political and territorial powers, negotiating precisely the extent (possible or permissible) to which each can authentically claim to be speaking and acting on behalf of most people, both in terms of absolute numbers and in terms of their most vital interests, opinions, will or needs. Since it is the case that public participation in terrestrial politics is predominantly conducted through the media (although the traditional apparatus of political parties, local activism and associative democracy still continue inside the envelope of the mediasphere), and since in addition 'media' now means television before other forms such as newspapers, it follows that television has become implicated in civic issues in new and complicated ways.

Looking at the rest of the world through television, it is inevitable that differences can be both celebrated and erased, recognized and removed, insisted upon and ignored. So there's a curious 'toggle' switching between television as a teacher of 'identity' among its audiences, and as a teacher of 'difference' among the same population. It seems to me that this 'toggle' switch is itself historical – it was set to 'identity' first, promoting what I've called 'cultural citizenship' and identity politics (during the era of 'golden-age' broadcast television), and to 'difference' more recently, promoting 'DIY' citizenship and semiotic self-determination. It follows from what I've argued above that both types of citizenship may be found in social circulation simultaneously; some groups may have moved beyond 'cultural citizenship' and identity politics to 'DIY citizenship' and semiotic self-determination, while others are still struggling for identity and see newer developments as irrelevant or dangerous. For instance, some sections of the women's movement and feminist theory, and some thinking within the politics of sexual orientation in the gay and lesbian movements and queer theory, have moved beyond 'identity politics', while many ethnic groups, including first peoples, are still struggling for their identity and for the rights of 'cultural citizenship' to be recognized. Television has, it seems to me, moved historically in a similar way, from the promotion among its audiences of an 'addressee position' based on common *identity* and 'cultural citizenship' during its first half-century, to a more recent acceptance of *difference* in its audiences, promoting 'DIY citizenship'.

Various semiotic developments can be explained by this schema. For instance, in the area of factual television and actuality reporting, I would argue that a definite move can be observed during the television era from news or journalism as a discourse of power to news or journalism as a discourse of identity. Concomitantly, the 'object' of news was once the decision-maker, now it is the celebrity. News was once about security (i.e. national security – defence and war, policing and civil order) and was based on conflict. Now it is about personal comportment and is based on confession.

In drama and other TV genres such as chat shows (both celebrity-guest and audience-talk shows), as well as in advertisements, television has grown in importance as a promoter of difference understood as 'neighbourliness'. Even when the audience is treated to the pathological side of neighbourly conduct – not least in the riveting new genre of 'neighbours from hell' documentaries – the overall perspective is to post a level of civility, tolerance and acceptance of difference that is being breached in whatever spectacular way in any one show. Hospital dramas tend to pivot around neighbourliness; the hospital standing for the local community, and the doctor/nurse/patient/administrator relationships standing for neighbourly ones. Just as people tend to choose both sexual partners and enemies from neighbours (not from near family or far strangers in both cases), so hospital dramas find sexual and other tensions inside the virtual community of the fictional hospital. They share the unspoken presumption of neighbourliness with recent genres like the 'world's most gruesome police-chase videos' and 'world's funniest home-video clips'. What's regarded as dramatic, uncivil or funny in each genre is directly related to the audience's sense of virtual community, since dramatic conflict/romance, moralistic discourses about getaway cars or amusing ruptures to family and bodily equilibrium can only work for the audience on a prior presumption of neighbourliness and civility in personal, social and domestic comportment. This is cultural citizenship on show.

Meanwhile, the cumulative growth of a new form of citizenship raises socio-political as well as semiotic questions. If there are citizens, then traditional citizenship theory will be looking for some kind of formal, contractual or legislative relationship with a state – citizens of media are presumably 'subject' to some institution which is doubtless seeking to lead them, to take power in their name, to mobilize them in one cause or another. 'Someone' is usually taken to be the much-maligned media corporation: the 'mogul' or 'baron' – in the present era often personified by Rupert Murdoch – whose 'power' is deemed to derive from their subjection of populations to their political and cultural agenda, rather than from their economic or corporate dominance as such.

Rupert Murdoch's career has indeed spanned the change from cultural to DIY citizenship: News International, his corporate vehicle, has shifted progressively from print (originally the Adelaide *News*), to broadcast-network television (Fox), then to non-broadcast television (Sky, Star) without abandoning the earlier forms (he retains newspaper titles in several continents, although he has closed the *News*). Meanwhile his own citizenship moved from 'identity' (he's a native of Australia) to 'DIY' (he took US citizenship to comply with federal ownership regulations). However, despite the alarming extent to which this individual is demonized and held to be personally responsible for the lives and politics of whole populations, I don't think it is Rupert Murdoch who explains the phenomena of 'cultural' and 'DIY' citizenship, or the 'use' of television as a transmodern teacher, that I've been trying to explain, but precisely the reverse. It is television's propensity to establish new versions of community that explains Rupert Murdoch. He has simply ridden the regulatory wave as governments and media organizations have coped with the democratization of media semiosis. In short, my model of citizenship is more interested in the process of citizenship formation among the populations that might be collectivized as citizens of whatever community, than in the formal relationship between any one citizen and any one 'state' or power. In this I am following the tradition of thinking about cultural citizenship that is derived from cultural criticism – the Arnoldian, Leavisite tradition which was developed by Hoggart and Williams – rather than social and political theories of citizenship, which focus on the civic rights and obligations that take legislative form. In my schema, Rupert Murdoch and all the other moguls, barons and 'kings of the world' who from time to time proclaim themselves sovereign *over* the people are certainly important figures in the landscape, but they're all temporary usurpers: more important is the truly sovereign community in whose name they operate – the populations among whom relationships, decisions and ideas are negotiated and arbitrated. Hence cultural citizenship is better seen as a historical activity among audiences, not as a conspiracy by corporate raiders. It is in process of formation – being made to mean something – long before it can be institutionalized and legislated. In my view 'cultural citizenship' is at a late stage of rights-formation, moving into formal legislative existence in a number of contexts, while DIY citizenship is much more recent, fleeting and of uncertain outcome. But it can be seen as 'citizenship' nonetheless, because semiotic self-determination is 'claimed' as a 'right' and 'taught' as a mode of civility or neighbourliness by those within its purview. It is – or could be – the citizenship of the future; decentralized, postadversarial, international, based on self-determination not state coercion right down to the details of identity and selfhood. Its model is the 'remote control' exercized by television audiences, and its manifestations include fan cultures, youth cultures, taste constituencies, consumer-sovereignty movements and those privatizations of previously 'public' cultures that succeed in democratization without politicization: extending to everyone membership of the republic of letters that was once reserved for literate/clerical elites.

The progressive fragmentation of sources of television, as the medium very slowly evolves from broadcast to non-broadcast (cable and satellite) forms, and from free-to-air to subscriber services, and from one-way transmission to various types of interactivity (ranging from the phone-in to full computer compatibility), and from broadcasting seen as 'national culture' to television as part of consumer choice, means that technologies of communication are evolving from what may be recognized as a *national semiosis* model in the period of broadcast network television, to a *semiotic self-determination* model in the post-identity era of DIY citizenship.

No wonder critics are concerned. But as always, advertisers are quick to see the positive aspect of such developments. There are many advertising campaigns, for international brand names in particular, that promote DIY citizenship in a field of 'identity-within-difference'; recognizing 'cultural citizenship' and identity, but playing with it. One such is on air as I write; a British television commercial (TVC) for Coca-Cola. It features an Aboriginal boy from what looks like the central desert of Australia, who is found at the beginning of the ad within his 'identity' group, painted up in traditional patterns and dancing traditional movements alluding to a corroborree. As the TVC progresses, refreshing water/Coke begins to abound, having the effect of transporting the boy directly from premodernity to 'DIY citizenship': the white paint is washed off the tribal bodies, the boy's own body gets a red T-shirt, emu-steps turn to breakdancing and clap-sticks turn to a bottle of Coke. The TVC alludes, consciously or otherwise, to the South African film *The Gods Must Be Crazy* (Jamie Uys, 1984), but it is also clearly promoting a worldwide citizenship of people of colour as the Aboriginal boy breaks into the urban rhythms of African America, while suggesting to the predominantly Anglo-Celtic but also multicultural British audience that their semiotic self-determination allows them access to and pleasure in these other identities, and indeed promotes respect and fellow-feeling for the co-consumers of Planet Coke. In this the advertisement is by no means alone. McDonalds TVCs in Australia play with the very same ideas, including the use of Aboriginal characters as part of their world community of Citizens of the Golden Arches. Benetton has for over a decade been promoting its United Colors; and internationally branded goods from IBM ('solutions for a small planet') to Microsoft ('where do you want to go today?'), from cars to beer, vie with each other to promote – to *teach* – cultural identity and semiotic difference all at once. As I write, Benetton is running an advertising campaign celebrating the fiftieth anniversary of the Universal Declaration of Human Rights. The print media advertisement features some of O. Toscani's familiar 'united colors' multicultural portraits, surrounding an excerpt from the Declaration: 'ALL HUMAN BEINGS ARE BORN FREE AND EQUAL IN DIGNITY AND RIGHTS (art. 1)' (*Vogue* (UK), April 1998: 68–9). It is in the spaces created by commercial culture, sponsors of highly capitalized innovation in the mediasphere, i.e. in upscale advertising, that the connections between culture, difference, identity and human rights are being visualized and made both appealing and accessible in the era of semiotic self-determination and DIY citizenship. The idea that a company specializing in the sale of franchises for clothes shops may also be a radical, avant-grade producer of cutting-edge ideas about citizenship and social relations in an international media economy still jars with many commentators; but it is at least arguable that the 'message' of the United Nations is getting across at least as effectively via Benetton as it is via formal schooling. Popular commercial media are certainly not outside the process of citizen-formation. They may even be making a good job of teaching its latest potentialities, to a public that can participate in the communicational exchange of ideas about selfhood and citizenship, rights and differences, without any requirement to buy a sweater (much less a franchise for a Benetton shop). Advertising on television and elsewhere is now a fully emancipated component of the general mediasphere, a bastion of what I will call, in deference to other recent Government-Education-Media hybrids like 'infotainment' and 'edutainment,' **democratainment**.

From civil, political and social to cultural citizenship

What forms of citizenship do these new forms (cultural and DIY) overlay? In a classic account, T.H. Marshall (1992, first published 1950: 8, 10) argued that the history of citizenship in modernity comprises three evolving components, each one building on rather than supplanting the one before. These are:

1   **civil citizenship** – Enlightenment rationality leading to individual rights and the 'bourgeois freedoms' (freedom of accumulation, contract, labour and exchange: see Macpherson, 1973);
2   **political citizenship** – the ascendancy of 'representative' (as opposed to direct) democracy and government by consent expressed in the vote;
3   **social citizenship** – welfare and education understood as rights.

Marshall's plan is explained by John Chesterman and Brian Galligan's helpful summary in their book on indigenous citizenship:

> According to Marshall's influential account, which has shaped modern thinking on citizenship, there are three main components of citizenship, or three kinds of human rights, which have developed cumulatively during the last three centuries: the civil element, which developed largely in the eighteenth century, consisted of the rights necessary for individual freedom, such as the right to freedom of speech and the right to own property; the political element, which largely arose during the nineteenth century, entailed the right to take part in political processes, most importantly as a voter; and the social element, which has received its greatest definition during the twentieth century, was the third and least easily defined category, to which Marshall most closely connected the educational system and social services. This social element covered a range of rights, from one's right to a modicum of economic security to the 'right to share to the full in the social heritage and to live the life of a civilised human being according to the standards prevailing in the society'.
>
> (Chesterman and Galligan, 1997: 5)

Chesterman and Galligan, tracing the history of Aboriginal citizenship in Australia, are at pains to point out that indigenous people throughout the modern period have been 'specifically excluded from certain rights in all three of Marshall's categories'. So while it is clear that a cumulative progression from civil to political to social rights of citizenship can indeed be seen to underlie the history of industrializing western commercial democracies since the Enlightenment, it was by no means a universal history, even for the inhabitants of the countries involved. A similar caveat would have to be made for women, non-heterosexual identities, various ethnic groups and colonized peoples, and children; their 'progress' is not necessarily in convoy with that of the white adult European male who is the 'universal' subject of civic discourse since the American, French, Industrial and Russian Revolutions. However, it is among the disenfranchised or unenfranchised so-called 'minorities', such as indigenous people, that a fourth type of citizenship has clearly and now irrevocably arisen:

4   **cultural citizenship**, or identity, as in 'identity politics'.

Chesterman and Galligan concede that 'new understandings of citizenship' have been informed by, for instance, the recognition of Aboriginal rights, and that 'these less formal social and cultural aspects of citizenship and community structures, practices and values are crucially important' (Chesterman and Galligan, 1997: 5), although in their own study they leave the articulation of 'cultural aspects of citizenship' to the experts, who in this case are Aboriginal people themselves:

> There have been two great themes to our struggle: citizenship rights, the right to be treated the same as other Australians, to receive the same benefits, to be provided with the same level of services; and indigenous rights, the collective rights that are owed to us as distinct peoples and as the original occupiers of this land. *Lois O'Donoghue, chairperson of the Aboriginal and Torres Strait Islander Commission*, 1996.
>
> (Quoted in Chesterman and Galligan, 1997: 193)

Lois O'Donoghue's distinction between 'citizenship rights' and 'indigenous rights' points to something more than the particular circumstances of indigenous people in Australia. It is a version of a much more general tendency which has gathered pace globally since Marshall's tripartite model of citizenship was used to describe mid-century Europe, namely a tendency towards the articulation of cultural citizenship and identity rights as a separate category from social, political or civil citizenship. 'Indigenous citizenship' stands therefore for a fourth type of 'cultural' or 'identity' citizenship more generally; 'collective rights that are owed' to any group as 'distinct peoples', be they ethnically/territorially organized as with Aboriginal people, or 'virtual' communities, as with women, children/youth or even 'mass' media audiences. David Trigger says that this kind of ('indigenous') 'cultural citizenship . . . would imply that real moral weight should be accorded to world views and practices that are at times inconsistent with predominant sentiments' (Trigger, 1998: 164).

'Mass' media audiences have been the focus of public and cultural policy since there were masses to mediate. They were for decades regarded as relatively undifferentiated, unknowable, by turns desirable (redeemable) and threatening (revolutionary). The technologies of communication characteristic of the twentieth century have been designed to reach them and regulate them, influence them and stop them being influenced. Oddly enough, these great unknowable masses that have stalked the pages of social and media theory, government legislation and cultural criticism since the nineteenth century have themselves been the locus of the development of the form of citizenship based not on sameness (undifferentiated mass), but on difference. The so-called 'masses' – the citizen-consumer audiences of 'mass society' – are historically the site whence the fourth type of citizenship has arisen, taking *difference* to the point where it can be claimed, and increasingly recognized, as a human right.

I am arguing, indeed, that a theoretically influential and historically significant 'model' of modern humanity – the model of unknowable and undifferentiated sameness among the industrialized, urban, popular classes – has completely collapsed in the very place where it was most expected and most feared; the 'mass' audience. Television is far and away the most 'mass' of the mass media, its audiences are still (despite computer-based and non-broadcast new technologies) the biggest collective communities our species has yet called into being, and it is still the site where advertisers and politicians most desire what social scientists most *fear*: an undifferentiated viewer (buy ours!; vote for us! . . . will they buy that?; vote for them?). But it is here, in the cultural sphere of privatized, individuated, mediated consumption, where audiences gather to partake of *mass* entertainment, that the form of citizenship that most *denies* massness has pitched its tent most securely.

References

Ang, Ien (1996, first published 1984) 'The battle between television and its audiences'. In *Living Room Wars*. London: Routledge, 19–34.
Chesterman, John and Galligan, Brian (1997) *Citizens without Rights: Aborigines and Australian Citizenship*. Cambridge: Cambridge University Press.
Ellis, John (1982) *Visible Fictions*. London: Routledge & Kegan Paul.
Enzensberger, Hans Magnus (1970) *Raids and Reconstructions: Essays on Politics, Crime and Culture*. London: Pluto Press.
Hall, Stuart and Whannel, Paddy (1964) *The Popular Arts*. London, Melbourne, Sydney, Auckland, Bombay, Toronto, Johannesburg, New York: Hutchinson Educational.
Hartley, John (1987) 'Invisible fictions: television audiences, paedocracy, pleasure'. *Textual Practice* 1: 2, 121–38.
—— (1996) *Popular Reality: Journalism, Modernity, Popular Culture*. London: Arnold.
Hoggart, Richard (1960) 'The uses of television'. *Encounter* 76, January (vol. XIV, no. 1), 38–45.
Jenkins, Henry (1992) *Textual Poachers*. London: Routledge.
Laclau, Ernesto anief Mouffe, Chantal (1985) *Hegemony and Socialist Strategy: Towards a Radical Democratic Politics*. Trans Winston Moore and Paul Cammack. London: Verso.

MacPherson, C.B. (1973) *Democratic Theory: Essays in Retrieval*, Oxford: Oxford University Press.

Marshall, T.H. (1992, first published 1950) 'Citizenship and social class'. In T.H. Marshall and Tom Bottomore, *Citizenship and Social Class*. London: Pluto Press.

Miller, Toby (1997) *The Avengers*. London: BFI Publishing.

Trigger, David (1998) 'Citizenship and indigenous responses to mining in the Gulf country'. In Nicholas Peterson and Will Sanders (eds) *Citizenship and Indigenous Australians: Changing Conceptions and Possibilities*. Cambridge: Cambridge University Press.

Tulloch, John and Jenkins, Henry (1995) *Science Fiction Audiences: Watching Dr Who & Star Trek*. London: Routledge.

PART SEVEN

Transforming Television

IN A RECENT REVIEW essay, American television scholar Lynn Spigel pointed to the defining paradox of contemporary television studies. Television studies has finally come of age as a field of research and teaching. After thirty years, she writes, "a growing body of literature has emerged that . . . now recognizes itself as a (loosely) organized protocol for understanding television as a cultural, social, political, aesthetic and industrial form." However, Spigel continues, "just at the moment when a body of literature seems somewhat 'there' (or 'there' enough to be called television studies), the whole question of TV's future—and with that the future of television studies—is shaking things up again. For some this can be anxiety provoking, for other liberating, for still others both."[1]

The "whole question of TV's future" to which Spigel refers is bound up with rapid change occurring across a variety of areas: technology (the shift from analog to digital modes of imaging, sound recording, data transmission and storage; internet applications; computer software and hardware development; etc.), international and national commercial and communication policy (the regulation or deregulation of telephony, satellite, cable, terrestrial broadcasting, media ownership and concentration, copyright, etc.), and corporate strategies (mergers of/alliances among equipment manufacturers, software developers, internet providers, computer and peripheral manufacturers, terrestrial broadcasters, film studios, cable and/or satellite services, etc.). It is clear that "television" has been and is being transformed as a result, but what is not clear—and this is where the future of television *studies* comes in—whether "television" will survive in a way that warrants its continuing to be the object of a field of scholarly study in relation to which university courses and books such as this one will be organized.

The force of these changes on television seems to be both centrifugal and centripetal. On the one hand, it would seem, television is being pulled apart and its uses, "contents," and technologies spun out into an increasing number and variety of other forms that are in some ways like television but clearly distinguishable in some respects from what we've understood *as* television in the past. If we play a DVD of a movie through a television set are we "watching television"? What if we play the same DVD on a portable DVD player with an LCD display? Is the outer orbit of television described by our watching a broadcast television program streamed over the internet? Or would television's gravitational force be strong enough also to pull into its orbit the experience of watching the output of five webcams placed in the home of a family in Almere, the Netherlands, and using the web to turn their lights on and off? Does the television program *Law and Order* make it on the syllabus of a television studies course but the video game of the show fall into some other curriculum?

On the other hand, many see the future of television and television studies to hinge on the fulfillment of the dream of technological convergence, in which media and media experiences which are now separate from one another will merge into a new, integrated, technological system and replace what we know as "television" in the process. Predictions of the imminent realization of convergence can be found throughout the trade and popular press since the early 1990s. As Mark Poster notes in his essay in this part, as early as 1993 an article in *Time* magazine predicted that new technologies would "force the merger of television, telecommunications, computers, consumer electronics, publishing and information services into a single interactive information industry." Seven years later, *Scientific American* is just as confident, but it is still waiting for those last few technical and legal obstacles to be overcome before television is supplanted by "d-entertainment":

> Music, movies, television, video games and the World Wide Web are morphing into a single entity. As these previously distinct media switch from essentially analog means of production (like celluloid film) and distribution (like delivery vans) to all-digital ones, their products are converging into one big stream of digital data. Call it d-entertainment. It will come to us on our TV screens, PCs, wristwatches and dashboard displays— anywhere, anytime. And once a few more technical and legal issues are worked out, we'll not only be able to enjoy it, we'll be able to create it and distribute it, too.[2]

It may be that in five years a book entitled *The Television Studies Reader* will seem as outmoded as *The Typewriter Studies Reader*, and courses on d-entertainment or that conveniently hollow designation "new media" will have replaced courses on television. Indeed, at its spring 2002 annual meeting members of the Society for Cinema Studies (the major international professional organization for university teachers of cinema studies) discussed changing its name to the Society for Cinema and Media Studies to reflect two decades of work among some of its members on television, radio, and other "new media." One participant in a plenary session suggested that the term "media studies" was already out of date. "Software," he argued, better reflected the scope of the field's current and future object of study and its manifestation across media, platforms, and technologies. To date, however, the Society for Cinema and Media Studies has yet to change its name to the Society for Software Studies.

The essays in this section were not chosen to catalogue the "new" technologies that will produce a post-television media environment, nor are they predictions of the state of television-to-come. Such is the pace and unpredictability of television's transformation that accounts of the next new thing have a shelf life shorter than the time it takes to publish them in collections such as this one. Rather, we gather under the heading "Transforming Television" some essays that encourage us to shift the frames within which we think about what television "is" (and is not), has been, and might be. They also encourage us to think about the relationship between television and the technologies with which its future seems, at this point at least, to be linked: computers, the internet, and digital media of various sorts.

As you read and think about television's future, there are a few things you might keep in mind. First, just because a technology is developed that allows television to be changed in a particular way, that doesn't mean it *will* be changed or in the way anticipated. The future of television depends not only upon technological innovation but also upon a host of other factors: government regulation and trade policies, business practices, legal issues (patent, copyright, antitrust), and the sometimes unpredictable ways a new technology is actually used by consumers. An interesting survey conducted in the US in the fall of 2002 showed that, in the short-term, at least, television and the internet are increasingly sharing the same household space, but are used for different purposes. The study found that nearly half of all "wired" adults in the US have a TV set and a PC in the same room, and nearly half of them frequently surf the net while the TV set is on. But the co-presence of the two technologies and their simultaneous use is, to this point at least, resulting in multitasking rather than integration: most internet surfing behavior is unrelated to TV viewing.[3]

Remember that for half a century the manufacturers and marketers of television technology have had a vested interest in promoting television as an ideal sensory and social experience that lies just over the next technological horizon and toward which every innovation (no matter how small) brings us one step closer. The discourse on the technological reinvention of television long predates the computer and internet era. Bigger screens, color, better picture quality, multiple sets for the same household, remote controls, portability, greater channel receiving capacity, stereo sound, and the use of the television set for something other than watching broadcast programming (video games, VCRs, DVDs, home videos, etc.) have all been touted as innovations that would profoundly affect our experience of television.

Keep in mind that the impact of these and other technological innovations has been extremely uneven—across and within national television cultures. Any generalizations about the current state of "television" and predictions of the effects of technological change upon "television" must take into account both the early-adopters of new technologies and those who still haven't figured out how to set the clock on the VCR. The transformation of television is taking place in relation both to those with the money and inclination to invest in the latest technology and those for whom television still means a few broadcast channels viewed on a twelve-inch black-and-white set. In the general introduction to this collection it was suggested that any definition of "television" is relative to the experience of the person making the definition. What television will "be" in the future begs the question: *to whom* will it be whatever it will become? So, rather than trying to draw a circle around some technologies and experiences in order to distinguish what *is* television from what is not (or is not yet) television, we would prefer that you think about television's future in terms of your own experience of it.

In his essay in Part Six (Watching Television), John Hartley observes that marketers and pundits tend to ignore the present moment of television and to be fixated on the projection of a brave new television world just about to emerge just over the technological horizon. But, he reminds us, "television in its 'classic' broadcast form is still culturally, if not technologically, pre-eminent. Once the promoters of newness have passed on to new excitements, television is still there—just as its own predecessors, cinema, the press and books are thriving despite television's own much-feared expansion." Furthermore, as was argued in the general introduction, compared with the experience of television in most countries only fifteen years ago, the experience of television for many has already been transformed by the very technologies that we expect to be revolutionized by the next wave of technological change: the VCR, remote control, digital recording/storage/display, cable and satellite transmission, etc. Change, in other words, is not something about to happen, but something that has been a part of the experience of television since its introduction.

Norwegian scholar Arild Fetveit's essay begins by posing a paradox. As anyone who has used image editing software to add horns and a beard to Uncle Ralph's Christmas photo knows, digital imaging technology makes it possible to manipulate photographic images to the point that the credibility of the "original" is undermined. A further elaboration of digital image generation/ manipulation endows a range of media forms—from print and television ads to local television newscasts and Hollywood films—with the capacity to produce "real-seeming" images of things, people, creatures, and places that don't exist outside the purpose and the technologies for and with which they were produced. By the same token, Fetveit argues, broadcasters around the world have found significant audience interest in genres that "depend more heavily upon the eviden-tial force of the photographic image than any previous form: *reality TV.*" At the same time that digital technologies call into permanent question the truthfulness of any photographic image (and here Fetveit includes live TV transmissions, video-taped images, and film images in the category of the "photographic image"), a genre of television becomes prominent that relies upon our belief in the image as evidence of *something* that did occur in front of the camera. "How," he asks, "are we to make sense of this? Are we, in some sense, at a turning point in visual culture?"

Fetveit then sets this apparent paradox within a history of theoretical arguments regarding the status of the photographic and cinematic image. As early as the mid-nineteenth century, the photograph was seen by some to possess a special truth status by virtue of what Fetveit calls its "indexical" relationship to the thing photographed. Because the photographic image is created by the exposure of the film to the same light that strikes the object in front of the camera, the resulting image attests to the presence of that object (the profilmic event, as he calls it) in a way that is analogous to a thermometer reading attesting to the temperature of the medium in which it is placed. However, as he notes, photographs "cannot account for their own production process very eloquently; they cannot tell us where, when, and how they are taken." Filmmakers (Fetveit uses the example of Russian documentarist Dziga Vertov here) discovered that the photographic/ cinematic image could be used in an illustrative or symbolic fashion as well: the image could be made to stand for something outside itself. As one critic of Vertov put it, a shot of a man shown skiing into the distance can be made into a "symbol of the departing past."

Thus, long before *Cops* or *Jurassic Park* there was an "unresolvable tension" between two uses of the photographic image: the illustrative (or iconic) and the indexical (or evidentiary). It is, he says, "within this very fabric that digital manipulation and reality TV now seem to confront each other." One of the appeals of reality TV, he suggests, might be that it serves as an antidote to the digital manipulation of the image in visual culture at large. Could it be that it is in those moments when the evidentiary pull of the television image is strongest (the phenomenon of "liveness" that Bourdon discusses in his essay in Part Four: Modes of Television section that, as the host of the show *Real TV* puts it, "real TV happens."

Jon Dovey's essay on camcorder culture is another of those pieces that might have been placed in several parts of the *Reader*: it would work well with pieces in Part Three: Modes of Television and Part Four: Making Television. Furthermore, its emphasis on the "private, domestic domain" of the camcorder video sets up an interesting dialogue with the essays in Part Two (Spaces of Television). Here, however, it picks up and amplifies the discussion of the kinds of video that Fetveit examines in his essay: video recorded by amateur camcorder enthusiasts as well as by surveillance cameras.

Like Fetveit, he sees the sudden prominence of camcorder and surveillance video footage in the television culture of the 1990s (a "sudden viral contamination") as related to its indexical, evidentiary capacities: "the low grade video image has become *the* privileged form of TV 'truth telling,' signifying authenticity and an indexical reproduction of the real world. . . ." Also like

Fetveit, Dovey frames his arguments in relation to the history of cinematic representation. In the late 1950s and early 1960s, filmmakers began to adapt film production technology developed for military use in World War II (light-weight reflex-view cameras and portable quarter-inch tape audio recorders) for documentary purposes. This technology facilitated a style of filmmaking called Direct Cinema or *cinema verité*, which claimed to set up a much more direct relationship between viewer and filmed event than was possible through more traditional documentary modes. Rather than foregrounding the role of the filmmaker as intermediary between event and viewer (through an on-camera presence, interviews with subjects, or voice-over narration), Direct Cinema filmmakers rejected such devices.

Dovey argues that although the technologies responsible for the camcorder might seem to follow in a straight historical line of development from that which made Direct Cinema possible, the miniature, low-cost, highly mobile, and user-friendly technologies of the camcorder have encouraged a very different relationship among videomaker, presentational style, and viewer. Instead of a style that hides the identity of the filmmaker and denies the effect of his or her subjectivity upon the film (as was the case with Direct Cinema), Dovey argues that "the contemporary video documentary is often nothing *but* an inscription of [the videomaker's] presence within the text. Everything about it, the hushed whispering voiceover, the incessant to-camera close-up, the shaking camera movements, the embodied intimacy of the technical process, appears to reproduce experiences of subjectivity. We feel closer to the presence and the process of the film-maker." Dovey would complicate Fetveit's argument, then, by insisting that in the home video, the video diary and other contemporary forms the institutional "third-person" anonymity that we associate with professionally produced television is replaced by a first-person subjectivity: " 'us-ness' rather than otherness, me as opposed to them." Dovey's discussion of amateur video and surveillance video might also be read together with Eric Freedman's essay in Part Four on the autobiographical impulse in community television.

Will Brooker's essay argues that even if technological convergence is still over the horizon, there are other modes of "convergence" that are changing our experience of television. As media scholar Henry Jenkins has argued, the availability of multiple and complementary electronic media (television *plus* computer games, the internet, CD players, VCRs, DVD players, MP3 players, etc.) encourages a kind of cultural convergence around multitasking and around particular media texts. At the same time, media producers and marketers are increasingly exploring the possibilities of what Disney CEO Michael Eisner once called "synergistic brand extension" and what cultural commentators call media convergence: producing and cross-promoting media and non-media products across a range of "platforms." As a result of both types of convergence, Brooker (Chapter 36) argues,

> We are at a point where we have to reconsider what it means to engage with a television programme. . . . where the text of the TV show is no longer limited to the television medium. We need a new word for the process, just as we had to settle on the term 'surfing' in the mid-1990s.

Taking as his case study US and British fans of the teen drama *Dawson's Creek*, Brooker explores the implications of the tendency of some television programs to "overflow" the bounds of television as a medium and television viewing as an activity. Through the show's elaborate official website, *Dawson's Creek* is constructed not just as a weekly television viewing experience, but as a continuous and unbounded opportunity for viewer interaction and participation.

We include two essays in this Part and hence in this collection that would appear to have little to do with television: the essays by Mark Poster and Don Slater both deal with the internet. We offer them here not because we wish to extend the definition of "television" to encompass the internet or because we see the internet as that point of technological convergence at which television necessarily morphs into its future form. Rather, these essays provide another techno-logical perspective from which both television and the relationship between television and "new media" might be viewed.

Mark Poster's essay is a chapter from his 2001 book *The Information Subject*, although this particular chapter on virtual reality, the internet, and postmodern subjectivity was written in the mid-1990s. He describes an internet still in its infancy and in the process of its own transform-ation—from a vehicle for exchanging text messages to a multi-media form. Remember: Netscape and Yahoo! were not launched until 1994; Java and cable modems not until a year or so later. The most recent figures for worldwide internet usage Poster had access to at the time of writing (1993) estimated some 30 million users (the estimate at the end of 2002 stood at over 600 million), and many of the features of the internet that we now regard as constitutive of it as an experience (its friendly graphical interface and video and audio streaming, among them) were still mere potentialities. Nevertheless, Poster sees the internet and various other computer applications technologies to be culturally and socially transformative, heralding a new media era. And, if this is the case, the question for Poster becomes: how can the sweeping changes stimulated by wide-spread computer access and the internet be understood?

The barrier to understanding these new technologies and their social and cultural implica-tions, he argues, lies principally in viewing what is a postmodern phenomenon through the lens of modernity. The transition from feudal to modern societies entailed not only the ascendance of new economic, political, and social institutions (capitalism, the nation state, democracy) but also the emergence of a new subjectivity to go along with them: a notion of the self as a rational, stable, independent, coherent individual. As Poster puts it, modernity fosters "the 'reasonable man' of the law, the educated citizen of representative democracy, the calculating 'economic man' of capital-ism, the grade-defined student of public education." Perhaps, he continues, a postmodern society is emerging "which nurtures forms of identity different from, even opposite to, those of modern-ity"—forms of identity that are underwritten by new electronic communication and represen-tational technologies. For example, both the internet and virtual reality computer programs have helped to foster what Poster calls a "simulational culture" "in the sense that the media often changes the things that it treats, transforming the identity of the original. . . . In the second media age 'reality' becomes multiple." The multiple realities made possible by electronic technologies blur the distinction between "virtual" and "real" and encourage a corresponding postmodern subjectivity that is "unstable, multiple, and diffuse."

Nearly a decade separate Poster's reflections on the transformative potential of the second media age and Don Slater's 2002 review of scholarship and commentary on the internet. Perhaps thinking here of Poster, Slater notes that until the late 1990s scholarly discourse on the internet tended to view it as constituting a new "unified 'cyberculture' with patterns of sociality that seemed automatically to flow from the nature of the technology itself." Studies of the internet constructed an implicit or explicit dichotomy between the "online" world and the "offline" world, with the former seen as producing or sustaining new identities, new kinds of relationships, new communities. Slater sets as his task in this essay to assess how this online/offline distinction has colored thinking about the nature and impact of new electronic technologies such as the internet. Rather than asking what social processes, identities, and forms of association are unique to the internet and the new media age, Slater suggests that we might ask how people actually use these technologies. Ethnographic studies of internet use, he argues, demonstrate that the online/offline distinction "played little if any role in people's use of or experience of the Internet: people integrated the various Internet media into existing social practices and identities."

Although representing divergent approaches to understanding the implications of "new technologies" for television, both Poster and Slater encourage us to think about relationships among media forms. Does television represent, as Poster would seem to imply, a technology and set of institutions inextricably linked to modernity and to the "first" media age? Do various media forms inevitably foster particular ways of knowing, identities, forms of association? Or, as Slater concludes, do the qualities of each medium, including "new" ones emerge only "through their particular appropriations"?

Notes

1 Lynn Spigel, "Television Studies for 'Mature' Audiences," *International Journal of Cultural Studies* 3: 3 2000, pp. 407–20.
2 Mark Fischetti, "The Future of Digital Entertainment," *Scientific American* 283: 5 2000.
3 Matt Richtel, "In That Place Where TV and the Net Almost Meet," *New York Times*, September 16, 2002, p. C-3. The survey was conducted by comScore Media Metrix.

Chapter 34

ARILD FETVEIT

REALITY TV IN THE DIGITAL ERA
A paradox in visual culture?

It's like they say. The picture's worth a thousand words. The video camera's worth a million words really.

(Police officer in *Real TV*)

More real than the real, that is how the real is abolished.

(Jean Baudrillard)

T HE ADVENT OF DIGITAL MANIPULATION and image generation techniques
has seriously challenged the credibility of photographic discourse.[1] At the same time, however, we are experiencing a growing use of surveillance cameras and a form of factual television
that seems to depend more heavily on the evidential force of the photographic image than any
previous form: *reality TV*.

The simultaneity of the digital "revolution in photography" and the proliferation of visual
evidence seems paradoxical.[2] It seems as if we are experiencing a weakening and a strengthening
of the credibility of photographic discourses at the same time. How are we to make sense of this?
Are we, in some sense, at a turning point in visual culture? And, if so, does this entail a
strengthening or a weakening of the evidential credibility of photographic images? Or is there a
third option available? The aim in this article is to historicize and conceptualize this possible
change in visual culture and to suggest plausible explanations for the proliferation of reality TV in
the digital era.

I will first present a conceptual framework for assessing changes in credibility for photographic discourses before historicizing this credibility briefly. Then I discuss the use of visual
evidence in reality TV and the impact of digitalization. I conclude by suggesting some explanations
concerning the initial paradox, the most important one emphasizing the increasingly discourse-
specific trust in photographic images and consequently, the need to complement a general technical understanding of photographic images with knowledge of different photographic practices.

Histories of photographic images

In order to suggest a conceptual framework for understanding changes in the credibility of
discourses based upon photographic images, I find it useful to look at an argument advanced by
John Tagg and later developed by Martin Lister.[3] These writers warn against placing too much
emphasis on the common characteristics of photographic images. Rather than thinking of photography as a singular medium with unifying characteristics, they encourage us to recognize that there

are numerous uses of photography and that the medium changes significantly according to the discourse it is used within. Presenting Tagg's view, Lister claims that,

> it is more helpful to think of "photographies" which have different "histories" than it is to think of a singular medium with a singular, grand and sweeping history. The conventional history of photography has been written like The History of Literature or Art. It would be better understood as like a history of writing. By which Tagg means that it is better understood as a technique which is employed in many different kinds of work.[4]

I think Tagg and Lister are right in warning against a too monolithic view of photographic images. A view that is too heavily based upon unique technical features will tend to neglect the amount of convention invested in photographic practices. However, the reverse danger also exists. By emphasizing issues of convention too strongly, the unique iconical/indexical relation to the profilmic—which prepares the ground for the use of photographic evidence—is overlooked. Tagg makes himself guilty of this in claims like the following: "That a photograph can come to stand as *evidence* . . . rests not on a natural or existential fact, but on a social, semiotic process."[5] This conventionalism dismantles any idea of a common technological core unifying photographic practices in different areas. It dissolves photography into a set of faintly related conventional practices constituted by the different conventions at work in the various fields of use.

I want to argue that we should neither opt for a wholesale technologically and existentially based view nor a wholesale conventionalist one. Rather, we ought to see photographic practices as fundamentally based upon existential features involving the iconical/indexical relation to the profilmic but also as strongly invested with conventions. Further, we should be aware that to the extent to which we believe in a common core in photography, changes in our trust in one type of photographic discourse might affect our trust in another. Thus digital manipulation of photographic images within one area might not only affect our trust within that particular area, it might also lead to a declining trust in other uses of photographic images and to an undermining of credibility for photographic discourses in general. The picture I am drawing here is one in which we can conceive of trust in discourses based upon photographic images as existing on two levels:

- trust in discourses based upon photographic images in general
- trust in specific discourses based upon photographic images: documentary film, nature photography, reality TV, news photography, photography used in advertising, and so on[6]

This general framework for writing on the history of photographic images suggests that we can write both the *history* and *histories* of photography—and moreover, it suggests that relationships between these levels might be interesting to explore. It should also be noted that in our understanding of photographic discourses, a historical shift of balance between these two levels is conceivable. At one point in time we may think of photographic practices as fairly unified, but the development of more diversified practices may prompt us to ask questions of trust on a more discourse-specific level.

Before coming to the present changes in credibility, I shall present a brief account of some earlier changes in this field. This might give a better background for understanding the present situation.

The growth of credibility

A suitable point of departure would be 1839, when the techniques of two of the inventors of photography, William Henry Fox Talbot and Louis Jacques Mandé Daguerre, were first disclosed. Both viewed photography as a tool that was able to produce visual evidence. Talbot characterizes photographic images as unique since they "have been obtained by the mere action of Light upon sensitive paper. They have been formed or depicted by optical and chemical means alone, and without the aid of anyone acquainted with the art of drawing."[7] They are unique, he adds, since an effect is produced "having a general resemblance to the cause that produced it."[8] Talbot thereby prefigures present semiotic conceptions of photography as based upon an iconic/indexical relation to the thing photographed. He goes on to suggest that the images might be accepted in court as "evidence of a novel kind."[9] This view parallels that of Daguerre's representative, the physicist M. François Arago, who argued that the French government should purchase Daguerre's patents on the grounds of their artistic and scientific uses. He argued that the camera would join "the thermometer, barometer, and hygrometer," as well as the telescope and microscope as scientific instruments, and that it will provide "faithful pictorial records" of events.[10] Although early photography was first of all used for making portraits, the evidential power of these images was not neglected. This is apparent not least in the early portraits of criminals.[11]

According to Tagg, a considerable change due to technical development occurred toward the end of the century:

> In the decades of the 1880s and the 1890s . . . photography underwent a double technical revolution, enabling, on the one hand, the mass production of cheaply printed half-tone block and, on the other hand, the mass production of simple and convenient photographic equipment, such as the hand-held Kodak camera.[12]

The half-tone plates that were introduced enabled the mass production of photographs in books, magazines, and newspapers. Light and inexpensive cameras made photography much more accessible. Both prepared the ground for an increased use of the camera for purposes of surveillance.[13] However, it is important to keep in mind that the early introduction of double exposure, composite images and other photographic tricks prefiguring film effects made for a complicated field where both issues of what photography should be and issues of its evidential quality was contested.[14]

Though the technical means for using photography in books and magazines were available, according to André Bazin, a "feeling for the photographic document developed only gradually."[15] He supports this claim by pointing to the rivalry between photographic reporting and the use of drawing in the illustrated magazines of 1890 to 1910, with drawings often preferred on account of their dramatic character.[16] The notion that a feeling for the photographic document *developed gradually* is interesting. One way to think of this is that there was an increasing emphasis on the documentary or evidential quality of the images, adding to their illustrative qualities. Another way to conceive of this development would be to see it as a result of a gradual *adoption* of the photographic technology within new areas. This cumulative adoption within different areas of use might then effect a strengthening of the general credibility of photographic evidence. Thus we get interplay between a discourse-specific level and a general level as suggested in the framework above.

The invention of cinema in the 1890s adds new dimensions to the array of visual evidence: time and movement. However, it also invites fictional uses where the evidential, in a sense, is relieved. Without going into the complexities of this, let me point to some major turns in the development of visual evidence within film. Though the first films derived much of their appeal from the sheer fascination with authentic footage, the first powerful interest for the evidential seems to evolve in the 1920s with Dziga Vertov's program for a "true cinema": Kino Pravda. Much as a reaction to fiction, the lives of people were to be caught "unawares." Still, Vertov was criticized for not going far enough, since he edited his films in a way that made it difficult to identify time and place of the events filmed. In 1926, Viktor Shklovsky said that "newsreel material is in Vertov's treatment deprived of its soul—its documentary quality."[17] He also complained that "there is no precise determination of the [shots] . . . The man who departs on broad skis into the snow-covered distance is no longer a man but a symbol of the departing past. The object has lost its substance and become transparent, like a work by the Symbolists."[18] This critique eloquently illustrates a possible spectrum open to actuality footage between the illustrative and symbolic on the one side and the evidential on the other. Later changes in the view of credibility can be understood partly in view of such a spectrum.

Though the term documentary film suggests a genre based on the documentary power of photographic images, manipulations, re-creations and fakeries were prevalent in these films throughout the 1930s.[19] Thus the illustrative and symbolic function of the images was dominant. After World War II, however, actuality material was strongly preferred over dramatizations (perhaps due to the impact of the authentic war footage).[20] Thus, the evidential function of the images was considerably strengthened.

Prefiguring today's reality TV, an even stronger emphasis on the evidential came with the advent of lightweight camera equipment featuring synchronic sound recording in the late 1950s.[21] Increased camera access allied with an epistemological optimism to establish a new documentary aesthetic, strongly based upon observation and interviews, often documenting events as they unfolded through an "objective," "fly on the wall" technique.[22] On the face of it, much of today's reality TV seems to embody aspirations both from Vertov's Kino Pravda to catch life "unawares," and from the verité movements of the 1960s to give an objective view of life as it unfolds. Thus, the evidential aspirations of photographic discourses is powerfully carried on—if not stretched to its limits—in reality TV.

I have suggested that a belief in the evidential powers of photographic images might grow through (1) the adoption of photographic techniques in novel areas, and through (2) the shift of emphasis from the illustrative to the evidential power of the images used. The history of photography is filled with examples of the first, with the adoption of photography in illustrated magazines (as pointed to by Bazin) being just one of them. The latter movement is exemplified in the critique of Vertov and, later, in the growing demands for authenticity within documentary film first after World War II, then with the coming of lightweight equipment. Though photomontage, retouching, and other non-evidential manifestations of photography have been around since the first days of photography, in general I think it is fair to say that the evidential view of photography has gained a strong position through the years. However, inherent in the fabric of photographic images seems to lie an unresolvable tension between the illustrative and the evidential, the iconic and the indexical—and it is within this very fabric that digitalization and reality TV now seem to confront each other. The former exerts a pull in the direction of the illustrative and the iconic, the latter in the direction of the evidential and the indexical.

Visual evidence in reality TV

Concepts like "reality TV," "reality show," "reality programming," and "neo-vérité" have been used to designate this recent trend in television, showing us dramatic moments from police work, rescue operations, accidents, and so forth.[23] Cops and LAPD: Life on the Beat show us police at work;

programs like *Crimewatch UK* re-create unsolved crimes in order to enlist the audience as assistants to the police;[24] *I Witness Video* and *Real TV* show dramatic (and sometimes funny) moments caught on tape. Though some of the reality TV programs employ re-creations—notably *Rescue 911* and *Crimewatch UK*—most rely on visual evidence of the following kinds:

- authentic footage from camera crews observing arrests or rescue operations
- footage from surveillance videos
- recordings (often by amateurs) of dramatic accidents and dangerous situations

Both *COPS* and *LAPD* are based on the recordings of a one-camera unit "riding along" with the police in the patrol car. The chaotic and rough sound track, saturated with white noise from police radios and accidental environmental sounds, testifies to the authenticity of the recordings, as does the ragged movements of the handheld camera. The footage in *COPS* is further authenticated by a voice-over in the opening of the program claiming that "*COPS* is filmed on location with the men and women of law enforcement." In long takes, displaying the action as it unfolds, we are presented with chases, arrests, and police inquiries. Though the camera has good access to events, we might still have a hard time figuring out what is happening through sheer observation. This is solved by having one police officer brief another in front of the camera. In *LAPD*, voice-over narration is also used, which facilitates a higher pace.

Formats that rely on amateur and surveillance videos are often structured around a single and unique moment caught by camera: a dramatic car crash, a robbery caught by a surveillance camera, or even airplanes colliding in midair. This moment, when "real TV happens," as the announcer in *Real TV* phrases it, is the evidential jewel around which the segment is built.[25] The dramatic footage is often supported by testimonies from people involved. In most cases, we get an account from a surviving victim looking back at the incident. We can also find interviews with friends and family, with accidental eyewitnesses, and in some cases with police or rescue workers. These elements surround and explain the dramatic footage. Repetition and slow motion are often used to help us inspect the visual evidence.

In an episode from the Norwegian version of *Real TV*, we see amateur videos from an air display featuring two MIG 29s doing impressive loops.[26] When the airplanes demonstrate a twin loop, they get too close, and the wing of the leader slices the other plane. As the planes collide, we hear the narrator of *Real TV* say: "During a fatal moment, the overwhelming view of the two gracious airplanes is transformed into an inferno in the air. The cameras capture every single moment." Then we meet two eyewitnesses. First, the announcer for the air display comments on the accident as we see it once more: "In a fraction of a second, these two graceful jets were flaming pieces of rubbish, falling out of the sky." Then a clip from an interview with a fireman is inserted, in order to remind us of the danger and to prolong the suspense: "Looking at the stage of the wreckage—if you would have been in there, there wouldn't have been a lot left of you," he says. We see the crash again, this time in slow motion and from a slightly different angle, as the narrator comments, "but in this video you can see the pilots eject themselves the second after the collision." Two circles are drawn above the planes in order to guide our vision. We can see two faint dots shooting out from the planes before we see the parachutes opening, bringing the pilots safely to the ground.[27]

Here the evidential power of the cameras that capture "every single moment" has become the main issue. The focus is not so much on presenting a story of an air crash as on presenting the audio/visual evidence that shows us what really happened in that decisive moment when the planes crash. The function of the camera is close to that of the scientific instrument, measuring out the concrete details of a particular instant. The format heavily propagates a belief in visual evidence. However, the strong presence of the verbal explanation pointing out what is going on in the footage should not be neglected. The "visual evidence" is not merely visual. Walter Benjamin makes an interesting prediction when commenting on increased camera access in the 1930s:

> The camera will become smaller and smaller, more and more prepared to grasp fleeting, secret images whose shock will bring the mechanism of association in the viewer to a halt. At this point captions must begin to function . . . Will not captions become the essential component of pictures?[28]

Benjamin's observation on the relationship between the visual and the verbal is surprisingly well fitted to reality TV featuring authentic recordings of dramatic events. Much of the blurred and chaotic images at the height of drama seem to need powerful support from linguistic sources for us to make sense of them. The description of what we see helps us to choose the suitable level of perception; it helps to focus not simply our gaze but also our understanding.[29]

The focus on presenting audio/visual evidence as much as "the story" is one of the features that distinguishes reality TV from earlier attempts to "catch the real." This focus also leads to an emphasis on the visible surface of the world rather than on deeper symbolic aspects. Whereas Vertov set out "to fix and organize the individual characteristic phenomena of life into a whole, an extract," reality TV opts for an exploration of the visible surface of the here and now, avoiding abstract, symbolic montage and often pointing to its own status as visual evidence.[30] The goal is "to capture that real TV moment," and audience members are advised to keep a camcorder in the trunk of their cars because you "never know when real TV might happen."[31] Similarly, the producers of *Cops* are looking for "amazing, unusual, exciting or weird videotapes. Crazy arrest, angry suspects, hot pursuits and bloopers from in car cameras" [sic].[32] What we get is evidential photography paired with an aesthetics of "liveness," a dramaturgy geared toward keeping alive the question "what happens next?" and often "Will the good guys make it?" – "Will the bad guys fry?" Then the putatively objective eye of the camera provides the answer for us to see. And the TV station will not let us have serious doubts: "Yes, they will."[33] Our two pilots survived against all odds and thereby inscribed themselves into the mythic core of reality TV. The deepest fascination with the evidential—when slow motion and repetition serve a close scrutiny of the footage— seems to occur when death is only inches away.

Nonetheless, how can this almost frantic obsession with the evidential powers of the camera survive in a digital era? Does not digitalization do away with visual evidence?

Digitalization and visual evidence

Photographic images cannot account for their own production process very eloquently; they cannot tell us where, when, and how they are taken. Though we are often successful in our guesses on issues like these, our only way of knowing is by way of a truthful account from the producer or some other person who knows. Any serious use of visual evidence has to rely on such knowledge. This means that, in order to be held credible, visual evidence is reliant upon more or less explicit verbal descriptions and personal/institutional warrant that the description is true. Provided that this is taken care of, that the technology works and the people using it are doing what they are supposed to, cameras will still serve their purposes in monitoring us on the street, in the bank, and in prison as they also will surveille physical experiments in the sciences and the inside of our bodies under surgery.

Whereas descriptions of images used for scientific purposes tend to be explicit, standardized, and detailed, the opposite is normally the case for images used in the media. Here we are informed about the status of the recordings either through genre convention or through network and program style. Our belief that television news mainly features authentic recordings, and that some networks tend to stick more firmly to such a policy than others, is established this way. Claims might also be more explicitly stated, like the claim that *Cops* is "filmed on location," or that we see "the pilots eject themselves the second after the collision" in a *Real TV* episode. In the last case we get an interpretation of the footage and no explicit statement about its authenticity, since this is regarded as self-evident. However, later developments of digital techniques have made such assumptions less evident.

The development of computer programs for manipulation and generation of images has made it, at times, very hard to see whether we are looking at ordinary photographic images or images that have been altered. In the latter case, iconicity is sustained whereas indexicality—the causal relation between the profilmic (what was in front of the camera) and the image—partly disappears. In most cases the relationship is still there, but we might have a hard time deciding which parts of an image originate from the profilmic event and which parts are digitally generated or manipulated. Thus the evidential power of composite and digitally manipulated images is practically lost. It is also important to note that digitalization has substantially expanded the spectrum of photographic techniques available—especially within the increasingly blurred boundaries between painting and photography—though the different practices employed may not be detectable in the images themselves. This makes us more heavily reliant upon the truthfulness of the claims made about photographic images.[34]

We should also note that the impact of "the digital revolution in photography" is contingent upon the use of these techniques within different areas. In some genres, digital manipulation techniques are used extensively; in others such techniques are more or less banned. People engaged in the production of factual discourses like news and documentary tend to shy away from digital imagery whereas those who create commercials and fiction films employ such techniques more freely. Negotiating institutional standards is an important part of adapting to the new situation. Such negotiations have taken place in the press, in television news, and wildlife photography, just to mention a few areas.[35] Some argue pragmatically that what is important is that the truth be told not whether the images are authentic, have been subjected to color adjustments, have had disturbing objects removed, or other manipulations done to them. Others seem to think that any conduct transgressing what goes on in a traditional darkroom setting will ruin the credibility not only of the images but also of what is being told.

There have been efforts to communicate the status of the images explicitly by marking manipulated images with "M," but it seems that a more implicit communication has gained the upper hand. There might be limits to the audiences' interest in metacommunication, and besides, arguments have also been advanced against the "M."[36] Following other factual discourses, producers of the reality TV formats discussed here are also careful not to give the impression that their programs have been subjected to image manipulation or that they contain footage that is not authentic.[37]

More research on these institutional negotiations would be welcome. What are the arguments used? Where are the limits drawn? How do agents position themselves in order to protect the credibility of their discourse and distance themselves from less credible discourses? It would also be interesting to know more about how changes in one discourse may bleed over and affect another or affect the credibility of photographic discourses on a more general level.[38]

But let us leave these questions now and turn to some less palpable dimensions of this change within visual culture.

A psychological loss

The dissemination of indexicality does not only represent an undermining of evidential power. On a deeper psychological level, it can be argued that it also comes to represent a loss of contact with the world. This is because photographic images come with a promise to provide a certain sense of connectedness. By way of the light rays emanating from the person photographed, the image becomes inscribed with traces from that person: it becomes a relic. As Bazin puts it, a "transference of reality from the thing to its reproduction" takes place.[39] And more than sheer information, what we seem to be attracted to in these images is a form of presence.

> A very faithful drawing may actually tell us more about the model but despite the promptings of our critical intelligence it will never have the irrational power of the photograph to bear away our faith . . . No matter how fuzzy, distorted, or discoloured, no matter how lacking in documentary value the image may be, it shares, by virtue of the very process of its becoming, the being of the model of which it is the reproduction; it *is* the model.[40]

This deep psychological fascination with the sense of connectedness, of closeness to something infinitely remote, is also what Barthes takes as his point of departure in *Camera Lucida*. Looking at a photograph of Napoleon's youngest brother, Jerome, taken in 1852, Barthes realizes with amazement, "I am looking at eyes that looked at the Emperor."[41] This sense of connectedness (which in Barthes's phrasing makes the representation disappear and replaces it with the object itself) is an important source of fascination with photographic images. When indexicality is disseminated, this sense of connectedness is also partly lost.

Pursued to a more global level, this is a loss concerning our sense of contact with reality through audio/visual representations. From a McLuhanesque point of view, the media are "extensions of man," prosthetic devices that extend our perceptive apparatus. From this perspective, the loss of indexicality could be interpreted as a powerful refiguration of these extensions, implicating our perceptive apparatus. In this refiguration, representations based upon the iconic/indexical are being replaced by representations sustaining the iconic, but losing the causal connection to reality. Thus, to the extent that indexicality is lost, we might not only lose evidential power, but we might come to feel a sense of losing touch with reality, of being stranded in the world of the simulacrum.

From technological to institutional trust

In view of all this, how can we make sense of our initial paradox, the simultaneous loss of faith in photographic images and the proliferation of reality TV and visual evidence? Rather than a general strengthening or weakening of the evidential credibility of photographic images, I think we are witnessing an *increased compartmentalization of credibility*; a shift of emphasis from general assessments of credibility to more discourse-specific judgements. I am not claiming that a compartmentalized understanding of photographic images is something entirely new, but I believe it is being strengthened currently. A move in our understanding of photography from a general and technically defined level to a more discourse-specific level reliant upon discourse-specific practices and institutional warrant permits the coexistence of reality TV and digital manipulation, since different discursive practices are guided by different rules.

This brings us back to Tagg and Lister. If we regard our initial paradox as solved, I think it is at the price of accepting that the common technological core unifying photographic images across different formats and practices has become less important to us. Thus our understanding of these images has moved some steps in the direction Tagg and Lister are suggesting. With increasingly different practices, now expanded by the advent of digital techniques, our understanding of and trust in photographic images must more than ever take varying practices and conventions into account. Thus the credibility of photographic discourses becomes less reliant on an overarching trust in the technology of photography and more dependent upon institutional warrant.

This compartmentalization may go a long way in explaining why the coexistence of digital manipulation and reality TV is no contradiction, but it does not provide an explanation for the obsession with visual evidence and reality expressed in reality TV. Obviously, institutional changes and economical drives should not be forgotten, but I also think the interest for reality TV is feeding upon less tangible aspects of the current changes.

The ambiguous longing for the real

In a deeper psychological sense, the proliferation of reality TV could be understood as a euphoric effort to reclaim what seems to be lost after digitalization.[42] And what seems lost is not only a belief in the evidential powers of photography but as much a sense of being in contact with the world by way of indexicality. The powerful urge for a sense of contact with the real is inscribed in much of the reality TV footage. The rough quality of the handheld footage draws attention to the issue of contact itself, to what Jakobson calls the phatic function of discourse.[43]

The reality depicted in these formats is most of the time one where other lives are at stake; either people survive accidents that could have been fatal or the danger is provided by police hunting assumed criminals. What most powerfully conveys a sense of reality is, perhaps, the presence of death. It is also where the real ends. In a sense, death cannot be represented, but we still cannot stop representing it.[44] On reality TV, however, death is only depicted when the surviving numbers are astonishing. After all, a major theme in these programs seems to be the good citizen escaping death and the bad citizen being confined.

Reality TV comes with a unique promise of contact with reality, but at the same time it promises a secure distance. Too much reality is easily dispensed with by a touch on the remote control. It is not reality, it is reality *TV*, reality *show*.[45] Kevin Robins points to a "tendency to replace the world around us with an alternative space of simulation."[46] He sees reality TV as "anticipating, ahead of any technological transformation, the experience of . . . virtual-reality systems."[47] He develops this comparison by maintaining that virtual reality "is inspired by the dream of an alternative and compensatory reality . . . so attractive because it combines entertainment and thrills with comfort and security."[48]

This view suggests a complex scenario in which developments in visual culture interact with both technical and socio-political issues. From this perspective, digital manipulation hardly represents any threat against reality TV since both bring us closer to simulation anyway, though admittedly in different ways. I think Robin's analysis is suggestive, particularly the sociological and political perspectives that it yields. It points to an increasing compartmentalization of society in which we build up "safe environments" where we no longer need to share physical space with the underprivileged, where the more problematic aspects of reality are locked out. With its focus on rescuing us from nature and technology gone awry and protecting us from criminals, reality TV could easily be interpreted as conveying an ideology tailored to such a development.

However, I think we should hesitate somewhat toward plainly talking about "simulation," both in regard to digitized photography and reality TV. A partial loss of indexicality does not bring about a state of simulation, at least not in the sense of a generalized suspension of referentiality. After all, the referential image was not invented by Talbot and Daguerre, though, admittedly, their effort of bringing together the iconical and the indexical has powerfully come to shape what we understand by "representing reality." Furthermore, rather than simply claiming that reality TV represents simulation, I suggest that we should see it as a representation of reality that is not very useful for developing our understanding of what goes on in the world.[49]

What is at stake here could be reconceptualized as a tension between modes of representation, modes that reflect different views on what reality is, or, perhaps more precisely, different views on which aspects of reality should be represented. Shklovsky, in his critique of Vertov, wanted less symbolism and general statements and more concrete accounts. Reality TV seems to have taken us further in such a direction than we have ever been before. Now Robins, however, in the tradition of Plato, Brecht, Benjamin, and others, wants to take us back. This seems like an ongoing struggle within the very fabric of photography—reflecting a similar tension within our understanding of reality—where no level between the symbolic and the concrete is "the right one" except according to the purposes and interests we might have. However, in a culture where critical and independent documentaries have a hard time competing with more flashy reality-oriented programming, it is in our interest not to allow reality TV too much influence on what "reality" should be on our television screens.[50]

Conclusion

I have argued that the coexistence of digital manipulation and visual evidence testifies to a transmutation in our visual culture. This is a change in which the credibility of photographic images has become less dependent upon technology and more based upon institutional warrant. Thus we have recently seen efforts to negotiate and communicate standards for photographic discourses. These changes require us to place greater emphasis on the differences between photographic practices and less upon the technical features that unite them. Such a move, from the idea of trust as linked to the technology itself and toward placing it in a larger techno-institutional complex, largely resolves our initial paradox originating from the simultaneous proliferation of digital imagery and visual evidence.

Reality TV itself might be read partly as a symptom of unsettled issues in this transmutation. More precisely, it might express a longing for a lost touch with reality, prompted by the undermining and problematizing of indexicality. Not only does reality TV powerfully reclaim the evidential quality of photography said to be lost after digitalization, it is also obsessed with conveying a sense of connectedness, of contact with the world—a trait that also, albeit on a less tangible psychological level, might seem to be weakened in an era where silicon has replaced the silver of Daguerre and Talbot.

Acknowledgment

Thanks to *Rådet for anvendt medieforskning*, *Handlingsplanen mot vold i bildemediene*, and *Institusjonen Fritt Ord* for supporting my research on reality TV financially. I also want to thank Arnt Maasø, Andrew Morrison, John Corner, James Friedman, Carol J. Clover, and Kiersten Leigh Johnson for helpful comments and suggestions. Thanks also to *Network for Speculative Media Research*. This article has been slightly revised since its original publication in *Media, Culture and Society* 21, 6 (November 1999): 787–804 and its first reprint in *Reality Squared: Televisual Discourse on the Real*, ed. James Friedman (New Brunswick, NJ and London: Rutgers University Press, 2002): 119–37.

Notes

1   I prefer talking about the credibility of "photographic discourses" rather than "photographic images" because it makes no sense to say that an image as such is credible or not. Only when the image is used within a discursive context does it make sense to talk about credibility.

2   Fred Ritchin, *In Our Own Image: The Coming Revolution in Photography* (New York: Aperture, 1990).

3   John Tagg, *The Burden of Representation: Essays on Photographies and Histories* (London: Macmillan, 1988), and Martin Lister, ed., introduction to *The Photographic Image in Digital Culture* (London: Routledge, 1995), 1–26.

4   Lister, *The Photographic Image*, 11.

5   Tagg, *The Burden of Representation*, 4.

6   This picture could be rendered in several different ways. For example, we could easily add a third level: either technologically based—photography, film, television, computer—or based on cultural function—entertainment, information.

7   William Henry Fox Talbot, *The Pencil of Nature* (London: Longman, Brown, Green and Longmans, 1844), n.p.

8   Ibid.

9   Ibid.

10 François Dominique Arago, "Report," in *Classic Essays on Photography*, ed. Alan Trachtenberg (New Haven, CO: Leete's Island Books, 1980), 17, 23.

11 It is hardly surprising that the possibilities of the new instrument were soon discovered by the legal apparatus. According to Alan Sekula, "The Body and the Archive," in *The Contest of Meaning: Critical Histories of Photography*, ed. Richard Bolton (Cambridge MA: MIT Press, 1989), 342–89, photographic documentation of prisoners became institutionalized in the 1860s. Susan Sontag notes in *On Photography* (New York: Penguin Books, 1979) that the Paris police were using cameras eagerly in the roundup of Communards in June 1871 (5). A substantial growth in the uses of photographic evidence by the police followed the development of Sir Edward Henry's system of identification by means of fingerprints in 1901. It soon became apparent that the only way to record fingerprints discovered at the scene of a crime was by way of photography (Tagg, *The Burden of Representation*, 75–6).

12 Ibid., 66.

13 Tagg argues that the "democratisation" and proliferation of photography following this "double technical revolution" set the stage for a far-reaching pictorial revolution: "the political axis of representation had been entirely reversed. It was no longer a privilege to be pictured but the burden of a new class of the surveilled" (ibid., 59).

14 James Lastra, in "From the Captured Moment to the Cinematic Image: A Transformation in Pictorial Order," in *The Image in Dispute: Art and Cinema in the Age of Photography*, ed. Dudley Andrew (Austin: University of Texas Press, 1997): 263–91, points to debates about whether "combined negatives of two or more exposures might still be considered 'photographs,' in light of the proliferation of single-exposure snapshots" (264), citing titles like W. K. Burton, "Combination Printing: Is It Legitimate In Photography?" *Pacific Coast Photographer* 2, no. 5 (June 1893), 318–20; H. P. Bowditch, "Are Composite Photographs Typical Pictures?" *McClure's Magazine* 3 (September 1894), 331–34; and W. deW. Abney, "Are Instantaneous Photographs True?" *International Annual of Anthony's Photographic Bulletin* 2 (1889), 256–57.

15 André Bazin, *What is Cinema?* 2 vols. (Berkeley: University of California Press, 1967), I: 11.

16 Ibid.

17 Viktor Shklovsky, "Where is Dziga Vertov Striding?" in *The Film Factory: Russian and Soviet Cinema in Documents 1896–1939*, ed. Richard Taylor and Ian Christie (Cambridge, MA: Harvard University Press, 1988), 152.

18 Ibid., 153.

19 Eric Barnouw, *Documentary: A History of the Nonfiction Film* (Oxford: Oxford University Press, 1984).

20 See Bazin, *What is Cinema?* I: 155–6.

21 This is not the first time sound plays an important role in bringing film closer to tangible reality. With the advent of sound, newsreels like Fox's *Movietone News* were praised for bringing the world closer, and Warners' *Jazz Singer* (1927) for bringing new life to the screen. However, the coming of sound was also heavily deplored by people like Pudovkin, Eisenstein and Arnheim, who felt that the highly developed abstract and symbolic montage of the silent film was threatened by the blunt closeness to reality brought about by sound.

22 Brian Winston, in *Claiming the Real: The Documentary Film Revisited* (London: British Film Institute, 1995), sees this as a very unfortunate development: "A hundred and thirty years or so after François Arago claimed the camera for science, the documentary purists, essentially American direct cinema proponents, implicitly reasserted that claim on behalf of the lightweight Auricon and the Eclair. In such hands the camera was nothing more than an instrument of scientific inscription producing evidence objective enough to be 'judged' by a spectator" (151). The problem with this, as Winston further argues, is that research, analysis and social meaning is abandoned in favor of "emotionalism and aesthetic pleasure" (ibid., 154).

23 Intimate talk shows are also often referred to as "reality TV." Though they obviously form part of a general turn toward "reality" within television entertainment, I prefer to reserve the term for programs depicting physical drama on location rather than emotional drama produced in the studio. Formats like *Big Brother* are also referred to as "reality TV," though a more suitable name would be "experiment TV." *Big Brother* is a social (Darwinist) experiment where ten participants agree to be locked up in a specially designed house for one hundred days and be voted out one by one. In order to secure the sterility of the experiment, the participants have never before met, and they have no contact with the world outside, no telephone, newspaper, radio, or television. Cameras and microphones observe them day and night in every room.

Whereas the intimate talk shows of Jerry Springer and Ricki Lake mostly trigger negative feelings through emotionally violent confrontations, *Big Brother* is also designed to produce romance and sex. With the right casting and the proper impulses and restrictions, this social laboratory will produce "real life soap characters" that quarrel, insult, bond and seduce each other in front of large television and internet audiences. The attraction is largely premised on a promise of pornography, and the format is constantly tuned in order to secure delivery (casting a stripper [Norwegian version] or a go-go dancer [French version], having no single bedrooms and perhaps no single beds [German version] are among the means used to incite close encounters).

It can be argued that *Big Brother* further interrogates issues at stake in the reality TV of violent drama. On one level it is dramatizing and normalizing our lives as fully surveilled and incarcerated. On another level it pushes the interrogation of authenticity on from the level of the image and onto the subjects photographed whose "authenticity" is strongly thematized by participants themselves as well as marketed by producers.

On a more general level *Big Brother* is like a herald announcing a new creative imagery in television production (with television, internet and telephone fully integrated). The matrix of this new creativity is the surveillance of a human experiment. Put ten young people in a house for a hundred days (*Big Brother*). Put four young couples on a tropical island and have beauties (among them a former Playboy model and Miss Georgia 2000) try to tempt them into committing adultery (*Temptation Island*). Watch obese people try to earn their weight loss in gold (*The Big Diet*). Perhaps the deeper experiment here is one in which some people are tested for their willingness to subject themselves to possible humiliation in order to be on television and obtain a momentary "reality stardom"—others are tested for how well they adapt to a peeping tom and cannibalist gaze. Television itself is tested for its ability to transform what we would otherwise think of as perverse into something "ordinary" and "normal".

24 The format used in *Crimewatch UK* is employed in local productions throughout the Nordic countries. The various programs are called *Øyenvitne* (Norwegian TV2), *Station 2* (Danish TV2), *Efterlyst* (Swedish TV 3), and *Polisii TV* (Finnish YLE TV 2).

25 *Real TV*, which in Norway is broadcast as *Fra Virkeligheten* (TV2), also contains more evolving events with longer takes, as did its predecessor *I Witness Video*, in Norway called *Videovitne* (TV Norge). However, these more slowly evolving segments, containing the rescue of animals or showing people doing "weird" things, do not raise issues of evidence in the same way as the dramatic footage of possible death (which most of the time turn out to be footage of survival).

26 Broadcast by Norwegian TV2 on March 5, 1998. In the Norwegian version, the host, John Daly, is replaced by Richard Kongsteien (who used to host *Øyenvitne*).

27 Although our attention is first and foremost directed toward the visual elements, excerpts of authentic sound occasionally also become the focus of special attention. In the example above, as the planes collide, we hear a vague sound, a bit like voices. The speaker says: "That's the sound of 150,000 people drawing their breath in, and gasping at what they've seen, myself included."

28 Walter Benjamin, "A Short History of Photography," in *Classic Essays on Photography*, 215. Working from similar assumptions as Benjamin's, Roland Barthes, in his "Rhetoric of the Image," in *Image, Music, Text*, ed. Stephen Heath (London: Fontana, 1977), 32–51, develops the concepts "anchorage" and "relay" when

trying to describe the function of the linguistic message with regard to the iconic. When the linguistic message dominates, Barthes talks of "anchorage." When the iconic and the linguistic are equally import-ant, the linguistic message functions as a "relay." He further claims that "in every society various techniques are developed intended to fix the floating chain of signifieds in such a way as to counter the terror of uncertain signs; the linguistic message is one of these techniques" (39).

29   The use of replay and slow motion is perhaps greater in sports than any other programming. Decisive moments of failure or achievement can be experienced again and again, extracted from the normal flow of time and projected into the sphere of slow motion for detailed scrutiny and aesthetic admiration. Another place where the aesthetics of slow motion is prevalent is in ultraviolent film scenes. Reality TV seems able to provide a common ground, bringing sport, violent events, and visual evidence together. The present example, the MIGs crashing in an air display, comes close to a merger of these elements.

30   Dziga Vertov, "Fiction Film Drama and the Cine-Eye: A Speech," in *The Film Factory*, 115.

31   URL: http://www.realtv1.com/ (February 15, 1997).

32   http://www.tvcops.com/page_cops.html (February 15, 1997).

33   In the formats where the material has been edited, keeping in line with network policy represents no problem. Another matter is live reports. Thursday afternoon on April 30, 1998, in front of a live television audience, a man protesting against HMOs on an LA freeway set his truck on fire and killed his dog before blowing his head off with a shotgun. Since this happened between 3 and 4 pm, a fair amount of children also got to watch as their programming was interrupted too. This incident might induce a change in policy when it comes to transmitting such events live.

34   Again, there is some hesitation (see note 14) toward using the word "photography" in relation to digitally manipulated images, but though terms like "hyper-photography," "post-photography," and "digital pho-tography" have been introduced, I believe the established designations are likely to prevail. More specified designations, as well as metacommunication about how the images were produced, will be required when the audience is frustrated or when those making the images want to distinguish their practices from others.

35   Whereas the issues seem to be resolved within news departments (with a slightly more conservative result in print media than in television), debates within wildlife photography might not be that settled. The March–April 1997 issues of *American Photography* ran a discussion about the norms of photography related to Barbara Sleeper and Art Wolfe's book *Migrations: Wildlife in Motion* (Hillsboro OR: Beyond Words Publishing, 1994) in which Wolfe has digitally enhanced about one third of the pictures. He claims it to be art while his critics call it fake documentation.

36   Søren Kjørup argues in "Billedmanipulation: Og den indexikalske teori om fotografiet," in *Mediegleder: Et festskrift til Peter Larsen*, ed. Jostein Gripsrud (Oslo: Ad Notam Gyldendal, 1993), 161–74, against the marking of manipulated images since this might support unrealistic beliefs in the evidential power of other images.

37   The importance of authenticity was strongly emphasized in a personal interview with John Langley, the executive producer of *Cops* (March 4, 1997). The same attitude was expressed by Andrew Jebb, the producer of *LAPD*, in a personal interview (March 3, 1997). It is interesting to note that Jebb gave a substantially lower estimate of the amount of "B-roll" (footage that is not authentic) used than his coworkers did in a less formal meeting (same date). This illustrates the importance for these producers to underline the "realness" of their products.

38   The proliferation of digitized imagery in advertising does not seem to affect our trust in documentary discourses too much. But when more of the discourses involving photographic images come to involve digital techniques, I believe our general trust might be affected—and eventually also our way of relating to documentary photography.

39   Bazin, *What is Cinema?* 1: 14.

40   Ibid.

41   Roland Barthes, *Camera Lucida: Reflections on Photography* (New York: Hill and Wang, 1981), 3.

42   Jean Baudrillard talks in *Simulacra and Simulations* (Ann Arbor: The University of Michigan Press, 1994) about a "[p]anic-stricken production of the real and of the referential" when the simulacrum replaces referential discourses (7).

43   Roman Jakobson, "Linguistics and Poetics," in *Modern Criticism and Theory: A Reader*, ed. David Lodge (London: Longman, 1988), 32–61.

44   As Vivian Sobchack says in "Inscribing Ethical Space: Ten Propositions On Death, Representation, and Documentary," *Quarterly Review of Film Studies* 9, no. 4 (1984),

> nonbeing is not visible. It lies over the threshold of visibility and representation. Thus, it can only be pointed to . . . The classic 'proof' of the excess of death over its indexical representation was the fascination exerted by the Zapruder film of John Kennedy's assassination; played again and again, slowed down, stopped frame by frame, the momentum of death escaped each moment of its representation (287).

Nonetheless, as Bill Nichols indicates in *Blurred boundaries: Questions of meaning in contemporary culture* (Bloomington: Indiana University Press, 1994), we don't give up: "at death's door, we find documentary endlessly, and anxiously, waiting. It hovers, fascinated by a border zone it cannot ever fully represent" (48).

45 *Reality show* is in fact the better term, whereas *experiment TV* is more fitting for the recent vogue of experiment formats like *Big Brother*. Both terms suggest more precisely what is at stake in the formats. I argue this at greater length in "Det kannibalske øje: virkelighetsshow, eksperimentfjernsyn og den nye kreativitet i fjernsynsunderholdningen," *MedieKultur* 34, 2002, 14–27.

46 Kevin Robins, "The Virtual Unconscious in Postphotography," in *Electronic Culture: Technology and Visual Representation*, ed. Timothy Druckrey (New York: Aperture, 1996), 159.

47 Kevin Robins, *Into the Image: Culture and Politics in the Field of Vision* (London: Routledge, 1996), 121–22.

48 Ibid.

49 Documentaries address issues of crime in quite another way than does reality TV. It can be useful to compare the representation of crime in *Cops* and *LAPD* to that offered in PBS *Frontline* documentaries like *Snitch* (Ofra Bikel 1999), *Drug Wars* (Martin Smith and Lowell Bergman 2000), *Real Justice* (Ben Gale and Ben Loeterman 2000) and *LAPD Blues* (Michael Kirk and Rick Young 2001). A comparison could, for example, focus on differences in the information projected, on the level of generality of the claims made, on the role of stereotypes, and on attitudes toward the police and those who are arrested (see http:// www.pbs.org/wgbh/pages/frontline/programs/categories/c.html for more details on the documentaries mentioned).

50 See John Corner, *Television Form and Public Address* (London: Edward Arnold, 1995) and *The Art of Record: A Critical Introduction to Documentary* (Manchester: Manchester University Press, 1996); and Richard Kilborn, "Shaping the Real: Democratization and Commodification in UK Factual Broadcasting," *European Journal of Communication* 13, no. 2 (June 1998), 201–18, for discussions on how commercial pressures and "reality" orientation affects current documentary production. It is also worth posing the question whether the ideology of reality TV has contributed to a stricter view of what should be admitted in documentary filmmaking resulting in fines to U.K. filmmakers for "breach of public trust." See Brian Winston, *Lies, Damn Lies and Documentaries* (London: BFI Publishing, 2000). We need an even fuller assessment of this, and also of how the logic of reality TV bleeds into news and wildlife programming.

Chapter 35

JON DOVEY

CAMCORDER CULTS

[. . .]

THE USE OF MATERIAL GENERATED through [camcorder and surveillance] technologies by network TV has contributed significantly to the institutionalisation of [. . .] new privatised, localised and embodied modes of address [in documentary].

First of all, the low grade video image has become *the* privileged form of TV 'truth telling', signifying authenticity and an indexical reproduction of the real world; indexical in the sense of presuming a direct and transparent correspondence between what is in front of the camera lens and its taped representation. Secondly, the camcorder text has become the form that most relentlessly insists upon a localised, subjective and embodied account of experience. Finally, the video text has become the form that represents better than any other the shifting perimeters of the public and the private. Video texts shot on lightweight camcorders uniquely patrol, re-produce and penetrate the boundaries between the individual subject and the public, material world.

Video, technology and cultural form

This reading of video texts is part of a wider discussion of the relationships between technology and cultural form. The 'common sense' history of these developments is that the proliferation of new low gauge videotape formats (previously V8, Hi8, S-VHS and now the various low gauge digital formats) in easy-to-shoot camcorder form aimed at the domestic consumer has 'caused' an explosion of new video based forms of TV; in other words a technologically determined account of video-based cultural forms. This explanation reproduces the conventional accounts of the development of Direct Cinema in the late 1950s and early 1960s. Such accounts privilege the development of lightweight 16mm cameras with crystal sync audiotape recorders that together facilitated a newly mobile practice for film-makers.[1]

The argument here runs that the sudden further miniaturisation of the means of the production of broadcast quality images has revived the project of the Direct Cinema pioneers to 'capture' a raw unmediated reality. Ricky Leacock, speaking in 1961, describes the problem of Direct Cinema as being 'How to convey the feeling of being there.'[2] – superficially this 'feeling of being there' might be taken as the code of camcorder culture.

However, this simple explanation, that technology equals cultural form, does not tell the whole story – either in the case of Direct Cinema or in the contemporary profile of the camcorder documentary. In the case of the historical parallel of Direct Cinema the technology argument fails to address why those particular film texts were chosen as possible subjects by producers during the 1960s. Lightweight technology of itself could conceivably have had a near infinity of possible applications; there was nothing intrinsic to the technology that predetermined that [documentary film maker Don] Pennebaker would create the 'rockumentary' or that [Frederick] Wiseman would examine American institutions. Particular films were chosen for specific historical reasons which had as much to do with markets and funding, and hence with wider cultural currents, as with mere technology. It would be fruitful for instance to pursue an analysis that linked the Direct Cinema claim to 'get behind the scenes' of reality in the political and cultural spheres, in films like *Primary*, or *Meet Marlon Brando*,[3] with the first stirring of a wider cultural awareness that reality itself was being pre-packaged, managed and directed into a series of 'scenes' through the diffusion of mass media by the end of the 1950s.

Similarly in the case of the camcorder – the spread of low gauge video-based forms of programming on mainstream TV occurs within a cultural context that determines the ends to which technology will be put. In this case miniaturisation and mobility appear to have the effect not of effacing the presence of the film-maker (as in Direct Cinema) but of emphasising it. The contemporary video document is often nothing *but* an inscription of presence within the text. Everything about it, the hushed whispering voiceover, the incessant to-camera close-up, the shaking camera movements, the embodied intimacy of the technical process, appears to reproduce experiences of subjectivity. We feel closer to the presence and the process of the film-maker. This presence has taken on precisely structured forms, has begun to develop its own grammar.

Nonetheless, the technology itself has not determined the stress on subjectivity expressed through video documentary forms. These expressions of subjectivity are to be found across a range of media (print journalism, literature, the Web) and are not exclusive to the technologies of video, film or the medium of TV. It is rather that the regime of truth generated by and for contemporary western culture *requires* subjective, intimate, exposing expression as dominant form. The camcorder has technical characteristics that lend themselves to this work – we have witnessed the emergence of a medium whose time has come.

In further evidence against the commonsense argument of pure technological determinism, it is also worth nothing that low gauge, lightweight, easy-to-use video technologies have actually been circulating since Sony first marketed the half-inch reel-to-reel video system to domestic consumers in 1964. Whilst it is true that none of the pre-1990 systems approached the combination of ease of use and broadcast quality imaging that is now available, nevertheless an enormous variety of video-based texts was produced by artists and documentarists who were fascinated by the relaxed, domestic, intimate and confessional styles that video seemed to offer.[4] However, crucially, none of this work achieved dominance in popular culture – indeed the gates of mainstream TV were kept firmly locked against such strange incursions from the margins which would have wholly threatened the impartial, balanced, objective regime of factual TV. The situation now is almost entirely reversed, with the former regime of balance and impartiality squeezed into quality threshold ghettos of the schedules by an explosion of wobblyscope TV. My point is that this change is not purely technological in character. Such texts have been circulating in 'alternative channels' for more than two decades, but it was not until the 1990s that they became part of mainstream TV.

Video virus

For commentators like me, involved with the cultures of video since the 1970s, TV's sudden viral contamination by camcorder and surveillance footage is startling. In the UK major primetime network programmes such as *You've Been Framed*, *Video Diaries*, *Undercover Britain*, *Emergency 999*, *Private Investigations*, *Horizon*, *Video Nation*, *Living With the Enemy*, *Caught on Camera* have all been based on the use of low-gauge camcorders or even smaller fibre optic-based minicams. Nor have the effects of the technology been confined to major TV projects. Camcorder footage has infiltrated itself into every corner of TV: *This Morning*'s Richard and Judy invited us to send in home videos of our ghastly domestic interiors for ritual humiliation and decor advice; kids' shows like *Alive and Kicking* or *As Seen On TV* invite children to submit homemade tapes; corporations like General Accident and Radion spent thousands on reproducing camcorder style for use in their advertising campaigns.

It is necessary to identify how camcorder cultures more generally have impacted upon TV production and to think about the kinds of televisual forms that have developed. Looking across the schedules of UK network TV in the mid-1990s, low-gauge video recordings formed a substantial part of four categories of programming: those based on happenstance amateur footage, surveillance derived programmes, covert 'camera in a bag' investigative films, and self-made diary projects.

In the first category of happenstance video, the 'lucky recording', the long running and amazingly successful *You've Been Framed* and *America's Funniest Home Videos* are the most obvious examples of video 'reality slap-stick'. The contemporary update of *Candid Camera* with the crucial and telling difference that there the gags were all staged, carefully setup situations to exploit the innocent victim – now these programmes rely upon video clips whose authenticity is guaranteed by the appearance of being happenstance 'accidental' recordings. This appearance of the lucky recording is of course carefully maintained; shows like this have very weak narrative structures relying upon a succession of very short clips in which the context of the events depicted is absent. Although we are encouraged to send in our clips for a small cash fee, many of the clips screened are acquired on an international market that exists for this kind of material. This market in effect functions as a kind of cartel through which video pratfalls circulate on a global scale. Video slapstick programmes, more than any other, have led to audiences becoming familiar with the exhibition of domestic video recordings in the mass media TV context.

Happenstance camcorder tapes are also the basis of the darker accident- and disaster-based genre of reality programme. Programmes like *Caught on Camera, Disaster*, and many of the growing natural disaster programmes like *The Wonders of Weather*, rely upon camcorder clips sent in by 'amateurs' or participants in the events portrayed. One of the distinguishing features of programmes like this, in common with other video reality work, is the way in which the narrative structure of the programme is skewed to rely on the video clip. Whereas in a conventional documentary structure actuality footage is used as evidential context in support of an argument or narrative, here the actuality passes beyond evidence linked to some wider signifying pattern to being the *raison d'être* for the whole programme. The voyeuristic gaze threatens to overwhelm the narrative structure of the conventional documentary. The video clip is more reality fetish than evidence, as it is replayed over and over, slowed down, grabbed, processed, de- and re-constructed for our entertainment and horror. The video clip here stands for a reality (of horror) that cannot be known but which must at the same time be contained. As Bill Nichols writes: 'A fascination with that which exceeds the grasp prepares the way for fetishism.'[5]

Video recordings of a different kind form the basis for programmes like *Police Camera Action*, *Crimewatch, America's Most Wanted* and the video chart-topper *Police Stop Video*. Here the emphasis is on the re-use of police or security guard generated surveillance materials. Whilst the *Crimewatch*-type programmes rely largely upon the static point of view of the surveillance camera, other programmes in this genre use a variety of different mobile cameras, such as from helicopters, in car, and hand-held, to tell their tales of miscreants successfully brought to book.

In the US these genres are more highly developed. The news tabloids like *Hard Copy* and *A Current Affair* will screen camcorder footage sent in by 'amateurs', and include both disaster and 'true life' crime stories within their purview. This has led to the growth of a whole sector of semi-professional camcorder news journalists (a.k.a. ambulance chasers), who keep their scanners tuned to the emergency services frequencies and their camcorders on standby in the hope of recording images they can sell either to network or local tabloid news programmes. Local stations in the US pay between $35 and $150 an item but with syndication and always the chance of a scoop semi-pro video journalists see the opportunity to make money. Reginald Blumfield taped a murder at the start of the LA riots, got himself a media lawyer and sold the footage to *A Current Affair* for $12,000.[6]

Undercover and covert video taping forms the basis for another substantial strand of UK factual TV. Channel Four's *Undercover Britain* and Granada's *Disguises* are substantial investigative network programmes that use reporters going 'undercover' in role, with hidden camcorders or minicams to gather incriminating evidence of the film's subjects. Bad landlords, exploitative employers, slaughterhouses, doctors, all have fallen victim to the video entrapment approach. Like programmes which rely upon surveillance footage, such films have raised numerous ethical questions to do with consent and fair dealing with their subjects. However, they are based on what appears to be a compulsive paradox (to which I will return in the discussion of pornography that appears below) – journalistic set-ups and scams are shown to reveal an essential 'truth' about some otherwise hidden aspect of society. The combination of voyeurism and public service righteousness that they elicit has so far proved an unassailable *de facto* argument for the continued development of such shows. [. . .]

The self-made documentary portrait has been one of the biggest 'growth' areas on TV facilitated by the camcorder. *Video Diaries* was originally developed as an access programme for 'ordinary members of the public' by the BBC's Community Programmes Unit but has been widely imitated.[7] Travelogues, music shows, feature films, all have succumbed to the apparent charm, simplicity and authenticity of the self-made tape. The video diary is perhaps the most widely successful and immediately recognisable camcorder-based genre in popular culture. The 1998 season of BBC *Video Diaries* included films by a disabled Member of Parliament, an explorer's self-made account of crossing the Antarctic, the story of a mental health worker dealing with his own personal difficulties, a diary made by a journalist on the trail of kidnapped hostages in Kashmir and a diary made by a thirteen-year-old musical prodigy suffering from Asperger's syndrome. These programmes were all editorially controlled by the diarists – still the only space in UK broadcast where this is possible. The diarist is offered basic camera instruction – they go off and shoot anything between 10 and 200 hours of footage which is then cut back at the BBC in consultation with the diarist. Whereas in the past the 'access' principle revolved around the idea of excluded or marginalised groups, here it functions as a way of getting interesting and unusual individuals to tell their own stories in first person form. This is perhaps another example of a significant change, from group identification and affinity to individualised identity and paradox. I will return to the video diary text in more detail below.

Finally, the camcorder has had an impact on the already existing industry of factual TV production. The availability of broadcast quality miniature cameras is changing working practices. The physical effects of the apparatus within this model cannot be underestimated. Using an object not much bigger than a Walkman it is possible to produce broadcast quality image and sound. These changes immeasurably alter the dynamics of the social event of recording. The apparatus, including the usual two to four person crew, is less visible, reduced to a single person with a single object which is small enough to allow the operator's body and face to remain in visual and physical interactive contact with the subjects of the film. All documentaries are recordings not of the subjects or the 'pro-filmic events' but of the interactions between the apparatus, including the crew, and the subject. Here the quality of that interaction is fundamentally altered, from one predicated on a subject outnumbered and physically intimidated by the apparatus to one based upon a more equal footing. The quality of the resulting interaction is less formal, more casual, more like a chat with a friend than an audition or job interview. That is not to argue that either performance or power relations are transcended. The register of performance changes from a more public to a more private mode. Simply, it becomes more intimate. Power relations certainly change, but the fact remains that the formal aspects of the diary that contribute to a strongly embodied sense of authorial presence militate against the more equal status of the participants in the event.

The UK explorer and expeditionary Benedict Allen has revived a popular TV tradition of anthropological films with his camcorder-shot diary accounts of journeys in Africa, Mongolia and the Amazon. In his work there *is* a different quality to the recordings of indigenous peoples. In an episode with Mongolian nomadic peoples I was struck by the sense of their ease and familiarity with the recording apparatus. These are yurt dwellers, whose traditional dress is hybridised with western sunglasses or a Walkman, their nomadism these days just as likely to use a four-wheel-drive as a horse. There is at least the possibility of a complicity with the viewer in a mutual bemusement at the plight of the very British pukka presence with a camcorder in their lives – however, it is only Allen who finally holds the camera and speaks the narration.[8]

Mosaic Films' 1997 *United Kingdom* series is probably the clearest consistent example of these effects of the technology on existing 'mainstream' documentary practice. Mosaic appear to have commodified the camcorder for post-Sony industrial film production. They developed a production model in which 40 film-makers were paid tiny sums to go out and shoot footage (over which they would have no final editorial control) in a process designed to whittle the original 40 down to a manageable fifteen. Film-makers were paid in incremental tranches the longer they were able to retain their place in the competitive production process. The film-makers go out and, because of the low costs involved, are able to spend longer in the company of the subjects. The camcorder is here deployed as a research tool as well as production apparatus, so shooting is at a high ratio. The tapes are then sent back to 'base' and cut by highly experienced documentary editors. Many of the finally screened programmes were excellent pieces of observational film-making, in which the 'state of the nation' aspiration of the documentary project is revived. However, even in this restatement of the Direct Cinema tradition the different apparatus has shifted the ground – there is an intimacy between film-maker, subject and technology that has a different quality to a 16mm film-based production. The entire *mise-en-scène* is more casual, less formal, more fluid than even the handheld 16mm camera.

The kind of uses that TV makes of the camcorder add up to a new, popular visual demotic characterised by authenticity, fluidity, subjectivity and emotionalism. Forms of the written word display similar tendencies particularly where they are mediated online. Kevin Kelly, the editor of digital culture magazine *Wired*, observed of Internet writing in 1994,

> Thoughts tend toward the experiental idea, the quip, the global perspective, the inter-disciplinary synthesis, and the uninhibited, often emotional response. I-Way thought is modular, non linear, malleable, co-operative. Many participants prefer Internet writing to book writing as it is conversational, frank, and communicative rather than precise and over written.[9]

Kelly's description of the difference between book writing and Internet writing seems to me very close to the difference between conventionally structured factual TV and the emergent visual demotic of camcorder culture on TV. 'Conversational, frank and communicative', 'uninhibited, often emotional', these are also qualities that characterise the camcorder-based TV programme, particularly those based in the diaristic autobiographical format.

Zero degree simulation

These developments, both in quantity and quality, defy explanation within the terms defined for video criticism by commentators to date – nowhere in the admittedly limited academic exegesis of the cultures of video is an explanation for this phenomenon to be found.[10] The reasons for this absence are largely historical, in two senses. Firstly, that the majority of critical writing about video was done at a time when video practice retained its marginal, alternative and crucially 'new' character. The peak period of these 'alternative' cultures of video, the late 1970s to the late 1980s, was also the period of the first articulations of the moment of postmodernism. The quality of writing about video has been deeply implicated within both the idea of the 'new' and within emergent debates around postmodernism. Secondly, in the sense that video is no longer a 'new' media technology – its position at the experimental forefront of media development has been taken by digital media and the emergence of cybercultures. When 'new' media replace existing media then the latter have a tendency to find definition in language and form as all the apparent possibilities of being 'new' get foreclosed. This is precisely the case of video in the 1990s. Video was a 'new' technology for 20 years. All kinds of uses were made of it during this time, none of them becoming dominant mainstream applications. Much of the same extraordinary fluidity of possible form is currently manifest in digital cultures whereas video culture appears to have solidified around a set of practices characterised by extreme indexicality in signification, intimacy and exposure.

The points made by Frederic Jameson in his chapter on video in *Post-modernism, or, The Cultural Logic of Late Capitalism* (Verso, 1991) are crucial in this respect, not because they offer us a direct explanation for the 'success' of the video text in the 1990s, but on the contrary because of the way they signally fail to do so. For Jameson the 'medium I have in mind as the most likely candidate for cultural hegemony today . . . is clearly video, in its twin manifestations as commerical television and experimental video, or "video art" '. Leaving aside for a moment the somewhat confusing elision of video into commercial television, Jameson goes on to conclude,

> Now reference and reality disappear altogether, and even meaning – the signified – is problematized. We are left with that pure and random play of signifiers that we call postmodernism, which no longer produces monumental works of the modernist type but ceaselessly reshuffles the fragments of pre-existent texts, the building blocks of older cultural and social production, in some new and heightened bricolage: metabooks which cannibalize other books, metatexts which collate bits of other texts – such is the logic of post modernism in general, which finds one of its strongest and most original, authentic forms in the new art of experimental video.[11]

Significantly this conclusion is based on a textual analysis of a 1979 tape called *AlienNATION* which was heavily based in bricolage, collage and a distinctive style of video montage that combined seemingly random borrowings from mainstream TV images combined with self-generated footage. Throughout the 1980s video art works relied heavily upon postproduction, upon editing for their effects – this was partly at least technology driven.[12] During this period comparatively sophisticated video editing equipment became available outside of the institutions of TV production for the first time. A powerful strand of video art relied upon postproduction as a way of deconstructing and providing meta-commentary on TV 'flow'. Whilst some of this work did indeed make its point by having none, by demonstrating *in extremis* how TV rendered invisible the 'referent and reality itself' there was also a significant body of work (my own included) which deconstructed TV in order to reconstruct alternative 'counter-hegemonic' positions.[13]

However, by the beginning of the 1990s the cycle of production possibilities had moved on and we can observe video texts returning to optically based practices, to the production of work that was based in pointing a camera at a 'referent' in the real world. This is of course partly due to the increasing availability of camcorders, but also perhaps due to exhaustion with the surface pleasures of postmodern media and a desire to find meaning in first person, viscerally indexical representations; to create meanings based in real worlds of competing, subjective, embodied experience.

In the context of Jameson's analysis the rash of video reality texts of the 1990s can be seen in two ways. Either, as I have implied above, as a reaction *against* the loss of referentiality that characterised 'high postmodernism' and a flight into the specific localised meanings of an individually experienced subjectivity. Alternatively it may be possible to extend Jameson's cosmology: 'the referent', he writes, 'or the objective world, or reality . . . still continue to entertain a feeble existence on the horizon like a shrunken star or red dwarf'. In these terms the contemporary dominance of video realities represents a final efflorescence, an ultimate supernova explosion of referentiality before its slow digital degradation into virtual half-life.

It is clear that far from a 'pure and random play of signifiers' camcorder and surveillance video tapes have become the pre-eminent signs of an indexical truthfulness. When we see the 'amateur video' caption on broadcast news we are meant to understand amateurishness as guarantor of truth, in the sense of being 'unmediated' raw data, 'captured' outside of the usual institutional procedures of news production. In this usage 'amateur' comes to mean somehow more truthful than the unlabelled 'professional'. The appeal of the 'wobblyscope' video text is surely that it *appears* to cut through the institution of the simulacrum (whilst at the same time taking its place in its palette of textures). This sense of video as reality text resonates through its many different TV manifestations.

If we accept for the time being that this sense of 'the authentic' is part of viewer response to video texts it is worth considering for a moment how this sense has been derived. Where and how do we experience video in our daily lives? Because video has a profile outside of broadcast TV it must carry with it some characteristics of this identity when it 'crosses over' into the mass medium. In this context I want to discuss domestic camcorder use, surveillance and pornography.

Reality porn

The pleasures of the camcorder begin in the private, domestic domain with the intimate and subjective experience of the 'closed circuit'. When we encounter camcorder footage on TV the memory of the domestic home movie context is an active part of our reception. This connotation brings certain qualities to the image, signified by its actual texture and form: grainy, badly lit, wobbly, with poor sound.

The fact that the camcorder footage can be replayed immediately (as opposed to analogue stills or Super 8) has a major effect on the way that video is used in the home. No sooner have the last *vol-au-vents* been consigned to the bin after the christening than the kids have got the video of the day's events in the VCR and the whole event is replayed for the entertainment of the immediate participants. The video is both an authenticating part of the whole process as well as an entertainment in its own right. The pleasures of domestic camcorder culture are all about defining our own individual family identities around a TV screen that usually pumps out bland, homogenised otherness; representations of other lives and other families that could never match the specific delights afforded by our own personalised, intimate, closed circuit production. The pleasures of identification more than make up for the technical failures and lack of narrative coherence of the home movie.

What is on offer here is first person rather than third person, 'us-ness' rather than 'otherness', me as opposed to them. The important quality here is subjectivity. The camera is actually an accepted part of the event itself: it is not outside, controlling and structuring, in the way a stills photographer might orchestrate a scene, it is inside the action, part of the flow, both provoking events and recording them.

My argument is that our experience of the domestic context is surely part of how we respond to the low-gauge video image when it appears on TV. It is somehow more friendly than the high-gloss image of the usual TV style more intimate, less pretentious, more comfortable in all its obvious failings.[. . .]

Added to this sense of informality is the quality of indexical accuracy derived from our experience of video as a mechanism of surveillance. In addition to our domestic familiarity with video we are also familiar with it as surveillance from our own everyday experience of the ubiquitous CCTV systems. At a theoretical level Mark Poster has elaborated a concept of the 'Super Panopticon' in which we all become willing participants in a complex web of different orders of surveillance processes.[14] This hypothesis is empirically backed up by the research that has been undertaken into public attitudes toward CCTV systems.[15] Such studies appear to show that by and large we have bought the idea that 'only the guilty have anything to fear', that we trust public authorities' use of surveillance technologies, and therefore by extension that we trust the reliability of the evidence which they produce. We have an investment in the process of social surveillance.

At one level this trust is extraordinary. Extraordinary in the sense that citizens do not object to such unprecedented visual surveillance on the grounds of civil liberties but also extraordinary in the sense that the quality of the visual images produced by video surveillance is so poor. Compared to, say, a 35mm slide the resolution and discernible detail from a surveillance camera is appalling. Equally we have enough evidence to know that surveillance systems don't always prevent crime, but can displace it. However, we also have the memory of powerful and disturbing images produced by surveillance whose association is sheer terror. Such images range from the everyday crime and violence featured in Reality TV to the recordings taken of the abduction of Jamie Bulger in the UK or the shooting of Latasha Harlins that preceded the King verdict riots in Los Angeles in 1992. The power, significance and 'truthfulness' of surveillance images have embedded themselves in the cultural body with the force of image sequences that have become immensely powerful signifiers of urban terror.

The trust that we appear to place in such systems may also connect with our sense of them as indexical image-machines employed in the service of the logic of social administration rather than in either their efficacy or accuracy. *Der Riese* (Michael Klier, 1984, Germany, 73 mins) is a feature-length documentary film made up entirely of footage from surveillance cameras. It makes an extraordinary portrait of the objects of surveillance in our society and by extension of its disciplinary structures. Places of public transportation, open public spaces like malls, anywhere in which money changes hands, anywhere in which private property is to be protected. What the surveillance cameras reveal is the interconnected disciplinary strands of social administration enforced within a regime of sight. *Der Riese* locates CCTV surveillance as an intrinsic part of the fabric of social control, suggesting how its role in social administration creates credibility for its evidential status.

The other crucial aspect revealed by this film is the machinic quality of the images. When the camera moves, it moves in a way that is more robotic than human, in a series of right-angled lurches and scans. Moreover the surveillance camera records in real time, continuous takes with no cuts, machine time itself, in a direct correspondence not only to the objects which it registers but also to clock time, signified by the date and time running continuously in the frame. These mechanical aspects of the surveillance camera suggest that perhaps the spread of surveillance imagery is a restatement of earlier notions about the essential truthfulness of mechanical image production.[16]

These aspects of the surveillance image – its association with disturbing images, its implication in the maintenance of social order, its mechanical qualities – create the notion of its indexicality and accuracy. Using the force of these associations producers have discovered that given the right packaging surveillance footage can make compelling TV. [. . .] [The] contexts of domesticity and surveillance are both in play in the way that the video text works on TV.

These contexts at first appear mutually incompatible. The domestic use of video signifying intimacy, embodied subjectivity; in contrast surveillance video is precisely *dis*embodied, objective. Yet it seems to me that it is exactly this combination that lends the camcorder programme its force. When I look at these shows I am recruited to the process of surveillance in its 'super panopticon' sense, positioned like the security guard or the cop behind the bank of monitors as patriarchal authority, *as well as* engaged by the pleasures of voyeurism. By voyeurism I mean here the pleasure of seeing that which was not meant to be seen or that which has been previously *unseen*. The combination of quasi-scientific accuracy and voyeuristic pleasure is compelling.

Processes of pleasure and desire can no longer be excluded from the discussion of factual TV or documentary. This is more than just acknowledging that such texts are now produced as part of the 'infotainment' business. The combinations of intimacy and indexicality that I have described above create a particular form of video voyeurism in which powerful pleasures and fears are stirred, pleasures and fears which seem to suggest pyschoanalytically inflected modes of interpretation rather than more conventional approaches to documentary studies.

A clue to understanding how these processes operate might be found in the amateur video pornography market that took off in the wake of camcorder availability. Accurate statistics on the size of this market are understandably hard to come by. The *Guardian* newspaper quoted the business magazine *US News and World Report*, stating that the US porn market was worth more than $8 billion in 1996.[17] In the same piece the author Alix Sharkey asserts that 'amateur' porn constitutes 25 per cent of all the hard core videotapes in circulation. The alt.culture website 'amateur porn' page suggests that the amateur market is worth $3 billion a year (Dec. 1998). Whatever the precise scale of the genre it is clear that home-made pornography has made a massive impact on the sex trade. There appear to have been two aspects to this impact: firstly, people from outside the industry using their camcorders to record sexual activity for pleasure and profit, the authentic 'real thing'; secondly, a whole new sub-genre of professionally made tapes that seek to emulate the amateur feel of the first category. (Just like developments on mainstream TV, for every minute of genuine happenstance shock video there are ten minutes of reconstructed packaged imitation.)

Pornographic narratives have always sought to engage the user through a semblance of realism. We are invited to participate in a fantasy that has some everyday, credible basis before the sex actually begins. The text acknowledges the necessity of a realist starting point for the fantasy to work. Then the performers are paid to make the sex look 'real' – to act particularly coded versions of genuine pleasure and arousal. So 'realism' has always had a significant role in pornographic narrative and, perhaps, by extension, in sexual fantasy.

This is at once obvious and paradoxical. Narrative and fantasy both require a credible, realist point of identification before taking the viewer off into impossible fantasy fulfilment. They must be both 'real' and 'unreal'. In the case of pornography it is also necessary to consider what role power plays. Power, domination, subjection and pleasure are intimately linked in porn. The simplest analysis suggests that the (male) viewer assumes sexual empowerment through identification with the narrative. This identification appears to be strengthened by the amateur porn text – here the 'actors' are giving up, of their own volition, their sexual experience for your sexual pleasure. The ironic distances negotiated by our suspension of disbelief in the clearly fictional porn fantasy are here foreshortened through the grammar of subjective identification created by the video text. In this context the scopophilic pleasures of the 'real' become undeniable – enormous numbers of men are paying for intensified sexual pleasure by buying porn that advertises itself not as weak narrative fantasy but as reality itself.

This pleasure is a powerful, residual part of the many interpretative equations that we enter into across the range of 'realist' texts. I cite the case of amateur porn because such pleasures are here at their most clear – however, I would argue that voyeurism is an important part of my pleasure in all kinds of factual programming and documentary film-making. With some notable exceptions this field of pleasure has been excluded from discussion of factual media,[18] appearing, if at all, at the margin of the 'discourses of sobriety' as that which must be repressed and resisted if the mission of public service media is to survive. Yet, [. . .] to deny the significance of pleasure, desire and voyeurism in the dynamic of contemporary factual media appears like a wilfully mistaken blind spot.

Pleasure, voyeurism and sex have their own particular roles in the history of video technology. This is obvious at a commonsense, everyday level. Domestic video cameras have a habit of finding their way into the bedroom at some point. If a camera is brought into an uninhibited social group, sexual innuendo will almost certainly be one of the discourses it generates. The first Sony domestic video system was marketed as 'The Creepy Peepy' – a kind of mass-market miniaturised *Peeping Tom* sales pitch. In one of the first TV ads for the product a middle-aged man appears against a black background with a seven- or eight-year-old and the equipment set up. 'Sing,' he commands and the little girl duly obliges. 'Are you ready to see yourself now?' 'Sure, Daddy' – the child's entry into language under the control of the patriarchal technology could hardly be more clear. This is territory more fully explored in Atom Egoyan's *Family Viewing* (Canada, 1987, 86 mins) in which the teenage protagonist's father is erasing footage of the absent mother with images of him having sex with his new lover, Freud's 'primal scene' literally erasing the (video) presence of the mother. Van, the teenager, obsessively replays the home movies of his mother in an attempt to revisit the lost plenitude of mother love. In an echo of Freud's Oedipal account of the father the final video image of the lost mother through a window is literally cut off from the audience by Van's father walking in front of the lens. *Family Viewing* is part of a tradition of cinematic accounts of the camera as object of phallic power that begins with *Peeping Tom* (dir. Michael Powell, UK, 1960, 106 mins). Here the murderer, Mark, has been brought up only by his father who conducted sadistic psychic experiments on his son which were all recorded on film. Again these flashback sequences imply the primal scene of adult sex. Mark as a little boy is filmed by his father watching lovers on a park bench. Here the camera has become an object of sadistic phallic power – Mark uses the home movie camera as a murder weapon, adapting it to unleash a blade at his victims, thus ensuring that their last terrorised moments are recorded. In *sex, lies and videotape* (Steven Soderbergh, 1989, USA, 100 mins) the James Spader hero, Graham, is impotent, gaining sexual satisfaction from the confessions he elicits from women with his Hi8 camera. In *Sliver* (Philip Noyce, 1993, USA, 100 mins) the lead male character is a voyeur who has had the entire apartment block wired so that it becomes a private surveillance theatre of intimacy, desire and transgression. The connection between male dysfunction and the phallic camera is underscored in these films through the astonishing frequency of unresolved mother/son relationships in their plot lines. Van's mother in *Family Viewing* has mysteriously disappeared in his childhood,

Mark's mother in *Peeping Tom* died in his infancy, the hero of *Sliver* could only relate to his mother, a 'soap' star, through the TV screen. Here then the desire to 'capture' reality is configured as an attempt to neutralise the Oedipal fears aroused by separation from the mother.

My point is that the pleasures of voyeurism are closely tied to the success of the video reality text on mainstream TV, that along with my understanding of video as a medium of intimacy and an accurate surveillance machine I take voyeuristic pleasure in seeing other people's 'real' sex represented, and that some of the same drive is involved in seeing other people's 'real' beatings, crimes, medical traumas, emotional confessions, exposures and so on. In this Freudian reading the drive to feel 'connected' to reality through the video image rehearses the compulsion and repulsion cycle of the Oedipal process.

This ambivalent cycle of desire and repulsion is central; when watching camcorder- or surveillance-based texts I often find myself experiencing that cycle of desire and dissatisfaction which constitutes the attenuated pleasures of pornography. In Nichols's words,

> Ambivalence derives from the dependence on the other for a sense of identity which, in its imaginary coherence or autonomy, denies the centrality of the other upon whom it is dependent. In pornography this ambivalence involves a paradoxical desire for a pleasure that is not one, is not fully available. Pornography sets out to please but not please entirely. It affords pleasure but not the pleasure that is (only) represented. The pleasure that is represented remains deferred, perhaps indefinitely, in favour of its (fetishistic) representation. The result is a gendered viewing subject caught up in a desire for this oscillatory pleasure *per se*. The completion of desire is deferred in favour of perpetuating a set of staged representations of desire (for more pornography).[19]

If, to paraphrase, pornography works by offering the viewer unobtainable desire, what is on offer when the video text produces images of deviance, everyday accident, horror and 'human interest' stories? The documentary text has traditionally operated by 'othering' and exoticising its subjects, in a cycle of desire for possession and marking of difference. The psychic charge of the intimacy-producing videocamera reproduces simultaneously the desire for possession as well as the marking of difference. 'Look at that! Thank goodness that's not me!' Desire for the real is bound up with a repulsion from what is not 'normal' or safe.

I have been arguing that the video text on TV in its contemporary form is characterised by associations of intimacy, a perception of accuracy and patterns of voyeuristic pleasure. [. . .] The camcorder [. . .] video text [. . .] is a document from a domestic habitat, indexical surveillance and a voyeuristic experience. [. . .] The video text uses these charateristics [. . .] to reflect on a fundamental cultural development: how to make a public voice for the individual private subject.
[. . .]

Notes

1   See, for example, Erik Barnouw, *Documentary: The History of Non-Fiction Film*, 2nd edition (Oxford University Press, 1983).
2   Richard Leacock quoted in Brian Winston, *Claiming the Real* (British Film Institute, 1995), p. 149.
3   For example, *Primary*, dir. Richard Leacock (1960) and *Meet Marlon Brando*, dir. Maysles Brothers (1965).
4   See Michael Renov, 'Video confessions' in Erika Suderburg and Michael Renov (eds), *Resolutions: Contemporary Video Practices* (University of Minnesota Press, 1996).
5   Bill Nichols, *Blurred Boundaries* (Indiana University Press, 1994), p. 73.
6   Fenton Bailey, 'Neighbourhood Watch', *TV WEEK* (11 September 1992).
7   See Jon Dovey, 'Old dogs and new tricks' in Tony Dowmunt (ed.), *Channels of Resistance* (British Film Institute, 1994), pp. 163–74.

8   Benedict Allen, *The Edge of Blue Heaven*, BBC, 1998.
9   Kevin Kelly, *Guardian*, 20 June 1994.
10 For example, Doug Hall and Sally Jo Fifer (eds), *Illuminating Video* (Aperture, 1991); Frederic Jameson, *Post Modernism, or, The Cultural Logic of Late Capitalism* (Verso, 1991); Sean Cubitt, *Videography* (Macmillan, 1993) and *Timeshift* (Routledge, 1991); Mike Wayne, *Theorising Video Practice* (Lawrence and Wishart, 1997); Suderburg and Renov, *Resolutions*; Ron Burnett, *Cultures of Vision: Images, Media and the Imaginary* (Indiana University Press, 1995); Julia Knight (ed.), *Diverse Practices* (University of Luton Press, 1996).
11 Frederic Jameson, *Postmodernism, or, The Cultural Logic Of Late Capitalism* (Verso, 1991), p. 96.
12 See George Barber's essay 'Scratch and after – Edit suit technology and the determination of style in video art' in Philip Hayward (ed.), *Culture, Creativity and Technology in the Late Twentieth Century* (John Libbey, 1991).
13 See, for example, *Death Valley Days*, Gorilla Tapes, 1984.
14 See Chapter 3 in Mark Poster, *The Mode of Information* (Polity, 1990).
15 See, for instance, T. Bennett and L. Gelsthorpe, *Public Attitudes Towards CCTV in Cambridge*, Report to Cambridge City Council (University of Cambridge Institute of Criminology, October 1998).
16 Winston, *Claiming the Real*, p. 254.
17 Alix Sharkey, 'The Land of the Free', *Guardian Weekend* (22 November 1997).
18 Bill Nichols, 'The ethnographer's tale' in *Blurred Boundaries* (Indiana University Press, 1994) and M. Renov, 'Towards a poetics of documentary' in *Theorising Documentary* (Routledge, 1993).
19 Bill Nichols, *Blurred Boundaries*, p. 74.

Bibliography

Barber, George, (1991) in Philip Hayward (ed.), *Culture, Creativity and Technology in the late Twentieth Century* (John Libby).
Barnouw, Erik, (1983) *Documentary: The History of Non-Fiction Film*, 2nd edition (Oxford University Press).
Burnett, Ron, (1995) *Cultures of Vision: Images, Media and the Imaginary* (Indiana University Press).
Cubitt, Sean, (1991) *Timeshift* (Routledge).
—— (1993) *Videography* (MacMillan).
Dovey, Jon, (1994) 'Old dogs and new tricks' in Tony Dowmunt (ed.), *Channels of Resistance* (British Film Institute).
Hall, Doug and Sally Jo Fifer, (1991) *Illuminating Video: An Essential Guide to Video Art* (Aperture).
Jameson, Frederic, (1991) *Postmodernism, or, The Cultural Logic of Late Capitalism* (Verso).
Knight, Julia (ed.), (1996) *Diverse Practices* (University of Luton Press).
McLuhan, Marshall and Quentin Fiore, (1967) *The Medium is the Message* (Penguin).
Nichols, Bill, (1994) *Blurred Boundaries* (Indiana University Press).
Poster, Mark, (1990) *The Mode of Information* (Polity).
Renov, Michael (ed.), (1993) *Theorising Documentary* (Routledge).
Suderburg, Erika, and Michael Renov (eds), (1996) *Resolutions: Contemporary Video Practices* (University of Minnesota Press).
Wayne, Mike, (1997) *Theorising Video Practice* (Lawrence and Wishart).
Winston, Brian, (1995) *Claiming the Real* (British Film Institute).

Chapter 36

WILL BROOKER

LIVING ON *DAWSON'S CREEK*
Teen viewers, cultural convergence, and television overflow

Introduction: audience attachments

A T THE TIME OF WRITING, I am a regular viewer of the BBC2 series *Attachments*, which is based around a fledgling dotcom company called Seethru.co.uk. After watching the episode where Soph is punished by her boss for her article 'Hell Is Other People Shagging', I went to the seethru.co.uk website, which treats Soph and her colleagues as 'real' people, with no mention of BBC2 or *Attachments*. On the front page I was able to read the full article, which could only be glimpsed in the actual episode. I then took part in a quiz compiled by Reece, the series' womanizing programmer, and sent a semi-ironic mail to the character pointing out that he'd misspelled a *Star Wars* reference. Following the Seethru links page took me to a site for the Tourette's Syndrome Barbie and another which featured photomontaged cartoons of Mr T versus Airwolf.

At what point, then, did the show 'end' for me? Technically, I stopped watching television at 9.45 pm, but I was engaging with the characters and narrative of the show for at least an hour afterwards, even to the point of sending a mail to a non-existent programmer. Was I still 'taking part' in *Attachments* when I followed the suggested links to Barbie and Mr T? If I revisit the site three evenings a week to check on developments – the bulletin boards, at least, are continually evolving – is it still appropriate to say that, for me, *Attachments* is only 'on' at 9pm on a Tuesday evening, on BBC2?

We are at a point where we have to reconsider what it means to engage with a television programme, to 'follow' a specific show. Already, shows such as *Attachments* – there are, as I shall discuss later, several other examples – present us with a situation where the text of the TV show is no longer limited to the television medium. We need a new word for the process, just as we had to settle on the term 'surfing' in the mid-1990s. In watching, experiencing, engaging, or living with *Attachments* as I do, I am witness to more than just the sometimes bizarre mélange of television flow which dazed Raymond Williams in the 1970s (Williams, 1974); indeed, I am not just a bewildered observer, but am becoming part of the broader text. *Attachments* has deliberately 'overflowed' the bounds of television, and through its simulacrum of a website has let itself merge into the vast diversity of the internet. And so my experience of its characters, situation, and plot has also become integrated with the sites I jump to from Seethru, the MP3s that its characters recommend, the discussions with 'real life' visitors I have on its bulletin board, and even the mail I received a few days later from 'Reece'.

Sites such as these raise important questions about the experience of watching television, and the concept of the television audience. To what extent has the nature of watching television changed due to dedicated websites that offer an immersive, participatory experience? To what extent does this participation depend on audience gender, ethnicity, age, and socioeconomic class? This article takes up these questions through a case study of the Warner Brothers television teen drama *Dawson's Creek* and its viewers.

Questions around convergence

The concept of 'overflow' can be linked to the notion of 'convergence', which emerged as a discourse in cultural studies during the late 1990s (see Jenkins, 1998). What I am discussing here is not technical convergence, the coming-together of various media forms – DVD, internet, TV, rewritable CD – in a single 'black box', but media and cultural convergence. As Henry Jenkins defines it, cultural convergence is associated with the practice of fans using numerous media at the same time, while media convergence implies producers marketing a text across various media platforms. Media convergence constitutes a 'structured interactivity', cultural convergence a participatory community. Media convergence implies cynical marketing strategies, cultural convergence a creative poaching (Jenkins, 2000). Jenkins comments wryly:

> Anyone who wants to see what [cultural] convergence looks like should visit my house and watch my adolescent son, sprawled on the living room rug, watching a baseball game on our big-screen television, listening to techno on his CD-player, and writing email to his friends or doing homework on his laptop.
>
> (Jenkins, 1998: n.p.)

Taking an institutional perspective, Susan Murray has described the ways in which 'post-network television and the New Hollywood' attempt to cross-market shows and movies to the teenage audience, using young stars as the link between different products. For instance, Warner Brothers included a lengthy promotion of the movie *Teaching Mrs Tingle* in the breaks between *Dawson's Creek* segments, based on their common star Katie Holmes (Joey), while Sarah Michelle Gellar was used in a similar 'media alliance' to promote the movie *Cruel Intentions* on the back of her starring role in *Buffy, the Vampire Slayer*. In the trailers for the new season of WB shows, characters from *Dawson's Creek* interacted with the cast of the less-established series *Charmed*. These alliances often expanded further, again using the star image to tie together diverse media forms; American Eagle was designated the 'official' clothing line for *Dawson's Creek*, while magazines such as *Teen People* were offered interviews with the shows' stars in another mutually-beneficial arrangement (Murray, 2000: n.p.).

The audience research which follows is framed by a number of points which arise from this existing work on convergence.

First, we should note that Jenkins' concept of convergence, illustrated by the anecdote about his son, clearly implies a certain level of privilege. Jenkins' son, according to the article, has his own laptop and CD-player, while the family owns a 'big-screen television'. It seems relevant to ask whether, for instance, a working class black teenager in south-east London has the same opportunities to practice cultural convergence.

Secondly, much of the *Dawson's Creek* official merchandise is intended for a North-American market. American Eagle and J. Crew clothes are not, to my knowledge, available in the UK, and it is worth asking how the availability of the spin-off product affects the level of participation in the wider discourse. The series itself is shown in the UK months after its US screening, and as part of Channel 4's mix-and-match Sunday morning schedules rather than in the coherent, heavily-branded flow of the WB network. This shift in context surely weakens any possibility of media alliance between *Dawson's Creek* and related WB shows – in the UK, *Buffy* is shown on BBC2 on Tuesday evenings and *Sabrina* on ITV's Saturday morning show *SM: TV*, while *Charmed* has a Saturday night slot on Channel 5, thus disrupting any sense of a cohesive WB package. The timelag, meanwhile, weakens any chance of intentional synchronization and cross-marketing between *Dawson's Creek* broadcasts and the release of a movie starring one of the show's actors such as *Go, Skulls, Teaching Mrs Tingle, Varsity Blues* or *Final Destination*. The 'top-down' structure of media convergence which WB seems cannily to build around *Dawson's Creek* in the US will, therefore, translate very differently to the UK audience.

Thirdly, we should consider the fact that, according to Murray, *Dawson's Creek* merchandise is aimed almost exclusively at girls; boys are not considered 'ancillary buyers', open to the promotion of associated merchandise (Murray, 2000: n.p.). The sponsorship of dawsonscreek.com's *Summer Diaries* by gilettegirlz.com, and Stayfree's extensive promotion of it'smybody.com on capeside.net would support this view of the show's intended audience.[1] An additional factor in this research, then, is the role of gender in shaping audience response to, and participation in, the wider culture of *Dawson's Creek*.

Fourthly, Jenkins' distinction between media and cultural convergence invites further analysis with reference to audience response. It could be argued that the official *Dawson's Creek* network, by linking to fan sites which in turn include fiction and song lyrics, problematizes Jenkins' strict division between owner-produced and fan-produced convergence. The official site itself could be seen to encourage creativity and community through its bulletin boards, 'slam books', and e-postcards, even if we bear in mind Murray's point (Murray, 2000: n.p.) that the site's in-house surveys are used to collect demographic information about viewers. On the other hand, perhaps these interactive forums and the generous links to fan pages merely suggest a sophisticated process of incorporation on the part of the producers. By providing bulletin boards and showcasting a token selection of fan artefacts, the WB site is, it could be argued, effectively keeping fans in its own playground and containing resistance by drawing 'folk' culture inside its corporate boundaries. We can begin to address this issue by asking viewers whether they engage solely with the 'official' secondary texts of *Dawson's Creek*, or whether – like the active fans of so many shows from *The X-Files* through *Batman* to *Starsky and Hutch* (see Brooker, 2000; Jenkins, 1992; Lavery et al., 1996) – they are still inspired to create their own.

Finally, I shall ask what the wider cultural discourse which constitutes *Dawson's Creek* implies for television studies in terms of convergence and overflow. Rather than watching *Buffy*, it now seems, the teenage viewer in particular is now invited to live *Buffy*, as the TV show is expanded beyond regular weekly episodes into a lifestyle experience. Rather than 'becoming' Buffy herself, the viewer is offered the place of Buffy's confidante, knowing the character intimately and immersing herself in the protagonist's life, just as the female viewer of *Dawson's Creek* is invited to place herself in the position of Dawson or Pacey's girlfriends: dressing the part, learning their secret passions, playing their favourite CDs, and inhabiting their environment. However we articulate the offered relationship, it is clear that this wider discourse has consequences for the way we study television.

The *Dawson's Creek* experience

A couple of clicks from the front page of the official show website, dawsonscreek.com, takes the visitor to capeside.net, which constructs a simulacrum of the show's fictional locale as if it were a real place with a web presence. This painstaking illusion is so rich in detail – banner advertisements for Screen Play video and the *Entre Nous* restaurant, library opening times, quotes from Bible classes at the Church of the Nazarene – that only the scattered appearance of character names like Dawson, Pacey, and Joey among the reviews and college articles marks it as anything other than a genuine tourist promotion.[2] Capeside.net is a virtual theme park built around the show; like Disney's Frontierland or a reconstructed Shaker village, the site draws its visitors into the *Dawson's Creek* Experience, letting them roam free in the characters' local area network.

In addition to this virtual tour of the show's location, dawsonscreek.com links to a 'slam book' where visitors are invited to fill in questions about themselves – ambitions, current crush, favourite movie – and pass the survey on to friends. Crucially, each slam book has already been filled in by the show's core characters, so that readers are immediately privy to the information that Pacey's ex-girlfriend, Andie McPhee, has read *The Story of O* and that Dawson considers *Helmets of Glory* the worst movie of all time. Again, the fan is drawn into a simulation; rather than merely reading about characters, she enjoys the illusion of participating in their lives and interacting with them as friends. Indeed, the 'Summer Diaries' feature, a Flash spin-off from the main site which, as the name suggests, offers access to the handwritten personal journals of Dawson and his crew, invites the visitor to catch up with 'your friends on Capeside', rather than admitting their status as fictional characters. Even when the series is over, then, the Capeside narrative continues; the internet permits the illusion that the characters have ongoing lives between episodes, and pulls it off convincingly.[3]

More conventionally, the internet visitor to dawsonscreek.com is offered e-postcards for mailing to friends, bulletin boards to discuss plot developments between episodes and online merchandising such as *Dawson's Creek* bucket hats and T-shirts.[4] Again, it seems significant that the Capeside High School T-shirts, which bear the fictional school's logo, are sold with a worn, 'distressed' finish; not only does the wearer effectively transform herself into a student at Dawson's school, but it immediately looks as if she and her shirt have an authentic history within the show.[5] In a further blurring of the boundaries between fan and character, the J.Crew clothing site is recommended by fans as the place to 'get the clothes they use on the show'; visitors to the online catalogue can pick out a capsule wardrobe of casual basics identical to Joey's or a check button-down shirt like Pacey's.[6] At least one newspaper article has already picked up on this crossover and run a feature on *Dawson's Creek* fashion, with advice on where to find lookalike outfits.[7]

The track listing of every song included in each episode also promotes a commitment to, and immersion in, the characters' world which goes beyond mere weekly viewing, however regular. To re-experience the soundtrack of episode 221, 'Ch-ch-ch-changes', for example, fans would have to buy seven different songs,[8] although the process is made more convenient through two official soundtrack albums. Again, in the break between shows or series, the viewer is encouraged to follow the characters' wider narrative through spin-off novels such as *Calm Before the Storm* and *Double Exposure*, marketed at US$4.99 from the WBStore.

Finally, the official WB website is canny enough to include links not just to its sister shows – *Buffy* features prominently – but also to fan pages, at least one of which has evolved into a small community with parodic song lyrics, satirical bulletin board comment, and archives of romantic fan fiction. *I Hate Jen*, named after the show's resident femme fatale, offers Jen's Theme Song – 'Oh, I'm just a girl, ruin everyone's life, I hate my Grams cause she hides my knives' – and encourages the visitor to contribute bitchy comments along the lines of 'do you ever wish that while Jen is biting her lip, she will one day bite too hard and her teeth will go right through her lips and get stuck like that forever?'[9]

In short, the *Dawson's Creek* fan may still find her key pleasures in the developing television narrative, but the TV show is clearly being marketed within a far wider multimedia context. While fans must return to this week's episode for reference, the show is apparently intended to serve as the starting point for further activity rather than as an isolated, self-contained cultural artefact. Instead of waiting for the next instalment, the fan is invited to extend the show's pleasures, to allow the show into her everyday life beyond the scheduling framework. Instead of a weekly, hour-long television episode, *Dawson's Creek* is constructed as an ongoing experience: watch the show again on video, join the bulletin board discussion, send Dawson e-postcards to a friend, read up on the series backstory in a US$5 novelization, go shopping for a blouse like Jen's, buy the song that was playing when Joey kissed Pacey, even write your own alternative ending and share it on a fan site.

The experience is there, for those viewers who have the technology and the inclination to immerse themselves in it. To reiterate, my audience research was designed to investigate the extent to which *Dawson's Creek* viewers actually follow the framework set up for them by WB, whether social factors affected their engagement, and whether they showed any signs of 'resistance' – in Jenkins' terms, an involvement in creative, homegrown cultural convergence, rather than simply lapping up the ready-made structures of media convergence around the show.

Research and findings

My research was based around two audience groups, who responded to the same survey. The first consisted of 27 American viewers, aged between 13 and 21 and attending college, junior high or high school in Maine. The entire American group, for reasons suggested below, was female. These participants were predominantly European-American, and came from what can broadly be identi-fied as a middle class family background: examples of their parents' profession included 'speech pathologists', 'doctor', 'lawyer', 'computer programmer and artist', 'accountants', 'financial advisers', 'computer analyst and school teacher', 'account manager and distribution manager for VW cars', and 'international business and interior decorator'.

This group of students spent an average of £20 on CDs, £50 on clothes and £10 on books per week. Three-quarters of them personally owned an internet-ready computer, and all but three had a mobile phone.

The second group comprises 40 viewers, aged between 12 and 18, from Kidbrooke School in south-east London. This group was half male, half female, more or less equally-divided between white, Asian, and black viewers, and the surveys suggest a predominantly working-class family background: 'loan collector and groundworker', 'salesman', 'fishmonger', 'army', 'dustwoman', 'fork truck driver', 'mum's fiancé works in insurance company', 'mum is a machienist [sic], dad works at a building site', 'dad electrtion [sic], mum carer', 'delivery man'.

In contrast to the American group, the majority of these students spent no more than £10 on CDs, with the same amount for clothes and books – that is, approximately £30 in total as opposed to the Americans' maximum of £80. A quarter of them had web access at home, and under half possessed a mobile phone.

Socioeconomic circumstance and participatory culture

Very few – 5 out of 40 – of the British viewers visit either the official or fanbased *Dawson's Creek* sites. There seems little involvement in the show through merchandise, though magazines are the most common purchase, with clothes and music in second place. The miscellaneous spin-offs include a 'pencle case' [sic] and a notebook.

Turning to the American respondents, there is a clear distinction in terms of participation in the internet-based culture of *Dawson's Creek*, though the level of involvement here is still lower than we might have imagined. Just over one-third of these respondents use the official site 'often' or 'occasionally' – one remarks 'I didn't know there was one' – and only 4 in 27 use fan sites. I shall address these points below.

These results enable us to draw some tentative links between socioeconomic circumstance and participation in the spin-off culture surrounding a show. The British viewers' lack of involvement with either official or fan websites around the show may be at least partly due to the fact that only a quarter of them have internet access at home. The average weekly budget of £10 for clothes, with most respondents spending under £10 on books and CDs, may explain why few of the British respondents engage with the show through spin-off merchandise. To buy a soundtrack album would require over a week's saving for most of these viewers, and so would imply a high level of dedication to the show.

The American viewers, on a markedly higher weekly budget, spend more on CDs and considerably more on clothes than their British counterparts in this study. Over two-thirds of the American respondents have bought music from the show, while over half have bought clothing which relates in some way to *Dawson's Creek*. By contrast, only 6 out of the 40 London viewers claimed to have bought *Dawson's Creek*-related clothing: one female respondent offers that she dresses 'like Jen', the other admits 'I dress like Jowy [sic] sometimes'. The contrast between British and American fans in terms of buying *Dawson's Creek*-related clothing is, as I shall suggest, to some extent related to national culture and availability.

Overall, then, it seems that the British viewers are limited by their budgets and restricted access to technology such as the internet, and so engage with the show through more inexpensive methods such as magazines, posters, pencil cases, or notebooks, and, as we shall see, through face-to-face group discussion about the characters. This kind of engagement with the show through related media – picking up a magazine, watching a TV show or video – allows an involvement in the characters and actors without any major financial commitment.

Dawson's Creek *and national cultural context*

As noted above, the difference in national context between the British and American viewers seemed most apparent in terms of viewers who related their involvement with the TV show to their choice of fashion. While it is generally assumed that British consumer culture is influenced by the US to the extent that the same products are available on both sides of the Atlantic, *Dawson's Creek* presents an exception in its cross-promotion with the US fashion companies J.Crew and American Eagle, which are seen by viewers as the *Dawson's Creek* house style.

For the American respondents, then, the clothing worn by actors in *Dawson's Creek* is far more likely to intersect with the fashions they already wear than it is for the London group. The US viewers who declared that they had bought clothing in the style of Jen or Joey often noted that they already wore fashions from American Eagle or J.Crew, and that they might be prompted to buy a specific item in the same style as the actress rather than attempting to copy her entire outfit.

> Joey's outfits resemble my style, so if I see her wearing something I like, I may be interested in buying something like it . . . J.Crew did a whole *DC* promotion using all the characters for models in their mail-order catalogs last year . . . I know some people who were definately [sic] more interested in buying those catalogs that season.

Other viewers echoed these comments, sometimes remarking on an overlap between the character and the viewer's preferences – 'Not purposely [sic], I do like AE and J.Crew though'; 'I wear similar clothes anyway but I don't buy them to look like Joey' – and sometimes identifying a specific influence – 'Um I probably have, to look like Joey. . . . LOL . . . JEN'; 'Joey, American Eagle type', 'Joey's hats'.

It seems, then, that American viewers may be more liable to see *Dawson's Creek* as a part of their everyday lives as consumers, due to the prominence of the show, and its characters in cross-promotions of which the J.Crew catalog is a prime example. These viewers effectively know where Joey/Katie Holmes shops for her hats, and so are able to extend their pleasures around the show to the shopping mall even if they tend to resist the idea of direct influence. On a similar level, some of these respondents stated that they had bought CD singles or followed up a specific artist – 'the Life's Bitch and Then You Die song', 'Shawn Mullins, Sophie B. Hawkins' – after having heard the music on the show. Rather than dedicated fandom, these responses speak of a more casual engagement with the show as a background presence in daily life, with *Dawson's Creek* serving as a source of occasional inspiration for shopping trips and Joey in particular figuring as a trusted role model in terms of fashion tastes.

I remarked above that *Dawson's Creek*'s immediate context in terms of American television scheduling is significantly different from its British context within Sunday morning's 'T4' schedule, and that cross-media marketing from *Dawson's Creek* to cinema will probably play more of a part in the American experience of Dawson's Creek than it does to the British, due to the timelag and the consequent difficulties in establishing effective cross-media 'alliances'.

This may have some bearing on the fact that over three-quarters of the Americans, compared to half the British group, stated that they would be inclined to watch a new TV show starring a *Dawson's Creek* actor, or go to a movie if it featured a member of the *Dawson's Creek* cast. The British viewers were more likely to follow the show's actors through print articles than through films and television. Again, I would suggest that the links between *Dawson's Creek* and related television and cinema may well be promoted more heavily within the American context, and that even when British viewers do finally have access to, say, *Teaching Mrs Tingle* – which reached screens in the US during August 1999 but was apparently never released in cinemas or on video in the UK – they are less likely to be aware of the *Dawson's Creek* connection.

Gender, community and stardom

'I have asked many of my male students about the survey, and they all basically laugh at me', my research assistant told me when I asked if she could find some male American respondents. 'None of my guy friends, or brothers for that matter, watch *Dawson's Creek* either. Maybe it just isn't a popular "guy" show in the US.' Offering surveys to volunteers among my own American students, I met with a similar response; no young men would complete the questionnaire.

It is possible, though, that *Dawson's Creek* does not have quite the same gendered associations for the British group as it seems to for Americans. One of the British male respondents mentioned that his discussion with friends about the show centred around 'how good it is and how I wish my life was like theres [sic]'. This point would need further investigation, but I think it feasible that *Dawson's Creek* may play slightly differently to a working class British audience, as a utopian slice of 'American' lifestyle rather than as a female-oriented melodrama, and so without the same stigma for male viewers.

That said, there was a marked distinction between the ways in which the British girls engaged with the show in contrast to their male peers. Almost half of the British viewers regularly watch the show in a group of 2–5 people or larger, and just over that amount discuss the show with friends afterwards; but all of those who watched with a group were female, and only two young men mentioned that they discussed the show. One of these respondents offered the comment above, that the show represented a kind of wish-fulfilment, while the other described his discussion as 'Argument [sic] I say it's rubbish, they disagree'.

The comments from young women who watch and discuss *Dawson's Creek* with friends suggest an engagement with the show as part of a young female community. Topics include 'the relaship [sic] between Pacey (Joshua Jackson) and Joey (Katie Holmes)'; 'who's the best looking or who has a nice personality'; 'who our favorete [sic] person is and what we like about them', 'how sad that episode was', 'Pacey's love life'. The show seems to prompt a pleasurable discussion of boys and relationships, focused particularly around Pacey/Joshua Jackson.

This pattern of engagement was echoed by the American viewers, although the ritual of watching in a group and extending the show's pleasures through group discussion has clearly become far more established with these young women. Twenty-three out of 27 watch with a group of 2–5 people or more, and 25 talk about the show afterwards. The topics are neatly summarized by one respondent:

> [W]ho did what and why . . . how much we hate a character (normally Jen or that Eve girl that was on for a few shows), who we think should be with who (Joey with Dawson vs Joey with Pacey, etc) or how cute we think Pacey is, and what we would do to be with him . . . normal girl talk).

Other responses are along much the same lines: 'How hot Pacey is!!!', 'What Pacey did on the show and how dumb Dawson usually is', 'Joey's looks and fashion sense', 'the plots . . . and often times how they apply to our everyday lives', 'how awesome Pacey is.'

The type of discussion is, as with the London group, typically or stereotypically 'female' – romance, fashion, 'bitching' about female characters and admiring male stars – 'normal girl talk'. It is echoed in a comment from later in the survey, where a viewer offers that she would buy a magazine with a *Dawson's Creek* article 'if it is about love life, secrets'. What emerges most strongly, however, is a focus on Pacey/Joshua Jackson as perhaps the main source of intertextual pleasures around *Dawson's Creek*.

Just as Joey is the show's role model in terms of fashion, Pacey is the favoured object of desire for this American group and seems to provide the main reason for much of their wider consumption and intertextual involvement around the show. As such, these responses support Susan Murray's suggestion that the alliances within and between 'post-network television and the New Hollywood' are built around star personae, with young actors such as Joshua Jackson, Katie Holmes and Sarah-Michelle Gellar promoted as the link between TV shows, movies, and magazines.

Viewers offered, for example, with regard to the question about related TV and movies, that they would watch a TV series 'only if Pacey was on it!', that they 'would buy a magazine or see a new movie only if it had Josh in it', that they went to see *Cruel Intentions* 'b/c Pacey is in it (he is so cute!)'.

Note that these viewers, who are representative of the group as a whole – 16 respondents offered Pacey as a reason for trying a new film, series or magazine – tend to refer to Joshua Jackson by his character name even when he takes on a completely different role. One viewer added that she wanted to see 'the new movie with Pacey in it (I can't remember the name right now)'; the guarantee of seeing Pacey apparently provides enough reason to see the film even if you don't know anything else about it.[10]

Media convergence, cultural convergence

Only five out of the 40 British viewers used what the survey designated 'official' websites, and only three visited fan sites. Among the American viewers, who had a greater access to the internet at home, just over one-third used the official *Dawson's Creek* sites.

These respondents specify that they visit the sites: 'to read about the storylines and characters', 'if we are really behind, we sometimes get online to find out what is happening. Also, to find the names of songs that were on specific shows', 'to find lyrics to their songs', 'to read about the stars', 'only when looking for Josh Jackson pics'. Only one respondent noted that she used the internet to discuss *Dawson's Creek* on message boards and chat-rooms, as well as for background reading about the stars, characters and plotlines.

This suggests a view of the internet sites as very much of secondary importance to the show itself, rather than on an equal level. The sites seem to be used as an information resource; hence perhaps the preference for the official site, which is presumably seen as more professional and reliable. Unless the viewer has missed the show for any reason, and so has to catch up on actual plot – in which case the internet becomes essential – the sites are apparently seen as back-up reference for secondary information on actors, lyrics or characters, with primary focus remaining on the show itself.

As such, the internet can be seen as having a similar relationship to the primary *Dawson's Creek* text as do magazines related to the show. Both media provide supplementary information or pictures about the actors and characters, but in no way threaten to supplant or replace weekly viewing.

In a sense, this response seems to indicate that even the American viewers have not fully immersed themselves in the *Dawson's Creek* 'experience' which the official sites construct around the show. Although these viewers have clearly incorporated *Dawson's Creek* to some degree into their everyday lives, through a pleasurably gossipy oral community and through the shared, though not universal, tendency to follow up music, fashions, magazines, and movies which relate in some way to the show, they have not yet reached the point where they visit the website for a daily fix between broadcast episodes,[11] or treat the online *Dawson's Creek* as anything like equivalent to the actual programme. I will address this point in my conclusion.

What we should note, however, is the extent to which these viewers' participation in the wider culture of *Dawson's Creek* is shaped from 'above', and based around what Jenkins would designate 'media convergence'. These young women are, essentially, following the pattern which was cannily mapped out by WB and its media alliances. They know that Joey wears American Eagle and J.Crew, they know that Pacey is in *Skulls* and Dawson in *Varsity Blues*, they know that the show's music is available on two soundtracks, and they show no signs of resisting as their participatory culture is neatly structured for them, with intertextual spin-offs and cross-promotions clearly linked up and signposted like stores in a shopping mall.

I should mention that there was a whole section of my survey dedicated to 'fan' culture. It asked respondents whether they had ever written stories about *Dawson's Creek* characters – often, occasionally or never – and what they were about; it asked the same questions around song lyrics, poems, artwork and websites. Of the 67 young viewers who completed the survey, 66 checked the 'never' box and left the section blank. The one exception was a 12-year-old boy from Kidbrooke School – the one who watched the show wishing his life was 'like theirs' – and who offered that he writes stories about the characters – 'but only romance stories'.

In terms of media convergence versus cultural convergence – 'structured interactivity' as opposed to the 'folk' art which Jenkins (1992) and others have identified within fandom – the results from these groups of young viewers lead us to what might seem a pessimistic conclusion. Although the group viewings and discussions do seem to draw on the show as part of a specifically-female bonding, and may provide a way into conversation about relationships, identity, family, and romance (see also Gillespie, 1992), in general these viewers seem to be content to engage with the show through consumerism rather than creativity.

Of course, such a comparatively small sample cannot be taken as anything like a general rule, but it does sound a note of caution against an overenthusiastic celebration of the fan-based participatory culture exhibited by sites such as *I Hate Jen*. There clearly exist lively, homemade sites which encourage visitors to contribute songs, images, and group-written stories based around *Dawson's Creek*, but we have to bear in mind that even those viewers who visit such sites, let alone participate in them, may well be in the minority.

In a general sense, I think this research reminds us that we should be careful not to take 'fans' – those who produce the artefacts we see online, in 'zines, at conventions – as equivalent to the less active but far larger group of 'viewers'. The young women whose engagement with *Dawson's Creek* extends to buying J.Crew hats and Joshua Jackson pillowcases may provide less material for academia than those who write filk songs about the characters, but I would suggest that they are more representative of the show's audience.

Conclusions

The results of my relatively small-scale research seem to confirm that the extent to which television viewers practice cultural convergence, engaging with a television text across several media, will depend to some degree on gender, national context, and socioeconomic background. I noticed no clear distinction between viewers of different ages or ethnicity in my results, and so have not discussed those issues here; but I have little doubt that these factors also have an influencing role in some cases. If we were to compare the responses of high school students with those of young adults in full-time employment, or look at the various responses to a TV show which is more popular with African-American teenagers than with whites, I am sure that distinctions would emerge.

I have also suggested that, for perhaps the majority of viewers, participation in a TV show's extra-textual discourse may be confined to what Jenkins called media convergence, rather than folk art – although as noted above, we could argue that posting bulletin board messages on an official site, like shopping for outfits or browsing through magazines, constitutes a kind of creative bricolage, albeit within a consumerist framework.

My results suggest that the internet is still used as a secondary reference, supplementary to the main text of the TV show, and even among more privileged viewers with online access at home, was only used by one-third of the respondents. Nevertheless, I feel that this represents a significant change in the way viewers experience television. Five years ago, I would surmise, very few teenage girls would have considered using the internet to supplement their enjoyment of a television drama.

We are not yet witnessing a seismic shift in what it means to watch television: but I am sure that we are witnessing the beginning of that shift. While I wrote this paper, the official site dawsonscreek.com added a new feature to its front page, inviting visitors to investigate Pacey's computer hard drive; a simulacrum of the character's desktop opens on the viewers' screen, and she has access to his mails, internet favourites, even the deleted items in his trashcan. This feature is a significant move towards the concept of the internet site as integral to the ongoing *Dawson's Creek* narrative, rather than just as an online encyclopedia. By double-clicking on Pacey's icons we can discover that he failed last semester's courses, has junked an invitation to consult his personal tutor and is receiving mail from his ex-girlfriend Andie, who offers to 'be there for him' while Joey is away for work.

This use of the website as extended primary text, providing key information on plot and character, is echoed by recent examples in the British media whereby television shows interlock and interact with their associated websites. Occasionally the hierarchy shifts completely, as in the case when the shock eviction of Nick Bateman on the UK's *Big Brother* was screened on webcam hours before it could be broadcast on television. At other times, visitors to the website actively influence the direction of the television series, as with *Jailbreak*,[12] whose contestants were helped to escape through viewers' emails to the official site.

As discussed above, *Attachments* integrates the dedicated Seethru website into its televised narrative, and vice versa; one of its fictional characters, Soph, recently posted an appeal on the site's discussion boards for visitors to contribute articles and features, effectively inviting the programme audience to become active participants in creating Seethru. At least two of the contributors to Seethru's bulletin boards have now been employed as part-time writers and programmers for the website, thus becoming, in a sense, real-life equivalents to the fictional cast of programmers (see Brooker, 2002).

This article offers a number of cautions. We cannot necessarily construct a notion of audience or audience response from the website itself; as this research has shown, their patterns of engagement will be shaped by a number of social and cultural factors. Even those privileged viewers who are regularly online, with both access and disposable income to follow the structures of media convergence which the producers have built around the show, are still likely to engage with it selectively. Just because a dedicated website has set up a fully-immersive experience does not mean that the majority of viewers are using it as anything more than a reference book in-between screenings of what remains, for them, the primary text. These websites suggest an ideal visitor and viewer, a diehard fan who lives the experience of a show rather than merely watching it. As such, they are currently ahead of actual audience involvement, and offer a more exciting vision of convergence than that suggested by my audience research. Fans, we have to remember, are an active minority. The response of keen but uncommitted viewers is less dramatic than we might have expected or hoped.

That said, the experience of following a favourite TV show has already changed for many viewers. The structures are there to enable an immersive, participatory engagement with the programme that crosses multiple media platforms and invites active contribution; not only from fans, who after all have been engaged in participatory culture around their favoured texts for decades, but also as part of the regular, 'mainstream' viewing experience. It will happen, increasingly, and we will need new terms to discuss the shifting nature of the television audience. The concept of overflow helps to establish this new vocabulary.

Notes

1 Intriguingly, both gillettegirlz.com and it'smybody.com adopt a 'lifestyle' approach similar to that used by WB in promoting Dawson's Creek; the actual shaving and sanitary protection products are subtly recommended as part of dating, fashion and health advice.

2 See, for instance, 'Summer . . . But What's A Vacation', by Joey Potter, at http://www.capeside.net/capenet/episodes/114/opinion/index2.html, and Dawson Leery's virtual tour of Potter's Bed and Breakfast, linked from http://www.capeside.net/business.html

3 The slam book and Summer Diaries are accessed from dawsonscreek.com, and have no specific URL of their own.

4 The merchandise is available from http://www.wbstore.com, which links to WB's official site http://www.dawsons-creek.com

5 The use of the female pronoun throughout is intentional; the Dawson's Creek viewers I surveyed for this

research were predominantly female, and the show's websites, as discussed above, seem to be targeted at young women.

6 For the J.Crew catalog, see http://www.jcrew.com/index.jhtml. The recommendation to 'get the clothes they use on the show' is from My Dawson's Creek Homepage, http://geocities.com/television-city/studio/9642/

7 'Dawson's Style', T2, teenage section of *Daily Telegraph*, 6 May 2000.

8 See http://www.dawsons-creek.com/music

9 See http://www.ihatejen.com/ihj/song.shtml and http://www.ihatejen. com/ihj/true.shtml

10 The full response mentioned that this viewer had seen 'Varsity Blues b/c of James Van der Beek' and 'Go = Joey was in it'. James Van der Beek is, significantly, not referred to as Dawson, and Joey's appearance in *Go* seems to be noted as incidental.

11 Compare with TheForce.net's slogan 'your daily dose of Star Wars'; some fans, clearly, are expected to log on every day for a hit of information.

12 Channel 5's *Jailbreak*, hosted by comedian Craig Charles, involved teams of contestants who were treated as prisoners and whose objective was to break out by avoiding guards, finding door codes and negotiating hidden passages. Participants were given limited access to viewers' emails, and if information passed on by a viewer directly helped someone to escape, they shared in the prize money.

References

Brooker, Will (2000) *Batman Unmasked: Analysing a Cultural Icon*. London: Continuum.

Brooker, Will (2002) 'Overflow and Audience', in Will Brooker and Deborah Jermyn (eds) *The Audience Studies Reader*. London: Routledge.

Gillespie, Marie (1992) *Television, Ethnicity and Cultural Change*. London: Routledge.

Jenkins, Henry (1992) *Textual Poachers*. London: Routledge.

—— (1998) 'The Poachers and the Stormtroopers: Cultural Convergence in the Digital Age', University of Michigan: posted on the Red Rock Eater News Service, http://www.tao.ca/wind/rre/0480.html (July).

—— (2000) 'Quentin Tarantino's Star Wars? Parody and Appropriation in an Age of Cultural Convergence', paper presented at the Society for Cinema Studies Conference, 10 March, Chicago.

Lavery, David, Marla Cartwright and Angela Hague (eds) (1996) *Deny All Knowledge: Reading the X-Files*. London: Faber & Faber.

Murray, Susan (2000) 'A Crash Course in Cross-Over Stardom: Teen Stars in Film and Television', paper presented at the Society for Cinema Studies Conference, 10 March, Chicago.

Williams, Raymond (1974) *Television: Technology and Cultural Form*. London: Fontana.

Chapter 37

MARK POSTER

POSTMODERN VIRTUALITIES

O N THE EVE OF THE TWENTY-FIRST century there have been two innovative discussions about the general conditions of life: one concerns a possible "postmodern" culture and even society; the other concerns broad, massive changes in communications systems. Postmodern culture is often presented as an alternative to existing society, which is pictured as structurally limited or fundamentally flawed. New communications systems are often presented as a hopeful key to a better life and a more equitable society. The discussion of postmodern culture focuses to a great extent on an emerging new individual identity or subject position, one that abandons what may in retrospect be the narrow scope of the modern individual with its claims to rationality and autonomy. The discourse surrounding the new communications systems attends more to the imminent technical increase in information exchange and the ways this advantage will redound to already existing individuals and already existing institutions. My purpose in this chapter is to bring these two discussions together, to enact a confrontation between them so that the advantages of each may redound to the other, while the limitations of each may be revealed and discarded. My contention is that a critical understanding of the new communications systems requires an evaluation of the type of subject it encourages, while a viable articulation of post-modernity must include an elaboration of its relation to new technologies of communication. Finally I shall turn to the issue of multiculturalism in relation to the postmodern subject in the age of the mode of information.

For what is at stake in these technical innovations. I contend, is not simply an increased "efficiency" of interchange, enabling new avenues of investment, increased productivity at work and new domains of leisure and consumption, but a broad and extensive change in the culture, in the way identities are structured. If I may be allowed a historical analogy: the technically advanced societies are at a point in their history similar to that of the emergence of an urban, merchant culture in the midst of feudal society in the Middle Ages. At that point practices of the exchange of commodities required individuals to act and speak in new ways,[1] ways drastically different from the aristocratic code of honor with its face-to-face encounters based on trust for one's word and its hierarchical bonds of interdependency. Interacting with total strangers sometimes at great distances, the merchants required written documents guaranteeing spoken promises and an "arms length distance" attitude even when face to face with the other, so as to afford a "space" for calculations of self-interest. A new identity was constructed, gradually and in a most circuitous path to be sure, among the merchants in which a coherent, stable sense of individuality was grounded in independent, cognitive abilities. In this way the cultural basis for the modern world was begun, one that eventually would rely upon print media to encourage and disseminate these urban forms of identity.

In the twentieth century electronic media are supporting an equally profound transformation of cultural identity. Telephone, radio, film, television, the computer and now their integration as "multimedia" reconfigure words, sounds and images so as to cultivate new configurations of individuality. If modern society may be said to foster an individual who is rational, autonomous, centered, and stable (the "reasonable man" of the law, the educated citizen of representative democracy, the calculating "economic man" of capitalism, the grade-defined student of public education), then perhaps a postmodern society is emerging which nurtures forms of identity different from, even opposite to, those of modernity. And electronic communications technologies significantly enhance these postmodern possibilities, Discussions of these technologies, as we shall see, tend often to miss precisely this crucial level of analysis, treating them as enhancements for already formed individuals to deploy to their advantage or disadvantage.[2]

The communications "superhighway"

One may regard the media from a purely technical point of view, to the extent that it is possible, evaluating them in relation to their ability to transmit units of information. The question to ask, then, is how much information with how little noise may be transmitted at what speed and over what distance to how many locations? Until the late 1980s technical constraints limited the media's ability in these terms. To transmit a high quality image over existing (twisted pair copper wire) phone lines took about ten minutes using a 2,400 baud modem or two minutes using a 9,600 baud modem. Given these specifications it was not possible to send "real time" "moving" images over the phone lines. The great limitation then of the first electronic media age is that images could only be transmitted from a small number of centers to a large number of receivers, either by air or by coaxial cable. Until the end of the 1980s an "economic" scarcity existed in the media highways that encouraged and justified, without much thought or consideration, the capitalist or nation-state exploitation of image transmission. Since senders needed to build their own information roads by broadcasting at a given frequency or by constructing (coaxial) wire networks, there were necessarily few distributors of images. The same economies of technology, it might be noted in passing, applied to processes of information production.

Critical theorists such as Benjamin, Enzensberger and McLuhan[3] envisioned the democratic potential of the increased communication capacity of radio, film and television. While there is some truth to their position, the practical model for a more radical communications potential during the first media age was rather the telephone. What distinguishes the telephone from the other great media is its decentralized quality and its universal exchange-ability of the positions of sender and receiver. Anyone can "produce" and send a message to anyone else in the system and, in the advanced industrial societies, almost everyone is in the system. These unique qualities were recognized early on by both defenders and detractors of the telephone.

In the recent past the only technology that imitates the telephone's democratic structure is the Internet, the government-funded electronic mail, database and general communication system.[4] Until the 1990s, even this facility had been restricted largely to government, research and education institutions and some private industry and individuals who enroll in private services (Compuserve, Prodigy) which are connected to it. In the last few years Internet has gained enormously in popularity and by the mid-1990s boasts thirty million users around the world.[5] But Internet and its segments use the phone lines, suffering their inherent technical limitations. Technical innovations in the late 1980s and early 1990s, however, are making possible the drastic reduction of earlier constraints. The digital encoding of sound, text and image, the introduction of fiber optic lines replacing copper wire, the ability to transmit digitally encoded images and the subsequent ability to compress this information, the vast expansion of the frequency range for wireless transmission, innovations in switching technology, and a number of other advances have so enlarged the quantity and types of information that may soon be able to be transmitted that a qualitative change, to allude to Engels's dialectical formula, in the culture may also be imminent.

Information superhighways are being constructed that will enable a vast increase in the flow of communications. The telephone and cable companies are estimating the change to be from a limit of sixty or so one-way video/audio channels to one of five hundred with limited bidirectionality. But this kind of calculation badly misses the point. The increase in transmission capacity (both wired and wireless) will be so great that it will be possible to transmit any type of information (audio, video or text) from any point in the network to any other point or points, and to do so in "real time," in other words quickly enough so that the receiver will see or record at least 24 frames of video per second with an accompanying audio frequency range of twenty to twenty thousand Hertz. The metaphor of the "superhighway" attends only to the movement of information, leaving out the various kinds of cyber*space* on the Internet, meeting places, work areas, and electronic cafes in which this vast transmission of images and words becomes places of communicative relation. The question that needs to be raised is "will this technological change provide the stimulus for the installation of new media different enough from what we now have to warrant the periodizing judgment of a second electronic media age?" If that is the case, how is the change to be understood?

A discourse on the new communications technology is in process of formation, one which is limited largely by the vision of modernity. The importance of the information superhighway is now widely recognized, with articles appearing in periodicals from the specialized 'zines (*Wired* and *Mondo 2,000*) to general journals (*Time, Forbes* and *The Nation*). Essays on the new technology vary from breathless enthusiasm to wary caution to skepticism. Writing in *Time*, Philip Elmer-Dewitt forecasts: "The same switches used to send a TV show to your home can also be used to send a video from your home to any other—paving the way for video phones . . . The same system will allow anybody with a camcorder to distribute videos to the world. . . ."[6] Key to the new media system is not only the technical advances mentioned above but also the merger of existing communication technologies. Elmer-Dewitt continues, ". . . the new technology will force the merger of television, telecommunications, computers, consumer electronics, publishing and information services into a single interactive information industry" (pp. 52–3). Other observers emphasize the prospects of wireless technology. Writing in *Forbes*, George Gilder predicts the spread of this system: ". . . the new minicell replaces a rigid structure of giant analog mainframes with a system of wireless local area networks . . . these wide and weak [replacing broadcasting based on "long and strong"] radios can handle voice, data and even video at the same time . . . the system fulfills the promise of the computer revolution as a spectrum multiplier . . . [the new system will] banish once and for all the concept of spectrum scarcity . . ."[7] Whether future communications media employ wired, wireless or some combination of the two, the same picture emerges of profound transformation.

Faced with this gigantic combination of new technology, integration of older technologies, creation of new industries and expansion of older ones, commentators have not missed the political implications. In *Tikkun*, David Bollier underlines the need for a new set of policies to govern and regulate the second media age in the public interest. President Bill Clinton and Vice-President Al Gore have already drawn attention to the problem, stressing the need for broad access to the superhighway, but also indicating their willingness to make the new developments safe for the profit motive. For them the main issue at stake is the strength of the United States in relation to other nations (read especially Japan) and the health of the industries involved. Bollier points to wider concerns, such as strengthening community life, supporting families and invigorating the democratic process.[8] At this point I want to note that Bollier understands the new media entirely within the framework of *modern* social institutions. The "information superhighway" is for him a transparent tool that brings new efficiencies but by itself changes nothing. The media merely redound to the benefit of or detract from familiar institutions—the family, the community, the state.

If Bollier presents a liberal or left-liberal agenda for politics confronted by the second media age, Mitchell Kapor, former developer of Lotus 1–2–3, offers a more radical interpretation. He understands better than Bollier that the information superhighway opens qualitatively new political opportunities because it creates new loci of speech: ". . . the crucial political question is 'Who controls the switches?' There are two extreme choices. Users may have indirect, or limited control over when, what, why, and from whom they get information and to whom they send it. That's the broadcast model today, and it seems to breed consumerism, passivity, crassness, and mediocrity. Or, users may have decentralized, distributed, direct control over when, what, why, and with whom they exchange information. That's the Internet model today, and it seems to breed critical thinking, activism, democracy, and quality. We have an opportunity to choose now."[9] With Kapor, the interpretation of the new media returns to the position of Enzensberger: socialist or radical democratic control of the media results in more freedom, more enlightenment, more rationality; capitalist or centralist control results in oppression, passivity, irrationality. Kapor's reading of the information superhighway remains within the binaries of modernity. No new cultural formations of the self are imagined or even thought possible. While the political questions raised by Bollier and Kapor are valid and raise the level of debate well beyond its current formation, they remain limited to the terms of discussion that are familiar in the landscape of modernity.

The political implications of the Internet for the fate of nation-state and the development of a global community also require attention. The dominant use of English on the Internet suggests the extension of American power, as does the fact that e-mail addresses in the United States alone do not require a country code. The Internet normalizes American users. But the issue is more complex. In Singapore, English serves to *enable* conversations between hostile ethnic groups, being a neutral "other." Of course, vast inequalities of use exist, changing the democratic structure of the Internet into an occasion for further wrongs to the poorer populations. Even within the high-use nations, wealthy white males are disproportionate users. Yet technologies sometimes spread quickly and the Internet is relatively cheap. Only grassroots political mobilization on this issue will ensure wide access.[10]

In some ways the Internet undermines the territoriality of the nation-state: messages in cyberspace are not easily delimited in Newtonian space, rendering borders ineffective. In the Teale-Homolka trial of early 1994, a case of multiple murders including sexual assault and mutilation, the Canadian government was unable to enforce an information blackout because of Usenet postings in the United States being available in Canada.[11] In order to combat communicative acts that are defined by one state as illegal, nations are being compelled to coordinate their laws, putting their vaunted "sovereignty" in question. So desperate are national governments, confronted by the disorder of the Internet, that schemes to monitor all messages are afoot, such as the American government's idea to monopolize encryption with a "Clipper Chip" or the FBI's insistence on building surveillance mechanisms into the structure of the information super-highway.[12] Nation-states are at a loss when faced with a global communication network. Technology has taken a turn that defies the character of power of modern governments.

The effortless reproduction and distribution of information is greeted by modern economic organizations, the corporations, with the same anxiety that plagues nation-states. Audio taping was resisted by the moguls of the music industry; video taping by Hollywood; modems by the telephone industry giants. Property rights are put in doubt when information is set free of its material integument to move and to multiply in cyberspace with few constraints. The response of our captains of industry is the absurd one of attempting vastly to extend the principle of property by promulgating new "intellectual property laws," flying in the face of the advance in the technologies of transmission and dissemination. The problem for capitalism is how to contain the word and the image, to bind them to proper names and logos when they flit about at the speed of light and procreate with indecent rapidity, not arborially, to use the terms of Deleuze and Guattari, as in a centralized factory, but rhyzomically, at any decentered location. If that were not enough to daunt defenders of modern notions of property, First Amendment issues are equally at risk. Who, for example, "owns" the rights to and is thereby responsible for the text on Internet bulletin boards: the author, the system operator, the community of participants? Does freedom of speech extend to cyberspace, as it does to print? How easy will it be to assess damages and mete out blame in a communicative world whose contours are quite different from those of face-to-face speech and print? These and numerous other fundamental questions are raised by Internet communications for institutions, laws and habits that developed in the very different context of modernity.

Reality problematized

Before turning to the issue of the cultural interpretation of the second media age, we need to consider a further new technology, that of virtual reality. The term "virtual" was used in computer jargon to refer to situations that were near substitutes. For example, virtual memory means the use of a section of a hard disk to act as something else, in this case, random access memory. "Virtual reality" is a more dangerous term since it suggests that reality may be multiple or take many forms.[13] The phrase is close to that of "real time," which arose in the audio recording field when splicing, multiple-track recording and multiple-speed recording made possible "other times" to that of clock time or phenomenological time. In this case, the normal or conventional sense of "time" had to be preserved by the modifier "real." But again the use of the modifier only draws attention to non-"reality" of clock time, its non-exclusivity, its insubstantiality, its lack of foundation. The terms "virtual reality" and "real time" attest to the force of the second media age in constituting a simulational culture. The mediation has become so intense that the things mediated can no longer even pretend to be unaffected. The culture is increasingly simulational in the sense that the media often changes the things that it treats, transforming the identity of originals and referentialities. In the second media age "reality" becomes multiple.

Virtual reality is a computer-generated "place" which is "viewed" by the participant through "goggles" but which responds to stimuli from the participant or participants. A participant may "walk" through a house that is being designed for him or her to get a feel for it before it is built. Or s/he may "walk" through a "museum" or "city" whose paintings or streets are computer-generated but the position of the individual is relative to their actual movement, not to a predetermined computer program or "movie." In addition, more than one individual may experience the same virtual reality at the same time, with both persons' "movements" affecting the same "space." What is more, these individuals need not be in the same physical location but may be communicating information to the computer from distant points through modems. Further "movements" in virtual reality are not quite the same as movements in "old reality": for example, one can fly or go through walls since the material constraints of earth need not apply. While still in their infancy, virtual reality programs attest to the increasing "duplication," if I may use this term, of reality by technology. But the duplication incurs an alternation: virtual realities are fanciful imaginings that, in their difference from real reality, evoke play and discovery, instituting a new level of imagination. Virtual reality takes the imaginary of the word and the imaginary of the film or video image one step further by placing the individual "inside" alternative worlds. By directly tinkering with reality, a simulational practice is set in place which alters forever the conditions under which the identity of the self is formed.

Already transitional forms of virtual reality are in use on the Internet. MUDs or Multi User Domains have a devoted following. These are conferences of sorts in which participants adopt roles in a neo-medieval adventure game. Although the game is played textually, that is, moves are typed as sentences, it is highly "visual" in the sense that complex locations, characters and objects interact continuously. In a variant of a MUD, LambdaMOO, a database contains "objects" as "built" by participants to improve upon the sense of reality. As a result, a quasi-virtual reality is created by the players. What is more, each player adopts a fictional role that may be different from their actual gender and indeed this gender may change in the course of the game, drastically calling into question the gender system of the dominant culture as a fixed binary. At least during the fictional game, individuals explore imaginary subject positions while in communication with others. In LambdaMOO, a series of violent "rapes" by one character caused a crisis among the participants, one that led to special conferences devoted to the issue of punishing the offender and thereby better defining the nature of the community space of the conference. This experience also cautions against depictions of cyberspace as utopia: the wounds of modernity are borne with us when we enter this new arena and in some cases are even exacerbated. Nonetheless, the makings of a new cultural space are also at work in the MUDs. One player argues that continuous participation in the game leads to a sense of involvement that is somewhere between ordinary reality and fiction.[14] The effect of new media such as the Internet and virtual reality, then, is to multiply the kinds of "realities" one encounters in society.

The postmodern subject

The information superhighway and virtual reality are communications media that enrich existing forms of consumer culture. But they also depart or may depart from what we have known as the mass media or the "culture industry" in a number of crucial ways. I said "may depart" because neither of these technologies has been fully constituted as a cultural practice; they are emergent communications systems whose features are yet to be specified with some permanence of finality. One purpose of this chapter is to suggest the importance of some form of political concern about how these technologies are being actualized. The technical characteristics of the information superhighway and virtual reality are clear enough to call attention to their potential for new cultural formations. It is conceivable that the information superhighway will be restricted in the way the broadcast system is. In that case, the term "second media age" is unjustified. But the potential of a decentralized communications system is so great that it is certainly worthy of recognition.

Examples from the history of the installation and dissemination of communications technologies are instructive. Carolyn Marvin points out that the telephone was, at the onset, by no means the universal, decentralized network it became. The phone company was happy to restrict the use of the instrument to those who registered. It did not understand the social or political importance of the universality of participation, being interested mainly in income from services provided. Also the example of Telefon Hirmondó, a telephone system in Budapest in the period before World War I, is worth recalling. The Hungarians used the telephone as a broadcast system, with a published schedule of programming. They also restricted narrowly the dissemination of the technology to the ruling class. The process by which the telephone was instituted as a universally disseminated network in which anyone is able to call anyone else occurred in a complex, multi-leveled historical articulation in which the technology, the economic structure, the political institution, the political culture and the mass of the population each played interacting roles.[15] A similarly complex history will no doubt accompany the institution of the information super-highway and virtual reality.

In *The Mode of Information* I argued that electronic communications constitute the subject in ways other than that of the major modern institutions. If modernity or the mode of production signifies patterned practices that elicit identities as autonomous and (instrumentally) rational, postmodernity or the mode of information indicates communication practices that constitute subjects as unstable, multiple and diffuse. The information superhighway and virtual reality will extend the mode of information to still further applications, greatly amplifying its diffusion by bringing more practices and more individuals within its pattern of formation. No doubt many modern institutions and practices continue to exist and indeed dominate social space. The mode of information is an emergent phenomenon that affects small but important aspects of everyday life. It certainly does not blanket the advanced industrial societies and has even less presence in less developed nations. The information superhighway and virtual reality may be interpreted through the poststructuralist lens I have used here in relation to the cultural issue of subject constitution. If this is done, the question of the mass media is seen not simply as that of sender/receiver, pro-ducer/consumer, ruler/ruled. The shift to a decentralized network of communications makes senders receivers, producers consumers, rulers ruled, upsetting the logic of understanding of the first media age. The step I am suggesting is at least temporarily to abandon that logic and adopt a poststructuralist cultural analysis of modes of subject constitution. This does not answer all the questions opened by the second media age, especially the political ones which at the moment are extremely difficult. But it permits the recognition of an emergent postmodernity and a tentative approach to a political analysis of *that* cultural system; it allows the beginning of a line of thought that confronts the possibility of a new age, avoiding the continued, limiting exclusive repetition of the logics of modernity.

Subject constitution in the second media age occurs through the mechanism of interactivity. A technical term referring to two-way communications, "interactivity" has become, by dint of the advertising campaigns of telecommunications corporations, desirable as an end in itself, so that its usage can float and be applied in countless contexts having little to do with telecommunications. Yet the phenomenon of communicating at a distance through one's computer, of sending and receiving digitally encoded messages, of being "interactive" has been the most popular application of the Internet. Far more than making purchases or obtaining information electronically, com-municating by computer claims the intense interest of countless thousands.[16] The use of the Internet to simulate communities far outstrips its function as retail store or reference work. In the words of Howard Rheingold, an enthusiastic Internet user, "I can attest that I and thousands of other cybernauts know that what we are looking for, and finding in some surprising ways, is not just information but instant access to ongoing relationships with a large number of other people."[17] Rheingold terms the network of relations that come into existence on Internet bulletin boards "virtual communities." Places for "meeting" on the Internet, such as "the Well" frequented by Rheingold, provide "areas" for "public" messages, which all subscribers may read, and private "mailbox" services for individual exchanges.

The understanding of these communications is limited by modern categories of analysis. For example, many have interpreted the success of "virtual communities" as an indication that "real" communities are in decline. Internet provides an alternative, these critics contend, to the real thing.[18] But the opposition "virtual" and "real" community contains serious difficulties. In the case of the nation, generally regarded as the strongest group identification in the modern period and thus perhaps the most "real" community of this era, the role of the imaginary has been funda-mental.[19] Pre-electronic media, like the newspaper, were instrumental in disseminating the sign of the nation and interpellating the subject in relation to it. In even earlier types of community, such as the village, kinship and residence were salient factors of determination. But identification of an individual or family with a specific group was never automatic, natural or given, always turning, as Jean-Luc Nancy argues, on the production of an "essence" which reduces multiplicity into fixity, obscuring the political process in which "community" is constructed: ". . . the thinking of community as essence . . . is in effect the closure of the political."[20] He rephrases the term community by asking the following question: "How can we be receptive to the *meaning* of our multiple, dispersed, mortally fragmented existences, which nonetheless only make sense by existing in common?" (p. xl). Community for him, then, is paradoxically the absence of "community." It is rather the matrix of fragmented identities, each pointing toward the other, which he chooses to term "writing."

Nancy's critique of community in the older sense is crucial to the understanding of the construction of self in the Internet. For his part Nancy has chosen to deny the significance of new communications technologies, as well as new subaltern subject positions in his understanding of community.

> The emergence and our increasing consciousness of decolonized communities has not profoundly modified [the givens of community], nor has today's growth of unprecedented forms of being-in-common—through channels of information as well as through what is called the 'multiracial society'—triggered any genuine renewal of the question of community (p. 22).

Nancy denies the relation I am drawing between a postmodern constitution of the subject and bidirectional communications media. The important point, however, is that in order to do so he first posits the subject as "multiple, dispersed, mortally fragmented" in an ontological statement. To this extent he removes the question of community from the arena of history and politics, the exact purpose of his critique of the essentialist community in the first place. While presenting an effective critique of the essentialist community, Nancy reinstates the problem at the level of the subject by ontologizing its inessentialism. My preference is rather to specify the historical emergence of the decentered subject and explore its links with new communications situations.

We may now return to the question of the Internet and its relation to a "virtual community." To restate the issue: the Internet and virtual reality open the possibility of new kinds of interactivity such that the idea of an opposition of real and unreal community is not adequate to specify the differences between modes of bonding, serving instead to obscure the manner of the historical construction of forms of community. In particular this opposition prevents asking the question of the forms of identity prevalent in various types of community. The notion of a real community, as Nancy shows, presupposes the fixed, stable identities of its members, the exact assumption that Internet communities put into question. Observers of and participants in Internet "virtual communities" repeat in near unanimity that long or intense experience with computer-mediated electronic communication is associated with a certain fluidity of identity. Rheingold foresees huge cultural changes as the effect of Internet use on the individual: ". . . are relationships and commitments as we know them even possible in a place where identities are fluid? . . . We reduce and encode our identities as words on a screen, decode and unpack the identities of others" (p. 61). In bulletin boards such as the Well, people connect with strangers without much of the social baggage that divides and alienates. Without visual cues about gender, age, ethnicity and social status, conversations open up in directions that otherwise might be avoided. Participants in these virtual communities often express themselves with little inhibition and dialogues flourish and develop quickly. Yet Rheingold attributes the conviviality of the Well and the extravagant identity transformations of MUDs to "the hunger for community that has followed the disintegration of traditional communities around the world" (p. 62). Even for this advocate of new communications technologies, the concept of a real community regulates his understanding of the new interactivity. While there may be some truth to a perspective that sees "virtual communities" as compensations for the loss of real communities, I prefer to explore the new territory and define its possibilities.

Another aspect to understanding identity in virtual communities is provided by Stone. Her studies of electronic communication systems suggest that participants code "virtual" reality through categories of "normal" reality. They do so by communicating to each other as if they were in physical common space, as if this space were inhabited by bodies, were mappable by Cartesian perspective, and by regarding the interactions as events, as fully significant for the participants' personal histories.[21] While treatment of new media by categories developed in relation to earlier ones is hardly new, in this case the overlap serves to draw closer together the two types of ontological status. Virtual communities derive some of their verisimilitude from being treated as if they were plain communities, allowing members to experience communications in cyberspace as if they were embodied social interactions. Just as virtual communities are understood as having the attributes of "real" communities, so "real" communities can be seen to depend on the imaginary: what makes a community vital to its members is their treatment of the communications as meaningful and important. Virtual and real communities mirror each other in chiasmic juxtaposition.

Narratives in cyberspace

Electronic mail services and bulletin boards are inundated by stories. Individuals appear to enjoy relating narratives to those they have never met and probably never will meet. These narratives often seem to emerge directly from people's lives but many no doubt are inventions. The appeal is strong to tell one's tale to others—to many, many others. One observer suggests the novelty of the situation: "technology is breaking down the notion of few-too-many communications. Some communicators will always be more powerful than others, but the big idea behind cyber-tales is that for the first time the many are talking to the many. Every day, those who can afford the computer equipment and the telephone bills can be their own producers, agents, editors and audiences. Their stories are becoming more and more idiosyncratic, interactive and individualistic, told in different forums to diverse audiences in different ways."[22] This explosion of narrativity depends upon a technology that is unlike print and unlike the electronic media of the first age: it is cheap, flexible, readily available, quick. It combines the decentralized model of the telephone and its numerous "producers" of messages with the broadcast model's advantage of numerous receivers. Audio (Internet Talk Radio) and video (The World-Wide Web using Mosaic) are being added to text, enhancing considerably the potentials of the new narratives. There is now a "World-Wide Web" which allows the simultaneous transmission of text, images and sound, providing hypertext links as well. The implications of the Web are astounding: film clips and voice readings may be included in "texts" and "authors" may indicate their links as "texts." In addition, other related technologies produce similar decentralizing effects. Such phenomena as "desktop broadcasting," widespread citizen camcorder "reporting" and digital filmmaking are transgressing the constraints of broadcast oligopolies.[23]

The question of narrative position has been central to the discussion of postmodernity. Jean-François Lyotard has analyzed the change in narrative legitimation structures of the premodern, modern and postmodern epochs. Lyotard defines the postmodern as an "incredulity" toward metanarratives, especially that of progress and its variants deriving from the Enlightenment.[24] He advocates a turn to the "little story," which validates difference, extols the "unpresentable" and escapes the overbearing logic of instrumentality that derives from the metanarrative of progress. Any effort to relate second media age technologies with the concept of the postmodern must confront Lyotard's skepticism about technology. For Lyotard, it must be recalled, technology itself is fully complicit with *modern* narrativity. For example, he warns of the dangers of "a generalized computerization of society" in which the availability of knowledge is politically dangerous:

> The performativity of an utterance . . . increase proportionally to the amount of information about its referent one has at one's disposal. Thus the growth of power, and its self-legitimation, are now taking the route of data storage and accessibility, and the operativity of information (p. 47).

Information technologies are thus complicit with new tendencies toward totalitarian control, not toward a decentralized, multiple "little narrativity" of postmodern culture.

The question may be raised, then, of the narrative structure of second media age communications: does it or is it likely to promote the proliferation of little narratives or does it invigorate a developing authoritarian technocracy? Lyotard describes the narrative structure of tribal, premodern society as stories that (1) legitimate institutions, (2) contain many different forms of language, (3) are transmitted by senders who are part of the narrative and have heard it before and listeners who are possible senders, (4) construct a non-linear temporality that foreshortens the past and the present, rendering each repetition of the story strangely concurrent, and, most importantly, (5) authorize everyone as a narrator. Modern society, Lyotard argues, derives its legitimacy from narratives about science. Within science language (1) does not legitimate institutions, (2) contains the single language form of denotation, (3) does not confirm addressee as possible sender, (4) gains no validity by being reported, and (5) constructs "diachronic" temporality. These contrasting characteristics may serve, as Lyotard wishes, to indicate the "pragmatics" of language. It would be interesting to analyze the role of technologies in the premodern and modern cases, and especially the change, within the modern, from print to broadcast media.

In any case, for Lyotard, the postmodern little narrative refunctions the premodern language game, but only in limited ways. Like the tribal myth, the little narrative insists on "the heteromorphous nature of language games" (p. 66); in short, it validates difference. Unlike older narrative forms, the little narrative emphasizes the role of invention, the indication of the unknown and the unexpected. Lyotard looks to certain developments in the natural sciences for his examples of such postmodern narratives, but we may turn to the Internet and to the developing technology of virtual reality. As we have seen, the Internet seems to encourage the proliferation of stories, local narratives without any totalizing gestures, and it places senders and addressees in symmetrical relations. Moreover these stories and their performance consolidate the "social bond" of the Internet "community," much like the premodern narrative. But invention is central to the Internet, especially in MUDs and virtual reality: the production of the unknown or paralogy, in Lyotard's term, is central to second media age communications. In particular the relation of the utterance to representation is not limited to denotation as in the modern language game of science, and indeed the technology encourages a lightening of the weight of the referent. This is an important basis for the instability of identity in electronic communications, leading to the insertion of the question of the subject and its construction. In this spirit, Katherine Hayles defines the "revolutionary potential" of virtual reality as follows: "to expose the presuppositions underlying the social formations of late capitalism and to open new fields of play where the dynamics have not yet rigidified and new kinds of moves are possible."[25]

For the new technologies install the "interface," the face between the faces; the face that insists that we remember that we have "faces," that we have sides that are present at the moment of utterance, that we are not present in any simple or immediate way. The interface has become critical to the success of the Internet. To attain wide appeal, the Internet must not simply be efficient, useful or entertaining: it must present itself in an agreeable manner. The enormous problem for interface design is the fear and hostility humans nourish toward machines and toward a dim recognition of a changing relation toward them, a sharing of space and an interdepend-ence.[26] The Internet interface must somehow appear "transparent," that is to say, appear not to be an interface, not to come between two alien beings, and also seem fascinating, announcing its novelty and encouraging an exploration of the difference of the machinic. The problem of the Internet, then, is not simply "technological" but para-machinic: to construct a boundary between the human and the machinic that draws the human into the technology, transforming the technol-ogy into "used equipment" and the human into a "cyborg," into one meshing with machines.[27]

In Wim Wenders's recent film "Until the End of the World" (1991), several characters view their own dreams on videotape, becoming so absorbed in what they see that they forget to eat and sleep. The characters sit transfixed before their viewing devices, ignoring everyone around them, disregarding all relations and affairs. Limited to the micro-world of their own dreams the char-acters are lost in a narcissistic stupor. And yet their total absorption is compelling. Visual represen-tations of the unconscious—no doubt Wenders has film itself in mind—are irresistible compared to everyday reality, a kind of hyper-reality.

One can imagine that virtual reality devices will become as compelling as the dream videos in Wenders's film. Virtual reality machines should be able to allow the participant to enter imagined worlds with convincing verisimilitude, releasing immense potentials for fantasy, self-discovery and self-construction. When groups of individuals are able to interact in the same virtual space, the possibilities are even more difficult to conceive. One hesitates to suggest that these experiences are commensurate with something that has been termed community. Yet there is every reason to think that virtual reality technologies will develop rapidly and will eventually enable participation through the Internet. Connected to one's home computer, one will experience an audiovisual "world" generated from a node somewhere in the Internet, and this will include other participants in the same way that today one can communicate with others on bulletin boards in videotext. If such experiences become commonplace, just as viewing television is today, then surely reality will have been multiplied. The continued Western quest for making tools may at that point retro-spectively be reinterpreted in relation to its culmination in virtual reality. From the club that extends and replaces the arm to virtual reality in cyberspace, technology has evolved to mime and to multiply, to multiplex and to improve upon the real.

Multiculturalism and the postmodern media age

If the second media age constitutes subjects in a postmodern pattern, critics have ascribed similarities between the politics of multiculturalism and the culture of postmodernity. Political positions surrounding issues of ethnicity and race are various and complex. But commentators have noted a filiation between Lyotard's critique of pluralism in favor of the different and the multiculturalists' parallel attack on liberal pluralism. In this connection, two questions are para-mount: (1) what is the relation of the second media age to ethnicity? and (2) what is the relation between the multiculturalist critique of modernity and the challenge to it by the second media age?

In many respects, the dissemination of second media age communications systems is likely to dispense with the question of ethnicity with the same disregard as has the first media age. In the absence of an effective anti-racist political movement, dominant institutions tend to be constructed as if white were the only race, Anglo-Saxon the only ethnicity and Christianity the only religion. Participation in the information superhighway and virtual reality will most likely be accessible to and culturally consonant with wealthy, white males. In these respects the media reflect the relations of force that prevail in the wider community. At another level, one may ask if these media intrinsically favor one group over another. Is virtual reality, for example, somehow white or somehow masculine? I believe these questions are important to raise but that they cannot be answered at present beyond a few brief remarks. The new technologies, even after two decades of the new social movements, are likely to have been conceived, designed and produced by white males. In that respect they are likely to conform at some level to the cultural peculiarities of that group. The best example of this may be found in video games. Beyond this uncomfortably vague statement, one cannot at present say much more. The technoculture of the second media age largely remains to be constructed.

With respect to the second question—the relation of multiculturalist and second media age resistances to the modern—there is more to be said. Multiculturalists claim some affinity with critiques of the modern that depart from the poststructuralist rejection of the Enlightenment view of the subject. The rational, autonomous individual who pre-exists society, as Descrates and Locke maintained, emerges after the critique by poststructuralists as a Western cultural figure associated with specific groups and practices, not as the unquestioned embodiment of some universal. One may argue that such attributes ought to be desired or realized by everyone. But then that argument is one among others and has no presumptive claims to priority over any other figuration of the subject. Multiculturalists also desire to relativize Western values, to remove the patina of universalism from what is no more than another ethnocentrism. In such critiques I can see no important difference in the poststructuralist and multiculturalists positions, both of which can be coordinated with the type of non-modernist subjects constituted by the new media.

Multiculturalists, postcolonialists and subaltern theorists sometimes further claim certain privileges for the subject position of the "minority" or "third world person" not simply as that of the oppressed but as affirming the ethnic characteristics of the group. In my view such cultural politics are not critical of the modernist position but simply shift the values or relative worth of two terms in the binary opposition autonomous rational universal/particularist non-rational other. To the extent that placing value on ethnicity promotes a recentering of the subject and supports the foundationalism or essentialism of the group in question, then the subject position so articulated has little to do with postmodernity or the second media age.[28] In "On the Jewish Question," Marx long ago effectively analyzed the limitations of such special pleading for an antiauthoritarian politics.[29] For the chief characteristics of the resistance of the new media to modernity lie in their complication of subjecthood, their denaturalizing the process of subject formation, their putting into question the interiority of the subject and its coherence. I believe these traits of the postmodern may contribute to a critique of the modern, may help to undermine the fundamental cultural configuration of modernity, whereas the type of multiculturalism that celebrates a particular ethnicity does not achieve that end. These hopeful possibilities are by no means guaranteed by the dissemination of second media age technologies and the articulation of a commensurate cultural formation.

Proponents of multiculturalism sometimes claim that poststructural theory and concepts of postmodern culture systematically limit the understanding of non-Western ethnicity by configuring it as the Other. While the "post" theories may be effective in a cultural critique of Western logocentrism, they argue, such a critique runs aground to the extent that Western identity is bound up with non-Western identity both at the levels of imperialist politics and economics as well as in the cultural domain. No doubt this argument effectively indicates a limitation of poststructuralism, one which postcolonial discourse may contribute to correcting. Indeed interpretations of ethnicity often go far in this direction, such as Rey Chow's formulation: "Ethnicity signifies the social experience which is not completed once and for all but which is constituted by a continual, often conflictual, working-out of its grounds" (p. 143). In this case multiculturalism is a process of subject constitution, not an affirmation of an essence. As the second media age unfolds and permeates everyday practice, one political issue will be the construction of new combinations of technology with multiple genders and ethnicities. These techno-cultures will hopefully be no return to an origin, no new foundationalism or essentialism, but a coming to terms with the process of identity constitution and doing so in ways that struggle against restrictions of systematic inequalities, hierarchies and asymmetries.

The relation of the second media age to multiculturalism is likely, then, to be profoundly ambivalent: to some extent both contribute to a critique of modernity and therefore to the dominant forms of oppression; on the other hand the new media will no doubt work against the solidification of ethnic identity and, it would appear to me, that traditionalists in the multiculturalist camp are unlikely to look with favor on the information superhighway and virtual reality. As these technologies emerge in social space the great political question will be what forms of cultural articulation they promote and discourage. One needs to keep in mind the enormous variability of the technology rather than assume its determining powers. The example of contemporary Singapore, where a policy implementing advanced information technologies is promulgated by an authoritarian regime, should serve as a warning against overly sanguine expectations.

Notes

1   See Jean-Christophe Agnew, *Worlds Apart: The Market and the Theater in Anglo-American Thought, 1550–1750* (New York: Cambridge University Press, 1986), for an analysis of the formation of this subject position and its particular relation to the theater. Jürgen Habermas, in *The Structural Transformation of the Public Sphere*, trans. Thomas Burger (Cambridge: Polity Press; Cambridge, MA: MIT Press, 1989), offers a "public sphere" of coffee houses, salons and other agora-like locations as the arena of the modern subject, while Max Weber, in *The Protestant Ethic and the Spirit of Capitalism*, trans. Talcott Parsons (New York: Macmillan, 1958), looks to Calvinist religion for the roots of the same phenomenon.
2   See, for example, the discussion of new "interactive" technologies in the *New York Times* on December 19, 1993. In "The Uncertain Promises of Interactivity," Calvin Sims restricts future innovations to movies on demand, on-line information services, interactive shopping, "participatory programming," video games and conferencing systems for business (p. 6F). He omits electronic mail and its possible expansion to sound and image in networked virtual reality systems.
3   I have not discussed the work of Marshall McLuhan simply for lack of space and also because it is not as directly related to traditions of critical social theory as is Benjamin's, Enzensberger's and Baudrillard's. Also of interest is Friedrich Kittler's "Gramophone, Film, Typewriter," *October*, 41 (1987–8), pp. 101–18, and *Discourse Networks: 1800/1900*, trans. Michael Metteer (Stanford University Press, 1990).
4   For an excellent essay on the economics of the Internet and its basic structural features, see Hal Varian, "Economic FAQs About the Internet," which is available on the Internet at listserver@essential.org (send message: subscribe tap-info [your name]) and in the Fall 1994 issue of *Journal of Economic Perspectives*.
5   Kevin Cooke and Dan Lehrer, "The Whole World is Talking," *The Nation* (July 12, 1993), p. 61.
6   Philip Elmer-Dewitt, "Take a Trip into the Future on the Electronic Superhighway," *Time* (April 12, 1993), p. 52.
7   George Gilder, "Telecosm: the New Rule of Wireless," *Forbes ASAP* (March 29, 1993), p. 107.
8   David Bollier, "The Information Superhighway: Roadmap for Renewed Public Purpose," *Tikkun* 8: 4 (1993), p. 22. See also the cautionary tone of Herbert Schiller in "The 'Information Highway': Public Way or Private Road?," *The Nation* (July 12, 1993), pp. 64–6.
9   Mitchell Kapor, "Where Is the Digital Highway Really Heading?: The Case for a Jeffersonian Information Policy," *Wired* 1: 3 (1993), p. 55.
10   For the implications of the Internet on world affairs, see Majid Tehranian, "World With/Out Wars: Moral Spaces and the Ethics of Transnational Communication," *The Public* (Ljubljana) forthcoming.

11   For one report, see Craig Turner, "Courts Gag Media at Sensational Canada Trial," *Los Angeles Times* (May 15, 1994), p. A4.
12   Robert Lee Hotz, "Computer Code's Security Worries Privacy Watchdogs," *Los Angeles Times* (October 4, 1993), pp. A3, 22.
13   Many writers prefer the term "artificial reality" precisely because they want to underscore the privilege of real reality. Needless to say this substitution will not cure the problem.
14   Julian Dibbell, "A Rape in Cyberspace," *The Village Voice* (December 21, 1993), pp. 36–42. I am indebted to Rob Kling for making me aware of this piece.
15   Carolyn Marvin, *When Old Technologies Were New: Thinking About Electric Communication in the Late Nineteenth Century* (New York: Oxford University Press, 1988), especially pp. 222ff.
16   For interesting examinations of this practice, see Mark Dery, ed., "Flame Wars: The Discourse of Cyberculture," *South Atlantic Quarterly* 92: 4 (1993).
17   Howard Rheingold, "A Slice of Life in my Virtual Community," in Linda Harasim, ed., *Global Networks: Computers and International Communication* (Cambridge, MA: MIT Press, 1993), p. 61.
18   See Rheingold's comments, for example: ". . . I believe [virtual communities] are in part a response to the hunger for community that has followed the disintegration of traditional communities around the world" ("Virtual Community," p. 62).
19   See Benedict Anderson, *Imagined Community: Reflections on the Origin and Spread of Nationalism* (New York: Verso, 1983).
20   Jean-Luc Nancy, *The Inoperative Community*, trans. Peter Conner *et al.* (Minneapolis: University of Minnesota Press, 1991), p. xxxviii. See also the response by Maurice Blanchot in *The Unavowable Community*, trans. Pierre Joris (Barrytown, NY: Station Hill Press, 1988).
21   Allucquére Roseanne Stone, "Virtual Systems," in *Incorporations*, ed. Jonathan Crary and Stanford Kwinter (Cambridge, MA: MIT Press, 1992), p. 618.
22   Jon Katz, "The Tales They Tell in Cyber-Space are a Whole Other Story," *Los Angeles Times* (January 23, 1994), p. 2: 1.
23   See *Mondo 2,000*, 11 (1993), pp. 34 and 106.
24   Jean-François Lyotard, *The Postmodern Condition: A Report on Knowledge*, trans. Geoff Bennington and Brian Massumi (Minneapolis: University of Minnesota Press, 1984), p. xxiv.
25   N. Katherine Hayles, "The Seductions of Cyberspace," in Varena Conley, ed., *Rethinking Technologies* (Minneapolis: University of Minnesota Press, 1993), p. 175.
26   Claudia Springer in "The Pleasure of the Interface," *Screen* 32: 3 (1991), pp. 303–23, is especially insightful on this question.
27   Katherine Hayles, "Virtual Bodies and Flickering Signifiers," *October 66* (Fall 1993), pp. 69–91, interprets these "different configurations of embodiment, technology and culture" through the binary pattern/randomness rather than presence/absence.
28   For an excellent statement of this problem, see Rey Chow, *Writing Diaspora* (Bloomington: Indiana University Press, 1993), especially chapters 1 and 2. See also an important alternative view in David Lloyd, "Ethnic Cultures, Minority Discourse and the State," in Peter Hulme, ed., *Colonial Discourse/Postcolonial Theory* (Manchester: Manchester University Press, 1994), pp. 221–38.
29   Karl Marx, "On the Jewish Question," in Robert Tucker, ed., *The Marx-Engels Reader* (New York: Norton, 1978), pp. 26–52.

Bibliography

Agnew, J.C. (1986) *Worlds Apart: The Market and the Theatre in Anglo-American Thought*, New York: Cambridge University Press.
Anderson, B. (1983) *Imagined Community: Reflections on the Origin and Spread of Nationalism*, New York: Verso.
Blanchot, M. (1988) *The Unavowable Community*, P. Joris (trans.), Barrytown, NY: Station Hill Press.
Bollier, D. (1993) "The Information Superhighway: Roadmap for Renewed Public Purpose," *Tikkun* 8 (4): 22.
Chow, R. (1993) *Writing Diaspora*, Bloomington: Indiana University Press.
Cooke, K. and Lehrer, D. (1993) "The Whole World is Talking," *The Nation*, 12 July: 61.
Derry, M. (ed.) (1993) "Flame Wars: The Discourse of Cyberculture," *South Atlantic Quarterly* 92 (4).
Dibbell, J. (1993) "A Rape in Cyberspace," *The Village Voice*, 21 December: 36–42.
Elmer-Dewitt, P. (1993) "Take a Trip into the Future on the Electronic Superhighway," *Time*, 12 April: 50.
Gilder, G. (1993) "Telecosm: the new Rule of Wireless," *Forbes ASAP* 29 March: 107.

Habermas, J. (1989) *The Structural Transformation of the Public Sphere*, T. Burger (trans.), Cambridge: Polity Press.
Hayles, K. (1993) "Virtual Bodies and Flickering Signifiers," *October* 66: 69–91.
Hayles, N.K. (1993) "The Seductions of Cyberspace" in V. Conley (ed.) *Rethinking Technologies*, Minneapolis: University of Minnesota Press.
Hotz, R.L. (1993) "Computer Code's Security Worries Privacy Watchdogs," *Los Angeles Times* 4 October: A3-22.
Kapor, M. (1993) "Where is the Digital Highway Really heading?: The Case for a Jefferson Information policy," *Wired* 1 (3): 55.
Katz, J. (1994) "The Tales They Tell in Cyber-Space are a Whole Other Story," *Los Angeles Times* 23 January: 2 1.
Kittler, F. (1987–88) "Gramophone, Film, Typewriter," *October* 41: 101–18.
—— (1990) *Discourse Networks: 1800/1900*, M. Metteer (trans.), Stanford: Stanford University Press.
Lloyd, D. (1994) "Ethnic Cultures, Minority Discourse and the State" in P. Hulme (ed.) *Colonial Discourse/Postcolonial Theory*, Manchester: Manchester University Press: 221–38.
Lyotard, J.F. (1984) *The Postmodern Condition: A Report on Knowledge*, G. Bennington and B. Massumi (trans.), Minneapolis: University of Minnesota Press.
Marvin, C. (1988) *When Old Technologies Were New: Thinking About Electric Communication in the Late Nineteenth Century*, New York: Oxford University Press.
Marx, K. "On The Jewish Question" in R. Tucker (ed.) *The Marx-Engles Reader*, 1978, New York: Norton.
Nancy, J-L. (1991) *The Inoperative Community*, P. Conner *et al.* (trans.), Minneapolis: University of Minnesota Press.
Rheingold, H. (1993) "A Slice of Life in my Virtual Community" in L. Harasim (ed.) *Global Networks: Computers and International Communication*, Cambridge MA: MIT Press.
Schiller, H. (1993) " 'The Information Highway': Public Way or Private Road?," *The Nation* 12 July: 64–6.
Sims, C. (1993) "The Uncertain Promises of Interactivity," *New York Times*, 19 December: 6F.
Springer, C. (1991) "The Pleasure of the Interface," *Screen* 32 (3): 175.
Stone, A.R. (1992) "Virtual Systems" in J. Crary and S. Kwinter (eds) *Incorporations*, Cambridge MA: MIT Press.
Turner, C. (1994) "Courts Gag Media at Sensational Canada Trial," *Los Angeles Times* 15 May: A4.
Weber, M. (1958) *The Protestant Ethic and the Spirit of Capitalism*, T. Parsons (trans.), New York: Macmillan.

Chapter 38

DON SLATER

SOCIAL RELATIONSHIPS AND IDENTITY ONLINE AND OFFLINE

THE VERY IDEA OF APPROACHING the new media in terms of a sharp distinction between the online and the offline has given research in this area a peculiar profile. In contrast to the typically panicked reception of older new media technologies (telephone, television), fearful of their ill effects on social relationships and identities, the Internet has posed the possibility of entirely new relationships and identities, constituted within new media, and in competition with ostensibly non-mediated, older forms of relationship. In this respect, the new media have been studied less as media that are used within existing social relations and practices, and more as a new social space which constitutes relations and practices of its own. The research agenda from this point of view focuses not on the characteristics and uses of these media as means of communication but rather on the kinds of social life and cultures that they are capable of sustaining, and how these specifically online socialities relate to the 'offline world'. Even more broadly, the 'online' side of this distinction has often been understood not simply in terms of what its 'inhabitants' do but as something like a unified 'cyberculture' with patterns of sociality that seem automatically to flow from the nature of the technology itself.

This kind of language characterized the early literature on the Internet, to a greater or lesser extent, up to the late 1990s, though it is now in decline. As a result, the burden of this chapter is not so much to present what has been 'discovered' about the difference between online and offline, or their impact on each other. Rather, it needs to show how and why that distinction has coloured the new media research agenda, and how and why it is being deconstructed. That is to say, the distinction has not been sustained, and is probably more symptomatic of an historical period than fruitful as a methodological presumption. Moreover, it is possible that the reasons the distinction has not been sustained have as much to do with actual changes in the nature and social place of the new media as they have to do with analytical weaknesses in the distinction itself.

Distinguishing life online

Christine Hine (2000) distinguishes between regarding the Internet as a culture and as a cultural artefact. The latter perspective, as developed through the sociology of science and technology, involves investigating the co-configuration of objects and social contexts, and hence considering how a technology may be interpreted as to its social and technical potentials. In this case, one is looking at how a means of communication is used within an offline social world. On the other hand, to study the Internet as culture means regarding it as a social space in its own right, rather than as a complex object used within other, contextualizing spaces. It means looking at the forms of communication, sociality and identity that are produced within this social space, and how they are sustained using the resources available within the online setting. Mark Poster (1995a; 1995b) has made a related distinction between the Internet as a tool, and hence part of a modernist orientation to the new media as something used instrumentally within wider social projects; and the Internet as a postmodern space of transformation, in which the subject of communication is transformed within the process of communicating. Poster usefully contrasts different uses and media within the Internet (e-mail used at the office is not likely to have the same identity implications as intense involvement in a MUD [multi-user dungeon]), but his distinction, like Hine's, implies that both analysts and participants can orient themselves to what might otherwise be just another medium as if it were a meaningful social space or cyberspace. There is a strong argument that, although past media have also seemed to constitute new forms and spaces of sociality, even virtualities (McLuhan, 1974; Standage, 1999), they have quickly been absorbed into everyday practices as utilities, or that they lacked some qualities that render the new media more capable of sustaining complex social spaces. Certainly, it is this feature of the Internet – mythologized as 'cyberspace' – that has been considered unique and revolutionary to new media, and therefore its key characteristic to be investigated. It is not a medium but a place to be or to dwell.

Ironically, early studies of computer-mediated communications emphasized how their apparent lack of online cues as to offline settings and identities resulted in an impoverished and anarchic asociality, reflected in poor social order and group efforts (see, for example, Baym, 2002; Hine, 2000; Jones, 1995). The irony is that this detachment from offline context is precisely what grounded the greatest claims for online sociality as both a vehicle for liberating social order and facilitating group effort. The latter is exemplified not just by mundane intranets, but also by the kind of shareware and open source software efforts that led a Microsoft employee to acknowledge that Linux could mobilize the 'combined IQ of the Internet' to solve its technical problems.

The claim that the new media sustain online social spaces that can be inhabited and investigated relatively independently of offline social relations has been advanced on quite various grounds, and from the earliest days of the Internet. We can summarize them in terms of four properties: virtuality, spatiality, disembedding and disembodiment. Each of these emphasizes a radical disjuncture between online and offline relationships and identities. However, we need to be clear from the outset that each of these dimensions has often been put forward as a characterization of the new media: they are generally stated as if they were intrinsic properties of the media themselves, and hence ways of investigating their specificity as new mediations of social life. The problem, as we will discuss later, is that they attempt to specify the properties of the new media independently of the particular social uses and networks in which they are embedded, as things in themselves from which particular uses (or effects) naturally flow. Two obvious fallacies arise from this. The first is a technological determinism. The second is an assumption that the Internet is a unified phenomenon, whereas it is in fact quite a diversity of software and hardware technologies which can be used differently and in different combinations. Quite simply: the use of ICQ or other chat systems by Indonesian parents as opposed to American teenagers is likely to be determined by more than simply the technology; while the same American teenagers or Indonesian parents may regard ICQ as opposed to websites completely differently with respect to virtuality, spatiality and so on.

Virtuality

First, the ideas of virtuality and simulation evoke the construction of a space of representation that can be related to 'as if' it were real, and therefore effects a separation from, or even replacement of, the 'really real'. It therefore contrasts with several terms that might characterize the offline world: 'real', 'actual' and 'material' being the central ones (Shields, 2000). The extreme point of virtuality, which exercised much of the early literature, is the idea of 'virtual reality': a space of representations in which all one's senses are exposed to coordinated representations such that the experience is completely immersive (though not mistaken for a 'real' one) and the participant can respond to stimuli as if to a real world that behaves consistently, in a rule-governed, non-arbitrary manner. Paradoxically, this literal notion of virtual reality as immersive multimedia (for example, Springer, 1991) was contemporary with an Internet whose virtuality was almost entirely textual, immersive not because of its sensory but rather because of its social and intellectual character: cybersex, for example, was a virtual reality not because it literally simulated sexual experiences but because it allowed for absorbing interactive narratives based on the quasi-presence of the other and their participation in constructing a text. Moreover, this sense of the online as a virtual space was largely exemplified by MUDs and MOOs which in fact descended very directly from offline role-playing fantasy games in which a limited number of rules could constitute a bounded, shared world and generate an unpredictable infinity of behaviours which nonetheless made sense as part of a consistent shared reality (Fine, 1983). We might also compare the notion of virtuality with theories of film realism, which also focus on the textual generation of internally consistent and hence absorbing worlds (Kuhn, 1982; MacCabe, 1985).

Hence, the focus moved from the virtual as simulation to the virtual as a coherent social space, and one in which new rules and ways of being and relating could emerge precisely because of the separation from the constraints of the 'really real'. We can flesh this out through the remaining three terms: spatiality, disembedding and disembodiment.

Spatiality

Closely related to virtuality was the apparent ability of the new media to constitute a place, or places. 'Cyberspace' captures the sense of a social setting that exists purely within a space of representation and communication – software, the network – and therefore does not map clearly onto offline spaces. At the same time, cyberspace itself can, and indeed must, be mapped.

Virtuality is a spatially ambiguous experience. *Where* is cyberspace? It exists entirely within a computer space, distributed across increasingly complex and fluid networks. An experience of early Internet users was the difficulty of understanding that clicking on a hypertext link could take you to a file anywhere in the world – it could be on your own computer or in another hemisphere – and it did not matter: a new and integrated space was being encountered whose coordinates related to a different physics. Indeed, the spatiality of cyberspace largely resides in the connections which make up the network. However, the boundaries of the network are themselves ambiguous and converge with other technologies, relations and information. Hence, some of the literature (Imken, 1999) prefers to talk of the 'matrix' to indicate an extended electronic and informational space that is considerably wider than the Internet, and one less easily split into offline and online. The spatial qualities of the online are in any case highly variable and contradictory (Crang, 1997). For example, on the one hand there is a stress on its complexity, its seemingly inexhaustible range and speed of movement, its unmappability (Dodge and Kitchen, 2000), which seem to render it a space to explore or discover but never comprehend. This enhances metaphors of the online as a truly new domain. On the other hand, the representations through which the virtual is constructed and experienced are famously domestic and simplifying. Far from the abstract data representations which inhabited Gibson's (1984) original vision of cyberspace, the real virtual is talked about in terms of rooms, places, sites; and accessed through browsers and portals intended to make the space coherent in terms of individual and largely consumerist interests.

Finally, the network organization of new media itself implies a new kind of spatiality which might be separate from yet transformative of offline social organization. Based on point-to-point communication rather than broadcast models, the new media appear both as non-hierarchical and as evading offline hierarchies. There appears to be an inexorable technological push in the direction of horizontal connections which are uncontrollable: for example, there is the rise of peer-to-peer networking (e.g. Gnutella) in which connections are entirely distributed to individual users, thereby bypassing any central organizing technical or social institution and hence any physical, real-world location that can be held accountable.

Disembedding and community

The most obvious feature of computer-mediated communications is that it allows communications between people who are spatially dispersed. The important factor in a chat room is not where in the world you are, but how you are using the communicative facilities at your disposal. The irrelevance of geographical position to Internet communication is often referred to as 'disembedding'. For example, in using a MUD or a chat facility such as ICQ one is effectively removed or separated from one's immediate locale ('disembedded'), which becomes irrelevant to the ongoing interaction. At the same time, the MUD or ICQ channel constitutes a new context of communication. It is inhabited by people who may be widely dispersed, but they share a context, rules and often a history of communication, and can properly treat their interactions as real, as having consequences (at least within the Internet context) and as valued.

The notion of 'disembedding' arose prior to and outside new media debates as a characterization of central features of modernity. In the work of Giddens (1990) and Thompson (see also Slevin, 2000), in particular, it is related to two communications-related developments: time-space compression, whereby increasing speed of interconnection (whether by penny post or electronic instant messaging) shortens the effective social distance between any connected points; and time-space distanciation, in which local times and spaces are melded into increasingly homogeneous global units of measurement which coordinate highly dispersed activities to a unified beat (attempts to establish a single 'Internet time' are a very literal version of this, characteristically the initiative of a private watch-making corporation, Swatch). In fact, it could be argued that the most prestigious model for understanding the Internet in these terms long predated it: Marshall McLuhan's (1974) idea of 'the global village'. McLuhan argued that electronic media (radio and television in his time) created a sense of simultaneity: an event portrayed on TV was happening in every living room where a TV was turned on, at the same time. This, along with the properties of the specific media, produced new forms of involvement and participation in which, as in the village, everyone could be present at the same event at the same time. Time was obliterated and spatial separation no longer had any impact on communication. The Internet added to the simultaneous reception of television the interactivity of online social relations (Kitchen, 1998: 15). The apparent annihilation of space online promotes a sense of co-presence, that people can be present to each other in a way that corresponds to face-to-face interaction. To the extent that this copresence is a function of the technology, it makes sense that it is socially enacted through media-specific communicative conventions, for example, flaming, smilies or 'netiquette' (e.g., Danet, 1998).

The notion of disembedding gave rise to one of the largest sets of claims about life online: that new media could sustain communities whose existence was largely or entirely virtual. Rheingold (1993), for example, argued that cyberspace was capable of constituting all the diversity of offline interaction and exchange:

There is no such thing as a single, monolithic, online subculture; it's more like an ecosystem of subcultures, some frivolous, others serious. The cutting edge of scientific discourse is migrating to virtual communities, where you can read the electronic pre-preprinted reports of molecular biologists and cognitive scientists. At the same time, activists and educational reformers are using the same medium as a political tool. You can use virtual communities to find a date, sell a lawnmower, publish a novel, conduct a meeting.

This disembedding could be seen as highly positive in many respects. Above all, the process of disembedding could be interpreted as freeing one from the confines of one's immediate location, empowering participants to connect with anyone from anywhere in the world on the basis of common interests or pleasures. A specifically postmodern politics and sociality was enacted in these elective communities, mobile sociality or neotribes (Bauman, 1990; Maffesoli, 1996). This capacity for online community could be variously framed: as transcending and overcoming the fragmented and anomic character of contemporary offline life through the postmodern equivalent of utopian communities; as reinvigorating qualities such as democracy, debate and self-organization in offline life (e.g. the use of the Internet to foster political participation, knowledge and accountability); as vying with offline life by claiming greater reality or value; or, negatively, as contributing to processes that drain offline sociality of its remaining communality (by replacing, disembodying, mediating, increasing fragmentation).

Disembodiment and identity

Just as going online seemed to detach one from place, it also seemed to detach one from the body. 'Disembodiment' signifies that a person's online identity is apparently separate from their physical presence, a condition associated with two features: textuality and anonymity. Although new channels of communication such as voice over IP and video conferencing are becoming available on the Internet, most communication between people has thus far been textual, at most complemented by some graphics. In a chat channel a person is only known to others through what they type and their claims about themselves cannot be verified or contradicted by their body and its expressions. Indeed, the phrase 'you are what you type' summed up the sense that a person's online performance of identity had to be taken at face value, if only because there is no other information to go on. This conspicuously includes such visible markers of sex, 'race' and age which, in offline interactions, fix identities in bodies. At the same time, online presence is apparently disembodied in the broader sense that it can be detached from other ways in which offline presences are held stable and accountable: names, addresses, one's past relationships and biography as they are fixed through e.g. law, credentials, memberships (including marriages). Simply, online identities are potentially anonymous with respect to one's offline identity, to which it might be very difficult to trace one's online performance.

Hence, much experience and discussion of online relationships is framed by the simple issue of deception and authenticity: on what basis should one believe that anyone online is who they claim to be; and can relationships that are plagued by this degree of doubt (or gullibility) be treated as serious and 'real' relationships? The alternative position, which characterizes the 'cyberlibertarianism' that dominated much of the early experience of new media disembodiment, is to treat it as an occasion to deconstruct the entire notion of authenticity, particularly in so far as it involves fixing the reality of identities through their embodiment (a manoeuvre that is fundamental to essentialisms such as racism and sexism). In this reading, the new media provide a space for four kinds of separation and liberation from prior identities and relationships: first, one can perform whatever identity one chooses (I can be a man, a woman or an extraterrestrial toad); second, one can create entirely new identities that are impossible or inconceivable in offline worlds constrained by social and bodily physics (famously, I can be one of seven different sexes on Lambda-MOO); third, because all presences online are textual they are also self-evidently *perform-ances*, and therefore one can be liberated from the concept of authenticity itself, and enter a different ethics and politics, that of performance; and, finally, this ethics and politics, in its most prevalent version, is carried out by 'cyborg' or 'hybrid' identities: they are defined not by a fixed and monadic individualization but rather by fluidity and interconnection. Cyberspace appeared as the site of a sociology of the future, in which identities are mobile, fluid and openly experienced as performative rather than authentic.

This programme is incomprehensible if not related to poststructuralist traditions, particularly in their conjunction with feminism. That is to say, new media spaces appeared as locations in which to practise and observe operations of deconstruction and performativity that long predated them, as will be discussed below.

Investing in life online

All of these claims need careful critique and qualification, as we will argue. However, it is also crucial to recognize that the online/offline distinction that they underwrite is not simply an academic one: it also has a powerful cultural and political status. A wide range of constituencies have had a considerable investment in establishing the alterity and newness of the new media as a social space. The very notion of 'cyberspace' was a screen onto which were projected many potent fears and hopes.

First, historical accounts of early Internet users reveal a strange counter-cultural world that comprised remnants and echoes of 1960s libertarian counter-culture; the emergent nerd culture of university engineering and computer science departments; and an unusually wide range of youth subcultures (including games subcultures) (Kitchen, 1998; Turkle, 1984). This very charac-terization of the origins of 'cyberculture' should cast doubt on the online/offline distinction. Cyberculture did not spring out of the intrinsic characteristics of new media, but arose from possibilities in virtuality that were recognized by games-playing cultures (e.g. 'Doom' and 'Quake', but also pre-Internet, BBS experiences of online poker; and before that 'Dungeons and Dragons'); science fiction and fantasy (cyberpunk); fashions in subcultural music and dress such as techno, rave, postpunk grunge and feminist music (e.g. riotgrrrls); new decentralized models of political organization; and many more. 'Cyberculture' was never a unified online culture but a highly diverse amalgam of cultural conjunctures, not all of which originated in the new media.

What these loose strands of cyberculture certainly converged around was an ethos that focused on a wide range of (often incompatible) freedoms. Net libertarianism involved a claim to total freedom in two senses: the civic sense of the right to any kind of speech, interaction and association, and an opposition to all censorship (which, unlike in offline life, seemed to be technologically guaranteed under the notion that the net treats censorship as 'noise' and routes itself around it, rendering itself invulnerable to offline sources of regulation and prohibition); and the sense of the free circulation of things, without conventional property rights or *prices* (Ross, 1998; Slater, 2000b). The latter was exemplified in such notions as the Internet as a 'gift economy' (an inexorable wave of the future that would engulf the older offline economy e.g., Barbrook, 1999), and in a disregard for intellectual property rights in favour of shareware and open systems. As in any libertarianism, the net version could bring together populisms of the far right and left in an agreed opposition to any form of hierarchy, governmental or corporate. There could be no clearer or wilder invocations of the online world as a place of freedom and alterity than John Perry Barlow's famous Declaration of Independence of Cyberspace or the fight against the Communications Decency Act. It is no surprise that this libertarianism, like so many previous ones (Brown, 1997; Ross, 1998), saw itself as inhabiting a new frontier territory or Wild West, embracing a claim to defend a new *space* (Rheingold, 1993, subtitled his book *Homesteading on the Electronic Frontier*). It was both ungoverned (or self-governed) and in principle ungovernable by any but its own inhabitants.

Second, cyberspace as different converged with another agenda: new economy and the dematerialization of economic relations and flows. Again, it is ironic that postmoderns and business consultants alike, and odd figures in between such as *Wired*'s Kevin Kelly or Demos's Geoff Mulgan, could all assert that the new media constituted a vanguard socioeconomic space in which the principles of the future could be discerned: connectivity (or 'connexity', as Mulgan (1998) put it), networking, disintermediation, dematerialization, etc. Online would come to engulf and overtake the offline.

Third, as indicated above, the online/offline distinction offers the space for a practical exploration or even realization of an intellectual trajectory that draws on poststructuralism, postmodernism and (post)feminism. The agenda is to deconstruct the notion of real and authentic identities (particularly notions which anchor them in nature, reason or the body) in favour of a model of identity as performance. As a corollary it has generally involved an embrace of decentring or fragmentation: if a depth model of real identities generated by a core reality is rejected as oppressive and false, then an embrace of fluid identities defined by shifting associations, connections and boundaries constitutes both a politicoethical strategy and a new kind of truth. For example, both Butler (1990; 1993) and Haraway (1990) are centrally concerned with the critique of conventional politics of representation which presumes 'real' identities ('woman', 'black', 'gay') that can be more or less truthfully represented (in politics or discourses). New media point to other forms of representation and corresponding organization in which people identify themselves through performances structured by their interaction with constantly changing, and not necessarily human (machines, networks, objects), others. Haraway's 'cyborg' has wide currency as the hero of new media politics: an ever monstrous structure because it challenges the authenticity of all identities by existing, fluidly, at the borders between them. A further step, exemplified by Sadie Plant's (1995; 1996; 1997) work, has been to identify this performative and connective model of identity, and its privileged enactment online, as an essentially feminine modality, and hence interpret the Internet as a fundamentally feminine space, a femininity evoked and discerned through metaphors of weaving, networking and diffusion. Indeed, Plant's imagery was largely a rendering of Irigaray's brand of psychoanalytic feminism, transferred from the act of writing to the interactivity of the new media. In all these versions, new media appear as a space apart from offline life from which can be launched both critiques of the conventional world and explorations of alternative ways of being, acting and relating.

This political-intellectual investment in a separable cyberspace is highly paradoxical, particularly in respect to the issue of bodies and identities. Amidst much celebration of a deconstruction or liberation from identities fixed in bodies, often traced to modern materialism and scientism, cyberlibertarianism nonetheless also seems to proclaim the technical realization of the Enlightenment dream of mind/body dualism, and a liberation of mind from body (Lupton, 1995), a separation which is experienced as both pleasure and terror (Hayles, 1999). Moreover, in consonance with the same Enlightenment relation to the world, cyberspace seems to promise a technical mastery, or transcendence, of mind over body, in which you can really be whatever you conjure up or type; the limits of offline physicality are escaped and remade by mind and desire. Several authors have interpreted this extravagant fantasy as a compensatory and escapist response to experiences of fragmentation and loss of control within people's broader social life. Robins (1995:

136), for example, argues that in much cyberutopian and cyborg literature, cyberspace appears as a place untouched by 'the social and political turbulence of our time', to which its inhabitants respond either by conjuring up a 'unified subjectivity', fusion and unmediated community, or alternatively by celebrating the dissolution of all unities as an occasion for pleasure, play and fantasies of creative mastery and total gratification.

This paradoxical relationship of online transcendence to offline fragmentation seems somewhat confirmed by the widespread observation that much, if not most, online behaviour does not conform to cyberlibertarian expectations. That is to say, it may well be that poststructuralist deconstructions and postmodern diagnoses of bodies and identities are completely correct, as are the hopes they place in practices which alter the terms of identity performance, but this does not mean that actual new media users are in fact engaged in anything like this. Springer (1996) and Bassett (1997) both offer an analysis in which the experience of disembodiment not only does not produce experimental identities but actually results in hypergendered performances. In the MUD self-descriptions analysed by Bassett, although participants were offered a wide choice of genders (far more than two) they almost invariably described themselves in hypermasculine or hyperfeminine terms. If anything, the lack of constraint on online performance provided an occasion to realize, in fantasy, the most conventional offline gender aspirations. Slater's (Rival et al., 1998; Slater, 1998; 2000a and b) work replicates this finding of conventionality: the concern of participants in an apparently unconstrained social scene for sexually explicit fantasies and representations was overwhelming the maintenance of a conventional normativity which included both ethical conservatism and sexual boundaries drawn from the conventions of offline pornography (homophobic, woman as sexually insatiable); moreover, even where there was creative exploration of sexuality it was highly regulated and strategically wedded to issues of authenticity (performance was treated as untruth). Claudia Springer analyses the hypergendering of identities not only in cyberspace but also in popular culture generally as a reaction to the problematization of the body and sexuality that is completely opposite to that expected by cyberutopians: it is precisely because the production of unambiguously sexed and heterosexual bodies is at the centre of social identities (not just sexual but national, racial and so on) that any problematization of the body will provoke fear and retrenchment. The body is indeed becoming more problematic as the essential ground of identity: it really is becoming more cyborg and merged with technology, revealed as performance, reconstructed through feminism and new sexualities. It is precisely *because* various new technologies such as the Internet make the body problematic that people exaggerate, rather than abandon, gender. The response is not an embrace of new possibilities but an attempt to act out these threatened identities on an intensified scale through a renewed assertion of mind over body. None of this should be surprising on the basis of a more reasonable reading of Butler (and Haraway) than is typical of much of the more utopian literature. Butler's work, after all, stresses the regulation of performance through discourses and powers such as compulsory heterosexuality, which bolt the entire normativity of sexuality-gender-sex in place, and might be expected to do so ever more urgently as this regulatory structure is technologically challenged.

Virtuality as practice

Much discussion of online social relations and identities seems to seek a highly generalized answer, and therefore tends to technological determinism: the impression is that by virtue of going online one is automatically involved in new social processes. It can be quite difficult to avoid this kind of logic. For example, Baym, (2002) argues against the early research assumption that media characteristics will have determining effects on interaction, asserting that 'there are many other contributors to online interpersonal dynamics'. This apparently uncontroversial statement unfortunately entirely misses the problem about arguing from media characteristics: how can we possibly identify the properties of a medium independently from how people use and understand these facilities? (The case of short text messaging on mobile phones will surely count as the classic case: this 'medium characteristic' simply *did not exist* – for the phone designers, telecoms companies, industry analysts and government regulators – until it was 'discovered' apparently spontaneously by hordes of teenagers.) Reducing 'media characteristics' to one 'variable' amongst others simply underwrites, rather than deconstructs, the crude positivism of such approaches. How can 'media characteristics' be counted as one variable lined up alongside 'contexts, users and the choices those users make' when I, for one, cannot identify the former except as it emerges through the latter? Baym instead treats 'users' perceptions of CMC and their 'desires' as just another variable (however 'central') rather than as a core analytical issue. Moreover, Baym treats the move from the earlier assumption to current research as if it were a move from simplistic thinking to an appreciation of diversity, which also misses the point. The problem was not that the earlier approaches were simplistic, and that complexifying them by throwing in more 'variables' would solve anything. Rather, what we need are more rich and integrated accounts of the social relations which generate and might make sense of these 'variables'. Such integrated accounts will only emerge from deep ethnographic studies of particular social groups with real histories, and cannot emerge from abstract, mechanistic and culturally impoverished social psychological typologies of 'group differences'.

What is really required, therefore, is a move from asking about 'the nature of online relationships and identities', to asking the entirely different question: 'What do people do online?': the former already presumes a difference and a specificity (it presumes 'media characteristics'), the latter is an open-ended investigation. Above all, it leaves open the possibility that the relationship between online and offline social processes is an issue *for participants* or users and that they may come up with quite different responses to it. Hence, concepts like 'virtuality' or 'cyberspace' can be treated as (one possible) result of people's practices.

The classic example of this approach is also one of the earliest: Sherry Turkle's (1995) *Life on the Screen* gives a view of fairly extreme involvement in simulated environments – MUDs and MOOs – which are bounded and contained but allow for intense attachment to constructed identities, both of self and other. At the limit point, 'real life' (RL) is simply one 'window' on the screen, equal in investment and validity to any of the virtual lives going on in other (mudding) windows. What is interesting about Turkle's work is that, largely by virtue of her psychological orientation and interview-based material, she focuses less on presumed intrinsic features of the media and much more on how (and indeed why) participants construct and invest in these online lives. She construes these involvements as a developmental or therapeutic stage in the overall development of a participant's identity and social capacities. The value of immersive online participation to the participant is linked to the notion of a 'moratorium': a time, and in this case space, in which actions are protected from the realities of consequences, commitments and accountability (at least to outside agents: there is clearly an often intense ethics internal to the scene). Participants in her account may not be aware of the therapeutic or strategic function of their involvement: it's simply an absorbing game, played with gusto. On the other hand, interviews consistently raise a sense of liberation from the confines of real-world identities which are often self-characterized as inadequate – shy, geeky, unattractive, unassertive, etc. The projective space of online life is a relief.

Turkle is therefore observing how participants are using certain communicative potentials and constructing social spaces according to the need for a strategic separation from real life. Her work has a clearly normative dimension: identification with online life has a therapeutic potential but this is entirely compromised when participants confuse online experimentation with real life and as it were refuse to re-emerge. In contrast to much cyber-culture which refuses to give greater ontological, ethical or social status to 'real life', Turkle is clear that the distinction is essential to mental health.

From Turkle's book one can build up a very simple and common-sense view of a normative relation between online and offline experiences and their valuation by participants: immersive experiences, in which identity and sociality are treated with deep seriousness, give way to, for example, more instrumental uses of the Internet, clearly integrated into everyday life (Poster, 1995a); or playful uses of virtual spaces but with greater irony, less involvement or seriousness.

In this approach, virtuality is not a premise or assumed feature of the Internet; on the contrary, it is a social accomplishment – something that participants may or may not choose to do or to value, and which they need to accomplish through highly reflexive skills in using the communicative potentials of the various Internet media. The important questions then become: why and when do participants choose to construct 'cyberspaces' as separate from other spheres of social action, and to what extent; how do they accomplish this; and how do they understand the ensuing relationships?

We might contrast the world Turkle investigates with Miller and Slater's (2000) ethnography of Internet use in relation to Trinidad. By starting from people's practice, rather than presumptions about media characteristics such as virtuality, it became clear that the online/offline distinction played little if any role in people's use or experience of the Internet: people integrated the various Internet media into existing social practices and identities. For example, rather than using the Internet as a vehicle of disembedding from local context and Trinidadian identity, they consistently used it as a means of enacting and furthering their 'Trinidadianness'; indeed, it was the site for a considerable intensification of their awareness of themselves as 'Trini'. Entirely online relationships were often treated as being in the same plane as offline relationships, and were integrated with them; or relationships (e.g. amongst schoolchildren) were pursued seamlessly from offline to online and back again. On the other hand, we were able to interpret the Trinidadian use of the Internet as part of a desire to overcome the virtuality of Trinidad *prior* to the Internet. As a highly diasporic country, as well as one forged through dislocations of slavery, indentured labour and economic and political migration, it was always an identity that had to be constructed virtually, over distance, as an idea or 'imagined community' (Anderson, 1986). The Internet was widely experienced as a highly mundane tool for sustaining Trinidadian relationships and identities in very concrete ways: a family dispersed across several continents could use e-mail to keep a constant, everyday contact and hence sense of a 'house-hold' that was previously impossible; Trinidadians living 'away' could perform key aspects of their culture in chat rooms (the verbal banter of 'ole talk'; the fluid sociality of 'liming'). Hence, far from being virtual, Trinidadian use of the Internet aimed at realizing concretely a *previously* virtual identity (Slater, 2002).

The minimal place of the online/offline distinction in Trinidad is not an argument against this distinction as such (any more than the cyber literature can sustain an argument for it). Rather it is an argument that virtuality is one possible, but not necessary, emergent feature of people's assimilation of a new medium, and has to be established empirically in any given case. It is also crucial to recognize that the question of virtuality and the status of online identities and relationships are frequently a matter of extensive, articulate and reflexive discussion amongst participants in particular Internet settings. For example, Slater (1998; 2000a and b) looked at complex understandings and negotiations over the meaning and value of online relationships and 'objects'. One of the most vivid case studies of reflexive understandings of the ambiguity of online realities is Julian Dibbell's (1994; 1998) 'rape in cyberspace' article. The female-presenting avatar of a long-term female participant in a MUD is textually 'raped' by a male-presenting character. The woman involved is extremely upset and at the same time feels distinctly odd about being upset over a virtual event, something occurring in a purely textual space with no bodily or offline consequences. She is absolutely clear that this was not a real rape, and should not be treated as such; she is equally clear that as a virtual event it has serious consequences for herself and for the online social order in which she and others have made significant personal and social investments. This involvement in the virtual is socially new and unexplored: its meaning has to be framed both in its own right (much of the discussion is about how the MUD responded as an online community) and in relation to other realities. Finally, Dibbell's article posed the issue of the textuality of online life. Libertarian arguments are frequently based on a radical separation between what one says/portrays and what one physically does (e.g. pornography as textual space of fantasy is something other than an act of rape). Investment in virtuality seriously clouds this issue in that the constituted reality of the place arises from texts as shared actions: they do not represent something else, but constitute something new. The question Dibbell's article raised is about the ambiguous status of that something. (For a further discussion of the framing of online 'rape' in relation to different brands of online feminism, see Ward, 2000.)

Methodologies

The lines are drawn between the online and the offline as much by methodology as by theory, politics and culture. As previously indicated, the question originally addressed to the new media was, ironically, whether or not they were so situationally impoverished as to render them unfit for sociality; and comparison with face-to-face interaction, as if it were a normative standard ('pure', 'unmediated'), persists. Hence, methodological tools for investigating the means for achieving sustained interaction and understanding have been crucial. As it became apparent that interaction not only was sustained but evinced a seemingly unique and emergent culture specific to these media as social spaces, the research agenda became extremely skewed towards phenomena that were, by definition, internal to online relationships and identities. Some of this research has focused on analysis of the textuality of interaction (e.g. Danet, 2001, looks at the playful use of signs, graphics, timing, indexical references and staging in what she treats literally as theatrical performance). There has been a great interest in phenomena such as smilies and netiquette which attempt to, respectively, compensate for absent physical cues and regulate interaction in situationally appropriate ways. The conversational and contextually detached character of chat has also been ripe for ethnomethodological treatment, though less than one might expect.

However, the overwhelmingly dominant approach has been loosely ethnographic or participant observation in character. This has significantly been in part a result of the fact that the literature was generated by both academics and non-academics who were themselves learning the new media by exploring them and therefore could not (or would not) detach their analysis from the participation that generated it. More than this, however, the claim that CMC settings can sustain rich, durable and new forms of sociality invites the claims to community we have already investigated and, following closely on their heels, the correlate claim that ethnography is the way to study community. Ethnography carries with it assumptions about community and bounded social spaces that both seemed appropriate to the Internet and at the same time framed it in a very particular way, as a social space that could be examined in its own right, as internally meaningful and understandable in its own terms. The invocations to both community and ethnography arose very early indeed and arose in similar spaces (examples might include: Reid, 1991; Bruckman and Resnick, 1993; Jones, 1995; Reid, 1995; Baym, 1996; Hamman, 1996; Kling, 1996; Agre and Schuler, 1997; Borden and Harvey, 1998; van Dijk, 1998; Markham, 1998; Cherny, 1999; Smith and Kollock, 1999): MUDs, virtual communities such as the WELL and crossovers such as

LambdaMOO. Ethnography meant participation in online communities, often supported by online interviews, with a view to learning online ways of being and doing: just as with a bounded face-to-face community, one could understand the history, language, rules and values of a newsgroup or MUD by participating in it. This version of online ethnography took literally the extrapolation of 'community' to 'cyberspace', and therefore made two assumptions that rested on a radical separation between online and offline: that online sociality really had this kind of cultural coherence; and that either describing or accounting for it entirely in its own terms was a valid and fruitful enterprise. The first assumption seemed to presume what had to be established (cultural coherence), and the second accepted a very limited notion of explanation.

It is well to point out that just as claims to community invited ethnography, so too the choice of ethnography could *presume* the existence of online community. Ethnography as a methodological tradition of hermeneutic engagement with lived cultures is always already wedded to the notion of a bounded community in which such cultures are grounded. There are interesting ironies here: in the early literature, ethnography was closely linked to the claim that online life could be investigated as an integral culture or social order in its own right; later uses of the term have pointed in exactly the opposite direction, to the need to contextualize online within offline (Hakken, 1999; Miller and Slater, 2000; 2002). The relation between ethnography and the online/offline distinction was further complicated by the deconstruction within anthropology of the very notion of a community that could be treated as bounded and 'other' to the observer (Clifford and George 1986; Clifford, 1988). In so far as the idea of virtual community either draws on romantic notions of a bounded community, or is contrasted with it (virtual communities replace or displace real organic face-to-face community), it adopts a version of community that is no longer current in the study of offline ones. The objects of contemporary ethnography are not bounded communities inhabited by people who are quite separate from 'us'. Rather they are distributed, multi-sited cultures, which are already highly mediated (rather than organic, face-to-face) and in profound contact with 'others' rather than bounded and pristine. This also means that both online and offline the relation between culture and place is not something that can be assumed (here's a culture: now study it); rather the complex construction of relations between culture and place are central to what an ethnography has to study. How does its object come to be defined in the first place?

These critiques have a two-pronged implication for ethnographies of online life. On the one hand, they cut the ground from under the assumption that Internet communities exist in any unproblematic sense or that we can know in advance what one is and then study it. On the other hand, they open up the field to notions of ethnography that are far more appropriate to the Internet as an object. A clear and sophisticated example is Christine Hine's *Virtual Ethnography* (2000), which tries to investigate the formation of an online network of participants in a political issue (the Louise Woodward affair) as an emergent and fluid property of social practices. For example, she highlights what could be termed a dialectical relationship between Internet as culture and as cultural artefact. Hine describes the various Internet media (newsgroups, WWW) as 'potentially diverse but locally stabilized' (2000: 12). The stability of these media as cultural artefacts is partly bound up with the fact that participants regard them as a social space in which they reflexively monitor their own and others' performances. One's sense of what a good website or newsgroup communication is depends on monitoring what other people are doing *online* as well as on the place of these technologies in one's offline life. Her study looks at how:

> The Internet has routinely been employed by its users to monitor their own interpretations in the light of other users' interpretations. It has been treated as a performative

space in which users need to act appropriately. Through this, the technology is stabilized by users themselves. The social relations which form on the Internet stabilize the technology and encourage its users to understand it in particular ways

(2000: 12)

Nonetheless, the question of whether a purely online ethnography is methodologically defensible is fraught. On the one hand, the grounds for rejecting it are often seriously wrong-headed. For example, they often rest on misguided and romantic comparison with face-to-face interaction. This has a long history within ethnography: the authenticity and even heroic encounter of the ethnographer with the Other is treated as a direct and unmediated relationship with their brute reality. Yet it is obvious that physical presence is no guarantee of truth, nor is mediated presence necessarily untrue – especially if that is what one is actually studying. This connects with a second issue, the veracity and verification of claims made online: informants may lie about various aspects of their identity, undetectably. This is obviously a more serious problem in a context which is famous for identity play, in which distortion of identity has little negative consequence for participants. In fact, however, it is entirely unclear and unproved that this is a good characteriza- tion of cyberspace in general: it is precisely what needs to be studied, not presumed (see Baym, 2002). So long as it is presumed by critics of any online study, it can mean applying far higher standards of reliability to investigating this object as opposed to others. One could question every returned form in a mailed survey as to whether the respondent really was a man, or a teenager, etc. The common-sense assumption would be that doubt only arises where there is some reason to lie or pretend. In the case of cyber ethnographies, similarly, questions arise where there might be some point in lying about one's gender, and where the truth or falsity of that claim has some bearing. A simple example: if one is studying how a particular discursive space is organized in cyberspace, the gendering of the performed identities might be crucial, but not their offline identities. On the other hand, if one were trying to understand *why* certain performances arose, then actual genders might be crucial. And the fact that it is crucial to the researcher is still to be distinguished from the question of whether it is salient to the participants and therefore might give grounds for doubt. The point here is not to argue for or against giving anyone the benefit of the doubt but simply to say that – as in any research situation – the researcher has to make judgements and rules on the basis of situation-specific knowledge and thinking.

The crucial methodological question about the online/offline relationship, however, lies at another level: questions about the adequacy of descriptions and explanations. Do we need offline information in order to make sense of so-called online sociality? And the answer is: it depends on the question. An investigation into the question of 'How are cyberspaces sustained?' is obviously capable of widely different constructions. Rather like the distinction between macro- and micro- sociology, at one extreme, it might take in the political economy of access, differential IT skills and the kinds of material and symbolic power that enable only some people to participate, under particular social conditions, hence structuring the kinds of communication and sociality that go on there. At the other extreme, we can legitimately bracket these questions in order to describe (rather than explain) the mechanisms by which those who are able to participate sustain an internally coherent sociality, following them outwards to other media, or offline, as this seems ethnographically relevant. The relationship between online and offline is therefore methodologic- ally negotiable in terms of criteria of relevance and levels of analysis.

Finally, it is worth pointing out that ethnographically the distinction between offline and online does not clearly map onto the distinction between actual and virtual (as discussed further, below). Participants may treat some of their online activity as virtual, some as real. For example, it is a commonplace of using the new media that in one window one may be telling someone about what is happening in another window; the former is accorded a reality status from which the participant can comment on the 'virtual' action going on in the latter. Rather than a single online/offline or virtual/real distinction, what we are dealing with is more in line with Goffman's (1986) frame analysis.

Deconstruction and convergence of online and offline

The issue for this chapter has not been the 'effects' of the online on the offline or vice versa. Rather, the issue is how the distinction between the two has been constitutive of so many understandings of the Internet and its sociological significance and social innovation. What has been interesting is that both proponents and critics of the Internet have largely encountered it as something which stands outside offline realities. This focus has had good and bad points. On the one hand, it focuses attention on the media-specific and is a way of unearthing the radical potentials of the new technology (shall we become posthuman?); on the other hand, these very gains have also been losses in trying to understand and explain how the new potentials are actually used, for that requires attention to the continuities between the offline and online: a focus on the conditions and contexts of Internet use.

The implication of this discussion is that virtuality should be investigated not as a property of new media (indeed, any media) but rather as a possible social accomplishment of people using these media. The important questions are *whether* new media users make a distinction between online and offline, and if they do, *when* and *why* do they do it, and *how* they accomplish it practically. It is the making of the distinction that needs studying, rather than assuming it exists and then studying its consequences. An obvious corollary of regarding virtuality as practice is that any boundary drawn between online and offline will always be contingent, variable and unstable. This is true both historically and within specific interactions. We will take up this contingency under three different aspects: first, connections between communicative channels; second, the relation between medium and context; and third, changing social structures.

Use of the online/offline distinction often assumes, bizarrely, an opposition between CMC on the one hand and face-to-face, embodied interaction on the other. At the same time, there is an assumption that 'virtuality' maps onto the former, 'reality' onto the latter. This is obviously far too simple: conversations and MUDs hardly exhaust the communicative contexts of modernity. In fact, new media exist within a far wider mediascape that already blurs the online/offline distinction in diverse ways. For example, in Slater's sexpics research, informants who engaged in cybersex relationships often also engaged in phone sex. This could mean that virtuality is not restricted to being online, but can embrace, and even link, several media (the same point is made by those who cannot see any difference between penpals and cyber-relationships). Conversely, people moving from Internet chat to phone sex could regard this as a move from the virtual to the real. The move to telephone was seen as rendering the relationship more embodied and 'real': the 'grain of the voice' gave an authenticity to the other's presence, but also allowed verification of some identity claims (yes, she really is a woman, doesn't seem to be American, sounds like she could be twenty-something). Finally, different media within 'the Internet' might be integrated with other media in different ways in different relations to the online/offline distinction: erotic use of IRC was compatible with entirely non-sexual use of e-mail and ICQ (or, more often, people set up separate accounts, channels, lists, etc. for different activities).

That is to say, first, virtuality does not adequately capture the variety of online/offline contexts, and does not map onto them in a stable way. Second, even the term 'online' might not map consistently onto a single media technology. The telephone could legitimately be seen as part of the online experience in some circumstances, and that experience might or might not be regarded as a virtual one. This complexity is obviously compounded both by technical change and by users' increasingly sophisticated assimilation of new media into everyday life. For example, the merging of the PDA and the mobile phone, or of Internet and television, or of telephone and computer through voice over IP, might make it impossible to use the term 'online' meaningfully in the sense that was employed by the first generation of Internet research. These real potentials for convergence might be argued *either* to broaden what we mean by online, or – quite the opposite – to reduce any sense of 'the online' by integrating new media into a broader mediascape. This blurring of the online/offline distinction by producers reconfiguring technologies is complemented by users' often unpredictable ways of relating technologies to everyday life (as well as their own re-programming of technologies).

To move to the second aspect, we can also put this in broader methodological terms. The relationship between online and offline is sometimes interpreted as the relationship between phenomenon and context. Hence putting the Internet in context might mean placing the online into the offline (e.g. Hakken, 1999). This can be quite reductive: the offline is treated as that which makes sense of, or explains, the online. Again, this would seem to travesty both ethnography and most contemporary science studies (e.g., Bijker and Law, 1992; Latour, 1999; Silverstone and Hirsch, 1992; see Miller and Slater, 2002). Putting the online into the offline reifies both: it assumes a thing called the Internet and a thing called society, or community, or social relations, and at best investigates how one affects the other. The point developed above is to break down the dualism and see how each configures the other. We might take as an example a place that looks like a self-evident context in which the offline meets the online: the cybercafé. And yet the cybercafé is not a simple context in which the new media are used; it is in fact a diverse social field which reconfigures the Internet in different ways and is in turn reconfigured by it. For example, Wakeford (1999) examines the production of different Internets in terms of the different socialities enacted by different kinds of cybercafés, in particular in relation to gender. We can compare this with Miller and Slater (2002), in which two different cybercafés involved the construction of quite different relations between the online and offline. In the first, the Internet was largely regarded as a tool of community development and skilling which prioritized offline projects and relationships and focused on the instrumental use of websites, multimedia software and e-mail. In the second, the focus was on extensive sociality through chat systems: online and offline relationships seemed to exist on one seamless plane. Different contexts, different Internets; but also, different Internets, different contexts.

Finally, while various forms of convergence and interpenetration of media and contexts destabilize the online/offline distinction, there are also powerful regulatory forces operating on it. For example, many of the central political measures which are currently reformulating Internet use are being implemented specifically *in order* to remove the distinction between online and offline identities and social relations. Commercial and political use of the Internet requires that online participants are established as legal subjects with rights and responsibilities. Their unity as legal subjects needs to be verified through such things as electronic signatures and encryption; secure means of payment and financial verification (e.g. credit card transactions); definition and enforcement of copyright, taxation and the honouring of contracts. In contrast to cyberlibertarian discourses, it seems clear that the potential to establish multiple, mobile, fragmented identities, and to treat them as real, is in fact decided by offline regulatory regimes and generally in the direction of legal fixity. That is to say, the general tendency is to to assimilate online to offline and erase the distinction. The reality status of an on-line relationship is therefore complex in any particular instance and subject to broader institutional/legal arrangements. Offering your credit card number and clicking 'submit' makes for a legally binding transaction, as 'real' as if it were face to face. On the other hand it would be hard to imagine law courts awarding palimony to an online sexual partner after the relationship ended. Or not just now; there is a widely shared prophetic assumption, which might be self-fulfilling, that relationships which are treated as virtual today will become increasingly accepted and end up being regarded as real and binding. This may be true, but we need to understand the particular social grounds upon which ontological, legal or ethical status is accorded to such relationships.

Business organization, taking up the possibilities of e-commerce, also seems to move in the direction of integrating online and offline. The term 'clicks and mortar' – denoting a company that has both online and offline presence, both websites and shops – indicates that firms are having to rethink their relationship rather than assume their separation. Some companies are concerned to translate their offline symbolic and material capital (brand name and stock) into a significant online presence; others move in the opposite direction, capitalizing on web-based reputation and turnover. As in general, virtuality is a matter of social practices, and in the case of e-commerce the existence of an online/offline distinction may well be the result of marketing strategy: for example, there are new online banks that erase visible connection to the well-established offline banks that own them, in order to attract a different clientele. Similarly, the buzzword of 'disintermediation' is about using web-based facilities to bring consumers directly into the management systems of the firm: querying inventory, order tracking, customer services and so on. Although this invokes the rhetoric of a frictionless, dematerialized economy and virtual relationships, it is a very material knitting of the consumer into communications systems, which happen to cut out the 'middlemen' and hence massively reduce transaction costs. On the other hand, the fact that much political and commercial regulation moves in the direction of integrating online and offline does not mean that it simply reduces the online to *pre-existing* offline relations and identities.

Conclusion

The line of argument advanced here is certainly not specific to Internet studies: radio, television and telephone have equally to be understood through their particular appropriations. Television watched by an isolated Euro-American couch potato is arguably rather more virtual, for example, than a television in the communal setting of a Mexican taverna or a student common room. Further, as noted above, there is some evidence that new forms of mediation are historically first experienced as 'virtual' in that they seem to replace or mediate other forms of mediation which have historically been established as 'real'. Why *do* people seem to think that telephones are more real than internet chats? At the same time, the enormous social salience of notions of virtuality and cyberspace in relation to the Internet indeed seems to point to something media specific. Not media-specific characteristics, but rather (as noted earlier) a historically and geographically locatable convergence of politics with an investment in defining the Internet as a 'space apart'.

It seems perfectly valid to treat the online/offline distinction as part of a transitional phase for both users and researchers. It was a way for both to think through the communicative potentials and specificities of a range of new media in the process of seeing how to assimilate them into a wide range of social practices and institutions. It is more than likely that the online/offline distinction will be regarded as rather quaint and not quite comprehensible inside ten years. Users and researchers are already well advanced in the process of disaggregating 'the Internet' into its diversity of technologies and uses, generating a media landscape in which virtuality is clearly not a feature of the media but one social practice of media use amongst many others.

Moreover, as we have stressed throughout, the shift away from 'virtuality' is not merely a matter of research agendas, but also of the evolving practices of users as well as of commercial and legal regulatory structures. Real social diversity and change in the shaping of the online/offline distinction means that there is a desperate need, firstly, for ethnographic research that is attentive both to rich particularity and 'holistic' understanding of social relationships; and, secondly, for comparative and historical ethnography. It is fairly pointless to look abstractly for correlations between the variables of media 'characteristics' and communicative practices when participants are busily redefining both across times and places.

References

Agre, P.E. and Schuler, D. (eds) (1997) *Reinventing Technology, Rediscovering Community: Critical Studies in Computing as a Social Practice*: Ablex.

Anderson, B. (1986) *Imagined Communities*. London: Verso.

Barbrook, R. (1999) *The hi-tech Gift economy* http://www.firstmonday.dk/issus/issue3 12/barbrook/index.html

Bassett, C. (1997) 'Virtually gendered: life in an online world', in K. Gelder and S. Thornton (eds), *The Subcultures Reader*. London: Routledge.

Bauman, Z. (1990) *Thinking Sociologically*. Oxford: Basil Blackwell.

Baym, N. K. (1996) 'The Emergence of Community in Computer-Mediated Communication', in R. Shields (ed.), *Cultures of Internet: Virtual Spaces, Real Histories, Living Bodies*. London: Sage: 138–63.

—— (2002) 'Interpersonal Life Online', Sonia Livingstone and Leah Lievrouw (eds), *The Handbook of New Media: The Social Shaping of ICTS*. London: Sage, 67–76.

Bijker, W. E. and Law, J. (eds) (1992) *Shaping technology/building society: Studies in Sociotechnical change*. Cambridge, MA: MIT Press.

Borden, D. L. and Harvey, K. (eds) (1998) *The Electronic Grapevine: Rumor, Reputation and Reporting in the New On-Line Environment*. Mahwah, NJ: L Erlbaum Associates.

Brown, S.L. (1997) 'The free market as salvation from government: the anarcho-capitalist view', in J.G. Carrier (ed.), *Meanings of the Market: the Free Market in Western Culture*. Oxford: Berg.

Bruckman, A. and Resnick, M. (1993) *Virtual professional community: Results from MediaMoo*. ftp media.mit.edu in pub/MediaMoo/Papers/Media Moo3 cyberconf.

Butler, J. (1990) *Gender Trouble: Feminism and the Subversion of Identity*. London: Routledge.

—— (1993) *Bodies That Matter*. London: Routledge.

Castells, M. (1996) *The Rise of Network Society*. Oxford: Blackwell.

Cherny, L. (1999) *Conversation and community: Chat in a virtual world*, Stanford, CA: CSLI Publications.

Clifford, J. (1988) *The Predicament of Culture: Twentieth Century Ethnography, Literature and Art*. London: Harvard University Press.

Clifford, J.M. and George, E. (eds) (1986) *Writing Culture: the Poetics and Politics of Ethnography*. London: University of California Press.

Crang, P. (1997) 'Introduction: Cultural turns and the (re)constitution of economic geography', in R. Lee and J. Wills (eds), *Geographies of Economies*. London: Arnold.

Danet, B. (1998) 'Text as Mask: Gender, Play and Performance on the Internet', in S.G. Jones (ed.), *Cybersociety 2.0: Revisiting Computer-Mediated Communication and Technology*. London: Sage.

—— (2001) *Cyberpl@y: Communicating Online*. Oxford: Berg.

Dibbell, J. (1994) 'A rape in cyberspace; or, how an evil clow, a Haitian trickster spirit, two wizards, and a cast of dozens turned a database into a society', in M. Dery (ed.), *Flame Wars: the Discourse of Cyberculture*. London: Duke University Press.

—— (1998) *My Tiny Life: Crime and Passion in a Virtual World*. New York: Henry Holt.

Dijk, J. V. (1998) 'The reality of virtual communities', *Trends in Communication* 1(1): 39–63.

Dodge, M. and Kitchen, R. (2000) *Mapping Cyberspace*. London: Routledge.

Fine, G. A. (1983) *Shared Fantasy: Role-Playing Games as Social Worlds*. Chicago: University of Chicago Press.

Gibson, W. (1984) *Necromancer*. London: Gollanz.

Giddens, A. (1990) *The Consequences of Modernity*. Cambridge: Polity.

Goffman, E. (1986) *Frame Analysis*. Northeastern University Press.

Hakken, D. (1999) *Cyborgs@Cyberspace*. New York: Routledge.

Hamman, R. (1996) *Cyborpasms: Cybersex Amongst Multiple-Selves and Cyborgs in the Narrow-Bandwidth Space of America Online Chat Rooms*, University of Essex.

Haraway, D. (1990) 'A manifesto for cyborgs: science, technology and socialist feminism in the 1980s', in L. Nicholson (ed.), *Feminism/Postmodernism*. London: Routledge.

Hayles, N.K. (1999) *How We Became Posthuman: Virtual Bodies in Cybernetics, Literature, and Informatics*. Chicago: University of Chicago Press.

Hine, C. (2000) *Virtual Ethnography*. London: Sage.

Imken, O. (1999) 'The convergence of virtual and actual in the Global Matrix', in M. Crang, P. Crang and J. May (eds), *Virtual Geographies: Bodies and Spaces, Relations*. London: Routledge.

Jones, S.G. (ed.) (1995) *CyberSociety: Computer-Mediated Communication and Community*. London: Sage.

Kitchen, R. (1998) *Cyberspace: the World in the Wires*. Chichester: Wiley.

Kling, R. (1996) 'Social Relationships in Electronic Forums. Hangouts, Salons, Workplaces and Communities', *CMC Magazine*, 3(7).

Kuhn, A. (1982) *Women's Pictures: Feminism and Cinema*. London: Routledge & Kegan Paul.

Latour, B. (1999) *Pandora's Hope*. Cambridge: Harvard University Press.

Lupton, D. (1995) 'The embodied computer/user', in M. Featherstone and R. Burrows (eds), *Cyberspace, Cyberbodies, Cyberpunk: Cultures of Technological Embodiment*. London: Routledge.

MacCabe, C. (1985) 'Realism and the cinema: notes on some Brechtian themes', in T. Bennett, S. Boyd-Bowman, C. Mercer and J. Woollacott (eds), *Popular Television and Film*. London: BFI.

Maffesoli, M. (1996) *The Time of the Tribes*. London: Sage.

Markham, A. (1998) *Life Online: Researching Real Experience in Virtual Space*. London: Sage.

Marvin, C. (1988) *When Old Technologies Were New*. New York: Oxford University Press.

McLuhan, M. (1974) *Understanding Media*. London: Abacus.

Miller, D. and Slater, D. (2000) *The Internet: an Ethnographic Approach*. London: Berg.

—— (2002) 'Cybercafés', in M. Johnson (ed.), *Internet Ethnographies*. Oxford: Berg.

Mulgan, G. (1998) *Connexity: Responsibility. Freedom, Business and Power in the New Century*. London: Vintage.

Plant, S. (1995) 'The future looms: weaving women and cybernetics', in M. Featherstone and R. Burrows (eds), *Cyberspace, Cyberbodies, Cyberpunk: Cultures of Technological Embodiment*. London: Routledge.

—— (1996) 'On the matrix: cyberfeminist solutions', in R. Shields (ed.), *Cultures of Internet: Virtual Spaces, Real Histories, Living Bodies*. London: Sage.

—— (1997) *Zeros and Ones: Digital Women and the New Technoculture*. London: Fourth Estate.

Poster, M. (1995a) *CyberDemocracy: Internet and the Public Sphere*. Available at: http://www.hnet.uci.edu/mposter/writings/democ.html.

—— (1995b) 'Postmodern virtualities', in M. Featherstone and R. Burrows (eds), *Cyberspace, Cyberbodies, Cyberpunk: Cultures of Technological Embodiment*. London: Routledge.

Reid, E. (1991) *Electropolis: Communication and Community of Internet Relay Chat*.

—— (1995) 'Virtual worlds: culture and imagination', in S. G. Jones (ed.), *Cybersociety: Computer-Mediated Communication and Community*. London: Sage.

Rheingold, H. (1993) *The Virtual Community: Homesteading on the Electronic Frontier*. Reading, MA: Addison-Wesley.

Rival, L., Slater, D. and Miller, D. (1998) 'Sex and sociality: comparative ethnography of sexual objectification', *Theory, Culture and Society*, 15 (3–4): 295–322.

Robins, K. (1995) 'Cyberspace and the world we live in', in M. Featherstone and R. Burrows (eds), *Cyberspace, Cyberbodies, Cyberpunk: Cultures of Technological Embodiment*. London: Routledge.

Ross, A. (1998) *Real Love: in Pursuit of Cultural Justice*. New York: New York University Press.

Shields, R. (2000) 'Performing virtualities: virtual spaces?', *Space and Culture* 4 (5).

Silverstone, R. and Hirsch, E. (eds) (1992) *Consuming Technologies: Media and Information in Domestic Spaces*. London: Routledge.

Slater, D.R. (1998) 'Trading sexpics on IRC: embodiment and authenticity on the internet', *Body and Society*, 4 (4): 91–117.

—— (2000a) 'Consumption without scarcity: exchange and normativity in an internet setting', in P. Jackson, M. Lowe, D. Miller and F. Mort (eds), *Commercial Cultures: Economies, Practices, Spaces*. London: Berg. pp. 123–42.

—— (2000b) 'Political discourse and the politics of need: discourses on the good life in cyberspace', in L. Bennett and R. Entman (eds), *Mediated Politics*. Cambridge: Cambridge University Press.

—— (2001a) 'Making things real: ethics and order on the Internet', *Theory, Culture and Society* Special issue: Sociality/Materiality.

—— (2002) 'Modernity under construction: building the Internet in Trinidad', in P. Brey, T. Misa and A. Rip (eds), *Modernity and Technology: The Empirical Turn*, Boston: MIT Press.

Slevin, J. (2000) *The Internet and Society*. Cambridge: Polity.

Smith, M. and Kollock, P. (eds) (1999) *Communities in Cyberspace*. London: Routledge.

Springer, C. (1991) 'The pleasure of the interface', *Screen*, 32 (3).

—— (1996) *Electronic Eros: Bodies and Desire in the Postindustrial Age*. Austin, TX: University of Texas Press.

Standage, T. (1999) *The Victorian Internet: the Remarkable Story of the Telegraph and the Nineteenth Century's On-line Pioneers*. London: Penguin.

Thompson, J.B. (1995) *The Media and Modernity: A Social Theory of the Media*. Cambridge: Polity.

Turkle, S. (1984) *The Second Self: Computers and the Human Spirit*. London: Grafton.

—— (1995) *Life on the Screen: Identity in the Age of the Internet*. New York: Simon & Schuster.

Wakeford, N. (1999) 'Gender and the landscapes of computing in an Internet cafe', in M. Crang, P. Crang and J. May (eds), *Virtual Geographies: Bodies and Spaces, Relations*. London: Routledge.

Ward, K. (2000) 'The emergence of the hybrid community: rethinking the physical/virtual dichotomy', *Space and Culture* 4/5.

Suggestions for further reading
Compiled by Caroline Dover

Anthologies, textbooks and monographs

Abercrombie, N. (1997) *Television and Society*, Cambridge: Polity.
Abercrombie, N. and Longhurst, B. (1998) *Audiences*, London: Sage.
Adorno, T. (1991) *The Culture Industry*, London: Routledge.
Alasuutari, P. (ed.) (1999) *Rethinking the Media Audience: The New Agenda*, London: Sage.
Allen, R.C. (1985) *Speaking of Soap Operas*, Chapel Hill: University of North Carolina Press.
Allen, R.C. (ed.) (1992) *Channels of Discourse, Reassembled* (2nd edn), London and New York: Routledge.
Allen, R.C. (ed.) (1995) *To Be Continued: Soap Opera Around the World*, London: Routledge.
Altman, R. (1999) *Film/Genre*, London: British Film Institute.
Alvarado, M. and Buscombe, E. (1978) *Hazel: The Making of a TV Series*, London: British Film Institute.
Anderson, A. (1997) *Media, Culture and the Environment*, London: University College Press.
Anderson, C. (1994) *Hollywood TV: The Studio System in the Fifties*, Texas: University of Texas Press.
Ang, I. (1991) *Desperately Seeking the Audience*, London: Routledge.
Ang, I. (1996) *Living Room Wars: Rethinking Media Audiences for a Postmodern World*, London: Routledge.
Bacon-Smith, C. (1992) *Enterprising Women: Television Fandom and the Creation of Popular Myth*, Philadelphia: University of Pennsylvania Press.
Baehr, H. and Dyer, G. (eds) (1987) *Boxed In: Women and Television*, London: HarperCollins.
Bagdikian, B. (2000) *The Media Monopoly* (6th edn), Boston: Beacon.
Barker, C. (1999) *Television, Globalisation and Cultural Identities*, Buckingham: Open University.
Barker, M. and Petley, J. (eds) (2001) *Ill Effects: The Media/Violence Debate*, London: Routledge.
Barthes, R. (1977) *Image-Music-Text*, S. Heath (trans.), London: Fontana.
Baym, N.K. (1999) *Tune In, Log On: Soaps, Fandom and On-line Community*, Thousand Oaks, CA: Sage Publications.
Bell, D. (2001) *An Introduction to Cybercultures*, London: Routledge.
Bell, D. and Kennedy, B.M. (eds) (2000) *The Cybercultures Reader*, London: Routledge.
Benjamin, W. (1973) *Illuminations*, London: Fontana.
Bignell, J. (1997) *Media Semiotics: An Introduction*, Manchester: Manchester University Press.
Bocock, R. (1993) *Consumption*, London: Routledge.
Bolter, J.D. and Grusin, R. (1999) *Remediation: Understanding New Media*, Cambridge, MA: MIT Press.
Bonner, F. (2003) *Ordinary Television: Analyzing Popular TV*, Thousand Oaks, CA: Sage Publications.
Bourdieu, P. (1984) *Distinction*, London: Routledge.
Bourdieu, P. (1993) *The Field of Cultural Production: Essays on Art and Literature*, Cambridge: Polity.
Boyd-Barrett, O. and Newbold, C. (eds) (1995) *Approaches to Media: A Reader*, London: Arnold.
Branston, G. and Stafford, R. (eds) (1999) *The Media Student's Book* (2nd edn), London: Routledge.
Briggs, A. and Burke, P. (2001) *A Social History of the Media: From Gutenberg to the Internet*, Cambridge: Polity.
Brooker, P. and Brooker, W. (1997) (eds) *Postmodern Afterimages: A Reader in Film, Television and Video*, London: Arnold.

Brooker, W. and Jermyn, D. (eds) (2003) *The Audience Studies Reader*, London: Routledge.
Brunsdon, C. (2000) *The Feminist, the Housewife, and the Soap Opera*, Oxford: Oxford University Press.
Brunsdon, C., D'Acci, J. and Spiegel, L. (eds) (1997) *Feminist Television Criticism: A Reader*, Oxford: Oxford University Press.
Bruzzi, S. (2000) *New Documentary: A Critical Introduction*, London: British Film Institute.
Buckingham, D. (1996) *Moving Images: Understanding Children's Emotional Responses to Television*, Manchester: Manchester University Press.
Buckingham, D. (2000) *The Making of Citizens: Young People, News and Politics*, London: Routledge.
Buckingham, D. (ed.) (2002) *Small Screens: Television for Children*, London: University of Leicester Press.
Buckingham, D., Davies, H., Jones, K. and Kelley, P. (1999) *Children's Television in Britain: History, Discourse and Policy*, London: British Film Institute.
Burns, T. (1977) *The BBC: Public Institution and Private World*, London: Macmillan.
Buscombe, E. (ed.) (1999) *British Television: A Reader*, Oxford: Oxford University Press.
Butler, J. (1990) *Gender Trouble: Feminism and the Subversion of Identity*, London: Routledge.
Butler, J.G. (1994) *Television: Critical Methods and Applications*, Belmont: Wadsworth Publishing Company.
Byars, J. (1991) *All That Hollywood Allows: Re-reading Gender in 1950s Melodrama*, London: Routledge.
Caldwell, J. (1995) *Televisuality: Style, Crisis and Authority in American Television*, New Brunswick, NJ: Rutgers University Press.
Caldwell, J. and Everett, A. (eds) (2003) *New Media*, New York: Routledge.
Carroll, N. (1996) *Theorizing the Moving Image*. Cambridge: Cambridge University Press.
Casey, B., Casey, N., Calvert, B., French, L. and Lewis, J. (eds) (2001) *Television Studies: The Key Concepts*, London: Routledge.
Caughie, J. (2000) *Television Drama: Realism, Modernism and British Culture*, Oxford: Oxford University Press.
Coleman, M.R. (ed.) (2002) *Say It Loud! African-American Audiences, Media and Identity*, London: Routledge.
Corner, J. (1995) *Television Form and Public Address*, London: Arnold.
Corner, J. (1996) *The Art of Record*, Manchester: Manchester University Press.
Corner, J. (1999) *Critical Ideas in Television Studies*, Oxford: Oxford University Press.
Corner, J. and Pels, D. (eds) (2003) *Media and the Restyling of Politics*, London: Sage.
Corner, J., Schlesinger, P. and Silverstone, R. (eds) (1997) *International Media Research*, London: Routledge.
Cottle, S. (ed.) (2003) *Media Organisations and Production*, Thousand Oaks, CA: Sage Publications.
Couldry, N. (2000) *The Place of Media Power: Pilgrims and Witnesses of the Media Age*, London: Routledge.
Couldry, N. (2002) *Media Rituals: A Critical Approach*, London: Routledge.
Creeber, G. (2001) *The Television Genre Book*, London: British Film Institute.
Crisell, A. (1997) *An Introductory History of British Broadcasting*, London: Routledge.
Cruz, J., and Lewis, J. (eds) (1994) *Viewing, Reading, Listening: Audiences and Cultural Reception*, Boulder, Colorado: Westview Press.
Cubitt, S. (1998) *Digital Aesthetics*, London: Sage.
Cunningham, S. and Jacka, E. (1996) *Australian Television and International Mediascapes*, Cambridge: Cambridge University Press.
Cunningham, S. and Miller, T. (1994) *Contemporary Australian Television*, Kensington: UNSW Press.
Cunningham, S. and Sinclair, J. (eds) (2000) *Floating Lives: The Media and Asian Diasporas*, St. Lucia, Queensland: University of Queensland Press.
Cunningham, S. and Turner, G. (eds) (1993) *The Media in Australia: Industries, Texts and Audiences*, Sydney: Allen & Unwin.
Curran, J. (2002) *Media and Power*, London: Routledge.
Curran, J. and Gurevitch, M. (eds) (1991) *Mass Media and Society*, London: Edward Arnold.
Curran, J. and Seaton, J. (1997) *Power Without Responsibility: The Press and Broadcasting in Britain* (5th edn), London: Routledge.
D'Acci, J. (1994) *Defining Women: Television and the Case of Cagney & Lacey*, Chapel Hill: University of North Carolina Press.
Dahlgren, P. (1995) *Television and the Public Sphere: Citizenship, Democracy and the Media*, London: Sage.
Davis, G. (1988) *Breaking Up the ABC*, Sydney: Allen & Unwin.
Dayan, D. and Katz, E. (1992) *Media Events*, Cambridge, MA: Harvard University Press.
De Certeau, M. (1984) *The Practice of Everyday Life*, Berkeley: University of California Press.
Dickenson, R., Ramaswani, H., and Olga, L. (eds) (1999) *Approaches to Audiences*, London: Arnold.
Doty, A. (1993) *Making Things Perfectly Queer*, Minneapolis: University of Minnesota.
Dovey, J. (2000) *Freakshows: First Person Media and Factual Television*, London: Pluto.

Dowmunt, T. (ed.) (1993) *Channels of Resistance: Global TV and Local Empowerment*, London: British Film Institute.

Downing, J. (1996) *Internationalizing Media Theory*, London: Sage.

Downing, J., Mohammadi, A. and Sreberny-Mohammadi, A. (eds) (1995) *Questioning the Media: A Critical Introduction*, Thousand Oaks, CA: Sage Publications.

Doyle, G. (2002) *Understanding Media Economics*, London: Sage.

Du Gay, P. (ed.) (1998) *Production of Culture/Cultures of Production*, London: Sage/Open University.

Durham, M.G. and Kellner, D.M. (eds) (2001) *Media and Cultural Studies: Keyworks*, London: Blackwell.

During, S. (ed.) (1999) *The Cultural Studies Reader* (2nd edn), London: Routledge.

Elliot, P. (1972) *The Making of a Television Series*, London: Constable.

Ellis, J. (1982) *Visible Fictions: Cinema, Television, Video*, London: Routledge & Kegan Paul.

Ellis, J. (2002) *Seeing Things: Television in the Age of Uncertainty*, London: IB Tauris.

Evans, J. and Hall, S. (eds) (1999) *The Visual Culture Reader*, London: Sage/Open University.

Fairclough, N. (1995) *Media Discourse*, London: Arnold.

Feuer, J. (1995) *Seeing Through the Eighties: Television and Reaganism*, London: British Film Institute.

Feuer, J., Kerr, P. and Vahimagi, T. (eds) (1984) *MTM: "Quality Television"*, London: British Film Institute.

Fishman, M. and Cavender, G. (1998) *Entertaining Crime: Television Reality Programmes*, New York: Aldine De Gruyter.

Fiske, J. (1987) *Television Culture*, London: Methuen.

Fiske, J. (1989) *Reading the Popular*, Boston, MA: Unwin Hyman.

Fleming, D. (ed.) (2001) *Formations: 21st Century Media Studies*, Manchester: Manchester University Press.

Franklin, B. (ed.) (2001) *British Television Policy: A Reader*, London: Routledge.

French, D. and Richards, M. (eds) (2000) *Television in Contemporary Asia*, Thousand Oaks, CA: Sage Publications.

Friedman, J. (ed.) (2002) *Reality Squared: Televisual Discourse on the Real*, New Jersey: Rutgers University Press.

Garnham, N. (1978) *Structures of Television*, London: British Film Institute.

Garnham, N. (1990) *Capitalism and Communication: Global Culture and the Economics of Information*, London: Sage.

Gauntlett, D. (1997) *Video Critical: Children, the Environment and Media Power*, London: John Libbey Media.

Gauntlett, D. (ed.) (2000) *Web Studies: Rewiring Media Studies for the Digital Age*, London: Arnold.

Gauntlett, D. (2002) *Media, Gender and Identity*, London: Routledge.

Gauntlett, D. and Hill, A. (1999) *TV Living: Television, Culture and Everyday Life*, London: Routledge.

Gavin, N. (ed.) (1998) *Media, Economy and Public Knowledge*, London: Cassell.

Geraghty, C. (1991) *Women and Soap Opera: A Study of Prime Time Soaps*, London: Polity.

Geraghty, C. and Lusted, D. (eds) (1998) *The Television Studies Book*, London: Arnold.

Gerbner, G., Mowlana, H. and Schiller, H.I. (eds) (1996) *Invisible Crises: What Conglomerate Control of Media Means for America and the World*, Boulder, CO: Westview Press.

Giddens, A. (1990) *The Consequences of Modernity*, Cambridge: Polity.

Giddens, A. (1991) *Modernity and Self-Identity: Self and Society in the Late Modern Age*, Cambridge: Polity.

Giddens, A. (2000) *Runaway World: How Globalisation is Shaping Our Lives*, London and New York: Routledge.

Gillespie, M. (1995) *Television, Ethnicity and Cultural Change*, London: Routledge.

Ginsberg, F., Abu-Lughod, L. and Larkin, B. (eds) (2002) *Media Worlds: Anthropology on New Terrain*, Berkeley: University of California Press.

Gitlin, T. (1994) *Inside Prime Time* (2nd edn), London: Routledge.

Glasgow Media Group (1982) *Really Bad News*, London: Writers and Readers.

Glynn, K. (2000) *Tabloid Culture: Trash Taste, Popular Power, and the Transformation of American Television*, Durham, NC and London: Duke University Press.

Golding, P. and Harris, P. (eds) (1997) *Beyond Cultural Imperialism: Globalization, Communication and the New International Order*, Thousand Oaks, CA: Sage Publications.

Goodwin, P. (1999) *Television Under the Tories*, London: British Film Institute.

Gray, A. (1992) *Video Playtime: the Gendering of a Leisure Technology*, London: Routledge.

Gray, A. (2002) *Research Practice for Cultural Studies*, Thousand Oaks, CA: Sage Publications.

Gray, H. (1995) *Watching Race: Television and the Struggle for 'Blackness'*, Minnesota: University of Minnesota Press.

Gripsrud, J. (1995) *The Dynasty Years: Hollywood Television and Critical Media Studies*, London: Routledge.

Gripsrud, J. (ed.) (1999) *Television and Common Knowledge*, London: Routledge.

Gunter, B. (1995) *Television and Gender Representation*, London: John Libbey.

Gunter, B. and McAleer, J. (1990) *Children and Television: The One-Eyed Monster?*, London: Routledge.

Habermas, J. (1989) *The Structural Transformation of the Public Sphere*, T. Burger (trans.), Cambridge: Polity.

Hagen, I. and Wasko, J. (eds) (2000) *Consuming Audiences?: Production and Reception in Media Research*, Cresskill, NJ: Hampton Press.

Hall, S. (ed.) (1997) *Representation: Cultural Representations and Signifying Practices*, London: Sage/Open University Press.

Hall, S., Hobson, D., Lowe, A. and Willis, P. (eds) (1981) *Culture, Media, Language*, London: Hutchinson.

Hallam, J. (2000) *Nursing the Image: Media, Culture and Professional Identity*, London: Routledge.

Hamamoto, D.Y. (1994) *Monitored Peril: Asian Americans and the Politics of Television*, Minneapolis: University of Minnesota Press.

Haralovitch, M. B. and Rabinovitz, L. (eds) (1999) *Television, History, and American Culture: Feminist Critical Essays*, Durham, NC and London: Duke University Press.

Harries, D. (ed.) (2002) *The New Media Book*, Berkeley: University of California Press/British Film Institute.

Hartley, J. (1982) *Understanding News*, London: Methuen.

Hartley, J. (1992) *Tele-ology: Studies in Television*, London: Routledge.

Hartley, J. (1998) *Uses of Television*, London: Routledge.

Hartley, J. (2002) *Communication, Cultural and Media Studies: The Key Concepts*, New York: Routledge.

Hartley, J. and Pearson, R. (eds) (2000) *American Cultural Studies: A Reader*, Oxford: Oxford University Press.

Hebdige, D. (1988) *Hiding in the Light*, London: Comedia.

Hendershot, H. (1998) *Saturday Morning Censors: Television Regulation Before the V-chip*, Durham, NC: Duke University Press.

Herman, E.S. and Chomsky, N. (1988) *Manufacturing Consent: The Political Economy of the Mass Media*, New York: Pantheon.

Hesmondhalgh, D. (2002) *The Cultural Industries*, London: Sage/Open University.

Highmore, B. (ed.) (2002) *The Everyday Life Reader*, London: Routledge.

Hills, M. (2002) *Fan Cultures*, London: Routledge.

Hine, C. (2000) *Virtual Ethnography*, London: Sage.

Hobson, D. (1982) *Crossroads: The Drama of a Soap Opera*, London: Methuen.

Hobson, D. (2002) *Soap Opera*, Cambridge: Polity.

Hodge, R. and Trip, D. (1986) *Children and Television: A Semiotic Approach*, Cambridge: Polity.

hooks, b. (1992) *Black Looks: Race and Representation*, Toronto: Between the Lines.

hooks, b. (1994) *Outlaw Culture: Resisting Representations*, New York: Routledge.

Jameson, F. (1998) *The Cultural Turn: Selected Writings on the Postmodern, 1983–1998*, London: Verso.

Jenkins, H. (1992) *Textual Poachers: Television Fans and Participatory Culture*, New York: Routledge.

Jhally, S. and Lewis, J. (1992) *Enlightened Racism: The Cosby Show, Audiences and the Myth of the American Dream*, Boulder, CO: Westview Press.

Kaplan, A.E. (1990) *Rocking Around the Clock: Music TV, Postmodernism and Consumer Culture*, New York: Methuen.

Karim, H. K. (ed.) (2003) *The Media of Diaspora*, New York: Routledge.

Keane, J. (1991) *The Media and Democracy*, Cambridge: Polity.

Kellner, D. (1995) *Media Culture. Cultural Studies, Identity, and Politics Between the Modern and the Postmodern*, London: Sage.

Kilborn, R. and Izod, J. (1997) *An Introduction to Television Documentary*, Manchester: Manchester University Press.

Kolar-Panov, D. (1997) *Video, War and the Diasporic Imagination*, London: Routledge.

Lacey, N. (1998) *Image and Representation: Key Concepts in Media Studies*, Basingstoke: Macmillan.

Langer, J. (1998) *Tabloid Television: Popular Journalism and the 'Other News'*, London: Routledge.

Lee, M. and Solomon, N. (1990) *Unreliable Sources*, New York: Lyle Stuart.

Lembo, R. (2000) *Thinking Through Television*, Cambridge: Cambridge University Press.

Levinson, P. (1999) *Digital McLuhan*, London: Routledge.

Levrouw, L.A. and Livingstone, S. (eds) (2002) *Handbook of New Media: Social Shaping and Consequences of ICTs*, London: Sage.

Lewis, J. (1991) *The Ideological Octopus: Explorations into the Television Audience*, London: Routledge.

Lewis, L. (ed.) (1992) *The Adoring Audience: Fan Culture and Popular Media*, London: Routledge.

Liebes, T. and Curran, J. (eds) (1998) *Media, Ritual and Identity*, London: Routledge.

Livingstone, S. (1998) *Making Sense of Television: The Psychology of Audience Interpretation* (2nd edn), London: Butterworth-Heinemann.

Livingstone, S. (2002) *Young People and New Media: Childhood and the Changing Media Environment*, London: Sage.

Livingstone, S. and Lunt, P. (1994) *Talk on Television: Audience Participation and Public Debate*, London: Routledge.

Lull, J. (1990) *Inside Family Viewing: Ethnographic Research on Television Audiences*, London: Routledge.

Lull, J. (ed.) (2000) *Culture in the Communication Age*, London: Routledge.

Ma, E.K.W. (1999) *Culture, Politics, and Television in Hong Kong*, London: Routledge.

Mackay, H. (ed.) (1997) *Consumption and Everyday Life*, London: Sage.

Mackay, H. and O'Sullivan, T. (eds) (1999) *The Media Reader: Continuity and Transformation*, London: Open University/Sage.

Mankekar, P. (1999) *Screening Culture, Viewing Politics: An Ethnography of Television, Womanhood, and Nation in Postcolonial India*, Durham, NC and London: Duke University Press.

Manovitch, L. (2002) *The Language of New Media*, Cambridge, MA: MIT Press.

Marshall, J. and Werndly, A. (2002) *The Language of Television*, London: Routledge.

Martin-Barbero, J. (1993) *Communication, Culture and Hegemony*, London: Sage.

Mattelart, A. (2003) *The Information Society: An Introduction*, Thousand Oaks, CA: Sage Publications.

Maxwell, R. (ed.) (2001) *Culture Works: The Political Economy of Culture*, Minneapolis: University of Minnesota.

McCarthy, A. (2001) *Ambient Television: Visual Culture and Public Space*, Durham, NC: Duke University Press.

McChesney, R. (1999) *Rich Media, Poor Democracy: Communication Politics in Dubious Times*, London: Sage Publications.

McGuigan, J. (1992) *Cultural Populism*, London: Routledge.

McLuhan, E. and Zingrone, F. (eds) (1995) *Essential McLuhan*, London: Routledge.

McLuhan, M. (2001) *Understanding Media* (reprint), London: Routledge.

McNair, B. (1999) *News and Journalism in the UK*, London: Routledge.

McQuail, D. (1997) *Audience Analysis*, London: Sage.

McQuail, D. (ed.) (2002) *McQuail's Reader in Mass Communication Theory*, London: Sage.

McRobbie, A. (1994) *Postmodernism and the Popular*, London: Routledge.

Meehan, E. R. and Riordan, E. (2002) *Sex and Money: Feminism and Political Economy in the Media*, Minneapolis: University of Minnesota Press.

Mellencamp, P. (ed.) (1990) *Logics of Television: Essays in Cultural Criticism*, Bloomington: Indiana University Press.

Meyrowitz, J. (1985) *No Sense of Place: The Impact of Electronic Media on Social Behaviour*, New York: Oxford University Press.

Miller, D. and Slater, D. (2000) *The Internet: An Ethnographic Approach*, Oxford: Berg.

Miller, T. (2001) *Globalization and Sport: Playing the World*, London: Sage.

Miller, T. (ed.) (2002) *Television Studies*, Berkeley: University of California Press/British Film Institute.

Millington, B. and Nelson, R. (1986) *'Boys From the Blackstuff': The Making of TV Drama*, London: Comedia.

Moores, S. (1995) *Satellite Television and Everyday Life: Articulating Technology*, London: John Libbey.

Moores, S. (2000) *Media and Everyday Life in Modern Society*, Edinburgh: Edinburgh University Press.

Moran, A. (ed.) (1992) *Stay Tuned: An Australian Broadcasting Reader*, Sydney: Allen & Unwin.

Moran, A. (1998) *Copycat TV: Globalisation, Program Formats and Cultural Identity*, Luton: University of Luton Press.

Moran, J. M. (2002) *There's No Place Like Home Video*, Minneapolis: University of Minnesota.

Morley, D. (1986) *Family Television: Cultural Power and Domestic Leisure*, London: Comedia.

Morley, D. (1992) *Television, Audiences and Cultural Studies*, London: Routledge.

Morley, D. (2000) *Home Territories: Media, Mobility and Identity*, London: Routledge.

Morley, D. and Brunsdon, C. (1999) *The Nationwide Television Studies*, London: Routledge.

Morley, D. and Chen, K. (eds) (1996) *Stuart Hall: Critical Dialogues in Cultural Studies*, London: Routledge.

Morley, D. and Robins, K. (1995) *Spaces of Identity: Global Media, Electronic Landscapes and Cultural Boundaries*, London: Routledge.

Morley, D. and Robins, K. (eds) (2001) *British Cultural Studies: Geography, Nationality and Identity*, Oxford: Oxford University Press.

Morse, M. (1998) *Virtualities*, Bloomington: Indiana University Press.

Mosco, V. (1996) *The Political Economy of Communication*, London: Sage.

Mulvey, L. (1989) *Visual and Other Pleasures*, Basingstoke: Macmillan.

Mumford, L. S. (1995) *Love and Ideology in the Afternoon: Soap Opera, Women and Television Genre*, Bloomington: Indiana University Press.

Neale, S. (2000) *Genre and Hollywood*, London: Routledge.

Neale, S. and Krutnik, F. (1990) *Popular Film and Television Comedy*, London: Routledge.

Nelson, R. (1997) *TV Drama in Transition: Forms, Values and Cultural Change*, London: Macmillan.
Newcomb, H. (ed.) (2000) *Television: The Critical View* (6th edn), New York: Oxford University Press.
Newcomb, H. and Alley, R. (1983) *The Producer's Medium: Conversations with Creators of American Television*, New York: Oxford University Press.
Nichols, B. (1994) *Blurred Boundaries*, Bloomington: Indiana University Press.
O'Regan, T. (1993) *Australian Television Culture*, Sydney: Allen & Unwin.
O'Sullivan, T. and Jewkes, Y. (eds) (1997) *The Media Studies Reader*, London: Arnold.
O'Sullivan, T., Dutton, B. and Rayner, P. (1998) *Studying the Media: An Introduction*, London: Arnold.
Paget, D. (1998) *No Other Way To Tell It: Dramadoc/Docudrama on Television*, Manchester: Manchester University Press.
Palmer, P. (1986) *The Lively Audience: A Study of Children Around the TV Set*, Boston: Allen and Unwin.
Philo, G. (1990) *Seeing and Believing: The Influence of Television*, London: Routledge.
Poster, M. (ed.) (1988) *Jean Baudrillard: Selected Writings*, Cambridge: Polity.
Poster, M. and Aronowitz, S. (2001) *The Information Subject*, Amsterdam: G+B Arts International.
Radway, J. (1984) *Reading the Romance: Women, Patriarchy and Popular Literature*, Chapel Hill: University of North Carolina Press.
Robbins, D. (2000) *Bourdieu and Culture*, London: Sage.
Robins, K. (1996) *Into the Image: Culture and Politics in the Field of Vision*, London: Routledge.
Robins, K. and Webster, F. (1999) *Times of the Technoculture: From the Information Society to the Virtual Life*, London: Routledge.
Roscoe, J and Hight, C. (2001) *Faking It: Mock-documentary and the Subversion of Factuality*, Manchester: Manchester University Press.
Rose, B.G. (ed.) (1985) *TV Genres: A Handbook and Reference Guide*, Westport: Greenwood Press.
Ruddock, A. (2001) *Understanding Audiences*, London: Sage.
Sakr, N. (2002) *Satellite Realms: Transnational Television, Globalization and the Middle East*, London: IB Taurus.
Scannell, P. (ed.) (1991) *Broadcast Talk*, London: Sage.
Scannell, P. (1996) *Radio, Television and Modern Life*, London: Blackwell.
Scannell, P. Schlesinger, P. and Sparks, C. (eds) (1992) *Culture and Power: A Media, Culture and Society Reader*, London: Sage.
Schiller, D. (2000) *Digital Capitalism: Networking the Global Market System*, Cambridge, MA: MIT Press.
Schiller, H.I. (1996) *Information Inequality: The Deepening Social Crisis in America*, New York: Routledge.
Schlesinger, P. (1978) *Putting 'Reality' Together*, London: Constable.
Schudson, M. (1995) *The Power of News*, Cambridge, MA.: Harvard University Press.
Sconce, J. (2000) *Haunted Media: Electronic Presence from Telegraphy to Television*, Durham, NC: Duke University Press.
Seale, C. (2003) *Media and Health*, London: Sage Publications.
Seiter, E. (1999) *Television and New Media Audiences*, Oxford: Oxford University Press.
Seiter, E., Borchers, H., Kreutzner, G. and Warth, E. (eds) (1989) *Remote Control: Television, Audiences and Cultural Power*, London: Routledge.
Shattuc, J. (1997) *The Talking Cure: Women and TV Talk Shows*, New York: Routledge.
Shohat, E. and Stam, B. (1994) *Unthinking Eurocentrism: Multiculturalism and the Media*, London and New York: Routledge.
Silverstone, R. (1985) *Framing Science: The Making of a BBC Documentary*, London: British Film Institute.
Silverstone, R. (1994) *Television and Everyday Life*, London: Routledge.
Silverstone, R. (1999) *Why Study the Media?*, London: Sage.
Silverstone, R. and Hirsch, E. (eds) (1992) *Consuming Technologies: Media and Information in Domestic Spaces*, London: Routledge.
Sinclair, J. (1999) *Latin American Television: A Global View*, Oxford: Oxford University Press.
Sinclair, J., Jacka, E. and Cunningham, S. (eds) (1995) *New Patterns in Global Television: Peripheral Vision*, New York: Oxford University Press.
Smith, A. (ed.) (1998) *Television: An International History*, Oxford: Oxford University Press.
Sparks, C. (1998) *Communism, Capitalism and the Mass Media*, London: Sage.
Spigel, L. (1992) *Make Room for TV: Television and the Family Ideal in Postwar America*, Chicago: University of Chicago Press.
Spigel, L. (2001) *Welcome to the Dreamhouse: Popular Media and Postwar Suburbs*, Durham, NC: Duke University Press.

Sreberny-Mohammadi, A. (1999) *Include Me In: Rethinking Ethnicity on Television: Audience and Production Perspectives*, London: BSC/ITC.

Sreberny-Mohammadi, A., Winseck, D., McKenna, J. and Boyd-Barrett, O. (eds) (1997) *Media in Global Context: A Reader*, London: Arnold.

Stevenson, N. (2002) *Understanding Media Cultures* (2nd edn), London: Sage.

Storey, J. (ed.) (1998) *Cultural Theory and Popular Culture: A Reader* (2nd edn), Harlow: Longman.

Streeter, T. (1996) *Selling the Air: A Critique of the Policy of Commercial Broadcasting in the United States*, Chicago: University of Chicago Press.

Strinati, D. (2000) *An Introduction to Studying Popular Culture*, London: Routledge.

Thomas, L. (2002) *Fans, Feminisms and 'Quality' Media*, New York: Routledge.

Thompson, J.B. (1995) *The Media and Modernity: A Social Theory of the Media*, Cambridge: Polity.

Thussu, D.K. (2000) *International Communication: Continuity and Change*, London: Arnold.

Thwaites, T., Davis, L. and Mules, W. (2002) *Introducing Cultural and Media Studies: A Semiotic Approach*, Basingstoke: Palgrave.

Torres, S. (ed.) (1998) *Living Color: Race and Television in the United States*, Durham, NC: Duke University Press.

Tracey, M. (1998) *The Decline and Fall of Public Service Broadcasting*, Oxford: Oxford University Press.

Tulloch, J. (1990) *TV Drama: Agency, Audience and Myth*, London: Routledge.

Tulloch, J. (2000) *Watching Television Audiences: Cultural Theories and Methods*, London: Arnold.

Tulloch, J. and Alvarado, M. (1983) *Doctor Who: The Unfolding Text*, London: Macmillan.

Tulloch, J. and Jenkins, H. (1995) *Science Fiction Audiences: Watching Doctor Who and Star Trek*, London and New York: Routledge.

Tulloch, J. and Moran, A. (1986) *A Country Practice: 'Quality Soap'*, Sydney: Currency Press.

Tulloch, J. and Turner, G. (eds) (1989) *Australian Television: Programs, Pleasures and Politics*, Sydney: Allen & Unwin.

Tumber, H. (ed.) (1999) *News: A Reader*, Oxford: Oxford University Press.

Tumber, H. (ed.) (2000) *Media Power, Professionals and Policies*, London: Routledge.

Tunstall, J. (1977) *The Media are American*, New York: Columbia University Press.

Tunstall, J. (1993) *Television Producers*, London: Routledge.

Turkle, S. (1995) *Life on Screen: Identity in the Age of the Internet*, New York: Simon and Schuster.

Turner, G. and Cunningham, S. (eds) (2000) *The Australian TV Book*, Sydney: Allen & Unwin.

Turner, G., Bonner, F. and Marshall, P.D. (2000) *Fame Games*, Cambridge: Cambridge University Press.

Van Zoonen, L. (1994) *Feminist Media Studies*, London: Sage.

Wang, G., Servaes, J. and Goonasekera, A. (eds) (2000) *The New Communications Landscape: Demystifying Media Globalization*, London: Routledge.

Wasko, J., Phillips, M. and Meehan, E.R. (2001) *Dazzled by Disney? The Global Disney Audiences Project*, London: Leicester University Press.

White, M. (1992) *Tele-Advising: Therapeutic Discourse in American Television*, Chapel Hill: University of North Carolina Press.

Wieten, J., Murdock, G. and Dahlgren, P. (eds) (2000) *Television Across Europe: A Comparative Introduction*, London: Sage.

Williams, R. (1963) *Culture and Society*, London: Penguin.

Williams, R. (1974) *Television, Technology and Cultural Form*, New York: Schocken Books.

Williamson, J. (1978) *Decoding Advertisements: Ideology and Meaning in Advertising*, London: Marion Boyers.

Winston, B. (1995) *Claiming the Real: Documentary Film Revisited*, London: British Film Institute.

Winston, B. (1998) *Media, Technology and Society*, London: Routledge.

Winston, B. (2000) *Lies, Damn Lies and Documentaries*, London: British Film Institute.

Zook, K.B. (1999) *Color by FOX: The Fox Network and the Revolution in Black Television*, New York: Oxford University Press.

Selected journals

Editorial Note: We have chosen not to include journal articles in this selected bibliography, but rather to indicate a wide range of English language international journals that publish articles in television studies, and related areas. We hope readers will use this list to facilitate compiling up to date and subject specific lists of academic articles. Readers looking for references to specific journal articles can also browse the reference lists at the end of each individual article in this collection.

Camera Obscura: Feminism, Culture and Media Studies. Bloomington, IN: Indiana University Press.
Communication and Media Studies. London and Thousand Oaks, CA: Sage Publications
Communication Research. London and Thousand Oaks, CA: Sage Publications.
Communication Review. London and New York: Taylor and Francis.
Communication Theory. Oxford: Oxford University Press.
Communications Abstracts. London and Thousand Oaks, CA: Sage Publications.
Communications: The European Journal of Communication. Berlin: Quintessenz Verlag
Comparative American Studies. London and Thousand Oaks, CA: Sage Publications.
Continuum: Journal of Media and Cultural Studies. Abingdon: Carfax.
Convergence: the Journal of Research into New Media. Luton: John Libbey Media.
Critical Quarterly. Oxford: Blackwells.
Critical Studies in Media Communication. Annandale, Va.: National Communication Association.
Cultural Studies. London and New York: Routledge.
Discourse and Society. London and Thousand Oaks, CA: Sage Publications.
Emergences: Journal for the Study of Media and Composite Cultures. Abingdon: Carfax.
Ethnicities. London and Thousand Oaks, CA: Sage Publications.
European Journal of Communication. London and Thousand Oaks, CA: Sage Publications.
European Journal of Cultural Studies. London and Thousand Oaks, CA: Sage Publications.
Feminist Media Studies. London CA: Routledge.
Feminist Theory. London and Thousand Oaks, CA: Sage Publications.
Film Quarterly. California: University of California Press.
Gazette: the International Journal for Communication Studies. London and Thousand Oaks, CA: Sage Publications.
Historical Journal of Film, Radio and Television. Abingdon: Carfax.
Hollywood Quarterly. Berkeley, California: University of California Press.
Information, Communication and Society. London and New York: Taylor and Francis.
International Journal of Cultural Studies. London and Thousand Oaks, CA: Sage Publications.
Journal of African Cultural Studies. Abingdon: Carfax.
Journal of American Culture. Oxford: Blackwells.
Journal of Broadcasting and Electronic Media. Washington D.C.: Broadcast Education Association.
Journal of Communication Inquiry. London and Thousand Oaks, CA: Sage Publications.
Journal of Communication. Oxford: Oxford University Press.
Journal of Consumer Culture. London and Thousand Oaks, CA: Sage Publications.
Journal of Contemporary Ethnography. London and Thousand Oaks, CA: Sage Publications.
Journal of Intercultural Studies. Abingdon: Carfax.
Journal of Language and Social Psychology. London and Thousand Oaks, CA: Sage Publications.
Journal of Latin American Cultural Studies. Abingdon: Carfax.
Journal of Material Culture. London and Thousand Oaks, CA: Sage Publications.
The Journal of Media Economics. Mahwah, N.J.: Lawrence Erlbaum.
Journal of Popular Culture. Oxford: Blackwells.
Journal of Popular Film and Television. Washington D.C.: Heldreef Publications.
Journal of Spanish Cultural Studies. Abingdon: Carfax.
Journal of Visual Culture. London and Thousand Oaks, CA: Sage Publications.
Media History. Abingdon: Carfax.
Media International Australia. Brisbane, Australia: Australian Key Centre for Cultural and Media Policy.
Media Studies Journal. New York: Freedom Forum Media Studies Centre.
Media, Culture and Society. London and Thousand Oaks, CA: Sage Publications.
Men and Masculinities. London and Thousand Oaks, CA: Sage Publications.
New Media and Society. London and Thousand Oaks, CA: Sage Publications.
Nordicom Review. Goteborg: Nordicom.
Parallax. London and New York: Routledge.
Race and Class. London and Thousand Oaks, CA: Sage Publications.
Representations. Berkeley: University of CA Press.
Screen. Oxford: Oxford University Press.
Sight and Sound. London: British Film Institute.
Social Semiotics. Abingdon: Carfax.
Social Text. Durham, NC: Duke University Press.
South Asian Popular Culture. London and New York: Routledge.

Space and Culture. London and Thousand Oaks, CA: Sage Publications.
Television and New Media. London and Thousand Oaks, CA: Sage Publications.
Theory, Culture and Society. London and Thousand Oaks, CA: Sage Publications.
Time and Society. London and Thousand Oaks, CA: Sage Publications.
The Velvet Light Trap. Austin, TX: University of Texas Press.

Index

advertising 60–4, 71, 144, 190–1, 226–39, 244, 289–90, 303–7, 394–7, 498–9, 529–30
Allen, R. C. 127, 152, 168, 242–57, 471–2, 509, 514, 516
Altman, R. 175
America's Funniest Home Videos 345–6, 559
Americanisation 84, 111–14
Ang, I. 52, 115–26, 134, 247, 390, 462, 470, 517
Attachments 561, 579
Attallah, P. 11
audience research 8, 461–78, 573
authenticity 183, 200, 212, 306, 337, 412, 546–9, 559–61, 600–1

Barthes, R. 115, 123–4, 191, 229–30, 550, 555
Baym, N. K. 603–4
Bazin, A. 303, 545–6, 550
Beauty And The Beast 301–2
Benjamin, W. 337, 345, 500, 548, 552, 582
Bennett, T. 9, 56
Big Brother 23, 166, 168, 270–1, 281, 311–21, 370, 579
Blumler, J. 35, 37–8, 41–2, 46
Bobo, J. 477–8
Bollywood 23, 154, 156, 273
Booth, W. C. 238
Bourdieu, P. 53, 117–19, 178, 462, 469–74, 481–2

broadcasting institutions 27–32, 36, 41–2, 166, 206–7
Brunsdon, C. 3, 6–8, 179, 311, 385–6, 406, 428, 464, 471–3
Buckingham, D. 244, 248, 475, 479–93
Buffy The Vampire Slayer 510–15, 521, 571–2
Butler, J. 377–9, 470, 602–3

cable television 13–14, 82, 343, 431
Cagney and Lacey 94–5, 110
Caldwell, J. 166, 183, 269–70, 293–312
camcorder technology 219–22, 286, 291, 548, 557–67
Candid Camera 427, 559
capitalism 92, 148, 503, 584–5
cartoons 475, 481
Caughie, J. 9
censorship 72–4, 355, 359, 601
Centre for Contemporary Cultural Studies 8–9, 463–4
children and television 3–4, 58, 70–4, 391, 475–6, 479–92
Chion, M. 186
Christianity 359–60, 393–4, 396–7, 409–10
cinema 20–1, 74, 113, 227, 359–61, 545–6
circulation 42, 357–8, 420
citizenship 152–3, 421, 426, 433–4, 524–32
class 8, 52–3, 57–8, 246, 253, 423, 425–6, 428, 450–2, 466–7, 470–4, 481–2
Clifford, J. 434, 476
Collins, R. 11, 30, 33–51, 108, 135, 372, 460
comedy 231–2, 259–60, 442, 445, 486–8

commercial television 6, 52–60, 80–5, 343
commissioning 281–4
community television 343–51
consumption 134, 398, 461–78
content analysis 245, 466
convergence 135–7, 312, 569–71, 577, 578–9, 609–11
COPS 222, 538, 547, 548–9
copyright 155, 260–1, 285, 358–9, 610
Corner, J. 3, 182, 189, 190, 196–7, 207, 226–312, 314, 327, 552
Coronation Street 246, 250, 252–3, 290, 332–42, 485, 491
Cosby Show, The 260, 264, 372, 442–56, 465–6
Couldry, N. 106, 271, 318, 332
crime 4, 559–60
cult television 509–22
cultural capital 54, 469–72, 482
cultural identity 38–40, 134, 530
cultural imperialism 119, 133–4, 137, 357, 365, 443
cultural industries 61, 135
cultural studies 8–9, 59, 171–2, 245–8, 380–1, 462–4
Cunningham, S. 107–9, 151–62, 460
Curran, J. 433, 464
current affairs 82, 146

D'Acci, J. 371, 373–88, 390
Dallas 112–17, 119, 121–2, 126, 243–4, 247, 442, 462
Dawson's Creek 469–580
Dayan, D. 184, 217, 418, 424, 433
daytime television 242, 422
De Certeau, M. 121, 336, 346
democratisation 291, 422
diaspora 154–5, 157–60, 434, 443–4, 453
digital television 20, 136 29, 304–5, 543–52, 561–3, 582
Disney 101–3, 288, 332, 539, 572
distribution 81, 135, 282–3, 362
Doctor Who 510–14, 519–21
documentary 185–90, 196–208, 220–1, 311–12, 315–16, 544–6, 557–61
Doty, A. 379–80
Dovey, J. 163, 165, 312, 538–9, 557–68
drama 95–100, 197–207, 354, 361–3
drama documentary/docudrama 196–207, 222

DVD 16–20, 268, 281, 535, 539
Dynasty 117, 243, 249, 442, 448

Eastenders 244, 246, 250, 253, 264, 288, 333
Eco, U. 185
economics and finance 81, 147, 249, 250, 281–3, 307
educational television 57
effects, see media effects
Ellen 377, 389, 392–3, 397–8
Ellis, J. 221–2, 268–9, 275–92, 526
encoding and decoding 121, 465, 380–1
entertainment 42, 45–6, 56–61, 156, 477
ER 281, 286, 410–11
ethics 46–7, 206, 601
ethnicity 153–6, 379, 428–34, 591–3
ethnography 8–9, 462, 470, 476–8, 605–9
everyday life 9, 22, 238–9, 248, 275–6, 339, 420–4, 461, 463, 475, 610

fans 318–19, 509–22, 569–70
feminism 92–3, 99, 101–3, 378–9, 602–3
Feuer, J. 171, 205
film theory 8, 464
Fiske, J. 8–9, 115, 122, 247, 379
format 87, 210–14, 258–60, 276–7, 351, 370, 510–13, 518
Foucault, M. 174, 178, 470, 474, 497
Fraser, N. 43, 152, 425–7
Frasier 280–1, 389, 391–2, 487
Friends 391–2, 411

game shows 264–5, 312, 491
Garnham, N. 41–2, 46, 151
gay representation 254, 343, 346–51, 379, 383–4, 389–99, 409
gender 243, 245, 247–8, 314, 373–85, 425–6, 465–70, 491, 518, 571, 575–6, 603, 608
Geraghty, C. 246, 251, 335
Giddens, A. 141, 328–9, 599
Gillespie, M. 119, 430, 443, 462
Gilroy, P. 430, 444, 453
Gitlin, T. 152–3
globalisation 433
Gray, A. 383, 462, 468–70
Gray, H. 382, 415
Gripsrud, J. 473–517
Guiding Light, The 252

Habermas, J. 42–7, 139–41, 151–2, 322, 355, 424–7
Hall, S. 121–2, 246, 381, 420, 443, 461, 464, 468
Hartley, J. 7, 9, 152–3, 156, 188, 190, 370, 459, 460, 482, 491, 524–34
hegemony 56, 115–16, 119, 126, 131, 467–8
Herman, E. S. 60, 142, 145, 447–8
Hermes, J. 126, 426, 470
high culture/low culture 39, 59, 473, 482
Hine, C. 596, 607
history of television 21
Hobson, D. 244, 246–7, 471
Hodge, B. 475–6
Hollywood 15, 89, 111–26
home videos 345–6
horror 511
Hostages 196–205
Hutchison, D. 31, 66–78
hybrid formats 102, 311, 319–20, 530

I Love Lucy 5
ideology 157, 350, 420–1, 463, 465, 473
institutions, see broadcasting institutions
interactivity 312, 529, 570–1, 577, 587–9
Internet 413, 519–20, 540–1, 569–79, 581–93, 596–612
intertextuality 173–4, 363, 518–20

Jameson, F. 113, 562–3
Jenkins, H. 318, 472, 518–19, 539, 570–1, 573, 577–8
Jhally, S. 450, 465–7

Kant, I. 44–6
Katz, E. 118–19, 184, 217, 418, 424
Kolar-Panov, D. 155

LAPD 546–7
Lewis, J. 30, 52–65, 450, 465–7
Livingstone, S. 270, 322–31, 426–7
Lull, J. 475
Lunt, P. 270, 322–31, 427

Martin-Barbero, J. 420
Marxism 155–6, 463–4, 503
masculinity 99, 375–85, 425–7, 469–70, 603
mass culture 5, 45–6, 53, 56

McChesney, R. 52, 54–5, 59–60, 115, 142, 145, 372, 447–8
McGuigan, J. 152, 156
McLuhan, M. 582, 599
McRobbie, A. 462
media effects 3–6, 70–3, 467, 609
media law 39, 67–75
media literacy 7, 526
Meehan, E. 31, 92–104
melodrama 94–6, 255, 363, 469–70
migration 89, 153–4, 157, 356, 420, 444, 605
Miller, D. 454, 605, 610
modernity 140–1, 248, 527, 581–7, 599
Modleski, T. 245, 247, 471
Moonlighting 302
Moores, S. 430
Moran, A. 10, 23, 168, 258–66
Morley, D. 134–6, 247, 371–2, 383, 418–41, 443, 445, 453, 462–5, 468–70
Morse, M. 209–25, 370, 423
MP3 539
multinational corporations 115, 358
music industry 358, 443
music video 156–8, 190–1

Nancy, J. 588
narrative 7, 114, 120, 123–6, 172–3, 242–4, 250–5, 511, 513, 589–91
nationalism 155, 361
Nationwide 247, 428, 430, 464–5
Neighbours 113, 244, 249, 443
Newcomb, H. 4
news, television 209–22, 549
newspapers 67, 145–6, 288
Nichols, B. 559, 567

O'Regan, T. 9–10, 14, 22–3, 31, 79–91
Oprah 327, 426
ownership 60–1, 80–2, 92–3, 101–2, 146–7, 284, 358, 529

Paul Kent Show, The 346
photography 543–6, 548–51
pleasure 6–9, 121–2, 232–4, 244–8, 360–1, 469, 472–3, 488, 563–7, 572–3
policy 34–6, 40–2, 52–64, 70–5, 83–5, 97, 140–1, 532
political economy 9, 116

popular culture 7–8, 154–5, 158–9, 245, 361–3, 444, 473, 482
pornography 14, 72–3, 563
Poster, M. 564, 581–95, 597
Postmodernism 472, 562–3
post-production/editing 186–8, 190–1, 204, 287–8, 296–7
Press Complaints Commission 69
privacy 67, 69–70, 205, 326
private sphere 420–1
production 259, 275–91, 293–307, 344, 358, 361–3, 381–3, 561
public access television 140, 211, 219–20, 330, 343–51, 357–61, 560
public service broadcasting 33–47, 53–64, 85, 279
public sphere 42–7, 139–49, 151–6, 215, 322, 329–30, 355–7, 359–61, 418, 424–34
PVR 16–17
pyschoanalysis 7, 490–1, 602

qualitative research 461–78
quantitative research 463
Quiz shows 10, 55, 88, 174, 176–7

race 382–3, 429–32, 442–54, 466–7, 591–2
radio 54–5, 80, 146–7, 242, 356, 419–20
Radway, J. 462, 468, 470
ratings 83, 93–103, 262–3, 390–3, 515
Real TV 538, 547, 549
Reality Television 311–12, 382, 543–52
regulation 13, 34, 60–4, 79–85, 144, 147, 262, 446–8
religion 407–8, 411–12
representation 8, 206, 350, 373–85, 398, 427, 429–32, 451–4, 602
ritual 333, 337–41, 419, 422
Ritzer, G. 142
Robins, K. 134–6, 443, 445, 551–2, 602
Room 101 259
Roque Santeiro 255
Roscoe, J. 23, 281, 311–21
Ross, K. 443

satellite television 34, 448
Scannell, P. 419–24, 427–9, 503
scheduling 20, 95, 251, 282, 480, 518
Schiller, H. 113, 115–19, 122–3

Science Fiction 232, 509–13
Scientific Advisory Committee on Television and Social Behaviour 4
Seinfeld 389, 391–3
Seiter, E. 8, 458, 461–78, 481
semiotics 237, 463–4
sex 69, 72–3, 484, 565–7
Shklovsky, V. 546, 552
Shutz, A. 18
Sinclair, J. 107–8, 130–8, 154
Slater, D. 596–614
Smith, J. 339
soap opera 7, 117, 120–1, 242–55, 316, 471, 513, 517–18
Sopranos, The 13, 21, 416
Sparks, C. 108, 139–50, 372, 460
Spigel, L. 3, 5
sponsorship 54, 283, 289–90
Sreberny, A. 430–1
Star Trek 511–12, 520–1
Structuralism and Post-structuralism 171, 247
Survivor 168, 270, 311

talk shows 98, 168, 187, 210, 214–15, 250, 323, 344, 423, 426–7
taste 38, 45–6, 56, 72, 178, 233, 471, 479–92
telenovelas 133, 242–3, 248–50, 254–5
textual analysis 172–3, 464–5, 509, 513
Thompson, J. O. 233–4
Touched By An Angel 402–3, 410–14, 416
Tracey, M. 39
transnationalism 34, 132, 155, 354, 360, 433–4, 442–4
Tripp, D. 475–6
Tulloch, J. 9
Tunstall, J. 111
Turkle, S. 604–5
Turner, G. 10, 26

uses and gratifications 461–4, 468, 474–5

VCD 16

video art 290–1
video recorder 14–16, 80, 193, 249, 469, 537
Viola, B. 291
violence 4–5, 70–5, 490

Walkerdine, V. 476–7
war 144, 199, 213–14, 216
Wearing, G. 291
Wernick, A. 237
West Wing, The 21, 515
Wheel Of Fortune 262, 276
Who Wants To Be A Millionaire 23

Williams, R. 142, 246, 529, 569
Winston, B. 300

X-Files, The 263

Zook, C. 383